Neuromechanics
of
HUMAN
MOVEMENT

THIRD EDITION

Roger M. Enoka, PhD
University of Colorado at Boulder

Human Kinetics

Library of Congress Cataloging-in-Publication

Enoka, Roger M., 1949-
 Neuromechanics of human movement / by Roger M. Enoka--3rd ed.
  p. cm.
 Previous editions published under title: Neuromechanical basis of kinesiology.
 Includes bibliographical references and index.
 ISBN 0-7360-0251-0
 1. Kinesiology. 2. Human mechanics. I. Enoka, Roger M., 1949- Neuromechanical
basis of kinesiology. II. Title.

 QP303.E56 2001
 612.7'6--dc21   2001024108

ISBN: 0-7360-0251-0

The cover images are reprinted from *De Motu Animalium* by Giovanni Alfonso Borelli, 1680, RB 4500, volume 1 and from "Textura del sistema nervioso del hombre y vertbrado," by Ramón Y Cajal, 1899-1904, Madrid, Moya.

This book is a new edition of *Neuromechanical Basis of Kinesiology,* second edition, published in 1994 by Human Kinetics.

Acquisitions Editor: Loarn D. Robertson, PhD; **Developmental Editor:** Renee T. Thomas; **Assistant Editor:** Amanda S. Ewing; **Copyeditor:** Joyce Sexton; **Proofreader:** E.T. Cler; **Indexer:** Craig Brown; **Permission Managers:** Dalene Reeder, Whitney Havice; **Graphic Designer:** Fred Starbird; **Graphic Artist:** Yvonne Griffith; **Photo Manager:** Clark Brooks; **Cover Designer:** Keith Blomberg; **Art Manager:** Craig Newsom; **Illustrator:** Argosy; **Printer:** Edwards

Printed in the United States of America   10 9 8 7 6 5 4 3 2 1

Human Kinetics
Web site: www.humankinetics.com

United States: Human Kinetics, P.O. Box 5076, Champaign, IL 61825-5076
800-747-4457
e-mail: humank@hkusa.com

Canada: Human Kinetics, 475 Devonshire Road Unit 100, Windsor, ON N8Y 2L5
800-465-7301 (in Canada only)
e-mail: orders@hkcanada.com

Europe: Human Kinetics, Units C2/C3 Wira Business Park, West Park Ring Road
Leeds LS16 6EB, United Kingdom
+44 (0) 113 278 1708
e-mail: hk@hkeurope.com

Australia: Human Kinetics, 57A Price Avenue, Lower Mitcham, South Australia 5062
08 8277 1555
e-mail: liahka@senet.com.au

New Zealand: Human Kinetics, P.O. Box 105-231, Auckland Central
09-523-3462
e-mail: hkp@ihug.co.nz

To Bonny, Maro, Joel, and Seth

Contents

Preface

In August 1996, I moved from a research position at the Cleveland Clinic Foundation to the professoriate at the University of Colorado at Boulder. In this capacity, I was expected to continue an extramurally funded research program and to contribute to the teaching mission of the university. I was assigned the responsibility of teaching the undergraduate class in biomechanics that was required for students majoring in kinesiology. I designed a course based on the second edition of this text. As had happened at the University of Arizona, I was once again confronted by the questions of students. It soon became obvious that a third edition of the text was necessary. Fortunately, the publisher was willing to undertake such a project and, with the encouragement of Dr. Loarn Robertson and Renee Thomas at Human Kinetics, what you have before you is the result of this endeavor.

The purpose of this text is to provide a scientific foundation for the study of human movement. In the tradition of Etienne-Jules Marey, the focus is on the integration of concepts and principles from biology and physics. The intent was to provide a valuable resource for the teaching of senior undergraduate students and beginning graduate students and to supply a reference for professionals. Based on comments and questions from students and colleagues, both locally and internationally, the third edition of the text has been revised in three significant ways. First, the conceptual structure of the previous edition has been retained but some of the material has been reorganized, especially in part I (on biomechanics) and part II (on the motor system). Chapter 2 now focuses on the forces due to body mass and those due to the surroundings; chapter 3 addresses the forces within the body; and chapter 4 provides examples on running, jumping, and throwing. Similarly, chapter 6 examines topics related to the function of the single-joint system, whereas chapter 7 expands these concepts to multi-joint systems.

Second, a substantial set of ancillary material has been prepared for instructors who use the text in teaching. The ancillary material includes an Instructor Guide, a Test Bank, and a set of PowerPoint slides. The Instructor's Guide describes approaches that could be used to teach a class in biomechanics for undergraduate students or a survey course in neuromuscular physiology for beginning graduate students. The guide includes a description of the content in each chapter, some suggestions on teaching strategies, examples of course syllabi, a set of lecture outlines for the biomechanics class, examples of questions for reading quizzes, sample laboratory exercises, examples of exams, and additional questions that can be used on exams. The test bank contains about 500 questions and answers that could be used by an instructor; these include multiple-choice questions and problems to be solved. The set of PowerPoint slides includes most of the figures in the text.

Third, the content of the text has been enhanced and updated. For example, most of the figures from the second edition of the text have been redrawn, and a number of new figures have been included in the third edition. The number of figures in the nine chapters has been increased from 281 to 367, with many of these available to instructors as PowerPoint slides. Similarly, the number of references have been expanded from 1055 in the second edition to about 1500 in the third edition. The citations included in the text represent the state of the relevant literature as it existed in November 2000.

Despite these revisions, it is likely that the text contains various strengths and weaknesses, depending on the interests of the reader. Nonetheless, I am hopeful that you will find the third edition of *Neuromechanics of Human Movement* a valuable resource.

Acknowledgments

The second edition of this text featured the drawings of the Renaissance physiologist Giovanni Alfonso Borelli (1608-1679). One of his classic drawings is on the cover of that text. For the third edition, however, I have chosen to highlight the work of Etienne-Jules Marey (1830–1904), whose contributions to the analysis of human movement have largely been ignored over the last several decades. Marey was a physician-trained scientist whose methods of recording movement revolutionized our understanding of time and motion. His contributions had a significant impact on art, aviation, cinematography, ergonomics, medicine, photography, physical education, and physiology (Braun, 1992).

Marey was born in Beaune, France, at a time of considerable progress in medicine, when, for example, physiology was establishing itself as a discipline distinct from anatomy. Although Marey eventually achieved the recognition of his peers with appropriate academic honors, his viewpoints contrasted with those that prevailed at the time. Three examples illustrate the significance of his ideas:

■ Vitalism. Marey opposed the popular notion of vitalism, which held that life was a result of special organic forces that could not be reduced to physics and chemistry. Marey was a mechanist who believed that physiology, which he regarded as the study of life functions, could be explained by physicochemical laws. Much of his work sought to emphasize the association between physics and physiology.

■ Vivisection. Marey objected to the practice of vivisection because it modified what it was supposed to study, which meant that the results could represent only a partial, or even a false, view of the normally intact system. Instead, he devised ways to measure movement with minimal interference by the observer.

■ Schémas. Marey espoused the idea that a phenomenon could be understood only when it could be simulated—something he accomplished with schémas. These provided the ultimate proof of his analyses.

Marey combined these ideas with his passion for gadgets. He designed and constructed a number of instruments that, for the first time, characterized the temporal and spatial relations underlying movement and the forces necessary to produce them. The most enduring legacy of Marey, who originally wanted to be an engineer, is the instruments that he invented. These included cardiographs to measure the movement of the cardiovascular system; thermographs to measure and inscribe the intensity and duration of heat changes in the body; pneumographs to study the respiratory system; myographs to study the phases and speeds of voluntary muscle contractions and the actions of heat, cold, anemia, and fatigue, as well as the effects of various positions; pressure sensors to record the pressure between the ground and the person or animal moving over the ground; and chronophotographs to capture displacement and time on a single photographic image. These instruments enabled Marey to provide precise and quantitative measurements of movements by and within the body.

Reprinted from the Collège de France.

Marey's work had a substantial impact on his contemporaries in many fields (Braun, 1992; Dagognet, 1992). As a reminder of these contributions, the current text includes a number of figures from the work of Marey.

In the third edition of this text, I have retained the original conceptual organization but have rearranged some of the topics. This reorganization was largely due to the comments made in a detailed critique by Claire Farley on the second edition. In addition, I have received a number of constructive comments from graduate students, postdoctoral fellows, and colleagues: Sophie De Serres, Monika Fleshner, Sandra Hunter, Rodger Kram, Douglass Laidlaw, Tim Noteboom, Mark Rogers, John Semmler, and Mickey Taylor. Much of the impetus for the revision, however, came from the questions posed by undergraduate and graduate students in the Department of Kinesiology and Applied Physiology at the University of Colorado. For all of these contributions, I am most grateful.

Credits

Figure 1.17 From "Load and skill-related changes in segmental contributions to a weightlifting movement" by R.M. Enoka, 1988, *Medicine and Science in Sports and Exercise, 20*, p. 185. Copyright 1988 by Lippincott, Williams, & Wilkins. Reprinted by permission.

Figure 1.31 From "Surface EMG for the noninvasive characterization of muscle," by R. Merletti, A. Rainoldi, and D. Farina, 2001, *Exercise and Sport Sciences Reviews, 29*, pp. 20–25. Copyright 2001 by Lippincott, Williams & Wilkins. Adapted by permission.

Figure 1.36 From "Relationships of the Surface Electromyogram to the Force, Velocity, and Contraction Rate of the Cineplastic Human Biceps" by C.W. Heckathorne and D.S. Childress, 1981, *American Journal of Physical Medicine, 60*, p. 6. Copyright 1981 by Williams & Wilkins. Adapted by permission.

Figure 2.9 Data from "Muscular and Non-muscular Moments of Force in the Swing Limb of Masters Runners" by S.J. Phillips & E.M. Roberts. In *Proceedings of the Biomechanics Symposium* (pp. 256–274) by J.M. Cooper & B. Haven (Eds.), 1980, Bloomington, IN: Indiana State Board of Health. Adapted by permission.

Figure 2.10 From "A Biomechanical Analysis of the Contribution of the Trunk to Standing Vertical Jump Take-offs" by D. I. Miller. In *Physical Education, Sports and the Sciences* (p. 357) by J. Broekhoff (Ed.), 1976, Eugene, OR: Microform. Adapted by permission.

Figure 2.13 From "In-Shoe Pressure Distribution for Running in Various Types of Footwear" by E. M. Hennig and T. L. Milani, 1995, *Journal of Applied Biomechanics, 11*, p. 303. Copyright 1995 by Human Kinetics.

Figure 2.14 From "Ground Reaction Forces in Distance Running" by P.R. Cavanagh and M.A. Lafortune, 1980, *Journal of Biomechanics, 13,* pp. 397-406.

Figure 2.24 Adapted from Peter J. Brancazio, *SportScience,* (Simon & Schuster, 1984).

Figure 2.25 From "Upper extremity function in running. II: Angular momentum considerations" by R.N. Hinrichs, 1987, *International Journal of Sport Biomechanics, 3,* pp. 259, 261. Copyright 1987 by Human Kinetics Publishers, Inc. Adapted by permission.

Figure 2.26 Reprinted from *Journal of Biomechanics, 10,* Hay et al., "A Computational Technique to Determine the Angular Momentum of the Human Body" pp. 269-277. Copyright 1977, with permission from Elsevier Science.

Figure 3.2 From "Bone-on-bone forces at the ankle joint during a rapid dynamic movement" by V. Galea and R.W. Norman in *Biomechanics IX-A* (p.72) by D.A. Winter et al. (Eds.), 1985, Champaign, IL: Human Kinetics. Copyright 1985 by Human Kinetics Publishers, Inc. Adapted by permission.

Figure 3.3 Reprinted from *Journal of Biomechanics, 30,* Duda et al., "Internal Forces and Moments in the Femur During Walking", pp. 933-941. Copyright 1997, with permission from Elsevier Science.

Figure 3.4 From "Physiological Changes in Skeletal Muscle as a Result of Strength Training" by D.A. Jones, O.M. Rutherford, and D.F. Parker, 1989, *Quarterly Journal of Experimental Physiology, 74,* p. 245. Copyright 1989 by The Physiological Society. Adapted by permission.

Champaign, IL: Human Kinetics. Copyright 1998 by William C. Whiting and Ronald F. Zernicke. Reprinted by permission.

Figure 5.15a Reprinted from *Brain Research, 307,* B. Ulfhake and J.-O. Kellerth, "Electrophysiological and Morphological Measurements in Cat Gastrocnemius and Soleus ∝-Motoneurones", p. 170. Copyright 1984, with permission from Elsevier Science.

Figure 5.18 From "Structure and Function in Vertebrate Skeletal Muscle" by S.E. Peters, 1989, *American Zoologist, 29,* p. 222. Copyright 1989 by The Society for Integrative and Comparative Biology. Adapted by permission.

Figure 5.19 From "Functional Anatomy of the Association Between Motor Units and Muscle Receptors" by B. R. Botterman, M. D. Binder, and D. G. Stuart, 1978, *American Zoologist, 18,* p. 136. Copyright 1978 by The Society for Integrative and Comparative Biology. Adapted by permission.

Figure 5.21 From "Response Profiles of Human Muscle Afferents During Active Finger Movements" by N. A. Al-Falahe, M. Nagaoka, and A. B. Vallbo, 1990, *Brain, 113,* p. 330. Copyright 1990 by Oxford University Press. Adapted by permission of Oxford University Press.

Figure 5.22 From "Proprioceptive feedback and movement regulation" by A. Prochazka, 1996, in *Handbook of Physiology: Sec 12,* L.B. Rowell and J.T. Sheperd (eds.), pp. 59-127, New York: Oxford University Press. Copyright 1996 by Oxford University Press. Adapted by permission.

Figure 5.23 From "Response Profiles of Human Muscle Afferents During Active Finger Movements" by N. A. Al-Falahe, M. Nagaoka, and A. B. Vallbo, 1990, *Brain, 113,* p. 339. Copyright 1990 by Oxford University Press. Adapted by permission of Oxford University Press

Figure 6.5 From *Skeletal Muscle: Form and Function,* by A.J. McComas, 1996, Champaign, IL: Human Kinetics. Copyright 1996 by Alan J. McComas. Adapted by permission.

Figure 6.7 From "Mechanisms of Muscular Fatigue" by R.H. Fitts and J.M. Metzger. In *Principles of Exercise Biochemistry* (p. 250) by J. R. Poortmans (Ed.), 1993, Basel: Karger. Copyright 1993 by S. Karger AG. Adapted by permission.

Figure 6.8 From "Muscle" by J.C. Rüegg, 1983, *Human Physiology* (p. 37) by R.F. Schmidt and G. Thews (Eds.), New York: Springer-Verlag. Copyright 1983 by Springer-Verlag. Reprinted by permission.

Figure 6.10 From "On the relationships between membrane potential, calciumtransiet and tension in single barnacle muscle fibres" by C.C. Ashley and E.B. Ridgeway, 1970, *Journal of Physiology, 209,* p. 111. Copyright 1970 by the Physiological Society. Adapted by permission.

Figure 6.13 From "In Vivo Measurement of human wrist

extensor muscle sarcomere length changes" by R.L. Lieber, F.J. Loren and J. Fridén, 1994, *Journal of Neurophysiology, 71,* pp. 874-881. Copyright 1994 by The American Physiological Society. Reprinted by permission.

Figure 6.20 From "Mechanics of Human Isolated Voluntary Muscle" by H.J. Ralston, V.T Inman, L.A. Strait, and M.D. Shaffrath, 1947, *American Journal of Physiology, 151,* p. 615. Copyright 1947 by the American Physiological Society. Adapted by permission.

Figure 6.21 From "Morphological basis of skeletal muscle power output" by V.R. Edgerton, R.R. Roy, R. J. Gregor and S. Rugg, in *Human Muscle Power* (p.55) by N.L Jones, N. McCartney and A.J. McComas (Eds.), 1986, Champaign, IL: Human Kinetics. Copyright 1986 by Human Kinetics Publishers, Inc. Adapted by permission.

Figure 6.24 From "Isometric Torque-Angle Relationship and Movement-Related Activity of Human Elbow Flexors: Implications for the Equilibrium-Point Hypothesis" by Z. Hasan and R.M. Enoka, 1985, *Experimental Brain Research, 59,* p. 447. Copyright 1985 by Springer-Verlag, Inc. Adapted by permission.

Figure 6.27 From "Effects of Electrical Stimulation on Eccentric and Concentric Torque-Velocity Relationships During Knee Extension in Man" by S.H. Westing, J.Y Seger, and A.Thorstensson, 1990, *Acta Physiological Scandinavica, 140,* p. 19. Copyright 1990 by Scandinavian Physiological Society. Adapted by permission.

Figure 6.28 From "Measurement of Maximal Short-Term (Anaerobic) Power Output During Cycling" by A.J. Sargenat and A. Boreham. In *Women and Sport* (p. 122) by J. Borms, M. Hebbelinck, and A. Venerando (Eds.), 1981, Basel: S. Karger AG. Copyright 1981 by S. Karger AG, Basel. Adapted by permission.

Figure 6.32 From "Injury to Skeletal Muscle Fibers of Mice Following Lengthening Contractions" by K.K. McCully and J.A. Faulkner, 1985, *Journal of Applied Physiology, 59,* p. 120. Copyright 1985 by The American Physiological Society. Adapted by permission.

Figure 6.33 From "Effect of stretching on the elastic characteristics and the contractile component of frog striated muscle" by G.A. Cavagna and G. Citterio, 1974, *Journal of Physiology, 239,* p. 5. Copyright 1974 by Cambridge University Press. Adapted by permission.

Figure 6.34 From "Shortening of Muscle Fibres During Stretch of the Active Cat Medial Gastrocnemius Muscle: the Role of Tendon Compliance" by R.I. Griffiths, 1991, *Journal of Physiology (London), 436,* pp. 225, 229. Copyright 1991 by Cambridge University Press. Adapted by permission.

Figure 6.40 From "Anatomy and Innervation Ratios in Motor Units of Cat Gastrocnemius" by R.E. Burke and P. Tsairis, 1973, *Journal of Physiology, 234,* p. 755. Copyright 1973 by Cambridge University Press. Adapted with permission.

Figure 6.41 From *Skeletal Muscle: Form and Function* by A.J. McComas, 1996, Champaign, IL: Human Kinetics. Copyright 1996 by A.J. McComas. Adapted by permission.

Figure 6.47 From "Unusual Motor Unit Firing Behavior in Older Adults" by G. Kamen and C.J. DeLuca, 1989, *Brain Research, 482,* p. 137. Copyright 1989 by Elsevier Science Publications. Reprinted by permission.

Figure 6.48 Reprinted from *Trends in Neurosciences, 7,* by R.M. Enoka and D.G. Stuart, "Henneman's 'Size Principle': Current Issues", p. 227. Copyright 1984, with permission from Elsevier Science Publications.

Figure 6.50 From "Discharge Frequency and Discharge pattern of Human Motor Units During Voluntary Contraction of Muscle" by R.S. Person and L.P. Kudina, 1972, *Electroencephalography and Clinical Neurophysiology,32,* p. 473. Copyright 1972 by Elsevier Publishing Co., Inc. Adapted by permission.

Figure 6.52 From "Preservation of Force Output through Progressive Reduction of Stimulation Frequency in Human Quadriceps Femoris Muscle" by S.A. Binder-Macleod and T. Guerin, 1990, *Physical Therapy, 70,* p.622. Copyright 1990 by The American Physical Therapy Association, Inc. Adapted by permission.

Figure 6.53 From "Contractile Properties of Single Motor Units in Human Toe Extensors Assessed by Intraneural Motor Axon Stimulation" by V.G. Macefield, A.J. Fuglevand and B. Bigland-Ritchie, 1996, *Journal of Neurophysiology, 75,* pp. 2509-2519. Copyright 1996 by The American Physiological Society. Adapted by permission.

Figure 6.58 Reprinted from *Trends in Neurosciences, 14,* by P.B.C. Matthews, "The Human Stretch Reflex and the Motor Cortex" p. 88. Copyright 1991, with permission from Elsevier Science.

Figure 6.60 From "Anatomy and innervation ratios in motor units of cat gastrocnemius" by R.E. Burke and P. Tsairis, 1973, *Journal of Physiology, 234,* p. 755. Copyright 1973 by Cambridge University Press. Adapted by permission.

Figure 6.64 Figure from "Evidence of Phase-Dependent Nociceptive Reflexes During Locomotion in Man" by P. Crenna and C. Frigo, 1984, in *Experimental Neurology, 85,* p. 341. Copyright 1984 by Academic press, reproduced by permission of the publisher.

Figure 6.67 From "Adapting Relfexes Controlling the Human Posture" by L.M. Nashner, 1976, *Experimental Brain Research, 26,* pp. 62,65, 66. Copyright 1976 by Springer-Verlag, Inc. Adapted by permission.

Figure 6.68 From "Properties of Postural Adjustments Associated with Rapid Arm Movements" by P. J. Cordo and L. M. Nashner, 1982, *Journal of Neurophysiology,47,* p. 296. Copyright 1982 by The American Physiological Society. Adapted by permission.

Figure 7.1 From "Strategies for Muscle Activation During Isometric Torque Generation at the Human Elbow" by T.S. Buchanan, G.P. Rovai, and W.Z. Rymer, 1989, *Journal of Neurophysiology,62,* p. 1209. Copyright 1989 by The American Physiology Society. Adapted by permission.

Figure 7.6 From "The Unique Action of Bi-Articular Muscles in Leg Extensions" by G.J. van Ingen Schenau, M.F. Bobbert, and A.J. Van Soest. In *Multiple Muscle Systems: Biomechanics and Movement Organization* (p. 647) by J.M. Winters and S.L.-Y. Woo (Eds.), 1990, New York: Springer-Verlag. Copyright 1990 by Springer-Verlag New York. Adapted by permission.

Figure 7.10 From "Body Segment Contribution to Sport Skill Performance: Two Contrasting Approaches" by D.I. Miller, 1980, *Research Quarterly for Exercise and Sport, 51,* p. 225, a publication of the American Alliance for Health, Physical Education, Recreation and Dance, 1900 Association Drive, Reston, VA 22091. Reprinted by permission.

Figure 7.22 From "Motor Systems" by R.F. Schmidt. In *Human Physiology* (p. 93) by R.F. Schmidt and G. Thews (Eds.), 1983, New York: Springer-Verlag. Copyright 1983 by Springer-Verlag. Adapted by permission.

Figure 7.23 From "The Functional Organization of the Motor System in the Monkey. II. The Effects of Lesions of the Descending Brain-Stem Pathways" by J.H. Lawrence and H. G. J. M. Kuypers, 1968, *Brain, XCI,* p. 26. Copyright 1968 by Oxford University Press. Adapted by permission.

Figure 7.25 From *Control of Voluntary Human Movement* (p. 241) by J.C. Rothwell, 1987, Kent, United Kingdom: Croom Helm. Copyright 1987 by John C. Rothwell. Adapted by permission.

Figure 7.31 From "Once more on the equilibrium-point hypothesis (λModel) for motor control" by A.G. Feldman, 1986, *Journal of Motor Behavior, 18,* pp. 17-54. Copyright 1986 by Heldref Publications. Adapted by permission. And from *Neurophysiological basis of movement,* by M.L. Latash, 1998, Champaign, IL: Human Kinetics. Copyright 1998 by Mark L. Latash. Adapted by permission.

Figure 7.33 From "Principles Underlying Single-Joint Movement Strategies" by G.L. Gottlieb, D.M. Corcos, G.C. Agarwal, and M.L. Latash, *Multiple Muscle Systems* (p. 241), by J.M. Winters and S.L.-Y. Woo (Eds.), 1990, New York: Springer-Verlag. Copyright 1990 by Springer-Verlag New York, Inc. Adapted by permission.

Figure 7.34a From "Once More on the Equilibrium-Point Hypothesis (λModel) for Motor Control" by A.G. Feldman,

1986, *Journal of Motor Behavior*, *18*, p. 21. Copyright 1986 by Heldref Publications. Adapted by permission.

Figure 7.36 From "Shift of Activity From Slow to Fast Muscle During Voluntary Lengthening Contractions of the Triceps Surae Muscles in Humans" by A. Nardone, and M. Schieppati, 1988, *Journal of Physiology*, *395*, p. 368. Copyright 1988 by Cambridge University Press. Adapted by permission.

Figure 7.37 From "Selective Recruitment of High-Threshold Human Motor Units During Voluntary Isotonic Lengthening of Active Muscles" by A. Nardone, C. Romanò, and M. Schieppati, 1989, *Journal of Physiology*, *409*, p. 456. Copyright 1989 by Cambridge University Press. Adapted by permission.

Figure 8.3 From "Chronic Transformation of Muscle in Spasticity: A Peripheral Contribution to Increased Tone" by A. Hufschmidt and K.H.Mauritz, 1985, *Journal of Neurology, Neurosurgery, and Pyschiatry*, *48*, p. 678. Copyright 1985 by Journal of Neurology, Neurosurgery, and Psychiatry. Adapted by permission.

Figure 8.4 From "Chronic Transformation of Muscle in Spasticity: A Peripheral Contribution to Increased Tone" by A. Hufschmidt and K.H. Mauritz, 1985, *Journal of Neurology, Neurosurgery, and Psychiatry*, *48*, p. 678. Copyright 1985 by Journal of Neurology, Neurosurgery, and Psychiatry. Adapted by permission.

Figure 8.8 From "The Viscoelastic Properties of Muscle-Tendon Units" by D.C. Taylor, J. Dalton, A.V. Seaber, and W.E. Garrett, 1990, *American Journal of Sports Medicine,18*, pp. 303,304. Copyright 1990 by the American Orthopaedic Society for Sports Medicine. Adapted by permission.

Figure 8.11 From "Biomechanical Comparison of Stimulated and Nonstimulated Skeletal Muscle Pulled to Failure" by W.E. Garrett, M.R. Safran, A.V. Seaber, R.R. Glisson, and B.M. Ribbeck, 1987, *American Journal of Sports Medicine, 15,* p. 452. Copyright 1987 by the American Orthopaedic Society for Sports Medicine. Adapted by permission.

Figure 8.13 From "Fatigue of Intermittent Submaximal Voluntary Contractions: Central and Peripheral Factors" by B.Bigland-Ritchie, F. Furbush, and J.J. Woods, 1986, *Journal of Applied Physiology, 61,* p. 424. Copyright 1986 by the American Physiological Society. Adapted by permission.

Figure 8.14 From "Fatigue of Submaximal Static Contractions" by B. Bigland-Ritchie, E. Cafarelli, and N.K. Vøllestad, 1986, *Acta Physiologica Scandinavica, Suppl. 556,* p. 138. Copyright 1986 by the Scandinavian Physiological Society. Adapted by permission.

Figure 8.15 From "Intramuscular Pressure, EMG and Blood Flow During Low-Level Prolonged Static Contraction in Man" by G. Sjøgaard, B. Kiens, K Jørgensen, and B. Saltin, 1986, *Acta Physiologica Scandinavica*, *128*, p. 479. Copyright 1986 by the Scandinavian Physiological Society. Adapted by permission.

Figure 8.17 From "Force and EMG Signal Patterns During Repeated Bouts of Concentric and Eccentric Muscle Actions" by P.A. Tesch, G.A. Dudley, M.R. Duvoisin, B.M. Hather, and R.T. Harris, 1990, *Acta Physiologica Scandinavica, 138,* p. 266. Copyright 1990 by the Scandinavian Physiological Society. Adapted by permission.

Figure 8.21 From "Impairment of Neuromuscular Propagation During Human Fatiguing Contractions at Submaximal Forces" by A. J. Fuglevand, K. M. Zackowski, K. A. Huey, and R. M. Enoka, 1993, *Journal of Physiology*, *460*, p. 556. Copyright 1993 by the Physiological Society. Adapted by permission.

Figure 8.26 Figure from "Estimation of Weights and Tensions and Apparent Involvement of a Sense of Effort" by D. I. McCloskey, P. Ebeling, and G. M. Goodwin, 1974, *Experimental Neurology*, *42*, p. 226. Copyright 1974 by the Academic Press, reproduced by permission of the publisher.

Figure 8.27 From "Post-Tetanic Potentiation of Response in Monosynaptic Reflex Pathways of the Spinal Cord" by D.P.C. Lloyd. Reproduced from *The Journal of General Physiology,* 1949, vol. 33, p. 149 by copyright permission of The Rockefeller University Press.

Figure 8.29 Figure from "Prolongation of Twitch Potentiating Mechanism Throughout Muscle Fatigue and Recovery" by S. H. Garner, A. L. Hicks, and A. J. McComas, 1989, *Experimental Neurology*, *103*, p. 280. Copyright 1989 by Academic Press, reproduced by permission of the publisher.

Figure 9.4 From "Muscle Strength and Its Development: New Perspectives" by R. M. Enoka, 1988, *Sports Medicine, 6*, P. 149. Copyright 1988 by ADIS International Ltd. Adapted by permission.

Figure 9.5 Delitto A, Brown M, Strube MJ, Rose SJ, Lehman RC: Electrical Stimulation of Quadriceps Femoris in an Elite Weight Lifter: A Single Subject Experiment. *Int J Sports Med* 1989; 10: 187-197. Georg Thieme Verlag. Adapted by permission.

Figure 9.9 From "Specificity in Strength Training: A Review for the Coach and Athlete" by D.G. Sale and D. MacDougall, 1981, *Journal of Applied Sports Sciences, 6,* p. 90. Copyright 1981 by the Canadian Association of Sport Sciences. Adapted by permission.

Figure 9.11 From "Dynamic Variable Resistance and the Universal System" by F. Smith, 1982, *National Strength & Conditioning Association Journal, 4,* pp. 14-19. Copyright 1982 by the National Strength & Conditioning Association. Adapted by permission.

Figure 9.14 From "Changes in force, Cross-Sectional Area, and Neural Activation During Strength Training

Introduction

It is generally agreed that the Greek philosopher Aristotle (384–322 B.C.) was the first to systematically study human movement. Several of his treatises described the actions and geometric characteristics of muscles. Although the system Aristotle devised for explaining motion did contain some contradictions, his pioneering efforts laid the foundation for the subsequent work of Galen (131–201), Galileo (1564–1643), Borelli (1608–1679), Newton (1642–1727), and Marey (1830–1904). The work of these philosophers and scientists has led us to view human motion as the consequence of the interaction between muscles and the external forces imposed by the surroundings on the body. For as Aristotle wrote, "The animal that moves makes its change of position by pressing against that which is beneath it" (Aristotle, 1968, p. 489). This statement emphasizes that the study of movement must focus on (a) characterizing the physical interaction between an animal and its surroundings and (b) determining the way in which the animal organizes the physical interaction (pressing). Within this framework, the events we call movements can be regarded as the consequences of an interaction between a biological system and its surroundings. Several factors, including the following, influence this interaction (see also Higgins, 1985):

- The structure of the environment—shape and stability
- The field of external forces—orientation relative to gravity, movement speed
- The structure of the system—bony arrangement, net muscle activity, segmental organization of the body, scale or size, motor integration (such as the need to provide postural support)
- The role of the psychological state—degree of attentiveness, motivation
- The task to be performed—the framework for the organization of the movement

This perspective is captured by Higgins (1985): "Movement is inseparable from the structure supporting it and the environment defining it" (p. 144).

The goal of this text is to examine the neuromechanics of human movement; we define **neuromechanics** as the interaction between the nervous system and the mechanical properties of the body. The organization of the text is based on the Aristotelian model through a focus on the notion that movement involves an interaction between an animal and its surroundings—that is, the integration of concepts and principles from biology and physics. Accordingly, the text has been organized into three parts that examine the mechanical basis of movement (part I), develop a biological model with which to emphasize the control of movement (part II), and characterize the adaptive capabilities of the motor system (part III).

Part I, "The Force-Motion Relation," examines the *mechanical* basis of movement and discusses selected principles of physics as they relate to biomechanics and the study of movement.

Part II, "The Motor System," develops a *biological* model with which to emphasize the control of movement as an interaction between the nervous system and skeletal muscle.

Part III, "Adaptability of the Motor System," characterizes the acute adjustments and chronic adaptations of the motor system in response to various forms of physical activity.

The intent of this text is to provide a scientific basis for the study of human movement. Therefore, the ideas and principles presented in the text are discussed in scientific terms, and more attention is paid to precise definitions and measurements than is commonly done in everyday conversation. Also, this text uses metric units of measurement (appendix A), which are preferred because of their precise definitions and common usage in science.

Part I

The Force-Motion Relation

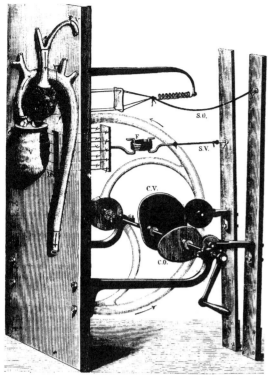

Reprinted from Marey, 1875.

M ovement has long been a source of fascination for individuals from numerous disciplines. But as the frontiers of science have expanded, it has become apparent that movement has as its basis complex biological and mechanical interactions. To encompass this breadth, many of us study movement from neurophysiological and biomechanical perspectives—an approach that is called a neuromechanical focus. Because **biomechanics** is defined as *the application of the principles of mechanics to the study of biological systems*, a neuromechanical focus combines concepts and principles from both biology (neurophysiology) and physics (biomechanics).

Part I describes the mechanical interaction between the world in which movement occurs and the body parts that are moved (biomechanics). The discussion includes an introduction to the terms and concepts commonly used to describe motion, a description of the various forces involved in human movement, and demonstrations of the biomechanical techniques used to analyze motion. Al-

though many of these aspects of the force-motion relation are illustrated with a variety of numerical examples that can be bewildering, the student is encouraged to focus on the systematic application of the various equations and methods.

Objectives

The goal of this text is to describe movement as the interaction of the human body with the physical world in which we live. In part I, the aim is to define the biomechanics of human movement. The specific objectives are

- to describe movement in precise, well-defined terms;
- to define force;
- to consider the role of force in movement; and
- to demonstrate the biomechanical techniques that are used to analyze movement.

Chapter 1

Reprinted from Marey, 1889.

Describing Motion

Although it is not difficult to appreciate the aesthetic qualities or the difficulty of a movement such as a triple-twisting, backward one-and-a-half somersault dive, it is another matter to describe the movement in precise terms. The accurate and precise description of human movement is accomplished by the use of the terms *position, velocity,* and *acceleration.* Such a description of motion, one that ignores the causes of motion, is known as a **kinematic** description. These kinematic terms are often used in everyday language, but without concern for or knowledge of their precise meanings. In biomechanics, as in any scientific endeavor, the observations and principles that emerge are only as good as the concepts and definitions on which they are based. The complexity of movement makes it important, indeed crucial, that our analyses rely on the rigorous definitions of these motion descriptors. To emphasize this need, we precede our discussion of kinematics with some reminders on the essentials of measuring physical quantities.

Measurement Rules

The scientific method requires that we agree on a measurement system and that we perform calculations with sufficient accuracy to have confidence in the result. The most commonly used measurement system is the metric system. The international metric system is known as the SI system (for *Le Système Internationale d'Unites*), comprising seven independent base units from which all other units of measurement are derived. The seven base units are length (m), mass (kg), time (s), electric current (A), temperature (K), amount of substance (mol), and luminous intensity (cd).

SI System

For part I of the book, which is about biomechanics, we are mainly interested in the fundamental quantities of length, mass, and time and their derivatives. **Length** is measured in meters (m), with one meter defined as the length of the path traveled by light in a vacuum during a time interval of 1/299,792,458 of a second. **Mass** is measured in kilograms (kg), with one kilogram defined as the quantity of matter contained in the reference preserved at the International Bureau of Weights and Measures at Sevres, France. **Time** is measured in seconds (s); one second is determined with an atomic clock as the duration of 9,192,631,770 periods of the radiation corresponding to the transition between the two hyperfine levels of the ground state of the cesium-133 atom.

In addition to the seven base units of measurement, there is a supplementary unit to measure angle. The unit of measurement is the radian (rad). As shown in figure 1.1, an angle is defined as the ratio of an arc length *(s)* to the radius of a circle (r). When the ratio has a value of 1, then the angle *(θ)* is equal to one radian (~57.3°). To become familiar with measuring angles in radians, recognize that a right angle is equal to 1.57 rad, that when the arm is extended the elbow joint is at an angle of 3.14 rad, and that one complete circle is 2π rad.

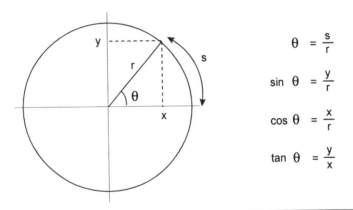

Figure 1.1 Definition of a radian.

Because it is convenient for numbers to range from 0.1 to 9999, prefixes (table 1.1) can be attached to the units of measurement to represent a smaller or larger amount of the unit. For example, to express long distances (e.g., marathon—26 miles, 385 yd), it is more economical to state the distances in thousands of meters. The prefix kilo (k) represents 1000; thus, 1 km = 1000 m. A marathon race, therefore, covers a distance of approximately 42.4 km. Similarly, prefixes referring to parts of a meter can be used for small distances. For example, there are 1,000,000 micrometers (μm) in one meter (1 μm = 0.000,001 m). The diameter of a muscle fiber is most appropriately expressed in micrometers, with a typical value of 55 μm.

Changing Units

Sometimes it is necessary to change the unit of measurement from another system (e.g., English units) to the SI system. Appendix A lists SI units and a number of common conversion factors for this purpose, and appendix B lists all the conversion factors. To convert a quantity from one measurement system to another, treat the units as arithmetic quantities. For example, to convert your height (say 5 ft 8 in.) to SI units, get the conversion factor from appendix B and then perform the conversion:

$$(68 \text{ in.}) \cdot \left(\frac{0.0254 \text{ m}}{1 \text{ in.}} \right) = 1.73 \text{ m}$$

Table 1.1 Prefixes Used With SI Units of Measurement

Prefix	Symbol	Power		
yetta	Y	1,000,000,000,000,000,000,000,000	=	10^{24}
zetta	Z	1,000,000,000,000,000,000,000	=	10^{21}
exa	E	1,000,000,000,000,000,000	=	10^{18}
peta	P	1,000,000,000,000,000	=	10^{15}
tera	T	1,000,000,000,000	=	10^{12}
giga	G	1,000,000,000	=	10^{9}
mega	M	1,000,000	=	10^{6}
kilo	k	1,000	=	10^{3}
hecto	h	100	=	10^{2}
deca	d	10	=	10^{1}
—	—	1	=	10^{0}
deci	d	0.1	=	10^{-1}
centi	c	0.01	=	10^{-2}
milli	m	0.001	=	10^{-3}
micro	μ	0.000,001	=	10^{-6}
nano	n	0.000,000,001	=	10^{-9}
pico	p	0.000,000,000,001	=	10^{-12}
femto	f	0.000,000,000,000,001	=	10^{-15}
atto	a	0.000,000,000,000,000,001	=	10^{-18}
zepto	z	0.000,000,000,000,000,000,001	=	10^{-21}
yocto	y	0.000,000,000,000,000,000,000,001	=	10^{-24}

Similarly, for converting a speed from miles per hour (mph) to meters per second (m/s), the conversion would proceed as follows:

$$(65 \text{ mph}) \cdot \left(\frac{1 \text{ h}}{3600 \text{ s}}\right) \cdot \left(\frac{1609 \text{ m}}{1 \text{ mile}}\right) = 29.1 \text{ m / s}$$

The advantage of using these procedures is that you will be less likely to invert a conversion factor if you pay attention to canceling units. If you are not familiar with SI units, then become acquainted by remembering reference values (e.g., height, weight) rather than memorizing conversion factors. For example, to judge whether or not a movement is fast, compare the speed of the movement to the average speed (10 m/s) of a person who runs 100 m in 10 s. Similarly, remember your height in meters as a reference for distance and your body mass in kilograms as a standard for mass.

When converting units of measurement for area, remember that the conversion factor must be squared. For example, to convert cm^2 to m^2, visualize a square that has sides of 1 m in length, which means 100 cm along each side. The area of the square is $100 \times 100 \text{ cm}^2$ or 1 m^2. Thus, there are 10,000 cm^2 in 1 m^2; that is, 1 $m^2 = 100^2 \text{ cm}^2$. Similarly, when converting units of measurement for volume, the conversion factor must be raised to a power of three.

Accuracy and Significant Figures

When we measure a physical property of an object, we obtain an estimate of its true value. The closeness of the estimate to the true value indicates the **accuracy** of the measurement. The accuracy depends on the resolution of the measurement device. For example, if we measure the body mass of an individual whose actual mass is 79.25 kg, then we need a scale that can measure one-hundredths of a kilogram to get an accurate estimate. The digits in a number that indicate the accuracy of a measurement are known as the **significant figures.** The number 79.25 has four significant figures, 79.3 has three, and 79 has two. In biomechanics, it is common to use three significant figures for most measurements.

For performing calculations, two practices concerning significant figures are usually followed. First, for adding or subtracting, the number of digits to the right of the decimal point in the answer should be the same as for the term in the calculation that has the least number of digits to the right of the decimal point. Similarly, for multiplying or dividing, the answer should have the same number of significant figures as the least-accurate term in the calculation. Second, when calculations involve small differences, greater accuracy is required in order to estimate the difference to three significant figures. For example, if one group of subjects took 1.2503 s to perform a movement and another group took 1.2391 s, then the difference between the two groups would be 0.0112 s. To find the difference between the two groups to three significant figures (0.0112), it was necessary to measure movement time to five significant figures.

Motion Descriptors

Movement involves the shift from one position to another. It can be described in terms of the size of the shift (displacement) or the rate at which it occurs (velocity and acceleration).

The **position** of an object refers to its location in space relative to some baseline value or axis. For example, the term *3-m diving board* indicates the position of the board above the waterline. Similarly, the height of a high-jump bar is specified relative to the ground; the position of the finish line in a race is indicated with respect to the start; the third and fifth positions in ballet refer to the position of one foot relative to the other; and so on. When an object experiences a change in position, it has been displaced and **motion** has occurred. Motion cannot be detected instantaneously; rather detection relies on comparison of the object's position at one instant in time with its position at another instant. *Motion, therefore, is an event that occurs in space and time.*

When an object is described as experiencing a **displacement**, the reference is to the spatial (space) element of motion, that is, the change in position of the object. Alternatively, an account of both the spatial and temporal (time) elements of motion involves the term *velocity* or *speed*. Velocity tells how fast and in what direction, whereas speed defines how fast. Because it has both magnitude and direction, **velocity** is a vector quantity that defines the change in position with respect to time. It indicates how rapidly the change in position occurred and the direction in which it took place. **Speed** is simply the magnitude of the velocity vector and, as such, does not concern the direction of the displacement. Because displacement refers to a change in position, velocity can be described as the time rate (derivative) of displacement. In calculus terminology, velocity is the derivative of position with respect to time.

Figure 1.2 represents two observations, separated in time by 3 s, of the vertical position of an object above some baseline value. The change in vertical position over this 3-s period is 2 m; therefore, the rate of change in position is 2 m in 3 s, that is, 2 m/3 s or 0.67 m/s. Thus the average velocity of the object moving from position 1 to position 2 is 0.67 m/s, where m/s refers to meters per second (this unit of measurement can also be expressed as $m \cdot s^{-1}$). Stated more explicitly,

$$velocity = \frac{\Delta \text{ position}}{\Delta \text{ time}} \qquad (1.1)$$

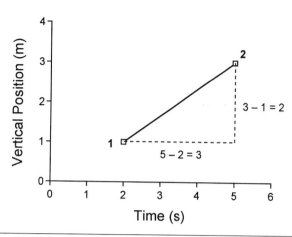

Figure 1.2 A position-time graph.

where Δ (delta) indicates a *change* in some parameter. Graphically, velocity refers to the slope of the position-time graph. Because a line graph (such as figure 1.2) depicts the relation between two (or sometimes more) variables, *a change in the **slope** of the line as it becomes more or less steep indicates a change in the relation between the variables.* The slope of the line is determined numerically by subtracting an initial-position value from some final position (Δ position) and dividing the change in position by the amount of time it took for the change to occur (Δ time). Slope, therefore, refers to the rate of change in a variable such that the steeper the slope, the greater the rate of change; and conversely, the lesser the slope, the slower the rate of change.

Throughout this text, many concepts are presented in the form of graphs. Typically, a graph shows the relation between at least two variables. Figure 1.2, for example, shows the relation between position and time. The relation can be indicated as the line, or data points, plotted on the graph. The main feature of a graph is to show the trend or pattern of the relation between the variables; more precise quantitative data are presented as tables or sets of numerical values. In evaluating a graph, first determine the variables involved (i.e., those on the axes) and then examine the relation between the variables. The relation between position and time in figure 1.2 is relatively straightforward; it can be represented by a single measurement, the slope of the line.

Vertical displacement can vary not only in *magnitude* (i.e., size) but also in *direction* (i.e., up-down). Figure 1.3 illustrates some of these alternatives by showing the position of an object at five instances in time. Use of Equation 1.1 produces velocities of 0.75, 1.50, 0, and –1.00 m/s for movement of the object from position 1 to 2, from position 2 to 3, from position 3 to 4, and from position 4 to 5, respectively. These values are plotted in figure 1.4. The steeper the slope of the position-time graph (e.g., position 2 to 3 = 1.50 m/s vs. position 1 to 2 = 0.75 m/s), the greater the velocity (figure 1.4). Conversely, a downward slope (e.g., position 4 to 5) indicates a negative velocity. The absence of a change in position (e.g., position 3 to 4) represents a zero velocity (i.e., no change in position). This example illustrates an important point about velocity: when the sign of the velocity value (positive, negative, or zero) changes, the movement has changed direction. Furthermore, when the direction of a movement changes, the velocity-time graph must pass through zero. Figure 1.4 indicates that an object initially moved in one direction (arbitrarily called the positive direction—note the positive slope in figure 1.3), then was stationary (zero velocity), and finally moved in the other direction (negative slope). Because velocity has both magnitude and direction, it is a vector quantity.

It is not sufficient to describe motion only in terms of the occurrence and rate of a displacement. For example, a ball held 1.23 m above the ground and dropped will reach the ground 0.5 s later. The change in position is 1.23 m, and the average velocity is 2.46 m/s (i.e., 1.23 m/0.5 s). But the ball does not travel with a constant velocity; the velocity changes over time. Starting

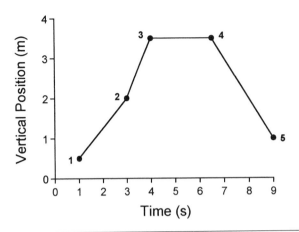

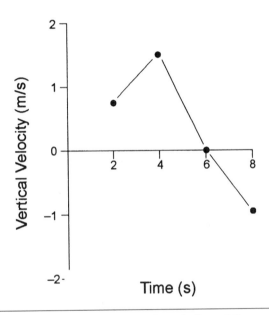

Figure 1.3 The variation in velocity associated with unequal changes in magnitude and direction in a position-time graph.

Figure 1.4 Average velocities of the displacements shown in figure 1.3.

with a zero velocity at release, the speed of the ball increases to a value of 4.91 m/s just prior to contact with the ground. This rate of change in velocity is referred to as **acceleration;** that is, acceleration is the derivative of velocity with respect to time or the second derivative of position with respect to time. The acceleration that the ball experiences while it falls is constant and has a value of 9.81 m/s². If the velocity of an object is measured in meters per second (m/s), then acceleration indicates the change in meters per second each second (m/s²). Consequently,

$$\text{acceleration} = \frac{\Delta \text{ velocity}}{\Delta \text{ time}} \qquad (1.2)$$

Because velocity is defined as the change in position with respect to time, velocity can be represented graphically as the slope of the position-time graph. Similarly, acceleration can be indicated as the slope of the velocity-time graph. For example, suppose we relabel figure 1.3 as a vertical velocity-time graph. If point 2 has the coordinates of 2.0 m/s and 3 s and point 3 has the coordinates of 3.5 m/s and 4 s, the rate of change from point 2 to point 3—the acceleration—can be calculated with Equation 1.2 as follows:

$$\text{acceleration} = \frac{3.5 - 2.0}{4 - 3} \frac{m/s}{s}$$

$$= 1.5 \text{ m/s/s (or m/s}^2 \text{ or m·s}^{-2})$$

Similarly, the acceleration from points 1 to 2, from points 3 to 4, and from points 4 to 5 is 0.75, 0, and –0.83 m/s^2, respectively. As with velocity, acceleration can have both magnitude and direction and hence is a vector quantity.

The acceleration experienced by the ball when it is dropped from a height of 1.23 m is due to the gravitational attraction between two masses, planet Earth and the ball. The force of **gravity** produces a constant acceleration of approximately 9.81 m/s^2 at sea level; this is usually written as –9.81 m/s^2 to indicate the downward direction. In general, an object acted upon by a force will be accelerated. A constant force (i.e., gravity) applied to an unsupported object produces a constant acceleration; conversely, the absence of a force means that the object is at rest or is traveling at a constant velocity (i.e., no acceleration). Because acceleration can be depicted as the slope of the velocity-time graph, it should be possible to visualize the shape of the velocity-time graph when an object is accelerating and when it is not. When the object accelerates, the slope of the velocity-time graph is nonzero. Conversely, when the object does not accelerate, the velocity-time graph has a zero slope.

Example 1.1
Kinematics of the 100-m Sprint

As an example of the relations among position, velocity, and acceleration, consider the kinematics of a person running the 100 m sprint as fast as possible. When a person performs this event, the displacement (the horizontal difference in position between the start and the finish) is 100 m. To describe the kinematics of the performance, however, we need to determine the position of the runner, for example, by the location of the hip joint, at various points in time during the race. One way to do this is to videotape the runner. If the frame rate of the video camera is set at 10 frames per second, then we can determine the position of the runner every 100 ms during the race. If the person runs the 100 m in 10.8 s, we will have about 109 measurements of horizontal position along the 100-m track, each at a known point in time. We can then plot these data as a position-time graph.

In a position-time graph, the change in position between any two consecutive data points represents the displacement that occurs during the selected interval. Is the displacement of the runner for each time interval during a 100-m race constant? If it were, then the shape of the position-time graph would be a straight line. The data in figure 1.5*a* show that the distance-time relation is not quite a straight line, especially at the beginning of the race. This deviation from linearity is amplified in the velocity- and acceleration-time graphs, which are derived from the distance-time graph.

From figure 1.3, we know that the slope of the position-time graph tells us about the velocity of the runner. Before we determine velocity, however, think about how you would expect the velocity of the runner to change during the race. It seems reasonable to expect that at the beginning of the race the runner's velocity would increase from zero to some maximum value that the runner would attempt to sustain. Look now at the position-time data in figure 1.5*a:* the slope starts off low, then increases, and finally becomes constant. With the application of Equation 1.1 to each interval, we can determine the velocity-time data for the runner and then graph these data in figure 1.5*b*. Similarly, we can derive the

(continued)

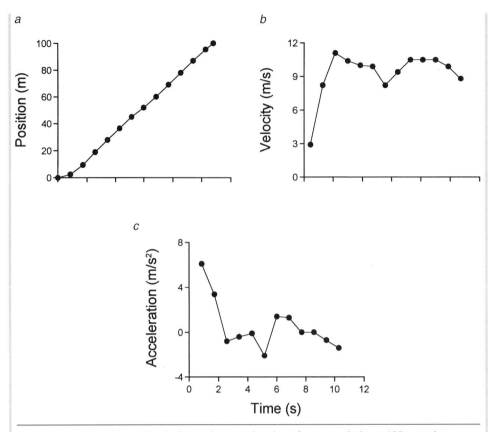

Figure 1.5 *(a)* Position, *(b)* velocity, and *(c)* acceleration of a runner during a 100-m sprint.

acceleration-time graph for the runner. The expected shape of the graph can be estimated from the slope of the velocity-time graph. When velocity changes a lot in an interval, then the runner's acceleration is relatively large for that interval. Conversely, when there is no change in velocity in an interval, the runner does not accelerate. On the basis of Equation 1.2, the acceleration-time data for each interval can be determined and graphed as in figure 1.5c.

Constant Acceleration

When acceleration is constant, motion can be described with some simple equations. These equations can be used to find the velocity of an object or the distance it has moved after it has experienced a certain amount of acceleration. From the elementary definitions of velocity (Equation 1.1) and acceleration (Equation 1.2), we can derive algebraic expressions involving time *(t)*, position *(r)*, velocity *(v)*, and acceleration *(a)*. In these equations of motion, v_i and v_f refer to initial and final velocities, respectively, at the beginning and end of selected time intervals; r_i and r_f similarly refer to the initial and final positions for each interval; and *t* indicates the duration of the interval. Because acceleration is constant, the average $(\bar{a})$ and instantaneous *(a)* values are the same and yield the following:

$$a = \frac{\Delta \text{ velocity}}{\Delta \text{ time}}$$

$$a = \frac{v_f - v_i}{t}$$

$$v_f = v_i + at \tag{1.3}$$

For example, when a ball is dropped from a height of 1.23 m, it will reach the ground 0.5 s later with a final velocity of –4.9 m/s. According to Equation 1.3, the variables that influence final velocity are the initial velocity (v_i) of the ball, its acceleration (a), and the duration of the fall (t). In this example, v_i is zero, a is the acceleration due to gravity (–9.81 m/s²), and t is 0.5 s. Suppose you want to determine the final velocity of a pitched baseball as it crosses the plate. What would you need to know? As with the ball-drop example, we would need to know v_i, a, and t. The major difficulty would be in determining a, because other forces, in addition to gravity, influence the motion of the ball and cause a to vary as a function of time. Under such conditions, we can determine a by deriving it numerically from film or video images of a movement. Alternatively, a can be measured directly with an instrument known as an accelerometer.

We can use a similar approach to determine how far an object will be displaced (Δr) after a given amount of acceleration. The equation is derived from our definition of velocity,

$$\text{average velocity} = \frac{\Delta \text{ position}}{\Delta \text{ time}}$$

$$\frac{v_f + v_i}{2} = \frac{r_f - r_i}{t}$$

Substitute Equation 1.3 for v_f:

$$r_f - r_i = \left(\frac{v_i + at + v_i}{2}\right) t$$

$$r_f - r_i = \left(\frac{2v_i + at}{2}\right) t$$

$$r_f - r_i = v_i t + \tfrac{1}{2} at^2 \tag{1.4}$$

This equation indicates that the change in position (displacement) of an object depends on three variables: its initial velocity (v_i), the acceleration (a) it experiences, and time (t). This relation can be used to determine the change in position of an object during a movement. For example, consider an individual who dives off a 10-m tower; by varying the value of t from 0 to 1.5 s in 0.1-s increments, we can determine the change in position $(r_f - r_i)$ for each 0.1-s interval and thereby obtain the trajectory (position-time graph) of the diver during the performance. The initial velocity of the diver is zero so that Equation 1.4 reduces to

$$r_f - r_i = \tfrac{1}{2} at^2$$

for this problem. If we assume that the effects of air resistance are so small that we can ignore them, then the acceleration is simply that due to gravity and is constant during the dive. We can determine the set of position-time data (as in table 1.2) that represents the trajectory of the diver by doing a number of calculations using Equation 1.4 and incrementing the value of t each time by 0.1 s.

In a similar way we can derive an equation to determine the final velocity as a function of displacement (Equation 1.5) rather than time (Equation 1.3).

$$\text{average velocity} = \frac{\Delta \text{ position}}{\Delta \text{ time}}$$

$$\frac{v_f + v_i}{2} = \frac{r_f - r_i}{t}$$

In this expression, t is unknown, so we rearrange Equation 1.3 to express t as the dependent variable $[t = (v_f - v_i)/a]$ and substitute for t.

Table 1.2 Calculation of Velocity and Acceleration From a Set of Position-Time Data

	Position (m)	Time (s)	Velocity (Δ position/Δ time) (m/s)	Acceleration (Δ velocity/Δ time) (m/s²)
1	0.00	0.000		
		0.050	(0.59 – 0.00)/(0.100 – 0.000) = 5.9	
2	0.59	0.100		(3.6 – 5.9)/(0.150 – 0.050) = –23.0
		0.150	(0.95 – 0.59)/(0.200 – 0.100) = 3.6	
3	0.95	0.200		(1.0 – 3.6)/(0.255 – 0.150) = –34.7
		0.225	(1.00 – 0.95)/(0.250 – 0.200) = 1.0	
4	1.00	0.250		(–1.0 – 1.0)/(0.275 – 0.225) = –40.0
		0.275	(0.95 – 1.00)/(0.300 – 0.250) = –1.0	
5	0.95	0.300		(–3.6) – [–1.0])/(0.350 – 0.275) = –34.7
		0.350	(0.59 – 0.95)/(0.400 – 0.300) = –3.6	
6	0.59	0.400		(–5.9 – [–3.6])/(0.450 – 0.350) = –23.0
		0.450	(0.00 – 0.59)/(0.500 – 0.400) = –5.9	
7	0.00	0.500		(–5.9 – [–5.9])/(0.550 – 0.450) = 0.0
		0.500	(–5.9 – 0.00)/(0.600 – 0.500) = –5.9	
8	–0.59	0.600		(–3.6 – [–5.9])/(0.650 – 0.550) = 23.0
		0.650	(–0.95 – [–0.59])/(0.700 – 0.600) = –3.6	
9	–0.95	0.700		(–1.0 – [–3.6])/(0.725 – 0.650) = 34.7
		0.725	(–1.00 – [–0.95])/(0.750 – 0.700) = –1.0	
10	–1.00	0.750		(1.0 – [–1.0])/(0.775 – 0.725) = 40.0
		0.775	(–0.95 – [–1.00])/(0.800 – 0.750) = 1.0	
11	–0.95	0.800		(3.6 – 1.0)/(0.850 – 0.775) = 34.7
		0.850	(–0.59 – [–0.95])/(0.900 – 0.800) = 3.6	
12	–0.59	0.900		(5.9 – 3.6)/(0.950 – 0.850) = 23.0
		0.950	(0.00 – [–0.59])/(1.000 – 0.900) = 5.9	
13	0.00	1.000		

$$\frac{v_f + v_i}{2} = \frac{r_f - r_i}{(v_f - v_i)/a}$$

$$\frac{v_f + v_i}{2} = (r_f - r_i)\frac{a}{v_f + v_i}$$

$$2a(r_f - r_i) = (v_f + v_i)(v_f - v_i)$$

$$2a(r_f - r_i) = (v_f^2 - v_i^2)$$

$$v_f^2 = v_i^2 + 2a(r_f - r_i) \qquad (1.5)$$

When the initial velocity for an interval is zero, such as for the object beginning at rest, then the equations can be simplified:

$$v_f = at$$

$$r_f - r_i = \tfrac{1}{2}at^2$$

$$v_f^2 = 2a(r_f - r_i)$$

Example 1.2
Penalty Kick in Soccer

When a player takes a penalty kick in soccer, the goalie stands stationary in the middle of the goal (7.32 m wide) with the ball placed on the penalty spot (11 m in front of the goal). Suppose that a player makes a penalty kick such that the ball leaves her foot with an initial velocity of 63 mph and travels along the ground into the goal just inside the goalpost with a final velocity of 54 mph.

A. What are the initial velocity and the final velocity of the ball in SI units?

$$v_i = 63 \text{ mph} \times 0.447 \ \frac{\text{m/s}}{\text{mph}} = 28.2 \text{ m/s}$$

$$v_f = 54 \text{ mph} \times 0.447 \ \frac{\text{m/s}}{\text{mph}} = 24.1 \text{ m/s}$$

B. What is the length of the path traveled by the ball from the penalty spot to the goal?

$$\Delta r = \sqrt{\left(\frac{7.32}{2}\right)^2 + 11^2}$$

$$\Delta r = 11.6 \text{ m}$$

C. What is the average acceleration of the ball between the initial and final velocities?

$$v_f^2 = v_i^2 + 2a(r_f - r_i)$$

$$a = \frac{v_f^2 - v_i^2}{2(\Delta r)}$$

$$a = \frac{24.1^2 - 28.2^2}{2 \times 11.6}$$

$$a = -9.07 \text{ m}/\text{s}^2$$

D. How much time does the goalie have to reach the ball from the moment it leaves the player's foot until it enters the goal?

$$\text{average velocity} = \frac{\Delta r}{\Delta t}$$

$$t = \frac{\Delta r}{\bar{v}}$$

$$t = \frac{11.6}{\left(\dfrac{28.2 + 24.1}{2}\right)}$$

$$t = 0.444 \text{ s}$$

Example 1.3
Calculation of Velocity and Acceleration

Kinematic analyses are usually based on a set of position-time data that are obtained with a recording device such as a movie camera or a video camera. A film or video record of a movement represents a set of still images (frames) that are subsequently projected individually onto a measuring device; the locations of selected landmarks with respect to some reference are then determined. The instrument used in this procedure, called a **digitizer,** is capable of determining the *x-y* coordinates of the selected landmarks. Once we have a set of position-time data, we can use Equations 1.1 and 1.2 to determine the average velocity and acceleration between each position measurement. Table 1.2 provides an example of this procedure.

The 13 position values listed in table 1.2, each recorded at a different instant in time, represent the vertical path that an object travels over a 1-s interval. The object rises above an initial position (0.0 m) to a height of 1.0 m before being displaced by an equal amount (–1.0 m) below the original position and finally returning to 0.0 m. We calculate the velocity of the object during this motion by applying Equation 1.1 to the intervals of time for which position information is available. For example, from table 1.2 we can select the intervals of 0.0 to 1.0 s, 0.0 to 0.25 s, or 0.0 to 0.1 s. If we apply Equation 1.1 to each of the intervals, the average velocity for each interval will be

$$0.0 - 1.0 = \frac{0.0 - 0.0}{1.0 - 0.0}$$

$$= 0 \text{ m/s}$$

$$0.0 - 0.25 = \frac{1.0 - 0.0}{1.25 - 0.0}$$

$$= 4 \text{ m/s}$$

$$0.0 - 0.1 = \frac{0.59 - 0.0}{0.1 - 0.0}$$

$$= 5.9 \text{ m/s}$$

Similarly, if we measure the position only at the times of 0.0, 0.5, and 1.0 s, we will get the impression that the object has not moved. Clearly, the smaller the intervals of time we measure, the more closely the calculated velocity will match that experienced by the object. However, economy of effort and measurement error suggest that we do not want to measure too frequently and that there must be some intermediate value. Most human movements can be measured adequately with frame rates that range from 50 to 100 frames per second, which correspond to intervals of 0.1 to 0.2 s between consecutive data points.

Table 1.2 shows velocity as determined for each interval between the position data. For example, the displacement during the first interval (0.59 – 0.0 = 0.59 m) was divided by the time elapsed during the interval (0.1 – 0.0 = 0.1 s) to yield the velocity for that interval (0.59/0.1 = 5.9 m/s). The calculated value (5.9 m/s) represents the *average* velocity over that interval and consequently is recorded at the midpoint in time of the interval (0.05 s). Similarly, the first acceleration value (–23.0 m/s²), which was determined with Equation 1.2, is listed at the midpoint in time (0.10 s) of the first velocity interval (0.05 to 0.15). By this procedure *the average value of velocity is determined for each position interval, and the average acceleration is calculated for each velocity interval.* Thus, from a set of 13 position-time observations, we calculate 12 velocity-time and 11 acceleration-time values.

The graphical relation between a motion descriptor (e.g., position or velocity) and its rate of change has already been mentioned. Further evidence of these relations is provided in table 1.2. When position increases (positions 1 to 4 and 10 to 13), velocity is positive; when position decreases (positions 4 to 10), velocity is negative. A similar dependency exists between the slope (increase or decrease) of velocity and the sign of the acceleration values. These relations are shown in figure 1.6.

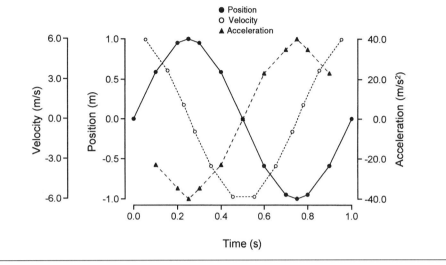

Figure 1.6 Graph of the kinematic data derived in table 1.2.

Up and Down

When an object is thrown, kicked, or hit into the air, or when a human jumps into the air, the motion of the center of mass is predictable and is characterized by a set of rules that are derived from the equations of motion (Equations 1.3, 1.4, and 1.5). Such airborne objects are often referred to as **projectiles.** Projectile motion has the following characteristics:

■ The effect of gravity is to cause the trajectory to deviate from a straight line into a curved path that can be described as a **parabola.**

■ When the release height and landing occur at the same level, the time taken for the object to reach the peak of its trajectory will be identical to the time taken to go from the peak to the landing.

■ The vertical velocity of the projectile (v_v) will change from an upward value (positive) at release, to zero at the peak of the trajectory (when it changes direction), to downward (negative) when the object returns to the ground.

■ The only significant force that the object experiences while in the air will be that due to gravity, and this will cause a vertical acceleration of –9.81 m/s².

■ Because there is no force acting in the horizontal direction, the horizontal acceleration of the object will be zero, which means that the object's horizontal velocity (v_h) will remain constant. Consequently, the horizontal distance traveled by the object can be determined as the product of horizontal velocity and the flight time of the object.

■ The flight time will depend on the vertical velocity at release and the height of release above the landing surface.

Although the trajectory of an object is parabolic, the shape of the parabola depends on the velocity—both magnitude and direction—at release. Three different parabolas are shown in figure 1.7. On the basis of the rules just presented, we can describe the velocity vector at selected instances throughout the trajectory; this is shown for the javelin in figure 1.7. Its trajectory is characterized by a constant horizontal velocity, a positive vertical velocity on the upward phase, a negative vertical velocity on the downward phase, and zero vertical velocity at the peak of the trajectory. The vertical velocity has the greatest absolute value at the beginning and the end of the flight. These features apply to such projectiles as a shot during the shot put, a gymnast performing a vault, a high jumper clearing the bar, and a basketball player performing a jump shot.

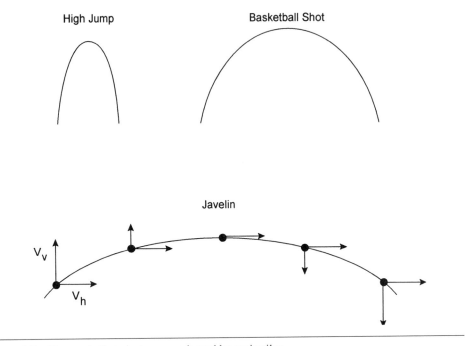

Figure 1.7   The parabolic trajectory experienced by projectiles.

Example 1.4
Trajectory of a Ball

Let us consider a ball thrown at an angle of 1.05 rad with respect to the horizontal from a height of 2.5 m above the ground, with a resultant velocity along the line of projection of 6 m/s. For solving problems of projectile motion, it is convenient to begin with a sketch of initial conditions (figure 1.8).

A. How long does the ball take to reach its highest point? The trajectory is parabolic, so the ball will continue going up until the vertical velocity has a value of zero (where $\bar{a}$ = average acceleration and the initial vertical velocity = 6 sin 1.05 = 5.2 m/s).

$$\bar{a} = \frac{\Delta v}{\Delta t}$$

$$\bar{a} = \frac{v_f - v_i}{t}$$

$$-9.81 = (0 - 5.2)/t$$

$$t = -5.2/-9.81$$

$$t = 0.53 \text{ s}$$

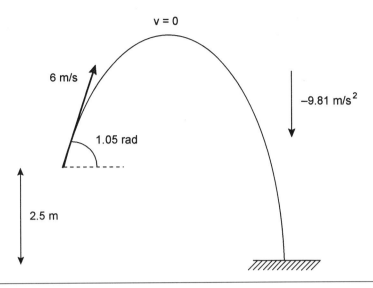

Figure 1.8   Initial conditions for the projectile motion of a ball.

B. How high (vertically) does the ball get? The height reached depends on the vertical component of the release velocity plus the height above the ground at which the ball is released. We already know the following: vertical velocity at release (5.2 m/s), vertical velocity at the peak of the trajectory (0 m/s), vertical acceleration (–9.81 m/s²), release height (2.5 m), and time to reach the peak (0.53 s). We also know that average velocity = $\bar{v}$.

$$\bar{v} = \frac{\Delta r}{\Delta t}$$

$$\frac{5.2 + 0}{2} = \frac{\Delta r}{0.53}$$

$$\Delta r = \frac{0.53(5.2 + 0)}{2}$$

$$\Delta r = 1.38 \text{ m}$$

Total height = Δr + release height

$$= 1.38 + 2.5$$

Height = 3.88 m

C. What is the vertical velocity of the ball just before it hits the ground? To answer this question, we consider the second part of the trajectory, from the peak down to contact with the ground. The initial velocity is 0 m/s, and the ball falls 3.88 m from the peak to the ground while it experiences an acceleration of –9.81 m/s², which enables us to use Equation 1.5:

$$v_f^2 = v_i^2 + 2a(\Delta r)$$

$$v_f^2 = 2 \times -9.81 \times 3.88$$

$$v_f^2 = -76.1$$

$$v_f = -8.73 \text{ m/s}$$

(Note that negative = downward.)

(continued)

D. How long does it take the ball to reach the ground from the peak? Because we know v_i, v_f, and a, we can determine the time taken for the ball to reach the ground by using Equation 1.3:

$$v_f = v_i + at$$

$$-8.73 = 0 + 9.81\,t$$

$$t = \frac{-8.73}{-9.81}$$

$$t = 0.89\ s$$

E. How long does the ball spend in flight?

$$t = t_{up} + t_{down}$$

$$t = 0.53 + 0.89$$

$$t = 1.42\ s$$

F. What horizontal distance does the ball travel (how far is it thrown)? In contrast to the previous calculations, this one uses the horizontal, as opposed to the vertical, information. Because we were given the velocity at release, we can determine the horizontal velocity at release ($v_i = 6 \cos 105 = 3$ m/s). We also know that in the absence of significant air resistance, the horizontal velocity is constant because it experiences no horizontal acceleration.

$$\bar{v} = \frac{\Delta r}{\Delta t}$$

$$\frac{v_i + v_f}{2} = \frac{\Delta r}{t}$$

$$\frac{3 + 3}{2} = \frac{\Delta r}{1.42}$$

$$\Delta r = 1.42 \times 3$$

$$\Delta r = 4.24\ m$$

This example demonstrates that the time of flight for a projectile depends on the vertical velocity at release (or takeoff) and the release height. The vertical velocity at release determines the height reached by the projectile and the time taken to reach the maximum height. Because parabolic trajectories are symmetrical, the time taken to return to the release height is identical to that taken to reach the peak point. If the landing height is different from the release height, however, we must also consider the time taken to travel this extra distance in determining the total flight time.

When the goal of a projectile event is to maximize the horizontal displacement, it is necessary to choose the correct combination of flight time (vertical velocity + release height) and horizontal velocity. This involves selecting the **optimum** angle of release (or takeoff). The necessary angle depends on the relative positions of the release and landing heights. When the release and landing heights are identical, then the optimum angle of release is 0.785 rad (45°). But when the landing height is lower than the release height, the optimum angle of projection is less than 0.785 rad. When the landing height is above the release height, the optimum angle of projection is greater than 0.785 rad. Furthermore, as the velocity of release increases for a particular release height, the more closely the optimum angle approaches 0.785 rad. Similarly, as release height increases while the release velocity remains constant, the lower (below 0.785 rad) the optimum angle of projection (Hay, 1993).

Example 1.5

Takeoff Angle in the Long Jump

An experienced athlete performing a long jump for maximum distance can achieve a take-off velocity of about 9.95 m/s. The takeoff angle *(θ)* used by the athlete will determine the maximum height achieved, the time spent in the air, and the horizontal distance (figure 1.9). If we assume that the takeoff and landing heights are approximately the same, then the equations for projectile motion can be rearranged to yield:

$$\text{Height} = \frac{1}{2a} \, (v_i \sin \theta)^2$$

$$\text{Flight time} = \frac{2}{a} \, (v_i \sin \theta)$$

$$\text{Distance} = \frac{2 \, v_i^2}{a} \, (\sin \theta) \, (\cos \theta)$$

where *a* is the acceleration due to gravity and v_i is the takeoff velocity. We can use these equations to plot the effect of takeoff angle on each of the variables. Figure 1.9 indicates that vertical height and flight time are maximum when the takeoff velocity is completely vertical (θ = 1.57 rad). However, the distance jumped is maximal at a takeoff angle of 0.785 rad.

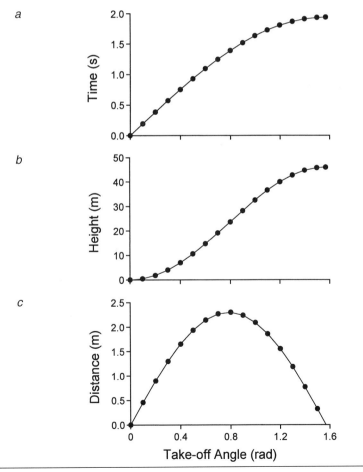

Figure 1.9 *(a)* Flight time, *(b)* vertical height, and *(c)* horizontal distance as a function of takeoff angle for the long jump.

Graphic Connections

Because velocity and acceleration are derived from position, the three measures are related when plotted on a graph. Figure 1.10 shows these connections based on the changes in thigh angle of a runner for one stride (defined as one complete cycle, from left foot toe-off to left foot toe-off in this example). Thigh angle is an **absolute angle** that is measured with respect to the right horizontal, and its measurement is indicated in the upper panel of the figure (the measured angle is for the limb with the filled-in shoe). The angle is measured in *radians* (1 rad = 57.3°), the SI unit for angle.

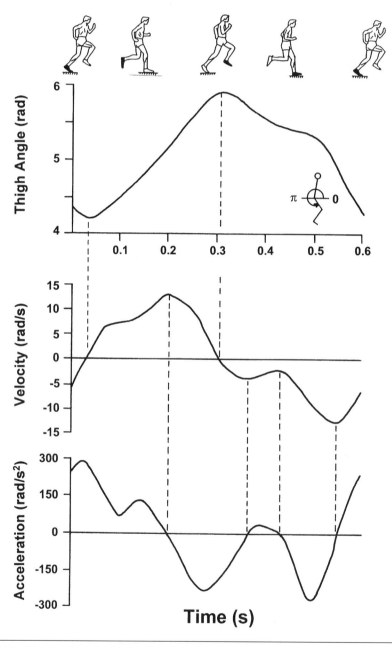

Figure 1.10 The angular velocity as a function of time can be graphically derived from the angular position-time graph, and the angular acceleration-time graph can be derived from the angular velocity-time graph.

To show these connections, we graph thigh angle as a function of time and then derive the velocity- and acceleration-time graphs. The first step is to identify the relative *minima* and *maxima* in the position-time graph. Any (and there may be several) peaks (maxima) and valleys (minima) in the curve should be noted. These points denote instants at which the rate of change has a value of zero. That is, for a small Δt at the peak or the valley the Δr is zero, which indicates that the slope of the graph is neither upward (positive) nor downward (negative) but zero. In figure 1.10, the thigh angle-time function has one minimum and one maximum. From these points of zero slope, and thus zero velocity, a perpendicular line is extended to the time axis of the velocity-time graph to mark the locations in time at which velocity is zero. In figure 1.10 these occur at about 0.03 and 0.30 s, respectively.

The second step in the derivation is to determine the slope of the position-time graph between these maxima and minima. The slope of the graph will be the same (i.e., positive or negative) between these points because, as points of zero velocity, they identify the location in time when the position-time curve changes its slope (i.e., changes direction). In each interval between the minima and maxima, the slope may become more or less steep, but it will remain either upward (positive) or downward (negative). In the thigh angle-time figure, there is one minimum and one maximum; there are therefore three such intervals (i.e., from the beginning of the movement to the minimum, from the minimum to the maximum, and from the maximum to the end of the movement). The slopes of the position-time graph associated with these intervals are negative, positive, and negative, respectively. Thus the velocity-time graph has values (positive or negative) similar to the slope of the thigh angle-time function for each interval. For example, for the first interval, from the beginning of the movement to the minimum, both the position-time slope and the velocity values are negative. Because a negative velocity value is associated with a downward position-time slope, the negative velocities in figure 1.10 indicate a *backward* rotation of the thigh (i.e., a reduction in the measured angle). In total, the velocity-time graph of figure 1.10 indicates two intervals of backward thigh rotation separated in time by an interval of forward thigh rotation. The variation in the magnitude of the velocity over time indicates how the speed of this rotation varies, whereas the sign (positive or negative) indicates the direction (forward or backward) of rotation.

The derivation of the acceleration-time relation from the velocity-time graph is accomplished by the same two-stage procedure: (a) identification of the relative minima and maxima and (b) determination of the slope during the identified intervals. From figure 1.10, the velocity-time curve contains four minima and maxima, and thus there are four instances at which the acceleration-time graph crosses zero. The resulting acceleration-time relation is a five-interval alternating positive-negative curve. The interpretation of an acceleration-time graph is generally more complicated than that for position- and velocity-time graphs. In figure 1.10, a positive acceleration indicates an acceleration of the thigh in the forward direction; during the first acceleration interval, the thigh rotates first backward and then forward (seen from the velocity-time graph), but throughout this interval the thigh accelerates in the forward direction. This example indicates that displacement and acceleration do not always act in the same direction. Furthermore, *it is not possible to tell the direction of acceleration from the direction of a movement.*

For example, consider the motion of a ball that a juggler tosses into the air and then catches. The motion of the ball is represented by a parabolic position-time graph in which position is represented as the vertical position above the juggler's hand. What is the shape of the acceleration-time graph? The answer is simple. We could determine the answer using the technique shown in figure 1.10; but an object in free fall, such as a ball tossed into the air, experiences a constant acceleration of -9.81 m/s^2. Although the ball moves up and down when tossed into the air, this displacement does not provide any intuitive clue about the direction of the acceleration that the ball experiences.

By the graphical technique outlined in this section, we are unable to know the precise magnitude of the rate of change in a variable. This procedure is **qualitative** in nature; it merely gives a positive or negative sign for the rate of change and possibly an approximate value. In contrast, table 1.2 indicates a **quantitative** approach by which we can more accurately determine the values of the derivatives. A qualitative analysis tells us what type or kind, whereas a quantitative analysis tells us how much.

Scalars and Vectors

Quantities that convey magnitude and direction are called **vectors:** for example, displacement, velocity, acceleration, force, momentum, and torque. Those variables that are defined by a magnitude only are called **scalars:** for example, mass, length, speed, time, temperature, and work. To distinguish between these two quantities, the variables that represent vectors are indicated in a bold font throughout the text. Vectors can be represented graphically as an arrow with a certain length and direction. The position vector (**r**) in figure 1.11*a*, for example, shows that an object is located 15 m from an origin with a direction of 0.4 rad relative to the horizontal. The direction of a vector is sometimes referred to as its **line of action** (figure 1.11*b*). As long as the magnitude of the vector remains constant, it can slide along its line of action without changing its mechanical action.

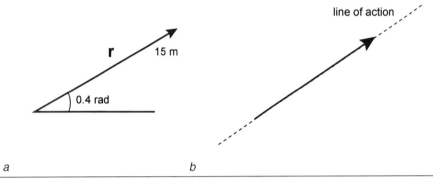

Figure 1.11   Characteristics of a position vector include *(a)* magnitude and direction, and *(b)* line of action.

Often in biomechanics we want to determine the net effect of several vectors or want to determine the effect of a vector in several different directions. These two procedures can be accomplished graphically with the **parallelogram law of combinations.** For example, figure 1.12 shows how we can find the net force (**F**$_r$) acting on an object due to the action of two forces (**F**$_p$ and **F**$_q$). This involves constructing a parallelogram with the vectors **F**$_p$ and **F**$_q$ and then drawing the diagonal of the parallelogram, which represents the resultant effect. Note that the tails (opposite the arrowheads) of the three vectors originate from the same point. The combination of two or more vectors into a single resultant vector is called **composition;** that is, the procedure is to compose the resultant. This association can be represented by the addition of the two vectors,

$$\mathbf{F_r} = \mathbf{F_p} + \mathbf{F_q}$$

The converse procedure, called **resolution,** is to take a vector and resolve it into one or more components. It is often useful, for example, to deal with vector components that are perpendicular to one another, such as in the *x* and *y* directions. Given a vector **V** (magnitude and direction), its *x* and *y* components can be determined using standard trig functions (figure 1.12):

$$V_y = V \sin \theta \qquad\qquad V_x = V \cos \theta$$

Conversely, if we are given the components V_x and V_y, we can determine the magnitude and the direction of the resultant *(V)* by the following relations:

$$V = \sqrt{V_x^{\,2} + V_y^{\,2}}$$

$$\theta = \tan^{-1} \frac{V_y}{V_x}$$

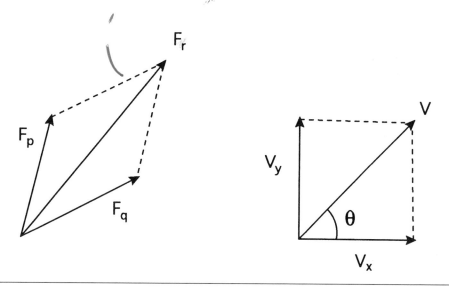

Figure 1.12 Vector parallelograms.

Example 1.6
Net Muscle Force

Figure 1.13 illustrates how composition is used to determine the resultant effect of coactivating different parts of the pectoralis major muscle. Figure 1.13*a* indicates the direction and magnitude of the force exerted by the clavicular $(F_{m,c})$ and sternal $(F_{m,s})$ portions of the pectoralis major muscle. Suppose that the clavicular component exerts a force of 224 N, which is directed at an angle of 0.55 rad above the horizontal, and that the sternal component has a magnitude of 251 N and acts 0.35 rad below the horizontal. To compose the resultant, we add these two components head to tail by sliding either one of the vectors along its line of action (figure 1.13*b*) and then joining the open ends (open tail to open head) to produce the resultant vector (figure 1.13*c*).

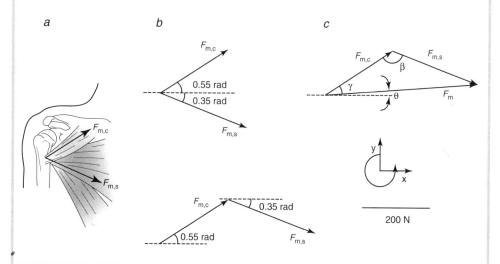

Figure 1.13 Geometric composition of the resultant muscle force (F_m) due to activation of both the clavicular $(F_{m,c})$ and sternal $(F_{m,s})$ components of the pectoralis major muscle. (*a*) Orientation of the two vectors; (*b*) graphic addition of the two vectors; and (*c*) calculation of the resultant vector.

(continued)

The magnitude of the resultant can be obtained by applying the law of cosines, which enables us to determine the length of one side of a triangle provided we know the length of the other two sides and the angle between them. The equation to determine the magnitude of F_m would be:

$$F_m^{\ 2} = F_{m,c}^{\ 2} + F_{m,s}^{\ 2} - (2 \times F_{m,c} \times F_{m,s} \times \cos \beta)$$

$$F_m = \sqrt{224^2 + 251^2 - (2 \times 224 \times 251 \times \cos 2.24)}$$

$$F_m = 428 \text{ N}$$

By applying the law of sines we can determine the magnitude of angle γ:

$$\frac{\sin \beta}{F_m} = \frac{\sin \gamma}{F_{m,s}}$$

$$\gamma = \sin^{-1}\left[F_{m,s} \times \frac{\sin \beta}{F_m} \right]$$

$$= \sin^{-1}\left[251 \times \frac{\sin 2.24}{4278} \right]$$

$$\gamma = 0.478 \text{ rad}$$

Because $F_{m,c}$ is at an angle of 0.55 rad with respect to the horizontal, the direction of F_m is

$$\theta = 0.55 - \gamma$$

$$\theta = 0.072 \text{ rad}$$

Right-Hand Coordinate System

Movement is a relative phenomenon; it involves the displacement of an object from one point in space to another point. To describe a movement, therefore, it is necessary to specify the location of the object at any point in time. This is typically done with a set of *xyz*-axes (figure 1.14). The *x, y,* and *z* directions are perpendicular to each other with the positive directions defined in the following way. Curl the fingers of your right hand in the direction of rotating the positive *x*-axis onto the positive *y*-axis; then the direction of your extended thumb indicates the positive *z*-axis. For this reason, this configuration of the *xyz*-axes is known as the *right-hand coordinate system.*

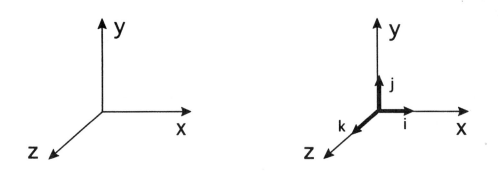

Figure 1.14   Right-hand coordinate system and unit vectors.

To specify a vector in the right-hand coordinate system, we state that it has so many units in the x direction, so many in the y direction, and so many in the z direction. This idea is abbreviated with the use of the terminology **i, j,** and **k,** which are known as unit vectors. The symbol **i** represents the x direction, **j** refers to the y direction, and **k** indicates the z direction. A vector described by the expression $-286\mathbf{i} + 812\mathbf{j} + 61\mathbf{k}$ has a component of 286 units in the negative x direction, another component of 812 units in the y direction, and a component of 61 units in the z direction. The magnitude of the vector can be determined with the Pythagorean theorem:

$$V = \sqrt{(-286)^2 + 812^2 + 61^2}$$
$$V = 863$$

Coordinate systems such as the xyz-axes can be fixed in space or can be fixed to an object that moves in three-dimensional space. In biomechanics, we often use both types of coordinate systems. When describing gross movements, however, we typically use an xyz system that is attached to the center of mass of the body with the y-axis going in the head-to-toes direction, the x-axis going front to back, and the z-axis going side to side. Movements can occur in any of the three planes *(x-y, x-z,* or *y-z)* or about the three axes *(x, y,* and *z)*. The x-y plane is referred to as the **sagittal** plane, and it divides the body into right and left. The x-z plane is known as the **transverse** plane, and it divides the body into top and bottom. The y-z plane is described as the **frontal** plane, and it divides the body into front and back. The three axes are usually given functional names based on the type of movement that would be performed when a person rotated about the axis. On the basis of this convention, the x-axis is referred to as the **cartwheel** axis, the y-axis as the **twist** axis, and the z-axis as the **somersault** axis.

Vector Algebra

When describing physical systems and the interaction of their components, we often manipulate vectors in algebraic expressions. The addition and subtraction of vectors are simple procedures in that we add or subtract the **i, j,** and **k** terms separately. For example, let us add $\mathbf{F}_p$ and $\mathbf{F}_q$:

$$\mathbf{F}_p = 10\mathbf{i} + 28\mathbf{j} + 92\mathbf{k} \text{ and } \mathbf{F}_q = 3\mathbf{i} - 11\mathbf{j} + 46\mathbf{k}$$
$$\mathbf{F}_p + \mathbf{F}_q = (10 + 3)\mathbf{i} + (28 - 11)\mathbf{j} + (92 + 46)\mathbf{k}$$
$$\mathbf{F}_p + \mathbf{F}_q = 13\mathbf{i} + 17\mathbf{j} + 138\mathbf{k}$$

Multiplication, however, is a more involved procedure. Actually, there are two procedures: scalar products and vector products. (Although the procedures are more commonly known as *dot* and *cross* products, the terms *scalar* and *vector* seem more appropriate as they define the type of product.) The distinction between the two procedures, scalar (dot) and vector (cross) products, has to do with the character of the result, that is, whether it is a scalar or a vector quantity.

The definition of a **scalar product** is given by the expression

$$\mathbf{d}\cdot\mathbf{F} = dF \cos \theta \qquad (1.6)$$

The dot product (notice the dot between **d** and **F**) of the two vectors **d** and **F** is calculated as the magnitude of **d** *(d)* times the magnitude of **F** *(F)* multiplied by the cosine of the angle *(θ)* between the two vectors (figure 1.15*a*). This procedure gives the magnitude of **F** that is directed along **d** multiplied by the magnitude of *d*. The magnitude of **F** directed along **d** is shown in figure 1.15*b* as the base of the right triangle (i.e., the side that equals **F** cos *θ*). Thus the scalar product is just **d** times **F** cos *θ*.

The multiplication of vectors with the scalar product is appropriate for calculating scalar quantities. One example is the calculation of work, where work is defined as the product of force and displacement (distance). Both force and displacement are vectors. The rigorous

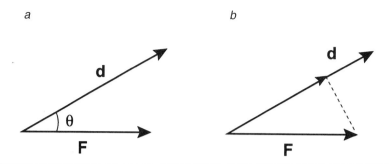

Figure 1.15   The scalar product of two vectors involves *(a)* determining how much of **F** acts in the same direction as **d** and *(b)* then multiplying the two terms.

definition of work (a scalar quantity derived by the scalar product) is that it equals the component of force in the direction of the displacement times the magnitude of the displacement.

Alternatively, when two vectors are multiplied and the product is a vector (magnitude and direction), the procedure is called the vector (cross) product. This is given by the expression

$$\mathbf{r} \times \mathbf{F} = rF \sin \theta \qquad (1.7)$$

which reads "**r** cross **F** is equal to the magnitude of **r** *(r)* times the magnitude of **F** *(F)* multiplied by the sine of the angle *(θ)* between the two vectors." This states that the magnitude of a vector product is equal to the product of two vector magnitudes and that the direction is along the axis about which the rotation of vector **r** onto vector **F** occurs (i.e., cross from **r** to **F**). This means that the direction of the product is always perpendicular to the plane that contains the other two vectors and is located at the base (intersection) of the two vectors. This relation is illustrated in figure 1.16.

Vector products can involve such combinations as position and force, position and angular velocity, and position and momentum. For example, the vector product of position **(r)** and force **(F)** is torque **(τ)**, as shown in figure 1.16. This product represents a rotary or angular force, whose magnitude depends on the size of the force and the distance (moment arm) of its line of action from the axis of rotation. The direction of the torque vector is along the axis about which the object would rotate due to the action of the force. That is, torque is equal to the product of force and the moment arm. For example, if a net muscle force and the distance to its line of action are located in the plane of this page, then the direction of the net muscle torque will be perpendicular to the page. In general, the direction of such a product can be either toward or away from you and depends on the directions of the two vectors that contributed to the product. Because it is difficult to show three-dimensional directions on a page, vectors that

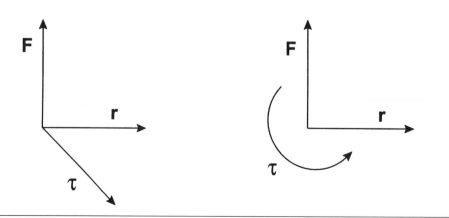

Figure 1.16   The vector product of **r** and **F** is the vector **τ**.

are perpendicular to the page are often drawn as curved arrows. Figure 1.16 shows torque (**τ**) drawn as a curved arrow, which the right-hand rule indicates as a vector that comes out of the page.

Linear and Angular Motion

In the preceding discussion, you may have noted that displacement was indicated with either of the two units of measurement, meters (m) or radians (rad); the distinction between the two is that of **linear** and **angular** motion, respectively. Linear motion refers to an equivalent displacement in space of all the parts of the object. Conversely, when all the parts of the object do not experience the same displacement (Δ position), the motion has included some rotation (angular displacement). A combination of linear **(translation)** and angular **(rotation)** motion in a single plane is called **planar** motion and involves rotation about a point that is itself moving. In most movements, our body segments undergo both linear and angular motion.

A *meter,* the unit of measurement for linear motion, is defined as the length of the path traveled by light in a vacuum during about one three-hundred thousandths of a second. A *radian* is the ratio of arc length to the radius of the circle (figure 1.1). When the arc length equals the radius, the ratio has a value of 1, and the object has rotated 1 rad (57.3°). For example, consider a discus throw by an athlete whose arm length from the shoulder to the discus has a value of 63 cm. As the arm rotates about a twist axis through the shoulder joint, the discus moves in a circular path. When the discus has moved along its path 63 cm (equal to the length of the arm and thus equal to the radius of the circle), the arm and the discus have been rotated through an angle of 1 rad.

The commonly used symbols and associated units of measurement for linear and angular position, velocity, and acceleration are outlined in table 1.3. As you can see, the symbols are usually Latin letters for linear terms and Greek letters for angular terms.

Angle-Angle Diagrams

In measuring human movement, we usually graph some variable (e.g., thigh angle, ball height) as a function of time. Because human movement is accomplished by the rotation of body segments about one another, it is often more instructive to examine the relation between two angles during a movement. Such graphs, called **angle-angle diagrams** (Cavanagh & Grieve, 1973; Marey, 1879), usually plot a **relative angle** (i.e., the angle between two adjacent body segments) against the absolute angle of a body segment (i.e., the angle relative to a reference in the surroundings).

Figure 1.17 shows two angle-angle diagrams for part of a weightlifting movement (the clean and jerk) in which the barbell was lifted from position 1 through position 10. The trunk-knee diagram shows that the movement comprises three distinct phases: (a) positions 1 to 5, slight

Table 1.3 Linear and Angular Symbols and the SI Units of Measurement

	Linear			Angular	
	Symbol		Unit	Symbol	Unit
	Scalar	Vector			
Position	r	**r**	m	θ (theta)	rad
Displacement	Δr	Δ**r**	m	$\Delta\theta$ (theta)	rad
Velocity	v	**v**	m/s	ω (omega)	rad/s
Acceleration	a	**a**	m/s^2	α (alpha)	rad/s^2

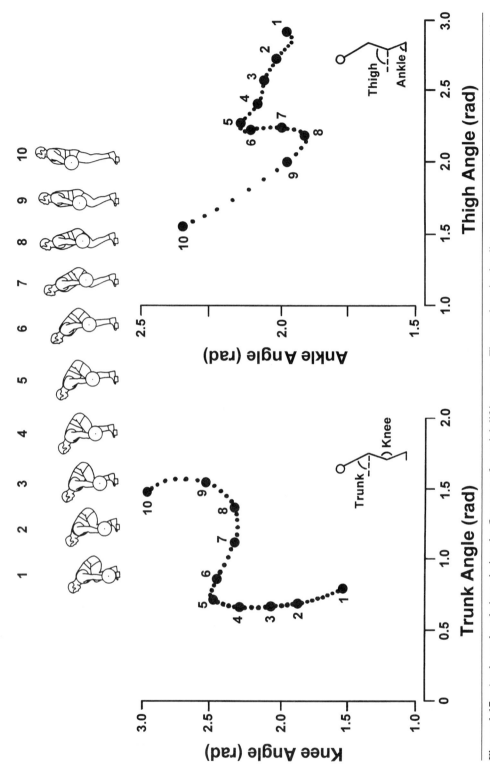

Figure 1.17 Angle-angle relations during the first part of a weightlifting event. The numbers in the diagrams correspond to the positions of the lifter indicated at the top of the figure.
Reprinted from Enoka, 1988.

forward rotation of the trunk and extension of the knee joint; (b) positions 5 to 8, backward rotation of the trunk and flexion of the knees; and (c) positions 8 to 10, some backward-forward trunk rotation and knee joint extension. Similarly, the thigh-ankle angle-angle diagram comprises three phases: (a) forward thigh rotation and ankle plantarflexion; (b) constant thigh angle and ankle dorsiflexion; and (c) forward thigh rotation and ankle plantarflexion. Examination of the phases composed of the numbered set of positions in figure 1.17 shows the extent to which the three phases for the two angle-angle diagrams coincide; the movement is accomplished by coordinated displacements about the joints of the leg. In figure 1.17 there is a constant 10-ms interval between each dot; so the greater the distance between the dots, the greater the velocity of movement.

Angular Kinematics

Because human movement typically involves both translation and rotation, it is necessary to know the relations between the linear and angular measures of position, velocity, and acceleration. When a rigid body of fixed length (r) rotates about a point from position 1 to position 2 (figure 1.18a), the displacement (s) experienced by the end of the rigid body is given by Equation 1.8:

$$s = r\theta \tag{1.8}$$

The linear velocity (v) of the end of the rigid body is determined as the rate of change in s with a direction that is tangent to the circular path.

$$\frac{\Delta s}{\Delta t} = \frac{\Delta(r\theta)}{\Delta t}$$

Because r has a fixed magnitude and does not change over time, this expression reduces to

$$\frac{\Delta s}{\Delta t} = \frac{r\Delta\theta}{\Delta t}$$
$$v = r\omega \tag{1.9}$$

Equation 1.9 indicates that the linear velocity (v) of any point on a rigid body is equal to the product of the distance from the axis of rotation to that point (r) and the angular velocity of the rigid body (ω). For different points along a rigid body, therefore, both r and v vary. As anyone who has been part of a rotating human chain on skates knows, the person farthest from the axis of rotation experiences the greatest linear velocity. Furthermore, the direction of the linear velocity vector $(\mathbf{v})$ is tangent to the path of the rigid body (figure 1.18b).

The variables $\mathbf{r}$, $\mathbf{v}$, and $\boldsymbol{\omega}$ are vectors and have both magnitude and direction. The magnitude and direction of $\mathbf{r}$ and $\mathbf{v}$ are straightforward, as shown in figure 1.18b. When a vector is shown as a curved arrow, its direction is actually perpendicular to the page and is located at the axis of rotation. In figure 1.18b, $\boldsymbol{\omega}$ is directed out of the page. Equation 1.9 is the scalar form of the relation between linear and angular velocity. The vector relation is indicated in Equation 1.10:

$$\mathbf{v} = \boldsymbol{\omega} \times \mathbf{r} \tag{1.10}$$

Equation 1.10 states that linear velocity $(\mathbf{v})$ is equal to the cross product $(\times)$ of angular velocity $(\boldsymbol{\omega})$ and position $(\mathbf{r})$. The cross product is a vector operator that is used to multiply vectors, the result (product) of which is a vector that is perpendicular to the plane of the original vectors. The $\boldsymbol{\omega}$ vector is perpendicular to the plane of motion.

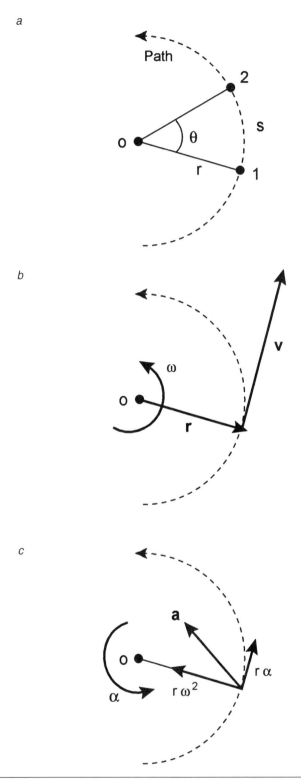

Figure 1.18 Relations between the linear and angular motion of a rigid body of fixed length *(r)* rotating about a fixed axis: *(a)* position, *(b)* velocity, *(c)* acceleration. The vectors **ω** and **α** are perpendicular to the page.

To determine the relation between linear and angular acceleration, we need to use Equation 1.10 to account for the change in both magnitude and direction of each velocity vector ($\mathbf{v}$ and $\boldsymbol{\omega}$):

$$\frac{\Delta \mathbf{v}}{\Delta t} = \frac{\Delta(\boldsymbol{\omega} \times \mathbf{r})}{\Delta t}$$

$$\mathbf{a} = \left(\boldsymbol{\omega} \times \frac{\Delta \mathbf{r}}{\Delta t}\right) + \left(\frac{\Delta \boldsymbol{\omega}}{\Delta t} \times \mathbf{r}\right)$$

$$= (\boldsymbol{\omega} \times \mathbf{v}) + (\boldsymbol{\alpha} \times \mathbf{r})$$

$$\mathbf{a} = \boldsymbol{\omega} \times (\boldsymbol{\omega} \times \mathbf{r}) + (\boldsymbol{\alpha} \times \mathbf{r})$$

In scalar terms, the magnitude of linear acceleration (a) can be determined by

$$a = \sqrt{\left(r\omega^2\right)^2 + (r\alpha)^2} \tag{1.11}$$

The term $r\omega^2$ accounts for the change in direction of $\mathbf{v}$, and the term $r\alpha$ represents the change in magnitude of $\mathbf{v}$ (figure 1.18c). Because the direction of $\mathbf{v}$ changes during angular motion, $r\omega^2$ is never zero; but $r\alpha$ may be zero if the magnitude of $\mathbf{v}$ is constant, which occurs in uniform circular motion. Recognize also that from the scalar relation between linear and angular velocity (Equation 1.9), we can derive a relation for linear acceleration for uniform circular motion ($r\alpha = 0$).

$$a = \frac{v^2}{r} \tag{1.12}$$

Sometimes the $r\omega^2$ term is referred to as the normal or radial component (a_n) and the $r\alpha$ term as the tangential component (a_t) of linear acceleration; these names indicate the direction of each component relative to the path of the rigid body. When the motion is planar (fixed axis of rotation), the lines of action of $\boldsymbol{\omega}$ and $\boldsymbol{\alpha}$ are collinear (lie on the same line) at the axis of rotation.

Example 1.7
Kicking a Football

A kicked football leaves the foot of a punter with a vertical velocity (v_v) of 25.9 m/s and a horizontal velocity (v_h) of 14.2 m/s.

A. What is the magnitude of the resultant linear velocity?

$$v = \sqrt{v_v^2 + v_h^2}$$

$$v = \sqrt{25.9^2 + 14.2^2}$$

$$v = 29.5 \text{ m/s}$$

B. What is the direction (an angle relative to the horizontal) of the resultant linear velocity?

$$\tan \theta = \frac{v_v}{v_h}$$

$$\theta = \tan^{-1} \frac{v_v}{v_h}$$

$$\theta = 1.07 \text{ rad}$$

(continued)

C. If the leg (hip-to-ankle length = 0.53 m) is straight at the moment of contact with the ball, what is the angular velocity of the leg?

$$v = r\omega$$

$$\omega = \frac{29.5}{0.53}$$

$$\omega = 55.7 \text{ rad / s}$$

D. What is the value of the acceleration component that accounts for the change in direction of the linear velocity?

$$r\omega^2 = 0.53 \times 55.7^2$$

$$r\omega^2 = 1644 \text{ m/s}^2$$

Example 1.8
Kinematics of an Elbow Movement

An elbow extension-flexion movement is performed slowly in a transverse plane passing through the shoulder joint (figure 1.19). The movement begins with the upper arm raised to the side so that it is horizontal, with an angle of 0.70 rad (40°) between the upper arm and forearm. In one continuous movement of moderate speed, the upper arm is held stationary while the elbow joint is extended horizontally to 3.14 rad (180°) and then flexed back to the starting position (0.70 rad).

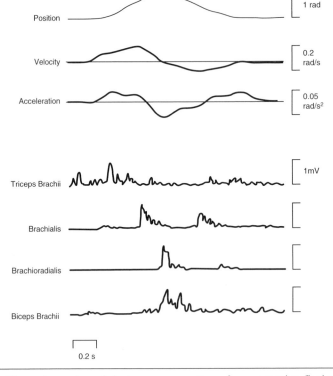

Figure 1.19   Kinematic graphs and electromyogram patterns for an extension-flexion movement of the forearm-hand segment about the elbow joint. The kinematic features of the movement are determined by the net muscle activity.

A. What is the shape of the position-time graph for this movement?

Because the upper arm remains stationary while the forearm rotates about the elbow joint, a graph of elbow angle over time should adequately describe the movement (top trace in figure 1.19).

B. When is angular velocity zero?

The velocity is zero when there is no angular displacement—at the beginning and end of the movement and, for an instant, when the direction of the movement changes from extension to flexion, that is, when elbow angle is at a maximum. The velocity-time graph (second trace in figure 1.19) indicates that when velocity is positive (above zero), the elbow is extending; when the velocity is negative, the elbow is flexing. Thus a change in the sign of velocity (e.g., positive to negative) indicates a change in the direction of movement.

C. When is angular acceleration zero?

The angular acceleration is zero when the value of angular velocity is at its maximum and minimum, which occurs twice in figure 1.19—that is, when the slope of the velocity-time graph is zero.

D. Why does the acceleration-time graph (third trace in figure 1.19) have three phases?

As we discuss in chapters 2 and 3, the acceleration experienced by a system (the forearm-hand in this example) depends on the forces acting on the system. Because this movement is controlled by the muscles that cross the elbow joint, the three phases of the acceleration graph can be explained by the net muscle activity. For the first part of the movement, the arm accelerates in the direction of extension (positive acceleration in this example). In the middle phase of the movement, the arm accelerates in the direction of elbow flexion. The movement concludes with a final phase of acceleration in the direction of elbow extension. As indicated by the records of muscle activity (electromyogram) in the four lower traces of figure 1.19, acceleration in the direction of elbow extension is due to activation of the elbow extensor muscle (triceps brachii), while acceleration in the direction of elbow flexion is associated with activation of the elbow flexor muscles (brachialis, brachioradialis, and biceps brachii). Note that the angular acceleration-time graph cannot be predicted directly from the elbow angle-time graph.

Curve Fitting and Smoothing

All measures of movement contain some error due to limitations in the technology and inaccurate measurements by the person doing the analysis. Consider, for example, a ball that is tossed straight up into the air, with its trajectory recorded on videotape. The ball rises to some peak height and then falls to the ground (figure 1.20). As we have discussed previously, the vertical velocity of the ball is zero at the peak of the trajectory, and the vertical acceleration is a constant -9.81 m/s^2 for the duration of the trajectory. A motion analysis system, however, will incorrectly estimate that the ball experiences a nonconstant vertical acceleration (bottom graph in figure 1.20). The reason for this discrepancy is that the measurement of ball position by the system contains small measurement errors that are magnified when the derivatives (velocity and acceleration) are determined. Errors in the measurement of position are compounded about 20 times by the time acceleration is calculated from the original position data.

To minimize such error propagation, measured data can be manipulated by processes known as *curve fitting* and *smoothing*. Curve-fitting techniques involve deriving a mathematical function to represent a data set. Common curve-fitting procedures include polynomial functions, cubic spline functions, and Fourier series. Alternatively, curve-smoothing techniques

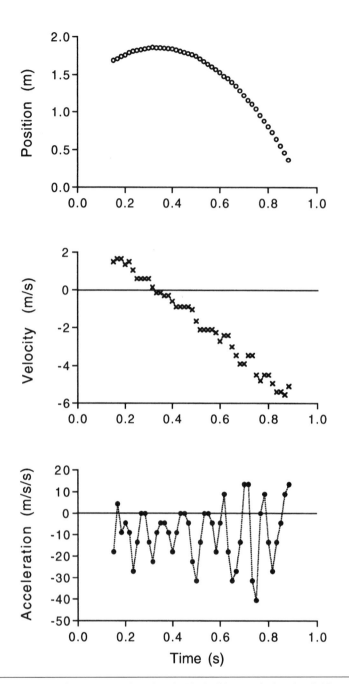

Figure 1.20 Kinematics of a ball tossed into the air. The ball leaves the hand at 0.15 s and reaches the ground at 0.88 s. The position of the ball is measured with a videotape recorder, and the position-, velocity-, and acceleration-time curves are determined by a motion analysis system.

use averaging procedures to reduce irregularities in a data set. Biomechanists often perform curve smoothing by using a digital filter. These techniques have the following forms:

$$x(t) = a_0 + a_1 t + a_2 t^2 + \ldots + a_n t^n \tag{1.13}$$

$$x(t) = a_0 + \sum_{i=1}^{n} \left[a_i \, cos \left(\frac{2\pi t}{T} \cdot i \right) + b_i \, sin \left(\frac{2\pi t}{T} \cdot i \right) \right] \tag{1.14}$$

$$x'(i) = a_0 x_i + a_1 x_{i-1} + a_2 x_{i-2} + b_1 x'_{i-1} + b_2 x'_{i-2} \tag{1.15}$$

Polynomial Functions

The simplest type of mathematical function to represent a set of data is the equation for a straight line. Data sets that can be represented by a straight line are described as linear functions. The general form of the equation for a straight line is

$$y = mx + b$$

where y is the dependent (outcome) variable, m corresponds to the slope of the line, x is the independent (predictor) variable, and b indicates the y-intercept. When m has a value of 1 and b is equal to 0, the equation reduces to the line of identity. The effect of m is to change the slope of the line and can even be negative. The line of best fit for a set of data is commonly determined by **regression analysis,** which is a statistical procedure that minimizes the differences between the line and the data.

When a straight line cannot represent a data set, we use nonlinear functions. For example, we can use an expression in which the independent variable is raised to a power. The shape of the function depends on the power used and can be modified by adding several terms together, multiplying the terms with coefficients, and including constants in the expression. A sum of terms that are powers of a variable is known as a polynomial function (Equation 1.13). For example, the function $x^3 + 3x^2 - 8x$ is a third-degree polynomial; second-degree polynomials are known as quadratic functions, and third-degree polynomials are referred to as cubic functions. As with the straight line, an appropriate polynomial expression for a set of data can be determined by regression analysis.

Polynomials are sometimes used to represent the change in a kinematic variable as a function of time. For example, a position-time relation may be represented by a fifth- or seventh-degree polynomial (Wood, 1982)—that is, equations in which the terms can be raised to the fifth or seventh power. Once such a data set is represented by a polynomial, it is a simple matter to determine the velocity- and acceleration-time functions for the data because this involves taking the first (velocity) and second (acceleration) derivatives of the position-time function. However, fitting a single polynomial function to an entire set of position data generally does not produce sufficiently accurate derivatives (Wood, 1982). One alternative is to use several polynomial functions, each representing a different part of the data, and then combine these functions to describe the entire data set.

Fourier Analysis

Any signal can be represented by a set of sine and cosine terms; such a set is known as a **Fourier series** (Equation 1.14). To understand how a combination of sine and cosine terms can be derived to represent a signal, it is necessary to review some basic properties of these functions. The functions $y = sin\ x$ and $y = cos\ x$ complete one revolution when x varies from 0 to 6.28 (2π) rad (figure 1.21a). The peak values for y are ± 1 for both functions, although they occur at different locations in the cycle. Three features of these basic functions can be changed:

1. The number of cycles completed in one revolution—to vary this, a coefficient other than 1.0 is placed in front of the x term. Figure 1.21b shows that the expression $y = sin\ 2x$ contains two cycles of the function in one revolution (2π rad). Cycle rate is expressed in terms of frequency: the completion of one cycle in 1 s is described as a frequency of 1 Hz. Similarly, the completion of two cycles in 1 s represents a frequency of 2 Hz.

2. The peak-to-peak amplitude of the function—to vary this, a coefficient other than 1.0 is placed in front of the sine or cosine term. Figure 1.21c indicates that the expression $y = 2\ sin\ x$ represents a function whose peak values are two times ± 1.0. Similarly, when the coefficient is less than 1.0, the peak values are less than ± 1.0.

3. The phase of the function—when sine and cosine functions are added, the basic function has peak values greater than ± 1.0 and its phase is shifted along the x-axis; that is, the angles at which the function is zero are shifted along the x-axis (figure 1.21d).

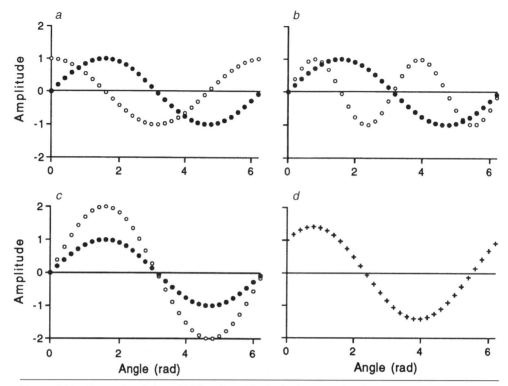

Figure 1.21 Properties of sinusoidal functions. The basic sine (•) and cosine (○) functions *(a)* complete one cycle per revolution (2π rad) with peak-to-peak values of ±1.0. However, the number of cycles per revolution *(b)* and the amplitude *(c)* can be varied by the inclusion of coefficients in the function or by the addition of sine and cosine terms *(d)*. The functions shown are *(a)* y = sin x and y = cos x; *(b)* y = sin 2x; *(c)* y = 2 sin x; *(d)* y = sin x + cos x.

The derivation of the Fourier series (Equation 1.14) for a particular signal that varies as a function of time involves the following steps:

■ *Mean*—calculate the mean value (a_0) of the signal so that the sinusoidal function varies about the correct absolute value.

■ *Fundamental*—use regression analysis to obtain the single sine + cosine term that best describes how the signal varies over time during one cycle (figure 1.22). The sine and cosine functions are evaluated at set points in time (*t*), which are normalized to the total time (*T*) it takes for one cycle to be completed. The functions can be evaluated with a constant Δt between data points (e.g., 0.1 s), such as occurs when the data are obtained with a video camera.

■ *Harmonics*—derive the multiple cycles (harmonics) of the fundamental (figure 1.22). We accomplish this by placing integer coefficients (1, 2, 3 . . . n) in front of the *x* term (figure 1.21*b*). These coefficients are included in Equation 1.14 as the *i* term in parentheses. The number of harmonics (*n*) needed to describe a signal depends on its smoothness; the more peaks and valleys in the signal, the greater the number of harmonics that will be required for the Fourier series to match the data set.

■ *Weighting coefficients*—adjust the amplitude of each harmonic with coefficients (a_i, b_i) that alter the peak-to-peak amplitude of each sine and cosine term (figure 1.21*c*). Typically, the coefficients decrease as harmonic number increases, which means that higher harmonics contribute less to replicating the signal (figure 1.23*b*). The weighting coefficients are defined as:

$$a_i = \frac{2}{T}\int_0^T x(t)\cos\frac{2\pi t}{T}i \cdot dt$$

$$b_i = \frac{2}{T}\int_0^T x(t)\sin\frac{2\pi t}{T}i \cdot dt$$

The amplitude of the harmonic (c_i) is then determined as the square root of the sum of squares of the weighting coefficients, and the phase (θ_i) of the harmonic is given by the inverse tangent of the coefficients:

$$c_i = \sqrt{a_i^2 + b_i^2}$$

$$\theta_i = \tan^{-1} \frac{a_i}{b_i}$$

■ *Sum the terms*—add the weighted harmonics to the mean value to produce an expression that comprises a series (Σ) of sine and cosine terms (figure 1.23c). For example, the series (n = 5) for the function shown in figure 1.23c is:

$$x(t) = a_o + \left[a_1 \sin\left(\frac{2\pi i}{T} \cdot t\right) + b_1 \cos\left(\frac{2\pi i}{T} \cdot t\right) \right]_{i=1}$$

$$+ \left[a_2 \sin\left(\frac{2\pi i}{T} \cdot t\right) + b_2 \cos\left(\frac{2\pi i}{T} \cdot t\right) \right]_{i=2}$$

$$+ \left[a_3 \sin\left(\frac{2\pi i}{T} \cdot t\right) + b_3 \cos\left(\frac{2\pi i}{T} \cdot t\right) \right]_{i=3}$$

$$+ \left[a_4 \sin\left(\frac{2\pi i}{T} \cdot t\right) + b_4 \cos\left(\frac{2\pi i}{T} \cdot t\right) \right]_{i=4}$$

$$+ \left[a_5 \sin\left(\frac{2\pi i}{T} \cdot t\right) + b_5 \cos\left(\frac{2\pi i}{T} \cdot t\right) \right]_{i=5}$$

$$x(t) = 4.8332$$
$$+ \left[-0.4936 \sin(12.414\, t) - 0.0478 \cos(12.414\, t) \right]$$
$$+ \left[0.0285 \sin(24.828\, t) + 0.065 \cos(24.828\, t) \right]$$
$$+ \left[-0.0178 \sin(37.241\, t) + 0.0942 \cos(37.241\, t) \right]$$
$$+ \left[-0.0195 \sin(49.655\, t) + 0.0105 \cos(49.655\, t) \right]$$
$$+ \left[0.0074 \sin(62.069\, t) + 0.0046 \cos(62.069\, t) \right]$$

Note that the amplitude of the fundamental is greater than the amplitudes of the harmonics $(i = 2$ to $5)$ (figure 1.23b), which is evident in the function just presented by the decrease in the weighting coefficients (a_i and b_i terms).

Once a series has been determined, such as for a position-time measurement, the function can be differentiated to derive the velocity- and acceleration-time functions (Equations 1.16 and 1.17, respectively). These equations, based on the differentiation of Equation 1.14, have the following general forms:

$$\dot{x}(t) = \sum_{i=1}^{n} \left\{ \left[-a_i \sin\left(\frac{2\pi t}{T} \cdot i\right)\left(\frac{2\pi}{T} \cdot i\right) \right] + \left[b_i \cos\left(\frac{2\pi t}{T} \cdot i\right)\left(\frac{2\pi}{T} \cdot i\right) \right] \right\} \qquad (1.16)$$

$$\ddot{x}(t) = \sum_{i=1}^{n} \left\{ \left[-a_i \cos\left(\frac{2\pi t}{T} \cdot i\right)\left(\frac{2\pi}{T} \cdot i\right)^2 \right] + \left[-b_i \sin\left(\frac{2\pi t}{T} \cdot i\right)\left(\frac{2\pi}{T} \cdot i\right)^2 \right] \right\} \qquad (1.17)$$

One of the important applications of a Fourier analysis is to determine the *frequency content of a signal.* This is accomplished by determining the frequency of the fundamental (number of

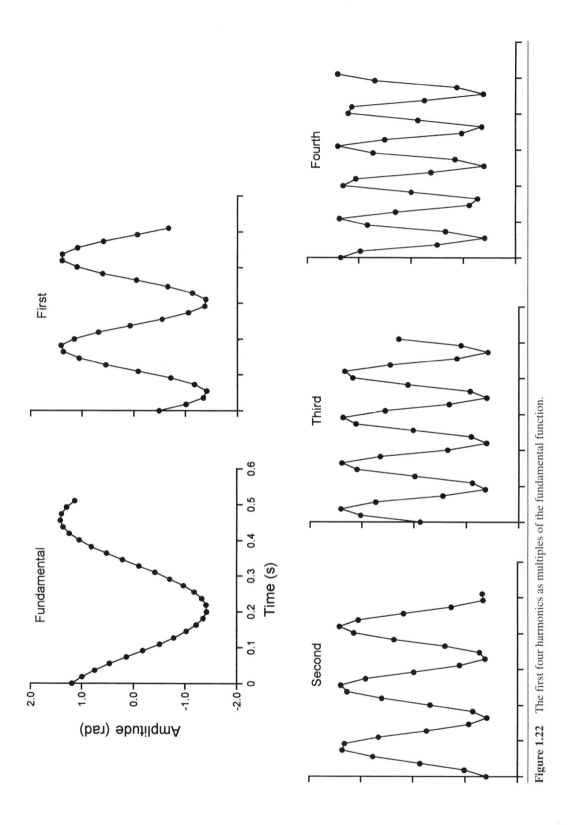

Figure 1.22 The first four harmonics as multiples of the fundamental function.

38

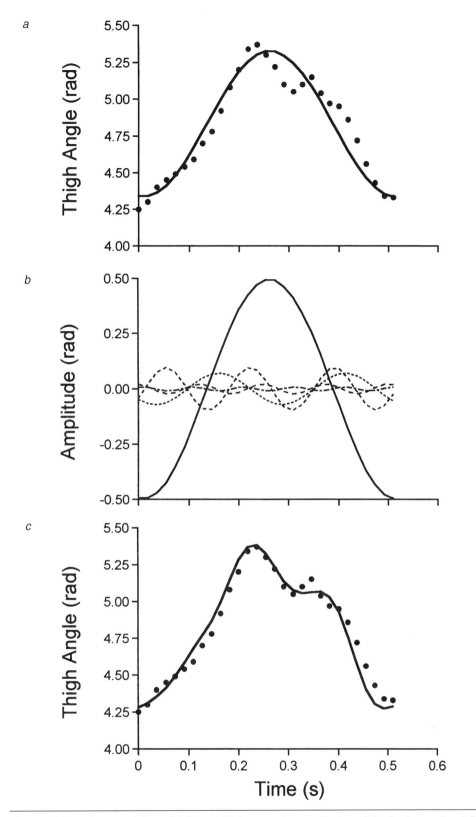

Figure 1.23 Influence of the weighting coefficients on the contribution of the fundamental and first four harmonics: *(a)* the original data (filled circles) and the fundamental; *(b)* the weighted contribution of the fundamental and first four harmonics to the Fourier series; *(c)* the approximation of the thigh-angle data by the first five terms in the Fourier series.

cycles per second), the number of harmonics necessary to represent the signal, and the weighted amplitude of each harmonic. The outcome is the transformation of a signal from the **time domain** to the **frequency domain** (figure 1.24). For example, a sine wave at a constant frequency is represented as a single data point with a given power or amplitude in the frequency domain (f_o). Similarly, the addition of two sinusoids (the second with three times the frequency of the first) appears as two data points (f_o and $3f_o$), each with a different amplitude (peak-to-peak value), in the frequency domain. Many biological signals (e.g., the electromyogram) require many sinusoids (sine + cosine terms) in the Fourier series and therefore contain many frequencies from a lower limit (f_1) to an upper limit (f_2). A common range used with the electromyogram is 10 Hz to 500 Hz. The representation of a signal in the frequency domain is often referred to as the **power density spectrum** because it characterizes the relative amplitude (power) of each frequency over the chosen range of frequencies. In general, the more peaks and valleys that exist in a signal, the greater the range of frequencies in the signal and therefore the greater the upper limit in the power density spectrum. The frequency content provides information about the rapidity of the fluctuations in the signal, which is sometimes useful to know when we are comparing the effects of various factors on biological processes.

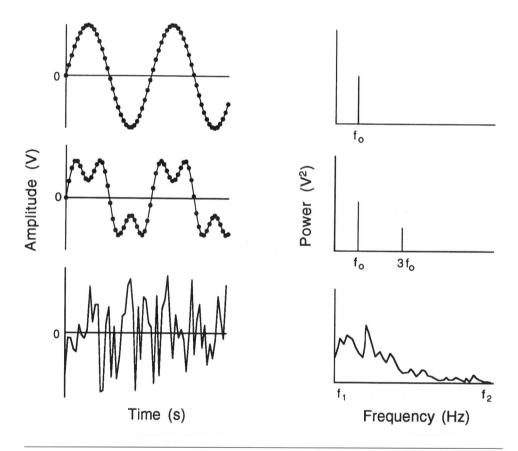

Figure 1.24 Transformations (Fourier) of signals from the time domain (left column) to the frequency domain (right column).

From "Transformations (Fourier) of signals from the time domain to the frequency domain" by D.A. Winter, 1990, *Biomechanics and Motor Control of Human Movement* (New York: Wiley), 28. This material is used by permission of Jossey-Bass, Inc., a subsidiary of John Wiley and Sons, Inc.

Example 1.9
Time and Frequency Domains

We can examine the relation between a time-domain signal and its frequency-domain version by reconstructing the time-domain signal from the components of the power density spectrum. This process is shown in figure 1.25, with the signal of interest being the horizontal acceleration of a person running the 100 m sprint (figure 1.5). The acceleration of the runner is shown in the upper left panel of figure 1.25, and the power density spectrum derived from the acceleration data is shown in the upper right panel. Six peaks (A-F) have been identified in the power density spectrum.

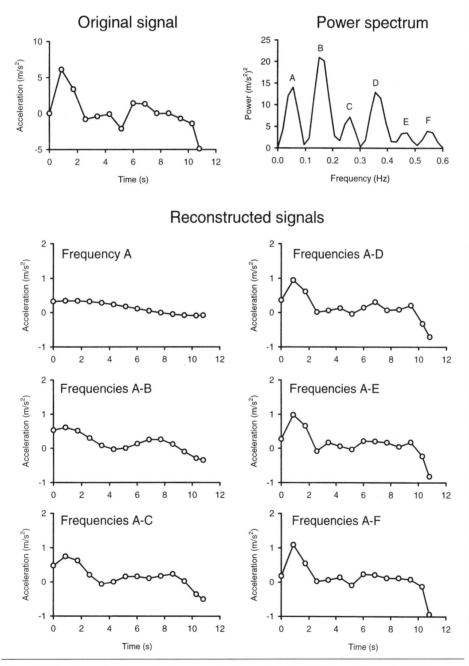

Figure 1.25   Reconstruction of a time-domain signal (acceleration) from the peaks in its power density spectrum.

(continued)

The remainder of figure 1.25 represents the time-domain signal as it was reconstructed from various combinations of the peaks in the power density spectrum. The graph labeled "Frequency A" indicates the amount of the acceleration record that is represented by peak A in the power density spectrum. The function in the graph was obtained by using the frequency (sinusoid) and amplitude (power) of the peak (A). Similarly, the other graphs show the functions that result from summing several of the peaks (frequency + amplitude). The lower right panel represents the sum of the six peaks in the power density spectrum, which can be compared with the original acceleration-time data (upper left panel). This analysis indicates that the acceleration data can be represented reasonably well by the first four peaks in the power density spectrum.

Example 1.10
Comparison of Power Density Spectra

The rate of fluctuations in a record determines the range of frequencies required in the power density spectrum. Acceleration-time data, for example, have a greater rate of fluctuations than do position-time data and thus require higher-frequency sinusoids for their frequency-domain representation. Figure 1.26 shows the position and acceleration of the index finger as it performed a slow abduction and adduction movement. The subject lifted a light load with a concentric contraction of the hand muscle (first dorsal interosseus) and lowered it with an eccentric contraction. The subject was asked to perform the task as steadily as possible by lifting and lowering the load with a constant velocity (slope of the position-time graph). Despite this instruction, the task was accomplished with fluctuations in both the position and acceleration records. Because the rate of fluctuations was greater for the acceleration-time data, the corresponding power density spectrum spanned a greater range of frequencies.

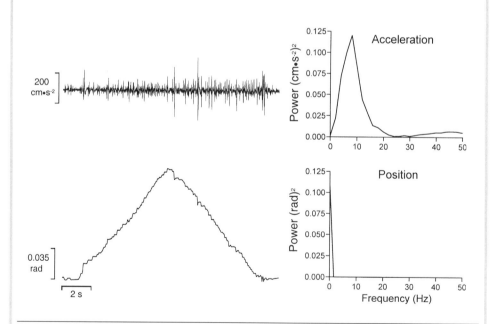

Figure 1.26   Position and acceleration data in the time domain (left column) and frequency domain (right column) for a slow (12 s) abduction followed by adduction of the index finger.

Data from Laidlaw, Bilodeau, and Enoka, 2000.

Digital Filter

The digital filter is an example of a smoothing technique (see chapter 2 in Winter, 1990). Unlike the Fourier analysis, the digital filter does not allow us to derive an equation to represent a signal. Rather, the digital filter provides an averaging technique that reduces unwanted components in a signal. Typically, these components result from measurement errors and will severely contaminate the estimates of velocity and acceleration from position-time data (Winter, Sidwall, & Hobson, 1974).

Previously we considered the frequency content of signals (Fourier analysis) when we saw how every signal can be represented by a fundamental sinusoid and its harmonics (multiples of the fundamental). Higher-order harmonics account for the high-frequency content (sharp edges and peaks) of a signal (figure 1.26). When the position of an object is measured from a video image, the measurement includes a true estimate of the position of the landmark in addition to errors due to such effects as camera vibration, distortions in the videotape and projection system, and inaccurate placement of the cursors. These error terms (referred to as noise) are generally random and are located in the high-frequency region of a power spectrum. Digital filters represent numerical techniques that can modify the region of the power spectrum in which the noise is thought to be located (figure 1.27).

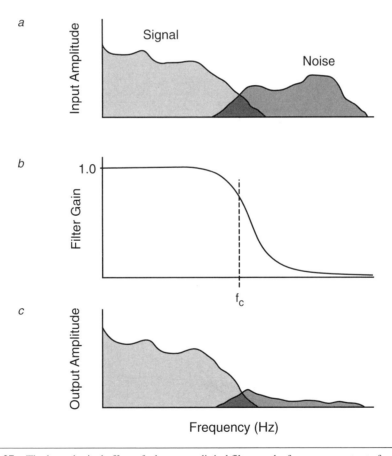

Figure 1.27   The hypothetical effect of a low-pass digital filter on the frequency content of a signal. *(a)* An original input signal contains both desired information (signal) and noise. The noise is generally located in the higher-frequency region of the power spectrum (frequency-amplitude graph). *(b)* The effect of a digital filter on the amplitude of different frequencies. At the cutoff frequency (f_c), the amplitude of the original signal is reduced to about 70% of its original value. *(c)* Power density spectrum (amplitude-frequency graph) of the signal once it has been passed through the digital filter.

The key step in the digital-filter procedure is to identify the frequency that separates the desired signal from the noise; this is referred to as the **cutoff frequency** (f_c). Unfortunately this is not a simple matter, because the frequencies of the desired signal and noise overlap to some extent (figure 1.27a). *The digital filter is a numerical procedure that manipulates the frequency spectrum of an input signal to produce an output signal containing a substantially attenuated frequency content above f_c.* The numerical effect of a digital filter is shown in figure 1.27b, where the frequencies are either left untouched (below f_c) or are reduced (above f_c). The cutoff frequency is defined as the frequency at which the amplitude of the output signal is reduced to 70% of its input value; that is, the power in the signal at that frequency is reduced by one-half. The hypothetical effect of this procedure is shown in figure 1.27c (compare the amplitude-frequency graph of the input [$x(f)$] in figure 1.27a to the output [$x'\pi(f)$] in figure 1.27c).

A commonly used digital filter (Butterworth, second order) has the following form:

$$x'(i) = a_o x_i + a_1 x_{i-1} + a_2 x_{i-2} + b_1 x'_{i-1} + b_2 x'_{i-2}$$

where:

x	= unfiltered (input) original data
$x\pi$	= filtered output data
i	= ith frame of data
$i-1$	= one frame before the ith frame of data
a_o, a_1, a_2, b_1, b_2	= filter coefficients

From this expression, it should be apparent that the output [$x'\pi(i)$] is a weighted average of the immediate (i) and past ($i-1$, $i-2$) unfiltered data plus a weighted contribution from the past filtered output ($i-1$, $i-2$).

To implement a digital filter, we need to determine the values of the coefficients (a_o, a_1, a_2, b_1, b_2). However, this requires that we first specify f_c. Perhaps the most comprehensive procedure available to determine f_c is the **residual analysis** (Winter, 1990). This involves comparing the difference (residual) between filtered and unfiltered signals over a wide range of cutoff frequencies and choosing an f_c that minimizes both signal distortion and the amount of noise that passes through the filter. For many human movements, an f_c of 6 Hz is generally adequate. Once f_c has been determined, we can obtain the coefficients by calculating the ratio of the sampling frequency (f_s, frames per second) to f_c. For an f_c of 6 Hz and with use of video data obtained at 60 Hz, the ratio is 10 and the coefficients are:

$$a_0 = 0.06746$$
$$a_1 = 0.13491$$
$$a_2 = 0.06746$$
$$b_1 = 1.14298$$
$$b_2 = -0.41280$$

The digital-filter coefficients for different f_s/f_c ratios are available in Winter, 1990.

Example 1.11
Calculating Filter Coefficients

The coefficients for a Butterworth filter can be calculated with a simple algorithm based on f_s and f_c. For example, given an f_s of 200 Hz and a desired f_c of 8 Hz:

$$S = \sin\left(\pi \times \frac{8}{200}\right) = 0.1253$$

$$C = \cos\left(\pi \times \frac{8}{200}\right) = 0.9921$$

$$SC = \frac{S}{C} \qquad = 0.1263$$

$$K = 2SC \times \sqrt{0.5} \quad = 0.1787$$

$$L = SC^2 \qquad = 0.0160$$

$$M = 1 + K + L \qquad = 1.1946$$

From these parameters, the coefficients can be calculated:

$$a_i = \frac{L}{M} = 0.0134$$

$$a_2 = 2\frac{L}{M} = 0.0268$$

$$a_3 = \frac{L}{M} = 0.0134$$

$$b_1 = 2\frac{1-L}{M} = 1.6474$$

$$b_2 = \frac{K - L - 1}{M} = -0.7009$$

The final consideration is to correct any unwanted distortion that the digital filter introduces in the filtered data. This effect is a phase distortion that can be observed as a shift of a sine wave along the horizontal axis; if one cycle equals 2π rad, then a phase distortion of $\pi/2$ rad is equal to a shift of the sine wave by one-quarter of the cycle. This is the magnitude of the phase distortion that is introduced by a second-order Butterworth filter. To remove the phase distortion, we need to pass the data through the digital filter twice—once in the forward direction and once in the backward direction. The forward direction means beginning with the real first data point; the backward direction means beginning with the last data point. The forward, then backward, filtering of data with a second-order filter results in the application of a fourth-order, zero-lag filter.

Once the position-time data have been smoothed with a digital filter, the derivatives (velocity and acceleration) can be determined using a numerical procedure called **finite differences.** The process involves using the smoothed position data *(x)* to calculate both velocity (Equation 1.18) and acceleration (Equation 1.19) as functions of time:

$$\dot{x}(i) = \frac{x_{i+1} - x_{i-1}}{2(\Delta t)} \tag{1.18}$$

$$\ddot{x}(i) = \frac{x_{i+1} - 2x_i + x_{i-1}}{(\Delta t)^2} \tag{1.19}$$

The effect of a fourth-order Butterworth filter is shown in figure 1.28. The position-time data of a ball tossed into the air (figure 1.20) were passed through the filter ($f_c = 6$ Hz), and the vertical acceleration of the ball was estimated by finite differences (Equation 1.19). The actual acceleration of the ball was about -9.81 m/s^2, which was closely approximated by the acceleration data derived from the filtered position-time coordinates (figure 1.28).

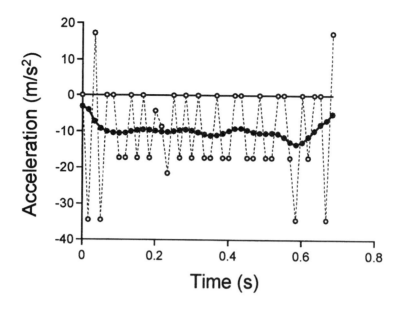

Figure 1.28 The vertical acceleration of a ball tossed into the air, as estimated from the unfiltered (○) and the filtered (●) position-time data.

Electromyography

The moment-to-moment control of muscle force by the nervous system is accomplished by electrical signals that are sent from motor neurons to muscle fibers. These signals, which are known as action potentials, can be recorded as they propagate along the sarcolemma of muscle fibers, from the neuromuscular junction to the ends of the fibers. Such a recording is referred to as an **electromyogram** (EMG; *myo* = muscle) (Dumitru, 2000; Duchêne & Goubel, 1993; Loeb & Gans, 1986; Stålberg & Falck, 1997). Electromyogram measurements are used by clinicians to diagnose problems in the neuromuscular system, by ergonomists to determine the requirements of job-related tasks, by physiologists to identify the mechanisms involved in various adaptations within the neuromuscular system, and by biomechanists to estimate muscle force.

Recording and Measurement

The measurement of EMG is made with probes known as **electrodes.** These measure the change in voltage (potential) associated with propagating action potentials. Electrodes can vary in size and material—for example, large (30 cm²) rubber-carbon pads, small (4-mm diameter) silver-silver chloride disks, and fine wires (25-μm diameter). For recording an EMG signal, the electrodes can be placed on the skin over a muscle (surface EMG), under the skin but over the muscle (subcutaneous EMG), or in the muscle between outside muscle cells (intramuscular EMG). The size and location of the electrode determine the composition of the recording, which can range from the action potential of a single motor unit to many superimposed action potentials (figure 1.29). Electrodes placed on the skin provide a global measure of action-potential activity in the underlying muscle, whereas fine-wire electrodes placed in the muscle are able to record single action potentials in a few adjacent muscle fibers.

A common arrangement used to record whole-muscle activity is to place one pair of electrodes, each with a diameter of about 8 mm and separated by about 1.5 cm, on the skin over the muscle. Measurement of the EMG with a pair of electrodes is known as a **bipolar** recording. The electrical signal recorded by each electrode (due to the flux of Na$^+$ and K$^+$

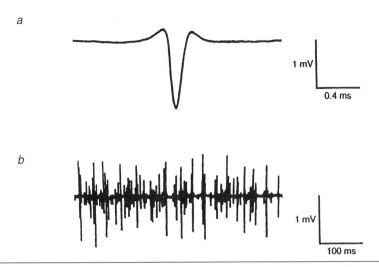

a

1 mV

0.4 ms

b

1 mV

100 ms

Figure 1.29 Electromyogram records of *(a)* one and *(b)* many action potentials. Notice the difference in the time scale for the two records.

ions across the sarcolemma) is transmitted to a processing device that measures and amplifies the signal. The measurement procedure consists of two steps. First, the voltage (potential difference) between the signal detected by each electrode and the ground electrode is determined. Second, the *difference* between the voltage measured by each electrode is calculated and amplified by the device, and the output is a voltage-time signal that we call the EMG (figure 1.30). Because an action potential propagating along a sarcolemma arrives at each electrode of a bipolar pair at a slightly different time (ms), the difference between the two measurements often appears as a biphasic or triphasic action potential (figure 1.30*a*). Alternatively, an EMG can be recorded with a single electrode, to produce what is known as a **monopolar** recording, and the output is the voltage between the electrode over the muscle and a ground electrode (Lateva & McGill, 2001). Monopolar recordings are used to measure the absolute magnitude of the voltage but are easily contaminated by activity in other muscles.

The placement of two electrodes in a bipolar pair has a marked effect on the amplitude of the recorded signal (Merletti, Rainoldi, & Farina, 2001). The critical distances are the spacing of the electrodes and the location of the electrodes relative to the neuromuscular junctions. To illustrate these effects, figure 1.31*a* shows the EMG recorded by eight different pairs of electrodes placed over a set of activated muscle fibers. The neuromuscular junctions are located in the middle of the fibers and span an area known as the **innervation zone.** Each muscle fiber is activated at the neuromuscular junction; this results in the propagation of action potentials in each direction toward the ends of the fiber. The scheme shown in figure 1.31*a* can be used to interpret the actual EMG records made from biceps brachii when it was contracting at 70% of maximum (Merletti et al., 2001). These data indicate the following points:

- The amplitude of the recorded signal is low for small interelectrode distances because the potential detected by each electrode in the pair is relatively similar—compare traces 1 and 3 with trace 8.

- When the electrodes span the innervation zone (trace 2), the amplitude is low because the electrodes record symmetrical potentials propagating in each direction.

- The EMG amplitude for a large interelectrode distance (traces 6 and 7) will be less than that for smaller distances (traces 3 and 4) if the electrodes span the innervation zone.

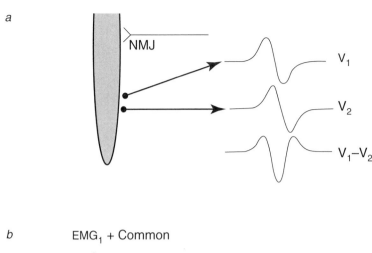

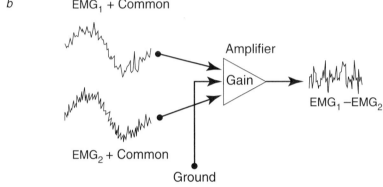

Figure 1.30 Bipolar recording of an EMG signal: *(a)* at the single action-potential level, the difference $(V_1 - V_2)$ between the voltage detected by each electrode results in a triphasic action potential; *(b)* at the level of many action potentials, the difference between the voltage detected by each electrode results in the rejection (by subtraction) of signals that are common to both electrodes.

■ If one electrode pair is placed over the innervation zone (trace 4), the EMG amplitude can be similar for a signal recorded with a smaller interelectrode distance (trace 3) because the innervation zone contributes minimally to the differential recording.

■ The greatest amplitude is recorded when the interelectrode distance is relatively large and the electrodes are placed on the same side of the innervation zone (trace 8). The optimum interelectrode distance depends on the length of the muscle fibers.

We must consider these relations when we are interested in the amplitude of the EMG signal.

A typical bipolar arrangement of electrodes on the skin over a muscle can detect muscle fiber action potentials within 1 to 2 cm of the electrodes (Fuglevand, Winter, Patla, & Stashuk, 1992; Roeleveld, Stegeman, Vingerhoets, & van Oosterom, 1997). Furthermore, the recording volume of the electrodes does not change with an increase in the size of the electrodes (Fuglevand et al., 1992; Jonas, Bischoff, & Conrad, 1999). As a consequence, one pair of electrodes cannot measure the entire activity of a muscle, at least for most muscles in the human body. To obtain a more complete record of the EMG for a muscle, it is necessary to use either an array of electrodes distributed over the surface (Chanaud, Pratt, & Loeb, 1987; Clancy & Hogan, 1995; Emerson & Zahalak, 1981; Thusneyapan & Zahalak, 1989) or a needle electrode with a large recording area (**macro EMG**) that is placed inside the muscle (Lateva & McGill, 2001; Stålberg, 1980, 1986). These strategies are used when an accurate measurement of the amount of muscle activation is necessary to control a neuroprosthesis or to assess changes in the activation of muscle by the nervous system, for example, after participation in a strength-training program.

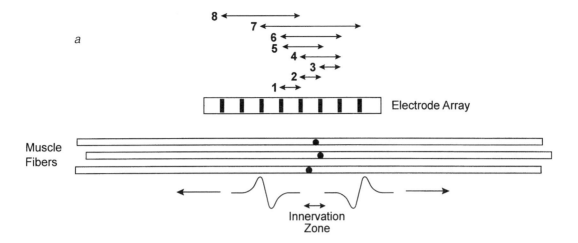

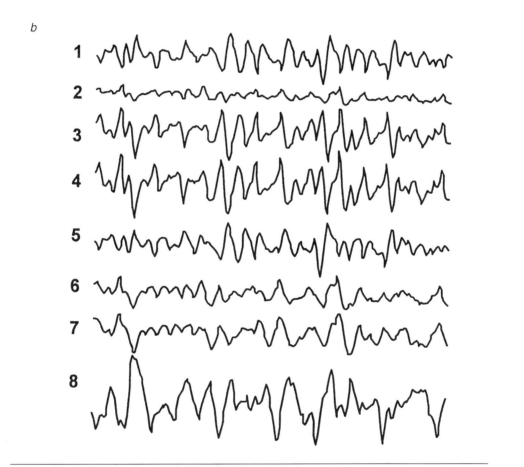

Figure 1.31 Electrode location influences EMG amplitude. *(a)* Eight electrodes are arranged in an array and placed over some muscle fibers. There is 10 mm between each electrode. The lines above the electrode array indicate eight different combinations of electrodes that were used to make bipolar recordings of the EMG signal. The interelectrode distances are 10 mm for pairs 1, 2, and 3; 20 mm for pairs 4 and 5; 30 mm for pair 6; 40 mm for pair 8; and 50 mm for pair 7. *(b)* Electromyogram activity recorded with an electrode array placed on the skin over biceps brachii. Traces 1 to 8 correspond to the electrode pairs shown in *a*.

Adapted from Merletti et al., 2001.

In contrast to global EMG measures, it is sometimes desirable to record the activity of the individual components, the action potentials of a single motor unit (Stålberg, Nandedkar, Sanders, & Falck, 1996). The most common procedure is to insert some fine wires (diameter = 10-50 μm) into the muscle with a hypodermic needle. The wires are insulated except for the ends, which serve as the detection surface. Recordings made with intramuscular fine-wire electrodes are typically used only to study motor unit activity at low forces, usually less than 20% of maximum (however, cf. Duchateau & Hainaut, 1990; Van Cutsem, Duchateau, & Hainaut, 1998). An alternative approach, which can discriminate motor unit potentials up to maximum force, involves the use of a needle electrode and a computer-based discrimination system. The needle electrode, called a **concentric needle electrode,** contains one to four thin wires inside the barrel of a needle (Stålberg et al., 1996). The wires are connected to the barrel of the needle and present small (diameter = 25-75 μm) detection surfaces to the surrounding tissue (Kamen, Sison, Du, & Patten, 1995). The recorded signals are stored in a computer, and subsequently a **decomposition** algorithm is used to discriminate the action potentials of several motor units during the contraction (LeFever & De Luca, 1982; LeFever, Xenakis, & De Luca, 1982). Examples of motor unit recordings are shown in chapters 6 and 9.

Although it is relatively easy to record the EMG activity of a muscle, it is just as easy for the signal to be contaminated by activity from other sources (Winter, Fuglevand, & Archer, 1994). The EMG signal can be contaminated by such things as movement of the electrodes and cables, activity in distant muscles **(volume conduction)**, and electromagnetic radiation in the surroundings (power cords, fluorescent lights, electric machinery). The two most common strategies used to minimize these effects are to obtain bipolar recordings and to limit the range of frequencies included in the recording. Bipolar recordings achieve this effect by a process known as **common mode rejection** (Winter, 1990), in which signals that are common to both electrodes get eliminated by subtraction. For example (figure 1.30*b*), the voltage detected by electrode 1 comprises an EMG signal (EMG_1) and the common activity from other sources (Common). Similarly, the voltage detected by electrode 2 consists of EMG_2 and the common signal. The output of the measuring device (an amplifier) is a voltage (V_o) that represents the difference between the two electrode signals times the multiplication factor (gain) set on the amplifier:

$$V_o = G\big[(EMG_1 + common) - (EMG_2 + common)\big]$$

$$V_o = G(EMG_1 - EMG_2)$$

where G represents the gain, which is typically set from 100 to 10,000. By this means, bipolar recordings are able to provide information about local muscle activity.

The other mechanism that can be used to reduce extraneous activity from an EMG recording is signal filtering. This process involves restricting the frequency range of the recorded signal. In this sense, a **filter** is a device that modifies the frequency content of a signal. There are basically four options (figure 1.32): (1) low-pass filter—retains only the low-frequency data; (2) high-pass filter—keeps the high-frequency data; (3) band-pass filter—eliminates frequencies below and above specified values so that the data comprise a desired band of frequencies; (4) band-stop filter—reduces the presence of a specified frequency or range of frequencies in the signal (e.g., 60 Hz). We implement these filters by setting a cutoff frequency above or below which we would like the other frequencies modified (figure 1.27). For example, if the cutoff frequency for a low-pass filter is set at 250 Hz, then frequencies in the signal above this value will be reduced. Similarly, if a band-pass filter had its cutoff frequencies set at 20 and 100 Hz, then the frequency components in the input signal below and above these values would be reduced (figure 1.33*c*).

Analysis and Interpretation

Most often, we measure the activity of many motor units that are concurrently active during a task. This type of EMG record is referred to as an **interference EMG** (Fuglsang-Frederiksen, 2000; Sanders, Stålberg, & Nandedkar, 1996) because it consists of many superimposed action

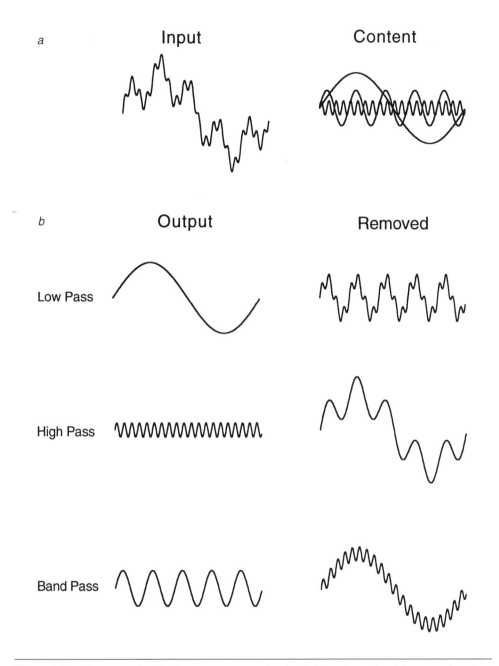

Figure 1.32 Filters can alter the frequency content of a signal: *(a)* an input signal that comprises three sine waves (content = 1, 5, and 20 Hz); *(b)* the output of low-, high-, and band-pass filters and the frequencies that were removed by each filter.

potentials (figures 1.29 and 1.33*a*). Because action potentials detected by EMG electrodes comprise positive and negative phases that fluctuate about a central line of zero voltage (isoelectric line), the superimposition of many action potentials in the interference EMG results in an irregular signal.

There are several procedures available to quantify the interference EMG (Fuglsang-Frederiksen, 2000; Loeb & Gans, 1986; Merletti & Lo Conte, 1997; Sanders et al., 1996). The two most commonly used procedures are rectification and integration. As shown in figure 1.34, **rectification** consists of taking the absolute value of the EMG signal; an electronic module can be used to remove or to flip over the negative phases (below the isoelectric line) of the

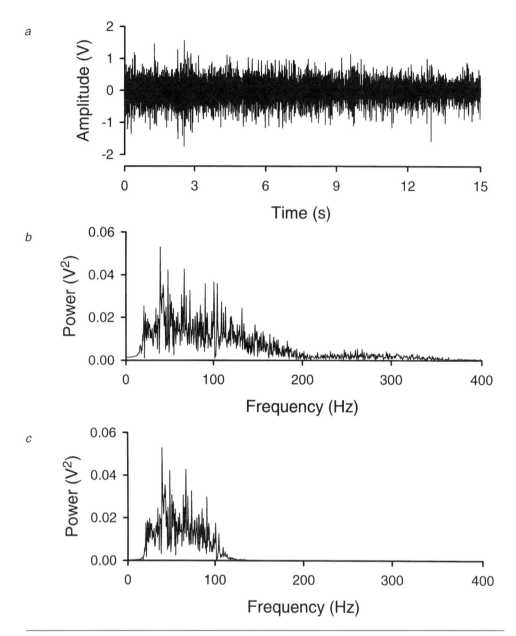

Figure 1.33   Original and processed EMG signals recorded from a hand muscle performing a steady contraction. *(a)* The original signal was recorded as an interference EMG and *(b)* then subjected to a **Fast Fourier Transformation** (FFT) to determine the power density spectrum. *(c)* When the interference EMG was passed through a band-pass filter (fourth-order, zero-lag Butterworth; 20-100 Hz), the power density spectrum was modified due to the effects of the filter.

interference EMG. Then the sharp peaks (high frequencies) that are present in the rectified EMG can be smoothed by **integration,** an electronic process that consists of filtering the EMG to reduce the high-frequency content of the signal. After the interference EMG has been rectified and integrated, the EMG can be quantified by measuring the amplitude of the integrated EMG. The outcome of this quantification procedure is an EMG signal that parallels the change in force (figure 1.34).

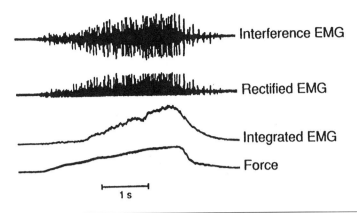

Figure 1.34 An interference EMG is rectified and integrated, and the resulting integrated EMG closely parallels the force due to the muscle activity during an isometric contraction.

An alternative procedure to estimate the amplitude of the interference EMG is to calculate the root-mean-square *(rms)* value. The calculation is performed with the following equation:

$$\text{EMG}_{\text{rms}} = \sqrt{\frac{1}{N}\sum_{i=1}^{N}x_i^{2}} \qquad (1.20)$$

where x_i is the *i*th sample of the interference EMG and N is the number of samples in the interval of interest. For comparison, the average amplitude is determined with the equation:

$$\text{average EMG} = \frac{1}{N}\sum_{i=1}^{N}|x_i| \qquad (1.21)$$

The average EMG provides information about the area under the signal, whereas the EMG$_{\text{rms}}$ reflects the mean power in the signal. For a given EMG recording, the absolute values of these amplitude estimates will differ, but the variations during the contraction will be highly correlated.

When an integrated EMG is compared with the force exerted by muscle, there is a close association between the two (Bigland-Ritchie, 1981; Fuglevand, Winter, & Patla, 1993). This association, however, is limited to isometric conditions in which the muscle contracts without changing its overall length. Under these conditions, there is a linear or a curvilinear relation between the integrated EMG and force (Lawrence & De Luca, 1983). This means that the magnitude of the EMG provides a reasonable estimate of the force exerted by muscle (figure 1.35). When muscle length changes (figure 1.36), however, the location of the electrodes relative to the active muscle fibers changes, causing a change in the EMG that is unrelated to the input received by the muscle from the nervous system (Gerilovsky, Tsvetinov, & Trenkova, 1989; Inman, Ralston, Saunders, Feinstein, & Wright, 1952). For this reason, it is difficult to quantify EMG under anisometric conditions (Bigland-Ritchie, 1981; Calvert & Chapman, 1977; Milner-Brown & Stein, 1975: cf., however, Hof & van den Berg, 1981a, 1981b, 1981c, 1981d).

One of the limitations of the interference EMG is the variability in the recording when the same task is performed by different subjects or by the same subject on different days. The two principal reasons for this variability are that the recording conditions change each time the electrodes are attached and the recording volume of the electrodes is usually less than the muscle mass involved in the task. To reduce the variability due to changes in the recording condition, the amplitude of the interference EMG is usually expressed relative to some standard value, a procedure known as **normalization.** The most common standard is the

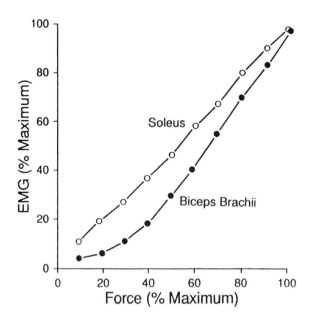

Figure 1.35 Relation between the integrated EMG and force for the soleus and biceps brachii muscles during an isometric contraction. Both EMG and force have been normalized to their respective maximum values.

Data from Bigland-Ritchie, 1981.

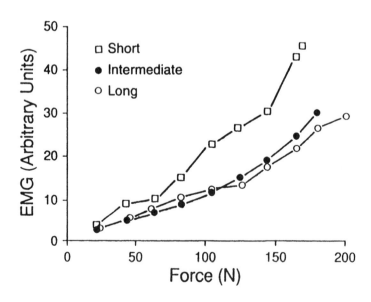

Figure 1.36 Measurement of EMG and force for biceps brachii at various lengths. The subject was a below-elbow amputee, and the muscle was attached to a force transducer.

Adapted from Heckathorne and Childress, 1981.

interference EMG recorded during a maximum voluntary contraction (MVC). Alternatively, the amplitude can be expressed relative to the response evoked in muscle by electrical stimulation (Keen, Yue, & Enoka, 1994) or relative to the EMG recorded during a reference task (Mathiassen, Winkel, & Hägg, 1995). The latter procedure is often used in ergonomic settings, for example in the study of work-related musculoskeletal disorders.

The interference EMG recorded during an activity is typically graphed as a function of time and quantified by rectification and integration. This is referred to as a *time-domain analysis.* An alternative approach, the *frequency-domain analysis,* is to determine the frequency content of the EMG signal (figure 1.33). Theoretically, there are three features of an EMG signal that can influence its frequency content (Hermens, v. Bruggen, Baten, Rutten, & Boom, 1992): the discharge rate of motor units, the relative timing of the action potentials discharged by different motor units, and the shape of the action potentials. The most significant factor is the shape of the action potentials, whereas discharge rate has a minimal influence. Because the interference EMG contains hundreds of action potentials with varying shapes (Hulliger, Day, Guimaraes, Herzog, & Zhang, 2001), the frequency content of the signal spans a range of frequencies (e.g., 2-200 Hz). One of the main reasons that action-potential shape varies is the difference in distances between the active muscle fibers and the electrodes. When the shapes of the action potentials in the interference EMG change, so does the frequency content of the EMG signal. This often happens in a fatiguing contraction as the action potentials decline in amplitude and increase in duration and the power density spectrum shifts to the left. Shifts in the power density spectrum are typically characterized by changes in the mean or median frequency. The **mean frequency** represents the central value of the frequency spectrum, whereas the **median frequency** is the frequency that divides the spectrum into two halves based on the energy content of the signal. For most purposes, the mean and median frequencies provide comparable information (Merletti, Knaflitz, & De Luca, 1990). When the power density spectrum shifts to the left in a fatiguing contraction, this produces a decrease in the mean and median frequencies of the spectrum.

Acoustomyography

A muscle contraction is based on the electrical activation of muscle by the nervous system. As a muscle contracts, however, it makes sounds that can be recorded with an appropriate microphone. The first report of muscle sounds was made in 1663 (cited in Oster, 1984). We do not generally hear these sounds, because they occur at a frequency that is below the normal capacity of the human ear (~40 Hz). The mean frequency is about 10 Hz at low forces and increases to about 22 Hz during an MVC, compared with a mean frequency of about 60 Hz for an EMG measured during a moderate-force contraction (Maton, Petitjean, & Cnockaert, 1990; Orizio, Perini, Diemont, Figini, & Veicsteinas, 1990; Stokes & Cooper, 1992). These sounds are probably due to the lateral movements of muscle fibers as they contract (Ouamer, Boiteux, Petitjean, Travens, & Salès, 1999). Because sound represents a series of pressure waves, it can be recorded, and it produces a signal that is similar to the interference EMG. Also, the sound signal can be analyzed with the same techniques used for the EMG (e.g., rectification and integration). The technique of recording muscle sounds is referred to as **acoustomyography** (AMG); it is also referred to as sound myography (SMG), phonomyography (PMG), and the mechanomyogram (MMG).

As with the EMG, the AMG is directly related to muscle force under isometric conditions; there appears to be a quadratic, not linear, relation between AMG and muscle force (Maton et al., 1990; Stokes, Moffroid, Rush, & Haugh, 1988). Correlation analyses, however, show that the EMG and AMG vary independently of one another as torque increases and then decreases, and that AMG varies more than EMG. There are also significant differences between the EMG and AMG when submaximal contractions are sustained until exhaustion. For moderate-intensity contractions (60-80% MVC), the EMG at the end of the contraction is greater than at the beginning, whereas the final AMG values are less than at the beginning (Orizio, Perini, &

Veicsteinas, 1989). Furthermore, the AMG signal appears to be related more to the range of change in muscle force rather than the absolute value of the force (Bichler, 2000). These observations indicate that the EMG and AMG signals contain some different information about a muscle contraction.

Summary

This chapter provides the foundation for the study of human movement. It examines the rigorously defined relations among position, velocity, and acceleration and establishes the concepts and definitions that are necessary to describe movement in precise terms. The study of kinematics has its foundation in physics, yet the application to human movement typically tests the limits of our understanding of these relations. Without a clear understanding of these principles, it is difficult to proceed to the next levels in the study of human movement. The key concepts include the relations among position, velocity, and acceleration, which are emphasized with several numerical and graphical examples, and the association between linear and angular motion. In addition, the chapter describes the procedures commonly used in biomechanics to process kinematic data and the technique used to measure the electrical activity in muscle during a contraction.

Suggested Readings

Hamill, J., & Knutzen, K.M. (1995). *Biomechanical basis of human movement*. Baltimore: Williams & Wilkins, chapters 8 and 9.

McGinnis, P.M. (1999). *Biomechanics of sport and exercise*. Champaign, IL: Human Kinetics, chapters 2, 3, 5, 6, and 9.

Nigg, B.M., MacIntosh, B.R., & Mester J. (2000). *Biomechanics of biology and movement*. Champaign, IL: Human Kinetics, chapter 1.

Watkins, J. (1999). *Structure and function of the musculoskeletal system*. Champaign, IL: Human Kinetics, chapter 1.

Winter, D.A. (1990). *Biomechanics and motor control of human movement*. New York: Wiley, chapters 2 and 8.

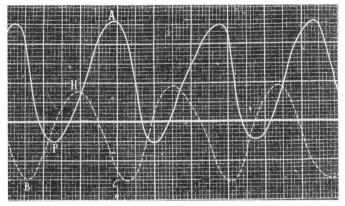

Chapter 2

Reprinted from Marey, 1889.

Movement Forces

Force is a concept that is used to describe the *physical interaction* of an object with its surroundings. It can be defined as an agent that produces or tends to produce a change in the state of rest or motion of an object—that is, it accelerates the object. For example, a ball sitting stationary (zero velocity) on a pool table will remain in that position unless it is acted upon by a force. Similarly, a person gliding on ice skates will maintain a constant velocity unless a force changes the motion—that is, the speed (magnitude) or the direction. The study of motion that includes consideration of force as the cause of movement is called **kinetics.**

Laws of Motion

Isaac Newton (1642–1727) characterized the relation between force and motion with three statements, known collectively as the *laws of motion*. These laws, which are referred to as the laws of inertia, acceleration, and action-reaction, were originally formulated for particles but are also relevant for rigid bodies, such as human body segments (Nigg & Herzog, 1994).

Law of Inertia

A particle will remain in a state of rest or move in a straight line with constant velocity, if there are no forces acting upon the particle.

More simply, *a force is required to stop, start, or alter motion.* This law is evident in a weightless (micro-gravity) environment, for example, when astronauts toss objects to one another or perform somersaults. In a gravitational world, however, forces act continuously upon bodies, and a change in motion occurs when there is a *net imbalance* of forces. In this context, the term *body* can refer to the entire human body, or just part of the human body (e.g., thigh, hand, torso), or even some object (e.g., shot put, baseball, Frisbee).

To appreciate fully the implications of this law, it is necessary to understand the term **inertia.** The concept of inertia relates to the difficulty with which an object's velocity is altered. **Mass,** expressed in grams (g), is a measure of the amount of matter composing an object and is a quantitative measure of inertia. Consider two objects of different mass but with the same amount of motion (similar velocities). It is more difficult to alter the motion of the more massive object; hence it has a greater inertia. Because motion is described in terms of velocity, the inertia of an object is a property of matter that is revealed only when the object is being accelerated—that is, when there is a change in velocity.

According to the law of inertia, an object in motion will continue in uniform motion (constant amplitude and direction of velocity) unless acted upon by a force. This means that the tendency of an object in motion is to travel in a straight line. For example, consider a ball tied to a string and swung overhead in a horizontal plane. When the string is released, will the trajectory of the ball be a straight line or a curved line? To answer this question, we invoke Newton's law of inertia. If no force acts on an object, then the object will, because of its inertia, travel in a straight line. Once the individual releases the string, no horizontal force acts on the ball and so it will travel in a straight line. But then how can a pitched ball in baseball or softball be made to deviate from a straight line? According to the law of inertia, other forces (e.g., air resistance, gravity) must act on the ball once it has been released. Remember, the trajectory of a projectile will be a straight line unless it is influenced by gravity or air resistance.

Because linear motion is represented as a constant velocity, in both magnitude and direction, a force must be present when an object travels along a curved path. This force prevents the object from following its natural tendency of traveling in a straight line. Although the length of the velocity vector may be constant, its direction changes continuously during angular motion. This change of direction is caused by an inwardly directed force known as **centripetal force.** Centripetal force (F_c) is defined as

$$F_c = \frac{mv^2}{r} \tag{2.1}$$

where m = mass, v = velocity, and r = the radius of the curved path. In Equation 2.1, what would happen to F_c if the speed of the ball (v) remained constant, the length of the string (r) stayed the same, and the mass of the ball increased? Centripetal force (F_c) would have to increase in order to satisfy these conditions. Conversely, F_c would decrease if the ball mass (m) and velocity (v) remained constant, while the length of the string (r) increased.

Law of Acceleration

A particle acted upon by an external force moves such that the force is equal to the time rate of change of the linear momentum.

The term **momentum** (G) describes the quantity of motion possessed by a body and is defined as the product of mass (m) and velocity (v). A runner with a mass of 60 kg moving at a horizontal speed of 8 m/s possesses a momentum of 480 kg·m/s. Thus

$$G = mv \tag{2.2}$$

and the rate of change in momentum can be written as

$$\frac{\Delta G}{\Delta t} = \frac{\Delta(mv)}{\Delta t}$$

Because m does not change in human movement, the applied force (F) is proportional to the product of mass and the rate of change in velocity ($\Delta v/\Delta t$ = acceleration),

$$F = \frac{\Delta G}{\Delta t} = m\frac{\Delta v}{\Delta t}$$

$$F = ma \qquad\qquad (2.3)$$

Thus Equation 2.3 is the algebraic expression of Newton's law of acceleration and states that force is equal to mass times acceleration. Conceptually, this is a cause-and-effect relation. The left-hand side *(F)* can be regarded as the cause because it represents the physical interactions between a system and its surroundings. In contrast, the right-hand side reveals the effect because it indicates the kinematic effects *(ma)* of the interactions on the system. Equation 2.3 is the most direct way to measure the force that is applied to an object.

Law of Action-Reaction

When two particles exert force upon one another, the forces act along the line joining the particles, and the two force vectors are equal in magnitude and opposite in direction.

The law of action-reaction implies that every effect that one body exerts on another is counteracted by an effect that the second body exerts on the first. This interaction between bodies is described as a force. For example, consider a person performing a jump shot in basketball. During the act of jumping, the person exerts a force against the ground, and the ground responds simultaneously with a reaction force (the ground reaction force) on the jumper. The law of action-reaction indicates that the forces between the jumper and the ground (i.e., the effect of the jumper on the ground and of the ground on the jumper) are equivalent in magnitude but opposite in direction. The consequence of this interaction, as specified by the law of acceleration *(F = ma)*, is that each body (i.e., the basketball player and the ground) experiences an acceleration that depends on its mass.

The law of action-reaction provides the foundation for many devices that are used to measure force. Examples include strain gauges, spring balances, piezoelectric crystals, and capacitors. When a force is applied to one of these devices, the device is deformed microscopically, and the amount of the deformation can be calibrated as units of force (newtons). The deformations include stretch (strain) for a strain gauge, displacement for a spring balance, electrical charge for a piezoelectric crystal, and electric current for a capacitor. If we want to use one of these devices, it has to be calibrated through application of known forces (e.g., weights) and measurement of the resulting deformation, which is often recorded as a voltage. The outcome of a calibration procedure is a graph that shows the relation between force and deformation. Subsequently, when an unknown force deforms the sensor, the deformation can be converted to force through application of the calibration factor.

Free Body Diagram

In the analysis of human motion, many variables influence performance. To reduce the complexity of a chosen analysis, biomechanists draw a **free body diagram.** A free body diagram defines the extent of the analysis and identifies the significant forces involved in the action. It is usually drawn as a stick figure, along with a set of coordinates, with the forces indicated as arrows. The stick figure part of the diagram indicates the system involved in the analysis. Identifying an appropriate system, which typically varies from one problem to another, is one of the greatest difficulties that beginning students encounter in the analysis of human movement.

As an introduction to this technique, we examine several different free body diagrams and consider the ways in which it is possible to define a system as a basis for the analysis of human movement. The actual forces that can be included in a free body diagram are described in more detail in the next two chapters. In general, however, when a system is in equilibrium and the free body diagram includes only two forces, they must be equal, opposite, and **collinear.** When such a free body diagram includes three or more forces, they must be **concurrent** (i.e., their lines of action must converge and intersect at a point); otherwise one of the forces would exert an unbalanced effect on the system (Meriam & Kraige, 1987).

For the first example, suppose that we want to determine the magnitude and direction of the ground reaction force experienced by a runner (figure 2.1*a*). According to the law of action-reaction, when the runner pushes on the ground, the ground will push back; we want to know how hard the ground pushes back. The first step is to specify and draw the system, which is the runner's body (figure 2.1*b*). The next step is to identify all the external forces acting on the system with arrows of correct length (magnitude) and direction and to label them appropriately (figure 2.1*c*). The forces shown in figure 2.1*c* represent air resistance (F_a), weight or gravity (F_w), and ground reaction force (F_g). In general, the forces will include the weight of the system and forces arising from contact with the surroundings (e.g., ground reaction force, air resistance).

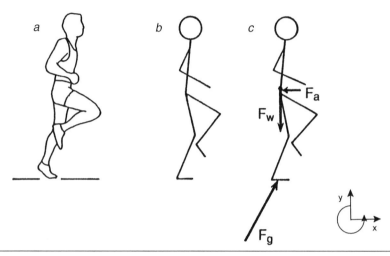

Figure 2.1 Derivation of a free body diagram from *(a)* a real-life figure to *(b)* the identification of the system and *(c)* the inclusion of the forces imposed on the system by its surroundings.

Free body diagrams show only the forces acting on the system and not those within the system. For example, the free body diagram in figure 2.1*c* does not show any muscle forces across the knee joint, even though the quadriceps femoris muscle is undoubtedly contracting; this is not shown because the muscle force is internal to this system. If, however, the aim of an analysis is to examine muscle activity across a joint during a movement, as we will do in chapter 3, then a different system must be defined. If we consider a particular interaction, such as the muscle activity associated with a particular movement, we must define the system so that the interaction occurs between the system and its surroundings. We need to specify the system so that we can see the agent causing the interaction. In the case of determining muscle activity, this involves figuratively cutting through the desired joint (e.g., knee joint). Around each joint are a variety of tissues that include muscle, joint capsule, ligaments, and so forth. We usually distinguish the effects of muscle from those of the other tissues. Consequently, when we draw a free body diagram that involves cutting through a joint, we identify a net muscle force (the resultant muscle force) and a force that accounts for the contact between adjacent body segments (the joint reaction force). Let us return to the example outlined in figure 2.1. For examining the effects of the muscles across the knee joint at the instant shown in figure 2.1*b*, the appropriate free body diagram is shown in figure 2.2.

As another example of defining a system, suppose the situation arises in which a weight lifter begins to develop back pains after several months of training. An appropriate analysis might include determining how much force is exerted by the muscles that extend the back and hip during a movement. Because this force is greatest at the beginning of the movement, the analysis would focus on the weight lifter at this position (figure 2.3*a*). The object of the analysis would be to calculate a muscle force, so we must define the system to identify the muscle

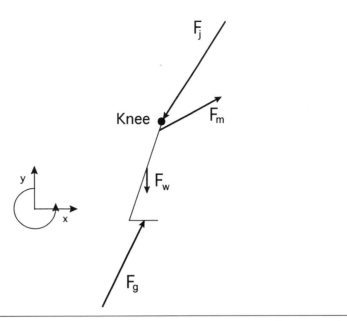

Figure 2.2   Free body diagram of a system (shank + foot) upon which four external forces are acting.

F_g = ground reaction force; F_j = joint reaction force; F_m = resultant muscle force; F_w = weight.

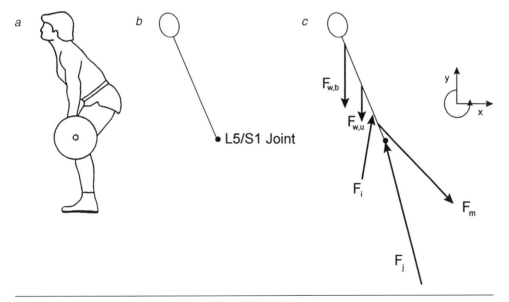

Figure 2.3   The derivation of a free body diagram to analyze part of a weightlifting movement: *(a)* whole-body diagram of the weight lifter; *(b)* system used to expose the forces across the L5-S1 intervertebral joint; *(c)* free body diagram showing the interactions between the system and its surroundings.

effect on the free body diagram. This involves figuratively cutting through the L5-S1 intervertebral joint so that the system becomes either the part of the weight lifter above the joint plus barbell or the part of the weight lifter below the joint. In the former instance, the stick figure would simply include a circle for the head and a line for the trunk and arms (figure 2.3*b*).

The next step is to illustrate all the interactions, drawn as force vectors (arrows), between the system (upper body of the weight lifter plus the barbell) and the surroundings. First, one of the most obvious forces is that due to gravity—that is, the weight of the barbell $(F_{w,b})$ and the weight of the upper body of the lifter $(F_{w,u})$. The direction of the weight vectors is always vertically downward. Second, because we cut through a joint, we must show both the resultant muscle force (F_m) and the joint reaction force (F_j) on the free body diagram. The joint reaction force (F_j) represents the reaction of the adjacent body part to the forces exerted on it by the system. Although the direction of F_m is reasonably straightforward in that it opposes the rotation produced by the load (i.e., the weight vectors), the direction of F_j is usually unknown and is arbitrarily drawn as a compressive force acting into the joint. If the system is in equilibrium, the forces directed to the right must be balanced by forces that are directed to the left; forces directed upward must be counteracted by forces that go downward; and forces that produce clockwise rotations must be balanced by forces that cause counterclockwise rotation. That is, the forces must be concurrent. Another force appropriate for this free body diagram is the force due to the pressure in the abdominal cavity (intra-abdominal pressure, F_i); this force tends to cause extension about the hip joint (Andersson, Örtengren, & Nachemson, 1977; Eie & Wehn, 1962; Rab, Chao, & Stauffer, 1977). This reflexively controlled force functions as a protective mechanism and has a significant role in lifting activities (Marras, Joynt, & King, 1985). These five forces $(F_{w,b}, F_{w,u}, F_j, F_m, F_i)$ represent the major interactions between this system and its surroundings. The appropriate free body diagram is shown in figure 2.3c. Once a free body diagram has been correctly drawn, it is possible to apply the law of acceleration directly.

From these examples, you should understand why it is necessary to draw a free body diagram and how we do this. The purpose of a free body diagram is to establish the conditions for an analysis. There are two steps in drawing a free body diagram. First, define the system you need in order to answer the question, which usually involves drawing a stick figure of the system. This is often the most difficult step. Second, identify all the ways in which the defined system interacts with its surroundings. These interactions are included on the free body diagram as force vectors. How we know which forces should be included on a free body diagram is discussed throughout chapters 2 and 3.

Torque

All human motion involves the rotation of body segments about their joint axes. These actions are produced by the interaction of forces associated with external loads and muscle activity. In particular, *human movement is the consequence of an imbalance between the components of these forces that produce rotation.* The capability of a force to produce rotation is referred to as **torque** or **moment of force.** Torque represents the rotational effect of a force with respect to an axis: the tendency of a force to produce rotation.

Torque is a vector that is equal to the magnitude of the force times the perpendicular distance between the line of action of the force and the axis of rotation. This distance, known as the **moment arm,** may be expressed as a scalar or a vector quantity. As a scalar quantity, it is the magnitude of the distance between the line of action and the axis of rotation. As a vector quantity, it is specified as being directed from the axis of rotation to the line of action of the force. Algebraically,

$$\boldsymbol{\tau} = \mathbf{r} \times \mathbf{F} \qquad (2.4)$$

where $\boldsymbol{\tau}$ = torque, $\mathbf{r}$ = moment arm, and $\mathbf{F}$ = force. Because the moment arm is a perpendicular distance, it is the shortest distance from the line of action of the force to the axis of rotation. The direction of the torque vector is perpendicular to the plane in which the force and the moment arm exist. As explained in chapter 1, when two vector quantities are multiplied and the product is a vector, the direction of the product is always perpendicular to the plane in which the other two vectors are located; this procedure is called the **cross product** or **vector product.** Torque, as a vector product, will usually be directed out of or into the page.

For graphic convenience, torque is often represented as a curved arrow in the same plane as the moment arm and force vectors. We can determine the direction of the curved arrow by applying the **right-hand-thumb rule,** as shown in figure 2.4. This involves drawing the vectors to be multiplied so that their tails are connected. To determine a torque vector, the moment

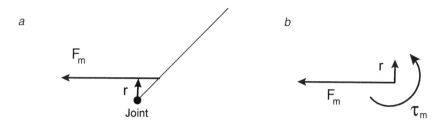

Figure 2.4 Use of the right-hand-thumb rule to determine the direction of a muscle torque (τ_m) vector. *(a)* Muscle torque is the product of a moment arm (r) and a muscle force (F_m). *(b)* Realignment of r and F_m so that their tails contact and the direction of τ_m can be determined with the right-hand-thumb rule.

arm and force vectors of the free body diagram (figure 2.4*a*) must be translated so that their tails contact but without changing the directions of the two vectors (figure 2.4*b*). Then the right hand, with thumb extended, is used to indicate the vector product. Take your right hand and point the fingers in the direction of **r** so that the palm faces the direction of **F**$_m$; then curl the fingers from the direction of **r** to the direction of **F**$_m$ (**r** × **F**$_m$) and extend the thumb. The extended thumb indicates the direction of the torque vector (τ_m). Consequently, a counterclockwise direction corresponds to a vector coming out of the page, which we usually call the positive direction. The extended thumb indicates the axis about which the rotary force acts.

Torque, or moment of force, is always determined with respect to a specific axis (as indicated by the moment arm) and therefore must be expressed with reference to the same axis. To discuss the rotary effect of load or a muscle force, we need to indicate the point about which the rotation will occur. Because torque is calculated as the product of a force and a distance, the units of measurement are newtons times meters (N · m).

Example 2.1
Influence of Moment Arm

As an example of the role of torque in human movement, consider an individual who sits on a bench and performs a knee extension exercise. The person is rehabilitating a knee injury and has a mass that can be attached to the shank to vary the difficulty of the exercise. Would it require more effort to perform the exercise if the mass were attached at the ankle or if it were attached at the middle of the shank?

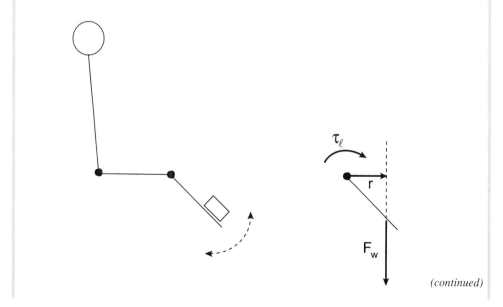

(continued)

This exercise involves the muscles around the knee joint, which must be activated to exert a torque that can displace the load. The magnitude of the muscle activity, therefore, depends on the load. In this instance, the load is a torque about the knee joint due to the mass of the system (attached mass + shank and foot mass) and is obtained from the following relation:

$$\tau_l = \mathbf{r} \times \mathbf{F}_w$$

where τ_l is the load torque, $\mathbf{r}$ is the moment arm, and $\mathbf{F}_w$ is the weight of the system ($\mathbf{F}_w = mg$, where m is the mass of the system and g is the acceleration due to gravity). If you use the right-hand-thumb rule to perform the vector product ($\mathbf{r}$ cross $\mathbf{F}$), what is the direction of τ_l? On the basis of the description of figure 2.4, point the fingers of your right hand in the direction of $\mathbf{r}$ and then curl them in the direction of $\mathbf{F}_w$, and your extended thumb will indicate the direction of τ_l. The result should tell you that τ_l is a vector pointing into the page, which indicates the axis about which the rotary force (torque) has its effect.

Because the weight of the system does not change in this example, τ_l varies with the moment arm ($\mathbf{r}$). So the question becomes, is $\mathbf{r}$ greater when the mass is attached to the ankle or to the midshank? Where is $\mathbf{r}$? The moment arm is defined as the perpendicular distance from the line of action of the force vector to the axis of rotation (knee joint). At any point in the range of motion of the exercise, $\mathbf{r}$ is longer when the mass is attached at the ankle compared with the midshank, which means that τ_l is greater with the mass attached to the ankle. This example demonstrates that one way to vary the load when exercising is to manipulate the moment arm.

Forces Due to Body Mass

Once we define a system with a free body diagram, we are able to consider the interactions (forces) that are likely to occur between a system and its surroundings. In general, the forces that act on the human body are those due to body mass and those due to contact with the surroundings. These forces are distributed throughout the human body and can be estimated with techniques that we will examine in this and the next chapter.

Gravity

Newton characterized gravity in a statement known as the **law of gravitation:** *All bodies attract one another with a force proportional to the product of their masses and inversely proportional to the square of the distance between them.* That is,

$$F \propto \frac{m_1 m_2}{r^2} \tag{2.5}$$

where m_1 and m_2 are the masses of two bodies and r is the distance between them.

These forces of attraction between objects are generally regarded as negligible in the study of human movement, with the exception of the attraction between Earth and various objects. **Weight** is an expression of the amount of gravitational attraction between an object and Earth. As a force, it is measured in newtons (N). Weight varies proportionately with mass—the greater the mass, the greater the attraction—but the two are separate quantities. Weight is a force (a derived quantity) whereas mass (a base measure in the SI system) is a measure of the amount of matter. Because weight represents the interaction between an object and Earth, the magnitude of the interaction depends on their respective masses and the distance between them; therefore, gravity decreases as altitude increases above sea level. This accounts for one of the advantages of performing at high altitude in events in which the contestant must overcome gravity (e.g., long jump, shot put, weightlifting).

We can determine the *magnitude of the total-body weight vector* by reading the value from a weight scale. The validity of this procedure can be demonstrated with a simple analysis based on Newton's law of acceleration (Equation 2.3),

$$\Sigma F = ma$$

which states that the sum (Σ = Sigma) of the forces (F) produces an acceleration (a) of the system that depends on the mass (m) of the system. Because gravity acts only in the vertical direction (y), the analysis can be confined to this direction. The forces acting on a person standing on a weight scale include the weight (F_w) of the person, which is directed downward and indicated as negative, and the vertical component of the ground reaction force $(F_{g,y})$, which is directed upward and indicated as positive. The decision to label F_w negative and $F_{g,y}$ positive is quite arbitrary; however, it is essential to distinguish these differences in direction. To this end, each free body diagram should be accompanied by a reference axis (coordinate system) that shows the positive directions of each component (figure 2.5): positive vertical (y), horizontal (x), and rotation directions.

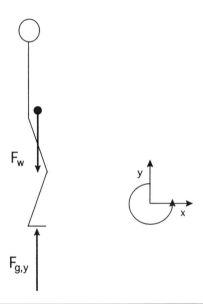

Figure 2.5   Free body diagram of the whole body.

The appropriate free body diagram is shown in figure 2.5, and the analysis is as follows:

$$\Sigma F_y = ma_y$$

$$-F_w + F_{g,y} = ma_y$$

$$F_w = F_{g,y} - ma_y$$

Because the person is stationary, $a_y = 0$. Thus, in scalar terms,

$$F_w = F_{g,y} - 0$$

$$F_w = F_{g,y}$$

The *direction of the weight vector* is always vertically downward toward the center of the Earth; the vector originates from a point referred to as the center of mass. The **center of mass**

(CM) represents a balance point, a location about which all the particles of the object are evenly distributed. It is an abstract point that moves when the body segments are moved relative to one another. The CM can even be located outside the physical limits of the system, as would be the case, for example, when a diver assumes a pike position. We discuss the techniques used to determine CM location in chapter 3.

Segmental Analysis

Like many forces encountered in the analysis of human movement, weight is a distributed force with the net effect shown at a central location. For example, a free body diagram shows the contact between a player's head and a soccer ball as occurring at a point, although it is distributed over a large part of the forehead. Similarly, the CM of the object is the point about which the mass of the object is evenly distributed. Accordingly, when the mass of the object is redistributed, which usually happens in human movement, the location of the CM also moves.

To determine the location of the whole-body CM during movement, biomechanists use a procedure known as *segmental analysis*. This approach considers the human body as a set of rigid bodies (segments) and deals with them individually (figure 2.6). A segmental analysis involves estimating the mass and the location of the CM for each body segment and then using this information to determine CM location for the whole body. This procedure is discussed in chapter 3. At this point, we introduce the database on segmental masses and CMs, which represents the magnitude and location of the weight vector for the various segments of the human body.

Several groups of investigators have dissected cadavers to derive regression equations to estimate various **anthropometric** (measurements of the human body) segmental dimensions (e.g., Chandler, Clauser, McConville, Reynolds, & Young, 1975; Dempster, 1955). As described by Miller and Nelson (1973), this database is not extensive and consists mainly of measurements made on older Caucasian males. Fortunately, additional databases on children, adolescents, and women are emerging in the literature (Ackland, Blanksby, & Bloomfield, 1988; Jensen, Doucet, & Treitz, 1996; Matsuo, Ozawa, Goda, & Fukunaga, 1995). Some of the data derived from one of the most comprehensive cadaver studies (n = 6), that performed by Chandler et al. (1975), are reported in tables 2.1 and 2.2. These data consist of regression equations to estimate segmental weights and CM locations (table 2.1) as well as actual values for segmental moments of inertia about the three axes (table 2.2).

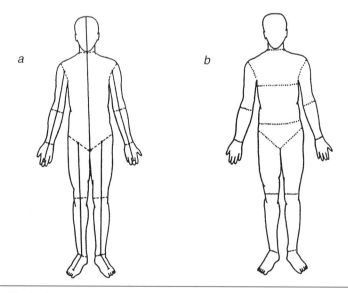

Figure 2.6   The body segment organization used in two studies: *(a)* Chandler, Clauser, McConville, Reynolds, and Young, 1975—the 14 segments comprised the head, trunk, upper arms, forearms, hand, thighs, shanks, and feet; *(b)* Zatsiorsky and Seluyanov, 1983—the 16 segments included the head, upper torso, middle torso, lower torso, upper arms, forearms, hands, thighs, shanks, and feet.

Table 2.1 Regression Equations Estimating Body Segment Weights and Locations of the Center of Mass

Segment	Weight (N)	CM location (%)	Proximal end of segment
Head	$0.032\ F_w + 18.70$	66.3	Vertex
Trunk	$0.532\ F_w - 6.93$	52.2	C1
Upper arm	$0.022\ F_w + 4.76$	50.7	Shoulder joint
Forearm	$0.013\ F_w + 2.41$	41.7	Elbow joint
Hand	$0.005\ F_w + 0.75$	51.5	Wrist joint
Thigh	$0.127\ F_w - 14.82$	39.8	Hip joint
Shank	$0.044\ F_w - 1.75$	41.3	Knee joint
Foot	$0.009\ F_w + 2.48$	40.0	Heel

Note. Body segment weights are estimated from total-body weight (F_w), and the segmental center-of-mass (CM) locations are expressed as a percentage of segment length as measured from the proximal end of the segment.

Table 2.2 Whole-Body Moments of Inertia ($kg \cdot m^2$) About the Somersault, Cartwheel, and Twist Axes

Position	Somersault	Cartwheel	Twist
Layout	12.55	15.09	3.83
Open pike (arms out to side)	8.38	8.98	4.79
Closed pike (fingers touching toes)	8.65	6.60	3.58
Tuck	4.07	4.42	2.97

Table 2.1 presents regression equations for estimating segment weight from total-body weight and for estimating CM location for each segment based on the measurement of segment length. For example, if an individual weighed 750 N, then

$$trunk\ weight = 0.532 \times 750 - 6.93$$
$$= 392\ N$$

which accounts for 52% of total-body weight. Similarly,

$$hand\ weight = 0.005 \times 750 + 0.75$$
$$= 4.5\ N$$

which represents about 0.6% of total-body weight. The segment boundaries used by Chandler et al. (1975) are shown in figure 2.6a. Table 2.1 can also be used to estimate CM location. If the length of an individual's thigh (hip-to-knee distance) is 36 cm, then, according to Chandler et al., the CM for that thigh is located at 39.8% of that distance from the hip joint:

$$CM\ location = 36 \times 0.398$$
$$= 14.3\ cm\ from\ the\ hip\ joint$$

Because human motion is based on the rotation of body segments about one another, the distribution of mass in a segment is as important to know as its mass. The distribution of mass can be quantified by a parameter known as the moment of inertia. The **moment of inertia** is the angular equivalent of inertia (mass) and represents *a measure of the resistance that an object offers to a change in its motion about an axis.* The moment of inertia *(I)* is defined as

$$I = \sum_{i=1}^{n} m_i r_i^2 \tag{2.6}$$

where *n* indicates the number of elements (particles or segments) in the system, m_i represents the mass of each element of the system, and r_i is the distance of each element from the axis of rotation. Equation 2.6 is useful for systems that comprise a relatively small number of mass elements. For objects that have a continuous distribution of matter, however, the same relation should be expressed as an integral.

$$I = \int r^2 \, dm \tag{2.7}$$

Equation 2.7 is used for a system that has a large number of small mass elements *(dm)*, such as the particles that compose the human body or a body segment. The integral states that *I* is calculated by summing the products of two terms, the mass of each element and the square of its distance (r^2) from the axis of rotation. The mass elements refer to the parts into which the object can be divided.

Both Equations 2.6 and 2.7 provide a measure of the mass distribution about an axis of rotation. The distribution of mass is usually characterized with reference to three orthogonal (perpendicular) axes that are referred to as the principal axes of rotation. In the analysis of human movement, these axes are often defined as the somersault (side to side), cartwheel (front to back), and twist (longitudinal) axes. Table 2.2 lists estimates of the moment of inertia about the three principal axes for the human body in different positions (Miller & Nelson, 1973). Note that the moment of inertia declines as the mass of the body is brought closer to the axis of rotation; for example, for each body position the moment of inertia is least about the twist axis.

From such measurements as those listed in table 2.2, it is possible to estimate whole-body moment of inertia about any axis of rotation used in human movement. We accomplish this with the **parallel axis theorem.** This theorem states that the moment of inertia about an axis of rotation (I_o) is equal to the sum of the moment of inertia about any parallel axis and a transfer term (md^2). In biomechanics, we often use moments of inertia that have been measured relative to the CM (I_g) and determine the value about another parallel axis (Equation 2.8),

$$I_o = I_g + md^2 \tag{2.8}$$

where *m* represents the mass of the system and *d* is the distance between the two parallel axes. For example, the parallel axis theorem can be used to calculate the whole-body moment of inertia about a transverse axis (somersault axis) passing through the hands of a gymnast (71.2 kg) who is performing stunts on a high bar.

$$I_{hands} = 12.55 \text{ kg·m}^2 + \left[71.2 \text{ kg} \times (1.02 \text{ m})^2 \right]$$
$$= 12.55 + 74.08 \text{ kg·m}^2$$
$$= 86.6 \text{ kg·m}^2$$

where 12.55 kg·m^2 is the moment of inertia about the transverse axis passing through the whole-body CM in a layout position (table 2.2) and 1.02 m^2 is the distance from the CM to the hands (the axis of rotation).

Example 2.2
Calculating the Moment of Inertia

Determine the mass distribution for a system that has four weights connected by a massless wire with its CM *(g)* located at 0.57 m from the proximal end *(o)*.

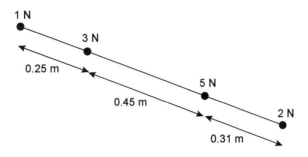

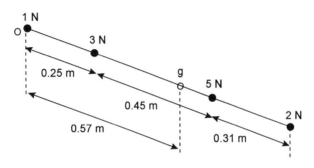

A. Use Equation 2.6 to calculate the moment of inertia of the system about its center of mass *(I_g)*.

$$I_g = \sum_{i=1}^{4} m_i r_i^2$$

$$I_g = m_1 r_1^2 + m_2 r_2^2 + m_3 r_3^2 + m_4 r_4^2$$

$$I_g = \frac{1}{9.81}0.57^2 + \frac{3}{9.81}0.32^2 + \frac{5}{9.81}0.13^2 + \frac{2}{9.81}0.44^2$$

$$I_g = 0.0331 + 0.0313 + 0.0086 + 0.0395$$

$$I_g = 0.1125 \text{ kg·m}^2$$

B. Use Equation 2.6 to calculate the moment of inertia of the system about the proximal end *(I_o)*.

$$I_o = \frac{3}{9.81}0.25^2 + \frac{5}{9.81}0.70^2 + \frac{2}{9.81}1.01^2$$

$$I_o = 0.0191 + 0.2497 + 0.2080$$

$$I_o = 0.4768 \text{ kg·m}^2$$

(continued)

C. Use the answer from part A and the parallel axis theorem (Equation 2.8) to determine the moment of inertia of the system about the proximal end.

$$I_o = I_g + \mathrm{md}^2$$

$$I_o = 0.1125 + \frac{11}{9.81} 0.57^2$$

$$I_o = 0.1125 + 0.3643$$

$$I_o = 0.4768 \text{ kg·m}^2$$

One way to determine the moment of inertia for an object such as the whole body or a body segment is to use the **pendulum method.** This involves measuring the magnitude of the moment of inertia for the object about the suspension point and then using the parallel axis theorem to calculate the moment of inertia about its CM. To use this method you must know the location of the CM and the distance between the CM and the suspension point. The pendulum method consists of suspending an object from a fixed point, setting it in motion by shifting it slightly from its resting position, and measuring the time one period of oscillation takes. The moment of inertia about the suspension point (I_o) is given by

$$I_o = \frac{F_w \cdot h \cdot T^2}{4\pi^2} \tag{2.9}$$

where

F_w = weight of the object

h = distance between the CM and the suspension point

T = period of one oscillation

Once I_o has been determined, I_g can be found by using the parallel axis theorem.

In addition to estimates of mass and CM location, the cadaver studies have yielded segmental moments of inertia. Because there is low variability in these data across specimens, they are typically reported as mean values (table 2.3) (Chandler et al., 1975).

Table 2.3   Segmental Moments of Inertia (kg·m²) About the Somersault, Cartwheel, and Twist Axes

Segment	Somersault	Cartwheel	Twist
Head	0.0164	0.0171	0.0201
Trunk	1.0876	1.6194	0.3785
Upper arm	0.0133	0.0133	0.0022
Forearm	0.0065	0.0067	0.0009
Hand	0.0008	0.0006	0.0002
Thigh	0.1157	0.1137	0.0224
Shank	0.0392	0.0391	0.0029
Foot	0.0030	0.0034	0.0007

To supplement the segmental data derived from cadavers, some investigators have used *mathematical modeling* procedures. With this approach, the human body is represented as a set of geometric components, such as spheres, cylinders, and cones (Hanavan, 1964, 1966; Hatze, 1980, 1981a, 1981b; Miller, 1979; Yeadon, 1990). One of the first to use this approach was Hanavan (1964, 1966). Figure 2.7*a* shows the Hanavan model, which divides the human body into 15 simple geometric solids of uniform density. The advantage of this model is that only a few simple anthropometric measurements (e.g., segment lengths and circumferences) are required to personalize the model and to predict the CM and moment of inertia for each body segment. However, three assumptions typically used in modeling body segments limit the accuracy of the estimates: segments are assumed to be rigid; the boundaries between the segments are assumed to be distinct; and segments are assumed to have a uniform density. In reality, there can be substantial displacement of the soft tissue during movement; the boundaries between segments are fuzzy; and the density varies within and between segments.

Hatze (1980) developed a more detailed model of the human body (figure 2.7*b*). Hatze's hominoid consists of 17 body segments and requires 242 anthropometric measurements for individualization. The model subdivides the segments into small mass elements of different geometrical structures; this allows the shape and density fluctuations of a segment to be modeled in detail. Furthermore, no assumptions are made regarding bilateral symmetry, and the model differentiates between men and women, adjusting the densities of certain segmental parts according to the value of a special subcutaneous fat indicator. The model is able to account for changes in body morphology, such as those due to obesity and pregnancy, and can accommodate children. Indeed, the model has been used to estimate the mass, CM, and moment of inertia for the limb segments of infants (Schneider & Zernicke, 1992). Although acquisition of the input for the model (242 anthropometric measurements) is time consuming, the output of the model provides accurate estimates of volume, mass, CM location, and moments of inertia for the identified body segments. Typical estimates for two male subjects are indicated in table 2.4. One unique feature of this model is the approach used to represent the trunk and shoulder segments (figure 2.7*b*).

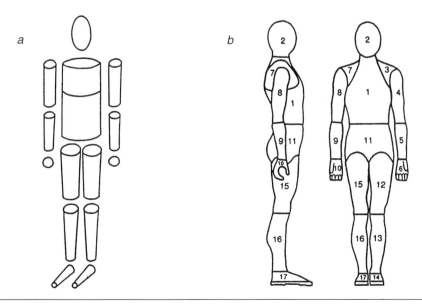

Figure 2.7 Models of the human body: *(a)* the Hanavan model of the human body; *(b)* the 17-segment hominoid of Hatze (1980). The 17 segments are 1, abdomino-thoracic; 2, head; 3, left shoulder; 4, left upper arm; 5, left forearm; 6, left hand; 7, right shoulder; 8, right upper arm; 9, right forearm; 10, right hand; 11, abdomino-pelvic; 12, left thigh; 13, left shank; 14, left foot; 15, right thigh; 16, right shank; 17, right foot.

Table 2.4 Segmental Parameter Values for Two Male Subjects Computed With the Hatze Model

Segment	Subject F.B. (23 yrs)			Subject C.P. (26 yrs)		
	Volume	CM location	I_{zz}	Volume	CM location	I_{zz}
Head-neck	4.475	0.517	0.0303	4.537	0.516	0.0337
Abdomino-thoracic	19.111	0.439	0.3117	19.803	0.444	0.3302
Left shoulder	1.438	0.727	0.0047	2.042	0.706	0.0080
Right shoulder	1.890	0.711	0.0071	2.121	0.699	0.0084
Left upper arm	2.110	0.432	0.0196	2.123	0.437	0.0203
Right upper arm	2.021	0.437	0.0168	2.340	0.428	0.0229
Left forearm	1.023	0.417	0.0067	1.223	0.413	0.0086
Right forearm	1.190	0.404	0.0079	1.313	0.412	0.0093
Left hand	0.453	0.515	0.0011	0.416	0.533	0.0010
Right hand	0.446	0.531	0.0011	0.417	0.524	0.0010
Abdomino-pelvic	8.543	0.368	0.0399	9.614	0.395	0.0541
Left thigh	8.258	0.479	0.1475	8.744	0.473	0.1653
Right thigh	8.278	0.480	0.1415	8.729	0.466	0.1702
Left shank	3.628	0.412	0.0615	3.856	0.420	0.0798
Right shank	3.686	0.417	0.0663	3.798	0.417	0.0747
Left foot	0.887	—	0.0041	1.032	—	0.0051
Right foot	0.923	—	0.0042	1.055	—	0.0051

Note. Volume = computed segment volume (L); CM location = distance from proximal end of segment (proportion of segment length, where 0.500 indicates 50% of segment length); I_{zz} = moment of inertia about the somersault (zz) axis through the CM. Segment densities were abdomen = 1000 + 30 i_m, head = 1120, neck = 1040, and arms and legs = 1080 + 20 i_m kg/m³, where i_m = 1 for men and 0 for women.

Another technique available for determining body segment parameters is based on recently developed imaging procedures such as computed tomography and magnetic resonance imaging (Engstrom, Loeb, Reid, Forrest, & Avruch, 1991; Martin, Mungiole, Marzke, & Longhill, 1989). An example of this approach is the use of *radioisotopes* to measure the intensity of a gamma-radiation beam before and after it passes through a body segment. The principle involves scanning a subject's body and obtaining the surface density and dimensions of the body segments subjected to the radiation. Zatsiorsky and colleagues (Zatsiorsky & Seluynov, 1983; Zatsiorsky, Seluyanov, & Chugunova, 1990a, 1990b) performed this procedure on 100 men (age = 24 ± 6 years; height = 1.74 ± 0.06 m; mass = 73 ± 9 kg) and 15 women (age = 19 ± 4 years; height = 1.74 ± 0.03 m; mass = 62 ± 7 kg). The segmental data on these young adults were subsequently adjusted by de Leva (1996), and the results are listed in tables 2.5 and 2.6. The proximal ends of the segments are similar to those used by Chandler et al. (1975) (table 2.1), with the exceptions of the trunk and upper torso (suprasternale), midtorso (xyphion), and lower torso (omphalion). The end of the hand segment was defined as the third knuckle, between the metacarpal and the finger.

Table 2.5 Segment Length, Mass, and Center-of-Mass (CM) Location for Young Adult Women (W) and Men (M)

Segment	Length (cm)		Mass (%)		CM location (%)	
	W	M	W	M	W	M
Head	20.02	20.33	6.68	6.94	58.94	59.76
Trunk	52.93	53.19	42.57	43.46	41.51	44.86
Upper torso	14.25	17.07	15.45	15.96	20.77	29.99
Middle torso	20.53	21.55	14.65	16.33	45.12	45.02
Lower torso	18.15	14.57	12.47	11.17	49.20	61.15
Upper arm	27.51	28.17	2.55	2.71	57.54	57.72
Forearm	26.43	26.89	1.38	1.62	45.59	45.74
Hand	7.80	8.62	0.56	0.61	74.74	79.00
Thigh	36.85	42.22	14.78	14.16	36.12	40.95
Shank	43.23	43.40	4.81	4.33	44.16	44.59
Foot	22.83	25.81	1.29	1.37	40.14	44.15

Table 2.6 Segmental Moments of Inertia ($kg \cdot m^2$) for Young Adult Women (W) and Men (M) About the Somersault, Cartwheel, and Twist Axes

Segment	Somersault		Cartwheel		Twist	
	W	M	W	M	W	M
Head	0.0213	0.0296	0.0180	0.0266	0.0167	0.0204
Trunk	0.8484	1.0809	0.9409	1.2302	0.2159	0.3275
Upper torso	0.0489	0.0700	0.1080	0.1740	0.1001	0.1475
Middle torso	0.0479	0.0812	0.0717	0.1286	0.0658	0.1212
Lower torso	0.0411	0.0525	0.0477	0.0654	0.0501	0.0596
Upper arm	0.0081	0.0114	0.0092	0.0128	0.0026	0.0039
Forearm	0.0039	0.0060	0.0040	0.0065	0.0005	0.0022
Hand	0.0004	0.0009	0.0006	0.0013	0.0002	0.0005
Thigh	0.1646	0.1995	0.1692	0.1995	0.0326	0.0409
Shank	0.0397	0.0369	0.0409	0.0387	0.0048	0.0063
Foot	0.0032	0.0040	0.0037	0.0044	0.0008	0.0010

Example 2.3
Performing a Segmental Analysis

Let us briefly consider a segmental analysis of the weight lifter depicted earlier in the "Free Body Diagram" section. To determine the contribution to the movement made by the muscles crossing the knee, we first decide how many segments to use to represent the lifter (figure 2.8a). In the movement, shown at the top of figure 1.17, the arms do not bend at the elbow, so we can consider the arms as one segment. And because the movement is confined to the sagittal $(x$-$y)$ plane, we assume that the left and right sides of the body are more or less doing the same thing. These simplifications allow us to reduce our free body diagram from the maximum of 15 to 17 segments (based on Hanavan's and Hatze's models) down to 6 segments. Furthermore, the whole-body stick figure will become six separate systems, one for each segment (figure 2.8b); this is the essence of a *segmental analysis*.

Next we draw the appropriate free body diagram (figure 2.8c). This includes identifying the system and determining the location (CM) and magnitude of the weight vector $(F_{w,s})$. Because we want to determine the net muscle force across the knee joint $(F_{m,k})$, we use the shank as the system. Both the CM location and the magnitude of the weight vector can be estimated from the data in table 2.1. According to table 2.1, the CM for the shank is located at 41.3% of shank length from the knee joint. If the shank of the weight lifter measured 36 cm, then the CM would be situated 14.9 cm (36 $\times$ 0.413 = 14.9) from the knee. Similarly, the magnitude of the weight vector is determined as a function of total-body weight. For an 800-N weight lifter, the weight of one shank would be 33.5 N (0.044 $\times$ 800 − 1.75 = 33.5). Finally, the other forces acting on the system, which we have not described yet, must be added to the free body diagram.

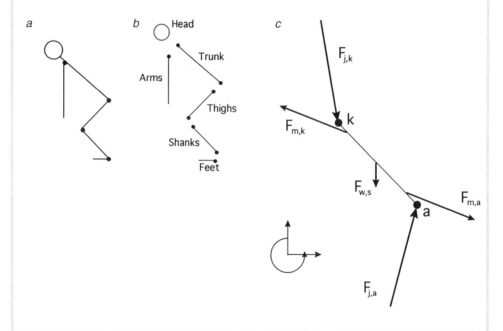

Figure 2.8 Free body diagram of a weight lifter: *(a)* whole-body stick figure; *(b)* segmental components; *(c)* free body diagram of the shank. $F_{j,a}$ and $F_{j,k}$ = ankle and knee joint reaction forces; $F_{m,a}$ and $F_{m,k}$ = ankle and knee resultant muscle forces; $F_{w,s}$ = weight of the shank.

Inertial Force

Newton told us that a moving object continues to move in a straight line and at a constant speed unless it is acted on by a force (law of inertia). The object's resistance to any change in its motion is called its *inertia. An object in motion can, due to its inertia, exert a force on another object.* To demonstrate this effect, place one of your forearms in a vertical position (hand pointing upward) with the upper arm horizontal. Relax the muscles of your forearm that cross the wrist joint. Slowly begin to oscillate your forearm about the elbow joint in a small arc in a forward-backward direction. As the movement becomes more vigorous, you should notice that your hand begins to flail, particularly if your forearm muscles are relaxed. You suspect that the motion of your hand is caused by the motion of the forearm, and you are correct. The forearm (because of its motion) has exerted an inertial force on the hand and caused the motion of the hand; this interaction is also known as a **motion-dependent effect.** This simple example emphasizes the mechanical coupling that exists between the components of a linked system, such as that between our body segments.

The hammer throw provides an extreme example of the inertial force. We learned in the section on projectile motion (chapter 1) that the distance a person can throw an object depends on the object's speed and the angle and height at which it is released. For example, the world-record performance for a hammer throw is 86.3 m, which required a release velocity of 29.1 m/s (65 mph) at the optimal angle of release (0.78 rad, 45°). To achieve this release speed, the athlete performed five revolutions while traveling across a 2.13-m-diameter ring. The athlete applied two forces to the hammer during this procedure: (a) a pulling force that provided an angular acceleration to increase the speed of rotation and (b) a centripetal force to maintain the angular nature of the motion. Brancazio (1984) estimated that to achieve a release velocity of 29.1 m/s, the athlete provided an average pulling force of about 45 N throughout the event and a centripetal force of about 2.8 kN at release.

Because forces act in pairs (action-reaction), the hammer must exert a force on the thrower (inertial force) of 2.8 kN at release. You can quite easily visualize this motion-dependent effect of the hammer by imagining what would happen to the athlete if he forgot to let go of the hammer but instead held on past the release point. As soon as the centripetal force exerted by the athlete on the hammer declined below 2.8 kN, the inertial force of the hammer, due to its motion, would cause the athlete to be dragged out of the throwing circle.

Motion-dependent effects are significant in many of our everyday activities, such as running, kicking, and piano playing. In running, for example, the motion of the thigh can quite readily affect the motion of the shank (Piazza & Delp, 1996). Figure 2.9 shows the changes that occur in knee angle and resultant muscle torque (rotary force exerted by muscle) about the hip and knee joints during the swing phase of a running stride (Phillips & Roberts, 1980). The net muscle torque about the hip joint is essentially biphasic: it has a flexor direction (shown as a positive torque) for the first half of the swing phase and then acts in an extensor direction for the second half of the swing phase. The flexor hip torque accelerates the thigh in a forward direction, while the extensor torque accelerates the thigh in a backward direction. Similarly, the resultant muscle torque about the knee joint (dashed line in figure 2.9) appears biphasic, with an intermediate period of a zero torque. However, whereas the hip torque has a flexor-extensor sequence, the resultant muscle torque about the knee has an extensor-flexor sequence. Thus a net hip flexor torque is associated with a net knee extensor torque, and the latter part of the swing phase comprises a sequence of net hip extensor and knee flexor torques.

The role of the resultant muscle torque about the knee joint becomes clearer when we consider how knee angle changed during the swing phase. We can do this by comparing the two graphs in figure 2.9. Knee angle first decreased and then increased during the swing phase (knee angle graph in figure 2.9). When the knee joint flexed (first half of the swing phase), this was controlled by a resultant extensor torque about the knee joint; that is, *flexion was controlled by the extensor muscles.* This condition represents a lengthening of the active muscles (extensors, quadriceps femoris) and is referred to as an eccentric or lengthening contraction.

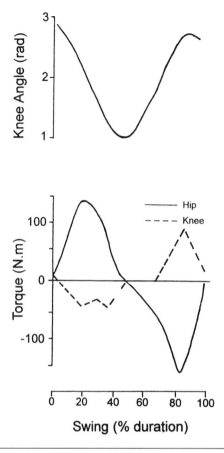

Figure 2.9 Knee angle and resultant muscle torques about the hip and knee joints during the swing phase of a running stride. The subject ran at 5.1 m/s. Knee angle was measured as the relative angle between the thigh and the shank. Positive torques indicate a net muscle force in the direction of flexion.

Adapted from Phillips and Roberts, 1980.

Similarly, during the phase of the knee joint extension, there was a resultant flexor (hamstrings) torque about the knee joint. This means that extension of the knee joint was controlled by an eccentric contraction of the knee flexor muscles; knee flexion was controlled, not by the knee flexors, but by the knee extensors, and vice versa.

Most movements that we perform involve eccentric contractions. The function of eccentric contractions is to control the effect of a load on the body. In this instance, the load was the inertial force exerted by the thigh on the shank. By using the muscles that cross the hip joints, subjects are able to cause the knee joint to flex and to extend. The muscles that cross the knee joint are used to control the effect of the thigh inertia force on the shank; the eccentric contractions serve to brake the forward and backward rotation of the shank. This example illustrates that the inertial force exerted by one body segment on another is an important consideration in the analysis of human movement (Bizzi & Abend, 1983; Phillips, Roberts, & Huang, 1983; Putnam, 1991). We will return to this concept in chapter 3 when we discuss intersegmental dynamics.

Forces Due to the Surroundings

The other major class of forces that we must consider in the analysis of human movement involves those that are imposed on the body by the surroundings. These include the reaction force provided by the ground and other support surfaces, as well as the interaction between the body and the fluid (air, water) in which the movement occurs.

Ground Reaction Force

The **ground reaction force** describes the reaction force provided by the support surface on which the movement is performed. It is derived from Newton's law of action-reaction *to represent the reaction of the ground to the accelerations of all the body segments*. The ground reaction force can be measured with an instrument known as a force platform, which essentially operates like a scale for measuring weight. Researchers began using this technique in the 1930s (Elftman, 1938, 1939; Fenn, 1930; Manter, 1938), although the idea had been proposed some time previously (Amar, 1920; Marey, 1879).

One important difference between a force platform and a weight scale is that the force platform can measure the ground reaction force in three dimensions, and it can do so quickly with minimal distortion of the signal. The resultant ground reaction force can be resolved into three components whose directions are functionally defined as vertical (upward-downward), forward-backward, and side to side. These components represent the reaction of the ground to the actions of the person that are transmitted through the feet to the ground and that correspond to the acceleration of the body in these respective directions. The extent to which any body segment influences the ground reaction force depends on its mass and the acceleration of its CM. For example, Miller (1990) estimates that the trunk and head account for about 50% of a runner's acceleration whereas each leg contributes about 17% and the arms about 5%.

An instructive example of the association between the ground reaction force and the relevant movement kinematics is shown in figure 2.10. The movement is the vertical jump. The height of a vertical jump depends on the magnitude of the vertical velocity at takeoff, which in turn is determined by the vertical component of the ground reaction force. For the performance

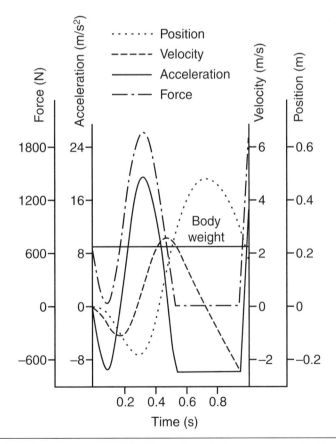

Figure 2.10   The vertical components of the kinematics and kinetics associated with a vertical jump. The position, velocity, and acceleration data are for the center of mass of the jumper. The force record corresponds to the vertical component of the ground reaction force $(F_{g,y})$.

Adapted from Miller, 1976.

shown in figure 2.10, the subject began from an upright position and then lowered her CM by approximately 0.2 m before changing direction (velocity crosses zero and goes from negative to positive) and moving upward to the takeoff position. Takeoff occurred when the vertical component of the ground reaction force fell to zero (time = 0.53 s). The subject was in the air for about 0.41 s, during which time her center of gravity was raised 0.49 m from the starting position. Recall that figure 2.10 indicates the net effect of the interaction between the subject and the ground; accordingly, the kinematics describe the motion of her total-body CM.

In this vertical jump, the peak downward velocity (acceleration = 0) occurred about midway during the downward movement (time = 0.19 s), and the peak upward velocity (positive values; acceleration = 0) occurred just prior to takeoff. The ground reaction force was zero and the vertical component of acceleration had a value of –9.81 m/s² (i.e., the effect of gravity at the jumper's CM) during the flight phase. As expected from our discussion of kinematics in chapter 1, changes in acceleration preceded changes in position. As noted previously in the context of Newton's law of acceleration, the ground reaction force and the acceleration graphs parallel each other. Initially, the acceleration of the system (total-body CM) was zero, and the ground reaction force was equal to body weight. As the body segments began to accelerate, the system acceleration changed, and the ground reaction force changed in parallel but oscillated about the body-weight line. The ground reaction force record consisted of four phases: (a) an initial phase in which the ground reaction force was less than body weight (negative acceleration); (b) a phase in which the ground reaction force was greater than body weight (positive acceleration); (c) the flight phase, in which the ground reaction force was zero (acceleration = –9.81 m/s²); and (d) the impact phase, in which the jumper returned to the ground.

Figure 2.11 illustrates the vertical component $(F_{g,y})$ of the ground reaction force associated with walking and with running. These data indicate the manner in which $F_{g,y}$ changed from the instant of foot contact with the ground (time zero on the abscissa) until the instant that the same foot left the ground (the time at which $F_{g,y}$ returns to zero). This interval is known as the stance or support phase. $F_{g,y}$ is nonzero only when the foot is in contact with the ground and changes continuously throughout this period of support. Recall from the discussion of weight that the magnitude of the weight vector is equivalent to $F_{g,y}$ when the system (body) is not accelerating in the vertical direction. Accordingly, when $F_{g,y}$ differs from body weight, the system experiences a vertical acceleration; when $F_{g,y}$ is greater than body weight, the vertical acceleration of the CM is upward; and when $F_{g,y}$ is less than body weight, the vertical acceleration of the CM is downward.

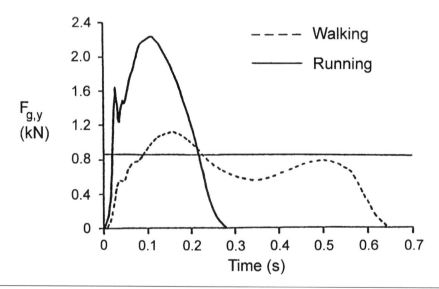

Figure 2.11 Vertical component of the ground reaction force $(F_{g,y})$ during the period of support in walking (dashed line) and running (solid line). The foot was placed on the ground at time zero and left the ground when $F_{g,y}$ returned to zero.

Because the ground reaction force represents the reaction of the ground to the action (acceleration of the CM) of the runner, the movement of the runner while the foot is on the ground is reflected in the ground reaction force (figure 2.12). A runner in the nonsupport phase of a stride experiences a downward acceleration (due to gravity) of 9.81 m/s², which means that when the foot contacts the ground there is an upward-directed vertical component $(F_{g,y})$ to counteract the downward motion of the runner (De Wit, De Clercq, & Aerts, 2000; Yingling, Yack, & White, 1996). Furthermore, when the foot contacts the ground it is initially in front of the runner's CM, which causes the ground to respond with a backward-directed (braking) horizontal component $(F_{g,x})$. As the runner's CM passes over the support foot, the horizontal component changes direction so that it acts forward (propulsion). The side-to-side component $(F_{g,z})$ is more difficult to explain, but it has a lesser magnitude and is more variable than $F_{g,x}$ and $F_{g,y}$. However, $F_{g,z}$ is correlated (r = 0.71) with the position of the foot relative to the midline between the feet during contact with the ground (Williams, 1985).

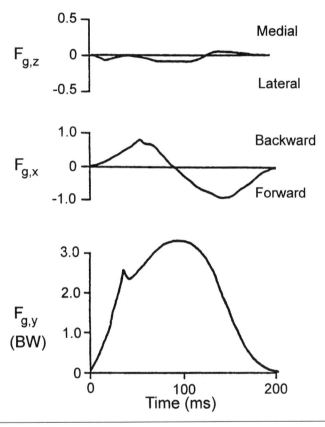

Figure 2.12 Generalized force-time curves for the three components of the ground reaction force during the support phase of a running stride. The forces are expressed relative to body weight (BW).

Example 2.4

Calculating the Resultant Ground Reaction Force

Suppose the runner depicted in figure 2.1c experienced the following ground reaction force components at one point in time during the stance phase:

Forward-backward $(F_{g,x})$	−286 N	(positive = forward)
Vertical $(F_{g,y})$	812 N	(positive = upward)
Side to side $(F_{g,z})$	61 N	(positive = lateral)

(continued)

A. Draw a diagram of the two components and the resultant force in each of the *sagittal* (divides body into left and right), *frontal* (divides body into front and back), and *transverse* (divides body into upper and lower) planes.

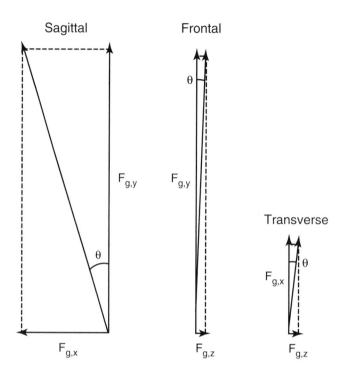

B. Calculate the magnitude and direction for each of these resultants.

Sagittal plane:

$$\text{magnitude} = \sqrt{F_{g,x}^{\,2} + F_{g,y}^{\,2}}$$
$$= \sqrt{(-286)^2 + 812^2}$$
$$= 861 \text{ N}$$
$$\text{direction} = \tan^{-1}\frac{286}{812}$$
$$= 0.34 \text{ rad relative to the vertical}$$

Frontal plane:

$$\text{magnitude} = \sqrt{F_{g,x}^{\,2} + F_{g,z}^{\,2}}$$
$$= \sqrt{(812)^2 + 61^2}$$
$$= 814 \text{ N}$$
$$\text{direction} = \tan^{-1}\frac{61}{812}$$
$$= 0.07 \text{ rad relative to the vertical}$$

Transverse plane:

$$\text{magnitude} = \sqrt{F_{g,x}{}^2 + F_{g,z}{}^2}$$
$$= \sqrt{(-286)^2 + 61^2}$$
$$= 292 \text{ N}$$
$$\text{direction} = \tan^{-1}\frac{61}{286}$$
$$= 0.21 \text{ rad relative to the horizontal}$$

C. Use the Pythagorean relation to determine the magnitude of the resultant (F_g) ground reaction force.

$$F_g = \sqrt{F_{g,z}{}^2 + F_{g,y}{}^2 + F_{g,x}{}^2}$$
$$= \sqrt{(-286)^2 + 812^2 + 61^2}$$
$$F_g = 863 \text{ N}$$

Center of Pressure

Figure 2.12 shows the three components of the resultant ground reaction force vector that act on the foot during the stance phase of running. This force, however, does not act at a single point but rather is distributed over part of the foot. This is obvious when you focus on how your foot touches the ground as you walk and run. The distribution of force over an area is measured as pressure, which has the unit of measurement of pascal (Pa; 1 Pa = 1 N/m²). One way to measure the pressure distribution under the foot during the stance phase is to place a number of small pressure transducers in a shoe that a subject can wear while walking or running (Cavanagh & Ae, 1980; Hennig, Cavanagh, Albert, & Macmillan, 1982; Hennig, Valiant, & Liu, 1996). Figure 2.13 shows such measurements. In this study, eight pressure transducers were placed in the shoe: two under the heel, two under the midfoot, three under the forefoot, and one under the big toe. The sequence of diagrams in figure 2.13 shows the distribution of pressure at these locations for various times (10-250 ms) after the foot first contacted the ground. For the first 50 ms of foot contact, the pressure was greatest under the heel and reached a peak value of ~1000 kPa at 30 ms. In the two middle records (70 and 90 ms), the pressure was more or less evenly distributed over much of the foot. Thereafter, the pressure was greatest under the forefoot.

The peak pressure experienced at different locations on the foot during walking and running varies across individuals. The factors that influence the variations in pressure include both structural features of the foot and details of the motion. Morag and Cavanagh (1999) examined the correlations between peak plantar pressure and eight sets of these structural and functional measures during walking. It was possible to explain approximately 50% of the variance in peak pressures under the rearfoot, the midfoot, the head of the first metatarsal, and the hallux with multiple regression equations that used various subsets of the structural and functional measures. The structural factors were the dominant predictors for peak pressure under the midfoot and the head of the first metatarsal, whereas both structural and functional factors were important at the heel and hallux.

When we measure the ground reaction force with a force platform, the magnitude of the force represents the sum of the pressure distributed under the foot. The location (point of

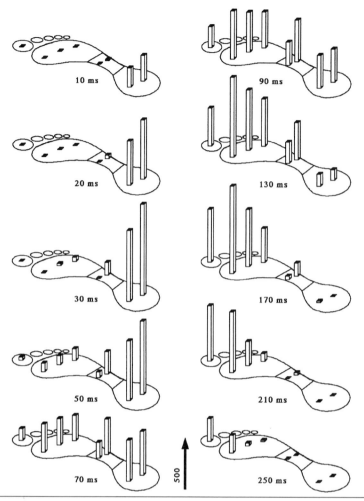

Figure 2.13   Pressure distribution at eight locations under the foot for a subject running at 3.3 m/s.
Reprinted from Hennig and Milani, 1995.

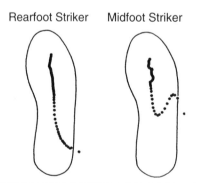

Figure 2.14   The displacement of the center of pressure (point of application of the ground reaction force vector) during the stance phase of a running stride (4.5 m/s).
Reprinted from Cavanagh and Lafortune, 1980.

application) of the ground reaction force under the foot corresponds to the **center of pressure.** It is simply the central point of the pressure exerted on the foot. Cavanagh and Lafortune (1980) characterized runners as either midfoot or rearfoot strikers; this distinction referred to the initial location of the center of pressure on the foot when the foot first contacted the ground (figure 2.14). For midfoot strikers, the initial location of the center of pressure was on the lateral border in the middle of the foot. For rearfoot strikers the initial location of the center of pressure was on the rear of the foot. For both types of runners, however, the center of pressure soon shifted to the central part of the foot and ended up under the big toe as the foot left the ground.

Friction

The resultant of the two horizontal components of the ground reaction force *($F_{g,x}$ and $F_{g,z}$)* represents the friction, or **shear force** *(F_s)*, between the shoe and the ground. It is the reaction of the ground to the forces exerted in the horizontal plane by the person or object. Friction is important in locomotion because it provides the basis for the horizontal progression of the CM. Recall that the three components of the ground reaction force represent the acceleration of the total-body CM, which is the sum of the individual body segment CM accelerations in all three directions. F_s corresponds to the acceleration of the total-body CM in the two directions located in the horizontal plane (i.e., the forward-backward and side-to-side directions).

In general, the maximum friction force is determined by the magnitude of the force that is normal (perpendicular) to the surface, which for the ground reaction force is $F_{g,y}$, and a coefficient (μ) that characterizes the contact (rough-smooth, dry-lubricated, static-dynamic) between the two objects (figure 2.15):

$$F_{s,max} = \mu F_{g,y} \tag{2.10}$$

For a given shoe-ground contact, the friction coefficient differs depending on whether the shoe is stationary relative to the ground (static, μ_s) or is moving (dynamic, μ_d). Because μ_s is greater than μ_d, F_s reaches greater values when the shoe does not move or slide on the ground; hence it is more difficult to make a rapid turn once the shoe begins to slip on the ground. We determine the magnitude of μ between shoes and surfaces experimentally by calculating the ratio of F_s to $F_{g,y}$ at the point in time just before the shoe moves relative to the ground. With this approach, μ_s has been reported to range from 0.3 to 2.0, with 0.6 for a cinder track and 1.5 for grass (Nigg, 1986; Stucke, Baudzus, & Baumann, 1984); and μ_d ranges from 0.003 to 0.007

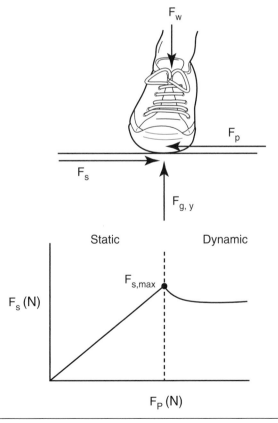

Figure 2.15   Factors that influence the magnitude of the friction force (F_s, shear force).
Data from Miller and Nelson, 1973.

during racing on ice skates (de Koning, de Groot, & van Ingen Schenau, 1992). When F_s is less than maximum, however, friction is simply equal to the resultant force in the horizontal plane.

When a shoe contacts the ground, the friction force (F_s) depends on the magnitude of the pushing force (F_p) exerted by the shoe on the ground (figure 2.15): (a) static—when the shoe does not slip, $F_s = F_p = \sqrt{F_{g,x}^2 + F_{g,z}^2}$; (b) maximum—the peak friction force $(F_{s,max})$ occurs just prior to the moment when the shoe slips on the ground, when $F_s = \mu_s F_{g,y}$; (c) dynamic—once the shoe slips on the ground, then F_s varies as a function of $\mu_d F_{g,y}$. These characteristics indicate that, for a given shoe-ground condition as represented by μ, friction increases with $F_{g,y}$, and because $F_{g,y}$ is predominantly influenced by body weight (F_w), the amount of friction is often greater for heavier individuals. Furthermore, as long as the shoe does not slip on the ground, the friction force is smaller than the maximum possible $(F_{s,max})$.

Example 2.5
Friction on a Sled

Determine the acceleration of a person sledding down a snow-covered slope $(\mu_d = 0.085)$ that is inclined (θ) above the horizontal at 0.6 rad.

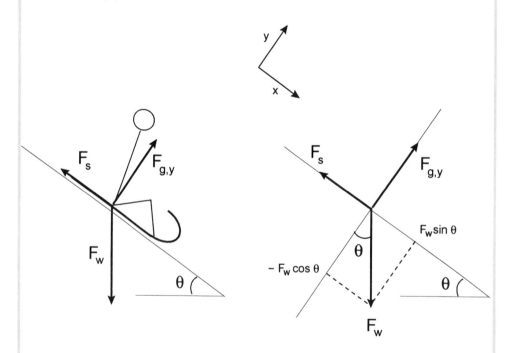

As shown in the figure, the system (person + sled) experiences two forces: gravity (weight) and the ground reaction force. When we consider the effects of friction, the ground reaction force is usually resolved into two components, one acting along the surface (F_s) and one perpendicular or normal to the surface $(F_{g,y})$. To determine the acceleration of the system, we can use Newton's law of acceleration:

$$\mathbf{F}_w + \mathbf{F}_{g,y} + \mathbf{F}_s = m\mathbf{a}$$

As we will discuss in more detail later, one way to solve such problems is to consider each direction $(x$ and $y)$ separately. According to the coordinate system in the figure, the forces acting in the x direction include F_s $(\mu_d F_{g,y})$ and a component of the system weight $(F_{w,x} = mg \sin \theta$, where g = the acceleration due to gravity). In the y direction, the forces are $F_{g,y}$ and a component of the system weight $(F_{w,y} = mg \cos \theta)$.

$$mg \sin \theta - \mu_d F_{g,y} = ma$$

$$F_{g,y} - mg \cos\theta = 0$$

$$F_{g,y} = mg \cos \theta$$

The identity for $F_{g,y}$ can be inserted into the equation for the x direction; then we can divide through by the mass of the system and derive an expression for a:

$$mg \sin \theta - \mu_d \, mg \cos \theta = ma$$

$$a = g \sin \theta - \mu_d g \cos \theta$$

$$a = g \, (\sin \theta - \mu_d \cos \theta)$$

$$a = 9.81 \, [\sin 0.6 - (0.085 \times \cos 0.6)]$$

$$a = 9.81 \, [0.5646 - (0.085 \times 0.8253)]$$

$$a = 4.85 \, \text{m/s}^2$$

Fluid Resistance

Both human motion (e.g., ski jumping, cycling, swimming, skydiving) and projectile motion (e.g., the flight of a discus or golf ball) can be profoundly influenced by the fluid (gaseous or liquid) medium in which they occur (Hubbard, 2000). This phenomenon, known as **fluid resistance,** occurs because the fluid opposes the motion of the object. This interaction causes the object to experience two main effects. One effect, a **drag force,** opposes the forward motion of the object. The other effect, a **lift force,** usually exerts an upward force on the object. The drag force is drawn on a free body diagram with a direction parallel to the direction of the fluid flow around the object; the lift force is perpendicular to the direction of the fluid flow (figure 2.16). The net fluid resistance is the resultant of the drag and lift forces.

The interaction between the fluid and the object is typically schematized as in figure 2.17, where the fluid is shown flowing around a stationary object. The schematized lines of fluid flow are referred to as **streamlines;** they conceptually represent consecutive layers of particles in the fluid. One streamline, or layer, is adjacent to the object; another streamline lies on top of this, another on top of that, and so forth. The streamline closest to the object is referred to as the **boundary layer.** By studying the motion of the streamlines, it is possible to identify two main

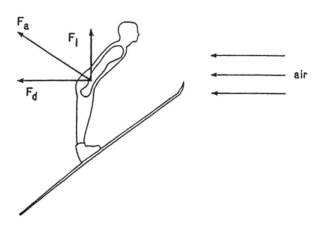

Figure 2.16 The air resistance encountered by a ski jumper. The air is shown moving relative to the jumper. The resultant air-resistance vector (F_a) is resolved into two components, drag (F_d) and lift (F_l).

factors that contribute to the drag force experienced by the object: one is related to the different velocities of the streamlines, and the other depends on the extent to which the relative motion of the streamlines is disturbed.

First, when a dye is placed in the fluid, it is apparent that the streamlines can move at different velocities. Typically, the streamline touching the object (boundary layer) has the lowest velocity because it is slowed down by the effect of friction between the layer of particles and the object; this effect is known as **friction drag** or **surface drag.** The amount of surface drag depends on the smoothness of the object's surface. The rougher the surface of the object, the greater the friction and thus the greater the surface drag. Concern for surface drag is evident in many sports, including swimming, cycling, and rowing. This is the reason that many swimmers shave body hair, wear caps, and don full body suits and the reason that cyclists experiment with exotic materials and designs for clothing.

Second, when the streamlines move around an object, they may remain uniform or may become non-uniform; uniform flow is referred to as **laminar flow** (figure 2.17*a*), and non-uniform flow is called **turbulent flow** (figure 2.17*b*). When the flow is turbulent, there is a pressure differential from the front to the back of the object; this exerts a force on the object that is known as **pressure drag** or **form drag.** The pressure is greater on the leading side of the object, and the front-to-back difference increases as the flow becomes more turbulent. This is why designers often streamline an object in order to minimize the tendency for the fluid flow to become turbulent. Since the 1984 Los Angeles Olympics, cyclists' helmets have become more pointed in the rear because such a design reduces airflow turbulence. Furthermore, the surface texture of an object, such as the dimples in a golf ball, can influence the width of the turbulent wake and hence decrease the pressure drag experienced by the object. The golf ball dimples decrease the width of the wake and pressure drag by delaying the point along the object at which the streamlines become turbulent. The net effect is that for a given golf swing, a dimpled golf ball can be driven 239 m, whereas a smooth golf ball travels only 46 m (Townend, 1984).

In addition to pressure and surface drag, a third factor that influences the drag component of fluid resistance is **wave resistance.** The presence of waves decreases the average proportion of the object's body that is out of the water and therefore increases fluid density. Wave resistance probably sets the upper limit on the speed of surface ships and may be important at the higher velocities associated with competitive swimming. The resistive effects of waves are probably attributable to the uneven density of the fluid (water vs. air) that the swimmer encounters. The current practice in pool design is to minimize wave turbulence with specially designed gutters and lane markers.

When an object moves through a fluid, it always experiences a drag force, and the pressure drag is usually much greater than the surface drag. In addition, an object can also experience a lift force. This occurs when the object has an asymmetrical shape (e.g., an airfoil), when it is inclined at an angle relative to the fluid flow (angle of projection), or when it is spinning. In the case of an airfoil (or nonzero angle of projection), the path that the particles must travel over the top side of the airfoil is greater than that traveled by the particles on the underside (figure 2.17*c*). As a result, the streamline traveling the greater distance around the object (top side) travels at a greater velocity, and the pressure on that side of the object is less than on the other side. This creates a pressure differential in the up-down direction across the object. This effect is known as **Bernoulli's principle,** which states that fluid pressure is inversely related to fluid velocity. When the pressure on the top side of the airfoil is less because the velocity of the streamlines is greater, there is a net force that pushes the airfoil upward. This effect is known as lift force (F_l) and represents the fluid-resistance force that acts perpendicular to the direction of fluid flow (figure 2.16).

Similarly, a projectile that spins about an axis not in the same direction as the fluid flow creates a pressure gradient across itself by influencing the velocity of the streamlines. For example, if a baseball has a counterclockwise spin as it passes through the air, the streamlines flowing in the counterclockwise direction have a greater velocity (due to reduced surface drag) than those flowing in the clockwise direction, and thus the pressure on the left side of the ball is lower. This creates a pressure gradient across the baseball from right to left and causes the baseball to curve to the left (figure 2.18). These effects on the trajectory of a projectile are due

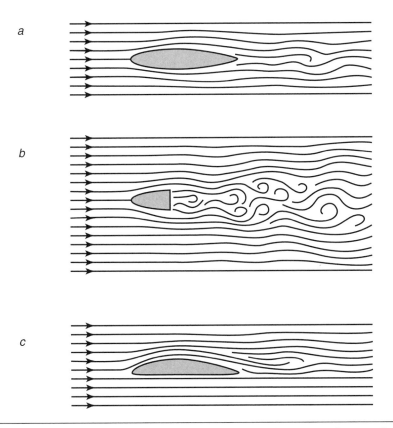

Figure 2.17 Tracings of smoke streamlines show the air traveling *(a)* around a streamlined object, *(b)* around the same object after it was cut in half, and *(c)* around an airfoil.

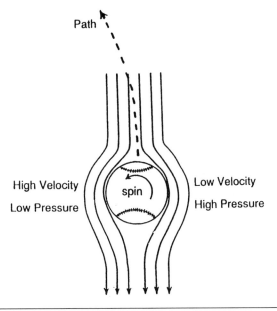

Figure 2.18 The effect of the lift component of air resistance on the trajectory of a baseball. The baseball has a spin in the counterclockwise direction, which will cause it to curve to the left.

to the lift component of air resistance. This effect, sometimes referred to as the Magnus force, causes baseballs to curve, golf balls to slice, and tennis balls to drop. For most projectile motion, however, the magnitude of the Magnus force is much smaller than the lift forces caused by shape asymmetries and a nonzero angle of projection.

Magnitude of Fluid Resistance

The magnitude of the fluid-resistance vector due to pressure drag can be determined from

$$F_f = kAv^2 \qquad (2.11)$$

where k is a constant, A represents the *projected area* of the object, and v refers to the velocity of the fluid relative to the object. The projected area is a silhouette view of the frontal area of the object as it moves through the fluid. The constant k is an abbreviation for the terms $0.5\rho C_D$ for drag and $0.5\rho C_L$ for lift; ρ accounts for fluid density; C_D distinguishes the effects of laminar and turbulent flow; and C_L is proportional to the angle between fluid flow and the orientation of the object. We can determine the net drag force by substituting values for the term $0.5\rho C_D$; C_D ranges from 0.4 for a smooth sphere to ~1.1 for an adult male running in an upright posture. Similarly, the lift force can be determined with the expression $0.5\rho C_L$; C_L for a discus ranges from 0.1 for a 0.03-rad (2°) angle of projection to 1.2 for a 0.45-rad (26°) angle of projection.

Consider the action of the air-resistance vector on the runner (Hill, 1928) in figure 2.1*c*. The constant k is about 0.72 kg/m³ for a runner moving through air ($0.5\rho C_D = 0.5 \times 1.2$ kg/m³ $\times$ 1.2). The projected area of the runner is approximately 0.45 m² (Shanebrook & Jaszczak, 1976), which compares with estimated values of 0.27 m² for a skier in a semi-squat position and 0.65 m² for a skier in an upright position (Spring, Savolainen, Erkkilä, Hämäläinen, & Pihkala, 1988). If the runner had a speed of 6.5 m/s and experienced a tailwind of 0.5 m/s, then the relative velocity *(v)* would be 6.0 m/s. Thus

$$F_f = 0.72 \times 0.45 \times 6.0^2$$
$$= 11.7 \text{ N}$$

Calculations by Shanebrook & Jaszczak (1976) indicated that at middle-distance running speeds (approximately 6 m/s), up to 8% of the energy expended by the runner is used in overcoming air resistance, whereas at sprinting speeds this value can be up to 16% of the total energy expenditure. Drafting (shielding) can abolish 80% of this cost. During running at 6.0 m/s, drafting behind another runner is equivalent to increasing speed by about 0.1 m/s. Similarly, 80% of the power generated by a cyclist traveling on level ground at 8.05 m/s (18 mph) is used to overcome air resistance (Gross, Kyle, & Malewicki, 1983). Cyclists can reduce power output by about 30% and still sustain the same speed when drafting behind another cyclist.

Ward-Smith (1985) has calculated the effects of head winds and tailwinds on performance times in a 100-m sprint:

Wind speed (m/s)	Head wind (s)	Tailwind (s)
1	+0.09	–0.10
3	+0.26	–0.34
5	+0.38	–0.62

With a 3-m/s head wind, 100-m time would be increased by 0.26 s, whereas a 3-m/s tailwind would decrease the time by 0.34 s. The effects of the head wind and tailwind at a similar speed are asymmetrical because of the differences in relative velocity; recall from Equation 2.11 that a doubling of the relative velocity causes a fourfold increase in the fluid resistance.

The drag acting on a swimmer has been estimated by measuring the propulsive force exerted by a subject swimming at a constant velocity (Vorontsov & Rumyantsev, 2000). Under these conditions, the acceleration of the swimmer is zero, and thus the forces acting on the swimmer are balanced. In the horizontal direction, the propulsive force is equal to the resistive force (drag). With this method, the average drag experienced by a swimmer during the front crawl has a value of 53 N at a constant speed of 1.48 m/s (van der Vaart et al., 1987).

Terminal Velocity

Because the relative velocity in Equation 2.11 is a squared term, it is the single most important factor influencing air resistance. A sky diver represents an interesting example of the interaction among the variables in Equation 2.11. After the sky diver has jumped from the airplane, his speed increases up to some terminal value. To determine the value of terminal velocity, let's begin with a diagram (figure 2.19).

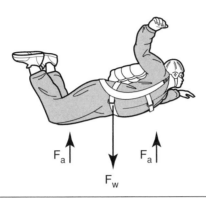

Figure 2.19   The forces experienced by a sky diver during free fall.

When the sky diver jumps out of the airplane, the system (sky diver, parachute, and associated equipment) is accelerated, due to gravity (F_w), toward the ground. But the downward acceleration of the system is only briefly equal to the value for gravity (-9.81 m/s^2), because as system speed increases, the opposing effect of air resistance increases. We know from Equation 2.11 that the magnitude of air resistance increases as the square of relative velocity: thus, as v increases, so does the force due to air resistance. The speed of the system continues to increase (i.e., acceleration is nonzero) until the force due to air resistance is equal to the weight of the system (i.e., the acceleration due to gravity). After the two forces become equal, speed remains constant, and the system has reached a *terminal velocity*. Because velocity remains constant (i.e., zero acceleration) and the system is in equilibrium at terminal velocity, the forces must be balanced. Thus

$$F_w = F_f$$

Further, because we have defined F_f (Equation 2.11),

$$F_w = kAv^2$$

we can rearrange this relation to determine the terminal velocity:

$$v = \sqrt{\frac{F_w}{kA}}$$

If $k = 0.55$ kg/m^3, $A = 0.36$ m^2, and $F_w = 750$ N, then

$$v = \sqrt{\frac{750}{0.55 \times 0.36}}$$

terminal velocity $= 61.6$ m/s (138 mph)

Despite being in free-fall conditions, experienced sky divers are able to perform somersaults, cartwheels, and other sorts of movements. How can they do this? Sky divers experience two forces as they fall: weight and air resistance (figure 2.19). Both of these forces are distributed forces; that is, they are distributed over the entire system but are drawn as acting at one or two points. The weight vector is always drawn as acting at the CM. Similarly, the force due to air resistance has a central balance point: the center of pressure for air resistance. By moving his limbs, a sky diver can alter his projected area and shift the center of pressure for air resistance so that the vector does not pass through the CM. If the line of action of the air-resistance vector is not collinear with the weight vector, then the air resistance exerts a rotary force (torque) about the CM and causes the sky diver to experience angular motion. The skydiver can stop the angular (but not linear) motion by aligning the lines of action of the two vectors.

Example 2.6

Air Resistance During Sky Diving

A sky diver experiences at least four phases during a jump: (a) an initial phase of acceleration from the moment of leaving the plane until reaching terminal velocity; (b) a phase of terminal velocity; (c) a phase of decreased vertical velocity immediately after the parachute opens; and (d) a final phase of free fall (constant velocity) with the parachute opened and the skydiver preparing to land. Draw a velocity-time graph that represents these four phases. Graph the air resistance as a function of time to show how the air resistance changes to produce the velocity-time graph.

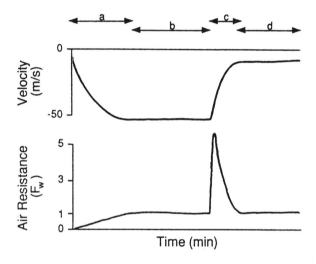

From these graphs, we can answer a number of questions about the experiences of the sky diver.

    A. Why does velocity increase during phase a? This happens because the forces acting on the sky diver $(F_w$ and $F_a)$ are not balanced and there is a net force in the downward direction.

    B. Why is velocity constant in phase b? The reason is that F_w and F_a are equal in magnitude but opposite in direction, so there is no net force acting on the sky diver. In the absence of a net force, the motion of a system remains constant (Newton's law of inertia).

    C. Why does velocity decrease in phase c? It decreases because of the marked increase in F_a. This occurs because the sky diver opens the parachute, increasing the projected area (Equation 2.11) and therefore F_a.

    D. Why is the constant velocity in phase d less than that in phase b? The reason is that the magnitude of F_a required to oppose F_w is achieved at a lower relative velocity, due to the larger projected area of the sky diver and parachute.

Buoyancy

When submerged in a fluid, an object experiences an upward-directed force known as the **buoyancy force.** As described by Archimedes, the magnitude of the buoyancy force (F_b) is equal to the weight of the fluid displaced by the object. We can determine this by calculating the product of the volume of the object (V_o) and the specific weight of the fluid (γ); specific weight refers to the weight for a standard volume of fluid.

$$F_b = V_o \gamma \qquad (2.12)$$

For example, a person floating in a pool and displacing 0.064 m³ of water (20° C; $\gamma = 9810$ N/m³) experiences a buoyancy force of 628 N. When stationary, this person assumes a position in the water at which the magnitude of the buoyancy force is equal to body weight; that is, buoyancy force and weight have equal magnitudes but opposite directions. The line of action for the buoyancy force acts vertically upward through the center of the volume for the part of the object that is submerged. When å0= person is in a floating position (i.e., the forces are balanced), the lines of action for the buoyancy force and the weight vector are coincident. When this person becomes active, as in swimming, the significant forces include weight, buoyancy force, and fluid resistance. During swimming at a constant speed (acceleration = 0), these forces must be coincident.

Momentum

One of the fundamental principles of motion is Newton's law of acceleration, which essentially says that the motion of an object remains constant unless it is acted upon by a force. In the formulation of this law, the motion of an object was quantified as momentum. If you think of two people running, what might you measure to determine who has more motion? Is it simply the faster person who has more motion? No, the answer also depends on the size of each person. It is the combination of speed and size that we use to express the amount of motion that a person has. We call this combination momentum, and calculate it as the product of mass and velocity. Momentum is a vector quantity whose direction is the same as the direction of velocity. As with several other physical quantities we have considered, we distinguish between **linear momentum (G)** and **angular momentum (H)**. By definition, the unit of measurement for linear momentum is kg·m/s (mass × velocity), and the unit of measurement for angular momentum is kg·m²/s (moment of inertia × angular velocity).

Impulse

Newton's law of acceleration states that when a force acts on an object, it changes the momentum of the object. In the analysis of human movement, however, it is necessary to extend this idea. The reason is that forces are not applied instantaneously but rather over an interval of time. For example, figure 2.20 shows the vertical component of the ground reaction force $(F_{g,y})$ that is applied to the foot of a runner during the stance phase of running. An impulse is defined graphically as the area under a force-time curve, numerically as the product of the average force (N) and time (s), and mathematically as the integral of force with respect to time (Equation 2.13),

$$\text{Impulse} = \int_{t_1}^{t_2} \mathbf{F} dt \qquad (2.13)$$

where t_1 and t_2 define the beginning and end of the force application. For example, if the average force $(F_{g,y})$ in figure 2.20 was 1.3 kN and the time of application was 0.29 s, the impulse would be 377 N · s. Thus, the magnitude of an impulse can be altered by varying either the average force or its time of application.

   If Newton's law of acceleration is interpreted to focus on intervals of time rather than instants of time, the law indicates that *the application of an impulse will result in a change in the*

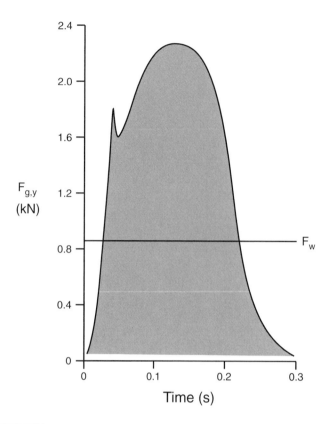

Figure 2.20 Graphic representation of an impulse as an area (shaded) under a force-time curve.

momentum of the system. This is the basis of the impulse-momentum approach to the analysis of motion, which can be stated as

$$\int_{t_1}^{t_2} \mathbf{F}dt = \Delta \mathbf{G} \tag{2.14}$$

Furthermore, the derivation of the impulse-momentum relation from Newton's law of acceleration confirms this interpretation:

$$\sum \mathbf{F} = m\mathbf{a}$$

$$\sum \mathbf{F} = m\frac{\left(\mathbf{v}_f - \mathbf{v}_i\right)}{t}$$

$$\sum \mathbf{F}t = m\left(\mathbf{v}_f - \mathbf{v}_i\right)$$

$$\sum \mathbf{F}t = \Delta m\mathbf{v} \ \ \text{or} \ \ \overline{F} \cdot t = \Delta m\mathbf{v} \tag{2.15}$$

where the term $\sum \mathbf{F}t$ represents the area under a force-time curve (figure 2.20) and is equivalent to the product of the average force and its time of application ($\overline{F} \cdot t$). Equation 2.15 suggests that if the magnitude of the impulse is known, its effect on the momentum of the system can be calculated. Conversely, if the change in momentum can be measured, it is possible to determine the applied impulse.

Example 2.7

Spiking a Volleyball

By videotaping a person spiking a volleyball and measuring the mass *(m)* of the ball, we can determine the impulse applied to the ball. From the videotape it would be necessary to measure both the velocity of the ball before *(v_b)* and after *(v_a)* contact and the total time the hand is in contact with the ball *(t_c)*. For one performance of this skill, we obtained

$$v_b = 3.6 \text{ m/s}$$
$$v_a = 25.2 \text{ m/s}$$
$$m = 0.27 \text{ kg}$$
$$t_c = 18 \text{ ms}$$

Equation 2.15 is applied as follows:

$$\overline{F} \cdot t = \Delta m\mathbf{v}$$
$$= m\Delta \mathbf{v}$$
$$= m(v_b - v_a)$$
$$= 0.27(25.2 - 3.6)$$
$$\overline{F} \cdot t = 5.83 \text{ N·s}$$

Because we know the contact time *(t_c)*, we can determine the average force ($\overline{F}$) exerted by the spiker during the contact:

$$\overline{F} \cdot t = 5.83 \text{ N·s}$$
$$= \frac{5.83}{t_c}$$
$$= \frac{5.83}{0.018}$$
$$\overline{F} = 324 \text{ N}$$

Thus, although the impulse appears to be small (5.83 N·s), the brief duration of the force application results in forces that are quite substantial ($\overline{F} = 324$ N). Incidentally, the time of contact with the volleyball in this example is quite similar to those (10-16 ms) recorded during the kicking of a ball (Asami & Nolte, 1983).

Example 2.8

Momentum Depends on Average Force and Contact Time

In most contact events, such as spiking a volleyball, the momentum of an object is altered by the application of relatively high forces for brief periods of time. There are instances, however, in which the change in momentum is accomplished through the application of smaller forces for longer periods. As an example (Brancazio, 1984) of these two strategies, consider the distinction between the consequences of one person's (mass = 71 kg) jumping off a 15-m building onto the pavement and the consequences of another person's (mass = 71 kg) diving

(continued)

off a 15-m cliff into the ocean. In each instance the individual will have a speed of about 17.3 m/s just prior to contact and a linear momentum of 1228 kg·m/s. Eventually, however, the speed (and thus momentum) of each person will reach zero. The jumper will experience large forces (probably fatal) for a brief interval upon contact with the pavement. The diver, however, will encounter smaller forces, due to contact with the water, over a longer period of time. Nonetheless, the change in momentum for each individual will be the same (ΔG = 1228 kg/m/s). The impulse (area under the force-time curve) provided by the landing surface will be identical for the two landings, although the shapes of the two force-time curves will be quite different.

Figure 2.21 shows the reaction force provided by the landing surface for the two jumps. For the landing onto the pavement, the upward-directed vertical component of the ground reaction force is a consequence of the structural properties of the pavement. If this ground reaction force was applied for 25 ms, then the average force ($\overline{F}$) required to change the linear momentum from 1228 kg · m/s to zero would be 49,120 N. For the water landing, the reaction force is due to a fluid-resistance drag force (Equation 2.11) and a buoyancy force (Equation 2.12). The drag force is influenced by the density of water (998 kg/m^3), a drag coefficient (~0.1), the projected area (~0.07 m^2), and the relative velocity (17.3 m/s at first contact). For this example, the drag force would reach a peak value of about 1000 N soon after contact with the water but then would decline to zero as the relative velocity decreased. The buoyancy force depends on the volume of water that is displaced; when a person is floating in water, the magnitude of the upward-directed buoyancy force is equal to body weight. So during the landing, the buoyancy force would increase from zero, at first contact with the water, up to body weight when the person was floating in the water at the end of landing. The combined effect of the drag force and the buoyancy force would be something like that shown in figure 2.21. The key feature of this example, however, is that each individual will experience the same net vertical impulse to change the same quantity of linear momentum; therefore, the area under each curve in figure 2.21 should be equal.

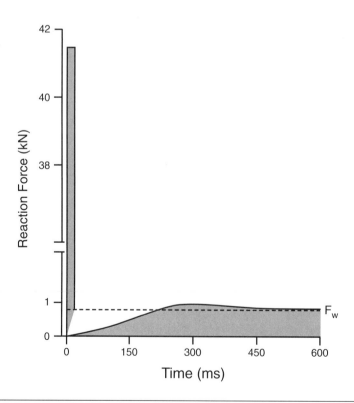

Figure 2.21   The reaction forces provided by pavement (briefer impulse) and water in landing from a 15-m jump.

Example 2.9
Forward Momentum in Running

Whenever an impulse is applied to a system, the momentum of the system changes in proportion to the net impulse. Furthermore, the effect on momentum is confined to the direction of the impulse. Consider the forward-backward component $(F_{g,x})$ of the ground reaction force during the support phase of running (figure 2.12). The graph illustrates that the runner experiences two forward-backward impulses during support. Initially $F_{g,x}$ is directed backward, creating a retarding or braking impulse; then $F_{g,x}$ changes direction, eliciting a propulsive impulse. Because these impulses act in opposite directions, the change in momentum that the runner experiences in the x direction depends on the difference between the braking and propulsion impulses. When the individual is running at a constant speed (no change in momentum), the two impulses are equal. For a runner to increase speed, however, the propulsive impulse must exceed the braking impulse; to decrease speed, the braking impulse must be greater than the propulsion impulse. These relations are shown in figure 2.22. The change in momentum due to the ground reaction force is equal to the difference between the initial (before stance) and final (after stance) values for momentum.

Because impulses in locomotion and other such activities are influenced by the weight of the individual, it is common practice to normalize the impulses and to express them as a proportion of the body-weight impulse. For example, if a runner weighs 630 N and experiences a braking impulse of 15.8 N·s that lasts for 0.1 s, then the braking impulse is 0.25 times the body-weight impulse ($15.8/[630 \times 0.1] = 0.25$). Munro, Miller, and Fuglevand (1987) reported braking and propulsive impulses of 0.15 to 0.25 times body-weight impulse with runners traveling at 3.0 to 5.0 m/s. These impulses increased with running speed.

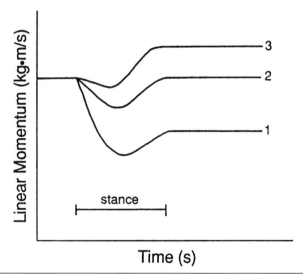

Figure 2.22   Change in the forward-backward linear momentum of a runner in response to (1) a braking impulse that is larger than the propulsive impulse; (2) equivalent braking and propulsive impulses; and (3) a propulsive impulse that is larger than the braking impulse.

Collisions

A **collision** is a brief contact between objects in which the force associated with the contact is much larger than other forces acting on the objects. When a tennis ball collides with a racket, for example, the contact force is much larger than the gravitational and air-resistance forces that the ball and racket experience. Many of our physical activities involve collisions, such as those between athletes (e.g., rugby, martial arts), between a participant and an inanimate object (e.g., handball, soccer), and between inanimate objects (e.g., badminton, golf, hockey).

When two objects collide, they exert equal and opposite forces on each other. This occurs because a force represents a physical interaction in the form of a push or a pull. When two objects are involved in the collision, they both experience the same force. And because the contact associated with the collision is the same for the two objects, the impulse applied to each object, as well as the change in momentum experienced by each object, is the same. So in a collision there is a conservation of linear momentum. This means that the sum of the linear momenta of the two objects (A and B) before the collision is the same as the sum of the linear momenta after the collision:

$$\left(m_A \mathbf{v}_A\right)_{before} + \left(m_B \mathbf{v}_B\right)_{before} = \left(m_A \mathbf{v}_A\right)_{after} + \left(m_B \mathbf{v}_B\right)_{after} \tag{2.16}$$

The left-hand side of Equation 2.16 represents the momentum of the system before the collision, and the right-hand side indicates the momentum after the collision. Because mass does not usually change in human movement, this equation can be rearranged to show that the change in momentum of object A is equal to the change in momentum of object B (Equation 2.17). Hence, the change in velocity experienced by each object is inversely proportional to its mass (Equation 2.18).

$$\left(m_A v_A\right)_{before} - \left(m_A v_A\right)_{after} = \left(m_B v_B\right)_{after} - \left(m_B v_B\right)_{before}$$

$$m_A\left(v_{A,before} - v_{A,after}\right) = m_B\left(v_{B,after} - v_{B,before}\right)$$

$$m_A \Delta v_A = m_B \Delta v_B \tag{2.17}$$

$$\frac{\Delta v_A}{\Delta v_B} = \frac{m_B}{m_A} \tag{2.18}$$

For example, consider hitting a tennis ball with a racket. After contact between the ball and the racket (the collision), the velocity of the ball is usually much greater than the velocity of the racket. The difference in the velocity of the ball and the racket is determined by the ratio of their masses. Hence the advantage of size (mass) in contact sports such as football and wrestling.

One important feature of collisions is whether or not they are **elastic;** that is, do the objects bounce off one another, or do they remain joined after the collision? If the collision is elastic, then each object preserves most of its kinetic energy (velocity after the collision is nonzero). In an inelastic collision, the colliding objects stick together.

The *elasticity* of a collision is indicated by the **coefficient of restitution** *(e)*:

$$\text{coefficient of restitution} = \frac{\text{speed after collision}}{\text{speed before collision}}$$

A perfectly elastic collision has a coefficient of restitution equal to 1, which indicates that the speed (velocity) after the collision is identical to that before the collision. However, for most collisions in human movement, the coefficient of restitution is less than 1. The coefficient of restitution of a ball is usually measured by dropping the ball from a known height onto the ground and determining how high it rebounds. If a ball dropped from a height of 1.0 m rebounds to 0.5 m, then the coefficient of restitution is 0.5. Selected coefficients of restitution for various balls at an impact speed of 24.6 m/s (55 mph) include the following: softball, 0.40; tennis ball, 0.55; golf ball, 0.58; basketball, 0.64; soccer ball, 0.65; Superball, 0.85. The coefficient of restitution tends to decrease as the speed of the collision increases.

The coefficient of restitution quantifies the extent to which a perfect collision is modified by the material properties of the objects involved in the collision. After a bat contacts a ball, the velocities of the ball and the bat depend not only on the mass of each but also on the coefficient of restitution. The coefficient of restitution represents the constant of proportionality between the speed before the collision and the speed after the collision. For example, consider the contact of a baseball and a bat, which is described by the equations that define the coefficient of restitution and the conservation of momentum:

$$\text{speed after collision} = -e \text{ (speed before collision)}$$

$$v_{B,a} - v_{b,a} = -e\left(v_{B,b} - v_{b,b}\right) \tag{2.19}$$

where B represents the bat and b indicates the ball. If we assume that the velocity vectors of the ball and the bat are collinear (lie in the same line as shown in figure 2.23), rearrangement of Equation 2.19 allows us to specify the velocity of the bat $(v_{B,a})$ and the ball $(v_{b,a})$ after contact:

$$v_{b,a} = v_{B,a} + e\left(v_{B,b} - v_{b,b}\right) \tag{2.20}$$

$$v_{B,a} = v_{b,a} - e\left(v_{B,b} - v_{b,b}\right) \tag{2.21}$$

To determine the velocity of the bat after the collision $(v_{B,a})$, we next substitute Equation 2.20 into the expression for the conservation of linear momentum (Equation 2.16).

$$m_B v_{B,b} + m_b v_{b,b} = m_B v_{B,a} + m_b v_{b,a}$$

$$m_B v_{B,b} + m_b v_{b,b} = m_B v_{B,a} + m_b\left[v_{B,a} + e\left(v_{B,b} - v_{b,b}\right)\right]$$

$$v_{B,a}\left(m_b + m_B\right) = m_b v_{b,b}\left(1+e\right) + v_{B,b}\left(m_B - m_b e\right)$$

$$v_{B,a} = \frac{m_b v_{b,b}\left(1+e\right) + v_{B,b}\left(m_B - m_b e\right)}{m_b + m_B} \tag{2.22}$$

Similarly, we can derive an expression for $v_{b,a}$ by substituting the expression for $v_{B,a}$ with Equation 2.20:

$$m_B v_{B,b} + m_b v_{b,b} = m_B v_{B,a} + m_b v_{b,a}$$

$$m_B v_{B,b} + m_b v_{b,b} = m_B\left[v_{b,a} - e\left(v_{B,b} - v_{b,b}\right)\right] + m_b v_{b,a}$$

$$v_{b,a}\left(m_b + m_B\right) = m_B v_{B,b}\left(1+e\right) + v_{b,b}\left(m_b - m_B e\right)$$

$$v_{B,a} = \frac{m_B v_{B,b}\left(1+e\right) + v_{b,b}\left(m_b - m_B e\right)}{m_B + m_b} \tag{2.23}$$

Equations 2.22 and 2.23 represent the general case for the velocity of a bat $(v_{B,a})$ and ball $(v_{b,a})$ after a collision. Typically, however, ball velocities are rarely collinear before $(v_{b,b})$ and after $(v_{b,a})$ impact, and the directions of $v_{b,b}$ and $v_{b,a}$ are usually opposite (i.e., toward and away from the batter). We accommodate the non-collinearity of the ball and bat velocities by inserting a cosine term next to $v_{b,b}$ in Equations 2.22 and 2.23 (see Townend, 1984, p. 142 for an example).

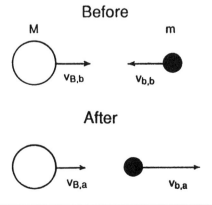

Figure 2.23 Mass and velocity of the bat (B) and ball (b) before $(v_{B,b}, v_{b,b})$ and after $(v_{B,a}, v_{b,a})$ a collision.

Example 2.10
A Ball-Bat Collision

Let us apply these ball-bat equations to determine the velocity of the baseball and the bat after a hit:

Mass of bat (m_B)	= 0.93 kg (30 oz)
Mass of ball (m_b)	= 0.16 kg (5 oz)
Velocity of ball before impact $(v_{b,b})$	= –38 m/s (85 mph)
Velocity of bat before impact $(v_{B,b})$	= 31 m/s (70 mph)
Coefficient of restitution (specified in rules)	= 0.55

A. Calculate the velocity of the baseball and bat after the hit.

$$v_{B,a} = \frac{m_b v_{b,b}(1+e) + v_{B,b}(m_B - m_b e)}{m_b + m_b}$$

$$v_{B,a} = \frac{-6.08(1+0.55) + 31(0.93 - 0.088)}{0.16 + 0.93}$$

$$v_{B,a} = 15.3 \text{ m/s}$$

and

$$v_{b,a} = \frac{m_B v_{B,b}(1+e) + v_{b,b}(m_b - m_B e)}{m_B + m_b}$$

$$v_{b,a} = \frac{28.8(1+0.55) + (-38)(0.16 - 0.51)}{0.16 + 0.93}$$

$$v_{b,a} = 53.3 \text{ m/s}$$

B. Would such a hit produce a home run in baseball? Assume that the angle of the ball's trajectory after it leaves the bat is 0.785 rad, and ignore the effects of air resistance. To find the horizontal distance that the ball will travel, we need to use the equations of motion that were introduced in chapter 1. First, we find out how long the ball will be in the air by using the *y*-direction information.

$$\bar{a} = \frac{\Delta v}{\Delta t}$$

$$t_{up} = \frac{v_f - v_i}{\bar{a}}$$

$$t_{up} = \frac{0 - 53.3 \sin 0.78}{-9.81}$$

$$= 3.82 \text{ s}$$

$$t = 2 \times t_{up}$$

$$t = 7.64 \text{ s}$$

Next, we can find the horizontal distance the ball will travel. Because we are ignoring the effect of air resistance, the horizontal velocity remains constant.

$$\bar{v} = \frac{\Delta r}{\Delta t}$$

$$\Delta r = 53.3 \cos 0.78 \times 7.64$$

$$\Delta r = 287 \text{ m } (940 \text{ ft})$$

C. It is highly unlikely that the ball would be hit a distance of 287 m. Because the numbers used in the calculations are within the range of those observed in baseball, the calculated distance suggests that we are missing an important factor in the analysis. Perhaps we need to consider the effect of air resistance, which does influence the actual trajectory of a baseball. How can we do this? We could use Equation 2.11, which provides a direct method for calculating the magnitude of the air resistance. However, there is a simpler way to estimate the effect of air resistance. We could assume that the effect of the air resistance is to cause a linear decrease in the horizontal velocity of the ball throughout its trajectory; thus, $v_i = 37.9$ m/s, $v_f = 0$ m/s.

$$\bar{v} = \frac{\Delta r}{\Delta t}$$

$$\Delta r = \frac{37.9 + 0}{2} \times 7.64$$

$$= 145 \text{ m } (475 \text{ ft})$$

This distance for the hit is more reasonable, but it would still be a home run.

Although these calculations of ball and bat velocities after impact rely on the application of standard techniques from physics, they may actually underestimate the effect of the collision. The critical variables affecting velocity after a collision are the coefficient of restitution, the velocity before contact, and mass. Whereas the preceding example used the actual mass of the ball and the bat, the mass of the bat may be larger due to Plagenhoef's concept of the *effective striking mass*. According to this concept, the effective striking mass of an implement, such as a bat, is greater than its actual mass due to the connection between the implement and the person holding it. However, little attention has been given to the extent to which the mass of the baseball bat is supplemented because of its connection to the rigid links of the athlete.

Another aspect of ball-bat collisions, which is related to the effective striking mass, is the notion of a *sweet spot*. Contact in a ball-bat collision is said to occur at the sweet spot when no reaction force is felt at the hands. Three theories seek to account for the sweet spot: the center of percussion, the natural frequency node, and the coefficient of restitution (Brancazio, 1984). Of these, the explanation provided by the **center of percussion** seems to be the most popular. When a ball contacts a bat, the location along the bat where no reaction force ($\mathbf{F}_r$) is felt at the hands is referred to as the center of percussion. When a force ($\mathbf{F}_c$) is applied at the CM of the bat, the bat experiences only linear motion (figure 2.24*a*). However, when the force is not applied at the CM, the bat experiences both linear and angular motion (figure 2.24*b*). When this happens, there is a point where the linear translation and the angular rotation cancel and the bat does not move. The contact point that produces a stationary pivot point is the center of percussion (figure 2.24*c*). It is located distal on the bat to the CM. The location of the ball contact on the bat relative to the centers of mass and percussion determines the nature of the reaction force at the hands (figure 2.24*c*).

Angular Momentum

When we analyze angular motion, we do so in terms of the torques acting on the system. Torque represents the rotary effect of a force and is calculated as the vector product of a moment

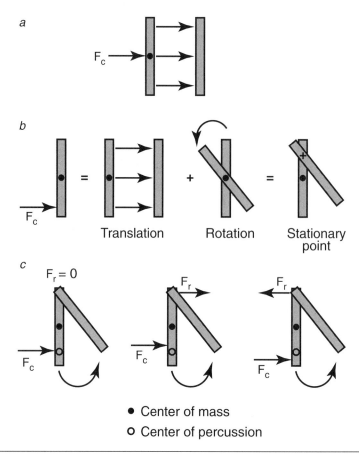

Figure 2.24 The effect of a force applied to a bat on the motion of the bat: *(a)* a contact force (**F**$_c$) applied at the center of mass; *(b)* **F**$_c$ applied at a place other than the center of mass; *(c)* **F**$_c$ applied at the center of percussion.

Adapted from Brancazio, 1984.

arm (**r**) and force (**F**). A synonym for torque is moment of force. In a similar vein, angular momentum (**H**) is derived as the moment of linear momentum (**r** × **G**). Angular momentum describes the quantity of angular motion and is calculated as the product of moment of inertia *(I)* and angular velocity (**ω**). For example, the angular momentum of the bat in figure 2.24*b* after the application of **F**$_c$ would be 0.258 kg·m²/s, calculated as the product of the bat's moment of inertia (0.05 kg·m²) and its subsequent angular velocity (5.2 rad/s). Because the direction of **H** is the same as that for **ω**, **H**$_{bat}$ would be out of the page in figure 2.24*b*.

The impulse-momentum relation also applies for angular motion. In this context, however, the impulse is the area under the torque-time curve (left-hand side of Equation 2.24).

$$\int_{t_1}^{t_2} (\mathbf{r} \times \mathbf{F})\, dt = \mathbf{H} \tag{2.24}$$

Again considering the bat in figure 2.24*b*, which experienced a Δ**H** of 0.258 kg·m²/s, we know that the angular impulse was 218 N·m·s. The angular impulse applied to the bat was due to the torque (**r** × **F**$_c$) about the axis of rotation (CM of the bat) applied over an interval of time. The moment arm (**r**) was the perpendicular distance from the line of action of **F**$_c$ to the axis of rotation.

Example 2.11
Arm Action During Running

When a person runs, the upper body and lower body rotate in opposite directions about the twist axis during a single stride. This motion can be quantified as the angular momentum about the twist axis. When the left foot is on the ground, the upper body has an angular momentum in the downward direction (same direction as angular velocity), and the lower body has an angular momentum in the upward direction (figure 2.25). The net result is a relatively small angular momentum for the total body in the upward direction. The angular momentum experienced by the lower body is a result of the angular impulse (left-hand side of Equation 2.24) due to the ground reaction force. Because the foot is not placed beneath the twist axis when we run, the resultant of the forward-backward and side-to-side components (**F**) exerts a torque about the twist axis. The perpendicular distance from the line of action of this resultant and the twist axis is **r** in Equation 2.24. To prevent whole-body angular motion (nonzero angular momentum) about the twist axis, the runner responds to the angular impulse provided by the ground reaction force to the lower body by contracting the trunk muscles and generating an opposing angular momentum for the upper body; that is, the arms and trunk rotate in the opposite direction to the legs. This interaction is shown in figure 2.25*b:* for the first 40% of the stride, the left foot is in contact with the ground,

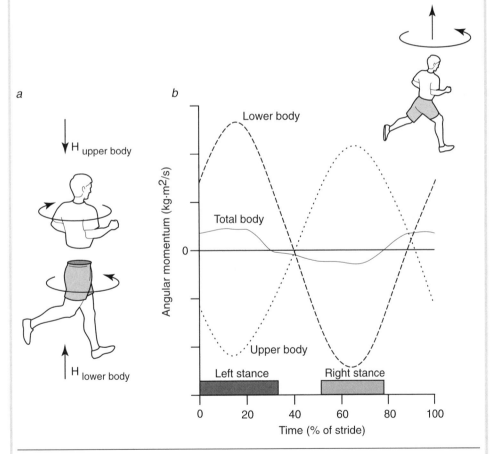

Figure 2.25 Angular momentum about the twist axis during a single running stride: *(a)* two-segment model of a runner; *(b)* angular momentum for the upper body, lower body, and total body.

Adapted from Hinrichs, 1987.

(continued)

producing a positive angular momentum in the vertical direction ($\mathbf{H}_y$) for the lower body, while concurrently the upper body is rotated with a negative $\mathbf{H}_y$. In the second part of the stride, the converse occurs while the right foot is in contact with the ground. The primary function of arm motion during running, therefore, is to counteract the angular momentum of the legs about the twist axis (Hinrichs, 1987; Hinrichs, Cavanagh, & Williams, 1987).

Because the human body does not behave as a single rigid body, such as the bat, it is necessary to consider the motion of each body segment when calculating angular momentum. This requires a **linked-system** analysis, in which we calculate the angular momentum of each segment about its CM (local angular momentum) and then determine the angular momentum of the CM for each segment about the system (whole body) CM (remote angular momentum). This relation has the following form:

$$\mathbf{H}^{S/CS} = \mathbf{H}^{B1/C1} + \mathbf{H}^{B2/C2} + \mathbf{H}^{B3/C3} + \dots \text{(local terms)} \qquad (2.25)$$

$$\mathbf{H}^{C1/CS} + \mathbf{H}^{C2/CS} + \mathbf{H}^{C3/CS} + \dots \text{(remote terms)}$$

where

$$\mathbf{H} = \text{angular momentum}$$

$$B1 = \text{body segment 1}$$

$$C1 = \text{center of mass for segment 1}$$

$$CS = \text{center of mass for the system}$$

$$S = \text{system}$$

$$/ = \text{with respect to}$$

Local terms (e.g., $\mathbf{H}^{B1/C1}$) have the form $I_g\omega$, whereas remote terms (e.g., $\mathbf{H}^{C1/CS}$) consist of the vector (cross) product $\mathbf{r} \times m\mathbf{v}$, which represents the moment of linear momentum relative to the system CM.

Figure 2.26 shows an example of the time course of angular momentum of the whole body as determined by a linked-system analysis (Hay, Wilson, Dapena, & Woodworth, 1977). In this example, a gymnast performed a vault that included periods in which he contacted either the ground or the vaulting horse and periods when he was not in contact with either. As we would expect from the impulse-momentum relation (Equation 2.24), the angular momentum of the gymnast changed when he contacted his surroundings and remained constant during the flight phases. The change in angular momentum was caused by an angular impulse due to the ground reaction force. As we discussed previously, the angular impulse represents the area under a torque-time curve, with the torque being the rotary effect of the ground reaction force about the CM of the gymnast. On the basis of the figure of the gymnast on the takeoff board in figure 2.26, would the ground reaction force pass behind or in front of his hips (CM) to produce the desired angular momentum? Because he rotated forward, the line of action of the ground reaction force must pass behind the hips and produce an angular momentum vector directed into the page.

Miller and Munro (1985) analyzed body segment contributions to the performance of a springboard dive. They calculated local and remote angular momenta for each body segment during the takeoff phase of various dives performed by Greg Louganis. The dives ranged from forward to reverse somersaults and from a straight (layout) dive to multiple somersaults (up to three and a half). Because angular momentum is conserved during the flight phase of a dive, the quantity of angular momentum generated during the takeoff phase determines the performance options available to the diver. From 79% to 93% of the angular momentum needed for

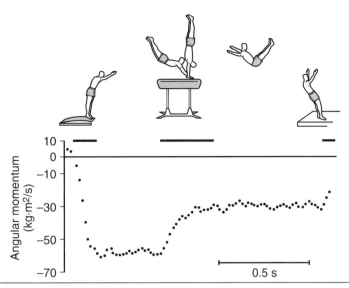

Figure 2.26 Angular momentum of a gymnast during a vault. The lines at the top of the graph indicate when the gymnast was in contact with the ground or the vaulting horse.

Reprinted from Hay, Wilson, Dapena, and Woodworth, 1977.

each dive (-70 to $57 \text{ kg m}^2/\text{s}$) was obtained from remote angular momentum, that is, was due to the motion of the body segments about the CM of the diver. The contribution from local angular momentum (i.e., due to the motion about segmental centers of mass) was more substantial in forward dives than in reverse dives. And the relative contributions of the body segments differed across the dives, with distinctions between forward- and reverse-somersault dives and between straight and multiple-somersault dives.

Conservation of Momentum

When the left-hand side of Equation 2.24 is zero, so too is the right-hand side. If an object's momentum does not change ($\Delta\mathbf{H} = 0$), then it must remain constant and is described as being conserved. Momentum can be conserved in either the linear or angular direction, and not necessarily at the same time. This is evident in such activities as gymnastics (e.g., Dainis, 1981; Nissinen, Preiss, & Brüggemann, 1985) and diving (e.g., Bartee & Dowell, 1982; Frohlich, 1980; Stroup & Bushnell, 1970; Wilson, 1977), and is classically demonstrated as the air-righting reaction in which the cat (as well as other animals) always lands on its feet when it is dropped from a low height (Kane & Scher, 1969; Laouris, Kalli-Laouri, & Schwartze, 1990; Magnus, 1922; Marey, 1894).

Example 2.12
Angular Momentum Is Conserved During a Dive

Once a springboard diver has left the board, she will experience two forces, weight and air resistance (figure 2.27). Let us consider the effect of these forces on her linear (**G**) and angular (**H**) momentum. From the impulse-momentum relation we have

$$\text{impulse} = \Delta \text{ linear momentum}$$

$$\overline{F} \cdot t = \Delta\, G$$

$$\overline{F} \cdot t = \Delta\, mv$$

(continued)

Because the average force includes the effect of weight (F_w) and air resistance (F_a), $\overline{F}$ is not zero, and there is a change in linear momentum; that is, $\Delta mv \neq 0$. Therefore, linear momentum does not remain constant. In contrast, consider the effect on angular momentum:

$$\text{angular impulse} = \Delta \text{ angular momentum}$$

$$(\overline{F} \times r) \cdot t = \Delta H$$

$$(\overline{F} \times r) \cdot t = \Delta I\omega$$

The **angular impulse** is equal to the product of the average torque $(\overline{F} \times r)$ and its time of application, where r is the moment arm from the line of action of each force to the axis of rotation (the CM). Because both F_w and F_a act through the CM in figure 2.27, the moment arm for each is equal to zero and thus there is no torque about the CM during the dive. The absence of a torque means that the right-hand side of the equation $(\Delta I\omega)$ is equal to zero and therefore momentum does not change but remains constant. This represents an example of the conservation of momentum.

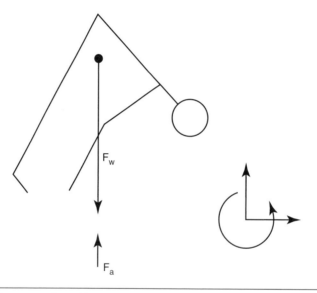

Figure 2.27   Forces experienced by a diver during free fall. F_a = air resistance; F_w = weight.

Because angular momentum is equal to the product of moment of inertia and angular velocity, any change in one parameter (i.e., moment of inertia or angular velocity) will be accompanied by a complementary change in the other parameter when angular momentum is constant. For example, suppose a diver performs a multi-somersault event in the pike position. If, during the dive, it becomes apparent that the diver will not make the appropriate number of revolutions, then the diver will assume a tuck position, which will (because **H** remains constant) be accompanied by an increase in the speed of rotation. The moment of inertia (I_g) of the diver about the somersault axis passing through the CM is about 7.5 kg·m^2 in the pike position, as opposed to 4.5 kg·m^2 in the tuck position. If, in the pike position, the diver has an angular velocity (ω) of 6 rad/s, then on changing to a tuck the speed will increase to 10 rad/s such that the product of the two parameters $(H = I_g\omega)$ will remain constant ($H = 45$ kg·m^2·s^{-1}). Specifically,

Pike $H = 7.5 \text{ kg} \cdot \text{m}^2 \times 6 \text{ rad} / \text{s}$

             $H = 45 \text{ kg} \cdot \text{m}^2 \cdot \text{s}^{-1}$

Tuck $H = 4.5 \text{ kg} \cdot \text{m}^2 \times 10 \text{ rad} / \text{s}$

             $H = 45 \text{ kg} \cdot \text{m}^2 \cdot \text{s}^{-1}$

and thus angular momentum *(H)* remains constant. The diver could also slow the speed of rotation by increasing the moment of inertia, in this case by assuming a greater layout position. This exchange between angular velocity and moment of inertia in order to conserve angular momentum during a dive is illustrated in figure 2.28.

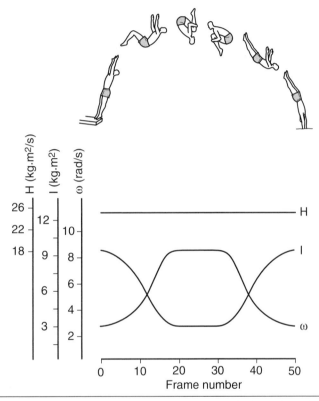

Figure 2.28   The conservation of angular momentum is accompanied by reciprocal changes in moment of inertia and angular velocity during a backward one-and-a-half somersault dive.

From J.G. Hay, *The Biomechanics of Sports Techniques*, 4/E (p. 155). Copyright © 1993 by Allyn & Bacon. Adapted by permission.

Example 2.13
Initiating a Twist in Diving

The impulse-momentum relation can also be used to explain how a diver is able to *initiate a twist* even though no force is available to assist in the maneuver. Figure 2.29 shows a diver performing a somersault in a layout position; the angular momentum of the diver ($\mathbf{H}_g$) is acting at the CM. According to the right-hand rule, the diver is preparing to perform a forward somersault. To initiate the twist, the diver rotates his arms about a cartwheel axis passing through his chest so that the right arm goes above the head and the left arm crosses his trunk (figure 2.29*b*). Because his arms rotate about a cartwheel axis, this does not alter

(continued)

$\mathbf{H}_g$ about the somersault axis. However, rotation of the arms generates an angular momentum in one direction about a cartwheel axis ($\mathbf{H}_{g,arms}$) that is counteracted (to keep $\mathbf{H}_g$ about the cartwheel axis zero) by an equivalent angular momentum of the trunk in the opposite direction about the cartwheel axis ($\mathbf{H}_{g,trunk}$) ($\mathbf{H}_{g,arms} + \mathbf{H}_{g,trunk} = 0$). Following this action-reaction maneuver, his arms are displaced as shown in figure 2.29*b*, and his trunk is inclined to the left of vertical by an angle θ. Because he is in free fall, the angular momentum remains constant at the value that he possessed when he left the board. Now, however, because his orientation has changed, $\mathbf{H}_g$ has components about both the somersault and twist axes relative to his body; the direction of $\mathbf{H}_g$ remains constant, but the axes move with the diver (figure 2.29*c*). The component of $\mathbf{H}_g$ about the twist axis *($H_{g,t}$)* is equal to $H_g \sin θ$, and the component about the somersault axis *($H_{g,s}$)* can be determined as $H_g \cos θ$.

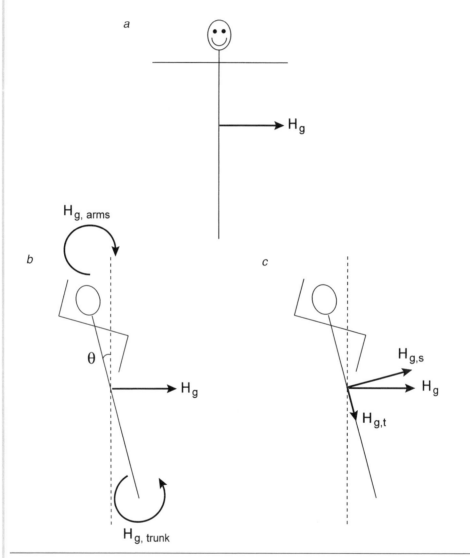

Figure 2.29   Initiation of a twist during a dive. *(a)* Orientation of the diver and H_g at takeoff; *(b)* rotation of the arms causes the body to tilt relative to the vertical; *(c)* the tilt causes H_g to have components about both the twist and the cartwheel axes.

For example, consider the tilt angle (θ = angle of trunk inclination to the left of vertical) that is necessary to execute a forward layout dive with a full twist from a 3-m diving board. Assume that no twist is initiated from the board. In this example, the diver has 30 kg·m²/s about the somersault axis at the moment of takeoff; $I_{g,s}$ represents the moment of inertia of the diver about the somersault axis passing through the CM; $I_{g,t}$ indicates the moment of inertia of the diver about the twist axis passing through the CM; and t is the time taken to perform the dive. The following initial conditions are given: H_g = 30 kg·m²/s; $I_{g,s}$ = 14 kg·m²; $I_{g,t}$ = 1 kg·m²; and t = 1.5 s.

$$H_{g,t} = I_{g,t}\omega_t$$

$$30 \sin \theta = 1 \times \frac{2\pi}{1.5}$$

$$\theta = \sin^{-1} \frac{4.19}{30}$$

$$\theta = 0.14 \text{ rad}$$

Given these initial conditions, the diver will need to tilt by 0.14 rad to complete a full twist in the dive. How much rotation about the somersault axis would accompany a tilt of 0.14 rad?

$$H_{g,s} = I_{g,s}\,\omega_s$$

$$30 \cos 0.14 = 14\,\omega_s$$

$$29.7 = 14\,\omega_s$$

$$\omega_s = 2.12 \text{ rad/s}$$

$$\frac{\Delta\theta}{t} = 2.12 \text{ rad/s}$$

$$\Delta\theta = 3.18 \text{ rad}$$

Thus, a tilt angle (θ) of 0.14 rad will result in a full-twisting, one-half (3.18 rad) somersault dive.

Yeadon (1993e) found that seven of eight divers performing the reverse 1.5 somersault dive with 2.5 twists obtained most of the twist from asymmetrical movements of the arms and hips during the aerial phase of the dive. However, about one-third of the tilt was derived from actions performed while the diver was in contact with the diving board.

Example 2.14
How Do Cats Land on Their Feet?

The impulse-momentum relation can also be used to understand the air-righting reaction, the so-called cat twist—the ability of cats (and other animals) to land on their feet when they are dropped from a low height in an upside-down position. This is an interesting issue because it raises the question how a cat can "acquire" angular momentum and perform the twist if there is no initial angular momentum and no angular impulse to cause a change in angular momentum.

One explanation (figure 2.30) of this feat is based on a muscle contraction-induced conservation of angular momentum for the upper and lower body (Hopper, 1973). As shown in

(continued)

figure 2.30*a*, the cat is modeled as a two-segment system comprising an upper (G_1) and a lower (G_2) body segment that are linked by a set of muscles *(PQ)*. In this scheme, the twist is initiated by a contraction of the muscles linking the upper and lower body *(PQ)*, which causes the two segments $(G_1$ and $G_2)$ to rotate (as indicated by the arrows) about their respective longitudinal axes. These rotations can be represented by angular momentum vectors, one for each segment $(\mathbf{H}_1$ and $\mathbf{H}_2)$, as shown in figure 2.30*b*. By the right-hand rule, $\mathbf{H}_1$ is directed diagonally downward, while $\mathbf{H}_2$ is directed diagonally upward. Hence, $\mathbf{H}_1$ and $\mathbf{H}_2$ have components in both the horizontal and vertical directions. The angular momentum components in the vertical direction cancel; but those in the horizontal direction sum to nonzero and indicate a positive angular momentum to the right, which reveals a rotation that will enable the cat to twist and to land on its feet.

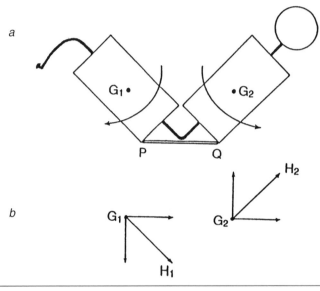

Figure 2.30 Model of a cat performing the air-righting reaction. (*a*) The two-segment model; (*b*) the angular momentum experienced by each segment.

Data from Hopper, 1973.

Work

A force applied to an object not only changes the momentum of the object but also, if it displaces the object, does work on the object. **Work** *(U)* is a scalar quantity that is calculated as the product of the displacement experienced by the object and the component of the force acting in the direction of the displacement (Equation 1.6). The unit of measurement for work is the joule (J; 1 J = 1 N·m). Work can be represented graphically as the area under a force-position (displacement) curve. This is a useful way to analyze movement when the force varies as a function of position. For example, when a person pulls on a linear spring and stretches it, the work done on the spring can be displayed as a force-length graph (figure 2.31*a*). The force needed to stretch the spring increases as a linear function of the amount of stretch. Because of this relation, the amount of work that must be done on the spring to stretch it by 1 mm is much greater at longer lengths; this is evident by the larger shaded area at the longer length (figure 2.31*b*).

Work can be positive or negative. When the force acts in the same direction as displacement, the work it does is positive. Conversely, when the force acts in the direction opposite the direction of displacement, the work it does is negative. For example, when a person lifts a barbell by using the elbow flexor muscles, the muscles perform **positive work** by pulling on

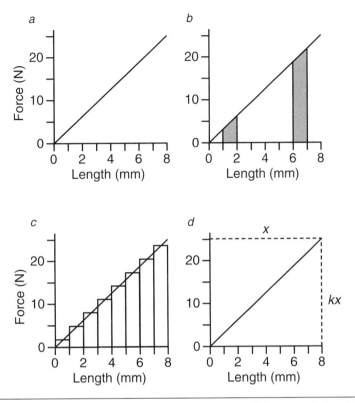

Figure 2.31 *(a)* The force applied to a spring increases linearly as it is stretched, *(b)* which means that the work done to stretch it by 1 mm is greater at longer lengths. *(c)* The area under the curve can be determined by calculating the amount of work represented by each of the eight rectangles and then summing the values for all the rectangles or *(d)* by taking one-half of the rectangle that has the sides of *kx* (force) and *x* (length).

the forearm to lift the load so that the force and displacement occur in the same direction. When the person lowers the barbell, however, the muscles perform **negative work** because the force exerted by the elbow flexor muscles still pulls on the forearm, while the displacement occurs in the opposite direction. When a muscle does positive work, it performs a concentric or shortening contraction. Conversely, when a muscle does negative work it does an eccentric or lengthening contraction. The metabolic energy required to perform negative work is much less than that required for an equivalent amount of positive work.

We can calculate the work performed by the force by measuring the area under the force-position curve. Mathematically, this involves taking the integral of force with respect to position.

$$U = \int F \, dr \tag{2.26}$$

Numerically, however, we can determine the area by dividing it into many small rectangles (figure 2.31*c*), calculating the amount of work represented by each rectangle, and then summing the rectangles.

$$U = \sum_{i=1}^{N} F_i \, \Delta x \tag{2.27}$$

where N = the number of rectangles and Δx = the width of the rectangles. The procedure shown in figure 2.31*c* involves determining the height *(F)* of each rectangle, multiplying the height by the width (Δx), and summing the values for all eight rectangles. It should be obvious from figure 2.31*c* that the thinner the rectangles, the closer the estimated area will be to the actual area.

When the displacement experienced by an object is not linear but instead follows a curved path, which often occurs in human movement, the work done by the force is determined slightly differently. The procedure is to divide the path into many small segments, over which both the force and the displacement can be considered to be linear; calculating the work for each segment; and then summing the segments. This is represented as the line integral (Equation 2.28) and involves taking the dot product of the force vector with a particular path (Δr), where the number of Δr segments is sufficient to cover the entire path of the object.

$$U = \int \mathbf{F} \cdot d\mathbf{r} \tag{2.28}$$

Kinetic Energy

In the time domain, we can determine the amount of motion an object has by calculating its momentum. In the length (position) domain, however, an object's motion is quantified as **kinetic energy** *(E$_k$)*. Kinetic energy is a scalar quantity that depends on the mass of the object and its velocity (Equation 2.29). As with many other quantities, it has both linear ($\frac{1}{2} mv^2$) and angular ($\frac{1}{2} I\omega^2$) terms.

$$E_k = \tfrac{1}{2} mv^2 + \tfrac{1}{2} I\omega^2 \tag{2.29}$$

The unit of measurement for energy, like that for work, is the joule (J; 1 J = 1 N·m = 1 kg·m²/s²). The kinetic energy that a volleyball has after being served by a player, for example, could include both linear and angular terms or just linear, depending on whether or not the ball has any spin. A volleyball traveling at 73 mph (32.6 m/s) and rotating at 48 rpm (revolutions per minute; 5.02 rad/s) has the following amount of kinetic energy:

$$E_k = \tfrac{1}{2} mv^2 + \tfrac{1}{2} I\omega^2$$
$$= \left(0.5 \times 0.27 \times 32.6^2\right) + \left(0.5 \times 0.002 \times 5.02^2\right)$$
$$= 143 + 0.025$$
$$E_k = 143 \text{ J}$$

As in this example, the magnitude of the linear component is often much larger than that of the angular component in most activities we perform. In a more complex activity, such as running or cycling, the kinetic energy of the body depends on the linear and angular terms for all the body segments.

In parallel with the impulse-momentum relation (Equation 2.15) in which an impulse changes the momentum of an object, the work-energy theorem states that the change in kinetic energy of an object is equal to the amount of work done on the object.

$$\Delta E_k = U \tag{2.30}$$

Because of this relation, energy is sometimes defined as the capacity to do work.

Example 2.15
Work by the Knee Extensor Muscles

When a person performed a knee extension exercise on an isokinetic dynamometer, he exerted a torque with his knee extensor muscles that displaced the lever arm of the dynamometer by 1.57 rad (figure 2.32). If we determine the area under the torque-angle graph, this will indicate how much work his leg did on the lever arm and how much the kinetic energy of the lever arm changed.

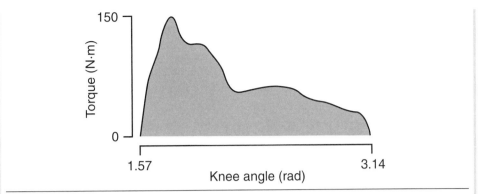

Figure 2.32   A torque-angle graph for one repetition of a knee extension exercise performed on an isokinetic dynamometer.

Potential Energy

When work is done on an object, its kinetic energy is not only changed but it is also displaced. For most movements that we perform, the displacement often occurs against an opposing force, such as gravity and friction. If the direction of the opposing force never changes, as is the case with gravity, then displacement against the force provides the object with energy that can be used when the displacement-producing force is removed. This energy is known as **potential energy.** The two main forms that occur in human movement are gravitational $(E_{p.g})$ and strain or elastic $(E_{p.s})$ potential energy. Gravitational potential energy represents the energy that an object has because of its mass and its location in a gravitational field.

$$E_{p.g} = mgh \tag{2.31}$$

where g is the acceleration due to gravity and h is the vertical height above a baseline location, such as the ground. The $E_{p.g}$ of an object comes from the negative work done by gravity when the object is displaced to its location (h); the work is negative because gravity acts downward while the displacement is upward. Because h is the vertical location, the actual path (linear or not) taken to achieve this location has no effect on either the $E_{p.g}$ of the object or the negative work done by gravity.

The other form of potential energy that concerns us is **strain** or **elastic energy.** One example of this is a spring. As described in figure 2.31, the force exerted by an ideal spring is a linear function of the amount of stretch that it experiences; the greater the stretch, the greater the force exerted by the spring. The slope of the line indicates the stiffness (k) of the spring. The more difficult it is to stretch a spring, the greater is its stiffness. The stiffness of the spring in figure 2.31 is 3.13 N/mm (25 N/8 mm). The stiffness of a spring (or of such tissues as tendon and ligament) depends on its material properties, which determine the resistance that it offers to any increases in its length. When a spring is stretched, the work is done on the spring by the stretching force and can be visualized as the area under the force-length graph (figure 2.31d). This area is one-half of the rectangle that has the amount of stretch (x) as the length of one side and the force (kx) as the length of the other side. This area represents the potential energy that the stretched spring has to do work.

$$E_{p.s} = \tfrac{1}{2}kx^2 \tag{2.32}$$

Example 2.16

Work Done on Elastic Bands

A physical therapist directing the rehabilitation of a patient recovering from knee surgery prescribes some knee extension exercises that involve a therapeutic elastic band. The stiffness of the band is 22 N/cm.

A. Calculate the force exerted by the band when it is stretched by 5 cm and 13 cm.

$$F_5 = kx$$
$$= 22 \text{ N / cm} \times 5 \text{ cm}$$
$$= 110 \text{ N}$$
$$F_{13} = kx$$
$$= 22 \text{ N / cm} \times 13 \text{ cm}$$
$$= 286 \text{ N}$$

B. Draw a force-deformation graph that shows the elastic force provided by the therapeutic band.

C. On the same graph, draw a line to show the force-deformation graph when two bands are used.

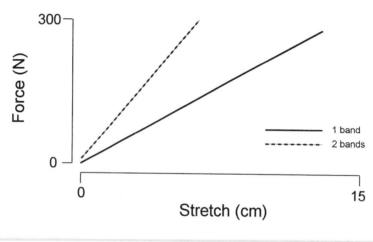

Conservation of Mechanical Energy

Equation 2.30 indicates that the work done on an object changes the kinetic energy of the object. From the discussion of potential energy, however, we know that the work done on an object overcomes two types of forces: those that exert a constant opposing effect (e.g., gravity) and those that are not constant (e.g., friction, air resistance). Hence, we can rewrite Equation 2.30 by representing the work done by these two types of forces:

$$\Delta E_k = U_c + U_{nc}$$

where U_c indicates the work done by constant opposing forces and U_{nc} represents the work done by the nonconstant opposing forces. Because U_c corresponds to potential energy acquired by the object, this equation becomes:

$$\Delta E_k = \Delta E_p + U_{nc}$$
$$\Delta E_k + \Delta E_p = U_{nc} \tag{2.33}$$

When there are no nonconstant opposing forces acting on an object, the left-hand side of Equation 2.33 becomes zero and we have a condition in which the sum of the changes in kinetic and potential energy is zero. That is, the sum of kinetic and potential energy is constant. This represents the law of **conservation of mechanical energy** (Equation 2.34).

$$E_k + E_p = \text{constant} \qquad (2.34)$$

Example 2.17
Exchange of Potential and Kinetic Energy

Consider a 60-kg (mass) acrobat about to leap off a 10-m tower. Assume that U_{nc} is zero. The acrobat has a potential energy of 5.88 kJ. The instant the acrobat leaves the tower, there is no supporting surface to provide a ground reaction force; and because of gravity, the acrobat will fall and there will be a conversion of energy from one form to another. The fall of the acrobat can be described as a change of energy from potential $(E_{p,g})$ to kinetic $(E_{k,t})$. Because the acceleration due to gravity is constant, the speed of falling increases with the distance covered in the fall. This correlates with an increasing conversion from potential to kinetic energy, in accordance with Equation 2.34.

Consider the energy of the acrobat after she has fallen 4 m. At this position, her potential energy is 3.53 kJ, a decrease of 2.35 kJ. Her kinetic energy $(E_{k,t})$ can be determined by

$$E_{k,t} = \tfrac{1}{2}mv^2$$

To calculate her kinetic energy after she has fallen 4 m, we need to determine her velocity (v) at that point. We can calculate velocity by using Equation 1.4 to determine the time (0.9043 s) it took for her to fall 4 m and then using the definition of acceleration:

$$a = \frac{\Delta v}{\Delta t}$$

$$a = \frac{v_f - v_i}{t}$$

$$-9.81 = \frac{v_f - 0}{0.9045}$$

$$v_f = -8.86 \text{ m/s}$$

where v_i and v_f refer to the initial (at the beginning of the fall) and the final (at 4 m) velocities, respectively. The final-velocity value (–8.86 m/s) can then be used to determine her kinetic energy at 4 m.

Alternatively, because $E_{k,t} = \tfrac{1}{2}mv^2$ and we know how much $E_{p,g}$ has been reduced (2.35 kJ) due to the law of conservation of mechanical energy, we can determine v by rearranging this relation:

$$E_{k,t} = \tfrac{1}{2}mv^2$$

$$v = \sqrt{\frac{2 \times E_{k,t}}{m}}$$

$$v = \sqrt{\frac{2 \times 2350}{60}}$$

$$v = \sqrt{78.33 \text{ m}^2/\text{s}^2}$$

$$v = 8.85 \text{ m}/\text{s}$$

(continued)

Using either method, we obtain a magnitude for the final velocity of about 8.85 m/s. Thus as the acrobat begins to fall, the kinetic energy changes from zero to a value of 2.35 kJ after 4 m—an increase that matches the decrease in potential energy.

Example 2.18
Jumping on a Trampoline

A child, jumping on a trampoline, depresses the trampoline bed by 0.72 m. If the child weighs 391 N and the trampoline has a stiffness of 18 N/cm, how high will the child jump?

$$E_k + E_{p.g} + E_{p,s} = \text{constant}$$

This is an energy transformation problem in which the potential strain energy is transformed to potential gravitational energy. Because E_k is zero at both the bottom of the bounce and the peak height reached, the equation becomes

$$E_{p.g} = E_{p,s}$$

$$mgh = \tfrac{1}{2} kx^2$$

$$h = \frac{\tfrac{1}{2} kx^2}{mg}$$

$$h = \frac{\tfrac{1}{2} \times 1800 \times 0.72^2}{391}$$

$$h = 1.19 \text{ m}$$

Power

In many short-duration athletic events (e.g., sprinting, Olympic weightlifting, arm wrestling, vertical jump) and even in some activities of daily living (e.g., recovering from a stumble), the rate at which muscles can produce work, referred to as power production, is the critical performance variable. Power production is measured as the amount of work done per unit time. **Power** ($\bar{P}$) can be determined as the work done *(U)* divided by the amount of time (Δt) it took to perform the work, or as the product of average force ($\bar{F}$) and velocity ($\bar{v}$):

$$\bar{P} = \frac{U}{\Delta t}$$

$$\bar{P} = \frac{\bar{F} \cdot \Delta r}{\Delta t}$$

$$\bar{P} = \bar{F} \cdot \bar{v}$$

As a measure of the rate of work performance, power is a scalar quantity that is measured in watts (W); 1 kW (1.36 horsepower) is the metabolic power corresponding to an oxygen consumption of about 48 ml/s. Because work represents a change in the energy of the system, power can also be written as *the rate of change in energy* (Ingen Schenau & Cavanagh, 1990).

$$\bar{P} = \frac{U}{\Delta t} = \frac{\Delta E}{\Delta t} = \bar{F} \cdot \bar{v}$$

The duration for which an activity can be sustained decreases exponentially as the power requirements of the activity increase (Lakomy, 1987).

Because power is defined as the rate of performing work, we can calculate it either by using the force and displacement associated with the work done or by using the change in mechanical energy (potential and kinetic) that enables the work to be done. Furthermore, these calculations can be applied to the whole body, can be applied to one body segment, or can be summed from the multiple segments in a limb (Arampatzis, Knicker, Metzler, & Brüggemann, 2000; Hatze, 1998). There is some debate among biomechanists, however, on the physical meaning of the power calculations applied to the whole-body CM (Ingen Schenau & Cavanagh, 1990). In contrast, the more common application in human movement is to evaluate the instantaneous power about selected joints during a movement (DeVita, Torry, Glover, & Speroni, 1996). This calculation, as presented in chapter 3, is typically performed with the angular equivalents of force and velocity. For example, the joint power during a movement is often estimated as the product of torque (τ) and angular velocity (ω).

Example 2.19
Muscle Power for an Elbow Movement

Because power can be determined as the product of force and velocity and because acceleration and force are proportional to each other, we can obtain the power-time profile associated with the movement by multiplying the velocity and acceleration curves. When velocity and acceleration have the same sign (positive or negative), *power is positive and represents an energy flow from the muscles to the arm.* Conversely, *when power is negative* (i.e., velocity and acceleration have opposite signs), *energy flows from the arm to the muscles.* These conditions are known as **power production** and **power absorption,** respectively, indicating energy flow from and to the muscles.

With regard to the elbow extension-flexion movement in chapter 1 (figure 1.19), positive velocity (greater than zero) indicates elbow extension, positive acceleration represents an extension-directed force, and positive power (production) represents energy flowing from the appropriate muscles to the system (forearm-hand). The power-time curve is determined by multiplying the velocity and acceleration (force) graphs. When the velocity or acceleration graph crosses zero (i.e., changes sign), so does the power curve. The resulting power-time graph for the elbow extension-flexion movement is depicted as a four-epoch event (figure 2.33). The first two epochs, power production and absorption, respectively, occur during elbow extension (see velocity-time graph) and represent periods of positive and negative work. During positive work, the muscles do work on the system; during negative work, the system (due to its inertia) does work on the muscles. A similar sequence (power production, then absorption) occurs during the flexion phase of the movement.

This example emphasizes the correlation between the concepts of positive and negative work, power production and absorption, and concentric and eccentric muscle activity. As shown in the lower panel of figure 2.33, the elbow extension-flexion movement is associated with a four-phase power-time profile. The epochs of power production correspond to periods of positive work and therefore concentric muscle activity. Recall that in chapter 1 we determined that this movement involved the following sequence of activity: concentric extensor, eccentric flexor, concentric flexor, and eccentric extensor. According to this scheme, therefore, power absorption is related to negative work and eccentric muscle activity.

(continued)

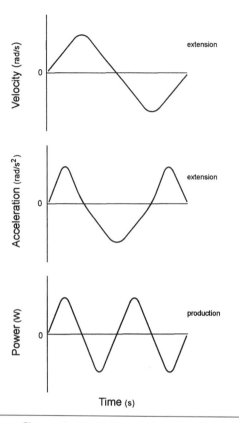

Figure 2.33 Power-time profile associated with the muscles across the elbow joint during the elbow extension-flexion movement shown in figure 1.19. Positive velocity represents an extension movement; positive acceleration indicates acceleration in the direction of extension; and positive power (production) refers to the power produced by the system.

Example 2.20
Power in Jumping

For some athletic endeavors, the ability of an individual to produce power is a significant criterion for success. This capability can be assessed through measurement of the performance of an individual during a vertical jump for maximum height (Sayers, Harackiewicz, Harman, Frykman, & Rosenstein, 1999), although there are some limitations to the accuracy of this procedure (Hatze, 1998). By simply measuring either the height that the CM is raised or the vertical impulse from the ground reaction force during the takeoff phase, we can estimate the average power produced by the individual during the jump. An assessment based on *kinematics* uses the equations of motion and the principles of projectile motion that were discussed in chapter 1. Consider the trajectory of an individual (mass = m) from the peak of a vertical jump to the landing. The height of the jump (r = the distance the CM is raised) can be determined with Equation 1.4:

$$r = v_i t + 0.5 a t^2$$

$$r = 0.5 \times 9.81 \times t^2$$

$$t = \sqrt{\frac{r}{4.9}}$$

where t = one-half of the flight time. From Equation 1.1, the average velocity is defined as

$$\bar{v} = \frac{\Delta r}{\Delta t}$$

and substituting for t

$$\bar{v} = \frac{\Delta r}{\sqrt{r/4.9}}$$

$$\bar{v} = \sqrt{r \cdot 4.9}$$

From the definition of power $(F \times v)$, the average power $(\bar{P})$ during the descent phase for the individual (which is the same as that during the ascent phase and comes from the actions of the jumper during the takeoff phase) can be determined as

$$\bar{P} = (9.81 \cdot m) \cdot \sqrt{r \cdot 4.9} \qquad (2.35)$$

Another way to determine average power is based on the *kinetics* of the vertical jump. This involves measuring the vertical impulse from the ground reaction force and using the impulse-momentum relation (Equation 2.15).

$$\text{impulse} = \Delta \text{momentum}$$

$$\int F_{net} \, dt = m \cdot \Delta v$$

$$\Delta v = \frac{\int F_{net} dt}{m}$$

This expression indicates that the takeoff velocity $(\Delta v = v_f)$ is equal to the *net* vertical impulse divided by the mass of the individual. To determine the net vertical impulse, we measure the area under the force-time curve for the ground reaction force and then subtract from this the body-weight impulse (body weight times the duration of the takeoff phase). Because initial velocity (v_i) is zero, average velocity $(\bar{v})$ can be calculated as:

$$\bar{v} = \frac{v_i + v_f}{2}$$

$$\bar{v} = \frac{v_f}{2}$$

$$\bar{v} = \frac{\int F_{net} \, dt}{2 \, m}$$

The average force $(\bar{F})$ exerted during the takeoff phase of the jump is calculated by dividing the absolute impulse $(\int F_{g,y} \, dt)$ by the duration of the takeoff phase:

$$\bar{F} = \frac{\int F_{g,y} \, dt}{t}$$

Average power produced by the jumper can be determined from:

$$\bar{P} = \bar{F} \cdot \bar{v}$$

$$\bar{P} = \frac{\int F_{g,y} \, dt}{t} \cdot \frac{\int F_{net} \, dt}{2 \, m} \qquad (2.36)$$

(continued)

The advantage of Equation 2.36 is that the average power can be estimated from the measurement of the vertical component of the ground reaction force and the mass of the individual. However, a more accurate measurement of average power can be achieved if we consider the change in mechanical energy during the takeoff phase for the jump (Hatze, 1998):

$$U = \tfrac{1}{2}mv^2 + mgh$$

where v = the velocity of the CM at takeoff and h = the vertical displacement of the CM from the start of the jump (crouch position) to the takeoff. Because the takeoff velocity can be obtained from jump height $\left(v = \sqrt{2\,g\,r}\right)$, the equation can be rewritten as:

$$U = \tfrac{1}{2}mv^2 + mgh$$
$$U = mgr + mgh$$

where m = jumper's mass, g = acceleration due to gravity, r = height that the CM is raised, and h = CM displacement during the takeoff phase. Average power can then be calculated as the work done divided by the duration (t) of the takeoff phase:

$$\overline{P} = \frac{m\,g(r+h)}{t} \tag{2.37}$$

These measurements, although more involved than those for Equation 2.36, can also be made from measurement of the vertical component of the ground reaction force (Hatze, 1998).

Summary

This chapter is the first of two to address the forces associated with human movement. Our approach is based on Newton's laws of motion and an analysis technique known as the free body diagram. Because human movement involves the rotation of body segments about one another, the concept of a rotary force (torque) and the relevant calculations are introduced. After these introductory sections, the chapter deals with the forces experienced by the human body during movement. These are categorized into forces due to body mass (gravity and inertial force) and forces due to the surroundings (ground reaction force, fluid resistance). The last part of the chapter describes the effects of these forces on the mechanical actions of the body, which are quantified as momentum and work. With these techniques, the motion of an object is characterized in terms of its momentum or its mechanical energy.

Suggested Readings

Hamill, J., & Knutzen, K.M. (1995). *Biomechanical basis of human movement*. Baltimore: Williams & Wilkins, chapters 10 and 11.

McGinnis, P.M. (1999). *Biomechanics of sport and exercise*. Champaign, IL: Human Kinetics, chapters 3, 4, and 6-10.

Nigg, B.M., MacIntosh, B.R., & Mester, J. *Biomechanics of biology and movement*. Champaign, IL: Human Kinetics, chapter 14.

Watkins, J. (1999). *Structure and function of the musculoskeletal system*. Champaign, IL: Human Kinetics, chapter 1.

Winter, D.A. (1990). *Biomechanics and motor control of human movement*. New York: Wiley, chapters 3, 4, and 5.

Chapter 3

Photograph courtesy of Cinémathèque Française.

Forces Within the Body

The motion of an object, which is described in terms of position, velocity, and acceleration, is characterized as the consequence of the interaction between the object and its surroundings. This interaction is commonly represented as a force. In chapter 2 we considered the forces due to body mass and those due to the surroundings that can be imposed on the human body to change its momentum or its mechanical energy. The forces involved in human movement, however, include not only these interactions but also the mechanical interactions within the musculoskeletal system. To examine these musculoskeletal forces, we draw free body diagrams and apply Newton's laws of motion to each body segment that participates in the movement. In chapter 2, this approach was described as a segmental analysis. The purpose of chapter 3 is to describe the properties of the musculoskeletal forces that are encountered in such an analysis and to present the procedures used to estimate the magnitudes and directions of these forces.

Musculoskeletal Forces

Through application of Newton's law of acceleration to a segmental analysis of the human body, it is possible to determine the magnitude and direction of forces inside the human body. We call these interactions **musculoskeletal forces**. To accomplish this we draw a free body diagram that ends at a joint; this allows us to include these forces as external effects acting on a system (e.g., figures 2.1, 2.2, and 2.3). Whenever we draw a free body diagram that includes part of the body and ends at a joint, we need to include a joint reaction force and a muscle force. The joint reaction force is typically drawn as a force acting into the joint; this represents the reaction of the adjacent body segment to the compressive force in the joint. The muscle force is usually shown acting back across the joint to represent the net pulling action of the muscles that cross the joint. In addition, when the free body diagram ends anywhere in the trunk, we need to include a force due to the pressure inside the abdomen or the thorax.

Joint Reaction Force

When a system for a free body diagram is defined so that it ends at a joint, the concept of a **joint reaction force** (F_j) is invoked *to represent the reaction of the adjacent body segment to the forces exerted by the identified system.* This is a three-dimensional force that has one component normal to the joint surface and, like the ground reaction force, two components that are tangential to the surface. The normal component is typically directed into the joint surface and represents a compressive force. The two tangential components compose the shear force that acts along the joint surface.

The joint reaction force can be influenced by any effect included on the free body diagram. Examples are forces transmitted from one end of the segment to the other end (e.g., ground reaction force), forces due to joint-related soft-tissue structures (e.g., ligaments, joint capsule), and the forces exerted by the muscles. The magnitude of these forces can be large. Although the magnitude of the forces transmitted by soft tissues, especially the ligaments, has been controversial, it now appears that these forces can be significant and that they vary over the range of motion of the joint (Mommersteeg, Huiskes, Blankevoort, Kooloos, & Kauer, 1997; Shelburne & Pandy, 1997).

The most significant and consistent contributor to the joint reaction force is the force due to muscle activity (Duda, Schneider, & Chao, 1997; Lu, Taylor, O'Connor, & Walker, 1997). When a muscle contracts, the tangential component of the muscle force vector is transmitted into the joint as a compressive force. Given that muscles have a shallow angle of pull, most of the muscle force is directed along the tangential component. For example, Lu et al. (1997) found that when subjects stood in an upright position and performed isometric contractions with the hip flexor, extensor, abductor, and adductor muscles, the tangential force along the femur was ~20 times greater than the perpendicular (normal) force measured at the ankle. For these contractions, the hip muscles exerted average forces of ~2000 N.

It is difficult to measure F_j experimentally, and it usually involves an invasive procedure. For example, Bergmann, Graichen, and Rohlmann (1993) implanted force transducers to measure the hip joint force in two patients who had been fitted with hip joint prostheses. When these patients walked on a treadmill at 1.1 m/s, their joint reaction forces at the hip varied during a stride as shown in figure 3.1. The vertical component was directed downward (compression) with a peak magnitude of three times body weight; the side-to-side component was directed medially with a peak magnitude of about body weight; and the forward-backward component was directed first forward and then backward with a peak magnitude of about 0.5 times body weight.

In most studies, however, the magnitude of F_j is usually estimated by determining all the other forces on a free body diagram and assuming that the remaining effect is due to F_j; this procedure is known as a *residual analysis*. We can use a residual analysis, for example, if the system is in equilibrium, which means that all the forces acting on the system must be balanced. Alternatively, it is possible to use various mathematical procedures, such as minimizing muscle stress, to estimate the magnitude of F_j. An, Kwak, Chao, and Morrey (1984) used such an approach on the elbow (humeroulnar) joint when a perpendicular load was applied at the wrist. When the joint was moved over a range of motion from complete extension to a right angle, F_j at the wrist was 6 to 16 times greater than the load. When the loads encountered in normal daily activities were considered, this meant that values for F_j equal to 0.3 to 0.5 times body weight were commonly encountered at the elbow joint.

Values for F_j have been estimated by residual analysis for such activities as standing, moving from sitting to standing, walking, running, weightlifting, and landing from a drop (summarized in Harrison, Lees, McCullagh, & Rowe, 1986). Even the common task of going from an erect posture to a squat position and then rising again is associated with large joint reaction forces. For this task, the maximum compression component of the tibiofemoral joint reaction

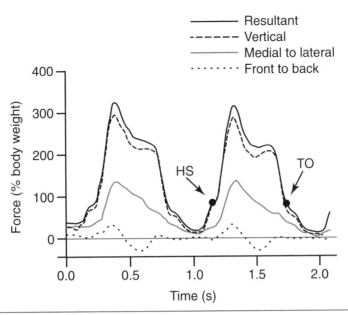

Figure 3.1   Joint reaction forces at the hip joint for two stance phases (HS = heel strike; TO = toe-off) during walking on a treadmill.

Data from Bergmann et al., 1993.

force ranged from 4.7 to 5.6 times body weight, whereas the shear component ranged from 3.0 to 3.9 times body weight (Dahlkvist, Mayo, & Seedhom, 1982). Power lifters experience maximum compressive forces of 17 times body weight and maximum shear forces of 2.3 times body weight at the L4-5 joint during the performance of the dead lift (Cholewicki, McGill, & Norman, 1991). Results such as these emphasize that the joint reaction force varies over the range of motion and that it can have a substantial magnitude, especially in comparison with the loads that the limbs encounter in daily activities.

An alternative approach to residual analysis for estimating F_j is to measure acceleration and use inverse dynamics to determine joint forces and torques (Bogert, Read, & Nigg, 1996). Attaching four accelerometers at known locations to the trunks of individuals made it possible to estimate the joint reaction force at the hip during walking, running, and skiing (Bogert, Read, & Nigg, 1999). The peak forces, in terms of body weight (F_w), averaged about 2 times F_w for walking at 1.5 m/s, 5 times F_w for running at 3.5 m/s, 4 to 7 times F_w for alpine skiing, 4 times F_w for cross-country skiing, and 7 to 13 times F_w for skiing moguls. Such information indicates the range of forces that a hip prosthesis must be able to withstand in an active individual.

Example 3.1
Absolute Magnitude of the Joint Reaction Force

The *joint reaction force* is usually determined from the *net* forces between adjacent body segments. To determine the absolute magnitude of the joint reaction force, however, it is necessary to consider each force rather than calculating a net effect. An interesting example of the difference between the net and absolute effects was provided by Galea and Norman (1985) in a study of the muscle actions across the ankle joint during a rapid ballet movement, a spring from flat feet onto the toes. In this analysis, the model used to perform these calculations (figure 3.2*a*) took into account the major muscles crossing the ankle joint and therefore those that contributed to the muscle-dependent component of the joint reaction

(continued)

force. The muscles included extensor hallucis longus, tibialis anterior, flexor hallucis longus, peroneus longus, and gastrocnemius/soleus. For the calculations, the force exerted by each of these muscles was estimated based on its EMG, length, and rate of change in length (Hof, 1984; Hof & van den Berg, 1981a, 1981b, 1981c, 1981d).

Once Galea and Norman (1985) had estimated a force for each muscle, the forces were grouped (figure 3.2b) into those that contributed to a plantarflexor force $(F_{m,pf})$ and those that contributed to a dorsiflexor force $(F_{m,df})$. The absolute force was calculated as the tangential component of the $F_{m,pf}$ vector *plus* the tangential component of the $F_{m,df}$ vector. The net joint reaction force (figure 3.2c), however, was calculated as the tangential component of the resultant muscle force (F_m), where F_m is the *difference* between $F_{m,df}$ and $F_{m,pf}$. For one subject, Galea and Norman calculated a net joint reaction force due to muscle activity of 732 N during the movement and an absolute joint reaction force of 6068 N, which is a huge difference.

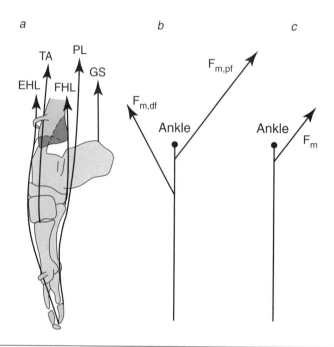

Figure 3.2   Muscles that are active across the ankle joint during a full pointe: *(a)* lines of action of the involved muscles; *(b)* separation of the muscular effects into those that exert dorsiflexor (df) and plantarflexor (pf) torque; *(c)* resultant muscle force.

Adapted from Galea and Norman, 1985.

EHL = extensor hallucis longus; TA = tibialis anterior; FHL = flexor hallucis longus; PL = peroneus longus; GS = gastrocnemius/soleus.

Muscle Force

In the segmental analysis of human movement, **muscle force** is often the most significant component included on a free body diagram. When the system defined in a free body diagram ends at a joint, the muscle force vector is shown as acting back across the joint to represent the pulling effect of the muscle on the segment. This vector usually represents the net muscle activity about a joint.

Because muscles can exert only a pulling force on a segment, opposing sets of muscles (agonists and antagonists) control movement about a joint. For example, the movement of elbow extension-flexion is controlled by one muscle group that causes acceleration in the extension direction (elbow extensors) and another group that causes acceleration in the flexion direction (elbow flexors).

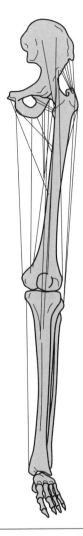

Figure 3.3 Lines of action of 24 muscles in the human leg.

Reprinted from Duda, Schneider, and Chao, 1997.

The muscle force vector can be represented as an arrow and described in terms of its magnitude and direction. In a segmental analysis, the force is represented by a line of action that extends between its proximal and distal attachments. Figure 3.3 shows an example for 24 muscles in the human leg; this model was used to estimate the joint reaction force at the hip (Duda et al., 1997). In this scheme, the application of force is represented as acting at a point, which is reasonable for most muscles (Brand et al., 1982). If the attachment site is substantial (e.g., trapezius, pectoralis major), a muscle may be represented by several lines of action (van der Helm & Veenbaas, 1991). Obviously, care must be taken to determine the lines of action as accurately as possible (Nussbaum, Chaffin, & Rechtien, 1995).

Magnitude of Muscle Force

Both the magnitude and direction of the muscle force vector are difficult to measure. To measure the magnitude of muscle force directly, we must measure the force transmitted by the tendon. In an isolated-muscle experiment, this measurement involves connecting the tendon to a force transducer (Ralston, Inman, Strait, & Shaffrath, 1947). In human experiments, in which the tendon is not detached from the bone, we can measure muscle force by placing a buckle transducer on the tendon. This is a surgical procedure that involves threading a tendon through an E-shaped buckle. When a buckle transducer was placed on the Achilles tendon during cycling, Gregor, Komi, and Jarvinen (1987) measured peak tendon forces of about 700 N in the right Achilles tendon for subjects pedaling at a rate of 90 rpm while producing 265 W of power. More recently, Komi and colleagues have developed a technique of inserting an optic fiber (0.5-mm diameter) through a tendon to measure the tendon force during various activities (Finni, Komi, & Lukkariniemi, 1998).

Most human subjects, however, are not willing to volunteer for such invasive procedures, and it is necessary to use more indirect techniques to assess muscle force. Much of the information available on the magnitude and direction of muscle forces has been derived from indirect estimates. One common approach has been to determine the **cross-sectional area** of muscle from sections made perpendicular to the orientation of the muscle fibers and to use this information to estimate muscle force (Fick, 1904). Cross-sectional area, a measurement of the end-on view of the area at the level at which the section (cut) has been made, indicates the number of force-generating units (myofibrils) that are lying *in parallel* in the muscle. These measurements can be obtained through dissection of cadavers or through use of imaging procedures on volunteers (ultrasound, computed tomography, magnetic resonance imagery) (Kawakami et al., 1994; Narici, Roi, & Landoni, 1988).

The relation between the cross-sectional area of a muscle and its maximum force is shown in figure 3.4. There is a linear relation between these two variables for both men and women; this means that the maximum force is greatest for the individuals with the largest cross-sectional areas. The slope of the regression line is referred to as **specific tension** or **normalized force** and varies from 16 to 60 N/cm^2 across studies, with a nominal value of 30 N/cm^2 (Edgerton, Apor, & Roy, 1990; Kanda & Hashizume, 1989; Lieber & Fridén, 2000; McDonagh & Davies, 1984; Roy & Edgerton, 1992).

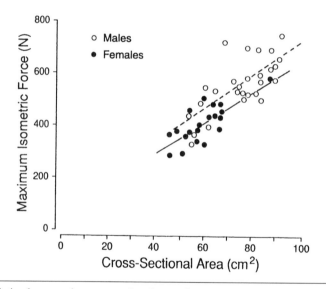

Figure 3.4   Relation between the cross-sectional area of quadriceps femoris and the maximum force it could exert during an isometric contraction.

Adapted from Jones, Rutherford, and Parker, 1989.

Despite this association, the cross-sectional area of muscle accounts for only about 50% of the variance in strength across individuals. Five factors that often contribute to this variation are (a) the use of a single measurement of cross-sectional area when, for most muscles, cross-sectional area varies along the length of the muscle (Kawakami, Abe, Kuno, & Fukunaga, 1995; Narici et al., 1988); (b) the need to identify all of the muscles that contribute to the force; (c) the difficulty associated with keeping the antagonist muscles silent during performance of a maximum contraction with the agonist muscles; (d) the assumption that the entire muscle mass can be activated (Kandarian & Williams, 1993; Kandarian & White, 1990); and (e) the variation in muscle architecture (the way muscle fibers are organized), which appears to modulate the estimated specific tension (Fukunaga, Roy, Shellock, Hodgson, & Edgerton, 1996). Because of these limitations, the measurement of muscle force relative to cross-sectional area at the whole-muscle level should be referred to as *normalized muscle force* rather than specific tension, which indicates the intrinsic force capacity of muscle. The term "specific tension" should be reserved for measurements made at the single-fiber level.

Given an accurate estimate of specific tension, the maximum force a muscle (F_m) can exert is estimated from

$$F_m = \text{specific tension} \times \text{cross-sectional area} \qquad (3.1)$$

If biceps brachii has a cross-sectional area of 5.8 cm² (table 3.1), then on the basis of a specific tension of 30 N/cm² we estimate that it can develop a maximum force of 174 N. Together, the maximum force that could be exerted for the elbow flexor muscles would be 657 N based on the cross-sectional data listed in table 3.1. However, Edgerton et al. (1990) report that the largest cadaver in their sample of four had a cross-sectional area of 34.7 cm² and therefore could have exerted a maximum force with the elbow flexor muscles of 1297 N. In addition to the data available on the muscles that cross the elbow joint (table 3.1), there are data for most other muscle systems, such as the hip, leg, and wrist (Brand, Pedersen, & Friederich, 1986; Clark & Haynor, 1987; Häkkinen & Keskinen, 1989; Leiber, Fazeli, & Botte, 1990; Murray, Buchanan, & Delp, 2000).

One issue of interest to muscle physiologists is whether specific tension can vary. Is it possible, for example, for the cross-sectional area of a muscle in two individuals to be the same but the maximum force to be different? Specific tension is a functional measure (the intrinsic force capacity) of the number of myofibrils per unit of cross-sectional area. Theoretically, therefore, specific tension would vary when the density of the myofibrils changes, as might occur when a muscle fiber swells or when the myofibrils are packed more closely together. There is some evidence, based on single-fiber measurements, that specific tension can vary with physical activity (Kawakami et al., 1995; Riley et al., 2000) and is different across fiber types. For example, Larsson, Li, Berg, and Frontera (1996) found that the specific tension of muscle fiber segments taken from the vastus lateralis muscle of volunteers decreased by 40% after six weeks of bed rest. Similarly, the specific tension of type II muscle fibers appears to decline with age (Larsson, Li, & Frontera, 1997). Furthermore, specific tension can vary across muscle fiber types and can be different for the same fiber type in different muscles. Harridge et al. (1996) found the specific tension of type IIa muscle fibers to be 22.3 N/cm² in soleus and

Table 3.1 Summary Data on Cross-Sectional Areas (CSA) and Moment Arms for the Elbow Flexor and Extensor Muscles

	CSA (cm²)	Predicted force (N)	Moment arm (cm)	Torque (N · m)	Torque (% maximum)
Biceps brachii	5.8	174	3.8	6.6	31
Brachialis	7.4	222	2.9	6.4	30
Brachioradialis	2.0	60	6.1	3.7	17
Pronator teres	3.6	108	1.6	1.7	8
Extensor carpi radialis longus	3.1	93	3.0	2.8	13
Triceps brachii	23.8	714	—	—	—

Note. Predicted force was estimated by multiplying the CSA values by a specific tension of 30 N/cm². Torque was determined as the product of predicted force and moment arm. The % maximum data indicate the contributions of the respective elbow flexor muscles to the total elbow flexor torque.

Data are from Edgerton et al., 1990.

vastus lateralis and 38.6 N/cm^2 in triceps brachii, while it was 22.6 N/cm^2 for type I fibers in triceps brachii. Similarly, at the whole-muscle level, the maximum force capacity normalized to cross-sectional area appears to differ among muscles. The ankle plantarflexor muscles, for example, exhibit a maximum normalized force that is twice as large as that of the dorsiflexor muscles (Fukunaga et al., 1996).

In contrast to estimating the maximum force capacity of muscle based on its cross-sectional area, we can use EMG to estimate muscle force during a contraction. Recall from chapter 1 that under isometric conditions, the magnitude of the EMG is highly correlated with muscle force (Bigland & Lippold, 1954; Lawrence & De Luca, 1983). Although this association is less direct for anisometric conditions (Calvert & Chapman, 1977; Milner-Brown & Stein, 1975), there are algorithms for estimating the magnitude of the muscle force from the EMG (Hof, Pronk, & van Best, 1987; Hof & van den Berg, 1977; Marras & Sommerich, 1991a, 1991b). The most typical strategy in using EMG to estimate muscle force is to measure the EMG signal during a maximum voluntary contraction and then to normalize subsequent EMG recordings to this maximum. With this approach we can describe the quantity of EMG during a particular movement as a percentage of the value recorded during a maximum voluntary contraction. Unfortunately, the most commonly used method of recording the EMG makes it an unreliable measurement for comparison across days or between subjects. Nonetheless, normalized EMG measurements often provide useful information about the magnitude of muscle activity.

Direction of Muscle Force

When a muscle force is included on a free body diagram, the force vector should be drawn so that it is directed back across the joint. We can think of the muscle as pulling on the body segment so that it rotates the segment about the joint. Most joint systems in the human body are designed as third-class levers in which the muscle force applied to the skeleton and the load experienced by the limb lie on the same side of the joint, with the point of application of the force being proximal to the load. This type of design maximizes the linear velocity of the endpoint of the lever ($v = r\omega$) but requires large muscle forces to control the motion of the lever about the fulcrum.

The angle between the muscle force vector and the skeleton is referred to as the **angle of pull.** Although the angle of pull of a muscle is generally shallow when a joint is in its anatomical resting position, the angle does change over the range of motion and can become substantial. When the elbow joint is at a right angle (1.57 rad), for example, the angles of pull of the muscles that cross the elbow joint are 1.4 rad for biceps brachii, 1.2 rad for brachialis, 0.4 rad for brachioradialis, 0.2 rad for pronator teres, and 0.05 rad for triceps brachii (An et al., 1984).

Example 3.2

Muscle and Load Torques During Knee Extension

Consider a person recovering from knee surgery who does seated knee extension exercises with a weighted boot. The exercise involves sitting at the end of an exercise bench and raising the lower leg (shank + foot) from a vertical (knee angle = 1.57 rad) to a horizontal position and then lowering the leg again. What torques about the knee joint (K) would be involved in this exercise? Figure 3.5 depicts the appropriate system, from the knee joint down to the toes, as well as the four forces—joint reaction force (F_j), resultant muscle force (F_m), limb weight (F_w), and boot weight (F_l)—that represent the interaction of this system with its surroundings. The first step in determining the torques is to draw the moment arms (a, b, c). This involves extending the line of action for each force and then drawing a perpendicular line from the line of action to the axis of rotation (figure 3.5b). Because the line of action for the joint reaction force passes through the axis of rotation, its moment arm, and therefore its torque about the knee joint, is equal to zero. Thus, for the system indicated in

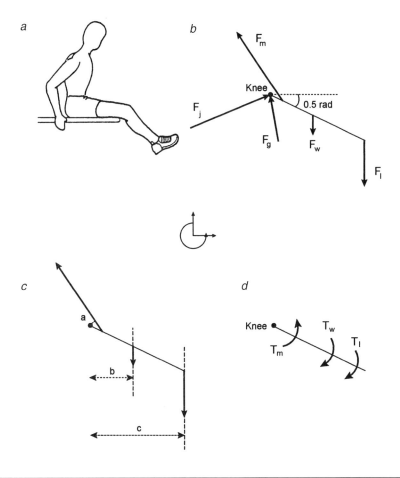

Figure 3.5   Free body diagram of the leg of a person performing leg extension exercises: *(a)* whole-body diagram; *(b)* free body diagram of the lower leg; *(c)* the forces that exert a torque about the knee joint; *(d)* the three torques produced by these forces.

figure 3.5, there are three forces that produce a torque about the knee joint. Figure 3.5*c* shows the resultant muscle torque (τ_m), the torque due to the weight of the boot (τ_l), and the torque due to the weight of the leg (τ_w). The torque due to the total load is determined as the sum of τ_l and τ_w. The direction of the curved torque arrow is the same as that of the rotation caused by the torque.

Now suppose that the person performing this exercise has an 80-N weight attached to the ankle, a body weight of 700 N, and a resultant muscle force with a magnitude of 1000 N and an angle of pull of 0.25 rad; calculate the three torques about the knee joint. We also know that the distance along the shank from the muscle force vector to the knee is 5 cm and that the length of the shank (knee to ankle) is 26 cm. The simplest approach for now is to calculate each of these torques separately. First, let us determine the torque produced by the resultant muscle force about the knee joint and draw a diagram that shows F_m and its moment arm *(a)*. As we discussed in chapter 2, torque is calculated as the product of a force and its moment arm, which is the shortest distance from the line of action of a force vector to the axis of rotation.

(continued)

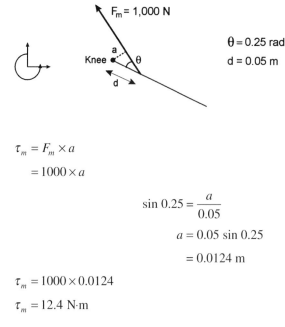

$$\tau_m = F_m \times a$$
$$= 1000 \times a$$

$$\sin 0.25 = \frac{a}{0.05}$$
$$a = 0.05 \sin 0.25$$
$$= 0.0124 \text{ m}$$

$$\tau_m = 1000 \times 0.0124$$
$$\tau_m = 12.4 \text{ N·m}$$

The torque due to the weight of the limb can be determined in a similar manner. We can also take the opportunity to review the methods we learned in chapter 2 to estimate the weight and center-of-mass location of body segments. The weight of the shank and foot can be estimated from the combined shank and foot regression equations in table 2.1. Similarly, from table 2.1 we can determine that the center-of-mass location (i.e., point of application for the weight vector) for the lower leg (shank + foot) is at a distance of 43.4% of shank length, as measured from the knee joint. We begin by drawing a diagram that shows F_w and its moment arm *(b)*. Once these two variables have been determined, we can calculate the torque due to the weight of the system (τ_w).

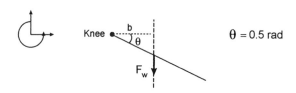

$$d = 0.36 \times 0.434$$
$$= 0.156 \text{ m}$$
$$F_w = (0.044 \times 700 - 1.75) + (0.009 \times 700 + 2.48)$$
$$= 37.8 \text{ N}$$

$$\tau_w = F_w \times b$$
$$= 37.8 \times b$$

$$\cos 0.5 = \frac{b}{d}$$
$$b = 0.156 \cos 0.5$$
$$b = 0.14 \text{ m}$$

$$\tau_w = 37.8 \times 0.14$$
$$\tau_w = 5.2 \text{ N·m}$$

The torque about the knee joint due to the ankle weight (τ_l) can be determined in a similar manner.

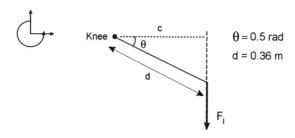

$$\tau_l = F_l \times c$$
$$= 80 \times c$$

$$\cos 0.5 = \frac{c}{0.36}$$
$$c = 0.36 \cos 0.5$$
$$c = 0.32 \text{ m}$$

$$\tau_l = 80 \times 0.32$$
$$\tau_l = 25.3 \text{ N·m}$$

We can determine the net torque about the knee joint in this example by summing the magnitudes and taking into account the direction of each torque (i.e., counterclockwise indicated as positive). As discussed previously, we can determine the direction of each torque vector with the right-hand-thumb rule. In the present example, the forces F_w and F_l produce clockwise rotation and thus are identified as negative torques.

To ascertain the net effect of these forces on the system, we sum (Σ) the moments of force (torques) about the knee joint (τ_K):

$$\Sigma \ \tau_K = \left(F_m \times a\right) - \left(F_w \times b\right) - \left(F_l \times c\right)$$
$$= 12.4 - 5.2 - 25.3$$
$$\Sigma \ \tau_K = -18.1 \cdot \text{m}$$

The net torque, therefore, has a magnitude of 18.1 N·m and acts in a clockwise direction. Does this mean that the leg is being lowered? No, the clockwise direction of the torque vector says nothing about the direction of the limb displacement. Recall from chapter 1 that a ball tossed into the air first goes up and then goes down while experiencing a downward acceleration throughout the entire trajectory. Similarly, a negative torque (acceleration) provides no information on the displacement about the knee joint. The leg could be going up or down while experiencing a net torque about the knee joint that acts in a clockwise direction. We need to have position, velocity, and acceleration (torque) information to get a complete description of the motion.

Moment Arm

Because torque is equal to the product of force and moment arm (figure 2.4), the rotary effect of a force can be altered by either factor. As we just discussed, muscles generally have a shallow angle of pull and are located close to the joint about which they exert a torque. Because the angle of pull is shallow, anatomical moment arms are typically short. But moment

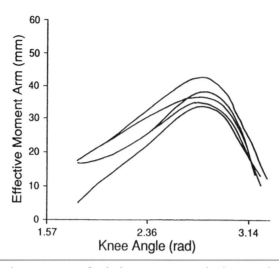

Figure 3.6 The effective moment arm for the knee extensor mechanism over the range of motion from a right angle to complete extension.

Adapted from Grood, Suntay, Noyes, and Butler, 1984.

arms change throughout the range of motion, as shown for the knee extensors in figure 3.6. Because strength is a measure of the capacity of muscle to exert torque, it is influenced not only by the size of the muscle (muscle force) but also by differences in the moment arm from the muscle force vector to the joint. Based on the moment arm values in figure 3.6, if the force exerted by the knee extensors is constant over the indicated range of motion, then strength will be maximum at a knee angle of about 2.8 rad when the moment arm is greatest.

Data from An, Hui, Morrey, Linscheid, and Chao (1981) indicate that the moment arms for the major elbow flexor muscles double as the elbow goes from a fully extended position to 1.75 rad (100°) of flexion. In contrast, the moment arm for triceps brachii (elbow extensor) decreases by about one-third over the same range of motion (table 3.2). Similar observations have been made for other arm muscles (Loren et al., 1996; Murray et al., 2000; Pigeon, Yahia, & Feldman, 1996), for muscles that cross the hip joint (Németh & Ohlsén, 1986), and the ankle and knee joints (Herzog & Read, 1993; Rugg, Gregor, Mandelbaum, & Chiu, 1990; Spoor, van Leeuwen, Meskers, Titulaer, & Huson, 1990).

Table 3.2 Moment Arms (cm) Associated With the Elbow Flexor and Extensor Muscles in Full Extension and in 1.75 rad of Flexion With the Hand in Two Positions (Neutral and Supinated)

	Elbow extended		Elbow flexed	
Muscle	Neutral	Supinated	Neutral	Supinated
Flexor				
Biceps brachii	1.47	1.96	3.43	3.20
Brachialis	0.59	0.87	2.05	1.98
Brachioradialis	2.47	2.57	4.16	5.19
Extensor				
Triceps brachii	2.81	2.56	2.04	1.87

Note. Data from An et al., 1981.

Example 3.3

Moment Arm Changes Influence the Point of Failure During Push-Ups

Let us examine the significance of the variation in a moment arm over a range of motion. Consider an individual who performs push-ups to exhaustion. The prime mover for push-ups is the elbow extensor muscle, triceps brachii. Suppose this muscle is maximally active as the individual approaches exhaustion and, on the basis of the cross-sectional data presented previously, is exerting a force of 714 N. According to the data in table 3.2, the moment arm for the triceps brachii is about 2.81 cm with elbow extended (figure 3.7a) and about 2.04 cm with elbow flexed to 1.75 rad (figure 3.7b). This variation in moment arm length is indicated as a change in the length of d in figure 3.7c. Because of this variation, the maximum torque would be approximately 14.1 N·m for the extended position and 10.2 N·m for the flexed position. That is, in the flexed position the torque due to the triceps brachii force, the prime mover for the exercise, is less than in the extended position.

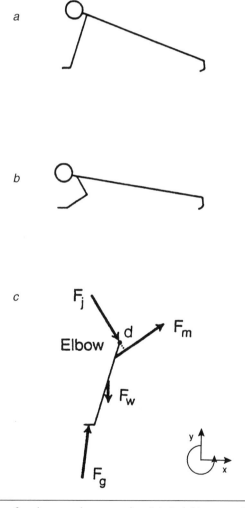

Figure 3.7 A person performing a push-up exercise: *(a)* straight-arm position; *(b)* bent-arm position; *(c)* free body diagram that isolates the resultant muscle force *(F_m)* about the elbow joint. The net torque *(τ_m)* about the elbow joint is equal to the product of F_m and the moment arm.

(continued)

Consequently, failure to perform any more push-ups is more likely to occur in the flexed position, where the maximum torque is least. In this case, failure occurs because of an inability to raise body weight, a constant load, up and down. A similar rationale applies to the point of failure during pull-ups to exhaustion. The moment arms for the elbow flexor muscles are minimal with complete elbow extension; and, if the muscle force is reasonably constant throughout the range of motion, that is the point at which failure occurs.

Tendon and Ligament Elasticity

The movements we perform are a consequence of the forces applied to the skeleton by our muscles. The work done by muscles, however, depends not only on the activity of the cross-bridges within the sarcomeres but also on the elasticity of the tendon. When a muscle is activated by the nervous system, the force it exerts is transmitted to the skeleton by the tendon and is modified by the material properties of the tendon (Fukunagaet al., 2001; Kubo, Kanehisa, Kawakami, & Fukunaga, 2000). Similarly, the forces experienced by articulating surfaces can be influenced by the material properties of the ligaments that encompass the joint.

Like all biological tissue, tendon and ligament can be stretched. When this occurs, the molecular composition and structure of the tissue resist the stretch and exert an elastic force on the skeleton. For tendon, the stretch can be caused either by a passive increase in the joint angle or by an active shortening of the muscle fibers. For ligament, the stretch occurs when some mechanical action causes a distraction of the articulating surfaces. When the magnitude of the stretch is relatively small (within the range of A to B in figure 3.8), the elastic force can be represented by the relation for an ideal spring (Hooke's law):

$$F_e = kx \tag{3.2}$$

where F_e = elastic force, k = spring stiffness, and x = amount of stretch. Equation 3.2 is an equation for a straight line, which has an intercept of zero and a slope of k. The slope corresponds to the stiffness of the tissue. According to Equation 3.2, the elastic force exerted by tendon or ligament is proportional to the amount of stretch. The proportionality constant (k) of a tissue depends on both the composition and the organization of its constituents.

When young adults exerted a near-maximum force with the triceps surae muscles, the stiffness of the Achilles tendon averaged 306 N·m/rad (Hof, 1998). Under these conditions, the muscle-tendon length shortened by about 28 mm (8% of tendon + aponeurosis length) during a maximum isometric contraction. For high-force eccentric contractions of the triceps surae

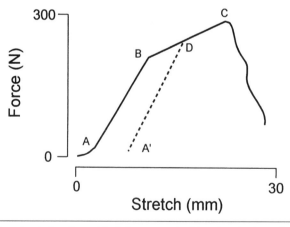

Figure 3.8　Force-length relation for an ideal tissue stretched into its plastic region.

muscles, the Achilles tendon might be stretched by as much as 10% of its resting length (Hof, 1998). Such findings underscore two features of muscle function. First, some of the work performed by the cross-bridges is used to stretch the tendon, which then functions as a more rigid connector between the muscle and the skeleton. For this reason, larger muscles have thicker (cross-sectional area) tendons (Loren & Lieber, 1995). Second, the elasticity of tendons enables them to store and release energy, which can significantly reduce the metabolic cost of performing some movements (Alexander, 1997; Biewener & Roberts, 2000; Fukunaga et al., 2001; Roberts, Marsh, Weyand, & Taylor, 1997).

There is a limit to how far tendon and ligament can be stretched without alteration of their properties. It is obviously possible to stretch a ligament far enough that it breaks (point C in figure 3.8). Based on in vitro measurements, rupture occurs in tendon (extensor digitorum longus) when it is stretched by about 15% of its initial length (Schechtman & Bader, 1997) and in ligament (medial collateral) after a stretch of about 20% (Liao & Belkoff, 1999). With less substantial stretches (between points B and C in figure 3.8), there are structural changes in the tissue, and the elastic force does not vary as described by Equation 3.2. To distinguish between small and large stretches, the force-length relations of tendon and ligament are usually divided into an elastic region and a plastic region. In the **elastic region** (between points A and B in figure 3.8), the tissue essentially behaves like an ideal spring, and the elastic force is described by Equation 3.2. When a stretch extends beyond the yield point (point B in figure 3.8) and into the **plastic region** (between points B and C in figure 3.8), the structure of the tissue is altered and the slope of the force-length relation changes. The imposed reorganization of the constituents in the tissue is described as a plastic change because it induces long-term changes in the structure of the tissue. For example, if the tissue is stretched to point D (figure 3.8) and then released, the tissue will assume a new resting length (point A') that is longer than the initial length (point A) because of plastic changes in its structure. The controlled lengthening of connective tissue into its plastic region will increase its resting length, which expands the range of motion about a joint.

The force-length relation of tendon and ligament varies, both between tissue types and among different structures of the same tissue type. Many of these differences are due to variation in cross-sectional area and length. For example, the stiffness of two ligaments with the same length varies according to the difference in cross-sectional area; a ligament with twice the cross-sectional area has twice the stiffness. Similarly, the stiffness of two ligaments with the same cross-sectional area varies on the basis of differences in length; a ligament that is twice as long as another has one-half the stiffness. For this reason, the comparison of tendon and ligament properties across conditions and subjects is based on normalized values, which are expressed as a stress-strain relation (figure 3.9). **Stress** (Pa) represents the force applied per unit area of the tissue, where area is measured in the plane that is perpendicular to the force vector (cross-sectional area). Strain (%) indicates the change in length of the tissue relative to its initial length. Stress and strain characterize the intrinsic force capacity and extensibility of tendon and ligament. The slope of the elastic region of a stress-strain relation is quantified as the **modulus of elasticity** (E), which is defined as the ratio of stress (σ) to strain (ε) and represents the normalized stiffness of the tissue.

$$E = \frac{\sigma}{\varepsilon} \qquad (3.3)$$

Normalization of the force-length relation as a stress-strain curve, however, does not account for all the differences between various structures. The elastic modulus for mammalian tendon, for example, varies from about 0.8 to 2 GPa, with an average value of 1.5 GPa (Bennett, Ker, Dimery, & Alexander, 1986). Some of this variability can probably be explained by the location on the stress-strain curve where the slope (modulus) is measured. For example, Loren and Lieber (1995) found no difference in the elastic modulus among the muscles that cross the wrist when the slope was measured at the maximum force the muscle could exert. These values

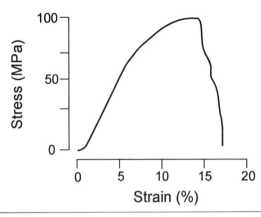

Figure 3.9 Stress-strain relation for an extensor digitorum longus tendon. Strain indicates the change in length of the tendon relative to its initial length [$(\Delta l/l) \times 100$], whereas stress represents the force per unit area (N/m^2 = Pa).

Data from Schechtman and Bader, 1997.

ranged from 0.438 GPa for extensor carpi radialis longus to 0.726 GPa for extensor carpi radialis brevis. However, when the modulus was measured at forces less than maximum, there were significant differences among tendons, which suggested differences in material properties between tendons at low forces.

Example 3.4
Tendon Properties

As indicated by the stress-strain normalization procedure, tendons vary in thickness (cross-sectional area) and length. The major determinant of these differences appears to be the magnitude of the physiological loads experienced by the tendon. This is evident, for example, if we compare the stress-strain relation of two tendons that differ in size.

	Extensor carpi radialis brevis tendon	Achilles tendon
Maximum muscle force (N)	58	5000
Tendon length (mm)	204	350
Tendon thickness (mm^2)	14.6	65
Elastic modulus (MPa)	726	1500
Stress (MPa)	4.06	76.9
Strain (%)	2.7	5
Stiffness (N/cm)	105	2875

These two tendons have similar values for strain and somewhat similar values for stress at the maximum muscle force, but the Achilles tendon is much stiffer than the tendon of the wrist extensor muscle.

Intra-Abdominal Pressure

The pressure inside the abdominal cavity varies in the course of our daily activities. It can range from low values that cause air to flow into the lungs to high values that make the trunk rigid. The magnitude of the intra-abdominal pressure and trunk rigidity are controlled by the activity of the trunk muscles. The principal muscles are those that surround the abdominal cavity, including the abdominal muscles anteriorly and laterally (rectus abdominis, external and internal obliques, and transversus abdominis), the diaphragm above, and the muscles of the pelvic floor below (Hodges & Gandevia, 2000).

Intra-abdominal pressure is increased by closing the epiglottis and activating these muscles; fluctuations in the intra-abdominal pressure tend to parallel most closely changes in the EMG activity of the transversus abdominis muscle (Cresswell, Grundström, & Thorstensson, 1992). Voluntarily pressurizing the abdominal cavity, which we do when lifting heavy loads or anticipating high-impact forces, is referred to as the **Valsalva maneuver.** In most activities we perform, however, the diaphragm and abdominal muscles are activated automatically and the **intra-abdominal pressure** is altered without a need for voluntary (conscious) intervention. When the trunk muscles are activated, both the **intra-thoracic** and the intra-abdominal pressures increase. The pressures in these two cavities tend to change in parallel during many activities, with the intra-abdominal pressure usually being greater (Harman, Frykman, Clagett, & Kraemer, 1988). The force generated by intra-abdominal pressure is determined as the product of the pressure and the cross-sectional area of the cavity (smallest transverse section), with the force acting at the center of pressure (Daggfeldt & Thorstensson, 1997).

Intra-abdominal pressure has been proposed as a mechanism to reduce the load on back muscles during lifting tasks (Cholewicki, Juluru, & McGill, 1999; Daggfeldt & Thorstensson, 1997; Morris, Lucas, & Bressler, 1961). Pressurization of the abdominal cavity provides a force that causes the trunk to be extended about the hip joint. This effect is indicated in figure 3.10. Imagine a three-segment system that comprises a base (pelvis), an upright (trunk) component, and an upper support (diaphragm). Between these elements is an inflated balloon (intra-abdominal cavity). When the system is pushed forward about the hip, the balloon is compressed and the pressure inside the balloon increases (figure 3.10b). When the system is released, the pressure inside the balloon pushes the system back to an upright position. Similarly, the intra-abdominal pressure provides a force (F_i) that acts through the diaphragm to oppose hip flexion loads (figure 3.10c). For example, if the person shown in figure 3.10c lifted a load of 91 kg $(F_{w,l})$ without increasing the intra-abdominal pressure, the back and hip muscles (F_m) would have to exert a force of 8223 N, and the joint reaction force (F_j) would be 9216 N just to support the load. However, if this lifter increased his intra-abdominal pressure to 19.7 kPa (force of 810 N), then F_m would be reduced to 6403 N, and F_j would decrease to 6599 N (Morris et al., 1961).

Intra-abdominal pressure can be measured with a pressure transducer that is attached to a catheter and inserted into the abdominal cavity through the nasal cavity. Figure 3.11 provides an example of such a recording during the squat lift, an event in the sport of power lifting (Harman et al., 1988). In this lift, the lifter began from an erect position and lowered the load until the thighs were parallel to the ground (the trunk, knee, and thigh angles reached minimum values); the lifter then returned to an erect posture. Because the load (weight of the lifter and the barbell) was 2200 N, the vertical component of the ground reaction force $(F_{g,y})$ fluctuates about this value. $F_{g,y}$ values less than 2200 N indicate that the system was accelerating downward; conversely, values greater than 2200 N depict an upward acceleration of the system. The increase in intra-abdominal pressure tends to coincide with values greater than 2200 N when the load (system acceleration) on the trunk muscles is greatest.

As a pressure in a confined volume, the intra-abdominal pressure exerts a force over the surface area of the abdominal cavity. The force that the intra-abdominal pressure exerts on the trunk is usually estimated as the product of intra-abdominal pressure and the surface area of the diaphragm, which Morris et al. (1961) estimated to be about 0.0465 m^2 for an adult. If this estimate is combined with the peak intra-abdominal pressure of 25 kPa shown in figure 3.11, then the force acting on the diaphragm due to the intra-abdominal pressure would have been approximately 1163 N during the squat lift. Clearly, this is a significant force in terms of human movement.

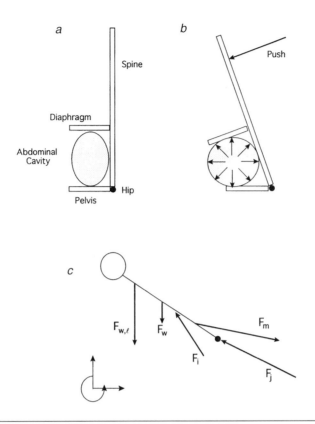

Figure 3.10   The effect of intra-abdominal pressure on the trunk: *(a)* a three-segment system with the intra-abdominal cavity represented as a balloon; *(b)* increase in pressure inside the balloon when the trunk is pushed forward; *(c)* a free body diagram that includes the force due to the intra-abdominal pressure.

Figure 3.11 indicates that the magnitude of the intra-abdominal pressure varies during a movement. One factor that appears to contribute to this variation is whether the load is being lifted or lowered. For example, when subjects pulled against an *isokinetic* dynamometer, the intra-abdominal pressure was greater during the concentric phase of the lift (hip extension) compared with the eccentric phase (hip flexion), even though the force exerted by the hands was greater during the eccentric phase (Cresswell et al., 1992). Furthermore, the magnitude of the intra-abdominal pressure can be supplemented by the use of a weightlifting belt, which can increase the intra-abdominal pressure during lifting activities (Harman, Rosenstein, Frykman, & Nigro, 1989; Lander, Hundley, & Simonton, 1992; McGill & Norman, 1993).

Despite the correlation between various movements and changes in intra-abdominal pressure, there is some controversy over the functional role of this mechanical effect (Marras & Mirka, 1992). It has been proposed, for example, that one effect of intra-abdominal pressure is to reduce the compressive forces that act on the intervertebral disks. However, Nachemson, Andersson, and Schultz (1986) have shown that although the Valsalva maneuver does increase the intra-abdominal pressure, it can also increase the pressure on the nucleus of the L3 disk for some moderate tasks. Nonetheless, for the most strenuous task, in which the subjects leaned forward 0.53 rad while holding an 8-kg load in outstretched arms, a Valsalva maneuver increased the intra-abdominal pressure from 4.35 kPa to 8.25 kPa and reduced the **intradiscal pressure** from 1625 kPa to 1488 kPa. Such a mechanism would reduce the pressure exerted on intervertebral disks during manual labor.

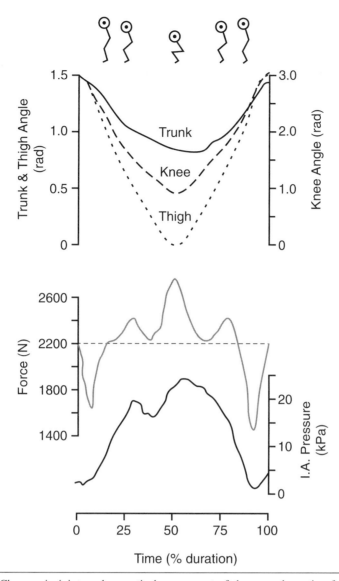

Figure 3.11 Changes in joint angles, vertical component of the ground reaction force, and intra-abdominal pressure during a squat lift by a weight lifter. Trunk and thigh angles are indicated as absolute angles relative to the horizontal such that when vertical, the angles are 1.57 rad. The knee angle is a relative angle between the thigh and shank.

Adapted from Lander, Bates, and DeVita, 1986.

Static Analysis

Now that we have discussed musculoskeletal forces, we have considered all the forces that we might need to include on a free body diagram. The three categories of forces are those due to body mass (gravity and inertial force), those due to the surroundings (ground reaction force and air resistance), and musculoskeletal forces (joint reaction force, muscle force, and the force due to intra-abdominal pressure). Our next task is to consider the formal procedures that we use to determine unknown forces after we have drawn a free body diagram.

When we apply Newton's law of acceleration ($\Sigma \mathbf{F} = m\mathbf{a}$) to study the motion of an object, we commonly distinguish among movements in which acceleration is zero and those in which it is not zero. When acceleration is zero, the right-hand side of the equation is zero, which means that the sum of the forces acting on the object is equal to zero. This condition is referred to as a **static** because acceleration is zero and all the forces are balanced. When this occurs, the object has zero acceleration, which means that it has a constant velocity; that is, it is either stationary or moving at a constant speed.

In a static analysis, the sum of the forces in any given direction is zero ($\Sigma \mathbf{F} = 0$), and the sum of the torques is also equal to zero ($\Sigma \tau_o = 0$). At most, there are three independent scalar equations available to solve statics problems in which the movement is confined to a single plane:

$$\Sigma\ F_x = 0 \tag{3.4}$$

$$\Sigma\ F_y = 0 \tag{3.5}$$

$$\Sigma\ \tau_o = 0 \tag{3.6}$$

Equations 3.4 and 3.5 refer to the sum (Σ) of the forces in two linear directions (x and y) that are perpendicular to one another. Equation 3.6 represents the sum of the torques about point o, which may or may not be the center of mass of the system.

When performing a static analysis, we need to follow a number of steps. These include drawing a free body diagram, writing the equation to be used, expanding the equation to include all the forces shown on the free body diagram, and then solving for the unknown term. The following examples demonstrate these procedures.

Example 3.5
Finding the Magnitude and Direction of an Unknown Force

Consider the rigid body in figure 3.12*a*, which is in equilibrium ($a = 0$) and upon which are acting three known forces and one unknown force. What is the magnitude of the unknown force? The first step is to draw a free body diagram. Although figure 3.12*a* indicates all the forces acting on the rigid body and does constitute a free body diagram, the most conve-

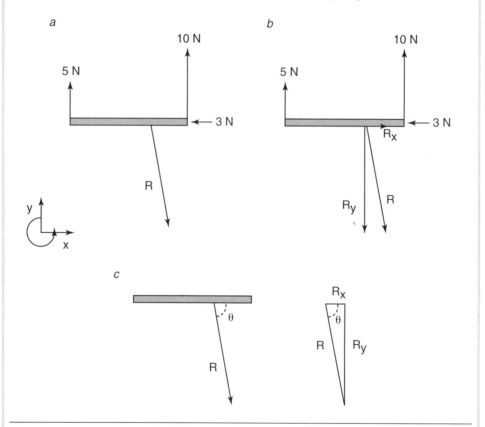

Figure 3.12   Distribution of forces acting on a rigid body: *(a)* free body diagram; *(b)* resolution of **R** into *x* and *y* components; *(c)* calculation of the direction and magnitude of **R.**

nient form is shown in figure 3.12*b*. A free body diagram must include a coordinate system, which indicates the positive linear and angular directions. For most of our problems this will include the *x-y* directions and a rotation. In figure 3.12*b*, the positive *x* direction is to the right, the positive *y* direction is up, and the positive rotation is counterclockwise. This is the most common convention. This means that any horizontal force directed to the right will be regarded as positive, and any to the left will be indicated as negative. The declaration of the horizontal-vertical directions is also an indication that only forces in these directions can be handled in the analysis and thus any force (e.g., **R**) not in either direction must be *resolved* into such directions (figure 3.12*b*).

The second step in the analysis is to write the equation of motion, which will be one of the versions of Newton's law of acceleration (Equations 3.4 to 3.6). The actual equation needed depends on the question. For example, if we want to determine the magnitude of a force in the *x* direction, then we should use Equation 3.4, which focuses on this direction. Once the equation has been written, the third step is to expand the equation based on the forces identified in the free body diagram. This step, which represents the second line of the solution, should identify the magnitude and direction of the forces acting in the chosen direction (*x, y,* or a rotation). So to determine the magnitude of R_x, we should proceed as follows:

$$\Sigma\ F_x = 0$$

$$R_x - 3 = 0$$

$$R_x = 3\ N$$

Note that in this example, the direction of the unknown force (R_x) is indicated as positive on the second line of the solution. This direction comes from the free body diagram (figure 3.12*b*). There are two forces acting on the rigid body in the *x* direction: one in the negative *x* direction with a magnitude of 3 N and the other in the positive *x* direction with an unknown magnitude. Because the system is in equilibrium, the calculation shows that the two forces are equal in magnitude but that the directions are opposite.

Now we do the same procedure in the *y* direction. Again, we begin by writing the necessary equation; then we expand the equation from the free body diagram, and finally we solve for the unknown variable.

$$\Sigma\ F_y = 0$$

$$5 + 10 - R_y = 0$$

$$R_y = 15\ N$$

According to figure 3.12*b*, there are three forces acting in the *y* direction. The direction of all three forces is known. Because the system is in equilibrium and the magnitude of two forces is known, we are able to determine the magnitude of the unknown force (R_y).

Once we have determined R_x and R_y, we can find the magnitude and direction of **R** (figure 3.12*c*). The magnitude of the resultant (R) can be determined by the Pythagorean relation:

$$R = \sqrt{R_x^2 + R_y^2}$$

$$= \sqrt{3^2 + 15^2}$$

$$R = 15.3\ N$$

This result, however, specifies only the magnitude of the resultant, not its direction. We can actually indicate the direction of **R** relative to several references; for example, we could determine the angle relative to a horizontal (R_x) or a vertical (R_y) reference. Let us calculate the direction of **R** relative to the system (figure 3.12*c*). By the parallelogram rule, *R* is the

(continued)

diagonal of the rectangle, which has R_x and R_y as its sides. Thus R_x, R_y, and R represent the sides of a triangle and we can determine θ as:

$$\cos\theta = \frac{R_x}{R} \qquad \sin\theta = \frac{R_y}{R} \qquad \tan\theta = \frac{R_y}{R_x}$$

Accordingly,

$$\cos\theta = \frac{R_x}{R}$$

$$\theta = \cos^{-1}\frac{R_x}{R}$$

$$\theta = \cos^{-1}\frac{3}{15.3}$$

$$\theta = \cos^{-1}0.1961$$

$$\theta = 1.37 \text{ rad}$$

The answer to the question is that **R** has a magnitude of 15.3 N and is directed to the right at an angle of 1.37 rad below the horizontal.

Example 3.6
Calculating a Net Muscle Torque

A person sitting on an exercise bench has a light load attached to his ankle while performing a knee extension exercise. Suppose we want to estimate the magnitude of the force exerted by his knee extensor muscles (quadriceps femoris) when he holds the load stationary in the middle of the range of motion. We can do this by performing a static analysis because the forces would have to be balanced to hold the load stationary.

For estimating the muscle force about the knee joint during the knee extension exercise, the free body diagram must include the knee joint at one end (figure 3.13). The most common way to draw the free body diagram for this analysis is to have the foot and shank

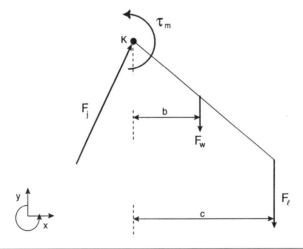

Figure 3.13   Free body diagram of the shank and foot of an individual performing a knee extension exercise.

compose the system and then to show how the surroundings interact with this system. In this type of analysis, the muscle force (F_m) and the joint reaction force (F_j) indicate separate effects of the surroundings (the rest of the body) on the system. The object of the static analysis is to determine the magnitude and direction of the resultant muscle torque about the knee joint (K), given a specific value for the resultant muscle force (F_m). Figure 3.13 shows two moment arms ($b = 0.11$ m and $c = 0.32$ m), the joint reaction force (F_j), the system (shank + foot) weight $(F_w = 41$ N), and the weight of the load $(F_l = 80$ N). Suppose the individual has to hold the limb at an angle of 0.5 rad below the horizontal: What resultant muscle torque (τ_m) must the person generate to accomplish this task?

The first step is to construct the free body diagram (figure 3.13). This involves defining the system, drawing the system as a simplified diagram such as a stick figure, and showing how the system interacts with its surroundings. These interactions can include forces due to body mass, forces due to the surroundings, and forces due to the musculoskeletal system. The second step is to select the appropriate equation (Equations 3.4 to 3.6). When we are asked to determine angular effects, as in this example, we should choose Equation 3.6 to sum the torque about the somersault axis through the knee joint.

$$\Sigma \, \tau_K = 0$$

The third step is to expand the equation, which is the second line of the solution. In this example, there are three forces $(F_w, F_l,$ and $F_j)$ and one torque (τ_m) acting on the system, as indicated by the vectors in figure 3.13. By choosing point K (the knee joint) as the point about which to sum the torques, we can ignore the joint reaction force because its line of action passes through this point, and its moment arm is therefore zero. Consequently,

$$\Sigma \, \tau_K = 0$$

$$\tau_m - \left(F_w \times b\right) - \left(F_l \times c\right) = 0$$

$$\tau_m = \left(F_w \times b\right) + \left(F_l \times c\right)$$

$$= \left(41 \times 0.11\right) + \left(80.0 \times 0.32\right)$$

$$= 4.51 + 25.276$$

$$\tau_m = 30.1 \text{ N·m}$$

This analysis indicates that when the shank-foot is held in the middle of the range of motion for the exercise, the weight of the system (F_w) and the load attached to the ankle (F_l) exert a torque of 30.1 N · m about the knee joint. To hold the shank-foot stationary, the net muscle torque must equal the magnitude of this load torque.

Example 3.7
Solving for Two Unknown Forces

A student sits at the end of an exercise bench and uses a rope-pulley apparatus to strengthen her quadriceps femoris muscle group with an isometric exercise. Let's determine the musculoskeletal forces at the knee joint. Again, the first step is to draw the free body diagram. To calculate the musculoskeletal forces at the knee joint, one end of the free body diagram must be the knee joint. The simplest system comprises the shank and the foot, from the knee (K) joint down to the toes (figure 3.14). The forces that must be included on the free body diagram are the weight of the system (F_w), the musculoskeletal forces $(F_m$ and $F_j)$, and the

(continued)

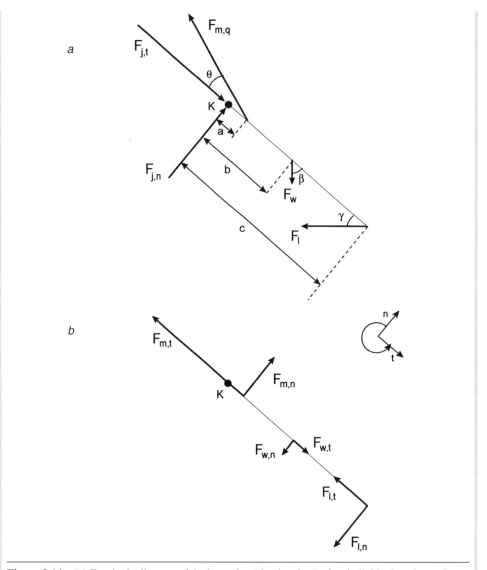

Figure 3.14 (*a*) Free body diagram of the lower leg (shank + foot) of an individual as she performs an isometric exercise to strengthen her quadriceps femoris muscle group. (*b*) The forces can also be resolved into normal (n) and tangential (t) components.

load due to the apparatus (F_l). Her leg weighs 30 N, and the center of mass of the system is 20 cm from the knee joint. She applies a force of 100 N to the rope-pulley apparatus, which is attached to an ankle cuff at a distance of 45 cm from her knee joint. The muscle force (quadriceps) vector acts back across the knee joint with an angle of pull (θ) of 0.25 rad and a point of application that is 7 cm from the knee joint. The joint reaction force (F_j) is shown as two components, one in the normal $(F_{j,n})$ direction and the other in the tangential $(F_{j,t})$ direction. The free body diagram shows the system at an angle of 0.7 rad below the horizontal, which means that the angle of F_w (β) is 0.85 rad and the angle of F_l (γ) is 0.7 rad.

The next step is to write an equation for the calculation. Because this problem has two unknowns $(F_m$ and $F_j)$, we must choose an equation that does not include both terms. Thus we will choose Equation 3.6. If we sum the torques about point *K*, we can momentarily ignore F_j because the moment arm from its line of action to *K* is zero. This involves summing the torques about point *K* due to the weight of the system (F_w) and the load exerted by the rope-pulley apparatus (F_l) and setting these equal to the torque associated with the quadriceps femoris muscle activity $(F_{m,q})$. This equality exists because the person is performing an isometric contraction, which means that the forces are balanced and the system is in equilibrium. So we perform the calculation by writing the equation (1st line) and then expanding the equation to include all the torques acting on the system about point K (2nd line). Recall that a force will exert a torque about a point if its line of action does not pass through the point. The magnitude of each torque is calculated as the product of the force and its moment arm. The moment arms for $F_{m,q}$, F_w, and F_l are:

$$F_{m,q} \qquad a \sin \theta = 7 \sin 0.25$$
$$= 1.7 \text{ cm}$$

$$F_w \qquad b \sin \beta = 20 \sin 0.87$$
$$= 15.3 \text{ cm}$$

$$F_l \qquad c \sin \gamma = 45 \sin 0.70$$
$$= 29.0 \text{ cm}$$

The calculation proceeds as follows:

$$\sum \tau_K = 0$$
$$\left(F_{m,q} \times a \sin \theta \right) - \left(F_w \times b \sin \beta \right) - \left(F_l \times c \sin \gamma \right) = 0$$
$$\left(F_{m,q} \times 1.7 \right) - \left(30 \times 15.3 \right) - \left(100 \times 29.0 \right) = 0$$
$$\left(F_{m,q} \times 1.7 \right) = \left(30 \times 15.3 \right) + \left(100 \times 29.0 \right)$$
$$\left(F_{m,q} \times 1.7 \right) = 459 + 2889$$
$$F_{m,q} = \frac{3358}{1.7}$$
$$F_{m,q} = 1975 \text{ N}$$

To determine the magnitude of $F_{j,n}$ and $F_{j,t}$, we need to resolve each force into its normal and tangential components (figure 3.14b) and then sum the forces in each direction. The components are:

$$F_{m,n} = F_{m,q} \sin 0.25$$
$$= 1975 \sin 0.25$$
$$= 489 \text{ N}$$
$$F_{w,n} = F_w \sin 0.87$$
$$= 30 \sin 0.87$$
$$= 23 \text{ N}$$
$$F_{l,n} = F_l \sin 0.70$$
$$= 100 \sin 0.70$$
$$= 64 \text{ N}$$
$$F_{m,t} = F_{m,q} \cos 0.25$$
$$= 1975 \cos 0.25$$
$$= 1914 \text{ N}$$
$$F_{w,t} = F_w \cos 0.87$$
$$= 30 \cos 0.87$$
$$= 19 \text{ N}$$
$$F_{l,t} = F_l \cos 0.70$$
$$= 100 \cos 0.70$$
$$= 77 \text{ N}$$

(continued)

These values represent the magnitudes of the normal and tangential components as they are shown in figure 3.14*b*. The magnitude of the *tangential* component of the joint reaction force is determined as:

$$\Sigma F_t = 0$$

$$F_{j,t} - F_{m,t} + F_{w,t} - F_{l,t} = 0$$

$$F_{j,t} = F_{m,t} - F_{w,t} + F_{l,t}$$

$$= 1914 - 19 + 77$$

$$F_{j,t} = 1972 \text{ N}$$

The magnitude of the *normal* component can be found in a similar manner:

$$\Sigma F_n = 0$$

$$F_{j,n} + F_{m,n} - F_{w,n} - F_{l,n} = 0$$

$$F_{j,n} = -F_{m,n} + F_{w,n} + F_{l,n}$$

$$= -489 + 23 + 64$$

$$F_{j,n} = -402 \text{ N}$$

The magnitude of $F_{j,n}$ is determined as negative 402 N. This does not mean that it is a negative force but rather that its direction is incorrect on the free body diagram. If the force is calculated as negative, this means that the direction of force is actually opposite to that indicated on the free body diagram. When the free body diagram was drawn, we were told that the system was in equilibrium. This means that the forces in each direction must add to zero. For the tangential direction, we assumed that $F_{j,t}$ was acting in the positive direction; this turned out to be correct. Also, we assumed that $F_{j,n}$ would have to act in the positive direction in order for the system to be in equilibrium. But this was incorrect, as indicated by the negative value that we calculated for $F_{j,n}$. The calculation indicates that $F_{j,n}$ acts in the negative direction in order for the system to be in equilibrium. Now that we know the magnitude of $F_{j,n}$ and $F_{j,t}$, we can determine the magnitude of the resultant joint reaction force (F_j) with the Pythagorean relation:

$$F_j = \sqrt{F_{j,n}^2 + F_{j,t}^2}$$

$$= \sqrt{402^2 + 1972^2}$$

$$F_j = 2013 \text{ N}$$

Thus, when a 100-N load is applied at the ankle, the knee joint experiences a joint reaction force that is 20 times larger than the load.

Finally, we can calculate the direction of the resultant joint reaction force with respect to the axis of the shank as

$$\tan \theta = \frac{F_{j,n}}{F_{j,t}}$$

$$\theta = \tan^{-1} \frac{F_{j,n}}{F_{j,t}}$$

$$\theta = \tan^{-1} \frac{402}{1972}$$

$$\theta = 0.2 \text{ rad}$$

The resultant joint reaction force, therefore, has a magnitude of 2013 N and is directed 0.2 rad below the longitudinal axis of the shank.

Example 3.8
Locating the Balance Point

A rigid body of uniform density, which weighs 20 N and has a length of 22 cm, has a load suspended from each end (figure 3.15a). At one end the load is 30 N, and at the other end the load is 60 N. To balance the rigid body on an extended finger, what is the magnitude of the force that we must exert with the finger, and where should the finger be placed? To answer this question, the first step is to draw a free body diagram. The rigid body has a uniform density, which means that the center of mass is located in the middle of the object. So we know the magnitude and direction of three forces acting on the rigid body. For the rigid body to balance on a finger, the finger must exert a force equal in magnitude but opposite in direction so that the forces are all balanced. With this information, we can draw the free body diagram (figure 3.15b). Once we have the free body diagram, we can choose an equation, expand it, and solve for the finger force:

$$\Sigma F_y = 0$$
$$-30 - 20 - 60 + \text{finger force} = 0$$
$$\text{finger force} = 110 \text{ N}$$

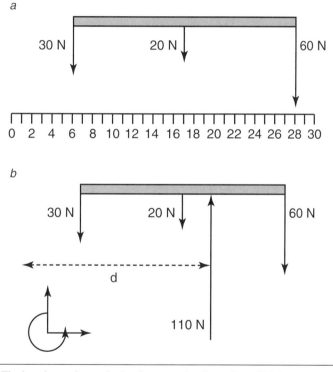

Figure 3.15 The location and magnitude of an opposing force that will balance a loaded rigid body: *(a)* the system; *(b)* the free body diagram.

Because the loads at each end of the system are not equal, the balance point (finger location) will not be in the middle of the rigid body. The balance point is essentially a fulcrum, in which the loads on one side pull the rigid body in one direction while those on the other side pull it in the other direction. The balance point, therefore, is the location about which the torques in each direction are equal so that the rigid body does not rotate. This is the definition of the center of mass (CM); it is the point (a location) about which the mass of

(continued)

the system is evenly distributed. Because the balance point (center of mass) represents the location about which the system is in equilibrium, it can be found through use of a static analysis. To find the balance point, we can sum the torques about the origin of the scale in figure 3.15 and find where the 110-N force must be located for the rigid body to be balanced.

$$\Sigma \ \tau_o = 0$$

$$-(30 \times 6) - (20 \times 17) + (110 \times d) - (60 \times 28) = 0$$

$$d = \frac{(30 \times 6) + (20 \times 17) + (60 \times 28)}{110}$$

$$d = 20 \ cm$$

So, to balance the rigid body shown in figure 3.15a, it is necessary to exert an upward force of 110 N that is applied at 20 cm along the scale.

Example 3.9
Center of Mass for the Human Body

The same approach as described in Example 3.8 can be used to find the location of the CM of a system that comprises several different parts, such as the human body. The approach involves using Equation 3.6 to find the point about which the mass of the system is evenly distributed—that is, the balance point. The location of the balance point depends on the relative positions of the different parts in the system. For the human body, this means the locations of the individual body segments.

To demonstrate this technique, let us determine the location of the total-body CM of a gymnast about to perform a backward handspring (figure 3.16). The necessary steps include the following:

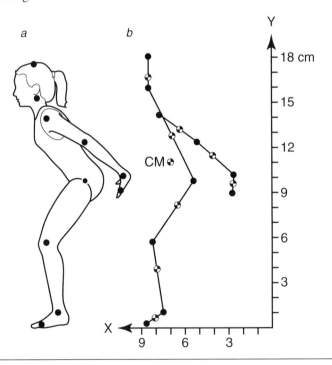

Figure 3.16   Location of whole-body center of mass (CM) as a function of the positions of the body segments: *(a)* limits of the respective body segments; *(b)* location of the segmental CMs as a percentage of segment length.

1. *Identify the appropriate body segments.* The human body can be divided into 14 to 17 parts for a segmental analysis (figures 2.6 and 2.7). The number of segments to be used in an analysis is determined by the number of joints that experience an angular displacement during the movement. If there is no rotation about the elbow joint, for example, then the arm (upper arm + forearm) can be represented as a single segment. For this example, we will use 14 segments: head, trunk, upper arms, forearms, hands, thighs, shanks, and feet. These segments are indicated in figure 3.16*a* by the marks over the joint centers that represent the proximal and distal anatomical landmarks for each segment.

2. *Connect the joint-center markers to construct a stick figure* (figure 3.16*b*).

3. From table 2.1, *determine the location of the CM for each segment as a percentage of segment length.* These lengths are measured from the proximal end of each segment (figure 3.16*b*).

Segment	CM location (%)	Proximal end
Head	66.3	Top of the head
Trunk	52.2	Top of the neck
Upper arm	50.7	Shoulder
Forearm	41.7	Elbow
Hand	51.5	Wrist
Thigh	39.8	Hip
Shank	41.3	Knee
Foot	40.0	Ankle

4. *Estimate segmental weights as a function of body weight (F_w)* (table 2.1). The gymnast weighs 450 N.

Segment	Equation		Weight (N)
Head	$0.032 \times F_w + 18.70$	=	33.10
Trunk	$0.532 \times F_w - 6.93$	=	232.47
Upper arm	$0.022 \times F_w + 4.76$	=	14.66
Forearm	$0.013 \times F_w + 2.41$	=	8.26
Hand	$0.005 \times F_w + 0.75$	=	3.00
Thigh	$0.127 \times F_w - 14.82$	=	42.33
Shank	$0.044 \times F_w - 1.75$	=	18.05
Foot	$0.009 \times F_w + 2.48$	=	6.53

5. *Measure the location of segmental CMs relative to an x-y axis* (figure 3.16*b*). The location of this axis is arbitrary and does not influence the location (with respect to the body) of the total-body CM; you can convince yourself of this by doing the calculation twice with the *x-y* axis in a different location each time.

(continued)

Segment	x-coordinate (cm)	y-coordinate (cm)
Head	8.6	16.8
Trunk	6.9	12.8
Upper arm	6.5	13.3
Forearm	4.2	11.5
Hand	2.8	9.6
Thigh	6.6	8.2
Shank	8.0	3.9
Foot	8.0	0.8

6. With the segmental weight *(F$_{w,s}$)* and location *(x, y)* data, *sum the segmental torques about the y-axis ($\Sigma\tau_y = F_{w,s} \times x$) and the x-axis ($\Sigma\tau_x = F_{w,s} \times y$)*. Double the limb segmental weights to account for both limbs.

Segment	x (cm)	y (cm)	F$_{w,s}$ (N)	$\Sigma\tau_y$ (N·m)	$\Sigma\tau_x$ (N·m)
Head	8.6	16.8	33.10	284.7	556.1
Trunk	6.9	12.8	232.47	1604.4	2975.6
Upper arm	6.5	13.3	29.32	190.6	390.0
Forearm	4.2	11.5	16.52	69.4	190.0
Hand	2.8	9.6	6.00	16.8	57.6
Thigh	6.6	8.2	84.66	558.8	694.2
Shank	8.0	3.9	36.10	288.8	140.8
Foot	8.0	0.8	13.06	104.5	10.5
				3018.0	5014.7

7. *Find the location of the balance point.* This is the point that produces the same torque for total-body weight about the *x*- and *y*-axes as that due to the sum of the segmental effects. This procedure is the same as that used in Example 3.8. This similarity is shown in figure 3.17, which illustrates an end-on view of the gymnast, who is represented as a rectangular object. The arrows indicate the magnitudes of the segmental weight vectors (1 = head, 2 = trunk, 3 = upper arm, 4 = forearm, 5 = hand, 6 = thigh, 7 = shank, 8 = foot) and the total body weight vector *(F$_w$)* with the locations representing the *x*-coordinate for the CMs.

This final calculation uses Equation 3.6 to determine the *x*- and *y*-coordinates for F_w. The net torque due to segmental weights about the *x*- and *y*-axes (3018.0 N·cm and 5014.7 N·cm, respectively) is the same as the net torque due to total-body weight. Thus

$$F_w \times \text{moment arm} = \sum_{i=1}^{8} \left(F_{w,s} \times \text{moment arm}\right)_i$$

$$\text{moment arm} = \frac{\Sigma\left(F_{w,s} \times \text{moment arm}\right)}{F_w}$$

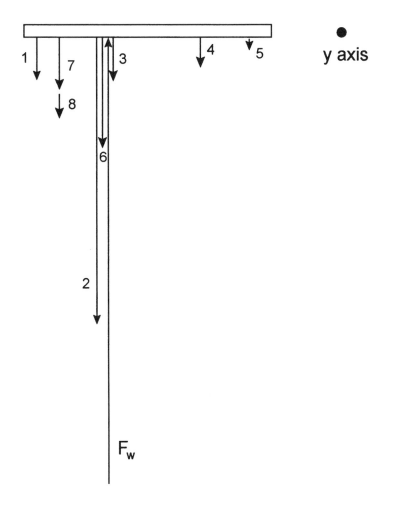

Figure 3.17 Location of segmental and total body weight vectors relative to the *y*-axis for the gymnast in figure 3.16.

To find the *x*- and *y*-coordinates for the total-body CM,

$$x = \frac{3018 \text{ N} \cdot \text{cm}}{450 \text{ N}}$$

$$= 6.71 \text{ cm}$$

$$y = \frac{5014.7 \text{ N} \cdot \text{cm}}{450 \text{ N}}$$

$$= 11.1 \text{ cm}$$

With these coordinates, the location of the total-body CM is indicated in figure 3.16*b* relative to the *x*- and *y*-axes established at the beginning of the example. These coordinates (6.71, 11.1) represent the point about which the mass of the system is evenly distributed (balanced).

Dynamic Analysis

A static analysis is the most elementary approach to the kinetic analysis of human movement. In contrast, when the system is subjected to unbalanced forces it will be accelerated, and this requires a more complicated type of analysis, known as a **dynamic analysis.** The general form of the three independent planar equations (Equations 3.4 to 3.6) used in the static approach also applies to the dynamic condition, with the exception that the right-hand side of the equations is now equal to the nonzero product of mass and acceleration. Hence, the scalar components and the angular term may be written as

$$\Sigma \ F_x = ma_x \qquad\qquad (3.7)$$

$$\Sigma \ F_y = ma_y \qquad\qquad (3.8)$$

$$\Sigma \ \tau_o = I_o \alpha + mad \qquad\qquad (3.9)$$

where $a = \sqrt{a_x^2 + a_y^2}$ and $\Sigma \ F = \sqrt{\left(\Sigma F_x\right)^2 + \left(\Sigma F_y\right)^2}$ in the x-y plane. As in the static case, these equations are independent and represent two linear directions (x and y) and one angular direction. In expanded form, Equation 3.7 states that the sum (Σ) of the forces (F) in the x direction is equal to the product of the mass (m) of the system and the acceleration of the system's CM in the x direction (a_x). Equation 3.8 similarly addresses forces and accelerations in the y direction. Equation 3.9 states that the sum of the torques *about point o* is equal to two effects, one related to the angular kinematics of the system and the other related to the linear kinematics of the system. The term for angular kinematics includes the product of the relevant moment of inertia (I_o) and the angular acceleration (α) of the system about the axis of rotation (o). The linear kinematics term includes the product of the mass of the system, the linear acceleration of the system CM (a), and the distance (d) between point o and the system CM.

The point o can be any point about which the moments are summed. Equations 3.7 to 3.9 are modified if point o is the CM or is a fixed point. If point o is the CM, then $d = 0$ and Equation 3.9 is reduced to $\Sigma \tau_g = I_g \alpha$. If point o is a fixed point, then $a = 0$ and the resultant of the applied forces is equal to $I_o \alpha$. If the system comprises a single rigid body, such as one body segment, and the moments are summed about the CM, then the resultant effect of the forces acting on the system with regard to a normal-tangential reference frame can be calculated as (Meriam & Kraige, 1987):

$$\Sigma \ F_n = mr\omega^2 \qquad\qquad (3.10)$$

$$\Sigma \ F_t = mr\alpha \qquad\qquad (3.11)$$

$$\Sigma \ \tau_g = I_g \alpha \qquad\qquad (3.12)$$

Because the right-hand side of Equations 3.7 to 3.9 is nonzero, the free body diagram of the system can be equated to a **kinetic diagram.** That is, by Newton's law of acceleration (**F** = m**a**), force (free body diagram) equals mass times acceleration (kinetic diagram). In this context, the free body diagram represents the left-hand side of the equation and the kinetic diagram the right-hand side. In this sense, the free body diagram defines the system and how it interacts (forces shown with arrows) with its surroundings. The kinetic diagram shows the effects of these interactions on the system—that is, how the interactions alter the motion of the system.

Example 3.10
Finding the Resultant Muscle Force

A volleyball player serves the ball using the overhand technique. This involves tossing the ball up in the air above the head and then striking the ball with a hand so that it travels over the net and into the opponents' court. Suppose we want to calculate the resultant muscle force about the center of mass at one point in time during the serve when the ball is in contact with the hand. As with a static analysis, the first step is to draw an appropriate diagram. For a dynamic analysis, this means both a free body diagram and a kinetic diagram. For this analysis we can define the system as the forearm and hand of the volleyball player so that the muscles crossing her elbow joint (F_m) appear as an external force (figure 3.18b). The forces that must be included on the free body diagram include the weight of the system (F_w), the contact force between the ball and the hand (F_b), and the musculoskeletal forces (muscle force $[F_m]$ and joint reaction force $[F_j]$). The kinetic diagram shows the effects of these forces on the system; this includes vectors for the three terms in Equations 3.7 to 3.9 (ma_x, ma_y, and $I_o\alpha$).

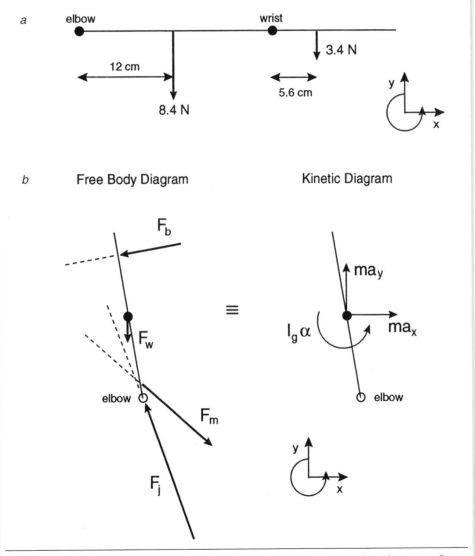

Figure 3.18   A dynamic analysis to determine the resultant muscle torque about the center of mass during a volleyball serve: *(a)* the weight and center-of-mass location of the forearm and hand segments; *(b)* the free body and kinetic diagrams for the forearm plus hand.

(continued)

The next step in the procedure is to identify the equation we will use. Because we are attempting to determine the resultant muscle torque about the center of mass, we should choose Equation 3.9 so that we can calculate angular effects. Before we can use this equation, however, we need to know more details about both the geometry of the system and the movement. This includes the location of the system CM and the moment of inertia about the system CM. Because we know that the volleyball player weighs 608 N, we can estimate the weight of her forearm as 8.4 N and the weight of her hand as 3.4 N from the anthropometric data in table 2.5. Also, because we know the length of her forearm (26 cm) and the length of her hand (7.5 cm), we can use table 2.5 to estimate that the forearm CM is located 12 cm from the elbow joint and that the hand CM is 5.6 cm from the wrist (figure 3.18*a*). To calculate the location of the system (forearm + hand) CM, we sum the torques about the elbow joint and perform a static analysis, as we did in figure 3.15. The system weight is 11.8 N, and the distance to the system CM from the elbow joint (*d*) can be determined as:

$$\Sigma \ \tau_{elbow} = 0$$

$$-(8.4 \times 12) + (11.8 \times d) - \left[3.4 \times (26 + 5.6)\right] = 0$$

$$d = \frac{(8.4 \times 12) + (3.4 \times 31.6)}{11.8}$$

$$d = 17.6 \ \text{cm}$$

Next, we need to determine the moment of inertia of the system about a somersault axis through its CM. From table 2.6, we can estimate the moment of inertia about the somersault axis for the forearm as 0.0039 kg·m² and for the hand as 0.0004 kg·m². To determine the moment of inertia for the system, we use the parallel axis theorem (Equation 2.8) to transfer the known value for each segment (forearm and hand) to the system CM. Because the system CM is located at 17.6 cm from the elbow, the transfer distance from the forearm CM to the system CM is 5.6 cm (17.6 – 12), and the transfer distance for the hand is 14 cm (31.6 – 17.6). Given that we estimated the mass of the forearm as 0.86 kg (8.4/9.81) and the mass of the hand as 0.35 kg (3.4/9.81), the moment of inertia of the system about a somersault axis passing through its CM (I_g) can be calculated as

$$I_g = \left[0.0039 + \left(0.86 \times 0.056^2\right)\right] + \left[0.0004 + \left(0.35 \times 0.14^2\right)\right]$$

$$= (0.0039 + 0.0027) + (0.35 \times 0.0196)$$

$$= 0.0066 + 0.0069$$

$$I_g = 0.0135 \ \text{kg·m}^2$$

We also need to know some kinematic details of the performance, which can be obtained with a motion analysis system. Suppose the video record indicated that the system (forearm + hand) was rotated 0.26 rad to the left of vertical, and a numerical analysis of the position-time data (e.g., table 1.2) yielded an angular acceleration for the system (α) of 489 rad/s². From the video record we can also determine that the moment arm for F_m (*a*) to the axis of rotation (*g*) was 8.2 cm, for F_b (*b*) it was 14.0 cm, and for F_j (*c*) it was 3.5 cm. Finally, other measurements indicated that, at the moment of interest, the contact force between the ball and the hand (F_b) was 290 N and that the joint reaction force (F_j) was 1821 N.

Given all this information, we can use figure 3.18*b* to write the equation of motion for a dynamic analysis (Equation 3.9), expand the equation (2nd line), and solve for F_m:

$$\sum \tau_g = I_g \alpha$$

$$\left(F_m \times a\right) + \left(F_b \times b\right) - \left(F_j \times c\right) = I_g \alpha$$

$$\left(F_m \times a\right) = I_g \alpha - \left(F_b \times b\right) + \left(F_j \times c\right)$$

$$F_m = \frac{I_g \alpha - \left(F_b \times b\right) + \left(F_j \times c\right)}{a}$$

$$F_m = \frac{\left(0.0135 \times 489\right) - \left(290 \times 0.14\right) + \left(1821 \times 0.035\right)}{0.082}$$

$$F_m = \frac{6.6 - 40.6 + 63.7}{0.082}$$

$$F_m = 363 \text{ N}$$

Although this example may seem relatively simple, it is usually difficult to determine the magnitude of the resultant muscle force using this method because it requires that we know the direction of the resultant muscle force and the magnitude and direction of the resultant joint force. The more common approach is to sum the torques about the joint, as described in the next example.

Example 3.11
Finding the Resultant Muscle Torque

In this example a weight lifter raises a barbell to his chest. Suppose that we are interested in determining the torque developed by the back and the hip extensor muscles when the barbell is about knee height. The first step is to draw the free body and kinetic diagrams. Because we want to determine a musculoskeletal force at the lumbosacral joint, one end of the system must include this joint. An appropriate system, as identified previously, would include the upper body from the lumbosacral *(LS)* joint to the head (figure 3.19). We can

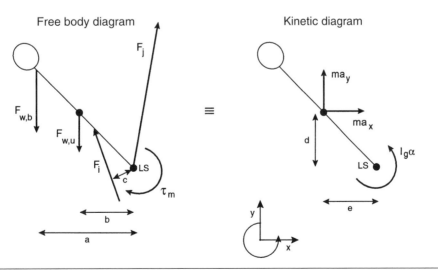

Figure 3.19 A dynamic analysis (free body diagram = kinetic diagram) of a weight lifter performing the clean lift.

(continued)

identify five forces that act on this system and that we should include on the free body diagram: the resultant muscle torque (τ_m) about the lumbosacral joint, the joint reaction force (F_j), the weight of the barbell $(F_{w,b})$, the weight of the system $(F_{w,u})$, and a force due to the intra-abdominal pressure (F_i). The kinetic diagram should include the three terms on the right-hand side of Equations 3.7 to 3.9. The typical approach is to draw these in the positive direction on the kinetic diagram and derive the equation based on these directions.

The next steps are to write the equation of motion, expand it, and solve for τ_m. As in the previous example, however, we need information about the performance before we can complete the calculation, specifically the following:

1. Estimates of the magnitudes of the three forces that produce moments about *LS*. The magnitude of $F_{w,b}$, which can be determined with a weight scale, is measured as 1003 N. The magnitude of $F_{w,u}$, which can be estimated from anthropometric tables (e.g., tables 2.1 and 2.5), is set at 525 N. The magnitude of F_i, which can be estimated from values published in the literature or can be measured with an intra-abdominal catheter and an estimate of diaphragm area, is assigned a value of 1250 N.

2. The mass of the system and its distribution. The mass of the system (upper body of the lifter) is estimated as 54 kg. The location of the system CM can be determined by the procedures outlined in Example 3.9 and is found to be 47 cm from *LS*. The moment of inertia of the system about its CM (I_g), which can be determined from known segmental values (e.g., table 2.6) and the parallel axis theorem, is estimated as 7.43 kg·m^2.

3. Kinematics of the movement (figure 1.17), as recorded from a video analysis. These measurements include the moment arms for the forces and the accelerations of the system. The moment arms are as follows: $F_{w,b}$ $(a = 38$ cm), $F_{w,u}$ $(b = 24$ cm), F_i $(c = 9$ cm), ma_x $(d = 40$ cm), and ma_y $(e = 24$ cm). The angular acceleration (α) of the system is 8.7 rad/s^2; the horizontal acceleration (a_x) of the system CM is 0.2 m/s^2; and the vertical acceleration (a_y) is -0.1 m/s^2.

With this information, we can calculate the magnitude of the resultant muscle torque (τ_m) about the lumbosacral *(LS)* joint by using Equation 3.9.

$$\Sigma \, \tau_{LS} = I_g\alpha + mad$$

$$\left(F_{w,b} \times a\right) + \left(F_{w,u} \times b\right) - \left(F_i \times c\right) - \tau_m = I_g\alpha - ma_xd - ma_ye$$

$$\tau_m = \left(F_{w,b} \times a\right) + \left(F_{w,u} \times b\right) - \left(F_i \times c\right)$$

$$-I_g\alpha + ma_xd + ma_ye$$

$$\tau_m = (1003 \times 0.38) + (525 \times 0.24)$$

$$-(1250 \times 0.09) - (7.43 \times 8.7)$$

$$+(54 \times 0.2 \times 0.40)$$

$$+(54 \times [-0.1] \times 0.24)$$

$$\tau_m = 381 + 126 - 113 - 65 + 4 - 1$$

$$\tau_m = 332 \text{ N·m}$$

The weightlifting event discussed in this example takes an experienced athlete about 0.4 s to complete. If we record the event at 100 frames per second, we will have 40 frames of video that contain relevant information on the event. To completely describe the time course of τ_m, it is necessary to perform the calculation just shown for each frame of data. The result is a set of instantaneous torques that can be plotted as a torque-time curve for the movement. An example for the knee joint is shown in figure 3.20; the data represent the mean torque about the knee joint for a group of 15 experienced weight lifters as they lifted a barbell (1141 N, which was 1.5 times body weight) to chest height. The graph indicates that the resultant muscle torque about the knee joint reached maximal values of about 100 and 50 N·m in the extensor and flexor directions, respectively, and that the direction fluctuated between extensor and flexor during the movement. This torque-time graph corresponds to the angle-angle diagram shown in figure 1.17.

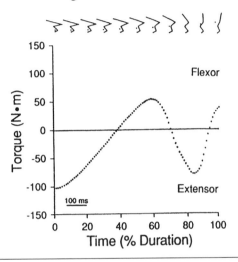

Figure 3.20   Resultant muscle torque about the knee joint during the clean lift in weightlifting. Reprinted from Enoka, 1983.

Example 3.12
When Is a Movement Fast?

An issue that often arises in the study of human movement is whether a dynamic analysis is necessary or whether the movement is slow enough that it can be assumed to be **quasistatic**— that is, whether we can analyze it using static techniques. Rogers and Pai (1990) examined this issue in a simple movement that involved a human subject moving from double- to single-leg support, as occurs when an individual is about to start walking. In the initiation of a step, body weight is shifted from two-legged support to single-leg support while the other leg flexes at the knee. This is accomplished by an increase in the activity of the lateral hip muscles of the flexing leg, an increase in the vertical component of the ground reaction force under the flexing leg, and a shift of the center of pressure toward the single-support leg (Rogers & Pai, 1990). Because the ground reaction force, as we discussed in chapter 2, represents the acceleration of the individual's CM, Rogers and Pai sought to determine how well the change in the vertical component of the ground reaction force under the flexing leg could be determined using a static analysis.

   To answer this question, we first draw a free body diagram for the analysis. We do not need to draw a kinetic diagram because we are going to perform a static analysis to see how well we can predict the measured ground reaction force. The free body diagram involves the front view of a person with a ground reaction force acting on each foot and the weight of the system (figure 3.21). Next we must write an equation and then expand it using the information on the free body diagram. To find out whether a static analysis is sufficient to

(continued)

estimate the ground reaction force acting on the flexing leg, we can sum the torques about the point o and estimate the magnitude of $F_{y,f}$

$$\Sigma\ \tau_o = 0$$

$$\left(F_{y,f} \times d_2\right) - \left(F_w \times d_1\right) = 0$$

$$F_{y,f} = \frac{F_w \times d_1}{d_2}$$

Because F_w is constant, $F_{y,f}$ can be predicted as the ratio of changes in d_1 and d_2. To obtain the data necessary to test this prediction, Rogers and Pai (1990) had subjects stand on two force platforms, one foot on each, in order to measure the vertical component of the ground reaction force and its point of application (center of pressure) on each foot. In addition, they used a motion analysis system and a segmental analysis to determine the location of the total-body CM; d_1 represents the distance between the vertical projection of F_w and the point of application of $F_{y,s}$. The results are shown in figure 3.22. Focus on the graphs that show the change in $F_{y,f}$ with time: the solid line represents the actually measured $F_{y,f}$; the dashed line indicates the estimated $F_{y,f}$ based on the quasistatic analysis; and the shaded area represents the difference between the two. In figure 3.22, the graphs on the left are for a rapid step initiation (leg flexion), whereas those on the right are for a slow step initiation. The results indicate that a quasistatic analysis is appropriate for this task when it is performed slowly but

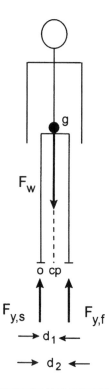

Figure 3.21　Quasistatic model used to predict the vertical component of the ground reaction force during step initiation.

Adapted from Rogers and Pai, 1990.

cp = center of pressure; d_1 = distance between cp and $F_{y,s}$; d_2 = distance between cp and $F_{y,f}$; $F_{y,f}$ = vertical component of the ground reaction force beneath the flexing leg; $F_{y,s}$ = vertical component of the ground reaction force beneath the single-support leg; F_w = body weight; g = center of mass; and o = point of application of $F_{y,s}$.

not when it is performed at normal or fast speeds. Similarly, slow lifts can be examined with a quasistatic analysis (Toussaint, van Baar, van Langen, de Looze, & van Dieën, 1992), but a quasistatic analysis is not appropriate for determining when a person will take a step after an unexpected disturbance (Pai, Rogers, Patton, Cain, & Hanke, 1998).

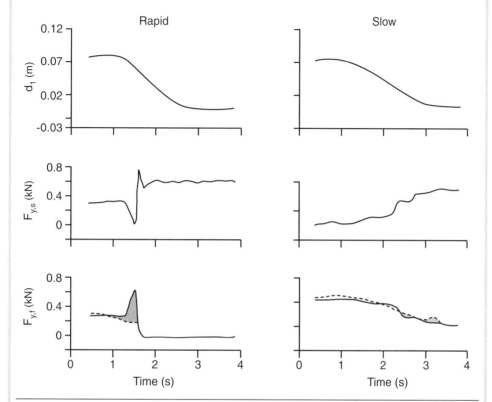

Figure 3.22 Changes in d_1, $F_{y,s}$, and $F_{y,f}$ with time during the step-initiation task when it is performed rapidly (left) and slowly (right).

Adapted from Rogers and Pai, 1990.

A dynamic analysis can, in general, proceed in either of two directions. Given information on the forces and torques, we can determine the associated kinematics; or given the kinematics, we can determine the underlying forces and torques. These two approaches are referred to as **forward dynamics** and **inverse dynamics,** respectively. The *inverse dynamics approach* involves obtaining the derivative of position-time data to yield velocity- and acceleration-time data (Elftman, 1939)—for example, measuring position and calculating joint forces. The principal disadvantage of this method is that errors embedded in the position-time data are greatly magnified by the time the data have been processed to yield acceleration (Hatze, 2000). In contrast, the *forward dynamics approach* involves the integration (in the calculus sense) of forces and torques (or accelerations) to produce the related kinematic information—for example, measuring acceleration and calculating velocity and position. The main difficulty associated with this technique is the need to accurately specify initial conditions. An alternative technique involves the use of features from both the inverse and forward approaches. In this method, measurements of position, linear acceleration, and angular velocity are combined to provide reliable estimates of link kinematics and joint loads (Ladin & Wu, 1991; Wu & Ladin, 1993).

Calculation of the net torque exerted about the hip by the weight lifter in Example 3.11 used the inverse dynamics approach; in that example we proceeded from the kinematics of the movement, along with some force information, to determine an unknown torque. It has been suggested that the nervous system uses inverse dynamics when it plans movements (Hollerbach & Flash, 1982). In this scheme, the nervous system determines the *desired* kinematics for a movement and then uses inverse dynamics to calculate the muscle torques needed to produce these kinematics. The complexity of these calculations, however, makes it unlikely that the nervous system organizes movements in this manner (Hasan, 1991).

Bobbert, Schamhardt, and Nigg (1991) used inverse dynamics with reasonable accuracy to estimate the magnitude of the vertical component of the ground reaction force during the support phase of running. They used four video cameras to obtain the kinematic information needed to determine the vertical acceleration of the CM of each body segment and then combined this with body segment mass data (Clauser, McConville, & Young, 1969) to calculate the vertical inertia force (mass $\times$ acceleration) for each segment. The inertia forces for each segment were summed to calculate $F_{g,y}$, which was then compared with the measured $F_{g,y}$. With this technique, the magnitude of the initial peak in the $F_{g,y}$-time graph was estimated with less than 10% error, and its time of occurrence was estimated within 5 ms. To achieve such accuracy in the estimation of forces, however, it is necessary to acquire extremely accurate kinematic data (Bobbert et al., 1991; Hatze, 2000; Ladin & Wu, 1991).

Intersegmental Dynamics

Because human movement typically involves the motion of more than one body segment, the cumulative motion of all the involved body segments determines the kinematics experienced by each body part. For example, consider an individual about to punt a football for distance. This task clearly involves the coordinated motion of the thigh, shank, and foot segments: the motion of the contact point on the foot (m) depends on the relative motion of the foot, shank, and thigh segments (figure 3.23a). The displacement of point m (s_M) is given by

$$s_M = s_{M/A} + s_{A/K} + s_{K/H} + s_H \qquad (3.13)$$

where the expression $s_{M/A}$ refers to the displacement of the metatarsals relative to the ankle joint, and the subscripts A, K, and H represent the ankle, knee, and hip, respectively. According to this equation, the displacement of the metatarsals depends on four displacement terms: the displacement relative to the ankle joint, the displacement of the ankle joint relative to the knee joint, the displacement of the knee joint relative to the hip joint, and the absolute displacement of the hip joint.

Similarly, if each segment also has an angular velocity (ω) and acceleration (α), then the magnitudes of the linear velocity (v) and acceleration (a) of the metatarsals depend on the relative kinematics of each segment in combination with the absolute kinematics of the hip joint. The angular velocity and acceleration of each segment are shown in figure 3.23b. A parallel equation to the one shown for s_M can be developed for v_M:

$$v_M = v_{M/A} + v_{A/K} + v_{K/H} + v_H$$

Because linear and angular velocity are related by the equation $v = r\omega$, then

$$v_M = r_f\omega_f + r_s\omega_s + r_t\omega_t + v_H \qquad (3.14)$$

where r_f corresponds to the distance from the ankle to the metatarsals, r_s indicates the length of the shank, and r_t represents the length of the thigh (figure 3.23a). The direction of each term is tangent to the path traced by the relevant anatomical landmark (figure 3.23c): $r_f\omega_f$ is tangent to the path of the metatarsals; $r_s\omega_s$ is tangent to the path of the ankle (the endpoint of the shank); and $r_t\omega_t$ is tangent to the path of the knee (the endpoint of the thigh).

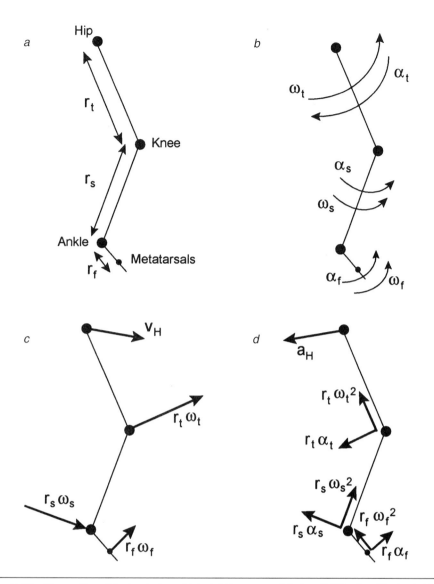

Figure 3.23   Kinematics of the leg during a kick. *(a)* Geometry of the leg. *(b)* The foot (f), shank (s), and thigh (t) each experience an angular velocity (ω) and acceleration (α) as the extremity moves to contact the ball at the metatarsals. The foot rotates about the ankle *(A)*, the shank about the knee *(K)*, and the thigh about the hip *(H)* joint. *(c)* The kinematic factors that influence the linear velocity of the metatarsals. *(d)* The kinematic variables that affect the linear acceleration of the metatarsals.

The acceleration of the metatarsals (a_M) also depends on the acceleration of the involved segments (figure 3.23d) and, based on the relation between linear and angular acceleration, can be written as:

$$a_M = a_{M/A} + a_{A/K} + a_{K/H} + a_H$$

$$a_M = \sqrt{\left(r_f\omega_f^2\right)^2 + \left(r_f\alpha_f\right)^2} + \sqrt{\left(r_s\omega_s^2\right)^2 + \left(r_s\alpha_s\right)^2} + \sqrt{\left(r_t\omega_t^2\right)^2 + \left(r_t\alpha_t\right)^2} + a_H \qquad (3.15)$$

where $r\omega^2$ represents the change in direction of v for a segment and $r\alpha$ indicates the change in magnitude of v. An important feature of this relation is that the acceleration of each segment in this system is influenced by *the acceleration of all the other segments*. For example, rearrangement of Equation 3.15 indicates that the acceleration of the shank during the football punt is dependent on the angular acceleration of the foot and thigh and the linear acceleration of the hip and a_M:

$$r_s\omega_s^2 + r_s\alpha_s = a_M - r_f\omega_f^2 - r_f\alpha_f - r_t\omega_t^2 - r_t\alpha_t - a_H$$

This equation can be used to determine the linear acceleration of any point along the shank (e.g., CM, ankle joint), where r represents the distance from the knee to the point of interest. Miller and Munro (1984) used this approach to determine the contributions of the different body segments to the height achieved during the flight phase of a springboard dive.

This kinematic coupling between segments occurs because of the dynamic interactions between segments. On the basis of what we know about the relation between force and acceleration ($\mathbf{F} = m\mathbf{a}$), these interactions between the accelerations of the body segments indicate that there must be *interactive forces between body segments during human movement*. The study of **intersegmental dynamics** examines these motion-dependent interactions between segments (Feltner & Dapena, 1989; Hoy & Zernicke, 1986; Phillips, Roberts, & Huang, 1983; Piazza & Delp, 1996; Putnam, 1991).

As an example of these effects, consider the interactions between the thigh and shank during a kick. Figure 3.24*a* shows the two-segment system and its orientation, which can be defined by four coordinates: the *x*- and *y*-coordinates of the hip *(h)* joint, and the angles of the thigh *(θ_t)* and shank *(θ_s)*. Each segment has a weight vector ($\mathbf{F}_{w,s}$ and $\mathbf{F}_{w,t}$), and there are resultant joint forces ($\mathbf{F}_{j,k}$ and $\mathbf{F}_{j,h}$) and resultant muscle torques ($\boldsymbol{\tau}_{m,k}$ and $\boldsymbol{\tau}_{m,h}$) acting about the knee and hip joints, respectively. To determine the motion-dependent effects, we need to express the resultant joint forces in terms of kinematic variables (position, velocity, and acceleration) and derive an expression for the resultant muscle torques. We begin by writing the dynamic equation of motion for the shank.

$$\sum \mathbf{F} = m\mathbf{a}$$
$$\mathbf{F}_{j,k} + \mathbf{F}_{w,s} = m_s \cdot \mathbf{a}_s \tag{3.16}$$

where m_s is the mass of the shank and $\mathbf{a}_s$ is the linear acceleration of the shank CM. Because we are dealing with a linked, two-segment system, $\mathbf{a}_s$ can be expressed in the form of Equation 3.15:

$$\mathbf{a}_s = \mathbf{a}_h + \left(\boldsymbol{\alpha}_t \times \mathbf{r}_{k/h}\right) + \left(\boldsymbol{\omega}_t \times \boldsymbol{\omega}_t \times \mathbf{r}_{k/h}\right) + \left(\boldsymbol{\alpha}_s \times \mathbf{r}_{s/k}\right) + \left(\boldsymbol{\omega}_s \times \boldsymbol{\omega}_s \times \mathbf{r}_{s/k}\right) \tag{3.17}$$

and this expression (Equation 3.17) can be inserted into Equation 3.16 and rearranged to solve for $\mathbf{F}_{j,k}$.

$$\mathbf{F}_{j,k} = m_s\mathbf{a}_h + m_s\left(\boldsymbol{\alpha}_t \times \mathbf{r}_{k/h}\right) + m_s\left(\boldsymbol{\omega}_t \times \boldsymbol{\omega}_t \times \mathbf{r}_{k/h}\right) + m_s\left(\boldsymbol{\alpha}_s \times \mathbf{r}_{s/k}\right) + m_s\left(\boldsymbol{\omega}_s \times \boldsymbol{\omega}_s \times \mathbf{r}_{s/k}\right) - \mathbf{F}_{w,s}$$
$$\tag{3.18}$$

where h = hip, s = shank, t = thigh, k/h = the distance from the knee to the hip, and s/k = the distance from the shank CM to the knee.

To derive the expression for the resultant muscle torque about the knee ($\boldsymbol{\tau}_{m,k}$), we write the moment-of-force equation for the shank about its CM.

$$\sum \boldsymbol{\tau}_{g,s} = I_{g,s}\boldsymbol{\alpha}_s$$
$$\boldsymbol{\tau}_{m,k} + \left(\mathbf{r}_{k/s} \times \mathbf{F}_{j,k}\right) = I_{g,s}\boldsymbol{\alpha}_s \tag{3.19}$$

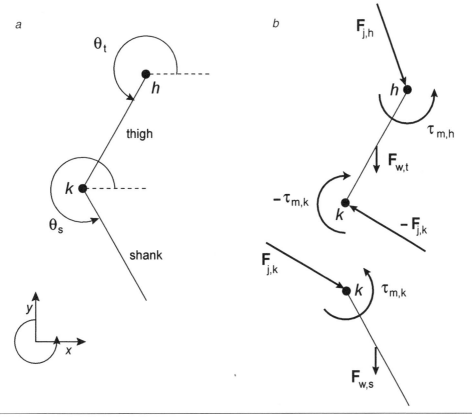

Figure 3.24 The *(a)* position and *(b)* free body diagram of a two-segment system (thigh + shank).

In the final step, Equation 3.19 is rearranged to solve for $\tau_{m,k}$; Equation 3.18 is substituted for the joint reaction force $(F_{j,k})$ in Equation 3.19; and the expression is changed from vector to scalar variables:

$$
\begin{aligned}
\tau_{m,k} = &\left(r_s \cos \varphi\, m_s\, l_t\, \alpha_t \right) && [r\alpha \text{ of thigh}] \\
&+ \left(r_s \sin \varphi\, m_s\, l_t\, \omega_t^2 \right) && [r\omega^2 \text{ of thigh}] \\
&+ \left(r_s^2\, m_s\, \alpha_s \right) && [r\alpha \text{ of shank}] \\
&+ \left(r_s \sin \theta_s\, m_s\, a_x + r_s \cos \theta_s\, m_s\, a_y \right) && [\mathbf{a} \text{ of hip}] \\
&+ \left(I_{g,s}\, \alpha_s \right) && [\text{shank inertia torque}] \\
&+ \left(r_s \cos \theta_s\, m_s\, g \right) && [\text{shank weight}]
\end{aligned}
$$

where φ = knee angle $(\theta_t - \theta_s)$, l_t = length of the thigh, g = acceleration due to gravity, r_s = distance from the knee joint to the shank CM, and $I_{g,s}$ = the moment of inertia of the shank about a somersault axis through its CM. This final equation indicates that the resultant muscle torque about the knee joint can be expressed in terms of five motion-dependent effects and one gravity-dependent effect (shank weight). From this equation, the relative significance of each motion-dependent effect throughout a movement can be determined (Putnam, 1991).

Similar procedures can be used to identify the motion-dependent effects for the thigh. Again, we begin by writing the moment-of-force equation for the thigh relative to its CM.

$$\sum \boldsymbol{\tau}_{g,t} = I_{g,t}\boldsymbol{\alpha}_t$$

$$\boldsymbol{\tau}_{m,h} - \boldsymbol{\tau}_{m,k} + \left(\mathbf{r}_{h,t} \times \mathbf{F}_{j,h}\right) - \left(\mathbf{r}_{k,s} \times \mathbf{F}_{j,k}\right) = I_{g,t}\boldsymbol{\alpha}_t \qquad (3.20)$$

As for the shank, we derive expressions for $\mathbf{F}_{j,h}$ and $\mathbf{F}_{j,k}$ in terms of kinematic variables (e.g., Equation 3.17) and substitute these into Equation 3.20. The expressions for $\mathbf{F}_{j,h}$ and $\mathbf{F}_{j,k}$ will contain effects due to the linear acceleration of the segment endpoint (hip), the change in direction ($r\omega$) and magnitude ($r\alpha$) of the linear velocity of the thigh and shank, and segment weight. The result is an expression for the resultant muscle torque about the hip joint ($\tau_{m,h}$) that includes one gravity-dependent variable (weight) and seven motion-dependent variables (Putnam, 1991).

$$
\begin{aligned}
\tau_{m,h} = {} & \left(r_s \cos\varphi \, m_s \, l_t + l_t^2 m_s\right)\alpha_t + \left(r_s \sin\varphi \, m_s \, l_t\right)\omega_t^2 \\
& + \left(l_t \cos\varphi \, m_s \, r_s + r_s^2 m_s + I_{g,s}\right)\alpha_s - \left(l_t \sin\varphi \, m_s \, r_s\right)\omega_s^2 \\
& + \left(r_t \sin\theta_t \, m_t + l_t \sin\theta_t \, m_s + r_s \sin\theta_s \, m_s\right)\alpha_x \\
& - \left(r_t \cos\theta_t \, m_t + l_t \cos\theta_t \, m_s + r_s \cos\theta_s \, m_s\right)\alpha_y \\
& - \left(r_t \cos\theta_t \, m_t + l_t \cos\theta_t \, m_s + r_s \cos\theta_s \, m_s\right)g + \left(I_{g,t} + r_t^2 m_t\right)\alpha_t
\end{aligned}
$$

where r_t = the distance from the hip joint to the thigh CM.

An important goal of this analysis is to determine the magnitude of the motion-dependent effects. Figure 3.25a provides such a comparison by showing the time course of the resultant muscle torque about the knee joint and the resultant motion-dependent torque exerted by the thigh on the shank during the kick. This graph shows that the effect of thigh motion on the shank is as large as that due to the muscles that cross the knee joint. The motion-dependent torque exerted by the thigh on the shank is negative for about the first 60 ms of the kick; the negative direction means that the thigh accelerated the shank in a backward-rotation direction. For most of the kick, the thigh motion accelerated the shank in a forward direction.

By a similar analysis it is possible to identify the effect of shank motion on the thigh. As described by Putnam (1991), the effect of shank motion on the thigh is not simply a mirror image of the effect of thigh motion on the shank. The shank is the distal segment in this two-segment system, whereas the thigh is the proximal segment with the shank on one end and the hip joint at the other. The shank experienced four motion-dependent effects, while the thigh was subjected to six. As with the thigh-on-shank interaction, we are interested in the magnitude of the shank-on-thigh motion-dependent effect. Figure 3.25b shows the net torque acting on the thigh due to the motion of the shank. Once again, the magnitude of the motion-dependent torque is large compared with that of the resultant muscle torque about the hip joint. Even though the resultant muscle torque was in the direction of flexion for the entire movement, which is consistent with the EMG activity (Dörge et al., 1999), the thigh accelerated in the direction of extension toward the end of the kick. The main point of this example is to empha-size that the muscle- and motion-dependent torques act in *opposite* directions for most of the kick. The net effect is that the thigh accelerates in the forward direction for about the first half of the kick and then accelerates in the backward direction for the remainder of the kick. Fur-thermore, the net effect has a smaller magnitude than the absolute torque exerted by either the muscle activity or the motion-dependent effect. To achieve this net effect, however, the pri-mary function of the muscles about the hip joint during a kick is to counteract the motion-dependent effects between the shank and thigh.

One conclusion that can be made from the study of intersegmental dynamics is that the motion of a body segment can exert significant torques on the other segments in the system.

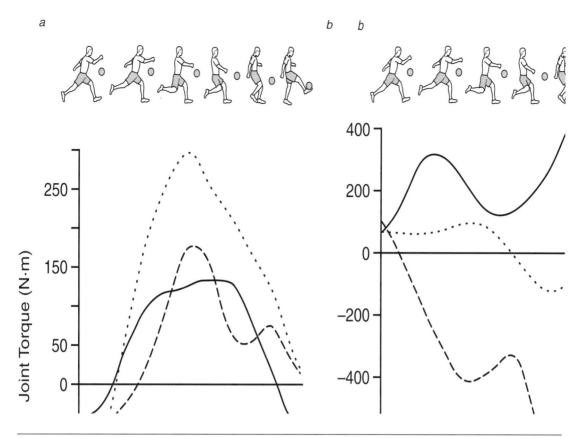

Figure 3.25   Motion-dependent effects during a kick: *(a)* the resultant muscle torque about the knee joint (solid line), the motion-dependent torque exerted by the thigh on the shank (dashed line), and the net effect (dotted line) of all torques acting on the shank; *(b)* the resultant muscle torque about the hip joint (solid line), the motion-dependent torque exerted by the shank on the thigh (dashed line), and the net effect (dotted line) of all the torques acting on the thigh.

Adapted from Putnam, 1983.

These effects are substantial for whole-limb, rapid movements such as kicking and throwing, but are also significant even in finger movements (Darling & Cole, 1990). Consequently, the control of movement by the nervous system must accommodate these motion-dependent effects (Gribble & Ostry, 1999; Sainburg, Ghez, & Kalakanis, 1999; Smith & Zernicke, 1987). The means by which the nervous system knows about these motion-dependent effects, however, appear complex (Koshland & Smith, 1989a, 1989b).

Joint Forces, Torques, and Power

On the basis of these descriptions of the characteristics of the musculoskeletal forces and the techniques for determining the magnitude and direction of each force, we can compare the relative contributions of different muscle groups to the performance of a movement. It is possible, for example, to determine the net joint reaction force and the net muscle torque acting at various joints in a subject at a particular point in the performance of a movement (Example 3.13). By extension, we can perform these calculations for the duration of a movement and compare the performance among groups of individuals and after various interventions (Example 3.14). It is even possible to estimate the distribution of the musculoskeletal forces among the structures that compose a joint if we ascertain the relative activity of the involved muscles (Examples 3.15 and 3.16).

Example 3.13

Segmental Analysis of Joint Forces and Torques

Because human movement is the result of the muscle-controlled rotation of body segments about one another, we are frequently interested in determining the quantity of muscle activity that contributes to the rotation. We can accomplish this by treating the human body as a series of connected rigid links (body segments) and performing a dynamic analysis on each segment. Three sets of information are required:

1. The kinematics (position, velocity, and acceleration) of the body segments

2. Estimates of the mass and the mass distribution (CM location and moment of inertia) of the segments

3. A known boundary constraint, such as the ground reaction force or a load acting on a segment

We begin the analysis with the body segment that includes the boundary constraint (the foot, in the case of the ground reaction force) and then back-calculate through the body, one segment at a time, to determine the net forces and torques acting about each joint. With this segmental analysis, we can determine the musculoskeletal forces and torques at the ankle, knee, and hip joints at one point in a weightlifting movement (Enoka, 1983). The analysis involves four steps. First, we define the system and its orientation. Second, we separate the human body into an appropriate number of rigid segments. Third, we draw the free body diagram and the kinetic diagram for each body segment. Fourth, we derive and solve the equations of motion (Equations 3.7, 3.8, and 3.9) for each segment, beginning with the segment that includes the known boundary constraint. For this weightlifting example, the system includes the legs in the configuration shown in figure 3.26.

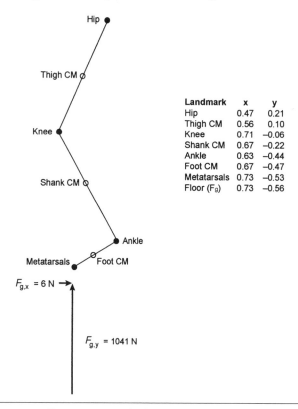

Landmark	x	y
Hip	0.47	0.21
Thigh CM	0.56	0.10
Knee	0.71	−0.06
Shank CM	0.67	−0.22
Ankle	0.63	−0.44
Foot CM	0.67	−0.47
Metatarsals	0.73	−0.53
Floor (F$_g$)	0.73	−0.56

Figure 3.26 The *x-y* coordinates (meters) of selected landmarks in the middle of the weightlifting movement.

CM = center of mass.

Because the purpose of the analysis is to determine the musculoskeletal forces at the ankle, knee, and hip, the leg should be separated into the foot, shank, and thigh for the analysis. We can obtain estimates of the mass distribution for these segments from the tables included in chapter 2. Furthermore, assume that a video-based motion analysis has provided estimates of the angular and linear accelerations of each segment at the instant of interest in the movement:

		Thigh	Shank	Foot
I_g	(kg·m^2)	0.12337	0.04706	0.00398
Mass	(kg)	8	3	1
α	(rad/s^2)	0.32	–9.39	–3.41
a_x	(m/s^2)	2.34	1.56	–0.36
a_y	(m/s^2)	–1.96	–1.64	–0.56

The next step is to draw the free body and kinetic diagrams for each segment. We should begin with the foot (figure 3.27) because that is the segment for which we have some boundary information (ground reaction force).

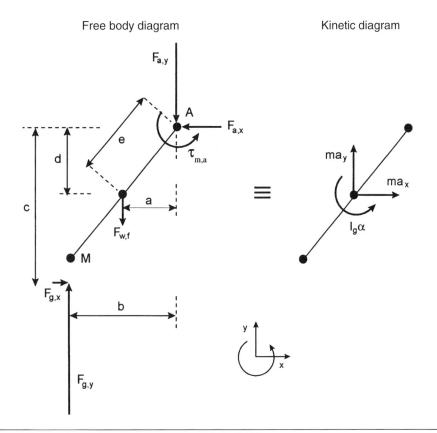

Figure 3.27 Free body diagram and kinetic diagram for the foot. The free body diagram (left) shows the forces *(F)* acting on the foot at the metatarsals *(M)*, the distances from the line of action of each force to the ankle joint *(A)*, and the net muscle torque *($\tau_{m,a}$)* about the ankle joint. The forces include the ground reaction force *($F_{g,x}$, $F_{g,y}$)*, the weight of the foot *($F_{w,f}$)*, and the joint reaction force *($F_{a,x}$, $F_{a,y}$)*. The kinetic diagram shows the horizontal inertia force *(ma_x)*, the vertical inertia force *(ma_y)*, and the inertia torque *($I_g\alpha$)* about the CM *(g)*.

(continued)

From the free body diagram (figure 3.27), we can derive the three equations of motion and solve for the unknown terms, which are the x and y components of the net joint reaction force at the ankle and the net muscle torque about the ankle:

$$\Sigma\, F_x = ma_x$$
$$-F_{a,x} + F_{g,x} = ma_x$$
$$-F_{a,x} = -F_{g,x} + ma_x$$
$$= -6 + (1 \times -0.36)$$
$$F_{a,x} = 6.36 \text{ N}$$

$$\Sigma\, F_y = ma_y$$
$$F_{g,y} - F_{a,y} - F_{w,f} = ma_y$$
$$F_{a,y} = F_{g,y} - F_{w,f} - ma_y$$
$$= 1041 - (1 \times 9.81) - (1 \times -0.56)$$
$$F_{a,y} = 1031 \text{ N}$$

$$\Sigma\, \tau_A = I_g\alpha + (ma_x \times d) - (ma_y \times a)$$
$$\tau_{m,a} + (F_{w,f} \times a) - (F_{g,y} \times b) + (F_{g,x} \times c) = I_g\alpha + (ma_x \times d) - (ma_y \times a)$$
$$\tau_{m,a} = (F_{g,y} \times b) - (F_{g,x} \times c) - (F_{w,f} \times a) + I_g\alpha +$$
$$(ma_x \times d) - (ma_y \times a)$$
$$= (1041 \times 0.10) - (6 \times 0.12) - (9.81 \times 0.04) +$$
$$(0.00398 \times -3.41) + (1 \times -0.36 \times 0.03) -$$
$$(1 \times -0.56 \times 0.04)$$
$$= 104.1 - 0.72 - 0.392 - 0.014 - 0.011 + 0.022$$
$$\tau_{m,a} = 103 \text{ N·m}$$

Once the musculoskeletal forces at the ankle are known, we proceed to the next segment in the system, the shank (figure 3.28). We can derive the three equations of motion and solve for the x and y components of the net joint reaction force at the knee and the net muscle torque about the knee:

$$\Sigma\, F_x = ma_x$$
$$F_{a,x} - F_{k,x} = ma_x$$
$$F_{k,x} = F_{a,x} - ma_x$$
$$= 6.36 - (3 \times 1.56)$$
$$F_{k,x} = 1.68 \text{ N}$$

$$\Sigma\, F_y = ma_y$$
$$F_{a,y} - F_{k,y} - F_{w,s} = ma_y$$
$$F_{k,y} = F_{a,y} - F_{w,s} - ma_y$$
$$= 1031 - (3 \times 9.81) - (3 \times -1.64)$$
$$F_{k,y} = 1006 \text{ N}$$

$$\Sigma \ \tau_K = I_g\alpha + \left(ma_x \times d\right) - \left(ma_y \times a\right)$$

$$\tau_{m,k} - \tau_{m,a} - \left(F_{w,s} \times a\right) + \left(F_{a,y} \times b\right) + \left(F_{a,x} \times c\right) = I_g\alpha + \left(ma_x \times d\right) + \left(ma_y \times a\right)$$

$$\tau_{m,k} = \tau_{m,a} + \left(F_{w,s} \times a\right) - \left(F_{a,y} \times b\right) - \left(F_{a,x} \times c\right) +$$

$$I_g\alpha + \left(ma_x \times d\right) + \left(ma_y \times a\right)$$

$$= 103 + \left(29.4 \times 0.04\right) - \left(1031 \times 0.08\right) -$$

$$\left(6.36 \times -0.38\right) + \left(0.04606 \times -9.39\right) +$$

$$\left(3 \times 1.56 \times 0.16\right) + \left(3 \times -1.64 \times 0.04\right)$$

$$= 103 + 1.18 - 82.5 - 2.42 - 0.43 +$$

$$0.749 - 0.197$$

$$\tau_{m,k} = 19.4 \ \text{N·m}$$

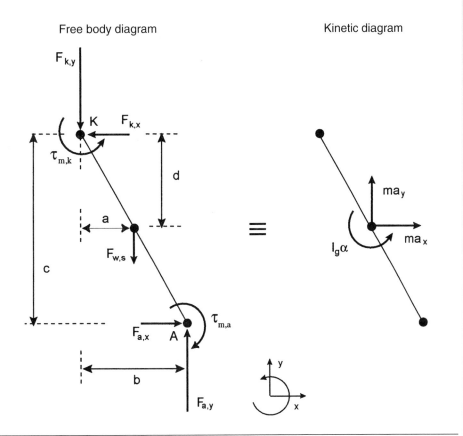

Figure 3.28 Free body diagram and kinetic diagram for the shank. The free body diagram (left) shows the forces *(F)* acting on the shank, the distances from the line of action of each force to the knee joint *(K)*, and the net muscle torque *($\tau_{m,k}$)* about the knee joint. The forces include the weight of the shank *($F_{w,s}$)* and the joint reaction forces at the ankle *($F_{a,x}$, $F_{a,y}$)* and the knee *($F_{k,x}$, $F_{k,y}$)*. The kinetic diagram shows the horizontal inertia force *(ma_x)*, the vertical inertia force *(ma_y)*, and the inertia torque *($I_g\alpha$)* about the CM *(g)*.

(continued)

Once the musculoskeletal forces at the knee are known, we proceed to the next segment in the system, the thigh (figure 3.29). We can derive the three equations of motion and solve for the x and y components of the net joint reaction force at the hip and the net muscle torque about the hip:

$$\Sigma\, F_x = ma_x$$

$$F_{k,x} - F_{h,x} = ma_x$$

$$F_{h,x} = F_{k,x} - ma_x$$

$$= 1.68 - (8 \times 2.34)$$

$$F_{h,x} = -17\ \text{N}$$

The value of –17 N means that $F_{h,x}$ has a magnitude of 17 N but it is actually acting in the opposite direction to that drawn on the free body diagram.

$$\Sigma\, F_y = ma_y$$

$$F_{k,y} - F_{h,y} - F_{w,t} = ma_y$$

$$F_{h,y} = F_{k,y} - F_{w,t} - ma_y$$

$$= 1006 - (8 \times 9.81) - (8 \times -1.96)$$

$$F_{h,y} = 943\ \text{N}$$

$$\Sigma\, \tau_H = I_g \alpha + (ma_x \times d) - (ma_y \times a)$$

$$\tau_{m,h} - \tau_{m,k} + (F_{w,t} \times a) - (F_{k,y} \times b) + (F_{k,x} \times c) = I_g \alpha + (ma_x \times d) - (ma_y \times a)$$

$$\tau_{m,h} = \tau_{m,k} - (F_{w,t} \times a) + (F_{k,y} \times b) - (F_{k,x} \times c) + I_g \alpha + (ma_x \times d) - (ma_y \times a)$$

$$= 19.4 - (78.5 \times 0.09) + (1006 \times 0.24) - (1.68 \times 0.27) + (0.12337 \times 0.32) +$$

$$(8 \times 2.34 \times 0.11) - (8 \times -1.96 \times 0.09)$$

$$= 19.4 - 7.07 + 241 - 0.454 + 0.039 + 2.06 + 1.41$$

$$\tau_{m,h} = 256\ \text{N·m}$$

The major point of this example is to demonstrate how to determine musculoskeletal forces in the human body at one instant in the course of a movement. To perform such an analysis, we need to know the forces due to body mass, the forces due to the surroundings, and the kinematics of the system. For this specific movement, the magnitude of the joint reaction force in the x direction was much smaller than that in the y direction, which increased modestly in the distal-to-proximal direction. The magnitude of the net muscle torque, however, was quite different across the ankle, knee, and hip, with the greatest value at the hip. Be careful not to interpret these data as representing the absolute magnitude of the muscle action about each joint; these data correspond to the net effect. To determine the relative activity among the muscles about a joint, it is necessary to make additional measurements, such as EMG recordings of muscle activity.

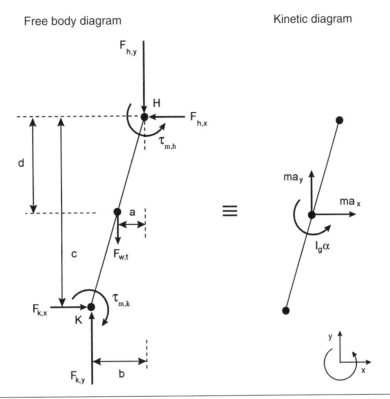

Free body diagram   Kinetic diagram

Figure 3.29   Free body diagram and kinetic diagram for the thigh. The free body diagram (left) shows the forces *(F)* acting on the thigh, the distances from the line of action of each force to the hip joint *(H)*, and the net muscle torque $(\tau_{m,h})$ about the hip joint. The forces include the weight of the thigh $(F_{w,t})$ and the joint reaction forces at the knee $(F_{k,x}, F_{k,y})$ and the hip $(F_{h,x}, F_{h,y})$. The kinetic diagram shows the horizontal inertia force (ma_x), the vertical inertia force (ma_y), and the inertia torque $(I_g \alpha)$ about the center of mass *(g)*.

Example 3.14
Joint Torque and Power During Walking

With the procedure described in the preceding example, it is possible to calculate the musculoskeletal forces at one point in time during a movement. To obtain a complete description of the movement, it is necessary to repeat these calculations approximately 100 times over the course of the movement. DeVita, Hortobágyi, and Barrier (1998) used such an approach when evaluating the effectiveness of an aggressive rehabilitation protocol for patients recovering from surgical repair of the anterior cruciate ligament (ACL).

The analysis focused on a comparison of the torque and power at the ankle, knee, and hip joints during walking. DeVita et al. (1998) compared the performance of patients after three weeks and six months of rehabilitation with that of healthy control subjects. The data required for such a comparison included estimates of body mass distribution, the measurement of a boundary condition, and the kinematics of the leg. The mass, CM location, and

(continued)

moment of inertia for the foot, shank, and thigh were estimated using some of the cadaver data and mathematical models described in chapter 2. The kinematic data were obtained with a motion analysis system that was employed to determine the position of the lateral malleolus, lateral femoral condyle, greater trochanter, and shoulder. These landmarks were used to determine the relative angles between the foot and shank (ankle joint), the shank and the thigh (knee joint), and the thigh and the trunk (hip joint). The position data were smoothed with a second-order, Butterworth digital filter, and the angles at the ankle, knee, and hip joints were then determined. Angular velocity was calculated by the finite-differences method (chapter 1).

After six months of rehabilitation, DeVita et al. (1998) found that the angular kinematics of the patients were almost identical to those of the healthy control subjects. At the three-week point, however, the patients presented with greater flexion and a lesser range of motion than normal at the ankle, knee, and hip joints. These adaptations were also evident in the profiles of the net torque about the three joints (figure 3.30). After three weeks of reha-

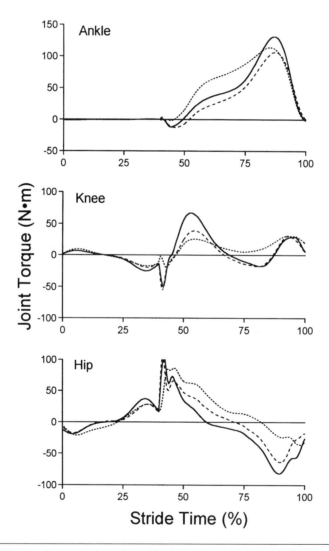

Figure 3.30 Net muscle torque about the ankle, knee, and hip joints during walking for patients after three weeks (dotted line) and six months of rehabilitation (dashed line) and for healthy control subjects (solid line). Positive torque indicates an extensor (and plantarflexor) torque. The foot was on the ground (stance phase) from 40% to 100% of stride time.

bilitation, the net torques during the stance phase were greater at the ankle and hip joints and less at the knee joint compared with the values at six months, which were rather similar to the data for the healthy control subjects. These results suggest that the patients initially compensated for the intervention by diverting activity away from the knee joint to the ankle and hip joints. Even after six months of rehabilitation, the patients exhibited a lesser net torque about the knee joint at about 50% to 60% of stride time and a greater net torque about the hip joint over the same interval. Despite these differences, when the torques were summed about the three joints, producing a value corresponding to the net support torque (Winter, 1983), there were no differences between the patients at six months and the healthy subjects (figure 3.31).

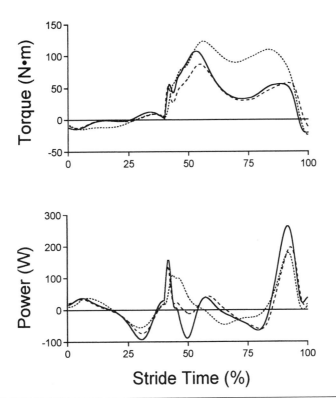

Figure 3.31   Summed torque and power about the ankle, knee, and hip joints within a single stride during walking. The data are for patients after three weeks (dotted line) and six months of rehabilitation (dashed line) and for healthy control subjects (solid line). Positive torque indicates an extensor (and plantarflexor) torque; positive power represents power production, and negative power corresponds to power absorption. The foot was on the ground (stance phase) from 40% to 100% of stride time.

   As with the torque profiles (figure 3.30), the joint power at the ankle, knee, and hip joints was significantly different in the patients after three weeks of rehabilitation but became more similar to that of healthy control subjects after six months of rehabilitation (figure 3.32). For example, the positive work (area under the power-time curve) done at the hip from 40% to 80% of stride time by the patients at three weeks was decreased by 44% after six months of rehabilitation. Similarly, the amount of negative work done at the knee joint (power absorption due to an eccentric contraction) increased with the duration of rehabilitation. Neither the positive work done at the hip nor the negative work done at the knee fully

(continued)

recovered even after six months of rehabilitation. The scale on the vertical axes in figure 3.32 indicates that the magnitude of power was greatest at the ankle joint and least at the hip joint. As a result, the summed power (figure 3.31) was dominated by the power about the knee and ankle joints. The summed power comprised alternating phases of power production and absorption, with the peak power production occurring just prior to toe-off. After six months of rehabilitation, the summed power for the patients was essentially similar to that for the healthy subjects except at around 50% of stride time.

The interesting feature of this analysis, however, is that although the summed joint torques and powers were similar between healthy control subjects and the patients after six months of rehabilitation, there remained significant differences between the two groups at the level of the individual joints. This result suggests that the patients developed a coping strategy to deal with an impaired knee joint mechanism. Similarly, the use of a functional knee brace by individuals recovering from ACL injury also alters the joint kinetics during both walking and running (DeVita, Blankenship, & Skelly, 1992; DeVita, Torry, Glover, & Speroni, 1996).

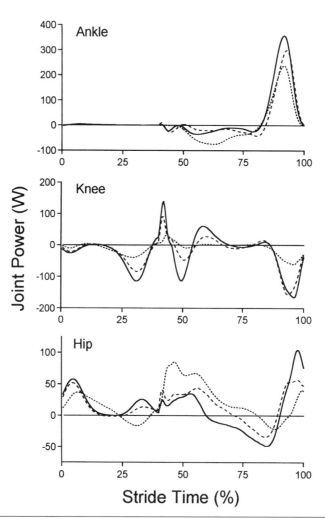

Figure 3.32 Net power about the ankle, knee, and hip joints during walking for patients after three weeks (dotted line) and six months of rehabilitation (dashed line) and for healthy control subjects (solid line). Joint power was calculated as the product of angular velocity and joint torque; positive power indicates production of power by muscles that cross the joint whereas negative power represents the absorption of power. The foot was on the ground (stance phase) from 40% to 100% of stride time.

Example 3.15
Joint Reaction Force in the Knee

Whereas the previous two examples dealt with the net mechanical action at various joints, the third example shows how it is possible to estimate absolute effects. In this example we compare the joint reaction force at the knee joint during a squat lift and a knee extension exercise (Escamilla, Fleisig, Zheng, et al., 1998). In the rehabilitation literature, these activities are described as closed and open kinetic chain exercises, respectively (Blackard, Jensen, & Ebben, 1999). The major difference between such exercises is the point of application and direction of the force exerted by the surroundings; in this example, these correspond to the ground reaction force for the squat lift and the contact force with the machine for the knee extension exercise.

As in Examples 3.13 and 3.14, a motion analysis system was used to measure the kinematics of each movement in the sagittal plane, and the contact force was measured with a force transducer placed between the subject and the surroundings (i.e., ground or machine). These data were then used to perform a dynamic analysis and to determine the musculoskeletal forces at the knee joint. In this study, however, these forces included the sum of the individual muscle forces, the net ligament force, and the contact force between the femur and the tibia (Zheng, Fleisig, Escamilla, & Barrentine, 1998). To achieve this level of detail, it was necessary to estimate the force exerted by each of the major muscles that cross the knee joint and to resolve the joint reaction force into a normal compressive component and a ligament force (figure 3.33).

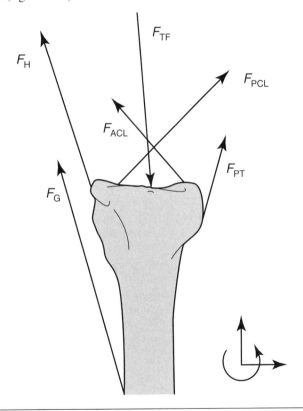

Figure 3.33   Forces acting on the tibia.

F_{acl} = tensile force of the anterior cruciate ligament; F_g = tensile force exerted by the gastrocnemius muscle; F_h = tensile force exerted by the hamstring muscles; F_{pt} = tensile force of the patella tendon; F_{pcl} = tensile force of the posterior cruciate ligament; and F_{tf} = compressive force due to tibiofemoral contact.

(continued)

Estimates of the force exerted by each muscle during the two tasks were based on the EMG activity of the muscle (figure 3.34). The muscles were quadriceps femoris (rectus femoris and the three vasti), medial hamstrings (semimembranosus and semitendinosus), and gastrocnemius. The force of each muscle was estimated from the following relation:

$$F_m = c \ k \ A \ \sigma \, \text{EMG}$$

where c = weighting coefficient, k = a factor that accounted for the effect of a change in muscle length on the force exerted by the muscle, A = cross-sectional area, σ = specific tension, and EMG = the amount of muscle activity normalized to the value during a maximum voluntary contraction. Once the summed muscle force was determined (sum of agonist and antagonist muscles), the difference between this value and the resultant force was set equal to the sum of the tibiofemoral contact force and the ligament force. The tibiofemoral contact force was assumed to act perpendicular to the articulating surface of the tibia. The ligament force, however, was derived from the shear component of the joint reaction force and the line of action of the ligament force. To calculate the ligament force, the shear component of the joint reaction force was multiplied by the cosine of the angle for the line of action for the ligament based on functions reported by Herzog and Read (1993).

For the knee extension exercise, the subject pushed against a pad that contacted the lower shank. The range of motion was about 1.57 rad, beginning with the knee joint flexed at a right angle. While the range of motion was also about 1.57 rad at the knee joint for the squat lift, the subject began from an erect position with the knee joint extended (3.14 rad). Because of these different starting positions, knee angle changed from left to right for the knee extension exercise and from right to left for the squat lift in figure 3.34. As a result, figure 3.34a shows that the EMG for quadriceps femoris was low at the beginning of each movement and increased as the knee was extended; that is, the load was raised. A similar EMG pattern was recorded for gastrocnemius (figure 3.34d) but not for the other two antagonist muscles (figure 3.34b and c). There was greater coactivation of the biceps femoris and hamstrings during the squat lift.

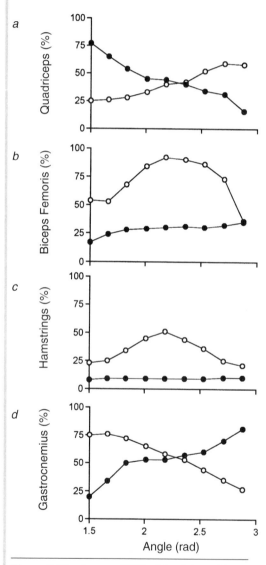

Figure 3.34   Average EMG of the (a) quadriceps femoris, (b) biceps femoris, (c) medial hamstrings, and (d) gastrocnemius muscles during the knee extension phase of the squat lift (open circles) and the knee extension exercise (filled circles). The EMG data are normalized to the values recorded during a maximum voluntary contraction.

Data from Escamilla, Fleisig, Zheng, et al., 1998.

The net extensor torque about the knee joint changed with a parabolic-like shape over the range of motion for the knee extension exercise (figure 3.35*a*). For the squat lift, however, the extensor torque increased almost linearly throughout the lift. The tibiofemoral compressive force was lowest at the beginning of each exercise but increased to similar levels (~3000 N) by about the middle of the range of motion (figure 3.35*b*). Because the tibiofemoral force was based on the absolute activity of the agonist and antagonist muscles, it was about three times greater than the compressive component of the net joint reaction force. The compressive force was greatest when the knee joint approached complete extension during the knee extension exercise, but the peak values occurred in the middle of the range of motion during the squat lift. In contrast, the ligament force was generally greatest when the knee joint was flexed. For the entire squat lift and for most of the knee extension exercise, the ligament force was provided by the posterior cruciate ligament (figure 3.35*c*). The peak ligament force was twice as great during the squat lift, and remained greater than the peak value for the knee extension exercise over most of the range of motion. Such comparisons indicate the effects of different exercises on the musculoskeletal forces.

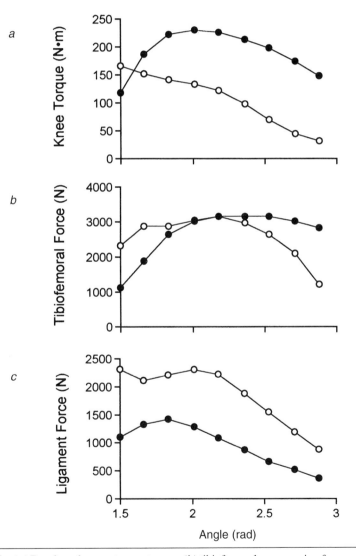

Figure 3.35 *(a)* Resultant knee extensor torque, *(b)* tibiofemoral compressive force, and *(c)* ligament force during the knee extension phase of the squat lift (open circles) and the knee extension exercise (filled circles). A positive ligament force indicates tension in the posterior cruciate ligament, whereas a negative ligament force indicates tension in the anterior cruciate ligament.

Data from Escamilla, Fleisig, Zheng, et al., 1998.

Example 3.16
Modeling of Knee Forces

More detail about the distribution of forces within a joint can be obtained by performing modeling studies. For example, Pandy and Shelburne (1997) developed a sagittal-plane model of the human knee to examine load sharing between the muscles, ligaments, and bones during isometric exercises. These were the key features of the model (Shelburne & Pandy, 1997):

- The geometry of the distal femur was based on cadaver data.
- The tibial plateau and patellar facet were represented as flat surfaces.
- The ligaments and capsule of the knee joint were modeled as 11 elastic elements.
- Eleven muscles crossed the knee joint, with each muscle represented by a Hill-type model (chapter 6) and attached to an elastic tendon.

With such a model, it was possible to estimate the forces experienced by the different structures in the joint over its entire range of motion in response to varying levels of muscle activation. Figure 3.36 shows an example of such forces experienced by the ACL. The results indicate that the ACL force increased with the level of activation of the quadriceps femoris but that the range of motion over which the force acted remained the same for the different levels of activation. The model also demonstrated that coactivation of the hamstring muscles decreased the ACL force and the range of motion over which the ACL ligament was loaded. However, coactivation of the hamstrings increased the anterior force due to tibiofemoral contact and thus the anterior force applied by the patellar tendon.

Because the model has a few limitations, some of the predictions differ from experimental measurements (Pandy & Shelburne, 1997). Nonetheless, the advantage of modeling studies is that they can provide much more detail over a greater range of physiological conditions than can be examined experimentally. Furthermore, models can always be refined to obtain a better fit with existing experimental data, and then the predictions can be extrapolated to conditions that have not yet been tested.

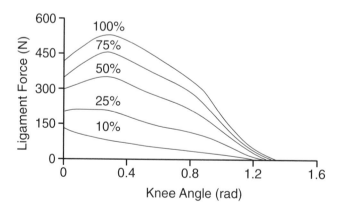

Figure 3.36   Anterior cruciate ligament force associated with isolated contractions of the quadriceps femoris. The knee joint is completely extended at 0 rad.

Data from Pandy and Shelburne, 1997.

Summary

This chapter focuses on the mechanical interactions that occur inside the human body when we perform movements. The purpose of the chapter is to describe the characteristics of these interactions, introduce the techniques used to analyze them, and provide detailed examples of how these within-body interactions can be estimated. We refer to the interactions as musculoskeletal forces, and four main ones are identified: joint reaction force, muscle force, elasticity of tendon and ligament, and the force due to intra-abdominal pressure. These forces occur among adjacent body segments and are associated with the rotation of one body segment relative to its neighbors. The first part of the chapter provides a description of the four musculoskeletal forces and explains how the magnitude and direction of each are estimated in the analysis of human movement. The second part of the chapter introduces the formal analysis techniques employed in biomechanics. Known as static and dynamic analyses, these are used to determine the quantitative details of a movement, including the magnitude and direction of unknown musculoskeletal forces. The final part of the chapter presents several detailed examples of use of these techniques to determine the force, torque, and power at selected joints in the human body during movement.

Suggested Readings

Hamill, J., & Knutzen, K.M. (1995). *Biomechanical basis of human movement.* Baltimore: Williams & Wilkins, chapter 12.

McGinnis, P.M. (1999). *Biomechanics of sport and exercise.* Champaign, IL: Human Kinetics, chapters 4, 12-14.

Nigg, B.M., MacIntosh, B.R., & Mester, J. *Biomechanics of biology and movement.* Champaign, IL: Human Kinetics, chapter 16.

Watkins, J. (1999). *Structure and function of the musculoskeletal system.* Champaign, IL: Human Kinetics, chapters 2 and 4.

Winter, D.A. (1990). *Biomechanics and motor control of human movement.* New York: Wiley, chapters 4 and 5.

Chapter 4

Reprinted from Marey, 1879.

Running, Jumping, and Throwing

Human movement can take a variety of forms, ranging from transporting the center of mass to the expression of emotions. Although there is some literature on the use of biomechanics to develop a taxonomy of postures and movements used in various activities, such as dance, the most common application of biomechanics has been to study the fundamental features of such activities as running, jumping, and throwing. The purpose of this chapter is to describe some of the biomechanical characteristics of these movements, which provides an opportunity to review and apply the concepts presented in chapters 1 to 3.

Walking and Running

Human gait involves alternating sequences in which the body is supported first by one limb, which contacts the ground, and then by the other limb. Human gait has two modes, walking and running. One distinction between these two modes lies in the percentage of each cycle during which the body is supported by foot contact with the ground. When we walk, there is always at least one foot on the ground; and for a brief period of each cycle, both feet are on the ground. Accordingly, walking can be characterized as an alternating sequence of single and double support. In contrast, running involves alternating sequences of support and nonsupport, with the proportion of the cycle spent in support varying with speed. For both walking and running, however, each limb experiences a sequence of support and nonsupport during a single cycle. The period of support is referred to as the **stance phase,** and nonsupport is known as the **swing phase.** The stance phase begins when the foot contacts the ground (footstrike), and ends when the foot leaves the ground (toe-off). Conversely, the swing phase extends from toe-off to footstrike. Gait cycles are usually defined relative to these events. For example, one complete cycle, such as from left foot toe-off to left foot toe-off, is defined as a **stride** (figure 4.1).

The stride contains two steps (figure 4.1). A **step** is defined as the part of the cycle from the toe-off (or footstrike) of one foot to the toe-off (or footstrike) of the other foot. Within a stride, there are four occurrences of footstrike and toe-off, two events for each limb. These are right footstrike, right toe-off, left footstrike, and left toe-off. Figure 4.1 shows the stance (shaded areas) and swing (open rectangles) for the right (R) and left (L) legs

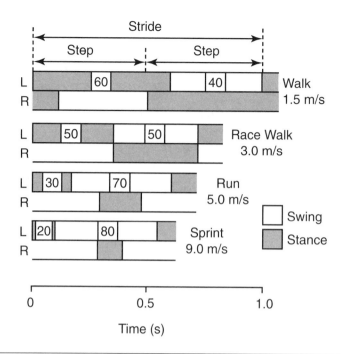

Figure 4.1   The events and phases characterizing walking and running gaits (R = right, L = left). The numbers in various rectangles indicate the relative duration (% stride) of that stance or swing phase.

Data from Vaughan, 1984.

during walking, race walking, running, and sprinting. During walking, each foot is on the ground (stance phase) for about 60% of the stride and off the ground (swing phase) for 40%. The duration of the stance phase decreases to 50% for race walking, 30% for running, and 20% for sprinting.

The absolute duration of the stride decreases with speed for both walking and running (figure 4.2a). The reduction in stride time is attributable mainly to a decrease in stance time, as the duration of the swing phase does not change much with speed (figure 4.2b). Although the speed-related decline in the absolute duration of the stance phase is greater with walking, the decrease in the relative duration (% stride time) is greater for running (figure 4.2c).

Stride Length and Rate

Running speed depends on two variables, stride length and stride rate (Vaughan, 1984; Weyand, Sternlight, Bellizzi, & Wright, 2000). For example, running speed increases if stride length remains constant and stride time decreases (i.e., stride rate increases). Similarly, speed increases if stride rate remains constant and stride length increases. Within certain limits, a number of length-rate combinations will produce a desired speed. The average combinations are shown in figure 4.3. For example, an individual running at a speed of 8 m/s uses a stride rate

of about 1.75 Hz and a stride length of about 4.6 m. Figure 4.3 illustrates that, on average, a runner increases speed over the range from 4 to 9 m/s by increasing stride rate continually, although more slowly (the slope is not that steep) at lower velocities, but does not increase stride length after about 8 m/s. Notice that the contribution of changes in stride length and stride rate to running velocity are different at low and high velocities; this is apparent by the differences in the slopes of the two curves (stride length and rate) at different velocities.

Based on the average data shown in figure 4.3, it appears that initial increases in running speed depend more on increases in stride length than on increases in stride rate. The relative contributions of stride length and stride rate are more obvious when the data are plotted in an *x-y* graph (stride rate vs. stride length), such as figure 4.4. For this graph, four subjects were studied while running at several speeds that ranged from 4 to 9 m/s. Each subject ran at 5 to 12 constant speeds using self-selected combinations of stride length and stride rate. Stride length was measured from footprints and stride rate from foot switches that indicated the stance phase. The combination chosen by each subject for a given speed is plotted as a small dot on figure 4.4.

Subject SU ran at speeds that ranged from 4.3 to 8.5 m/s. His initial changes in speed (4.3 to 7.0 m/s) were due to a combined increase in stride length (3.2 to 4.4 m) and stride rate (1.4 to 1.7 Hz). Based on the slope of the

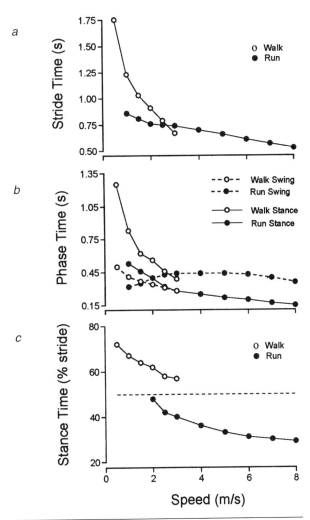

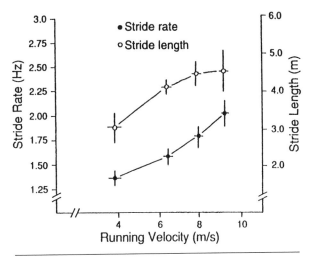

Figure 4.3 Average values of stride length and stride rate at four running velocities.

Data from Luhtanen and Komi, 1978.

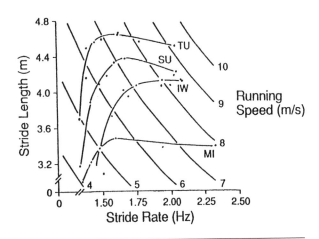

Figure 4.4 The relations among stride rate, stride length, and running speed.

Data from Saito, Kobayashi, Miyashita, and Hoshikawa, 1974.

Figure 4.2 *(a)* Changes in stride time and *(b)* the absolute and *(c)* relative durations of the stance and swing phases with speed for walking and running.

Adapted from Nilsson, Thorstensson, and Halbertsma, 1987 (part b).

length-rate relation over this range, changes in stride length were more significant for these initial increases in speed. Subsequently, SU increased speed (from 7.0 to 8.5 m/s) by slightly decreasing stride length (about 20 cm) and substantially increasing stride rate (from 1.7 to 2.0 Hz). In general, the trained runners (Subjects TU, SU, and IW) increased stride length up to 7.0 m/s, whereas the untrained runner (MI) did so only up to about 5.5 m/s. All four runners, however, achieved initial increases in speed (up to ~6.0 m/s) mainly by increasing stride length. Clearly, the combination of stride length and rate chosen to achieve a desired speed varies among runners. Furthermore, it seems that anthropometric variables (e.g., stature, leg length, limb segment mass) are not the primary determinants of preferred stride frequency and length (Cavanagh & Kram, 1989). The typical explanation given for this strategy (i.e., change in stride length rather than rate) is that it requires less energy to

lengthen the stride within reasonable limits than to increase stride rate (Cavagna, Mantovani, Willems, & Musch, 1997; Martin, Sanderson, & Umberger, 2000).

Angle-Angle Diagrams

Increases in stride length are accomplished by altering the kinematics of the limbs. The changes needed include both the range of motion about a joint (quantity) and the pattern of displacement (quality). For example, figure 4.5 shows that angular displacement about the knee joint increases as the runner goes from a walk to a run, and that the stance phase (indicated by the shaded horizontal bar) includes only knee flexion during a sprint but both

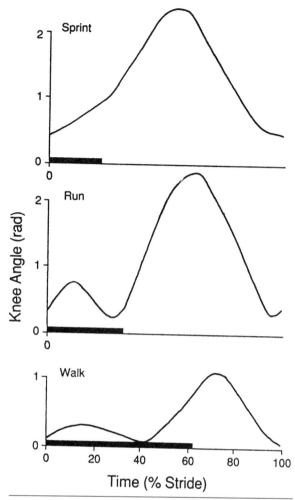

Figure 4.5 Knee angle during a stride for a sprint, run, and walk. A knee angle of 0 rad indicates complete extension. The shaded bar indicates the stance phase, from footstrike (left end) to toe-off (right end).

Adapted from Vaughan, 1984.

flexion and extension during walking and running. Similarly, as running speed increases, there is an increase in arm motion, which includes an increase in the range of motion about both the shoulder and elbow joints.

These changes in the quantity and quality of displacement with speed can be characterized with angle-angle diagrams (Hershler & Milner, 1980a, 1980b; Marey, 1879; Miller, 1978). When you examine angle-angle diagrams, the two features to focus on are the shape of the diagram and its location relative to reference angles. Figure 4.6 shows a typical thigh-knee angle-angle diagram for a person running at a moderate speed. The angles included on the diagram are indicated by the stick figure in the lower right portion of the figure. As described in chapter 1, these comprise an absolute angle (thigh angle with respect to the forward horizontal) and a relative angle (knee angle as the included angle between the thigh and

the shank). Three reference angles are included on the diagram, one for the thigh and two for the knee. The reference angle for the thigh is $3/2\ \pi$ rad, which indicates when the thigh is vertical. The reference angles for the knee indicate an extended knee joint (π rad) and the knee joint flexed to a right angle ($\pi/2$ rad). According to the location of the thigh-knee diagram in figure 4.6, the thigh rotates in front of and behind the thigh-vertical position, while the knee is never completely extended but is flexed to more than a right angle.

The shape of an angle-angle diagram indicates the relation between the included angles throughout the movement. For cyclic activities, the diagram indicates the angles during a single cycle, which corresponds to one stride for walking and running. These angles change in a counterclockwise direction on the thigh-knee diagram for walking and running. The interpretation of the shape of the diagram is aided by the possibility of including the location of specific events, such as footstrike and toe-off, on the diagram. Figure 4.6 includes the location of footstrike and toe-off for both the right and left legs. Because figure 4.6 shows the thigh and knee angles for the left leg, the stance phase includes the region for left footstrike (LFS) to left toe-off (LTO). The inclusion of right footstrike (RFS) and right toe-off (RTO) indicates the thigh and knee angles of the left leg when these events occurred.

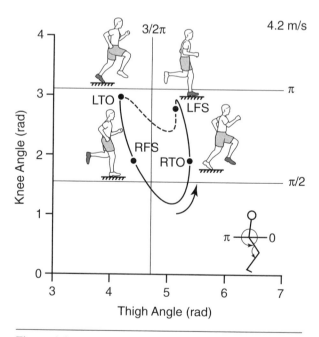

Figure 4.6 Thigh-knee diagram of the left leg of a person running at 4.2 m/s. The left foot has the black shoe.

Reprinted from Enoka, Miller, and Burgess, 1982.

LFS = left footstrike; LTO = left toe-off; RFS = right footstrike; RTO = right toe-off.

The shape of the thigh-knee diagram from left leg footstrike to toe-off (stance phase—dotted line) comprises two parts. First, the knee angle decreases (flexion) while the thigh angle does not change. Second, the knee angle increases (extension) while the thigh angle decreases (backward rotation). From left leg toe-off to footstrike (swing phase—solid line), the angular displacement again comprises two distinct parts. First, from LTO to the minimum knee angle, the thigh angle increases (forward rotation) and the knee angle decreases (flexion). Second, from the minimum knee angle through to LFS, the knee angle increases (extension) while the thigh rotates slightly forward and then backward.

Although it is sometimes useful to dissect the angular displacement of an angle-angle diagram, the most useful feature of this type of diagram is as a template for comparing the coordination of a movement across conditions and between subjects. In contrast to this typical thigh-knee diagram, the three graphs for subjects with below-knee amputations depicted in figure 4.7 indicate a substantial difference during the stance phase (i.e., the region from LFS to LTO). Specifically, the amputee thigh-knee diagrams reveal a knee joint pattern of a constant angle followed by flexion rather than the normal flexion-extension sequence evident in figure 4.6. Because figure 4.7 shows the thigh-knee diagrams for the prosthetic limbs of the below-knee amputees, the pattern of the graphs is perhaps not surprising. This failure to flex the knee during stance, shown in figure 4.7 by the lack of a decrease in the knee angle immediately after footstrike, means that the amputees just used their limbs as a rigid

strut about which to rotate while the prosthetic foot was on the ground. This type of graphic display could be used in a clinical setting to monitor a rehabilitation program aimed at modifying this strategy so that the gait would appear more symmetrical. Similarly, angle-angle diagrams can be used to indicate the reduced coordination of various patient populations, such as those with cerebellar ataxia (Palliyath, Hallett, Thomas, & Lebiedowska, 1998).

Angle-angle diagrams have also been used to represent the kinematics of the arms during running. Because the motion of the arms is frequently not confined to the sagittal plane during running, imaging techniques that can capture three-dimensional motion are necessary. With use of these techniques, the displacement of the upper arm about the shoulder and the relative angle between the upper and lower arms (elbow angle) for an individual running at 11.4 m/s have the form shown in figure 4.8. A positive shoulder angle indicates flexion (forward of vertical) and a negative one represents extension (backward of vertical), whereas an elbow angle of 0 rad corresponds to complete extension. The amplitude and timing of the displacement vary as a function of running speed (Lusby & Atwater, 1983).

Although figure 4.8 includes information on the timing of the displacement at the two angles, an angle-angle diagram can present this information more succinctly (figure 4.9). Essentially, the pattern of displacement about the shoulder and elbow joints is confined to the upper right and lower left quadrants of the angle-angle diagram. The upper right quadrant represents concurrent shoulder

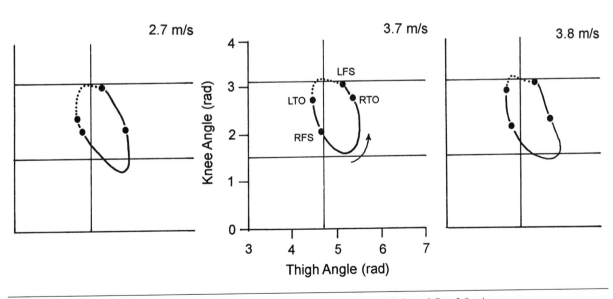

Figure 4.7 Thigh-knee diagrams for three below-knee amputees running at speeds from 2.7 to 3.8 m/s.

Reprinted from Enoka, Miller, and Burgess, 1982.

LFS = left footstrike; LTO = left toe-off; RFS = right footstrike; RTO = right toe-off.

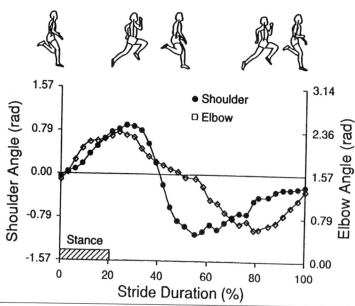

Figure 4.8   Displacement about the right shoulder and elbow joints during a sprinting stride. A shoulder angle of 0 rad indicates a vertical position of the upper arm; positive angles correspond to forward rotation (flexion). An elbow angle of 0 rad represents complete extension.

Reprinted from Li and Atwater, 1984.

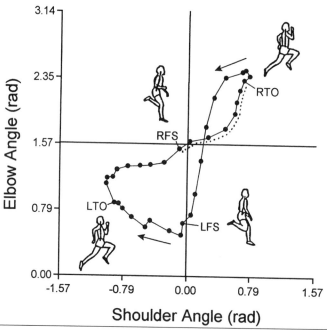

Figure 4.9   Shoulder-elbow angle-angle diagram based on the data shown in figure 4.8.
Reprinted from Li and Atwater, 1984.

LFS = left footstrike; LTO = left toe-off; RFS = right footstrike; RTO = right toe-off.

and elbow flexion, whereas the lower quadrant indicates concurrent shoulder and elbow extension. The stance phase of the right leg (RFS to RTO) is accompanied mainly by concurrent extension at the two joints. But the pattern is not one of a tight coupling of the two actions (i.e., flexion or extension), because there are instances in which opposing motion occurs at the two joints. Can you see where this occurs in figure 4.9? One example is in the phase from LFS to LTO when the shoulder extends and the elbow flexes. The shoulder-elbow angle-angle diagrams, like those for the leg, provide a qualitative means to evaluate the coordination of the movement.

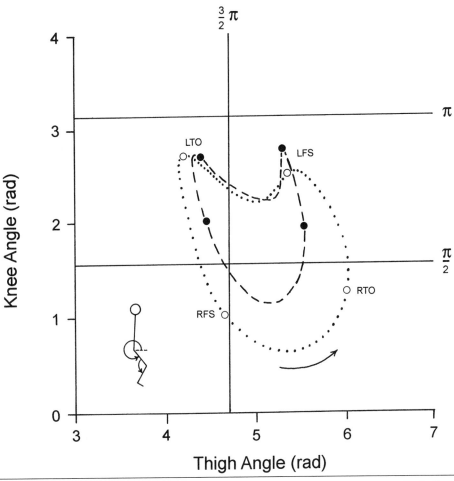

Figure 4.10   Thigh-knee angle-angle diagrams for a person running at 3.9 m/s (dashed line) and at 7.6 m/s (dotted line). Data from Miller et al., 1979.

LFS = left footstrike; LTO = left toe-off; RFS = right footstrike; RTO = right toe-off.

Another useful feature of these cyclic angle-angle diagrams is that, in addition to shape comparisons, the size of the diagram indicates the range of motion experienced at each joint during the event. For example, we would expect increases in stride length as a runner increases speed to be due to changes in the range of motion (amount of motion) at various lower-extremity joints. Figure 4.10 confirms this expectation by showing that as speed increases (3.9 to 7.6 m/s), the amount of rotation of the thigh and about the knee joint increases; the larger angle-angle diagram represents the faster speed.

Ground Reaction Force

The ground reaction force represents the response of the ground (support surface) to the actions of the body segments. It represents the resultant effect of these actions and so corresponds to the acceleration experienced by the center of mass of the body.

As shown in figure 2.11, the $F_{g,y}$ curve has two peaks for walking but usually a single peak for running (Alexander, 1984b). The reason for this difference is the action of the leg during the stance phase. When we run, the knee flexes during the first part of the stance phase (figure 4.6) to counter the downward displacement of the center of mass, which reaches a minimum near the middle of the stance phase. Subsequently, the knee extends to project the body upward by the end of the stance phase. Throughout the stance phase of running, however, the knee extensor muscles (quadriceps femoris) and the plantarflexor muscles (soleus and gastrocnemius) are active (Dietz, Schmidtbleicher, & Noth, 1979; Mero & Komi, 1987); this accelerates the center of mass in an upward direction. Because the entire stance phase comprises net muscle activity in the direction of extension, the reaction of the ground is a single-peaked curve.

In walking, in contrast, the knee joint essentially remains extended; the knee joint flexes only slightly (figure 4.5). For simplicity, we can assume that the knee remains extended, which means that the leg is used as a rigid strut during the stance phase; this is known as the **inverted-pendulum model** of walking. As a consequence, the center of mass (approximately the hip joint) follows the arc of a circle during the stance phase as the leg rotates about the ankle joint (Alexander, 1984b). When the hip joint is over the foot, therefore, the center of mass is at its maximum height, and the forward horizontal velocity is at a minimum, but not zero (figure 4.11). This produces a minimum in the $F_{g,y}$ curve in the middle of the stance phase. So during running, the center of mass reaches a minimum vertical position near the middle of

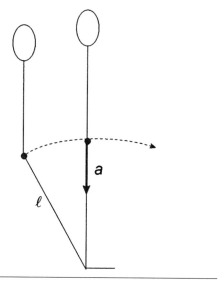

Figure 4.11 Path of the hip joint during the stance phase of walking, based on the simplification that the leg (*l*) remains straight.

Data from Alexander, 1984b.

the stance phase whereas it reaches a maximum at about the same point during walking (Cavagna, Thys, & Zamboni, 1976). This is another way to distinguish between the two gaits (McMahon, Valiant, & Frederick, 1987). Overweight individuals often "run" without an aerial phase; and when most people run slowly or when they run in place, the stance phase constitutes more than 50% of the stride time. Yet clearly, by the center-of-mass definition they are still running.

Munro et al. (1987) characterized some of the changes in running gait as the speed of 20 men increased from 3.0 to 5.0 m/s. They found that, on average, the stance time decreased from 270 to 199 ms, the peak $F_{g,y}$ increased from 2.51 to 2.83 times body weight, and the average force during the stance phase increased from 1.4 to 1.7 times body weight. These results indicated that speed was increased from 3.0 to 5.0 m/s by applying a greater $F_{g,y}$ over a shorter duration (figure 4.12). The average force for both the braking and propulsion directions of $F_{g,x}$ also increased with running speed, although the *net* forward-backward impulse was zero because the running speeds were constant. Similar findings were reported by Nilsson and Thorstensson (1989) over the range from 1.0 to 6.0 m/s and by Weyand et al. (2000) over a range from 6.2 to 11.1 m/s.

Given the association between stance duration and the peak value of $F_{g,y}$ (figure 4.12), Breit and Whalen (1997) examined the relation between temporal measures of foot-ground contact and the ground reaction force. For 218 walking steps and 199 running steps, they found that the magnitude of the ground reaction force components increased with gait speed. There was a strong association between the magnitude of the peak forces (vertical and forward-backward components) and the reciprocal of stance duration for both walking (0.91-2.34 m/s) and run-

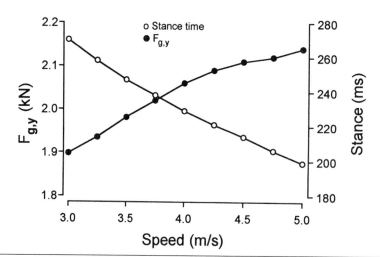

Figure 4.12 Change in the maximum $F_{g,y}$ and stance time with running speed.

ning (1.78-5.9 m/s). The best predictor of the peak verti-cal force $(F_{g,y})$, expressed relative to body weight (BW), was the ratio of stride duration (T) to stance duration (t_c). The regression equation for running was:

$$\text{peak } F_{g,y} \text{ (BW)} = 0.856\frac{T}{t_c} + 0.089 \qquad (4.1)$$

As explained by Breit and Whalen (1997), this is a useful relation because it enables us to estimate the daily loading history of the musculoskeletal system by mea-suring durations rather than the ground reaction force.

Example 4.1
Maximum Walking Speed

The inverted-pendulum model of leg function (figure 4.11) during walking provides a reasonable estimate of the maximum walking speed that a human can achieve (Alexander, 1984b). Suppose the center of mass has a constant linear velocity v and the length of the leg is denoted by l, then the angular velocity of the leg can be obtained from Equation 1.9:

$$\omega = \frac{v}{l}$$

Furthermore, the acceleration experienced by the hip joint (center of mass) during the stance phase is equal to the effect that causes the hip to move along the arc of a circle. This is the component of accelera-tion that accounts for the change in direction of the linear velocity vector, which produces Equation 1.12:

$$a = \frac{v^2}{l}$$

From the peak vertical position of the hip joint (hip over the foot) through to toe-off, the maximum verti-cal acceleration experienced by the center of mass is that due to gravity (g). Thus,

$$g = \frac{v^2}{l}$$
$$v \le \sqrt{gl}$$

For an adult with a leg length (hip to ground) of 0.85 m (McMahon et al., 1987), this equation sug-gests that the maximum walking speed is

$$v = \sqrt{9.81 \times 0.85}$$
$$v = 2.9 \text{ m/s}$$

This value is slightly faster than the acknowledged speed (2.0 m/s) when adults switch from a walk to a run. Furthermore, the model also explains why people with shorter legs, such as children, cannot walk as fast as adults.

Walk-Run Transition

On the basis of the inverted-pendulum model of walking (Alexander, 1984b; Cavagna, Heglund, & Taylor, 1977), the major force acting on the body during walking is grav-ity, which causes the center of mass to be accelerated downward (a in figure 4.11) throughout the stance phase. This provides a centripetal force (Equation 1.12) that enables the center of mass to follow a circular path dur-ing the stance phase. This centripetal force is equal to body mass (m) times acceleration

$$\text{Centripetal force} = \frac{mv^2}{l} \qquad (4.2)$$

as described in Example 4.1. Thus, the maximum speed at which we can walk (v) and still maintain the circular path for the center of mass is limited by gravity.

$$\frac{mv^2}{l} \le mg$$

The ratio of these two forces is defined as the **Froude number,** which is described as dimensionless speed (Kram, Domingo, & Ferris, 1997).

$$\text{Froude number} = \frac{mv^2/l}{mg} = \frac{v^2}{gl} \qquad (4.3)$$

We cannot walk at Froude numbers greater than 1.0, because that would mean the centripetal force would exceed the gravitational force. Interestingly, many bipeds, including humans and birds, prefer to switch from a walk to a run at a Froude number of ~0.5 (Gatesy & Biewener, 1991). This indicates that the different speeds (v) at which bipeds change from a walk to a run depend mainly on differences in leg length (l).

To test this simple model, Kram et al. (1997) deter-mined the speed of the walk-run transition when they approximated a reduction in the acceleration due to grav-ity. They accomplished the gravity reduction by partially supporting body weight with a suspension harness. Based on the definition of a Froude number (v^2/gl), the speed of the walk-run transition (v) should decrease if the accel-eration due to gravity declines so that the Froude num-ber remains constant at ~0.5. The results of the experi-ment indicated that the transition speed did decline with

Table 4.1   Speed of the Walk-Run Transition for Variations in Acceleration Due to Gravity

Gravity (g)	Transition speed (m/s)	Froude number	Predicted speed (m/s)
1.0	1.98	0.45	1.98
0.8	1.84	0.49	1.77
0.6	1.65	0.53	1.54
0.5	1.55	0.56	1.40
0.4	1.39	0.56	1.25
0.2	1.18	0.83	0.89
0.1	0.97	1.13	0.63

Note. The predicted transition speed was based on a Froude number of 0.45 and a leg length (λ) of 0.89 m.

Data from Kram et al., 1997.

a reduction in the acceleration due to gravity *(g)*, but only down to *g* values of 0.4 (table 4.1). Kram et al. (1997) found that at the lowest *g* values, the acceleration due to the swinging arms and legs contributed significantly to the task of walking, so gravity was not the only force acting on an individual (Donelan & Kram, 2000). As a consequence, it appears that the inverted-pendulum model provides a reasonable explanation of the walk-run transition, although other factors can also influence the transition.

Leg Spring Stiffness

Running and hopping have been characterized as actions that enable an individual to move along the ground much like a bouncing ball (Cavagna, Saibene, & Margaria, 1964; Farley, Houdijk, van Strien, & Louie, 1998). To accomplish such an action, our legs behave as if they were springs, such that the human body can be modeled as a **spring-mass system** (Arampatzis, Brüggemann, & Metzler, 1999; McMahon & Cheng, 1990). The spring is compressed during the first half of the stance phase and rebounds during the second half (figure 4.13). Although the leg spring model gets shorter during the stance phase, the actual anatomical springs (i.e., tendons) in fact get longer. The rotation of the leg segments, in combination with the connective tissue, acts like compression springs but is not actually compressed. The mechanical characteristics of the spring are expressed as leg stiffness (Example 4.2). The magnitude of leg stiffness, which we can adjust, influences the duration of the stance phase and the vertical displacement of the center of mass during the stance phase. This capability enables a person to

use a range of stride rates and stride lengths to run at a given speed (Farley & Gonzalez, 1996). Furthermore, subjects tend to change leg stiffness when running on surfaces of different stiffness (e.g., concrete floor vs. rubber mats) so that the total vertical stiffness (leg stiffness + surface stiffness) remains constant. Regulation of the total vertical stiffness enables a person to use similar running mechanics on different surfaces, such as a constant stance-phase duration, stride rate, and vertical displacement of the center of mass (Ferris, Louie, & Farley, 1998; Ferris, Liang, & Farley, 1999).

Leg stiffness in running depends on the level of muscle activity and the geometry of the leg when the foot contacts the ground. The effect of varying muscle activity is to alter the stiffness at a joint. Previously we discussed linear springs, such as tendons, ligaments, and therapeutic bands. There are also angular springs, which are usually referred to as **torsional springs.** A common example of a torsional spring is a snapping mousetrap. These springs resist angular displacement because of their property of angular stiffness (κ). For example, when muscles perform eccentric contractions, they resist the angular displacement caused by a load and therefore act as torsional springs. This occurs during the first half of the stance phase of running when the leg spring is compressed

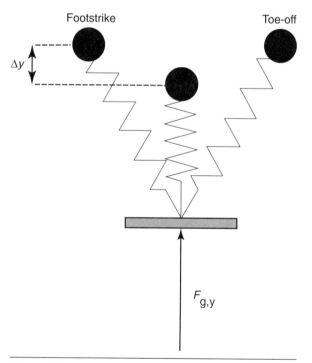

Figure 4.13   A spring-mass model of the human body at three points during the stance phase of running. The large filled circles represent body mass; the spring indicates the leg. Compression of the leg spring is indicated by the vertical displacement (Δy) of body mass.

Data from Ferris et al., 1998.

and the leg extensor muscles (ankle, knee, and hip) perform eccentric contractions. Because of this relation, leg stiffness depends on the quantity of muscle activity about each joint, which we can determine by performing a dynamic analysis (chapter 3) to calculate the resultant muscle torque (Arampatzis et al., 1999).

The other factor that influences leg stiffness in running is the orientation of the leg at footstrike. By varying leg geometry, this alters the perpendicular distance (moment arm) from the line of action of the ground reaction force vector to each of the major joints (McMahon et al., 1987). The product of the ground reaction force and moment arm corresponds to the load that the muscles must counteract (Glitsch & Baumann, 1997). Figure 4.14 shows that increasing knee flexion by 0.35 rad (20°) at footstrike results in a markedly different load torque about the knee and hip. For a given joint stiffness, for example, a greater load torque (ground reaction force × moment arm) produces a greater angular displacement. This occurs during Groucho running, which involves an exaggerated knee flexion posture (McMahon et al., 1987).

To examine the relative contributions of joint stiffness and leg geometry to variation in leg stiffness, Farley et al. (1998) studied humans hopping on surfaces of different stiffness. The behavior of the leg spring was charac-

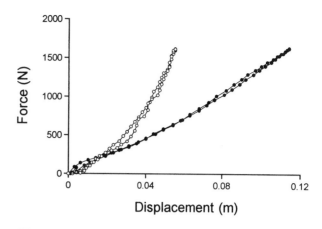

Figure 4.15 The change in leg length and the vertical component of the ground reaction force for a subject hopping in place on two surfaces with differing stiffness (filled circles = most stiff; open circles = least stiff).

Data from Farley et al., 1998.

terized by plotting the vertical component of the ground reaction force against the change in leg length. The bottom left corner of the graph (figure 4.15) represents the moment that the foot contacted the ground, after which the length of the leg spring decreased and $F_{g,y}$ increased. Peak $F_{g,y}$ occurred when the leg spring was maximally compressed. The slope of this relation (Δl and $F_{g,y}$) indicates the stiffness of the leg spring (N/m). The stiffness of the leg spring was least when subjects hopped on the stiffest surface. For the subject shown in figure 4.15, leg stiffness went from 14.3 kN/m on the stiffest surface to 29.4 kN/m on the least-stiff surface.

To determine how subjects changed leg stiffness, Farley et al. (1998) calculated joint stiffness when the subjects hopped on the different surfaces. **Joint stiffness** was determined as the ratio of the change in resultant muscle torque to the angular displacement (N·m/rad):

$$\kappa = \frac{\Delta \tau_m}{\Delta \theta} \qquad (4.4)$$

On the basis of experimental measurements and a computer model, the investigators found that the stiffness of the ankle joint had the greatest effect on leg stiffness for this task. Ankle stiffness changed from 396 N·m/rad on the stiffest surface to 687 N·m/rad on the least-stiff surface, accounting for 75% of the change in leg stiffness. Farley et al. also found that subjects flexed the knee by 0.16 rad when going from the least to the most stiff surface; this changed the moment arm for $F_{g,y}$ relative to the knee joint from 0.001 m to 0.054 m. This change in leg geometry caused the leg stiffness to change from 17.1 to 22.2 kN/m. Of these two factors, changes in the stiffness of the ankle joint had the greater effect on the variation

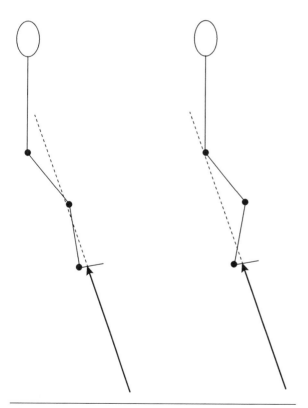

Figure 4.14 Changes in leg geometry at footstrike alter the load torque about each joint.

in leg stiffness, at least for hopping in place. The role of leg geometry may be more significant in running, where it appears that stiffness about the knee joint has the greatest effect on changes in leg stiffness (Arampatzis et al., 1999).

Example 4.2
Spring Stiffness of the Leg

The calculation of leg stiffness for such studies as those shown in figure 4.15 involves the application of rules from geometry, trigonometry, and calculus to a few experimental measurements (Ferris et al., 1998). The required measurements include leg length (l; distance from the greater trochanter to the ground), the vertical component of the ground reaction force ($F_{g,y}$), and the speed of the runner (v). From these data, it is possible to determine leg stiffness (k_{leg}) from Equation 3.2:

$$k_{leg} = \frac{\text{peak } F_{g,y}}{\Delta l} \qquad (4.5)$$

where peak $F_{g,y}$ refers to the maximum amplitude of the vertical component of the ground reaction force and Δl indicates the change in leg length from footstrike to the middle of the stance phase. The change in leg length corresponds to the extent to which the spring is compressed (figure 4.13); this can be calculated from the following geometric relations.

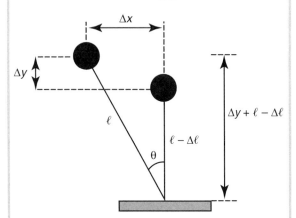

The length of the leg in the midstance position is equal to leg length (l) minus the length the leg has shortened due to flexion at the ankle, knee, and hip joints (Δl). The angle (θ) represents the angular displacement of the leg about the ankle joint from footstrike through to midstance. From trigonometry we have,

$$\cos \theta = \frac{\Delta y + l - \Delta l}{l}$$
$$\Delta l = \Delta y + l - l \cos \theta$$

This expression is for the simplest case, when an individual runs on a rigid surface; if the surface is not rigid, then an additional Δy term must be added to account for the compliance of the surface (Ferris et al., 1998). The vertical displacement of the center of mass (Δy) can be determined by double integration (calculus) of the vertical acceleration of the center of mass, which was obtained from $F_{g,y}$ after subtraction of the subject's weight and division by body mass (figure 2.5). θ can be determined from

$$\theta = \sin^{-1} \frac{\Delta x}{l}$$

The horizontal displacement of the center of mass (Δx) can be calculated with Equation 1.1. This involves multiplying the average horizontal velocity (v) by one-half of the stance-phase duration, that is, the time it took for the leg to rotate from footstrike through to midstance. The duration of the stance phase can be measured from the ground reaction force record. With these procedures, it is possible to determine the average spring stiffness of the leg during the stance phase of running.

Energy Fluctuations

Most often when we walk or run, we pay little attention to either the length or the rate of the strides that we use to achieve a particular speed. If we do experiments with different combinations of stride length and rate, it becomes obvious that there is one combination that seems to require the least effort to achieve the desired speed. To assess the validity of this perception, biomechanists determine the energy costs needed to perform the work of walking and running at different speeds.

Most of the work done during walking and running is used to displace the center of mass in the vertical (U_v) and forward (U_f) directions (Cavagna et al., 1976). These two components are sometimes referred to as **external work,** to distinguish them from the work (internal) done to move the limbs (Fenn, 1930). The mechanical energy used to perform external work is derived from the kinetic (E_k) and potential ($E_{p,g}$) energy of the center of mass. In the vertical direction, the amount of work done (U_v) depends on the change in both $E_{k,v}$ and $E_{p,g}$. In the forward direction, however, the amount of work done (U_f) depends only on the change in $E_{k,f}$. Because the fluctuations in $E_{k,v}$ are so small compared with those of the other two energy terms, $E_{k,v}$ is often neglected. Thus the total mechanical energy of the center of mass (E_{cm}) is mainly due to the sum of $E_{p,g}$ and $E_{k,f}$ (figure 4.16).

One of the features that distinguishes walking and running is the trajectory of the center of mass during the stance phase. The vertical position of the center of mass reaches a maximum in midstance during walking but a minimum at the same point during running. This distinction influences the contributions of the energy fluctuations to the external work done on the center of mass.

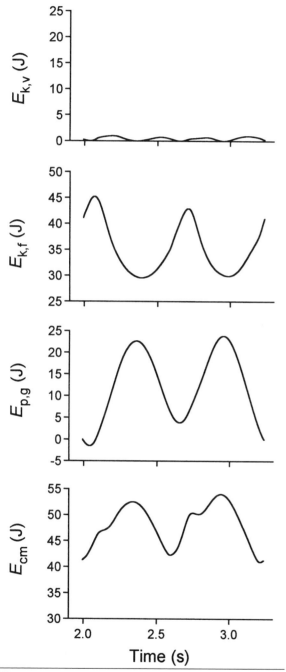

Figure 4.16 Fluctuations in mechanical energy of the center of mass within one stride (two support phases) during walking. Note that the gravitational potential energy ($E_{p,g}$) reaches a minimum when the forward kinetic energy ($E_{k,f}$) is at a maximum, resulting in a sum (E_{cm}) that fluctuates less than the individual components. Fluctuations in E_{cm} indicate the external work done on the center of mass.

Data from Griffin, Tolani, and Kram, 1999.

When the knee is kept extended and the leg is used as a strut during walking, $E_{p,g}$ reaches a maximum and $E_{k,f}$ achieves a minimum at midstance (Cavagna & Franzetti, 1986). The fluctuations in $E_{p,g}$ and $E_{k,f}$ are inversely related (figure 4.16); and, as with the exchange of energy in Example 2.17, some of the change in $E_{p,g}$ results from the forward motion of the body ($E_{k,f}$) and some of the change in $E_{k,f}$ is produced by changes in the vertical position of the center of mass ($E_{p,g}$). Because of this interaction, human walking has been described as an inverted pendulum in which the center of mass rises to a peak during the stance phase and then falls forward (Cavagna et al., 1976; Cavagna, Willems, & Huglund, 2000).

The amount of energy that is exchanged between potential and kinetic energy can be quantified as the percentage of energy that is recovered (% recovery). To calculate this we subtract the external work from the work done in the vertical and forward directions (Cavagna et al., 1976):

$$\% \text{ recovery} = \frac{U_v + U_f - U_e}{U_v + U_f} \cdot 100 \qquad (4.6)$$

The amount of mechanical energy recovered during walking at intermediate speeds is about 65%, compared with < 5% in running (Cavagna et al., 1976). The % recovery is greatest when U_v and U_f are similar, which occurs at intermediate walking speeds. At lower ($U_v > U_f$) and higher ($U_v < U_f$) speeds, the external work increases and the % recovery declines. Similarly, when reductions in gravity are simulated by means of partial support of body weight, the % recovery decreases as the amount of body-weight support increases, and the speed at which maximum recovery occurs declines with an increase in support (Griffin, Tolani, & Kram, 1999).

Example 4.3

Ground Reaction Force and Energy Fluctuations

The energy fluctuations during walking and running can be calculated based on the measurement of the ground reaction force during the stance phase (Cavagna, 1975). We know from chapter 2 that the necessary equations are:

$$E_{p,g} = mgh$$
$$E_{k,f} = \tfrac{1}{2}mv_f^2$$

For the fluctuations in gravitational potential energy ($E_{p,g}$), we need to obtain the mass of the subject (m), the acceleration due to gravity (g), and the position of

(continued)

the subject's center of mass *(h)* throughout the stance phase. For the fluctuations in the forward kinetic energy $(E_{k,f})$, we need *m* and the forward velocity (v_f) of the center of mass during the stance phase.

From Newton's law of acceleration *(F = ma)*, we know that the acceleration of the center of mass depends on the mass of the person and the forces acting on the body; that is,

$$a = \frac{F}{m}$$

In the forward-backward direction during walking and running, the only significant force acting in this direction is the ground reaction force $(F_{g,x})$. As a result, the forward velocity of the center of mass in this direction (v_x) can be obtained by integrating the forward-backward acceleration:

$$v_x(t) = \int \frac{F_{g,x}}{m} dt + c \qquad (4.7)$$

where *c* represents the integration constant, which is the average velocity of the person's center of mass, and the limits of integration are the beginning and end of the stance phase. Once the velocity of the center of mass has been determined in the forward-backward direction, the kinetic energy of the center of mass in this direction can be calculated as a function of time:

$$E_{k,f}(t) = \frac{m}{2}\left[v_x(t)\right]^2 \qquad (4.8)$$

Similarly, the vertical position of the center of mass *(h)* can be obtained from the double integration of acceleration in the vertical direction. Because there are two significant forces in the vertical direction, the term for acceleration is a little more involved:

$$v_y(t) = \int \frac{F_{g,y} - F_w}{m} dt + c_1 \qquad (4.9)$$

In this instance, c_i is set so that the average vertical velocity is zero over one stride. Variations in vertical height *(h)* are obtained from the integration of $v_y(t)$.

$$h(t) = \int v_y dt + c_2 \qquad (4.10)$$

and c_2 is set so that the average displacement is zero. Fluctuations in the potential energy due to gravity $(E_{p,g})$ of the center of mass are calculated from

$$E_{p,g}(t) = mgh(t) \qquad (4.11)$$

These procedures are shown graphically in figure 4.17.

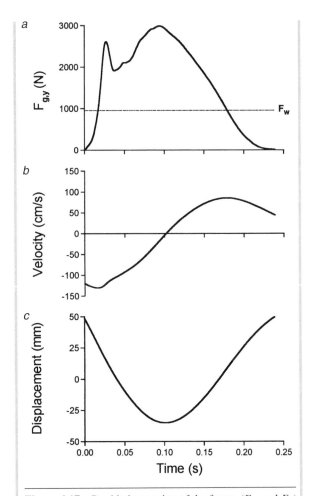

Figure 4.17   Double integration of the forces $(F_{g,y}$ and $F_w)$ acting in the vertical direction during *(a)* the stance phase of running to yield *(b)* the vertical velocity of the center of mass and then *(c)* the vertical position of the center of mass.

Energy Cost

If we run a short distance several times at various speeds, it is evident that the rate at which we consume energy increases as we run faster. This is obvious by the increases in heart rate, ventilation rate, and the rate of oxygen consumption when we run faster. The increase in the rate of energy expenditure appears to be due mainly to the increase in the intensity of muscle activity that is needed to run faster. In general, the muscle activity during walking and running serves two major functions: to support body weight and to generate a propulsive impulse (Kram, 2000). Because the magnitude of the vertical component of the ground reaction force is much greater than the forward-backward component (figure 2.12), most of the metabolic energy expended during running is used to support body weight.

Three types of experiments have been performed to determine the contributions of body-weight support to the metabolic energy needs during locomotion. These studies have included measuring the metabolic cost of locomotion (rate of oxygen consumption) when extra mass is added, when gravity is reduced, and when species of different size locomote at various speeds (Cavagna et al., 2000; Farley & McMahon, 1992; Kram & Taylor, 1990; Taylor, Heglund, McMahon, & Looney, 1980). The general conclusion from these studies is that the magnitude of the vertical component of the ground reaction force is a major determinant of the metabolic cost during running at a constant speed. For example, when Farley and McMahon (1992) simulated a reduction in gravity by providing partial support of body weight, they found a linear relation between the metabolic cost of running (≤ 3 m/s) and the average amplitude of the vertical component of the ground reaction force.

Similarly, the amount of time that the leg muscles have to generate the necessary force seems to be directly related to the metabolic cost of locomotion. Kram and Taylor (1990) measured the rate of oxygen consumption and stance time when various species ran at a range of steady state speeds. The animals ranged from kangaroo rats (32 g) to ponies (141 kg). Kram and Taylor found, as expected, that the rate of oxygen consumption increased with running speed. Furthermore, as we noted previously with humans (figure 4.12), stance time decreased with running speed. The ratio of these two measures, which represents a **cost coefficient,** was nearly constant across speed. This meant that much of the increase in metabolic cost was explained by the decrease in stance time—that is, the intensity of muscle activity.

As Chang and Kram (1999) point out, however, when we run with a tailwind or into a head wind, it is obvious that there is a change in the metabolic cost of running. To examine this effect, Chang and Kram applied horizontal forces to runners on a treadmill that aided or impeded the task of running at a constant speed (3.3 m/s). The effect of this intervention was to modify the relative magnitudes of the braking and propulsive impulses in the forward-backward direction. The force that impeded running was similar to a head wind, which caused an increase in the propulsive impulse (figure 4.18). Conversely, a force that aided the runner was similar to a tailwind and produced an increase in the braking impulse. By comparing the rate of oxygen consumption with changes in the propulsive impulse, Chang and Kram concluded that the muscle activity associated with generating the propulsive impulse accounts for about 30% of the metabolic energy we use when running at slow speeds.

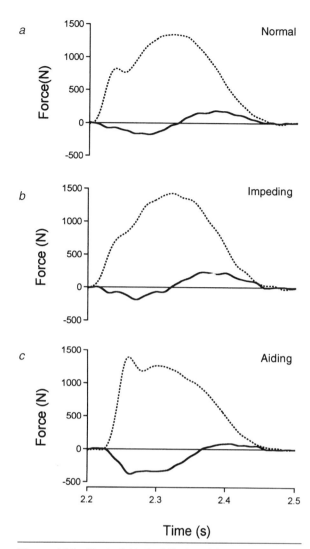

Figure 4.18 Vertical (dashed line) and forward-backward (solid line) components of the ground reaction force during running at 3.3 m/s under *(a)* normal conditions, *(b)* with an impeding horizontal force, and *(c)* with an aiding horizontal force. The magnitudes of the braking (negative) and propulsion (positive) impulses change with the presence of applied horizontal forces.

Data from Chang and Kram, 1999.

Gait Disorders

Because orthopedic and neurological impairments are often expressed as movement disturbances before they can be detected by the physical signs and symptoms obtained in a clinical examination, many institutions have established movement-disorders clinics to assist with the management of patients (Hallett et al., 1994). A central feature of such clinics is the biomechanical assessment of gait, often including the measurement of whole-body kinematics, the recording of EMG activity from leg muscles, and the evaluation of contact forces between the feet and the ground. The performance of patients can be compared with that of healthy persons, and inferences can be made about the locus of the impairment in the motor system (Dietz, 1997).

Much is known about the control of locomotion by the nervous system (Grillner, 1981; Pearson & Gordon, 2000a; Rossignol, 1996, 2000; Wetzel & Stuart, 1976), and this facilitates the identification of sites that might be responsible for a movement disorder. Neuronal circuits located in the spinal cord generate the essential rhythm of locomotion. The rhythm comprises alternating activation of the flexor and extensor muscles of the leg. The output generated by these circuits specifies the timing and intensity of the muscle activity required for the movement. These stereotypic patterns of muscle activity are modulated by information that is sent back to the spinal cord from peripheral sensory receptors to ensure that the activation pattern can accommodate variations in the surroundings. Furthermore, descending commands from more rostral parts of the nervous system (e.g., brainstem, cerebellum, and motor cortex) can modify both the stereotypic patterns and the sensory feedback.

Studies on patients with Parkinson's disease, spasticity, and paraplegia illustrate the utility of this approach (Dietz, 1997). Parkinson's disease comprises an impairment of the basal ganglia, a group of nuclei involved in planning movements that project to locomotor centers in the brainstem. The function of the basal ganglia is impaired in Parkinson's disease because of the depletion of a neurotransmitter (dopamine). One of the earliest signs of the disease is a decrease in the speed of locomotion and a reduction in the range of motion about the joints of the legs. The result is a rigid and poorly modulated gait that comprises small, shuffling steps. From these signs, it is evident that the dysfunction involves a problem with the regulation by descending commands and a reduced modulation by sensory feedback. Not only can gait studies be used as a diagnostic tool; they can also be used to monitor the effectiveness of various therapeutic interventions. For patients with Parkinson's disease, gait studies can provide an evaluation of L-dopa medication (Blin, Ferrandez, Pailhouse, & Serratrice, 1991), which facilitates the replacement of the missing neurotransmitter.

Spasticity is a disorder that results from a lesion in the brain or spinal cord. The symptoms of spasticity include exaggerated reflexes, clonus, and muscle hypertonia. Clonus involves the repeated rapid contraction and relaxation of a passively stretched muscle, whereas muscle hypertonia refers to the reflex resistance of a muscle to stretch, which varies with the speed of the stretch. The physical signs of spasticity are largely unrelated to a patient's disability, which is a movement disorder (Dietz, 1997; Perry, 1993). For example, studies on functional limb movements have shown no relation between the exaggerated reflexes and the movement disorder (Berger, Quintern, & Dietz, 1984; Powers, Marder-Meyer, & Rymer, 1989). In walking, patients with spasticity exhibit a lower amplitude and reduced modulation of activation in the calf muscles. The stereotypic pattern of muscle activation required for locomotion appears to be intact in these patients, whereas the modulation by sensory feedback is impaired. Therapy should focus on training the residual motor functions and preventing secondary complications, such as muscle spasms (Dietz, 1997; Young, 1994). Furthermore, surgical interventions should be based on the outcome of gait analyses rather than clinical exams (Perry, 1993).

The final example involves locomotor training of patients with paraplegia due to partial or complete spinal cord transections. In these patients, the connections between the rostral centers of the nervous system and the generator circuits in the spinal cord are disrupted. Nonetheless, with appropriate training (Edgerton, Roy, de Leon, Tillakaratne, & Hodgson, 1997; Rossignol, 2000), patients with paraplegia are often able to improve muscle activation during assisted locomotion. The typical strategy involves suspending patients in a harness over a treadmill so that the legs do not have to support the entire weight of the body. Over the course of several months, patients with paraplegia can learn to modulate the timing of activity in leg muscles to resemble that of healthy individuals, although the amplitude remains reduced. Patients with an incomplete paraplegia can learn to perform unsupported stepping movements on the ground (Dietz, Colombo, Jensen, & Baumgartner, 1995). The benefits experienced by patients with complete paraplegia include an enhancement of cardiovascular function and reduced symptoms of spasticity. Such training appears to be a necessary adjunct for developing therapies, including pharmacologic interventions and tissue implants (de Leon, Hodgson, Roy, & Edgerton, 1998a, b).

Jumping

A jump is a movement that causes the center of mass to be projected upward and the feet of the performer to leave the ground. Jumps can be organized to achieve several different goals, such as the maximum height that the hands can reach, the maximum horizontal distance that can be covered, the maximum height that the center of mass can be raised, and the maximum time that can be spent off the ground. These goals correspond to such actions as rebounding in basketball; the long jump in athletics and the standing broad jump; the high jump in athletics; and performances in gymnastics, diving, and dance. In terms of biomechanics, these movements can be categorized into those that seek to maximize the vertical velocity of the center of mass at takeoff, those designed to maximize the horizontal distance, and those that involve somersaults and twists during the flight phase. As examples of these movements, we will examine the vertical jump, the long jump, and springboard diving.

The Vertical Jump

When a person is asked to jump and reach as high as possible with the hands, the typical strategy involves a technique called the **countermovement jump.** The person begins from an upright erect position and then performs a small-amplitude downward movement that involves flexion at the hip, knee, and ankle; this is followed by a rapid extension of the legs and a forward and upward rotation of the arms about the shoulders. This strategy is called a countermovement jump because it begins with an initial movement in the opposite direction; that is, the jumper first moves downward even though the goal is to maximize the upward vertical velocity at takeoff.

The kinematics of the jumper's center of mass during a countermovement jump are shown in the column on the left in figure 4.19. The upward and downward displacements of the center of mass are obvious in the velocity-time graph (figure 4.19b). As we discussed in chapter 1, a negative velocity indicates a downward displacement of the center of mass whereas a positive velocity represents an upward displacement. Accordingly, the velocity-time graph shows that the center of mass experiences a downward-upward-downward pattern of displacement during the jump. The peak positive velocity occurs at the instant the jumper leaves the ground.

Similarly, the jumper's center of mass first accelerates downward, then upward, and finally downward (figure 4.19c). However, this pattern includes two phases when the acceleration is constant. First, acceleration has a value of zero at the beginning of the jump, which means that the two vertical forces (body weight and ground reaction force) acting on the jumper are balanced. Second, acceleration is constant at about -10 m/s^2 during the flight

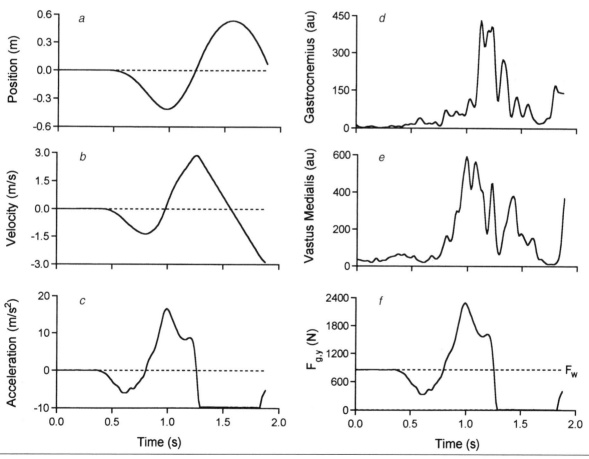

Figure 4.19   Kinematics, EMG, and ground reaction force for the vertical jump. The three panels on the left indicate the *(a)* position, *(b)* velocity, and *(c)* acceleration of the center of mass during a countermovement jump performed by an elite athlete. The top two panels on the right show the EMG of the *(d)* gastrocnemius and *(e)* vastus medialis muscles, measured in arbitrary units (au). *(f)* The bottom panel on the right represents the vertical component of the ground reaction force.

Data provided by Maarten F. Bobbert, PhD.

phase of the jump, which indicates the effect of gravity on the center of mass of the jumper. When acceleration is not constant, the ratio of the vertical component of the ground reaction force to the force due to gravity (body weight) changes. Negative accelerations, therefore, indicate intervals in which the vertical component of the ground reaction force is less than body weight. Conversely, positive accelerations represent intervals in which the vertical component of the ground reaction force is greater than body weight.

This association between the vertical acceleration of the center of mass and the vertical component of the ground reaction force can be observed in figure 4.19c and f. The shape of the two graphs is the same; they differ only in the values on the y-axis. If body weight (F_w) is subtracted from $F_{g,y}$, then $F_{g,y}$ fluctuates about F_w just as the acceleration varies about zero. This comparison suggests that when we are interpreting graphs of the vertical component of the ground reaction force, variation in $F_{g,y}$ about F_w provides information about the direction of the vertical acceleration experienced by the center of mass.

The EMGs of two muscles that contribute significantly to the countermovement jump are shown in figure 4.19d and e. These two muscles produce an extensor (plantarflexor) torque about the ankle joint (gastrocnemius) and an extensor torque about the knee joint (vastus medialis). These muscles, and their synergists, control both the downward and the upward displacement of the center of mass during the takeoff phase. The initial downward displacement is achieved by a reduction in the level of muscle activation so that the extensor torque is less than the effect of gravity. This involves an eccentric contraction by these muscles. To accelerate the center of mass upward, however, the effect of the muscle activity must be greater than gravity. This is apparent in figure 4.19e in the increase in the EMG of vastus medialis at about the time $F_{g,y}$ begins to exceed F_w. Also note that muscle activation proceeds in a proximal-to-distal sequence (vastus medialis before gastrocnemius), as has been reported for the EMGs of several leg muscles during the countermovement jump (Bobbert & Ingen Schenau, 1988).

To identify the critical variables that determine the height an individual can jump, biomechanists compare performances in the countermovement and squat jumps. In contrast to the countermovement jump, the squat jump has no initial downward displacement, and the jump begins from the crouched position. When experienced volleyball players perform these two jumps, they are able to jump about 3 to 11 cm higher with the countermovement jump (Bobbert, Gerritsen, Litjens, & Soest, 1996; Ravn et al., 1999). A key difference between these two jumps lies in the types of contractions performed by the knee and ankle extensor muscles. These muscles perform an eccentric and then a concentric contraction in the coun-

termovement jump, but an isometric followed by a concentric contraction in the squat jump. A typical explanation for the superior performance of the countermovement jump is that the initial eccentric contraction maximizes muscle force at the beginning of the push-off phase, that is, the interval involving upward displacement of the center of mass (Bobbert et al., 1996). This effect is most evident at the hip joint, where the resultant muscle torque reaches a peak value of about 313 N·m during the countermovement jump compared with 183 N·m during the squat jump (Fukashiro & Komi, 1987).

The maximum height that a person can reach in the vertical jump depends primarily on the amplitude and timing of the muscle activity in the legs (Ravn et al., 1999). One way to compare performances in the countermovement and drop jumps is to do a dynamic analysis (chapter 3) and determine the resultant muscle torque about the hip, knee, and ankle joints. Such a data set is shown in figure 4.20, where the resultant muscle torque is graphed as a function of angular velocity at each joint. A negative angular velocity indicates flexion at the joint, and a positive torque represents an extensor muscle torque. Because the squat jump does not include an initial downward movement, there was no flexion at the three joints. For the countermovement jump, however, there was an initial flexion at each joint that involved eccentric contractions, that is, flexion combined with extensor muscle activity. At all three joints, the peak torque occurred at the transition from the eccentric to the concentric contraction—consistent with the concept that the initial eccentric contraction maximizes the muscle force at the onset of the push-off phase. The greatest difference between the two jumps occurred at the hip joint, where the peak torque was much greater during the countermovement jump.

Despite the obvious superiority of the countermovement jump over the squat jump in the maximum vertical height that can be achieved, there is no consensus among biomechanists and muscle physiologists on the reason for this difference (Ingen Schenau, Bobbert, & Haan, 1997).

The Long Jump

The purpose of the long jump is to maximize the horizontal distance between the takeoff and the landing positions. The two principal factors that contribute to this distance are the displacement of the center of mass and the lean of the body at takeoff and at landing. Leaning forward at takeoff and backward at landing adds distance to the displacement of the center of mass and increases the jump distance. The primary determinant, however, is the horizontal distance that the center of mass can be displaced. When experienced athletes perform the long jump, for example, 90% of the distance achieved is due

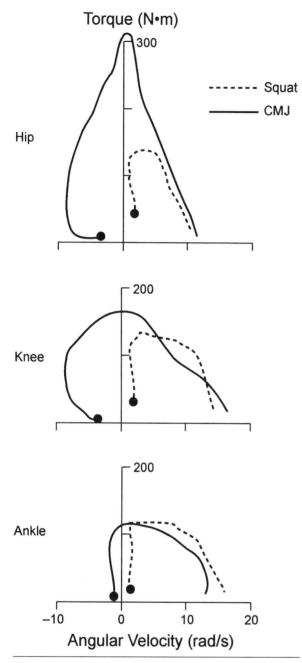

Figure 4.20 Resultant muscle torque and angular velocity at the hip, knee, and ankle joints during the countermovement jumps (CMJ) and squat jumps performed by a single subject. Positive torque indicates extensor activity. Each trial began from the filled circle.

Data from Fukashiro and Komi, 1987.

to the displacement of the center of mass, and 5% is due to the lean at each of the takeoff and landing positions (Hay, Miller, & Cantera, 1986).

According to the laws of projectile motion, the horizontal displacement of the center of mass is greatest when the takeoff angle is 0.785 rad (45°), which requires that the horizontal and vertical velocity of the center of mass be similar at takeoff. However, the takeoff angle is less than this optimum value whether the long jump is performed with a running approach or from a stationary position. The takeoff angle is about 0.35 rad (20°) with the running approach and 0.51 rad (29°) from a standing position (Hay et al., 1986; Horita, Kitamura, & Kohno, 1991; Kakihana & Suzuki, 2001). The reason for this discrepancy is that individuals can achieve a much greater horizontal velocity than vertical velocity (Brancazio, 1984). The horizontal and vertical velocities are around 9.0 and 3.2 m/s for the running long jump and 3.27 and 1.83 m/s for the standing long jump.

The horizontal distance achieved in a long jump depends on the time the jumper is in the air, which is determined by the vertical velocity at takeoff. This does not involve converting horizontal velocity to vertical velocity but rather performing actions that accelerate the jumper's center of mass in the upward direction during the takeoff phase. One concise way to characterize these actions is with angle-angle diagrams. Figure 4.21 shows the relative angular displacements of the thigh, shank, and foot segments of an athlete during the last stance phase (takeoff) of a running long jump (Kakihana & Suzuki, 2001). The thigh-knee angle-angle diagram (figure 4.21a) indicates a displacement profile similar to those we observe during running (figure 4.6). After the foot contacted the ground (TD, touchdown), the stance phase comprised two parts. First, the knee flexed while thigh angle did not change. Second, the thigh rotated backward while the knee extended. The shank and ankle, on the other hand, exhibited the converse behavior (figure 4.21b). The first part of the stance phase comprised backward rotation of the shank and flexion (dorsiflexion) of the ankle; the second part involved extension (plantarflexion) of the ankle while shank angle did not change much.

The timing of the angular displacements for the leg segments can also be examined in a velocity-time graph. Figure 4.21c shows the angular velocity for the thigh (an absolute angle) and the knee and ankle (relative angles) during the takeoff phase of a running long jump. A negative angular velocity indicates that the thigh segment was rotating backward and that the knee and ankle joints were flexing. According to figure 4.21c, the thigh segment of the athlete rotated backward for the entire duration of the stance phase while the knee and ankle joints flexed for about the first half of takeoff and then extended. Figure 4.21c also indicates the timing of the change in direction of angular displacement from flexion to extension; the change in direction at the knee joint preceded that at the ankle joint.

To characterize the actions necessary to maximize long-jump distance, Kakihana and Suzuki (2001) compared

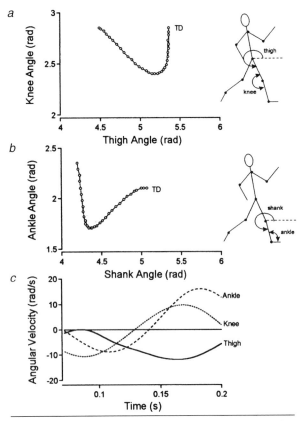

Figure 4.21 Angular kinematics of the support leg during the last stance phase of a running long jump: *(a)* thigh-knee angle-angle diagram; *(b)* shank-ankle angle-angle diagram; *(c)* angular velocity of the thigh, knee, and ankle angles. The data are from a single subject who was an Olympic-caliber sprinter. The thigh and shank angles are absolute segment angles; the knee and ankle represent the joint angles between the adjacent segments.

Data from Kakihana and Suzuki, in press.

TD = touchdown.

Table 4.2 Takeoff Characteristics for Long Jumps Performed With 3-, 5-, and 9-Step Approaches by an Accomplished Athlete

	3 step	5 step	9 step
Distance jumped (m)	2.63	2.80	4.22
Takeoff duration (ms)	153	131	124
Touchdown velocity (m/s)			
Horizontal	4.82	6.19	7.37
Vertical	–0.31	–0.29	–0.10
Takeoff velocity (m/s)			
Horizontal	4.46	5.71	6.85
Vertical	2.26	2.54	3.01
$F_{g,y}$ impulse (N·s)	291	293	319
$F_{g,x}$ impulse (N·s)			
Backward (braking)	46	51	88
Forward (propulsion)	7	8	8

Note. $F_{g,y}$ = vertical component of the ground reaction force; $F_{g,x}$ = forward-backward component of the ground reaction force.

the performances of two athletes when they used three-, five-, and nine-step approaches for a running long jump. Some of the details of the performances by the more accomplished athlete are listed in table 4.2. As you might expect, he jumped farther as the approach distance increased, due to greater horizontal and vertical velocity of his center of mass at takeoff. Although the kinematics of the support leg did not differ markedly, the magnitude of the ground reaction force and the amplitude of the muscle activity increased with the distance jumped.

With the three-step approach, the shape of the vertical component of the ground reaction force $(F_{g,y})$ was similar to that measured during running (figure 4.22). For the five- and nine-step approaches, however, the magnitude of the first peak (the "impact" maximum) increased to values that were about 10 times greater than body weight

(F_w) (Hatze, 1981a). This peak occurred about 10 to 15 ms after the foot contacted the ground. In contrast, the forward-backward component of the ground reaction force $(F_{g,x})$ was not similar to those measured during running, due to the pronounced braking impulse. During running at a constant speed, for example, the braking and propulsion impulses have similar magnitudes so that the net horizontal impulse is close to zero. As indicated in table 4.2, however, the braking impulse during the long jump increased from 46 to 88 N·s with approach distance, while the propulsion impulse did not change much. The greatest increase in the braking impulse appears to have been due to a large peak in the backward component, which coincided with the peak in the $F_{g,y}$ record (figure 4.22).

Because the ground reaction force represents the reaction of the ground to the actions of the athlete while his foot was on the ground, the variation in $F_{g,y}$ and $F_{g,x}$ must be accompanied by changes in the amount of muscle activity. This is indicated by variation in the rectified and averaged EMGs for several muscles of the support leg for the three approach distances (figure 4.23). In these records, ▼ indicates touchdown of the foot and ▲ represents the moment when the foot left the ground. The muscles that experienced the greatest increase in activity across the three approach distances were vastus medialis, tibialis anterior, and lateral gastrocnemius. In addition to the differences in EMG amplitude, the timing of the muscle activity also changed as more of the EMG occurred prior to foot touchdown with the nine-step approach. Such information can often help explain why one person can jump farther than another (Kakihana & Suzuki, 2001).

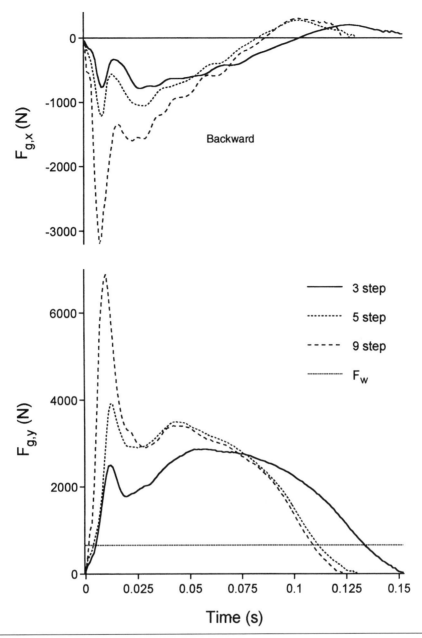

Figure 4.22 Vertical *(F_{g,y})* and forward-backward *(F_{g,x})* components of the ground reaction force during the takeoff phase for the long jump. Three trials of data are shown: one each for a three-, five-, and nine-step approach.

Data from Kakihana and Suzuki, in press.

Because the line of action of the ground reaction force vector does not pass through the jumper's center of mass for most of the takeoff phase, the jumper has some angular momentum during the flight phase of the jump. It is the magnitude and duration of the backward component of $F_{g,x}$ during the takeoff phase that cause the line of action of the ground reaction force to pass behind the center of mass for most of the takeoff phase (Kakihana & Suzuki, 2001). This generates angular momentum in the direction of a forward somersault; that is, the jumper experiences an angular impulse about his center of mass. This effect can be visualized as the ground reaction force times the moment arm from its line of action to the center of mass, which acts over the duration of the takeoff phase. The jumper controls the forward angular momentum by rotating the legs and arms during the flight phase. These actions must be sufficient to prevent the athlete from performing a forward somersault while placing the body in a pike-like position for landing.

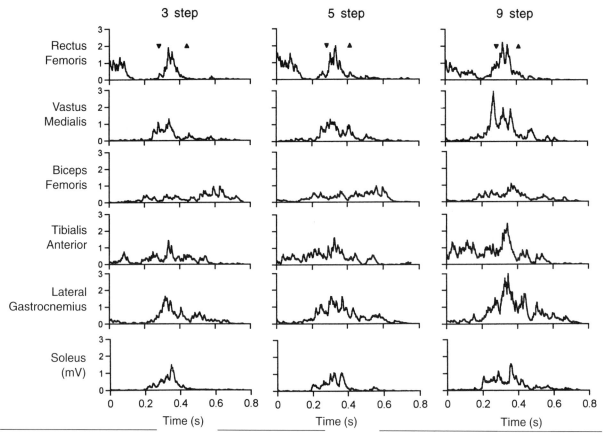

Figure 4.23 Rectified and averaged EMG signals from six leg muscles during the takeoff phase for long jumps with three-, five-, and nine-step approaches. The takeoff phase occurred between ▼ and ▲.

Data from Kakihana and Suzuki, in press.

In athletic competition, the length of the approach must be adequate for the athlete to obtain a horizontal velocity of about 10 m/s at the beginning of the takeoff phase. Once this speed has been achieved, the challenge is to obtain as much vertical velocity at takeoff as possible while minimizing the decline in horizontal velocity. This constraint leaves the athlete with approximately 100 ms to increase the vertical velocity of the center of mass, which limits the distance of the jump.

Springboard Diving

In addition to the jumps designed to maximize the vertical and horizontal displacements of the center of mass, there are jumps that enable individuals to perform rotations while in the air. These jumps, which are included in such activities as dancing, diving, freestyle skiing, gymnastics, skating, and trampolining, require the performer to generate sufficient angular momentum during the takeoff phase to accomplish the desired rotation. Many of the principles associated with these types of movements can be illustrated through examination of some of the features of springboard diving (Miller, 2000).

There are four main types of springboard dives: forward, reverse, backward, and inward (figure 4.24). These dives differ in the number of steps taken prior to the takeoff phase, the direction the diver faces relative to the board, and the direction of the rotations about the somersault axis. The *forward* dive involves several steps in the approach, with the diver facing away from the board and the somersaults occurring in the forward direction. The *reverse* dive also involves several steps in the approach and the diver facing away from the board, but the somersaults occur in the backward direction. The *backward* dive is performed from a standing position with the diver facing toward the board, and the somersaults are done in the backward direction. The *inward* dive is also performed from a standing position with the diver facing the board, but the somersaults occur in the forward direction.

Each dive can comprise up to five phases: approach, hurdle, takeoff, flight, and entry. The approach occurs only in the forward and reverse dives and corresponds to the initial steps taken by the diver. The hurdle refers to the movements performed by the diver to raise and lower the whole-body center of mass prior to the takeoff phase. For the dives with an approach phase (forward and re-

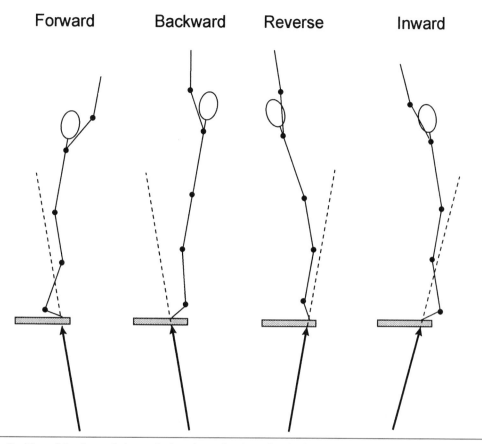

Figure 4.24 Position of the diver relative to the board reaction force for the four types of springboard dives.
Data from Miller, 1981.

verse dives), the diver rotates the thigh of one leg forward as if performing a high step up, and the diver's feet leave the board. For the dives performed from a standing position (backward and inward dives), the diver's feet remain in contact with the board during the hurdle while the arms are raised and the ankles are extended, then flexed, to raise and lower the center of mass. The takeoff phase involves the final depression and recoil of the springboard, which projects the diver into the flight phase and then the entry phase into the water.

Reaction Force

Probably the most critical component of the dive is the takeoff phase, in which the board provides a reaction force on the feet of the diver. The takeoff phase involves two actions by the diver: pressing down on the board and lifting up off the board. These actions cause the board first to be depressed and then to recoil from the imposed load. As the board is depressed, it stores strain or elastic energy, which it returns to the diver when it recoils. When the board is depressed, the center of mass of the diver is displaced downward and reaches a minimum at the transition from the depression to the recoil (figure 4.25). Accordingly, the center of mass has a downward (nega-

tive) velocity during depression of the board and an upward velocity during the recoil. The diver's upward velocity peaks just prior to the moment the toes leave the board. For most of the takeoff phase, however, the center of mass of the diver experiences an acceleration in the upward (positive) direction due to the reaction force provided by the board. In addition to these vertical kinematics, the reaction force must include a horizontal component that enables the diver to clear the end of the board. The horizontal velocity of the diver at the end of the takeoff phase is about 0.5 to 1.0 m/s (Miller, 1981).

As the board recoils, the position of the diver relative to the reaction force provided by the board determines the direction of the diver's angular momentum vector during the flight phase. The effect of the reaction force is to exert a torque about the diver's center of mass, which can be visualized as the product of the force and its moment arm relative to the center of mass. Figure 4.24 shows the different body positions that are required to perform the four types of dives. For the forward dive, for example, the reaction force exerts a torque about the center of mass in the direction of forward rotation. Because the magnitude and direction of the reaction force change throughout the takeoff phase, the effect of the reaction force is

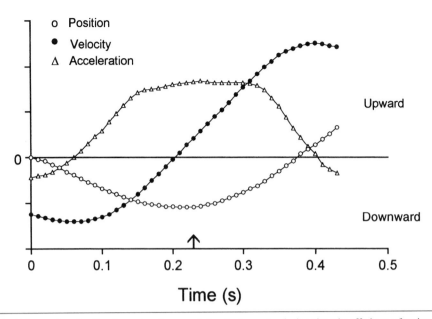

Figure 4.25 Vertical kinematics of a diver's center of mass relative to the water during the takeoff phase of an inward 2.5-somersault dive in the tucked position. The up arrow on the *x*-axis indicates the transition of the board from the depression to the recoil.

Data from Miller, 1981.

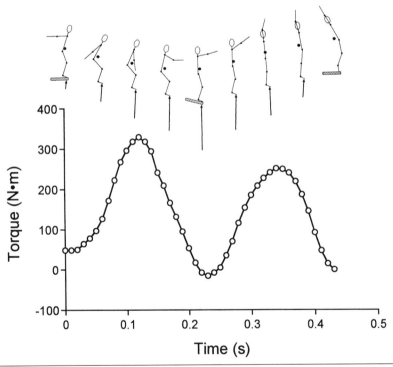

Figure 4.26 Torque about a diver's center of mass due to the reaction force during the takeoff phase for a reverse 2.5-somersault dive. The largest dot on each stick figure indicates the position of the center of mass. The arrow at the diver's feet represents the reaction force exerted by the board.

Data from Miller, 1981.

graphed as the torque relative to the center of mass over the course of the takeoff phase. Such a torque-time graph is shown for a reverse 2.5-somersault dive (figure 4.26); the positive torque indicates a backward rotation during the flight phase. The middle stick figure at the top of

figure 4.26 indicates maximum depression of the board. For both the depression and recoil parts of this dive, the diver experienced a torque that produced a backward rotation; that is, the line of action of the reaction force vector passed in front of the diver's center of mass.

Angular Momentum

Based on the impulse-momentum relation (chapter 2), the effect of the diver's actions during the takeoff phase can be quantified as the area under the torque-time curve, which represents the impulse applied to the diver by the board. The impulse during the recoil of the board determines the magnitude and direction of the angular momentum vector during the flight phase. To perform forward somersaults during the flight phase, for example, the diver needs to experience an impulse that will produce such rotation, which is characterized by an angular momentum vector pointing to the diver's left. Accordingly, the direction of the angular impulse is different for dives that involve forward (forward and inward) and backward (backward and reverse) somersaults (figure 4.27).

Once a diver leaves the board, the only significant force acting on the diver is gravity. This means that the linear momentum of the diver changes during the flight phase but the angular momentum of the diver remains constant (Example 2.12). As a consequence, the magnitude and direction of the angular momentum obtained by the diver during the takeoff phase do not change during the flight phase. This whole-body angular momentum could have components in the somersault, twist, and cartwheel directions (Yeadon, 1993b). The somersault component, for example, would act along the somersault axis passing through the center of mass, with the direction to the left for forward somersaults and to the right for backward somersaults. Recall that the direction of the angular momentum vector is perpendicular to the plane in which the rotation occurs.

Although angular momentum remains constant during the flight phase, this does not mean that the speed of the angular rotations cannot change. A constant angular mo-

mentum means that the product of the moment of inertia *(I)* and angular velocity *(ω)* for the whole body is constant. Consequently, when *I* changes, *ω* changes also. For example, when a diver goes from a tuck to a layout position, *I* decreases about the somersault axis and thus the speed of the somersault increases. Divers use this interaction to control the orientation of the body for the entry phase of the dive.

While the angular momentum for the whole body remains constant during the flight phase, the angular momentum for individual body segments can change. As stated in Equation 2.25, the angular momentum of each body segment comprises two terms: local and remote angular momentum. The local angular momentum *(Iω)* refers to the angular momentum of the segment relative to its own center of mass. The remote angular momentum (**r** × *m***v**) corresponds to the effect of segment center of mass about the whole-body center of mass. If the angular momentum of a body segment changes during a dive, then the angular momentum of another body segment must change by an equal magnitude but in the opposite direction so that the net angular momentum about the whole-body center of mass remains constant. For example, when a diver goes from a pike position to a layout position, the upper body rotates backward while the lower body rotates in the forward direction. Similarly, when a diver rotates the arms about a cartwheel axis through the chest to initiate a twist (Example 2.13), the trunk and legs rotate in the opposite direction so that the two angular momentum vectors cancel (Yeadon, 1993c).

The most difficult dives involve various combinations of somersaults and twists. While the angular momentum

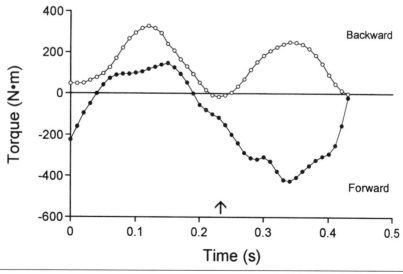

Figure 4.27 Torque about a diver's center of mass due to the reaction force during the takeoff phase for a reverse 2.5-somersault dive (open circles) and a forward 3.5-somersault dive (filled circles). The up arrow indicates the transition between the depression and recoil of the board. Positive torques produced a backward somersault.

Data from Miller, 1981.

needed for the somersaults must be obtained from the springboard, the angular momentum for the twists can come either from the board or from asymmetrical movements of the arms, chest, or hips about the sagittal plane during the flight phase (Yeadon, 1993a). However, both computer simulations (Yeadon, 1993d) and performance measurements (Yeadon, 1993e) indicate that most of the twist is produced by the movements performed during the flight phase. Elite performances in springboard diving, therefore, seem to require the generation and control of angular momentum during both the takeoff and flight phases and at the same time adherence to strict requirements on the orientation of the body.

Throwing and Kicking

The throw and the kick are two of the basic elements of human movement. Although the purpose of both is *to project an object so that it has a flight phase,* the distinction between the two is the manner in which the body imparts the flight phase to the object. In a throw, the object is supported by a limb, usually the hand, and displaced through a range of motion while the limb increases the *quantity of motion,* or momentum, of the object. Typically several body segments, in a proximal-to-distal

sequence, contribute to the momentum of the object (Putnam, 1991). Although the kick is also characterized by a proximal-to-distal involvement of body segments, it differs from a throw in that it is a striking event in which the momentum of the object is increased by a brief impact between a limb and the object (Elliott, 2000). In this section we consider some features of throws and kicks.

Throwing Motion

While the throw can be characterized by the progressive contribution of the body segments to the momentum of the object to be projected (with a constant mass, the change in momentum corresponds to a change in velocity), the task can be accomplished with a variety of motions. These different forms include the overarm throw (e.g., baseball, cricket, javelin, darts), the underarm throw (e.g., bowling, softball pitch), the push throw (e.g., shot put), and the pull throw (e.g., discus, hammer). The kinematics of the throwing motion are typically three-dimensional, especially when the throw is for maximum distance or speed (Escamilla, Fleisig, Barrentine, Zheng, & Andrews, 1998; Feltner, 1989; Feltner & Dapena, 1986, 1989; Feltner & Taylor, 1997). For example, the contributions of the body segments to the overarm throw (figure 4.28) include displacements

Figure 4.28   Sequence of a typical baseball pitch.
Reproduced from Feltner and Dapena, 1986.

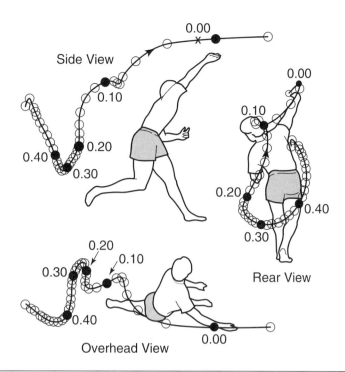

Side View

0.00

0.10

0.20

0.40

0.30

0.00

0.10

0.20

0.40

0.30

Rear View

0.20

0.10

0.30

0.40

Overhead View

0.00

Figure 4.29 Three views of the path of the ball during an overarm throw. The ball was released at 37.3 m/s (83.5 mph), and the instant of release is indicated as the final shaded-ball position (0.00). Prior to release, the shaded-ball positions indicate intervals of 100 ms. These measurements were obtained from a film (64 frames/s) of the movement.

Adapted from Atwater, 1977.

in the vertical, side-to-side, and forward-backward directions (figure 4.29). In contrast, when the task requires accuracy, such as in throwing a dart or shooting a free throw in basketball, the throwing motion is generally planar; and the strategy, especially for beginners, is to minimize the number of body segments involved in the movement.

The sequence of a typical baseball pitch is shown in figure 4.28. A qualitative inspection of this sequence indicates that the movement involves the progressive contribution of the body segments, beginning from the base of support and progressing through to the hand. The baseball pitch consists of two phases (figure 4.28): (a) positions *a* through *k*—the velocity of the ball is increased mainly by the action of the legs; and (b) positions *l* through *u*—the velocity of the ball is increased by the action of the trunk and arms. The second phase, which produces the greater increase in the velocity of the ball, involves the progressive increase in the angular velocity of the body segments in the following order: pelvis, upper trunk and upper arm, forearm, and hand (Atwater, 1979). This means that the peak angular velocity of the pelvis occurs before that of the upper trunk and upper arm, the peak angular velocity of the upper trunk and upper arm occurs before that of the forearm, and so on. In this progression of segmental activity, which is also seen in striking movements such as the kick, proximal

segments begin to rotate before the distal segments, and the proximal segments begin to slow down before the distal segments have reached peak angular velocity. The result of this proximal-to-distal progression is that the velocity of the ball does not increase substantially until the last 100 ms of the movement (Atwater, 1970).

In addition to this proximal-to-distal sequence, the overarm throw involves an extensive range of motion for the arm (Escamilla, Fleisig, & Barrentine, 1998). These displacements occur at the shoulder, elbow, and wrist joints but are most extensive about the shoulder joint. Because of its geometry, the shoulder joint is capable of displacement about three separate axes of rotation: rotation about an anterior-posterior axis, which is referred to as abduction-adduction; rotation about a side-to-side axis, which is known as flexion-extension; and rotation about a longitudinal axis, which is described as external-internal rotation. Figure 4.30 shows that during a baseball pitch there are about 1.57 rad of elbow flexion-extension, 1.57 rad of external rotation, and 1.0 rad of internal rotation. Position *p* in figure 4.28 shows the arm in the position of maximum external rotation. This extreme position probably causes many of the arm injuries that baseball pitchers sustain.

The proximal-to-distal sequence of muscle activity has been observed in many throwing and striking motions: for example, baseball pitch, handball throw, javelin

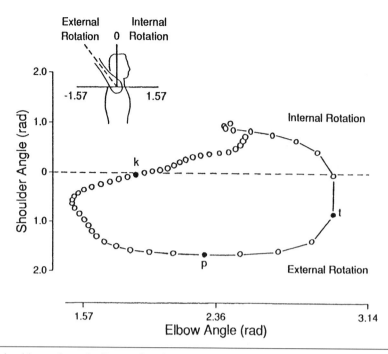

Figure 4.30   Elbow-shoulder angle-angle diagram for a baseball pitch. The interval between data points is 5 ms; the farther apart the data points, the faster the movement. The data points at *k, p,* and *t* correspond to positions identified in figure 4.28.
Reproduced from Feltner and Dapena, 1986.

throw, penalty shot in water polo, shot put, tennis serve, and volleyball spike. To examine the role of this sequential activity in throwing, Alexander (1991) developed three simple models that each had one proximal and one distal muscle. The models were of a push throw, an underarm throw, and an overarm throw. For the push throw, the proximal muscle was the knee extensors, and the distal muscle was the elbow extensors. For the underarm throw, the proximal muscle was the shoulder flexors, and the distal muscle was the elbow flexors. For the overarm throw, the proximal muscle was those that control horizontal adduction, and the distal muscle was the internal rotators. For all three models, Alexander found that when activation of the proximal muscle preceded that of the distal muscle, the performance was enhanced. The mechanical energy of the projectile at release (push throw) and the speed at release (underarm and overarm throws) were maximal at a specific delay between activation of the proximal and distal muscles. These results suggest that the sequencing of muscle activation is important for such tasks as throwing and kicking and that learning these sequences is necessary for becoming skilled with these tasks.

Kicking Motion

The kick can be described as a striking skill in which a flight phase is imparted to an object as the result of a

brief impact between a limb (or implement) and the object. By this criterion, we include as striking skills such activities as kicking a ball, hitting a volleyball, and striking a projectile in racket and bat sports. As with the throw, the motion underlying a striking skill can vary depending on the objectives of the activity; these goals can be related to horizontal distance, time in the air, accuracy, or the speed of the movement. For many striking skills (e.g., soccer kick, punt, volleyball serve, tennis serve), the motion is similar to that for the overarm throw and involves a proximal-to-distal sequence of body segment contributions to the velocity of the endpoint (hand, foot, implement) that will strike the projectile. For example, during kicking of a ball, the thigh reaches a peak positive (forward) angular velocity before the shank and decreases its angular velocity, while that for the shank continues to increase through to contact with the ball (figure 4.31). Luhtanen (1988) describes a similar sequence for the upper arm, forearm, and hand during a volleyball serve.

Because striking skills alter the momentum of the projectile through an impact, an important difference between a throw and a kick is the rigidity of the limb during contact with the ball. When performing striking skills, athletes frequently manipulate the rigidity of the limb to influence the impact with the object. For example, the change in ball velocity during a kick is greater when the lower leg is more rigid at impact. This is accomplished

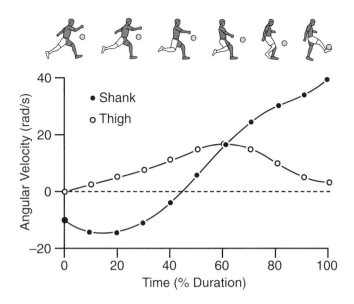

Figure 4.31 Angular velocity of the thigh and shank of the kicking leg during the final step of a kick.

Adapted from Putnam, 1991.

by contracting the muscles in the foot and those that cross the ankle joint so that the foot is more rigidly attached to the shank. Another example of variation in rigidity is seen in the underhand pass (bump, dig) in volleyball. This skill requires that the individual allow the volleyball to bounce off the ventral surface of the forearms with a prescribed trajectory. Skillful players accomplish this task by varying the rigidity of the arms and thereby determining the extent to which the ball will bounce off the forearms. Similarly, the strings on rackets can be strung to various levels of tightness; this represents one factor that contributes to rigidity in racket sports.

Summary

This chapter applies the principles and concepts described in chapters 1 to 3 to the basic forms of human movement: walking, running, jumping, throwing, and kicking. Human locomotion comprises alternating phases of support (stance) and nonsupport (swing), whose durations change with speed. The displacement of the limbs during walking and running is most succinctly characterized with angle-angle diagrams, and the interaction of the foot with the ground is quantified by measurement of the ground reaction force. Because of differences in the activity of leg muscles, the path followed by the center of mass during the stance phase differs between walking and running. In the stance phase of walking, there is little knee flexion, which provides an explanation for the speed at which humans prefer to switch from a walk to a run and for the fluc-

tuations in mechanical energy. In the stance phase of running, there is greater modulation of muscle activity, which varies the stiffness of the leg during the stance phase and the energy cost of locomotion. These characteristics provide the foundation for the clinical evaluation of gait. Similar analyses are applied to jumping and throwing, which have different performance goals. In jumping, the object is to project the center of mass upward so that the feet leave the ground. The different trajectories experienced by the center of mass for the different types of jumps are a consequence of variations in the ground reaction force. In throwing and kicking, the goal is to apply an impulse to an object so that it has a flight phase. Throws tend to involve actions in which forces are applied by a limb over a relatively long duration. The impulses applied in kicks involve much briefer contact times. For both throws and kicks, however, the limb motion involves a coordinated sequence of proximal-to-distal muscle activity. The examples presented in this chapter indicate the strategies that can be used to describe and understand the biomechanical details of most movements.

Suggested Readings

Farley, C.T., & Ferris, D.P. (1998). Biomechanics of walking and running: Center of mass movements to muscle action. *Exercise and Sport Sciences Reviews, 26*, 253–285.

Winter, D.A. (1990). *Biomechanics and motor control of human movement*. New York: Wiley, chapter 5.

Part I
Summary

At the beginning of part I, a number of specific objectives were listed to help us achieve the goal of defining the mechanical bases of movement. Completing part I should have helped you do the following:

- Understand the definitions of and relations (numeric and graphic) among position, velocity, and acceleration, which comprise the kinematic variables used to describe movement

- Know how to read a graph carefully and how to interpret the relation between the two or more variables shown on the graph

- Appreciate the relations between linear and angular motion

- Realize that many of the details of projectile motion can be determined from the definitions of position, velocity, and acceleration

- Consider force as a concept used to describe an interaction between two objects and understand that the magnitude of the interaction can be determined using Newton's laws, particularly the law of acceleration

- Be able to use a free body diagram to define conditions of an analysis and to use the free body and mass acceleration diagrams as a graphic version of Newton's law of acceleration

- Conceive of torque as the rotary effect of a force for which torque is defined as the product of force and moment arm

- Identify the ways in which the human body interacts with its surroundings to influence movement

- Recognize that force acting over time (impulse) causes a change in the momentum (quantity of motion) of a system

- Acknowledge that the performance of work (force $\times$ distance) requires the expenditure of energy and that the work can be done by the system (positive) or on the system (negative)

- Perceive power as a measure of the rate of doing work or the rate of using energy

- Comprehend the concept of musculoskeletal forces that occur within the body as body segments rotate about one another

- Perform static and dynamic analyses to estimate the magnitude and direction of the musculoskeletal forces

- Distinguish the kinematic and kinetic descriptions of running, throwing, and kicking

- Differentiate the biomechanical characteristics of walking and running

- Note the mechanical energy fluctuations and the energy cost of human locomotion

- Appreciate the role of biomechanics in the clinical evaluation of gait

- Grasp the significance of variations in the ground reaction force in determining the details of a movement, such as the height, distance, and rotations that occur during a jump

- Be able to distinguish between throws and kicks

- Understand that the sequencing of muscle activity is critical in throwing and kicking

Reprinted from Marey, 1879.

Part II

The Motor System

Human movement is a complex phenomenon. To examine the neuromechanical bases of movement, we simplify many of the biological details of the human body. For example, in part I, "The Force-Motion Relation," we assumed that the force exerted by muscle acts at points on rigid body segments and causes the involved body segments to rotate about pinned, frictionless joints. Such simplifications allowed us to address some of the basic concepts associated with the study of movement.

Part II continues this focus by describing the **single-joint system** (figure II.1) as a model of the basic biological elements of the human body that are necessary to produce movement. This model includes six elements: bone, synovial joint, muscle, tendon, neuron, and sensory receptor. With this scheme, movement can be represented as the activation of muscle by motor neurons to control the rotation of adjacent body segments, which is monitored by sensory receptors. Subsequently, the fidelity of the model can be improved by incorporating a few hundred motor neurons and multiple muscles.

In part II, we shall first review simplified descriptions of these six elements (chapter 5—"Single-Joint System Components"), then consider several interactions be-

tween the elements that underlie movement (chapter 6—"Single-Joint System Function"), and finally examine the organization and control of multiple single-joint systems (chapter 7—"Multi-Joint Systems").

Objectives

The goal of this text is to describe movement as the interaction of a biological model (a simplified version of humans) with the physical world. In part I, we examined the biomechanics of movement, focusing on the relation between force and motion. The aim of part II is to define a biological model and to describe how it works. Specific objectives include the following:

- To describe the single-joint system and explain why it is an adequate model for the study of the basic features of movement
- To list the details of the structural characteristics of the six components of the single-joint system
- To explain the means by which information is transmitted rapidly throughout the system

209

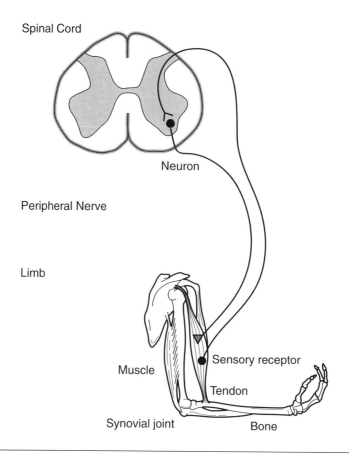

Figure II.1   The six components of the single-joint system.

- To outline the link between the neural signal and muscle contraction
- To define the mechanical characteristics of the force-generating units
- To characterize the basic neuromuscular unit of the system
- To describe the strategies used by the nervous system to control muscle force
- To examine the neuroanatomical basis and the role of afferent information in the operation of the system
- To consider the organization and control of multiple single-joint systems

Photograph courtesy the Collège de France.

Single-Joint System Components

Although it is anticipated that you will have encountered most of the material in this chapter in introductory human anatomy and physiology courses, the material is presented here to emphasize a functional focus. Indeed, perhaps the most important task in chapter 5 is to emphasize that *the morphological and mechanical features of the single-joint system elements are determined largely by the functions they serve.* To this end, the chapter focuses on the morphological and mechanical characteristics of the single-joint system components with some mention of their adaptive capabilities. Because the components are all living tissue, they adapt to the demands that they experience; for example, muscle size increases with strength training, bone strength decreases during space flight, and sensory receptors become less sensitive with age. Subsequent chapters deal with the interactions among the elements of this system in the production of movement.

Bone

Many different tissues provide a structural framework for the single-joint system. These tissues, known as connective tissue, comprise living (cells) and nonliving (intercellular material) substances that are bathed in tissue fluid. The cells (e.g., fibroblasts, macrophages, fat cells, and mast cells) perform functions necessary for the maintenance of the tissue. The intercellular material, which includes the proteins collagen, elastin, and reticulum and forms the matrix in which the cells live, determines the physical characteristics of the tissue. These materials form the basis of bone, tendon, and ligament.

The 206 bones in the human body perform several functions essential to the production of movement. They (a) provide mechanical support as the central structure of each body segment, (b) act as a lever system to transfer muscle forces, (c) produce red blood cells, and (d) serve as an active ion reservoir for critical ions (calcium, phosphorus, sodium, potassium, zinc, magnesium). Bone is a living tissue consisting of a protein matrix (mainly collagen) upon which calcium salts (especially phosphate) are deposited. These minerals give bone its solid consistency. Water accounts for 20% of the wet weight of bone; the protein matrix, which is mainly osteocollagenous fibers, represents 35%; and the bone salts account for 45%. The osteocollagenous fibers determine the strength and resilience of bone.

Although bone is often classified as cancellous (or trabecular) or cortical (or compact), the biomechanical properties of the two types are similar, differing only in their degree of porosity and density. For example, the density of human femoral cortical bone is 1.85 g/cm^3 compared with 0.3 g/cm³ for tibial trabecular bone. Cancellous bone is less dense (and hence weaker) and comprises trabeculae that are oriented in the direction of the forces commonly experienced by the bone. The microstructure of cortical bone is composed of cylindrical lamellae, whereas the shapes of the lamellae for cancellous bone are more irregular. Cancellous bone is composed of trabecular struts and marrow-filled cavities; the material properties depend on the trabecular struts, while the structural properties are influenced by both the struts and the cavities. The mechanical properties of cortical bone depend on the porosity, the level of mineralization, and the organization of the solid matrix (Rho, Kuhn-Spearing, & Zioupos, 1998). The mechanical properties of bone vary between sites on a bone, between bones, and among individuals. However, there is less variation in the properties of compact bone than in those for cancellous bone.

The basic structural unit of bone is the **osteon** (or Haversian system), which consists of a series of concentric layers of mineralized matrix that surround a central canal

(Haversian) containing blood vessels and nerves (figure 5.1). A typical osteon has a diameter of about 200 μm. Osteons often are aligned parallel to the long axis of the bone. However, the collagen fibers that compose the lamellae appear to have different orientations (transverse, longitudinal, oblique) in adjacent lamellae (Rho et al., 1998). The collagen fibers comprise many collagen fibrils, which are composed of collagen molecules and associated bone salts.

Bone As a Material

In the study of bone biomechanics, bone is examined as a material, as a structure, and as a system (Kaplan et al., 1994; Roesler, 1987). The material properties of bone are generally characterized by the **load-deformation relation**. In this scheme, a load is applied to the tissue, and the ensuing deformation (change in length) is measured. Different loads can be applied to bone to identify such features as its strength, stiffness, and ability to store

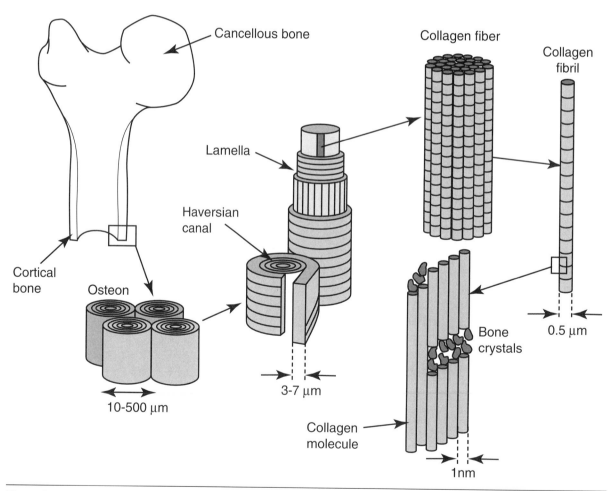

Figure 5.1   The structure of bone down to the collagen molecule.
Data from Rho et al., 1998.

energy. Because the size and shape of bones vary, the typical approach when determining the material properties of bone is to perform measurements that are independent of size. To do this, we measure the normalized load and the normalized deformation. This involves expressing the load relative to the size of the bone specimen and the deformation relative to the initial length of the specimen. These measurements are usually made with specialized devices designed to measure the material properties of biological tissues, such as bone. As we discussed in chapter 3, normalized load is described as *stress* (σ), and normalized deformation is called *strain* (ε). Stress is measured as force per unit area (MPa or MN/m^2), whereas strain indicates the change in length as a function of the initial length (%). Such measurements describe the intrinsic material properties of bone, which can be determined for different types of loads such as those applied in the tension, compression, shear, and bending directions.

Note that the tension and compression directions are normal (perpendicular) to the end of the bone (specimen) and that the shear direction is tangential; tensile loads tend to elongate a specimen whereas compressive loads tend to shorten and widen the specimen.

To determine the stress-strain relation for a bone specimen under a tensile load, the specimen is placed in a device and then stretched. This device measures the pulling forces applied to the specimen and the change in length that it experiences with each pulling force. The resulting stress-strain relation for human cortical bone is shown in figure 5.2a. For this idealized relation, low stresses produce small strains, and high stresses result in greater strains. The slope of the stress-strain relation indicates the normalized stiffness of the specimen. For the relation shown in figure 5.2a, the stiffness (slope of the stress-strain relation) varies with the applied stress. As we discussed in chapter 3, the region of high stiffness is

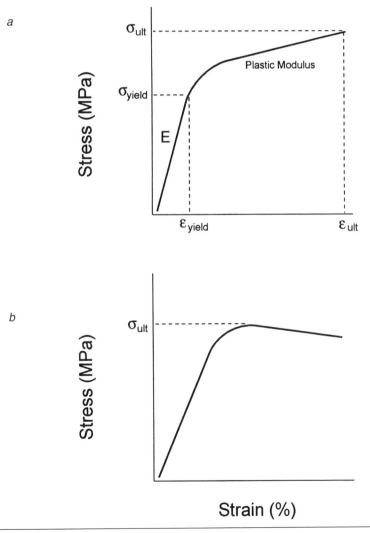

Figure 5.2 Idealized stress-strain relation for human cortical bone subjected to *(a)* tension and *(b)* compression loads.
Data from Carter and Spengler, 1978.

called the *elastic region* whereas the region of lower stiffness is described as the *plastic region*. When a stress is applied to a specimen and then released, the specimen will return to its original length if the stress was within the elastic region, but it will return to a longer length if the stress extended into the plastic region. This suggests that the specimen behaves as an elastic band when stretched within the elastic region but experiences changes in its structure when stretched into the plastic region. The elastic region, therefore, indicates how much energy the specimen can store and return without experiencing adverse mechanical effects.

To characterize the material properties of bone, it is necessary to measure the slope of the elastic region (*E;* elastic modulus), the stress and strain values that distinguish between the elastic and plastic regions (σ_{yield}, ε_{yield}), the slope of the plastic region, and the ultimate stress and strain the specimen can bear (σ_{ult}, ε_{ult}). Figure 5.2 shows how these properties are represented on the stress-strain curve by peak values, inflection points, and slopes. Actual data for these parameters are presented in table 5.1 for the human femur and tibia as a function of age (Burstein, Reilly, & Martens, 1976).

Bone As a Structure

In contrast to the material properties of bone, the structural properties of bone are determined by its geometry.

The femur of an adult, for example, is stronger than the femur of a child, largely due to differences in size. Similarly, because the femur typically encounters longitudinal forces, it offers the greatest resistance to compression loads, is weakest in response to shear (side to side) loads, and has an intermediate strength for tension loads. Measurements indicate that the human femur has a strength (σ_{ult}) of 132 MPa when a tensile force is applied along the length of the bone (longitudinal) but a strength of only 58 MPa for tensile forces acting perpendicular (normal) to the bone. Similarly, the femur has a compressive strength of 187 and 132 MPa for longitudinal and perpendicular forces, respectively (Cowin, 1983). In engineering terms, bone has a **safety factor** of between two and five; that is, bones are two to five times stronger than the forces they commonly encounter in the activities of daily living (Alexander, 1984a; Biewener, 1991; Konieczynski, Truty, & Biewener, 1998).

From these types of measurements it is apparent that the stress a bone can withstand depends significantly on its size (cross-sectional area). Consequently, bones that are subjected to large stresses must have large cross-sectional areas, which would mean that they have a greater mass and impose a greater energy demand on the system during movement. However, the structure of bone, especially long bones, has evolved to achieve a compromise between strength (resistance to imposed loads) and mass (Kaplan et al., 1994). Consider the cross-

Table 5.1 Stress-Strain Characteristics for Human Bone Subjected to a Tension Load

	Age (years)	σ_{yield} (MPa)	σ_{ult} (MPa)	Elastic modulus (GPa)	Plastic modulus (GPa)	ε_{ult}	Energy (MPa)
Femur	20-29	120	140	17.0	0.75	0.034	3.85
	30-39	120	136	17.6	0.64	0.032	3.55
	40-49	121	139	17.7	1.00	0.030	3.19
	50-59	111	131	16.6	0.89	0.028	2.84
	60-69	112	129	17.1	0.98	0.025	2.65
	70-79	111	129	17.1	0.98	0.025	2.65
	80-89	104	120	15.6	1.08	0.024	2.23
Tibia	20-29	126	161	18.9	1.17	0.040	4.36
	30-39	129	154	27.0	0.91	0.039	5.77
	40-49	140	170	28.8	1.39	0.029	4.09
	50-59	133	164	23.1	1.21	0.031	4.19
	60-69	124	147	19.9	1.20	0.027	3.05
	70-79	120	145	19.9	1.18	0.027	3.27
	80-89	131	156	29.2	1.43	0.023	2.96

Note. Modified from Burstein et al., 1976.

sectional geometry of the middle section of a long bone. It has a ring design in which bone surrounds a marrow core. The amount of bone in the ring depends on the outside and inside diameters of the ring—the periosteal and endosteal diameters, respectively. The thickness of the ring of bone depends on the difference in the two diameters. Currey and Alexander (1985) suggest that the optimal design for marrow-filled bones for terrestrial mammals is one in which the ratio of the cross-sectional radius to ring thickness is about 2.0. Such a ratio produces a high ultimate strength and resistance to impact loads for a given quantity of bone mass.

Bone As a System

The structural properties of bone emphasize that function has a major effect on the cellular organization and hence the mechanical characteristics of bone. As the stress-strain patterns vary, so do the mechanical properties and cellular organization of bone. **Wolff's law** characterizes this relation as follows: "Every change in the . . . function of bone . . . is followed by certain definite changes in . . . internal architecture and external confirmation in accordance with mathematical laws" (Carter, 1984, p. 1). Some studies related to this law have focused on bone as a structure and have attempted to identify appropriate parameters by which the structure and geometry of bone can be described. Other studies, however, have focused on the processes by which bone adapts to its environment; these represent the study of *bone as a system*. The processes experienced by bone include growth, reinforcement, and resorption, which are collectively termed **remodeling** (Burr, 1997; Kaplan et al., 1994; Lanyon & Rubin, 1984). The time required for one complete cycle of remodeling (replacement of all structures) seems to be about 10 to 20 years for limb bones of the adult human (Alexander, 1984a).

Remodeling represents a balance between bone absorption by osteoclasts and bone formation by osteoblasts. The balance between these processes changes continually and is influenced by such factors as physical activity (stress-strain loads), age, and disease. Several reports in the literature have documented the remodeling of bone with changes (increases and decreases) in activity (Biewener & Bertram, 1993; Carter, Beaupré, Giori, & Helms, 1998; Konieczynski et al., 1998; Mikic & Carter, 1995). For example, Shumskii, Merten, and Dzenis (1978) found a greater deposition and density of bone in the tibia of athletes compared with control subjects. Similarly, MacDougall et al. (1992) found that bone density was greater in the lower legs of men who ran 15 to 20 miles per week compared with those who ran less than 10 miles per week. Furthermore, the normalized cross-sectional area of the tibia and fibula increased with mileage and was significantly greater in men who ran 40 to 50 miles per week compared with control subjects. Even weight lifters (6 years' experience) have been reported to show an increase in bone mineral density at weight-bearing sites (lumbar spine, trochanter, femoral neck) but not at non-weight-bearing sites (midradius) (Colleti, Edwards, Gordon, Shary, & Bell, 1989). Moreover, bone mineral content can increase even after as little as six weeks of exercise (Beverly, Rider, Evans, & Smith, 1989).

The critical mechanical variable that promotes bone formation is the strain experienced by the bone when it is loaded (Konieczynski et al., 1998). The features of strain that seem to influence bone formation include its amplitude, direction, rate of change in length, and the frequency of the strain cycles. Many studies have shown that bone formation occurs only with the application of relatively large but brief, repetitive forces; these are often referred to as **impact loads.** Such loads presumably maximize the magnitude of the strain and the strain rate (rate of increase in length) experienced by the bone (Giddings, Beaupré, Whalen, & Carter, 2000). Additionally, the direction of the cyclically applied load appears to influence the orientation of the osteons and therefore the strength of the bone in the direction of the applied loads.

In contrast to the bone formation that occurs in response to impact loads, the removal of this stimulus has the converse effect. For example, one of the major problems experienced by astronauts during extended flights is the loss of bone tissue (Zernicke, Vailis, & Salem, 1990). The micro-gravity conditions of space flight cause bone **demineralization,** the excessive loss of salts from the skeleton (Anderson & Cohn, 1985; Loitz-Ramage & Zernicke, 1996; Morey, 1979), presumably due to the absence of our typical gravitational environment. This raises two concerns: bone is weaker and therefore more susceptible to fracture during strenuous activities (e.g., extravehicular activity), and bone seems to have difficulty recovering from an episode of demineralization when the astronauts return to a normal-gravity environment. For these reasons, NASA (National Aeronautics and Space Administration) has been interested in exercise programs that might limit the loss of bone tissue during **weightlessness.** Studies indicate that bone remodeling is best induced by loads that are applied intermittently rather than in a sustained, continuous manner (Lanyon & Rubin, 1984). Furthermore, the magnitudes of the joint forces have a greater effect on bone mass than does the number of loading cycles (Whalen, Carter, & Steele, 1988).

Whereas few of us will experience a loss of bone tissue due to weightlessness, our bones will decline in mass and strength as a function of age (Hernandez, Beaupré, & Carter, 2000; Snow-Harter & Marcus, 1991). This effect, known as **osteoporosis,** involves an increase in the porosity of bone that results in a decrease in its density and strength and an increase in its vulnerability to fracture. Men and women appear to lose cortical bone at about the same rate, but women lose trabecular (cancellous) bone, especially after menopause, at a much greater rate (Kaplan et al., 1994). For several years after menopause, the rate of bone resorption is greater than the rate of bone formation, producing a calcium imbalance and a loss of bone mass. This adaptation appears to predispose older women to an increased risk of fractures from falls, which is associated with high rates of mortality and morbidity. Appropriate countermeasures appear to include the performance of physical activities that enhance bone formation (e.g., exercises that impose impact loads on the skeleton), the use of hormonal treatments (Christiansen, 1992), and nutrition counseling (especially concerning calcium intake) (Hernandez et al., 2000).

Attempts to determine the mechanisms that control remodeling have included the study of the electrical properties of bone (Otter, McLeod, & Rubin, 1998; Ryaby, 1998). Apparently, when a stress is sufficient to cause bone collagen fibers to slip relative to one another, this action generates electrical potentials in bone. This generation of electrical potentials due to pressure has been referred to as the **piezoelectric** effect of bone. Scientists have attempted to establish a relation between the mechanical stress experienced by bone and the associated electrical effects as a physical explanation of Wolff's law. It has been shown, for example, that weak electrical currents can induce the formation of a callus (Marino, 1984). One practical consequence of this phenomenon has been the use of electric and magnetic stimulation to enhance fracture healing, especially for those fractures where nonunion seems doubtful (Brighton, 1981; Vander Molen, Donahue, Rubin, & McLeod, 2000). Some investigators have even used the electrical stimulation of bone to attempt to impede the onset of osteoporosis.

Synovial Joint

The 206 bones in the human body form about 200 articulations, which are generally classified into three groups: the fibrous joint, the cartilaginous joint, and the synovial joint. The fibrous joint is relatively immovable and includes such articulations as the sutures of the skull and the interosseus membranes between the radius and ulna or between the tibia and fibula. The cartilaginous joint is slightly movable and includes the sternocostal joint, intervertebral disks, and pubic symphysis articulations. The synovial joint is freely movable and includes the hip, elbow, and atlantoaxial joints. Because the synovial joint most closely approximates the frictionless, pinned joint of the rigid-link model, it is taken as the joint component of the single-joint system.

The synovial joint serves two functions: it provides mobility of the skeleton by permitting one body segment to rotate about another, and it transmits forces from one segment to another. These interactions, which involve the contact of adjacent bones, are controlled by a number of structural features that include articular cartilage, joint capsule, synovial membrane, ligaments, and the geometry of the bones. The surfaces of the bones that form the joint are lined with **articular cartilage,** a dense white connective tissue with an ultimate compressive stress of about 5 MPa. Articular cartilage has no blood vessels, lymph channels, or nerves. It contains chondrocytes, which are cells that maintain the organic component of the extracellular matrix, and a dense network of fine collagen fibrils in a concentrated solution of proteoglycans. The chondrocytes account for about 10% of the volume of articular cartilage. Water is the most abundant component of articular cartilage, accounting for 65% to 80% of the weight of the tissue. The collagen fibrils, proteoglycans, and water determine the biomechanical behavior of articular cartilage (Mankin, Mow, Buckwalter, Iannotti, & Ratcliffe, 1994).

Two forms of lubrication (Mow, Proctor, & Kelly, 1989) protect articular cartilage: (1) boundary lubrication—absorption of the glycoprotein lubricin by the surface of the articular cartilage; and (2) fluid-film lubrication—a thin film of lubricant that causes separation of the articulating surfaces. Boundary lubrication seems to be important when the contact surfaces sustain high loads for long periods of time. In contrast, fluid-film lubrication seems more important when the loads are low and variable and the contact surfaces move at high speeds relative to one another. Synovial joints are capable of self-lubrication, whereby fluid is exuded in front of and beneath the moving contact of the articular cartilage but is reabsorbed as the load passes (Mow et al., 1989). The flux of fluid across the articular cartilage probably serves to provide nutrients for the chondrocytes.

The function of articular cartilage is to allow relative motion of opposing joint surfaces with minimal friction and wear, and to modify the shape of the bone to ensure better contact with its neighbor (Mankin et al., 1994). To this end, articular cartilage behaves as a water-filled sponge. Like the other connective tissues, articular cartilage is a **viscoelastic** material, which means that when it is subjected to a constant load or a constant deformation, its response (mechanical behavior) changes over time (force relaxation, creep, hysteresis). This response can include changes in the thickness of articular cartilage due to the stress-related flux of water. Articular cartilage is thicker in more active individuals and increases in thickness when an individual goes from a resting to an active state. Articular cartilage can become specialized, such as at the temporomandibular and knee joints, and develop intra-articular disks or menisci that enlarge the contact areas of the articulating surfaces. The loads experienced by articular cartilage are supported by the collagen-proteoglycan matrix and by the resistance offered by fluid flow through the matrix (Ahmed & Burke, 1983).

The articulating surfaces of the synovial joint are enclosed in a **joint capsule,** which attaches to the bones of the joint and thus separates the joint cavity from surrounding tissues. The internal aspect of the capsule, as well as those areas of the articulating bones that are not covered with articular cartilage, are lined with **synovial membrane,** a vascular membrane that secretes synovial fluid into the joint cavity. The synovial fluid provides nourishment for the articular cartilage and lubricates the articular cartilage. The joint capsule is a loose structure that surrounds the entire joint and, in some places, fuses with capsular ligaments, which are typically thought to keep the articulating surfaces in close proximity. Like articular cartilage, the joint capsule and associated ligaments adapt to alterations in the pattern of activity. For example, one of the common adaptations associated with limb immobilization is a transient decrease in the range of motion about a joint due to alterations in the structure of the joint capsule and ligaments. Apparently, connective tissue has a tendency to adapt to the shortest functional length; when a joint is immobilized, the capsule and ligaments shrink, and new tissue is synthesized to accommodate the shorter length. These changes result in a reduction in the mobility at the joint. Such immobilization may even contribute to the development of osteoarthritis (Videman, 1987).

In general, there is a trade-off between the mobility of a joint and its stability; the most mobile joints tend to be the least stable. **Joint stability** is defined as the ability of a joint to maintain an appropriate functional position throughout its range of motion. Joint stability depends on three factors: (a) the shape of the articular surfaces and their geometric interaction; (b) the restraint provided by ligaments, joint capsule, and other periarticular structures; and (c) the action of the muscles that cross the joint. These three factors determine the number of **degrees of freedom** at a joint, that is, the number of axes about which motion can occur. A synovial joint may have from one to three degrees of freedom, with the axes passing through the joint from side to side, from front to back, or from end to end. The only motion possible at the humeroradial joint (elbow) is in the flexion-extension plane (Engin & Chen, 1987), which is rotation about an axis that passes side to side through the joint. In contrast, the hip and shoulder (glenohumeral) joints have three degrees of freedom (Engin & Chen, 1986, 1988; Högfors, Sigholm, & Herberts, 1987), which means that the joint structure permits rotation about each of the axes. Motion at these joints can occur in the flexion-extension plane, in the abduction-adduction plane, and in rotation about a longitudinal axis. A summary of the quality and quantity of motion possible at some of the major joints in the human body is provided in table 5.2. The ranges of motion are relative to the anatomical reference position—standing upright with the arms extended and palms facing forward.

Ligament

Ligaments contribute significantly to the stability of the synovial joint (Fu, Harner, Johnson, Miller, & Woo, 1993; Nigg & Herzog, 1994; Wilson, Feikes, & O'Connor, 1998). The primary function of a ligament is to attach articulating bones to one another across a joint. At joints with many degrees of freedom and a large range of motion, there are usually multiple ligaments that resist distracting forces in various directions. For example, the knee joint includes four ligaments: the anterior cruciate ligament, posterior cruciate ligament, medial collateral ligament, and lateral collateral ligament. The anterior and posterior cruciate ligaments resist anterior and posterior displacement of the tibia, respectively. Similarly, the medial collateral ligament resists valgus angulation (knock-knee) and external rotation of the tibia, while the lateral collateral ligament resists varus angulation (bow-leg) and internal rotation of the tibia (Hsieh & Draganich, 1998). When one of the knee joint ligaments is damaged, it is common practice to brace the knee joint during rehabilitation so that the ligaments experience less strain. For example, knee braces reduced the strain experienced by the anterior cruciate ligament when patients went from a seated position to standing and when the knee joint was subjected to internal and external rotation (Beynnon et al., 1997).

Ligaments insert directly into bone or into the periosteum and comprise fibers (collagen, proteoglycans, fibronectin, elastic, and actin) that are oriented in many different directions. The major protein present in ligament is collagen, which exists in fibrillar form and enables ligaments to resist tensile forces. Collagen comprises about 75% of the dry weight of a ligament. The strength of a collagen fiber appears to depend on its diameter, which can vary from 10 to 1500 nm. Furthermore, the load-deformation characteristics of ligament depend on the number of adjacent (side by side) collagen fibers and on the length of the fibers (Butler, Grood, Noyes, & Zernicke, 1978; Woo et al., 1994). The cross-sectional area of the ligament indicates the number of adjacent collagen fibers. Doubling the cross-sectional area of a ligament without changing the length of the fibers would double the strength and the stiffness of the ligament (slope of the load-deformation curve). Conversely, doubling the length of the collagen fibers would halve the stiffness of the ligament.

Table 5.2 Motion at the Major Joints of the Human Body

Joint	Articulating surfaces	Degrees of freedom	Range of motion
Spine	Atlantooccipital	Flexion-extension Lateral flexion	0.3 rad 0.2 rad
	Atlantoaxial	Flexion-extension Rotation (longitudinal)	0.2 rad 0.8 rad
	C3–C7	Flexion-extension Lateral flexion Rotation (longitudinal)	0.7 rad flexion, 0.7 rad extension 0.8 rad to each side 0.9 rad
	Thoracic	Flexion-extension Lateral flexion Rotation (longitudinal)	0.06–0.2 rad 0.06–0.16 rad 0.16 rad
	Lumbar	Flexion-extension Lateral flexion Rotation (longitudinal)	0.3 rad 0.1 rad 0.03 rad
Shoulder	Glenohumeral, acromioclavicular, sternoclavicular, scapulothoracic	Flexion (sagittal plane) Extension (sagittal plane) Flexion (transverse plane) Extension (transverse plane) Abduction (frontal plane) Adduction (frontal plane) Internal-external rotation	3.14 rad 0.8 rad 2.4 rad 0.8 rad 3.14 rad 0.8 rad 3.14 rad (arm abducted and elbow at 1.57 rad)
Elbow	Humeroulnar, humeroradial	Flexion-extension Hyperextension	2.5 rad 0.2 rad
	Proximal radioulnar, humeroradial	Pronation-supination	0.9 rad pronation, 0.8 rad supination
Wrist	Radiocarpal, intercarpal	Flexion-extension Radial-ulnar deviation	1.1 rad flexion, 0.9 rad extension 0.3 rad radial, 0.5 rad ulnar
Hip	Femoral head-acetabulum	Flexion-extension Abduction-adduction Internal-external rotation	2.1 rad flexion, 0.3 rad extension 0.8 rad abduction, 0.4 rad adduction 0.8 rad in each direction
Knee	Tibiofemoral	Flexion-extension Hyperextension Internal-external rotation Abduction-adduction	2.3 rad 0.2 rad 0.7 rad internal, 0.5 rad external (knee at 1.57 rad) < 0.1 rad (knee at 0.5 rad)
Ankle	Tibiotalar, fibulotalar, distal tibiofibular	Flexion-extension	0.2–0.4 rad dorsiflexion, 0.4–0.6 rad plantarflexion
Foot	Subtalar	Inversion-eversion	0.3 rad inversion, 0.1 rad eversion
	Intertarsal and tarsometatarsal	Dorsi-, plantarflexion	0.3 rad dorsiflexion, 0.9 rad plantarflexion
	Metatarsophalangeal	Flexion-extension	0.5 rad flexion, 1.5 rad extension

Note. The sagittal plane divides the body into left and right; the frontal plane distinguishes front and back; the transverse plane separates the body into upper and lower; and longitudinal refers to rotation about a longitudinal axis. The range-of-motion data represent average values for young adults.

When differences in cross-sectional area and length are removed, the material properties of ligament are reasonably consistent and can be characterized by a stress-strain curve (figure 5.3). The initial strain that a ligament experiences at low tensile forces is due to flattening of the collagen crimp (toe region of the stress-strain curve); that is, at rest the collagen fibers have a wavy appearance until the stretch becomes too great (failure). After the initial strain, ligament behaves like an elastic band when stretched (linear region). However, the material properties vary with time. As is the case for other connective tissues, both the stress and strain experienced by a ligament decline over time. When a ligament is stretched and is held at this new length, the stress on the ligament decreases with time; this property is known as **force relaxation.** Conversely, when a ligament is stretched and the stress is maintained, the length of the ligament gradually increases; this property is known as **creep.** These reductions in stress and strain are due to the viscous and elastic properties of ligament.

When subjected to excessive forces, a ligament will rupture. The rate at which a ligament is stretched influences the location of the rupture (Nigg & Herzog, 1994). Although a ligament appears capable of healing (Woo et al., 1994), it will not recover its preinjury capabilities. Similarly, the material and structural properties of ligament change with exercise, immobilization, and aging.

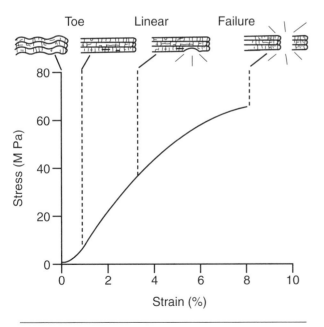

Figure 5.3 Idealized stress-strain relation for collagenous tissue. The tissue can experience only a small change in length before it sustains some damage.

Adapted from Butler, Good, Noyes, and Zernicke, 1978.

Muscle

Muscles are molecular machines that convert chemical energy, initially derived from food, into force. The properties of muscle include (a) irritability—the ability to respond to a stimulus; (b) conductivity—the ability to propagate a wave of excitation; (c) contractility—the ability to modify muscle length; and (d) adaptability—a limited growth and regenerative capacity. Histology identifies three types of vertebrate muscle: cardiac, smooth, and skeletal. Only skeletal muscle is considered in the single-joint system analysis of human movement. Skeletal muscle comprises fused cells with well-defined striations. With the exception of some facial muscles, skeletal muscles act across joints to rotate body segments and thus produce movement. The properties of muscle, therefore, have a major influence on the movement capabilities of humans. For the single-joint system, muscle represents the motor that produces movement.

Muscle contains many identifiable elements. Our focus is on the function of muscle and the processes by which that function is achieved. Two critical processes of muscle function include *(a) the relation between the sarcolemma and the sarcoplasmic reticulum* and *(b) the components of the sarcomere.* These processes are associated with the connection between the nervous system and muscle (sarcolemma-sarcoplasmic reticulum) and the force that muscle can exert (sarcomere).

Gross Structure

Muscle fibers are linked together by a three-level network of collagenous connective tissue. **Endomysium** surrounds individual muscle fibers; **perimysium** collects bundles of fibers into fascicles; and **epimysium** ensheathes the entire muscle (figure 5.4a and b). This connective tissue matrix, which exists throughout the entire muscle and not just at its ends, connects muscle fibers to tendon and hence to the skeleton (Huijing, 1999; Tidball, 1991). Because of this relation, muscle fibers and connective tissue (including tendon) operate as a single functional unit. Sometimes using the term "musculotendinous unit" emphasizes this relation; however, in this text the term *muscle* denotes both the contractile tissue and the associated connective tissue (including tendon).

Muscle fibers vary from 1 to 400 mm in length and from 10 to 60 μm in diameter. The cell membrane encircling each set of myofilaments that composes a muscle fiber is known as the **sarcolemma.** As a plasma membrane, the sarcolemma provides active and passive selective transport across the membrane, an essential property of excitable membranes. Because of this property, the sarcolemma allows some material to pass through (passive transport) and actually helps other material to

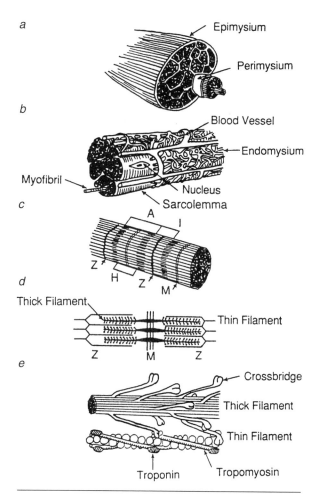

Figure 5.4 Organization of skeletal muscle from the gross to the molecular level. Note the levels of connective tissue within muscle, the bands and zones that comprise the sarcomere, and the molecular components of the thick and thin filaments: *(a)* whole muscle; *(b)* a group of muscle fibers; *(c)* one myofibril; *(d)* a sarcomere; *(e)* one thick and one thin filament.

Reprinted from Pitman and Peterson, 1989.

pass through (active transport). The sarcolemma is about 7.5 nm thick. The fluid enclosed within the fiber by the sarcolemma is known as **sarcoplasm.** Within the sarcoplasm are fuel sources (e.g., lipid droplets, glycogen granules), organelles (e.g., nuclei, mitochondria, lysosomes), enzymes (e.g., myosin adenosinetriphosphatase [ATPase], phosphorylase), and the contractile apparatus (bundles of myofilaments arranged into myofibrils).

In addition, the sarcoplasm contains an extensive, hollow, membranous system that is functionally linked to the surface sarcolemma and that assists the muscle in conducting commands from the nervous system. This membranous system includes the sarcoplasmic reticulum, lateral sacs (terminal cisternae), and transverse (T) tubules (figure 5.5). The **sarcoplasmic reticulum** runs

longitudinally along the fiber, which places it parallel to and surrounding the myofibrils. At specific locations along the myofibril, the sarcoplasmic reticulum bulges into **lateral sacs.** Perpendicular to the sarcoplasmic reticulum and associated with the lateral sacs are **transverse tubules,** which are branched invaginations of the sarcolemma. As we shall consider in more detail later, the connection between the sarcoplasmic reticulum and the transverse tubules aids in the rapid communication between the sarcolemma and the contractile apparatus.

Sarcomere

Skeletal muscle fibers can be regarded as a series of repeating units, each of which comprises the same characteristic banded structure. This unit, the **sarcomere,** includes the zone of a myofibril from one Z band to another (figures 5.4*d* and 5.5). The sarcomere is the basic contractile unit of muscle and comprises an interdigitating set of thick and thin contractile proteins (figure 5.4*d*). Thick filaments have a diameter of 12 nm compared with 7 nm for thin filaments. Similarly, thick filaments are slightly longer (1.6 μm) than thin filaments (1.27 μm). A **myofibril** is a series of sarcomeres that are added end to end. Each myofibril is composed of bundles of myofilaments (thick and thin contractile proteins) and has a diameter of about 1 μm. Because a sarcomere has a length of about 2.5 μm in resting muscle, a 10-mm myofibril represents 4000 sarcomeres added end to end.

The obvious striations of skeletal muscle are due to the differential refraction of light as it passes through the contractile proteins. The thick-filament zone (figure 5.4*c*), which includes some interdigitating thin filaments, is doubly refractive (i.e., forms two refracted rays of light from a single incoming ray) and comprises the dark band, called the **A band** (anisotropic). Within the A band is a zone that contains only thick filaments. Because this zone is clear of thin filaments, it is known as the **H band** (Hellerscheibe, or clear disk). The area between the A bands contains predominantly thin filaments and, because it is singly refractive, is called the **I band** (isotropic).

Each set of filaments (thick and thin) is attached to a central transverse band; the thick filaments attach to the **M band** (Mittelscheibe, or middle disk—the band located in the middle of the A band), and the thin filaments connect to the **Z band** (Zwischenscheibe, or between disk). A cross section through the A band shows that each thick filament is surrounded by six thin filaments, whereas a single thin filament can interact with only three thick filaments.

Myofilaments

The myofibril contains two myofilaments, known as thick and thin filaments. Each myofilament is composed of

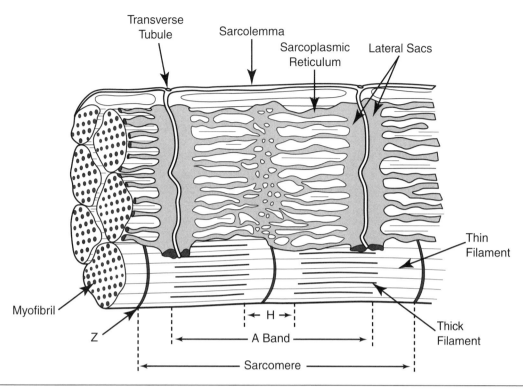

Figure 5.5   Alignment of the transverse tubules and sarcoplasmic reticulum with respect to the myofibrils. The figure shows six of the myofibrils that are part of a single muscle fiber.

Adapted from Bloom and Fawcett, 1968.

several proteins (figure 5.6). The structure of the thin filament is dominated by actin but also includes the proteins tropomyosin and troponin, which regulate the interaction between actin and myosin. Each thin filament is composed of two helical strands of fibrous actin (**F actin**) (figure 5.6a). Each F-actin strand is a polymer (i.e., chemical union of two or more molecules) of some 200 globular actin (**G actin**) molecules (figure 5.6b). A G-actin molecule is a protein containing about 374 amino acids.

Located in the groove of the F-actin helix are two coiled strands of **tropomyosin** (figure 5.6a and b). The structure of tropomyosin is referred to as a two-chain coiled-coil; each of these chains contains approximately 284 amino acids. The **troponin** (TN) complex has a globular structure that includes three subunits (figure 5.6b): the **TN-T** unit binds troponin to tropomyosin; **TN-I** inhibits four to seven G-actin molecules from binding to myosin when tropomyosin is present; and **TN-C** can reversibly bind Ca^{2+} ions as a function of calcium concentration. Troponin C has four binding sites, two for Ca^{2+} and two for Ca^{2+} or Mg^{2+}. Thus the thin filament has as its backbone two strands of actin molecules (F actin) upon which are superimposed (wrapped around or attached to) two-stranded (tropomyosin) and globular (troponin) pro-

teins. These proteins operate in much the same way during a muscle contraction; tropomyosin and troponin influence the activity of actin. For example, variations in the troponin and tropomyosin isoforms can cause changes in the relation between intracellular Ca^{2+} and muscle fiber tension (Galler, Schmitt, Hilber, & Pette; 1997; Schiaffiano & Reggiani, 1996), which is known as the **calcium-activation curve.**

A set of thin filaments that projects longitudinally into one sarcomere connects the Z-band region to another set, which projects in the opposite direction into the adjacent sarcomere. At this connection, each thin filament appears to be linked to its four closest neighbors. A region of considerable flexibility, the Z band changes its shape under different conditions. Z-band width can vary from one muscle fiber to another (e.g., different muscle fiber types), and it probably also varies as a consequence of training (Schroeter, Bretaudiere, Sass, & Goldstein, 1996; Sjöström, Kidman, Larsén, & Ängquist, 1982; Thornell, Carlsson, Kugelberg, & Grove, 1987).

The thick filaments contain myosin and several myosin-binding proteins: C protein, H protein, M protein, and myomesin (Schiaffino & Reggiani, 1996). Of the thick-filament proteins, the myosin molecule is the one we know the most about (Cooke, 1990; Irving & Piazzesi,

a

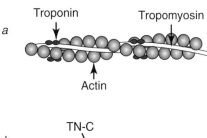

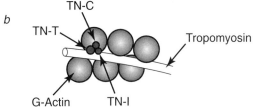

b

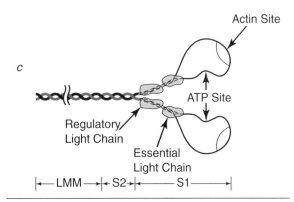

c

Figure 5.6   Organization of the myofilaments: *(a)* the thin filament; *(b)* troponin (TN) elements; *(c)* the myosin molecule.

Adapted from Whalen, 1985.

ATP = adenosine triphosphate; LMM = light meromyosin; S1, S2 = subfragments 1 and 2.

1997). It is a long, two-chain, helical structure that terminates in two large globular heads (figure 5.6*c*). Each globular head, which is ~17 nm long, has an adenosine triphosphate (ATP)- and an actin-binding site. With the aid of an enzyme (protease), the myosin molecules can be decomposed into **light meromyosin** (LMM) and **heavy meromyosin** (HMM) fragments. The HMM fragment can be further subdivided into **subfragments 1** and **2** (S1 and S2). Light meromyosin has a relatively low molecular weight (135 kilodaltons [kDa]), whereas HMM is heavier (335 kDa). The globular heads of the myosin molecule, which contain ATP- and actin-binding sites, are known as S1. The two binding sites are connected by a cleft. The remaining portion of HMM is called S2. The role of these four components (HMM, LMM, S1, and S2) in a muscle contraction has been examined extensively by muscle physiologists.

Because LMM binds strongly to itself under physiological conditions, approximately 400 myosin molecules aggregate to form the dominant element of the thick fila-

ment (Pepe & Drucker, 1979). The union is not random, but structured. The molecules are aligned in pairs, and the S1 element of each molecule is oriented to its partner at 3.14 rad (180°). The next pair is displaced by a translation of about 0.0143 μm and a rotation of 2.1 rad (120°). The result is an ordered alignment of myosin molecules in which the HMM projections (cross-bridges) encircle the thick filament (figure 5.4*e*). Each sarcomere actually contains two such sets of myosin molecules; however, because the S1 elements of the two sets point in opposite directions, the LMM fragments unite in the M band (figure 5.4*c*) to form a single filament.

The myosin molecule contains two hinge regions, that is, zones of greater flexibility. These occur at the LMM-HMM and S1-S2 junctions. In the resulting alignment, the HMM fragment can extend from the thick filament to within close proximity of the thin filament (figure 5.4*e*). Because of the ability of S1 to interact with actin, the HMM extension has been called the **cross-bridge.** The S1 region of HMM contains the sites that hydrolyze ATP and the motor domain that converts chemical energy to mechanical work (Lutz & Lieber, 1999). Each thick filament is surrounded by and can interact with six thin filaments because the cross-bridges encircle the thick filament. There are about 1600 thick filaments per μm² in human quadriceps femoris muscle (Claassen, Gerber, Hoppeler, Lüthi, & Vock, 1989).

The proteins that compose the contractile apparatus can be distinguished as the products of different genes. Eight multigene families contribute the major components of the sarcomere: myosin heavy chain, alkali light chain, DTNB (Dithionitrobenzoic acid) light chain, actin, tropomyosin, troponin C, troponin I, and troponin T (Gunning & Hardeman, 1991; Tsika, Herrick, & Baldwin, 1987). The first three of these components form the myosin molecule. Because proteins comprise sequences (chains) of amino acids, a protein with a high molecular weight (200 kDa) is referred to as a **heavy chain.** Conversely, a protein with a low molecular weight (<30 kDa) is identified as a **light chain.** And a given protein that is synthesized with a slightly different amino acid composition is known as an **isoform;** that is, there can be different isoforms (amino acid compositions) of the same protein that may or may not be the product of different genes (Babij & Booth, 1988). Isoforms are sometimes referred to as *isoenzymes.* There can be different isoforms of the myosin heavy chain and different isoforms of the light chain (table 5.3). Although the different heavy chain isoforms appear to have physiological significance, less is known about the functional consequences of differences in other contractile protein isoforms. However, isoforms of the contractile proteins do change during development and as a consequence of altered physical activity.

Table 5.3   Isoforms of the Contractile Proteins in Various Adult Skeletal Muscles

Gene family	Skeletal muscle	
	Slow	Fast
Myosin heavy chain	S	F_{2A}, F_{2B}, F_{2X}, F_{EO}, F_{SF}
Alkali light chain	1_{Sa}, 1_{Sb}	1_F, 3_F
Dithionitrobenzoic acid light chain	2_S, $2_{S'}$	2_F
Actin	α_{sk}	α_{sk}
α-actinin	S	F
Myosin-binding protein C	S	F
Tropomyosin	β, α_s	β, α_F
Troponin C	S	F
Troponin I	S	F
Troponin T	S	F

Note. S = slow; F = fast; F_{2A}, F_{2B} = correspond to the two fast-twitch fibers defined by histochemistry; F_{2X} = defined by anitbody staining and protein analysis; F_{EO} = found in adult extraocular muscle; F_{SF} = super-fast contractile proteins of jaw muscle.

Data from Gunning and Hardeman 1991; Schiaffino and Reggiani 1996.

The myosin molecule consists of two coiled heavy chains with light chains attached to the myosin heads (figure 5.6c). The isoforms differ in cardiac, smooth, and skeletal muscle. The heavy chains in skeletal muscle have a molecular weight of 220 kDa. There is a strong relation between the maximum velocity at which muscle fibers can shorten and the ATPase activity of the heavy chain isoform contained in the fiber (Schiaffino & Reggiani, 1996). There appear to be one slow and five fast heavy chain isoforms (table 5.3). Four light chains are attached to the globular heads, and these are distinguishable by molecular weight (~16-30 kDa), by whether or not they can be phosphorylated, and by the experimental agent (alkali or DTNB) that separates them from the heavy chain. As with the heavy chains, there appear to be different isoforms of the light chains for fast- and slow-twitch muscle fibers (table 5.3). Although the specific function of the light chains is unknown, they are necessary for contractile function and probably modulate the interaction between actin and myosin (Lowey, Waller, & Trybus, 1993).

Cytoskeleton

Since the initial proposal of the sliding filament theory of muscle contraction, it has become obvious that there must exist additional structures that facilitate the force-generating function of the myofilaments (Huijing, 1999; Monti, Roy, Hodgson, & Edgerton, 1999; Patel & Lieber, 1997; Sheard, 2000; Trotter, Richmond, & Purslow, 1995). These structures, which are termed the **cytoskeleton** (Cooke, 1985), are involved in the alignment of the thick and thin filaments and in the transmission of force from the sarcomeres to the skeleton. The cytoskeleton has been described as consisting of two lattices; the **endosarcomeric** cytoskeleton maintains the orientation of the thick and thin filaments within the sarcomere, and the **exosarcomeric** cytoskeleton maintains the lateral (side by side) alignment of the myofibrils (Patel & Lieber, 1997; Waterman-Storer, 1991).

The major components of the endosarcomeric cytoskeleton are the proteins **titin** and **nebulin.** Titin appears to provide a connection between the thick filaments and the Z band (figure 5.7a), which keeps the myofilaments aligned and contributes to the banding structure of skeletal muscle. Because the titin connection provides a continuous link along the sarcomere, it probably contributes significantly to the passive tension of muscle (Wang, McCarter, Wright, Beverly, & Ramirez-Mitchell, 1993). Nebulin appears to regulate the length of the thin filament and to influence the interaction between actin and myosin. Because the thin-filament proteins (actin, troponin, tropomyosin) can be of variable lengths, it has been proposed that nebulin sets the number of elements that should be connected (polymerized) and therefore determines the length of the thin filament. Nebulin may also, like troponin and tropomyosin, play a regulatory role in muscle contraction (Patel & Lieber, 1997).

The exosarcomeric cytoskeleton provides connections that transmit the force generated by actin and myosin to intramuscular connective tissues and the skeleton. The exosarcomeric proteins include the intermediate filaments and focal adhesions. The **intermediate fibers** are arranged longitudinally along and transversely across sarcomeres (figure 5.7b), between the myofibrils within a muscle fiber (figure 5.7c), and between muscle fibers (figure 5.7d). The intermediate fibers—which consist of such proteins as desmin, vimentin, and skelemin—are localized at the Z and M bands and connect each myofibril to its neighbor. The intermediate fibers are probably responsible for the alignment of adjacent sarcomeres and undoubtedly provide a pathway for the longitudinal and lateral transmission of force between sarcomeres, myofibrils, and muscle fibers. Much of the force generated by the contractile proteins is transmitted laterally (Monti et al., 1999; Street, 1983). Additionally, when myofibrils are added to a muscle fiber, as occurs with muscle hypertrophy, the intermediate fibers can align the new contractile proteins.

Focal adhesions connect myofibrils to the sarcolemma (figure 5.7c) and also connect muscle fibers to the

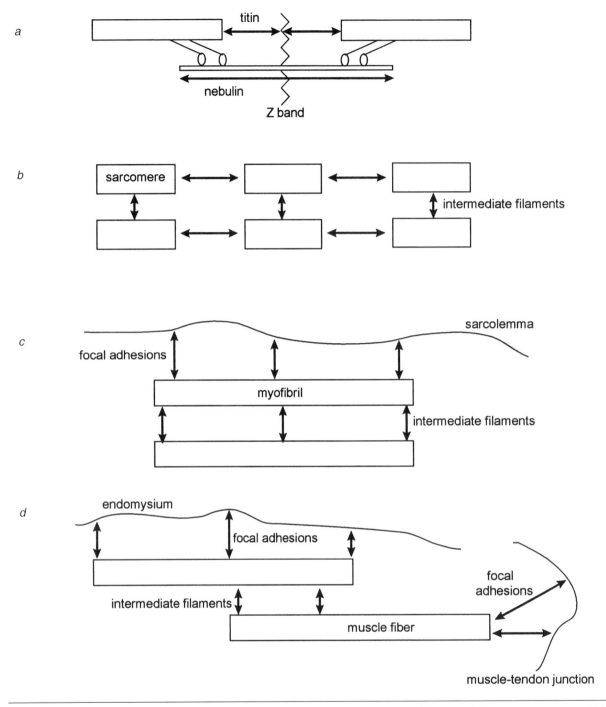

Figure 5.7 The cytoskeletal proteins (arrows) provide connections *(a)* between the myofilaments, *(b)* between sarcomeres within a myofibril, *(c)* between myofibrils and the sarcolemma, and *(d)* between muscle fibers and associated connective tissues.

Data from Patel and Lieber, 1997.

endomysium and the muscle-tendon junction (figure 5.7*d*). The major role of focal adhesions is to connect intracellular proteins to extracellular space; in muscle, focal adhesions are also known as costameres. Focal adhesions include a number of cytoskeletal anchor proteins: α-actinin, ankyrin, desmin, dystrophin, integrins, myonexin, paxillin, syntrophin, talin, and vinculin, some of which are shown in figure 5.8. One preliminary model of the focal adhesion (costamere) proposes that force is transmitted from α-actinin in the Z band to the talin-vinculin complex and then to the transmembrane integrins (Patel & Lieber, 1997). Dystrophin appears to be neces-

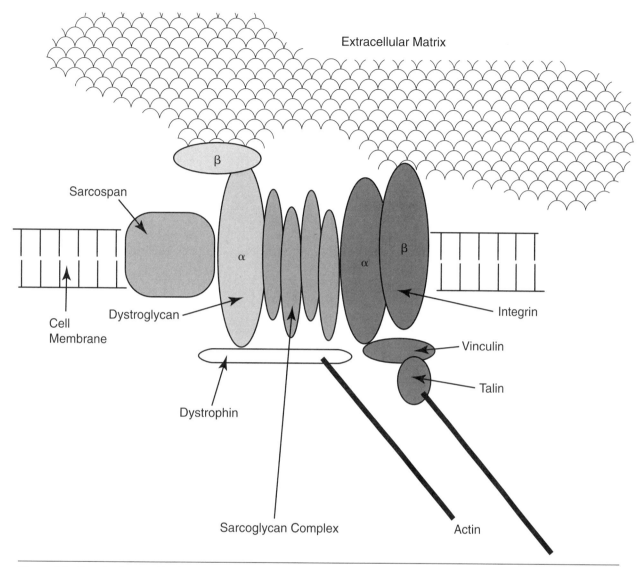

Figure 5.8   Proteins involved in the transmission of force from inside a muscle cell to the extracellular matrix.
Data from Monti et al., 1999.

sary to prevent mechanical damage (Petrof, Shrager, Stedman, Kelly, & Sweeney, 1993). From these descriptions, it should be apparent that much remains to be learned about the molecular basis of these systems.

Tendon

Tendon is a flexible band of collagen that connects muscle to bone. The primary functions of tendon are to transmit force from muscle to the skeleton and to store elastic energy. For the single-joint system, tendon is considered as an element distinct from muscle because it can have a significant influence on muscle function. Typically when the properties of biological tissues are discussed in textbooks, tendon and ligament are considered concurrently because of their similarities in morphology (Woo et al., 1994). In this chapter, however, the focus is on function; therefore the information on tendon is presented after that on muscle, while ligament is considered in conjunction with the synovial joint. Nonetheless, many of the structural details on tendon are also applicable to ligament.

Rarely does a muscle simply have one tendon at each end for attachment to the skeleton (figure 5.9). Rather, the connective tissue associated with tendon typically extends into the muscle where it becomes an **aponeurosis.** The aponeurosis is prominent in muscles that have a pennate structure; that is, the muscle fibers are aligned at an angle to the line of pull of the muscle (figure 5.9*a, c,* and *e*). Functionally there is no distinction between the tendon proper and the aponeurosis, as both are

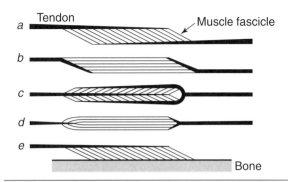

Figure 5.9 Five common arrangements of tendon and muscle (a toe). The tendons are shown as thick lines and the muscle fascicles as thin lines.

Adapted from Alexander and Ker, 1990.

involved in the transmission of force and the storage of elastic energy. Furthermore, the dimensions of a tendon can vary in length and breadth, and the attachment on bone can be focused or broad. Such differences influence the mechanical properties of tendon; for example, longer tendons have a greater capacity to store elastic energy (Biewener, 1998).

Tendon and ligament are dense connective tissues that contain collagen, elastin, actin, fibronectin, proteoglycans, water, and cells (fibroblasts). The components of the connective tissue matrix are synthesized and degraded by the fibroblasts. Approximately 86% of the dry weight of tendon and ligament consists of type I collagen (Woo et al., 1994), which is a fibrous protein that has considerable mechanical stability (Burgeson & Nimni, 1992). The **fibril** (figure 5.10) is the basic load-bearing unit of both tendon and ligament. The structure of the fibril, from the alpha chains of the triple helix to the packing of the tropocollagen molecules in the microfibril, is the same for tendon and ligament. The major distinction between the two connecting elements concerns *the way in which the fibrils are arranged.* In tendon, the fibrils are arranged longitudinally in parallel to maximize the resistance to tensile forces. In ligament, the fibrils are generally aligned in parallel with some oblique or spiral arrangements to accommodate forces in different directions.

The **triple-helix** structure of tropocollagen indicates that the molecule consists of three intertwined polypeptide chains (figure 5.11). Each polypeptide chain includes a sequence of about 1000 amino acids (mainly proline, hydroxyproline, and glycine) and is known as an *alpha chain*. The three-stranded tropocollagen molecules are then arranged end to end (in series), and five such rows are stacked in parallel (side by side) to form the **microfibril.** The adjacent tropocollagen molecules are staggered by one-quarter, which enables oppositely charged amino acids to be aligned. The collagen fibril, which is the basic load-bearing unit of tendon and ligament, consists of bundles of microfibrils held together by biochemical bonds (cross-linkages) between the collagen molecules; these cross-links occur both within and between

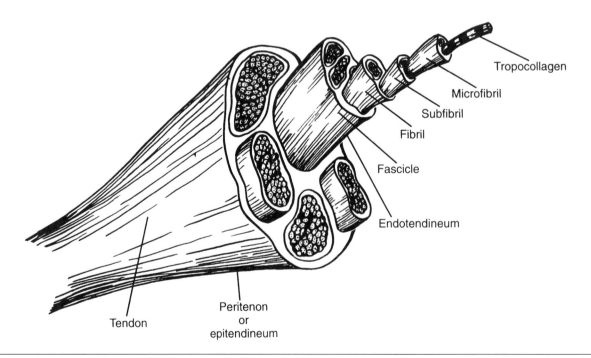

Figure 5.10 The hierarchical organization of tendon to the level of tropocollagen.

Reprinted from Whiting and Zernicke, 1998.

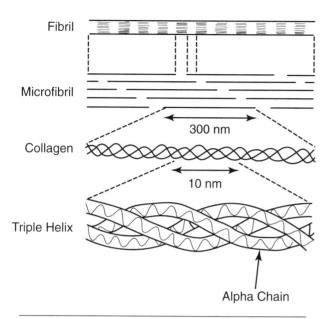

Fibril

Microfibril

Collagen

300 nm

10 nm

Triple Helix

Alpha Chain

Figure 5.11 The organization of collagen into the fibril.

the rows of collagen molecules in the microfibril. Because these **cross-links** bind the microfibrils together, *the number and state of the cross-links are thought to have a substantial effect on the strength of the connective tissue* (Bailey, Robins, & Balian, 1974; Woo et al., 1994). Thus the functional focus of tendon and ligament is the fibril, a collection of units (microfibrils) bound together by cross-links.

The connection between the myofibrils and the tendon is known as the **myotendinous junction.** The myofibrils and collagen fibers are attached in several layers of folds; this increases the resistance of the junction to rupture (Trotter, 1993). With this arrangement, the myofibrils and collagen fibers lie side by side and are connected by focal adhesions. Although muscle fibers transmit force along their sides as well as at their ends, the myotendinous junction appears well designed to resist shear forces. For example, microscopic analysis of junction ruptures indicates that the muscle fibers do not break in the folded region but instead at a short distance from this region (Trotter, 1993). At the other end of the tendon, the connection between tendon and bone is called the **osteotendinous junction.** The details of this attachment vary depending on whether the tendon connects to epiphysial bone or periosteum (Nigg & Herzog, 1994). Like the myotendinous junction, the osteotendinous junction is well designed to resist rupture.

Structural Properties

The mechanical properties of tendon and ligament are frequently characterized as a load-deformation relation

in response to a tensile load (Woo et al., 1994). As shown in figure 5.12, the resistance (force) offered by tendon and ligament varies nonlinearly as a function of tissue length; the steeper the graph, the greater the stiffness of the tissue. In these experiments, a specimen (e.g., ligament, tendon, ligament-bone) was obtained from a cadaver and mounted on a device that stretched the tissue at a prescribed rate (strain rate) to failure and measured the displacement (elongation or deformation) and force. Figure 5.12 shows the variation in length and peak force at failure for various specimens. For example, a medial patellar tendon-bone specimen was stretched 10 mm and exerted a peak tensile force of about 3 kN before it began to fail, whereas an anterior cruciate ligament-bone specimen was stretched 15 mm and exerted a peak tensile force of around 1.5 kN before failure.

The data shown in figure 5.12 are taken from a study that compared the mechanical properties of various collagenous tissues for use in reconstruction of articular cartilage at the knee joint (Noyes, Butler, Grood, Zernicke, & Hefzy, 1984). The gracilis tendon represents the tissue between the muscle and the tibial insertion. The fascia lata specimen was 7 to 10 cm wide and was taken from the middle of the thigh just proximal to the lateral femoral condyle. The data indicate that the patellar tendon-bone specimen was stronger than the anterior cruciate ligament-bone specimen, but both the patellar tendon and anterior cruciate specimens were stronger than those of the gracilis tendon and the fascia lata (figure 5.12).

Many of these differences among specimens can be explained by differences in their size. For example, suppose that two tendon specimens have the same length but that one has a cross-sectional area twice as large as the other. This difference in size will influence the force-deformation relation. The maximum deformation that each specimen could sustain before exhibiting damage

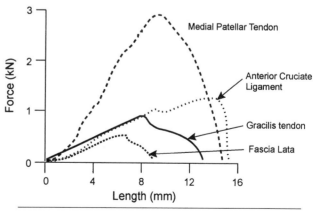

Figure 5.12 Load-deformation relations for connective tissue specimens stretched to failure.

Data from Noyes, 1977; and Noyes, Butler, Grood, Zernicke, and Hefzy, 1984.

would be the same. However, the strength of the two specimens would be different: the peak force (*y*-axis) would be twice as great for the specimen with the larger cross-sectional area. This difference would make the stiffness (slope of the graph) twice as great for the larger specimen. Similarly, suppose that two specimens have the same cross-sectional areas but that one is twice as long as the other. The peak force of each specimen would be the same, but the maximum deformation would be twice as long for the longer specimen. This difference would make the stiffness of the longer specimen one-half that for the shorter specimen. The sizes (cross-sectional area and length) of tendons and ligaments vary depending on their primary function (Shadwick, 1990).

Material Properties

When the load and deformation are normalized so that load is expressed per unit cross-sectional area (stress) and deformation is described as a percentage of the initial length (strain), the biomechanical properties of tissues can be compared as stress-strain relations. Figure 5.3 represents an idealized stress-strain relation for collagenous tissue, such as tendon and ligament. The stress-strain relation comprises three regions: toe, linear, and failure. The *toe region* corresponds to the initial part of the relation, in which the collagen fibers are stretched and straightened from a resting zigzag pattern. The toe region extends up to about 3% strain. The *linear region* represents the elastic capability of the tissue (figure 3.8); the slope of the relation in this region is referred to as the elastic modulus (or tangent modulus) and is steeper for stiffer tissues. The linear region goes up to about 6% to 10% strain, beyond which the tendon experiences structural changes (Woo et al., 1994). Beyond the linear region, the slope decreases as some of the fibers are disrupted in the *failure region.* When connective tissue experiences a strain of this magnitude (10-15%), the tissue undergoes plastic changes and there is a change in its resting length. When measured carefully, the ultimate stress (σ_{ult}) for tendon and ligament is generally in the range of 50 to 100 MPa, which means that the maximum load a tendon or ligament can bear largely depends on the cross-sectional area of the specific structure. The elastic modulus for tendon ranges from 0.8 to 2.0 GPa.

Because of the components in tendon and ligament, these tissues exhibit both elastic and viscous properties, which influence their dynamic response to various loads. For example, when a load is attached to a tendon, the resistance (force) offered by the tendon gradually declines over time; this behavior is known as the force-relaxation response (figure 5.13*a*). Furthermore, whereas the force declines during the application of a constant load, the length of the tendon gradually increases; this behavior is known as creep (figure 5.13*b*). When the load is released,

the tendon will shorten, as expected for an elastic material, but it will be longer than it was before the application of the load. These two behaviors (force relaxation and creep) also occur when a ligament or tendon is loaded repetitively.

Similarly, the resistance that a tissue offers to a stretch at a given velocity, which depends on its viscosity, decreases with prior activity. This property, known as **thixotropy,** is attributable to a transient physical change in the gel (proteoglycans and water) within the tissue. When viscosity decreases, such as after warm-up exercises, the

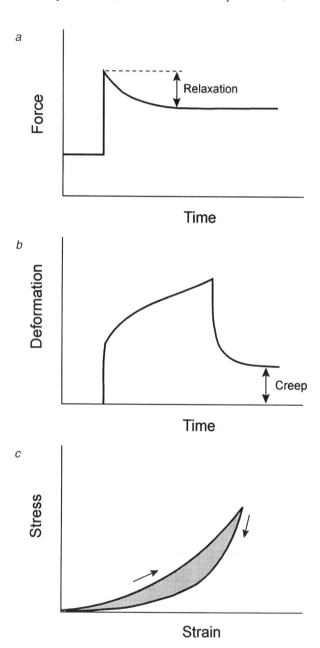

Figure 5.13 Material properties of tendon and ligament: *(a)* force-relaxation response, *(b)* creep response, and *(c)* hysteresis area (shaded).

tissue is able to accommodate higher-velocity stretches before it is damaged—hence the need for people to perform warm-up exercises before participating in strenuous physical activities. Similarly, for a given level of viscosity, tendon and ligament offer a greater resistance to fast stretches compared with slow stretches. As a consequence, when tensile loads are applied rapidly to a ligament-bone complex, the ligament is more likely to be damaged first, whereas for slow rates of stretch the ligament-bone connection is more likely to be compromised.

Because the primary function of tendon is to transmit force between muscle and bone, tendon is less viscoelastic than most other biological material. We can demonstrate this by measuring the hysteresis in a stress-strain relation. In this test, a load is applied to a specimen and then released, and the stress and strain are measured during the loading (up arrow) and unloading (down arrow) phases (figure 5.13c). For an elastic material such as a spring, the stress-strain relation is the same for the loading and unloading phases (figure 2.31). For biological material, however, the line for the unloading phase lies below that for the loading phase. The area between the two lines is known as the hysteresis area, which represents that amount of energy dissipated in the loading and unloading process. The hysteresis area for tendon ranges from 2.5% to 20% of the area under the loading phase of the stress-strain curve (Bennett, Ker, Dimery, & Alexander, 1986). This indicates that tendons are capable of storing and releasing strain (elastic) energy.

Adaptations

The material properties of tendon and ligament tend to decline with such conditions as reduced use (e.g., immobilization, bed rest), age, and steroid use, but increase with chronic exercise (Butler et al., 1978; Noyes, 1977; Woo et al., 1994). For example, when humans reach about 40 to 50 years of age, the connections between ligaments and tendons with bone are weaker, and there are more cross-links in tendon and ligament, making these tissues less compliant (Frank, 1996; Woo et al., 1994). Furthermore, exercise appears to increase the strength and stiffness of ligaments (Tipton, Matthes, Maynard, & Carey, 1975), but probably only by about 10% to 20% (Frank, 1996). Conversely, joint immobilization appears to decrease ligament strength and stiffness (Frank, 1996; Butler et al., 1978).

Neuron

We have thus far described four elements of the single-joint system: the rigid link (bone) that forms the structural basis of the system, a joint about which rigid links rotate, a motor (muscle) that can rotate a rigid link, and an element (tendon) that connects the motor to the rigid link. Next we consider the nervous system and its cellular components, which represent the element that controls the motor.

There are only two cell types in the nervous system: **neurons** and **neuroglia.** The neuron is characterized by a distinctive cell shape: an outer membrane (axolemma) capable of generating and conducting an electrical signal, and a unique structure (synapse) for the transfer of information. Less is known about the neuroglia, which are nine times more numerous than neurons. Neuroglia provide structural, metabolic, and protective support for the neurons and assist with repair after an injury (Kandel, 2000b). For example, three prominent functions that we know are performed or assisted by glial cells are myelination, phagocytosis, and metabolism. Myelination is accomplished by oligodendrocytes in the central nervous system (CNS) and by Schwann cells in the peripheral nervous system. In this process, the surface membrane of the glial cell (oligodendrocyte or Schwann cell) wraps around the axon, a branch of the neuron that is involved in sending out commands (figure 5.14). One consequence of this myelination is that the commands sent by the neuron travel at a much greater speed than without myelination. In phagocytosis, glial cells (microglia) are known to proliferate around damaged neurons (injured or degenerating) and to transform into large macrophages that remove the debris. The contributions of neuroglia to metabolism involve modulation of the ions, transmitters, and metabolites that are necessary for the normal function of neurons.

Although neurons are a morphologically diverse group of cells, their common function is performed in three

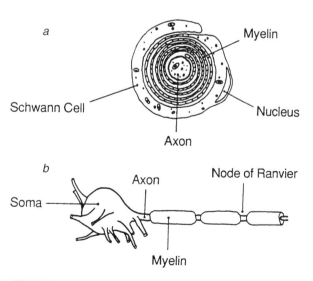

Figure 5.14   Myelination of an axon by a Schwann cell: *(a)* cross-sectional view of a Schwann cell ensheathing an axon; *(b)* an axon ensheathed by many Schwann cells, which provide an interrupted covering of myelin. The gaps in the myelin are known as nodes of Ranvier.

distinct phases: (a) the reception of information (input), (b) an evaluation of the input to determine whether an output signal should be transmitted, and (c) transmission of the output signal. A typical neuron has four morphological regions—dendrites, soma, axon, presynaptic terminal (figure 5.15)—that interact to accomplish these

a

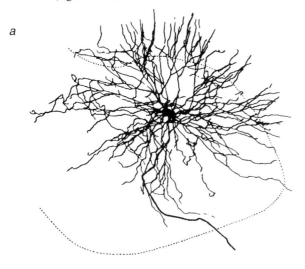

b

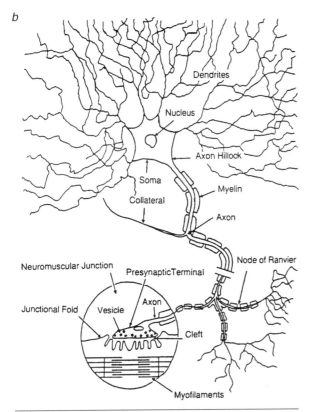

Figure 5.15 Morphological features of neurons. *(a)* A reconstruction of a motor neuron from the spinal cord of a cat shows a large dendritic tree surrounding a small soma and an axon exiting at the bottom of the figure. *(b)* An idealized (not to scale) neuron showing the four morphological regions: dendrites, soma, axon, and presynaptic terminal.

Reprinted from Ulfhake and Kellerth, 1984.

tasks (Palay & Chan-Palay, 1987). The **soma** (cell body) contains the apparatus (e.g., nucleus, ribosomes, rough endoplasmic reticulum, Golgi apparatus) needed for the synthesis of macromolecules. The **axon** is a tubular process that arises from the soma at the axon hillock. One of its functions is to serve as a cable for transmitting the output signal (Rall, 1987), which is an electrical event known as the **action potential.** The axon hillock, the most excitable portion of the axon, represents the site of initiation of the action potential. The axon usually gives off branches that are referred to as **collaterals.** Near its end, the axon divides into many fine branches that form functional contacts with the receptive surface of cells. These contacts are referred to as **synapses.** The ending of the axon involved in the synapse is identified as the **presynaptic terminal** and includes the means for transferring the output signal from the neuron to the effector cell. In neuron-to-neuron interactions, the most common receptive site is the **dendrites,** the other processes extending from the soma. Although synapses can occur between any neuronal parts (e.g., axodendritic, axosomatic, axoaxonic, dendrodendritic, dendrosomatic), about 80% of the input sites (synapses) are located on the dendrites.

Three functional classes of neurons are important in the single-joint system: afferent, interneuron, and efferent (figure 5.16). This scheme represents the flow of information from the surroundings (outside the single-joint system) into the CNS and ends with a response that is transmitted to muscle. **Afferent** neurons convey sensory information back into the CNS regarding stimuli that have been detected in the surroundings. We will examine the role of various sensory modalities in the control of movement when we discuss sensory receptors, the sixth element of the single-joint system. Afferent signals enter the CNS and act at both local and remote levels throughout the CNS. Simple reflexes are an example of local effects. An afferent signal enters the spinal cord and results in a response (output) from the same level of the spinal cord. **Interneurons** account for 99% of all neurons and represent the CNS component that modulates the interaction between input (afferent) and output (efferent) signals. Interneurons can elicit excitatory and inhibitory responses in other neurons. This modulation (excitation and inhibition) can occur directly, with the interneuron forming part of the circuit between the afferent and efferent neurons; or it can occur indirectly, with the interneuron altering the excitability of the connection between the afferent and efferent neurons (figure 5.16). In addition, the efferent neuron can receive input from other structures within the CNS, and the interneuron can also modulate this interaction.

Efferent neurons transmit the output signal (action potentials) from the CNS to the effector organ. In the single-joint system, the effector organ is muscle. Efferent neurons that innervate muscle are referred to as **mo-**

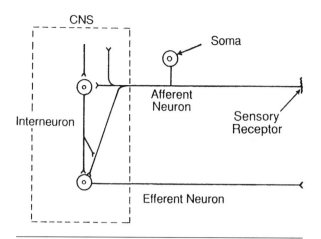

Figure 5.16 The three functional classes of neuron include the afferent neuron, interneuron, and efferent neuron.

CNS = central nervous system.

tor neurons. The somas of these neurons are located in the brain stem and in the gray matter of the spinal cord, and their axons exit the cord and are bundled together into peripheral nerves that course to the target muscles. Forty-three pairs of nerves (12 cranial and 31 spinal) in the human body leave the CNS and form the peripheral nervous system. The spinal cord is often described as a segmented structure in which the segments correspond to the vertebrae. Between each pair of vertebrae, a set of axons exits and another set enters on each side (left and right) of the cord. The axons belonging to efferent neurons exit the spinal cord in the **ventral** (front) **roots,** whereas the axons of the afferent neurons enter through the **dorsal** (back) **roots** (figure 5.17). Motor neurons have large-diameter, myelinated axons that traverse from the

spinal cord directly to skeletal muscle. The somas of the motor neurons are located in the ventral horn of the spinal cord.

In contrast to motor neurons that innervate skeletal muscle, some efferent neurons connect to cardiac muscle, smooth muscle, and glands. These neurons form the **autonomic nervous system.** They control such physiological processes as arterial blood pressure, gastrointestinal motility and secretion, perspiration, and body temperature. Most of these functions are not under voluntary control but instead are regulated by autonomic reflexes. Whereas motor neurons directly innervate skeletal muscle, there are two neurons in the autonomic nervous system between the CNS and the effector cell. One of these neurons has its soma in the CNS, and the other has its soma outside the CNS in cell clusters known as **autonomic ganglia.** On the basis of anatomical and physiological differences, the autonomic nervous system can be subdivided into sympathetic and parasympathetic divisions. In the **sympathetic** division, the cell bodies of the first neurons are located in the thoracic spinal cord, and the autonomic ganglia containing the cell bodies of the second neurons are usually located close to the spinal cord. In the **parasympathetic** division, the cell bodies of the first neurons reside in the brain and the sacral region of the spinal cord, and the autonomic ganglia containing the cell bodies of the second neurons are located within the effector organ.

As the axons of motor neurons exit the spinal cord in the ventral root, they form peripheral nerves that also contain axons of afferent neurons and neurons belonging to the autonomic nervous system. When the nerve reaches the muscle, it subdivides first into primary nerve branches and then into smaller branches until single axons

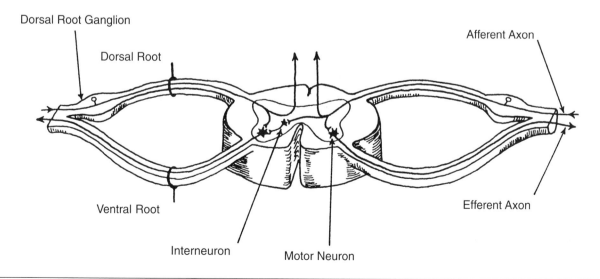

Figure 5.17 Segmental organization of the spinal cord. At the level of each vertebra in the spinal column, the spinal cord gives off a pair of dorsal and ventral roots to each side (right and left) of the body.

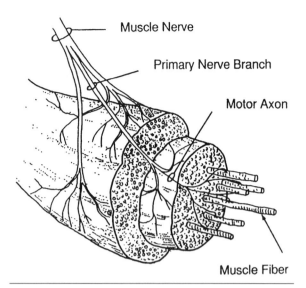

Figure 5.18 Subdivision of the muscle nerve down to the level of single axons that innervate single muscle fibers. The primary nerve branches can produce discrete activation of different parts of a muscle.

Adapted from Peters, 1989.

contact single muscle fibers (figure 5.18). The connection (synapse) between an axon and a muscle fiber is known as a **neuromuscular junction,** sometimes referred to as a *motor end plate.* Neuromuscular junctions are larger in fast-twitch muscle fibers but are depleted of neurotransmitter more rapidly when subjected to repetitive stimulation (Gertler & Robbins, 1978; Panenic & Gardiner, 1998). At the neuromuscular junction, the presynaptic membrane (axon) is separated from the postsynaptic membrane (muscle) by a 1- to 2-μm cleft. An action potential generated by the motor neuron is transmitted across this cleft by an electrochemical process in which the electrical energy embodied in the nerve action potential is converted to chemical energy in the form of a neurotransmitter. The excitation associated with the nerve action potential generates the release of a chemical neurotransmitter by the presynaptic terminal; this process is considered in more detail in chapter 6. At the neuromuscular junction, the neurotransmitter is **acetylcholine.** The neurotransmitter, in turn, causes a change in the permeability and the electrical status of the postsynaptic membrane such that the signal is converted to a muscle (sarcolemmal) action potential. Thus the energy contained in the action potential of the motor neuron is converted into chemical energy by the release of neurotransmitter and then back to electrical energy by the generation of the muscle action potential. By this process, the motor neuron represents the fifth element of the single-joint system and provides the ability to control the force exerted by muscle.

Sensory Receptor

Now we consider the sensory receptor, the sixth and final element of the single-joint system. The reason for including the first five elements in this biological model for the control of movement is intuitively obvious, but why include sensory receptors? The basic function of sensory receptors is to provide information to the system on its own state and that of its surroundings. This type of information flow, from the sensory receptors to the CNS, is sometimes referred to as **feedback;** it represents the transfer of information back to the CNS. *It appears as a general principle, both in engineering design and in biological systems, that the more maneuverable a system, the more feedback it requires to maintain its stability* (Hasan & Stuart, 1988). As a biological system, the human body is highly maneuverable in that we can perform all sorts of movements, which require considerable feedback to control. The number of afferent neurons that provide feedback information is much greater than the number of efferent neurons involved in activating muscle.

Sensory receptors convert energy from one form to another through a process known as **transduction.** Energy can exist in a variety of forms, such as light, pressure, temperature, and sound; but the common output of sensory receptors is electrochemical energy in the form of action potentials. The action potentials are transmitted centrally and used by the CNS to monitor the status of the musculoskeletal system. The human body contains many different types of sensory receptors, which can be distinguished on the basis of their location (exteroceptors, proprioceptors, interoceptors), function (mechanoreceptors, thermoreceptors, photoreceptors, chemoreceptors, nociceptors), and morphology (free nerve endings, encapsulated endings).

The single-joint system needs at least two types of information in order to control movement. It needs to know where it is and when it is disturbed by something that happens in its surroundings. This information is provided by **proprioceptors,** which detect stimuli generated by the system itself, and by **exteroceptors,** which detect external stimuli (Gandevia, 1996; Prochazka, 1996; Sanes, 1987). With this information, the single-joint system is able to organize a rapid response to a disturbance, to determine its position, and to distinguish between self-generated and imposed movements. Proprioceptors include muscle spindles, tendon organs, and joint receptors. Exteroceptors are included in the eyes, ears, and skin. The latter respond to temperature, touch, and pain.

Muscle Spindle

Provided that a muscle operates across a joint and is subject to unexpected loads, it will have a variable number of muscle spindles (6 to 1300) distributed throughout (Hasan & Stuart, 1984; Matthews, 1972). There are about 27,500 spindles in the human body, with 4000 in each arm and 7000 in each leg (Prochazka, 1996). Hand and neck muscles have the highest density of spindles. The spindles are fusiform shaped and lie in parallel with the skeletal muscle fibers (figure 5.19). The ends of the spindles, which vary in length from 0.5 to 10 mm, attach to the intramuscular connective tissue (endomysium and perimysium). Although the muscle spindle is a morphologically complex sensory receptor (Pearson & Gordon, 2000b; Prochazka, 1996; Proske, 1997), it is essentially

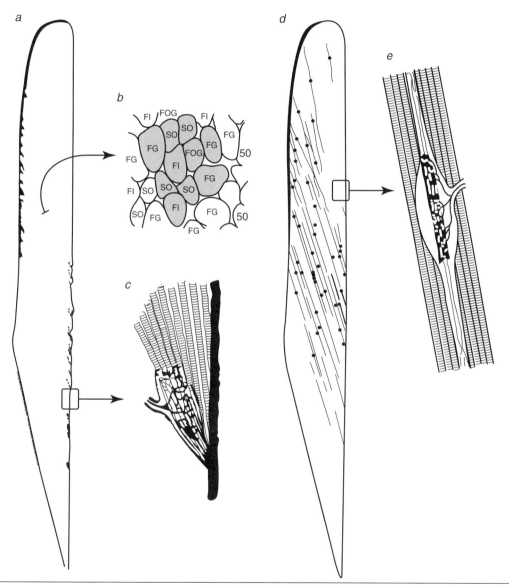

Figure 5.19   Distribution of the muscle spindle and tendon organ in the medial gastrocnemius muscle of the cat: *(a)* a longitudinal section of the muscle with tendon organs stained to indicate that the tendon organs are associated with the aponeurosis; *(b)* a cross section through the muscle showing the mixture of muscle fiber types; *(c)* enlarged view of a single tendon organ in series with skeletal muscle fibers; *(d)* a longitudinal section of the muscle showing the muscle spindle distribution throughout the belly of the muscle; *(e)* enlarged view of a muscle spindle showing its location in parallel with the skeletal muscle fibers.

Adapted from Botterman, Binder, and Stuart, 1978.

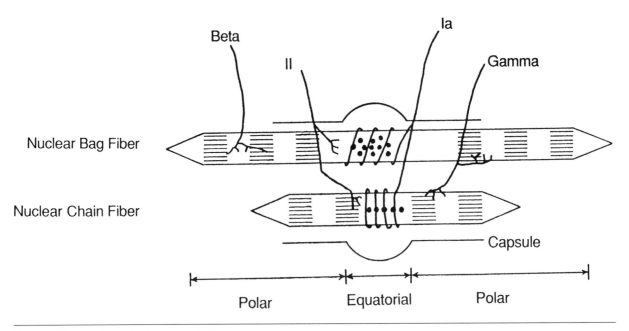

Figure 5.20 A schematized muscle spindle.

a collection of miniature skeletal muscle fibers (2-12) enclosed in a connective tissue capsule (figure 5.20). These smaller muscle fibers are referred to as **intrafusal** muscle fibers; those outside the muscle are called **extrafusal** fibers. Because of the greater myofilament content (cross-sectional area) of the extrafusal fiber, it can generate approximately 36 times more force than an intrafusal fiber. There are two types of intrafusal fibers, which differ as to the arrangement of their nuclei, their motor innervation, and their contraction speed. The nuclei of the **nuclear chain fiber** (~8 μm in diameter) are arranged end to end like the links in a chain, whereas those in the **nuclear bag fiber** (~17 μm in diameter and 8-10 mm long) cluster in a group. Both types of fiber, however, are devoid of myofilaments in the *equatorial* (central) region. The nuclear bag fiber is the longer of the two, extending at both ends beyond the capsule.

As a sensory receptor, the muscle spindle has an afferent supply over which the action potentials are transmitted to the CNS. In general, afferent axons are classified into four groups, primarily according to differences in axonal diameter. Group I axons have the greatest diameters, and Group IV the smallest; the larger the axon diameter, the faster the action potentials can be conducted (table 5.4). Each muscle spindle has a variable number (8 to 25) of Group I and II afferents. The larger of the two afferent axons, the **Group Ia afferent,** has an ending that spirals around the equatorial regions of both the nuclear chain and bag fibers (figure 5.20). The **Group II afferent** has a nonspiral ending that connects principally to

the chain fibers. Not all muscle spindles have Group II afferents, but they all have Group I afferents. The somas of the Group I and II afferent neurons are located in the dorsal root ganglion, close to the spinal cord (figure 5.17).

In addition to having an afferent system, the intrafusal fibers of the muscle spindle receive efferent input. In general, skeletal muscle fibers are innervated by three groups of motor neurons (α, β, γ), which can be distinguished by size and by the fibers that they innervate (table 5.4). The **alpha (α) motor neurons** are the largest and innervate the extrafusal muscle fibers; **gamma (γ) motor neurons** are the smallest and connect exclusively to intrafusal muscle fibers; and **beta (β) motor neurons** are intermediate in size and innervate both the extrafusal and intrafusal muscle fibers. Each spindle is innervated by 10 to 12 gamma motor neurons and a single beta motor neuron. The beta and gamma motor neurons contact the intrafusal fibers in their myofilament-rich *polar* regions. When an action potential is initiated at the axon hillock of a beta or gamma motor neuron and transmitted to a muscle spindle, the net effect is a contraction of the intrafusal fibers in their polar regions and a stretch of the equatorial region. The central stretch of the intrafusal fibers will be detected by the muscle spindle afferents (Groups I and II). This stretch heightens the sensitivity of the muscle spindle and can be sufficient to activate the afferents so that they generate action potentials that are transmitted to the CNS. Because the gamma and beta motor neurons can activate the muscle spindle (fusiform shape), they are sometimes known as **fusimotor** neurons.

Table 5.4 Classification of Nerve Fibers

Fiber type	Function[a]	Fiber diameter (μm)	Conduction velocity (m/s)
Efferent			
Aα	Skeletal muscle	15	100
Aβ	Skeletal muscle + muscle spindle	8	50
Aγ	Muscle spindle	5	20
B	Sympathetic preganglionic	3	7
C	Sympathetic postganglionic (unmyelinated)	1	1
Afferent			
Ia	Muscle spindle	13–20	80–120
Ib	Tendon organ	13–20	80–120
II	Muscle spindle	6–12	35–75
III	Deep pressure sensors in muscle	1–5	5–30
IV	Pain (unmyelinated), temperature	0.2–1.5	0.5–2

[a]Examples of functions served by the different classes of nerve fibers.

Communication within the afferent element of the single-joint system begins with the development of a **generator potential** by the sensing elements of the sensory receptors (Proske, 1997). For mechanoreceptors (e.g., muscle spindle, tendon organ, joint receptor), the generator potential is created by mechanical deformation of the sensory terminal. The generator potential is conducted along the axon to the trigger zone, and if the signal is large enough, an action potential is initiated. The most excitable portion of the afferent axon, the trigger zone, is located close to the sensing elements, usually within the capsule of the muscle spindle and the tendon organ. The action potential is transmitted centrally, where it impinges on various motor neurons and interneurons.

Muscle spindles provide information on *changes in muscle length* (Pearson & Gordon, 2000b; Prochazka, 1996; Proske, 1997). Because muscle spindles are arranged in parallel with skeletal muscle fibers, there are two ways in which the sensory receptor can be activated and thereby provide an afferent signal related to muscle length. The first way, just described, is for the gamma or beta motor neurons to cause the intrafusal muscle fibers to contract and stretch the equatorial region, where some of the Group I and II afferent endings are located. The second way in which the spindle is activated is by passive stretch of the entire muscle. The sensitivity of the muscle spindle, however, can be altered by gamma and beta motor neurons so that its response is greater to either absolute changes in muscle length or to the rate of

change in muscle length (Kakuda & Nagaoka, 1998; Taylor, Durbaba, Ellaway, & Rawlinson, 2000).

Example 5.1

Muscle Spindle Activity in Humans

Figure 5.21 shows examples of muscle spindle activity (Al-Falahe, Nagaoka, & Vallbo, 1990). The experiment measured the discharge of a single muscle spindle in the extensor digitorum muscle in the forearm of a human subject while a finger was moved sinusoidally either by the experimenter (figure 5.21a) or by the subject (figure 5.21b). To record the muscle spindle activity, a probe (an electrode) was placed in the muscle nerve; this technique is known as **microneurography** (Forster & Schmelz, 1996). The bottom trace in the figure shows the action potentials discharged by the muscle spindle during the two conditions. The second-to-bottom trace shows the discharge rate of the muscle spindle, which reached peak values of about 25 Hz. The third trace from the bottom shows the metacarpophalangeal joint angle, with an upward deflection indicating flexion and stretch of the extensor digitorum muscle. The top trace shows the electrical activity

(continued)

(EMG) in the extensor digitorum muscle; the muscle was electrically silent when the movement was imposed by the investigator but was active when the subject performed the movement. These data show that for both types of movement, imposed and active, the muscle spindle discharge increased when the extensor digitorum muscle was stretched during the flexion (upward) phase of the movement.

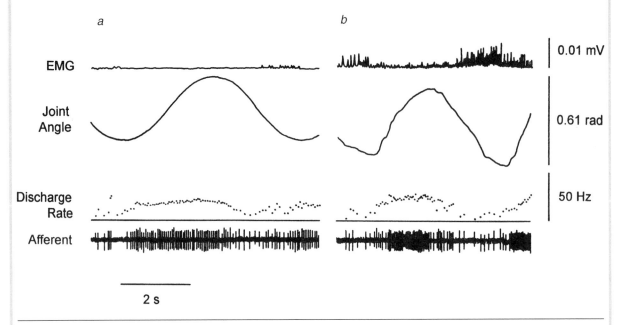

Figure 5.21 Discharge of a human muscle spindle during *(a)* a passive and *(b)* an active stretch (upward joint angle) of a forearm muscle.

Adapted from Al-Falahe, Nagaoka, and Vallbo, 1990.

This information on muscle stretch that is provided by the muscle spindle can serve at least two purposes. The information can help the CNS determine the position and orientation of the single-joint system, and it can signal a disturbance imposed on the system by its surroundings. We will examine these processes in chapter 6.

Tendon Organ

In contrast to the muscle spindle, the tendon organ is a relatively simple sensory receptor; it includes a single afferent and no efferent connections (Hasan & Stuart, 1984; Pearson & Gordon, 2000b). Tendon organs range in length from 0.2 to 1 mm. Few tendon organs are located in the tendon proper. Most are arranged around a few extrafusal muscle fibers as these connect with an aponeurosis of attachment (figure 5.19). Because of this location, the tendon organ is described as being in series with skeletal muscle fibers. The sensory terminal of the afferent neuron is contained within a capsule, and branches to encircle several strands of collagen in the myotendinous junction (figure 5.22). It is estimated that there are about 10 skeletal muscle fibers in a typical tendon organ capsule and that each of these muscle fibers is innervated by a different alpha motor neuron. Each motor unit can engage about six tendon organs. The afferent neuron associated with the tendon organ is referred to as the Group Ib afferent (table 5.4).

When a muscle and its connective tissue attachments are stretched, either through pulling of the muscle (passive stretch) or through activation of the skeletal muscle fibers (active stretch), the strands of collagen pinch and excite the Group Ib afferent (inset in figure 5.22). Because the tendon organ is activated in this way, it is described as a *monitor of muscle force*. The level of force necessary to excite a tendon organ depends on the mode of activation. Passive stretch requires a muscle force of 2 N, whereas the activity of a single muscle fiber (30-90 μN) is sufficient in active force conditions (Binder, Kroin, Moore, & Stuart, 1977).

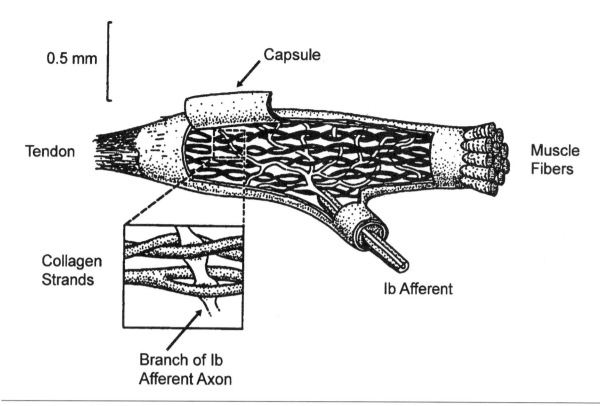

Figure 5.22 The tendon organ.

Adapted from Prochazka, 1996.

Example 5.2

Tendon Organ Activity in Humans

An example of the discharge of a tendon organ is shown in figure 5.23 (Al-Falahe et al., 1990). The microneurography technique was used to record the discharge of a single tendon organ located in the extensor digitorum muscle of a human volunteer. The subject performed a finger movement against a zero load (figure 5.23a) and against a light load (figure 5.23b). In each panel, the top trace records the angle of the metacarpophalangeal joint, with flexion of the joint and stretch of the muscle shown as an upward deflection. The middle trace indicates the discharge of the tendon organ, which achieved peak rates of about 40 Hz. The bottom trace shows the EMG (electrical activity) of the muscle performing the finger movement. Figure 5.23 shows how the discharge of a tendon organ parallels the EMG. Because there is a close association between muscle EMG and force, these data indicate that tendon organ discharge monitors the force exerted by muscle (Petit, Scott, & Reynolds, 1997).

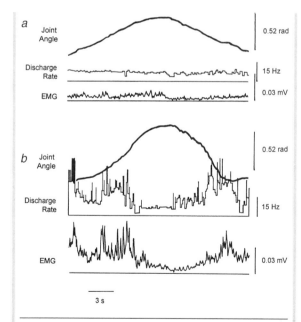

Figure 5.23 Discharge of a human tendon organ during finger movements against *(a)* a zero load and *(b)* a light load.

Adapted from Al-Falahe, Nagaoka, and Vallbo, 1990.

Joint Receptors

As with the muscle spindle and the tendon organ, joint receptors can function as mechanoreceptors and provide information for the single-joint system that is necessary for the control of movement (Burgess, Horch, & Tuckett, 1987; Gandevia, 1996). In contrast to the muscle spindle and the tendon organ, however, the joint receptor is not a single, well-defined entity. Rather, joint receptors vary in their location (e.g., joint capsule, ligament, loose connective tissue), type (e.g., Ruffini ending, Golgi ending, pacinian corpuscle, free nerve endings), and presumably function. These receptors are served by neurons with Group II, III, and IV afferents.

The **Ruffini endings** typically consist of two to six thinly encapsulated, globular corpuscles with a single myelinated parent axon that has a diameter of 5 to 9 μm. These receptors may be categorized as static or dynamic mechanoreceptors and are capable of signaling joint position and displacement, angular velocity, and intra-articular pressure (Johansson, Sjölander, & Sojka, 1991). **Pacinian corpuscles** are thickly encapsulated with a parent axon of 8- to 12-μm diameter. These receptors have low thresholds to mechanical stress and apparently detect acceleration of the joint (Bell, Bolanowski, & Holmes, 1994). **Golgi endings** are thinly encapsulated, fusiform corpuscles that are similar to tendon organs. The axon of the afferent neuron connected to the Golgi ending has a diameter of 13 to 17 μm. These receptors, which have high thresholds, monitor tension in ligaments, especially at the extremes of the range of motion. **Free nerve endings** are widely distributed and constitute the joint nociceptive system. They have small-diameter axons (0.5-5 μm) and are active when a joint is subjected to an abnormal mechanical stress or to chemical agents. These four types of joint receptors are able to provide the single-joint system with information about the position, displacement, velocity, and acceleration of movement as well as about noxious stimuli experienced by the joint (Dyhre-Poulsen & Krogsgaard, 2000; Johansson et al., 1991). However, joint receptors do not provide unambiguous signals of joint position (Gandevia, 1996). Nonetheless, when these receptor types are located in distinct anatomical regions, such as in the knee joint, they are capable of providing unique afferent information (Zimny & Wink, 1991).

The significance of joint receptors for the normal function of the single-joint system has been convincingly demonstrated by the effect of joint pathology on muscle activation. For example, when normal subjects are given a large experimental effusion in the knee joint (fluid injected into the joint space), the ability to activate the quadriceps femoris is greatly reduced, even in the absence of pain (Stokes & Young, 1984; Young, Stokes, & Iles, 1987). This inhibition of muscle activation depends on the volume of fluid added but can cause a 30% to 90% reduction in the maximal voluntary activation of quadriceps femoris. Conversely, the removal of fluid from the knee joint, for example after a meniscectomy, can markedly improve a patient's use of the muscle. In the absence of pain, chronic joint effusion can cause weakness and atrophy of muscle. Similarly, patients with old cruciate ligament tears typically exhibit a decrease in strength of both the quadriceps femoris and hamstrings (Grabiner, Koh, & Andrish, 1992; Johansson et al., 1991).

The axons innnervating joint receptors distribute their information extensively throughout the CNS, from the spinal cord up to the brain. At the level of the single-joint system, however, joint receptors seem to have a more potent effect on fusimotor neurons (gamma motor neurons) than on alpha motor neurons. Consequently, joint receptors are more likely to exert an effect on the single-joint system indirectly, by modulating the activity of the muscle spindle, than to do so directly by influencing the output of alpha motor neurons.

Cutaneous Mechanoreceptors

In contrast to the three sensory receptors already discussed in this section, cutaneous mechanoreceptors provide information exclusively on external events that influence the single-joint system. The cutaneous mechanoreceptors in the hand and foot, for example, provide important information on how we interact with our surroundings. There are about 17,000 mechanoreceptors in the skin of the human hand. A decline in somatosensory acuity, presumably involving cutaneous mechanoreceptors, contributes to the reduced control of posture among older adults and among patients with various pathologies (Cole, Rotella, & Harper, 1999; Horak, Shupert, & Mirka, 1989). In addition to mechanoreceptors, the skin includes thermoreceptors and nociceptors that can also influence the function of the single-joint system, even of the alpha motor neurons that are activated during the performance of a task.

Four types of cutaneous mechanoreceptors have been identified: Merkel disks, Meissner corpuscles, Ruffini endings, and pacinian corpuscles (Rothwell, 1994). The first two are found close to the surface of the skin whereas the latter two are deeper. The **Merkel disk** is sensitive to local vertical pressure and does not respond to lateral stretch of the skin. This receptor responds with a rapid initial discharge of action potentials that is quickly reduced to a slow steady rate. **Meissner corpuscles** are innervated by two to six axons, and each axon may innervate more than one corpuscle. The Meissner corpuscle is sensitive to local, maintained pressure, but its response (discharge of action potentials) fades rapidly. Ruffini endings are innervated by a single axon and respond to stretch of the skin over a wide area. This sensitivity, however, depends on the direction of the stretch; the ending will be excited with stretch in one direction and inhibited by stretch at a right angle to the preferred direction. The response of Ruffini endings adapts slowly to a sustained stretch. Pacinian corpuscles, the largest receptors in the skin, are innervated by a single axon. The pacinian corpuscle detects a rapidly changing pressure stimulus. These four cutaneous mechanoreceptors provide the single-joint system with the ability to detect stimuli applied to the skin over small and large areas, and for brief and sustained durations.

Summary

Because of the complexity of the human body, we have developed a simplified model of the components of the motor system that are essential for movement. This simplified model we call the *single-joint system.* This chapter reviews the properties of the six components of the single-joint system: bone, synovial joint, muscle, tendon, neuron, sensory receptor. The single-joint system is an extension of the concepts encountered in part I on the free body diagram, with the addition of components to control (muscle, tendon, and neuron) and monitor (sensory receptor) the rotation of the rigid body segments. Because these six components all comprise living tissue, they adapt to the physical stress encountered in the activities of daily living. The result is a dynamic system with continually changing properties.

Suggested Readings

Kalu, D.N. (1996). Bone. In L.B. Rowell & J.T. Shepherd (Eds.), *Handbook of physiology: Sec. 12. Exercise: Regulation and integration of multiple systems* (pp. 395–412). New York: Oxford University Press.

Kaplan, F.S., Hayes, W.C., Keaveny, T.M., Boskey, A., Einhorn, T.A., & Iannotti, J.P. (1994). Form and function of bone. In S.R. Simon (Ed.), *Orthopaedic basic science* (pp. 127–184). Park Ridge, IL: American Academy of Orthopaedic Surgeons.

Mankin, H.J., Mow, V.C., Buckwalter, J.A., Iannotti, J.P., & Ratcliffe, A. (1994). Form and function of articular cartilage. In S.R. Simon (Ed.), *Orthopaedic basic science* (pp. 1–44). Park Ridge, IL: American Academy of Orthopaedic Surgeons.

McComas, A.J. (1996). *Skeletal muscle: Form and function.* Champaign, IL: Human Kinetics, chapters 1, 2, and 4.

Nigg, B.M., & Herzog, W. (Eds.) (1994). *Biomechanics of the musculo-skeletal system.* New York: Wiley, chapter 2.

Whiting, W.C., & Zernicke, R.F. (1998). *Biomechanics of musculoskeletal injury.* Champaign, IL: Human Kinetics, chapter 2.

Woo, S. L-Y., An, K-N., Arnoczky, S.P., Wayne, J.S., Fithian, D.C., & Myers, B.S. (1994). Anatomy, biology, and biomechanics of tendon, ligament, and meniscus. In S.R. Simon (Ed.), *Orthopaedic basic science* (pp. 45–87). Park Ridge, IL: American Academy of Orthopaedic Surgeons.

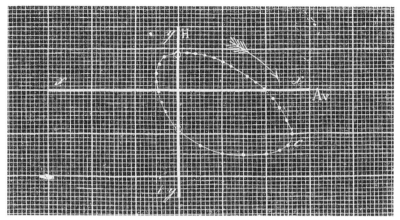

Reprinted from Marey, 1879.

Single-Joint System Function

In chapter 5 we characterized the six elements (bone, synovial joint, muscle, tendon, neuron, sensory receptor) of the single-joint system. In chapter 6 we consider how these elements interact to produce movement. This chapter addresses five key features of the operation of the single-joint system: (a) excitable membranes, the means by which information is transmitted rapidly throughout the system; (b) excitation-contraction coupling, the link between the neural signal and muscle contraction; (c) muscle mechanics, the biomechanical properties of muscle; (d) the motor unit, the basic functional unit of the single-joint system; and (e) feedback from sensory receptors, the role of afferent information in the function of the system.

Excitable Membranes

From the perspective of the single-joint system, movement is initiated by an activation signal that is sent from the nervous system to muscle. This signal must be trans-mitted along the axons of the involved neurons, across the neuromuscular junction to the muscle fiber, and into the muscle fiber to the contractile proteins. The property of the system that underlies this capability is the excitable membrane of the nerve and muscle cells; these membranes are known as the axolemma and sarcolemma, respectively. The physical process involves the movement of ions across the membrane, which produces an electrical signal (action potential) that travels along the membranes and eventually releases an excitation factor in the muscle fiber. To describe the generation and function of the electrical signals, we will examine the reason that membranes are excitable (steady state potential), the ionic basis of the action potential, and the generation of the action potential.

Steady State Potential

Excitable membranes comprise a lipid bilayer on or in which proteins are located; they are semipermeable in

241

that some lipid-soluble substances and smaller molecules can move through them. These membranes are referred to as **plasma membranes.** The membrane proteins—which account for about 50% to 70% of the membrane structure and serve structural, enzymatic, receptor, channel, and pump functions—are critical to the capability of the membrane to store, transmit, and release energy. The membrane is surrounded by intracellular (e.g., sarcoplasm, axoplasm) and extracellular fluids (figure 6.1), which contain variable concentrations of certain ions—notably sodium (Na^+), potassium (K^+), and chloride (Cl^-). The concentration ratio

(outside the cell with respect to the inside) differs for each of these ions (e.g., muscle cell of a warm-blooded animal, $Na^+ = 12.08$, $K^+ = 0.03$, $Cl^- = 30.00$) such that the net effect is a charge distribution (voltage or **electrical potential**) across the membrane. *The particular distribution of an ion represents an equilibrium between two forces, the electrical and concentration gradients.* The electrical force is due to the attraction of unlike charges and the repulsion of like charges. The concentration-gradient force causes ions to move from an area of high concentration to one that is lower in concentration.

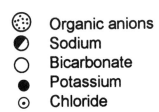

mM	Cations	mM
160	Potassium	4
10	Sodium	145
2	Calcium	5
26	Magnesium	2
198		156

	Anions	
3	Chloride	114
10	Bicarbonate	31
100	Phosphate	2
20	Sulfate	1
—	Organic acids	7
65	Proteins	1
198		156

Figure 6.1 Distribution of ions about a mammalian excitable membrane. The membrane has channels through which K^+ and Cl^- can move easily, Na^+ with difficulty, and A^- (negatively charged anions) not at all.

When a membrane is in a steady-state condition and not conducting a signal, the electrical potential across the membrane remains relatively constant and is called the **resting membrane potential.** The resting membrane potential is about 60 to 90 mV, and the inside is negative with respect to the outside. The ions involved in establishing the electrical potential represent just a few of those included in the intracellular and extracellular fluids. The ionic distribution across the membrane represents a balance between the positive and negative ions and the concentration-gradient force experienced by each ion. In the resting state, Na^+ is prevented from remaining in the cell by the pumping activity of a membrane-bound protein, known as the **Na^+-K^+ pump** (Clausen, 1996; Nielsen & Clausen, 2000), that transports Na^+ from the intracellular to the extracellular fluid. Coupled to the extracellular localization of Na^+, K^+ is held internally due to the activity of the Na^+-K^+ pump and an electrical attraction to various organic anions (A^-), which are negatively charged ions such as amino acids and proteins that are too large to cross the membrane. Thus, the activity of the Na^+-K^+ pump keeps Na^+ in the extracellular fluid and K^+ in the intracellular fluid. The charges provided by Na^+

(attraction) and A^- (repulsion) cause Cl^- to be concentrated in the extracellular fluid. *The distribution of these ions (Na^+ and Cl^- externally, K^+ and A^- internally) largely determines the steady state potential that exists across an excitable membrane.*

The forces acting on these ions (Na^+, K^+, and Cl^-), and the movement or flux of the ions across the membrane in a steady state condition, are schematized in figure 6.2. As described previously, the forces driving the ions across the membrane are due to concentration-gradient and electrical-charge effects (figure 6.2a). The magnitude of each force for the various ions is illustrated in figure 6.2a by the length of its arrow. For example, Na^+ has a greater extracellular concentration and thus experiences a concentration-gradient force that drives it inward. Because the membrane is electrically negative inside with respect to the outside, positive ions (Na^+ and K^+) experience an inward-directed electrical force, and the negative ions (Cl^-) experience an outward (upward)-directed force. We can determine the net force experienced by each ion by summing the concentration and electrical effects (figure 6.2b). For example, Na^+ is subject to inward concentration and electrical effects, which result in a large,

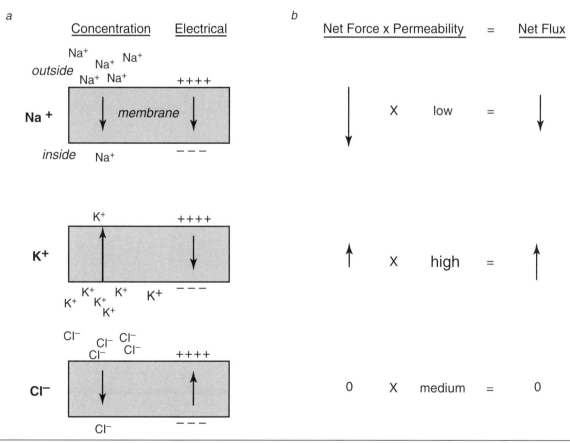

Figure 6.2 *(a)* The concentration-gradient and electrical-charge forces experienced by the Na^+, K^+, and Cl^- ions determine the net force that each ion experiences. *(b)* The quantity of an ion that crosses the membrane (net flux) depends on its net force and the permeability of the membrane to the ion.

From "Membrane Potential" by J. Koester. In *Principles of Neural Science (3rd ed.),* (p. 87) by E.R. Kandel, J.H. Schwartz, and T.M. Jessell (Eds.), 1991, New York: Elsevier Science Publishing Co., Inc. Copyright 1991 by Elsevier Science Publishing Co., Inc. Reproduced with permission of The McGraw-Hill Companies.

inward net force for Na⁺. By similar reasoning, K⁺ experiences a small, outward net force, whereas the concentration and electrical components for Cl⁻ cancel, resulting in a zero net force.

The net force for each ion combines with the permeability of the membrane to the ion to determine the net magnitude and direction of the flux for the ion at a steady state membrane potential. The ease with which an ion crosses a membrane (i.e., the permeability of the membrane to an ion) can be classified as low, medium, or high. Because of differences in permeability, the amount of an ion that crosses a membrane (net flux) depends on the combination of the net force experienced by that ion and its permeability. The result (figure 6.2*b*, net flux column) indicates that, *in steady state conditions, approximately equal quantities of Na⁺ and K⁺ cross the membrane, whereas Cl⁻ remains inside the cell.*

The potential that exists across a membrane under steady state conditions is most influenced by the relative permeability of the membrane to the various ions. Because these excitable membranes are most permeable to K⁺, the membrane potential is close to the potential (–95 mV) at which K⁺ is in equilibrium (no net force). If the concentrations of potassium in the intracellular $[K]_i$ and extracellular $[K]_e$ fluids are known, then the equilibrium potential for potassium (E_K) can be estimated with the **Nernst equation:**

$$E_K = \frac{RT}{F} \log_e \frac{[K]_e}{[K]_i} \quad (6.1)$$

$$= 61.5 \log_{10} \frac{[K]_e}{[K]_i}$$

$$= 61.5 \log_{10} \frac{160}{4.5}$$

$$E_K = -95 \text{ mV}$$

where R is the gas constant (1.99 cal/K/mol), T the temperature in degrees Kelvin, and F the Faraday constant (9.65 x 10⁴ coulombs/mol). In mammalian skeletal muscle, the resting membrane potential is about –90 mV. An increase in the concentration of K⁺ in the extracellular space produces a decrease in the potential across the membrane.

When Na⁺ leaks across the membrane, it is quickly returned to the extracellular space by the adenosine triphosphate (ATP)-driven activity of the Na⁺-K⁺ pump. One cycle of this process, however, involves the translocation of three Na⁺ ions and two K⁺ ions—that is, a net translocation of one positive ion to the extracellular space. The action of the pump has two effects. First, it maintains the concentration gradient of K⁺ across the membrane. Second, the net movement of positive ions contributes to the generation of the electrical potential across the

membrane, which is known as the **electrogenic** action of the pump (Nielsen & Clausen, 2000). Under steady state conditions, the electrogenic action of the Na⁺-K⁺ pump contributes about –5.6 mV to the resting membrane potential (McComas, 1996).

Example 6.1
Na⁺-K⁺ Pump Action

The Na⁺-K⁺ pump is a transmembrane molecule that moves three Na⁺ ions and two K⁺ ions across the membrane for each cycle of action. The molecule uses energy from ATP to perform this function. It has been estimated that each pump can split a maximum of 8000 molecules of ATP per minute (Clausen, Nielsen, Harrison, Flatman, & Overgaard, 1998). In the skeletal muscles of mammals, the concentration of Na⁺-K⁺ pumps is about 0.2 to 0.8 nmol/g wet weight, but this increases with strength training and endurance training (Green, Dahly, et al., 1999) and decreases under hypoxia (Green, MacDougall, Tarnopolsky, & Melissa, 1999). Under resting conditions, only about 5% of these pumps are active in exchanging Na⁺ and K⁺. When a muscle is activated, however, either by voluntary activation or by electrical stimulation, most of the Na⁺-K⁺ pumps become active (Hicks & McComas, 1989; Nielsen & Harrison, 1998). Nonetheless, the pumps seem unable to deal with the huge flux of ions that occurs with sustained excitation; this probably contributes to development of muscle fatigue (Clausen et al., 1998; Nielsen & Harrison, 1998; Sejersted & Sjøgaard, 2000; Sjøgaard, 1996; Verburg, Hallén, Sejersted, & Vøllestad, 1999).

Ionic Basis of an Action Potential

Despite the apparent stability of the resting membrane potential, it is possible to disrupt the ionic distribution and to change the membrane potential. For example, the movement of negative ions across the membrane to the outside, or the movement of positive ions to the inside, produces a decrease in the membrane potential, a change referred to as **depolarization**—that is, the membrane becomes less polarized or closer to zero. Conversely, the movement of negative ions internally or the deposition of additional positive ions externally causes the membrane to become **hyperpolarized** (more polarized).

The shift in ions across the membrane is due to changes that occur within the membrane. These changes can be induced chemically (e.g., by a neurotransmitter), electrically (e.g., by variations in membrane potential), or mechanically (e.g., by pinching or stretching of nerve endings) and are described as *gated* changes in membrane permeability. For example, although Na$^+$ crosses the membrane in the resting state with considerable difficulty, the permeability of the membrane to Na$^+$ can be altered by about 500-fold, making this crossing much easier. This change is referred to as an increase in Na$^+$ **conductance.**

Ions such as Na$^+$ and K$^+$ cross the membrane by moving through protein structures that are called **ion channels.** Once Na$^+$ can cross the membrane, it does so by moving down its concentration gradient (figure 6.2a) from the extracellular to the intracellular fluid. As the positive ions move inside the cell, the membrane becomes depolarized, which causes an additional increase in sodium conductance leading to a further depolarization, and so on. Such changes in Na$^+$ conductance are **voltage gated,** because changes in the electrical potential (voltage) lead to changes in conductance, which lead to further changes in the electrical potential, and so forth.

The opening and closing of an ion channel involves changing the structure of the protein. The structural change is transient and can be local or general, or involve the movement of a blocking particle. Several types of stimuli control the opening and closing of ion channels: these are ligand-gated channels, phosphorylation-gated channels, voltage-gated channels, and stretch or pressure-gated channels. Figure 6.3 shows examples of voltage-gated and ligand-gated channels. The ligand is a neurotransmitter; hence, the channel is identified as a **transmitter-gated** channel. In this model, Na$^+$ and K$^+$ ions are prevented from passing through voltage-gated channels by a blocking particle. It is the opening and closing of ion channels that control the generation of an action potential. The orientation of the blocking particle depends on the potential across the surrounding membrane. In the resting state (upper diagram in figure 6.3a), the particle is positioned so that it blocks the channel. As the potential across the membrane becomes depolarized, the particle shifts its position, and the channel is opened (lower diagram in figure 6.3a). Similarly, the transmitter-gated channel is closed in steady state conditions but opens when a neurotransmitter attaches to the channel and causes it to change its structure. Both Na$^+$ and K$^+$ can pass through the same transmitter-gated channel. In general, the transmitter-gated channels initiate the changes in membrane potential, which lead to the involvement of the voltage-gated channels.

Communication within the single-joint system is accomplished by transmitter- and voltage-gated changes in membrane potential. In general, these alterations are of two types: **synaptic potentials** and action potentials. Both types of potentials involve the same mechanism— an ionic shift across the membrane—but the synaptic potential essentially functions as a precursor to the action potential. Synaptic potentials have no threshold, and they decrease in amplitude as they are conducted along the

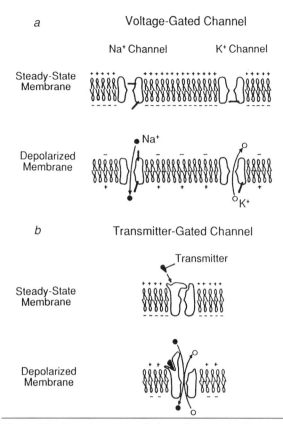

Figure 6.3 Function of gated channels in excitable membrane: *(a)* voltage-gated channel; *(b)* transmitter (ligand)-gated channel.

From "Directly Gated Transmission at the Nerve-Muscle Synapse" by E. R. Kandel and S. A. Siegelbaum. In *Principles of Neural Science* (3rd ed.) (p. 141) by E. R. Kandel, J. H. Schwartz, and T. M. Jessell (Eds.), 1991, New York: Elsevier Science Publishing Co., Inc. Copyright 1991 by Elsevier Science Publishing Co., Inc. Reproduced with permission of The McGraw-Hill Companies.

membrane. Action potentials involve a self-regenerative process, known as **propagation,** that minimizes changes in amplitude.

Physically, an action potential is a patch of membrane where the potential has been reversed so that the inside is positive with respect to the outside. It is possible to record an action potential in an experiment by placing a probe (an electrode) inside a cell (intracellular) and recording the potential inside the cell before, during, and after the action potential passes the electrode. With such an intracellular measurement, the action potential is recorded as a voltage-time event (figure 6.4). An action potential is characterized by four phases: depolarization, overshoot, repolarization, and hyperpolarization. The depolarization phase represents a decrease in the potential across the membrane. The overshoot corresponds to a complete reversal of the potential so that the inside is positive with respect to the outside. The **repolarization** phase indicates an increase in the potential across the membrane. The hyperpolarization phase, which is generally longer than the first three phases, represents an interval when the membrane potential is more negative than during steady state conditions.

These changes in membrane potential result from alterations in Na⁺ and K⁺ conductances (g_{Na} and g_K) that are temporally offset (figure 6.4b). Because Na⁺ and K⁺ are both positive ions, their simultaneous movement across the membrane would not alter the membrane potential. However, because the net Na⁺ influx occurs before the K⁺ efflux, and because the increased Na⁺ conductance lasts for only a short time, the membrane experiences first a depolarization and then a repolarization. At any instant in time, therefore, the membrane potential (V_m) is due to an imbalance in the Na⁺ and K⁺ conductances (figure 6.4b).

The number of ions of one species (e.g., Na⁺, K⁺) that cross the membrane depends on the driving force and the permeability of the membrane to that ion (i.e., Na⁺,

K⁺, Cl⁻). The change in permeability to Na⁺ occurs first; this depolarizes the membrane. This effect is terminated by the change in permeability of the membrane to K⁺, which drives the membrane potential in the opposite direction. At the conclusion of the action potential (~2.5 ms in figure 6.4b), for example, sodium conductance has returned to resting levels while potassium conductance remains greater than normal. At this point, therefore, K⁺ ions continue to efflux from the cell, which makes the inside of the cell more negative with respect to the outside; that is, the membrane becomes more polarized or hyperpolarized. Because this occurs after the action potential, it is referred to as the **afterhyperpolarization.** The afterhyperpolarization lasts for 50 ms to several seconds. The Na⁺-K⁺ pumps gradually reverse this ionic distribution by returning Na⁺ to the extracellular fluid and K⁺ to the inside. This action causes the membrane poten-

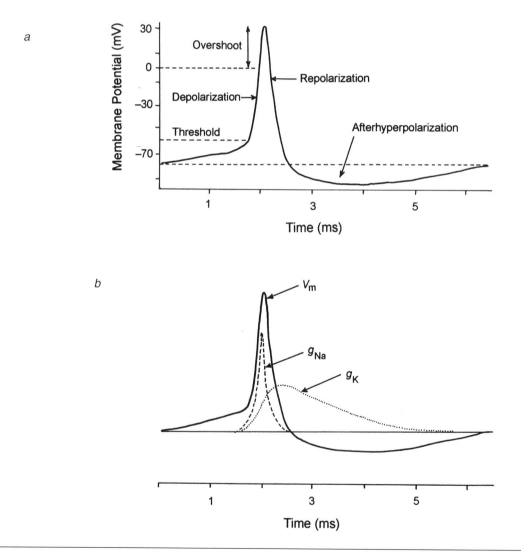

Figure 6.4 A schematic diagram of the action potential indicating the timing of its various *(a)* phases and *(b)* conductance changes.

g_{Na} = sodium conductance; g_K = potassium cunductance; V_m = membrane potential.

tial to return to steady state levels. In this recovery phase, the membrane is more polarized than normal, which makes it more difficult to generate another action potential; that is, there is a larger-than-normal difference between the membrane potential and the threshold level. This phase is known as the **refractory period.**

Once an action potential has been initiated in a motor neuron, it is propagated along the axon at speeds that are proportional to the diameter of the axon. The conduction velocities of motor axons range from 50 to 65 m/s in the median and ulnar nerves of humans and from 40 to 55 m/s in the tibial and peroneal nerves. The effect of axon diameter on conduction velocity is mainly due to the insulation of much of the surface area of the large axons, which limits the surface area involved in the ionic shifts. Instead, the action potential jumps from one node of Ranvier (noninsulated axolemma) to another; this is known as **saltatory conduction.** The presence of myelin, however, is somewhat fragile; and there are a number of neurological diseases that involve the focal or patchy destruction of myelin sheaths that is usually accompanied by an inflammatory response. These demyelinating diseases can affect myelin in the central nervous system (e.g., multiple sclerosis, encephalomyelitis, myelopathy) and the peripheral nervous system (e.g., Guillain-Barré syndrome, some types of neuropathies) and can impair the propagation of action potentials.

Generation of an Action Potential

An action potential is an **all-or-none** electrical command that is issued by a cell in response to the input that it receives. Both neurons and muscle fibers can generate action potentials. The inputs received by a neuron that underlie the generation of an action potential occur in the form of synaptic potentials, which can be either excitatory or inhibitory.

A neuron can have up to 10,000 synapses, which transmit input from such sources as peripheral sensory receptors, interneurons, and supraspinal centers. These synapses are distributed over the soma and the dendritic tree. When a neurotransmitter is released at a synapse, it generates a synaptic potential in the **postsynaptic** (receiving) neuron. The synaptic potential is conducted over the neuron, decreasing in amplitude as it travels along the membrane. The effect of the synaptic potential on neuron activity depends on its amplitude when it reaches the axon hillock, which is the transition region from the soma to the axon. The farther the synapse is from the axon hillock, the less effective the synaptic potential in shifting the membrane potential toward the **action potential threshold** of the neuron (trigger level for generation of an action potential; figure 6.4a). The neuron does not generate an action potential each time it receives a synaptic potential; rather, the generation of an action po-

tential is based on the sum of the synaptic potentials at the axon hillock. Because a neuron receives many excitatory and inhibitory synaptic potentials at the same time, the membrane potential fluctuates about some average steady state level. When the membrane potential in the region of the axon hillock deviates by 10 to 15 mV above the steady state level, the threshold level is reached and the neuron generates an action potential that is propagated along the axon to an effector cell. Thus, a neuron generates an action potential in response to the net effect of numerous, continuous inputs (synaptic potentials).

Synaptic potentials are generated and conducted by transmitter-gated changes in membrane conductance, whereas action potentials rely on voltage-gated changes in conductance. We can see this distinction if we consider the second example of action potential generation, that by the sarcolemma of the muscle fiber. This occurs at the neuromuscular junction (figure 5.15b), where the neurotransmitter is acetylcholine (ACh). When the axonal action potential reaches the synaptic bouton (nerve ending enlargement), it accelerates the release of ACh by promoting fusion of the vesicles with the terminal membrane (inside the axon). The action potential causes an increase in Ca^{2+} conductance in the axolemma of the synaptic enlargement, and the increase in intra-axonal Ca^{2+} facilitates vesicle fusion with the presynaptic membrane. This process of vesicular fusion and release of neurotransmitter is known as **exocytosis.** Measurements made on human muscle specimens suggest that 20 to 50 vesicles release ACh in response to an axonal action potential (McComas, 1996).

When ACh is released into the synaptic cleft, it diffuses across the cleft and attaches to a receptor on a transmitter-gated Na^+-K^+ channel. Once the channel is opened, Na^+ flows into the muscle cell and K^+ flows out, which leads to the generation of a synaptic potential known as the **end-plate potential.** Because the end-plate potential causes a modest depolarization of the sarcolemma, this leads to the opening of voltage-gated Na^+ channels, which further depolarizes the sarcolemma and shifts it toward threshold. Eventually, the sarcolemma, in the region of the neuromuscular junction, is depolarized enough so that threshold is reached, and a sarcolemmal action potential is generated and propagated along the excitable membrane. The time it takes for the transformation of the action potential from the nerve to the muscle is known as the **synaptic delay.** At the neuromuscular junction in mammals, the synaptic delay is about 0.2 ms (Eccles & Liley, 1959).

A unique feature of the neuromuscular junction is the amplitude of the end-plate potential. In contrast to most synaptic potentials, the end-plate potential typically results in the generation of a sarcolemmal action potential. The only time that the one-to-one association between the end-plate potential and an action potential appears to break down is during fatiguing contractions. There is probably no other synapse in the nervous system where a given input (synaptic potential) will invariably result in the generation of an action potential. The peak-to-peak amplitude of the end-plate potentials averages 1.4 mV in the extensor digitorum longus of mice, and this increases to an average of 1.8 mV after 12 weeks of running (Dorlöchter, Irintchev, Brinkers, & Wernig, 1991). The average amplitude of the sarcolemmal action potential in the rat diaphragm is around 84 mV (Metzger & Fitts, 1986).

Small amounts of the neurotransmitter ACh are released continuously at the neuromuscular junction. This spontaneous release of ACh elicits **miniature end-plate potentials,** which have amplitudes of about 0.7 mV in fast-twitch muscle fibers and 1.9 mV in slow-twitch muscle fibers (Lømo & Waerhaug, 1985). Interestingly, the frequency of the miniature end-plate potentials decreases with age in soleus but not in extensor digitorum longus (Alshuaib & Fahim, 1991). Because of the miniature end-plate potentials, the steady state potential of the postsynaptic sarcolemma fluctuates about an average value, as does the potential of the postsynaptic membrane of the neuron.

Example 6.2

Impairment of Action Potential Generation

The processes involved in the transformation of an axonal action potential into a sarcolemmal action potential are collectively referred to as **neuromuscular propagation.** One or more of these processes can be impaired under various conditions, such as with pharmacological agents, diseases that affect the neuromuscular junction, or prolonged exercise. For example, drugs that bind to the ACh receptor (suxamethonium, tubocurarine) or prevent the breakdown of ACh (anticholinesterase drugs) can be used to paralyze muscle during surgical procedures. Similarly, the toxin botulinum reduces the ability of the nerve terminal to release ACh (McComas, 1996).

The diseases that influence the neuromuscular junction are transmitted genetically and produce defects that range from faulty packaging of ACh to an impairment of the receptors and enzymes that manage ACh. *Myasthenia gravis,* for example, is an immunological disorder in which the ACh receptors are targeted by the immune system. The result is a reduction in the number of ACh receptors, which produces muscle weakness. The disorder usually occurs first in the ocular muscles, but can progress to involve swallowing, talking, and chewing. One unique feature of the disorder is that the muscle weakness can vary over

the course of a day and from day to day. The disorder can be detected by the presence of antibodies to the ACh receptor in the plasma and by electrophysiological tests. In a clinical examination, the disturbance of neuromuscular propagation can be detected through comparison of the timing of action potentials in two muscle fibers belonging to the same motor unit. In healthy individuals, there is a slight variation (<20 μs) in the arrival time of the action potentials in two muscle fibers; this variability is referred to as **jitter.** Patients with myasthenia gravis, however, experience a greatly enhanced jitter due to a decrease in the number of ACh receptors (figure 6.5).

The *Lambert-Eaton myasthenic syndrome* is another immune disorder that affects the neuromuscular junction. This condition results in a destruction of the voltage-gated Ca^{2+} channels in the presynaptic motor nerve terminal. Patients with this disorder experience a myasthenic-like weakness, but electrical stimulation of the nerve to the muscle evokes responses that increase in amplitude, in contrast to the decrease that occurs in patients with myasthenia. Such results suggest the impairment of a presynaptic process, apparently involving the presynaptic Ca^{2+} channels (McComas, 1996).

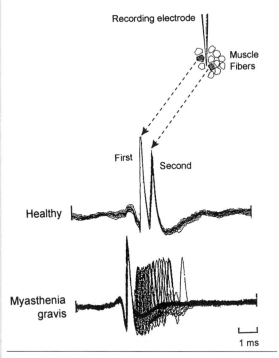

Figure 6.5 Jitter of action potentials in two muscle fibers belonging to the same motor unit. Superimposed recordings in a healthy subject indicate a slight variation in the timing of the second action potential relative to the first. Similar recordings in a patient with myasthenia gravis show a pronounced increase in the jitter, that is, a spread in the timing of the second action potential.

Adapted from McComas, 1996.

Synaptic Transmission and Integration

Most of the information related to human movement that is transmitted by excitable membranes is conveyed from one cell to another by chemical synapses. In this scheme, an active cell releases a neurotransmitter that diffuses a short distance and binds to membrane-bound receptors in the target cell. The result of this interaction, which will influence the potential of the postsynaptic membrane, depends on both the type of neurotransmitter and the receptor. Some interactions produce an inhibitory effect whereas others evoke an excitatory effect. For an inhibitory interaction, the typical response is an opening of channels for K^+ and Cl^- and a flux of these ions that causes the membrane potential to become more negative. This is known as an **inhibitory postsynaptic potential.** In contrast, an excitatory interaction opens Na^+ and K^+ channels so that there is a net influx of positive ions, which causes the membrane to become less negative; this is an **excitatory postsynaptic potential.**

Four types of substances can act as neurotransmitters: ACh, monoamines, amino acids, and peptides. *Acetylcholine* is widely distributed throughout the brain and spinal cord and is one of the major neurotransmitters in the efferent branch of the peripheral nervous system. The *monoamines* include the catecholamines (i.e., dopamine, norepinephrine, and epinephrine) and serotonin. The catecholamines typically exert an inhibitory action in the central nervous system, although norepinephrine has an excitable effect in the peripheral autonomic system. Serotonin is active in the neural pathways controlling consciousness and mood, with projections from higher centers to the brainstem and spinal cord. The *amino acids* (e.g., glycine, aspartate, glutamate, gamma-aminobutyric acid) exert a mixture of inhibitory and excitatory effects in the spinal cord and brain. The *peptides* that function as neurotransmitters include endorphins and enkephalins, which are involved in the suppression of pain transmission, and substance P, which is released by the endings of pain fibers in the spinal cord.

The effectiveness of a synaptic interaction depends on the amount of neurotransmitter released by the presynaptic cell and the responsiveness of the postsynaptic cell. The quantity of neurotransmitter that is released in response to an action potential depends on the availability of neurotransmitter, the membrane potential in the axon terminal, the amount of Ca^{2+} in the terminal, and the presence of presynaptic connections from other neurons. Some neurons form synapses on the axon terminals of other neurons, which can have inhibitory or excitatory effects on the response of the presynaptic terminal to the incoming action potential. Similarly, the responsiveness of the postsynaptic membrane can be altered by the action of substances known as **neuromodulators** (Binder,

Heckman, & Powers, 1996; Hoffmann, Jonsdottir, & Thorén, 1996; Katz, 1995). These cause biochemical changes in the neuron that alter its excitability to the current evoked by the action of the neurotransmitter and the receptor.

Because neurons have thousands of synapses, rarely is a single synapse active in isolation. Consequently, the input received by a postsynaptic neuron consists of the summed response of multiple synaptic potentials. Concurrent input received from multiple synapses adds by a process referred to as **spatial summation.** Inputs that arrive at slightly different times but that overlap in time are added by a process known as **temporal summation.** The response of the cell (e.g., neuron, muscle fiber) depends on the magnitude of these summed synaptic potentials at the most excitable region of the cell, where the action potentials are generated.

Axonal Transport

In discussion of the interaction between nerve and muscle cells, the axon is typically thought of as a tapering cylinder along which action potentials are propagated. The internal structure of the axon, however, comprises a complex system that is capable of transporting various chemicals in both directions along the axon. The transported material includes structural elements, proteins, RNA (ribonucleic acid), and amino acids. The intra-axonal displacement of these materials is known as **axonal transport** (Schwartz & De Camilli, 2000).

In comparison with the action potential, axoplasmic transport is slow, but nonetheless it provides critical interactions between the motor neuron and the muscle fibers that the motor neuron innervates. The transport system involves the fibrillar elements that compose the cytoskeleton of the neuron. These are microtubules, neurofilaments, and microfilaments, shown as the long cylinders in the axon of figure 6.6. **Microtubules,** which can be up to 0.1 mm in length and about 26 nm in diameter, are arranged longitudinally in the axon with polarity in the same direction. They comprise long polymers of tubulin dimers. Specific proteins regulate the stability and orientation of microtubules. **Neurofilaments** are comparable to the intermediate filaments in other cells, such as the muscle fiber, and include such proteins as vimentin, desmin, keratin, and glial fibrillary acidic protein. They have a diameter of 10 nm and are 3 to 10 times more abundant than microtubules. Like the microtubules, neurofilaments are oriented along the length of the axon. **Microfilaments** are similar to the thin filaments in muscle, comprising a two-stranded helix of actin polymers. Microfilaments have a diameter of about 4 nm.

Axonal transport along the cytoskeleton occurs in both directions and at two different speeds, fast and slow. Transportation away from the soma is known as **orthograde**

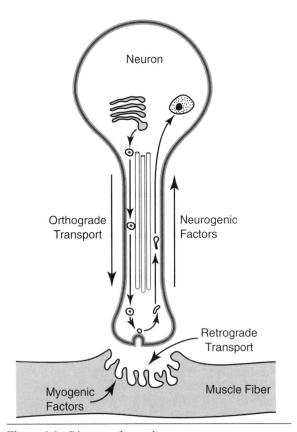

Figure 6.6   Diagram of axonal transport systems.
From "Synthesis and Distribution of Neuronal Protein" by J.H. Schwartz, 1985. In *Principles of Neural Science, 2nd ed.,* by E.R. Kandel and J.H. Schwartz, (Eds.), p. 42, New York: Elsevier. Reprinted by permission of The McGraw-Hill Companies.

transport (or anterograde transport), while that toward the soma is known as **retrograde transport** (figure 6.6). For example, an important step in the electrochemical transfer of information from the neuron to the muscle is the release of the neurotransmitter by the vesicle into the synaptic cleft. After a number of cycles, the vesicle membrane requires repair and is transported retrogradely back to the soma, where the membrane repair occurs; the vesicle is subsequently sent back to the neuromuscular junction via orthograde transport.

The fast orthograde transport of organelles occurs along the microtubules in a saltatory manner—that is, stop and go. The displacement is driven by molecular motors, which include the enzymes kinesin and cytoplasmic dynein. These motors are attached to the microtubules, and their manner of functioning appears to be qualitatively similar to that of the cross-bridge in muscle (Sheetz, Steuer, & Schroer, 1989; Schwartz & De Camilli, 2000). Each motor translocates organelles in only one direction. Kinesin drives orthograde transport, while cytoplasmic dynein supports retrograde transport. On the basis of measurements made with a laser beam, it has been estimated that a single kinesin molecule can exert a force of about 2 pN and can move organelles at about

0.5 to 2.0 μm/s. These motors can move organelles at speeds up to 410 mm/day in the orthograde direction and up to 200 mm/day in the retrograde direction.

The function of fast axonal transport is to move subcellular organelles along the axon. In contrast, slow axonal transport moves cytoskeletal elements and soluble proteins down the axon. Slow axonal transport displaces material either at 0.1 to 2 mm/day or at 2 to 4 mm/day. The slower component moves the proteins that make up the neurofilaments and the microtubules. The faster component transports actin (used to form the microfilaments), proteins such as neural myosin and clathrin, and some of the enzymes involved in intermediary metabolism.

Trophic Effects

While the critical role of axonal transport in maintaining neuronal integrity is obvious, this system also modulates the properties of the involved components. These effects occur in both directions and are known as nerve-muscle (neurogenic) and muscle-nerve (myogenic) trophism. For example, when a muscle is **denervated** (its nerve is cut), the changes involve a loss of muscle mass (atrophy); a degeneration of muscle fibers as nuclei migrate to the center of the fiber and the mitochondria disintegrate; decreases in the force output and the time course of the twitch; depolarization of the resting membrane potential within 2 h after denervation; an increase in the resting membrane resistance, reflecting a decrease in membrane permeability; alterations in the sodium channel structure; the spontaneous generation of sarcolemmal action potentials; the synthesis of extrajunctional ACh receptors; a reduction in the enzyme acetylcholinesterase; and the development of sprouts by intact motor axons. Although denervation causes the removal of both action potentials and axonal transport, the observation that the onset of these changes depends on how far the nerve is cut from the muscle strongly suggests a significant role for neurogenic factors in regulating the normal properties of the nerve-muscle system. Furthermore, **reinnervation** (reconnection of the nerve to the muscle) results in a reversal of these changes.

Similarly, disturbance of the axon has demonstrated the existence of *muscle-nerve* trophism (Lowrie & Vrbová, 1992). This can be shown by changes in the afterhyperpolarization phase of the motor neuron action potential (Czéh, Gallego, Kudo, & Kuno, 1978). When a drug (tetrodotoxin) that blocks axonal propagation but does not impair axonal transport is applied to an axon, the afterhyperpolarization phase changes if the axon is stimulated on one side of the block but not on the other. When the axon is artificially stimulated for 14 weeks on the motor neuron side of the block so that no action potential reaches the muscle, the afterhyperpolarization phase decreases in duration. In contrast, when the stimulation is applied on the muscle side of the block and the muscle is activated, the afterhyperpolarization phase does not change. This finding suggests that activation of the muscle, albeit with artificial stimulation, maintains the health of the motor neuron as displayed in the afterhyperpolarization phase of the action potential. Other electrophysiological properties of the motor neurons (e.g., action potential overshoot, resting membrane potential, axonal conduction velocity) also change after the axon is cut (Huizar, Kuno, Kudo, & Miyata, 1978). Furthermore, the development of a functional contact between the axon terminals of a motor neuron and muscle seems critical for the maturation of the neuron (Greensmith & Vrbová, 1996).

As a physiological process, axonal transport can adapt to altered patterns of usage. For example, Jasmin, Lavoie, and Gardiner (1987) examined the transport of the enzyme acetylcholinesterase from the soma to the neuromuscular junction in the motor neurons of rats following eight weeks of participation in either a swimming or a running program. **Acetylcholinesterase,** which is an enzyme found at the neuromuscular junction, terminates the activity of the neurotransmitter ACh. After eight weeks of exercise, the axonal transport of acetylcholinesterase had increased in the runners but not in the swimmers. This finding suggests that axonal transport can adapt to chronic changes in activity but that the adaptations are specific to the type of activity; motor neuron activity increased in both the runners and swimmers, yet only the runners exhibited a change in the axonal transport of this enzyme.

The rate of axonal transport can also decrease, as appears to happen with aging (Frolkis, Tanin, Marcinko, Kulchitsky & Yasechko, 1985). Older rats transport proteins inside the axon at a slower rate (200 mm/day) compared with adult rats (380 mm/day). Furthermore, when axonal transport is halted, there is less of a change in the resting membrane potential and excitability of single muscle fibers in older rats. This means that axonal transport plays less of a role in specifying some properties of muscle fibers in older rats. The slowing of axonal transport with age is a primary factor involved in neuronal aging.

Axonal transport also appears to be an important mechanism by which disease can invade the nervous system. Disease agents (viruses, bacteria) are taken up by vesicles during **pinocytosis** (the closure and release of the vesicle from the membrane after exocytosis) and become internalized inside the axon. Retrograde transport has been implicated in the movement of viruses (poliomyelitis and herpes) and the tetanus toxin (due to bacterial infection in the skin) from the periphery to the cell body (Ochs, 1987).

Axonal transport, therefore, represents a mechanism by which muscle can exert a neurotrophic effect on its motor neurons and by which motor neurons can influence the properties and health of the muscle fibers. As

with all physiological processes, axonal transport varies with activity and age.

Excitation-Contraction Coupling

At the neuromuscular junction, the neurotransmitter ACh takes less than 100 μs to diffuse across the synaptic cleft and attach to receptors on the postsynaptic membrane. The attachment of ACh to the postsynaptic receptors results in the opening of the transmitter-gated Na^+-K^+ channel and in the influx of Na^+ and efflux of K^+ from the muscle fiber. The movement of Na^+ and K^+ across the sarcolemma results in the development of the end-plate potential (synaptic potential) that can trigger the generation of a sarcolemmal action potential. The processes involved in the conversion of an axonal action potential into a sarcolemmal action potential are referred to as neuromuscular propagation.

Once the axonal action potential has been transformed into a sarcolemmal action potential, several processes convert the motor neuron command (action potential) into a muscle fiber force. These processes are known as **excitation-contraction coupling.** The steps involved in excitation-contraction coupling are indicated in figure 6.7: (1) propagation of the sarcolemmal action potential; (2) propagation of the action potential down the transverse (T) tubule; (3) coupling of the action potential to the change in Ca^{2+} conductance of the sarcoplasmic reticulum; (4) release of Ca^{2+} from the sarcoplasmic reticulum; (5) reuptake of Ca^{2+} by the sarcoplasmic reticulum; (6) Ca^{2+} binding to troponin; and (7) interaction of the cross-bridge (myosin) and actin. Most of these steps involve events that *permit* the interaction of actin and myosin (Ca^{2+} disinhibition), whereas only step 7 actually *involves* the interaction of actin and myosin (cross-bridge cycle).

Ca²⁺ Disinhibition

Under resting conditions, the thick and thin filaments are prevented from interacting by the regulatory action of troponin and tropomyosin, and Ca^{2+} is stored largely in the sarcoplasmic reticulum. Steps 1 to 6 in figure 6.7 identify the events involved in the removal of this inhibition. Essentially, these events enable the sarcolemmal action potential to trigger the release of Ca^{2+} from the sarcoplasmic reticulum and the subsequent inhibition of the regulatory action of troponin and tropomyosin. Because the net effect of this series of events is the removal, or inhibition, of inhibition, this process is referred to as **disinhibition.**

Ca^{2+} disinhibition begins with the muscle action potential as it is propagated along the sarcolemma at speeds

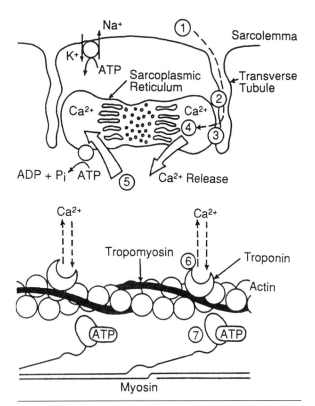

Figure 6.7 The seven steps involved in excitation-contraction coupling.

Adapted from Fitts and Metzger, 1993.

ATP = adenosine triphosphate; ADP = adenosine diphosphate; P_i = inorganic phosphate.

of up to 6 m/s. The sarcolemmal action potential is propagated down the T tubule and into the interior of the muscle fiber (Bastian & Nakajima, 1974); the inward spread of activation has been estimated to occur at a speed of about 70 μm/ms. The T-tubule action potential activates the dihydropiridine (DHP) channels that are distributed throughout the T tubules. These channels act as a voltage sensor that transmits a signal to the ryanodine receptors in the sarcoplasmic reticulum, through which Ca^{2+} is released from the sarcoplasmic reticulum. The mechanism by which the DHP channels span the 15 nm between the T tubule and the sarcoplasmic reticulum and contact the ryanodine receptors is unknown; it may involve a chemical connection, a mechanical signal, or an effect due to changes in Ca^{2+} concentration. Some evidence favors the mechanical connection between conformational (structural) changes in DHP channels and the ryanodine receptors (Ríos, Ma, & González, 1991; Ríos & Pizarró, 1988).

Figure 6.8 shows the role of Ca^{2+} in excitation-contraction coupling. In the resting state, the potential across the sarcolemma is negative with respect to the

outside; and most of the Ca^{2+} is stored in the terminal cisternae, which are the enlargements of the sarcoplasmic reticulum near the T tubules (figure 6.8a). The action potential is propagated down the T tubule and triggers an increase in the Ca^{2+} conductance (g_{Ca}) of the terminal cisternae, which corresponds to an opening of the ryanodine receptors. In the absence of an action potential, g_{Ca} is normally low so that Ca^{2+} has difficulty crossing the membrane of the sarcoplasmic reticulum. Once g_{Ca} has been increased, Ca^{2+} is able to move from the terminal cisternae down its concentration gradient through the ryanodine release channels and into the sarcoplasm (figure 6.8b). The quantity of ryanodine receptors is two- to threefold greater in fast-twitch fibers than in slow-twitch fibers, enabling a greater amount of Ca^{2+} to be released by each action potential (Damiani & Margreth, 1994). When the Ca^{2+} concentration in the sarcoplasm is above a threshold level (10^{-7} M), Ca^{2+} binds to the regulatory protein troponin that is attached to the actin filament. The binding of Ca^{2+} to troponin probably causes a structural change in the thin filament such that the myosin-binding site on actin is uncovered, and the two proteins (actin and myosin) are then able to interact (figure 6.9). The uncovering of the binding site may involve a transient rotation of the regulatory complex (troponin-tropomyosin).

The change in g_{Ca} is transient, and once the action potential has passed (figure 6.8c), g_{Ca} returns to a resting level and Ca^{2+} is returned to the sarcoplasmic reticulum by Ca^{2+} pumps (Ca^{2+} adenosinetriphosphatase [ATPase]) attached to the membrane of the sarcoplasmic reticulum. The enzyme Ca^{2+} ATPase pumps Ca^{2+} into the sarcoplasmic reticulum against a concentration gradient requiring the hydrolysis of one molecule of ATP for the translocation of two Ca^{2+} molecules. The rate at which Ca^{2+} is returned to the sarcoplasmic reticulum determines the rate of decline in force after the cessation of an action potential. Fatigued muscle, for example, exhibits a reduction in the rate of reuptake of Ca^{2+} (due to a decline in the activity of the Ca^{2+} pumps), which produces a decline in the rate of relaxation. This reuptake of Ca^{2+} lowers the concentration of Ca^{2+} in the sarcoplasm, which results in an inhibition of the activity of the enzyme (actomyosin ATPase) that regulates the interaction of actin and myosin.

The relative duration of these events is shown in figure 6.10. These data, which were measured on the large muscle fibers of the barnacle, comprised the potential across the excitable membrane, intracellular calcium contraction, and muscle force (Ashley & Ridgway, 1968, 1970). Calcium concentration was visualized through use of aequorin, which is a protein that luminesces when Ca^{2+} is present. Such measurements indicate that the mem-

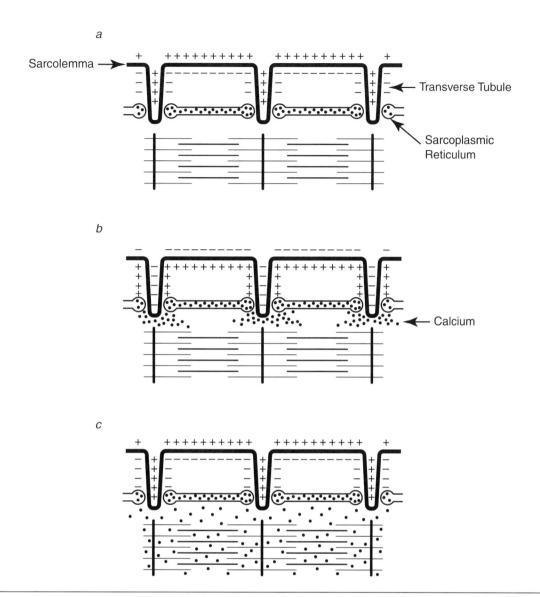

a

Sarcolemma →

Transverse Tubule

Sarcoplasmic
Reticulum

b

Calcium

c

Figure 6.8 Role of Ca²⁺ in excitation-contraction coupling. *(a)* Ca²⁺ is stored in the sarcoplasmic reticulum at rest, *(b)* released into the sarcoplasm in the presence of an action potential, and *(c)* returned to the sarcoplasmic reticulum after the action potential has passed.

Reprinted from Rüegg, 1983.

brane potential changes first, then calcium concentration, and finally muscle force. The duration of a typical action potential is much briefer than that shown in figure 6.10, which means that the duration of these events is briefest for the action potential and longest for the muscle force.

Cross-Bridge Cycle

The interaction of actin and myosin that occurs as a result of Ca²⁺ disinhibition is referred to as the cross-bridge cycle. Myosin is either weakly or strongly bound to actin, depending on the nucleotide that is attached to myosin

(Rayment, Holden, Whittaker, Yohn, Lorenz, Holmes, & Milligan, 1993; Warshaw, 1996). When either ATP or ADP·P_i is attached, myosin attaches to and detaches from actin (figure 6.11). When P_i is released, however, myosin undergoes a conformational change and is more strongly bound to actin. The myosin head exerts a force for several hundreds of milliseconds after the bound nucleotide is released (Ishijima et al., 1998). This conformational change represents the part of the cycle when work is performed and the thick and thin filaments slide relative to one another; this is often referred to as the power stroke of the cross-bridge cycle. The power stroke

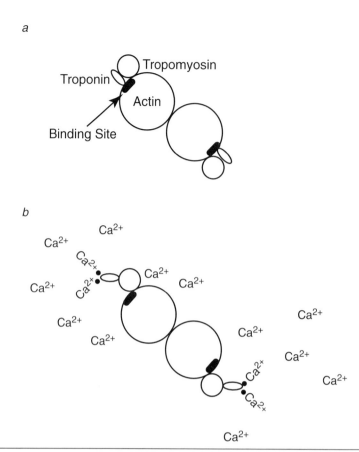

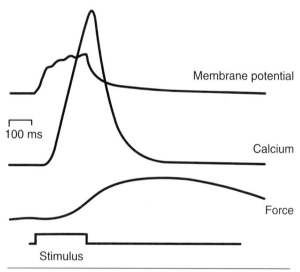

Figure 6.9   Scheme for the uncovering of the binding site on actin following the attachment of Ca^{2+} to troponin: *(a)* arrangement of the thin filament in the resting state; *(b)* uncovering of the binding site.

Data from Gergely, 1974.

Figure 6.10   A depolarization of the muscle membrane causes an increase in intracellular Ca^{2+} and a force exerted by the muscle fiber.

Adapted from McComas, 1996.

may involve closure of the cleft that divides the actin binding site (Volkmann, Hanein, Ouyang, Trybus, DeRosier, & Lowey, 2000). Displacement of the myosin head along an actin filament occurs with single mechanical steps of about 5.3 nm, and there are usually two to five successive steps during one biochemical cycle of ATP hydrolysis (Kitamura, Tokunaga, Iwane, & Yanagida, 1999). After the release of ADP, myosin remains strongly bound to actin in a rigor state until another ATP molecule attaches to myosin, when the myosin detaches and the cycle begins again. The rate of ATP hydrolysis varies about fourfold with muscle fiber type, being greatest for the fastest-contracting fibers (Steinen, Kiers, Bottinelli, & Reggiani, 1996). In a single power stroke for skeletal muscle, the force exerted between actin and myosin is in the range of 2 to 5 pN, and the displacement is in the range of 10 to 15 nm (Irving & Piazzesi, 1997; Warshaw, 1996). However, the connection between these mechanical events and the hydrolysis of ATP remains unclear (Rayment et al., 1993).

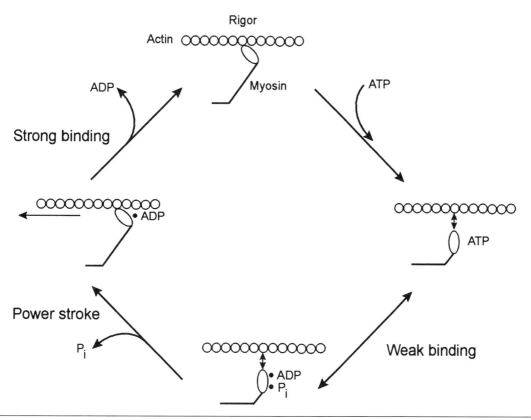

Figure 6.11   The cross-bridge cycle.

ATP = adenosine triphosphate; ADP = adenosine diphosphate; P_i = inorganic phosphate.

Because the displacement of the myosin head occurs while actin and myosin are connected, the thick and thin filaments slide past one another and exert a force on the cytoskeleton. The sliding of the filaments relative to one another has given rise to the **sliding filament hypothesis** of muscle contraction (Huxley & Niedergerke, 1954; Huxley & Hanson, 1954). The force exerted by muscle is usually explained as a consequence of the concurrent, but not synchronous, cycling of many cross-bridges following Ca^{2+} disinhibition; this is known as the **cross-bridge theory of muscle contraction** (Huxley, 2000; Huxley, 1957; Huxley & Simmons, 1971). Given that the filaments can slide by about 1000 nm and that the displacement associated with each power stroke is about 11 to 30 nm (Kitamura et al., 1999), each myosin head probably performs several attach-detach sequences during a single bout of activation. We describe this activity as a muscle contraction, where the term **contraction** refers to *the state of muscle activation in which cross-bridges are cycling in response to an action potential.* When the electrical events of the sarcolemma are finished, the permeability of the sarcoplasmic reticulum reverts to its normal low level; the Ca^{2+} pump (located in the membrane of the sar-

coplasmic reticulum) returns Ca^{2+} to the sarcoplasmic reticulum (figure 6.8*c*); and the inhibitory effect of the troponin-tropomyosin complex is reestablished.

Imaging a Muscle Contraction

Similar to the use of EMG to measure muscle action potentials, **magnetic resonance imaging** (MRI) has been used to record the contractile activity of muscle. A technique that can localize atomic nuclei, MRI can be used to study the structure and function of the single-joint system. Conceptually, the technique involves three steps: (1) exposing an object to a magnetic field that aligns chemical elements with odd atomic weights; (2) perturbing the alignment of these elements; and (3) measuring the rate, called the relaxation rate, at which atomic nuclei return to the initial alignment. The two principal relaxation rates are known as the longitudinal (T_1) and transverse (T_2) relaxation times. Increases in both T_1 and T_2 **relaxation times** have been correlated with increases in the water content of muscle and, as a result, have proved useful for the study of muscle activation, muscle soreness, and musculotendinous strains (Fleckenstein & Shellock, 1991; Meyer & Prior, 2000).

In a typical experiment, measurements are made of a body part before and after the performance of a prescribed task so that changes in T_1 and T_2 can be determined. By varying the details of the performance in repeat measurements, it is possible to determine associations between the relaxation times and such performance criteria as the work done and the magnitude of the force exerted by the subject. With this protocol, the MRI data can provide information on the cumulative effects of the exercise (crossbridge activity) but do not indicate the moment-to-moment activity during the performance. Changes in T_2 relaxation time, for example, appear to be related to an exercise-induced change in the intracellular water content of muscle fibers following a muscle contraction (Fleckenstein, Canby, Parkey, & Peshock, 1988; Fisher, Meyer, Adams, Foley, & Potchen, 1990). Although T_2 relaxation time can be influenced by extracellular water, intracellular pH, level of oxygenation in the blood, fluid viscosity, temperature, and intramuscular fat (Yue et al., 1994), exercise-induced changes seem to be caused by alterations in H_2O exchange or binding with proteins rather than either a relative increase in the extracellular fluid volume or a decrease in the paramagnetic solutes. For this reason, the measurement of changes in T_2 with physical activity is a technique that offers considerable potential for expanding our knowledge of muscle function.

An example of the application of this technology is shown in figure 6.12. These data indicate the relative use of the thigh muscles to perform brief bouts of high-intensity exercise on a cycle ergometer compared with a knee-extension device (Richardson, Frank, & Haseler, 1998). Muscle usage for these two exercises can be evaluated qualitatively through comparison of the intensity of the image after exercise (bottom row of images) with that before exercise. Lighter regions after exercise indicate a greater use of that muscle. From these images, we can determine that the knee extensor muscles were used most during the knee-extension exercise and that substantial activation of both the anterior and posterior compartments occurred during the cycling exercise. The magnitude of the change in intensity can be determined by calculating T_2 values. Richardson et al. found that there was a significant increase in T_2 of the four knee extensor muscles after the knee-extension exercise and a significant increase in T_2 for all 10 muscles after the cycling exercise (table 6.1).

Three observations underscore the usefulness of MRI for studying muscle function. First, there is a positive linear relation between the intensity of the T_2 signal and the intensity of a muscle contraction. This relation has been reported for shortening (concentric) and lengthening (eccentric) contractions and for several different muscle groups. For example, when a specific group of muscles moves a load and contracts concentrically, the oxygen consumption is greater and more motor units are recruited than when the muscles contract eccentrically to move the same load. As a consequence, the intensities

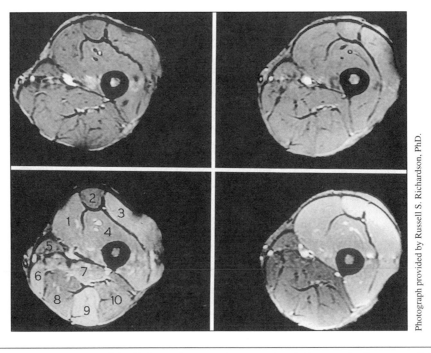

Photograph provided by Russell S. Richardson, PhD.

Figure 6.12 Magnetic resonance images of the thigh muscles at rest (upper row) and after exercise (bottom row). The images in the left column are from before and after exercise on a cycle ergometer. The images in the right column are from before and after exercise on a knee-extension machine. The lighter image after exercise indicates an increase in signal intensity, which is used to determine T_2 values. The muscles labeled on the bottom left image correspond to (1) vastus medialis, (2) rectus femoris, (3) vastus lateralis, (4) vastus intermedius, (5) sartorius, (6) gracilis, (7) adductor longus, (8) semimembranosus, (9) semitendinosus, and (10) biceps femoris.

Table 6.1 T_2 Values (ms) in Thigh Muscles Before and After Knee-Extension and Cycling Exercises

Muscle	Knee-extension exercise		Cycling exercise	
	Before (ms)	After (ms)	Before (ms)	After (ms)
Vastus medialis	27.7	32.6*	27.7	31.4*
Rectus femoris	27.3	37.4*	26.3	29.1*
Vastus lateralis	28.3	34.2*	27.5	33.0*
Vastus intermedius	28.8	32.0*	28.8	32.0*
Sartorius	30.2	29.4	26.8	31.4*
Gracilis	28.3	26.3	25.0	29.9*
Adductor magnus	29.0	28.6	27.9	33.5*
Semimembranosus	24.5	25.5	21.6	25.2*
Semitendinosus	26.1	27.0	24.7	29.3*
Biceps femoris	28.0	27.1	28.1	30.5*

Note. *Significant increase in T_2 after exercise.

Data from Richardson et al., 1998.

of both the EMG and the T_2 signal are less during the eccentric contraction (Adams, Duvoisin, & Dudley, 1992; Fisher et al., 1990; Jenner, Foley, Cooper, Potchen, & Meyer, 1994; Shellock, Fukunaga, Mink, & Edgerton, 1991). Second, the MRI measurement has enough spatial resolution to identify the subvolume of finger flexor muscles (flexor digitorum superficialis and flexor digitorum profundus) that control the activity of individual fingers (Fleckenstein, Watumull, Bertocci, Parkey, & Peshock, 1992). This capability enables researchers to determine the prevalence of functional compartmentalization within a single muscle and within a group of synergist muscles. It also makes it possible to determine whether a task involves coactivation of an agonist-antagonist set of muscles. However, the measurement is not reliable enough to allow the development of maps of muscle activation based on pixel-by-pixel estimates of T_2 (Prior, Foley, Jayaraman, & Meyer, 1999). Third, MRI signals may provide a technique to noninvasively determine the fiber-type composition of a muscle. A strength-training program for the knee extensor muscles resulted in a significant increase in the proportion of fast-twitch muscle fibers in the vastus lateralis muscle. This change in fiber-type proportion was highly correlated with increases in the T_1 and T_2 relaxation times (Kuno, Katsuta, Akisada, Anno, & Matsumoto, 1990). However, some experiments have cast doubt on the validity of this approach (Parkkola et al., 1993).

On the basis of the properties of excitable membranes, the nervous system is able to send a signal to muscle that results in activation of the contractile proteins. In describing the function of the single-joint system, we have so far focused on the biochemical and biophysical mechanisms that underlie its activation. We next consider the biomechanical properties of the system motor (muscle mechanics) and then its control by the nervous system.

Muscle Mechanics

While the force that a muscle exerts clearly depends on the amount of excitation provided by the nervous system, it is perhaps less obvious that muscle force also depends on the properties of the muscle itself. These muscular factors include the mechanical properties of muscle and the structural effects due to differences in muscle architecture. Although an action potential in a muscle fiber is an all-or-none event, the force exerted by a muscle fiber in response to a muscle fiber action potential is not always the same. The force depends on activation factors and on the mechanical properties of muscle.

Quasistatic Properties

For a given level of activation, the force that a muscle can exert depends on its length and on the rate of change in length (velocity). When these capabilities are measured experimentally, the muscle is placed at a certain length or its length is changed at a constant velocity, and the force is measured. The outcome is a single data point that, along with other data points, can be graphed to represent the appropriate relation. The force-length and force-velocity relations measured this way characterize the quasistatic properties of muscle; they do not, however, describe the force exerted by muscle during movement.

The force-length and force-velocity relations of muscle depend on the contractile properties of the muscle fibers, the organization of the fibers in the muscle, and the arrangement of the muscle around the joint. This section describes the quasistatic properties of muscles at each of these three levels.

Single-Fiber Level

The sliding filament hypothesis of muscle contraction states that the exertion of force by muscle is accompanied by the sliding of thick and thin filaments past one another. The most popular explanation for this phenomenon, the *cross-bridge theory of muscle contraction,* suggests that cross-bridges (S1 extensions) extending from thick filaments are able to attach to the thin filaments and then undergo a structural-chemical transition, thereby exerting a tensile force (Huxley, 2000; Piazzesi et al., 1999; Rayment et al., 1993). According to this scheme, the development of force depends on these cross-bridge attach-detach cycles; the greater the number of cycles occurring at the same time, the greater the force. And because force is exerted only during the attachment phase,

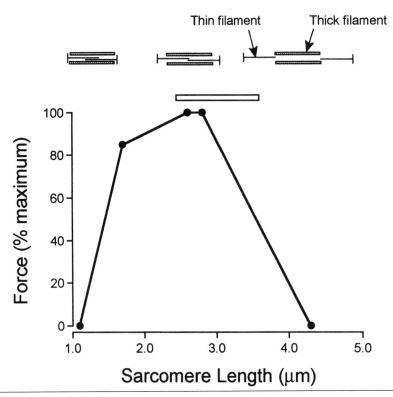

Figure 6.13 The force a muscle fiber can exert as a function of sarcomere length. The open bar at the top of the figure indicates how much sarcomere length changes over the physiological range of motion for the wrist extensor muscle.

Reprinted from Lieber, Loren, and Fridén, 1994.

the thick and thin filaments must be close enough to each other for the attachment to occur and thus for a force to be exerted.

As the *length* of the muscle changes and the thick and thin filaments slide past one another, the number of actin binding sites available for the cross-bridges changes. This leads to the observation that *tension varies with the amount of overlap between thick and thin filaments within a sarcomere* (Gordon, Huxley, & Julian, 1966). This effect is typically shown as a graph of muscle force as a function of sarcomere length (figure 6.13). At a sarcomere length of 4.3 μm, there is minimal overlap of the thick and thin filaments; sarcomeres do not get this long under normal conditions. At a sarcomere length of about 2.5 to 2.8 μm, there is maximum overlap between the cross-bridges and the binding sites on the thin filaments. As the filaments slide farther over one another and interfere with the available binding sites, the amount of **overlap of myofilaments** decreases and sarcomere length decreases to about 1.1 μm. The net result of this change in the number of potential cross-bridge attachments is that the force a muscle can exert will also vary with muscle length. Measurements made on a wrist extensor muscle (extensor carpi radialis brevis) during a surgical procedure showed that sarcomere length went from 3.4 μm in a flexed-wrist position to 2.6 μm in an extended-wrist position (Lieber, Loren, & Fridén, 1994). On the

basis of figure 6.13, this change in sarcomere length would be associated with an ~50% decline in the maximum force the sarcomere could exert.

To determine the force-velocity relation for a muscle fiber, the dissected fiber is placed in a bath and connected to a device that can apply a desired force to the fiber. Optical devices are used to measure sarcomere length and fiber length, both at rest and during the contraction. The fiber is activated with brief electric shocks and then released so that the velocity of the contraction can be measured. The velocity of the muscle contraction depends on the relation between the maximum isometric force capacity of the fiber (P_o) and the magnitude of the force applied to the fiber. For forces less than the isometric force, the fiber will shorten. Conversely, the length of the fiber will increase when the applied force is greater than the isometric force. For each applied force, a single velocity measurement is made. Figure 6.14 shows the velocity-force relation based on the measurement of velocity when the muscle fiber acted against 32 different forces (Edman, 1988).

The force-velocity relation for a single muscle fiber (figure 6.14) has three key features. First, there is an increase in the speed at which the muscle fiber shortens as the force decreases. Second, the force-velocity relation is reasonably flat around P_o, corresponding to a 2% change in muscle velocity for a 30% change in force.

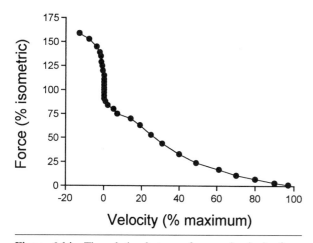

Figure 6.14   The relation between force and velocity for a single muscle fiber from a frog. Positive velocity indicates a shortening contraction, and negative velocity corresponds to a lengthening contraction.

Data from Edman, 1988.

Third, the force exerted by the fiber is greatest during lengthening contractions (negative velocity in figure 6.14): lengthening contractions occur only when the load is about 40% greater than P_o.

The maximum rate at which a muscle fiber can shorten (V_{max}) is limited by the maximum cycling rate of the cross-bridges. When expressed in fiber lengths per second, V_{max} correlates strongly with the quantity of the enzyme myofibrillar ATPase (Bárány, 1967; Edman, Reggiani, Schiaffino, & te Kronnie, 1988). Because this enzyme is responsible for controlling the splitting of ATP within the contractile system, increased amounts of the enzyme enhance the rate at which energy is made available for the cross-bridges. Furthermore, V_{max} remains constant over a range of sarcomere lengths and levels of activation (Edman, 1992).

The force that a muscle fiber can exert at various velocities can be explained by the cross-bridge theory of muscle contraction. The amount of work done by muscle during a contraction depends on the number of cross-bridge attachments and the average work done during each cross-bridge cycle. For shortening contractions, an increase in the speed at which the thick and thin filaments slide past one another causes some potential binding sites to be missed by cross-bridges and causes the average work done during the power stroke to decline because of a decrease in cross-bridge displacement. For lengthening contractions, the greater forces may be due to an increase in the quantity of Ca^{2+} released in response to activation, stretching of the less completely activated sarcomeres within each myofibril, or an increase in the average force exerted during each cross-bridge cycle. Furthermore, the detachment of a cross-bridge during a lengthening contraction occurs after the cross-bridge has

experienced a certain amount of stretch, and then the cross-bridge can reattach much more rapidly than during an isometric contraction (Lombardi & Piazzesi, 1990).

The contractile properties of muscle are often characterized with a **rheological model** (figure 6.15). Rheology is the study of the deformation and flow of matter (Whiting & Zernicke, 1998). Three elements are often included in these models: a linear spring (elasticity), a dashpot (viscosity), and a frictional element. Because the effect of internal friction is relatively small compared with those of the elastic (spring) and viscous (dashpot) properties of muscle and tendon, it is usually omitted from the model of muscle. The Hill model of muscle (figure 6.15) was first proposed in 1938 (Winters & Woo, 1990). The central component of the Hill model is the **contractile element** (CE), which often includes a dashpot and is characterized by the length-force and force-velocity relations. The CE is surrounded by two elastic elements that represent the elasticity of the connective tissue. These are indicated as springs in the model. The **series elastic element** (SE) and the **parallel elastic element** (PE) correspond to the passive effects of the connective tissue (Kawakami & Lieber, 2000), including the cytoskeleton, on the force exerted by the CE.

The Hill model can be used to explain why the peak force that a muscle exerts in response to a single stimulus (twitch) is less than that exerted in response to multiple stimuli (tetanus). The difference in force is attributable to two factors: the quantity of calcium released by the sarcoplasmic reticulum and the mechanical behavior of muscle. First, the single action potential that evokes a twitch does not release sufficient Ca^{2+} to uncover enough binding sites for maximum force. With a series of action potentials, there is a progressive accumulation of intracellular Ca^{2+} that eventually maximizes cross-bridge activity, and the force reaches maximum (Allen, Lee, & Westerblad, 1989). Second, the effect of Ca^{2+} on the muscle force is accompanied by a mechanical effect that can be explained by the Hill model (figure 6.15). The

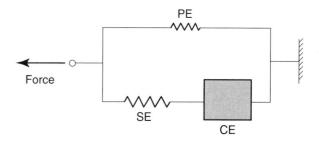

Figure 6.15   A Hill model of a single muscle fiber.

PE = parallel elastic element; SE = series elastic element; CE = contractile element.

state of activation of the contractile machinery reaches a maximum intensity within 4 ms after the action potential and is maintained at maximum for about 30 ms before it begins to decline (Hoyle, 1983). In response to this activation, the CE generates force, but this force is registered externally only by being transmitted through the SE. Because the SE functions as a spring, the slack must be stretched out of the SE before it will transmit any force exerted by the CE (Kawakami & Lieber, 2000). The characteristics of the SE are such that the state of activation of the CE has begun to decline in a twitch before the SE has been fully stretched.

More simplistically, the CE generates a certain quantity of force in response to a single action potential. Some of this force is used to stretch the SE, and the remainder can be measured externally. In contrast, during a tetanus the SE becomes fully stretched after the first 5 to 10 action potentials, so all the subsequent force exerted by the CE can be registered externally (Hoyle, 1983). In combination, the progressive intracellular accumulation of Ca^{2+} and stretch of the SE result in a tetanic force that is greater than the twitch force. Tetanic force is about two to seven times greater than twitch force in motor units of human hand muscles (Fuglevand, Macefield, & Bigland-Ritchie, 1999; Thomas, Bigland-Ritchie, & Johansson, 1991; Young & Mayer, 1981).

Whole-Muscle Level

The basic contractile properties of muscle, as characterized by the force-length and force-velocity relations of the single fiber, are influenced by the way in which the fibers are organized to form a muscle (Lieber & Fridén, 2000; Russell, Motlagh, & Ashley, 2000). There are three main effects of muscle design: length, width, and angle. We can describe these effects by considering a muscle that consists of three muscle fibers (figure 6.16). The three muscle fibers can be placed end to end (in series), side by side (in parallel), or at an angle to the line of pull of the muscle. When muscle fibers are arranged in series, this maximizes the range of motion (ΔL) and the maximum shortening velocity of the muscle. In contrast, an in-parallel arrangement maximizes the force (F) that the muscle can exert. However, when the fibers are aligned at an angle to the line of pull of the muscle, less than the maximum force that the fiber can exert contributes to the muscle force (figure 6.17).

To explain these effects of muscle design, we will consider what happens when each muscle is activated by the nervous system. For the **in-series** muscle, each muscle fiber experiences a change in length (Δl) in response to the activation. For a muscle that has three fibers arranged in series, the change in length (ΔL) for the muscle is equal

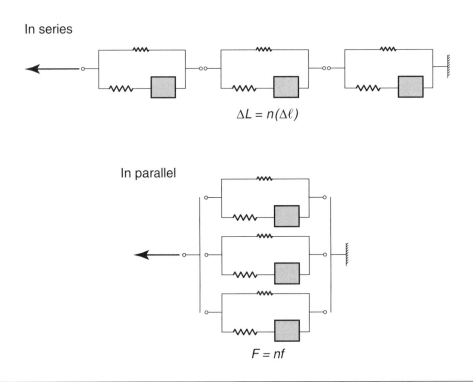

Figure 6.16 Influence of the in-series and in-parallel arrangement of three muscle fibers on the range of motion (ΔL) and maximum force (F) that a muscle can exert. Each muscle fiber is represented by a Hill model in the two schemes.

Single Fiber

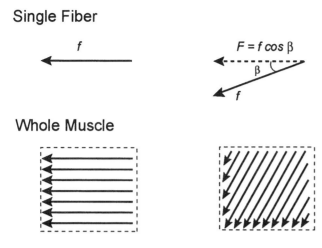

Whole Muscle

Figure 6.17   The angle of pennation (β) has an effect on the force exerted by both the single fiber and the whole muscle.

to three times Δ*l*. Consequently, the range of motion for a muscle depends on the number of fibers that are arranged in series. Similarly, the maximum velocity *(V)* of a contraction depends on the number of fibers *(n)* arranged in series ($\Delta V = n\Delta v$). In contrast, the maximum force that a muscle can exert is maximized by the **in-parallel** arrangement of muscle fibers. For a muscle with three fibers arranged in series, the force is equal to the average force exerted by the three fibers. When the fibers are arranged in parallel, however, the muscle force *(F)* is equal to the sum of the forces exerted by each fiber *(f)*; that is, $F = nf$. We encountered this relation earlier (chapter 3) in considering the cross-sectional area of muscle as an index of the maximum force that a muscle can exert (Roy & Edgerton, 1992).

The third feature of muscle design is the angle of **pennation** (β), which refers to the alignment of the muscle fibers at an angle to the line of pull of the muscle. When the angle of pennation is zero, the net force exerted by the fiber *(f)* acts in the direction of the whole-muscle force *(F;* figure 6.17). When the angle of pennation is not zero, however, the net force of the single fiber that acts in the direction of the line of pull for the muscle varies as the cosine of the angle of pennation. This description, however, can be misleading, because most of the force exerted by a fiber is transmitted laterally (Sheard, 2000). Nonetheless, at the level of the whole muscle it is probably reasonable to conceptualize the force as being transmitted in a longitudinal direction.

This raises the question of why most muscles have a nonzero angle of pennation. One reason is that for a given volume of muscle, more fibers can be placed in parallel when the pennation angle is not zero. This is shown in the bottom panel of figure 6.17: there are seven fibers in the volume when β = 0 and 13 fibers in the same volume when β ≠ 0. As a result, the pennated arrangement can exert a greater maximum force. The number of fibers that can be contained in a given volume is an important consideration because the volume available for various organs is often a limiting factor in biological design (Otten, 1988). For example, the muscles that control the fingers are located in either the hand or the forearm; those in the hand are small (restricted space), while those in the forearm are larger and stronger. If all the muscles that control the fingers were located in the hand, the hand would be bulky and more awkward for manipulation.

Example 6.3

Estimating the Number of In-Parallel Fibers

The in-parallel effect at the level of whole muscle is the same as that at the muscle fiber level; the greater the cross-sectional area (in-parallel content), the greater the maximum force the muscle can exert. Because of pennation, however, the measurement of cross-sectional area for the whole muscle is more difficult than that for a single muscle fiber. To get an accurate measurement of cross-sectional area, it is necessary to measure the area of a section made perpendicular to the long axis of each fiber. Consequently, measurement of whole-muscle cross-sectional area is not simply at the thickest part of the muscle but must take into account the angle of pennation. Such a measurement is referred to as the **functional** (or physiological) **cross-sectional area;** this is more accurate than estimating the maximum force that a muscle can exert by measuring anatomical cross-sectional areas (Lieber & Fridén, 2000; Narici, 1999).

Functional cross-sectional area (fCSA) can be calculated from knowledge of muscle volume, average pennation angle, and average fiber length:

$$fCSA = \frac{\text{volume } (\text{cm}^3) \cdot \cos \beta}{\text{fiber length } (\text{cm})} \qquad (6.2)$$

Muscle volume can be measured with an imaging technique such as MRI or computerized tomography, whereas estimates of pennation angle and fiber length are usually taken from published data (Lieber & Fridén, 2000). For the leg muscles included in figure 6.18, fCSA ranged from 1.7 cm² (sartorius, gracilis, extensor hallucis) to 58.0 cm² (soleus).

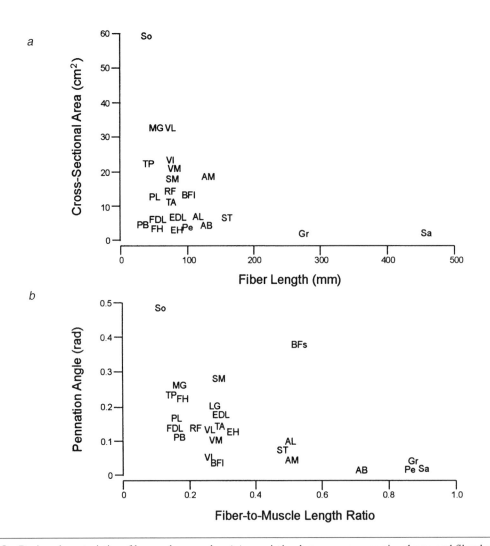

Figure 6.18 Design characteristics of human leg muscles: *(a)* association between cross-sectional area and fiber length; *(b)* relation between pennation angle and the ratio of fiber length to muscle length.

Data from Friederich and Brand, 1990; and Wickiewicz, Roy, Powell, and Edgerton, 1983.

AB = adductor brevis; AL = adductor longus; AM = adductor magnus; BFl = long head of biceps femoris; BFs = short head of biceps femoris; EDL = extensor digitorum longus; EH = extensor hallucis; FDL = flexor digitorum longus; FH = flexor hallucis; Gr = gracilis; LG = lateral gastrocnemius; MG = medial gastrocnemius; PB = peroneus brevis; Pe = pectineus; PL = peroneus longus; RF = rectus femoris; Sa = sartorius; SM = semimembranosus; So = soleus; ST = semitendinosus; TA = tibialis anterior; TP = tibialis posterior; VI = vastus intermedius; VM = vastus medialis; VL = vastus lateralis.

Muscles in the human body comprise a mixture of these three design features. Some muscles are long, some are wide, and most have fibers arranged with a nonzero angle of pennation. This distinction is apparent in measurements made on 25 leg muscles in five cadavers (figure 6.18); consult Roy and Edgerton (1992) and Lieber (1992) for similar data on arm muscles and Yamaguchi, Sawa, Moran, Fessler, and Winters (1990) for data on lower-extremity, trunk, upper-extremity, hand, and head-neck musculature. Although these measurements were made on preserved cadavers and are probably different from values for living tissue, the data do allow comparisons between muscles. The magnitude of the difference between muscle fibers in terms of in-series and in-parallel design can be substantial. In these specimens, fiber length ranged from 25 mm in soleus to 448 mm in sartorius (figure 6.18*a*). If we assume an average sarcomere length of 2.2 μm, then the average number of in-series sarcomeres ranged from 11,364 for soleus to 203,636 for sartorius.

Similarly, there are marked differences among muscles in the number of muscle fibers arranged in parallel, which is indicated by the measurement of cross-sectional area (figure 6.18*a*). For example, muscles that support an upright posture (e.g., knee extensors, ankle plantarflexors) are generally considered to be twice as strong as their antagonists. This would imply that the cross-sectional area of the antigravity muscles should be twice as large. Indeed, the cross-sectional area of quadriceps femoris is about double that for the hamstrings (87 vs. 38 cm²), and the value for the plantarflexors is substantially larger than that for the dorsiflexors (139 vs. 17 cm²). As shown in figure 6.18*a,* however, muscles that have large cross-sectional areas tend to have short muscle fibers. For example, the average muscle fiber in hamstrings is longer than an average one in quadriceps femoris (43,000 vs. 31,200 sarcomeres in series), and the average fiber length in the dorsiflexors is greater than that in the plantarflexors (29,300 vs. 15,200 sarcomeres in series). Consequently, although the hamstrings and dorsiflexors are weaker than their antagonists, they have a greater capability for change in length and rate of change in length (shortening velocity).

In most muscles, the ratio of fiber length to muscle length is less than 1, ranging from 0.08 in soleus to 0.85 for some leg (sartorius, pectineus, gracilis) and wrist (extensor carpi radialis longus) muscles. Most muscles have ratios in the range of 0.2 to 0.5 (figure 6.18*b*). Deviation of the ratio from 1, where a value of 1 indicates equal fiber and muscle lengths, is due to two in-series effects:

pennation and staggered fibers. Muscles with low ratios tend to have the fibers arranged with greater pennation angles (figure 6.18*b*). Conversely, muscles with pennation angles around zero have high ratios, which means that the fibers span most of the muscle length. The other in-series effect that can account for a fiber-to-muscle length ratio of less than 1 is the serial attachment of short **staggered fibers.** This effect can be demonstrated by plotting the longitudinal distribution of the muscle fibers that belong to a single motor unit (figure 6.19). This means that the force exerted by one motor unit is not transmitted from one end of the muscle to the other by its own fibers but rather is transmitted by the cytoskeleton and connective tissue (Huijing, 1999; Lieber & Fridén, 2000; Monti et al., 1999; Roy & Edgerton, 1992; Trotter, 1990).

The major effect of these design features on the force-length relation of muscle is attributable to the connective tissue that combines single fibers into whole muscles. As a consequence, the force exerted by muscle is not solely dependent on the *active* process of cross-bridge cycling and filament overlap. In addition, the connective tissue (e.g., endomysium, perimysium, epimysium, tendon) and cytoskeleton (figure 5.7) exert a *passive* force that combines with the cross-bridge activity. Because of this interaction, the force exerted by *muscle* is due to both the contractile (myofilaments) and structural (connective tissue and cytoskeleton) elements.

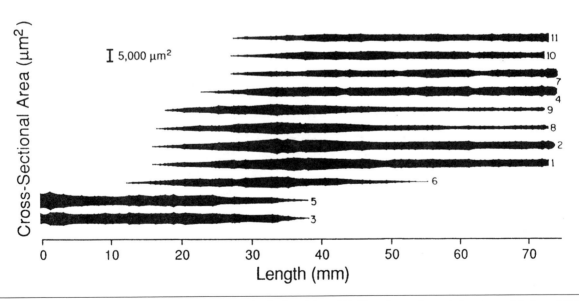

Figure 6.19 The cross-sectional area and relative longitudinal position of 11 fibers from a fast-twitch motor unit in the cat tibialis anterior muscle. On the length scale (*x*-axis), zero is the proximal end of the muscle.

Figure 6.20 illustrates the contributions of the active and passive components to total muscle force as muscle length varied over the range from the minimum contraction length to the maximum stretched length. This graph shows the **force-length relation** of whole muscle. These data were obtained by the direct measurement of muscle force in patients who had a special type of below-elbow prosthesis. Two forces were measured at each muscle length: one when the subject was resting and the other when the subject exerted a maximum voluntary force. When the subject remained relaxed, the passive force increased as the length of the muscle increased. When the subject performed a maximum voluntary contraction at each length, the force was due to both the passive (solid circles) and total (open circles) components and varied as shown in figure 6.20. The parabolic line, which was determined as the difference between the passive and total components, represents the change in force due to the active component as a function of muscle length. At shorter muscle lengths, all the force was due to the active component (cross-bridge activity), whereas at the longer lengths, most of the muscle force was due to the passive component. The actual shapes of these different components, however, vary among muscles (Baratta, Solomonow, Best, & D'Ambrosia, 1993), as should be expected from the differences in muscle design (figure 6.18).

As with the force-length relation, the force-velocity relation for muscle is influenced by muscle design. Whereas the maximum shortening velocity (V_{max}) for a single fiber depends primarily on the details of the myosin molecule (Schiaffino & Reggiani, 1996), V_{max} for

whole muscles depends on both the fiber-type composition of the muscle and the range-of-motion capacity of the muscle. In the cat hindlimb, for example, the tibialis anterior and tibialis posterior muscles each have about 20% type I fibers, yet V_{max} for tibialis anterior is 28.4 cm/s compared with 4.2 cm/s for tibialis posterior (Baratta, Solomonow, Best, Zembo, & D'Ambrosia, 1995). This difference in V_{max} is due to the greater range of motion for tibialis anterior (5.83 cm) compared with tibialis posterior (2.33 cm). This comparison indicates that muscle design can have a major effect on the force-velocity relation of whole muscle.

The classic description of the force-velocity relation for whole muscle (Equation 6.3) characterizes the decline in force as a function of shortening velocity with an equation for a rectangular hyperbola (Hill, 1938):

$$v = \frac{b\left(F_{m,o} - F_m\right)}{F_m + a} \qquad (6.3)$$

$$F_m v + av = bF_{m,o} - bF_m \qquad (6.4)$$

where

v = velocity of shortening

v_o = maximum velocity of shortening at $F_{m,o}$

$F_{m,o}$ = maximal isometric force

F_m = instantaneous muscle force

a = coefficient of shortening heat ($0.15F_{m,o}$ to $0.25F_{m,o}$)

b = constant $\left(a\dfrac{v_o}{F_{m,o}}\right)$

Equation 6.4 describes the force-velocity relation of muscle during a shortening contraction in terms of work and energy. The left-hand side of this equation ($F_m v + av$) corresponds to the rate of change in energy; the right-hand side ($bF_{m,o} - bF_m$) indicates the rate of doing work. Because muscle has some viscosity (fluid friction), the rate of energy utilization is not linearly related to the rate of work production. The term $F_m v$ represents the rate at which the contractile proteins do work (i.e., produce power) on the load, and the term av represents a damping element (due to viscosity) that makes rapid movements wasteful.

The interaction of these two terms ($F_m v$ and av) results in the increase and subsequent decline in power production as the velocity of contraction increases—that is, the power curves shown in figure 6.21*b*. Hill's equation (Equation 6.3) can be rearranged to determine muscle power ($F_m v$) explicitly:

$$F_m v = \frac{v\left(bF_{m,o} - av\right)}{v + b} \qquad (6.5)$$

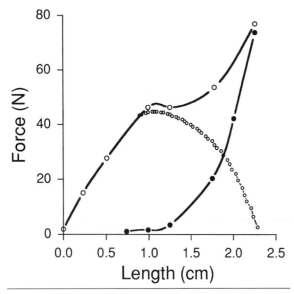

Figure 6.20 Contributions of the active (parabolic line) and passive (filled circles) elements to the total (open circles) muscle force-length relation.

Adapted from Ralston, Inman, Strait, and Shaffrath, 1947.

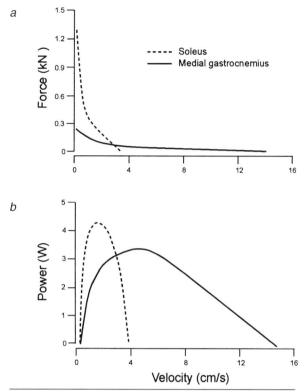

Figure 6.21 *(a)* Predicted force-velocity and *(b)* power-velocity relations for the soleus (dashed line) and medial gastrocnemius (solid line) muscles in humans. The force-velocity relation has a peak force at velocity = 0, and force then declines as velocity increases. In contrast, the power-velocity relation has a peak power at an intermediate velocity (1.0 cm/s for soleus, and 5.0 cm/s for medial gastrocnemius).

Adapted from Edgerton, Roy, Gregor, and Rugg, 1986.

On the basis of Equation 6.5 it is possible to demonstrate that power $(F_m v)$ is maximum when the muscle shortens at one-third of v_o or acts against a load that is one-third of $F_{m,o}$ (Josephson, 1993). Measurements of single muscle fibers, for comparison, indicate that peak power occurs when the load is about 20% of $F_{m,o}$ (Trappe et al., 2000).

Example 6.4
Muscle Architecture Influences Muscle Mechanics

The ability of muscle to generate power depends on its force capacity and shortening velocity. Because both cross-sectional area (an index of muscle force capacity) and contractile speed (as indicated by fast- and slow-twitch muscle fibers) vary between muscles, the ability to generate power differs across muscles. An example of this variation is shown in figure 6.21 for

the human soleus and medial gastrocnemius muscles. Although soleus has a much greater $F_{m,o}$ whereas medial gastrocnemius has a much greater V_{max}, the peak power produced by the two synergist muscles is similar but complementary, in that each occurs at a different region of the velocity-power domain (Wickiewicz, Roy, Powell, Perrine, & Edgerton, 1984).

Example 6.5
Isotonic Contractions Underestimate Muscle Function

One way to measure the force-velocity relation for a muscle is to disconnect one end from bone and attach it to a load, then activate the muscle supramaximally by stimulating its nerve and measure the force and velocity during the contraction. This procedure is referred to as isotonic loading: the load remains constant during the **isotonic contraction.** Different values for force and velocity are obtained when the load is varied (e.g., 3-75% $F_{m,o}$) between contractions; these measurements form the data set for the force-velocity curve (figure 6.21*a*). Subsequently, the power-velocity relation can be obtained by calculating power as the product of the force and velocity and plotting the product with the velocity values (figure 6.21*b*). With this isotonic-loading procedure it is possible to determine the force-velocity relation for shortening contractions and the power-velocity relation for power production.

Gregor and colleagues (figure 6.22) obtained the force-velocity and power-velocity relations for soleus by isotonic loading and compared them with values measured when a cat ran at about 2.2 m/s (cats can gallop at speeds up to 8 m/s) (Goslow, Reinking, & Stuart, 1973). To determine the force and velocity of soleus while the cat ran on a treadmill, a force transducer was placed on the soleus tendon and muscle length was measured from a video record of the movement. The force-velocity and power-velocity results for one cat during a step are shown in figure 6.22. When the foot contacted the ground (filled dot) and for some time thereafter, soleus performed a lengthening contraction (negative velocity), which was associated with a rapid increase in force to a peak value and the absorption of power (negative power). After the contraction reached zero velocity (isometric), soleus performed a shortening contraction (positive velocity) and produced power (positive power). Both the muscle force and power production during the movement (running at 2.2 m/s) were greater than the

(continued)

values measured during isotonic loading. This enhancement in muscle performance was probably due to the lengthening-shortening contraction that occurred during running as compared with the isometric shortening contraction examined in the isotonic-loading experiment (Monti et al., 1999). The comparison indicates that isotonic contractions underestimate the actual performance capabilities of muscle.

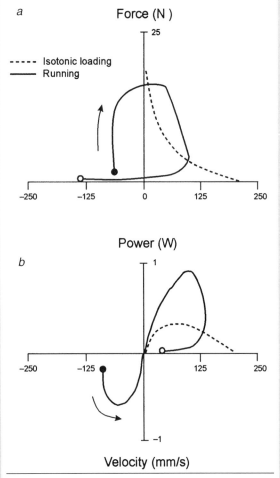

Figure 6.22   *(a)* Force-velocity and *(b)* power-velocity measurements for the cat soleus muscle. The isotonic-loading curves were measured experimentally and are compared with those measured during running at 2.2 m/s.

Data from Gregor et al., 1988.

Single-Joint System

At the next level of analysis, we consider the force-length and force-velocity relations for muscles that are attached to the skeleton. The two principal effects are those due to the moment arm and the contribution of multiple muscles to the net effect about a joint. In contrast to the situation at the single-fiber and whole-muscle levels, the significant mechanical action of muscle at this level is not the force it exerts but rather the torque produced about

the joint (Hoy, Zajac, & Gordon, 1990; Murray et al., 2000). As noted in chapters 2 and 3, this depends on the magnitudes of both muscle force and the moment arm relative to the joint. Similarly, the muscle torque about a joint is rarely due to the action of a single muscle, which means that the net effect depends on the relative contributions of several different muscles.

Because the force that a muscle exerts (figure 6.20) and its moment arm (figure 3.6) vary over the range of motion, the net muscle torque about most joints varies over the range of motion. For most muscles, variation in the moment arm depends on where the muscle is attached to the skeleton relative to the joint (van Mameren & Drukker, 1979). For example, figure 6.23*a* shows two similar muscles that differ in the location of the distal attachment. The distance from the proximal attachment to the joint *(p)* is the same for both muscles. The distance from the distal attachment to the joint for muscle *A* *(d$_a$)* is about one-half that for muscle *B* *(d$_b$)*, and the distances *p* and *d$_b$* are similar. As a result of this arrange-

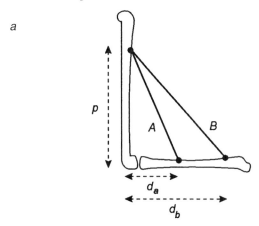

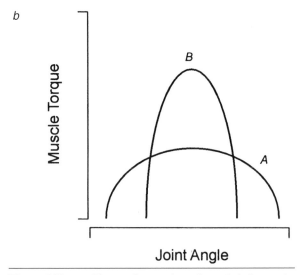

Figure 6.23   *(a)* The attachment sites of muscle influence its moment arm and *(b)* its torque-angle relation.

Data from Rassier et al., 1999.

ment, the moment arm for muscle *A* is about one-half of that for muscle *B* (Rassier, Macintosh, & Herzog, 1999). This difference in the attachment sites has a substantial effect on the **torque-angle relation** for each muscle; the torque-angle relation is equivalent to the force-length relation at the level of the single-joint system. The muscle with the shorter moment arm (muscle *A*) exerts torque over a greater range of motion, but the peak torque is less than that for the identical muscle with the longer moment arm (muscle *B*).

Example 6.6
An Indirect Estimate of the Variation in Moment Arm

As a muscle moves through its range of motion, there is a change in the moment arm from the muscle force vector to the joint. For the elbow flexor muscles, the moment arm is greatest in a midrange position (elbow angle about 1.57 rad) and least in full extension and full flexion. On the basis of this relation, we would expect the muscle force necessary to support a constant-torque load to vary inversely with the changes in the moment arm. That is, the resultant muscle torque must be constant over the range of motion to support a constant-torque load. However, recall that the resultant muscle torque is equal to the product of muscle force and moment arm. Thus, if the moment arm changes, muscle force must change in an inverse manner to maintain a constant product. This relation is difficult to assess directly, because both the moment arm and the muscle force are difficult quantities to measure. Instead, Hasan and Enoka (1985) examined the EMG and found that it varied in the manner that would be expected of muscle force given the change that occurs in the moment arm (figure 6.24). To support the constant load, therefore, muscle force (as indicated by the EMG) and moment arm varied inversely to achieve a constant muscle torque.

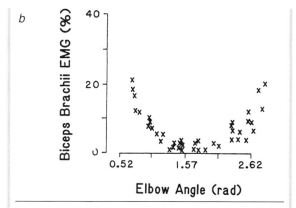

Figure 6.24 Electromyogram activity necessary for two concurrently active elbow flexor muscles—(*a*) brachioradialis and (*b*) biceps brachii—to support a constant-torque load over a substantial range of motion of the elbow joint. The EMG was measured as the average voltage needed to support the load and is expressed as a percentage of the maximum voluntary contraction.

Adapted from Hasan and Enoka, 1985.

Because both the moment arm from the muscle force vector to the joint axis and the muscle force change over the range of motion, the shape of the angle-torque relation depends on how these two variables (moment arm and force) change relative to one another. On the basis of cadaveric arm specimens, Lieber and colleagues measured the moment arms and estimated muscle forces for a number of muscles that cross the wrist joint (Loren et al., 1996). The data for three wrist extensor muscles show that moment arm and muscle force can change in different ways over the range of motion and produce different torque-angle relations (figure 6.25). For many joints in the human body, the net muscle torque varies over the range of motion and has a peak value at intermediate joint angles. Although the relative contributions of variations in moment arm and muscle force to the shape of the torque-angle relation are generally unknown, the percentage change in moment arm over the range of motion is usually greater than the change in muscle force. We can see this by comparing figure 6.25*a* and *b*.

Lieber (1992) characterizes these interactions by examining the ratio of muscle fiber length to moment arm length. The size of the ratio for a particular muscle indicates the extent to which the muscle contributes to the resultant muscle torque over the entire range of motion. When the ratio is high, the change in fiber length and thus sarcomere length is small relative to the angle-dependent change in moment arm. Recall from the length-tension relation of sarcomeres (figure 6.13) that the force exerted by a sarcomere remains greatest at intermediate sarcomere lengths. Consequently, for a high ratio of muscle fiber to moment arm, the muscle fiber remains at an intermediate length and remains capable of exerting

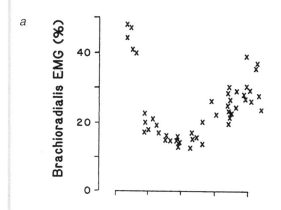

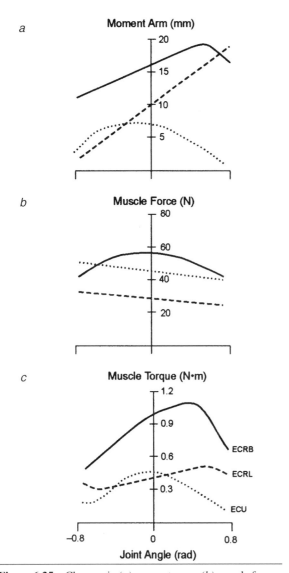

Figure 6.25 Changes in *(a)* moment arms, *(b)* muscle forces, and *(c)* muscle torques over the wrist joint range of motion for the muscles extensor carpi radialis brevis (ECRB), extensor carpi radialis longus (ECRL), and extensor carpi ulnaris (ECU). Negative joint angle corresponds to flexion relative to the neutral position of the wrist (0 rad).

Data from Loren et al., 1996.

maximal forces over a greater range of motion; this corresponds to a broad muscle length-tension relation. Lieber (1992) reports that muscles with a high ratio include gluteus maximus (80), sartorius (11), and extensor carpi radialis longus (11) whereas those with a low ratio include soleus (0.9), vasti (1.8), hamstrings (1.8), and dorsiflexors (3.1). This relation emphasizes that the entire architecture of a muscle, from sarcomere arrangement to joint organization, can influence the functional capabilities of the single-joint system (Lieber & Fridén, 2000).

The moment arm and multiple muscles around the joint also influence the force-velocity relation, which is ex-

pressed as the **torque-velocity relation** at the level of the single-joint system. The most common way to measure the torque-velocity relation in humans is to use a device known as an isokinetic dynamometer. This is an exercise machine in which the motion of a lever arm is controlled by a motor. The operator sets the angular velocity at which the lever will rotate over a prescribed range of motion. The individual being tested either pushes or pulls against the lever to test the capacity of a specific muscle group. Although the torque exerted by the limb may vary over the range of motion, the angular velocity of the movement will remain relatively constant; *isokinetic* means constant angular velocity, but not constant velocity for the muscle fascicles (Ichinose, Kawakami, Ito, Kanehisa, & Fukunaga, 2000). For determination of the torque-velocity relation, the person performs a series of **isokinetic contractions**, each at a different speed, and the net muscle torque at a specific joint angle is measured at each speed.

In addition to being able to set the magnitude of the angular velocity on an isokinetic dynamometer, it is also possible to set the direction. For example, in testing the knee extensor muscles it is possible to set the angular velocity on the machine so that the person will perform a concentric (shortening) or an eccentric (lengthening) contraction. This distinction is defined in figure 6.26. Under these conditions, the type of contraction a muscle performs depends on the ratio of the muscle torque (τ_m) to the load torque (τ_L). When the ratio is greater than 1, the muscle torque is greater and the muscle performs a

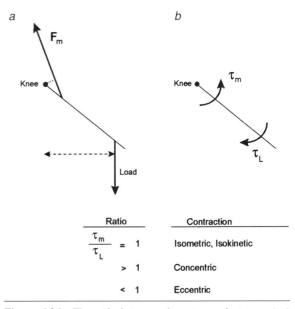

Figure 6.26 The ratio between the net muscle torque (τ_m) and the torque due to a load (τ_L) determines the type of muscle contraction. Each torque *(b)* is equal to the force multiplied by its moment arm relative to the joint *(a)*; the moment arms are indicated as dashed lines.

concentric contraction. In contrast, when the ratio is less than 1, which means that the load torque is greater, the muscle performs an eccentric contraction. When the ratio is equal to 1, the two torques are equal in magnitude and the limb does not accelerate; thus, velocity is constant at either zero (isometric) or some nonzero value (isokinetic).

To determine the torque-velocity relation for the knee extensor muscles, the person performs a series of isokinetic contractions, each one at a different angular velocity. Figure 6.27a shows a set of six trials (curves labeled i to vi) for both concentric and eccentric contractions. The torque exerted by the knee extensor muscles varied over the range of motion with a peak torque at a knee angle of about 2 rad (3.14 rad = complete extension). Because the muscle torque varies with knee angle, the torque at a specific knee angle was selected for each trial, and the data point was plotted on a torque-velocity graph. Figure 6.27b, for example, represents torque-velocity relations of the knee extensor muscles for three conditions: voluntary contractions, contractions evoked with electrical stimulation, and a combined voluntary and evoked contraction. For each condition, the torque-velocity relation is qualitatively similar to the force-velocity relation for single muscle fibers (figure 6.14). The muscle torque was greatest during eccentric contractions, and it decreased as the angular velocity increased during the concentric contractions. Because the muscle torque was greatest during the electrically evoked eccentric contractions (traces i and ii in figure 6.27a), it seems that it is difficult to achieve maximum activation of the muscles during voluntary eccentric contractions (Aagaard, Simonsen, Anderson, Magnusson, Halkjær-Kristensen, Dyhre-Poulsen, 2000; Komi, Linnamo, Silventoinen, & Sillanpää, 2000). The maximum eccentric torque for the knee extensor muscles has been estimated at 151% of maximum voluntary contraction torque (Webber & Kriellaars, 1997).

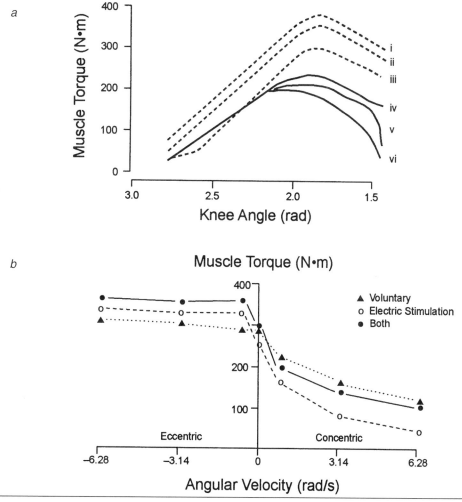

Figure 6.27 Torque-angle and torque-velocity relations for the knee extensor muscles during performance of isokinetic contractions: *(a)* knee extensor torque during voluntary activation (iii, iv), electrical stimulation (ii, vi), and combined activation (i, v) during eccentric (i, ii, and iii) and concentric (iv, v, and vi) contractions; *(b)* knee extensor torque at a knee angle of 1 rad as a function of knee angular velocity.

Adapted from Westing, Seger, and Thorstensson, 1990.

Muscles in Motion

The force-length and force-velocity relations of muscle, from the level of the single fiber to the single-joint system, define the quasistatic properties of muscles. They indicate the force a muscle can exert at a given muscle length or at a given constant rate of change in length (velocity) when the muscle is activated maximally. During performance of movements, however, muscle length changes at variable rates, activation is rarely maximal, and the load imposed on the muscle can change (Marsh, 1999). As a consequence, the force exerted by muscle often deviates from that described by quasistatic measurements (Gillard, Yakovenko, Cameron, & Prochazka, 2000).

Example 6.7
Changes in Muscle Activation and Load During Cycling

The power that propels a bicycle comes from the legs of the rider. Cyclists generate power by applying a force on the pedals that is transmitted to the ground and that, because of friction, causes the wheel to rotate relative to the ground. As with isolated muscle, the legs of the cyclist exhibit a force-velocity relation whereby the maximum force applied to the pedals decreases as crank velocity increases (figure 6.28*a*). By taking the product of the maximum force and crank velocity, it is possible to calculate the maximum power that can be produced at each crank velocity (figure 6.28*b*) (Zoladz, Rademaker, & Sargeant, 2000). As with isolated muscle, maximum power occurs at an intermediate velocity. For elite cyclists, optimum velocity appears to be about 110 rpm when the pedal force is about 500 N. Similarly, the crank velocity at which peak power occurs increases as the level of EMG activity increases. It is about 50 rpm at 100 W compared with 100 rpm at 400 W (MacIntosh, Neptune, & Horton, 2000).

When a cyclist encounters a resistance, such as a gust of wind or a hill, this has the effect of decreasing the propulsive force applied by the cyclist. As shown in the free body diagram of figure 6.29, the propulsive force is equal to the difference between the tangential components of the ground reaction force $(F_{g,t})$, air resistance $(F_{a,t})$, and weight vectors $(F_{w,t})$. As a result of the increased resistance and decreased propulsive force, the cyclist slows down and crank velocity decreases. This causes the power generated by the cyclist to decrease. To counteract this effect, the cyclist will change gears, which has the effect of increasing crank velocity, power production, and speed. This example demonstrates that gears on a bicycle allow the cyclist to manipulate the force-velocity relation

and to maintain a desired level of power production. It is an example of the changing conditions encountered by muscle in the performance of movement.

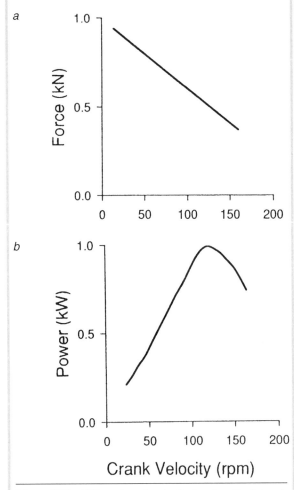

Figure 6.28   Effect of crank velocity (rpm) on the *(a)* peak force and *(b)* power applied to the pedals during cycling. Peak force declines as crank velocity increases, but peak power occurs at an intermediate crank velocity.

Adapted from Sargeant and Boreham, 1981.

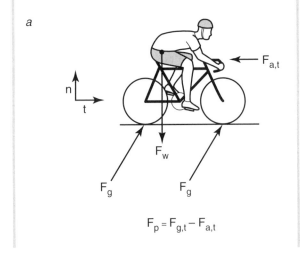

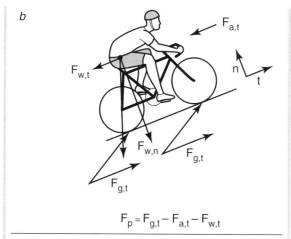

$$F_p = F_{g,t} - F_{a,t} - F_{w,t}$$

Figure 6.29 Free body diagram of a bicycle rider system. *(a)* The system traveling along level ground experiences a system weight *(F_{w,t})*, air resistance *(F_{a,t})*, and a ground reaction force *(F_{g,t})*. The propulsive force *(F_p)* acts in the direction in which the cyclist is progressing. *(b)* When the system travels up a hill, *F_{a,t}* and *F_{w,t}* now oppose the forward motion of the system while *F_{g,t}* assists it.

Activation Level

When the intensity of muscle activation is varied from low to maximal, both the magnitude of the muscle force and the shape of the torque-angle relation vary (figure 6.30). Marsh, Sale, McComas, and Quinlan (1981) used electrical stimulation of the tibialis anterior muscle at various frequencies to activate the muscle at different submaximal intensities. At the three lowest frequencies (1, 10, and 20 Hz), they found that the evoked torque increased as the ankle joint was moved into plantarflexion. At 30- and 40-Hz stimulation, however, they found a peak in the torque-angle relation at an intermediate joint angle. The shape of the 40-Hz curve was more similar to that achieved by maximal voluntary contraction of the dorsiflexor muscles. Similar effects have been observed in experiments on the length-force relation of isolated muscles (Rack & Westbury, 1969).

When isolated muscles are subjected to stimulation at different frequencies, which is one way to vary the level of muscle activation, there is a shift in the force-velocity relation. When shortening contractions are examined (figure 6.31*a*), the force-velocity relation is

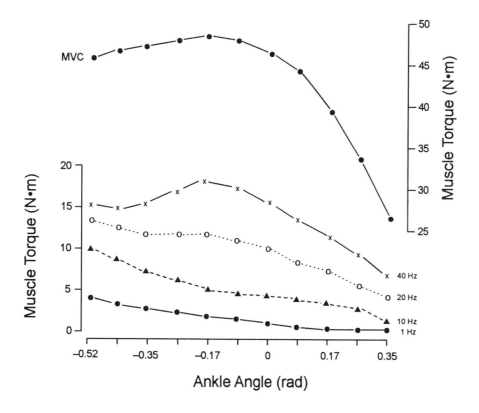

Figure 6.30 Torque exerted by the dorsiflexor muscles during submaximal evoked contractions and a maximum voluntary contraction (MVC). Negative angles designate plantarflexion. The evoked contractions involved electrical stimulation of the tibialis anterior muscle at various frequencies (1-40 Hz).

Data from Marsh et al., 1981.

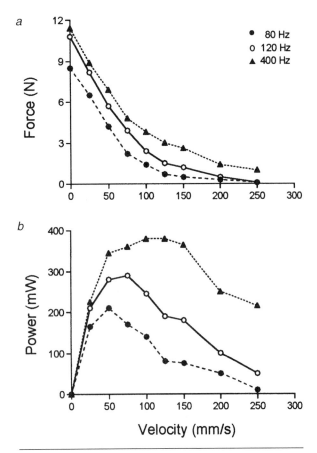

a

b

Figure 6.31 The *(a)* force-velocity and *(b)* power-velocity relations of rat medial gastrocnemius muscle when stimulated at different frequencies (80, 120, and 400 Hz).

Data from de Haan, 1998.

displaced upward with higher frequencies of stimulation. As a result, the force exerted by muscle is greater at a given shortening velocity. In contrast, submaximal frequencies seem to alter the shape of the velocity-force relation for lengthening contractions. When the cat soleus muscle was stimulated at 35 Hz, the evoked force was relatively constant at five different velocities during lengthening contractions, and the force was greatest during these contractions (Joyce, Rack, & Westbury, 1969). When the stimulus rate was reduced to 7 Hz, the force evoked during the lengthening contractions was less than that achieved during the isometric contraction. That is, the shape of the force-velocity relation changed from the 35- to the 7-Hz stimulation.

Even if variations in the stimulus frequency simply displace the force-velocity relation without altering its shape, they can change the shape of the power-velocity relation. From the force-velocity measurements made on the rat medial gastrocnemius muscle, de Haan (1998) calculated the power-velocity relations at different frequencies of stimulation (figure 6.31b). At higher stimulus frequencies, the power produced by the muscle was

greater at each velocity for the shortening contractions. In addition, the peak in the power-velocity relation occurred at faster velocities as the stimulus frequency was increased. These measurements and calculations indicate that variations in the level of muscle activation (stimulus frequency) can alter the magnitude and shape of the force-length and force-velocity relations of muscle.

Short-Range Stiffness

The force that a muscle can exert during constant-velocity contractions is greatest when the muscle is being forcibly lengthened (figures 6.14 and 6.27). Even in less constrained movements, this capacity of muscle is evident (Gillard et al., 2000). For example, it is easier to lower a heavy load with the elbow flexor muscles, which requires a lengthening contraction, than it is to lift the same load with a shortening contraction. The force that a muscle exerts during a lengthening contraction, however, can be quite variable (Kirsch, Boskov, & Rymer, 1994).

It is known, for example, that muscle force varies nonlinearly when an active muscle goes from an isometric to an eccentric contraction, that is, when an active muscle is forcibly lengthened. An example of this effect is shown in figure 6.32. In this experiment, the length of the extensor digitorum longus muscle was controlled while the nerve to the muscle was stimulated and the muscle force was measured (McCully & Faulkner, 1985). For the isometric contraction, length did not change, while force rose to a plateau during the stimulation. When length did change, however, the change in force did not closely parallel the change in length, as would occur with a linear spring. During the constant-velocity (constant slope of the length curve) shortening contraction, force declined, at first rapidly and then more slowly, from the isometric value. In contrast, during the constant-velocity lengthening contraction, the force increased, first rapidly and then more slowly. For a constant-velocity contraction, the slope of the force record indicates the stiffness of the muscle. During the lengthening (eccentric) contraction, stiffness was initially high (i.e., a large change in force for a small change in length) and then declined; this high initial stiffness is referred to as the **short-range stiffness** (Gillard et al., 2000; Rack & Westbury, 1974; Walmsley & Proske, 1981). It is greater in type I compared with type II muscle fibers (Malamud, Godt, & Nichols, 1996).

This behavior can be explained by the function of the cross-bridges. When a muscle is forcibly lengthened from an isometric contraction, the attached cross-bridges are stretched, and this increases the average force exerted by each cross-bridge. Fibers from frog muscles stretched in this way exhibited first a rapid increase in force and then a steady state force (Lombardi & Piazzesi, 1990). The steady state force that was achieved during the lengthening, which was about twice

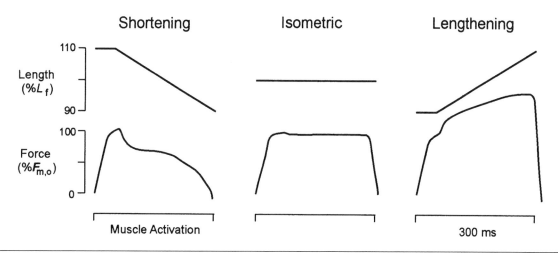

Figure 6.32 Change in muscle force during controlled changes in muscle length. Length is indicated as a percentage of muscle fiber length ($\%L_f$) at the resting length of muscle. Force is expressed as a percentage of the maximum isometric force ($\%F_{m,o}$). For each contraction, the muscle was stimulated at 150 Hz for 300 ms. After 100 ms of stimulation, muscle length was decreased (shortening), held constant, or increased (lengthening). Compare the force profile during the shortening and lengthening contractions with the isometric contraction.

Adapted from McCully and Faulkner, 1985.

the isometric force, occurred after the fiber had been stretched by ~20 nm per half sarcomere. The change in force at the beginning of the stretch depended on the velocity of the stretch; it increased continuously for slow stretches but increased and then decreased for fast stretches. By superimposing small stretches during the contraction, Lombardi and Piazzesi (1990) found that the stiffness of the fiber was 10% to 20% greater during the lengthening contraction than during the isometric contraction. They concluded that after the cross-bridges have been stretched by a certain amount they detach and reattach rapidly; the reattachment rate is ~200 times faster than during an isometric contraction. Thus, the short-range stiffness that appears at the beginning of a lengthening contraction is due to an increase in the average force exerted by each cross-bridge. Furthermore, as the lengthening contraction continues, the cross-bridges reattach quickly, again generating a greater average force.

Stretch-Shorten Cycle

A common pattern of muscle activation is *a lengthening-shortening contraction in which the active muscle is stretched before it shortens*. This is known as the **stretch-shorten cycle** (Ingen Schenau et al., 1997). It occurs in most movements that we perform, as in the knee extensor and ankle plantarflexor muscles after footstrike in running (figures 4.5 and 4.6); in the knee extensor muscles during kicking (figure 4.31); in the trunk and arm muscles during throwing; and in the hip, knee, and ankle extensor muscles during the countermovement jump (figures 4.19 and 4.20) and the long-jump takeoff

(figure 4.21) (Prilutsky, 2000). Perhaps the only common physical activity not to include the stretch-shorten cycle is swimming.

The advantage of the stretch-shorten cycle is that a muscle can perform more positive work if it is actively stretched before being allowed to shorten (Cavagna & Citterio, 1974; Fenn, 1924). The result is that *a greater quantity of work can be done during the shortening contraction than if the muscle simply performed a shortening contraction by itself.* The experimental evidence for this conclusion is based on the work done by an isolated muscle (figure 6.33). The experiment had two parts: (1) the muscle was first stretched and then stimulated before it was allowed to shorten and perform positive work (figure 6.33*a*); (2) next the muscle was first stimulated and then stretched before performing positive work (figure 6.33*b*). The results for each part of the experiment are shown as length-time, force-time, and force-length graphs. The critical comparison is contained in the length-force graphs. Phase c shows the change in force and length as the muscle performs work. Because work is defined as the product of force and displacement, the area under the force-length graph during phase c represents the work done during each part of the experiment. Clearly, the area under the curve is greater for the second part of this experiment, which consisted of the stretch (lengthening contraction) of an active muscle; this corresponds to the stretch-shorten cycle. Similarly, the enhanced performance of muscle in vivo compared with the value from experimental measurements (figure 6.24) has been attributed to the benefits of the stretch-shorten cycle (Monti et al., 1999).

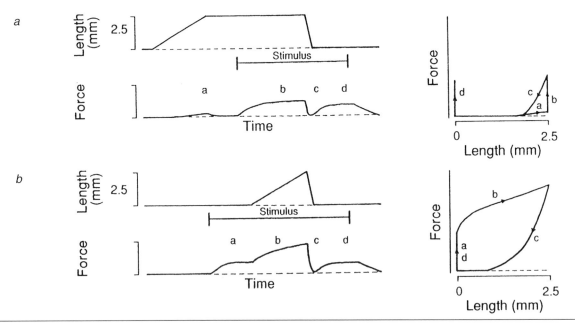

Figure 6.33 (a) Positive work done by an isolated muscle during a shortening contraction preceded by an isometric contraction and (b) a shortening contraction preceded by a lengthening contraction. The work done by the muscle (area under phase c of the length-force curve) is greater for the lengthening-shortening contraction (stretch-shorten cycle).

Adapted from Cavagna and Citterio, 1974.

Four mechanisms have been proposed to explain the greater positive work that a muscle can do with a stretch-shorten cycle: time to develop force, elastic energy, force potentiation, and reflexes. The first mechanism, time to develop force, has to do with the increased time that the muscle has to become fully activated when there is an initial lengthening contraction. Because the positive work is measured as the area under the force-length curve (figure 6.33), an increase in the muscle force at the beginning of the shortening contraction enhances the positive work that can be done. The second mechanism, elastic energy, involves the storage of elastic energy in the SE (figure 6.15) during the lengthening contraction and the subsequent use of this energy during the shortening contraction. From the work-energy relation (chapter 2), we know that an increase in the available energy will increase the amount of work that can be done. The third mechanism, force potentiation, suggests that the force from individual cross-bridges is enhanced as a consequence of the preceding stretch. However, this effect appears only at relatively long muscle lengths (Edman & Tsuchiya, 1996). The fourth mechanism concerns the stretch reflexes that can be evoked by the forced lengthening of the muscle at the beginning of the stretch-shorten cycle.

The role of these mechanisms in the enhancement of the positive work done by muscle in the stretch-shorten cycle is controversial (Ingen Schenau et al., 1997). It appears that the relative contribution of each mechanism varies across movements. Some research on this topic has involved a comparison of the countermovement and squat vertical jumps. The extra height that an individual can jump with the countermovement jump can be completely explained by the first mechanism, the extra time the muscles have to generate force prior to the beginning of the shortening contraction (Ingen Schenau et al., 1997). Other movements, however, such as those that involve a rapid stretch-shorten cycle, appear to be influenced by the elastic energy mechanism (Komi & Gollhofer, 1997; Reich, Lindstedt, LaStayo, & Pierotti, 2000; Zatsiorsky, 1997).

In contrast, force potentiation seems an unlikely contributor, while the role of reflexes remains controversial. Although it is possible to elicit a stretch reflex in a stretch-shorten cycle (Komi & Gollhofer, 1997; Nicol & Komi, 1998), the timing of the response is a problem. For example, it takes some time for the sensory receptors to be activated during the lengthening contraction, the afferent signal to be transmitted to the spinal cord, the reflex response to be transmitted back to the muscle, and the muscle to generate the force response. For this reason, it has been estimated by some (Ingen Schenau et al., 1997), but not by others (Dietz et al., 1979; Komi & Gollhofer, 1997), that a stretch-shorten cycle faster than 130 ms does not experience a contribution from the stretch reflex. Nonetheless, the rate of stretch experienced by muscles in many stretch-shorten cycles does seem to evoke a stretch reflex of sufficient magnitude to influence the force exerted by muscle during the shortening contraction (Komi & Nicol, 2000; Nicol & Komi, 1998; Voigt, Dyhre-Poulsen, & Simonsen, 1998). Furthermore, four weeks of training with hopping improved the excitability of short-latency stretch reflexes in the soleus muscle (Voigt, Chelli, & Frigo, 1998).

Some of the controversy over the mechanisms underlying the enhancement of performance with the stretch-shorten cycle is the consequence of an incomplete description of muscle function during the task. For example, assessment of the stretch-shorten cycle is usually based on whole-muscle measurements. However, the change in whole-muscle length, which includes the muscle fibers and tendon, *does not necessarily coincide with the change in length experienced by the muscle fibers* (Biewener, 1998; Fellows & Rack, 1987; Griffiths, 1991; Ito, Kawakami, Ichinose, Fukashiro, & Fukunaga, 1998; Roberts, Marsh, Weyand, & Taylor, 1997). When the medial gastrocnemius muscle of a cat is electrically stimulated to produce an isometric contraction, muscle fibers can shorten up to 28% of their resting length (figure 6.34*a*). For this to happen, the tendon must lengthen by an equivalent amount so that whole-muscle length remains constant (i.e., isometric). This tendon **compliance** (mm/N), which is the inverse of stiffness, is most evident in muscles with long tendons. Not only does this effect occur during electrical stimulation of muscle, it also occurs during voluntary movements such as walking. Figure 6.34*b* shows whole-muscle length, muscle-fiber length, and EMG for the medial gastrocnemius muscle of a cat during the step cycle. Prior to the foot contacting the ground (at vertical line), both whole-muscle and muscle-fiber length increased and then shortened; this is a typical concentric contraction. However, after foot contact there was an increase in whole-muscle length, which we would generally identify as an eccentric contraction, but a shortening of muscle-fiber length. The increase in whole-muscle length must have been accomplished by a stretch of the tendon. This shortening of muscle fibers during an eccentric contraction decreases with faster stretches, and can involve an increase of muscle-fiber length. It seems, therefore, that *during isometric and slow eccentric contractions the change in muscle-fiber length does not parallel the change in whole-muscle length in muscles with long tendons, at least for two-joint muscles.* Such observations suggest that some presumed stretch-shorten cycles do not actually involve a stretch of the active muscle fibers.

Despite the uncertain role of elastic energy as a general contributor to enhancement of the positive work done in the stretch-shorten cycle, there is general agreement that it can improve the economy of performance. This is most obvious for cyclic activities, such as walking, running, and hopping. For the support phase of these activities, the muscles have to perform a certain amount of

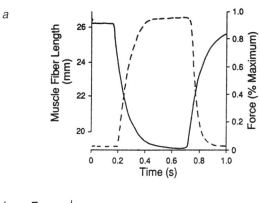

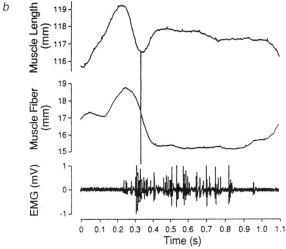

Figure 6.34 Change in muscle-fiber length during isometric and eccentric contractions. *(a)* An isometric contraction was elicited in a medial gastrocnemius muscle. Whole-muscle length remained constant, while muscle-fiber length decreased (solid line) and force increased (dashed line). Muscle-fiber length was measured with an ultrasound technique between two piezoelectric crystals. *(b)* An eccentric contraction in the medial gastrocnemius muscle after foot contact was associated with shortening of muscle-fiber length. Footstrike occurred at the vertical line. Following footstrike, whole-muscle length increased about 1.5 mm while muscle-length fiber decreased by about 2.0 mm.

Adapted from Griffiths, 1991.

positive work (Kram, 2000). With the stretch-shorten cycle, some energy can be added to the muscle by the stretch of the connective tissues, especially the tendon, that can then be used during the performance of the positive work. Because less metabolic energy (ATP) is used under these circumstances, the performance is more **economical;** that is, a given quantity of work is done with less energy. Hof (1998), for example, has estimated that in slow running, the calf muscles of humans absorb about 45 J of energy in the first half of the stance phase and generate about 60 J during the second half. The capability of muscle and tendon to store elastic energy and then use it to perform positive work is greatest in muscles with long tendons. Biewener (1998) reports that 92% to

97% of the work done by the plantaris and gastrocnemius muscles of the wallaby during hopping is recovered from elastic storage, compared with 60% for the turkey gastrocnemius muscle during trotting and 0% for the pigeon pectoralis muscle during flying. Similarly, the tendons of soleus, gastrocnemius, and plantaris in the cat contribute significantly to the work done by the muscles during walking and trotting (Prilutsky, Herzog, Leonard, & Allinger, 1996).

There appear to be two reasons for the common occurrence of the stretch-shorten cycle in most movements. First, it can enhance the positive work done by muscle during the shortening contraction. Second, it can lower the metabolic cost of performing a prescribed amount of positive work.

Example 6.8
Muscle Force in Humans

The measurement of muscle force in humans can be accomplished only with invasive techniques, which have been pioneered by Komi and colleagues (Komi, 1990, 1992). These procedures involve either the attachment of a force transducer to a tendon or the insertion of an optic fiber through a tendon (Finni et al., 1998; Fukashiro, Komi, Jarvinen, & Miyashita, 1995; Gregor, Komi, Browning, & Jarvinen, 1991; Komi et al., 1996). These procedures are performed under appropriate medical conditions. With such procedures, it is possible to estimate the tendon force during various activities. In addition to the force measurement, subjects are videotaped while they walk, run, hop, jump, and ride a bicycle so that changes in muscle length can be estimated. The results of one such experiment with two-legged hopping, in which tendon forces were measured with the optic fiber technique, are shown in figure 6.35. Changes in muscle length were estimated as a function of joint angles (Hawkins & Hull, 1990). The data represent Achilles tendon and patellar tendon forces, as well as the length changes of the triceps surae and quadriceps femoris muscles; negative velocity indicates lengthening of the tendon. When the foot contacted the ground, the force increased to a peak value of about 1.7 kN in the Achilles tendon and 2.2 kN in the patellar tendon. The peak forces occurred at the transition from the eccentric to the concentric contractions. Furthermore, Komi and colleagues have found that the relative magnitudes of the forces in the two tendons differ for hopping and jumping. Such measurements provide novel information about the in vivo function of muscles.

One of the limitations of these analyses is in the technique used to estimate the change in muscle

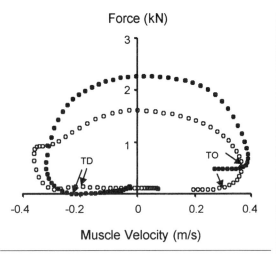

Figure 6.35 Changes in the Achilles tendon (open circles) and patellar tendon (filled circles) forces compared with muscle velocity of the triceps surae and quadriceps femoris muscles during two-legged hopping. Touchdown (TD) occurred at the left endpoint and toe-off (TO) at the right endpoint of the graph. The time between each data point was 5 ms.

Data from Finni, Komi, and Lepola, 2000.

length. Typically, the change in muscle length is assumed to parallel the angular displacement about the involved joints. This assumption has been examined in humans through comparison of changes in fascicle length, as detected with an ultrasound device, and joint angle. Ikegawa, Finni, and Komi (2000) found that the association between fascicle length (vastus lateralis) and knee joint angle varied with the level of muscle EMG during rapid eccentric contractions on an isokinetic dynamometer. There was a close association between the two displacements at low (25%) but not high (100%) levels of activation. Similarly, Kawakami, Muraoka, Ito, Kanehisa, and Fukunaga (2000) found a dissociation between changes in fascicle length (medial gastrocnemius) and ankle angle during the countermovement jump. These findings indicate that a significant proportion of the change in muscle length during forceful eccentric contractions is attributable to stretch of the tendon.

Shortening Deactivation

In contrast to the mechanisms that enhance muscle force in the stretch-shorten cycle, there are mechanisms that cause a depression of muscle force during performance of a shortening contraction (De Ruiter, De Haan, Jones, & Sargeant, 1998; Edman, 1996; Herzog, 1998). This effect has been observed in both single muscle fibers and whole muscles. The depression is measured by comparing the force a muscle can exert during an isometric contrac-

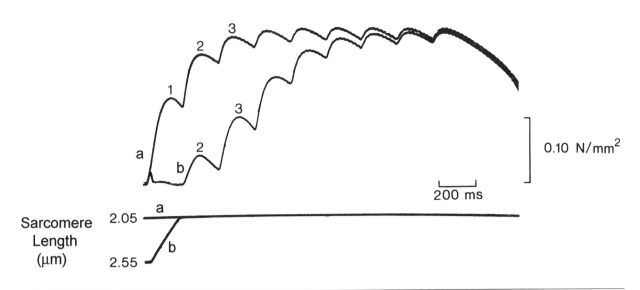

Figure 6.36 Force depression after a shortening contraction by a single muscle fiber.

Data from Edman, 1996.

tion with the force exerted when the muscle shortens to the same length and then performs an isometric contraction. Figure 6.36 compares the force exerted by a muscle fiber during an isometric contraction (trace a) with the force exerted after the fiber has shortened from a sarcomere length of 2.55 μm to 2.05 μm (trace b). Clearly, the force exerted by the fiber was depressed immediately after the shortening but eventually reached the same value as the isometric contraction; it takes about 1 to 1.5 s to overcome the force depression due to shortening. The force depression, which is called **shortening deactivation,** increases with the amount of shortening, is greater at slower speeds of shortening, and increases with the magnitude of the force (Herzog, 1998). However, there is no evidence of force depression when a fiber is stimulated to produce a fused tetanus (Edman, 1996).

The mechanism that causes force depression after a shortening contraction appears to involve deactivation of the myofilament system. There is some disagreement, however, about whether the mechanism is chemical or mechanical. Edman (1996) suggests that the shortening contraction causes a temporary decrease in the affinity for calcium at the binding sites. In contrast, Herzog (1998) notes that the force depression lasts too long (>5 s) to be attributable to a transient chemical effect and instead argues in favor of a mechanical effect. The mechanism involves a stress-induced inhibition of cross-bridge attachment in the new overlap region of the thick and thin filaments after the shortening (Maréchal & Plaghki, 1979). According to this scheme, the thin filament is stretched during the shortening contraction, and this reduces the availability of attachment sites on actin in the new overlap region. Whatever the mechanism, the force

depression that occurs after a shortening contraction has a sufficient magnitude and duration to influence many movements.

Work-Loop Analysis

Measurement of the force exerted or the power produced by muscle during movement is often quite different from that determined experimentally. To account for this difference, the work done or power produced by muscle during movement is often determined from direct measurements of muscle force and displacement. This is known as the **work-loop** method (Biewener & Roberts, 2000: Josephson, 1985, 1999). It involves subtracting the work done on muscle during a stretch (lengthening contraction) from the work done by muscle during the shortening contraction to determine the net work done.

An example of the procedure is shown in figure 6.37. The change in length experienced by a muscle, along with the force it exerts, is measured during a repetitive movement; two cycles of the movement are shown in figure 6.37a. These measurements are then plotted on a length-force graph. For the example in figure 6.37a, the length-force graph is interpreted in the counterclockwise direction. Beginning from the dot, the diagram has three phases: (1) length increases with little change in force; (2) force increases while length decreases slightly; and (3) both length and force decrease. In this example, the second phase corresponds to the lengthening contraction, and the third phase indicates the shortening contraction. Because work is equal to the product of force and displacement, the area under the length-force diagram indicates the work associated with the movement. The work experienced by the muscle, however, comprises the work

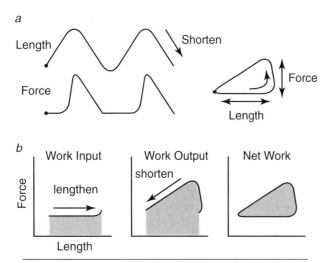

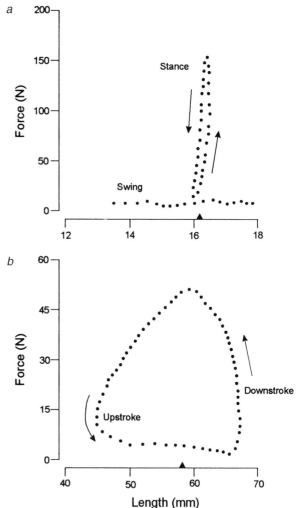

Figure 6.37 The work-loop method for determining the net work performed by muscle: *(a)* the length and force records used to construct the work loop; *(b)* the work loop displays the differences between the work input and the work output.

Data from Josephson, 1985.

done on it during the lengthening contraction (work input) and the work it does during the shortening contraction (work output). The net work done by the muscle is the difference between the two, or the area inside the length-force diagram.

The shape of a work loop varies across movements and among muscles. Two contrasting examples of a work loop are shown in figure 6.38. Each work loop indicates the variation in muscle length and force for a single cycle of a repetitive movement. Figure 6.38 shows hopping by a wallaby and flying by a pigeon. For the hopping movement (figure 6.38*a*), the length-force graph looks like an inverted T, with the vertical part corresponding to the stance phase and the horizontal part representing the swing phase. Such a shape indicates that muscle force was close to zero while muscle length changed substantially during the swing phase. In contrast, the muscle essentially performed an isometric contraction during the stance phase. The muscle did not do much work during hopping, as indicated by the small area between the up and down arrows during the stance phase.

The work done by the pectoralis muscle of the pigeon, however, was much more substantial (figure 6.38*b*). One cycle of the movement is divided into the upstroke and the downstroke. During the upstroke, the muscle lengthened while exerting a minimal force; thus, the work input during the lengthening contraction was minimal. For the downstroke, the muscle performed a shortening contraction while the force first increased and then decreased. The net work done by the muscle during flying was large and was due mainly to work output. According to Biewener (1998), the plantaris muscle of the wallaby has

Figure 6.38 Work loops for *(a)* the plantaris muscle of a wallaby during hopping and *(b)* the pectoralis muscle of a pigeon during flying. The triangle (▲) on the *y*-axis indicates the resting length of the muscle.

Data from Biewener, 1998.

a long tendon and is able to store elastic energy whereas the pectoralis muscle of the pigeon is not. Thus, the two muscles function quite differently during the performance of locomotor activities (Biewener & Roberts, 2000).

Motor Unit

Muscle force is graded through activation of the individual elements of the neuromuscular system, which are known as motor units. A **motor unit** is defined as *the cell body and dendrites of a motor neuron, the multiple branches of its axon, and the muscle fibers that it innervates.* Most skeletal muscles comprise a few hundred motor units (table 6.2) (McComas, 1991, 1996; Stein & Yang, 1990). Because each motor neuron innervates many

Table 6.2 Electrophysiological Estimates of the Number of Motor Units in Human Skeletal Muscles

Muscle	Number
Abductor hallucis longus	285
Biceps brachii	109
Biceps brachii + brachialis	357
Extensor digitorum brevis	143
Hypothenar muscles	263
Plantarflexors	381
Thenar muscles	208
Tibialis anterior	256
Vastus medialis	224

From McComas, 1998.

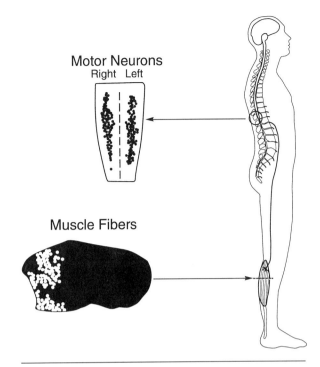

Figure 6.39 Motor neurons in the spinal cord send axons to innervate muscle fibers. Each motor neuron connects to several hundred muscle fibers.

muscle fibers, ranging from about 5 to 2000 in various muscles, a few hundred motor neurons are able to activate the thousands of fibers that compose each muscle.

Neural Component

The neural component of the motor unit, which consists of the motor neuron and its dendrites (figure 5.15), represents the final common pathway by which the commands from the nervous system are sent to muscle (Liddell & Sherrington, 1925). The motor neurons innervating skeletal muscle are located in the spinal cord and brainstem, and each motor neuron sends its axon via a peripheral nerve to the muscle fibers that it innervates. Figure 6.39 show two populations of motor neurons, one on the left and the other on the right side of the spinal cord, each of which innervates a muscle on the corresponding side of the body.

The features of the motor neuron that vary within a population include its morphology, excitability, and distribution of input. The morphological feature of the neural component that has received the greatest attention is motor neuron size. This feature is thought to be important because of its role in the activation of motor neurons. The size of a motor neuron can be indicated by the diameter of the soma, the surface area of the cell body, the number of dendrites arising from the soma, the diameter of the axon, and cell capacitance. On the basis of measurements of motor neurons in the cat, these properties seem to be correlated so that the largest motor neuron has the greatest value for each of these properties (Binder et al., 1996; Stuart & Enoka, 1983).

As initially reported by Henneman (1957), there is a strong correlation between the size of a motor neuron

and the order of activation. When Henneman evoked a stretch reflex in a muscle of a decerebrate cat, he noted that the order in which motor units were activated varied with action potential amplitude. Because action potential amplitude depends on axon diameter and thus cell size, he deduced that motor units were activated in the order of increasing size. Subsequent studies have continued to characterize motor neurons by placing a microelectrode inside the cell and measuring selected biophysical properties of the membrane. As summarized in table 6.3 for cat motor neurons, these properties include input resistance (MΩ), rheobase (nA), afterhyperpolarization duration (ms), and axonal conduction velocity (m/s). **Input resistance** is a measurement of the electrical resistance exhibited by a cell as the change in voltage it experiences in response to current injected by an intracellular microelectrode (Ohm's law). Small motor neurons tend to have a high input resistance, which results in a greater response (i.e., they are more excitable) to a given input. **Rheobase** is a measure of excitability as indicated by the amount of current that has to be injected into the motor neuron for it to generate an action potential. The rheobase for small motor neurons is much less than that for larger motor neurons. Afterhyperpolarization duration is the amount of time that the membrane potential during the trailing part of the action potential is less than its normal resting (steady state) value. The duration

Table 6.3 Distribution of Motor Neuron Properties Based on Differences in Size

	Large	Intermediate	Small
Morphology			
Cell diameter (μ)	63	60	58
Cell surface area (μ²)	11,290	10,470	10,160
Number of main dendrites	12	11	10
Axon diameter (μm)	7	7	6
Membrane properties			
Axon conduction velocity (m/s)	101	103	89
Input resistance (MΩ)	0.6	0.9	1.7
Rheobase (nA)	20	13	5
Afterhyperpolarization duration (ms)	19	22	44
Synaptic input			
Ia connectivity (%)	87	97	94
Ia EPSP amplitude (μV)	71	118	179
Recurrent inhibition amplitude (μV)	280	679	1173

Note. EPSP = excitatory post-synaptic potential.

Data for motor neurons innervating the cat medial gastrocnemius muscle (Stuart & Enoka, 1983).

of the afterhyperpolarization may influence the maximum rate at which a motor neuron can generate action potentials. The afterhyperpolarization is much briefer in motor neurons that supply fast-twitch muscle fibers compared with slow-twitch muscle fibers. **Conduction velocity** is the velocity at which action potentials are propagated along the axon, which varies with the diameter of the axon. These associations indicate that small motor neurons are more excitable but that they generate and propagate action potentials at a slower rate than larger motor neurons.

To understand the function of the motor unit, it is necessary to combine the information on the excitability of motor neurons with the details of the inputs they receive. Motor neurons have extensive dendritic trees, which receive about 80% of the input directed to the cell (figure 5.15). It appears, however, that the input from different sources can have a variable effect on the generation of an action potential by the motor neuron. This difference can be a consequence of the *number and location of synapses associated with each input system.* One way to assess the effect of different inputs is to use a microelectrode to determine the **effective synaptic current** (nA) generated in the motor neuron in response to a given input (Binder et al., 1996; Heckman & Binder, 1991). This measurement indicates the net effect of activating an input system and represents the signal that will be transmitted to the axon hillock where the action potential is generated. Synaptic inputs to populations of motor neurons exhibit three patterns of distribution (Heckman & Binder, 1990): (1) *least input* (smallest effective synap-

tic current) to the largest motor neurons—input from the Group Ia afferent of the muscle spindle; (2) *uniform input* to all motor neurons—inhibitory input from a muscle spindle located in an antagonist muscle and from an interneuron (recurrent inhibition from the Renshaw cell); and (3) *greatest input* to the largest motor neurons—input from a brainstem nucleus (red nucleus) and from a nerve (sural) containing feedback from cutaneous receptors. These observations suggest that the activation of a motor neuron depends not only on its intrinsic excitability but also on the type (distribution) of input that it receives. Furthermore, the distribution of input influences the rate at which the motor neurons in a population are recruited (Kernell & Hultborn, 1990).

Muscle Component

Although a muscle fiber is innervated by a single motor neuron, each motor neuron innervates more than one muscle fiber (figures 6.39 and 6.40). The number of muscle fibers innervated by a single motor neuron is referred to as the **innervation ratio** and varies from about 1:1900 (e.g., gastrocnemius, tibialis anterior) to 1:6 (e.g., extraocular muscles). That is, one motor neuron may innervate from 6 to 1900 muscle fibers. For example, the first dorsal interosseus muscle (a hand muscle) contains about 41,000 muscle fibers and 120 motor units; it has, on average, an innervation ratio of about 1:342 (table 6.4). In contrast, medial gastrocnemius has about 1,120,000 muscle fibers and 580 motor units, which yields an average innervation ratio of 1:1934 (Feinstein,

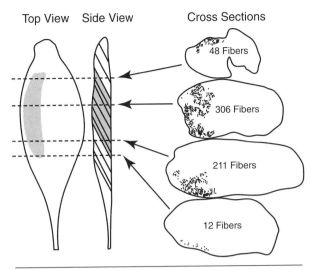

Top View   Side View   Cross Sections

48 Fibers

306 Fibers

211 Fibers

12 Fibers

Figure 6.40 The distribution of fibers in the medial gastrocnemius muscle is shown in longitudinal section on the left and in the cross-sectional views to the right. The muscle fibers belonging to the unit were confined to a subvolume of the muscle. Adapted from Burke and Tsairis, 1973.

Lindegård, Nyman, & Wohlfart, 1955). The range of innervation ratios in a muscle, however, is unknown (Enoka & Fuglevand, 2001). Each time a motor neuron is activated in the central nervous system, it elicits one or more action potentials in all of its muscle fibers (except under some fatiguing conditions); hence, the lower the innervation ratio, the lower the number of muscle fibers that are activated. The innervation ratio is also indicative of the number of times that an axon must branch in order to contact all of its muscle fibers.

Figure 6.40 shows the location of the fibers belonging to a single fast-twitch (type FR) motor unit in the medial gastrocnemius muscle of a cat. The motor unit had 500 muscle fibers. Such measurements have shown that fibers of a single motor unit occupy a specific region of the muscle. This territory can extend to up to 15% of the volume of the muscle, with a density of 2 to 5 muscle fibers per 100 belonging to the same motor unit (Burke, 1981). This means that a given region of a muscle contains muscle fibers from 20 to 50 different motor units. The territory of a motor unit in the cat tibialis anterior

Table 6.4 Anatomical Estimates of the Number of α Motor Axons and Muscle Fibers in Human Skeletal Muscles

Muscle	Specimen	α Motor axons	Number of muscle fibers	Innervation ratio
Biceps brachii[a,c]	Stillborn infants	774	580,000	750
Brachioradialis[e]	Male 40 yr	315	>129,200	>410
		350		
Cricothyroid[a,d]	Four adults	112	18,550	166
First dorsal interosseus[e]	Male 22 yr	119	40,500	340
First lumbrical[e]	Male 54 yr	93	10,038	108
	Female 29 yr	98	10,500	107
Opponens pollicis[a,c]	Stillborn infants	133	79,000	595
Masseter[b]	Male 54 yr	1452	929,000	640
Platysma[e]	Female 22 yr	1096	27,100	25
Temporalis[b]	Male 54 yr	1331	1,247,000	936
Medial gastrocnemius[e]	Male 28 yr	579	1,120,000	1934
	Male 22 yr		964,000	1634
Posterior cricoarytenoid[a,d]	Four adults	140	16,200	116
Rectus lateralis[f]	Two cadavers	4150	22,000	5
Tensor tympani[f]	Two cadavers	146	1100	8
Tibialis anterior[e]	Male 40 yr	445	250,200	562
	Male 22 yr		295,500	657
Transverse arytenoid[a,d]	Four adults	139	34,470	247

[a]Buchthal, 1961; [b]Carlsöö, 1958; [c]Christensen,1959; [d]Faaborg-Andersen, 1957; [e]Feinstein et al., 1955; [f]Torre, 1953.

muscle may range from 8% to 22% of a cross-sectional area, but in the soleus muscle the territory ranges from 41% to 76% (Bodine, Garfinkel, Roy, & Edgerton, 1988).

Not only is the territory of a single motor unit limited to a specific part of a muscle, but it also appears that different parts of a muscle can contain distinct populations of motor units. This observation has given rise to the concept of a **neuromuscular compartment** (Peters, 1989; Windhorst, Hamm, & Stuart, 1989). A *compartment* is defined as the volume of muscle supplied by a primary branch of the muscle nerve. A compartment contains a unique population of motor units, and the muscle fibers belonging to one motor unit are confined to a single neuromuscular compartment. The proportion of muscle fiber types can differ between the compartments of a single muscle. Neuromuscular compartments have been found in some, but not all, muscles. Because compartments can be activated independently, a single muscle, which is an anatomical entity, can consist of several distinct regions that each serves a different physiological function (English, 1984; English & Ledbetter, 1982; Fleckenstein et al., 1992). Also, the existence of compartments suggests that it can be misleading to infer the function of a muscle based solely on the location of its attachments. The analysis of muscle function must consider both the architecture and innervation pattern of the muscle.

The muscle biceps brachii is often cited as an example of a muscle with distinct neuromuscular compartments. It is innervated by three to six primary branches of the musculocutaneous nerve, and functionally, the motor units in biceps brachii appear to comprise two distinct populations. One population, which is located in the lateral aspect of the long head, is active when a flexion torque is exerted about the elbow joint. The other population is active when the torque about the elbow joint includes both flexion and supination components (ter Haar Romeny, Denier van der Gon, & Gielen, 1982; van Zuylen, Gielen, & Denier van der Gon, 1988).

Example 6.9
Number of Motor Units in a Muscle

The number of functioning motor units in a muscle can be estimated with electrophysiological techniques (Danbe, 1995; McComas, 1995). One common procedure involves applying electric shocks of varying intensity to a peripheral nerve and measuring the evoked responses in the muscle (figure 6.41*a*). The protocol begins with application of a weak shock that will generate an action potential in a single motor axon, which is recorded as a muscle action potential. Then

the intensity of the stimulus is increased slightly to activate another motor axon. By gradually increasing the stimulus intensity, the investigator is able to measure the evoked potentials from 11 to 20 motor axons (figure 6.41*b*). From this set, the average amplitude of the evoked response for a single motor unit is determined and compared with the response evoked by a maximal stimulus (figure 6.41*c*). The estimated number of functioning motor units is determined by dividing the amplitude of the maximal response by the average amplitude for the single motor units. Although the reliability of this technique has been questioned (Stein & Yang, 1990), it does appear an appropriate procedure to monitor changes in various patient populations (McComas, 1991).

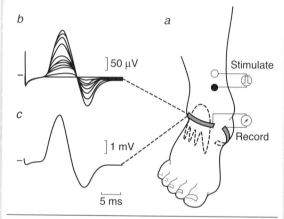

Figure 6.41   Electrophysiological technique for estimating the number of functioning motor units in a muscle: *(a)* stimulating electrodes placed over the nerve to evoke responses in the extensor digitorum brevis muscle; *(b)* set of responses evoked in single motor axons; and *(c)* the maximal evoked response.

Adapted from McComas, 1996.

Contractile Properties

Motor units can be compared with one another based on a number of physiological properties, including the discharge characteristics of the motor neuron, the speed of contraction, the magnitude of force, and the resistance to fatigue. Most comparisons are based on the contractile properties of the motor unit. Two methodologies are commonly used for evaluating these parameters, one direct and the other indirect. A *direct* evaluation refers to the physiological measurement of the motor unit properties. An *indirect* assessment is based on the histochemical, biochemical, and molecular measurement of characteristics that are related to contractile function. The direct physiological characterization of a motor unit is based on the discharge pattern of its action potentials and on its contractile properties. We consider the discharge characteristics later in the "Activation Patterns" section. For now, we focus on the contractile properties of motor units (figure 6.42).

Contractile Speed

The quantal contractile property of a motor unit is a **twitch.** This is the force-time response to a single input (figure 6.42*a*). Under normal conditions, the input is an action potential in response to an activation signal from the nervous system. In some experiments, however, the input is an electric shock that artificially generates an action potential. A twitch response is usually characterized by three measurements: the time from force onset to peak force **(contraction time),** the magnitude of the peak force, and the time it takes for the force to decline to one-half of its peak value **(half-relaxation time)** (figure 6.42*a*). Contraction time is used as a measure of the speed of the contractile machinery, although it mainly depends on the rate at which Ca^{2+} is released from the sarcoplasmic reticulum. If contraction time is long, the motor unit is described as a *slow-twitch* motor unit, whereas a brief contraction time indicates a *fast-twitch* motor unit (figure 6.42*b*).

Motor Unit Force

Motor units are rarely activated to produce individual twitches. Rather, the input typically comprises several action potentials, resulting in a series of twitch responses that overlap and produce a force that is greater than the twitch force. The force-time profile that consists of overlapping twitch responses is known as a tetanus (figure 6.42*c* and *d*). As the frequency of the action potentials increases, the tetanus changes from an irregular force profile **(unfused)** (figure 6.42*c*) to a smooth plateau **(fused tetanus)** (figure 6.42*d*). The rate at which the action potentials are sent from the motor neuron to the muscle fibers determines both the magnitude and the smoothness of the motor unit force.

The relation between activation rate and average tetanic force is known as the **force-frequency relation.** To determine the force-frequency relation for a motor unit, the unit must be activated with electric shocks at various rates and the evoked force measured. For the data shown in figure 6.43*a*, a tungsten microelectrode was inserted into a nerve to stimulate single motor units at various frequencies (2-100 Hz), and the force exerted by the motor units was measured. These data were then graphed to indicate the force-frequency relation for the motor units (figure 6.43*b*). This relation indicates, among other things, the rate at which the motor units must be activated to achieve maximal force (Fuglevand et al., 1999; McNulty, Falland, & Macefield, 2000; Thomas, Bigland-Ritchie, & Johansson, 1991). Similarly, if we record the discharge rate of action potentials during voluntary contractions, we can assess the proportion of the maximum force that the motor units exert.

Not only does the peak force during a tetanus vary with activation rate; so too can the shape of the tetanus. When the time between successive inputs is equal to 1.25 times the contraction time of the motor unit, the unfused tetanus may reach an initial peak and subsequently decline before returning again to the peak value. This behavior has been described as **sag** (figure 6.42*c* shows a slight sag after the fourth stimulus). In many mammalian muscles, fast-twitch motor units exhibit sag whereas slow-twitch units do not (Carp, Herchenroder, Chen, & Wolpaw, 1999). However, the sag property has not been

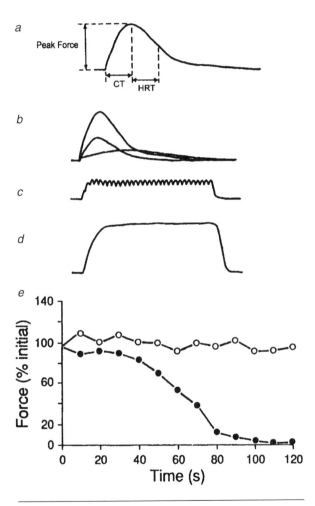

Figure 6.42 Twitch and tetanic responses of motor units in a cat hindlimb muscle: *(a)* motor unit twitch (contraction time [CT] = 24 ms; half-relaxation time [HRT] = 21 ms; peak force = 0.03 N); *(b)* twitch responses for fast- and slow-twitch motor units; *(c)* an unfused tetanus (stimulated at 28 Hz) for a fast-twitch unit (peak force = 0.42 N); *(d)* a fused tetanus (stimulated at 200 Hz) for the motor unit in *c* (peak force = 1.30 N); *(e)* fatigue test for fatigue-resistant and fatigable motor units.

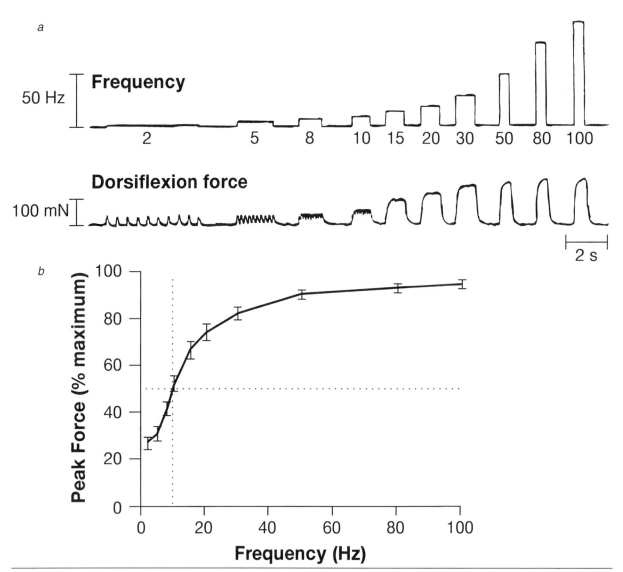

Figure 6.43 The force-frequency relation for motor units in human toe extensor muscles. *(a)* Motor units activated by intraneural stimulation (upper trace) evoked a force in the dorsiflexor muscles (lower trace); *(b)* force was normalized to the maximum value for each motor unit to produce the force-frequency relation for 13 motor units.

Data from Macefield, Fuglevand, and Bigland-Ritchie, 1996.

demonstrated in human motor units (Macefield, Fuglevand, & Bigland-Ritchie, 1996; Thomas, Johansson, & Bigland-Ritchie, 1991).

The capability of the motor unit to exert force is not measured from the twitch; it is assessed from the peak force of a single fused tetanus (figure 6.42*d*). The difference between the peak twitch force and the maximum force in a fused tetanus (referred to as P_o), known as the twitch-tetanus ratio, generally varies from 1:1.5 to 1:10. Thus, in a fused tetanus the force may be 1.5 to 10 times greater than the twitch force. Peak tetanic force for human motor units does not vary as a function of twitch contraction time, as it does in most other mammalian muscles. Rather, P_o can vary over a substantial range for

the same twitch contraction time, and conversely twitch contraction time can double with no systematic change in P_o (figure 6.44*a*). These data indicate that the peak force exerted by motor units in the human thenar muscle is not related to the twitch contraction time; that is, some fast-twitch motor units exert relatively low forces (Bigland-Ritchie, Fuglevand, & Thomas, 1998; Van Cutsem, Feiereisen, Duchateau, & Hainaut, 1997).

Fatigability

The force achieved in a single tetanus declines over time if the motor unit is required to produce a series of tetani. The ability of a motor unit to prevent such a decline indicates its *resistance to fatigue.* The time between the

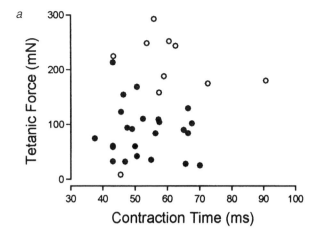

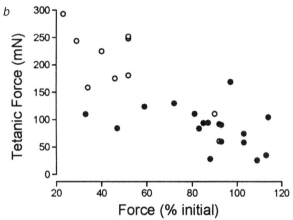

Figure 6.44 Relations between *(a)* maximum tetanic force and twitch contraction time and between *(b)* maximum tetanic force and the decline in force after a fatiguing contraction for motor units of human hand and arm muscles.

Data provided by Christine K. Thomas, PhD (•), and by Andrew J. Fuglevand, PhD (○).

onset of activation and the beginning of the decline in force differs markedly among motor units, and can be assessed by various fatigue tests. A standard fatigue test (Burke, Levine, Tsairis, & Zajac, 1973) designed for motor units in the cat hindlimb involves eliciting tetani for 2 to 6 min at a rate of one tetanus each second—each tetanus lasts for 330 ms and includes 13 stimuli. The ratio of the peak force exerted after two min of this stimulus protocol as compared with that exerted in the initial tetanus is used as an index of fatigue (figure 6.42*e*). This fatigue test seems to stress the connection between the electrical signal from the nervous system and the contraction of the muscle (Enoka & Stuart, 1992; Jami, Murthy, Petit, & Zytnicki, 1983). This test distinguishes motor units that are resistant to fatigue and those that are not. Fatigue-resistant motor units (types S and FR) have a fatigue index greater than or equal to 0.75 compared with an index of less than 0.25 for fatigable motor units

(type FF). An index of 0.25 indicates that after 2 min the force exerted by the unit will be only 25% of that measured at the beginning of the test. These data suggest that activation of the type S and FR motor units is more appropriate for sustained contractions because they are more resistant to fatigue.

Motor Unit Types

Based on the distributions of these contractile properties, it is often possible to identify different groups of motor units. Such classification schemes are based on the physiological properties of the motor units. For example, motor units in the hindlimb muscles of the cat can be classified into three groups based on sag in the unfused tetanus and resistance to fatigue (Burke, 1981): slow contracting, fatigue resistant **(type S);** fast contracting, fatigue resistant **(type FR),** and fast contracting, fast to fatigue **(type FF).** The type S motor units produce the least force and the type FF the greatest (table 6.5); type FF units have more muscle fibers (i.e., greater innervation ratio), and these are often the biggest fibers in the muscle. In contrast, motor units in human muscle do not appear to fit this scheme (Bigland-Ritchie et al., 1998; McComas, 1998; Van Cutsem et al., 1997). They can be distinguished based on differences in tetanic force and fatigability, but not contraction time (figure 6.44). For example, the most fatigue-resistant motor units in the human thenar muscle tend to produce a lesser tetanic force (figure 6.44*b*) (Fuglevand et al., 1999). The first motor units activated during a voluntary contraction performed by a human subject are weak and fatigue resistant, but they may be slow or fast contracting. It is not correct, therefore, to say that low-force contractions performed by humans are sustained by slow-twitch muscle fibers.

Although there is not a strong association between force and contraction speed for human motor units, there do appear to be both fast- and slow-twitch motor units in most human muscles. Twitch contraction times of human motor units have been reported to extend along a continuum from 20 to 72 ms (mean = 35 ms) for masseter, 35 to 85 ms (mean = 59 ms) for thenar muscles, 43 to 91 ms (mean = 57 ms) for long finger flexors and hand muscles, 50 to 107 ms (mean = 75 ms) for toe extensors, and 40 to 110 ms (mean = 76 ms) for medial gastrocnemius (Fuglevand et al., 1999; Garnett, O'Donovan, Stephens, & Taylor, 1978; Macefield et al., 1996; McNulty et al., 2000; Nordstrom & Miles, 1990; Thomas, Johansson, & Bigland-Ritchie, 1991). Differences in contraction speed among motor units are due to variations in the enzyme myosin ATPase (bound to one of the S1 heads), the rate at which Ca^{2+} is released from and taken up by the sarcoplasmic reticulum (Kugelberg & Thornell, 1983), and the architecture of the muscle (Monti et al., 1999).

Table 6.5 Motor Unit and Muscle Fiber Characteristics for Three Cat Hindlimb Muscles

	MG	FDL	TA
Number of muscle fibers	170,000	26,000	—
Number of motor units	270	130	—
Innervation ratio			
S	611	180	93
FR	553	132	197
FF	674	328	255
Mean tetanic force (mN)			
S	76	11	40
FR	287	53	101
FF	714	300	208
Muscle fiber area (μm^2)			
I	1980	1023	2484
IIa	2370	1403	2430
IIb	4503	2628	3293
Muscle fiber types (%)			
I	25	10	11
IIa	20	37	50
IIb	55	53	39

Note. MG = medial gastrocnemius; FDL = flexor digitorum longus; TA = tibialis anterior.

Modified from Bodine, Roy, Eldred, & Edgerton, 1987; Burke, 1981; and Dum & Kennedy, 1980.

One feature of contraction speed that may distinguish among human motor units is the activation rate required to achieve half the maximum force. Fuglevand et al. (1999) identified two groups of motor units when assessing the force-frequency relation (figure 6.43) of motor units in the long finger flexors and hand muscles. One group of motor units required an activation rate of 9 Hz whereas the other group needed 16 Hz to achieve half the maximum force. The average contraction times for the two groups of motor units were 66 ms and 46 ms, respectively. However, there was no difference in the fatigability of these two groups of motor units.

Muscle Fiber Types

In contrast to the use of direct physiological measurements to distinguish motor unit types, some classification schemes are based on histochemical, biochemical, and molecular properties of the muscle fibers (Pette, Peuker, & Staron, 1999). The histochemical and biochemical techniques involve determining the enzyme content of the muscle fibers. Because enzymes are the catalysts for chemical reactions, measuring the amount of enzyme provides an index of the speed or quantity of the reaction. Similarly, molecular techniques can be used

to determine the distribution of different isoforms of key molecules involved in a contraction. Thus *the aim of histochemical, biochemical, and molecular techniques is to measure mechanisms responsible for the various physiological properties* (e.g., contraction speed, magnitude of force, fatigue resistance). Once a correlation can be determined between a chemical reaction or the abundance of a molecule and a physiological response, the quantity of enzyme or molecule can be interpreted as a correlate of the physiological response. Typically, three types of enzymes are measured: one type indicates contractile speed (myosin ATPase is an index of the maximum velocity of shortening) (Bárány, 1967; Edman et al., 1988), whereas the other two represent the metabolic basis (aerobic vs. anaerobic) on which the muscle fiber produces its energy for contraction. Commonly assayed enzymes for aerobic metabolism are succinic dehydrogenase (SDH) and nicotinamide adenine dinucleotide-tetrazolium reductase (NADH-TR); for anaerobic capabilities the enzymes are phosphorylase and alpha-glycerophosphate dehydrogenase (α-GPD).

On the basis of these enzyme assays of muscle fibers, it is possible to classify the fibers into three groups. Two schemes can be used. One scheme, which classifies fibers solely on the basis of myosin ATPase, uses the names *types I, IIa,* and *IIb.* The distinction between **type I** and **type II muscle fibers** is based on the amount of ATPase activity remaining in the muscle fibers after preincubation in a solution with a pH of 9.4. Type I represents the slow-twitch, and type II the fast-twitch muscle fibers. Type II muscle fibers can be further separated into two groups (IIa and IIb) after preincubation in solutions with pHs of 4.3 (IIa) and 4.6 (IIb) (Brooke & Kaiser, 1974). The distinction between the muscle fiber types is shown in figure 6.45 with a myosin ATPase stain of a thin cross section of a cat hindlimb muscle. The other scheme— which uses enzymes for contraction speed (myosin ATPase), aerobic capacity (SDH or NADH-TR), and anaerobic capacity (phosphorylase and α-GPD)—employs the terms slow twitch, oxidative **(type SO);** fast twitch, oxidative-glycolytic **(type FOG);** and fast twitch, glycolytic **(type FG).**

One molecular technique that has been used to identify muscle fiber types assesses the distribution of the genetically defined isoforms of the myosin heavy chain (Bottinelli & Reggiani, 2000; Sant'ana Pereira, Wessels, Nijtmans, Moorman, & Sargeant, 1994; Staron & Pette, 1986). With this technique, the molecular components of a muscle fiber specimen can be separated by gel elec-

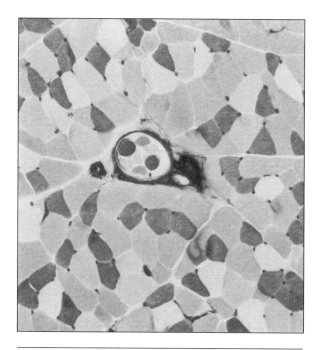

Figure 6.45 Photomicrograph of muscle fiber types in the tibialis posterior muscle of the cat hindlimb. The thin cross section of muscle was stained for myosin adenosine triphosphatase to show the distribution of type I (dark), IIa (white), and IIb (gray) fibers. In the middle of the photomicrograph is a muscle spindle, with its capsule and small intrafusal muscle fibers.

Photograph supplied courtesy of Dr. R.J. Callister.

trophoresis and the quantity of each element measured by densitometry. Based on myosin heavy chain (MHC) isoforms, three types of muscle fibers have been identified with this technique in human skeletal muscle: **MHC-I, MHC-IIa,** and **MHC-IId.** Although the human MHC-IIb gene and transcript have been identified (Schiaffino & Reggiani, 1996), type IIb fibers contain the MHC-IId (or MHC-IIx) isoform and not the MHC-IIb isoform (Ennion, Sant'ana Pereira, Sargeant, Young, & Goldspink, 1995; Smerdu, Karch-Mizrachi, Campione, Leinwand, & Schiaffino, 1994). There is a high correspondence between the histochemically determined I, IIa, and IIb fiber types and the MHC-I, MHC-IIa, and MHC-IId types identified by electrophoresis (Harridge et al., 1996; Sant'ana Pereira et al., 1994). A significant advantage of the molecular analysis is the possibility of identifying hybrid muscle fibers, that is, those comprising combinations of the MHC isoforms.

While many of the single-fiber characteristics described earlier in the chapter were determined with intact fibers from the frog, technical developments have made it possible to compare some of the properties of type-identified mammalian muscle fibers. The most common preparation is the **permeabilized fiber,** which involves the permeabilization of the outer membrane by the application of chemicals, the mechanical removal of the membrane, or freeze-drying. Although this preparation disrupts the normal integrity of the fiber, it has been used to compare some of the mechanical properties of the various fiber types. Several studies have shown, for example, that the contractile speed, as indicated by shortening velocity, varies with fiber type (table 6.6). Because permeabilized fibers swell during performance of these measurements, fiber diameter cannot be measured accurately, and so the estimated values for specific tension differ from the values obtained with intact fibers.

The measurement of motor unit properties in human muscle results in a less discrete classification scheme than that for muscle fibers (Bigland-Ritchie et al., 1998). There are at least four explanations for this discrepancy. First, it is possible that the measured biochemical and molecular characteristics are not strongly related to contractile function, but this seems unlikely (Booth & Baldwin, 1996; Edgerton, Bodine-Fowler, Roy, Ishihara, & Hodgson, 1996). Second, the muscle fibers of a motor unit may comprise a range of contractile properties, and we can measure only the net effect. There is evidence that the molecular composition of a muscle fiber can vary along its length (Bottinelli, Pellegrino, Canepari, Rossi, & Reggiani, 1999), so it seems possible that contractile function varies among the muscle fibers of a motor unit (Gordon & Pattullo, 1993). Third, the forces exerted by single muscle fibers might be modified in the transmission pathway from the fiber to the skeleton. The force

Table 6.6   Mechanical Properties of Type-Identified Fiber Segments From Human Vastus Lateralis Muscle

	I	I–IIa	IIa	IIa–IId	IId
v_o (fl/s)	0.264	0.521	1.121	2.139	2.418
v_{max} (fl/s)	0.317	0.638	0.718	0.936	1.286
Curvature	0.032	0.030	0.063	0.060	0.072
Cross-sectional area (μm^2)	9278	8569	7922	5492	6294
Specific tension (N/cm^2)	4.38	5.10	6.06	6.47	6.18

Note. v_o = unloaded shortening velocity, as determined with the slack test; fl/s = fiber lengths per second; v_{max} = maximum rate of shortening, as measured from the force-velocity relation; curvature = the curvature of the force-velocity relation, expressed as the ratio $a/F_{m,o}$ (Equation 6.3).

Data from Bottinelli, Canepari, Pellegrino, & Reggiani, 1996.

generated by contractile proteins, for example, is transmitted through the cytoskeleton and connective tissues before it is registered externally (Huijing, 1999; Monti et al., 1999; Patel & Lieber, 1997). This process might make the contractile properties of muscle fibers appear more similar than they in fact are. Fourth, experiments on humans have largely focused on low-threshold motor units; this could mask associations that exist across an entire population of motor units (Enoka & Fuglevand, 2001). Because of these possibilities, the classification scheme that should be used for human motor units is unclear.

Nonetheless, there does appear to be some association between muscle fiber typing and muscle function. When Monster, Chan, and O'Connor (1978) examined the extent of usage for 15 muscles during a normal 8-h working day, they found that muscles with a higher proportion of type I fibers were used more frequently. Presumably, muscles with a higher proportion of type I fibers (table 6.7) have a greater oxidative capability and are less likely to fatigue due to metabolic factors. Similarly, there appears to be a positive correlation between the proportion of fast-twitch fibers in biceps brachii and the maximum elbow flexor force (Nygaard, Houston, Suzuki, Jørgensen, & Saltin, 1983), and between the proportion of type I fibers and peak oxygen consumption (Mancini et al., 1989).

To explore this issue systematically, Harridge et al. (1996) obtained biopsy samples from three different muscles of human volunteers and measured the fiber-type distribution and physiological properties of segments from single muscle fibers. The muscles examined in this study were soleus (MHC-I = 70%), vastus lateralis (MHC-I = 47%), and triceps brachii (MHC-I = 33%). Across these three muscles, whole-muscle measurements of twitch contraction time (figure 6.46*a*), the rate of increase in tetanic force when the muscle was activated by electrical stimulation (figure 6.46*b*), and the fatigability

Table 6.7   Percentage of Type I Fibers in Human Skeletal Muscles

Muscle	Percentage
Obicularis oculi	15
Biceps brachii	38–42
Triceps brachii	33–50
Extensor digitorum brevis	45
Vastus lateralis	46
Lateral gastrocnemius	49
Diaphragm	50
Quadriceps femoris	52
First dorsal interosseus	57
Abductor pollicis brevis	63
Masseter	60–70
Tibialis anterior	73
Adductor pollicis	80
Soleus	80

after 2 min of intermittent electrical stimulation (figure 6.46*c*) were all associated with the proportion of the MHC-II fibers in the muscles. Although the MHC isoforms determine such physiological properties as the maximum shortening velocity and the maximum rate of tetanic force in single fibers, the associations shown in figure 6.46 suggest that the biochemical and molecular determinants of these other properties may covary with the MHC-determined fiber types. An important feature of these data, however, is the absence of significant associations within each muscle. It seems that when we are comparing the fiber-type proportions for a specific

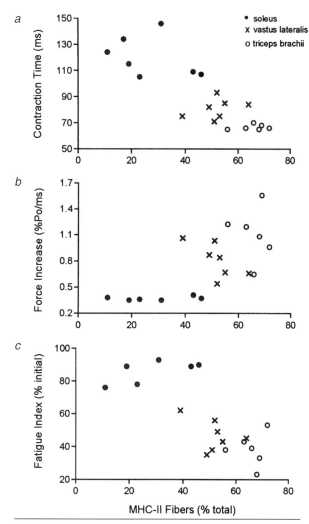

Figure 6.46 Associations among (a) the proportion of myosin heavy chain II (MHC-II) fibers and twitch contraction time, (b) rate of increase in tetanic force, and (c) fatigability for three human muscles.

Data from Harridge et al., 1996.

muscle across subjects, fiber-type differences can only partially explain the physiological differences.

Although motor unit and muscle fiber activity is often discussed in terms of the S-FR-FF motor unit scheme, this does not appear to be appropriate for human muscles. First, investigators have been unable to identify comparable motor unit types in human muscle (Fuglevand et al., 1999; Macefield et al., 1996; Sica & McComas, 1971; Thomas et al., 1991). Second, the first motor units activated in a voluntary contraction can be either slow twitch or fast twitch (Bigland-Ritchie et al., 1998; Van Cutsem et al., 1997). Third, the cross-sectional area of human muscle fibers often does not increase from type I to type IIb, as it does in many nonhuman muscles (table 6.5). The relative size of the different fiber types appears to vary among muscles and between men and women; type I fibers are often the same size or larger than type II fibers (Alway,

Grumbt, Stray-Gundersen, & Gonyea, 1992; Harridge et al., 1996; Miller, MacDougall, Tarnopolsky, & Sale, 1993). These findings suggest that much remains to be learned about the functional organization of motor units in humans.

Activation Patterns

The force that a muscle can exert is varied through alteration in the amount of motor unit activity (Kernell, 1992). This is accomplished by changing either the number of motor units that are active (motor unit recruitment) or the rate at which motor neurons discharge action potentials (discharge rate modulation).

Motor Unit Recruitment

In 1938, Denny-Brown and Pennybacker reported that the performance of a particular movement always appeared to be accomplished by the activation of motor units in a set sequence. Because the sequence of motor unit activation remains relatively fixed, it has been called **orderly recruitment.** As the force exerted by a muscle increases, additional motor units are activated, or **recruited;** and once a motor unit is recruited, it remains active until the force declines. In this scheme, shown in figure 6.47, motor unit 1 is recruited first and remains active as long as the force does not decrease. The increase in force occurs because of continuing recruitment of motor units (four more in figure 6.47) and increase in

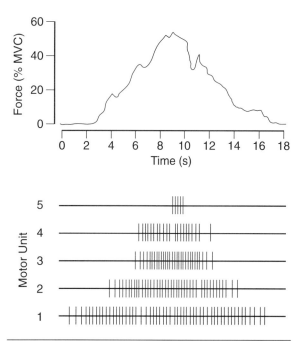

Figure 6.47 Recruitment and discharge pattern of five (of many) motor units during a muscle contraction in which force increased to 50% of maximum.

Reprinted from Kamen and DeLuca, 1989.

MVC = maximal voluntary contraction.

the activation rate of the recruited motor units. As the force is reduced, motor units are sequentially inactivated, or **derecruited,** in the reverse order; that is, the last motor unit recruited is the first derecruited.

The relative contribution of motor unit recruitment to muscle force varies between muscles. In some hand muscles, for example, all the motor units are recruited when the force reaches about 50% of maximum. In other muscles, such as biceps brachii, deltoid, and tibialis anterior, motor unit recruitment continues up to 85% of the maximum force (DeLuca, LeFever, McCue, & Xenakis, 1982a; Kukulka & Clamann, 1981; Van Cutsem et al., 1997). The increase in muscle force beyond the upper limit of motor unit recruitment is accomplished entirely through variation in the discharge rate of action potentials.

Orderly recruitment has been demonstrated in a wide variety of muscle groups and animal species for many different tasks. It appears to be the result of several physiological processes rather than a single mechanism. One factor underlying orderly recruitment is motor neuron size, which is indicated by the surface area of the soma and dendrites. This effect is known as the **Size Principle,** which states that *the recruitment order of motor units is determined by differences in motor neuron size.* According to the Size Principle, the motor unit with the smallest motor neuron is recruited first and the motor unit with the largest motor neuron is recruited last (Binder & Mendell, 1990; Cope & Pinter, 1995; Enoka & Stuart, 1984; Henneman, 1957, 1979). This organization appears to exist among the motor neurons that innervate one particular muscle (cf. however, Sokoloff, Siegel, & Cope, 1999). Such a group of motor neurons is referred to as a **motor neuron pool.**

The recruitment of motor units, however, does not depend solely on motor neuron size; it is also influenced by other motor neuron characteristics and by the organization of synaptic inputs on the dendrites and soma of the motor neurons in the pool. It appears that some morphological (e.g., number of dendrites, axon diameter, innervation ratio), membrane (e.g., input resistance, rheobase, afterhyperpolarization), and synaptic input (e.g., Renshaw cells, Group Ia afferent) characteristics vary with motor neuron size (figure 6.48) such that the smallest motor neurons can be excited most easily. Although we do not know exactly how each of these factors varies among motor neurons, it seems that there is a systematic variation because the *effective synaptic current* varies with input from different systems. Because the peak force a motor unit can exert covaries with size, recruitment by the Size Principle means that muscle force can be graded systematically (figure 6.49*a*).

Although the orderly recruitment of motor units has been shown to occur in many behaviors (Desmedt & Godaux, 1977; Person, 1993; Van Cutsem et al., 1998),

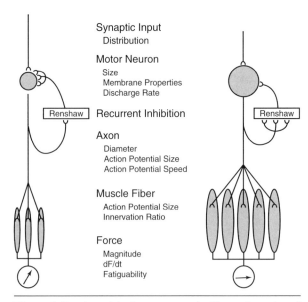

Figure 6.48   A model of two motor units illustrating selected morphological and physiological characteristics that correlate with motor neuron size.

Reprinted from Enoka and Stuart, 1984.

dF/dt = rate of change in force.

it can vary under some conditions. One well-studied example of an alteration in recruitment order at the whole-muscle level is the **paw-shake response.** This behavior is elicited in animals, such as cats, when a piece of tape sticks to a paw and the animal's response is to vigorously shake the paw in an attempt to remove the tape. The behavior involves a rapid alternating flexion and extension of the paw, which is controlled by the ankle flexor and extensor muscles. The extensor muscles include the slow-twitch muscle soleus and the fast-twitch muscle medial gastrocnemius. In normal activities, such as standing, walking, running, and jumping, the soleus and medial gastrocnemius are concurrently active; the force exerted by soleus remains relatively constant across tasks, while that exerted by medial gastrocnemius increases with the power demands of the task (Walmsley et al., 1978). In the paw-shake response, however, the slow-twitch soleus is preferentially inactivated, and the behavior is produced by activation of the fast-twitch muscles (Smith, Betts, Edgerton, & Zernicke, 1980). This change in recruitment among a group of synergist muscles is necessary so that the animal can move the limb rapidly to dislodge the irritant.

At the motor unit level, changes in recruitment order have been observed as a consequence of manipulation of sensory feedback (Garnett & Stephens, 1981; Kanda, Burke, & Walmsley, 1977) and during performance of lengthening contractions (Nardone, Romanò, & Schieppati, 1989). One way to demonstrate this effect is to determine the recruitment order of pairs of motor units

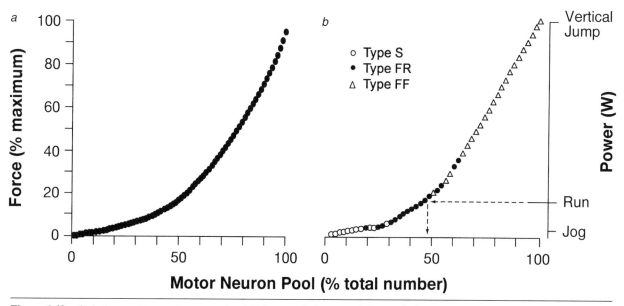

Figure 6.49   Orderly recruitment of motor units. *(a)* The cumulative sum of the tetanic forces produced by the 80 motor units in the cat peroneus longus muscle results in a gradual increase in muscle force (Kernell, Eerbeek, & Verhey, 1983). *(b)* Hypothetical model of motor unit recruitment (Walmsley, Hodgson, & Burke, 1978). Recruitment begins with the smallest motor neuron (at 0% of the pool) and continues until sufficient power is produced. The model suggests, for example, that it is necessary to recruit about 48% of the motor units in the pool to produce sufficient power to run. The model also indicates that there is some overlap in the recruitment order of the different types of motor units.

Type S = slow contracting, fatigue resistant; FR = fast contracting, fatigue resistant; FF = fast contracting, fast to fatigue.

in the absence and presence of a perceptible cutaneous sensation elicited by electrical stimulation of the skin. In the absence of the stimulus, one motor unit is recruited at a lower force than the other; that is, one has a lower **recruitment threshold.** In the presence of the cutaneous sensation, however, the unit with the higher recruitment threshold is activated first. Because the unit with the higher recruitment threshold probably exerts a greater force, this reversal of recruitment order represents the selective activation of stronger motor units. Such activation would be desirable if the cutaneous sensation required a rapid, forceful response. Similarly, the altered activation order of motor units during lengthening contractions is probably due to a change in the balance of the input received by the motor neuron pool (e.g., from muscle spindles, by presynaptic inhibition).

One advantage of orderly recruitment is that when a muscle is commanded to exert a force, the sequence of motor unit recruitment is determined by spinal mechanisms and does not have to be specified by the brain. Therefore, the command generated by the brain does not have to include information on which motor units to activate; this relieves the brain of the need to be concerned with this level of detail for the performance of movement. However, because recruitment order is predetermined, largely by spinal mechanisms, it is not possible to activate selective motor units.

The consequence of this predetermined order is that the motor units recruited for a task depend on the proportion of the motor neuron pool that is needed. A hypothetical model of this relation is shown in figure 6.49*b*. In this scheme, the proportion of motor units recruited depends on the power demands of the task. For example, jogging at a slow speed represents an activity in which the muscle power requirements are minimal. The model indicates that it is necessary to recruit only low-threshold motor units in order to jog. *Because recruitment order is fixed, the gradual increase in the power demands of a task involves the progressive recruitment of higher-threshold motor units.* When the power demands of the task are high, as for a vertical jump, the model indicates that both low- and high-threshold motor units are recruited in a prescribed order.

Discharge Rate

The force exerted by muscle is due to variable combinations of the number of active motor units (recruitment) and the rate at which the motor neurons discharge action potentials. When a motor unit is recruited and the force exerted by the muscle continues to increase, the rate at which the motor neuron discharges action potentials usually increases (figure 6.50). Although each motor unit action potential results in a motor unit twitch, when the action potentials occur close to one another, the twitches add together and exert a force that is greater than the twitch. The degree to which the twitches summate depends on the rate at which the action potentials are discharged, producing the force-frequency relation (figure 6.43). The increase in force when action potential rate goes from 5 to 10 Hz is not the same as that due to increasing the rate from 20 to 25 Hz, even though there is a difference of 5 Hz in each case. The greatest increase in force (steepest slope) occurs at intermediate discharge rates (9 to 12 Hz).

On the basis of the force-frequency relation, we can measure the rate at which a motor neuron discharges action potentials and infer the relative force that the motor unit exerts. For most tasks that have been examined, discharge rate is well below that necessary to evoke the maximum force for a motor unit. Because of technical limitations, most is known about motor unit discharge during low-force, isometric contractions. For such tasks, there is a concurrent increase in motor unit recruitment and discharge rate as the muscle force is increased (Monster & Chan, 1977; Person & Kudina, 1972, Seyffarth, 1940). Figure 6.50 illustrates this scheme by showing that a gradual increase and subsequent decrease in force were accomplished by the recruitment and derecruitment of motor units and a parallel variation in the discharge rate for the earliest-recruited motor units. Each thin line in figure 6.50 represents the activity of a single motor unit located in the rectus femoris muscle, with recruitment occurring at the left-most dot on each thin line. Motor unit 1, for example, was recruited at a force of about 18% of maximum with an initial discharge rate of 9 Hz, which increased to 15 Hz at the peak force. If the force-frequency relation for this motor unit was

similar to that shown in figure 6.43, then the motor unit would have exerted a peak force that was about 60% of maximum.

The rate at which a motor neuron discharges action potentials is never as consistent as that suggested by the thin lines in figure 6.50. We can determine the variability in discharge rate by calculating the instantaneous discharge rate between successive pairs of action potentials. We do this by measuring the action potentials discharged by a motor neuron, then taking the reciprocal of the duration between successive action potentials. The outcome of such a process is shown in figure 6.51 for a motor unit in a hand muscle. The scatter in the instantaneous discharge rate indicates the variability in the timing of action potential discharge. For example, the scatter is greater for the motor unit in figure 6.51 during the anisometric contraction compared with the isometric contraction. The variability in discharge rate is usually expressed as the coefficient of variation, which is a measure of normalized variability.

$$\text{Coefficient of variation} = \left(\frac{\text{standard deviation}}{\text{mean}} \right) \times 100$$

The coefficient of variation is typically about 20% for human motor units. The motor unit in figure 6.51 had a coefficient of variation of 12% for the isometric contraction, 18% during raising of the load (shortening contraction), and 24% during lowering of the load (lengthening contraction).

The minimum rate at which motor neurons discharge action potentials repetitively during voluntary contractions is about 5 to 7 Hz (Kudina & Alexeeva, 1992; Spiegel, Stratton, Burke, Glendinning, & Enoka, 1996; Van Cutsem et al., 1997). When discharge rate is measured while a muscle exerts moderate forces (~35% of maximum), the maximal discharge rates are greater for low-threshold motor units (Tanji & Kato, 1973; Monster & Chan, 1977, De Luca et al., 1982a). At high forces, some studies have shown that the high-threshold motor units have greater maximum discharge rates (Gydikov & Kosarov, 1974; Monster & Chan, 1977), while others have shown that the maximal discharge rate is greater for low-threshold motor units (Kamen et al., 1995). Maximum discharge rates, however, vary across muscles: mean rates of 35 to 40 Hz have been recorded for first dorsal interosseus, <35 Hz for extensor indicis, 25 to 35 Hz for adductor digiti minimi, 25 to 30 Hz for adductor pollicis, 29 Hz for deltoid, 20 to 25 Hz for biceps brachii and extensor digitorum communis, 11 Hz for soleus, and 33 Hz for tibialis anterior (Bellemare, Woods, Johansson, & Bigland-Ritchie, 1983; De Luca et al., 1982a; Freund, Büdingen, & Dietz, 1975; Kukulka & Clamann, 1981; Monster & Chan, 1977; Tanji & Kato, 1973; Van Cutsem et al., 1997). Relative to figure 6.43, these discharge rates

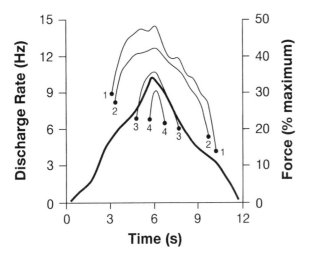

Figure 6.50 Modulation of discharge rate by four motor units during a gradual increase and then decrease in the force (thick line) exerted by the knee extensor muscles.

Adapted from Person and Kudina, 1972.

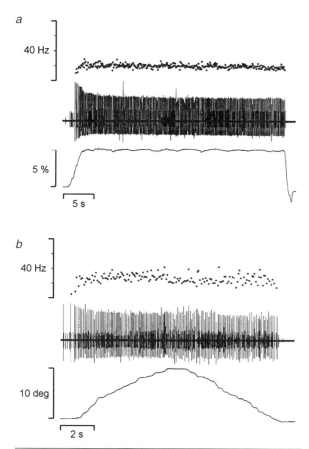

Figure 6.51 The action potentials discharged by a motor unit in a hand muscle when performing *(a)* an isometric contraction and *(b)* while raising and lowering a light load. The index finger exerted an abduction force that was 5% of maximum during the isometric contraction and lifted an equivalent inertial load during the anisometric contraction. The position trace in *b* indicates the angle of the metacarpophalangeal joint of the index finger in the abduction-adduction plane; the positive slope indicates lifting the load, and the negative slope corresponds to lowering the load.

Data from Laidlaw, Bilodeau, and Enoka, 2000.

suggest that the motor units were operating on the upper steep part of the force-frequency relation.

Discharge Pattern

The force exerted by a muscle depends not only on motor unit recruitment and the rate at which action potentials are discharged, but also on the pattern of action potential activity (Windhorst, 1988). *Discharge pattern* refers to the timing of action potentials, both those discharged by the same motor unit and those discharged by other motor units. There are at least four prominent effects of discharge pattern: muscle wisdom, double discharge, common drive, and motor unit synchrony.

Muscle wisdom refers to the change in motor unit discharge that occurs during fatigue. When an individual

sustains a fatiguing contraction at a high force, there is a decline in the rate at which motor unit action potentials are discharged (Bigland-Ritchie, Johansson, Lippold, Smith, & Woods, 1983; Dietz, 1978). The decrease in discharge rate, however, does not occur during either low-force, fatiguing contractions (Christova & Kossev, 1998; Garland, Enoka, Serrano, & Robinson, 1994; Maton & Gamet, 1989) or high-force contractions with muscles that have a high percentage of slow-twitch motor units (Macefield, Fuglevang, Howell, & Bigland-Ritchie, 2000). The gradual reduction in discharge rate is not due to an impairment of the processes associated with action potential generation and propagation; rather it is an adaptation that matches the neural activity to the changing conditions in the muscle (Enoka & Stuart, 1992). The adaptation appears to be controlled, at least partly, by changes that take place in the muscle; this is the reason the fatigue-related decline in discharge rate has been referred to as muscle wisdom. The significance of this effect is shown in figure 6.52, where the force elicited in the knee extensor muscles with a constant frequency of electrical stimulation is compared with that evoked by a declining frequency of electrical stimulation. Over the 60-s interval, the force declined less when the frequency of stimulation was reduced gradually than it did when the frequency remained constant (60 Hz). The physiological reason for this difference, however, remains unknown (Binder-Macleod, Lee, Russ, & Kucharski, 1998; Binder-Macleod & Russ, 1999).

Another discharge pattern is the **double discharge,** which refers to the discharge of two action potentials by a single motor unit within about 10 ms (Garland & Griffin, 1999). Human motor units typically discharge over the range from 7 to 35 Hz, which means intervals of about 30 to 140 ms between consecutive action potentials.

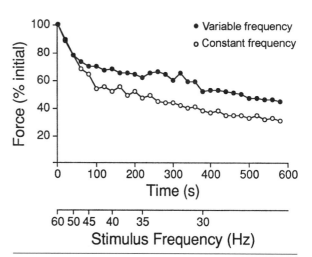

Figure 6.52 The submaximal force elicited in the knee extensor muscles by electrical stimulation.

Adapted from Binder-Macleod and Guerin, 1990.

When a motor unit is electrically stimulated at about 12 Hz (82-ms interval) and then a double discharge (10-ms interval) is interposed in the train of stimuli, there is a substantial increase in the force exerted by the motor unit (Burke, Rudomin, & Zajac, 1970; Sandercock & Heckman, 1997). For example, figure 6.53 shows the effect of a double discharge on the force of a single motor unit during an unfused tetanus. The motor unit in the extensor digitorum brevis muscle was stimulated twice with a train of 10 stimuli at 5 Hz, but one train began with two quick stimuli (10 ms apart) that mimicked a double discharge. The increase in force due to the double discharge is indicated as the shaded area. Furthermore, the force-time integral evoked by a train of 7 stimuli was greatest when the train began with a brief interval (5-15 ms) that was followed by longer intervals (>100 ms) corresponding to activation at 7 to 10 Hz (Thomas, Johansson, & Bigland-Ritchie, 1999).

The appearance of double discharges in a train of action potentials seems to change with the activation history of a muscle (Enoka & Fuglevand, 2001). For example, the occurrence of double discharges increases both after physical training and with aging. When subjects performed 12 weeks of dynamic training (10 sets of 10 contractions with loads that were ~35% of maximum), the incidence of double discharges in the tibialis anterior muscle increased (Van Cutsem et al., 1998). This was associated with an improvement in the ability to rapidly increase muscle force. In contrast, the incidence of double discharges in a hand muscle was greater in old compared with young adults and was associated with a reduced ability to perform steady contractions (Laidlaw et al., 2000). Although human motor units do not appear to use double discharges often during voluntary movements, there may be differences between muscles and tasks, such as whether the contractions are fatiguing and whether the task involves shortening and lengthening contractions (Bawa & Calancie, 1983; Griffin, Garland & Ivanova, 1998; Gydikov, Kossev, Kosarov, & Kostov, 1987).

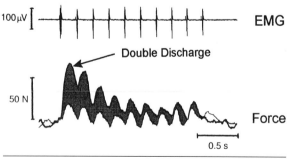

Figure 6.53   The EMG and force for a single motor unit evoked by two trains of 5-Hz stimulation. For one train (double discharge), an extra stimulus was imposed at the onset of the stimulus.

Adapted from Macefield et al., 1996.

In contrast to the double discharge, which refers to the consecutive action potentials discharged by a single motor unit, the effects of common drive and synchronization refer to the temporal relation of the action potentials among different motor units. **Common drive** describes the correlated variation in the average discharge rate of concurrently active motor units (De Luca, LeFever, McCue, & Xenakis, 1982b), which was first suggested by Henneman (1957, 1979). The *average* discharge rates covary at a rate of about 1 to 2 Hz; that is, the average discharge rates vary in parallel with a sinusoidal fluctuation of 1 to 2 Hz. The magnitude of the correlated discharge between motor units appears to change with tasks (De Luca & Mambrito, 1987). Although the inputs to the motor neuron pool that produce the common drive have not been identified, they appear to be different from those that mediate motor unit synchronization (Semmler, Nordstrom, & Wallace, 1997).

Whereas common drive is based on the measurement of average discharge rates, motor unit **synchronization** quantifies the amount of correlation between the timing of the individual action potentials discharged by concurrently active motor units. If the action potentials generated by one motor unit are completely random (independent in time) with respect to those generated by another motor unit, they are described as asynchronous. However, when the timing of the action potentials discharged by two motor units is not completely independent, the activity is described as synchronous. This effect is typically studied by recording the discharge of two motor units (figure 6.54) and statistically comparing the temporal occurrence of action potentials (Nordstrom, Fuglevand, & Enoka, 1992). The magnitude of the synchronization between pairs of motor units is variable and is influenced by such factors as the task that is examined, the motor units and muscles involved in the task, and the habitual physical activity that is performed by the individual (Bremner, Baker, & Stephens, 1991a, 1991b, 1991c; Farmer, 1998; Kamen & Roy, 2000; Schmied, Pagni, Sturm, & Vedel, 2000; Schmied, Vedel, & Pagni, 1994; Semmler & Nordstrom, 1995). For example, it is greater in the nondominant hand compared with the dominant hand of untrained individuals, greatest in strength-trained individuals, and least in skill-trained individuals (Semmler & Nordstrom, 1998). Furthermore, it is greater during anisometric contractions compared with isometric contractions (Semmler, Kutzscher, Zhou, & Enoka, 2000).

The correlated discharge of motor units requires the concurrent delivery of synaptic currents to the motor neurons. Although this can occur by chance, the systematic occurrence of correlated discharges needs either of two mechanisms (Farmer, Halliday, Conway, Stephens, & Rosenberg, 1997; McAuley & Marsden, 2000; Salinas & Sejnowski, 2000): (1) branched input from a common

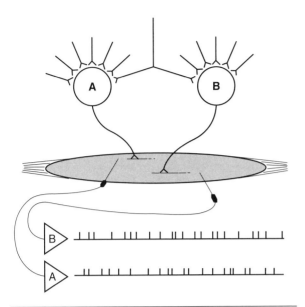

Figure 6.54 Timing of motor unit action potentials. The motor neurons of two motor units (A and B) are shown receiving many inputs, including one input that is common to both motor neurons. The action potentials discharged by the two motor units (shown below as tick marks) are recorded with wire electrodes inserted into the muscle. Although the action potentials discharged by the two motor units appear to be independent, there is a slight statistical correlation, and thus a degree of synchrony, that depends on the strength of the common input received by the two motor neurons.

source; or (2) modulation of independent synaptic input by a common oscillator. Both mechanisms provide **common input** that is sufficient to cause motor neurons to discharge action potentials at the same time (Farmer, 1998; Kirkwood, 1979; Kirkwood & Sears, 1991). Furthermore, the common input arises from supraspinal sources (Marsden, Farmer, Halliday, Rosenberg, & Brown, 1999; McAuley & Marsden, 2000; Schmied, Pagni, Sturm, & Vedel, 2000). Consequently, the amount of correlated activity, which is quantified as motor unit synchronization, provides an index of the relative proportion of common input received by motor neurons. Because of this association, motor unit synchronization is one of the few techniques that provides information about functional connections in patient populations (Baker, Davey, Ellaway, & Friedland, 1992; Datta, Farmer, & Stephens, 1991; Farmer et al., 1998; Schmied et al., 1995; Schmied, Pouget, & Vedel, 1999).

To examine the influence of motor unit synchronization on muscle function, computer simulations were used to estimate the EMG and force generated by a pool of motor neurons at several levels of steady state activation (Yao, Fuglevand, & Enoka, 2000). The effect of motor unit synchronization on the simulated EMG and force was examined by adjusting the timing of independently generated motor neuron action potentials to impose a degree of correlation between some of the action potentials discharged by different motor neurons. The simulations were for a hand muscle that comprised 120 motor units. The adjustments were selected to match the degree of synchronization measured experimentally (Kamen & Roy, 2000; Nordstrom et al., 1992; Semmler & Nordstrom, 1998). The output of the simulations comprised the surface-detected EMG and whole-muscle force of the motor units in response to 11 steady state levels of excitation: at 5% of maximum and then at 10% to 100% of maximum in 10% increments. Simply manipulating the timing of the action potentials discharged by the active motor units had a substantial influence on the output of the motor unit pool. Motor unit synchronization markedly increased the amplitude of the EMG, but not the average force, although it did increase the amplitude of the force fluctuations (figure 6.55).

Example 6.10
Motor Unit Synchronization and Strength

When an individual participates in a strength-training program, much of the increase in strength, especially in the first few weeks of training, is generally attributed to adaptations that occur in the nervous system (Semmler & Enoka, 2000). One of the most frequently cited neural factors that contributes to strength gains is motor unit synchronization. This possibility is based on the findings that strength-trained individuals exhibit higher levels of motor unit synchronization in hand muscles (Milner-Brown, Stein, & Yemm, 1973; Semmler & Nordstrom, 1998) and that the amount of synchronization increases when individuals participate in a strength-training program (Milner-Brown, Stein, & Lee, 1975). These associations, however, do not indicate that motor unit synchronization produces an increase in muscle force. On the contrary, computer simulations in which the timing of motor unit action potentials was manipulated indicated that variation in the level of motor unit synchronization does not alter muscle force during isometric contractions (Yao et al., 2000).

Alternatively, motor unit synchronization may not influence muscle force at all but simply be a consequence of the connections between motor neurons. For example, the level of synchronization is less among motor units in hand muscles of individuals who frequently perform movements requiring independent control of the fingers, for instance in the hands of musicians and in the dominant hand of control subjects

(continued)

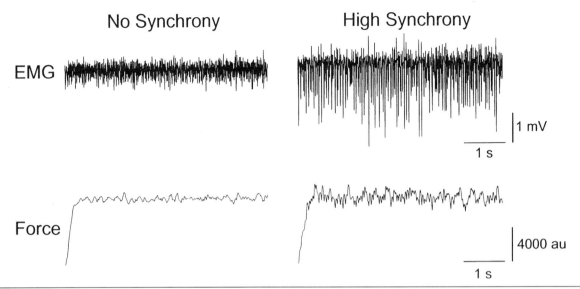

Figure 6.55   Comparison of simulated EMG (upper traces) and force (lower traces) for conditions of no synchrony (left) and high synchrony (right). The motor neuron pool was activated at 50% of maximum for both simulations.

Data from Yao et al., 2000.

(figure 6.56). In contrast, synchronization is greater in hand muscles that are not used to perform such fine movements. Although such findings likely reflect changes in the corticospinal control of muscle strength and independent finger movments (Heusler, Hepp-Reymond, & Dietz, 1998; Semmler & Enoka, 2000), variation in the amount of synchronization may be incidental to the strategies used by the sensorimotor cortex to control movement (Brown, 2000; Feige, Aertsen, & Kristeva-Feige, 2000; Halliday, Conway, Farmer, & Rosenberg, 1998).

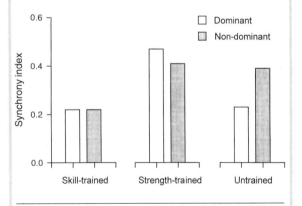

Figure 6.56   The strength of motor unit synchronization among motor units in a hand muscle of the dominant and nondominant arm for musicians (skilled), strength-trained individuals, and control subjects.

Data from Semmler and Nordstrom, 1998.

Influence of Task

The force that a muscle exerts depends largely on the number of motor units that have been recruited and the rate at which they are discharging action potentials. Most of our knowledge about the behavior of motor units, however, has been derived from experiments involving low-force isometric contractions. This limitation became a concern when it was found that the recruitment order of motor units in lateral gastrocnemius changed when subjects performed lengthening contractions compared with shortening contractions (Nardone et al., 1989). Since that time, there has been renewed interest in assessing the relative roles of motor unit recruitment and discharge rate modulation when muscles are used to perform various tasks (Enoka & Fuglevand, 2001).

In general, it appears that the recruitment order of motor units remains the same for isometric and anisometric contractions, including shortening and lengthening contractions (Laidlaw et al., 2000; Søgaard, Christensen, Jensen, Finsen, & Sjøgaard, 1996; Thomas, Ross, & Calancie, 1987). However, the distribution of activity among a group of synergist muscles and the modulation of discharge rate vary across types of contractions. For example, the activity of motor units in biceps brachii differed during stretching of an elastic band compared with releasing of the band (Kossev & Christova, 1998). When subjects used a shortening contraction to stretch the elastic band, the motor neurons initially discharged action potentials at a high rate and then at a lower constant rate to complete the task (figure

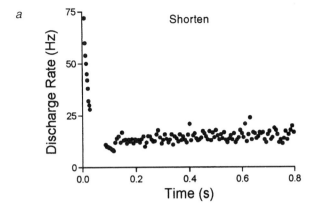

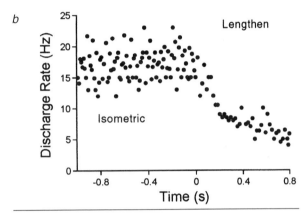

Figure 6.57 The instantaneous discharge rate of a motor unit in biceps brachii during stretching and releasing of an elastic band. (*a*) The muscle performed a shortening contraction to stretch the elastic band; (*b*) the muscle performed an isometric and a lengthening contraction to hold and release the band. Both the shortening and lengthening contractions began at 0 s. Several trials are superimposed in each graph.

Data from Kossev and Christova, 1998.

6.57*a*). However, release of the band with a lengthening contraction was accomplished with a gradual decrease in discharge rate (figure 6.57*b*). Because the whole-muscle EMG also declines during performance of a lengthening contraction, the active muscle fibers must experience greater stress with these types of contractions.

When the elbow flexor muscles were used to perform low-velocity contractions against a load imposed by a motor, the recruitment threshold of motor units in biceps brachii was lower during shortening and lengthening contractions compared with isometric contractions (Tax, Denier van der Gon, Gielen, & van den Tempel, 1989). For brachialis and brachioradialis, however, the recruitment thresholds were greater for the anisometric contractions than for the isometric contractions (Tax, Denier van der Gon, & Erkelens, 1990). Additionally, the initial discharge rate for motor units was greater for shortening

contractions and less for lengthening contractions compared with isometric contractions (Tax et al., 1990).

It appears that although the relative contributions of motor unit recruitment and discharge rate modulation to muscle force can vary across tasks, orderly recruitment of motor units remains consistent.

Feedback From Sensory Receptors

In the operation of the single-joint system, sensory receptors provide information that originates from a wide range of stimuli. This information is essential for normal movement. The process of **sensory perception** involves the detection of a stimulus by a receptor; conversion of the sensation into action potentials that describe the location, intensity, and modality of the stimulus; and interpretation of the signal by the central nervous system. To begin this process, a stimulus elicits a **receptor potential** in the afferent nerve terminals of a sensory receptor. This potential, which involves the flux of ions across the excitable membrane, is conducted along the axon to the trigger zone and will generate an action potential if it exceeds the threshold of the afferent. The number of action potentials that are generated, as well as the rate at which they are generated, usually depends on the magnitude of the receptor potential, which is proportional to the intensity of the stimulus. Although multiple consecutive stimuli increase the net receptor potential, the receptor becomes less sensitive to a constant stimulus (**adaptation**). The action potentials generated in the afferent axon are propagated into the central nervous system where they can evoke reflex responses, initiate automatic responses, and form the basis of perceptions about a movement.

In the absence of feedback from sensory receptors, movement is severely compromised. Studies of these deficits have been performed on experimental subjects by preventing feedback along afferent axons (**deafferentation**) and on patients who have lost the function of some sensory nerves because of a peripheral neuropathy. These studies have shown that it is possible to perform movements after deafferentation but that the movements are uncoordinated and inaccurate, especially in the absence of vision. For example, patients who have lost large-diameter sensory fibers have difficulty controlling multi-joint movements (Cole & Sedgwick, 1992; Sainburg, Ghilardi, Poizner, & Ghez, 1995). Hand movements are especially impaired by deafferentation (Prochazka, 1996).

Three types of afferent events are important in the control of movement: (1) exteroception, (2) proprioception, and (3) the consequences of action. This information is provided by two classes of sensory receptors: exteroceptors and proprioceptors. Exteroceptors, which detect external stimuli that impinge on the system, are distributed throughout the system, including the eyes, ears, and skin. The information provided by exteroceptors tells the system about the state of its external environment, including its location relative to its surroundings. Proprioceptors detect stimuli generated by the system itself (Sanes & Evarts, 1984), such as the mechanical variables associated with the activation of muscle, and are involved in the moment-to-moment control of movement (Gandevia, 1996; Prochazka, 1996). Proprioceptors include muscle spindles, tendon organs, and joint receptors. The information provided by exteroceptors and proprioceptors enables the system to organize a rapid response to a perturbation, to determine limb position, to differentiate between self-generated and imposed movements, and to guide movements.

Reflexes

The ability of sensory receptors to initiate rapid responses to perturbations is based on the existence of short-latency connections between the input (afferent signal) and the output (motor response or efferent output). Such input-output connections are termed reflexes (Pearson & Gordon, 2000b; Prochazka, Clarac, Loeb, Rothwell, & Wolpaw, 2000). The simplest neural circuit underlying a reflex involves a sensory receptor and its afferent innervation, as well as a group of motor units that receive input from the afferent. This circuit, however, can be embedded in the neural elements controlling a single muscle, can be distributed among a group of synergists (muscles that exert a similar mechanical action), can involve an interaction between an agonist-antagonist pair of muscles, or can require the coordination of muscles in contralateral limbs.

Reflexes have evolved as mechanisms that can protect the system against unexpected disturbances. When the system is perturbed, as by an unexpected stretch of a muscle, reflexes can generate a rapid response that will counteract the perturbation. The neural circuits that enable input-output connections to compensate for such disturbances perform a **negative-feedback** function; that is, the motor response tends to counteract the stimulus that initially activated the sensory receptor.

Stretch Reflex

The two main functions of muscle are to generate power and to react to perturbations. Muscle needs to be springlike in order to react appropriately; the stretch reflex helps the muscle achieve this capability. When a muscle experiences a brief, unexpected increase in length

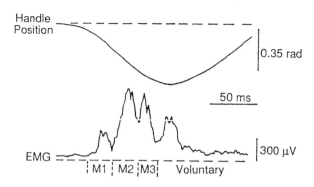

Figure 6.58 A stretch reflex that was elicited by an unexpected stretch (downward) of the extensor muscles that cross the wrist. M1, M2, and M3 correspond to distinct bursts of EMG activity that differ in their latency from the stimulus.

Reprinted from Matthews, 1991.

(a stretch), the response is known as the stretch reflex (Sinkjær, 1997). An example of a stretch reflex is shown in figure 6.58. In this example, a human subject was grasping a handle that was unexpectedly displaced, resulting in a stretch of the extensor muscles that cross the wrist. The stretch reflex is indicated as the EMG elicited in the extensor muscles. As figure 6.58 shows, the increase in EMG (response to stretch) begins soon after the onset of the handle displacement (stimulus). The stretch reflex consists of at least two components (Matthews, 1991). One component is the short-latency response (M1), which is mediated by a neural circuit limited to the spinal cord. The second component (M2) has a long latency and a more complex origin that may involve the motor cortex in the brain. A third component (M3) is occasionally observed.

Figure 6.58 shows that the various components of the stretch reflex all preceded the earliest voluntary EMG, which underscores the ability of reflexes to provide rapid responses to perturbations. Although the latencies for the stretch-reflex components can vary, the M1 component generally has a latency of about 30 ms and the M2 around 50 to 60 ms, and the earliest voluntary activity (EMG) will begin at 170 ms. When neurological disorders alter the stretch reflex (e.g., Parkinson's disease, hemiplegia, Huntington's disease, dystonia), it is usually the M2 component that is affected (Hallett et al., 1994).

The sensory receptor involved in the stretch reflex includes at least the muscle spindle, both its Group Ia and Group II afferents. The neural circuit involving the Group Ia afferent is shown in figure 6.59. Action potentials are generated in the muscle spindle afferents in response to muscle stretch and are propagated centrally to the spinal cord; there they elicit synaptic potentials in the motor neurons innervating the muscle where the spindle is located. In this instance, the motor neurons are described as **homonymous,** because they innervate the same muscle in which the sensory receptor (muscle spindle) is located. If the stretch is an adequate stimulus, a sufficient number of synaptic potentials are generated in the motor neuron to elicit an action potential that is propagated to the muscle and to evoke a contraction. The net effect of this input-output circuit is that the stretch (stimulus) will elicit a contraction (response) that minimizes the stretch; this type of negative-feedback response has also been referred to as a **resistance reflex.** The stretch reflex seems most capable of accommodating small disturbances in muscle length.

The input-output relations of the stretch reflex, however, can be modified (Hammond, Merton, & Sutton, 1956). Because of the possible involvement of the cortex in the stretch reflex (M2 response), the nervous system is able to modulate the response and spread it to muscles that have not been stretched, even antagonist muscles, if the activity is mechanically appropriate (Matthews, 1991). The net effect is that both the short- and long-latency components of the stretch reflex can be altered to meet the demands of the task.

A response related to the stretch reflex is the **tendon-tap reflex** (also known as the *tendon jerk*). It is common in clinical settings to elicit this response by striking the patellar tendon with an appropriate implement and assessing the vigor of the contraction. The tendon-tap reflex

represents a subset of the stretch reflex and involves only activation of the Group Ia afferent and the associated motor neuron output (Matthews, 1990). Because it is based on the monosynaptic connection of the Group Ia afferent, it is a rapid response with a latency of ~30 ms between striking the patellar tendon and recording the EMG in the quadriceps femoris muscles. The size of the tendon-tap reflex is used as an index of the combined effect of muscle spindle responsiveness, motor neuron excitability, and the level of inhibition (presynaptic) acting on the Group Ia afferents in the spinal cord.

Reciprocal-Inhibition Reflex

The central actions of the input from an unexpected stretch of a muscle can be diverse. An example of the divergence of the central actions is the effect that the Group Ia afferent input elicits in the motor neurons that innervate the antagonist muscle. As shown in figure 6.59, the Group Ia afferent branches when it reaches the spinal cord. One of these branches synapses with an interneuron, the **Ia inhibitory interneuron,** which can generate inhibitory postsynaptic potentials in the motor neurons of the antagonist muscle (Day, Marsden, Obeso, & Rothwell, 1984; Katz, Penicaud, & Rossi, 1991). In figure 6.59, the Ia inhibitory interneuron is shown with a filled-in synapse (inhibitory) on the motor neuron. This connection, which serves to lower the excitability of the motor neurons that innervate the antagonist muscle, is known as the **reciprocal-inhibition reflex.** Therefore, activation of muscle spindles in the quadriceps femoris

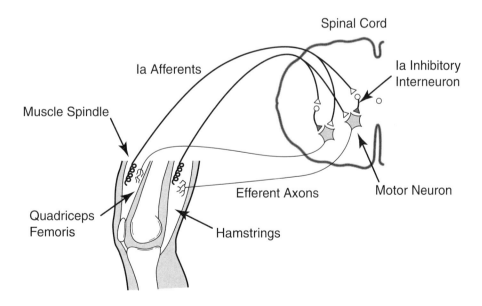

Figure 6.59   Neural circuits underlying the stretch and reciprocal-inhibition reflexes.

muscle (figure 6.59) elicits an excitation of the homonymous (quadriceps femoris) motor neurons but inhibits those of the antagonist (hamstring) muscles. Because the net muscle activity about a joint results from the difference in activity between an agonist-antagonist pair, the reciprocal-inhibition reflex increases the likelihood that the stimulus sensed in one muscle will elicit a meaningful response in that muscle. Reciprocal inhibition is altered in patients with Parkinson's disease and dystonia, and after a stroke (Hallett et al., 1994).

Withdrawal and Crossed-Extensor Reflexes

In addition to localized reflexes involving the muscle spindle and tendon organ, the repertoire of input-output connections includes those triggered by a variety of sensory receptors (e.g., cutaneous receptors, joint receptors, free nerve endings) with diverse responses. The withdrawal and crossed-extensor reflexes are examples of this diversity. When cutaneous receptors (Group III and IV afferents) sense a noxious stimulus, the response is to withdraw the site from the stimulus. If the stimulus is applied to the back of the leg, for example, the response will probably involve withdrawal of the leg away from the stimulus, hence the term **withdrawal reflex.** The response has a latency of about 100 ms. The withdrawal reflex was originally termed the flexion-withdrawal reflex (Sherrington, 1910), but has since been shown to involve other muscles besides flexors (Schouenborg, Weng, & Holmberg, 1994). The withdrawal reflex can be variable because it depends on which afferents are activated by the stimulus and is transmitted over polysynaptic pathways, which means that the input signal can be modified along its path (figure 6.60). The neural organi-

zation of the withdrawal reflex is rather focused; a noxious stimulus applied to different cutaneous regions elicits activation of different muscles with varying latencies, intensities, and durations (Andersen, Sonnenborg, & Arendt-Nielsen, 1999; Schouenborg et al., 1994).

The cutaneous afferents involved in the withdrawal reflex branch when entering the spinal cord and connect to many different neurons. The target neurons include the motor neurons that innervate the extensor muscles in the contralateral limb (figure 6.60) so that the withdrawal reflex is often accompanied by a **crossed-extensor reflex.** This response involves excitation of the motor neurons innervating extensor muscles and inhibition in the motor neurons of the flexor muscles in the contralateral limb. Thus, if one leg is withdrawn from a stimulus, the contralateral limb is extended to provide postural support.

Hoffmann Reflex

In contrast to the stretch, reciprocal-inhibition, and crossed-extensor reflexes, all of which can occur under normal movement conditions, the **Hoffmann reflex,** or H reflex, is an artificially elicited response. The H reflex is used to test the efficacy of transmission of an applied stimulus as it passes from the afferent fibers, through the motor neuron pool, to the efferent fibers. The H reflex is sometimes used as an approximate measure of the excitability of the motor neuron pool (Hallett et al., 1994), although it largely involves activation of low-threshold motor units (Buchthal & Schmalbruch, 1970; Trimble & Enoka, 1991). It is elicited by applying a single electrical shock (stimulus) to a peripheral nerve. Because the stimulus is a single shock, the response is a twitch in the muscle innervated by the stimulated nerve; the response can be measured as the EMG or force associated with the twitch. The H reflex is most commonly examined in soleus, but it can be elicited in such other muscles as quadriceps femoris, tibialis anterior, and muscles of the hand, foot, arm and forearm. For example, eliciting an H reflex in quadriceps femoris (figure 6.61) involves laying a subject in a supine position and placing the stimulating electrode over the femoral nerve just below the inguinal ligament. Because the H reflex relies on the selective activation of the Group Ia afferents, the correct positioning of the electrodes with respect to the nerve is critical and can be difficult to achieve in some subjects; this is especially true for quadriceps femoris.

The neural circuit for the H reflex is shown in figure 6.62. It involves the activation of the Group Ia afferents and the subsequent generation of action potentials in the motor neurons innervating the muscle. This is a population response that involves many Group Ia afferents as well as a number of motor units. The activation of the Group Ia afferents entails beginning with a low-intensity stimulus and slowly increasing it until action potentials are generated in the largest-diameter axons; in most

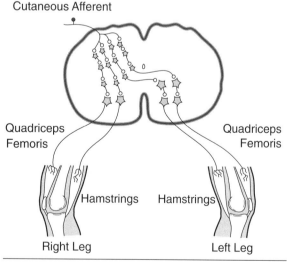

Figure 6.60 Neural circuit for the withdrawal and crossed-extensor reflexes.

Adapted from Burke and Tsairis, 1973.

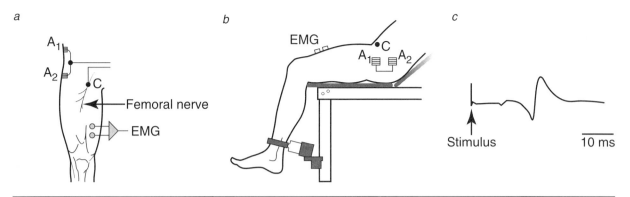

Figure 6.61 An H reflex elicited in quadriceps femoris: *(a)* location of the stimulating electrodes (C, cathode; A$_1$ and A$_2$, two anodes that are connected together); *(b)* position of the subject; *(c)* H reflex recorded as an EMG over vastus medialis.

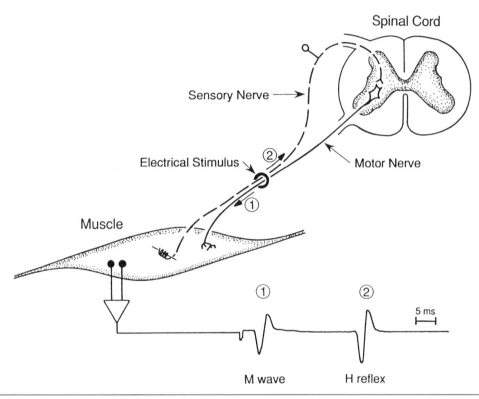

Figure 6.62 Circuit diagram for the H reflex. The electrical stimulus is applied over the peripheral nerve, and the response is measured in the muscle innervated by the nerve.

human subjects these are the Group Ia afferents and probably some Group Ib afferents. With activation of the Group Ia afferents, action potentials are propagated centrally to the spinal cord (2 in figure 6.62), where they elicit postsynaptic potentials in the motor neurons. The likelihood that these synaptic potentials will generate action potentials depends on the size of the synaptic potentials and the level of the membrane potential. The closer the membrane potential is to threshold for action potential generation, the more likely the stimulus (syn-

aptic potentials) is to elicit an action potential. If the membrane potential of more motor neurons is closer to threshold, then the stimulus will generate action potentials in more motor neurons, and the response (EMG and force) will be larger. For this reason, *the H reflex is used as an approximate test of the level of excitability of the motor neuron pool.*

Because the H reflex is influenced by the level of excitability in the motor neuron pool, even distant stimuli (e.g., loud and unexpected sounds) or remote muscle activity is sufficient to influence the response. For example, the H reflex elicited in the soleus muscle of a subject increases in amplitude if the subject voluntarily activates other muscles, such as those involved in clenching the teeth. The use of remote muscle activity to increase the excitability of a motor neuron pool is referred to as the **Jendrassik maneuver** (Pereon, Genet, & Guiheneuc, 1995). This effect has clinical applications. For example, a patient with weak leg muscles can be enabled to rise from a chair when a therapist provides resistance for the voluntary activation of arm and neck muscles by the patient, which can elicit a Jendrassik effect in the leg muscles.

Not only does the H reflex vary on a moment-to-moment basis because of such effects as the Jendrassik maneuver; it also varies as a result of chronic activity patterns (Mynark & Koceja, 1997; Nielsen, Crone, & Hultborn, 1993). For example, the H reflex elicited during a maximum voluntary contraction increased after a strength-training program (Sale, MacDougall, Upton, & McComas, 1983). This effect was interpreted as reflex potentiation due to a training-induced increase in motor neuron excitability. Similarly, Koceja and Raglin (1992) reported a decrease in the amplitude of the H reflex in a group of swimmers during an overtraining phase of their program, but a return to normal during the tapering phase.

When evoking the H reflex, the electrical stimulus is set at a low intensity that appears to involve the selective activation of slow-contracting motor units (Trimble & Enoka, 1991). Consequently, activity-induced changes in H-reflex amplitude probably reflect alterations in the excitability of low-threshold motor units. When the intensity of the electrical stimulus is gradually increased, the stimulus begins to generate action potentials in axons of smaller diameter. After the Group Ia afferents, the class of axons with the next-largest axon diameter is the alpha axons, which belong to the motor neurons. When action potentials are generated in the alpha axons, the response is a short-latency (5 ms) event, called the **M wave** (1 in figure 6.62). The M wave is elicited experimentally to probe the integrity of the circuit between the site of the stimulus (muscle nerve) and the site of recording (usually the muscle EMG); that is, the M wave tests the integrity of neuromuscular propagation (Bigland-Ritchie, Kukulka, Lippold, & Woods, 1982; Enoka & Stuart, 1992). When the electrical stimulus is maximal, this results in the synchronous activation of all the muscle fibers and represents the summed response of all their action potentials. But when measured with a conventional electrode arrangement (bipolar, 8-mm diameter, 1.5-cm interelectrode distance), the M-wave record does not represent the action potentials in the entire muscle but rather only those from muscle fibers that are in close proximity

to the electrodes (probably about 1-2 cm) (Fuglevand et al., 1992). This is the reason that M-wave amplitude is similar for small and large muscles (Hicks, Cupido, Martin, & Dent, 1992). Interestingly, M-wave amplitude declines with age, probably due to a reduction in the excitability of muscle fibers (Hicks et al., 1992).

Tonic Vibration Reflex

Like the H reflex, the tonic vibration reflex is an artificially elicited response that has both clinical and experimental uses (Lance, Burke, & Andrews, 1973). The neural circuit for this reflex is the same as that for the tendon-tap reflex. It involves the muscle spindle and the homonymous motor units activated by excitation of the muscle spindles. However, it appears that vibration activates both mono- and polysynaptic pathways. The muscle spindle is extremely sensitive to small-amplitude vibration that has a frequency of 50 to 150 Hz. Application of vibration to a muscle with a standard clinical vibrator provides an adequate stimulus to excite many muscle spindles and activate enough motor units to cause a muscle contraction, which results in an increase in the force and EMG during a submaximal contraction (figure 6.63). Furthermore, the vibration results in a decrease in the excitability of the motor neurons innervating the antagonist muscle through the reciprocal-inhibition circuit. However, the effect of vibration is complex (Kossev, Siggelkow, Schubert, Wohlfarth, & Dengler, 1999). Although vibration produces a reflex response (EMG and force), both the tendon-tap and H reflexes are depressed during vibration, and prolonged vibration can reduce maximum voluntary contraction force (Kouzaki, Shinohara, & Fukunaga, 2000).

Example 6.11

Application of Vibration in Rehabilitation

The tonic vibration reflex has been used in the rehabilitation of stroke (cerebral vascular accident) patients, especially for the restoration of motor function in the upper extremity (Bishop, 1974, 1975a, 1975b). The typical approach is to apply vibration to the synergy (extensor or flexor muscles) that is not dominant following the incident. For example, generally the flexor synergy (scapular retraction and elevation, shoulder abduction and external rotation, elbow flexion and supination, and wrist and finger flexion) predominates, and one rehabilitation strategy is to elicit brief bursts of activity in the antagonist muscles (extensor strategy) with the use of vibration. The vibration enables the therapist to provide a powerful

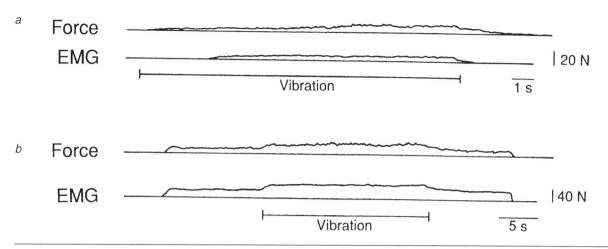

Figure 6.63 The tendon vibration reflex. *(a)* An active vibrator is placed over the tendon of biceps brachii and elicits an EMG in the muscle and a force that is exerted at the wrist. *(b)* The force and EMG associated with a submaximal contraction of biceps brachii can be enhanced by the use of a vibrator. Vibration was applied for the duration of the time indicated by the horizontal lines.

afferent input to the spinal cord and to manipulate the tonic activity between an agonist-antagonist set. With an appropriate selection of the stimulation site, it is possible to decrease the excitability of hyperactive motor neurons in one muscle and to increase the excitability of the hypoactive motor neurons in the antagonist. The therapeutic effect of vibration is enhanced by placing the muscles to be vibrated in lengthened positions and by positioning the patient appropriately; a supine position facilitates the effect of vibration on the extensor synergy, whereas a prone position is better for the flexor synergy. Treatment can be further enhanced through application of vibration to the involved muscles during the performance of functional activities. For example, a patient presenting with a flexor-synergy pattern in the upper extremity can have the vibration applied to the elbow extensor muscles while performing a reaching movement. Similarly, vibration of an antagonist muscle can be used to reduce the spasticity in an agonist muscle. The effect of vibration is to normalize movement in the clinic, but it may evoke only a transient adaptation that disappears when the patient leaves the clinic.

Because the Group Ia afferent also projects to supraspinal centers, the signals sensed by muscle spindles can be perceived. Vibration disrupts the information conveyed by the muscle spindle about muscle length and can, therefore, produce illusions about joint position (Gandevia, 1996). When muscle is vibrated, it is perceived to be at a longer length. For example, when the elbow flexor

muscles are vibrated at 100 Hz, elbow joint angle is perceived to be about 10° more extended than it actually is. Similarly, if the elbow flexor muscles are vibrated while a finger touches the nose, the nose appears to get longer. However, these illusions are not present when vibration is superimposed on a voluntary contraction. Such findings have indicated the important role played by muscle spindles in our sense of body position.

Example 6.12
Vibration Can Enhance Performance

While most applications of vibration have involved high frequencies and small amplitudes, some investigators have examined the effects of low-frequency (30-45 Hz), large-amplitude (3-6 mm) vibration on performance (Bosco, Cardinale, & Tsarpela, 1999; Issurin & Tenenbaum, 1999; Issurin, Liebermann, & Tenenbaum, 1994). A single session of this intervention has been found to produce acute increases in the strength and power production capabilities of elite and amateur athletes. In a typical vibration treatment, the subjects gripped the vibrator (2.8 kg) while standing with the elbow joint at an angle of 2.5 rad (Bosco et al., 1999). The arm was then vibrated (30 Hz, 6 mm) for five 60-s periods, with a 60-s rest between each period. The effect of the vibration on performance was measured as the average power produced by the elbow flexor muscles when rapidly lifting a load that

(continued)

was 5% of body mass. After vibration, the average power produced by the elite athletes increased by 13%, from 60 to 68 W. Furthermore, after a three-week training program the one repetition-maximum load increased by 50% for subjects who received the vibration compared with a 16% increase in subjects who performed conventional training (Issurin et al., 1994). In addition, the vibration produced a pronounced increase in flexibility.

Reflexes and Movement

The study of reflexes has, at least since the time of Sherrington (1857–1952), provided a dominant focus in studies on the neural control of movement. In this scheme, the motor neuron is represented as the central element to which afferent and supraspinal input is directed. The motor neuron is still regarded as the **final common pathway**—the route through which the commands are issued to muscle; but evidence suggests that the motor neuron is not the major integrating element for the control of movement. It appears that the *interneuron,* rather than the motor neuron, serves as the focal point of this integration (Baldissera, Hultborn, & Illert, 1981; Pearson, 1993; Windhorst, 1988). Most of the neural traffic from afferent and supraspinal sources converges on a number of different interneurons rather than going directly to the motor neurons. As a consequence of this pre-motor neuron convergence, the input (e.g., Group Ia input caused by the muscle stretch) can be altered before it is transmitted to the motor neurons. One effect of this arrangement is that input-output relations (e.g., reflexes) become less stereotyped and can vary depending on the nature of the other input converging on the interneurons (Fournier & Pierrot-Deseilligny, 1989). The main advantage of this scheme is that it allows greater flexibility in terms of the output that is evoked by a specific input.

An example of the flexibility associated with interneuronal convergence is the variation in a reflex that can occur with movement (Brooke et al., 1997; De Serres, Yang, & Patrick, 1995; Nashner, 1982; Rossignol, Julien, Gauthier, & Lund, 1981; Stein & Capaday, 1988; Yang & Stein, 1990), such as the withdrawal reflex during walking (Crenna & Frigo, 1984). A noxious stimulus applied to the skin over the calf muscles elicits a withdrawal reflex in the thigh muscles of the same leg (figure 6.64). The response, which is intended to remove the limb from the painful stimulus, can be measured as an EMG in the thigh muscles (vastus lateralis and biceps femoris). When a subject is walking, however, these same muscles are also needed to support the body in selected phases of the stride cycle. Consequently, at these times it would be inappropriate to withdraw the limb in response

to a noxious stimulus. The response to the painful stimulus must be modulated by the nervous system so that support is provided when necessary and the limb is withdrawn when it is mechanically possible. This modulation is shown in figure 6.64 for the biceps femoris muscle. The response (magnitude of the EMG) consists of short- and long-latency components. The short-latency component (57 ms) was greatest during the transition from stance to swing, whereas the long-latency component (132 ms) was greatest at the end of the swing phase. This same type of modulation has also been reported for the H reflex during walking (Crenna & Frigo, 1987; Sinkjær, 1997; Stein & Capaday, 1988) and running (Simonsen & Dyhre-Poulsen, 1999).

On the basis of such observations, it is apparent that reflexes are not fixed responses to a given stimuli; rather the input-output relation can vary. This means that the response, despite a constant stimulus, depends on the

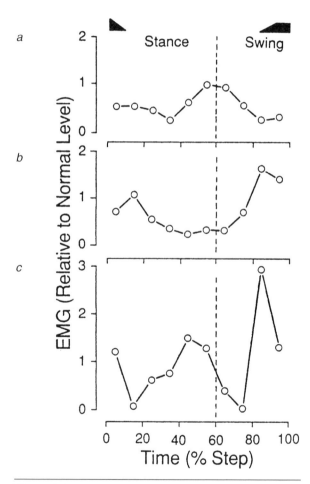

Figure 6.64 The EMG responses to a noxious stimulus are plotted relative to the normal level of EMG (1 = normal) during a walking step: *(a)* the short-latency response, *(b)* the long-latency response, *(c)* the combined response.

Reprinted from Crenna and Frigo, 1984.

subject's history of activity (e.g., stationary vs. active, swing vs. support, sedentary vs. active). For example, the spinal part of the stretch reflex (M1) is weak in most muscles during active movements, especially in comparison with the long-latency reflex (Bennett, De Serres, & Stein, 1996; Crago, Houk, & Hasan, 1976; Houk & Rymer, 1981; Marsden, Merton, & Morton, 1976; Melvill-Jones & Watt, 1971; Vallbo & Wessberg, 1993). In clinical and laboratory testing, therefore, it is necessary that the patient or subject assume a standardized position (e.g., sitting, lying) when the reflex is elicited.

Although there are many neural mechanisms that can modify a reflex, we know the most about two of these: recurrent inhibition and presynaptic inhibition. *Recurrent inhibition* is a local feedback circuit that can modify reflex responses through an interneuron called the **Renshaw cell** (Windhorst, 1988). The Renshaw cell can be activated by supraspinal input, by Group III and IV muscle afferents, and by a collateral branch of the alpha motor neuron axon (R in figure 6.65). In turn, the Renshaw cell generates an inhibitory postsynaptic potential in the same motor neuron and other interneurons.

The circuit involving the axon collateral, Renshaw cell, and motor neuron is referred to as **recurrent inhibition** (figures 6.48 and 6.65) (Windhorst, 1996). Recurrent inhibition from a given motor neuron pool is distributed to many other motor neuron pools but is weak or absent among pools innervating distal muscles (e.g., hand, foot) (Katz, Mazzocchio, Penicaud, & Rossi, 1993). Activation of recurrent inhibition results in, among other effects, a decrease in the excitability of motor neurons. Because large motor neurons give off more collateral branches to Renshaw cells but receive fewer synapses from Renshaw cells (figure 6.48), recurrent inhibition has a greater effect on the excitability of the smaller motor neurons. Furthermore, because the recurrent inhibition in a motor neuron pool increases during weak contractions but decreases during strong contractions (Fournier & Pierrot-Deseilligny, 1989; Nielsen & Pierrot-Deseilligny, 1996), recurrent inhibition is high when the smaller motor neurons are active and diminishes as larger motor neurons are recruited. Recurrent inhibition may also increase during fatiguing contractions (Löscher, Cresswell, & Thorstensson, 1996b).

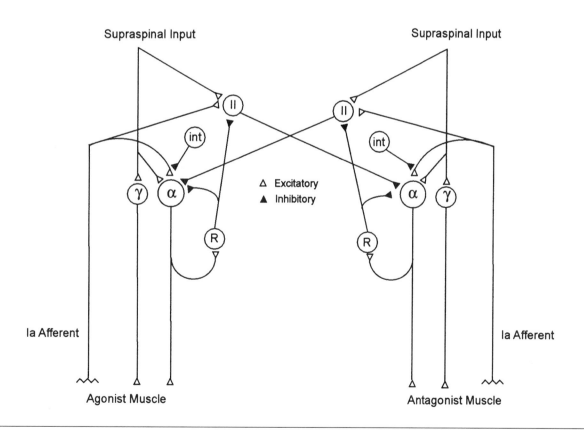

Figure 6.65 A simplified circuit diagram showing presynaptic inhibition of a Group Ia afferent by an interneuron (int), and recurrent inhibition through the Renshaw cell (R) and onto the alpha motor neuron (α) and the Ia inhibitory interneuron (II). The gamma motor neuron (γ) innervates the muscle spindle.

In addition to its effects on motor neurons, recurrent inhibition also generates inhibitory postsynaptic potentials in gamma motor neurons and in the Ia inhibitory interneuron (Hultborn, Lindström, & Wigström, 1979). The connection to the gamma motor neuron means that recurrent inhibition can modulate the excitability of the muscle spindle and therefore influence the input-output relation for the stretch reflex. The connection to the Ia inhibitory interneuron means that recurrent inhibition can inhibit (decrease the excitability of) the interneuron that mediates the reciprocal-inhibition reflex; this means that recurrent inhibition is able to inhibit the inhibition, which is disinhibition (figure 6.65). Recurrent inhibition, therefore, represents a significant element in the adaptability of reflexes.

Another way to modify reflexes is by a mechanism known as **presynaptic inhibition.** This involves modulation of an incoming afferent signal before it reaches the motor neuron. This interaction involves an interneuron that synapses on the afferent axon close to where it contacts the motor neuron and generates an inhibitory synaptic potential in the axon; thus, the interneuron modifies the afferent action potential before (presynaptic) it contacts the motor neuron (figure 6.65). Presynaptic inhibition, which reduces the action potential and the subsequent amount of neurotransmitter that is released at the afferent-motor neuron synapse, modifies the input-output relation so that for the same stimulus (muscle stretch) the response can vary (Fournier & Pierrot-Deseilligny, 1989). Much has been learned about this mechanism in studies of the adaptability of the stretch reflex (Matthews, 1990, 1991). This adaptability is achieved by imposing an inhibitory effect on the action potentials transmitted by the Group I and II afferents. Presynaptic inhibition contributes significantly to the modulation of reflexes during movement (Stein, 1995).

Acute and Chronic Adaptations

Not only can reflexes be modulated in terms of the moment-to-moment control of movement; the input-output relation can also be modified by the performance of different types of physical activity (Bawa & Sinkjær, 1999). For example, 20 min of running on a treadmill can reduce the amplitude of the H reflex in the triceps surae muscles (Bulbulian & Bowles, 1992). And the reduction is greater during downhill running (–10% grade) compared with level running; downhill running places a greater reliance on the eccentric contractions of leg muscles and produces delayed-onset muscle soreness.

A convincing example of **plasticity** resulting from long-term activity is the change that occurs in the stretch reflex and the H reflex with appropriate training (Evatt, Wolf, & Segal, 1989; Wolpaw & Carp, 1990; Wolpaw, Herchenroder, & Carp, 1993). In an extensive set of experiments, Wolpaw, Carp, and colleagues have shown that it is possible to train (for 80 days) a nonhuman primate to increase or decrease the reflex response (stretch or H) to a constant stimulus. To a given stretch (unexpected change in muscle length), the reflex EMG can be trained to increase or to decrease without changes in the background EMG before the stretch is applied. Furthermore, when the training is performed with one limb, the changes in the reflex response are present in the contralateral untrained limb (Wolf, Segal, Heter, & Catlin, 1995). These changes are probably due to adaptations that occur in those elements of the neural circuit that are accessible by supraspinal input. For the H and stretch reflexes, this includes the Group Ia synapse on the motor neuron and the motor neuron itself. Because the Group Ia synapse can be inhibited by presynaptic inputs from several supraspinal sites, this seems to be the most likely candidate for the long-term adaptation of the stretch and H reflexes (Wolpaw & Carp, 1990).

Automatic Responses

Feedback from sensory receptors is also important for a class of behaviors known as automatic responses. These behaviors are produced by neural circuits that are more complex than those associated with reflexes (Prochazka et al., 2000). Like reflexes, automatic responses are evoked by sensory feedback and occur at a short latency after the sensory stimulus is received by the central nervous system. These behaviors range from fight-or-flight responses associated with the preservation of life through to postural adjustments that precede the performance of a movement (Melvill Jones, 2000). Because of our interest in the control of movement, we will focus on the control of posture as an example of automatic responses.

Postural activity comprises muscle contractions that place the body in the necessary location from which a movement is performed. The contractions are based on feedback from somatosensory, vestibular, and visual sensors and can involve responses to perturbations as well as activity that precedes a movement (Dietz, 1992). In general, these automatic responses serve postural-orientation and postural-equilibrium functions (Horak & Macpherson, 1996). **Postural orientation** entails positioning the body relative to its surroundings, such as the line of gravity, and locating the body segments relative to one another. To understand the neural mechanisms involved in the control of postural orientation, studies have attempted to identify the body segment that remains in a relatively fixed location during a movement. For many tasks, such as those including movement of the arms and legs, it appears that muscles are activated automatically to maintain the trunk in a vertical orientation. In other tasks, however, such as those involving substantial whole-body movement, postural-orientation activity may be focused more on maintaining the position of the head. Because the magnitude and sequence of muscle contractions participating in these automatic responses can vary, the focal point chosen for postural orientation appears to vary across individuals and movements. The postural expectations related to a movement cause an individual to prepare a set of muscles to provide the automatic response; this is known as the **postural set.**

In addition to maintaining the orientation of the body, postural activity is also concerned with maintaining the orientation of body segments both within and between limbs (Hoy, Zernicke, & Smith, 1985; Zernicke & Smith, 1996). Consider, for example, the movement shown in figure 6.66a. The subject is asked to shake the forearm rapidly in a forward-backward motion while keeping the upper arm horizontal. This movement is accomplished by alternately activating the flexor and extensor muscles that cross the elbow joint. The movement also requires postural activation of shoulder muscles to stabilize the upper arm and to minimize the inertial effects of the forearm motion on other body segments. Furthermore, the muscles that cross the wrist need to be activated to control the motion of the hand, which could vary from an uncontrolled flail, to a slow wave, to no relative motion between the hand and the forearm.

The muscle contractions that contribute to **postural equilibrium** attempt to maintain the balance of the individual. These responses involve controlling the small displacements that occur during a steady posture, reacting to perturbations that disturb the position of the body, and anticipating a movement-related disturbance of balance. In an upright posture, the base of support is determined by the position of the feet and includes the area underneath and between the feet. A person in an upright posture is in *equilibrium* as long as the line of action of the weight vector remains within the boundaries of the base of support, and the person is *stable* as long as the musculoskeletal system can accommodate perturbations and return to an equilibrium position. When we stand in an upright posture, our bodies sway back and forth but we do not fall because of the automatic postural activity that maintains equilibrium.

A method commonly used to study the automatic reactions to postural disturbances is to have subjects or patients stand on a platform that can be moved suddenly in several different directions (Nashner, 1971, 1972). With the use of this protocol, investigators have identified several response strategies that depend on the type of perturbation experienced by the individual. When the support surface is moved suddenly, muscle contractions are evoked at a latency of 70 to 100 ms after the onset of the disturbance. These automatic responses can be modified by the direction and velocity of the disturbance, the initial position of the subject, the prior experience and expectations of the subject, and the task being performed by the subject (Horak & Macpherson, 1996). Two examples underscore the specificity of these automatic responses. When the support surface was perturbed so that the ankle was dorsiflexed and the calf muscles were stretched, the intensity of the automatic responses depended on whether the muscle activity was needed to maintain balance or not. For example, when the platform was translated backward, the EMG for the posterior leg muscles (soleus, hamstrings, and gastrocnemius) was larger than for the toes-up rotation (figure 6.67a). Similarly, the muscles that participate in the postural adjustment depend on the body segments that contact the surroundings; that is, the postural set depends on the initial conditions. When a subject was in an upright position and only the feet contacted the surroundings, the response to a perturbation was initiated in the leg muscles (figure 6.68). However, when the hands were used to provide support with the surroundings, the response to a perturbation was initiated in the arm muscles.

Not only are the automatic responses associated with postural equilibrium specific for each condition; they are also readily adaptable to meet changing needs. This property was demonstrated in a comparison of the EMG response of the calf muscles to perturbations involving backward translation and toes-up rotation of the support surface. In this experiment, the support platform was either translated backward or was rotated toes-up (figure 6.67). A common effect of both perturbations was to stretch the calf muscles. However, subjects knew immediately that it was necessary to activate the gastrocnemius muscle to

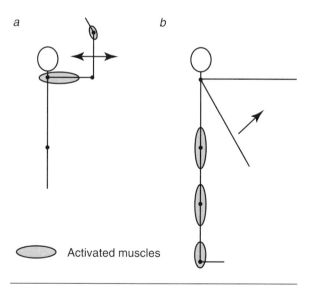

Activated muscles

Figure 6.66 Distribution of postural activity with rapid movements. *(a)* Rapid alternating flexion-extension at the elbow joint requires postural activation of the shoulder and wrist muscles to control the inertial effect due to forearm motion. *(b)* Rapid elevation of the arm to an extended horizontal position is preceded by postural activity in the legs.

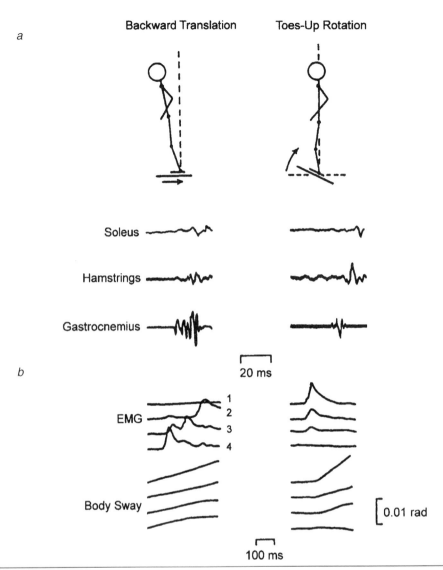

Figure 6.67   Postural responses of a subject when the support surface was translated backward (left column) or rotated in the toes-up direction (right column). *(a)* Although both perturbations induce dorsiflexion at the ankle, the intensity of muscle activation in the posterior leg muscles varied depending on their role in maintaining balance. *(b)* The EMG was necessary to maintain balance when the platfrom was translated backward, but not when the toes were rotated up. For both the EMG and body sway traces, Trial 1 is the top line and Trial 4 the bottom line.

Adapted from Nashner, 1982.

maintain stability in the translation condition and to activate tibialis anterior for the rotation condition (Gollhofer, Horstmann, Berger, & Dietz, 1989; Hansen, Woollacott, & Debu, 1988). The ability to switch between these two activation strategies may depend on our ability to sense the location of the total body weight vector relative to the base of support (Dietz, 1997).

The automatic responses evoked by the disturbance of one limb often occur in both limbs. For example, displacement perturbations of a single leg during stance, balancing, or gait typically evoke a bilateral postural response of similar latency in both legs (Dietz, 1992). The

bilateral response probably provides a more stable base from which to compensate for the perturbation. Similarly, when a hand holding a support object is perturbed, this can elicit an automatic postural response, such as an increased handgrip force, in the contralateral arm and hand (Marsden, Merton, & Morton, 1983). Such responses are automatic and are superimposed on other movements being performed by the nonperturbed limb. The appearance of automatic postural adjustments in muscles that are not perturbed suggests that these responses represent a coordinated and predetermined motor pattern.

Standing   Holding Handle

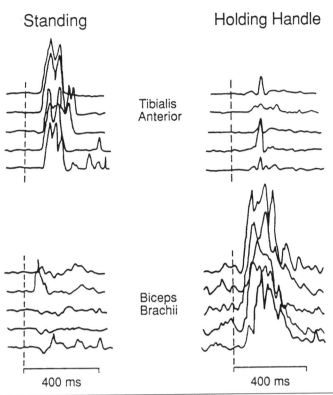

Tibialis
Anterior

Biceps
Brachii

400 ms   400 ms

Figure 6.68 Electromyogram response to a postural disturbance. The vertical line indicates the moment of forward translation of the support surface for the five trials in each set. The responses of tibialis anterior were greatest for the standing condition, whereas the biceps brachii activity was greatest when the subject held a handle.

Adapted from Cordo and Nashner, 1982.

The third group of automatic responses involved in the maintenance of postural equilibrium is known as **anticipatory postural adjustments.** Suppose an individual standing upright is asked to raise an arm as rapidly as possible to a horizontal position (figure 6.66b). This is a reaction-time task in which the movement is done as quickly as possible after a "go" signal. The anterior deltoid muscle is the prime mover for the task. The briefest reaction time between a "go" signal and the onset of muscle activity is about 120 ms. In this task, however, the hamstring muscles on the same side of the body are activated about 50 ms before the activation of the prime mover (Belen'kii, Gurfinkel, & Pal'tsev, 1967). The activation of the leg muscles serves at least two purposes: it serves as an anticipatory stabilization against the inertial effects of the subsequent arm movement, and it provides a rigid connection between the limb motion and the associated ground reaction force. By increasing the rigidity of the body segments not involved in the movement, the anticipatory adjustments can probably facilitate the subsequent movement, even to the extent of transferring energy through intersegmental dynamics. The presence of anticipatory adjustments depends on the task, the support provided by the surroundings, and the

health of the subject (Aruin, Forrest, & Latash, 1998; Aruin, Ota, & Latash, 2001; De Wolf, Slijper, & Latash, 1998). For example, patients with Parkinson's disease have difficulty combining anticipatory postural adjustment with intended (voluntary) movements (Rogers, 1991).

Automatic responses, such as those that help to establish postural orientation and maintain postural equilibrium, can be evoked by sensory feedback from the somatosensory system (muscle, joint, and cutaneous receptors), the vestibular system (semicircular canals and macular otoliths), and the visual system. The relative role of these different input systems varies across tasks and conditions, which partially accounts for the variability in the output (automatic) responses. While reflexes can be described as input-output relations produced by the spinal cord, automatic responses entail significant supraspinal modulation of the output evoked by a given input. For example, the coordination of postural adjustments involves at least the basal ganglia and cerebellum, and perhaps the cerebral cortex (Horak & Macpherson, 1996). This modulation can even include the suppression of automatic responses. The neural control of automatic responses is more complex than that of reflexes.

Example 6.13
Sensory Feedback and Hand Movements

In the spectrum of movement capabilities, a qualitatively different type of movement involves the exploration of our environment. This distinction is typified by the functions performed by the hands as compared with those of the arms and legs. The human hand and brain are close partners in our ability to explore the physical world and to reshape it. Both of these functions depend on accurate descriptions of mechanical events when objects come into close contact with the hand. Much of this information is provided by the mechanoreceptive afferents that innervate the hairless skin of the hand. These sensory receptors participate in a behavior that we call **active touch** (Johansson 1996, 1998; Phillips, 1986; Wing, Haggard, & Flanagan, 1996).

The role of cutaneous mechanoreceptors in the control of motor output has been explored in the study of grip-force responses to unexpected changes in load (Flanagan, Burstedt, & Johansson, 1999; Johansson, Riso, Häger, & Bäckström, 1992; Johansson, Häger, & Riso, 1992; Johansson, Häger, & Bäckström, 1992). When an object is squeezed between the index finger and the thumb in a pinch grip, an unexpected change in the pulling load elicits an *automatic adjustment* in the grip force after a brief delay. The latency of the grip-force response decreases (174 to 80 ms) as the rate of change in pulling load increases. The automatic response consists of two parts: the initial phase comprises a bell-shaped rate of change in force, and the second phase includes a slow increase in the rate of change in force (figure 6.69). Similar biphasic responses have been reported for isometric tasks, compensation for body sway elicited by translation of the support surface, and eye movements during smooth pursuit. The initial phase is a standard element that has a constant duration but an amplitude that varies with the rate of change in the pulling load. The second phase appears for longer-duration increases in grip force and is abolished if the index finger and thumb are anesthetized. This suggests that the second phase is *dependent on afferent feedback from mechanoreceptors in the hand.*

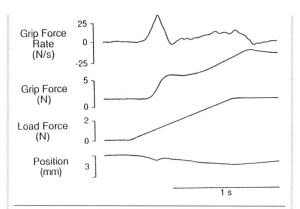

Figure 6.69   Automatic grip-force response to an unexpected change in the load force. A motor applied the load force, and the subject was required to prevent movement (or change in position). The rate of change in grip force (top trace) consists of two phases, an initial bell-shaped response followed by a more gradual change.

Data from Johansson, Riso, Häger, and Bäckström, 1992.

Kinesthesia

The sensory receptors that we discussed in chapter 5 not only contribute to reflexes and automatic responses but also produce perceptions about movement (Proske, Wise, & Gregroy, 2000). These sensations are referred to as kinesthesia or proprioception (Gandevia, 1996). Kinesthetic sensations, which are derived from the combination of input from different types of afferent fibers (e.g., skin, muscles and tendons, joint capsules, ligaments) and from centrally generated motor commands, include those concerning position and movement, effort and heaviness, and the perceived timing of movements. These sensations are necessary to match the motor commands sent to the single-joint system to the variable conditions that it encounters.

Position and Movement

Joint receptors were initially thought to provide the primary signal for the determination of joint position and movement. Now, however, input from the muscle spindle is considered to be more important (Gandevia, McCloskey, & Burke, 1992; Matthews, 1987; McCloskey, 1987), except in the hand, where joint, cutaneous, and muscle afferents provide critical kinesthetic information. Experiments have shown that humans can detect movements as slow as 2°/min at the knee, ankle, and finger joints. Information on joint position and movement is probably combined with knowledge of limb lengths to develop a perceptual map of the body segments, which is necessary for achieving absolute positions in three-dimensional space (Gandevia, 1996).

The use of muscle spindle input to determine joint position and movement is complicated by the existence of the fusimotor system and the possibility of activating the muscle spindle in the absence of a change in position. The central nervous system avoids this problem by subtracting the fusimotor activity from the muscle spindle signal. It accomplishes this by supplying sensory centers with information about the outgoing motor commands; this information is referred to as a **corollary discharge.** By this mechanism, the motor centers can tell the sensory centers about the timing and magnitude of fusimotor activity and thereby enable the system to determine joint position and movement from the muscle spindle feedback.

Effort and Heaviness

When a muscle is activated and used to lift a load, the central nervous system receives visual, cutaneous, muscle-receptor, and joint-receptor feedback that can be used to judge the weight of the load. This judgment is based on an estimate of the force that must be exerted to support the load. However, a number of experiments have demonstrated that the perception is influenced by central signals, perhaps from the sensorimotor cortex (Gandevia, 1996). In these experiments, conditions were manipulated so that even though the muscle force remained constant, the sense of effort increased. The interventions included weakening the muscle, reducing the excitability of the motor neurons, or fatiguing the muscle. To exert the same muscle force, therefore, the central drive to the spinal centers must have increased, and this was sensed as an increase in the effort associated with the task. Nonetheless, information on the force exerted by a muscle (e.g., feedback from tendon organs) is necessary, when combined with corollary discharges, to estimate the heaviness of an object.

Timing of Movements

Human subjects are able to identify two moments in time related to the onset of movement: the dispatch of a command to move, and the beginning of the actual movement. The perception that a command to move has been generated occurs before the onset of the EMG. This suggests that it is probably derived from the centrally generated command to move. In contrast, the perception that a movement has begun occurs after the beginning of EMG activity and is probably based on proprioceptive signals.

Role in Movement

In the performance of a movement, Hasan & Stuart (1988) propose that proprioceptive feedback has two roles: one concerns the interaction between the body and its surroundings, and the other modifies internally generated motor commands to accommodate musculoskeletal mechanics.

An important feature of the single-joint system is its ability to generate movement in a form that is *appropriate for its surroundings.* One role of proprioceptors is to assist the system in meeting this need. It is not sufficient, for example, that the single-joint system simply be capable of producing movement; it must do so within the constraints imposed by its surroundings. These constraints can include unexpected perturbations, limits on which limbs or muscles can be involved in a task, and the opportunity to facilitate a movement through segmental interactions (as described in the "Intersegmental Dynamics" section in chapter 3). Accordingly, proprioceptors can provide information that enables the single-joint system to accommodate the constraints imposed by the surroundings. This is accomplished by the use of assistance and resistance reflexes and by the selection of appropriate muscle synergies. Resistance reflexes are those responses that rely on proprioceptive feedback to resist unexpected disturbances due to some effect of the surroundings; the stretch reflex is a resistance reflex. In contrast, proprioceptors can provide information that is derived from the interaction between the single-joint system and its surroundings to assist a movement. In preparing to perform a movement, proprioceptors can provide feedback to stabilize the system relative to its surroundings and enhance the subsequent movement. Such adjustments are known as **assistance responses.** Furthermore, proprioceptors provide feedback that enables the system to select from among many options an appropriate group and sequence of muscle activity (**muscle synergy**) to accomplish a given task.

The second role served by proprioceptors is the *accommodation of musculoskeletal mechanics.* As discussed previously in this chapter, the ability of the single-joint system to produce movement depends not only on the excitation provided by the neural element but also on the mechanical properties of muscle and the geometry of the system. Proprioceptors can provide information that enables the nervous system to take into account these features of the system in order to generate an appropriate command for the performance of a movement. To achieve this goal, proprioceptors must provide information at the levels of a single muscle, a single joint, and several joints.

The force that a *single muscle* exerts is not constant for the same motor command. Muscle force depends on such mechanical properties as the length of the muscle and its rate of change. Unexpected changes in muscle length, therefore, disrupt the intended effect of a motor command. Proprioceptors can detect unexpected changes in muscle length and thereby minimize the effect of length on muscle force and enable the nervous system to control muscle force more precisely. A similar effect occurs at the level of a *single joint*. Because the moment arm for most muscles changes over their range of motion, muscle torque is frequently maximum at an intermediate position. Consequently, for a given motor command to generate a submaximal muscle force, the limb could move to either of two positions, one on either side of the maximum. To prevent this control problem, proprioceptive feedback may provide a signal that increases with joint angle so that the motor command will increase continuously over the range of motion, and each limb position will be defined uniquely. Finally, proprioceptors must provide feedback to assist with the control of *several joints*. Movement of a linked system, such as the human body, causes the motion of one body segment to exert an influence on all the other segments in the system (intersegmental dynamics). Proprioceptive feedback is critical for the system to interpret the nature of these interactions and to coordinate the activity of all the segments in the system.

Summary

This chapter describes five critical ways in which the six elements of the model of the motor system (the single-joint system) interact to produce movement. These topics include the ability of the nerve and muscle cells to transmit signals rapidly (excitable membrane), the way in which the nervous system controls muscle activity (excitation-contraction coupling), the biomechanical properties of the motor that drives the single-joint system (muscle mechanics), the basic functional unit of the motor system and its activation (motor unit), and the role of sensory information in the operation of the single-joint system (feedback from sensory receptors). Consideration of these topics emphasizes that, at the most fundamental level, movement involves the control of motor unit activity by the nervous system. In this chapter we examine how the nervous system controls motor unit activity and how the arrangement of motor units within a muscle influences the mechanical properties of the single-joint system. Furthermore, we consider the critical role of sensory feedback in enabling the activation of motor units to match conditions in the surroundings and thereby produce a purposeful movement.

Suggested Readings

Gardiner, P.F. (2001). *Neuromuscular aspects of physical activity*. Champaign, IL: Human Kinetics, chapters 1–2.

Jones, D.A., & Round, J.M. (1990). *Skeletal muscle in health and disease*. Manchester: Manchester University Press, chapters 1–4.

Lieber, R.L. (1992). *Skeletal muscle structure and function*. Baltimore: Williams & Wilkins, chapters 1, 2, and 3.

McComas, A.J. (1996). *Skeletal muscle: Form and function*. Champaign, IL: Human Kinetics, chapters 7–12.

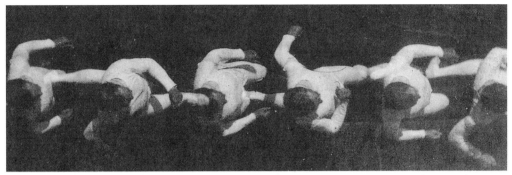

Reprinted from Braun, 1992.

Multi-Joint Systems

I n the previous two chapters of this text, we developed a model of the motor system that we called the single-joint system. With this model we were able to focus on some of the fundamental features (physiological and bio-mechanical) of the human body that enable us to generate movement. The human body, however, is much more than a single-joint system. We did not, for example, consider the role of two-joint muscles, why there are so many muscles around a joint, how a movement is initiated by the single-joint system, or how the system deals with intersegmental dynamics and coordination. Accordingly, the purpose of chapter 7 is to consider the human body as several single-joint systems and to examine the control of such multi-joint systems. We will accomplish this by looking at the organization of muscles and reflex connections in multi-joint systems, examining activation of the system by central pattern generators and supraspinal centers, and identifying some of the strategies used by the motor system to perform movement.

Muscle Organization and Activity

To expand the single-joint system into a model of the human body, it is necessary to enhance several of the system's features. First, recall the biomechanical description of the human body as a set of ~17 body segments that are linked together by soft tissues (chapters 2 and 3). This makes the human body a multi-segmented system, which means that motion of one body segment can influence all the other body segments. Second, the control of motion in multi-joint systems rarely involves a single muscle; rather, it requires groups of muscles. Furthermore, each muscle in such a set has unique biomechanical characteristics. Third, the coordinated motion of multi-joint systems involves neural connections that are distributed among muscles based on their common function. With these attributes, the single-joint system is expanded to become a more appropriate model of the human body.

Multiple Muscles

We emphasized in chapter 2 that human movement generally occurs because of an imbalance among the forces acting on the body, rather than because of the application of a single isolated force. For example, we do not typically activate a single muscle by itself to perform a movement but rather activate a group of synergist muscles or an agonist-antagonist set of muscles. This is necessary because each muscle can accelerate a segment in a limited number of directions, such as extension, flexion and supination, or abduction and flexion. As a consequence, joints with one degree of freedom require at least one pair of muscles (agonist and antagonist) but usually have many more. The use of multiple muscles to perform a function enhances the functional capabilities of the group because each muscle has different force-length, force-velocity, and torque-velocity characteristics.

For example, the elbow joint has one degree of freedom (flexion-extension), but it has a three-headed muscle that provides acceleration in the direction of extension (triceps brachii) and has three major muscles that provide acceleration in the direction of flexion (biceps brachii, brachialis, and brachioradialis). Although each of these three muscles can contribute to an elbow flexor torque, they are not equivalent "force generators" because they have different architectures and therefore different capabilities (Buchanan, Rovai, & Rymer, 1989; Ettema, Styles, & Kippers, 1998; Funk, An, Morrey, & Daube, 1987; Murray, Delp, & Buchanan, 1995; Zhang et al., 1998). We learned in chapter 6 that differences in muscle fiber length, muscle cross-sectional area, and muscle attachment points affect the range of motion, contraction velocity, maximum force, and shape of the torque-angle relation. Table 7.1 outlines some of the architectural differences among the three main elbow flexor muscles. This diversity exists at many joints throughout the body, such as at the ankle, knee, hip, vertebral column, and shoulder (figure 6.18).

Not only are there differences in the torque-angle relations for each of these elbow flexor muscles, but also variation in the attachment points enables a muscle to contribute to more than one mechanical action. For example, because of the location of its distal attachment, biceps brachii is able to contribute to both the net elbow flexor torque and the forearm supination torque. As a result of this dual capability, the two heads of biceps brachii can function independently (ter Haar Romeny et al., 1982; van Zuylen et al., 1988) and differently than the other two flexors. Buchanan et al. (1989), for example, have shown that for a variety of loads in the flexion-extension, internal-external rotation (varus-valgus), and supination-pronation directions at the wrist, there is a strong association between the activity of brachialis and brachioradialis but not between biceps brachii and brachioradialis. Increases in isometric supination torques were associated with increases in biceps brachii EMG but not brachioradialis EMG (figure 7.1). Conversely, increases in pronation torques were accomplished with increases in brachioradialis EMG but not biceps brachii EMG. When subjects exerted forearm supination-pronation torques, biceps brachii was typically most active when brachioradialis and brachialis were least active. With this diversity in design and associated function, the nervous system can vary the activation of synergist muscles depending on the details of the task (Graves, Kornatz, & Enoka, 2000; Hasan & Enoka, 1985; Nakazawa, Kawakami, Fukunaga, Yano, & Miyashita, 1993; Tal'nov, Serenko, Strafun, & Kostyukov, 1999; van Bolhuis & Gielen, 1997).

Table 7.1   Design Features of the Three Main Human Elbow-Flexor Muscles

| | Muscle length (cm) | Fiber length (cm) | Muscle CSA (cm²) | Distance to joint | | Moment arm (cm) |
				Proximal (cm)	Distal (cm)	
Biceps brachii	24.0	17.8	5.8	30	4	4.3
Brachialis	20.1	14.4	7.4	10	3	2.3
Brachioradialis	23.7	14.7	2.0	6	25	—

Note. The distance to the joint indicates the location of the center of the attachment point (proximal and distal) to the axis of rotation of the elbow joint. CSA = cross-sectional area.

The distance data were provided by Scott L. Delp, PhD. The moment arms were measured with the elbow joint at a right angle by Klein, Rice, & Marsh, 2000.

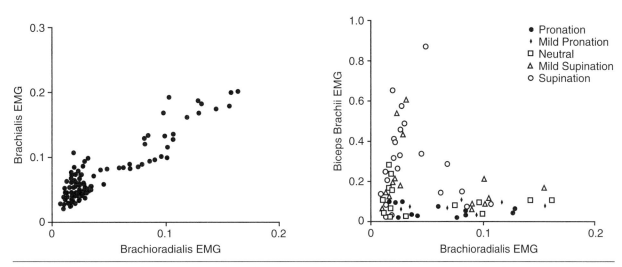

Figure 7.1 Comparison of changes in EMG activity (expressed in arbitrary units) among the three main elbow flexor muscles during the application of isometric torques at the wrist in the direction of forearm pronation and supination. Pronation torques resulted in covarying EMG in brachialis and brachioradialis. In contrast, EMG did not covary in biceps brachii and brachioradialis with different torques. A supination torque was accompanied by increases in biceps brachii EMG whereas a pronation torque was associated with increases in brachioradialis EMG.

Adapted from Buchanan, Rovai, and Rymer, 1989.

Example 7.1
Torques Due to Off-Axis Attachments

Rarely do muscles attach about a joint to produce an isolated function, such as extension or adduction. Rather, the attachments are slightly off axis to produce a diversity of actions. For example, Lawrence, Nichols, and English (1993) found that only one of the muscles (flexor digitorum longus) that cross the cat ankle joint produced an isolated function (figure 7.2). Two muscles (peroneus and tibialis posterior) exerted torques in the abduction-adduction plane with a minor component in the plantarflexion-dorsiflexion plane. All the other muscles, especially lateral gastrocnemius, medial gastrocnemius, and tibialis anterior, had significant components in both planes.

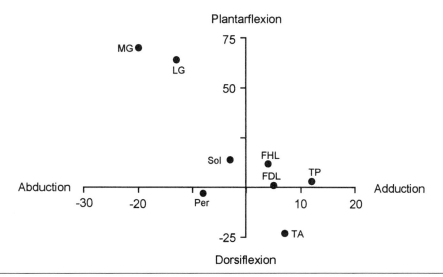

Figure 7.2 The torques (N·cm) exerted by muscles that cross the ankle joint in the cat. The muscles studied were flexor digitorum longus (FDL), flexor hallucis longus (FHL), lateral gastrocnemius (LG), medial gastrocnemius (MG), peroneus (Per), soleus (Sol), tibialis anterior (TA), and tibialis posterior (TP).

Data from Lawrence et al., 1993.

(continued)

Similarly, the direction of the torque exerted by the muscles that cross the human elbow joint have components in more than one plane, sometimes exerting torques about all three axes (i.e., somersault—flexion-extension; twist—supination-pronation; cartwheel—varus-valgus). These components were determined by electrical stimulation of each muscle at various joint angles throughout the range of motion (Zhang et al., 1998). The evoked torques for each muscle were normalized relative to the maximum torque the muscle exerted in the flexion-extension direction, and the data were averaged across a number of subjects. The forearm was kept in a neutral position. The two heads of biceps brachii exerted torques in the flexion and supination directions, which changed as a function of joint angle (figure 7.3). The other muscles had lesser components in the direction of pronation and supination, and these also changed with joint angle.

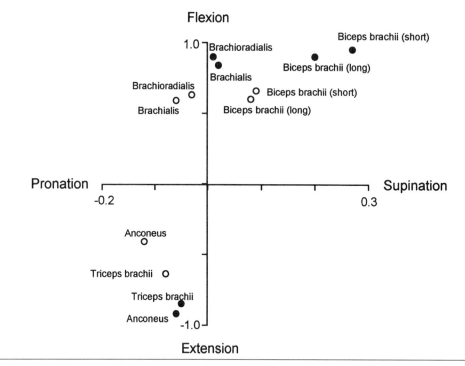

Figure 7.3   Normalized torques evoked by electrical stimulation in the muscles that cross the human elbow joint. The muscles studied were anconeus, the short and long heads of biceps brachii, brachialis, brachioradialis, and the lateral head of triceps brachii. The torques evoked in the two directions (flexion-extension and pronation-supination) were measured with the elbow joint at a right angle (•) and with the elbow flexed from complete extension by ~0.5 rad (o).

Data from Zhang et al., 1998.

Example 7.2

Tendon Transfers and Muscle Architecture

A tendon transfer is an orthopedic procedure designed to restore lost muscle function. It involves disconnecting the tendon of a healthy muscle from its normal attachment site and connecting it to the tendon of a muscle damaged by trauma, injury, or disease. For example, a common procedure is to transfer the tendon of flexor carpi ulnaris to the tendon of extensor carpi radialis longus in patients who have radial nerve palsy (Fridén & Lieber, 1998). To maximize the outcome of such an intervention, the donor muscle should have design characteristics (e.g., fiber lengths, attachment sites) similar to those of the muscle it is replacing (Delp, Ringwelski, & Carroll, 1994). This does not happen often; the wrist flexors, for example, have shorter muscle fibers than the wrist extensors (Lieber & Fridén, 1998). On the basis of intraoperative measurements of sarcomere length with a laser beam, Lieber and Fridén (1997) found that the range of motion experienced by flexor carpi ulnaris was completely different after the surgery than before (figure 7.4). Before the procedure, sarcomere length was maximal (4.16 μm) when the wrist was extended and was 3.48 μm when the wrist was in a neutral position. After the procedure, sarcomere length was maximal (4.82 μm) when the wrist was flexed and was 3.89 μm in the wrist-neutral position. This is not an optimal outcome, because force is maximal at sarcomere lengths of 2.6 to 2.8 μm (Fridén & Lieber, 1998). At sarcomere lengths of around 3.8 μm, the muscle can exert only about 28% of its maximum force. Such findings suggest guidelines that surgeons can use in choosing a length at which to attach a muscle in the tendon transfer procedure.

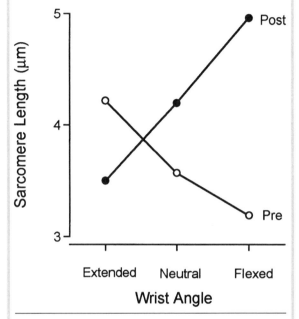

Figure 7.4 Sarcomere lengths in the flexor carpi ulnaris muscle at various wrist angles before and after a tendon transfer procedure.

Data from Lieber and Fridén, 1997.

Given that the magnitude and direction of the force exerted by each muscle are unique, the relative contribution of synergist muscles to a net force can vary across tasks. To study this issue, which is termed **force sharing,** we determine how the force is distributed or shared among the involved muscles. The most direct way to determine force-sharing patterns is to measure muscle forces in the course of normal motor behavior by placing force transducers on the tendons of selected muscles and recording the forces and the kinematics of the behavior (Walmsley et al., 1978). Most of these experiments have been performed on the hindlimb of the cat, where the properties of the involved muscles are substantially different. Figure 7.5 shows a typical set of data for a cat locomoting at various speeds, ranging from a walk to a trot (Herzog, 1996). Each trace comprises a loop and corresponds to the forces exerted by two muscles during

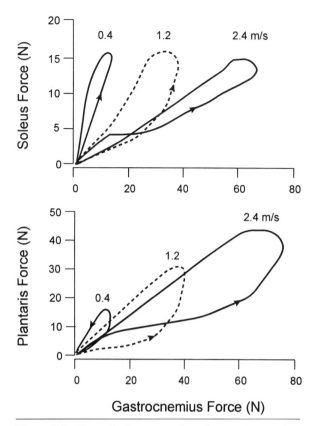

Figure 7.5 Force sharing among the soleus, gastrocnemius, and plantaris muscles of the cat during the step cycle at various speeds of locomotion.

Data from Herzog, 1996.

a single step cycle. The loops change with the speed of locomotion and are different for the two pairs of muscles. While the peak force exerted by soleus remained relatively constant across the three speeds, the peak forces exerted by both gastrocnemius and plantaris increased with speed (figure 7.5). These differences are consistent with the architecture and physiological properties of these muscles. On the basis of EMG measurements, it is likely that similar effects occur among synergist muscles in humans.

A somewhat different case of force sharing involves the distribution of forces among the fingers during various tasks (Leijnse, 1997). When subjects placed a hand on a table and pressed down with varying numbers of fingers, the force exerted by a single finger was related to that exerted by the other fingers but depended on how many other fingers were pressing down. When the exerted force increased from zero to maximum, the forces exerted by the involved fingers were linearly related, but the peak force exerted during a multi-finger task was less than the maximum during a single-finger task (Li, Latash, & Zatsiorsky, 1998). Furthermore, the variance in the total peak force over 10 trials was less than the sum of the variances for the individual fingers, which suggests that changes in the single-finger forces were compensated across the fingers. This coupling was also evident in the involuntary activation of fingers when they were not required to exert a force. These interactions can be explained by the existence of an association between the command signals for the muscles that control individual fingers, that is, a sharing of the required force among the fingers (Zatsiorsky, Li, & Latash, 1998). This coupling is facilitated by the distribution of the mechanical action of each motor unit in these muscles to several digits (Keen, Woodring, Schieber, & Fuglevand, 1998; Kilbreath, Raymond, Gorman, & Gandevia, 1998).

Two-Joint Muscles

One common variation in the points of attachment for a muscle is the number of joints that the muscle spans. For example, a significant number of muscles span two joints and thus are referred to as two-joint muscles (e.g., biceps brachii, rectus femoris). Two-joint muscles provide at least three advantages in the control of the musculoskeletal system.

■ *First, two-joint muscles couple the motion at the two joints that they cross* (Arsenault & Chapman, 1974; Fujiwara & Basmajian, 1975; Ingen Schenau, Bobbert, & Soest, 1990). For example, biceps brachii crosses both the elbow and the shoulder joints and thus contributes to both elbow and shoulder flexion. Because these two movements occur concurrently in many daily activities, it is useful to have a muscle that contributes to both actions. In addition, this coupling can be achieved by a reduction in the EMG of a one-joint muscle and an increase in the activity of the two-joint muscle. Yamashita (1988) found a reduction in the EMG of gluteus maximus (a one-joint hip extensor) and an increase in the EMG of semimembranosus (a two-joint hip extensor and knee flexor) during concurrent hip extension and knee extension. Zajac (1993) suggests that one-joint muscles produce the propulsive energy for a vertical jump while the two-joint muscles refine the coordination.

■ *Second, the shortening velocity of a two-joint muscle is less than that of its one-joint synergists* (Ingen Schenau, Bobbert, & Soest, 1990). For example, the shortening velocity of rectus femoris (two joint) during concurrent hip and knee extension is less than the shortening velocity of the vasti (one joint). Similarly, the shortening velocity of gastrocnemius (two joint) is less than the shortening velocity of soleus (one joint) during concurrent knee extension and plantarflexion. The advantage of a lesser shortening velocity is that the two-joint muscles are higher on the force-velocity relation (figures 6.21 and 6.27) compared with the one-joint muscle and hence are capable of exerting a force that is a greater proportion of the isometric maximum.

■ *Third, two-joint muscles can redistribute muscle torque, joint power, and mechanical energy throughout a limb* (Gielen, Ingen Schenau, Tax, & Theeuwen, 1990; Ingen Schenau, Bobbert, & Soest, 1990; Prilutsky, Petrova, & Raitsin, 1996; Prilutsky & Zatsiorsky, 1994; Toussaint et al., 1992). Figure 7.6 represents a model of the human leg comprising a pelvis, thigh, and shank with several one- and two-joint muscles. In this model,

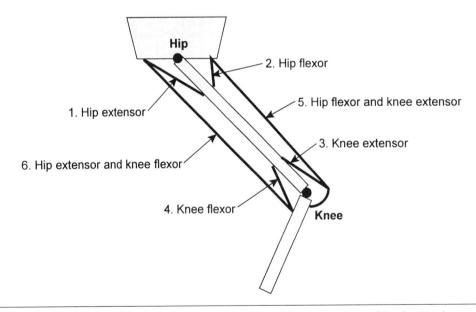

Figure 7.6 Model of the human leg with six muscles arranged around the hip and knee joints. Muscles 1 to 4 cross one joint while muscles 5 and 6 cross both joints.

Adapted from Ingen Schenau, Bobbert, and Soest, 1990.

muscles 1 and 3 are one-joint hip and knee extensors; muscles 2 and 4 are one-joint hip and knee flexors; and muscles 5 and 6 are two-joint muscles. These muscles can be activated in various combinations to exert extensor torques about the hip and knee joints. One option is to activate muscles 1 and 3, which are the two one-joint muscles that produce the extensor torques. Alternatively, it would be possible to activate muscle 5 along with muscles 1 and 3. Because muscle 5 (two joint) exerts a flexor torque about the hip joint and an extensor torque about the knee joint, concurrent activation of muscles 1, 3, and 5 will result in a reduction in the net torque at the hip but an increase in the net torque at the knee. Based on this interaction, the two-joint muscle (muscle 5) is described as redistributing some of the muscle torque and joint power from the hip to the knee. Conversely, activation of muscle 6 along with muscles 1 and 3 will redistribute torque from the knee to the hip.

Example 7.3
Pedal Force Direction Requires Activation of Two-Joint Muscles

The downstroke in cycling, in which the foot pushes the pedal down, involves concurrent extension at the hip and knee joints. Although the downstroke could be accomplished by activation of the one-joint hip and knee extensor muscles (gluteus maximus and the vasti), EMG measurements have shown that several of the two-joint muscles also participate in this task. For example, rectus femoris is active at the beginning of the downstroke whereas the hamstrings are active later (Gregor, Cavanagh, & LaFortune, 1985). The explanation for this pattern of activity is based on the direction of the force that is applied to the pedal (Ingen Schenau, 1990). At the beginning of the downstroke, the pedal force is directed downward and forward (figure 7.7a), requiring net extensor muscle torques about the hip and knee joints. The muscle torque about the knee, however, is much greater because of a longer moment arm (a) at the knee joint compared with the hip joint (b). Through coactivation of gluteus maximus and rectus femoris, the net muscle torque is kept small about the hip—which is necessary to keep the pedal force pointing forward—and an extensor torque is exerted about the knee joint by rectus femoris. The action of rectus femoris at the knee joint supplements that of the vasti, but can do so only because of the strong contraction by the gluteus maximus.

Later in the downstroke, the direction of the pedal force changes from forward to backward (figure 7.7b). The line of action of this backward-directed pedal

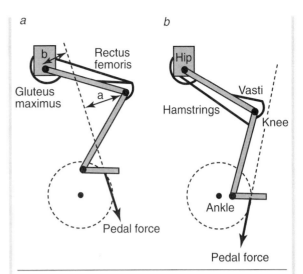

Figure 7.7 Model of the human leg during cycling at *(a)* the beginning and *(b)* middle of the downstroke phase. The direction of the pedal force depends on the muscles that contribute to the movement.

Data from Ingen Schenau, 1990.

force passes in front of the knee joint as a result of a net extensor torque about the hip joint and a net flexor torque about the knee joint. Coactivation of the two-joint hamstring muscles contributes to both the extensor torque about the hip and the flexor torque about the knee. At the knee joint, however, both the hamstrings and vasti are active, but with the hamstrings exerting the dominant effect and producing the requisite flexor torque about the knee. Coactivation of the vasti and the hamstrings increases the magnitude of the force exerted by the hamstrings, which is registered about both the knee and hip joints. By this mechanism, the net extensor torque about the hip is increased at this stage of the downstroke.

Resultant Muscle Torque

Because of this musculoskeletal organization, it is important to re-emphasize the concept of **resultant muscle torque** as the net effect of muscle activity about a joint. We learned in chapter 3 how to use Newtonian mechanics to calculate the resultant muscle torque for both static and dynamic conditions. With this approach, we defined a free body diagram, accounted for all the kinematic and kinetic effects acting on the system except the resultant muscle torque, and then calculated the resultant muscle torque as the residual effect. This provided an estimate of the net muscle activity and its contribution to the movement, which can be useful in the prescription of exercise and rehabilitation activities.

It is possible to determine the net muscle activity by a qualitative analysis of a movement. For example, consider a person lying supine on a bench and performing forearm curls (elbow flexion-extension movements) with a handheld weight (figure 7.8*a*). If the individual executes a *slow* movement throughout the full range of motion, we can determine the net muscle activity as the arm moves from position 1 through position 4, the muscle group primarily responsible for the movement, and the type of contraction being performed.

The load against which the muscle group acts is the weight held in the hand $(F_{w,h})$ plus the weight of the forearm-hand segment $(F_{w,s})$. The task involves rotation of the body segment and the weight around the elbow joint, which can be indicated by the free body diagram shown in figure 7.8*b*. The four forces acting on the system can be reduced to two torques (figure 7.8*c*), a load torque (τ_l) and a resultant muscle torque (τ_m); τ_l represents the effect of the two weights. We can determine the direction of the two torque vectors by visualizing the

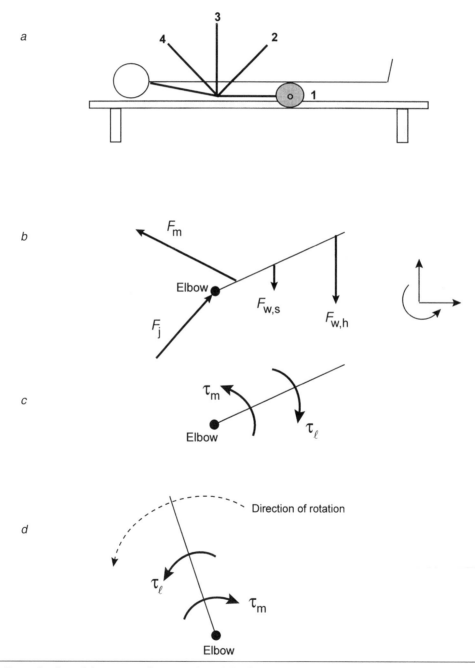

Figure 7.8 Determination of the pattern of net muscle activity for a slow movement. *(a)* A supine subject performs an elbow flexion-extension movement with a dumbbell in the right hand. *(b)* Free body diagram isolates the forearm-hand segment. *(c)* Resultant muscle and load torques. *(d)* The net muscle activity is based on comparison of the directions of the torques and the movement.

rotary effect of each force on the system; $F_{w,h}$ and $F_{w,s}$ will cause the system to rotate in a clockwise direction whereas F_m will produce a counterclockwise rotation.

From these diagrams we can determine the muscle group mainly responsible for the movement, as well as the type of contraction that it performs. The appropriate steps are to draw

1. the body segment in the approximate position,
2. the load torque vector (τ_l),
3. the resultant muscle torque vector (τ_m) in the direction opposite that of the load torque vector, and
4. the direction of rotation of the body segment.

For example, consider the movement of the forearm-hand segment in the forearm curl from position 3 to position 4. Note that the body segment is drawn not at either position 3 or position 4 but rather midway between the two positions (figure 7.8*d*). For *slow* movements, *the direction of the resultant muscle torque vector is opposite that of the load torque vector.* To determine the muscle group represented by the resultant muscle torque vector, imagine that there are no other forces or torques acting on the system and that the segment rotates in the same direction indicated by the resultant muscle torque vector. If this direction is one of extension, then the responsible muscle group is the extensors. Conversely, if the resultant muscle torque vector produces flexion, then the vector represents the flexor muscles. Alternatively, the direction of pull indicated by F_m will indicate which muscle group the vector represents.

By comparing the directions of the resultant muscle torque vector and the segment rotation, we can determine the type of contraction performed by the net muscle activity. If the directions of the resultant muscle torque vector and the segment rotation are the same, then the muscle group performed a concentric contraction. If the segment rotation and the resultant muscle torque are not acting in the same direction (as in the movement from position 3 to 4), then the net muscle activity is an eccentric contraction. Thus the movement from position 3 to position 4 is controlled by an eccentric contraction of the elbow extensors. In general, if an extensor muscle group produces extension or a flexor group causes flexion, the net muscle activity is a concentric contraction.

In contrast, flexion controlled by an extensor group or extension controlled by a flexor group represents an eccentric contraction. With use of these procedures, it is possible to determine qualitatively the net muscle activity for such slow movements as the forearm curl exercise over the entire range of motion (table 7.2).

This example of the forearm curl exercise with a person in a supine position emphasizes an important feature of the way we use our muscles. Suppose that the individual now moves from the supine position to an upright posture and performs a similar exercise, raising and lowering an extended arm between positions 1 and 2 (figure 7.9). What patterns of net muscle activity are necessary to complete this movement? Using the procedure just described, we can determine that the movement is controlled by the shoulder flexors, that is, both going from position 1 to 2 and going from position 2 to 1. The net muscle activity would be a concentric contraction to raise the load and a lengthening contraction to lower it. The difference in the patterns of activity between the supine and upright postures has to do with *the orientation of the individual (and hence the movement) relative to the direction of gravity.* For both the upright standing and supine examples, imagine a vertical line (gravity) that passes through the axis of rotation (shoulder and elbow, respectively). The major qualitative difference is that the movement never crosses this line in the upright exercise, whereas it does in the supine exercise. For *slow* exercises, crossing this line means changing the muscle group that controls the movement.

Movement Speed

The analysis employed in the preceding examples applies only to conditions that we call quasistatic, that is, those instances that are almost static and in which the acceleration of the system and its various parts is small (Miller, 1980; Toussaint et al., 1992). *Under quasistatic conditions we can approximate the mechanical state of the muscle by doing a static analysis* (i.e., $\Sigma F = 0$). This raises the issue of when a quasistatic state can be assumed and when it cannot. Alexander and Vernon (1975) have used a version of the quasistatic approach to calculate the resultant muscle torques about the ankle and knee joints during the stance phase of a jog. Others, however,

Table 7.2 Net Muscle Activity for the Forearm Curl Exercise Shown in Figure 7.8

Movement	$1 \longrightarrow 2$	$2 \longrightarrow 3$	$3 \longrightarrow 4$	$4 \longrightarrow 3$	$3 \longrightarrow 2$	$2 \longrightarrow 1$
Elbow flexors	C	C	—	—	E	E
Elbow extensors	—	—	E	C	—	—

Note. C = concentric contraction; E = eccentric contraction.

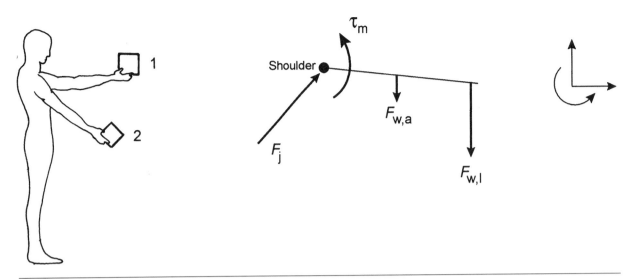

Figure 7.9 A shoulder flexion-extension movement. Because the load torque ($F_{w,a} + F_{w,l}$) acts in the same direction throughout the movement, the direction of the resultant muscle torque (τ_m) is constant throughout the range of motion.

have felt it necessary to perform a complete dynamic analysis (i.e., $\Sigma F = ma$) for such conditions (Mann, 1981; Miller & Munro, 1985).

Certainly a dynamic analysis is necessary for more vigorous activities, such as kicking (figure 7.10). To demonstrate that a quasistatic analysis is not appropriate for such a movement, let us perform a quasistatic analysis and then compare the results to those from a dynamic analysis. The four positions of the kicking leg (the one with the filled-in shoe) from figure 7.10 are superimposed onto one stick figure, first relative to the hip joint (figure 7.11a) and then with respect to the knee joint (figure 7.11b). Note that the position of the shank relative to the knee in figure 7.11 is the same as its original position in figure 7.10. Next, we determine the pattern of net muscle activity about the knee joint during the kick as we did for the forearm curl example (figure 7.8). Because the movement (positions 1 to 4) never crosses the vertical line that passes through the axis of rotation (knee), the load torque vector, and therefore the resultant muscle force vector, acts in the same direction throughout the movement; the net muscle activity is shown in table 7.3.

On the basis of this quasistatic rationale, the knee flexor muscles supposedly control the motion about the knee joint during the toe kick (figure 7.10). Our intuition tells us, however, that this is not reasonable. The obvious shortcoming of this analysis is the assumption that the movement is slow. Clearly, it is not slow! In chapter 2 we considered some of the forces commonly encountered in human movement. Recall that inertial forces are effects due to the motion of an object or segment. In fast movements, inertial forces are substantial, and they drastically

alter the pattern of muscle activity that is necessary for the control of movement (Putnam, 1983, 1991).

We can see the magnitude of the inertial effects by comparing the resultant muscle torque about the knee joint in figure 7.10 with that deduced through the quasistatic approach. Interpretation of the torque-angle graph (figure 7.10) begins in the lower right-hand corner and progresses in a counterclockwise direction. The graph indicates that except in the first part of the kick, the resultant muscle torque is due to the knee extensors and not the flexors as suggested by the quasistatic analysis. Most of the movement from position 1 to position 3, during which knee angle decreases, is controlled by an eccentric contraction of the knee extensor muscles. The resultant muscle torque reaches a peak value at the transition from the eccentric to the concentric contraction. From position 3 through to contact with the ball, the net activity involves a concentric contraction with the knee extensor muscles. These observations indicate that a quasistatic analysis, which ignores the effects due to acceleration, is inappropriate to reveal the pattern of net muscle activity for tasks such as a kick.

The information shown in figure 7.10 can be derived qualitatively through comparison of the resultant muscle torque and angular velocity graphs (figure 7.12). To illustrate this procedure, let us return to the example of horizontal extension-flexion at the elbow joint (figure 1.19). The first half of the movement involves extension (positive velocity) and the second half involves flexion, as indicated by the positive and negative phases of the velocity-time graph (figure 7.12). Furthermore, each velocity phase comprises two acceleration intervals, one

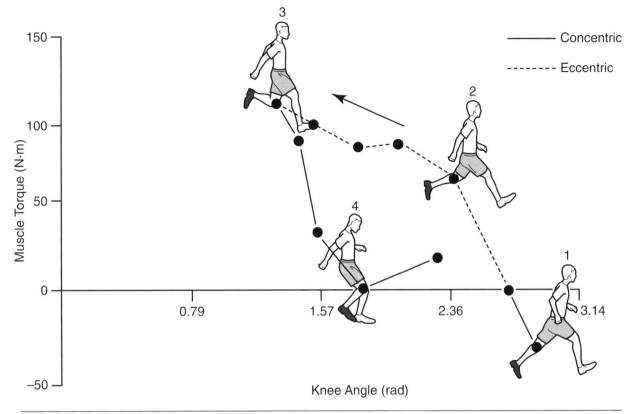

Figure 7.10 Resultant muscle torque about the knee joint of the kicking leg as a function of knee angle during the swing preceding ball contact in a fast kick of a soccer ball. The total time for the swing was 170 ms, with 17 ms between each of the large dots on the diagram. To interpret the graph, begin at the bottom right-hand corner and proceed in a counterclockwise direction from position 1 to 4.

Reprinted from Miller, 1980.

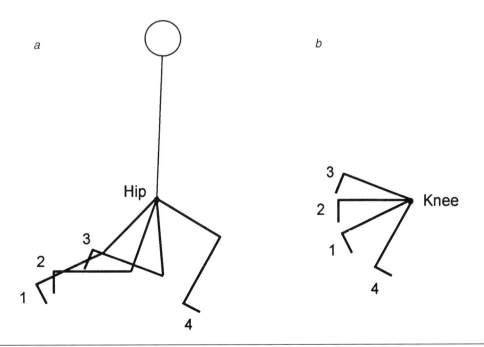

Figure 7.11 Angular displacement of the *(a)* leg relative to the hip and *(b)* the shank relative to the knee during the soccer kick shown in figure 7.10.

Table 7.3 Net Muscle Activity for the Soccer Kick Shown in Figure 7.10 Based on a Quasistatic Analysis

Movement	1 → 2	2 → 3	3 → 4
Knee flexors	C	C	E
Knee extensors	—	—	—

Note. C = concentric contraction; E = eccentric contraction.

positive and one negative, due to the net muscle activity about the elbow joint. In this example, the negative muscle torque corresponds to a flexor torque, and the positive values indicate an extensor torque. The exten-sion phase of the movement involves first an extensor torque and then a flexor torque. Displacement in the direction of extension while the extensors are active is achieved with a concentric contraction. Conversely, dis-placement in the direction of extension while the flexors are active involves an eccentric contraction of the flexor muscles (figure 7.12). Similarly, the flexion phase of the movement is accomplished with a concentric contraction of the flexor muscles and then an eccentric contraction of the extensor muscles. We arrived at this same pattern of net activity by other means in chapter 1 (Example 1.8).

This discussion of net muscle activity emphasizes an important consequence of musculoskeletal design. Be-cause of intersegmental dynamics (chapter 3), fast and

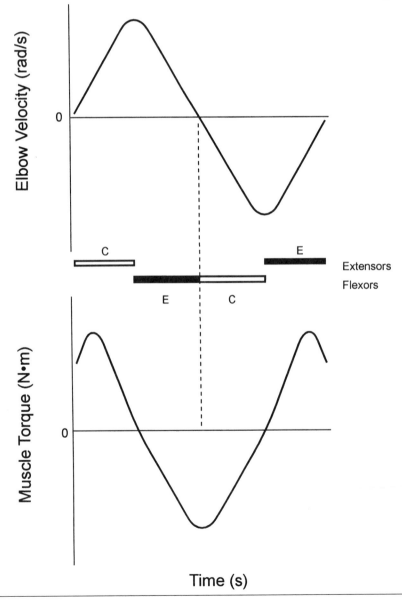

Figure 7.12 Deduction of the net muscle activity responsible for an elbow extension-flexion movement performed in a horizontal plane. Positive velocity represents extension at the elbow joint. Positive torque indicates a resultant torque by the extensor muscles.

C = concentric contraction; E = eccentric contraction.

slow movements are controlled differently by the nervous system; that is, the pattern of net muscle activity changes with movement speed in order to accommodate inertial effects between segments. Nonetheless, whether a movement is performed slowly or rapidly, the contribution of muscle is determined by the net activity among synergist and antagonist muscles.

Reflex Connections

Not only do reflexes exert significant effects at the level of the single joint (chapter 6), there are reflex connections at the level of multi-joint systems. Furthermore, sensory feedback is essential for the coordinated function of multi-joint systems (Nichols, 1994; Nichols, Cope, & Abelew, 1999). This necessity is underscored by studies on patients who have lost large-diameter sensory afferents; these afferents contribute to proprioception. When such individuals were asked to perform a motion similar to slicing a loaf of bread while the eyes were closed, the coordination of the arm was impaired compared with that of control subjects (Sainburg, Poizner, & Ghez, 1993). This was evident by deviation of the wrist motion from a straight line (figure 7.13). The information provided by the proprioceptive afferents appears to be necessary for the control of intersegmental dynamics (Sainburg et al., 1995).

In the development of the single-joint system, we described a number of reflexes. The implication was that every muscle or agonist-antagonist pair of muscles experiences these effects in response to an appropriate stimulus. Neurophysiological studies on reflex connectivity, however, indicate that such connections do not occur all the time (Jankowska & Odutola, 1980). Furthermore, the reflex connections from one joint to another, either in the same limb or to another limb, are variable among different species and appear to exist among functionally related muscles (Nichols, 1994). The following paragraphs describe examples of these interactions in humans for muscles that cross different joints within a limb, effects that act between limbs, and a whole-body response.

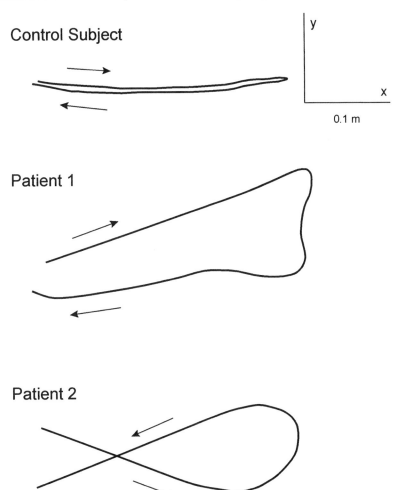

Figure 7.13 Kinematics of the wrist in a sagittal plane (x = forward-backward; y = up-down) during a slicing task.

Data from Sainburg et al., 1993.

Within a Limb

One way to identify the reflex connections between muscles in humans is to determine the effect of stimulating a peripheral nerve on the activity of single motor units in another muscle. The motor unit activity is measured by inserting an electrode into the muscle and recording the action potentials discharged by one motor unit during a low-force contraction. When the nerve to another muscle is stimulated, the effect on the motor unit is expressed as a change in its discharge of action potentials. The change could be either an increase (excitation) or a decrease (inhibition) in the motor unit activity.

When the stimulus applied to the peripheral nerve is a low-intensity electric shock, action potentials are generated in the Group Ia afferents (Meunier, Pierrot-Deseilligny, & Simonetta, 1993). These action potentials propagate back to the spinal cord and synapse directly onto motor neurons that innervate many muscles. The effect is to evoke excitatory postsynaptic potentials in the motor neurons, which increases the number of action potentials discharged by the motor neurons. This effect is known as Group Ia excitation. With such stimulation, there is often a delayed depression in the discharge of the motor unit, which is interpreted as recurrent inhibition (Meunier, Pierrot-Deseilligny, & Simonetta-Moreau, 1994). Recurrent inhibition is mediated through the Renshaw cell, an interneuron that evokes inhibitory postsynaptic potentials in motor neurons (figure 6.65).

When these stimuli were applied to the peripheral nerves listed in table 7.4, Meunier and colleagues (1994) found widespread effects on the discharge of motor units. In 25 comparisons, they found both Group Ia excitation and recurrent inhibition for 12 combinations of peripheral nerves and motor unit activity in other muscles (table 7.4). There were 5 combinations in which only Group Ia

excitation or recurrent inhibition was evoked. However, there were 8 combinations in which neither reflex was evoked. Most of these null effects involved the pretibial muscles (tibialis anterior) and the associated nerve (deep peroneal). These connections, at least from the femoral nerve to the soleus and tibialis anterior muscles, are of sufficient strength to influence the H reflex and the EMG activity (Meunier, Mogyoros, Kiernan, & Burke, 1996). Similar distributions, at least for the stretch reflex, appear to exist among muscles in the arm. A rapid stretch of the biceps brachii, for example, elicited responses in triceps brachii, pectoralis major, deltoid, and the hypothenar muscles (O'Sullivan, Eyre, & Miller, 1991).

Between Limbs

Reflex connections have been found between limbs on the same and different sides of the body and have been shown to involve several different types of sensory receptors. Furthermore, the between-limb effects can occur at both short and long latencies.

The tendon-tap reflex involves a short-latency contraction in response to a stretch of the muscle by a tap applied to its tendon. The magnitude of the response depends on the sensitivity of the muscle spindles and the excitability of the involved motor neurons. When a tap is applied to the patellar tendon just prior to a similar tap on the Achilles tendon, the magnitude of the evoked EMG and force is initially increased and then depressed (Koceja, 1995; Koceja & Kamen, 1991). This effect, which is interpreted as short-latency excitation and long-latency inhibition of the triceps surae motor neurons, is evoked by tendon taps to either the ipsilateral or the contralateral patellar tendons. Similarly, reciprocal inhibition evoked in flexor carpi radialis by electrical stimulation of the radial nerve is reduced by passive and active

Table 7.4 Distribution of Reflex Connections Among Muscles in the Human Leg

	Soleus	Medial gastrocnemius	Superficial peroneal	Deep peroneal	Femoral
Soleus	—	RI	Ia + RI	None	Ia + RI
Medial gastrocnemius	Ia + RI	—	Ia + RI	Ia	Ia + RI
Peroneus brevis	Ia	RI	—	Ia	Ia + RI
Tibialis anterior	None	None	None	—	Ia + RI
Quadriceps femoris	Ia + RI	Ia + RI	None	None	—
Biceps femoris	Ia + RI	Ia + RI	Ia + RI	None	None

Note. When peripheral nerves were stimulated (top row), the stimulus could evoke reflex responses in motor units that belonged to the muscles in the left column. The reflex responses studied were either excitation by Group Ia afferents (Ia) or recurrent inhibition (RI).

Data from Meunier et al., 1994.

movement of the contralateral arm (Delwaide, Sabatino, Pepin, & La Grutta, 1988).

The reflex connections between limbs not only involve the stretch or tendon-tap reflexes; they can also be evoked by stimulation of cutaneous receptors (Perl, 1957). The sural nerve comprises afferent fibers that innervate the skin overlying the lateral border of the foot and the lower leg. When an electric shock is applied to this area, the sensation depends on the intensity of the stimulus. Low-intensity stimuli are not noxious, but they evoke responses that tend to move the leg away from the stimulus. When such stimuli were applied to the foot of individuals running on a treadmill, EMG responses were widely distributed throughout both legs at a latency of about 80 ms (Tax, Wezel, & Dietz, 1995). The magnitude of the evoked responses varied throughout the step cycle, but independent of fluctuations in the EMG associated with running. Modulation of these responses in the two legs appeared to involve a compromise between preserving the cadence and maintaining balance. Similarly, Iles (1996) found that stimulation of the contralateral sural nerve increased presynaptic inhibition of Group Ia afferents from the soleus muscle and that the effect varied with the position of the ipsilateral foot.

Interlimb reflex connections also appear to exist between the arms and legs. For example, when subjects sat in a chair and rotated a foot about the ankle in the plantarflexion and dorsiflexion directions, the amplitude of the H reflex in flexor carpi ulnaris muscle varied (Baldissera, Cavallari, & Leocani, 1998). The modulation was such that the magnitude of the reflex was greatest when the foot was being plantarflexed. Because the flexor carpi ulnaris muscle contributes to flexion of the wrist, this modulation would tend to favor in-phase coordination of the foot and hand and to be less supportive for out-of-phase displacements.

Whole Body

Perhaps the classic example of a whole-body, reflex-like response is the **startle reaction.** This is the response of the body to an unexpected auditory stimulus; sometimes it can be evoked with visual, vestibular, or somesthetic stimuli (Bisdorff, Bronstein, & Gresty, 1994; Bisdorff et al., 1999; Hawk & Cook, 1997). It is typically described as a generalized flexion response that is most prominent in the face, neck, shoulders, and arms (Brown, 1995; Landis & Hunt, 1939), although it can also be evoked in the leg muscles of humans (Delwaide & Schepens, 1995). The startle reaction belongs to a class of behaviors known as escape responses (Ritzmann & Eaton, 1997).

The startle reaction appears to originate in the caudal brainstem and to involve a subcortical reflex loop (Brown, 1995; Davis, 1984). An early study showed that this reaction evokes rapid responses that begin with an eye blink

(40 ms) and can progress to include flexion at the neck (75-120 ms), trunk and shoulders (100-120 ms), elbows (125-195 ms), fingers (145-195 ms), and legs (145-395 ms) (Landis & Hunt, 1939). Subsequent studies have suggested that the eye blink response has two parts, an initial auditory blink reflex and the subsequent generalized startle reaction (Brown, 1995). The magnitude of the startle reaction is variable; it habituates with repeat stimuli, decreases in a dose-dependent way with ethanol, increases with fear and arousal, and can be modulated by supraspinal centers (Davis, 1984). The most effective stimulus is a brief, loud noise, such as 90 dB for ≤30 ms. The startle reaction is exaggerated in some clinical conditions, such as hyperekplexia.

The startle reaction can have a marked effect on voluntary movements (Nieuwenhuijzen, Schillings, Van Galen, & Duysens, 2000; Siegmund, Sanderson, & Inglis, 2000). For example, when a loud acoustic stimulus was randomly superimposed on reaction-time movements, the reaction time was shortened by one-half (Valls-Solé, Rothwell, Goulart, Cossu, & Muñoz, 1999). The reaction-time task involved flexion and extension of the wrist or rising up onto the toes in a standing posture. Under control conditions, the time from the "go" signal to the beginning of the response was 204 ms for the wrist movement and 244 ms for the foot movement. With the superimposition of the startle stimulus, the reaction time decreased to 104 ms for the wrist movement and 123 ms for the foot movement. Because the EMG pattern was similar for trials with and without the startle stimulus, Valls-Solé et al. (1999) concluded that each movement was triggered by activity at the subcortical levels.

Central Pattern Generators

Given that multi-joint systems comprise multiple muscles that span several joints and are connected by reflex circuits, it is reasonable to ask how the nervous system controls such a system. Among the fundamental elements that contribute to this task are the **central pattern generators,** which are neuronal circuits that produce coordinated motor patterns in the absence of sensory feedback and in response to brief or tonic inputs (Grillner & Wallen, 1985; Stein, Grillner, Selverston, & Stuart, 1997). Central pattern generators (CPGs) produce automatic movements, such as locomotion, respiration, swallowing, and defense reactions (Pearson & Gordon, 2000a). The motor pattern generated by a CPG is specific to the behavior it controls. To accomplish this diversity, CPGs vary in the organization, properties, and interactions among the constituent neurons; this enables the network to use one of several mechanisms to produce

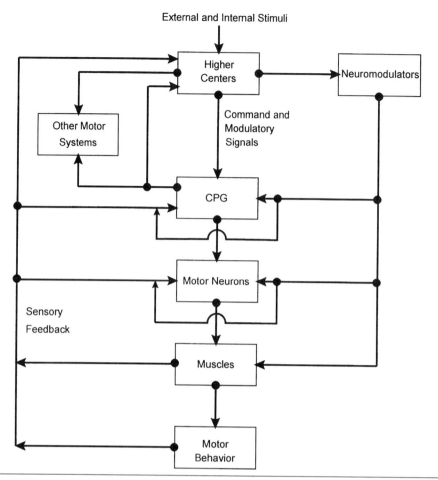

Figure 7.14 Flow of information through the nervous system that is necessary for movement.

Data from Selverston, Panchin, Arshavsky, and Orlovsky, 1997.

CPG = central pattern generator.

its characteristic bursts of action potentials (Calabrese, 1998; Kiehn, Hounsgaard, & Sillar, 1997).

The flow of information through the nervous system that produces motor behavior is shown in figure 7.14. The CPG is located between the higher centers and the motor neurons. It is typically activated by signals from command and modulatory neurons located in higher centers. The activity of the CPG, however, is also influenced by sensory feedback and by hormones (neuromodulation). Most is known about the structure and function of CPGs that control rhythmical movements, the classic example being locomotion. For such movements, the CPG must produce a rhythm that results in alternating activation of antagonistic muscles; it must be able to vary the frequency of the output; and it must shape the pattern of motor output.

One of the first models of a CPG was proposed by Brown (1911) to explain the motor pattern observed in the leg muscles of the cat during locomotion. Brown's model, which is known as the **half-center model,** com-

prises one set of CPG neurons that project to motor neurons innervating extensor muscles and another set that projects to motor neurons innervating flexor muscles (figure 7.15a). These two sets of neurons, or half centers, inhibit each other reciprocally so that when one half center is active, the other is inhibited. Apart from the intrinsic properties of the neurons generating the rhythm, two mechanisms are commonly used by CPGs to alternate activation among output neurons (half centers). One mechanism is delayed excitation of antagonistic neurons, which coexists with inhibitory connections. The other mechanism is a postinhibitory rebound, which refers to an increased excitability of the network neurons after a period of inhibition.

Since Brown's proposal, we have learned many details about the CPG components, such as the source of the rhythm, the types of neurons involved in the CPG, and the cellular interactions that define the motor pattern (Stein et al., 1997). Because of the complexity of the CPG, most of the details have emerged from studies

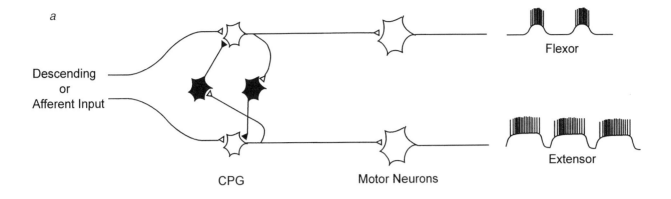

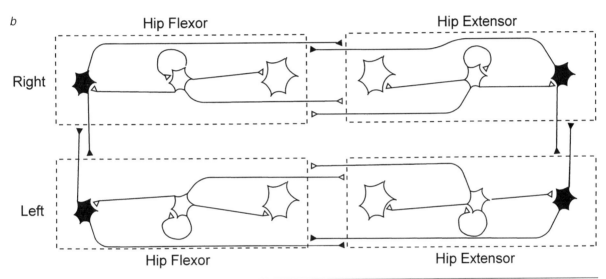

Figure 7.15 Organization of central pattern generators (CPGs). *(a)* The half-center model of Brown (1911), which represents reciprocal inhibition (filled-in neurons) between neurons that project to motor neurons innervating flexor and extensor muscles. The motor rhythm is shown as alternating bursts of action potentials in the nerves projecting to the antagonis muscles. *(b)* The CPG network that controls rostral scratching in the turtle. The CPG for each leg (right and left) and muscle group (flexor and extensor) is shown within the dashed lines. According to this scheme, the scratch behavior by one leg involves rhythmic activation of the hip flexor and extensor muscles, and interacts with the neurons controlling the other leg.

Data from Stein and Smith, 1997 (7.15b).

on CPGs with relatively fewer elements. These have included such systems as the heartbeat CPG in crustacea, the feeding and swimming CPGs in the mollusk, the pyloric and gastric CPGs in the crustacean stomatogastric system, the flight CPG in the locust, the swimming CPGs in the lamprey and leech, and the respiratory CPG in mammals. As an example, the CPG that produces a scratch behavior by one hindlimb of the turtle is shown in figure 7.15*b*. This behavior involves alternating activation of the hip flexor and extensor muscles, which requires interactions among interneurons (excitatory and inhibitory) and motor neurons that control both legs. Thus, when one leg is activated, the other is inhibited.

The existence of CPGs in humans seems certain on the basis of the observations of rhythmic reciprocal contractions and long-latency flexor reflexes in paraplegic patients, as well as fictive locomotor patterns in primates (Dimitrijevic, Gersaimenko, & Pinter, 1998). The evidence from such studies suggests that the CPG controlling limb movement is distributed along the spinal cord and is not a single entity (Gelfand, Orlovsky, & Shik, 1988; Kiehn & Kjaerulff, 1998; Saltiel, Tresch, & Bizzi, 1998).

Three features of the neurons that comprise a rhythm-generating network can be manipulated to produce a CPG: (1) cellular properties, (2) synaptic properties, and

(3) connections among the neurons (Stein et al., 1997). The fundamental rhythm produced by most CPGs depends on the endogenous pacemaker properties of **generator neurons** (Selverston et al., 1997). The rhythm is produced by the activation and inactivation of currents caused by the flux of ions (e.g., K^+, Na^+, and Ca^{2+}) across the membrane. The interactions among these currents can generate potentials with many different shapes. Because CPGs comprise a number of generator neurons, the temporal patterns of the motor output are determined by the membrane properties of the generator neurons and the interactions between these neurons. The shape of the motor output, however, depends on the interactions between the generator neurons and the output neurons of the network. In general, the number of neurons in the CPG depends on the complexity of the rhythm. For example, a CPG that produces only excitation has fewer elements than one that generates alternating activity in extensor and flexor muscles.

CPGs are activated by **command neurons,** which are located in higher centers (figure 7.14). Command neurons can initiate or suppress the activity of a CPG, usually by changing the membrane potential of the generator neurons. However, command neurons can also influence the intercellular connections within a CPG. Command neurons are activated whenever the animal senses a need for a particular behavior, for example to escape an external threat or to satisfy an internal state of motivation (e.g., hunger, thirst, and mating). Because command neurons can influence more than one CPG, the behavior that results from activation of a command neuron can vary depending on the context of the animal (Selverston et al., 1997).

Example 7.4
Central Pattern Generators Might Monitor the Kinematics of Limbs

Although the output of a CPG is a pattern of muscle activation, it is likely that the control variable is some feature of the motor behavior that is being elaborated. Because the muscles of a limb are probably controlled by different CPGs, they (CPGs) can be coupled with different timing relations to vary the details of a behavior. For example, varying the timing of CPG activity for human locomotion could change the speed of locomotion, change the gait from walking to running, or change the direction from forward to backward (Smith, Carlson-Kuhts, & Trank, 1998). Although the timing and magnitude of muscle activity vary across these conditions, the behavior is constrained by such requirements as the need to maintain balance and to minimize the expenditure of energy (Lacquaniti, Grasso, & Zago, 1999).

Despite the capabilities of the central nervous system (CNS), the task of controlling human locomotion appears to be overwhelming when considered in terms of CPGs controlling resultant muscle torques about the involved joints. This would involve controlling the action of individual muscles and dealing with intersegmental dynamics to produce the desired displacement of the center of mass. Alternatively, the CPGs could monitor the kinematics of the limb segments. One possibility is that CPGs control the elevation angles of the segments in the leg; the elevation angles correspond to the angle in the sagittal plane between the vertical and the body segment (Lacquaniti et al., 1999). The elevation angles for the thigh, shank, and foot covary during human walking such that a three-dimensional graph of the angles lies on a plane. The orientation of the plane changes with the relative timing of angular displacement among the segments. This association has been termed the **planar law of intersegmental coordination** (Bianchi, Angelini, Orani, & Lacquaniti, 1998; Grasso, Bianchi, & Lacquaniti, 1998). On the basis of this scheme, Lacquaniti and colleagues propose that the observed patterns of muscle activity are a consequence of the CPGs attempting to achieve the desired kinematic relations for a particular gait rather than simply producing alternating bursts of activity in antagonist muscles.

Sensory Modulation

Although CPGs are capable of generating a specific motor pattern, feedback from sensory receptors is absolutely necessary for a normal pattern in an intact behaving animal (Büschges & El Manira, 1998). From studies on the integration of sensory feedback into CPG function, four principles have emerged: (1) sensory feedback contributes to the generation and maintenance of rhythmic activity; (2) phasic sensory signals initiate the major phase transitions in intact motor systems; (3) sensory signals regulate the magnitude of ongoing motor activity; and (4) transmission in a reflex pathway can vary during a movement (Pearson & Ramirez, 1997).

Generation and Maintenance of Rhythm

When the CPG is disconnected from the muscles it controls, the output produced by the CPG is referred to as a **fictive** pattern; that is, no actual motor pattern is expressed in the muscles (figure 7.15*a*). In such preparations, the CPG can also be isolated from sensory feedback (deafferentated) and can be separated from higher centers (e.g., decerebrated or spinalized). The critical test of a CPG is that it must be able to generate a motor rhythm under these conditions. However, the CPG has to be activated artificially in these preparations, for example by electrical stimulation, by the introduction of pharmacologic agents, or by phasic afferent feedback. The ability to activate the isolated CPG with afferent feedback underscores the contribution that sensory feedback can make to the function of the CPG. Although the rhythm observed in a fictive preparation can be similar to that found in normal behavior, the motor pattern is typically quite different, because of modulation by afferent feedback.

In intact and behaving systems, there are a number of examples of the significant role of afferent feedback in shaping a motor rhythm. One example is chewing. Mastication in mammals is controlled by three jaw-closing muscles (temporalis, masseter, and pterygoid) and one jaw-opening muscle (digastric). The motor pattern used during mastication depends on the type of food that is being chewed. The motor pattern is controlled by a CPG located in the brainstem and appears to involve the intrinsic properties of trigeminal motor neurons (Lund, Kolta, Westberg, & Scott, 1998). Feedback from muscle spindles in the jaw-closing muscles and pressure receptors in the periodontum provide positive feedback during mastication, which increases cycle duration and the bursts of activity in the motor neurons. In contrast, the spindles are active during resting conditions when the

jaw-closing muscles are stretched, not when the jaw is closed. Thus, the muscle spindles and pressure receptors enhance and modify the motor pattern during the jaw-closing phase of mastication. Moreover, chronic musculoskeletal pain slows the rate of chewing movements and alters the associated motor pattern (Svensson, Houe, & Arendt-Nielsen, 1997).

Phase Transitions

One observation made by Sherrington (1910) was that afferent feedback appears to be critical in controlling the switch from the stance to the swing phase in locomotion. When cats walked on a treadmill, he noted that the switch from the stance phase to the swing phase depended on the amount of extension at the hip joint. Subsequently, in spinalized cats (CPG disconnected from higher centers) walking on a treadmill, Grillner and Rossignol (1978) found that blocking extension of the hip prevented the hindlimb from initiating the swing phase. As a result of stretching and vibrating various muscles during the step cycle, it seems that feedback from muscle spindles located in hip and ankle flexor muscles (pathway 5 in figure 7.16) is capable of resetting the locomotor rhythm (Hiebert, Whelan, Prochazka, & Pearson, 1996). This effect, however, occurred only during the stance phase and not the swing phase.

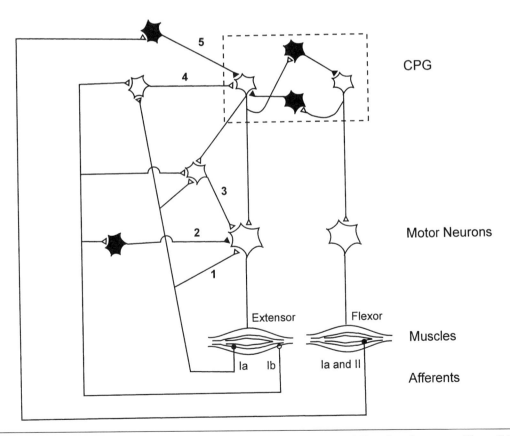

Figure 7.16   Some effects of afferent feedback from muscle spindles (Group Ia and II) and tendon organs (Group Ib) to motor neurons and the locomotor central pattern generator (CPG).

Data from Pearson, 1995; and Pearson and Ramirez, 1997.

The stance-to-swing transition during walking also appears to depend on feedback from Golgi tendon organs (Pearson & Ramirez, 1997). Tendon organs provide information on the force in a muscle. Under typical quiescent conditions, activation of tendon organs results in disynaptic inhibition of the motor neurons innervating the muscle in which the tendon organs reside (pathway 2 in figure 7.16). During locomotion, however, input from Group Ib afferents of extensor muscles produces excitation of the motor neurons that project to the extensor muscles (pathway 3 in figure 7.16). This has the effect of enhancing the extensor muscle activity during the stance phase. Electrical stimulation of Group Ib afferents from knee and ankle extensor muscles prolongs the stance phase in decerebrate cats (CPG disconnected from higher centers) walking on a treadmill (Whelan, Hiebert, & Pearson, 1995). These results suggest that the force in the extensor muscles must decline before the CPG will switch from the stance to the swing phase.

Magnitude of Motor Activity

One of the functions of feedback from large-diameter afferents is to enhance muscle activation during the various phases of the rhythm, for example, the stance phase of walking. Three pathways reinforce the activation of the extensor muscles during the stance phase of walking (Pearson & Ramirez, 1997). First there is the monosynaptic excitation from Group Ia afferents (pathway 1 in figure 7.16). Second, there is disynaptic excitation from Group Ia and Ib afferents to the extensor motor neurons (pathway 3 in figure 7.16). This pathway is opened by the CPG during locomotion. Third, there is polysynaptic excitation of the extensor half center of the CPG by feedback from Group Ia and Ib afferents (pathway 4 in figure 7.16). This reinforcement of muscle activity during the locomotor rhythm might be necessary to accommodate changes in the interaction between the limb and its surroundings, such as in walking up an incline, walking backward, carrying a heavy load, and walking into a head wind.

Modulation of Transmission in Reflex Pathways

Several times in this chapter, as well as in chapter 6, we noted that the magnitude of a reflex is not fixed but instead varies across tasks and within the different phases of a single task. When the locomotor CPGs are activated, for example, reflex pathways switch from a posture control mode to a movement control mode (Sinkjær, Andersen, & Larsen, 1996; Stephens & Yang, 1996). This can even lead to a reflex reversal, whereby the same sensory signal can bring about a completely opposite motor response. For example, displacement of a limb can evoke a resistance reflex when maintaining a posture but an assistance reflex during movement (Büschges & El Manira, 1998). Similarly, feedback by Group Ib afferents inhibits

motor neurons when holding a posture (pathway 2 in figure 7.16) but provides excitation during locomotion.

There are three mechanisms that can change the gain and sign (resistance or assistance) of reflex pathways. One is efferent modulation of proprioceptors, such as fusimotor control of the sensitivity of muscle spindles (Prochazka, 1989; Taylor et al., 2000). Another mechanism is presynaptic modulation of afferent pathways. Variations in the amplitude of monosynaptic reflexes in cats and H reflexes in humans during locomotion are mainly due to presynaptic inhibition of afferent feedback in the spinal cord (Gossard, 1996). The third of these mechanisms involves neuromodulatory substances that are released during a particular state. These alter transmission in reflex pathways (Burke, 1999; McCrea, Shefchyk, Stephens, & Pearson, 1995). Neuromodulators, which are usually amines or peptides, exert an effect through second messengers that can occur rapidly (within 10 ms) and produce a long-term change in the properties of the neuron (Dickinson, 1995). For example, substance P can alter transmission in the pathways of pulmonary reflexes during hypoxia, which results in an increase in the ventilatory drive to the respiratory muscles (Pearson & Ramirez, 1997). These mechanisms enable the system to match the efficacy of reflexes to its needs during rhythmic pattern generation.

Modulation by Chemicals and Steroids

One of the principles that has emerged in the study of CPGs is that they are not fixed circuits but are able to change to adapt the behavior. In addition to modulation by sensory feedback, it appears that the intrinsic properties of the neurons, as well as the synaptic connections between them, are regulated by inputs from modulatory neurons. For example, neuromodulators can change both the frequency of the locomotor pattern and the intensity of the muscle contractions (Sillar, Kiehn, & Kudo, 1997). The modulators include such chemicals as amino acids, amines, and peptides, which can alter the electrical properties of neurons in the CPG and can cause the release of neurotransmitters at presynaptic terminals within the CPG.

Two of the better-known modulators are serotonin (5-HT) and gamma-aminobutyric acid type B ($GABA_B$). The actions of the amine 5-HT include control of cellular conductances, transmitter receptors, and synaptic connections. For example, 5-HT can alter some of the voltage-gated conductances of motor neurons and thereby influence the timing and intensity of the discharge by motor neurons during locomotion (Sillar et al., 1997). The release of 5-HT that acts on the locomotor CPG is controlled by the raphe region in the brainstem; the activity of these neurons increases during motor behavior (Jacobs, 1994). Similarly, $GABA_B$ acts through metabotropic receptors to modulate synaptic transmission. It can presynaptically modulate synaptic transmission from inhibitory and excitatory interneurons, and postsynaptically it can reduce Ca^{2+} currents. Gamma-aminobutyric acid is supplied by neurons that are either intrinsic or extrinsic to the spinal cord.

Another class of neurons that can influence CPGs and behavior are the steroid hormones (Weeks & McEwen, 1997). Steroids are able to induce neuronal plasticity, such as dendritic remodeling, neurogenesis, neuronal death, and alterations in excitability and neuropeptide expression. Among vertebrates, the rat is the species in which the effects of steroids on the CNS are most commonly studied. Sex and steroid hormones, along with influencing development, can modify the structure and characteristics of neurons in the brain. For example, both sex and stress hormones can alter the structure and function of the hippocampus, which participates in contextual memory, spatial memory, and declarative memory (Weeks

& McEwen, 1997). The importance of these mechanisms is underscored by the findings that many of the molecular and cellular processes involved in steroidal modulation are conserved across species. These hormones play key roles in the construction, expression, and modulation of the neural networks that produce motor behavior.

Supraspinal Control

We now turn our attention to the higher centers referred to in figure 7.14. In addition to providing command and modulatory signals for CPGs, these centers provide activation signals for all the voluntary movements that we perform (Amaral, 2000a; Ghez & Krakauer, 2000). Many structures within the CNS contribute to the development of the motor neuron signals that activate muscle. There are three main levels of control: the spinal cord, the descending systems of the brainstem, and the motor areas of the cerebral cortex (figure 7.17). The spinal cord and

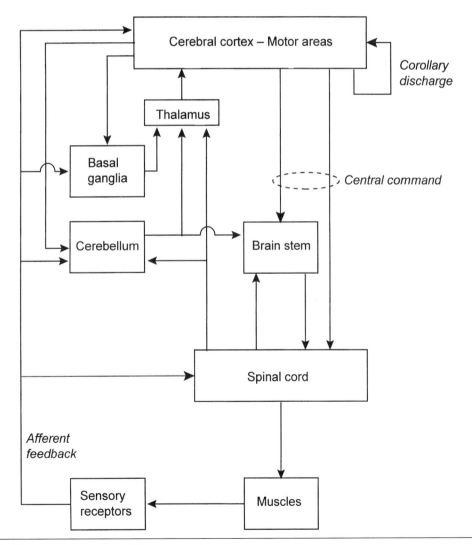

Figure 7.17   The major components of the motor system.

Data from Ghez, 1991b.

brainstem mediate reflexes and automatic behaviors, while the cortical motor areas initiate and control more complex voluntary movements.

The spinal cord contains neuronal networks that can produce reflexes and automatic behaviors independently of input from the brainstem and the cerebral cortex. Nonetheless, the function of these networks can be modified and controlled by descending input from these higher centers. For example, the brainstem integrates visual and vestibular information with somatosensory feedback, which is important in the control of posture. Similarly, the cerebral cortex can exert effects directly on the spinal networks, such as those controlling hand function, or through the descending systems of the brainstem. The direct projection from the cerebral cortex to the spinal cord is known as the **corticospinal tract.**

The flow of information through these three levels of control can be modified by two other supraspinal structures, the cerebellum and the basal ganglia. The cerebellum receives input from peripheral sensory receptors, the spinal cord, and the cerebral cortex; this enables it to compare the actual motor performance with the intended outcome. On the basis of this comparison, the cerebellum sends output to the brainstem and (via the thalamus) to the cerebral cortex that improves the match between the intended and actual motor behaviors. Similarly, the basal ganglia integrate input from many areas

of the cerebral cortex that is then used in the control of movement.

Cerebral Cortex

The cerebrum consists of left and right cerebral hemispheres connected by axon bundles known as **commissures.** The functions served by the two hemispheres are quite different. The outer shell of the cerebral hemisphere is a 3-mm layer of cortical neurons, known as the cerebral cortex, that represents a major integrating center of sensory input and motor output signals (Amaral, 2000a). The motor areas of the cerebral cortex are located immediately anterior and posterior to the central sulcus (figure 7.18). The three anterior components include the **primary motor area** (Brodmann's area 4), the **supplementary motor area** (area 6: between areas 4 and 8 on the medial surface), and the **premotor cortex** (area 6). The two posterior components are the **primary somatosensory cortex** (areas 1 to 3) and the **posterior parietal cortex** (areas 5 and 7). The traditional view of this organization, however, has been revised as a consequence of findings that the premotor cortex actually comprises six distinct and separate regions, each of which sends some projections directly to the spinal cord (Dum & Strick, 1996). The premotor areas are defined as those regions of the frontal lobe that have direct projections to the primary

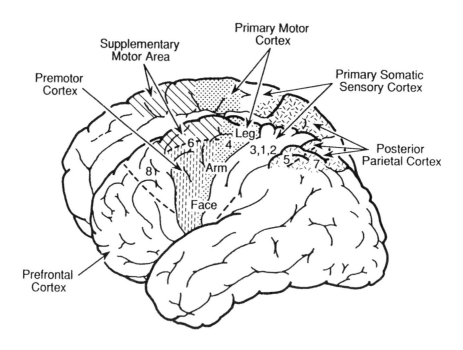

Figure 7.18   Regions of the left and right halves of the cerebral cortex.

From "Voluntary Movement" by C. Ghez. In *Principles of Neural Science, 3rd ed.,* p. 611, by E.R. Kandel, J.H. Schwartz, and T.M. Jessell (Eds.), 1991, New York: Elsevier Science Publishing Co., Inc. Reprinted by permission of the McGraw-Hill Companies.

motor cortex; they include two premotor areas on the lateral surface of the hemisphere and four premotor areas on the medial wall.

The input and output of the cerebral cortex has a **somatotopic** (body map) organization in which the cortical neurons influencing muscles and the sensory information from the various parts of the body are arranged in an orderly sequence (figures 7.18 and 7.19) (Amaral, 2000b; Roland & Zilles, 1996). Despite the orderliness of these maps, the same muscles can be activated with electrical stimulation from several distinct places in the primary motor cortex (Dum & Strick, 1996; Schieber & Hibbard, 1993). One of the differences between these multiple sites, such as for the hand, appears to be the projections that each receives. Nonetheless, single corticospinal neurons innervate a limited number of segments in the spinal cord, and the projections are organized topographically (figure 7.23). For example, corticospinal neurons that project to lower cervical segments are involved primarily in the control of distal arm movements, whereas those that project to upper cervical segments control the neck and proximal arm movements (He, Dum, & Strick, 1993). The movement of a single finger, however, is not achieved through activation of a single, discrete set of cortical neurons; rather, several different groups are involved (Sanes, Donoghue, Thangaraj, Edelman, & Warach, 1995; Schieber, 1995). These topographic maps are also found in other regions of the cerebral cortex (posterior parietal cortex, supplementary motor area, and premotor areas) and in the cerebellum and thalamus. Furthermore, the maps are not fixed but can be modified, for example after an injury or with physical training (Müller et al., 1997; Weiss et al., 1998).

As shown in figure 7.17, output from the motor areas of the cerebral cortex can act directly or indirectly on motor neurons. The direct action involves axons that originate in the frontal, prefrontal, and parietal cortex and project in the corticospinal and corticobulbar tracts. Axons in the corticospinal tract terminate on motor neurons in the spinal cord, while those in the **corticobulbar tract** end in cranial nuclei that innervate the facial muscles. About 43% of the axons in the corticospinal tract project to several different levels of the spinal cord and even to different motor nuclei (Cheney, Fetz, & Mewes, 1991; Dum & Strick, 1996). About one-third of the fibers in the corticospinal tract originate from area 4, one-third from area 6, and one-third from areas 1, 2, and 3 (figure 7.18). In the brainstem, at the level of the medulla, about three-quarters of the fibers in the corticospinal tract cross the midline and project in the **lateral corticospinal tract** to interneurons and motor neurons that control distal muscles on the contralateral side of the body. The remaining one-quarter of the fibers stay on the same side of the body and form the **ventral corticospinal tract,** which ends on interneurons that control axial muscles on both the left and right sides of the body.

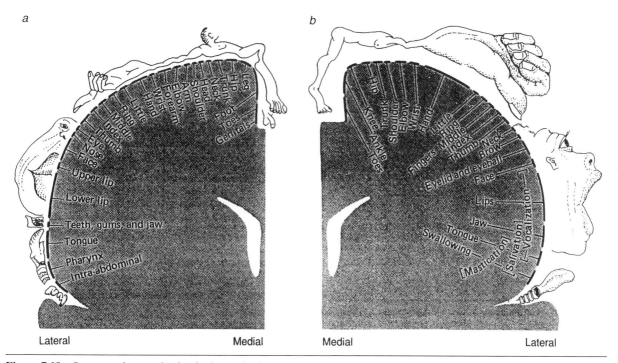

Figure 7.19   Somatotopic organization in the cerebral cortex: *(a)* sensory homunculus; *(b)* motor homunculus.

From "Touch" by E. R. Kandel and T. M. Jessell, 1991, in E. R. Kandel, J. H. Schwartz, and T. M. Jessell (Eds.), in *Principles of Neural Science* (3rd ed.). p. 372. Copyright 1991 by Elsevier Science. Adapted by permission of The McGraw-Hill Companies.

Across species, the number of projections from the primary motor cortex to motor nuclei in the spinal cord is correlated with manual dexterity. A number of axons in the corticospinal tract arise from the somatosensory and posterior parietal cortex. These projections terminate in the dorsal horn, where they modulate the flow of information from somatosensory pathways.

The primary motor cortex receives substantial input from area 5 (lateral portion) of the parietal cortex, modest input from area 2 of the primary somatic sensory cortex, a little input from areas 3a and 1 of the primary somatic sensory cortex, a little input from area 7 of the parietal cortex, and no input from area 3b (Dum & Strick, 1996). Areas 5 and 7 also send the most dense and widespread connections to the premotor areas. Projections from the premotor areas to the primary motor cortex are organized topographically. The motor areas of the cortex receive substantial input from the **ventrolateral thalamus,** which itself receives input from the basal ganglia and the deep cerebellar nuclei (figure 7.17). The output from the basal ganglia and the cerebellum does not go to the same parts of the thalamus, and different regions of the ventrolateral thalamus project to different parts of the primary motor cortex. Similarly, each thalamic nucleus provides the most substantial input to an individual premotor area. In addition to projections to the primary motor cortex and the spinal cord, the premotor areas have numerous interconnections, especially the supplementary motor area.

Voluntary Movement

Whereas the movements produced by the spinal cord and brainstem are largely predetermined, those generated by the cerebral cortex occur in response to a perceived need for the movements. Such actions are known as voluntary movements and are distinguished from reflex and automatic responses in that they can be interrupted by the performer (Prochazka et al., 2000). The performance of a voluntary movement is based on the generation of the intent or idea, the development of a plan of action, and execution of the plan (Kandel, 2000a; Krakauer & Ghez, 2000; Saper, Iversen, & Frackowiak, 2000). The posterior parietal cortex is mainly responsible for defining the intent; the premotor areas of the frontal cortex develop the plan; and the primary motor cortex sends out the command signals. The output from the motor cortex is often referred to as the **central command** and is transmitted both to lower neural centers (brainstem and spinal cord) and back to other supraspinal centers involved in the development of the plan (figure 7.17). The signal that is transmitted back to the supraspinal centers is known as the corollary discharge and provides a reference that enables the system to interpret incoming afferent signals. Because the corollary discharge is a copy of the efferent signal, it sometimes is called the **efference copy.**

Measurement of neuronal activity in both the primary motor cortex and the premotor areas has indicated that the discharge of action potentials by single neurons precedes the onset of EMG associated with simple movements (Dum & Strick, 1996). Many neurons in the primary motor cortex modulate their activity in association with various aspects of the force exerted during a task. This characteristic is common among corticospinal neurons that connect directly to motor neurons in the spinal cord (Cheney & Fetz, 1980; Dettmers et al., 1995). When monkeys performed wrist flexion and extension movements, Evarts (1968) found that different neurons were active during flexion compared with extension. The activity of some neurons, however, was more strongly related to coactivation of the antagonist muscle (Humphrey & Reed, 1983). There is some evidence of force-related activity among neurons in the premotor areas. While neurons in the primary motor cortex exhibit the greatest modulation of activity at low static forces, those in the premotor areas grade their activity over a greater range of forces. However, there does appear to be some difference in the activity of the neurons between isometric contractions and tasks that involve the displacement of a load (Sergio & Kalaska, 1998).

In studies of the activity of populations of neurons in the primary motor cortex, the activity was maximal for a preferred direction of movement (Georgopoulos, Kalaska, Caminiti, & Massey, 1982; Georgopoulos, Kettner, & Schwartz, 1988). Each neuron is most active when movements are performed in a specific direction and is silent when movements are performed in the opposite direction. Consequently, for a given movement, many neurons are active such that the direction of the movement corresponds to the *net* direction of all the active neurons. Each thin line in figure 7.20 indicates the preferred direction and the amount of activity for a single neuron in the primary motor cortex of a monkey during a reaching movement. The population vector, the net effect of all the individual neurons, is closely aligned with the direction of the reach. Because the population vector is expressed prior to movement onset and changes with the trajectory during a movement, Georgopoulos and colleagues suggest that the primary motor cortex determines the kinematic details of a movement (Georgopoulos, 1988). This direction-related activity has been found in premotor areas, deep cerebellar nuclei, area 5, area 2, and the basal ganglia (Dum & Strick, 1996). The sequence of activation, albeit with some overlap in time, appears to proceed from area 6, to area 4, to area 5, to area 2 (Kalaska & Crammond, 1992).

Roles of Motor Areas

Each motor area of the cerebral cortex has primary, but not exclusive, responsibility for selected aspects of movement generation (Krakauer & Ghez, 2000). Dum and

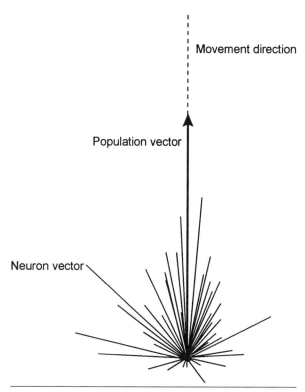

Movement direction

Population vector

Neuron vector

Figure 7.20 The population vector determined from neurons in the primary motor cortex corresponds to the direction of the movement.

Data from Georgopoulos, Caminiti, Kalaska, and Massey, 1983.

Strick (1996) have summarized the roles of the various areas with the following scheme.

■ *Preparation for a Motor Response.* By varying the time between the instructions for a task and the beginning of the task, investigators can assess which motor areas participate in the preparation to perform the task. Such activity has been found in both the primary motor cortex and the premotor areas, with the most activity in the supplementary motor area and the dorsal premotor area on the lateral surface of the hemisphere.

■ *Anticipation of Behavioral Events.* When there is a fixed time between the start of a trial and the onset of the movement, anticipatory activity gradually increases. This activity has been found in the dorsal premotor area.

■ *Signal-Related Activity.* Neurons in several premotor areas, especially the supplementary motor area and the dorsal premotor area, become more active after an instructional stimulus. This activity may be involved in forming associations between motor behavior and sensory stimuli.

■ *Visual Guidance of Movement.* Some tasks are characterized by the need for vision to detect a target, the location of which defines the appropriate motor response. Neurons in the ventral premotor area are critical in this behavior.

■ *Conditional Associations.* Tasks that require an interpretation of a stimulus, such as that *red* means *stop*, depend on neurons in the lateral premotor cortex (ventral and dorsal premotor areas).

■ *Self-Paced Movements.* Self-paced movements are internally generated rather than being a response to an external stimulus. With such tasks, it is possible to record slow changes in the electrical potential over the cortex; this effect is known as the readiness potential. Although there is no agreement on the origin of the readiness potential, it is likely to involve one of the premotor areas, such as the rostral cingulate motor area on the medial wall of the hemisphere.

■ *Sequential Movements.* Tasks that entail performing a sequence of movements, which is the most common of the motor behaviors, involve many cortical areas. Although many studies support a prominent role for the supplementary motor area in organizing such sequences, some investigators have not observed this activity. One of the reasons for this discrepancy is that the activity in the supplementary motor area declines with practice.

As you can see from this description of the observed associations between motor performance and the activity of neurons in the motor areas of the cerebral cortex, much remains to be learned about their specific roles in movement.

Example 7.5
Readiness Potential

One of the tools commonly used by both clinicians and experimentalists to study brain function is the **electroencephalogram** (Binnie & Prior, 1994), a technique that involves recording the electrical activity of cortical neurons. Electroencephalography (EEG) is based on the placement of electrodes on the scalp over the frontal, parietal, occipital, and temporal lobes of the cerebral cortex. The EEG represents the flow of currents in these regions. The frequency content of the EEG ranges from 1 to 30 Hz, with four distinct regions: delta waves (0.5 to 4 Hz), theta waves (4 to 8 Hz), alpha waves (8 to 13 Hz), and beta waves (13 to 25 Hz). The delta and theta waves are usually observed during various phases of sleep, whereas the alpha waves occur during relaxed wakefulness and the beta waves are associated with intense mental activity.

Electroencephalography has a number of clinical and experimental uses. For example, long-term monitoring can provide diagnostic information on patients with epilepsy (Binnie & Prior, 1994). In experimental settings, the EEG is often used to study brain activity prior to the performance of a movement. The

(continued)

EEG recorded under these conditions is called the **readiness potential;** sometimes this potential is also called the premovement or Bereitschafts potential (figure 7.21). The gradual increase in the EEG that comprises the readiness potential begins about 1 to 2 s before the onset of the movement and is maximal over the vertex. Because the readiness potential begins soon before the onset of the movement and is present whether the movement is executed or simply imagined, it probably corresponds to activity in the supplementary motor area (Cunnington et al., 1996).

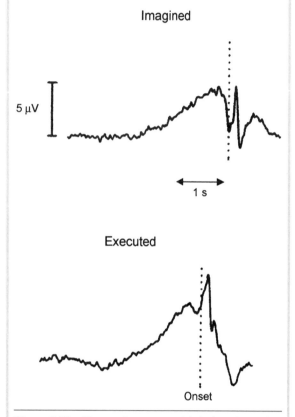

Figure 7.21 The readiness potential during the performance of imagined and executed finger movements.

Data from Cunnington, Iansek, Bradshaw, and Phillips, 1996.

Example 7.6
Electroencephalogram-Controlled Prosthesis

One application of the EEG signal is its use in driving various external devices, such as a cursor on a computer screen (Wolpaw, McFarland, Neat, & Forneris, 1991). This application has considerable potential as a means to enable persons with limited motor capa-

bilities. It can, for example, be used to provide a command signal for a prosthetic hand. To evaluate the functional capabilities of an EEG-driven prosthesis, Lauer, Peckham, and Kilgore (1999) trained three individuals to control the beta rhythm of the EEG so that it could move a cursor to various targets on a computer screen. The beta rhythm was extracted from an electrode array located over the frontal cortex. Two of the subjects were able-bodied, and one used a neuroprosthesis. All three individuals were able to accurately control the cursor within six training sessions, and the accuracy of the control signal was not disturbed by arm movements. Moreover, Lauer et al. (1999) developed an interface between the EEG signal and the neuroprosthesis that enabled the user to pick up and move an object, grasp and release a fork, and grasp and release a cup. The next challenge is to enable the user to exert a sustained force and to control force more precisely.

Brainstem

The brainstem comprises the medulla oblongata, pons, and mesencephalon (figure 7.22). The brainstem is largely responsible for the control of posture. It integrates information provided by the equilibrium organ (vestibular apparatus) and sensory receptors in the neck region, along with input from the cerebral cortex and cerebellum. The **medulla oblongata** is the continuation of the brain into the spinal cord and is the site where most of the cranial nerves enter and exit the brain. Several vital autonomic nuclei concerned with respiration, heart action, and gastrointestinal function are located in the medulla oblongata. The **pons** lies between the medulla and the mesencephalon (midbrain). A large bundle of crossing fibers lying on the lower aspect of the pons interconnects the brainstem and the cerebellum. The **mesencephalon** merges anteriorly into the thalamus and hypothalamus.

Distributed in the brainstem are at least three motor centers that send efferent fibers to influence the motor neurons of the spinal cord (figure 7.22). These motor centers include the red nucleus, lateral vestibular nucleus, and reticular formation. The **red nucleus** is located in the mesencephalon and gives rise to the **rubrospinal tract,** which crosses in the brainstem and influences contralateral spinal centers. The tract is arranged somatotopically (body map), meaning that the location of the axons in the tract depends on the motor neurons that they innervate. For example, axons of neurons in the dorsomedial part of the nucleus travel medially in the tract and innervate cervical segments. When stimulated alone electrically, the red nucleus mainly excites alpha and gamma motor neurons that innervate

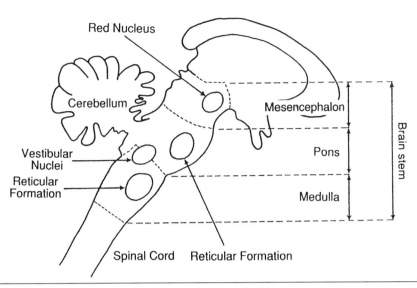

Figure 7.22 Components of the brainstem and the location of the motor centers.
Adapted from Schmidt, 1983.

flexor muscles and inhibits motor neurons that connect to extensor muscles. The red nucleus receives most of its input from the dentate nucleus (in the cerebellum) and the motor cortex. The **lateral vestibular nucleus** extends between the pons and medulla oblongata, with the neurons arranged somatotopically within the nucleus. The axons of cells located in this nucleus give rise to the **vestibulospinal tract,** which influences ipsilateral motor neurons. The effects of the lateral vestibular nucleus include excitation of alpha and gamma motor neurons that innervate extensor muscles and inhibition of motor neurons that connect to flexor motor neurons. The lateral vestibular nucleus receives input from the cerebellum and the equilibrium organ (labyrinth). The **reticular formation** produces two **reticulospinal tracts,** the *pontine* and *medullary* components. The reticulospinal tracts are diffuse—they have no somatotopic organization—and terminate along the length of the cord from the cervical to lumbar segments. The reticular formation receives input from the cerebral cortex, the fastigial nucleus (in the cerebellum), and ascending pathways of the spinal cord.

The **descending pathways** from supraspinal structures can be classified into three pathways: the corticospinal tract and two groups (A and B) of brainstem tracts (Kuypers, 1985). The crossed, pre-central sulcus component of the corticospinal tract largely terminates laterally on or near motor neurons that innervate *distal muscles* (figure 7.23). Some axons in the corticospinal tract terminate ventrally on or near motor neurons that innervate *axial* and *proximal muscles.* The corticospinal tract has a greater degree of topographic organization than either brainstem pathway. The postcentral sulcus component

of the corticospinal tract modulates incoming sensory information from the periphery, including that required for the control of movement.

The **Group A pathway** lies in the ventromedial brainstem and consists of the vestibulospinal, reticulospinal, and tectospinal tracts; the **tectospinal tract** arises from neurons in the superior colliculus, which is a mesencephalic area concerned with orientation to visual stimuli. The tectospinal tract probably contributes to the head- and neck-orienting reactions to visual stimuli (Rothwell, 1994). Activation of the Group A pathway provides postural support for goal-directed movement involving synergistic muscles, especially axial and proximal muscles. The Group A axons travel in the ventral and ventromedial funiculi of the spinal cord and *terminate bilaterally onto motor neurons that innervate axial and proximal muscles* (figure 7.23). The axons of the Group A neurons give off many collaterals, which seems necessary for coordinating the activity of many muscles.

The descending axons in the **Group B pathway** lie in the lateral brainstem and consist of the crossed rubrospinal and the crossed reticulospinal tracts. This pathway contributes to goal-directed motor activity by *influencing motor neurons that innervate distal flexor muscles.* The axons in this pathway have relatively few collaterals, and they end either directly on motor neurons or on short **propriospinal axons** of the spinal cord; propriospinal neurons are interneurons that convey information between spinal segments. The Group B axons travel in the contralateral dorsolateral funiculus of the spinal cord and terminate in the intermediate zone close to neurons that affect distal flexor muscles (figure 7.23).

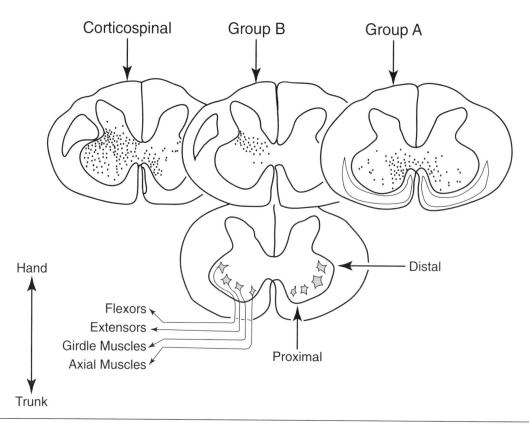

Figure 7.23   Termination zones of the three descending pathways. The upper three cross sections show the location of the terminations of the axons in the corticospinal tract, Group B pathway, and Group A pathway, respectively. The lower cross section indicates the topographic organization of the motor neurons in a cervical segment of the spinal cord.

Adapted from Lawrence and Kuypers, 1968.

Cerebellum

The **cerebellum** is located inferior to the cerebral hemispheres and posterior to the brainstem. It is an unusual structure because it contains over one-half of the neurons in the brain, is highly ordered, and has no direct efferent connections to the spinal cord or brainstem motor nuclei despite its involvement in the control of movement (Ghez & Thach, 2000). The cerebellum has two *hemispheres* and a middle region called the **vermis.** The cerebellum comprises an outer mantle of gray matter (cerebellar cortex), internal white matter, and three pairs of deep subcortical nuclei (fastigial, interpositus, dentate). The cerebellum receives input from the periphery (somatosensory and visual), brainstem (vestibular), and cerebral cortex. The entire output of the cerebellum is transmitted through the deep subcortical nuclei and the vestibular nucleus in three symmetrical pairs of tracts that *connect the cerebellum and the brainstem.* The cerebellum receives about 40 times more input than it delivers as output.

The cerebellum has three functional divisions, each of which receives input and sends output to distinct parts of the CNS (Ghez, 1991a). The three divisions are the spinocerebellum, cerebrocerebellum, and vestibulocerebellum (figure 7.24). The **spinocerebellum,** which includes the vermis and intermediate hemispheres, receives most of its sensory input from the spinal cord. The output from the vermis region of the spinocerebellum goes to the **fastigial nucleus,** whereas that from the intermediate hemispheres is directed to the **interpositus** (or interposed) **nucleus.** The **cerebrocerebellum,** which comprises the lateral hemispheres of the cerebellum, receives input from the cerebral cortex via the pons. The output goes initially to the **dentate nucleus** and then through the thalamus to the motor areas of the cerebral cortex. The **vestibulocerebellum** occupies the flocculonodular lobe and receives input from the **vestibular nuclei** in the medulla, and sends its output back to the same nuclei.

The input to the cerebellum arrives via two afferent systems, the mossy fibers and the climbing fibers, both of which are excitatory (figure 7.25). The **mossy fibers** originate in several brainstem nuclei and in the spinal cord, and comprise the spinocerebellar tract. The somatosensory information transmitted by the spinocerebellar tract projects to two somatotopic maps: one on the anterior lobe and the other on the posterior lobe (cf. however, Robinson, 1995). The **climbing fibers** originate in

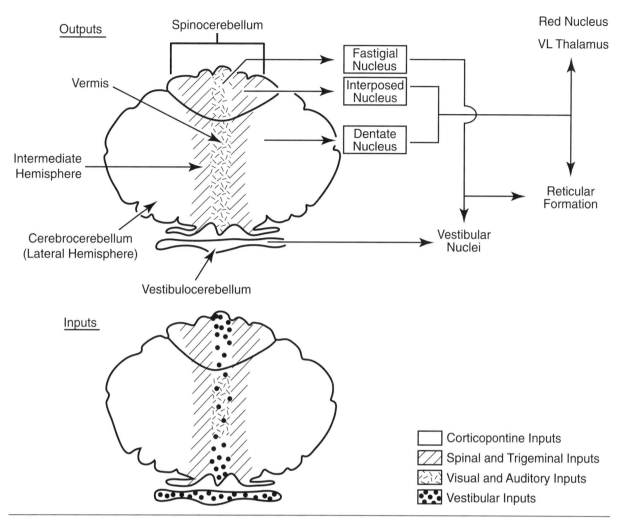

Figure 7.24   Three functional subdivisions of the cerebellum.

From "The cerebellum" by C. Ghez. In *Principles of neural science, 3rd ed.,* p. 633, by E.R. Kandel, J.H. Schwartz and T.M. Jessell (Eds.), 1991. New York: Elsevier Science. Reproduced with permission of The McGraw-Hill Companies.

the **inferior olive nucleus** of the medulla. Each climbing fiber projects to a **Purkinje cell** (these cells are the output neurons of the cerebellum) and is able to evoke an obligatory action potential. The axons of the Purkinje cells project downward to the cerebellar or vestibular nuclei.

The output provided by the Purkinje cells is inhibitory, which means that the cerebellum sends tonic inhibitory input to the three cerebellar nuclei. Most of the output from the cerebellum comes from the interpositus and dentate nuclei. The axons cross the midline of the brain and separate into ascending and descending tracts. The descending tract innervates the reticular formation in the pons and medulla. The ascending tract innervates the red nucleus and the ventrolateral part of the thalamus. This area of the thalamus sends projections to areas 4 and 6 of the cerebral cortex. There is also a loop from the red nucleus to the inferior olive and back to the cerebellum (climbing fibers).

Because the cerebellum is not directly involved in the perception of sensation and because damage to it does not cause paralysis, the cerebellum must function at the level between the sensory and motor systems. One approach that has been used to identify the role of the cerebellum in movement is to compare the timing of the activity in the cerebellar nuclei with the onset of a movement. These neurons do exhibit activity prior to the onset of movement. As indicated by such measurements, neurons in the dentate nucleus are involved in the initiation of a voluntary movement, while those in the interpositus nucleus discharge action potentials during the movement. Activity in the fastigial nucleus is related to the control of posture.

Despite these conclusions, there is less certainty about what details of a movement are most influenced by the cerebellum. Some evidence suggests that the neurons in the dentate nucleus indicate the onset of a movement while those in the interpositus nucleus contribute to the

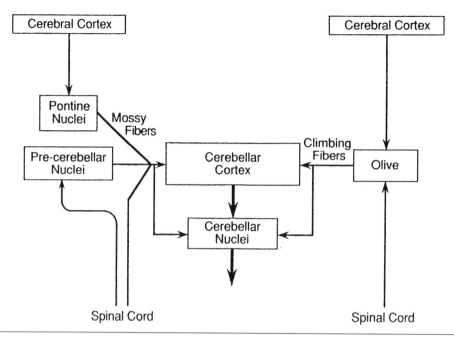

Figure 7.25 Afferent input to the cerebellum and output via the deep cerebellar nuclei.
Adapted from Rothwell, 1987.

control of muscle activity during a movement (Rothwell, 1994). Four sets of results complicate this interpretation. First, recordings from Purkinje cells and neurons in the cerebellar nuclei suggest that populations of cells indicate the direction of a movement (Fortier, Kalaska, & Smith, 1989), as has been found for neurons in the cerebral cortex. Second, recordings from Purkinje cells indicate that they control the activity of the antagonist muscle. Third, cerebellar neurons are active when slow movements are performed in either direction, in contrast to the single direction for a fast movement. Fourth, the output from neurons in the interpositus nucleus is not arranged somatotopically but rather comprises a set of domains that each influences a particular kind of movement (Robinson, 1995).

Because of these findings, there is no consensus on the precise features of movement that are of concern to the cerebellum. Due to the number of neurons in the cerebellum, the orderliness of its structure, and the consequences of cerebellar lesion, the cerebellum is assumed to contribute significantly to the control of movement. Rothwell (1994) has identified three theories of cerebellar function: timing device, learning device, and coordinator. As a *timing device,* the cerebral cortex initiates the movement by activating the agonist muscle, and the cerebellum stops the movement at the desired location. As a *learning device,* the cerebellum strengthens selected input-output connections so that, over time, less input is required to elicit the intended output. As a *coordinator,* the cerebellum coordinates muscle activity across sev-

eral joints so that the activity at different joints is scaled to produce the intended limb movement. The cerebellum appears to be interposed between the generation of the movement plan and the actual performance of the movement and thereby to modulate the activity of the muscles involved in the task.

Example 7.7
Cerebellar Disorders

A method frequently used to study lesions in the cerebellum is to cool a set of neurons and then measure the effect on performance. Such interventions produce impairments that are similar to the deficits exhibited by patients with cerebellar lesions (Rothwell, 1994). When the interpositus and dentate nuclei are cooled, simple movements—those performed in one plane about a single joint—show an increase in the reaction time and speed-dependent effects on their smoothness. For fast movements, there can be an overshoot of a movement to a target or delays at the turning points of a movement. Slow movements, however, are characterized by an **action tremor,** which comprises oscillations in the movement at a frequency of 3 to 5 Hz. Cooling of the fastigial nucleus impairs the ability to sit, stand, and walk.

Latash (1998) defines a number of terms that are used by clinicians to describe the abnormalities observed in patients with cerebellar disorders:

- **Kinetic tremor**—oscillations during movement

- **Intention tremor**—the large oscillations observed when a limb approaches the target

- **Postural tremor**—oscillations during a postural task

- **Dysmetria**—an inability to achieve a target position, due to either an overshoot (**hypermetria**) or an undershoot (**hypometria**)

- **Dysdiadochokinesia**—an inability to perform movements at a specified rhythm

- **Hypotonia**—a decrease in the resistance to passive joint motion

Many of the signs observed in patients with cerebellar disorders are referred to as **ataxia,** which means an impaired ability to execute voluntary movements.

Basal Ganglia

The basal ganglia represent five closely related nuclei: **caudate, putamen, globus pallidus, subthalamic nuclei,** and **substantia nigra** (DeLong, 2000). The caudate and putamen nuclei combine to form the **striatum,** whereas the globus pallidus has two parts, the internal and external segments. The basal ganglia receive a major input from the cerebral cortex and send most of their output, via the thalamus, back to the cortex (figure 7.26). The inputs to the basal ganglia are arranged topographically. Based on the number of projections from the striatum, the pathways are described as direct or indirect. The **direct pathway** involves the internal part of the globus pallidus and the substantia nigra, which project directly to the ventrolateral thalamus and then back to the cortex. The **indirect pathway** from the striatum involves the external part of the globus pallidus. The direct pathway results in excitation of cortical neurons whereas the indirect pathways produce inhibition.

As with the cerebellum, the functional role of the basal ganglia appears to reside between the sensory and motor systems. Most of the projections from the thalamus are directed to the premotor areas and the supplementary motor area. Many neurons in the basal ganglia are active during movement involving the contralateral side of the body. The basal ganglia are concerned with motor planning in that the output neurons code for various aspects of movement, such as direction, amplitude, and velocity, rather than the detailed activation of specific muscles and motor programs. The discharge of action potentials by most cells, however, does not begin until after the onset of movement. The possible role of the basal ganglia in movement is involvement in the processes of movement initiation and the sequencing of movement fragments.

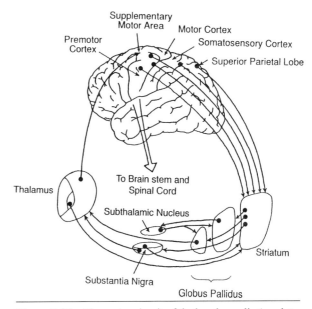

Figure 7.26 The motor circuit of the basal ganglia (caudate, putamen, globus pallidus, subthalamic nuclei, and substantia nigra).

From "The Basal Ganglia" by L. Côté and M.D. Crutcher. In *Principles of Neural Science, 3rd ed.,* p. 651, by E.R. Kandel, J.H. Schwartz, and T.M. Jessell (Eds.), 1991, New York: Elsevier Science Publishing Co., Inc. Adapted by permission of The McGraw-Hill Companies.

The basal ganglia can, for example, influence centrally initiated postural reactions, background postural tone, and peripherally triggered postural reactions.

Although the basal ganglia do not have direct connections with the spinal cord, a role for the basal ganglia in movement has been well documented by the study of patients with Parkinson's disease, Huntington's disease, and hemiballismus (Hallett, 1993). As described by Côté and Crutcher (1991), these diseases involve impairment of the basal ganglia and are characterized by (1) involuntary movements and tremor; (2) muscular **rigidity**—an increased resistance to movement about a joint; and (3) **bradykinesia**—poverty and slowness of movement including a prolonged reaction time. These studies suggest that the basal ganglia are important in adapting motor output to changing conditions, such as variation in the support provided by the surroundings, changes in the intent of a movement, and the performance of more than one task at a time.

Ascending Pathways

The human body contains a great diversity and number of sensory receptors. Those that have a more direct effect on movement were discussed in chapter 5 in the description of the single-joint system. The afferent signals from these sensory receptors enter the spinal cord through the dorsal root and synapse onto neurons at both the segmental and supraspinal levels. The groups of fibers that

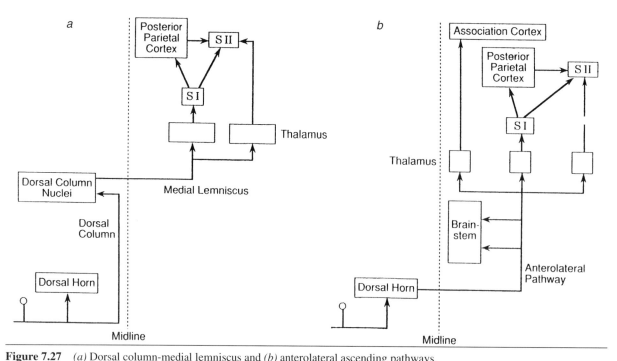

Figure 7.27 *(a)* Dorsal column-medial lemniscus and *(b)* anterolateral ascending pathways.

From "Anatomy of the Somatic Sensory System" by J. H. Martin and T. M. Jessell, 1991, in E. R. Kandel, J. H. Schwartz, and T. M. Jessell (Eds.), in *Principles of Neural Science* (3rd ed.). p. 359. Copyright 1991 by Elsevier Science. Adapted by permission of The McGraw-Hill Companies.

distribute the information to the supraspinal centers are referred to as **ascending pathways.** Somatic sensory information from the arms, legs, and trunk ascends through the thalamus to the cerebral cortex in two major pathways: the dorsal column-medial lemniscus pathway and the anterolateral pathway. Somatic sensory information includes afferent signals from mechanoreceptors, thermoreceptors, nociceptors, and chemoreceptors. Both ascending pathways send sensory information to the contralateral brain; however, they cross the midline at different points (figure 7.27). These two ascending pathways play a major role in **perception;** that is, the afferent signals reach cognitive awareness.

The **dorsal column-medial lemniscus pathway** distributes information on limb proprioception and tactile sensation, including touch and vibration sense. This pathway crosses the midline in the medulla and ascends through the brainstem as the medial lemniscus to the thalamus and the primary somatic sensory area of the cerebral cortex. The thalamus integrates and distributes most of the sensory and motor information going to the cerebral cortex. The thalamus receives input about somatic sensation, audition, and vision and transmits information to the cerebellum, basal ganglia, and cerebral cortex. The afferent axons in the dorsal column are arranged somatotopically, with input from the sacrum most medial and that from the neck most lateral. A somatotopic organization of the afferent input is preserved all the way to the primary (SI) and secondary (SII) somatic sensory cortices and to the posterior parietal cortex. The

information conveyed in the dorsal column-medial lemniscus pathway is not simply relayed from the sensory receptors in the periphery to the primary somatic sensory cortex; rather it is processed to varying degrees along the pathway.

The **anterolateral pathway** conveys information mainly about pain and temperature, with some tactile and proprioceptive information. The axons in this pathway cross in the spinal cord and ascend in the lateral part of the spinal cord to the reticular formation in the brainstem and the thalamus. The anterolateral pathway actually comprises three parts: the spinothalamic, spinoreticular, and spinocervical. The names describe the origin and termination of these parts. The **spinothalamic** and **spinoreticular** tracts carry noxious and thermal afferent signals. The **spinocervical** tract ends in an area of the midbrain containing neurons involved in the descending control of pain. The information in these three tracts is also sent to the primary and secondary somatic sensory cortices and to the posterior parietal cortex.

Although the two pathways project to the thalamus, the axons synapse on separate populations of neurons. Information from the various classes of sensory receptors remains segregated in the spinal cord, brainstem, and thalamus and does not interact until it reaches the somatic sensory areas of the cerebral cortex. The sensory information is distributed among several areas of the cerebral cortex and to subcortical areas where it influences the flow of information in descending pathways.

Example 7.8
Shocks to the Brain Evoke Muscle Responses

One way to determine the efficacy of ascending and descending systems is to measure **evoked potentials.** These are the electrical responses either in the brain or in muscle that are evoked by stimuli applied at the other end of the pathway. For example, an electric stimulus applied in the periphery evokes small brain potentials that can be averaged and then measured. These potentials can also be measured along the spinal cord with surface electrodes placed on the back. Similarly, electric or magnetic stimuli applied to the brain evoke muscle contractions, such as occurs with **transcranial magnetic stimulation** (Mills, 1991). This technique involves generating a magnetic field with a coil that is placed above the scalp (figure 7.28). The magnetic field passes through the scalp and skull and induces an electric current in the brain. The induced current probably activates presynaptic elements that project to output neurons, which then activate muscle. By moving the coil to different locations over the scalp, it is possible to evoke a response in various muscles throughout the body (Schieppati, Trompetto, & Abbruzzese, 1996).

By measuring the time it takes for the stimulus to evoke an action potential in a single motor unit, it is possible to identify the pathway activated by transcranial magnetic stimulation. The latency from the stimulus to the response in a hand muscle is about 25 ms, which means that the stimulus must have activated a monosynaptic pathway (Garland & Miles, 1997). Such measurements can provide useful information about various neurological conditions and neural circuits (Miles, 1999). An increase in the latency, for example, can suggest delays in central conduction, as is experienced by patients with multiple sclerosis, motor neuron disease, cervical myelopathy, and

Friedreich's ataxia. Delays in central conduction can be caused by a decrease in the number of axons in the corticospinal tract, demyelination of these axons, or a block of action potential propagation in these axons. Since the development of the magnetic stimulator in the early 1980s, the technique has been used to study projections from the motor cortex to the spinal motor neurons and to identify motor impairments such as weakness and spasticity in patients (Mills, 1991).

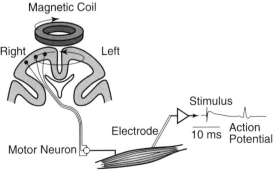

Figure 7.28 Transcranial magnetic stimulation can evoke an action potential in a single motor unit.

Data from Mills, 1991.

Movement Strategies

Because of the complexity of both the interactions among the supraspinal centers and the organization of the musculoskeletal system, there are many activation sequences and combinations of muscles that can be used to perform a desired movement. In fact, there are many more options available than are needed for most movements (Bernstein, 1984). What are the rules that the nervous system uses in order to choose from among these options? What strategies do we use to perform different movements? It seems desirable to have many degrees of freedom (skeletal, anatomical, and neural options) available when we are learning a new movement, but once we have learned the movement we use only a subset of the available options. The topic of *movement strategies concerns the study of the neural activation patterns that are associated with achieving different movement goals.*

Control Theories

The study of movement strategies has a long tradition of borrowing concepts from engineering, especially those from control systems theory (Houk, 1988; Prochazka, 1989; Prochazka et al., 2000). These ideas have been useful because at the most fundamental level, we can consider movement as an activity that is performed by muscles and controlled by the nervous system. From this perspective, the study of movement strategies involves identifying the control signals sent by the nervous system to muscle.

One important feature of the control signals that can be sent to muscle is the extent to which the command is influenced by feedback from sensory receptors. In the absence of feedback, the control signal is known as a **feedforward** command (figure 7.29). The use of feedforward commands requires that the controller know the state of the system and what is necessary to achieve the desired outcome (Kawato, 1999). Feedforward commands are used during fast movements, such as a rapid kick or throw, and can even be used by CPGs to produce automatic behaviors. However, if the conditions in which the movement is executed change during the performance, then it is desirable to adjust the command signals

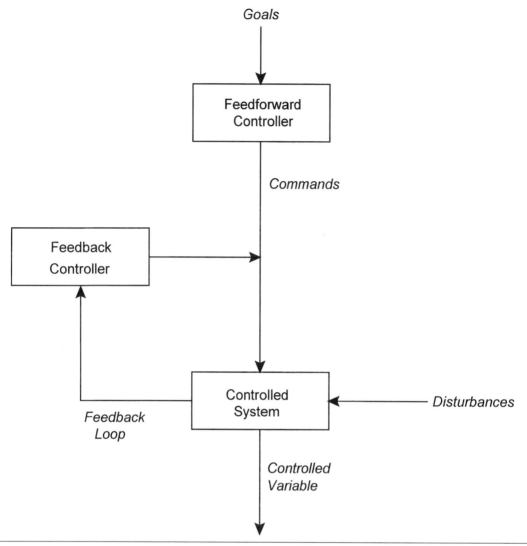

Figure 7.29   Feedforward and feedback control.

accordingly. This adjustment uses feedback from sensory receptors to modify the outgoing command signal to muscle; this process is known as **feedback** control (figure 7.29). The control signals, whether feedforward or feedback, may be used to keep the controlled variable constant; this is termed **regulation.**

The feedback signal may cause an adjustment in the command signal that removes the stimulus; this is known as negative feedback. This concept was introduced in chapter 6 in the discussion of resistance reflexes. For example, figure 6.58 shows that when a handle being held by a subject was unexpectedly displaced, the afferent feedback activated the stretched muscle to contract and thereby eliminate the stretch of the muscle. This is the stretch reflex. Alternatively, it is also possible for feedback to enhance the mechanical effect that evoked it. This is known as **positive feedback.** For example, the tendon organ, which responds to changes in

muscle force, usually provides negative feedback to the spinal cord. Under some conditions, however, the tendon organ can provide positive feedback, meaning that the afferent signals from this receptor cause an increase in muscle force (Pratt, 1995; Prochazka, Gillard, & Bennett, 1997).

Feedback control is effective only if the time between the stimulus in the periphery and the adjustment of the control signal is minimal. The time from the stimulus to the onset of the response is known as the **delay.** For many of the movements we perform, feedback signals are provided by muscle spindles and tendon organs, which transmit the information over the rapidly conducting Group Ia and Ib axons. As a result, the fastest responses (reflexes) we can produce occur in the order of milliseconds. Because of these delays, the fastest movements we perform are essentially over before the feedback is received by the controller.

In addition to the requirement of a minimal delay, feedback control requires that the size of the adjustment be matched to the stimulus. This association is expressed as the **gain** of the feedback loop.

$$\text{Gain} = \frac{\Delta \text{ control signal}}{\Delta \text{ controlled variable}} \qquad (7.1)$$

For the stretch reflex, the gain of the feedback loop is the amount of reflex-induced change in muscle length relative to the amount of stretch experienced by the muscle. The higher the gain, the greater the response relative to the stimulus. The size of the gain, however, depends on the delay in the feedback loop. If the delay is short, the gain cannot be high or it will cause the system to become unstable. When the gain is not high, however, the adjustment in the control signal will not compensate completely for the stimulus that evoked the feedback signal. In contrast, when the delay is long, the gain can be higher and the compensation will be more complete (Houk, 1988).

Servo Control

Many movements that we perform comprise various combinations of feedforward and feedback control. Perhaps the most common combination involves the adjustment of feedforward commands by continuous or intermittent feedback signals (figure 7.29). An alternative strategy is for the feedforward controller to send commands to the feedback controller and thereby generate command signals that are sent to the controlled system. Because the feedback loop attempts to keep the value of the controlled variable the same as that specified by the controller, this feedback scheme is called a **servo mechanism.** To accomplish this type of control, the feedforward controller functions as a **comparator.** It compares the magnitude of the controlled variable to the value specified by the high-level controller, and then adjusts the command signals sent by the low-level controller so that the two match (figure 7.30). The output of the comparator is known as the **error signal** because it depends on the difference between the command signal and the controlled variable.

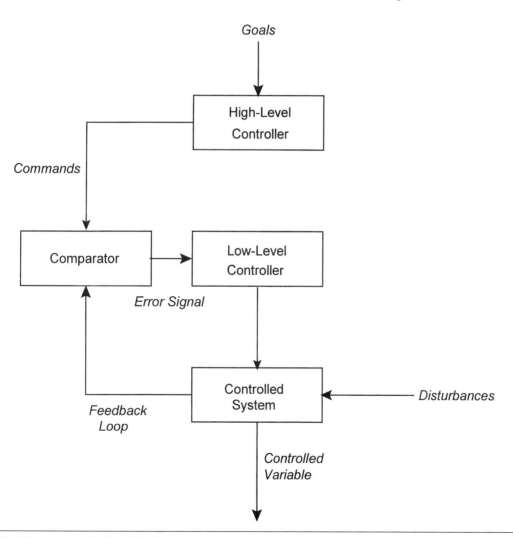

Figure 7.30 The servo mechanism of feedback control.

One of the earliest theories about the control of human movement was based on the servo mechanism. It was called the **servo hypothesis** (Merton, 1953). The hypothesis suggests that the control of muscle length is accomplished through the muscle spindle. The desired muscle length is established by a command signal that activates the gamma motor neurons, which sets the length of the fusimotor fibers in the muscle spindle. Functioning as a comparator, the muscle spindle compares the lengths of the fusimotor fibers and the skeletal muscle fibers. If the fusimotor fibers are shorter, this activates the sensory endings of the muscle spindle and thereby activates the motor neurons that innervate the muscle. Conversely, if the fusimotor fibers are longer, the excitation of the motor neurons will decline. The servo action of the muscle spindle is mediated by the **tonic stretch reflex,** which is a sustained muscle contraction in response to a slow stretch. The tonic stretch reflex enables muscles to behave somewhat like springs in that the resistance to stretch increases as the muscle continues to be stretched.

According to the servo hypothesis, muscle contractions are produced by error signals derived by muscle spindles. This hypothesis was discredited, however, when it was found that activation of the gamma motor neurons did not precede activation of the alpha motor neurons (Vallbo, 1971). Rather, alpha and gamma motor neurons appear to be activated at about the same time; this concurrent activation has become known as **alpha-gamma coactivation.** According to this scheme, voluntary movements are initiated by a combination of a feedforward command to alpha motor neurons and a signal to a servo mechanism that controls muscle length through the muscle spindle (Latash, 1998). Control of muscle length by such a mechanism, however, requires the gain of the tonic stretch reflex to be extraordinarily high so that any unexpected change in length is easily compensated by a reflex adjustment in the command signal to muscle. Because the gain of the tonic stretch reflex loop is not that high (Brooke et al., 1997), this does not seem to be a reasonable control strategy for voluntary movements.

Equilibrium-Point Hypothesis

At about the same time the concept of alpha-gamma coactivation was developed, an alternative control strategy was proposed that also involved reflex loops. According to this scheme, the length of a muscle depends on the interaction of the tonic stretch reflex and the magnitude of the load acting on the muscle. The tonic stretch reflex refers to the reflex activation of muscle due to changes in its length, which means that the force a muscle exerts increases as a function of its length. For a given command signal to a muscle, therefore, muscle length will change until the muscle force and the load force are balanced. This is the equilibrium-point hypothesis (Feldman 1966a, 1966b, 1986).

The central feature of this hypothesis is the association between muscle length and force for a constant command signal to the muscle. The association has a specific shape (figure 7.31), which an investigator can determine by unexpectedly changing the load and asking the subject not to change the command signal. When the subject is able to refrain from reacting to the change in load, the joint angle (muscle length) will change until a new equilibrium point is reached. If the load is changed several times, the emerging relation is called the **invariant characteristic** (figure 7.31a). Variations in muscle torque are a consequence of load-induced changes in muscle length that alters the reflex activation of the muscle through the tonic stretch reflex.

Although the shape of the invariant characteristic remains relatively constant for a set of muscles, its location on the x-axis can be varied by changing the threshold of the tonic stretch reflex (λ), which is known as the **lambda model.** This threshold, which is defined by the central command to the muscle, corresponds to the muscle length at which the alpha motor neurons will be activated by the tonic stretch reflex in response to changes in muscle length. In figure 7.31b, the threshold for one invariant characteristic is about 1.2 rad (filled circles); that for the other invariant characteristic is about 1.8 rad (open circles). A shift in λ can produce a change in muscle length without a change in muscle force (an isotonic contraction), a change in muscle force without a change in muscle length (an isometric contraction), or a change in both muscle length and force, as occurs with an elastic load (Latash, 1998).

Equilibrium-Trajectory Hypothesis

Whereas the equilibrium-point hypothesis was developed from single-joint movements, the **equilibrium-trajectory hypothesis** represents an extension to multi-joint movements (Latash, 1998). In this scheme, the CNS plans a movement by specifying a virtual trajectory for the working point of the multi-joint system (Hogan & Flash, 1987). For targeted movements, such as moving a limb from one position to another, the working point would be the part of the limb that is going to make contact with the target—for example, the hand in a reaching movement or the foot in a kick.

The trajectory for a multi-joint movement could be planned relative to several different reference points. For example, a reaching movement could be planned in terms of hand motion, joint rotations, or muscle forces. Hogan and Flash (1987) achieved the best match between the predicted and actual trajectories for a reaching movement when the trajectory was defined relative to the hand and the trajectory was as smooth as possible. Smoothness was accomplished by assuming that the CNS generates trajectories by minimizing the jerk (the derivative of acceleration with respect to time); this is known as the

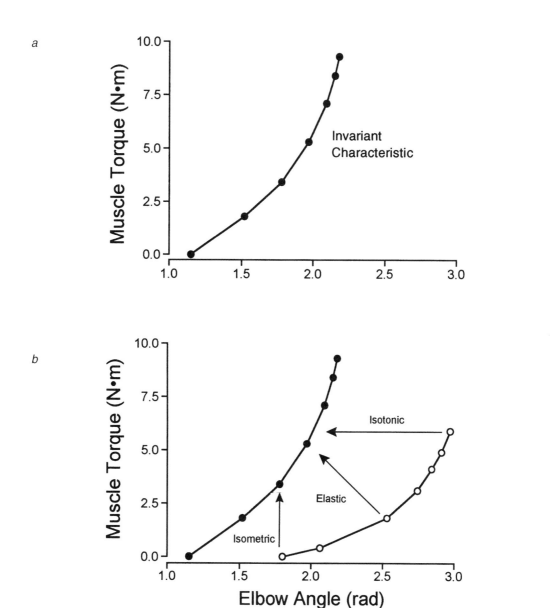

Figure 7.31   The invariant characteristic between muscle torque and joint angle *(a)* can be shifted along the joint angle axis *(b)* by changing the threshold of the tonic stretch reflex. When the command to a muscle changes, the muscle shifts to a new invariant characteristic.

Adapted from Feldman, 1986; and Latash, 1998.

minimum jerk principle. With this approach, the predicted trajectories for reaching movements were similar to those measured experimentally. The actual trajectory for the movement, however, deviated from the virtual trajectory because of such factors as intersegmental dynamics and changes in the forces exerted by the surroundings.

Patterns of Electromyogram Activity

One approach to identifying the strategies used by the nervous system to control voluntary movement is the study of simple movements. Usually these movements involve displacement in one plane about a single joint.

For example, a subject might be asked to flex the elbow joint rapidly in a horizontal plane, from an initial position to a final elbow angle (figure 7.32). To determine the control strategy for such a task, many investigators will compare the patterns of muscle activation (EMG) with the kinematics of the movement. When an individual performs such a goal-directed movement, the muscles that accelerate the limb often exhibit a **three-burst pattern of EMG.** These muscles are usually identified as the agonist, which accelerates the limb in the direction of motion, and the antagonist, which slows down the motion. The three-burst pattern of EMG comprises an initial agonist burst of EMG that is followed by a burst of antagonist EMG and a second burst

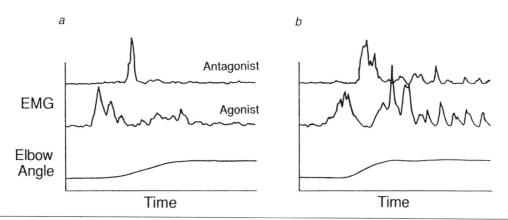

Figure 7.32 The three-burst pattern of EMG activity for an elbow flexion movement (0.50 rad). The EMG data are rectified and filtered: *(a)* a distinct sequence; *(b)* a movement displaying coactivation at the termination of the movement.

Adapted from Karst and Hasan, 1987.

of agonist EMG (Wachholder & Altenburger, 1926). These three bursts usually overlap in time, but the peaks occur in the order of agonist, antagonist, and agonist (figure 7.32).

When subjects are asked to vary the details of the task such as movement speed, the extent of the displacement, or the accuracy of the final position, the pattern of EMG activity will vary. The EMG measurements that can vary include the duration of each burst of activity, the EMG amplitude, the time between the onset of each burst of EMG, and the amount of coactivation at the end of the movement. For example, when just the speed of the elbow flexion movement is increased, this will involve an increase in the size of the first agonist burst of EMG, a decrease in the delay to the onset of the antagonist burst of EMG, an increase in the size of the antagonist burst, and an increase in the final level of coactivation (Corcos, Gottlieb, & Agarwal, 1989). Similarly, an increase in movement amplitude involves greater amplitude and duration of the first agonist burst, a longer delay to the onset of the antagonist burst, and variable effects on the size of the antagonist burst (Gottlieb, Corcos, & Agarwal, 1989).

Such findings led Gottlieb and colleagues to propose the **dual-strategy hypothesis** to account for the performance of goal-directed elbow flexion movements (Gottlieb et al., 1989; Corcos et al., 1989). The hypothesis explains variations in the EMG (agonist and antagonist) and resultant muscle torque in movements that involve different displacements, speeds, and loads. The hypothesis is based on a model of motor neuron excitation as a rectangular pulse that can be modulated by variation of its amplitude and duration to satisfy the expected torque requirements of the task (Almeida, Hong, Corcos,

& Gottlieb, 1995). Modulation of excitation amplitude produces a **speed-dependent strategy** that involves an increase in EMG and torque amplitude and a decrease in the latency to the onset of antagonist EMG (figure 7.33*a*). In contrast, modulation of excitation duration produces a **speed-independent strategy** that involves similar initial slopes for agonist EMG and resultant muscle torque, increasing EMG and torque durations, and an increase in the latency to the onset of the antagonist EMG (figure 7.33*b*). When subjects are required to perform a rapid task with certain time constraints, they choose the speed-dependent strategy. However, when subjects are free to choose movement speed they use the speed-independent strategy that entails selecting an excitation intensity (amplitude) and then matching that with the appropriate duration to achieve the desired movement (Gottlieb, Corcos, Agarwal, & Latash, 1990a).

The dual-strategy hypothesis was based on the notion that such movements are controlled by command signals sent directly to the alpha motor neurons. Furthermore, tests of this hypothesis require that measurement of the EMG signals be able to indicate the essential details of these command signals. The alpha motor neurons, however, receive afferent feedback from peripheral sensory receptors, which modifies the output of the motor neuron pool and thereby obscures some of the details of the central command (Latash, 1998). Recently, Gottlieb (1996) has proposed that the central command for voluntary movement involves a feedforward component to the alpha motor neurons, a negative feedback component for reflex effects, and a component that can modulate the contributions of the reflex mechanisms. The central feature of this scheme, however, is that movements are planned in terms of the muscle torques that must be exerted.

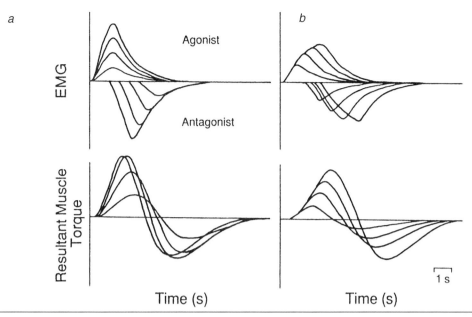

Figure 7.33 Simulated agonist and antagonist EMG and resultant muscle torque for a rapid elbow flexion movement over four trials. *(a)* For the speed-dependent strategy, amplitude of excitation increased over the four trials, *(b)* while for the speed-independent strategy, duration of excitation increased.

Adapted from Gottlieb, Corcos, Agarwal, and Latash, 1990.

Example 7.9
Neurological Disorders and the Three-Burst Pattern of EMG

The three-burst pattern of EMG has been studied in patients with motor disorders when they perform rapid arm movements about a single joint, such as the elbow or wrist (Berardelli et al., 1996). Abnormalities in the triphasic pattern often result in slow movements, irregular trajectories, and reduced accuracy. Some of the effects for various motor disorders are summarized in table 7.5.

On the basis of a comparison of these profiles with the characteristics of the triphasic EMG pattern for normal subjects, Berardelli et al. (1996) concluded as follows:

Table 7.5 Kinematics and EMG of Rapid Arm Movements in Patients With Motor Disorders

	Amplitude variability	Peak velocity	Agonist duration	Antagonist duration	Coactivation
Athetosis	Increased	Decreased	Prolonged	Prolonged	Yes
Dystonia	Increased	Decreased	Prolonged	Prolonged	Yes
Huntington's disease	Increased	Decreased	Prolonged	Prolonged	Yes
Cerebellar ataxia	Increased	Decreased	Prolonged	Prolonged	Normal
Upper MN syndrome	—	Decreased	Prolonged	Prolonged	Normal
Parkinson's disease	Normal	Decreased	Normal	Normal	Normal
Essential tremor	—	Normal	Normal	Normal	Normal

Note. MN = motor neuron; — = not studied.

(continued)

- The basal ganglia have a role in scaling the size of the first agonist burst of EMG, reinforcing the voluntary command, and inhibiting inappropriate EMG.
- The cerebellum contributes to the timing of the EMG bursts.
- The corticospinal tract influences the timing of the recruitment of motor units.

- Proprioceptive feedback is not necessary for the triphasic EMG pattern, but it does affect the accuracy of the trajectory and the final position.

Given the common appearance of the triphasic pattern in many movements, Berardelli et al. suggest that its measurement is useful for understanding the pathophysiology of motor disorders.

Coactivation

One of the features of EMG patterns that attracts attention is coactivation of agonist and antagonist muscles. At one level, it seems wasteful to coactivate agonist and antagonist muscles because actions depend on the net muscle torque. The frequent use of coactivation, however, suggests that there are specific advantages to such a strategy. One advantage is that *coactivation has the mechanical effect of making a joint stiffer and more difficult to perturb* (Baratta et al., 1988; Kornecki, 1992). The effect of coactivation on stiffness (N/m), which is defined as the *slope* of a force-length (or torque-angle) relation, can be illustrated by considering a set of invariant characteristics for agonist and antagonist muscles (figure 7.34a). Recall that an invariant characteristic repre-

sents the force-length (torque-angle) relation for muscle under the condition of a constant command and that the characteristic can be shifted along the *x*-axis by changing the threshold of the tonic stretch reflex (figure 7.31). The stiffness of the joint, indicated by the slope of the dashed line in figure 7.34*b,* depends on the invariant characteristics set by the command signals for the agonist and antagonist muscles. The stiffness can be varied over a large range and depends on which pair of invariant characteristics is selected (figure 7.34*a*).

Because coactivation increases the stiffness and hence the stability of a joint, this seems like a useful strategy when we learn novel tasks or when we perform a movement requiring a high degree of accuracy. For example, Person (1958) monitored the EMG of biceps and triceps brachii while training subjects over a two-week period

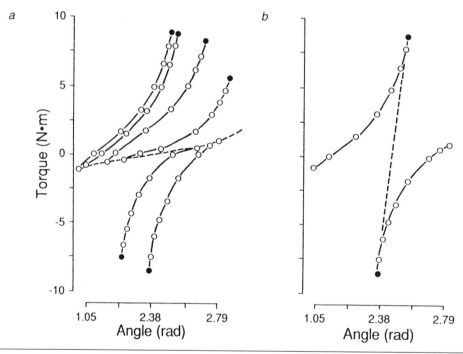

Figure 7.34 The stiffness at a joint depends on the net muscle activity. *(a)* Family of invariant characteristics for the elbow flexors (positive torques) and elbow extensors (negative torques). The dashed line represents the passive torque-angle relation. *(b)* The choice of appropriate invariant characteristics for the elbow flexors and extensors results in a net relation (dashed line) that has a greater slope and therefore a higher stiffness.

Adapted from Feldman, 1986.

to file and cut with a chisel. Over the course of the training, the EMG activity changed from a high level of coactivation to one of alternating activity with little coactivation. Similarly, strength training with isometric contractions appears to involve a reduction in the coactivation of the antagonist muscle within the first week of training (Carolan & Cafarelli, 1992). Furthermore, elite athletes exhibited reduced coactivation of the semitendinosus muscle compared with sedentary subjects when performing isokinetic contractions with the knee extensor muscles (Amiridis et al., 1996). However, six months of strength training the knee extensor muscles was accompanied by mixed declines in coactivation of the antagonist muscle (Häkkinen et al., 1998).

Skilled performance also involves some coactivation. There are at least four reasons why individuals might use coactivation for various tasks. First, for movements that involve changes in direction (e.g., extension to flexion), it is more economical to modulate the level of tonic activity in an agonist-antagonist set of muscles than to alternately turn them on and off. Hasan (1986) has suggested that under certain conditions coactivation will actually decrease the cost of performing the movement in terms of the effort involved in the task; some empirical observations support this suggestion (Engelhorn, 1983). Second, because coactivation increases the stiffness and hence the stability of a joint, this may be a desirable strategy when individuals lift heavy loads or loads about which they are uncertain. For example, old adults frequently coactivate the antagonist muscle when performing lengthening contractions (figure 7.35). Third, one of the capabilities of two-joint muscles is the transfer of

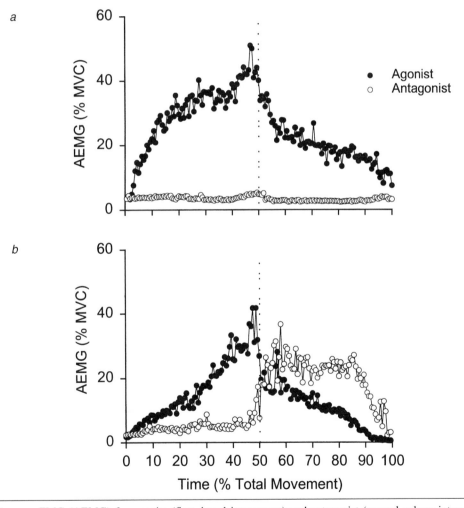

Figure 7.35 Average EMG (AEMG) for agonist (first dorsal interosseus) and antagonist (second palmar interosseus) muscles during abduction-adduction movements with the index finger. A load was raised slowly (0.06 rad/s) with a shortening contraction of the agonist during the first 50% of the movement, and lowered with a lengthening contraction of the agonist during the second 50%. Most young adults used the EMG pattern shown in *a*, whereas most old adults used the pattern in *b*, which involved heightened coactivation during the lengthening contraction.

Data from Burnett, Laidlaw, and Enoka, 2000.

MVC = maximal voluntary contraction.

power from one joint to another. As described previously, coactivation of a single-joint hip extensor (e.g., gluteus maximus) and a two-joint hip flexor (e.g., rectus femoris) has the net effect of increasing the extensor torque at the knee joint. Consequently, coactivation at the hip joint can result in an increase in the torque at the knee joint. This strategy may be useful in conditions requiring maximal force or for supplementing a fatigue-induced decline in muscle force (Dimitrijevic et al., 1992). Fourth, because of the divergence of inputs from cortical neurons to the spinal neurons, as well as the anatomical organization of motor units and muscles in the forearm and hand, fine movements of the fingers require complex patterns of coactivation (Kilbreath & Gandevia, 1994; Rose, Keen, Koshland, & Fuglevang, 1999; Sanes et al., 1995; Schieber, 1995).

Example 7.10
Coactivation Does Not Limit Performance in Stroke Patients

Individuals who experience a stroke exhibit varying degrees of residual motor function following the cerebrovascular accident. The remaining capabilities in the arm can be assessed by evaluating the ability of patients to perform such tasks as touching the opposite knee, placing the hand on the chin, and raising the arm overhead (Gowland, deBruin, Basmajian, Plews, & Burcea, 1992). The inability of a patient to perform one of these tasks is a consequence of the generation of an inadequate net muscle torque. Neurodevelopmental theory (Bobath, 1978) suggests that this inability is due to an inappropriate coactivation of muscle because of a failure to inhibit antagonist activity. It appears, however, that the problem has more to do with muscle weakness and insufficient motor unit activity than with heightened coactivation (Burke, 1988; Fellows, Kaus, Ross, & Thilmann, 1994; Gowland et al., 1992; Tang & Rymer, 1981). Moreover, persons with poststroke hemiplegia benefit from physical training during rehabilitation (Brown & Kautz, 1998).

Eccentric Contractions

When we use a muscle to displace a load, we can generate a muscle torque that is greater than the load torque; this enables the muscle to perform a concentric (shortening) contraction. Conversely, if the muscle torque is less than the load torque, the muscle will perform an eccentric (lengthening) contraction. Although we use both contraction modes frequently, the patterns of EMG activity can be quite different. For example, when subjects used the calf muscles to raise and lower loads, the EMG patterns during the eccentric contraction were different from those used during the concentric contraction (figure 7.36). Nardone and Schieppati (1988) found that the lifting phase involved mainly the soleus muscle, whereas the soleus activity was more variable during the lowering phase. When lowering the load, subjects exhibited either of two strategies: (1) primary use of lateral gastrocnemius (figure 7.36b) or (2) intermittent activation of soleus and some coactivation of lateral gastrocnemius (figure 7.36c).

In a subsequent study, Nardone et al. (1989) found that these eccentric contractions were associated with alterations in the recruitment order of motor units. Figure 7.37 shows motor unit activity in the lateral gastrocnemius muscle of a human subject during concentric and eccentric contractions. In the first trial (figure 7.37a), the intramuscular electrode detected no local motor unit activity during the slow concentric contraction (plantarflexion), but motor units were recruited during the eccentric contraction (negative slope of the position trace). In the second trial (figure 7.37b), the concentric contraction was performed more rapidly, and the same motor unit was recruited as in the slow eccentric contraction. These differences in recruitment order are consistent with the whole-muscle EMG records (bottom two traces in figure 7.37) during the concentric and eccentric contractions.

Alterations in the recruitment order of motor units, however, do not appear to be a general control strategy for eccentric contractions. For example, disturbances of recruitment order occur infrequently in eccentric contractions performed by hand and arm muscles (Bawa & Jones, 1998; Howell, Fuglevand, Walsh, & Bigland-Ritchie, 1995; Kossev & Christova, 1998; Laidlaw et al., 2000; Søgaard et al., 1996). Nonetheless, eccentric contractions do appear to be unique in several respects (Enoka, 1996). In terms of control strategies, the unique features of eccentric contractions are the reliance on afferent feedback to achieve a desired trajectory and the involvement of fewer motor units compared with a shortening contraction.

Because the muscle torque must be less than the load torque during an eccentric contraction, the command signals depend on afferent feedback to provide information on the progress of the movement. Accordingly, Schieber and Thach (1985) recorded differences in the discharge by Group Ia afferents of muscle spindles during eccentric contractions compared with concentric contractions (figure 7.38). For some trials, the peak discharge rate was greater during the eccentric contraction, but the discharge was always more sustained throughout the entire movement when compared with that in the concentric contraction. Because the predominant effect of feedback

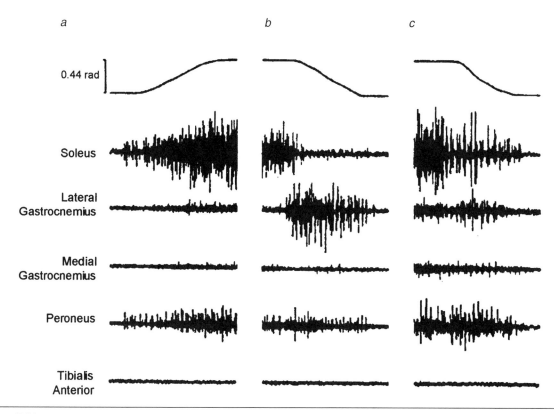

Figure 7.36 Patterns of EMG activity in muscles that cross the ankle joint during *(a)* lifting and *(b* and *c)* lowering of loads.
Adapted from Nardone and Schieppati, 1988.

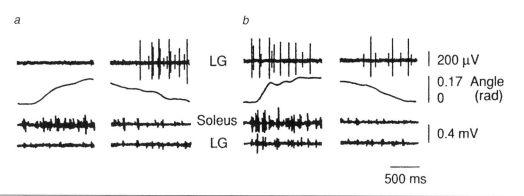

Figure 7.37 Motor unit activity in the lateral gastrocnemius (LG) muscle during concentric and eccentric contractions. The four traces (from top to bottom) represent intramuscular EMG, ankle position, soleus EMG, and lateral gastrocnemius EMG. When the ankle angle increased (upward), the muscles performed a shortening contraction *(a)* slowly and *(b)* quickly.
Adapted from Nardone, Romanó, and Schieppati, 1989.

by Group Ia afferents is excitatory on motor neurons and yet there was less EMG during the eccentric contraction, the integration of signals in the spinal cord was likely quite different for the concentric and eccentric contractions (Nardone et al., 1989). For example, Nichols et al. (1999) found that the greatest disturbance of coordination in walking due to disruption of sensory feedback occurred during walking down an incline, which involves eccentric contractions by the leg muscles (Abelew, Miller,

Cope, & Nichols, 2000). Furthermore, even the sign of a short-latency response to a cutaneous stimulus was reversed during an eccentric contraction compared with a concentric contraction (Haridas, Zehr, Sugajima, & Gillies, 2000).

The reduced EMG that occurs during eccentric contractions is a consequence of the greater force that muscles can exert during these contractions. Recordings with intramuscular electrodes indicate that fewer motor

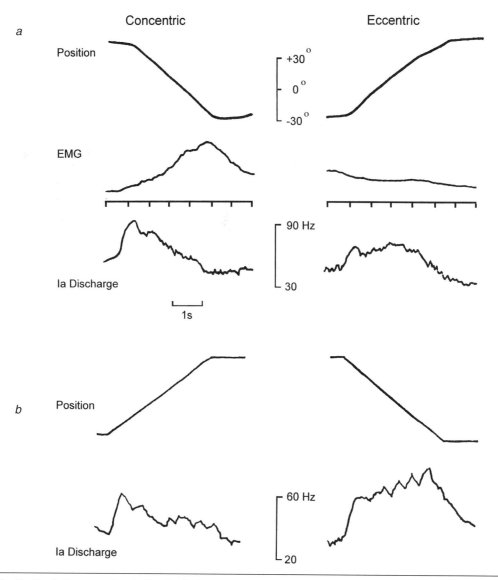

Figure 7.38   Feedback from muscle spindles (Ia discharge) during concentric and eccentric contractions performed with *(a)* wrist extensor and *(b)* flexor muscles by primates. The range of motion was 1.4 rad, and the contractions were performed against a light load. Data from Schieber and Thach, 1985.

units are recruited and that the average discharge rate is less during eccentric contractions (Kossev & Christova, 1998; Laidlaw et al., 2000). Furthermore, the discharge rate can be more variable during eccentric contractions, and this can influence the steadiness of the force exerted by muscle. For example, when subjects lifted light loads in the abduction-adduction plane with the index finger, the discharge rate of single motor units was more variable, and this was associated with reduced steadiness of the performance (Laidlaw et al., 2000). When the task involved forces that were 5% of maximum, the coefficient of variation for discharge rate was much greater during the eccentric contraction performed by old adults, and the performance was most unsteady (table 7.6).

Whereas accumulating evidence suggests that the control of eccentric contractions is different from that for concentric and isometric contractions, not all eccentric contractions are the same. For example, eccentric contractions that are used to lower inertial loads and release elastic loads are characterized by a muscle torque that is less than load torque, an increase in muscle fiber length, and a trajectory that is controlled and is dependent on afferent feedback. Important exceptions to these criteria are the eccentric contractions that occur during the stretch-shorten cycle and isokinetic contractions. In the stretch-shorten cycle, fiber length may not increase during the stretch (Fukunaga et al., 2001), and the trajectory represents the springlike response of the involved muscles

Table 7.6 Steadiness, Average EMG, and Discharge Rate of Motor Units During Contractions at 5% of Maximum

	Young			Old		
	Isometric	Concentric	Eccentric	Isometric	Concentric	Eccentric
Steadiness	46.0	0.22	0.21	75.0	0.28	0.43
EMG (% MVC)	7.70	11.3	5.26	12.2	17.7	12.1
Discharge rate						
Mean (Hz)	11.6	16.0	11.3	11.5	16.5	12.1
SD (Hz)	1.84	2.75	1.74	3.30	4.74	5.25
CV (%)	15.9	15.4	15.6	28.3	29.6	41.5

Note. Steadiness = standard deviation (SD) of force (isometric, measured in mN) or position (concentric and eccentric contractions, measured in degrees); CV = coefficient of variation; MVC = maximum voluntary contraction.

Data from Laidlaw et al., 2000.

rather than a feedback-dependent trajectory. Similarly, although the eccentric contractions performed on an isokinetic device may entail an increase in muscle fiber length, the task involves resisting the imposed load rather than producing a feedback-dependent trajectory. These distinctions are probably necessary to identify the unique control strategies underlying each task.

Movement Plans

There is a continuing debate in the research literature on how the CNS organizes movement. The discussion is often framed by the question, What is controlled by the nervous system to produce movement? Latash (1998) proposes that it is easier to say what is *not* controlled:

- Forces exerted by individual muscles
- Activation patterns of the involved muscles
- Net torques about single joints
- Angular displacements about single joints

To identify the variables that are controlled in a multi-joint system during movement, many investigators have examined reaching movements performed by humans. One consistent finding is that the path followed by the hand is usually close to a straight line (Morasso, 1981; Soechting & Lacquaniti, 1981). Investigators have attempted to determine why subjects choose one particular trajectory when there are so many to choose from. It is likely that the chosen trajectory is easiest, but how do we find out which variable determines whether or not a particular trajectory is easy? Is it a kinematic or a kinetic detail of the movement?

The minimum jerk principle is an example of a kinematic explanation for why a particular trajectory is chosen.

It proposes that the smoothest trajectory is chosen—that is, one in which jerk (the derivative of acceleration with respect to time) is minimized. In contrast, others have suggested that it is the kinetic details of the task that are minimized. Examples are the change in muscle force (Yamaguchi, Moran, & Si, 1995), muscle torque (Dornay, Uno, Kawato, & Suzuki, 1996; Kawato, Maeda, Uno, & Suzuki, 1990), or the kinetic energy (Soechting, Buneo, Herrmann, & Flanders, 1995). When subjects performed reaching movements in three-dimensional space to real targets or to the locations of remembered targets, the kinematics of the arm were consistent across a range of movement speeds, which suggested an optimization of kinetic variables (Nishikawa, Murray, & Flanders, 1999). Nonetheless, it is likely that both the kinematic and kinetic details are considered in the planning of a movement and that the relative weight of each depends on the context of the movement (Soechting & Flanders, 1998).

Summary

This chapter expands the model of the single-joint system to represent the human body as a set of such systems that are connected together. The result is a multi-joint system whose structure and control are more complex than those of a single-joint system. The structural complexities include multiple muscles around each joint, the existence of two-joint muscles, and widely divergent reflex connections. Control of multi-joint systems is achieved by multiple controllers that send command signals both from the local level and from remote locations. The local controllers are CPGs, whereas the remote controllers correspond to the supraspinal centers. In comparison to what is known about the organization and structure of the muscles and controllers of multi-joint systems, much less is known about the details of the command signals used by the controllers to produce movement. Despite considerable effort over the last 100 years, relatively little is known about the strategies used by the nervous system to perform various movements.

Suggested Readings

Latash, M.L. (1998). *Neurophysiological basis of movement.* Champaign, IL: Human Kinetics, chapters 9–12, 20, and 21.

Rothwell, J. (1994). *Control of human voluntary movement.* London: Chapman Hall, chapters 7, 9, 10, and 11.

Part II
Summary

The goal of part II (chapters 5–7) has been to define the structure and function of a biological model we have called the single-joint system. This model comprises the basic elements of the human body required to produce movement. As a result of reading these chapters, you should be familiar with the features and concepts related to the single-joint system, and in particular be able to do the following:

- Observe that the morphological and mechanical features of the single-joint system components are largely determined by the functions they serve

- Note the structural features of the six components of the single-joint system

- Understand why the single-joint system provides a reasonable model to study the control of movement

- Conceive of the means by which information is transmitted rapidly throughout the system

- Recognize the bidirectional effects of neurons and muscle fibers on each other

- Acknowledge the critical role of calcium in connecting the excitation from the nervous system to the contraction of muscle

- Realize that muscle does not exert the same force under all conditions for a constant excitation by the nervous system

- Differentiate the effects of muscle architecture on the force exerted by muscle

- Identify the quasistatic properties of muscle at the level of the single fiber, whole muscle, and single joint

- Appreciate the unique properties of muscle that are evident in an intact, behaving human

- Understand the mechanism that links the neural signal with muscle, resulting in a muscle contraction

- Realize that the motor unit is the basic functional unit of the system and describe its neural and muscular features

- Perceive the differences between the various types of muscle fibers and motor units

- Know that muscle force is controlled by the nervous system, which varies the activity of motor units for this purpose

- Comprehend the basic features of afferent feedback, including simple reflex circuits and automatic responses

- Acknowledge the contribution of afferent feedback to the sensations associated with movement

- Observe that it is necessary to combine several single-joint systems in order to represent more accurately the movement capabilities of the human body

- Recall that movement is a result of the net muscle action about a joint

- Consider central pattern generators as fundamental components of the nervous system involved in the control of multi-joint systems

- Discern the organization of higher centers in the nervous system and their role in the production of movement

- Distinguish among the control theories that attempt to explain how the nervous system organizes movement

- Regard the patterns of muscle activation as providing information about the strategies used to control movements

- Grasp the uncertainty that exists regarding the movement plans used by the nervous system

Part **III**

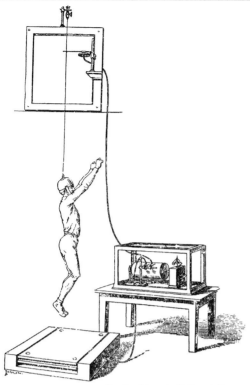

Reprinted from the Collège de France.

Adaptability of the Motor System

In this text, we have characterized human movement as an interaction between a biological system and its surroundings. In part I, we identified the concepts and principles that have been derived from physics for the study of motion. In part II, we developed a simple biological model that enabled us to examine the biological processes involved in the performance of movement. We called the model the single-joint system. It comprised two body segments and the elements necessary to control motion about a single joint. In chapter 7, this model was expanded to multi-joint systems that included more than two body segments, which enabled a more realistic representation of the movement capabilities of the human body. The neuromuscular elements involved in the production of movement are known as the **motor system.** Part III of the text describes the acute adjustments (chapter 8) and chronic adaptations (chapter 9) that are exhibited by the motor system.

Objectives

To conclude our study of the neuromechanics of human movement, we examine the adaptive capabilities of the motor system. The goal of part III is to describe the ways in which the motor system adapts to various types of physical stress. Specific objectives include the following:

- To explain the effect of altering core temperature on performance capabilities
- To indicate the techniques that have been developed to alter flexibility
- To outline the multifactorial basis of muscle fatigue and identify the processes that can be impaired in various tasks
- To examine the sensory adaptations that occur during fatiguing contractions
- To describe the potentiating capabilities of muscle
- To establish the principles of exercise prescription
- To define the performance characteristics of strength and power and the mechanisms that mediate changes in these parameters
- To document the adaptations that occur after periods of reduced activity
- To evaluate the changes that occur with aging and identify the physiological basis of these changes

Chapter 8

Reprinted from Marey, 1879.

Acute Adjustments

One prominent characteristic of the motor system is its adaptability. When subjected to an acute or chronic stress, the motor system can adapt to the altered demands of usage. These adaptations can be extensive, and they have been shown to influence all aspects of the system, both morphological and functional. In this chapter we consider the immediate (acute) response of the motor system to the stress associated with a single bout of physical activity. We will examine the effects of a warm-up; the techniques and mechanisms underlying the changes in flexibility; muscle soreness and damage; the mechanisms that cause muscle fatigue; the phenomenon of muscle potentiation; and the effects of arousal on performance.

Warm-Up Effects

Often when an individual undertakes a bout of physical activity, the initial activity includes light exercises to prepare the body for the ensuing stress. The purpose of the light exercises is to elicit a warm-up effect, which includes increasing core temperature and disrupting transient connective tissue bonds. The increase in core temperature will improve the biomechanical performance of the motor system, and the stretch may reduce the possibility of a muscle strain (Garrett, 1990; Stanish & Hubley-

Kozey, 1984). However, a regular program of stretching exercises does not produce a clinically relevant reduction in the incidence of lower-limb injury (Pope, Herbert, Kirwan, & Graham, 2000). The effects of a warm-up are different from those achieved with exercises designed to increase flexibility—that is, those intended to induce long-term increases in the range of motion about a joint.

Temperature

The warm-up has a significant effect on temperature-dependent physiological processes. The elevation of core temperature can increase the dissociation of oxygen from hemoglobin and myoglobin, enhance metabolic reactions, facilitate muscle blood flow, reduce muscle viscosity, increase the extensibility of connective tissue, and improve the conduction velocity of action potentials (Shellock & Prentice, 1985). Because of our focus on human movement, we are most interested in the effect of a warm-up on the ability of muscle to exert force, perform work, and produce power.

Muscle Function

Generally, performance in an activity such as the vertical jump is enhanced after a warm-up. This happens because the warm-up increases the maximum power that a muscle can produce (figure 8.1) and these activities

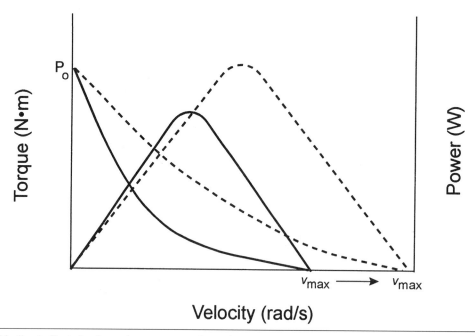

Figure 8.1 Idealized effect of a change in temperature due to a warm-up on the torque- and power-velocity relations. The power-velocity relations are bell shaped. An increase in temperature shifts V_{max} and the peak power to the right.

depend on the quantity of power produced by the muscles. The enhancement of jump performance following a warm-up is elicited by the effect of muscle temperature on contraction speed. For example, changes in temperature within the physiological range alter the maximum velocity of shortening ($12\% \cdot °C^{-1}$) but not the maximum isometric force (Binkhorst, Hoofd, & Vissers, 1977). Furthermore, changes in muscle temperature do not alter $F_{m,o}$ but do shift V_{max} to the right by 12% for each degree (°C) increase in temperature (figure 8.1). The net effect of the temperature-induced change in contraction speed is an increase in peak power. Conversely, reductions in muscle temperature decrease its work capacity (Wade et al., 2000).

When the change in temperature is substantial, muscle force can be influenced (Steinen et al., 1996). For example, Ranatunga, Sharpe, and Turnbull (1987) found that the maximum isometric force of a hand muscle remained relatively constant on cooling to 25° C but decreased by about 30% when cooling continued to ~12° C. Similarly, Bergh and Ekblom (1979) observed an increase in the maximum isometric torque of the knee extensor muscles from 262 N·m at 30.4° C to 312 N · m at 38.5° C ($2.4\% \cdot °C^{-1}$), with the temperature measured in the vastus lateralis muscle. Furthermore,

these changes increased vertical jump height by 44% (17 cm) and maximum power production in cycling by 32% (316 W).

The influence of temperature on muscle force is much less than the effect on the consumption of adenosine triphosphate (ATP) by muscle (figure 8.2). On the basis of measurements made on muscle fiber segments obtained by biopsy from the rectus abdominis and vastus lateralis muscles, Steinen et al. (1996) determined myofibrillar adenosinetriphosphatase (ATPase) activity (an index of ATP consumption) and force for the various muscle fiber types. Measurements were made at four different temperatures and normalized to the values obtained at 20° C. As indicated by the slope of the two lines in figure 8.2, the myofibrillar ATPase activity varied more than specific force over the temperature range examined. Although the data in figure 8.2 are for type IIa fibers, similar relations were observed for type I and type IId (IIb) fibers. The cost of force generation, however, when expressed as the ratio of ATP consumption to specific force, was least for type I fibers and greatest for type IId (IIb) fibers. Furthermore, the cost of force generation changed with temperature, as indicated by the difference in the slope of the two lines in figure 8.2.

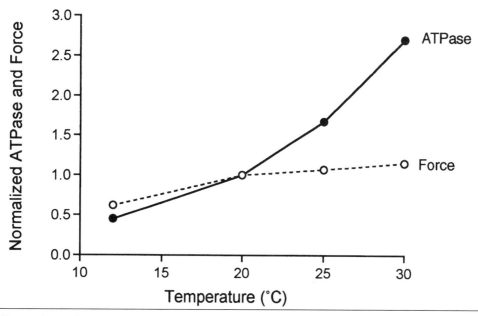

Figure 8.2 Changes in myofibrillar adenosine triphosphatase (ATPase) activity (mmol/l · s^{-1}) and force (N/mm^2) for type IIa fibers with temperature.

Data from Steinen et al., 1996.

Example 8.1

Warm-Up Effect Independent of Temperature

A preceding activity, such as that performed during a warm-up, can have an effect on the force capacity of muscle independent of changes in temperature. When single muscle fibers were stimulated to produce ten 400-ms tetani (stimulation at 70 Hz) with 4 s between each tetanus, the peak force increased by 10% (Bruton, Westerblad, Katz, & Lännergren, 1996). The increase in force lasted for about 15 min. The potentiation could not be attributed to augmentation of Ca^{2+} release or to changes in intracellular pH. The most likely explanation was the 40% reduction in inorganic phosphate (P$_i$), which can produce an 8% to 12% increase in tetanic force (Steinen, Roosemalen, Wilson, & Elzinga, 1990).

Techniques

Ingjer and Strømme (1979) found that the best strategy for inducing changes in muscle temperature, as measured by performance in a maximum-effort 4-min run on a treadmill, was to perform an *active-related warm-up* (see also O'Brien, Payne, Gastin, & Burge, 1997; Shellock,

1986; Shellock & Prentice, 1985). An *active* warm-up is one in which the changes in temperature result from muscle activity rather than from a passive external heat source, such as a warm bath or a heating pad. In a *related* warm-up, the muscles activated are the same as those subsequently used in the event. The increase in muscle temperature in an active-related warm-up depends on the intensity of the muscle contraction. When subjects performed isometric contractions (8-20 s in duration) with the quadriceps femoris muscles, Saugen and Vøllestad (1995) found that the increase in temperature in vastus lateralis was greatest for forces in the range of 30% to 70% maximum voluntary contraction (MVC). The increase in temperature ranged from 3.1 mK/s at 10% MVC to 14 mK/s at 70% MVC. The increase in temperature did not become greater with stronger contractions; this suggests that warm-up exercises should not exceed moderate intensities.

Ingjer and Strømme (1979) were able to raise the intramuscular temperature of the lateral part of quadriceps femoris from 35.9° C to about 38.4° C with both active and passive techniques. Nonetheless, they favored an active warm-up because a greater proportion of the energy expenditure during the treadmill run was provided by aerobic processes. Ingjer and Strømme suggest that the duration of the warm-up should be greater than 5 min and that the intensity should be equivalent to a 7.5-min/mile pace for a trained athlete or sufficient to cause perspiration and an increase in heart rate in an untrained individual. Stewart and Sleivert (1998) found that a warm-up at ~65% of maximum oxygen consumption for 15 min produces the greatest improvement in the range of motion and the subsequent anaerobic performance. Similarly, a warm-up at a moderate intensity and of long duration appears to be optimal for swimmers (Houmard et al., 1991). The increase in muscle temperature from such activities is lost by about 15 min after the warm-up; therefore, the time between the warm-up and the event should be no longer than 15 min.

Stiffness of Passive Muscle

In addition to elevating core temperature, warm-up exercises are used to increase the range of motion about a joint (Smith, 1994). Increases in core temperature, whether due to muscle contractions or a passive heat source, enhance the extensibility of the tissues around the joint. This effect is evident only while temperature is elevated.

It is the structural elements of muscle and tendon that resist the imposed increase in length during stretching exercises. As indicated by the force-length relation of muscle (figure 6.20), the passive resisting force of muscle increases with the amount of stretch. The resistance of passive muscle to stretch can be indicated on a torque-angle graph (figure 8.3c). For example, Hufschmidt and Mauritz (1985) measured the passive resistance of the plantarflexor muscles in healthy subjects and in patients with varying degrees of spasticity. They did this by using a torque motor to displace the ankle joint through a 0.35-rad range of motion (figure 8.3a), from 0.175 rad (10 degrees) of plantarflexion to 0.175 rad of dorsiflexion, and measuring the resistance exerted by the plantarflexor muscles through the foot (figure 8.3b). The area enclosed between the stretch and release phases of the torque-angle graph indicates the energy absorbed by the plantarflexor muscles during the task (figure 8.3c). Because spasticity involves changes in muscle that result in an increased passive resistance to angular displacement about a joint, patients who had exhibited spastic symptoms for more than one year had stiffer muscles (Hufschmidt & Mauritz, 1985). This increased stiffness was evident as an increase in the energy absorbed during the stretch and release, that is, the area of the loop in figure 8.3c. This effect is greater for the extensor (antigravity) muscles (Dietz, 1992).

The resistance that a passive muscle offers to an imposed stretch is indicated by the slope of the torque-angle relation, which corresponds to the stiffness of the muscle. Muscle stiffness increases as the duration between the consecutive stretches gets longer. For example, when the time between stretches of the passive plantarflexor

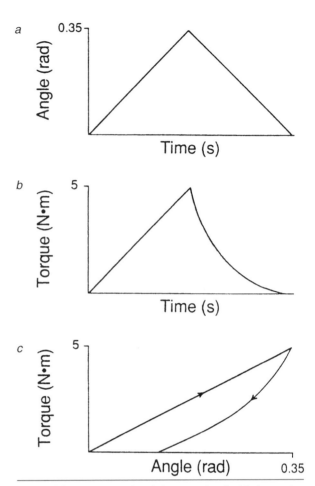

Figure 8.3 Torque-angle relation associated with the passive stretch and release of the plantarflexor muscles: *(a)* the increase (stretch) and decrease (release) in ankle angle during the stretch; *(b)* the passive torque exerted by the muscles during the stretch; *(c)* the resulting torque-angle relation, which does not overlap during the stretch and release phases.

Adapted from Hufschmidt and Mauritz, 1985.

muscles increased from 0 to 30 s, Hufschmidt and Mauritz (1985) found that the stiffness of the muscles increased. This is evident in figure 8.4 by the greater slope during the stretch, especially the initial part of the stretch. This effect—which has been observed in single muscle fibers, finger muscles, and the plantarflexor muscles—seems to involve an increase in muscle stiffness that occurs over a 30-min rest interval following muscle activation (Hufschmidt & Mauritz, 1985; Kilgore & Mobley, 1991; Lakie & Robson, 1988a). The increase in stiffness is greatest immediately after the activity and then becomes more gradual. The increased stiffness can be eliminated by active or passive movements but not by isometric contractions (Lakie & Robson, 1988a).

This history-dependent effect on stiffness is known as thixotropy (Campbell & Lakie, 1998; Proske, Morgan, & Gregory, 1993; Walsh, 1992). It is a property exhibited by various gels, such as muscle. In general, the gel

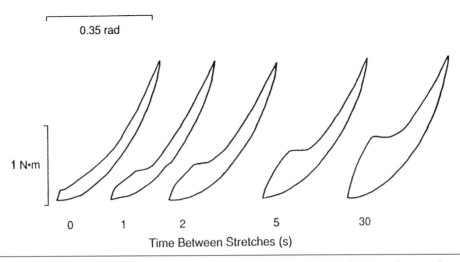

Figure 8.4 Effect of variable rest intervals on the torque-angle relation associated with the passive stretch and release of the plantarflexor muscles.

Adapted from Hufschmidt and Mauritz, 1985.

becomes more fluid when shaken, stirred, or otherwise disturbed, and it sets again when allowed to stand. The molecular rearrangement in muscle underlying thixotropy probably involves the development of stable bonds between actin and myosin filaments (Campbell & Lakie, 1998). With inactivity, the number of bonds increases, making the muscle stiffer. With a brief stretch or period of physical activity, however, most of the bonds are broken and muscle stiffness decreases (Hagbarth, Hagglund, Nordin, & Wallin, 1985; Lakie & Robson, 1988b; Wiegner, 1987). This can be accomplished by moving most major muscle groups through a complete range of motion (Wiktorsson-Möller, Öberg, Ekstrand, & Gillquist, 1983).

The time course of both muscle and joint (connective tissue) thixotropy should define the protocol for passive range-of-motion activities in patients who are immobile. However, measurements indicate that it takes 16 h of passive motion per day to prevent joint stiffness and that even this amount of activity does not maintain bone density (Gebhard, Kabo, & Meals, 1993). Such durations, however, are impractical for a therapist who typically uses several stretches, each lasting about 15 s, to maintain the range of motion about various joints; this is similar to the duration necessary to counteract the effects of inactivity (Roy, Pierotti, et al., 1998).

Muscle Tone

The thixotropic property of muscle endows it with a passive stiffness that resists changes in its length. Clinicians refer to this resistance to stretch by a relaxed muscle as **muscle tone.** The resistance to stretch can, of course, be supplemented by the stretch reflex, but this does not occur in a relaxed subject at low rates of stretch because the fusimotor system is not active enough to sensitize the muscle spindles to the stretch. Apparently, muscle tone is similar in relaxed healthy individuals and totally anesthetized patients (Rothwell, 1994).

Alterations in muscle tone can be used by clinicians to identify underlying pathologies. For example, reduced levels of muscle tone, known as **hypotonus,** are exhibited by patients who present with lesions in the cerebellar hemispheres and in persons who experience spinal transections. Rothwell (1994) suggests that hypotonus is probably due to a decreased excitability of the stretch reflex. Interestingly, muscle tone is reduced after low-frequency vibration (Walsh, 1992).

In contrast, an increase in muscle tone, referred to as **hypertonus,** is probably caused by low levels of motor neuron activity despite an attempt to relax. The two most common forms of hypertonus are spasticity and rigidity. **Spasticity** describes a pathologically induced state of heightened excitability of the stretch reflex (Latash, 1998). It occurs as a consequence of several different motor disorders, including brain trauma, spinal cord injury, and some systemic degenerative processes such as multiple sclerosis. Spasticity can be induced by a lesion in the central nervous system (primarily in the corticospinal tract) and by transection of the spinal cord. When a spastic muscle is stretched, it responds with a more vigorous stretch reflex than normal muscle. Furthermore, the exaggerated stretch reflex increases with the velocity of the stretch. Many mechanisms underlie spasticity, including changes in the excitability of motor neurons, postsynaptic hypersensitivity to a neurotransmitter, enlargement of motor unit territories by sprouting, and increases in the passive thixotropic properties of muscle. The symptoms associated with spasticity include increased passive resistance to movement in one direction, a hyperactive tendon-tap reflex, the adoption of a characteristic posture by the involved limb, an apparent inability to relax the involved muscle, and an inability to move the involved joint quickly or in alternating directions.

One misconception associated with spasticity is that the changes in muscle tone impair movement capabilities. This is not correct. Spasticity in an antagonist muscle is not the primary factor that impairs the ability of an agonist muscle to perform a movement. The impairment is attributable to an inability of the agonist muscle to recruit a sufficient number of motor units (McComas, Sica, Upton, & Aguilera, 1973; Sahrmann & Norton, 1977; Tang & Rymer, 1981). Consequently, the appropriate clinical protocol is to improve the activation patterns in the agonist rather than attempting to reduce the spasticity in the antagonist muscle. For example, the long-term application of transcutaneous electrical nerve stimulation to the common peroneal nerve significantly increased the dorsiflexion force (agonist), but not the plantarflexion force, and reduced clinical spasticity (Levin & Hui-Chan, 1992).

The other form of hypertonia is rigidity. Rigidity and spasticity have markedly different symptoms. The symptoms associated with rigidity include a bidirectional resistance to passive movement that is independent of the movement velocity and that occurs in the absence of an exaggerated tendon-tap reflex. The most common occurrence of rigidity is in Parkinson's disease and involves a persistent muscle contraction that appears in passive manipulation as a series of interrupted jerks (cogwheel rigidity).

Flexibility

Frequently no distinction is made between warm-up exercises and those designed to increase flexibility. When an individual performs warm-up exercises, the increase in core temperature enhances the passive extensibility of the tissues around the joint and increases the range of motion (Magnusson, Aagard, Simonsen, & Bojsen-Møller, 1998). If two individuals perform a set of warm-up exercises and then compare the range of motion about a joint, the person with the greater range of motion is more flexible at that joint (figure 8.5). Differences in flexibility between joints and individuals are due to long-term adaptations, not the changes that take place after a set of warm-up activities.

The research on flexibility training has focused on developing effective strategies to increase the range of motion and on identifying the factors that limit flexibility (Alter, 1996; Bandy, Irion, & Briggler, 1998; Gleim & McHugh, 1997; Hutton, 1992). There has been some disagreement over whether a range of motion is limited by an individual's ability to completely relax the involved

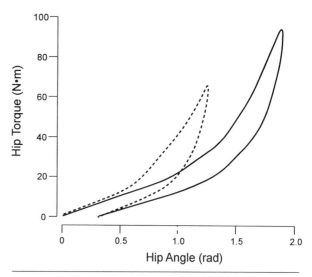

Figure 8.5 Torque-angle relation for two individuals during the straight-leg raise test. The measurements correspond to flexion of the hip and the extensor torque about the hip joint due to the passive properties of the joint tissues. The more flexible individual (solid line) was able to tolerate greater discomfort.

Data from McHugh, Kremenic, Fox, and Gleim, 1998.

muscles. Because the range of motion is usually much greater when a person is completely anesthetized, Walsh (1992) suggested that the inability to relax is a major limitation in the range of motion about a joint. Moreover, individuals who have **hypermobile** joints, often referred to as being double-jointed or as having lax joints (Alter, 1996), are characterized by a reduced stiffness of the joint tissues due to enhanced relaxation of the involved muscles (Walsh, 1992). Because such persons do not actually have two joints, it is more appropriate to describe this characteristic as a hypermobile joint, which indicates the reason for the enhanced range of motion.

Stretching Techniques

Based on the critical role of relaxation in flexibility, several techniques have been developed that purport to improve relaxation and thereby increase flexibility (Alter, 1996). Three of these exercises have been derived from a rehabilitation technique known as *proprioceptive neuromuscular facilitation* (PNF) (Knott & Voss, 1968). The **hold-relax** (HR) technique consists of an initial maximum isometric contraction of the muscle to be stretched (antagonist), followed by relaxation and stretch of the muscle to the limit of the range of motion. The **agonist-contract** (AC) stretch requires the assistance of a partner or a therapist (figure 8.6). The partner moves the participant's limb so that the joint is at the limit of rotation. The participant then contracts the agonist (e.g., quadriceps femoris) while the partner applies a force to the limb to stretch the antagonist muscle (e.g., hamstrings).

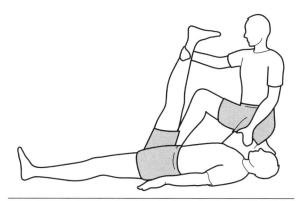

Figure 8.6 Partner-assisted flexibility training. An example of the hold-relax, agonist contraction technique in which the partner stretches the hamstrings maximally (hip flexion) while the individual concentrically contracts the quadriceps femoris muscles.

The **hold-relax, agonist contraction** (HR-AC) technique is a combination of the HR and AC techniques. For the example shown in figure 8.6, the HR-AC technique would involve an initial maximum isometric contraction of the hamstrings followed by a relaxation and stretch of the hamstrings; the hamstring stretch would be accomplished by manual assistance from the partner and by contraction of the quadriceps femoris.

The PNF stretches were designed on the basis of known connections and effects within the nervous system. The *HR technique* is intended to stretch the muscle while the alpha motor neurons are least excitable so that afferent input from the length detectors (muscle spindles) is least likely to elicit a stretch-evoked activation of muscle. To examine this possibility, both Hoffmann (H) and tendon-tap (T) reflexes have been measured immediately after isometric contractions. Recall from chapter 6 that the H reflex is used to test the level of excitability of the motor neuron pool, whereas the T reflex tests the combined effects of muscle spindle responsiveness, motor neuron excitability, and the level of presynaptic inhibition. Studies have shown that the amplitudes of both the H and T reflexes are depressed after an isometric contraction and that the depression of the T reflexes is greater than that of the H reflexes (Enoka, Hutton, & Eldred, 1980; Guissard, Duchateau, & Hainaut, 1988; Moore & Kukulka, 1991). These findings suggest that the excitability of both the muscle spindle and the motor neurons is decreased immediately after an isometric contraction and that this depression lasts about 10 s (Crone & Nielsen, 1989). Furthermore, the depression of the reflexes is similar for contractions that vary from 1 to 30 s in duration.

The rationale for the *AC technique* is to activate the reciprocal-inhibition reflex (chapter 6) onto the motor neurons that innervate the antagonist (muscle to be stretched) by contraction of the agonist muscle. In this scheme, voluntary activation of the agonist involves activation of both the alpha (α) and gamma (γ) motor neurons and the interneuron (I) that mediates the reciprocal-inhibition reflex (figure 8.7) (Nielsen, Kagamihara, Crone, & Hultborn, 1992). This interneuron is known as the Ia inhibitory interneuron (chapter 6). Activation of this interneuron causes action potentials to be transmitted to motor neurons that innervate the antagonist muscle, and subsequently causes a reduction in the excitability of these motor neurons. Consequently, the AC technique is presumed to involve an activation of the agonist muscle and, through reciprocal inhibition, a relaxation of the antagonist muscle. Etnyre and Abraham (1988) have shown that the plantarflexor muscles (e.g., soleus) are electrically silent (EMG), as would be expected with reciprocal inhibition, during performance of the AC stretch and contraction of the dorsiflexor muscles.

A number of studies have compared the effectiveness of the various stretching techniques (Condon & Hutton, 1987; Etnyre & Abraham, 1986; Guissard et al., 1988; Moore & Hutton, 1980; Wallin, Ekblom, Grahn, & Nordenborg, 1985). In general, the findings indicate that

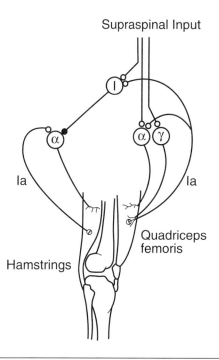

Figure 8.7 Neural pathways activated during the agonist-contract stretch of the hamstrings. Activation of the quadriceps femoris by supraspinal centers results in the concurrent activation of motor neurons innervating quadriceps femoris and the Ia inhibitory interneuron that mediates the reciprocal-inhibition reflex. This connection supposedly causes the antagonist (hamstrings) to relax during activation of the agonist (quadriceps femoris).

the improvement in flexibility with static stretching is similar to that achieved with ballistic stretching (Magnusson et al., 1998). However, ballistic stretches have the disadvantage that they are more likely to produce muscle soreness (Shellock & Prentice, 1985). When the tests of flexibility involve stretching to the physiological limit rather than with a constant torque, the PNF stretches (HR, AC, and HR-AC techniques) provide greater improvements in flexibility than static and ballistic stretches. There does not, however, seem to be a consistent difference among the three PNF techniques.

One issue that is unresolved from these studies on the PNF stretching techniques is the relative significance of the neural mechanisms in the improvement of flexibility. There can be two effects: one related to an improved tolerance of the stretch and the other involving a reduction in muscle activation. Accumulating evidence indicates that improvements in flexibility after one session or several weeks of training are mainly due to greater tolerance of the stretch. For example, improvement in the range of motion at the hip or knee joints due to tightness of the hamstrings was not associated with any change in passive stiffness or EMG but a willingness of individuals to tolerate greater discomfort (Halbertsma, van Bolhuis, & Göeken, 1996; Magnusson et al., 1998; Magnusson, Simonsen, Aagaard, Strensen, and Kjær, 1996; McHugh, Kremenic, Fox, & Gleim, 1998). The sensations associated with stretching a muscle to the limit of its range of motion are typically rather intense, so the posttraining improvement in flexibility must be associated with a reduction in the sensory feedback or an attenuated interpretation of these signals. The PNF stretches, particularly the contract-relax technique, enable individuals to tolerate greater stretches (Magnusson, Simonsen, Aagaard, Dyhre-Poulsen, et al., 1996).

In the absence of neural input, successive stretches can increase the length of a muscle-tendon unit (Taylor, Dalton, Seaber, & Garrett, 1990). In experiments that examined this effect, a leg muscle (extensor digitorum longus) was stretched from an initial force of about 2 N to a length that produced a passive force of 78 N and was held at this length for 30 s. This stretch cycle was repeated 10 times. Figure 8.8a indicates that the muscles had to be stretched to longer lengths in subsequent stretches in order to exert a force of 78 N; the total increase in length over the 10 stretches was about 3.5%. The converse protocol was also applied; the muscle was stretched by 10% and the force exerted in successive stretches was measured (figure 8.8b). These measurements indicate that in the absence of neural input, the load on a muscle-tendon unit due to its passive properties (connective tissue) decreases

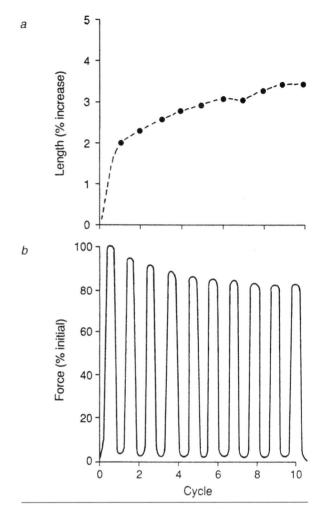

Figure 8.8   Stretch-induced changes in *(a)* length and *(b)* force of a muscle-tendon unit.

Adapted from Taylor, Dalton, Seaber, and Garrett, 1990.

with stretches to a prescribed length (Magnusson, Simonsen, Dyhre-Poulsen, et al., 1996). Despite this effect, the poststretch decline in passive muscle stiffness returns to baseline values within an hour (Magnusson, 1998).

After several decades of research on the topic of flexibility, however, many questions remain. For example, short-term studies have suggested that several weeks of training produces only transient changes in the passive stiffness of muscle and its associated tissues (Magnusson, 1998). However, practitioners of yoga provide compelling evidence that long-term stretching exercises can induce pronounced changes in the passive mechanical properties of these tissues. Examine, for example, the postures (asanas) that yogis practice and the ranges of motion that they can achieve (Iyengar, 1979). Mastery of the body in this discipline, however, is achieved only after many years of practice.

Muscle Soreness and Damage

Strenuous physical activity can have diverse effects on muscle, ranging from subcellular damage of muscle fibers to stretch-induced muscle injuries (strains). The subcellular damage, which most active individuals experience, frequently produces an inflammatory response and is associated with muscle soreness that begins hours after completion of the exercise. In contrast, strain injuries typically occur as an acute painful injury during high-power tasks and require clinical intervention.

Muscle Soreness

Because the perception of soreness is not evident until 24 to 48 h after the exercise, postexercise muscle soreness is called **delayed-onset muscle soreness.** This term distinguishes the postexercise soreness from the exertional pain that occurs during exercise (Asmussen, 1952, 1956). Delayed-onset muscle soreness is often quantified by asking individuals to rate the level of soreness on a 10-point scale. Alternatively, the sensation can be expressed as tenderness via measurement of the pressure that evokes a painful response (Edwards, Mills, & Newham, 1981). The clinical symptoms associated with delayed-onset muscle soreness include an increase in plasma enzymes (e.g., creatine kinase), myoglobin, and protein metabolites from injured muscles; structural damage to subcellular components of muscle fibers, as seen with light and electron microscopy; and temporary impairment of muscle function (Armstrong, 1990). The major sensation underlying delayed-onset muscle soreness is tenderness, which comprises a feeling of discomfort elicited by pressure (Howell, Chleboun, & Conaster, 1993; Jones & Round, 1997). When the muscle is at rest, there is no discomfort.

An individual experiences delayed-onset muscle soreness after performing unaccustomed activity, especially if it involves eccentric contractions (Fridén & Lieber, 1997; Gibila, MacDougall, Tarnopolsky, Stauber, & Elorriaga, 1995; McCully & Faulkner, 1985; Newham, 1988; Whitehead, Allen, Morgan, & Proske, 1998). Healthy individuals, for example, experience delayed-onset muscle soreness when resuming an activity after several weeks of inactivity. Although it is generally agreed that the soreness is due to subcellular pathology related to mechanical factors, there is no consensus on the factor responsible for the phenomenon (Morgan & Allen, 1999). Because eccentric contractions involve fewer motor units than concentric contractions to produce a given force, the active muscle fibers experience greater *stress* (force per unit area) that may disrupt the sarcolemmal, sarcoplasmic reticular, and myofibrillar structures (Child, Brown, Day, Saxton, & Donnelly, 1998; Warren, Hayes, Lowe, & Armstrong, 1993; Warren, Hayes, Lowe, Prior, & Armstrong, 1993; McCully & Faulkner, 1985). Alternatively, Fridén and Lieber (1992) propose that the amount of *strain* associated with the forced lengthening of the eccentric contractions is the more significant mechanical factor.

Whatever the mechanism responsible for delayed-onset muscle soreness, the postexercise effects include several functional impairments. The dominant effects include muscle weakness, a reduced ability to produce power, and a limited range of motion due to increased stiffness (Howell et al., 1993; Newham, Jones, & Clarkson, 1987; Rodenburg, de Boer, Schiereck, van Echteld, & Bär, 1994). In some individuals, strenuous eccentric exercise can produce exaggerated muscle weakness and swelling, which can require medical intervention (Sayers, Clarkson, Rouzier, & Kamen, 1999). This condition is known as **rhabdomyolysis.**

Muscle Fiber Damage

In an attempt to identify the mechanisms responsible for delayed-onset muscle soreness, physiologists often compare the time course of these sensations to the damage that occurs in the sore muscles (Salmons, 1997). The structural abnormalities evident after exercise include sarcolemmal disruption, dilated transverse (T) tubules, distortion of myofibrillar components, fragmented sarcoplasmic reticulum, lesions of the plasma membrane, cytoskeletal damage, changes in the extracellular myofiber matrix, and swollen mitochondria (Fridén, Kjörell, & Thornell, 1984; Lieber, Schmitz, Mishra, & Fridén, 1994; Stauber, 1989). Although such damage is apparent immediately after the exercise, changes also continue during the postexercise period when the soreness develops.

A common marker of muscle damage is the presence of the enzyme creatine kinase in the plasma, which indicates the turnover of proteins rendered dysfunctional by physical or oxidative stress (Evans & Cannon, 1991). The efflux of enzymes occurs by diffusion through exercise-induced holes in the plasma membrane of the muscle cell. The postexercise increase in the skeletal muscle enzymes in the circulation is related to the type and intensity of the exercise. It is greater with eccentric contractions than with concentric contractions, and it increases with exercise intensity. Interestingly, estrogen may directly influence the muscle cell membrane and reduce the efflux of skeletal muscle enzymes. Because of this effect, women tend to exhibit lower postexercise levels of circulating creatine kinase (Dop Bär, Reijneveld, Wokke, Jacobs, &

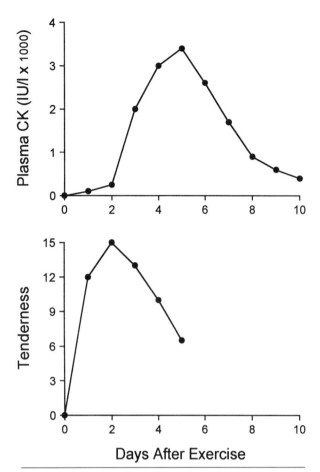

Figure 8.9 The time course of changes in plasma creatine kinase (CK) levels and tenderness of the involved muscles in the days after performance of 20 min of eccentric contractions (one every 15 s) with the elbow flexor muscles.

Data from Jones and Round, 1997.

Bootsma, 1997; Evans & Cannon, 1991), and female rats exhibit less structural damage than male rats after downhill running (Komulainen, Koskinen, Kalliokoski, Takala, & Vihko, 1999). However, peak levels of creatine kinase in the plasma occur at about five to six days after the exercise, compared with one to two days for the soreness sensations (figure 8.9). Furthermore, the postexercise effects decline with repeat bouts of exercise, but more quickly for the plasma levels of creatine kinase than for tenderness (Jones & Round, 1997). Such findings suggest that delayed-onset muscle soreness is not due to the damage of muscle fibers.

Muscle Weakness

One of the most consistent outcomes of an exercise protocol that induces delayed-onset muscle soreness is prolonged muscle weakness. For example, Howell et al. (1993) found that 5 to 15 repetitions of slowly (5-9 s) lowering a heavy load with the elbow flexor muscles re-

sulted in a 35% decrease in strength that was half recovered in about six weeks (figure 8.10*a*). Because of the magnitude of this effect, a number of researchers have attempted to identify the mechanisms responsible for muscle weakness after a protocol of eccentric contractions.

The potential mechanisms that could contribute to the muscle weakness after a bout of eccentric contractions include an inability to activate the motor units by voluntary command, depletion of metabolic substrates, damage and degradation of the contractile structures, and failure to activate the contractile structures. Because the weakness is also present in electrically evoked contractions (Child et al., 1998; Jones, Allen, Talbot, Morgan, & Proske, 1997), inadequate voluntary activation is not a central contributor to the weakness. Similarly, because the weakness can be induced after only a few eccentric contractions (Howell et al., 1993), depletion of metabolic substrates is not a major factor. Although numerous investigators have attempted to establish an association between muscle fiber damage and the postexercise weak-

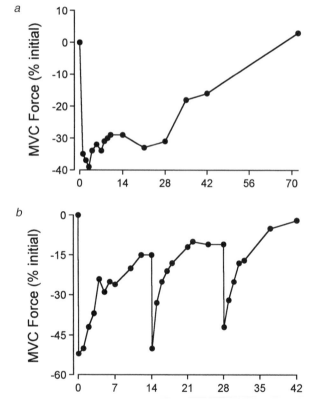

Figure 8.10 Muscle weakness after a protocol of eccentric contractions with the elbow flexor muscles. Weakness is expressed as the percentage reduction in maximum voluntary contraction (MVC) force. *(a)* Weakness after a single bout of eccentric contractions; *(b)* weakness after exercise at days 0, 14, and 28.

Data from Howell et al., 1983 (8.10a) and from Newham et al., 1987 (8.10b).

ness, the extent of the damage is usually minor, and the weakness is exhibited by single muscle fibers that are not damaged (Hesselink, Kuipers, Guerten, & Van Straaten, 1996; Morgan & Allen, 1999). Alternatively, the weakness appears to be due to an inability to activate the contractile structures, probably involving an impairment of excitation-contraction coupling (Ingalls, Warren, Williams, Ward, & Armstrong, 1998) as a consequence of overstretched sarcomeres (Morgan & Allen, 1999).

The muscle weakness that occurs after a bout of eccentric contractions seems to involve mechanisms different from those associated with the postexercise increases in tenderness and plasma creatine kinase. For example, when subjects performed eccentric contractions once every two weeks for a total of three sessions, there was a marked decrease in MVC force after each session (figure 8.10b), a lesser increase in tenderness after the second and third sessions, and no increase in plasma creatine kinase after the second and third sessions (Newham et al., 1987). It appears that several factors are involved in the consequences of physical activity that induces delayed-onset muscle soreness (Morgan & Allen, 1999).

Cause of Muscle Soreness

The sensation of tenderness appears to be triggered by the loss of cellular calcium homeostasis (Clarkson, Cyrnes, McCarmick, Turcotte, & White, 1986; Fridén & Lieber, 1997; Jackson, Jones, & Edwards, 1984) due to the activity-induced disruption of sarcomeres. A high intracellular calcium concentration activates proteolytic and lipolytic systems that initiate the degradation of cellular structures (Armstrong, 1990). Because this inflammatory process has a time course similar to that of the heightened tenderness (Lieber, Schmitz, et al., 1994) and there is an appropriate activation of the immune system (Malm, Lenkel, & Sjödin, 1999), the sensation of soreness is usually attributed to the inflammatory response.

Muscle Strain

In contrast to the microinjuries that often accompany delayed-onset muscle soreness, muscle can experience acute and painful events, such as cramps and strains. **Muscle cramp** is a painful, involuntary shortening of muscle that appears to be triggered by a variety of mechanisms, including both neural and muscular factors (Bentley, 1996; Bertolasi, De Grandis, Bongiovanni, Zanette, & Gasperini, 1993; Ross & Thomas, 1995). A strain is an injury that occurs because of an unexpected and substantial stretch of a muscle (Best, Hasselman, & Garrett, 1997). These strains, which are also referred to as *pulls* and *tears,* can be categorized as mild, moderate, or severe (Whiting & Zernicke, 1998). Mild strains in-

volve minor structural disruption, local tenderness, and minimal function deficit. Moderate strains comprise some structural damage, visible swelling, marked tenderness, and some impairment of function. Severe strains exhibit substantial structural damage that usually requires surgical intervention. Best et al. (1997) report that gradual increases in strain (from 13% to 23%) were accompanied by progressive impairment of contractile function, EMG amplitude, and tissue damage. They also noted that the disruption of muscle fibers preceded that of connective tissue.

Clinical reports indicate that these strains invariably occur at the muscle-tendon or the muscle-bone junction; muscle strains have been reported for medial gastrocnemius, rectus femoris, triceps brachii, adductor longus, pectoralis major, and semimembranosus (Best et al., 1997; Garrett, 1990). Muscles most prone to such an injury are the two-joint muscles (because they can be stretched more), muscles that limit the range of motion about a joint, and muscles that have a high proportion of type II muscle fibers (Garrett, Califf, & Bassett, 1984). Because of these factors, there is often one muscle within a synergistic group that is more prone to injury—for example, adductor longus in the hip adductors and rectus femoris in the knee extensors. Moreover, the injury most often occurs during powerful eccentric contractions, when the force can be several times greater than the maximal isometric force. The injury frequently involves bleeding with the subsequent accumulation of blood in the subcutaneous spaces. The most appropriate immediate treatment is to rest the muscle and to apply ice and compression (Best et al., 1997). Rehabilitation should include physical therapy to improve the range of motion and to prescribe *functional* strengthening exercises.

Experiments designed to identify the characteristics of the muscle strain injury have indicated that the disruption occurs near the muscle-tendon junction despite differences in the architecture of the muscles tested and the direction of the strain (Best et al., 1997). When different muscles were stretched passively (muscle not contracting), the strain injury did not occur after a constant fiber strain. However, there was no difference in the total strain to failure when a given muscle was stretched while it was passive versus when it was active (muscle activated by electrical stimulation). Nonetheless, muscle contraction can double the strain energy that the muscle can absorb during the stretch (Garrett, Safran, Seaber, Glisson, & Ribbeck, 1987). Figure 8.11a shows strain energy as the area under the force-length graph, with stretch-induced failure occurring at the peak force. In figure 8.11b, the strain energy (area under the curve) absorbed by the active muscle is about twice that absorbed by the passive muscle, although the peak force at failure is only about 15% greater in the active muscle. Because

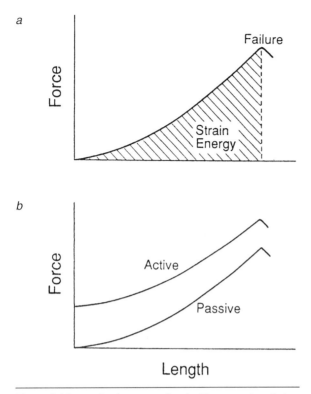

Figure 8.11   *(a)* Strain energy absorbed by a muscle unit during a stretch to failure. The stretch-induced failure occurred at the peak force. *(b)* More strain energy can be absorbed by the muscle when it is active compared with passive.

Adapted from Garrett, Safran, Seaber, Glisson, and Ribbeck, 1987.

of this effect, any factor, such as fatigue or weakness, that tends to reduce the contractile capability of muscle may predispose the muscle to a strain.

Muscle Fatigue

In everyday language, muscle fatigue refers to the acute impairment of performance due to physical activity. When assessed experimentally, muscle fatigue is often quantified as a reduction in the maximum force that a muscle can exert (Fitts, 1996; Gandevia, Enoka, McComas, Stuart, & Thomas, 1995). Although fatigue can be confused with muscle weakness and is a common complaint of patients with a variety of disorders, the term has a much more focused meaning in experimental studies. Within this context, the term fatigue should not be used to describe a perceived weakness of muscle or the endpoint of a performance (exhaustion). Rather, muscle fatigue encompasses the activity-related impairment of physiological processes that reduce muscle force. These effects begin soon after the onset of sustained physical activity.

Because the physiological processes involved in performance extend from the limbic system to the cross-bridge, numerous factors can contribute to the development of muscle fatigue. The last 100 years of study have clearly demonstrated that fatigue is not caused by the impairment of a single process but rather by several mechanisms, both motor and sensory, and that these vary from one condition to another. The variation in responsible mechanisms has been termed the **task dependency** of muscle fatigue (Bigland-Ritchie, Rice, Garland, & Walsh, 1995; Enoka & Stuart, 1992; cf. however, Walsh, 2000). One way to understand the physiology of muscle fatigue, therefore, is to identify the conditions that can impair the various processes and thereby contribute to muscle fatigue.

Task Dependency

When an individual performs a task, the requirements of the task (e.g., amount of force, muscles involved, duration of the activity) stress various physiological processes associated with the motor performance. As the task requirements change, so do the processes that experience the greatest stress. The task variables that influence the distribution of stress among the processes include the level of subject motivation, the neural strategy (pattern of muscle activation and motor command), the intensity and duration of the activity, the speed of a contraction, and the extent to which an activity is sustained continuously. The physiological processes that can be impaired by these variables include (1) activation of the primary motor cortex, (2) the central nervous system drive to motor neurons, (3) the muscles and motor units that are activated, (4) neuromuscular propagation, (5) excitation-contraction coupling, (6) the availability of metabolic substrates, (7) the intracellular milieu, (8) the contractile apparatus, and (9) muscle blood flow (figure 8.12).

Central Drive

The excitation provided by supraspinal centers is not impaired during high-force fatiguing contractions, but it can be during prolonged contractions. This limitation is expressed as an increase in the effort associated with the task, the appearance of tremor in the involved muscles, and the spread of activation to accessory muscles (Duchateau & Hainaut, 1993; Gandevia, 1998).

The maximality of the activation provided by the nervous system to muscle is typically assessed through comparison of the force exerted during an MVC with the force that can be elicited artificially by electrical stimulation (Allen, McKenzie, & Gandevia, 1998). This approach involves applying single shocks or a brief train of shocks to the nerve during a fatiguing contraction. The test has been applied to both sustained and intermittent contractions performed at both maximal and submaximal intensities. For example, when subjects performed a sustained 60-s MVC with a thumb muscle (adductor pollicis),

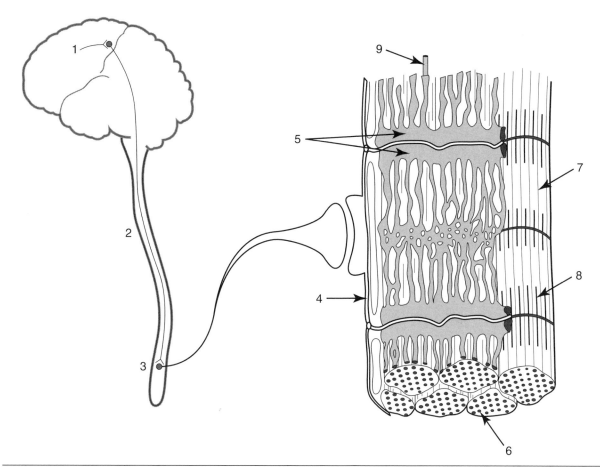

Figure 8.12   Potential sites that can contribute to muscle fatigue.

Data from Bigland-Ritchie, 1981.

the force declined by 30% to 50%, but this decrease in voluntary force could not be supplemented by an electric shock (Bigland-Ritchie et al., 1982). Similarly, the maximal voluntary and electrically elicited force declined in parallel (figure 8.13*a*) when subjects performed an intermittent (6-s contraction, 4-s rest) submaximal contraction (target force was 50% of maximum) with the quadriceps femoris (Bigland-Ritchie, Furbush, & Woods, 1986). In this experiment, the maximum voluntary and electrically elicited forces were elicited periodically during the submaximal contraction. The parallel decline in the voluntary and evoked forces suggests that the central drive remained maximal during these tasks.

In contrast, subjects exhibited substantial central fatigue when they could no longer sustain a force of 30% of maximum with the plantarflexor muscles even though the force could be evoked by electrical stimulation of the nerve innervating the muscle (Löscher, Cresswell, & Thorstensson, 1996a). After 60 s of electrical stimulation, during which time the central processes could recover, the subjects were able to continue the task with a voluntary contraction for another 400 s.

Two tests of artificial stimuli were applied to the muscle in the experiment shown in figure 8.13. One test consisted of a train of eight stimuli that were delivered at a rate of 50 Hz, which evoked a brief tetanus. The second test used was the **twitch superimposition** (Tw_s) test, which is also known as the twitch interpolation or the twitch occlusion test. The twitch superimposition test involves applying one to four supramaximal electric shocks to the nerve during an MVC and seeing whether or not the force increases (Allen et al., 1998). If the stimulus evokes additional force, then the central drive during the contraction is not maximal and the individual is deemed to be exhibiting **central fatigue.** Figure 8.14 shows that the magnitude of the evoked response depends on the level of force exerted by the subject. The ability of an individual to achieve maximal voluntary activation is quantified as (Allen, Gandevia, & McKenzie, 1995):

Voluntary activation (%) =

$$\left(\frac{1 - \text{superimposed twitch}}{\text{control twitch}} \right) \times 100$$

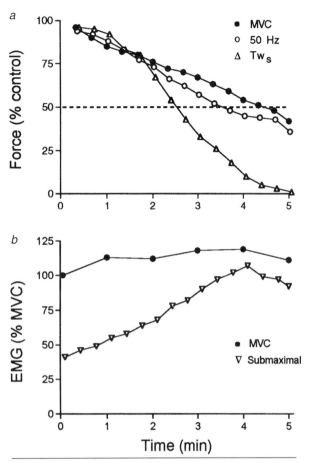

a

b

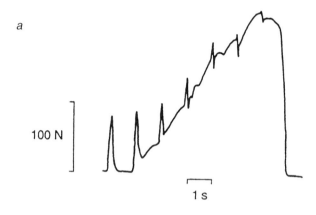

a

100 N

1 s

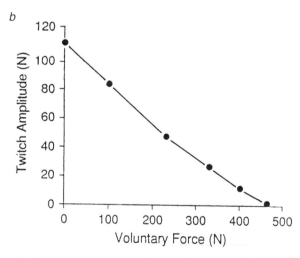

b

Figure 8.13 *(a)* Decline in maximum voluntary contraction (MVC) force and in the artificially elicited force (tetanus = 50 Hz, twitch = Tw$_s$) during a fatiguing contraction with the quadriceps femoris muscle; *(b)* change in the integrated EMG for quadriceps femoris during the MVC contractions and the intermittent submaximal contractions over the course of the task.

Adapted from Bigland-Ritchie, Furbush, and Woods, 1986.

(Bigland-Ritchie, Furbush, & Woods, 1986; Gandevia & McKenzie, 1985; Grimby, Hannerz, & Hedman, 1981). This inability appears as a deviation of the two force lines (MVC and 50 Hz) in figure 8.13*a* or as a decrease in the level of voluntary activation. A lack of motivation probably results in an inadequate central drive to the appropriate motor neurons. Second, some muscles are more difficult than others to activate maximally (Bigland-Ritchie, Furbush, & Woods, 1986; Milner-Brown & Miller, 1989; Thomas, Woods, & Bigland-Ritchie, 1989). For example, subjects in one study could maximally activate the tibialis anterior muscle, as assessed by twitch superimposition; but 10 of 17 men and 4 of 11 women could not maximally activate the plantarflexor muscles (Belanger & McComas, 1981).

Figure 8.14   The twitch superimposition method. *(a)* Decrease in the amplitude of the twitch force elicited by an electric shock as the voluntary force exerted by quadriceps femoris increased; *(b)* decline in twitch force as a function of voluntary force. The twitch was elicited at various levels of force during voluntary contractions. The maximum voluntary contraction (MVC) force was about 470 N.

Adapted from Bigland-Ritchie, Cafarelli, and Vøllestad, 1986.

where superimposed twitch is the amplitude of the evoked twitch, and the control twitch refers to the amplitude of the twitch evoked in a relaxed muscle. During the intermittent fatiguing contraction (figure 8.13*a*), the amplitude of the superimposed twitch force decreased to zero by the time the MVC force reached the target force (50% MVC). This meant that the central drive was maximal at the end of the fatigue test and that voluntary activation was 100%.

The tests that have been conducted on fatiguing contractions indicate that the neural drive to muscle provided by the central nervous system is not always maximal and that the reduction in central drive can be a factor that contributes to the decline in force. There are at least two examples of the inability of humans to generate an adequate central drive during fatiguing activity. First, subjects who are not motivated maximally do not exhibit a parallel decline in the voluntary and evoked forces

One way to identify the locus of the central impairment during a fatiguing contraction is to compare the forces evoked by stimulation of the brain and the peripheral nerve. When subjects sustained contractions at 20%, 30%, or 100% of maximum with the elbow flexor muscles, there was an increase in the magnitude of the EMG responses evoked by transcranial magnetic stimulation (Example 7.8) (Sacco, Thickbroom, Thompson, & Mastaglia, 1997; Sacco, Thichbroom, Byrnes, & Mastaglia, 2000; Taylor, Butler, Allen, & Gandevia, 1996). Because the evoked responses were not altered by manipulation of afferent feedback and because they paralleled the changes observed in response to stimulation of the corticospinal tract or peripheral nerve, the increase in the evoked EMG responses likely resulted from changes due to intrinsic cortical processes. As a consequence, the force evoked by transcranial magnetic stimulation increased with the duration of a sustained maximum contraction (Gandevia, Allen, Butler, & Taylor, 1996). However, the changes in cortical excitability recover quickly even though central fatigue persists, which suggests a significant role for central sites that provide input to the motor cortex (Gandevia, 1998; Gandevia et al., 1996; Sacco et al., 1997; Taylor, & Gandevia, 2001).

Other results that have indicated a role for central drive in limiting performance in sustained activities come from studies that manipulate the humoral factors circulating in the cerebrospinal fluid. In some experiments, pharmacological agents are infused into the cerebrospinal fluid of experimental animals (typically rats), and the effect on endurance time is assessed. The results indicate that some agents (e.g., amphetamine, which is a central nervous system stimulant) can increase the time to exhaustion, whereas other agents (e.g., 6-hydroxydopamine, a neurotoxin that destroys catecholaminergic fibers) decrease the time it takes to reach exhaustion (Bhagat & Wheeler, 1973; Heyes, Garnett, & Coates, 1985). In another experiment, the endurance time of men when cycling at 80% of the maximal rate of oxygen uptake was compared between control conditions and after infusion of a placebo or buspirone, which is an agonist for a brain serotonin receptor (Marvin et al., 1997). Serum prolactin was elevated significantly after administration of buspirone, which indicated an increased stimulation of the serotonin receptors in the hypothalamus. The ratings of perceived exertion were higher after infusion of buspirone, and endurance time decreased from 26 to 16 min. These observations suggest that humoral factors such as epinephrine and the neurotransmitter 5-hydroxytryptamine can play a significant role in sustaining the central drive during fatiguing tasks (Blomstrand, Celsing, & Newsholme, 1988; Chaouloff, Kennett, Serrurier, Merino, & Curson, 1986; Heyes, Garnett, & Coates, 1988). It appears, therefore, that the level of various hormones circulating in the

cerebrospinal fluid is important in the ability to sustain the central drive.

Neural Strategy

A resultant muscle force about a joint can be achieved by a variety of muscle activation patterns. This flexibility certainly exists among a group of synergist muscles and perhaps among the motor units within individual muscles (Fallentin et al., 1993; Semmler, Kutzscher, & Enoka, 1999; Sjøgaard, Kiens, Jørgensen, & Saltin, 1986; Tamaki et al., 1998). Because of this possibility, one option the motor system has for delaying the onset of force decline (fatigue) is to vary the contribution of synergist muscles to the resultant muscle force. Although this possibility is available only when the task requires submaximal forces, most activities of daily living involve such forces.

Varying levels of activation among synergist muscles were observed when subjects sustained an isometric knee extensor force at 5% of the MVC force for 1 h (Sjøgaard et al., 1986; Sjøgaard, Savard, & Juel, 1988). Despite the low intensity of the task, the subjects did experience fatigue as indicated by a 12% decline in the MVC force and an increase in the associated effort at the end of the hour. During the fatiguing contraction, the subjects were able to maintain a constant force (5% MVC) while the level of activity varied in rectus femoris and vastus lateralis (figure 8.15). This observation indicates that the neural drive to the muscles changed while the net output remained constant. Similarly, when the knee extensor muscles perform low-intensity, intermittent contractions to the endurance limit, there is a progressive increase in the coactivation of the knee flexor muscles (Psek & Cafarelli, 1993).

Another example of the interaction among synergists involves the effect of selectively fatiguing one muscle in a synergistic group (Sacco, Newberry, McFadden, Brown, & McComas, 1997). In this study, the lateral gastrocnemius muscle was fatigued by electrical stimulation while

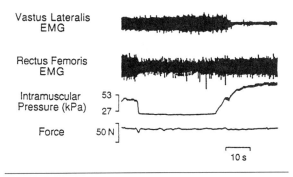

Figure 8.15 Variable contributions of vastus lateralis and rectus femoris to a sustained knee extensor force. Intramuscular pressure was measured in the rectus femoris muscle.

Adapted from Sjøgaard, Kiens, Jørgensen, and Saltin, 1986.

blood flow to the leg was occluded. Subsequently, subjects performed an MVC, and the EMG was depressed by 52% in the lateral gastrocnemius muscle and by 29% in the medial gastrocnemius. This finding suggests the presence of an inhibitory reflex connection from the fatigued muscle (lateral gastrocnemius) to a synergist muscle (medial gastrocnemius). Presumably, the accumulation of metabolites or the presence of anoxia in the fatigued muscle triggered sensory feedback that depressed the excitability of motor neurons innervating the synergist muscle.

Even when the muscles used to perform a task remain the same, variations in the activation of these muscles can produce differences in the rate of decline in force. For example, Rube and Secher (1990) examined the ability of subjects to perform an isometric leg extension task (concurrent knee and hip extension) with either one or two legs. Subjects were required to perform 150 MVCs for both conditions (one and two legs) before and after five weeks of strength training. The subjects were assigned to one of three groups: control group, one-legged training group, and two-legged training group. Both the one- and two-legged groups increased strength after five weeks of training. Furthermore, the rate of decline in force during the 150 contractions was less after training (figure 8.16). But the effect was specific to the training mode. The one-legged training group was less fatigable only during the one-legged task, and the two-legged training group was less fatigable only during the two-legged task. These data suggest that the neural strategy adopted during the one-legged task was different from that used during the two-legged task and that this difference influenced the fatigue experienced in each task.

The final example of whole-muscle activation patterns and fatigue involves the different types of muscle contractions. One of the unexpected findings on this topic is the apparent difference in fatigability of muscle for concentric and eccentric contractions. This difference is shown in figure 8.17. Subjects performed maximal contractions with the quadriceps femoris on an isokinetic device that was set with a 1.2-rad range of motion and a speed of 3.14 rad/s. The subjects performed three bouts of 32 contractions each for both the concentric and eccentric conditions, with a 60-s rest between each bout of exercise. Within each bout, the torque exerted during the

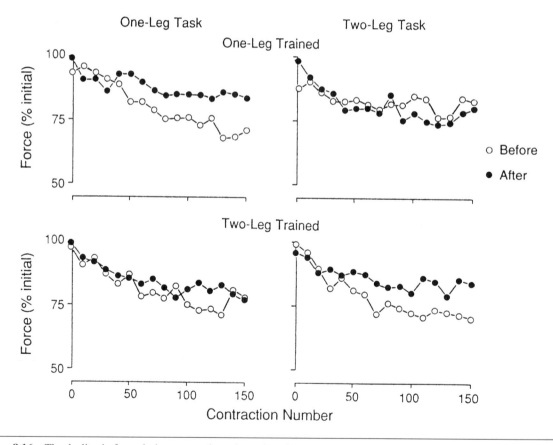

Figure 8.16 The decline in force during one- and two-legged performances of a leg extension task before and after five weeks of training. The upper row shows the results for the one-legged training group; the bottom row indicates the data for the two-legged training group. The rate of decline in force was less after training, but for the one-legged group during the one-leg task only and for the two-legged group during the two-leg task only.

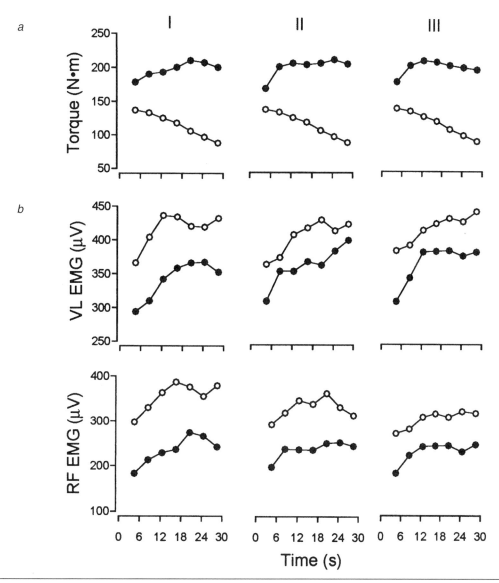

Figure 8.17 Changes in *(a)* torque and *(b)* EMG during concentric (open circles) and eccentric (solid circles) fatiguing contractions with the quadriceps femoris muscle. The EMG is shown for vastus lateralis (VL) and rectus femoris (RF).

Adapted from Tesch et al., 1990.

concentric contractions decreased while that for the eccentric contractions increased slightly (figure 8.17*a*). Furthermore, the integrated EMG for both vastus lateralis and rectus femoris was less during the eccentric contractions but increased during each bout for both the concentric and eccentric contractions (figure 8.17*b*). Thus, the association between the magnitude of the EMG and torque differed for the two types of contractions during the fatiguing protocol.

Although several investigators have found that the fatigue experienced with eccentric contractions is less than that for concentric contractions (Grabiner & Owings, 1999; Pasquet, Carpentier, Duchateau, & Hainaut, 2000; Rácz, Tihanyi, & Hortobágyi, 2000), others have found

no difference (Komi & Viitasalo, 1977; Linnamo, Bottas, & Komi, 2000). A critical factor here appears to be the speed of the eccentric contractions. Komi and colleagues used faster contractions, which probably caused muscle damage in addition to muscle fatigue. Most investigators, however, prefer to distinguish among the mechanisms that are responsible for muscle damage, muscle fatigue, and muscle weakness (Gandevia et al., 1995).

Motor Unit Behavior

The activity of motor units during a fatiguing contraction depends on the intensity and the type of contraction being performed. The average discharge rates of motor units in many muscles decline during a sustained MVC

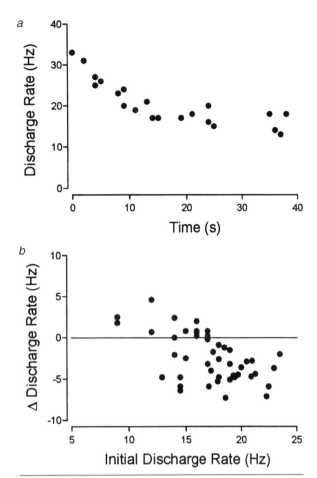

Figure 8.18 Changes in the discharge rate of motor units during fatiguing maximal and submaximal isometric contractions. (a) Discharge rates from 21 motor units during a maximal contraction with the adductor pollicis muscle (Bigland-Ritchie, Johansson, Lippold, Smith, & Woods, 1983); (b) the change in discharge rate of 45 motor units in biceps brachii after fatiguing contractions held at about 25% maximum voluntary contraction (Garland et al., 1994).

Data from Bigland-Ritchie, Johansson, Lippold, Smith, and Woods, 1983; and Garland et al., 1994.

(figure 8.18a) (Bigland-Ritchie, Johansson, Lippold, Smith, & Woods, 1983; Peters & Fuglevand, 1999). One exception appears to be the big toe extensor muscle, which comprises mainly slow-twitch motor units (Macefield et al., 2000). Similarly, the average discharge rate of motor units during submaximal isometric contractions does not change substantially (figure 8.18b). The discharge rate can increase, remain constant, or decrease; but the change is usually modest (Christova & Kossev, 1998; De Luca, Foley, & Erim, 1996; Garland et al., 1994; Maton & Gamet, 1989). Furthermore, the change in discharge rate appears to differ for isometric and anisometric contractions (Griffin, Ivanova, & Garland, 2000). As a consequence, the increase in EMG during a fatiguing contraction held at a submaximal force is largely due to the recruitment of additional motor units.

To assess the change in motor unit behavior during fatiguing anisometric contractions, one study had subjects produce displacements about the elbow joint with a trajectory similar to the force record in figure 8.19 (Miller, Garland, Ivanova, & Ohtsuki, 1996). The task involved a concentric contraction with the triceps brachii muscle to raise a load, a brief isometric contraction to hold the load, and an eccentric contraction to lower the load. The movement was performed in a transverse plane, and each subject completed 100 cycles of the task. For most motor units, there was an increase in the number of action potentials discharged during the concentric and eccentric contractions and an increase in discharge rate during the isometric contraction as fatigue developed. Moreover, some low-threshold motor units were occasionally derecruited during the eccentric contraction, which meant that the load was lowered by motor units with higher recruitment thresholds. This strategy is similar to that reported previously by Nardone et al. (1989) for motor units in the triceps surae muscle during performance of eccentric contractions (figures 7.36 and 7.37). However, the derecruitment of low-threshold motor units during eccentric contractions does not appear to be a general control strategy (Kossev & Christova, 1998; Laidlaw et al., 2000; Søgaard et al., 1996).

The ability of motor units to sustain an activity also depends on the proportion of the task that involves isometric contractions. For example, slow-twitch motor units can sustain an isometric force longer than fast-twitch motor units (Burke et al., 1973), and slow-twitch muscle (soleus) can sustain a greater force during isovelocity

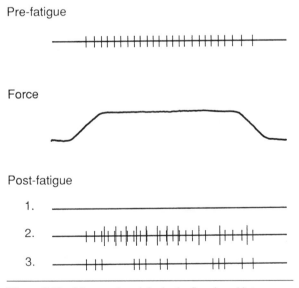

Figure 8.19 Motor unit activity in the first dorsal interosseus muscle during an isometric contraction performed before and after a fatiguing contraction. The force exerted during the task is shown in the middle trace.

Data from Enoka et al., 1989.

shortening contractions than fast-twitch (extensor digitorum longus) muscle (Brooks & Faulkner, 1991). However, fast-twitch muscle is able to sustain a greater power production for 5 min compared with slow-twitch muscle (Brooks & Faulkner, 1991). This difference in power output results from biochemical differences in the optimum velocity of shortening for slow- and fast-twitch muscle. Fast-twitch muscle has a higher optimum velocity of shortening, which combines with a lower sustained force to produce a greater power production. Undoubtedly this difference in the ability to exert force and to produce power has functional significance, because many movements rely on the ability of muscle to produce power rather than to exert a force.

Not only can motor unit activity change during a fatiguing contraction; there is also an acute effect of the fatigue state on motor unit activity during a standardized task (Enoka, Robinson, & Kossev, 1989). For example, the motor units used to achieve a submaximal target force after a fatiguing contraction can be different from those used before the fatiguing contraction, and the discharge rate is more variable (figure 8.19). Furthermore, the changes are usually greater for high-threshold motor units (Duchateau, Carpentier, & Hainaut, 1999). These findings indicate that there is some flexibility in motor unit recruitment based on the activation history of the muscle (Person, 1993).

An example of the adaptability of motor unit behavior is shown in figure 8.20. In this study, subjects sustained an isometric contraction with the elbow flexor muscles at a target force of 15% MVC both before and after the arm was placed in a cast for four weeks (Semmler, Kutzscher, & Enoka, 1999, 2000). Prior to the immobilization, the EMG increased progressively during the fatiguing contraction for all subjects (figure 8.20a). After the immobilization, however, subjects exhibited two distinct EMG patterns. Some subjects (5 of 6 men) used the same pattern as before immobilization. The other subjects (6 of 6 women and 1 of 6 men) used intermittent muscle activation with no progressive increase in EMG amplitude (figure 8.20b). Furthermore, there was no change in the endurance time of those subjects whose EMG pattern remained the same, whereas the endurance time of subjects who used the intermittent EMG increased by an average of 207%. The intermittent EMG pattern did not appear to involve the cumulative recruitment of motor units, as is typical; instead there was an apparent rotation of activity among a selected group of motor units. It is unclear whether or not such effects underlie the enhanced endurance capacity of women (Fulco et al., 1999; Hunter, Flagg, Fleshner, & Enoka, 2000).

Neuromuscular Propagation

Several processes are involved in converting an axonal action potential into a sarcolemmal action potential. Col-lectively, these processes are referred to as neuromuscular propagation. Sustained activity can impair some of the processes entailed in neuromuscular propagation, and this can contribute to the decline in force associated with fatigue. Potential impairments include a failure of the axonal action potential to invade all the branches of the axon (branch-point failure), a failure of excitation-secretion coupling in the presynaptic terminal, a depletion of neurotransmitter, a reduction in the quantal release of neurotransmitter, and a decrease in the sensitivity of the postsynaptic receptors and membrane (Krnjevic & Miledi, 1958; Kugelberg & Lindegren, 1979; Sieck & Prakash, 1995; Spira, Yarom, & Parnas, 1976).

The most common way to test for impairment of neuromuscular propagation in humans is to elicit M waves before, during, and after a fatiguing contraction. Recall that an M wave is measured by applying an electric shock to a nerve to generate action potentials in the axons of alpha motor neurons and determining the EMG response in muscle (figure 6.62). A decline in M-wave amplitude is interpreted as an impairment of one or more of the processes involved in converting the axonal action potential (initiated by the electric shock) into a muscle (sarcolemmal) action potential. Figure 8.21 shows an example of a decline in M wave immediately after a fatiguing contraction, as well as the eventual recovery of the M wave after 10 min of rest. This type of decline in M-wave amplitude tends to occur in long-duration, low-intensity contractions and less frequently in short-duration, high-intensity contractions (Bellemare & Garzaniti, 1988; Bigland-Ritchie et al., 1982; Fuglevand, Zackowski, Huey, & Enoka, 1993; Kranz, Williams, Cassell, Caddy, & Silberstein, 1983; Milner-Brown & Miller, 1986). Modeling studies suggest that impairment of neuromuscular propagation is one of several mechanisms that can contribute to the decline in force during these types of tasks (Fuglevand, Zackowski, Huey, & Enoka, 1993).

Excitation-Contraction Coupling

Under normal conditions, excitation by the nervous system results in the activation of muscle and the associated cycling of cross-bridges. Seven processes (Fitts & Metzger, 1988; Fitts, 1996) are involved in the conversion of the excitation (action potential) into a muscle fiber force (figure 6.7): (1) propagation of the action potential along the sarcolemma; (2) propagation of the action potential down the T tubule; (3) change in the Ca^{2+} conductance of the sarcoplasmic reticulum; (4) movement of Ca^{2+} down its concentration gradient into the sarcoplasm; (5) reuptake of Ca^{2+} by the sarcoplasmic reticulum; (6) binding of Ca^{2+} to troponin; and (7) interaction of myosin and actin and the work done by the cross-bridge.

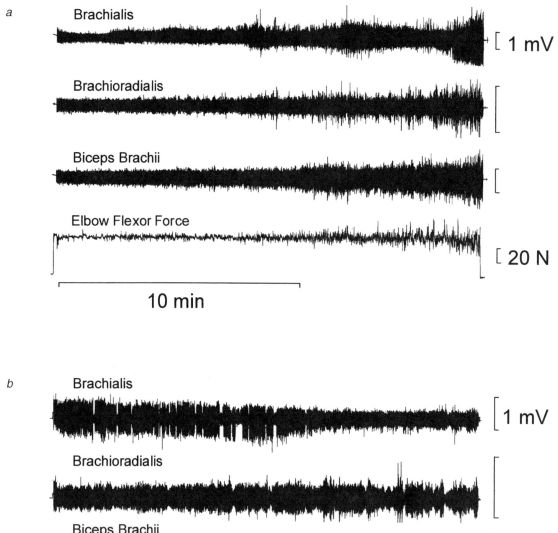

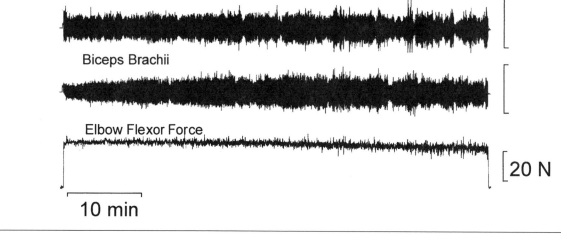

Figure 8.20   EMG activity for the brachialis, brachioradialis, and biceps brachii muscles during a submaximal fatiguing contraction *(a)* before and *(b)* after four weeks of casting.

Data from Semmler, Kutzscher, and Enoka, 1999.

Each of these processes can be influenced by many different factors. For example, opening of the Ca^{2+} release channels in the sarcoplasmic reticulum is facilitated by ATP, inhibited by Mg^{2+}, and probably influenced by P_i and pH. Impairment of excitation-contraction coupling, however, does not appear to contribute to the initial de-

velopment of fatigue (Allen et al., 1995; Edman, 1995). Rather, as fatigue progresses there is a decrease in the availability and efficacy of Ca^{2+} as an activation signal and also a decline in the force exerted by individual cross-bridges. These effects are distinguished as the **failure of activation** and **myofibrillar fatigue** (Edman, 1995).

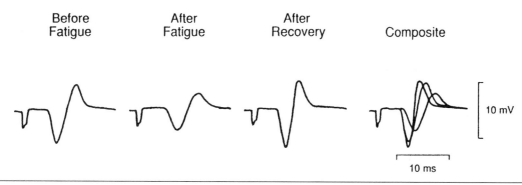

Figure 8.21   M waves elicited in a hand muscle (first dorsal interosseus) by stimulation of the ulnar nerve. M waves were elicited before and after a fatiguing contraction and after 10 min of recovery. The fatiguing contraction involved sustaining an isometric force at 35% of the maximum voluntary contraction force for as long as possible. M-wave amplitude declined immediately after the fatigue task but recovered quickly.

Adapted from Fuglevand, Zackowski, Huey, and Enoka, 1993.

Activation failure generally occurs later than myofibrillar fatigue during high-force contractions. It is caused by a decrease in the sensitivity of the myofibrils to Ca^{2+} and a reduction in the release of Ca^{2+} from the sarcoplasmic reticulum. Although the reduction in the sensitivity of the myofibrils to Ca^{2+} can be caused by the development of acidosis, it is possible to evoke the decrease in sensitivity in the absence of acidosis (Stephenson, Lamb, Stephenson, & Fryer, 1995; Westerblad, Allen, Bruton, Andrade, & Lännergren, 1998). Instead, the reduction in the release of Ca^{2+} from the sarcoplasmic reticulum involves an ATP-dependent component (Westerblad et al., 1998). Apart from the direct inhibition of the Ca^{2+} release channels by low concentrations of ATP, there are at least four ATP-sensitive sites that could contribute to the impairment of Ca^{2+} release: (1) sarcolemmal Na^+-K^+ ATPase pumps, which are required to prevent the gradual depolarization of the membrane; (2) sarcolemmal K^+ channels that open when ATP concentration is low, which may reduce the duration of action potentials; (3) sarcoplasmic reticulum Ca^{2+} ATPase, which is responsible for returning Ca^{2+} to the sarcoplasmic reticulum; and (4) processes that connect the T-tubule activation to the terminal cisternae of the sarcoplasmic reticulum. Alternatively, the extracellular accumulation of K^+ due to action potential activity appears capable of impeding the inward propagation of action potentials in some fatiguing contractions (Edman, 1996; Sejersted & Sjøgaard, 2000; Sjøgaard, 1996).

Myofibrillar fatigue is caused by the impairment of cross-bridge function that is evident as a decrease in both the isometric force and the shortening velocity (Edman, 1995). Experiments on single muscle fibers have indicated that the decline in cross-bridge force during fatigue at physiological temperatures is not due to acidification (Westerblad et al., 1998). By exclusion, myofibrillar fatigue is attributed to the accumulation of P_i ions (Edman, 1995; Westerblad et al., 1998). Similarly, the decrease in

shortening velocity appears to involve other factors besides H^+, perhaps the accumulation of adenosine diphosphate (ADP).

One way to demonstrate a role for the impairment of excitation-contraction coupling in the fatigue experienced by humans is to show that the decline in force cannot be ascribed to neural or metabolic factors. This has been done (Bigland-Ritchie, Cafarelli, & Vøllestad, 1986) for a task in which subjects performed a series of 6-s contractions with the quadriceps femoris muscle at a force level that was 30% of maximum. There was a 4-s rest between each 6-s contraction. The subjects performed this sequence for 30 min. The force exerted during an MVC declined in parallel to the electrically elicited force (figure 8.13a), which suggests that the subjects voluntarily exerted as much force as the muscle was capable of producing. There were no significant changes in muscle lactate, ATP, or phosphocreatine; and the depletion of glycogen was minimal and was confined to the type I and IIa muscle fibers. Consequently, the decline in MVC force could not be explained by an inadequate neural drive (the M waves were not reduced), acidosis, or lack of metabolic substrates. Additionally, the twitch response decreased more than the tetanus or MVC force; this is regarded as evidence of an impairment of excitation-contraction coupling. For these reasons, the decline in force is attributed to impairment of one or more processes associated with excitation-contraction coupling (Bigland-Ritchie, Cafarelli, & Vøllestad, 1986; Saugen, Vøllestad, Gibson, Martin, & Edwards, 1997).

Another experimental approach that has been used to demonstrate a role for the impairment of excitation-contraction coupling in muscle fatigue is to monitor the recovery from fatigue (figure 8.22). The experimenters compare the recovery of the force evoked with high (80 Hz) and low (20 and 1 Hz) rates of stimulation. Electric shocks delivered at 80 Hz provide a measure of the maximum force that can be evoked from the muscle

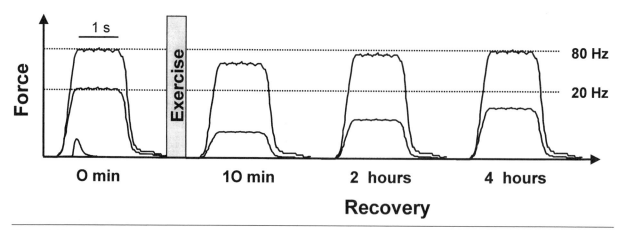

Figure 8.22　Recovery of muscle force after a fatiguing contraction. The maximum force capacity of muscle (adductor pollicis and quadriceps femoris) recovered much more rapidly than the force associated with submaximal contractions.

Data from Edwards, Hill, Jones, and Merton, 1977.

independent of the central nervous system. In contrast, the force evoked with lower rates of stimulation is influenced by the efficacy of excitation-contraction coupling; the role of excitation-contraction coupling is greatest at the lowest rates of stimulation. Figure 8.22 shows the time course of recovery for forces evoked in a hand muscle after the muscle was fatigued with a series of intermittent trains of stimuli at 20 Hz. A similar effect was observed in quadriceps femoris after performance of a series of maximal contractions.

The prolonged recovery of the force evoked by low frequencies of stimulation (1 and 20 Hz in figure 8.22) has been termed **low-frequency fatigue** (Edwards, Hill, Jones, & Merton, 1977; Fuglevand, Zackowski, Huey, & Enoka, 1993; Miller et al., 1987). Because the force depression persists in the absence of electrical and metabolic disturbances, it is attributed to an impairment of excitation-contraction coupling. Low-frequency fatigue can be caused by many different types of exercises (Jones, 1996) and likely involves one of three effects: (1) an increase in the intracellular concentration of Ca^{2+}, which reduces the release of Ca^{2+} from the sarcoplasmic reticulum and hence impairs excitation-contraction coupling (Chin & Allen, 1996; Favero, 1999); (2) a failure of coupling between T-tubule depolarization and the release of Ca^{2+} from the sarcoplasmic reticulum (Jones, 1996; Lännergren, Westerblad, & Bruton, 1996); and (3) precipitation of Ca^{2+} with P_i inside the sarcoplasmic reticulum (Fryer, Owen, Lamb, & Stephenson, 1995; Kabbara & Allen, 1999). The frequency-dependent depression of force suggests the use of caution regarding selection of the measurement used to quantify fatigue.

Metabolic Substrates

The development of muscle fatigue is clearly associated with changes that take place in the muscle. As summa-

rized by McComas (1996), fatigue produces many changes in active muscle fibers (table 8.1). Despite numerous experiments, however, it has not been possible to identify any single factor, including the acidification of muscle, that is principally responsible for the decline in force (Fitts, 1996).

Two critical factors in a muscle contraction are excitation of the muscle by the nervous system and the supply of metabolic energy to the cross-bridges. Although the ability to sustain a muscle contraction does not always depend on the availability of metabolic energy, for some tasks the depletion of metabolic substrate is associated with a decline in performance (Sahlin, Tonkonogi, & Söderlund, 1998). For example, when subjects exercised on a cycle ergometer at a rate of 70% to 80% of maximal aerobic power, exhaustion and the inability to sustain the forces necessary for the task coincided with the depletion of glycogen from the muscle fibers of vastus lateralis (Hermansen, Hultman, & Saltin, 1967). Similarly, when exercising subjects were fed glucose or had it infused intravenously, they were able to exercise longer (Coggan & Coyle, 1987; Coyle, Coggan, Hemmert, & Ivy, 1986). Consequently, the availability of carbohydrates determines how long motivated subjects can ride a cycle ergometer at 65% to 85% of maximal aerobic power (Broberg & Sahlin, 1989; Costill & Hargreaves, 1992; Hultman, Bergström, Spriet, & Söderlund, 1990; Sahlin et al., 1998). However, exhaustion from performing intermittent submaximal contractions (30% MVC) is not associated with either substrate depletion or the accumulation of P_i and H^+ (Vøllestad, 1995).

The products of energy metabolism are also known to influence muscle force. One popular candidate is H^+ concentration. Although H^+ can inhibit glycolysis, this interaction does not appear to be a major mechanism that causes the decline in force at physiological temperatures.

Table 8.1   Changes in Muscle Fibers During Fatigue

Mechanical	Electrical	Biochemical	
		Increased	Decreased
Decline in force	Early hyperpolarization	$[Na^+]$	$[K^+]$
Slowed force development	Late depolarization	P_i	PCr
Slowed relaxation	Slowed conduction	$[H^+]$	ATP hydrolysis
Decreased power production	Reduced EMG	Lactate	Ca^{2+} flux
		H_2PO_4	
		ADP	
		Basal Ca^{2+}	Ca^{2+} sensitivity
		H_2O	

PCr = phosphocreatine; H_2PO_4 = diprotonated phosphate; $[Na^+]$ = sodium concentration.

For example, reducing intracellular pH (7.0-6.6) in single, intact muscle fibers by increasing the CO_2 in the extracellular medium caused only a moderate decline in the number of attached cross-bridges, a decrease in the force exerted by each cross-bridge, and a reduction in the speed of cross-bridge cycling during shortening contractions (Edman & Lou, 1990; Lännergren & Westerblad, 1989; Westerblad et al., 1998). Similarly, high-intensity leg exercises that elevated the concentration of blood lactate did not reduce muscle glycogenolysis or glycolysis (Bangsbo, Madsen, Kiens, & Richter, 1996). It is probable that other products of ATP hydrolysis (e.g., Mg-ADP, P_i) contribute to the decline in force. An increase in the concentration of P_i, for example, can reduce the maximum isometric force but does not affect the maximum speed of shortening. Conversely, an increase in the concentration of Mg-ADP can cause a small increase in the maximum isometric force and a modest decline in the maximum speed of shortening (Chase & Kushmerick, 1988; Cooke, Franks, Luciani, & Pate, 1988). The task conditions under which these products might be important in muscle fatigue are not yet known.

Nonetheless, the metabolic consequences of physical activity do appear to influence performance and to differ across contraction types. Jones and colleagues compared muscle performance in isometric and anisometric contractions evoked in humans by electrical stimulation. In one study, the quadriceps femoris muscle was activated by stimuli applied to the femoral nerve to perform first an isometric contraction and then a shortening contraction (Jones, 1993). Although the contractions were performed one after the other, the decline in force was much greater for the shortening contraction (figure 8.23). In another study, a hand muscle was stimulated electrically, and the phosphorus metabolites were measured

by magnetic resonance spectroscopy (Cady et al., 1989) and compared with the change in force and power (Jones, 1993). Blood flow to the arm was occluded during the sequence of evoked contractions. As with the study on quadriceps femoris, the isometric force evoked in the hand muscle declined less than the peak power produced during the shortening contraction (figure 8.24). Consistent with this difference, more phosphocreatine was broken down and more lactate was accumulated during the shortening contraction (table 8.2). The metabolic cost was estimated at 9.3 mM ATP/s for the shortening contraction compared with 4.7 mM ATP/s for the isometric contraction. This difference in energy cost probably explains much of the difference in the fatigability of the two types of contractions.

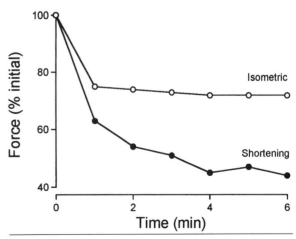

Figure 8.23   The force evoked by electrical stimulation of the quadriceps femoris muscle, first held isometric and then allowed to shorten against an isokinetic dynamometer (1.57 rad/s).
Data from Jones, 1993.

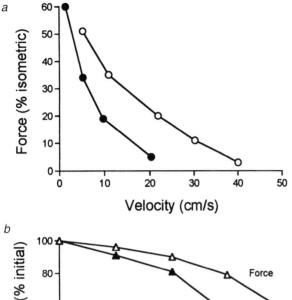

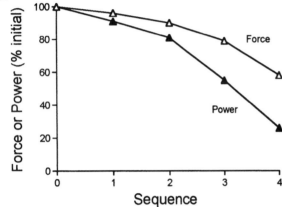

Figure 8.24 (a) Shift in the force-velocity relation and (b) reductions in the isometric force and peak power during a fatigue protocol performed with the adductor pollicis muscle. Each sequence of fatiguing contractions involved 1-s tetani at 50 Hz and comprised five isometric contractions followed by four shortening contractions against different loads. The sequence was repeated four times.

Data from Jones, 1993.

Blood Flow

Among the mechanisms that could contribute to fatigue, the impairment of blood flow to active muscle was one of the first to be identified. An increase in muscle blood flow with motor activity is necessary for the supply of substrate, the removal of metabolites, and the dissipation of heat. When a muscle is active, however, there is an increase in intramuscular pressure that compresses blood vessels and occludes blood flow when it exceeds systolic pressure. For example, when the knee extensor muscles sustain an isometric contraction for as long as possible at a submaximal force (5%-50% of the MVC), blood flow decreases with an increase in the level of the sustained force (Sjøgaard et al., 1988). It is not possible, however, to identify a specific force level at which blood flow in a muscle is occluded, because intramuscular pressure can vary markedly within a group of synergist muscles and even within a single muscle for a given contraction intensity. Nonetheless, blood flow is probably not significantly impaired for tasks that involve less than 15% of the MVC force (Gaffney, Sjøgaard, & Saltin, 1990; Sjøgaard et al., 1988). Conversely, when blood pressure is increased above the intramuscular pressure, there is a significant increase in endurance time for contractions in which the force is less than 60% of maximum (Fitzpatrick, Taylor, & McCloskey, 1996; Petrofsky & Hendershot, 1984).

In addition to this obvious effect of intramuscular pressure on muscle blood flow, an elevated blood flow (hyperperfusion) can decrease fatigue by a mechanism that is independent of oxygen or substrate delivery. A reduction in blood flow (ischemia) exerts an effect on mechanical performance that is independent of a reduction in the oxygen content of the blood (hypoxemia). The increase in blood flow associated with hyperperfusion

Table 8.2 Metabolite Contents of Adductor Pollicis at Rest and After Isometric and Shortening Contractions

	Rest	Isometric	Shortening
Inorganic phosphate	8.2 ± 0.3	19.9 ± 1.0	25.1 ± 1.0
Phosphocreatine	30.0 ± 0.6	18.3 ± 0.4	11.6 ± 0.9
ATP	8.2 ± 1.1	7.9 ± 0.4	7.5 ± 0.4
pH	7.18 ± 0.04	7.06 ± 0.01	6.78 ± 0.04
Δ lactate	—	± 7.5	± 18.3

Note. Data from Cady et al., 1989.

may improve the removal of metabolites and thereby diminish the inhibitory effect of metabolite accumulation (Barclay, 1986; Stainsby, Brechue, O'Drobinak, & Barclay, 1990). These findings indicate that the force capacity of muscle is sensitive to changes in arterial blood pressure (Wright, McCloskey, & Fitzpatrick, 2000).

Sensory Adaptations

Much less is known about the changes that occur in sensory processes than about those that occur in the motor system during fatiguing contractions. There have been some studies, albeit with conflicting observations, on the effects of fatigue on the sensitivity of large-diameter proprioceptive afferents. In addition, some attention has been directed to the sensory-based phenomena referred to as muscle wisdom and the sense of effort.

Afferent Feedback and Reflexes

Experiments on anesthetized animals have generally shown that fatigue enhances the sensitivity of muscle spindle afferents (Groups Ia and II) in response to single motor unit contractions (Christakos & Windhorst, 1986; Nelson & Hutton, 1985; Zytnicki, Lafleur, Horcholle-Bossavit, Lamy, & Jami, 1990). However, results from conscious humans indicate that fatigue is associated with a decline in fusimotor drive to muscle spindles (Bongiovanni & Hagbarth, 1990), a reduction in spindle discharge during sustained isometric contractions (Macefield, Hagbarth, Gorman, Gandevia, & Burke, 1991), and a decrease in the amplitude of the H reflex (Duchateau & Hainaut, 1993). The effects of fatigue on the Group Ib afferent of the tendon organ are also uncertain. In experimental animals, the sensitivity of tendon organs to motor unit contractions does not change during fatiguing contractions; tendon organ discharge varies linearly with motor unit force (Gregory, 1990). In contrast, the response of tendon organs to whole-muscle stretch has been reported to decline with fatigue (Hutton & Nelson, 1986), and there is a reduction in the inhibitory effect of Group Ib feedback on motor neurons (Zytnicki et al., 1990).

Despite the uncertain effects of fatigue on the proprioceptive afferents, some evidence suggests that fatigue enhances the reflex EMG and motor neuron responses to brief perturbations (Darling & Hayes, 1983; Windhorst et al., 1986). For example, in one experiment the torque and EMG response of the elbow flexor muscles to a stretch were examined when subjects exerted the same torque before and after a fatiguing contraction (Kirsch & Rymer, 1987). The joint was rapidly displaced by 0.5 rad before and after the fatigue task, which consisted of 20 repetitions of a 25-s isometric contraction to a force of 50% of maximum. Although the fatiguing contraction substantially reduced the force that the elbow flexor muscles could exert, the torque response to the muscle stretch was similar to that measured before the fatigue task. The ability of the subjects to respond with a comparable torque was due to the increase in the EMG response after the exercise. Because the stretch was applied 10 min after the end of the fatiguing contraction, the increase in EMG was interpreted as an increase in the stretch-elicited neural drive after the fatiguing contraction (see also Kirsch & Rymer, 1992).

In addition to modulating the activity transmitted by large-diameter afferents, fatiguing contractions activate the sensory receptors served by Group III and Group IV afferents (Garland & Kaufman, 1995). The receptors innervated by Group III afferents are sensitive to changes in both the mechanical state and the metabolic environment of the muscle, whereas the Group IV afferents are most sensitive to the chemical milieu in the muscle. Because the receptors innervated by these afferents are so numerous, small variations in activity are likely to have a large effect in the central nervous system. However, the timing of an effect from these afferents is unclear because discharge rate appears to decline for 30 s before it increases (Kaufman, Rybicki, Waldrop, & Ordway, 1983). Although not much is known about the central action of these afferents, feedback transmitted by small-diameter afferents during fatiguing contractions probably depresses the excitability of motor neurons (Duchateau & Hainaut, 1993).

Muscle Wisdom

The term muscle wisdom is used to describe an effect that has been observed in three types of experiments: stimulus rate, discharge rate, and relaxation rate. First, a muscle is better able to sustain a force elicited by electrical stimulation if the stimulus rate declines over time rather than remaining constant (figure 6.52) (Binder-Macleod & Guerin, 1990; Binder-Macleod & Russ, 1999; Marsden, Meadows, & Merton, 1983). Second, the discharge rate of motor neuron populations can decline during a fatiguing contraction (Bigland-Ritchie, Johansson, Lippold, Smith, & Woods, 1983; Dietz, 1978; Garland et al., 1994). Third, fatigue is associated with a progressive decrease in the rate of relaxation in force (Bigland-Ritchie, Johansson, Lippold, & Woods, 1983; Gordon, Enoka, Karst, & Stuart, 1990; Hultman & Sjöholm, 1983; Lännergren & Westerblad, 1991). Because the relaxation rate of the twitch decreases, the duration of the twitch response increases, and therefore the same degree of fusion in the force during a tetanus can be achieved with a lower rate of activation (figure 8.25). The change in relaxation rate occurs because of biochemical changes associated with excitation-contraction coupling. *Muscle wisdom, therefore, describes the ability of muscle to*

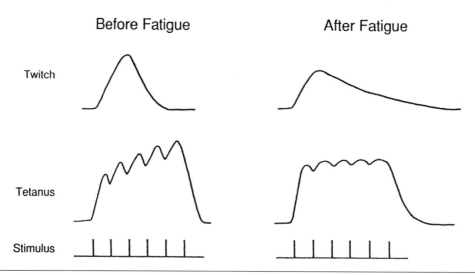

Figure 8.25   A fatiguing contraction is usually associated with an increase in the relaxation time of a twitch and an increase in the degree of fusion of an unfused tetanus.

reduce the discharge of its motor neurons to match the change in the reduction in its relaxation rate. This means that the activation is more economical.

There are at least three mechanisms that could decrease discharge rate during a fatiguing contraction (Enoka & Stuart, 1992). One is afferent feedback from peripheral receptors that inhibits the discharge of interneurons and motor neurons (Bigland-Ritchie, Dawson, Johansson, & Lippold, 1986; Seyffarth, 1940). This feedback might involve reflex inhibition by Group III and Group IV afferents and disfacilitation of Group Ia afferents (i.e., a reduction in fusimotor-controlled feedback from muscle spindles). A second mechanism is an adaptation in the excitability of motor neurons so that the same synaptic input elicits fewer action potentials (Kernell & Monster, 1982a, 1982b). Adaptation occurs as a consequence of an intrinsic biophysical property of the motor neuron membrane. A third mechanism is a decrease in the central drive to motor neurons. Recordings from cells in area 4 of the motor cortex of monkeys as they performed repetitive isometric torques showed that the output was modulated in concert with the EMG (Belhaj-Saif, Fourment, & Maton, 1996). This suggests that the discharge of motor neurons may be modulated by descending signals during fatiguing contractions. It is probable that all three mechanisms (sensory feedback, spinal neuron adaptations, descending modulation) can contribute to a fatigue-related decline in motor neuron discharge rate but that the relative contributions depend on the details of the task, especially duration (Enoka & Stuart, 1992).

Sense of Effort

The process of motor programming that is performed by the supraspinal centers results in a descending motor command known as the central command (chapter 7). In the performance of a movement, this signal is sent to lower neural centers (brainstem and spinal cord) and also back to the supraspinal centers as a corollary discharge to aid in the interpretation of incoming sensory information. The corollary discharge (figure 7.17) that projects to the primary somatosensory cortex provides the basis for the **sense of effort** (Jones, 1995). The sense of effort is a sensation that indicates the effort required to generate a specific muscle force. This sensation is independent of the mechanisms that impair the ability of muscle to exert a force. For example, imagine standing stationary in an upright position with a heavy load in one hand. After a few minutes, although you will still be able to support the load, you will notice that the task requires an increase in the effort necessary to do so. To continue supporting the load it is necessary to increase the descending command, which will lead to a greater corollary discharge and the perception of an increase in the effort associated with the task. For sustained submaximal contractions performed by a motivated subject, the effort will always increase before the force begins to decline.

The typical way to study effort during a fatiguing contraction is to have a subject perform a contralateral matching experiment. In this protocol, the subject exerts a sustained force with one limb (the test limb) and periodically indicates the effort associated with the task by performing a matching contraction with the other limb. The matching limb typically exerts a force until the sensations, or effort, are equal for the two limbs. The results of such an experiment are shown in figure 8.26. The filled circles indicate the matching force when the load was supported intermittently by the test arm. The line with open circles represents the estimated load by the matching arm when the test arm was supporting the load continuously for 10 min. The load was estimated once every 15 to 45 s by the

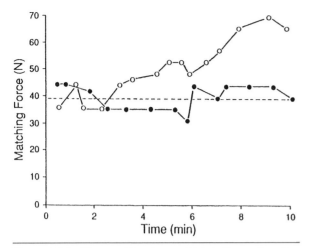

Figure 8.26   The matching force, which indicates the effort associated with the task, did not change when the load was supported intermittently (filled circles) but increased when the load was supported continuously (open circles).

Adapted from McCloskey, Ebeling, and Goodwin, 1974.

matching arm. The progressive increase in the matching force (open circles) when the test arm continuously supported a constant load indicates that the subject had to increase the effort during the fatiguing contraction.

Despite the prevalence of muscle fatigue as a prominent symptom in a wide variety of diseases of the central nervous system, minimal attention has been paid to the role of central nervous system pathology in fatigue (Jones & Killian, 2000). Some of this inattention is attributable to the difficulty associated with designing and interpreting appropriate psychophysical experiments. For example, which afferent signals are used to assess the effort associated with performance? Most evidence suggests that the sense of effort during a fatiguing contraction seems to rely predominantly on the corollary discharge (Cafarelli, 1988; Jones & Hunter, 1983), with feedback from peripheral receptors contributing to other sensations (e.g., sense of heaviness or tension). Studies on patients with effort syndromes and chronic fatigue syndrome suggest that the sense of effort may entail at least two components: one associated with the impairment of performance and another above the level of the motor cortex, wherein the perceived effort does not relate directly to motor performance (Lloyd, Gandevia, & Hales, 1991). These studies suggest the need for advanced psychophysical testing and therapy for such patients.

Example 8.2

Identifying the Cause of Fatigue in Patients

To identify the physiological mechanisms that underlie the fatigue experienced by patients presenting with

various conditions, clinical investigators often perform a battery of tests and compare the outcomes with those for healthy individuals. One example is multiple sclerosis, in which fatigue is a common and disabling symptom. When patients with multiple sclerosis performed a 45-s maximal contraction with a hand muscle, the force declined by 45% in patients but only by 20% in control subjects (Sheean, Murray, Rothwell, Miller, & Thompson, 1997). The strength of the hand muscle prior to the fatiguing contraction was similar for the two groups of subjects, and there was no difference in the effect of fatigue on contractile function. Furthermore, based on potentials evoked by transcranial magnetic stimulation, there was no impairment of the primary motor pathways or excitability of the motor cortex in the patients. These results led Sheean et al. (1997) to conclude that the fatigue experienced by the patients during this test was due to a decline in the activation of the primary motor cortex. A similar conclusion was reached in a study on patients with chronic fatigue syndrome (Lloyd et al., 1991). Interestingly, for the patients with multiple sclerosis there was no association between the magnitude of the force decline during the fatiguing contraction and their clinical symptoms. Furthermore, another study showed no association between cerebral abnormalities, as determined by magnetic resonance imaging, and neurological disability in patients with multiple sclerosis (van der Werf et al., 1998). These studies indicate the challenge faced by clinicians who attempt to associate signs and symptoms with laboratory measures of fatigue.

Muscle Potentiation

In contrast to the performance-reducing effects of fatigue, several acute mechanisms can enhance the output of the neuromuscular system (Hutton, 1984; McComas, 1996). After a brief period of activity, these mechanisms can increase both the electrical and mechanical output above resting values. Examples of these capabilities include the potentiation of monosynaptic responses, miniature endplate potentials, M waves, twitch force, and the discharge of muscle spindle receptors.

Monosynaptic Responses

It seems reasonable to assume that most processes in the motor system can be augmented by brief periods of activity. This is certainly true at the level of input-output relations for the spinal cord. Lloyd (1949) delivered single electric shocks to the muscle nerve of an experimental animal and measured the output in the ventral root. The experimental preparation is schematized in figure 8.27*a*. Because the ventral root was cut, the electric shock (stimulus) generated action potentials that were transmitted along the afferent axons and into the spinal cord. The synaptic input by the afferent axons activated motor neurons, and the monosynaptic response was measured in efferent axons (figure 8.27*a*). The input-output relation involved populations of afferent and efferent axons. The monosynaptic responses were measured before and after tetanic stimulation of the nerve (12-s duration at 555 Hz), shown at time zero in figure 8.27*b*. The tetanic stimulation increased the amplitude of the monosynaptic response by seven times, compared with the control value (before the tetanus). The potentiation of the monosynaptic response decayed over a 3-min interval (figure 8.27*b*). A similar effect has been reported for potentiation of the H- and tendon-tap reflexes after a brief period of high-frequency electrical stimulation (Hagbarth, 1962).

When Lloyd (1949) activated different afferent pathways after the tetanic stimulation, the potentiation was limited to the afferent pathway that received the tetanic stimulation. Therefore, the mechanism underlying the potentiation was presynaptic; that is, it was located before the synaptic contact with the motor neurons. Given the type of stimuli that elicit potentiation of the monosynaptic response, the mechanism probably involves Group Ia afferents (Hutton, 1984). The effects could include an increase in the quantity of neurotransmitter released, an increase in the efficacy of the neurotransmitter, or a reduction in axonal branch-point failure along the Group Ia afferents (Kuno, 1964; Lüscher, Ruenzel, & Henneman, 1979).

Miniature End-Plate Potentials

At the neuromuscular junction, the spontaneous release of neurotransmitter (acetylcholine) elicits miniature end-plate potentials in the postsynaptic membrane (see chapter 6). The miniature end-plate potentials are not constant events; the amplitude is greater for fast-twitch compared with slow-twitch muscle fibers, and the frequency can decline as a function of age (Alshuaib & Fahim, 1991; Lømo & Waerhaug, 1985). Similarly, a brief period of high-frequency stimulation can increase the amplitude and frequency of the spontaneously released miniature end-plate potentials (Pawson & Grinnell, 1990; Vrbová & Wareham, 1976). The increase in frequency lasts for a few minutes, whereas the increase in amplitude has been reported to last for several hours. Furthermore, the effect is greater at neuromuscular junctions where more neurotransmitter is released per unit length of the junction.

The mechanisms seem to involve activity-dependent increases in the sensitivity of the postsynaptic membrane and in the influx of Ca^{2+} into the presynaptic terminal. The increase in postsynaptic membrane sensitivity means that a quantum of neurotransmitter will elicit a greater response (amplitude of the synaptic potential) in the postsynaptic membrane. In addition, because Ca^{2+} is necessary for the fusion of vesicles to the presynaptic membrane and the subsequent release of neurotransmitter, a

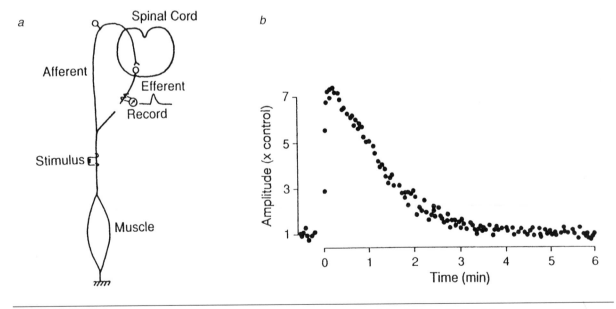

Figure 8.27 Potentiation of monosynaptic responses: *(a)* the experimental model and *(b)* amplitude of the monosynaptic response. Adapted from Lloyd, 1949.

greater influx of Ca^{2+} will lead to an enhanced frequency of spontaneous release of neurotransmitter.

M-Wave Amplitude

The processes involved in converting an axonal action potential into a sarcolemmal action potential are collectively referred to as neuromuscular propagation. One way to test the stability of neuromuscular propagation is to elicit M waves (figure 6.62). This test involves stimulating the muscle nerve and measuring the subsequent compound muscle action potential. Although M-wave amplitude can be reduced by presynaptic factors (e.g., branch-point failure, neurotransmitter depletion), only postsynaptic factors can increase M-wave amplitude. These factors include a reduction in the temporal dispersion of the muscle fiber action potentials and an increase in the amplitude of individual muscle fiber action potentials.

When a human subject performs a voluntary contraction or when a muscle is activated with electrical stimulation, there is often an initial transient increase in M-wave amplitude (figure 8.28). For example, when subjects performed 20 maximal contractions (3-s duration for each contraction, 1.5 s between contractions) with the thenar muscles, M-wave amplitude increased immediately after the first contraction and then reached a plateau at an average increase of about 24% (Hicks, Fenton, Garner, & McComas, 1989). Studies on single muscle fibers that were subjected to repetitive stimulation suggest that the increase in M-wave amplitude was at least partially due to an activity-dependent increase in the amplitude of muscle fiber action potentials (Hicks & McComas, 1989). It seems that activation increases the activity of the Na^+-K^+ pump, which lowers (hyperpolarizes) the resting membrane potential and produces a greater change in voltage (amplitude) across the membrane during an action potential. Therefore, at least some of the initial increase in M-wave amplitude at the onset of activity is due to an increase in the activity of the Na^+-K^+ pumps, and this seems to cause a modest increase in force (Enoka et al., 1992).

Post-Tetanic Potentiation

Perhaps the best known of the potentiation responses is the effect of prior activity on twitch force. The magnitude of the twitch force is extremely variable and depends on the activation history of the muscle. A twitch elicited in a resting muscle does not represent the maximal twitch. Rather, twitch force is maximal following a brief tetanus; this effect is known as **post-tetanic potentiation** of twitch force (Belanger, McComas, & Elder, 1983; Brown & von Euler, 1938; Schiff, 1858). The post-tetanic potentiation of twitch force can be substantial and can be elicited by either voluntary contractions or elec-

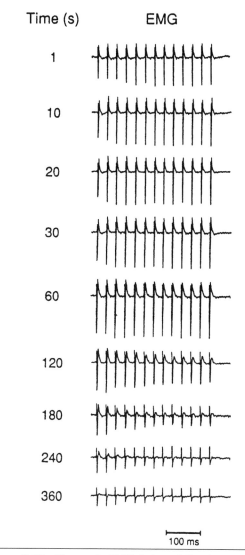

Figure 8.28   Changes in EMG during a 360-s fatiguing contraction involving electrical stimulation of a cat hindlimb muscle. The stimulus regimen consisted of 330-ms trains of 13 stimuli given once each second. The EMG represents the summed muscle action potentials (M waves) that were elicited by the electric shocks. The EMG amplitude increased during the first 60 s of the test and then declined.

Data from Enoka, Trayanova, Laouris, Bevan, Reinking, and Stuart, 1992.

trical stimulation. For example, when the ankle dorsiflexor muscles of human volunteers were intermittently stimulated with electric shocks, the potentiation of twitch force ranged from 29% to 150% after 20 to 40 s of stimulation (Garner, Hicks, & McComas, 1989) and by 5% to 140% after a 7-s tetanus at 100 Hz (O'Leary, Hope, & Sale, 1997). Furthermore, twitch force can be potentiated by both maximal and submaximal voluntary contractions (Vandervoort, Quinlan, & McComas, 1983). A special case of potentiation achieved with submaximal activation involves the progressive increase in twitch force when a series of twitches are elicited in close succession; this is known as the **staircase effect,** or **treppe** (Bowditch, 1871; Krarup, 1981).

At least two processes are involved in post-tetanic twitch potentiation (Grange & Houston, 1991; Vandervoort et al., 1983). An early potentiation occurs after brief contractions and decays relatively quickly. After a delay of about 60 s, a late potentiating process emerges, which reaches a peak at about 200 s and then decays to control levels after about 8 to 12 min of recovery. The mechanisms underlying these potentiation processes probably involve an alteration in calcium kinetics (Duchateau & Hainaut, 1986; O'Leary et al., 1997), the phosphorylation of myosin light chains (Grange, Vandenboom, Xeni, & Houston, 1998; Sweeney, Bowman, & Stull, 1993; Sweeney & Stull, 1990), and the force-velocity characteristics of the cross-bridges (Edman, Månsson, & Caputo, 1997; MacIntosh & Willis, 2000).

Potentiation of the submaximal force occurs in all three types of motor units (types S, FR, and FF). When motor units were activated with a stimulus that elicited a submaximal tetanic force, the potentiation (increase in peak force) was greater for the fast-twitch motor units (50-60% of control in types FR and FF) than for the slow-twitch motor units (20% of control in type S). However, the incidence of potentiation among the motor units was greater for the fatigue-resistant motor units (60%-75% for types S and FR) compared with the fatigable motor units (40% for type FF). Because the occurrence of potentiation was distributed across all three types of motor units, the mechanisms underlying potentiation differ from those that define motor unit type (Gordon, Enoka, & Stuart, 1990).

The study of post-tetanic twitch potentiation has emphasized that the processes of potentiation and fatigue occur concurrently, beginning from the onset of activation. For example, when the extensor digitorum muscle of rats was stimulated with a protocol that reduced the submaximal tetanic force to an average peak force of 36% of the control value, 50% of the muscles exhibited post-tetanic twitch potentiation (Rankin, Enoka, Volz, & Stuart, 1988). This effect was not observed for soleus. The coexistence of potentiation and fatigue has also been observed in the human quadriceps femoris muscle after a 60-s MVC (Grange & Houston, 1991).

A scheme for the interaction of these two processes and the net effect on twitch force during a specific protocol is shown in figure 8.29. In the experiment from which the scheme was devised, the ankle dorsiflexor muscles of human volunteers were electrically stimulated to elicit a 3-s submaximal tetanus once every 5 s for a duration of 180 s. Between the tetani, a twitch was elicited by a single electrical shock. For this particular protocol, twitch force increased and then decreased during the stimulation period and then subsequently increased and decreased during the recovery period. Garner et al. (1989) proposed that the time course of the change in twitch force was due to the interaction of the processes that mediate potentiation and fatigue.

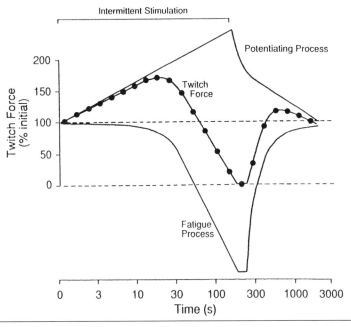

Figure 8.29 Coexistence of potentiation and fatigue and the net effect on the twitch force. When a muscle is stimulated electrically, the contraction elicits processes that both diminish (fatigue) and enhance (potentiate) the muscle force. The result is a nonlinear change in the amplitude of the twitch force.

Adapted from Garner, Hicks, and McComas, 1989.

The effect of preceding activity on tetanic force is less well known. When single muscle fibers were stimulated with 10 tetani separated by 4-s intervals, tetanic force first declined and then was augmented by about 10% after 5 min (Bruton et al., 1996). The enhancement of tetanic force lasted for about 15 min and was associated with a reduction in P_i but not a reduction in intracellular calcium concentration, a change in temperature, or a decrease in intracellular pH. Such an effect may contribute to the enhancing effects of a warm-up.

Postcontraction Sensory Discharge

In addition to the effects on motor processes, a brief period of intense activity can also influence sensory processes. One example of this effect is the increased neural activity that has been recorded in the dorsal roots of experimental animals after a contraction; this phenomenon has been termed the **postcontraction sensory discharge** (Hutton, Smith, & Eldred, 1973). The increase in the dorsal root activity is primarily due to an increase in muscle spindle discharge, mainly from the Group Ia afferents. Moreover, the postcontraction sensory discharge is abolished if the muscle is stretched immediately after the contraction. The mechanism responsible for this phenomenon is the development of stable cross-bridges in the intrafusal fibers. These cross-bridges develop during the muscle contraction and persist after the extrafusal fibers relax so that the muscle spindle is in a state of increased tension and the resting discharge is higher than before the contraction (Gregory, Morgan, & Proske, 1986; Hutton et al., 1973). Consequently, when the muscle is stretched, these cross-bridge bonds are broken and the postcontraction sensory discharge is abolished.

Because postcontraction sensory discharge increases the excitatory input to the motor neuron pool, it influences subsequent activity for up to 15 min, with a peak effect at 5 to 20 s after the contraction. For example, it enables the system to respond more rapidly and forcefully to subsequent perturbations of muscle length, influences kinesthetic sensations, and opposes the relaxation of muscle that may be desired for stretching maneuvers. The strength of postcontraction sensory discharge can be sufficient to increase the resting discharge of motor neurons (Suzuki & Hutton, 1976).

Example 8.3
Involuntary Arm Movements

The sensory inflow after a brief but intense voluntary contraction produces a phenomenon known as the **Kohnstamm effect** (Kohnstamm, 1915). We can demonstrate this effect by performing an MVC and then observing the postcontraction effects. For example,

stand in a door jamb with your arms extended and slightly abducted so that the back of the hands can push against the door frame. After a 15-s MVC, step forward and relax your arms. For most individuals, the arms will rise slightly due to postcontraction activation of the motor neurons innervating proximal arm muscles (Kozhina, Person, Popov, Smetanin, & Shlikov, 1996). The magnitude and direction of the Kohnstamm effect depend on the intensity and duration of the preceding voluntary activity (Sapirstein, Herman, & Wallace, 1937), and the effect is more readily expressed in proximal muscles.

Arousal

Arousal is described as an internal state of alertness. It is a component of several emotional responses, including fear and anxiety, and is mediated by the neuroendocrine system. Its physiological manifestations commonly include increases in blood pressure and heart rate; sweating; dryness of the mouth; hyperventilation; and musculoskeletal disturbances such as restlessness, tremor, and feelings of weakness (Bonnet, Bradley, Lang, & Requin, 1995; Hoehn-Saric, Hazlett, Pourmotabbed, & McLeod, 1997; Spielberger & Rickman, 1990). The arousal response is a product of several structures in the central nervous system, including the limbic system.

The level of arousal exhibited by an individual varies along a continuum from deep sleep to the fight-or-flight response. It can have a substantial effect on an individual's movements. For example, some studies have demonstrated that a moderate amount of arousal maximizes performance in motor learning tasks, such as throwing and shooting (Schmidt & Lee, 1999). This effect has been termed the **inverted-U hypothesis** (Raglin, 1992) and argues in favor of moderate levels of arousal when performance is critical. Furthermore, there are occasional reports in the news media of superhuman feats of strength that are attributed to heightened levels of arousal. Despite these observations, few studies have examined the associations between the physiological correlates of arousal and the neuromuscular details of performance.

Assessment of Arousal

Because arousal induces changes in several autonomic functions, one strategy to assess arousal is to measure the changes in selected physiological variables or the neuroendocrine factors that mediate the responses. The commonly measured physiological variables include heart rate, blood pressure, pupil dilation, and skin conductance due to sweating. The association between arousal and changes in these physiological variables, however, is not direct. Typically, there is a low correlation between changes in the physiological variables and variations in arousal. Furthermore, the physiological changes differ with the stressor used to manipulate arousal (Pacak et al., 1998; Raglin, 1992).

The neuroendocrine factors commonly associated with elevations in arousal include the catecholamines, adrenocorticotropic hormone, cortisol, growth hormone, and prolactin (Campeau et al., 1997; Pancheri & Biondi, 1990). There is a strong association between changes in arousal and modulation of these factors. Although an arousal response can begin within milliseconds of the presentation of an appropriate stimulus, the time before changes in the levels of the neuroendocrine factors can be detected is usually too long for an application to movement analysis. Most movements are completed within seconds, whereas the time course of detectable changes in the circulating levels of the neuroendocrine factors is on the order of minutes (Van Eck, Nicolson, Berkhof, & Sulon, 1996; Kirschbaum & Hellhammer, 1994).

As a supplement to measurement of the physiological and neuroendocrine variables, arousal can also be quantified by self-reports of the perceived level of arousal. Two common approaches are used: one determines an individual's anxiety, and the other estimates the moment-to-moment level of arousal. The assessment of anxiety usually involves having an individual complete a questionnaire that assesses both the average (trait anxiety) and the current (state anxiety) levels of anxiety (Spielberger, Gorsuch, Lushene, Vagg, & Jacobs, 1983). The scores indicate the extent to which the individual might be aroused by stress. The moment-to-moment level of arousal is measured with the visual analog scale, a 10-cm line anchored at each end with descriptive polar phrases, such as "Not at all anxious" on the left end and "Very anxious" on the right end (Cella & Perry, 1986; O'Connor & Cook, 1999). The comprehensive assessment of arousal in humans, therefore, requires the concurrent measurement of physiological variables, neuroendocrine factors, and perceived levels of anxiety.

Mechanism of Action

Although there is a consensus that arousal can influence motor performance, the mechanisms that mediate the effect are uncertain. One explanation suggests that as arousal varies so does the attention afforded by the individual to the task, which could produce a corresponding variation in performance (Raglin, 1992). Whatever the cognitive consequences of arousal, however, there must be some variation in the neural commands sent to muscle that cause changes in the performance. Little is known about the nature of these changes.

Because arousal involves an increase in the circulating levels of various neuroendocrine factors, it is likely that the neural activation patterns vary with the level of arousal. Two examples support this possibility. First, the endurance time of fatiguing tasks depends on the level of such factors as epinephrine and 5-hydroxytryptamine (5-HT, serotonin) (Blomstrand et al., 1988; Heyes et al., 1988). For example, the duration that subjects can cycle at 80% of the maximal rate of oxygen uptake is decreased after oral administration of an agent that enhances serotonergic activity (Marvin et al., 1997). This is not too surprising, as serotonin levels in the central nervous system have been implicated in the regulation of sleep, depression, anxiety, aggression, appetite, temperature, sexual behavior, and pain sensation (Birdsall, 1998). Furthermore, therapeutic administration of 5-hydroxytryptophan (5-HTP), an intermediate metabolite in the synthesis of serotonin, is effective in treating depression, fibromyalgia, binge eating with obesity, chronic headaches, and insomnia (Birdsall, 1998).

Second, some of the neurotransmitters that modulate the activity of the autonomic nervous system can act as neuromodulators and modify the function of the spinal circuits underlying motor performance (Dickinson, 1995; Katz, 1995; Marder, 1998). For example, numerous stressors can increase the activity of serotonergic neurons and thereby raise the extracellular levels of 5-HT (Chaouloff, Berton, & Mormede, 1999), which can alter the response of a neural network to synaptic drive (Singer & Berger, 1996). Variation in the level of serotonin can alter the activity of spinal motor neurons (Li Volsi, Licata, Ciranna, Caserta, & Santangelo, 1998), EMG activity during the performance of a choice reaction-time task (Rihet, Hasbroucq, Blin, & Possamai, 1999), and even the central pattern generators associated with locomotion (Feraboli-Lohnherr, Barthe, & Orsal, 1999; Jovanovic, Petrov, Greer, & Stein, 1996). These interactions indicate that it is necessary to examine the effects of arousal on motor performance in order to obtain a more complete understanding of the function of the nervous system.

Neuromuscular Function

Apart from examining the controversial inverted-U hypothesis as it applies to motor performance (Raglin, 1992; Schmidt & Lee, 1999), only a few studies have assessed the effects of arousal on selected aspects of performance. The aim in these studies has been to determine the effects of arousal on muscle strength, the steadiness of submaximal contractions, and the distribution of muscle activity. On the basis of these examples, it should be obvious that we know little about the effects of arousal on the details of muscle activation.

Maximum Force

A study performed by Ikai and Steinhaus (1961) is often cited as an example of the potentiating effect that arousal can have on the maximum force. In this study, subjects performed brief maximum isometric contractions with the elbow flexor muscles once each minute for 30 min. Occasionally and unexpectedly, one of the investigators discharged a firearm prior to an MVC. In addition, each subject was asked to shout loudly prior to the last MVC. For most subjects, the MVC force was greater after the loud noise associated with the discharge of the gun and with the shout. The effect of the loud noise, however, provides evidence of the potentiating effect of a startle response (Valls-Solé et al., 1999) and not an enhancement due to arousal. In contrast, the maximum force that individuals can exert during a handgrip did not increase after they participated in arousal-enhancing activities that included doing mental math problems and receiving electric shock (Noteboom & Enoka, 2000).

If arousal does have an effect on muscle strength, two distinct mechanisms might be involved: changes in either the contractility of muscle or the coordination of the involved muscles. Because motivated individuals can maximally activate a muscle by voluntary command under standard laboratory conditions (Allen et al., 1998), it seems unlikely that arousal can enhance the contractility of muscle. Similarly, the catecholamine epinephrine, which is secreted in greater amounts with increases in arousal, can potentiate twitch responses but not tetanic force (Marsden & Meadows, 1970; Williams & Barnes, 1989). In contrast, the modulatory effects of neuroendocrine factors on spinal networks might optimize coordination and increase the load that could be lifted with heightened arousal. This possibility needs to be examined.

Steadiness

When a person performs a fatiguing contraction at a submaximal force, the effort associated with sustaining the force increases and the force becomes more tremulous (figure 8.20a). Similarly, when arousal is manipulated by the application of a stressor, subjects have a reduced ability to exert a steady force. For example, Noteboom and Enoka (2000) compared the ability of subjects to exert a steady submaximal pinch force in the presence and absence of unexpected electric shocks of varying amplitude or while performing a mental math task. Arousal was assessed with the visual analog scale during both the control period (time points 1 to 4) and the application of each stressor (time points 5 to 7; figure 8.30a). Both the electric shock and the mental math task increased arousal. The effect of arousal on steadiness was quantified as the change in the standard deviation of the force fluctuations around the average force. At time points 6 and 7 in figure 8.30a, the change in steadiness was not different for the subjects in the control group, but the subjects in the two stressor groups were less steady (figure 8.30b). Furthermore, the effect on steadiness was much greater for the subjects in the

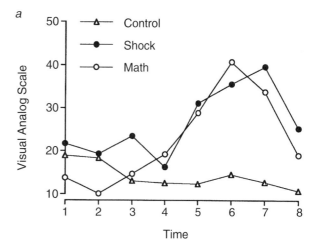

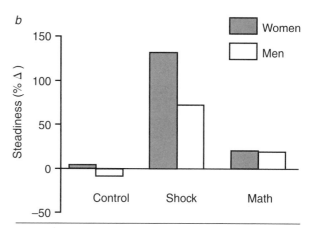

Figure 8.30 Level of arousal *(a)* in a control group of subjects and in subjects who either received electric shock or performed a mental math task and *(b)* the effect of changes in arousal on the steadiness of the force exerted during a pinch grip.

Data from Noteboom and Enoka, 2000.

electric shock group than for those in the matching group and was greater for the women compared with the men within the shock condition.

Overflow of Activation

When a person performs a task that requires a high level of effort, there is a spread of activation to other muscles besides those principally responsible for the task. For example, other muscles are typically activated during the performance of a strength task and in the course of a fatiguing contraction (Howard & Enoka, 1991; Moore, 1975; Ohtsuki, 1983; Zijdewind & Kernell, 2001). This spread of activation probably enhances the postural stability of the individual and enables the transfer of power across joints by two-joint muscles.

Increased levels of arousal also enhance the amount of muscle activation used to perform a task. For example, Weinberg and Hunt (1976) found that subjects with high levels of anxiety (an index of arousability), as compared with less anxious subjects, responded to negative feedback on performance by increasing the amount of muscle EMG during a throwing task. The change in EMG activity caused a decline in performance for the highly anxious subjects but an improvement in the performance of the less anxious subjects.

The effect of arousal on the spread of muscle activation has been used as the basis for some therapeutic interventions with patients. For example, many of the techniques utilized in PNF are based on the overflow of activation, which is referred to as **irradiation.** In a typical application, a patient is encouraged to perform a particular movement pattern against a maximum resistance, which spreads the activation to synergist muscles. Moreover, the basic PNF procedures recommend the use of strong verbal commands "to simulate a stress situation" and thereby enhance the spread of activation to the synergist muscles (Knott & Voss, 1968). Clinical experience suggests that patients have a greater capacity to involve impaired muscles under such conditions of heightened arousal.

Summary

This is the first of two chapters to examine the effects of physical activity on the motor system. The focus of this chapter is the immediate (acute) response of the system to the stress associated with a single bout of physical activity; the chapter addresses six topics that characterize the adaptive capabilities of the system: warm-up effects, flexibility, muscle soreness and damage, muscle fatigue, muscle potentiation, and arousal. First, we discuss warm-up effects and describe the influence of changes in temperature on the mechanical output of the system and on the passive stiffness of muscle and connective tissue. Second, we distinguish warm-up activities from those related to flexibility, and consider techniques that are used to alter flexibility and the factors that limit joint range of motion. Third, we examine the muscle soreness that occurs after strenuous activity. Delayed-onset muscle soreness occurs more frequently after eccentric than after concentric contractions. The consequences of such activity include an increase in the tenderness of muscle, elevated levels of plasma creatine kinase, and a temporary impairment of muscle function. Fourth, we consider the effects of sustained activity on the ability to exert force (muscle fatigue) and the perceived effort associated with the activity. Because the mechanisms that cause muscle fatigue vary with the details of the task, we attempt to identify the conditions under which the different mechanisms can be impaired and hence contribute to muscle fatigue. Fifth, we characterize the potentiating effects of acute activity on monosynaptic responses, miniature end-plate potentials, M-wave amplitude, post-tetanic twitch potentiation, and postcontraction sensory discharge. Sixth, we explore the effect of arousal on motor performance, including how it can be measured, why it is significant, and what is known about its effect on the neuromuscular details of performance. These examples, however, do not represent a complete summary of the acute adjustments of which the motor system is capable.

Suggested Readings

Gardiner, P.F. (2001). *Neuromuscular aspects of physical activity.* Champaign, IL: Human Kinetics, chapter 3.

McComas, A.J. (1996). *Skeletal muscle: Form and function.* Champaign, IL: Human Kinetics, chapter 15.

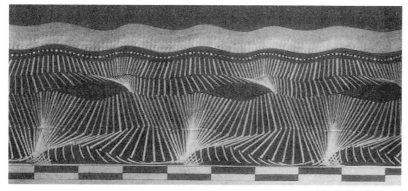

Photograph courtesy of the Collège de France.

Chronic Adaptations

In chapter 8, we examined the acute adjustments of the motor system in response to a single bout of physical activity. We learned that the adjustments can be extensive and that the response involves the processes and components of the system that are stressed by the activity. Chapter 9 addresses the cumulative (chronic) response of the motor system to the stress associated with long-term physical activity. We will examine the adaptations associated with strength and power training, reduced activity, recovery from injury, and aging.

Muscle Strength

The measurement of strength is used as an index of the force-generating capacity of muscle. In clinical and experimental settings, strength is commonly measured in one of three ways: as the maximum force that can be exerted during an isometric contraction, the maximum load that can be lifted once, or the peak torque during an isokinetic contraction (figure 9.1). The isometric contraction task is usually referred to as a maximum voluntary contraction (MVC), whereas the load that can be lifted once is known as the **one repetition-maximum load** (1-RM load). For the MVC task, strength is expressed as the maximum force exerted by a limb during the isometric contraction. For the 1-RM task, the load torque varies throughout the range of motion, and the maximum load that can be lifted depends on the ability of the muscles to exert a torque greater than the maximum-load torque. For the isokinetic task, the peak torque can be assessed during either a concentric or an eccentric contraction. Figure 9.1 shows an isokinetic task that involved a concentric contraction; the individual first pushed against the device to extend the knee and then pulled against the device to flex the knee. While the magnitude of the MVC force depends primarily on the size of the involved muscle, both the 1-RM load and the peak torque during an isokinetic contraction depend on both muscle size and the coordinated activation of muscles by the nervous system (Rutherford & Jones, 1986; Semmler & Enoka, 2000).

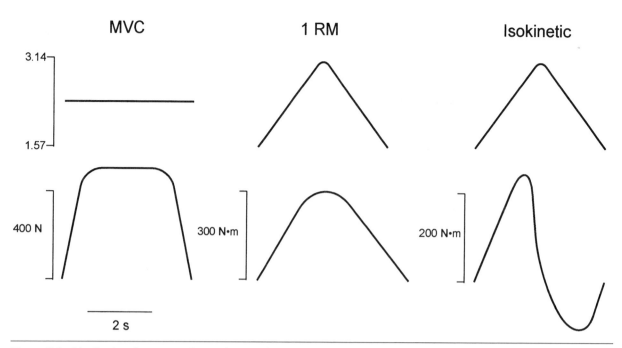

Figure 9.1   Idealized performances of a maximum voluntary contraction (MVC), a one repetition-maximum (1-RM) lift, and an isokinetic contraction with the knee extensor muscles. The upper row indicates knee angle (3.14 rad = complete extension). The lower row shows force for the MVC but the resultant muscle torque for the 1-RM and isokinetic tasks.

The strength gains experienced by an individual, therefore, depend on how strength is measured and on the exercises performed in the training program (Siff, 2000). Because of this association, we will discuss the training and loading techniques used in strength training before considering the adaptations that produce the increases in strength.

Training Techniques

The adaptations experienced by the motor system with repeated bouts of exercise depend on the specific tasks performed in the training program. As described in chapters 6 and 7, variation in an exercise task influences the motor units that are activated, coordination among the synergist muscles, the amount of postural support needed for the movement, and the type of sensory feedback received by the central nervous system (CNS). Because of these effects, the most effective training strategy is to match the exercise to the intended outcome. For these reasons, this section describes six training modalities that each have different strengths and weaknesses and thus should be prescribed according to the training goal.

Isometric Training

An isometric contraction (*iso* = constant, *metric* = whole-muscle length) was previously defined as a condition in which the torque due to the load is matched by a muscle-exerted torque that is equal in magnitude but opposite in direction. Although there is no change in whole-muscle length with an isometric contraction, the muscle fibers shorten (Griffiths, 1991; Ito et al., 1998). An exercise involves an isometric contraction when activating the muscle causes a body segment to push against an immovable object in the surroundings.

In the 1950s, Hettinger and Muller popularized isometric exercises as a fitness activity (Hettinger, 1961). Isometrics were touted as exercises that produce a good hypertrophic response and take little time, besides being economical. The scheme proposed by Hettinger and Muller was characterized by *consideration of threshold points, intensity levels, and the systematization of an exercise program.* For example, it was suggested for the elbow flexors that daily exercises at 40% to 50% of maximum would produce strength gains, at 20% to 30% of maximum would maintain the status quo, and at less than 20% of maximum would result in a loss of strength. The isometric scheme also entailed a trade-off between exercise duration and intensity; for durations of 1 to 2 s, the exercise had to be done at 100% of maximum to provide sufficient stress, whereas for a duration of 4 to 6 s the intensity could be lowered to 66% of maximum. Hettinger and Muller suggested that one 4- to 6-s contraction per day at 40% to 50% of maximum would produce the maximum gains in strength (e.g., 2% a week for the elbow flexors). Furthermore, Hettinger and Muller recognized that threshold values had to be reset periodically, and they encouraged rechecking the maximum value.

Although the ideas proposed by Hettinger and Muller have been challenged, the contribution was significant in that it emphasized a quantitative approach to exercise prescription. The popularity of isometric exercises has subsided in recent years, but such exercises are still advocated as part of a strength-training program. Furthermore, the effectiveness of exercises involving isometric contractions was shown to be equal to that of isokinetic contractions in evoking functional improvements in patients with chondromalacia patellae (Duncan, Chandler, Cavanaugh, Johnson, & Buehler, 1989). However, the strength gains achieved with isometric exercises reach a peak after about six to eight weeks, so training programs should be structured accordingly (Zatsiorsky, 1995).

For example, Kitai and Sale (1989) had six subjects perform 6 weeks of training with isometric exercises. The subjects trained three times a week by performing two sets of 10 repetitions. Each repetition was a 5-s maximal (100%) isometric contraction of the plantarflexor muscles with the ankle joint fixed at a right angle between the shank and the foot. Two contractions were performed each minute, and there was a 2-min rest between sets. The training resulted in an increase in strength (maximal isometric torque) of 18% (25.5 N·m) at the training angle and increases of 17% and 14% at adjacent (0.17 rad) plantarflexion and dorsiflexion angles. These increases in strength with isometric training are similar to values reported by other groups (Davies, Parker, Rutherford, & Jones, 1988; Garfinkel & Cafarelli, 1992). With a similar 16-week protocol, Alway, MacDougall, and Sale (1989) found that isometric training produced an increase of 44% in the maximum plantarflexor torque. Nonetheless, gains in isometric strength are poorly correlated with those achieved by a program of anisometric contractions (Wilson & Murphy, 1996).

Although most of the focus on isometric training has been on the gains achieved by the prime mover muscles, many other muscles perform isometric contractions during strength-training exercises to provide postural support for the task. The significant role of this postural activity is underscored by the effect of posture on the measured outcome of a strength-training program (Hortobágyi & Katch, 1990; Rasch & Morehouse, 1957; Rutherford & Jones, 1986). For example, the improvement in performance after eight weeks of weight training with the squat and bench-press lifts was evident only when the training and testing postures were similar (Wilson, Murphy, & Walshe, 1996). For the chest and arms, the subjects experienced an increase in the maximal bench-press load (12%), the bench-press throw (8%), and the isokinetic bench press (13%), but not the ground reaction force during a push-up test or the peak torque during horizontal arm adduction. These results indicate that the strength gains were specific to the training exercises,

resulting in a poor correlation between MVC force and performance but a moderate association between the rate of increase in force during an MVC and performance (Morrissey, Harman, & Johnson, 1995; Wilson & Murphy, 1996).

Anisometric Training

When a muscle is activated and the torque it exerts is different from the load torque, there is a change in muscle length and the muscle performs an **anisometric** contraction. This term encompasses both concentric and eccentric contractions, which involve a decrease or an increase in muscle length, respectively.

In the modern era of strength training, DeLorme (1945) was one of the first to prescribe exercising systematically. As a restorative aide (now known as a physical therapist), DeLorme devised an exercise scheme that could be used in a rehabilitation program. The DeLorme technique, known as **progressive-resistance exercises,** involves performing three sets of 10 repetitions in which the load is increased for each set. The load is based on the amount that can be lifted 10 times, which is referred to as the 10-RM load. The first set of 10 repetitions is done with one-half of the 10-RM load, the second set with three-quarters of the 10-RM load, and the final set with the full 10-RM load. The rationale behind this approach is that the first two sets serve as a warm-up for the maximum effort of the third set. The reverse protocol was proposed as the basis for the Oxford technique (Zinovieff, 1951), the rationale being that the second (75% 10-RM) and third (50% 10-RM) sets loaded the muscle while it was fatigued after performing the first, maximum-effort set. The DeLorme and Oxford techniques have been referred to as *ascending-* and *descending-pyramid loading,* respectively (McDonagh & Davies, 1984). There are, however, many combinations that can be used in a weight-training program (Fleck & Kraemer, 1987).

Because most exercises include both concentric and eccentric contractions, the 10-RM load does not provide a consistent stress for all phases of each repetition. From the torque-velocity relation (figure 6.27), we know that the torque a muscle can exert is greater for an eccentric contraction compared with a concentric contraction. Consequently, in a movement that involves alternating concentric and eccentric contractions, the capabilities of the concentric contraction limit performance and thus determine the 10-RM load. In addition, because the amount of exercise stress depends on the magnitude of the load relative to maximum capabilities, it is probably the concentric component of a concentric-eccentric sequence that experiences the greater stress and subsequent adaptation (Hortobágyi & Katch, 1990).

The greater forces associated with eccentric contractions have fostered an attitude that eccentric exercises should provide a more intense training stimulus and hence greater strength gains. However, it is not the absolute force that determines the quantity of the training stimulus, but rather the size of the force relative to maximum. Indeed, many studies have shown that concentric-only and eccentric-only exercise programs produce similar strength gains and enhancement of work capacity. Rather, training programs that use both concentric and eccentric contractions produce superior strength gains compared with either mode by itself (Colliander & Tesch, 1990; Dudley, Tesch, Miller, & Buchanan, 1991; Godard, Wygand, Carpinelli, Catalano, & Otto, 1998; Häkkinen, 1985). For example, a strength-training program involving isokinetic contractions with the knee extensor muscles produced an 18% increase in the peak torque for subjects who trained with concentric contractions and a 36% increase in peak torque for subjects who trained with concentric-eccentric contractions (Colliander & Tesch, 1990).

In contrast, some studies have shown that the relative increase in peak torque during an isokinetic contraction is greater after training with eccentric contractions compared with concentric contractions (Higbie, Cureton, Warren, & Prior, 1996), even when training has involved the same absolute load (Hortobágyi, Barrier, et al., 1996). For example, subjects who trained the knee extensor muscles with eccentric contractions for 12 weeks experienced a 46% increase in the peak torque compared with a 13% increase in peak torque exhibited by subjects who trained with concentric contractions (Hortobágyi, Hill, et al., 1996). Moreover, the strength gains achieved with either eccentric or concentric contractions are specific to the training mode (Aagaard, Simonsen, Trolle, Bangsbo, & Klausen, 1996; Morrissey et al., 1995). These researchers have attributed this difference to the unique properties of eccentric contractions, which include the following characteristics (Enoka, 1996):

■ *Cross-Bridge Activity.* The high stresses associated with eccentric contractions probably influence the behavior of individual cross-bridges and sarcomeres (Lombardi & Piazzesi, 1990). Detachment of the cross-bridge during an eccentric contraction appears to involve a mechanical disruption of the chemical actomyosin bond in contrast to the more orderly binding of adenosine triphosphate (ATP) and detachment that occur during the normal cross-bridge cycle. Because of differences in the quantity of contractile proteins and amount of filament overlap among sarcomeres, the maximum force that each sarcomere can exert varies along the length of a muscle. Consequently, the lengthening of a contracting muscle involves the stretching and popping of individual sarcomeres as each reaches its yield stress (Morgan, 1990; Morgan & Allen, 1999).

■ *Motor Unit Activity.* Submaximal concentric and eccentric contractions typically involve different contributions by synergist muscles that can include the activation of different motor units within the same muscle (Nakazawa et al., 1993; Nardone & Schieppati, 1988; Nardone et al., 1989). Furthermore, motor unit synchronization is enhanced during eccentric contractions; this suggests that the proportion of common input to pairs of motor units is greater during eccentric contractions compared with isometric and concentric contractions (Semmler, Kutzscher, Zhou, & Enoka, 2000).

■ *Maximality of Activation.* Although muscle force is greater during a voluntary eccentric contraction, the EMG is substantially less than during a concentric contraction. This suggests that individuals are incapable of maximally activating a muscle during an eccentric contraction (Higbie et al., 1996; Nakazawa et al., 1993; Kellis & Baltzopoulos, 1998; Pasquet et al., 2000; Tesch et al., 1990; Webber & Kriellaars, 1997; Westing, Cresswell, & Thorstensson, 1991). Furthermore, strength gains achieved with eccentric contractions often involve an increase in the EMG and muscle activation (Aagaard et al, 2000; Colson, Pousson, Martin, & Van Hoecke, 1999).

■ *Submaximal Activation.* Steady state running at a submaximal intensity on a treadmill at a level grade is associated with a constant level of oxygen consumption. In contrast, steady state downhill (–10% grade) running at the same intensity is accomplished by a gradual increase in oxygen consumption and in the EMG of leg muscles (Dick & Cavanagh, 1987). Downhill running involves a significant reliance on eccentric contractions of the leg muscles.

■ *Afferent Feedback.* There appear to be heightened levels of feedback from muscle spindles during eccentric contractions (Burke, Hagbarth, & Löfstedt, 1978; Scheiber & Thach, 1985). This may be necessary in order to achieve the precise match between the muscle and load torques that enables the individual to perform a controlled lowering of an inertial load with an eccentric contraction.

■ *Reflexes.* Level running at a submaximal intensity on a treadmill for 20 min produced a reduction in the amplitude of the soleus H reflex of 9%. Downhill running (–10% grade) at the same intensity reduced the H-reflex amplitude by 25% (Bulbulian & Bowles, 1992). Similarly, H reflexes were depressed (Nardone & Schieppati, 1988) and the sign of a cutaneous reflex was reversed (Haridas et al., 2000) during the lowering of an inertial load, which required an eccentric contraction.

■ *Contralateral Effects.* A fatigue protocol performed by the knee extensors of one leg increased the peak torque during maximal eccentric contractions carried out after the fatigue task by the knee extensors of the contralateral leg (Grabiner & Owings, 1999). There was no change in the peak torque for concentric contractions.

■ *Muscle Damage.* Delayed-onset muscle soreness is preferentially elicited by activity that involves eccentric contractions (Morgan & Allen, 1999; Salmons, 1997).

■ *Hypertrophy.* As compared with concentric contractions, eccentric exercises may provide a more effective stimulus for hypertrophy, which might be mediated by a differential control (transcription vs. translation) of protein synthesis (Booth & Baldwin, 1996; Williams & Neufer, 1996; Wong & Booth, 1990a, 1990b).

These differences underscore the need to match the details of a training program to the goals of the individual.

Accommodation Devices

Exercise machines in which the load is controlled by gear or friction systems (e.g., Cybex, Biodex), by hydraulic cylinders (e.g., Ariel, Kincom, Lido, Omnitron), or by pneumatic systems (e.g., Keiser) provide an *accommodating resistance.* These systems can generate a load equal in magnitude but opposite in direction to the force exerted by the subject. One consequence of the gear systems and of some hydraulic devices is *a movement in which the angular velocity of the displaced body seg-*

ment is constant, which results in an isokinetic contraction (Ichinose et al., 2000; Kaufman, An, & Chao, 1995).

An isokinetic contraction represents the dynamic condition (because muscle length changes) in which the quotient of muscle torque to load torque equals 1. When no net torque acts on the system, the acceleration of the system is zero, and velocity is constant. Obviously the muscle and load torques are not equal in magnitude at the beginning or the end of an isokinetic contraction; otherwise the movement would never start or stop. Isokinetic devices can be used to perform concentric and eccentric contractions (figure 9.2). For a concentric contraction, the individual pushes against the device, and power flows from the individual as work (positive) is done on the device. For an eccentric contraction, however, the individual must resist the load imposed by the device; power flows from the device to the individual, and the device does negative work on the individual.

Many investigators use isokinetic devices (figure 9.3*a*) to quantify the torque, work, and power output of muscle. Typically, they accomplish this by measuring the resistance provided by the machine (F_l in figure 9.3*b*) and expressing the effort in the appropriate units. A free body diagram of the system (figure 9.3*b*), however, indicates that the machine load is not the only factor affecting the

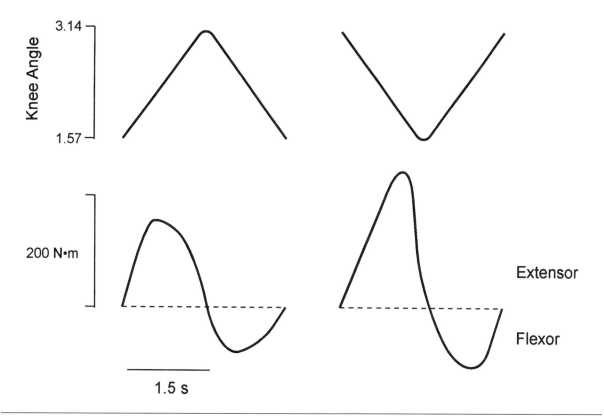

Figure 9.2 Concentric and eccentric isokinetic contractions. The upper row indicates knee angle (3.14 rad = complete extension) whereas the lower row shows the resultant muscle torque.

load torque; the weight of the limb must also be considered. Furthermore, the acceleration of the limb at the beginning and end of the task, which comprises an inertia force, can influence the estimated muscle torque (Iossifidou & Baltzopoulos, 1998). Winter, Wells, and Orr (1981) have demonstrated that neglecting the acceleration components (acceleration due to gravity and the acceleration of the limb to reach the speed of the machine) can lead to an error of 500% at the highest speeds in the determination of the amount of work performed by the muscles. However, these acceleration effects can be determined and incorporated into the appropriate calculations to allow more accurate measurements (Aagaard, Simonsen, Trolle, Bangsbo, & Klausen, 1994a; Gransberg & Knutsson, 1983; Kaufman et al., 1995; Iossifidou & Baltzopoulos, 1998; Kellis & Baltzopoulos, 1995). Without this correction, the torque exerted by the machine (F_l) is not a measure of the resultant muscle torque (τ_m).

One *disadvantage* of isokinetic devices is that they violate the principle of specificity. Natural movements rarely involve a constant angular velocity of a limb and hence are not isokinetic. Moreover, the maximum speed on many isokinetic devices (5 rad/s) is much less than the maximum angular velocity achieved during movements such as running, jumping, and throwing. These characteristics may explain why the peak torques exerted during isokinetic contractions at functionally relevant speeds are usually less than those achieved during less constrained movements. For example, the peak torque that the knee extensors can exert during a concentric contraction at 1.05 rad/s is about 160 N·m (Crenshaw, Karlsson, Styf, Bäcklund, & Fridén, 1995) compared with a peak torque of 300 N·m during the concentric phase of a vertical jump (Bobbert & Ingen Schenau, 1988). Similarly, a strength-training program that included the squat

lift resulted in significant gains in maximal squat load (21%), 40-m sprint time (2%), peak power during a 6-s cycle (10%), and vertical jump height (21%), but not peak torque during an isokinetic contraction (Wilson et al., 1996). Additionally, strength training with isokinetic contractions increases the peak torque during an isokinetic contraction but does not alter maximal kicking performance (Aagaard et al., 1996).

Despite these limitations, isokinetic training can produce adaptations comparable to those obtained with less constrained techniques, although these changes may be specific to the training speed and type of contraction (Aagaard et al., 1996; Kellis and & Baltzopoulos, 1995; Higbie et al., 1996; Morrissey et al., 1995; Seger, Arvidsson, & Thorstensson, 1998). For example, when subjects trained the knee extensors for 7 weeks on an isokinetic device at 3.14 rad/s, there were significant increases in peak torque (about 14%) for contractions from 0 to 3.14 rad/s but not at 4.2 and 5.2 rad/s (Lesmes, Costill, Coyle, & Fink, 1978). Similarly, subjects who trained for 10 weeks at 1.1 rad/s experienced a 9% increase (25 N·m) in peak torque, whereas those who trained at 4.2 rad/s had a 20% increase (30 N·m) in peak torque; each of these increases was specific to the training speed (Ewing, Wolfe, Rogers, Amundson, & Stull, 1990).

Isokinetic devices offer several *advantages*. One significant advantage is that a muscle group may be stressed differently throughout its range of motion. This accommodation is useful in rehabilitation settings (Kellis & Baltzopoulos, 1995). When one specific locus in a range of motion is painful, the patient can reduce the effort at this point yet exercise the joint system in the other nonpainful regions (Shirakura, Kato, & Udagawa, 1992). Furthermore, the patient can simply stop in the middle of an exercise without having to worry about controlling

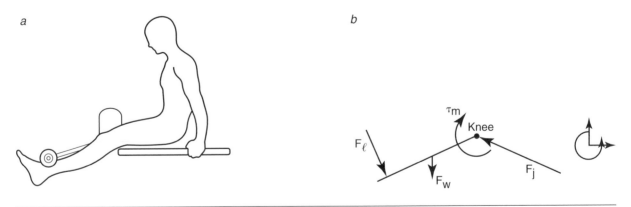

Figure 9.3   A subject performing an isokinetic knee extension exercise: (*a*) the isokinetic dynamometer; (*b*) a free body diagram of the forces acting on the shank.

F_j = joint reaction force; F_w = limb weight; F_l = machine load; τ_m = resultant muscle torque.

the load. Because of the accommodation property, the resistance provided by the device varies in proportion to the capabilities of the user over the range of motion. Isokinetic devices also provide substantial support for the user, removing the need to provide some of the stabilizing support that must be generated with other rehabilitation exercises.

In contrast to isokinetic devices, hydraulic and pneumatic systems provide an accommodating resistance but do not control movement speed. Hydraulic devices provide resistance as individuals exert a force against a leaky, fluid-filled chamber (Fothergill, Grieve, & Pinder, 1996; Pinder & Grieve, 1997). The resistance is manipulated by varying the diameter of the valve through which the fluid leaks from one chamber to another; the resistance is high when the diameter of the valve is small. The hydraulic system offers an accommodating resistance against which muscles can perform concentric contractions. The greater the force exerted by the individual, the greater the resistance provided by the device. However, movement speed increases as the applied force increases. Nonetheless, hydraulic devices can elicit strength gains comparable to those achieved with free weights. For example, Hortobágyi and Katch (1990) trained one group of subjects with free weights and another group with a hydraulic device for 12 weeks. The average improvements in the maximum bench-press and squat loads were 23% for subjects who trained with free weights and 20% for those who trained with a hydraulic device. Furthermore, changes in force, velocity, and power evaluated by isokinetic and hydraulic dynamometers were not different (~8%) for the two groups. Pneumatic systems also provide a variable resistance, via a compressor that alters the pressure and hence the resistance against which the individual works. The user can change the pressure rapidly, simply by depressing a button. One useful feature of pneumatic systems is that the pressure can be increased sufficiently to enable the performance of eccentric contractions; however, control of the device is minimal under these conditions.

Plyometric Training

In contrast to the isokinetic device, **plyometric** exercises were designed to train a specific movement pattern, the eccentric-concentric sequence of muscle activity associated with the stretch-shorten cycle. Most human movements involve the stretch-shorten cycle. Recall from chapter 6 that the advantage of the stretch-shorten cycle is that a muscle can perform more positive work after it has done an eccentric contraction than in the absence of a preceding eccentric contraction (figure 6.33). Four mechanisms have been proposed to account for the enhancement of positive work: time to develop force, elastic energy, force potentiation, and reflex augmentation.

Although there is no consensus on the dominant mechanism (Ingen Schenau et al., 1997), it is likely that the storage and utilization of elastic energy are significant in plyometric exercises, which involve rapid stretch-shorten cycles. An example of a plyometric exercise is hopping down a flight of stairs, on either one or two legs.

As mentioned in chapter 6, stretch-shorten cycles that are performed rapidly and that involve a small displacement during the stretch phase may not actually entail an eccentric contraction in the sense of the lengthening of active sarcomeres. Rather, the increase in muscle length may reflect a stretch of the tendon; nonetheless, this would contribute significantly to the positive work done by the muscle (Fukunaga et al., 2001; Roberts et al., 1997). The enhancement of performance due to the stretch-shorten cycle is maximized when the stretch phase has a small amplitude but high velocity and when there is no delay between the stretch and shorten phases (Cavagna, 1977; Edman, Elzinga, & Noble, 1978; Rack & Westbury, 1974).

Plyometric exercises are able to induce a training effect (Reich et al., 2000). For example, Blattner and Noble (1979) trained two groups of subjects for eight weeks, one group on an isokinetic device and the other with plyometric exercises. The two groups increased their vertical jump heights by about the same amount (5 cm) as a result of the training. Similarly, Häkkinen, Komi, and Alén (1985) found that jump training caused a minor increase in the maximal knee extensor force during an isometric contraction but a substantial increase in the rate of force development and an increase in the area of fast-twitch fibers. Although it is difficult to train experimental animals to perform jump training, Dooley, Bach, and Luff (1990) managed to train rats to perform 30 jumps a day, five days a week, for at least eight weeks. The jumps were estimated to be between 30% and 67% of the maximum height that the rats could achieve. The training produced some changes in the medial gastrocnemius muscle but not in the soleus. There was a 15% increase in the maximum tetanic force, a 3% increase in the maximum rate of force development, a 15% increase in fatigability, and a 4% decrease in the percentage of type IIa muscle fibers. Artificially evoked stretch-shorten cycles, however, can induce similar changes in the soleus muscle of rats (Almeida-Silveira, Pérot, & Goubel, 1996). These observations indicate that regular vertical jump exercises performed at a moderate intensity are able to induce adaptations in the involved muscles.

The advantage of plyometric exercises is that they enable an individual to train the stretch-shorten component of a movement, which is difficult to accomplish with any other technique. Nonetheless, plyometric exercises should not be the sole component of a training program but rather should be part of a more diverse program that addresses the strength, speed, endurance, and flexibility needs of the individual (King, 1993; Zatsiorsky, 1995).

Neuromuscular Electrical Stimulation

Reports from the Soviet Union in the 1960s suggested that the application of electric shocks to a muscle could result in strength gains (Elson, 1974; Zatsiorksy, 1995). Such procedures, which are referred to as **neuromuscular electrical stimulation,** involve artificially activating the muscle with a protocol designed to minimize the pain and discomfort associated with the artificial activation (Moreno-Aranda & Seireg, 1981a, 1981b, 1981c). Neuromuscular electrical stimulation has been used since the 18th century as a rehabilitation tool (Hainaut & Duchateau, 1992; Liberson, Holmquest, Scot, & Dow, 1961), but only since the 1970s has it been applied to noninjured active athletes as a supplement to conventional training.

Because the axolemma is more easily excited than the sarcolemma, the electric current that passes through a muscle to evoke a muscle contraction *generates action potentials in the intramuscular nerve branches rather than directly exciting muscle fibers* (Hultman, Sjöholm, Jäderholm-Ek, & Krynicki, 1983). Accordingly, the term "neuromuscular electrical stimulation" is preferable to "electromyostimulation" because it indicates that the artificial activation involves both the nerve and the muscle.

Neuromuscular electrical stimulation can be used either to supplement or to substitute for voluntary activation of muscle. When used as a supplement, it can enhance activation by increasing the excitation of muscle or by altering the motor units that participate in a task. The ability of an individual to maximally activate a muscle by voluntary command seems to vary across muscles (Belanger & McComas, 1981). Individuals appear capable of maximally activating the biceps brachii (Allen, McKenzie, & Gandevia, 1998; De Serres & Enoka, 1998; Gandevia, Herbert, & Leeper, 1998) and the thumb adductors (Herbert & Gandevia, 1996) but perhaps not quadriceps femoris (Nøregaard, Lykkegaard, Bülow, & Danneskiold-Samsøe, 1997; Stackhouse, Dean, Lee, & Binder-Macleod, 2000), the dorsiflexor muscles (Kent-Braun & Le Blanc, 1996), or the plantarflexor muscles (Cresswell, Löscher, & Thorstensson, 1995). For example, 600-ms trains at 100 Hz superimposed on the quadriceps femoris muscle during an MVC indicated deficits of 5% to 30% in maximum force (Strojnik, 1995). If the voluntary command does not evoke the maximum force that the muscle can exert, then neuromuscular electrical stimulation can probably overcome some of the deficit.

Alternatively, if the voluntary command is sufficient to achieve contraction maximality, then the effect of neuromuscular electrical stimulation might be to enhance the activation of high-threshold motor units. For example, when low-intensity neuromuscular electrical stimulation was applied over the triceps surae and quadriceps femoris muscles, the time to the peak twitch force decreased (Trimble & Enoka, 1991). This suggests that the neuromuscular electrical stimulation caused a faster-contracting population of motor units to be activated by the stimulus that evoked the twitch response (Buchthal & Schmalbruch, 1976). Accordingly, when electrical stimulation was applied over the motor point of tibialis anterior, the recruitment order for pairs of motor units varied about 30% of the time during voluntary contractions, compared with 6% in the absence of the stimulation (Feiereisen, Duchateau, & Hainaut, 1997).

The facilitative effect of neuromuscular electrical stimulation can be substantial. For example, Howard and Enoka (1991) examined the effect of right leg neuromuscular electrical stimulation on the MVC force of the left leg knee extensor muscles. Neuromuscular electrical stimulation of the quadriceps femoris of the left leg elicited a strong cutaneous sensation and a right leg force that was 40% of maximum. In addition, the right leg stimulation caused an average increase of 11% in the left leg MVC force. The increase in MVC force averaged 6% for young men who were recreationally active but 16% for young men who regularly performed weightlifting exercises. These results indicate that none of the subjects was able to achieve the maximum force by voluntary activation and that neuromuscular electrical stimulation applied to the contralateral limb evoked a facilitative effect. Such effects are presumably responsible for the therapeutic procedure of brushing the skin, which has been shown to increase the quadriceps femoris and biceps femoris EMG during an MVC (Matyas, Galea, & Spicer, 1986).

Neuromuscular electrical stimulation can be applied with a variety of protocols. The parameters that can be varied include stimulus frequency, stimulus waveform, stimulus intensity, electrode size, and electrode type. The simplest stimulus protocol is to apply a train of rectangular pulses (figure 9.4a). One limitation of this scheme, however, is that it requires a frequency of about 100 Hz to elicit the maximum force in a muscle, which is much more painful than stimuli at <50 Hz (Barr, Nielsen, & Soderberg, 1986). This problem can be circumvented with a protocol of high-frequency stimulation (10 kHz) that is modulated (i.e., turned on and off) at a lower frequency (50-100 Hz); this scheme is attributed to Kots (1971) and is shown in figure 9.4b. Moreno-Aranda and Seireg (1981a, 1981b, 1981c) tested such a protocol and found that the optimum regimen involved application of the stimulus for 1.5 s once every 6 s for 60 s, followed by a 60-s rest. The specific details of the optimum protocol probably differ among muscle groups. Nonetheless, this type of protocol minimizes the pain associated with the procedure and can elicit a force that is equivalent to the MVC force (Delitto, Brown, Strube, Rose, & Lehman, 1989).

In addition to varying stimulus frequency, it is also possible to use stimulus waveforms that have different shapes (figure 9.4c). There are two reasons for changing waveform shape. First, the shape of the stimulus waveform can influence the *comfort* associated with neuromuscular electrical stimulation. Commercially available clinical stimulators provide a variety of waveform shapes (e.g., rectangular, triangular, sinusoidal) that can deliver electric current in either a positive (monophasic) or a positive-negative (biphasic) pulse. Although there is no waveform shape that is universally preferred, subjects and patients do have individual preferences (Baker, Bowman, & McNeal, 1988; Delitto & Rose, 1986). This may be an important consideration in patient compliance with a prescribed protocol. Second, conventional stimulus waveforms (e.g., biphasic rectangular pulses) are known to alter *the recruitment order of motor units* (Fang & Mortimer, 1991c, Feiereisen et al., 1997; Trimble & Enoka, 1991). Although the altered recruitment order may be advantageous in strength training and for recovery from injury, it hastens the onset of fatigue in the functional electrical stimulation of paralyzed muscle (Fang & Mortimer, 1991a; Wise, Morgan, Gregory, & Proske, 2001). With the use of a quasitrapezoidal waveform and a tripolar stimulating electrode, Fang and Mortimer (1991b, 1991c) devised a technique to preferentially recruit fatigue-resistant motor units. The tripolar cuff electrode causes a differential block (action potentials cannot be propagated) by hyperpolarizing the membrane of large-diameter axons and enabling the small-diameter axons to be activated selectively.

Both the size and material of the electrode influence the efficacy of the stimulation. Large electrodes enable the current to be more readily disbursed throughout the muscle, which is essential for large muscles such as quadriceps femoris. Moreover, the current density (nA/cm^2) is less with large electrodes; this permits a greater amount of current to be passed without damaging the underlying tissue and thus minimizes the discomfort associated with the procedure. In addition to a large surface area, the electrode should have a low impedance—that is, a low resistance to the flow of electric current. Large carbonized-rubber electrodes seem particularly effective at meeting these needs (Lieber & Kelly, 1991).

As with neuromuscular electrical stimulation, the artificial generation of action potentials in the peripheral motor system can be achieved with **magnetic stimulation** (Lotz, Dunne, & Daube, 1989). Commercially available magnetic stimulators can induce an electric field and the flow of current, which will depolarize excitable membranes and generate action potentials. In contrast to the situation with neuromuscular electrical stimulation, however, the threshold for a motor response is lower than that for a sensory response with magnetic stimulation. Therefore, magnetic stimulation is less painful than electrical stimulation. Furthermore, the stimulus declines less over distance compared with electrical stimulation and thus the stimulus is more widespread.

Although there is some disagreement in the research literature concerning the maximum capabilities of neuromuscular electrical stimulation, there is no doubt that it is possible to increase strength in both healthy and injured muscle with this technique (Hainaut & Duchateau, 1992; Lieber, Silva, & Daniel, 1996; Miller & Thépaut-Mathieu, 1993; Thériault, Boulay, Thériault, & Simoneau,

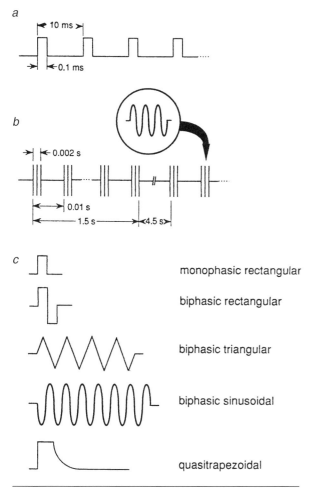

Figure 9.4 Selected stimulus regimens used in neuromuscular stimulation: *(a)* a conventional train of low-frequency (100 Hz) rectangular stimuli with a pulse width of 0.1 ms; *(b)* a pattern of high-frequency stimulation (10-kHz sine wave) that is modulated at a low frequency (100 Hz) with 0.01 s between trains of stimuli; *(c)* waveform shapes commonly used with neuromuscular electrical stimulation. The biphasic waveforms vary about a zero line.

Adapted from Enoka, 1988.

1996). A common approach is to use the Kots protocol (stimulus frequency of 2500 Hz modulated in 50-Hz bursts), with 10 repetitions in each of 15 to 25 training sessions. A single repetition lasts 60 s and comprises 10 s of stimulation and 50 s of rest. The stimulus intensity is set at the maximum tolerable level. The increase in strength (isometric contraction) ranges from 0.6% to 3.6% per session, with an average of about 1.6% per session. This is comparable to the strength gain that can be achieved with other training modalities (Hainaut & Duchateau, 1992).

Neuromuscular electrical stimulation hastens the onset of muscle fatigue. This effect has often been attributed to stimulation-induced changes in the activated motor units; specifically, more fatigable motor units become involved in the task with the application of electrical stimulation. Nuclear magnetic resonance studies, however, have shown that energy metabolism is different for a task achieved with voluntary contractions compared with electrically evoked contractions (Ratkevicius, Mizuno, Povilonis, & Quistorff, 1998; Vanderthommen et al., 1999). When moderate forces (<40% MVC) were sustained with leg muscles, ATP turnover was greater, intracellular pH was lower, and muscle blood flow was increased when the force was sustained by electrical stimulation. The elevated metabolic demand was probably due to a reduction in the number of motor units that contributed to the task because the electric current did not activate the entire muscle (Adams, Harris, Woodard, & Dudley, 1993).

In many training studies that have used neuromuscular electrical stimulation, the maximum intensity of current tolerated by the subjects is about 60 mA (Laughman, Youdas, Garrett, & Chao, 1983). In a case study, however, Delitto et al. (1989) examined the enhancement of performance when training was supplemented with high-intensity stimulation (200 mA). The subject was a highly motivated and experienced weight lifter. He participated in a 140-day study that was divided into four phases of about one month each. The dependent variable was the maximum load that could be lifted in the clean and jerk, snatch, and squat lifts. In the second and fourth periods of training, the voluntary training regimen (3 h/day) was supplemented with neuromuscular electrical stimulation of the quadriceps femoris (2.5 kHz modulated at 75 Hz was delivered to evoke ten 11-s contractions per thigh in each session, for three sessions each week). The results indicate that performance in all three lifts improved substantially with the intervention (figure 9.5). This study suggests that the outcomes depend on the intensity of stimulation used in the protocol (Miller & Thépaut-Mathieu, 1993). However, athletes are generally reluc-

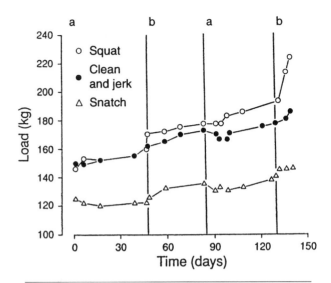

Figure 9.5   Changes in the maximum loads lifted by an experienced weight lifter for three lifts. During the b periods, the regular training of the weight lifter was supplemented with neuromuscular electrical stimulation of the quadriceps femoris.

Adapted from Delitto, Brown, Strube, Rose, and Lehman, 1989.

tant to use neuromuscular electrical stimulation as a supplement to training because the stress is applied during isometric contractions rather than during the movements for which they are training, which violates the principle of specificity (Zatsiorsky, 1995).

Training protocols that use electrical stimulation do not evoke the same adaptations in all motor units. The outcome depends on the amount of activity imposed on the motor unit (Kernell, Eerbeek, Verhey, & Donselaar, 1987; Kernell, Donselaar, & Eerbeek, 1987). This effect was demonstrated in a longitudinal study of six motor units residing in the thenar muscles of two subjects (Chan, Andres, Polykovskaya, & Brown, 1999). Each motor unit was subjected to three sessions of training each week for seven weeks. In each training session, the motor unit received 24,000 stimuli delivered in bursts that evoked 90% of the tetanic force (~40 Hz). The training effect for one motor unit is shown in figure 9.6; its twitch and tetanic forces increased, whereas there was no change in its fatigability. Other motor units, however, experienced a decrease in the twitch and tetanic forces and an improved resistance to fatigue. These divergent responses depended on the initial contractile speed and fatigue resistance of each unit. Furthermore, the adaptations had disappeared five weeks after the training.

Neuromuscular electrical stimulation is a useful modality in rehabilitation. Some investigators have suggested that it is easier to strengthen hypotrophic muscle with electrical stimulation than it is with voluntary acti-

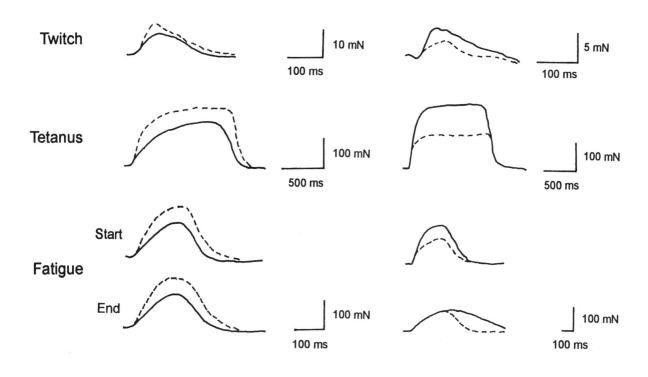

Figure 9.6 Twitch and tetanic forces of two motor units before (solid lines) and after (dashed lines) seven weeks of training with electrical stimulation. The fatigue index (ratio of tetanic force at the start and end of fatiguing contraction) did not change for the unit in the left column but did for the unit in the right column.

Data from Chan et al., 1999.

vation (Godfrey, Jayawardena, & Welsh, 1986; Williams, Morrissey, & Brewster, 1986). In the absence of a neural drive (patients with spinal cord injury), neuromuscular electrical stimulation can preserve muscle properties (Andersen, Mohr, Biering-Sørensen, Galbo, & Kjær, 1996; Kagaya, Shimada, Sato, & Sato, 1996). For example, stimulation (20 Hz) of tibialis anterior for 1 to 2 h over a six-week interval was sufficient to reduce the fatigability of the muscle (increased proportion of type I muscle fibers) and to increase contraction and relaxation times, but not to increase muscle fiber size or strength (Stein et al., 1992). Neuromuscular electrical stimulation can induce a substantial cardiorespiratory stress in paraplegic patients, and with several months of training there is a marked improvement in endurance capabilities (Petrofsky & Stacy, 1992). Neuromuscular electrical stimulation is at least as effective as voluntary exercise at minimizing the atrophy of quadriceps femoris and improving the restoration of gait in patients following reconstruction of the anterior cruciate ligament (Lieber et al., 1996; Snyder-Mackler, Ladin, Schepsis, & Young, 1991).

Example 9.1
The Russian Protocol

As described by Zatsiorsky (1995), the Russian protocol for neuromuscular electrical stimulation comprised the following routine:

- Carrier signal—sinusoidal or triangular
- Frequency—2.5 kHz
- Modulation—50 Hz
- Duty cycle—50%, with 10 ms on and 10 ms off
- Stimulus amplitude—at least sufficient to evoke a force that was equal to MVC force, or up to the level of tolerance
- Contraction time—10 s
- Rest between contractions—50 s
- Number of contractions—10 per day
- Training frequency—5 days per week for ≤25 training days

(continued)

When such a protocol was applied to both calf muscles of eight subjects (16-17 years) for 19 days, there were significant improvements in MVC force, vertical jump height, and calf circumference (figure 9.7).

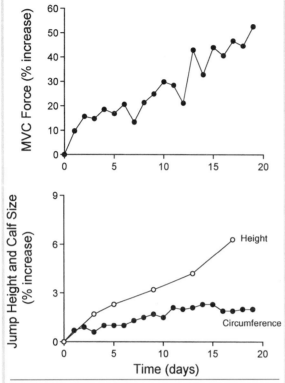

Figure 9.7   Increases in maximum voluntary contraction (MVC) force, vertical jump height, and calf circumference with neuromuscular electrical stimulation.

Data from Zatsiorsky, 1995.

Loading Techniques

Several issues are important to consider when one is deciding how to vary the load in order to induce strength gains; these include progressive-resistance exercises, the magnitude of the load, and the way in which the load varies over the range of motion.

Progressive-Resistance Exercises

The load used in strength training can be manipulated in a number of ways. DeLorme (1945) proposed varying the load systematically from one set of repetitions to another; this technique is known as *progressive-resistance exercises*. As indicated previously, DeLorme's technique involves three sets of repetitions of an exercise in which the load increases with each set. In conventional weight-training programs, this typically means increasing the weight of the barbell from one set to another. However, the torque exerted by muscle depends on the *size of the*

moment arm and the *speed of the movement* in addition to the magnitude of the external load (the amount of the barbell weight). As a consequence, progressive-resistance exercises can be accomplished without changing the size of the load (barbell weight) but simply by varying moment arm length or the speed of the movement. For example, figure 9.8*a* shows an individual in the middle of a bent-knee sit-up. This exercise involves using the abdominal and hip flexor muscles (Andersson, Nilsson, Ma, & Thorstensson, 1996) to raise and lower the upper body. As the four positions shown in figure 9.8*b* indicate, there

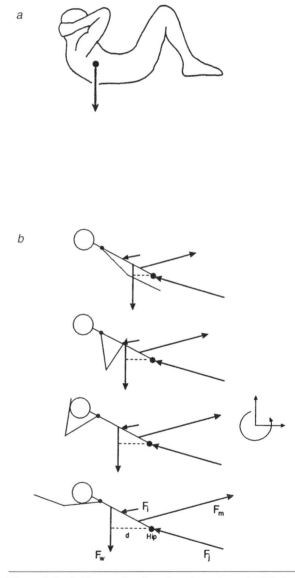

Figure 9.8   Subject performing a bent-knee sit-up. *(a)* Whole-body figure. *(b)* Changing arm position increases the moment arm (d) of the upper-body weight vector *(F_w)* with respect to the hip joint, and thus a greater muscle force *(F_m)* is required to perform the task. F_i and F_j represent the intra-abdominal pressure and the joint reaction forces, respectively.

are four variations of the exercise that involve placing the arms in different positions. The change in the arm position does not alter the weight of the upper body (F_w), but it does shift the center of gravity toward the head and thus increases the moment arm of the system weight relative to the hip joint (dotted line in figure 9.8*b*). The net effect is an increase in the force that the muscles must exert (F_m) to accomplish the movement.

This example (figure 9.8) underscores the general point that the demands imposed on a muscle vary as the posture assumed by the individual changes. This includes changing the relative angles between adjacent body segments and altering the orientation of the body relative to the force of gravity. For example, Zatsiorsky (1995) found that varying the forward lean of the trunk during the squat exercise had a substantial effect on the resultant muscle torque about the knee joint. Similarly, the location in the range of motion at which the load torque is maximum differs when an exercise is performed in a supine compared with a standing position. This feature of progressive-resistance exercises can be used to enhance the diversity of a training program.

Magnitude of the Load

When defining the concept of progressive-resistance exercises, DeLorme (1945) proposed that each of the three sets should include 10 repetitions. Currently, most strength-training programs advocate using from 1 to 8 repetitions in a set. The number of repetitions performed in a set generally determines the load that is lifted; as the load becomes heavier, fewer repetitions are performed. Heavier loads are assumed to increase the stress imposed on the involved muscle. However, this occurs only if the kinematics of the movement remain constant across loads. If an individual performs two squats, for example, one with a barbell weight of 500 N and the other with a weight of 1000 N, then the torque exerted by the knee extensors with the heavier load will be about twice that for the lighter load if the movement is performed in exactly the same way each time. When subjects lifted loads of 40%, 60%, and 80% of the 4-RM load, the kinematics of the movement were altered (e.g., there was more flexion at the hip during a squat), and the resultant muscle torque did not increase in proportion to the load (Hay, Andrews, & Vaughan, 1980; Hay, Andrews, Vaughan, & Ueya, 1983). In weightlifting and in rehabilitation, therefore, it is necessary to focus on the form of the movement to ensure that the appropriate muscles are involved in the task.

Because heavy loads tend to alter the kinematics of a movement, the most favored loads for strength training appear to be about 4 to 6 RM with four sets (three to six) of each exercise (Atha, 1981; Fleck & Kraemer, 1987; McDonagh & Davies, 1984; Sale & MacDougall, 1981). According to the scheme proposed by Sale and MacDougall

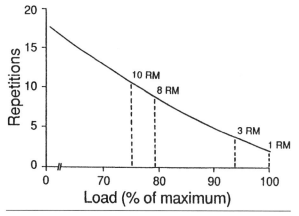

Figure 9.9 The relation between the number of repetitions in an exercise set (RM = repetition maximum) and the magnitude of the load as a percentage of maximum.

Adapted from Sale and MacDougall, 1981.

(1981), a 5- to 6-RM load would be about 85% to 90% of the maximum load (figure 9.9). In contrast, body builders use 8- to 12-RM loads with three to six sets done over several different parts of the range of motion about a joint to increase muscle mass and definition.

McDonagh and Davies (1984) summarized the effect of load with the following statements, which are based on studies that involved *untrained* subjects: loads less than 66% of maximum do not increase strength even with 150 contractions per day; loads greater than 66% of maximum increase strength from 0.5% to 1.0% each training session; and with loads of greater than 66% of maximum, as few as 10 repetitions per session can increase strength. Harre (1982) further suggested that beginners use loads of 60% to 80% of maximum with 8 to 10 repetitions in each set, and that elite athletes use loads of 80% to 100% of maximum with 2 to 5 repetitions per set. There is no difference for recreational weight lifters, however, in the gains in 1-RM load over 13 weeks for one set compared with three sets of repetitions (Hass, Garzarella, De Hoyos, & Pollock, 2000).

An alternative to manipulating the magnitude of the load during weightlifting is to vary the speed of the movement. Some investigators have compared the strength gains achieved with conventional weightlifting exercises to those that result from rapid movements (so-called explosive exercises). Because the maximum force that a muscle can exert declines as the speed of shortening increases (force-velocity relation), there is no obvious reason to suppose that rapid movements might provide a more effective training stimulus. Accordingly, Häkkinen and Komi (1986) found that knee extensor strength did increase in subjects following 20 weeks of weightlifting training (squat exercise) but that strength did not increase in another group of subjects who trained for a similar duration with rapid vertical jumps. In contrast, training of the elbow flexor muscles with heavy loads (90% of 1 RM) and with rapid movements (10% of 1 RM) produced comparable increases in muscle strength and the cross-sectional area of muscle fibers (Dahl, Aaserud, & Jensen, 1992). Several investigators have found that high-speed training improves the rate of force development (Van Cutsem et al., 1998; Young & Bilby, 1993).

Constant and Variable Loads

With the exception of isometric exercises, strength-training activities involve changing the length of an active muscle over a prescribed range of motion. Because the torque that a muscle can exert changes with joint angle (figures 6.25 and 6.27), it is necessary to indicate not only the size of the load but also the way in which the load changes over the range of motion. The main distinction is whether the load applied to the limb either remains constant or varies over the range of motion; these loading strategies are known as **constant-** and **variable-load** training, respectively. In general, free weights (i.e., barbells and dumbbells) provide constant loads whereas machines (e.g., Nautilus, Universal) provide loads that vary over a range of motion.

For example, consider the forearm curl exercise, which involves flexion, then extension of the elbow joint during the lifting of a load. With free weights (figure 9.10a), the load held by the individual remains *constant* through-

out the exercise and acts vertically downward. The magnitude and direction of the load vector (F_l) remain constant over the range of motion (figure 9.10a). With some machines, however, the load held in the hands *varies* over the range of motion (figure 9.10b). The load provided by the machine on the hands is a torque that corresponds to the product of the mass in the weight stack and the moment arm of the cam. Although the mass in the weight stack remains constant for the exercise, the cam is not circular, and so the moment arm varies over the range of motion. The moment arm is the distance from the axis of rotation of the cam to the point at which the cable leaves the cam and connects to the weight stack (figure 9.10b). The variable load is shown in the free body diagram as a change in the length of the load vector.

The effect of the two loading techniques on the resultant muscle torque over the range of motion is shown in figure 9.11. The resultant muscle torque about the elbow joint (τ_m) was determined for the constant- and variable-load tasks (figure 9.10) and compared with the MVC force that was determined with isometric contractions at several joint angles. The load used for the constant- and variable-load tasks was 60% of 4 RM. The main comparison, which relates to the touted advantage of variable-load devices, is that the resultant muscle torque during the variable-load exercise paralleled the change in MVC force. Hence, the involved muscle experienced a

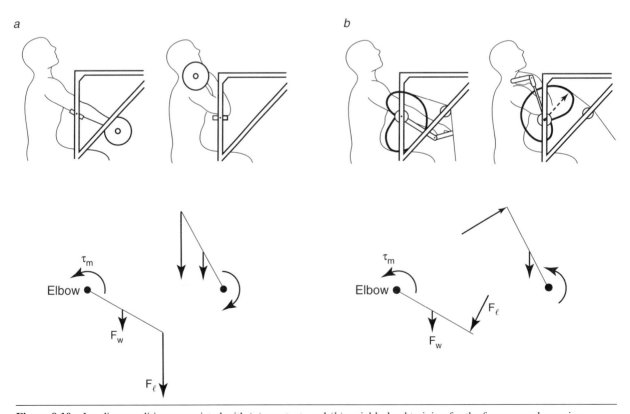

Figure 9.10 Loading conditions associated with *(a)* constant- and *(b)* variable-load training for the forearm curl exercise.

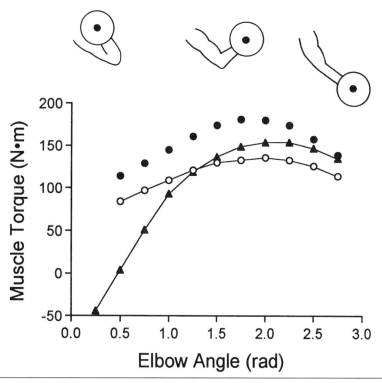

Figure 9.11   Resultant muscle torque about the elbow joint during a forearm curl exercise with a barbell (▲) and a Nautilus machine (○) in comparison with the MVC torque (●) that can be exerted over the range of motion.

Adapted from Smith, 1982.

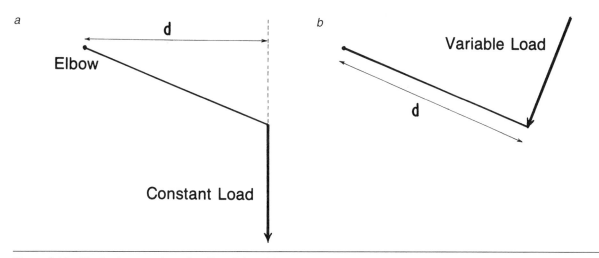

Figure 9.12   The load torque about the elbow joint with *(a)* a constant load or *(b)* a variable load held in the hands.

similar relative stress throughout the range of motion. In contrast, the resultant muscle torque for the constant load experienced a much greater change over the range of motion.

The reason for the difference is that the load applied to the hands is not the same as the load about the elbow joint. Specifically, the load torque about the elbow joint is the product of the load at the hands and the moment arm from the hands to the joint (figure 9.12). For the constant-load exercise, the moment arm varies from zero when the arm is vertical to a maximum when the forearm is horizontal. In contrast, the direction of the variable-load vector is approximately perpendicular to the arm over the range of motion, which means that the moment arm from the hands to the joint changes very little. Thus, contrary to the names, the load torque about the elbow joint varies more with the constant load than it does for the variable load.

Example 9.2
A Cam With Two Moment Arms

An alternative design for variable-load devices involves two moment arms, one related to the cable that goes to the weight stack and another related to the cable that goes to the lifter. In such designs, the two moment arms vary in a reciprocal manner, as dictated by the shape of the cam (figure 9.13). The variation in moment arms depends on the strength capability of an average adult throughout a given range of motion. At the location of greatest strength (figure 9.13*a*), the lifter's moment arm *(d)* is less than the load's moment arm *(e)*. Conversely, the lengths of the two moment arms are reversed in regions of least strength (figure 9.13*b*). With this scheme, the variable load (weight stack × moment arm) is greatest where the lifter is strongest. This enables the machine to provide a variable load that matches the strength capability of the average adult throughout a prescribed range of motion.

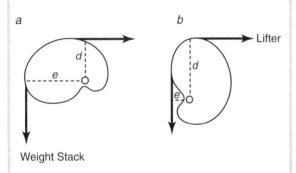

Figure 9.13 A variable-load cam that controls two moment arms. *(a)* Due to the shape of the cam, the moment arm for the cable going to the lifter is greater than that for the cable to the weight stack. *(b)* The converse occurs in a different location in the range of motion.

Data from Stone and O'Bryant, 1987.

Neuromuscular Adaptations

Changes in muscle strength are generally attributed to either neural or muscular factors. The principal muscular factor is muscle size (Lieber & Fridén, 2000). As indicated in figure 3.4, variation in the cross-sectional area of muscle between individuals can account for about 50% of the differences in strength. In addition, the efficacy of

force transmission from the sarcomeres to the skeleton likely varies among individuals due to differences in the cytoskeleton and associated connective tissue structures. Two lines of evidence, however, suggest that some differences in strength depend on other factors, perhaps involving the nervous system (Semmler & Enoka, 2000). These are the dissociation between changes in muscle size and strength and the specificity of the strength gains.

Dissociated Changes in Muscle Size and Strength

Two examples of dissociated changes are the timing of the adaptations and the strength gains that can be achieved without muscle activation. The timing example occurs during the early stages of a strength-training program when the increase in EMG precedes the muscle hypertrophy (Akima et al., 1999; Häkkinen, Alén, & Komi, 1985; Häkkinen & Komi, 1986; Rutherford & Jones, 1986). For example, figure 9.14 shows the time course of changes in the cross-sectional area of quadriceps femoris (as determined by magnetic resonance imaging, MRI), integrated EMG, and the maximum isometric force in response to 60 days of training and 40 days of detraining (Narici, Roi, Landoni, Minetti, & Ceretelli, 1989). Similarly, eight weeks of training increased the load that subjects could lift by 100% to 200%, but there were no changes in the cross-sectional areas of muscle fibers (Staron et al., 1994).

Dissociated changes in muscle size and strength have also been demonstrated with protocols that evoke an increase in muscle strength without even subjecting the

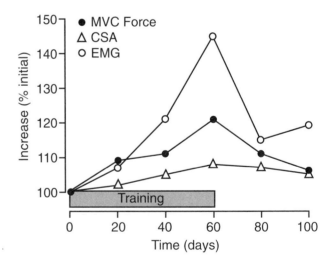

Figure 9.14 Changes in cross-sectional area (CSA) of the quadriceps femoris, integrated EMG of vastus lateralis during a maximum contraction, and the maximum voluntary contraction (MVC) force during isokinetic training and detraining.

Adapted from Narici, Roi, Landoni, Minetti, and Ceretelli, 1989.

muscle to physical training. This occurs, for example, when subjects train one limb and experience a strength gain in the contralateral limb. This effect is known as **cross education** (Semmler & Enoka, 2000; Zhou, 2000). Most studies examining cross education have indicated that when the muscles in one limb participate in a strength-training program, the homologous muscles in the contralateral limb experience an increase in strength despite the absence of activation during the training program and no change in muscle fiber characteristics. A cross-education effect even occurs when the training program involves neuromuscular electrical stimulation (Hortobágyi, Scott, Lambert, Hamilton, & Tracy, 1999). On average, the strength gain in the contralateral limb is about 60% of that achieved in the trained limb (figure 9.15).

A related effect occurs with imagined contractions. A four-week program of training with imagined MVCs increased the MVC force by 22% compared with a 30% increase for subjects who actually performed contractions during training (Yue & Cole, 1992). Furthermore, the cross-education effect was 11% for the subjects who performed imagined contractions and 14% for those who performed actual contractions. However, the subjects in this study were sedentary, and the muscle was an intrinsic hand muscle (abductor digiti minimi). When a similar protocol was performed on the elbow flexor muscles with subjects who were able to activate the muscles maximally by voluntary command, the imagined contractions

did not increase strength (Herbert, Dean, & Gandevia, 1998). The efficacy of imagined contractions, therefore, appears to depend on the involved muscles and the activity level of the individual.

Specificity of Strength Gains

If the strength of a muscle largely depended on its size, we would expect the maximum force exerted by a muscle to be the same whenever the muscle is activated maximally. This does not happen (Almåsbakk & Hoff, 1996; Wilson et al., 1996). In general, the improvement in strength is greatest when the training and testing modalities are the same and less when the modalities differ. For example, 12 weeks of training consisting of raising and lowering a load with the knee extensor muscles produced ~200% increases in 1-RM load but only ~20% increases in the isometric MVC force (Rutherford & Jones, 1986). Similarly, 20 weeks of training the elbow flexor muscles with a hydraulic resistance device increased the cross-sectional area of the involved muscles but task- and gender-dependent increases in strength (O'Hagan, Sale, MacDougall, & Garner, 1995). The increases in peak force on the hydraulic device at the speed used in training, as well as the increases in 1-RM load, were about 50% for men and 120% for women. In contrast, the peak torque exerted on an isokinetic dynamometer at four angular velocities did not change by much (<25% increase).

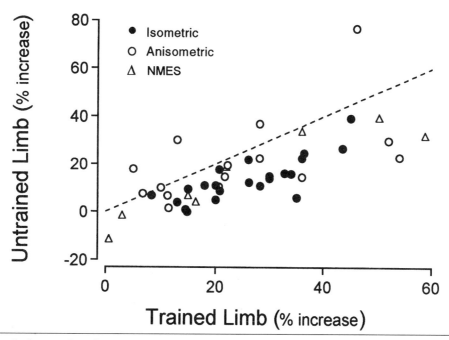

Figure 9.15 Results from studies of cross education show the range of associations between increases in strength for the trained and untrained limbs. Strength, measured as the MVC force, was increased by voluntary contractions or by neuromuscular electrical stimulation (NMES) in several different muscles. Most values lie below the line of identity (dashed line), which indicates that the increase in strength in the trained limb was greater than that in the untrained limb.

Adapted from Enoka, 1988.

The specificity of the strength gains is most pronounced for tasks that require more learning, such as less constrained movements (Chilibeck, Calder, Sale, & Webber, 1998; Rutherford & Jones, 1986; Wilson et al., 1996), those involving voluntary activation compared with electrical stimulation (McDonagh, Hayward, & Davies, 1983; Young, McDonagh, & Davies, 1985), and those involving eccentric contractions (Higbie et al., 1996). For example, 12 weeks of training the knee extensor muscles on an isokinetic dynamometer produced greater specificity in the subjects who trained with eccentric contractions than in those who trained with concentric contractions (figure 9.16). In addition, cross education was greater in subjects who used eccentric contractions (Hortobágyi, Lambert, & Hill, 1997) and even greater when the eccentric contractions were evoked with neuromuscular electrical stimulation (Hortobágyi et al., 1999).

The extensive literature on the specificity of training indicates that improvements in strength are often unrelated to changes in muscle size. Observations on specificity are usually interpreted as indicating a significant role for learning and coordination (Laidlaw, Kornatz, Keen, Suzuki, & Enoka, 1999; Rutherford & Jones, 1986).

Neural Factors

Based on the time course of the adaptations, phenomena such as cross education, and the specificity of training, it appears possible to obtain an increase in strength without an adaptation in the muscle, but not without an adaptation in the nervous system. Nonetheless, it has proved difficult to identify specific mechanisms that underlie these changes. Figure 9.17 indicates some potential sites within the nervous system where the adaptations may occur. The adaptations might involve activation maximality, coactivation of antagonist muscles, plastic-

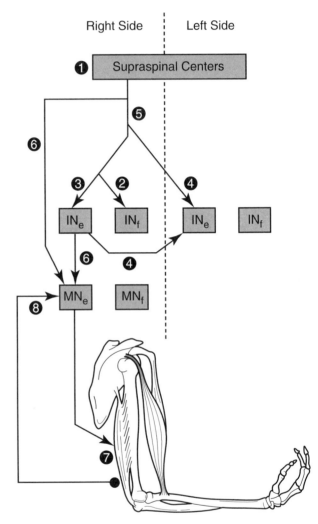

Figure 9.17 Potential sites of adaptations in the nervous system that might contribute to increases in strength: (1) enhanced output from supraspinal centers, as suggested by findings with imagined contractions; (2) reduced coactivation of antagonist muscles; (3) greater activation of synergist muscles; (4) enhanced coupling among spinal interneurons (IN) that produces cross education; (5) changes in descending drive that reduce the bilateral deficit; (6) shared input to motor neurons that increases motor unit synchronization; (7) greater muscle activation (EMG); and (8) heightened excitability and altered connections onto motor neurons (MN). The scheme indicates potential interactions between limbs (right and left sides) and between extensor (e) and flexor (f) muscles.

Data from Semmler and Enoka, 2000.

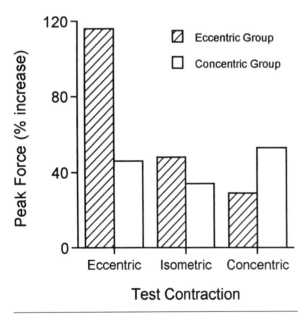

Figure 9.16 Specificity of the increases in peak force exerted by the knee extensor muscles on an isokinetic dynamometer. Some subjects trained with concentric contractions and others with eccentric contractions. Peak forces were measured for both groups of subjects while they performed eccentric, isometric, and concentric contractions.

Data from Hortobágyi, Hill, et al., 1996.

ity in the spinal cord, and coordination of the muscles involved in the task.

Activation Maximality   As represented by sites 1, 6, and 7 in figure 9.17, one neural adaptation that might contribute to strength gains is an increase in the neural drive to the muscle during an MVC (Fisher & White, 1999). This possibility has been examined by measuring changes in the EMG and testing the activation maximality with the twitch interpolation technique (figure 8.14). For example, the summed EMG for vastus lateralis and vastus medialis increased along with performance on isometric contractions, 1-RM lifts, and vertical jumps after six months of training (Häkkinen et al., 1998). Others, however, have found that improvements in strength are accompanied by task-specific increases in EMG, a non-monotonic change in EMG, or no change in EMG (Carolan & Cafarelli, 1992; Higbie et al., 1996; Hortobágyi, Barrier, et al., 1996; Keen et al., 1994; Laidlaw et al., 1999).

Furthermore, most investigators find that well-motivated, healthy subjects can activate limb muscles at close to maximum by voluntary command, as indicated by the twitch interpolation technique (Allen et al., 1998; De Serres & Enoka, 1998; Merton, 1954). Other measures, however, such as tetanic stimulation, MRI-based T_2 relaxation time, and the force-frequency relation of motor units, suggest that activation is not maximal during an MVC (Adams, Harris, et al., 1993; Enoka, 1995; Kent-Braun & Le Blanc, 1996). There remains some uncertainty, therefore, about whether activation is maximal during the measurement of strength.

Coactivation of Antagonist Muscles   The resultant muscle torque about a joint depends on the difference in the torque exerted by opposing muscles. Consequently, one way to increase strength is to reduce the size of the opposing muscle torque (site 2 in figure 9.17). Although activation of the antagonist muscle can decline with strength training and is less in elite athletes, the magnitude of the reduction is relatively minor compared with the improvements in strength (Amiridis et al., 1996; Carolan & Cafarelli, 1992; Häkkinen et al., 1998). Thus a reduction in coactivation of the antagonist muscles does not appear to contribute significantly to strength gains achieved by agonist muscles.

Spinal Cord Connections   Observations on cross education, the bilateral deficit, motor unit synchronization, and reflex potentiation suggest that adaptations at the level of the spinal cord are capable of contributing to increases in strength. Although cross education (site 4 in figure 9.17) occurs after training with imagined contractions, the effect is greater after training with actual contractions, especially electrically evoked contractions (Hortobágyi et al., 1999; Zhou, 2000). These comparisons suggest that the effect is dominated by interlimb interactions at the level of the spinal cord.

In contrast to the facilitative interlimb effects observed with cross education, the concurrent activation of both limbs typically causes a reduction in strength. The decline in force that occurs during an MVC under these conditions is referred to as a **bilateral deficit** (Howard & Enoka, 1991; Li, Latash, & Zatsiorsky, 1998; Ohtsuki, 1983; Secher, Rube, & Elers, 1988). The bilateral deficit (site 5 in figure 9.17) occurs when homologous muscles in two limbs or multiple fingers in the same hand exert an MVC. An example of a bilateral deficit is shown in figure 9.18 for a task that involved isometric contractions of the triceps brachii muscles with the elbow at about a right angle. Each column in figure 9.18 corresponds to one trial. In Trial 1 (left column), the subject

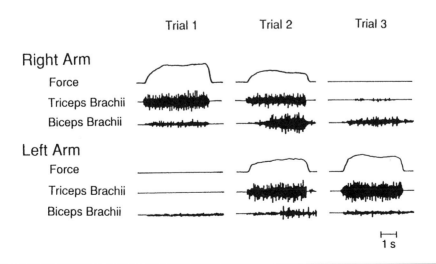

Figure 9.18   Maximum force and EMG of the elbow extensor muscles during maximum voluntary contractions performed with the right arm, both arms, and the left arm.

Adapted from Ohtsuki, 1983.

performed a maximum isometric contraction with the right arm. In Trial 2 (middle column), the subject concurrently activated the elbow extensors of both arms maximally. In Trial 3 (right column), the subject performed a maximum isometric contraction with the left arm. The critical feature of the graph is that both the maximum force exerted by each arm and the quantity of EMG were *less* during the bilateral contraction compared to the force and EMG during the single-limb trial. The reduction in force with a bilateral deficit averages about 5% to 10% of maximum but can be substantial (25-54%), especially during rapid contractions (Koh, Grabiner, & Clough, 1993).

Although most studies that have examined bilateral interactions have reported a bilateral deficit, it appears that bilateral interactions are modifiable with training (Secher, 1975; Taniguchi, 1998). For example, Howard and Enoka (1991) compared the maximum isometric force exerted during one- and two-limb knee extensor contractions and found a bilateral deficit for untrained subjects (–9.5%) and elite cyclists (–6.6%) but a **bilateral facilitation** for weight lifters (+6.2%). A bilateral facilitation means that the maximum isometric force occurred during the bilateral contraction rather than the unilateral contraction. This adaptation is presumably mediated by the long-term patterns of muscle activation that affect the descending drive to the interneuronal pools.

One of the most frequently cited examples of neural adaptations that accompany strength training is a change in the amount of motor unit synchronization (site 6 in figure 9.17). This property describes the amount of correlation between the discharge of various motor units. It is a measure of the temporal coincidence of action potentials from different motor units. A high degree of synchrony means that motor units tend to discharge action potentials at about the same time, which indicates enhanced patterns of shared synaptic input onto motor neurons (Datta & Stephens, 1990; Nordstrom et al., 1992; Sears & Stagg, 1976). This type of analysis has indicated that there is a modest degree of synchrony between motor units. The amount of synchronization, however, is greater among motor units in the hand muscles of individuals who consistently perform strength-training activities (Milner-Brown et al., 1975; Semmler & Nordstrom, 1998). Nonetheless, computer simulations suggest that increases in motor unit synchronization do not produce an increase in the force during isometric contractions (Yao et al., 2000).

Spinal cord adaptations have also been observed in the testing of reflexes (site 8 in figure 9.17). Electrical stimulation of a muscle nerve can evoke two reflex responses (V1 and V2) in addition to the M wave. Changes in the amplitude of V1 and V2 relative to M-wave amplitude are an index of reflex potentiation (Sale, 1988). Reflex potentiation has been found to occur in all muscles

tested, to be more pronounced in weight lifters than sprinters, to increase with strength training, and to decrease with limb immobilization (Sale, McComas, MacDougall, & Upton, 1982). Subsequent studies on operant conditioning of the stretch reflex and the H reflex suggest that much of the plasticity appears to be located in the spinal cord, to involve the motor neurons, and also to be expressed in the contralateral, untrained limb (Carp & Wolpaw, 1994; Wolpaw, 1994; Wolpaw & Lee, 1989).

These studies demonstrate that participation in a strength-training program can induce changes in the connections between motor neurons located in the spinal cord. However, the relative significance of these effects is unknown.

Coordination   Of all the potential neural factors, perhaps the most significant is the coordination of activity among the muscles involved in the strength task. This is the most likely explanation for the specificity of strength gains. For example, Rutherford and Jones (1986) trained a group of subjects for 12 weeks with a bilateral knee extension task. The subjects used a 6-RM load. Both the MVC force and the training load were recorded over the course of the training program. The relative changes in MVC force and training load are shown in figure 9.19. The increase in MVC force, which is evident as a shift along the *x*-axis, was 20% for the men and 4% for the women. In contrast, the training load increased, as shown by a shift along the *y*-axis, by 200% for the men and by 240% for the women. Because MVC force was tested with an isometric contraction whereas the training involved anisometric contractions, the greater increase in training load must have been due to an improvement in the coordination associated with the knee extension task. In a similar example, subjects who strength-trained a hand muscle for 8 weeks experienced a 33% increase in MVC force but only an 11% increase in the tetanic force evoked by electrical stimulation (Davies, Dooley, McDonagh, & White, 1985). Furthermore, when another group of subjects trained the muscle with electrical stimulation for 8 weeks, there was no change in the evoked tetanic force whereas the MVC force declined by 11%. Similarly, strength training has been shown to enhance the stability of coordination between fingers (Carroll, Barry, Riek, & Carson, 2001).

The adaptations that underlie task specificity could involve changes among the motor units in a single muscle, between muscles in a group of synergists, or whole-body postural mechanics. An example of within-muscle adaptations involves the steadiness of submaximal contractions. When subjects exert low forces or lift light loads with the fingers, arms, or legs, the fluctuations in force are greater for old adults (Galganski, Fuglevand, & Enoka, 1993; Laidlaw et al., 2000). After several weeks of strength training, however, the steadiness exhibited by old adults improves and becomes similar to that of young

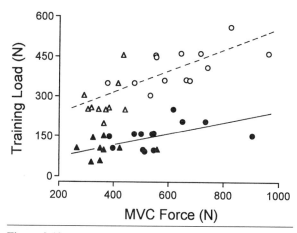

Figure 9.19 The relation between maximum voluntary contraction force and training load in men (circles) and women (triangles) before (filled symbols) and after (open symbols) a 12-week training program.

Adapted from Rutherford and Jones, 1986.

adults (Keen et al., 1994). The improvement in performance is not associated with a change in the distribution of motor unit forces but probably involves an adaptation related to the discharge rate of the activated motor units (Laidlaw et al., 2000). A similar example concerns the reduced volume of muscle that was activated to lift a submaximal load after participation in a strength-training program (Ploutz, Tesch, Biro, & Dudley, 1994).

An example of the interaction among synergists involves the ability of two-joint muscles to distribute net moments of force and to transfer power between joints (Ingen Schenau, Boots, de Groot, Snackers, & Woenzel, 1992). This capability is presented in figure 7.6. On the basis of this scheme, the two-joint muscles can redistribute some of the muscle torque and joint power from the hip to the knee or from the knee to the hip. Such interactions probably explain why weight lifters appear to perform extraneous contractions when lifting heavy loads, such as arching the back when performing a bench press or a knee extension exercise.

Alternatively, some proportion of a strength gain is likely attributable to the postural activity associated with a task. Because the human body is a linked mechanical system, it is necessary to orient the body segments and to set the base of support on which the movement is performed (Horak & Macpherson, 1996). The elbow flexor muscles, for example, could lift a handheld weight with the body in a variety of postures, including standing, sitting, prone, or supine positions. Such variations in posture appear to influence the outcome of a training program as indicated by studies on the specificity of strength gains. For example, eight weeks of strength training with the bench-press and squat lifts increased 1-RM load and vertical jump height by 21% and a 6-s test on a cycle ergometer by 10%, but there was no change in performance on an isokinetic dynamometer (Wilson et al.,

1996). The improvements in performance were greatest in the tests involving postures that were used during training. The significance of postural adaptations is often neglected in studies on strength training.

Although a compelling case can be made for a significant role of neural factors in strength gains, the specific mechanisms remain elusive. There is neither a consensus on individual mechanisms nor evidence on the relative significance of the various mechanisms.

Muscular Factors

In contrast to the uncertainties regarding the neural factors, there is no doubt that specific muscular factors contribute to differences in strength among individuals and across time. As we discussed in chapter 3, there is a strong correlation between MVC force and cross-sectional area (figure 3.4). This same relation also applies at the level of single motor units and muscle fibers. An increase in cross-sectional area of muscle size can be caused by **hypertrophy,** an increase in the cross-sectional area of individual muscle fibers, or by **hyperplasia,** an increase in the number of muscle fibers. Most experimental evidence suggests that the typical response of human subjects to strength training involves hypertrophy but that hyperplasia may occur under some conditions, which are not yet known (Antonio & Gonyea, 1993; Higbie et al., 1996; Hortobágyi et al., 1996; Kawakami et al., 1995; McCall, Byrnes, Dickinson, Pattany, & Fleck, 1996; Narici et al., 1996).

The magnitude of the training-induced increase in *cross-sectional area* depends on several factors, including the initial strength of the individual, the duration of the training program, and the training technique used. In novice subjects, 6 weeks of isometric training increased the cross-sectional area of the elbow flexor muscles (biceps brachii, brachioradialis) by about 5% (Davies et al., 1988), whereas 8 weeks of isometric training increased the cross-sectional area of the quadriceps femoris by 15% (Garfinkel & Cafarelli, 1992). Similarly, 60 days of isokinetic training at 2.1 rad/s with the knee extensors increased the cross-sectional area of the quadriceps femoris by 9% (Narici et al., 1989). Furthermore, 19 weeks of eccentric-concentric knee extensor exercises produced a greater increase in cross-sectional area than exercises that involved only concentric contractions (Hather, Tesch, Buchanan, & Dudley, 1991). In contrast, 24 weeks of dynamic training by experienced body builders failed to elicit an increase in the cross-sectional area of muscle fibers in biceps brachii (Alway et al., 1992).

The effect of strength training on the various muscle fiber types can also be diverse. For example, 16 weeks of isometric training with the triceps surae muscles did not alter the fiber-type proportions in either soleus or lateral gastrocnemius despite a 45% increase in MVC force (Alway et al., 1989). In contrast, 19 weeks of a knee extension exercise produced an increase in the proportion of type IIa muscle fibers and a decrease in the proportion of type IId (IIb) muscle fibers in vastus lateralis (Hather, Tesch, Buchanan, & Dudley, 1991). This even included a reduction in the type IId (IIb) myosin heavy chains (MHCs) (Adams, Hather, Baldwin, & Dudley, 1993), which appear to involve a change in the mRNA isoform expression (Caiozzo, Haddad, Baker, & Baldwin, 1996). Similarly, the 16-week isometric program increased the cross-sectional area of type I (20%) and II (27%) muscle fibers in soleus and the type II fibers (50%), but not the type I fibers, in lateral gastrocnemius. Furthermore, the increase in cross-sectional area of muscle fibers is greater for an eccentric-concentric program (type I, 14% increase; type II, 32% increase) than for a concentric program (type II, 27% increase) (Häkkinen, 1985). These observations show that not all the muscle fibers in an active group of synergist muscles experience the same training stimulus.

Although strength training can induce hypertrophy, differences in muscle size account for only about 50% of the differences in strength between individuals (Jones et al., 1989; Narici et al., 1996). This association is apparent in figure 3.4 as the scatter of the data points about the regression lines. This raises the question whether there are other changes, besides neural factors, that can occur in muscle to account for differences in strength. One possibility appears to be differences in normalized force (chapter 3). For example, muscle strength and size were measured for the elbow flexor and knee extensor muscles in men and women (table 9.1). Muscle strength was measured as the peak force exerted on an isokinetic device at an angular velocity of 1.0 rad/s, and the maximum anatomical cross-sectional area for each muscle group was measured with ultrasound. The normalized force, which indicates the force that can be achieved per unit of cross-sectional area, was similar between men and women for the elbow flexor muscles but different for the knee extensor muscles.

The data in table 9.1 demonstrate that the strength of a muscle depends partly on its size, as characterized by its cross-sectional area. The other muscular factor is specific tension (chapter 3), which represents the intrinsic force-generating capacity of the muscle fibers. On the basis of measurements made on segments of muscle fibers, specific tension has been found to vary with muscle fiber type, to decline selectively with aging, and to increase for some fiber types with sprint training (Bottinelli & Reggiani, 2000; Harridge et al., 1996, 1998; Larsson et al., 1996, 1997). For example, the specific tension of an average type II muscle fiber in vastus lateralis was greater than that for a type I muscle fiber in young and active old adults but not for sedentary old adults. Presumably, specific tension can change with participation in a strength-training program.

At least two mechanisms can account for variations in specific tension. These are the density of the myofilaments in the muscle fiber and the efficacy of force transmission from the sarcomeres to the skeleton. Because the force that a muscle can exert depends on the number of force-generating units that are in parallel (figure 6.16), differences in strength for muscles of the same size could be due to differences in the density of the myofilaments. Although myofilament density does not appear to change after six weeks of training with anisometric contractions (Claasen, Gerber, Hoppeler, Lüthi, & Vock, 1989), it may be a significant factor in longer-duration programs and different types of exercise protocols. Alternatively, specific tension could be influenced by variation in the structural elements that transmit force from the sarcomeres to the skeleton (Patel & Lieber, 1997; Sheard, 2000). This process involves the cytoskeletal proteins (figure 5.8), which could become more effective at transmitting force after participation in a strength-training program or less effective after a program of inactivity (Chopard, Pons, & Marini, 2001). One candidate, for example, could be the integrins, which serve as a link between the extracellular matrix and the cytoskeleton and appear to be an important component in the response of a cell to the mechanical signals in its surroundings (Carson & Wei, 2000).

Table 9.1 Normalized Forces for Strength Data

	MVC force (N)	CSA (cm^2)	Normalized force
Elbow flexors			
Men	130 ± 4	141 ± 0.4	9.2
Women	89 ± 4	91 ± 0.2	9.8
Knee extensors			
Men	477 ± 17	74 ± 2	6.5
Women	317 ± 15	62 ± 2	5.1

MVC = maximal voluntary contraction; CSA = cross-sectional area.

Note: Data from Kanehisa, Ikegawa, & Fukunaga, 1994.

Example 9.3
Strength-Training Strategies

We can appreciate the practical issues related to the development of strength compared with muscle mass if we compare the training strategies used by weight lifters and body builders. The goal of weight lifters is to increase the maximum load that can be lifted in prescribed events, whereas the goal of body builders is to increase muscle mass. As described by Garhammer and Takano (1992), weightlifting programs are based on the concept of periodization, which means that the training program is divided into several phases. The original model of periodization comprised a preparation phase and a competition phase. The preparation phase is characterized by high volume and low intensity, which means many repetitions and relatively light loads—for example, 6 to 15 training sessions a week, three to six exercises each session, with each exercise comprising four to eight sets of four to six repetitions. The competition phase, in contrast, would involve 5 to 12 training sessions a week, one to four exercises each session, with each exercise comprising three to five sets of one to three repetitions. A weight lifter may train five or six days a week with one to three sessions each day. The duration of each phase may last from several weeks to several months, and two or more complete cycles of preparation and competition may fit into a single training year.

In contrast, body builders tend to use lighter loads (6 to 12 RM) and to reach exhaustion in each set of repetitions (Tesch, 1992). Elite body builders use a split system with four consecutive days of training followed by a day off. The split system focuses on two or three major muscle groups in a training session (table 9.2). Each muscle group performs 20 to 25 sets of repetitions (6 to 12) for a total of 40 to 70 sets in a single session. Body builders use brief intervals (1-2 min) between sets of exercises. This training approach, which appears to maximize muscle hypertrophy, focuses on high volume (sets × repetitions × load) with each muscle group worked to failure. The physiological mechanisms responsible for these different effects are unknown.

Table 9.2 Split System Used by Body Builders

Day 1	Day 2	Day 3	Day 4	Day 5
Chest	Quadriceps	Back	Hamstrings	Rest
Triceps brachii	Calves	Biceps brachii	Shoulders	
		Abdominals		

Note. Scheme taken from Tesch, 1992.

Although it is widely accepted that muscle hypertrophy requires a change in the ratio of protein synthesis to degradation, the mechanisms controlling the ratio have not been clearly defined. The potential stimuli for muscle hypertrophy include hormonal, metabolic, and mechanical factors (Jones et al., 1989). *Hormonal stimuli* (e.g., insulin, growth hormone, testosterone) are unlikely to provide the key stimulus for hypertrophy because unlike the distribution of a hormone, the change in cross-sectional area can be limited to one muscle fiber type or one muscle. In addition, the increases in muscle size, strength, and muscle protein that occur with strength training are not further enhanced by the administration of growth hormone (Yarasheski et al., 1992). Nonetheless, hormones may have a permissive effect for other factors. A thyroid hormone (T3), for example, seems to have a significant effect on the expression of type I and IIa MHC (Caiozzo, Herrick, & Baldwin, 1991, 1992; Fitzsimons, Herrick, & Baldwin, 1990).

Activity that stresses *metabolic factors* tends to result in improvements in endurance rather than strength. However, there does appear to be some association between factors related to greater metabolite changes during exercise and the enhancement of muscle cross-sectional area. For example, greater training-induced increases in MVC force and cross-sectional area of the quadriceps femoris were associated with elevated changes in phosphate metabolites and pH (Schott, McCully, & Rutherford, 1995). These metabolite changes may directly stimulate protein synthesis or cause the release of local growth factors.

In contrast, evidence suggests that *mechanical stimuli* are important for muscle hypertrophy (Stamenovic & Wang, 2000; Vandenburgh, 1992). The mechanism by which this occurs involves the application of a mechanical stimulus (e.g., stretch, contraction) that leads to the release of a second messenger and the subsequent modulation of the rates of protein synthesis and degradation. For example, intermittent stretch of skeletal muscle cells in culture results in an increase in the synthesis of different prostaglandins that can modulate protein synthesis and protein degradation (Vandenburgh, Hatfaludy, Sohar, & Shansky, 1990). There are two classes of second messengers: (a) extracellular matrix molecules (e.g., proteoglycans, collagen, laminin, fibronectin) that surround cells, transmit the mechanical stimulus to the cell surface, and influence nuclear events and cell growth; and (b) stretch-induced alterations in plasma membrane-associated molecules (e.g., Na^+-K^+ adenosinetriphosphatase [ATPase], ion channels, phospholipases, G proteins) and associated cytoplasmic second messengers (e.g., prostaglandins, cyclic AMP, inositol phosphates, intracellular Ca^{2+}, protein kinase C).

Mechanical stimuli influence not only the quantity but also the quality of the protein that is synthesized (Booth & Baldwin, 1996). This is accomplished through regulation of the expression of genes that determines muscle fiber phenotype, which depends on the protein-isoform genes that are transcribed. Goldspink et al. (1992) examined this effect by determining the consequences of mechanical stimuli on the MHC genes (Goldspink et al., 1992). These genes encode the myosin cross-bridge and are different for slow- and fast-twitch muscle (table 5.3). Goldspink and colleagues concluded that the gene for the fast MHC is the default gene and that the expression of the slow MHC depends on the mechanical environment. For example, they found that stimulation regimes eliciting maximal force, especially when the protocol involved muscle stretch, were effective at resulting in the expression of the slow MHC and repressing the expression of the fast MHC. However, much remains to be learned about the connection between mechanical stimuli and the activation or repression of various muscle genes (Booth, Tseng, Flück, & Carson, 1998; Williams & Neufer, 1996).

In addition to a potential role of hormonal, metabolic, and mechanical factors in the hypertrophic response, developmental factors also determine muscular adaptations (Booth & Baldwin, 1996). Cells undergoing myogenesis in the absence of neural input develop distinct subpopulations of myotubes (which subsequently become mature muscle fibers) that have a limited capacity to change phenotype (Hoh, 1991; Hoh & Hughes, 1988). Moreover, this fiber-type differentiation produces muscle fibers that can respond to certain physiological perturbations (e.g., weight training, unloading, denervation) and those that do not respond—so-called *respond-*

ers and *nonresponders.* The exact proportions of these fiber types in different muscles and the variability between individuals remain to be determined. Consequently, a given training stimulus is unlikely to elicit the same hypertrophic response in all muscles or to be similar for different individuals (Thomis et al., 1998).

Muscle Power

At the beginning of this chapter, we noted that strength and power are measures of the output of the motor system. One useful way to distinguish between these two parameters is to consider the force-velocity relation of muscle (figures 6.14 and 6.27). The force-velocity relation is characterized as comprising four distinct regions: velocity = 0, force = 0, velocity > 0, and velocity < 0. Strength is usually defined as the point on the force-velocity curve where velocity is close to zero, whereas the power produced by the motor system corresponds to the region in which velocity ≠ 0.

The power that a muscle can produce depends on the product of muscle force and the velocity of shortening (figures 6.22 and 6.31). Power production is maximal when the muscle acts against a load that is about one-third of MVC force or when the muscle shortens at one-third of the maximum shortening velocity (chapter 6). Consequently any adaptation that increases the maximum force a muscle can exert or its maximum shortening velocity will increase the maximum power that it can produce (Siff, 2000). In this section, we consider the measurement of power production at various levels of the motor system and the chronic adaptations that occur with training.

Power Production and Movement

Success in many athletic endeavors depends on the ability of the performer to sustain power production at the highest level possible for the duration of the event. This is known as the **critical power** (Walsh, 2000). The maximum sustainable power is inversely related to the duration of the event. Despite this significant role for power production, it is one of the least-examined biomechanical parameters in the analysis of human movement. Some of this lack of attention can be attributed to the difficulty associated with measuring power and the abstract nature of the parameter. The next few sections provide examples that address these two issues.

Power Production and Whole-Body Tasks

The power produced by the motor system can be determined by a task performance (e.g., vertical jump, weightlifting), with the use of an ergometer, or by an isolated-muscle experiment. The evaluation of a task performance provides an index of whole-body power. The vertical jump is commonly used for this purpose. The average power produced during a squat jump, which involves only concentric contractions, can be estimated by kinematic or kinetic measurements as we discussed in chapter 2. These procedures can be performed quite quickly and are useful for monitoring the progress of athletes during a training program or for comparing the efficacy of various training strategies.

For both the kinematic and kinetic approaches, it is necessary to obtain estimates of the average power and average velocity during the movement. The kinematic approach involves calculating the average power during the descent of the flight phase, which must equal the power provided to the body during the takeoff phase. As indicated by Equation 2.35, the calculation requires only the mass of the individual *(m)* and the height to which the center of mass is raised *(r)*:

$$\overline{P} = (9.81 \cdot m) \cdot \sqrt{r \cdot 4.9}$$

The first term $(9.81 \cdot m)$ corresponds to the average force, and the second term $\left(\sqrt{r \cdot 4.9}\right)$ indicates the average velocity during the descent phase.

Alternatively, we can estimate the average power by performing a kinetic analysis, which is based on the vertical component of the ground reaction force (figure 9.20). As indicated in Equation 2.36, the calculation requires knowledge of the net impulse (shaded area in figure 9.20; $\int F_{net}\,dt$), the absolute impulse ($\int F_{g,y}\,dt$), the duration of the propulsive phase of the impulse *(t)*, and the mass of the individual.

$$\overline{P} = \frac{\int F_{g,y}\,dt}{t} \cdot \frac{\int F_{net}\,dt}{2\,m}$$

The first term indicates the average force and the second term the average velocity. Another kinetic approach is to use Equation 2.37, which is based on the change in mechanical energy (potential and kinetic energy).

$$\overline{P} = \frac{m\,g(r+h)}{t}$$

where *r* = jump height, *h* = vertical displacement of the jumper's center of mass during the takeoff phase, and *t* = the duration of the propulsive phase of the vertical impulse.

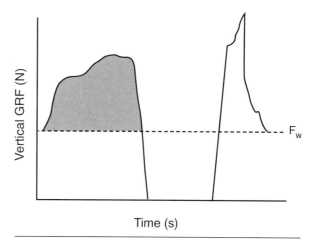

Figure 9.20   Vertical component of the ground reaction force (GRF) during a squat jump for maximum height. The net impulse is shown as the shaded area.

Example 9.4

A Comparison of the Three Techniques to Estimate Power

When an individual (87.2 kg) performed a squat jump for maximum height, he was able to raise his center of mass by 42.3 cm. Let us calculate the average power $(\overline{P})$ produced by the jumper using the three approaches.

First, the kinematic approach:

$$\overline{P} = (9.81 \cdot m) \cdot \sqrt{r \cdot 4.9}$$
$$= (9.81 \cdot 87.2) \cdot \sqrt{0.423 \cdot 4.9}$$
$$= 1232 \text{ W}$$

Second, the impulse-momentum (kinetic) approach:

$$\overline{P} = \frac{\int F_{g,y}\,dt}{t} \cdot \frac{\int F_{net}\,dt}{2\,m}$$
$$= \frac{510}{0.32} \cdot \frac{236}{(2 \times 87.2)}$$
$$= 2156 \text{ W}$$

Third, the mechanical energy (kinetic) approach:

$$\overline{P} = \frac{m\,g(r+h)}{t}$$
$$= \frac{855(0.423 + 0.567)}{0.32}$$
$$= 2645 \text{ W}$$

(continued)

These estimates vary due to the assumptions associated with each procedure. The mechanical energy approach is the most accurate (Hatze, 1998). The major source of error with the impulse-momentum approach is the estimate of average velocity, which in this example was estimated as 1.35 m/s when it was actually 1.82 m/s. The limitations of the kinematic approach are the assumptions regarding the symmetry of the trajectory.

For comparison, based on measurements of the torque-velocity relation, the maximum power produced by the plantarflexor muscles during the squat jump was calculated as 2499 W (Ingen Schenau, Bobbert, Huijing, & Woittiez, 1985). Similarly, Josephson (1993) estimated the maximum power for muscle to range from 5 to 500 W/kg, with the sustainable power ranging from 5 to 150 W/kg.

Another approach that can be used to determine power production, such as for weightlifting events, is to calculate the rate of change in mechanical energy (Garhammer, 1980). Because the quantity of work done can be determined from the change in energy, and power equals the rate of doing work, power can be calculated from the rate of change in energy.

$$P = \frac{\Delta \text{ energy}}{\Delta \text{ time}}$$

$$= \frac{E_{k,t} + E_{p,g}}{\Delta t}$$

$$P = \frac{0.5mv^2 + mgh}{\Delta t} \tag{9.1}$$

where $E_{k,t}$ refers to the maximum kinetic energy, $E_{p,g}$ represents potential energy, and time indicates the time to the maximum kinetic energy.

An example of this approach is provided in table 9.3, which indicates the power delivered to a barbell by a weight lifter during three lifts: (a) the clean, a movement that requires the displacement of the barbell from the floor to the lifter's chest in one continuous rapid motion; (b) the squat, a movement in which a lifter supports a barbell on the shoulders and goes from a standing erect position to a knee-flexed position (thighs parallel to the floor), then returns to standing; and (c) the bench press, a movement in which the lifter assumes a supine position and lowers the barbell from a straight-arm location above the chest down to touch the chest, then raises it back to the initial position. Data have been taken from the literature (clean—Enoka, 1979; squat—McLaughlin, Dillman, & Lardner, 1977; bench press—Madsen & McLaughlin, 1984) to illustrate the differences in power production for the three lifts (table 9.3).

These data suggest that the peak power delivered to the barbell is greatest during the clean and least for the bench press. This is interesting, because the squat and bench press are two of the three lifts that constitute the sport of power lifting. Indeed, these data suggest that success in the squat and bench-press lifts is not determined solely by power production but also depends on muscle strength.

Production of Power About a Single Joint

In contrast to estimating whole-body or whole-limb average power, an ergometer enables us to focus more specifically on one muscle group (Grabiner & Jeziorowski, 1992). An ergometer permits the measurement of the torque-angular velocity relation about a joint, and we can then use the data to calculate the associated power (Aagaard et al., 1994a, 1994b; De Looze, Bussmann, Kingma, & Toussaint, 1992) or even to determine a power loop (Stevens, 1993). For example, De Koning, Binkhorst, Vos, and van't Hof (1985) measured the torque-angular velocity relation about the elbow joint for three groups of subjects: untrained women, untrained men, and arm-trained males (i.e., track and field athletes, rowers, weight lifters, body builders, handball players,

Table 9.3   Power Delivered to a Barbell During the Three Types of Lifts

	Clean	Squat	Bench press
Barbell weight (N)	1226	3694	1815
Peak barbell velocity (m/s)	2	0.30	1.54
Height (m)	0.30	0.30	0.06
Time to $E_{k,t}$ (s)	0.35	1.30	0.70
$E_{k,t}$ (J)	250	17	219
$E_{p,g}$ (J)	368	1108	109
Power (W)	1766	865	469

$E_{k,t}$ = maximum kinetic energy; $E_{p,g}$ = potential energy.

Table 9.4 Elbow Flexor Strength (P_o), Maximum Angular Velocity (ω_{max}), and Peak Power for Arm-Trained Men and Untrained Men and Women

	Arm-trained men	Untrained men	Untrained women
P_o (N·m)	90.9 ± 15.6	68.5 ± 11.0	42.7 ± 6.9
ω_{max} (rad/s)	17.0 ± 1.6	16.6 ± 1.5	14.9 ± 1.3
Power (W)	253.0 ± 58.0	195.0 ± 46.0	111.0 ± 24.0

Values are given as mean ± standard deviation.

karate exponents, and tug-of-war competitors). The MVC force (P_o) varied in the order that you would expect: arm-trained men, untrained men, and untrained women. There was, however, only a small difference in the maximum angular velocity (ω_{max}) among the groups (table 9.4). Nonetheless, there was a significant difference among the groups in the peak power that the elbow flexor muscles could produce.

Another approach we can use to determine power production about a single joint is to perform a biomechanical analysis and calculate the product of torque and angular velocity about a joint (Enoka, 1988a; Winter, 1983). This approach requires a description of limb kinematics and data on a contact force, such as the ground reaction force or a pedal force. For example, we can determine the power that a subject can apply to the pedal of a cycle ergometer by calculating the product of pedal force and pedal velocity or by summing the joint power (torque × angular velocity) for the hip, knee, and ankle joints (Ingen Schenau, Woensel, Boots, Snackers, & de Groot, 1990). These two methods produce similar results and indicate the power produced by the leg throughout one complete pedal revolution (figure 9.21*a*). However, the individual joint powers provide additional information on the contribution of the three joints to the total leg power (figure 9.21*b*).

Power Production for Isolated Muscle

The power production capabilities of the motor system can also be measured at the level of the single muscle or muscle fiber. Brooks and Faulkner (1991), for example, compared the ability of slow-twitch muscle (soleus) and fast-twitch muscle (extensor digitorum longus) of mice to sustain isometric force and to sustain power production. The peak isometric force that extensor digitorum longus could exert was greater than that for soleus (363 vs. 273 mN). However, when force was normalized relative to muscle size (cross-sectional area), peak force was similar for the two muscles (24.5 N/cm² for extensor digitorum longus compared with 23.7 N/cm² for soleus). Nonetheless, extensor digitorum longus was more fatigable and experienced a more rapid decline in isometric

force with sustained activation; the maximum sustainable force was 1.38 N/cm² for extensor digitorum longus and 4.58 N/cm² for soleus. In contrast, when power production was expressed relative to muscle mass, the peak sustainable power was greater for extensor digitorum longus (9.1 W/kg) compared with soleus (7.4 W/kg). Although force declined more for extensor digitorum longus with sustained activation, the greater velocity of shortening resulted in a greater sustainable power. This observation suggests that type S and type FR motor units (see chapter 6) are important for the ability to sustain isometric force but that type FR and type FF motor units are more important for sustaining power production (see also Rome et al., 1988).

Peak power production has also been measured for segments of single muscle fibers taken from primates (Fitts, Bodine, Romatowski, & Widrick, 1998). Muscle samples were obtained by biopsy from soleus and medial gastrocnemius, and the contractile properties were measured in vitro. From measurements of the force-velocity relation, the peak power was calculated for type I and type II fiber segments from each muscle. The peak power was greater for the type II fibers when compared with the type I fibers; it was 5 times greater for the soleus fibers and 8.5 times greater for the medial gastrocnemius fibers. Fitts et al. found that the greater peak power of the type II fibers was due to a greater maximal shortening velocity and a lower curvature of the force-velocity relation. In addition, the maximal force (P_o) of the type II fibers in medial gastrocnemius was greater than that for type I fibers.

Eccentric-Concentric Contractions

Because power is defined as the rate of doing work, it can also be considered in terms of the *rate of change in energy* (table 9.3). Accordingly, the power that a muscle can produce depends on how quickly the energy is used to perform work. The principal source of energy for muscle is chemical energy (ATP). However, we have also discussed how muscle can use mechanical energy (elastic or strain energy) to perform positive work and produce power. This is accomplished during movement

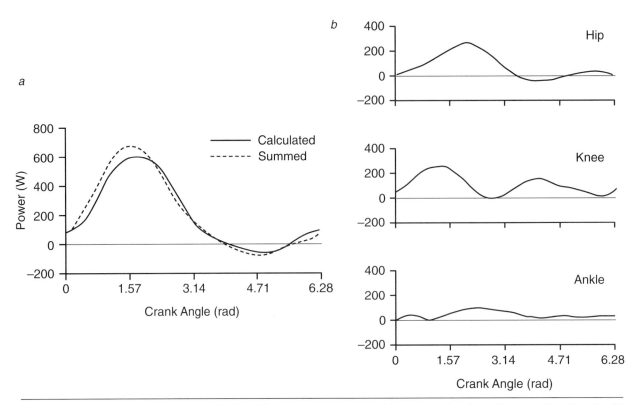

Figure 9.21 Power production during a single pedal cycle on an ergometer: *(a)* power produced as a function of crank angle; *(b)* joint power, which was calculated as the product of torque and angular velocity, for the hip, knee, and ankle as a function of crank angle.

Adapted from van Ingen Schenau, van Woensel, Boots, Snackers, and de Groot, 1990.

through the performance of an eccentric contraction before a concentric contraction. With such a combination, muscle is able to perform more positive work during the concentric contraction, and there is an increase in the power that is produced by the muscles (Takarada, Hirano, Ishige, & Ishii, 1997). This enhanced performance is attributed, at least partly, to the ability of muscle to store energy during the stretch (eccentric contraction) and subsequently to use some of this energy during the concentric contraction.

The height that an individual can reach in a vertical jump depends on how much power the muscles can produce. The most effective technique is the countermovement jump, which involves an eccentric-concentric contraction of the quadriceps femoris and triceps surae muscles. Many biomechanists suggest that the greater height achieved with the countermovement jump is influenced by the storage and utilization of elastic energy that occurs with an eccentric-concentric contraction (Ingen Schenau et al., 1997). This capability, however, depends on the architectural properties of the involved muscles and the kinematic details of the performance (Biewener & Roberts, 2000).

Power Production and Training

Because of the technical demands associated with measuring joint power, there are few studies on the effects of training on power production at the level of the single-joint system. Duchateau and Hainaut (1984) performed one such study on a hand muscle (adductor pollicis) of human volunteers. Two groups of subjects trained the muscle at a moderate intensity (10 repetitions) every day for three months. One group used maximum isometric contractions (5-s duration, once every minute), and the other group did rapid concentric contractions against a load of 30% to 40% of maximum. The moderate load for the dynamic contractions was chosen because we know that muscle produces maximum power when the contraction force is about one-third of maximum. Isometric training produced a greater increase in the maximum power and a shift in the force at which the maximum occurred.

The effects of the training protocols on the force-velocity relation were consistent with the principle of specificity. The group that trained with the greater loads (MVC force) experienced a significant increase in the

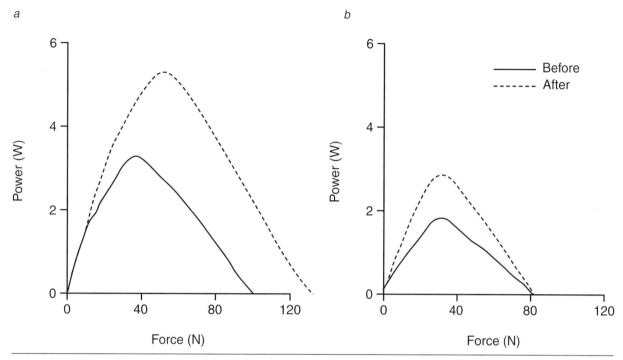

Figure 9.22   The effects of *(a)* isometric and *(b)* dynamic training on muscle power production.
Adapted from Duchateau and Hainaut, 1984.

MVC force, whereas the other group did not (figure 9.22). Surprisingly, the isometric group experienced a 51% increase in maximum power compared with a 19% increase for the dynamic group (figure 9.22). This finding suggests that the greatest increase in power is obtained with high-force rather than high-velocity training. A similar effect was found with the knee extensor muscles (Aagaard et al., 1994b). After 12 weeks of strength training, subjects who used a high resistance experienced increases in both strength and power production, whereas subjects who used a low resistance did not. In comparison, subjects who trained with loaded kicking movements experienced modest increases in net muscle torque and peak power at intermediate velocities.

The effect of training load was examined more systematically by comparing the effects of training the elbow flexor muscles with loads that were 15%, 35%, or 90% of 1-RM load (Moss, Refsnes, Abildgaard, Nicolaysen, & Jensen, 1997). The subjects, assigned to one of the three groups, trained three times a week for nine weeks. The outcome was expressed as the increase in peak power when lifting loads that ranged from 15% to 90% 1 RM as fast as possible. The 1-RM load increased by 6.6%, 10.1%, and 15.2% for the three groups (15%, 35%, and 90% 1 RM). The increase in peak power was modest with the lightest load, whereas it was greatest,

but with a high degree of specificity, for the group who trained with the heavy load (figure 9.23). In contrast, the increase in peak power was most consistent for the subjects who trained with a 35% 1-RM load. Similarly, Moritani (1992) found that training loads of 30% produced greater increases in power production than did loads of either 0% or 100%; these increases were accompanied by significant increases in the quantity of EMG and a decrease in the mean power frequency. These data suggest the strategy that an individual should choose depending on the goal of a training program (Wilson, Newton, Murphy, & Humphries, 1993).

The adaptations that occur with high-speed training using intermediate loads (~35% 1 RM) appear to involve an increase in the discharge rate of motor units. This was evident in subjects who trained the dorsiflexor muscles five times a week for 12 weeks (Van Cutsem et al., 1998). The training program increased MVC torque by 30%, the EMG during an MVC by 20%, and the rate of increase in torque of high-speed, submaximal contractions. The average values for motor units in the tibialis anterior muscle exhibited a decrease in recruitment threshold, an increase in twitch torque, and no change in contraction time. The faster high-speed contractions were probably attributable to an increase in the rate at which the first four action potentials were discharged at the

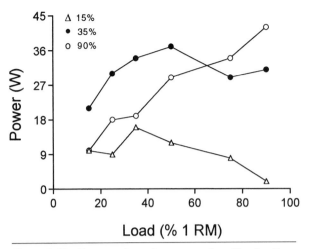

Figure 9.23 Increases in peak power produced by the elbow flexor muscles when lifting a range of loads after training with 15% (△), 35% (▲), or 90% (●) of the 1-RM load.

Data from Moss et al., 1997.

beginning of the contraction. These findings indicate that adaptations in the nervous system can contribute to improvements in performance with power training.

In terms of muscle mechanics, the peak power a muscle can produce depends on its maximum force, the maximum shortening velocity, and the curvature of the force-velocity relation (Fitts & Widrick, 1996). For example, six months of swim training by collegiate men increased the shortening velocity of type I fiber segments from deltoid by 20% (Fitts, Costill, & Gardetto, 1989). However, the shortening velocity of type II fiber segments decreased by ~45%. Results obtained from rats after a running program suggest that the increase in shortening velocity likely involves an increased expression of fast myosin light chains and an increase in ATPase activity (Schluter & Fitts, 1994). Alternatively, changes in fiber cross-sectional area have a significant effect on peak

power. For example, the peak powers of type I and type IIa fiber segments from the gastrocnemius muscle of elite master runners were less than those for age-matched control subjects (Widrick, Trappe, Costill, & Fitts, 1996). These differences, however, resulted from smaller cross-sectional areas of the fibers from the runners. The data accumulated by Fitts and colleagues demonstrate that several adaptations could occur at the level of muscle mechanics to alter the power production capability of muscle. The specific associations between training protocols and muscular adaptations remain to be determined.

Adaptation to Reduced Use

One popular technique used by experimentalists to identify the fundamental properties of the motor system is to perturb the system and measure the response. A typical perturbation is to alter the amount of activity performed by the system; this can involve either an increase or a decrease in the amount of activity. An assumption frequently expressed in the research literature is that the excitation of muscle by the nervous system is a critical factor in determining the properties of the muscle. As a consequence, a number of experimental models have been developed to alter the connection between the nervous system and muscle and, by subtraction, to determine the role of the nervous system in defining muscle properties (table 9.5). In this section, we consider three commonly used models of reduced use and examine the types of adaptations that have been observed with each model. Information on the other models is available elsewhere (Booth & Baldwin, 1996; Gordon & Pattullo, 1993; Lieber, 1992; Pette & Vrbová, 1992; Roy, Baldwin, & Edgerton, 1991). In addition, the profound effects of reduced use on the structural components of the neuromuscular system (e.g., bone,

Table 9.5 Experimental Models Used to Study the Effects of Changes in Physical Activity

	Neural	Muscle
Enhanced use	Electrical stimulation Exercise	Stretch Exercise Compensatory hypertrophy
Reduced use	Denervation Tetrodotoxin Curare Colchicine Rhizotomy Spinal transection Spinal isolation	Tenotomy Immobilization Hindlimb suspension Barbiturate sleep Bed rest Water immersion

articular cartilage, tendon, ligament) are not considered here, but there is also a substantial literature on these adaptations (Snow-Harter & Marcus, 1991; Wohl, Boyd, Judex, & Zernicke, 2000; Woo, Debski, Withrow, & Janaushek, 1999; Zernicke et al., 1990).

Limb Immobilization

Individuals who have an injured limb immobilized in a cast for a few weeks often experience a loss of muscle mass and function that is apparent upon removal of the cast. This adaptation is of obvious concern to the clinician, who would like to know how to minimize the loss of mass and function (Grimby, Gustafsson, Peterson, & Renström, 1980; Vandenborne et al., 1998; Veldhuizen, Verstappen, Vroemen, Kuipers, & Greep, 1993). However, the scientist regards this adaptation as an opportunity to characterize the changes that occur in the motor system with this type of stress (reduction in activity) and to identify the mechanisms that mediate these changes.

Reduction in Activity

Many studies have been performed on both animals and humans to examine the adaptations that occur with limb immobilization. A critical feature of all reduced-use protocols is the extent to which the intervention reduces activation of the involved muscles. When healthy humans had an arm immobilized in a cast, the activity of the elbow flexor muscles decreased modestly (Semmler, Kutzscher, & Enoka, 2000). This effect was quantified by measuring bursts of EMG activity for 24-h periods before and during immobilization (figure 9.24). In this study, the EMG activity of biceps brachii declined by 38% and that for brachioradialis decreased by 29% during four weeks of immobilization. Interestingly, this effect appeared to differ for men and women. The women had greater levels of EMG prior to immobilization and experienced a greater reduction in EMG during immobilization.

Multiple measures of EMG during immobilization (figure 9.25a) indicate that it declines steadily and then remains at the reduced level (Fournier, Roy, Perham, Simard, & Edgerton, 1983). However, the amount of the decline in EMG depends on the length at which the muscle is immobilized; the decline is greatest for short muscle lengths and negligible for long lengths. The integrated EMG decreased by 77% for soleus and 50% for medial gastrocnemius at the shortest lengths. These reductions in EMG were accompanied by a 36% loss of muscle mass for soleus and a 47% loss of muscle mass for medial gastrocnemius at the shortest lengths.

The amount of atrophy (loss of muscle mass) due to limb immobilization varies across studies. A reduction in muscle mass (wet weight) as high as 50% has been recorded (Fournier et al., 1983), and the decrease in muscle fiber cross-sectional area has been found to be as much as 42% (Nicks, Beneke, Key, & Timson, 1989) with a few weeks of limb immobilization. Others, however, have reported a modest reduction of 17% in wet weight (Robinson, Enoka, & Stuart, 1991) and a 14% decrease in the mean diameter of type I but not type II muscle fibers (Gibson et al., 1987) for a similar duration of immobilization. The atrophy is probably a consequence of both a decline in the rate of protein synthesis (Gibson et al., 1987) and a loss of muscle fibers (Oishi, Ishihara, & Katsuta, 1992).

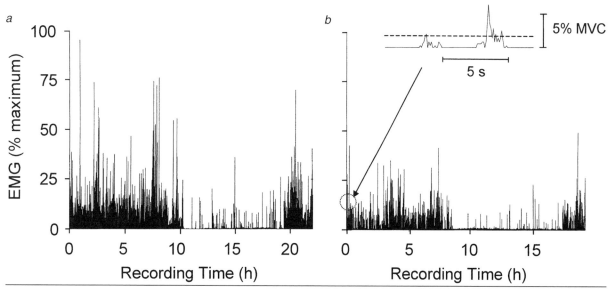

Figure 9.24 Electromyogram activity in biceps brachii of one individual *(a)* before and *(b)* during four weeks of arm immobilization. The recordings were based on bursts of EMG activity, which are shown in the inset.

Data from Semmler, Kutzscher, and Enoka, 2000.

MVC = maximum voluntary contraction.

a

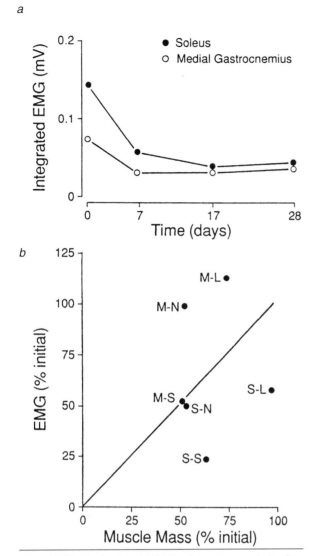

b

Figure 9.25 Reductions in EMG and muscle mass during four weeks of limb immobilization of the rat hindlimb: *(a)* decline in integrated EMG for the soleus and medial gastrocnemius muscles constrained to be at a short length; *(b)* relation between the decline in EMG and reduction in muscle mass.

Adapted from Fournier, Roy, Perham, Simard, and Edgerton, 1983.

S-S = soleus, short length; S-N = soleus, neutral length; S-L = soleus, long length; M-S = medial gastrocnemius, short length; M-N = medial gastrocnemius, neutral length; M-L = medial gastrocnemius, long length.

Despite the reduction in EMG and the muscle atrophy that have been reported to occur with limb immobilization, these results are difficult to interpret because of the dissociations between the decline in EMG and muscle atrophy and between muscle atrophy and loss of function. These effects are apparent in figure 9.25*b* as a deviation of the data points from the line of identity. Fournier et al. (1983) found no reduction in EMG for the medial gastrocnemius muscle when it was immobilized

at a neutral length, but the muscle experienced a 54% decline in mass. Similarly, rat soleus and medial gastrocnemius muscles experienced similar declines in wet weight (43-52%) at short and neutral lengths, whereas the decline in maximum isometric force at the short length was 72% to 77% compared with 45% at the neutral length (Simard, Spector, & Edgerton, 1982; Spector, Simard, Fournier, Sternlicht, & Edgerton, 1982). The decrease in maximum isometric force did not parallel the reduction in wet weight.

Some of the dissociation between muscle atrophy and the decline in force can be attributed to the definition of atrophy as the loss of mass. As discussed previously, the maximum force a muscle can exert is closely related to its cross-sectional area, not the quantity of muscle mass. When muscle atrophy is expressed in terms of cross-sectional area, there is a much tighter correlation with the decline in force (Hortobágyi et al., 2000; Lieber, 1992). However, another study showed that the cross-sectional area of type I and IIa muscle fibers declined by about 25%, whereas the maximum isometric force decreased by 40% for type FR and 52% for type S motor units (Nordstrom, Enoka, Callister, Reinking, & Stuart, 1995). Clearly, the remodeling that occurs in the neuromuscular apparatus during short-term immobilization is more complex than can be predicted by a linear relation between the decline in EMG, loss of muscle mass, and impairment of performance. It is likely that the altered neuromechanical conditions (e.g., fixed muscle length, continued isometric contractions, altered sensory feedback) are just as important as the reduction in neuromuscular activity in determining the nature of the adaptations.

Neuromuscular Adaptations

Given the absence of a simple relation between the decrease in activity and impairment of performance with limb immobilization, it has been difficult to develop a coherent view of the adaptations that occur with this intervention. The adaptations appear to extend from the genetic regulation of muscle mass to the descending control of muscle activation. For example, seven days of immobilization of the rat soleus muscle at a short length reduced muscle mass by 37%, depolarized muscle fiber membranes by 5 mV, decreased the frequency of miniature end-plate potentials by 60%, and reduced Na+-K+ transport across the membrane by 25% (Zemková et al., 1990). Similarly, three weeks of immobilization of the rat plantaris muscle at a long length increased the postsynaptic areas of junctional folds and clefts at the neuromuscular junctions of type I and type II muscle fibers (Pachter & Eberstein, 1986).

One observation that has been reported in numerous limb-immobilization studies is the **slow-to-fast conversion** of muscle fiber types. There is a decline in the proportion of slow-twitch, oxidative (type SO) muscle fibers and an increase in the proportion of fast-twitch, oxidative-glycolytic (type FOG) fibers (Fitts, Brimmer, Heywood-Cooksey, & Timmerman, 1989; Hortobágyi et al., 2000; Lieber, Fridén, Hargens, Danzig, & Gershuni, 1988; Oishi et al., 1992). For example, after one week of limb immobilization there was an increase in the quantities of mRNA for faster isoforms of the MHCs in the gastrocnemius, plantaris, and soleus muscles of the rat hindlimb (Jänkälä, Harjola, Petersen, & Härkönen, 1997). A similar effect has been observed in the vastus lateralis muscle of humans after three weeks of leg immobilization (Hortobágyi et al., 2000). The typical explanation for this adaptation is that the muscle fibers most affected by the immobilization are those whose activity is reduced the most, namely, the type SO muscle fibers. Despite the appeal of this rationale and its observation in muscles of the rat, dog, and human, studies on motor units in a cat hindlimb muscle have not shown a similar change in motor unit proportions or a differential reduction in cross-sectional area after several weeks of immobilization (Mayer et al., 1981; Nordstrom et al., 1995; Robinson et al., 1991). Nonetheless, the decline in force seems to be greatest in type S and FR motor units of cat hindlimb muscle (Petit & Gioux, 1993), which is consistent with the slow-to-fast hypothesis.

Limb immobilization has a profound effect on performance. The muscle atrophy results in a substantial loss of strength and an impairment with most activities of daily living (Imms, Hackett, Prestidge, & Fox, 1977; Imms & MacDonald, 1978). For example, six weeks of immobilization due to a fracture produced a 55% decline in the MVC force and a 45% reduction in the MVC EMG in a hand muscle (Duchateau & Hainaut, 1991). Six weeks of immobilization even appeared to inhibit the ability of subjects to generate a central drive that was sufficient for maximum activation of a hand muscle. Nonetheless, these changes did not impair the ability of the subjects to sustain their maximal force for 60 s. Similarly, others have found that three weeks of immobilization in a plaster cast produced a reduction in the electrically evoked (10%) and the MVC force (23%), but did not influence the fatigability of the triceps surae muscle in human volunteers (Davies, Rutherford, & Thomas, 1987).

The effect of immobilization on the fatigability of muscle differs for high- and low-force contractions. For example, the endurance time for an isometric contraction sustained at 65% MVC force by the elbow flexor muscles did not change after four weeks of limb immobilization, whereas the endurance time for a contraction at 20% MVC increased by 59% (Yue, Bilodeau, Hardy, & Enoka, 1997). Furthermore, this effect appears to be related to the gender of the individual. After four weeks

of limb immobilization, Semmler, Kutzscher, and Enoka (1999, 2000) found that the endurance time for an isometric contraction at 15% MVC force with the elbow flexor muscles increased by 207% for one group of subjects (mainly women) and did not change for the other group. As shown in figure 8.20, the increase in endurance time was associated with an unusual EMG during the fatiguing contraction.

The consequences of limb immobilization are also apparent at the level of the motor unit. Six to eight weeks of immobilization alters both the properties and behavior of motor units in human hand muscles (Duchateau & Hainaut, 1990). When recruitment threshold was expressed relative to maximum force, there was an increase in the number of high-threshold motor units in the immobilized muscle. However, the average force exerted by these units was less (figure 9.26a), and there was a decline in the peak-to-peak amplitude of the motor unit action potentials. Although recruitment order was not affected by the immobilization, there was an increase in the range of recruitment (figure 9.26b) and a decrease in the range of discharge rate modulation. This indicates a change in the activation strategy used to grade muscle force.

The magnitude of the strength loss after immobilization is greater than the amount of muscle atrophy. For example, Hortobágyi et al. (2000) found that the strength of the quadriceps femoris muscles decreased by 47% after three weeks of immobilization, whereas the average decrease in the cross-sectional area of the muscle fibers was 11%. This dissociation underscores the significant role of adaptations in the neural drive to muscle during limb immobilization (Duchateau & Hainaut, 1987; Yue et al., 1997). Nonetheless, when muscles, motor units, or muscle fibers are activated with electrical stimulation, there remains a discrepancy between the decline in force and the decrease in cross-sectional area. This finding suggests that some of the reduction in force must involve an adaptation in the mechanisms of force transmission within the muscle (Chopard et al., 2001; Patel & Lieber, 1997; Sheard, 2000).

Recovery of strength after immobilization appears to depend on the health of the person exposed to the intervention. Studies performed on healthy subjects indicate a complete recovery of muscle strength within a few weeks (Duchateau & Hainaut, 1987; Semmler, Kutzscher, & Enoka, 2000; Yue et al., 1997). Although recovery can occur in these individuals as a consequence of normal activities of daily living, it is facilitated by exercises that include eccentric contractions (Hortobágyi et al., 2000). In contrast, measurements performed on persons who were immobilized because of an injury or a surgical procedure indicate that it can take months for complete recovery (Grimby et al., 1980; Vandenborne et al., 1998).

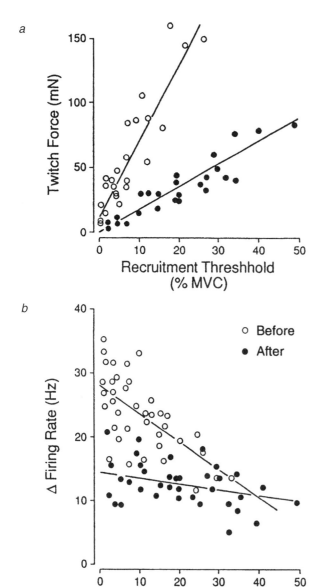

Figure 9.26 Immobilization-induced change in *(a)* motor unit twitch force and *(b)* range of discharge rate modulation as a function of recruitment threshold. Each data point corresponds to a single motor unit.

Adapted from Duchateau and Hainaut, 1990.

MVC = maximum voluntary contraction.

Limb Unloading

When astronauts were first sent into space, several models were developed to study the physiological adaptations that occur during spaceflight (Desplanches, 1997). One model involves suspending the hindlimbs of an animal off the ground for a few weeks so that the limbs are free to move but cannot touch the ground or any support surface (figure 9.27*a*). This experimental technique is

known as **hindlimb suspension.** The animal can perform many of its daily functions and experiences only minimal levels of stress, which are transient and variable between animals (Thomason & Booth, 1990). Similarly, one leg of a human can be placed in a sling to reduce the level of activity (figure 9.28) (Berg, Dudley, Häggmark, Ohlsén, & Tesch, 1991; Dudley et al., 1992). The individual ambulates using crutches and the nonsuspended leg. In addition, the thickness of the sole of the shoe worn on the nonsuspended leg is increased by about 10 cm to reduce the possibility that the suspended foot will strike the ground during ambulation.

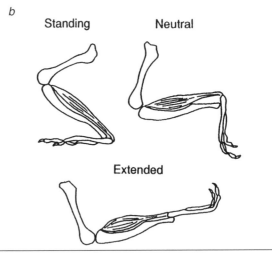

Figure 9.27 The hindlimb-suspension model. *(a)* A rat with its hindlimbs suspended off the ground. The rat can move around its cage by using its front legs. *(b)* Change in the range of motion for the soleus muscle during hindlimb suspension; the left image shows the minimum angle at the ankle joint during normal standing; the right image indicates the neutral position during hindlimb suspension; and the bottom image represents the maximum angle for both conditions.

Provided by Charles M. Tipton, PhD. (9.27*a*). Adapted from Riley et al., 1990 (9.27*b*).

three days of suspension but then recovers to control levels (Alford, Roy, Hodgson, & Edgerton, 1987; Riley et al., 1990). Paradoxically, the muscles atrophied during the period when EMG levels were normal (figure 9.29*b*), meaning that there is a dissociation between the levels of activity and the loss of muscle mass (figure 9.30). Numerous studies have indicated that the soleus muscle (slow-twitch ankle extensor) experiences greater atrophy than either its fast-twitch synergist (medial gastrocnemius, plantaris) or its antagonist (tibialis anterior, extensor digitorum longus) muscles. Furthermore, forelimb muscles experience heightened activity during hindlimb suspension (Allaf & Goubel, 1999).

The dissociation between EMG and muscle atrophy is probably attributable to an altered leg posture (figure 9.27*b*). In a weight-bearing stance, the range of motion at the ankle joint extends from about 0.5 rad to 3.14 rad. However, after a few days of suspension the ankle adopts a neutral angle of about 1.57 rad, which reduces its range of motion substantially. Also, recall that the EMG is affected by muscle length: for the same muscle force, the EMG is greater at shorter muscle lengths. Presumably, the forces exerted by the muscles are substantially reduced during hindlimb suspension despite the maintained levels of EMG.

A number of studies have shown significant reductions in neuromuscular function after short-term exposure to leg unloading. For example, six weeks of leg unloading reduces whole-muscle and fiber cross-sectional area (Dudley et al., 1992; Hather, Adams, Tesch, & Dudley, 1992). The cross-sectional areas of the vasti were reduced by 16%, those of the soleus by 17%, and those of gastrocnemius by 26%. Biopsies of the vastus lateralis muscle indicated reductions in cross-sectional area of

Figure 9.28   The leg unloading model.

Provided by Per A. Tesch, PhD.

Reduction in Activity

Four important ways in which the hindlimb-suspension model mimics spaceflight are a cephalic shift in fluid, loss of bone mineral content, decreased growth, and removal of the need for postural activity in the leg muscles. Despite the reduced need for hindlimb postural support, the EMG activity recorded in ankle muscles is not substantially depressed for the duration of the suspension period (figure 9.29*a*). The activity of soleus and medial gastrocnemius muscles is depressed for about the first

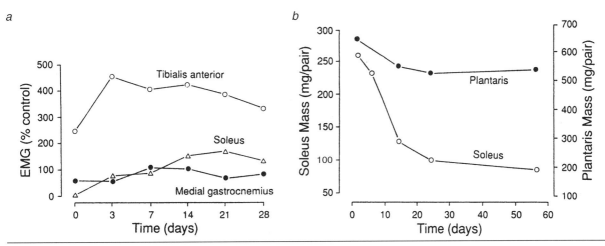

Figure 9.29   Results of 28 days of hindlimb suspension: *(a)* integrated EMG activity in three rat hindlimb muscles; *(b)* loss of mass in two muscles during 28 days of hindlimb suspension. Muscle mass is expressed in milligrams (mg) for the two hindlimb muscles of each animal.

Adapted from Thomason and Booth, 1990.

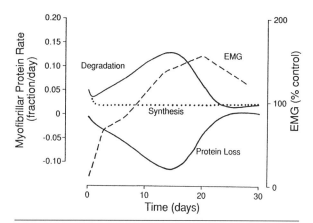

Figure 9.30 Time course of protein degradation, protein synthesis, protein loss, and integrated EMG activity in the rat soleus muscle during 28 days of hindlimb suspension. The net loss of protein is largely due to an increase in protein degradation despite an increase in EMG.

Adapted from Thomason and Booth, 1990.

12% for the type I fibers and 15% for the type II muscle fibers. Furthermore, skin temperature over the calf muscles was 4 °C cooler for the suspended leg, presumably due to a decreased blood flow through the less active limb (Berg & Tesch, 1996).

Neuromuscular Adaptations

Many animal studies have shown a preferential effect of hindlimb suspension on slow-twitch muscle (Esser & Hardeman, 1995; Fitts, Metzger, Riley, & Unsworth, 1986; Roy et al., 1991; Thomason, Herrick, & Baldwin, 1987). Consequently, investigators often focus on the effects elicited in soleus (Thomason & Booth, 1990). A few weeks of suspension produces a decline in the proportion of type I fibers in soleus with little effect on synergist (medial gastrocnemius) or antagonist muscles (tibialis anterior). The suspension produces a decrease in the concentration of myofibrillar and myosin proteins, with an increased appearance of the fast myosin isoforms. However, this effect occurs in some, but not all, type I muscle fibers of soleus (Gardetto, Schluter, & Fitts, 1989). There is a reduction in the proportion of muscle fibers that comprise only the MHC for type I fibers and an increase in the proportion that contain multiple isoforms of the MHCs for type II fibers (Oishi, Ishihara, Yamamoto, & Miyamoto, 1998). Consequently, there is a decrease in the proportion of slow-twitch motor units in the soleus muscle after a few weeks of hindlimb suspension (Leterme & Falempin, 1996). These adaptations, however, do not involve changes in the soma size or oxidative capacity of the innervating motor neurons (Ishihara, Oishi, Roy, & Edgerton, 1997).

Accompanying these changes in protein content and myosin isoforms are some changes in the metabolic

capabilities of the muscle fibers (Roy et al., 1991). The concentrations of enzymes involved in oxidative metabolism (succinate dehydrogenase and citrate synthase) increase in soleus with hindlimb suspension. But after several weeks of suspension, predominantly fast-twitch muscles (medial gastrocnemius, tibialis anterior) exhibit lower levels of some of the enzymes (succinate dehydrogenase) that characterize oxidative metabolism but not others (citrate synthase). In contrast, both type I and type II muscle fibers in extensor and flexor muscles either maintain or elevate the levels of enzymes (e.g., alpha glycerophosphate dehydrogenase) associated with glycolytic metabolism.

These quantitative and qualitative changes in protein and enzyme content with hindlimb suspension produce several adaptations in the mechanical properties of muscle. The maximum force capacity of the soleus muscle is reduced, but the decline is greater than would be anticipated based on the loss of muscle mass. This indicates a reduction in normalized force (Herbert, Roy, & Edgerton, 1988; McDonald & Fitts, 1995; Thomason & Booth, 1990), which involves a decrease in specific tension (Larsson et al., 1996; Riley et al., 2000; Thompson, Johnson, & Shoeman, 1998). At the muscle fiber level, type I muscle fibers from both soleus and medial gastrocnemius show a significant reduction in diameter and peak force, whereas the type IIa fibers from medial gastrocnemius exhibit a decline in diameter but no change in peak force (Gardetto et al., 1989). However, Leterme and Casasnovas (1999) found a decrease in the peak tetanic force of motor units in lateral gastrocnemius after 14 days of hindlimb suspension.

In contrast to these results obtained with rat muscle, there was no preferential fiber-type effect in humans after a 21% decrease in the strength of the knee extensor muscles due to six weeks of leg unloading (Dudley et al., 1992; Hather et al., 1992). The decrease in fiber cross-sectional area was 12% for type I fibers and 15% for type II fibers from vastus lateralis, and there was no change in the fiber-type proportions. Furthermore, there was a reduction in whole-muscle cross-sectional area of 17% for soleus and 26% for gastrocnemius. The muscle atrophy associated with leg unloading is associated with a decrease in the capacity for protein synthesis (Gamrin et al., 1998).

In addition to the changes in force capacity, there are alterations in contraction speed (Roy et al., 1991; Thomason & Booth, 1990). The soleus muscle becomes faster, which should be expected because of the shift in myosin isoforms and the reduction in the proportion of type I muscle fibers. This was evident by an increase in the maximum velocity of shortening (V_{max}) for the soleus muscle and some of its type I muscle fibers (Thompson et al., 1998). Not all of the muscle fibers indicated an increase in V_{max}, which is consistent with the change in myosin isoforms limited to a subpopulation of these muscle fibers (Gardetto et al., 1989). With this increase in V_{max} is a shift in the force-velocity relation to the right. Other effects on contraction speed include a reduction in both contraction time and half-relaxation time; these effects are probably related to changes in Ca^{2+} kinetics. Hindlimb suspension increases the Ca^{2+} concentration necessary to activate the contractile apparatus (Gardetto et al., 1989; McDonald & Fitts, 1995).

Similar to the observation reported for limb immobilization, a few weeks of hindlimb suspension does not alter the fatigability of the soleus muscle. The rat medial gastrocnemius muscle experiences a more complicated adaptation that involves no effect on fatigability after 7 days of suspension, but apparently the muscle becomes much more fatigable after 28 days of suspension (Winiarski, Roy, Alford, Chiang, & Edgerton, 1987). Similarly, the fatigability of motor units in rat lateral gastrocnemius did not change after 14 days of suspension (Leterme & Casasnovas, 1999). In contrast, a 6-day spaceflight increased the fatigability of the rat soleus muscle (Caiozzo, Baker, Herrick, Tao, & Baldwin, 1994), and four weeks of leg suspension reduced the work capacity of the knee extensor muscles (Berg, Dudley, Hather, & Tesch, 1993).

Because the decrease in muscle strength with limb unloading is greater than the amount of muscle atrophy, the intervention seems to impair the activation of muscle. For example, exercise-induced shifts in the signal intensity of magnetic resonance images (figure 6.12) indicate that greater volumes (50-130%) of the knee extensor muscles are activated to lift submaximal loads after five weeks of suspension (Ploutz-Snyder, Tesch, Crittenden, & Dudley, 1995). Similarly, the EMG of the knee extensor muscles associated with exerting a force of 30% to 45% MVC increased by 25% after 10 days of suspension (Berg & Tesch, 1996). This adaptation may be due to an impairment of excitation-contraction coupling rather than a reduced ability to maximally activate the muscle. The adaptations experienced by humans with leg suspension recover within a few days of normal activity (Berg & Tesch, 1996).

Spinal Transection

In contrast to limb immobilization and limb unloading, which represent models of restraint, **spinal transection** imposes a reduction in use by disconnecting parts of the nervous system from muscle. The separation is imposed in experimental animals at the level of the spinal cord, usually T12-T13. This disruption is referred to as an **upper motor neuron lesion** because it eliminates supraspinal control of the hindlimbs. This lesion is distinct from a **lower motor neuron lesion** in which the muscle is separated from all components of the nervous system (i.e., denervation).

Reduction in Activity

As described by Lieber (1992), spinal cord transection, which is also known as **spinalization,** produces an immediate flaccid paralysis in which the hindlimbs are dragged by the experimental animal. About three to four weeks after the spinalization, the muscles develop spasticity, which eventually leads to sustained extensor activity with no apparent voluntary activation of the muscles. In this paralyzed state, however, the neuromuscular system can still be activated; and, with appropriate support and afferent feedback, the animals can be trained to perform hindlimb locomotion on a treadmill (Gregor et al., 1988; Lovely, Gregor, Roy, & Edgerton, 1990). Furthermore, spinalization at two weeks of age eventually (after 5-6 months) produces a 75% reduction in the quantity of integrated EMG and a 66% decrease in the duration of activity in the soleus muscle. The effects are less pronounced for gastrocnemius and include no change in the quantity of integrated EMG but a 66% reduction in the duration of activity (Roy et al., 1991).

In humans who experience a spinal cord injury, many motor units in muscles that are deprived of descending control are active spontaneously. For example, Thomas (1997) found that motor units in thenar muscles of patients who had an injury at C7 or higher for more than a year exhibited spontaneous activity, which the patients were unable to control. The motor units discharged at low rates, in the range of 1 to 8 Hz, with occasional rapid bursts of activity. Thus, chronic paralysis does not eliminate activity in paralyzed muscle.

Neuromuscular Adaptations

As with limb immobilization and limb unloading, spinalization produces muscle atrophy with a preferential effect on slow-twitch muscle and a slow-to-fast conversion of muscle fiber types (West, Roy, & Edgerton, 1986). The conversion of fiber types and loss of muscle mass are most pronounced in single-joint muscles involved in postural support. Soleus and medial gastrocnemius atrophy by about 45% and 30%, respectively, by two weeks after spinalization. There is a decrease in the proportion of type I muscle fibers and an increase in type II fibers; these effects result in an increase in the proportion of type FR motor units in soleus and an increase of type FF and FI (intermediate, fast-twitch) motor units in medial gastrocnemius (Munson, Foehring, Lofton, Zengel, & Sypert, 1986). These changes include an increase in the expression of fast myosin isoforms, a decrease in the number of fibers in soleus that react with a slow MHC antibody, and an increase in myosin ATPase of 50% for soleus and 30% for medial gastrocnemius (Jiang, Roy, & Edgerton, 1990; Roy, Sacks, Baldwin, Short, & Edgerton, 1984). Furthermore, investigators found an increase in the proportion of fibers from the rat soleus muscle that included multiple MHC isoforms (Talmadge, Roy, & Edgerton, 1995). The adaptations were less pronounced in the tibialis anterior muscle (Pierotti, Roy, Hodgson, & Edgerton, 1994).

The slow-to-fast conversion of muscle fiber types also influences the activities of enzymes associated with oxidative and glycolytic metabolism (Castro, Apple, Staron, Campos, & Dudley, 1999; Roy et al., 1991). These effects, however, are complex because the magnitude of the metabolic adaptations at the single-fiber level depends on both the age at spinalization and the muscle fiber type as defined by myosin properties. For example, there appear to be different effects on citrate synthase and succinate dehydrogenase, two enzymes involved in the citric acid cycle. In contrast, spinalization does not seem to alter the relation between the glycolytic potential of a muscle fiber and its type as defined by myosin ATPase.

The physiological adaptations exhibited by spinalized muscles are consistent with the changes in contractile and metabolic proteins (figure 9.31). The slow-to-fast conversion in the cat soleus muscle is associated with a decrease in both time to peak force and half-relaxation time and an increase in V_{max}. The increase in the maximum velocity of shortening (V_{max}) is to be expected given the increase in myosin ATPase, the increase in proportion of type II muscle fibers, and the increased incidence

of fast myosin isoforms (Roy et al., 1984). The change in the time course of the twitch (time to peak force and half-relaxation time) probably reflects changes in Ca^{2+} kinetics. In the cat medial gastrocnemius muscle, there is no change in the time course of the twitch, but V_{max} increases due to the increase in myosin ATPase. In both slow- and fast-twitch muscle, there is an increase in glycolytic enzyme activity after spinal cord transection.

The fatigability of the soleus muscle is not affected by spinalization (Gordon & Pattullo, 1993). For medial gastrocnemius, however, fatigability can change depending on the age at spinal transection. For young animals there is no effect on the fatigability of medial gastrocnemius; but when an adult animal experiences a spinal transection, the medial gastrocnemius muscle becomes more fatigable. In humans, the effect of spinalization on fatigability changes with time. Soon after spinalization (≤6 weeks), there are minimal changes in the fatigability of the soleus or quadriceps femoris muscles (Castro et al., 1999; Gaviria & Ohanna, 1999; Gerrits et al., 1999; Shields, 1995). Patients who have been spinalized for more than a year, however, exhibit marked fatigability of these muscles.

Because the spinal transection model involves the removal of supraspinal control over spinal networks, there are changes in the properties and connectivity of spinal

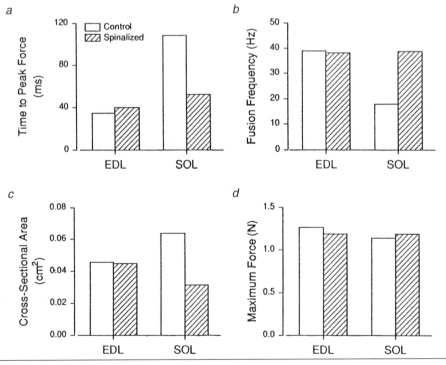

Figure 9.31 Contractile properties of soleus (SOL) and extensor digitorum longus (EDL) muscles in normal and spinalized rat hindlimbs: *(a)* time to reach the peak twitch force; *(b)* stimulus frequency at which the tetanic force became fused (smooth); *(c)* cross-sectional area; *(d)* maximum tetanic force. The greater effects occurred in the soleus muscle.

Adapted from Lieber, 1992.

cord neurons. For example, motor neurons that innervate the soleus muscle become less excitable and begin to resemble motor neurons that innervate fast-twitch muscle. The changes include a decrease in the afterhyperpolarization and an increase in rheobase (Cope, Bodine, Fournier, & Edgerton, 1986). There are, however, mixed reports on changes in the motor neurons that innervate the medial gastrocnemius muscle (Czeh et al., 1978; Foehring & Munson, 1990; Foehring, Sypert, & Munson, 1987a, 1987b), which appear to differ with motor unit type (Hochman & McCrea, 1994a). In contrast, paralysis that is induced by the application of tetrodotoxin, which does not involve sectioning the spinal cord, evokes changes in the twitch and tetanic responses of motor units in soleus but minimal changes in the motor neurons (Gardiner & Seburn, 1997).

The changes in motor neuron properties are accompanied by changes in segmental reflexes. In humans with cervical spinal cord lesions, it is possible to elicit interlimb responses not normally present in able-bodied individuals. For example, brief electric shocks to the lower extremities are sufficient to elicit unusual ipsilateral and contralateral upper-extremity responses (Calancie, 1991). The contralateral responses predominate and involve the response of motor units to light touch, individual hair movement, and thermal stimulation (Calancie, Lutton, & Broton, 1996). Furthermore, the excitatory postsynaptic potentials recorded in motor neurons to ankle extensor muscles after stretch are enhanced after six weeks of spinal cord transection (Hochman & McCrea, 1994a, 1994b, 1994c). Such adaptations may contribute to the development of spinal spasticity.

Muscle and motor unit properties after spinal cord injury in humans have been examined in muscles that are completely paralyzed and in those that retain some voluntary activity. Among 17 subjects who had a spinal cord injury at C7 or higher for more than a year, the strength of the paralyzed thenar muscles for half the subjects was similar to that of able-bodied subjects (Thomas, 1997). The contraction time of the evoked twitch response was not different between the injured and able-bodied subjects. However, the properties of the twitch and tetanic responses were much more variable in the spinal cord-injured subjects. Furthermore, the muscles of these individuals comprised fewer motor units that ranged in strength from exerting no detectable force to being five times stronger than normal (Thomas, 1997; Yang, Stein, Jhamandas, & Gordon, 1990).

Similar studies have been performed on the triceps brachii muscle in spinal cord-injured subjects who retain some voluntary control of the muscle. Maximum voluntary contraction force is significantly less in these individuals compared with able-bodied persons (Thomas, Tucker, & Bigland-Ritchie, 1998; Thomas, Zaidner,

Calancie, Broton, & Bigland-Ritchie, 1997). Although these muscles exhibit marked atrophy, they are also weak due to an impairment of the neural drive to the motor neurons (Thomas, Zaidner, et al., 1997). As observed in paralyzed muscle, the forces exerted by motor units in partially paralyzed muscle range from near zero to much stronger than normal. For example, 11% of the motor units in partially paralyzed triceps brachii generated normal EMGs but no measurable force; 65% of the units were similar to control units; and 24% were stronger than usual (Thomas, Broton, & Calancie, 1997). However, these motor units were activated voluntarily in order of increasing force, which is consistent with the orderly recruitment of motor units.

Motor Recovery From Injury

Although the neuromuscular system has remarkable adaptive capabilities, there are limits to the adaptations that can be expressed. There are limits, for example, to muscle plasticity (Pette & Vrbová, 1999). Moreover, it has long been recognized that the nervous system has minimal regenerative capabilities. To explore this feature of chronic adaptations, we consider the capabilities of the neuromuscular system to recover motor function after an injury to the peripheral nerve or a lesion in the CNS.

Peripheral Nervous System

It has been known for some time that the neuromuscular system is capable of some recovery of function after an injury to a peripheral nerve. Because neurons in the adult CNS are not capable of cell division, this recovery depends on the ability of the neurons to reinnervate appropriate targets. When an axon is cut, in a procedure known as **axotomy,** degenerative changes occur both in the axon distal to the lesion and in the neuron (figure 9.32). About two to three days after the axotomy, the soma begins to swell and may double in size, and the rough endoplasmic reticulum (stained as Nissl substance) breaks apart and moves to the periphery of the soma (figure 9.32b and c). The dissolution of the Nissl substance is referred to as **chromatolysis.** The process of chromatolysis lasts one to three weeks and seems to involve a massive resynthesis of the proteins necessary for regeneration of the axon and the formation of sprouts. If a sprout is able to invade the remaining myelin fragments (figure 9.32c) or newly generated Schwann cells, it is likely that reinnervation of the original target will occur. This is possible in the motor, sensory, and autonomic divisions of the peripheral nervous system. Invasion of the appropriate

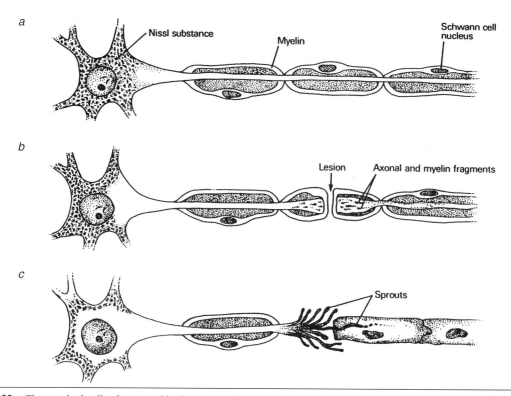

Figure 9.32 Changes in the distal axon and in the neuron after axotomy: *(a)* a normal soma and axon of a neuron; *(b)* two to three days after axotomy; *(c)* one to three weeks after axotomy.

From "Reactions of neurons to injury," by J.P. Kelly. In *Principles of Neural Science, 2nd ed.,* p. 187, by E.R. Kandel and J.H. Schwartz (Eds.), 1985, New York: Elsevier Science Publishing Co., Inc. Reproduced with permission of the McGraw-Hill Companies.

myelin fragment appears to be the most critical step in the recovery of function. Failure of reinnervation, however, results in degeneration of the axotomized neuron, the distal segment of the axon, and the target cell (McComas, 1996).

Because recovery depends on the ability of sprouts to reinnervate appropriate targets, the nature of the injury to a peripheral nerve is an important determinant in the extent of the recovery of function. In general, a complete transection of the nerve offers the worst prognosis; a partial denervation (sparing of some axons) is less severe; and a crush injury has only minimal long-term effects. Injuries that result in a transection of peripheral nerve trunks are usually accompanied by lasting motor and sensory deficits, which represent poor functional recovery (Cope, Bonasera, & Nichols, 1994; Scott, 1996). There are surgical techniques for resuturing a severed nerve with the aim of permitting regenerating axons to develop sprouts and reinnervate original targets. These procedures, however, typically result in a significant number of misdirected reinnervations (table 9.6). When this occurs, motor neurons that originally innervated one muscle now innervate another muscle. A test of this is to find a motor unit in a test muscle and then determine which muscle the subject must contract to activate the

motor unit (table 9.6). In one study on the first dorsal interosseus muscle, 39% of the motor units were reinnervated correctly; 11% of the motor units were reinnervated by axons that previously went to abductor digiti minimi (abducts the fifth finger), 22% by axons that previously innervated adductor pollicis (adducts the thumb), and 28% by axons that previously innervated other muscles (Thomas, Stein, Gordon, Lee, & Elleker, 1987).

An obvious consequence of these misdirected reinnervations is that the activation of a motor neuron pool does not lead to the selective activation of one muscle. For example, table 9.6 indicates that activating the motor neuron pool for first dorsal interosseus results in activation of at least the first dorsal interosseus (index finger abduction) and abductor digiti minimi (fifth finger abduction) muscles. Similarly, activation of the motor neuron pool for adductor pollicis (thumb adduction) will also activate both first dorsal interosseus and abductor digiti minimi. This reorganization obviously impairs motor coordination for fine movements. These misdirections also occur with sensory axons and make it difficult for patients to localize a sensory stimulus, although they can detect it. Furthermore, the intermingling of motor neurons and muscle fibers disrupts the relation between the force at

Table 9.6 Origin of Motor Axons in Reinnervated Muscles After Complete Transection of the Ulnar Nerve at the Wrist

	Abductor digiti minimi	First dorsal interosseus	Adductor pollicis	Others
Abductor digiti minimi	16 (34%)	15 (31%)	9 (18%)	8 (17%)
First dorsal interosseus	6 (11%)	22 (39%)	12 (22%)	16 (28%)

The first column indicates motor unit location, whereas the rows indicate the muscles in which the voluntary contractions were needed to activate the motor unit.

Note. Data are from Thomas et al., 1987.

which motor units are recruited (recruitment threshold) and the amplitude of the twitch force. The relation is frequently used as an index of orderly recruitment based on the Size Principle, whereby small units (low twitch forces) are recruited at low forces. The absence of a relation between recruitment threshold and twitch amplitude suggests a loss of the ability to recruit motor units according to size and to finely grade the force exerted by a muscle. Taken together, the misdirected reinnervations and loss of size-related recruitment indicate a poor coordination for fine movements. However, the recovery of function is sufficient for power movements.

Compared with the situation of a complete nerve transection, there is less impairment following recovery from a partial transection of the nerve close to the muscle. The principal recovery mechanism following a partial lesion is somewhat different from that associated with a complete transection; it still involves axonal growth and reinnervation, but the axons of surviving motor units develop sprouts to reinnervate the muscle fibers that have been denervated (Dengler, Konstabzer, Hesse, Schubert, & Wolf, 1989; Slawinska, Tyc, Kasicki, Navarrete, & Vrbová, 1998). This type of sprouting by surviving axons, referred to as **collateral sprouting,** appears to be confined to the distal region of the motor axon and to occur close to the target. Apparently all the motor units within a pool compensate for these types of nerve injuries by collateral sprouting (Rafuse, Gordon, & Orozco, 1992; Rafuse & Gordon, 1996). The number of additional fibers reinnervated depends on the size of the motor unit; larger motor units are capable of supporting a larger number of muscle fibers. Furthermore, the extent of the sprouting depends on the number of fibers that were denervated (figure 9.33). The greater the extent of the partial lesion and hence the number of muscle fibers that are denervated, the greater the amount of collateral sprouting and the greater the size of the surviving motor units. The performance of physical activity, such as running, can further enhance the tetanic force of already enlarged motor units (Seburn & Gardiner, 1996).

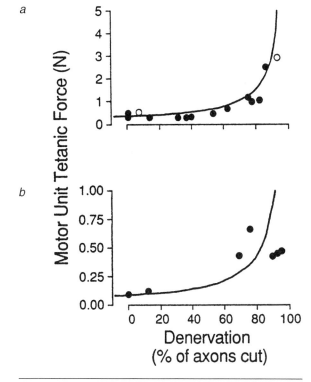

Figure 9.33 Tetanic force of motor units as a function of the degree of partial denervation (percentage of the nerve that was cut): *(a)* motor units in medial (filled circles) and lateral (open circles) gastrocnemius; *(b)* motor units in soleus.

Adapted from Rafuse, Gordon, and Orozco, 1992.

Collateral sprouting can account for up to about 80% of the motor neuron loss, with motor units capable of enlarging to about five times the original size (Gordon, Yang, Ayer, Stein, & Tyreman, 1993). These observations indicate that when as much as 80% of the peripheral nerve is cut, the neuromuscular system can recover the maximum force capability. This recovery could result from three mechanisms: an increase in the innervation ratio, an increase in the average cross-sectional area of muscle fibers, or an increase in the specific tension.

The most important mechanism appears to be an increase in the innervation ratio, which must be due to collateral sprouting (Rafuse & Gordon, 1998; Tötösy de Zepetnek, Zung, Erdebil, & Gordon, 1992). The potential for collateral sprouting does not depend on descending drive, because it occurs to the same extent when the spinal cord is transected above the level of the motor neuron pool.

Example 9.5
Denervation Changes Muscle Fiber Properties

When the nerve to a muscle is cut, the muscle loses its innervation; this is described as **denervation.** In addition to the changes that occur in the proximal and distal segments of the severed axons, the target cells of the motor axons—the muscle fibers—undergo a number of changes. As described in more detail by McComas (1996), these changes include the following:

- Denervation atrophy: the decrease in fiber size, which begins about three days after denervation, occurs in all fibers.

- Displacement of nuclei: the nuclei change shape and migrate from the outer membranes to the center of the fiber.

- Necrosis: some fibers degenerate and die after several months.

- Reduction in size: as the fibers atrophy, many organelles (e.g., mitochondria, sarcoplasmic reticulum) also decrease in size.

- Lowered enzyme activity: the activities of many, but not all, enzymes decrease so that the fibers appear more homogeneous.

- Decline in contractile properties: as a consequence of the fiber atrophy and decrease in enzyme activities, the amplitudes of the twitch and tetanus decline and the twitch becomes slower.

- Sarcolemmal adaptations: the resting potential of the sarcolemma decreases; the permeability to K+ and Cl– declines; the duration of the action potential increases; the sensitivity to acetylcholine is heightened; fibrillation potentials appear; the concentration of acetylcholinesterase decreases; and the fiber releases factors that promote sprouts in nearby motor axons.

The connection between motor neurons and muscle fibers can also be disrupted by **neuropathies,** which are disorders of peripheral nerves. These disorders can be acute or chronic and can involve the myelin sheath or the axon. Guillain-Barré syndrome, an autoimmune disorder that disrupts the myelination of peripheral nerves, is an example of an acute neuropathy. Chronic neuropathies can result from genetic diseases, metabolic disorders, intoxication, nutritional disorders, carcinomas, and immunological disorders.

Central Nervous System

Researchers disagree on the recuperative abilities of the CNS. Although most accept that the CNS is capable of reorganization, the evidence is scarce that the system can recover from injury. One example suggesting that the CNS is capable of reorganization is the **synaptogenesis** (formation of new synapses) that occurs with enhanced activity (Jones, Chu, Grande, & Gregory, 1999). For example, when electrodes were implanted in the thalamus of the cat and corticocortical connections were subjected to four days of stimulation, the results were an increased density of specific classes of synapses in layers II-III in the motor cortex, an increase in certain structural features of synapses, and alterations in the patterns of synaptic activity (Keller, Arissian, & Asanuma, 1992). It has been suggested that this reorganization underlies processes associated with motor learning and memory.

Other attempts to examine sprouting in the CNS have focused on the ability of the spinal cord to compensate for removal of selected inputs or pathways. Three classical preparations are used to examine CNS sprouting: the spared-root preparation, a hemisection model, and a deafferentation preparation. The **spared-root** preparation involves transection of all the dorsal roots supplying a hindlimb except one (usually L6). The animal recovers from the surgery and learns to reuse the limb. Once the motor recovery has been measured (weeks to months later), experiments are performed to determine the extent of the sprouting in the spinal cord by the spared dorsal root. The **hemisection** model involves removing one-half ("hemi") of the spinal cord at some appropriate level, and then monitoring both the recovery of function and subsequently the extent of sprouting in the spinal cord. The **deafferentation** preparation follows the same principle and measures the recovery of function and sprouting after transection of the dorsal (afferent) roots.

These are difficult experiments to perform, and there is no consensus on the results; some scientists conclude that the sprouting does occur and others suggest that it does not (Goldberger, Murray, & Tessler, 1993). Distinguishing between sprouting and unmasking is one difficulty, and accounting for interanimal variability is another. As is the case for the peripheral nervous system, there is some evidence that collateral sprouting occurs in the spinal cord with the spared-root preparation. There are also clear examples in which the recovery of function can be explained by unmasking (O'Hara & Goshgarian, 1991). **Unmasking** refers to the activation of a dormant neural pathway (or set of synapses) that is not needed until another (primary) pathway has been interrupted. Furthermore, because the evidence for sprouting relies on the measurement of synaptic density and because there is considerable variability in this parameter between animals, it is possible that evidence of sprouting is missed when data from different animals are combined rather than examined individually (Goldberger et al., 1993). Nevertheless, it appears that sprouting occurs continuously in the normal CNS, with synaptic connections degenerating and being renewed. This provides a potential mechanism for plasticity in the damaged nervous system.

One of the critical factors in CNS regeneration is the presence or absence of scar tissue. Crushing of the spinal cord causes massive glial and connective tissue scar from which recovery is minimal (Freed, de Medinaceli, & Wyatt, 1985). Sprouts cannot cross physical barriers such as scars, and this severely limits regeneration. Furthermore, the sprouts from damaged axons in the CNS are usually short, and this limits the range of regeneration. Scientists do not yet know why the regenerative capacity is so different in the peripheral and central nervous systems. Key elements appear to be the abundance of factors that promote sprouting, the presence of axon-elongation inhibitors, the expression of proteins that facilitate axon elongation, and the magnitude of the sequelae (glial cell formation, scar tissue, inflammation, and invasion by immune cells).

Example 9.6
Changes in Brain Activity

Typical examples of plasticity in the CNS include the adaptations that occur after either focal injury in the CNS (e.g., stroke) or alterations in the periphery (e.g., amputation, immobilization). The development of imaging technologies has enabled researchers to examine the changes that take place in the human brain. This can be accomplished with positron emission tomography (PET), which images the synthesis of compounds that contain a labeled isotope. For example, PET has been used to image the turnover of an agent that modulates synaptic transmission in the intact brain (Imahori, Fujii, Kondo, Ohmori, & Nakajima, 1999). The researchers compared turnover of the neuromodulator in patients after a focal lesion, due to either a stroke or a brain tumor, with activity in healthy subjects. They found that the early events in reorganization of the neural connections began in remote regions of the brain rather than in the areas close to the lesions. Presumably this activity indicates the activation of alternative pathways in an attempt to compensate for the damage.

Rehabilitation Strategies

Physical activity is an important component of a healthy lifestyle, especially for persons who have experienced a partial or complete lesion in the CNS. Apart from traditional activities that can be prescribed for individuals with spinal cord injuries (Noreau & Shephard, 1995), supplemental activity can involve functional electrical stimulation and assisted-locomotion training.

Functional electrical stimulation refers to the artificial activation of muscle with a protocol of electric shocks that enhances the function of muscle. Within the context of this chapter, the primary purpose of this procedure is to counteract the effects of inactivity (Gordon & Mao, 1994). The three major consequences of reduced activity for patients who experience CNS lesions are disuse atrophy, increased fatigability, and reduced bone density. Before functional electrical stimulation can be used to assist with activities of daily living, therefore, therapeutic interventions must attend to these deficiencies (Hartkopp, Murphy, Mohr, Kjær, & Biering-Sorensen, 1998; Scremin et al., 1999).

A variety of functional electrical stimulation protocols have been used on paralyzed muscle. These have evoked adaptations ranging from a change in the MHC composition of muscle fibers to increases in bone density, muscle force, and endurance (Andersen et al., 1996; Chilibeck, Jeon, Weiss, Bell, & Burnham, 1999; Kagaya et al., 1996; Rodgers et al., 1991). The adaptations evoked with electrical stimulation depend on the details of the stimulation protocol. For example, maintenance of the endurance capability of the tibialis anterior muscle in spinal cord-injured patients requires 1 to 2 h of stimulation (20 Hz) per day, but this amount does not alter muscle force (Stein et al., 1992). As one would expect, the effects of such imposed activity vary across the motor unit types. When identified single motor units in thenar muscles were stimulated at 30 to 50 Hz for about 30 min over a six-week period, the force of the slower, fatigue-resistant motor units increased whereas that for the faster, fatigable motor units declined (Chan et al., 1999). Conversely, the fatigue resistance of the slow-twitch motor units did not change, whereas that for the fast-twitch units increased. Along with numerous studies on the effects of long-duration, low-frequency stimulation, these findings indicate that the stimulation protocols designed to increase endurance invariably lead to a decrease in muscle force (Gordon & Mao, 1994; Pette & Vrbová, 1999).

Most studies that have examined the effect of functional electrical stimulation on paralyzed muscle have not imposed a load on the artificially activated muscles, which the strength-training literature indicates is necessary to achieve an increase in muscle force (Kern et al., 1999). For example, 8 weeks of a strength-training protocol applied to the quadriceps femoris muscle of patients about 46 weeks after complete spinal cord transection evoked an increase in muscle cross-sectional area of 20% (Dudley, Castro, Rogers, & Apple, 1999). The effect of the functional electrical stimulation was to reverse 48 weeks of muscle atrophy such that muscle size 54 weeks after the injury was the same as it had been 6 weeks after the injury. Similarly, Scremin et al. (1999) found that strength training with functional electrical stimulation increased the cross-sectional area of many thigh muscles and enabled the patients to progress to a cycling program. Moreover, functional electrical stimulation appears capable of activating a greater proportion of the muscle mass in these patients than it does in able-bodied persons (Hillegass & Dudley, 1999).

It has proved more difficult, however, to halt the marked loss of bone mass experienced by these patients. For example, months of cycle training with contractions evoked by functional electrical stimulation produce only modest changes in bone mineral density (BeDell, Scremin, Perell, & Kunkel, 1996; Mohr et al., 1997).

Studies on other populations, such as postmenopausal women, suggest that improvements in bone mass require weight-bearing activities in which the limbs are exposed to impact forces (Kaplan et al., 1994; Konieczynski et al., 1998; Snow-Harter & Marcus, 1991).

An alternative strategy that has produced impressive adaptations in neuromuscular function is **assisted-locomotion training** (Barbeau & Rossignol, 1987; Dietz, Colombo, & Jensen, 1994). This procedure, which involves training spinal cord-injured persons to walk on a treadmill, has been used with both paraplegic and quadriplegic patients. At the onset of the training program, an individual is placed in a harness to support some body weight (up to 60%), and therapists assist each leg with the transition from the stance phase to the swing phase. As the training progresses, the proportion of body-weight support is gradually reduced, and the EMG of the extensor leg muscles increases and becomes more similar to that observed in healthy individuals (figure 9.34). The magnitude of the training effect is greatest in persons with partial lesions that result in incomplete paralysis (Dietz, 1997).

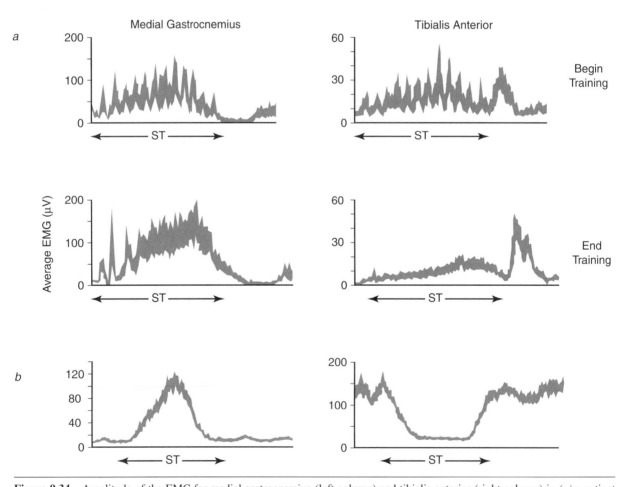

Figure 9.34   Amplitude of the EMG for medial gastrocnemius (left column) and tibialis anterior (right column) in *(a)* a patient with incomplete paraplegia and *(b)* a healthy subject while walking on a treadmill. Electromyograms are shown for the patient at the beginning and end of training. ST indicates the stance phase.

Data from Dietz et al., 1994.

These findings indicate that the isolated spinal cord is able to generate locomotor patterns and that it is able to adapt when presented with imposed loads. The magnitude of the adaptation experienced by patients with incomplete paraplegia can progress to unsupported stepping movements on the ground (Dietz et al., 1995). But whether or not the adaptations progress to this level, patients experience positive effects on the cardiovascular and musculoskeletal systems. For example, the symptoms of spasticity are reduced, and the activation of large muscles heightens the load and adaptations experienced by the cardiovascular system. Furthermore, passive exercise can attenuate disuse atrophy even after a complete transection of the spinal cord (Dupont-Versteegden, Houlé, Gurley, & Peterson, 1998).

The adaptive capabilities of the isolated spinal cord appear to be quite remarkable. For example, spinalized adult cats can be trained to stand or to perform stepping movements (Rossignol, 2000; Roy, Talmadge, et al., 1998). The training regimen involves about 30 min/day, five days per week, for 8 to 12 weeks. The adaptations exhibited by the involved muscles differ for the two training tasks, including the fiber type and MHC composition and the contractile properties (Roy et al., 1999). Figure 9.35 shows the effects of stand and step training on the contractile properties of the soleus, medial gastrocnemius, and tibialis anterior muscles. As suggested by these differential effects, a cat can learn to stand if it is trained to stand, whereas stand training has a minimal effect on the ability to step (de Leon et al., 1998a, 1998b; Edgerton et al., 1997). These results underscore the specificity of the adaptations and suggest the therapeutic strategies that should be most beneficial.

Adaptations With Age

Senescence is generally accompanied by a marked decline in the capabilities of the motor system. Although these changes can often be attributed to pathological processes, even healthy and vigorous elderly individuals experience reductions in performance capabilities that seem to represent the natural consequences of aging. In this section we describe some of the changes that occur in the motor system with age and then examine mechanisms that appear to mediate these adaptations.

Movement Capabilities of Older Adults

Throughout, this text has emphasized the concept that the motor unit represents the functional unit of the motor system. It represents the link between the nervous system and muscle. Because aging causes significant changes in motor unit properties, there are marked declines in most aspects of movement. These changes in-

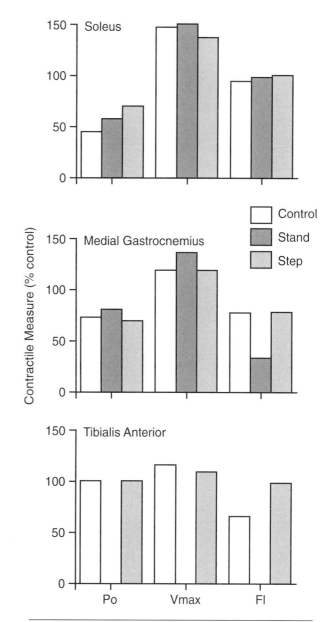

Figure 9.35 Changes in the contractile properties of three muscles of spinalized cats after several weeks of no training (Control), training in standing (Stand), or training in stepping (Step). The data are plotted relative to those for healthy cats.

Data from Roy et al., 1999.

P_o = maximum tetanic force; V_{max} = maximum shortening velocity; FI = fatigue index.

clude a decline in strength, a reduction in the magnitude of reflex responses, a slowing of rapid reactions, an increased postural instability and diminished postural control, decreased control of submaximal force, and reduced manipulative capabilities (Grabiner & Enoka, 1995). These effects are underscored, for example, by the decline in the world record performances that have been produced by older athletes (Holloszy & Kohrt, 1995;

Tanaka & Seals, 1997), and by the deterioration with age of such highly skilled acts as putting in golf (Smith et al., 2000).

Muscle Strength and Power

One of the most prominent effects of age on the motor system is the unavoidable decline in muscle mass and strength, which has been termed **sarcopenia** (Dutta, Hadley, & Lexell, 1997). The decline in strength has been observed in many different muscles (Holloszy & Kohrt, 1995; Hunter, White, & Thompson, 1998; Porter, Vandervoort, & Lexell, 1995; Reimers, Harder, & Saxe, 1998). In some muscles, the decrease in strength begins at about age 60 years (figure 9.36a), whereas for other muscles there is a constant decline with advancing age (figure 9.36b). For example, a longitudinal study on men found that MVC torque decreased by 16% to 30% over 12 years, except at fast speeds for the elbow extensor muscles (Frontera et al., 2000). The magnitude of the decline in strength, however, varies among individuals.

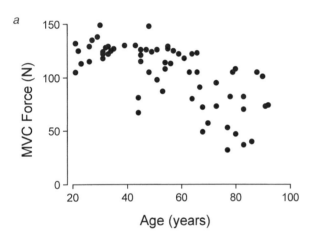

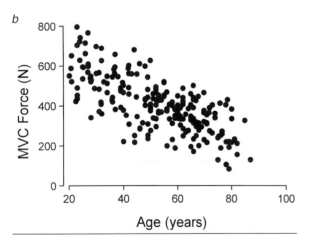

Figure 9.36 The decrease in maximum voluntary contraction (MVC) force for individuals of different ages for (a) the hand muscle adductor pollicis and (b) for quadriceps femoris.

Part a is adapted from Narici, Bordini, and Ceretelli, 1991; part b is from Hunter et al., 1998.

This is obvious in figure 9.36a by the increased scatter of the data points after age 60 years. The variable loss of strength suggests that the responsible mechanisms are activated to different degrees among individuals. The decline in strength, however, is not due to a reduced ability of older adults to achieve maximal activation of muscle during a voluntary contraction (De Serres & Enoka, 1998; Kent-Braun & Ng, 1999; Roos, Rice, Connelly, & Vandervoort, 1999).

The decrease in strength, however, is usually greater than the loss of muscle mass. For example, the cross-sectional area of muscle in a longitudinal study (Frontera et al., 2000) declined by 16.1% for the quadriceps femoris and by 14.9% for the knee flexor muscles compared with average strength reductions of 20% to 30%. Furthermore, the percentage decrease in strength (peak torque) was similar at low and fast speeds for the knee flexor and extensor muscles but not the elbow flexor and extensor muscles. As a result of this dissociation, muscle strength at the onset of the 12-year study and the changes in cross-sectional area were independent predictors of muscle strength at the end of the 12 years.

Despite the presence of sarcopenia, numerous studies have demonstrated that muscle strength can be enhanced in older adults after participation in appropriate training programs (Häkkinen et al., 1996; Lexell, Downham, Larsson, Bruhn, & Morsing, 1995). The strength gains can be substantial, especially in sedentary persons (Fiatarone et al., 1990; Lexell et al., 1995). Such adaptations, however, involve minimal changes in muscle size. For example, Lexell et al. (1995) found that 11 weeks of strength training by men and women increased 1-RM load for the knee extensor muscles by ~160%, but the cross-sectional area of the fibers in the vastus lateralis muscle showed no change. In contrast, an active lifestyle appears to reduce the amount of sarcopenia that is evident in muscles of older adults (Reimers et al., 1998) and to enhance physiological status (Bassey, 1998; Nakamura, Moritani, & Kanetaka, 1996).

Traditional strength-training programs, as discussed at the beginning of this chapter, typically involve lifting heavy loads in several sets of repetitions about three times a week. However, older adults can achieve impressive strength gains with variations in the traditional program. For example, twice-weekly training sessions enhance exercise adherence yet are sufficient to produce substantial increases in 1-RM load (figure 9.37) in both arm (arm curl, military press, and bench press) and leg (leg press) muscles (McCartney, Hicks, Martin, & Webber, 1996). Alternatively, a four-week training program that involved light loads and steady contractions was sufficient to increase 1-RM load, albeit the response was less than that achieved with heavy loads (Laidlaw et al., 1999). Older adults even experience an increase in muscle strength with tai chi training (Lan, Lai, Chen, & Wong, 1998). Such

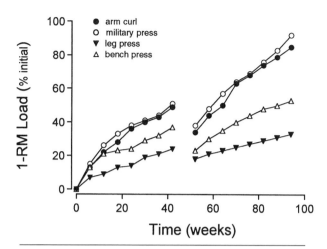

Figure 9.37 Increases in one repetition-maximum (1-RM) load over a two-year strength-training program. There was an eight-week break in the middle of the program.

Data from McCartney et al., 1996.

improvements likely involve adaptations in the nervous system, as the changes in muscle size are minimal.

In addition to the loss of muscle mass and strength with age, the contractile speed of many muscles is also less in older adults (Hunter et al., 1998; McCartney et al., 1996; McComas, 1996). This adaptation is evident as an increase in the contraction and relaxation time of the twitch, a decline in the speed of rapid contractions, and a reduction in the power that muscles can produce (De Vito et al., 1998; Doherty & Brown, 1997; Izquierdo et al., 1999; Metter, Conwit, Tobin, & Fozard, 1997; Thelen, Schultz, Alexander, & Ashton-Miller, 1996). Some investigators suggest that the decrease in power production capacity is more critical than the loss of strength. For example, the power that the leg extensor muscles can produce declines more rapidly than the strength of the knee extensor muscles, and there is a high correlation between peak power capacity and the power expended when climbing stairs (Bassey, 1997). Furthermore, the ability of older adults to recover from a stumble depends on the muscle power and coordination among the leg muscles (Robinovitch et al., 2000; Thelen et al., 1996, 2000). Strength training, however, can increase the power production of single muscle fibers in the vastus lateralis muscle of old men (Trappe et al., 2000).

Fatigability

In comparison to the effect of aging on strength, there is less certainty about the effect of age on the fatigability of muscle. A number of protocols have been used to examine this relation. The studies that have used voluntary activation of muscle have all shown no change in fatigability with age (Bemben, Massey, Bemben, Misner, & Boileau, 1996; Hicks et al., 1992; Laforest, St-Pierre, Cyr, & Guyton, 1990; Lindstrom, Lexell, Gerdle, &

Downham, 1997). The studies have involved submaximal and maximal contractions, isometric and dynamic contractions, and sustained and intermittent contractions as performed by hand and leg muscles. Other studies that have activated muscle with electrical stimulation have shown mixed results. There have been reports of no change, an increase, and a decrease in fatigability (Hunter et al., 1998). For example, 30 s of ulnar nerve stimulation at 20 Hz (Lennmarken, Bergman, Larsson, & Larsson, 1985) indicated an increased fatigability in elderly men (67 years) but not elderly women (63 years), whereas 30-Hz stimulation (Narici et al., 1991) demonstrated a decreased fatigability with age (70 male subjects, 20-91 years). These inconsistencies may be related to the variable occlusion of muscle blood flow during the different protocols (Hunter et al., 1998).

These findings suggest that, in general, the relative function of the neuromuscular system does not change much with advancing age. In absolute terms, however, the capability of most organ systems, including the cardiovascular and respiratory systems, declines with age (Lakatta, 1995; Sparrow & Weiss, 1995). These absolute decreases are evident by decreases in maximal oxygen consumption, peak heart rate, and the ability of muscles to extract and use oxygen, which reduce the absolute endurance capacity of older adults.

Reflex Responses and Rapid Reactions

The peak-to-peak amplitude of the H-reflex EMG decreases with age. Vandervoort and Hayes (1989) found that the H-reflex amplitude in soleus for a group of elderly women (82 years) was only 43% of that for younger women (26 years). This difference in H-reflex amplitude, however, could be explained by the reduction in muscle fiber excitability with age. The peak-to-peak amplitude of the M wave was also different for the two groups of subjects. Recall that the M wave represents the direct activation of muscle and provides an index of muscle fiber excitability (Hicks et al., 1992), whereas the H reflex involves the reflex activation of the motor neurons in the spinal cord. For the elderly group of subjects, the H-reflex stimulus resulted in the activation of 55% of the muscle fibers that contributed to the M wave, and for the younger subjects the proportion was 60%. Consequently, the proportion of the motor unit pool that was activated by the H-reflex stimulus did not differ with age.

Nonetheless, there are differences between young and old adults in the modulation of the H reflex across standing and prone positions. For example, young subjects decreased the normalized amplitude of the H reflex when going from a prone to a standing position, whereas old subjects did the opposite (Angulo-Kinzler, Mynark, & Koceja, 1998). In addition, there were differences due to age in the reflex amplitude and its modulation when the muscles performed submaximal contractions at various levels.

Differences have also been found between young (27 years) and old (75 years) subjects in the tendon-tap reflex elicited in the quadriceps femoris muscle (Burke, Kamen, & Koceja, 1989). In this study, a rubber-tipped implement struck the patellar tendon and elicited a tendon-tap reflex that was measured as the force exerted at the ankle. The amplitude of the reflex response was greater in the younger subjects (30 vs. 18 N) and occurred with a briefer latency (60 vs. 79 ms). The difference in the amplitude of the response might be related to the difference in strength between the two groups, but the difference in latency suggests an age-related difference in the detection, transmission, and processing of the stimulus. Recall that the tendon-tap reflex involves excitation of muscle spindles, propagation of afferent signals back to the spinal cord, activation of the alpha motor neurons, and excitation of the associated muscle fibers. It is unclear which of these processes change and contribute to the alteration in latency with age.

The study of rapid reactions to visual cues or sudden movements provides further clues on the neural adaptations that occur with aging. This effect can be quantified through measurement of the **reaction time,** which is the time from target displacement to the beginning of the response by the subject. For example, Warabi, Noda, and Kato (1986) compared the response time of eye and hand muscles to various target displacements. The response of the eyes was measured with an electrooculogram, and that of the hand was measured as the movement of a joystick. Both reaction times increased by similar amounts with age and were greatest for the larger target displacements. Because the motor components of these movements (e.g., peak velocity, duration, amplitude) were not altered with age, Warabi et al. (1986) concluded that the principal effect of age on the rapid-reaction task was an impairment of sensory processing. This conclusion is consistent with other reports of a decline in sensory capabilities with age (Dyck, Karnes, O'Brien, & Zimmerman, 1984; Klein, Fischer, Hartnegg, Heiss, & Roth, 2000; Stevens, Cruz, Marks, & Lakatos, 1998; Thelen, Brockmiller, Ashton-Miller, Schultz, & Alexander, 1998). Furthermore, the differential effects of age on the various components of the stretch reflex (figure 6.58) argue against a significant role for impairment of central processing in these changes (Corden & Lippold, 1996).

Older adults also exhibit slower responses when performing complex multi-component tasks. For example, the response time to make a sudden turn during walking was greater in old adults (Cao, Ashton-Miller, Schultz, & Alexander, 1997). Furthermore, women needed longer to make the turn than did men of the same age. Similarly, increases in the time taken to perform a step when falling forward reduce the likelihood that balance can be recovered (Robinovitch et al., 2000; Thelen, Wojcik, Schultz, Ashton-Miller, & Alexander, 1997). These studies indicate that all movements, from reflexes to multitask activities, become slower with advancing age.

Maintenance of Posture

Aging is typically accompanied by reductions in the ability to control both posture and gait (Hortobágyi & DeVita, 2000; Polcyn, Lipsitz, Kerrigan, & Collins, 1998; Rogers, Kukulka, & Soderberg, 1992; Schultz, 1992). These effects are most readily documented as a decline in the amount of walking and in the performance of the daily activities of living among elderly individuals. The adaptations that underlie these reductions are complex, and involve both motor and sensory processes. Alterations in the control of posture are significant because they influence the balance of an individual and influence the likelihood of accidental falls and injuries (Kannus et al., 1999). Furthermore, the concurrent loss of strength and reduction in balance exaggerate the functional impairments (Rantanen, Guralnik, Ferrucci, Leveille, & Fried, 1999).

Maintenance of an upright posture requires that an individual keep the projection of the weight vector within the base of support. This requires the involvement of several different processes: (a) sensory information to detect the orientation and motion of the individual, (b) selection of an appropriate response strategy to maintain balance, and (c) activation of the muscles that can overcome any postural imbalance. The sensory information can be derived from visual, somatosensory, and vestibular sources. Not all this information is necessary, and an individual can chose from among these sensory signals. Moreover, patients with deficits in one of these sensory systems can readily learn to rely on the other two. However, age seems to diminish the ability of an individual to select the appropriate sensory information (Hay, Bard, Fleury, & Teasdale, 1996; Horak, Shupert, & Mirka, 1989). This decline is accompanied by altered strategies to control the forward-backward displacement of the center of gravity (Collins, De Luca, Burrows, & Lipsitz, 1995) and the use of slower and larger responses to disturbances of balance (Gu, Schultz, Shepard, & Alexander, 1996; Nardone, Siliotto, Grasso, & Schieppati, 1995; Tang & Woollacott, 1998).

Although the maintenance of an upright posture appears to be a simple task, there are a number of impairments that can reduce this ability. Horak et al. (1989), for example, concluded that the reduced postural control of older adults could be caused by an abnormal selection of sensory information, poor detection of disequilibrium, abnormal selection of postural-adjustment response, prolonged latencies for rapid responses, reduced perception of stability limits, weakness of involved muscles, or impaired ability to coordinate activity among synergist muscles.

Because of the diminished control of posture that older adults exhibit, considerable attention has focused on the association between balance and falls in this population. The ability to maintain balance is often quantified from the displacement of the center of pressure during standing. The measures include the average displacement and the range of displacement of the center of pressure during leaning and swaying tasks. There is, however, no association between such measures of postural stability and the ability of an indⁱviᵈual to recover from a loss of balance (Owings, Pavol, Foley, & Grabiner, 2000). Rather, the ability to recover usually depends on the dynamics of the step response, which is reduced in older adults (Robinovitch et al., 2000). Importantly, appropriate interventions, such as tai chi, can significantly reduce the number of falls experienced by older adults (Lan et al., 1998; Wolf et al., 1996).

Control of Submaximal Force

In contrast to the more extensive literature on posture and gait in elderly subjects, much less is known about the effects of age on simpler movements and the behavior of motor units in the gradation of force (Erim, Beg, Burke, & De Luca, 1999; Laidlaw et al., 2000; Patten & Kamen, 2000). Although maximum capabilities decline with age (e.g., strength, flexibility, sensory perceptions), the consequences of these changes for the control of submaximal force are less well described. Some submaximal tasks have been examined, such as the control of isometric force and slow anisometric contractions, the kinematics of arm movements, and the control of grip force. For example, when subjects are asked to sustain a force at a constant, submaximal value for about 20 s, the force fluctuates about the target value (Galganski et al., 1993; Graves et al., 2000; Slifkin & Newell, 1999). Similarly, when subjects slowly lift and lower a load, the acceleration fluctuates about the zero line (figure 1.26). These fluctuations are used as an index of **steadiness** and occur despite attempts by the subjects to perform steady contractions. The fluctuations in force (standard deviation) and acceleration are quantified as the standard deviation and, to account for differences in strength, normalized relative to the target force (coefficient of variation) or the load ($m \cdot s^2/kg$). Figure 9.38 shows the steadiness results for young and old subjects lifting and lowering loads (2.5%, 5%, 20%, 50%, and 75% MVC) with the index finger. In general, the old subjects were less steady than young adults, especially when performing eccentric contractions with light loads. Similar results have been found for the elbow flexor and knee extensor muscles (Graves et al., 2000; Tracy, Pruitt, Butler, & Enoka, 2000). These data indicate that older adults are less able to perform steady submaximal contractions and that the decrease in steadiness is greater when performing anisometric contractions compared with isometric contractions. This impairment, however, disappears after participation in a strength-training program

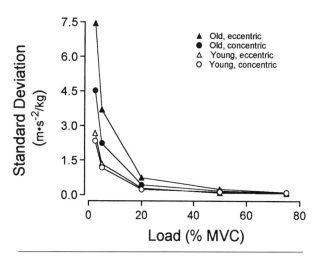

Figure 9.38 Standard deviation of normalized acceleration for the index finger during concentric and eccentric contractions performed by young and old adults.

Data from Burnett et al., 2000.

MVC = maximum voluntary contraction.

(Bilodeau, Keen, Sweeney, Shields, & Enoka, 2000; Keen et al., 1994; Laidlaw et al., 1999).

Another effect of age on the control of submaximal force involves the grip force during the manipulation of small objects (Cole, 1991). Subjects were instructed to lift a small object (1.7-cm width, 1.6-N weight) in a vertical direction about 5 cm, and the pinch force exerted by the thumb and index finger was measured. The slipperiness of the sides of the object could be altered. The elderly subjects exerted a force that was about 2 times greater than that of the young subjects and 2.5 times greater than the force needed to prevent the object from slipping. The excessive grip forces by the older subjects are due to an adaptation in tactile afferents that reduces hand sensibilies and to alterations in the glabrous skin that increase hand slipperiness (Cole et al., 1999). Clearly, performance capabilities for such tasks as manipulation depend on the maintained integrity of both sensory and motor systems.

Physiological Adaptations With Age

Throughout this text, movement has been presented as a phenomenon that involves the integration of numerous sensory and motor processes. Many of the processes that contribute to this phenomenon change with age. Some of the changes that occur with advancing age include:

- Death of motor neurons (Gardner, 1940; Tomlinson & Irving, 1977)
- Alterations in the morphological and biophysical properties of neurons (Liu et al., 1996; Zhang, Sampogna, Morales, & Chase, 1997)

- Slowing of the conduction velocity of action potentials (Falco, Hennessey, Braddom, & Goldberg, 1992; Wang, de Pasqua, & Delwaide, 1999; Xi, Liu, Engelhardt, Morales, & Chase, 1999)

- Decrease in the number of functioning motor units (Campbell, McComas, & Petito, 1973; Doherty, Vandervoort, Taylor, & Brown, 1993; Wang et al., 1999)

- Reduction in the frequency of miniature end-plate potentials (Alshuaib & Fahim, 1991)

- Enlargement of the innervation ratio (Kadhiresan, Hassett, & Faulkner, 1996; Kanda & Hazhizume, 1989; Masakado et al., 1994)

- Decrease in the amplitude of the M wave (Hicks et al., 1992)

- Coexpression of MHCs in muscle fibers (Andersen, Terzis, & Kryger, 1999)

- Increase in peak tension and prolongation of the twitch (Doherty & Brown, 1997)

- Altered calcium kinetics in the sarcoplasmic reticulum (Danieli-Betto et al., 1995; Margreth, Damiani, & Bortoloso, 1999)

- Decrease in the maximum shortening velocity and specific tension of muscle fibers (Degens, Yu, Li, & Larsson, 1998; Larsson et al., 1997)

- Reduction in oxidative enzyme activity (e.g., citrate synthase) in some muscles (Coggan et al., 1992; Houmard et al., 1998)

- Decline in tactile sensibility (Cole et al., 1999; Schmidt, Wahren, & Hagbarth, 1990)

This list is not complete; rather it provides an overview of the types of changes that are particularly relevant to the control of movement.

Among these changes, much interest has focused on the phenomenon of motor neuron death because of the functional consequences for movement. Two significant consequences include the decline in muscle mass due to the progressive atrophy and disintegration of denervated muscle fibers, and the development of collateral axonal sprouts that reinnervate some of the abandoned muscle fibers. The result of these processes is a decline in the number of motor units with age but an increase in the size (innervation ratio) of surviving motor units. The decline in motor unit number with age parallels the decrease in muscle strength (figure 9.36a).

The reinnervation of denervated muscle fibers by surviving motor units increases the innervation ratio of these units. Recall from chapter 6 that the force exerted by a motor unit depends on its innervation ratio, the average cross-sectional area of the muscle fibers, and the spe-

cific tension. Because of the increase in innervation ratio, the force exerted by single motor units increases as a function of age (Doherty & Brown, 1997; Galganski et al., 1993). This influences the ability of an individual to smoothly grade muscle force in two ways. First, there are fewer low-force motor units (Masakado et al., 1994). Typically a motor unit pool consists of many low-force units with an exponentially declining number of high-force units (Enoka & Fuglevand, 2001; Fuglevand, Winter, & Patla, 1993). The low-force units are important for finely controlled movements that involve submaximal forces. Second, the smoothness (absence of fluctuations) of the force exerted by a muscle depends on the force contributed by the most recently recruited motor unit (Allum, Dietz, & Freund, 1978; Christakos, 1982). Because motor units are recruited at low discharge rates that produce unfused tetani, the recruitment of a motor unit contributes fluctuations to the net force. Furthermore, the increase in motor unit force with age results in larger fluctuations with each motor unit recruited. As the average force increases, however, the relative contribution of the most recently recruited motor unit to the net force decreases (Fuglevand et al., 1993), which suggests that the effect of enlarged motor units on the force fluctuations is greatest at low forces. This is consistent with the observation that old adults are less steady, compared with young adults, when exerting low forces and lifting light loads.

Studies on the rat medial gastrocnemius muscle have shown a decrease in the proportion of type II muscle fibers and a reduction in tetanic force exerted by fast-twitch motor units in older rats (Kadhiresan et al., 1996; Kanda & Hashizume, 1989). Furthermore, the type S motor units in these muscles exerted a greater tetanic force, which resulted from an increase in the innervation ratio with no change in the average cross-sectional area of the muscle fibers or the specific tension. In humans, however, there does not appear to be a preferential loss of fast-twitch muscle fibers with advancing age. Rather, there is a reduction in the proportion of the muscle cross-sectional area that comprises fast-twitch muscle fibers due to a reduction in the diameter of the type II muscle fibers (Lexell & Taylor, 1991; Proctor, Sinning, Walro, Sieck, & Lemon, 1995). Furthermore, the changes can include an increase in the grouping, as opposed to a random distribution, of the different fiber types (Larsson, 1983). These findings suggest that aging is not associated with a preferential loss of motor neurons that innervate type II muscle fibers in humans.

Despite the magnitude of these changes with advancing age, accumulating evidence indicates that the quality of life experienced by older adults depends on the lifestyle that each one chooses. An active lifestyle, especially one that includes strength training, is associated with improvements in strength, less of a decrease in steadiness, and reduced levels of muscle atrophy. Furthermore, these attributes enable the older adult to maintain independence and to avoid many of the debilitating psychological changes that can accompany advancing age. Much remains to be learned, however, about the most appropriate training strategies for these individuals and the key physiological mechanisms that are responsible for the observed changes.

Summary

This is the second of two chapters examining the effects of physical activity on the neuromuscular system. This chapter focuses on the long-term (chronic) response of the system to the stress associated with altered levels of physical activity, presenting five topics that characterize the chronic adaptive capabilities of the system: muscle strength, muscle power, adaptation to reduced use, motor recovery from injury, and the changes that accompany advancing age. First, the concept of strength is defined; the training and loading techniques used to increase strength are presented; and the neural and muscular adaptations that accompany strength training are examined. Second, the concept of power production and its importance for movement are discussed, and the training techniques that can be used to increase power production are described. Third, we review the neuromuscular adaptations that occur when the level of physical activity is reduced, considering the examples of limb immobilization, limb unloading, and spinal transection. Fourth, we discuss the ability of the neuromuscular system to recover motor function after an injury to the nervous system. The capabilities of the peripheral and central nervous systems are distinguished, and two common rehabilitation strategies are described. Fifth, the movement capabilities of older adults are characterized and the adaptations that accompany advancing age are discussed. These examples are not intended to represent a complete summary of the chronic adaptive responses, but rather to illustrate the capabilities of the system.

Suggested Readings

Gardnier, P.F. (2001). *Neuromuscular aspects of physical activity.* Champaign, IL: Human Kinetics, chapters 5–6.

McComas, A.J. (1996). *Skeletal muscle: Form and function.* Champaign, IL: Human Kinetics, chapters 16, 17, 19, 21, and 22.

Part III
Summary

The goal of part III (chapters 8 and 9) has been to extend the concept of the single-joint system to describe the adaptive capabilities of the neuromuscular system. This description has focused on the acute adjustments (chapter 8) and chronic adaptations (chapter 9) of the system. As a result of reading these chapters, you should be familiar with the following features and concepts related to the motor system and be able to do the following:

- Realize the effect of altering core temperature on performance capabilities

- Conceive of the rationale for the techniques that have been developed to alter flexibility

- Identify the many factors that can contribute to muscle fatigue and acknowledge that performance can be impaired by different processes depending on the details of the task

- Understand the sensory adaptations that occur during fatiguing contractions

- Comprehend the various forms of muscle potentiation

- Know the performance characteristics of strength and power and the mechanisms that mediate changes in these capabilities

- Realize the extent of the adaptations that occur in the neuromuscular system with a reduction in the level of physical activity

- Acknowledge the ability of the motor system to recover some function following an injury to the nervous system

- Understand the procedures and limitations associated with two common rehabilitation techniques used with patients who have a spinal cord injury

- Identify the adaptations in motor function that occur with advancing age and the mechanisms that mediate these changes

SI Units

The abbreviation SI is derived from *Le Système Internationale d'Unites*, which represents the modern metric system. There are seven base units in this measurement system, from which the other units of measurement are derived.

Base

1. **Length**—meter (m)

   Defined as the length of the path traveled by light in a vacuum during 1/299,792,458 of a second.

   1 in. = 2.54 cm

   1 ft = 30.48 cm = 0.3048 m

   1 yd = 0.9144 m

   1 mile = 1609 m = 1.609 km

2. **Mass**—kilogram (kg): Defined as the mass of a platinum iridium cylinder preserved in Sevres, France.

   1 lb = 0.454 kg

   2.2 lb = 1 kg

Derived

Area—square meters (m^2): Two-dimensional measure of length.

   1 ft^2 = 0.0929 m^2

   1 acre = 0.4047 hectares (ha)

Volume—cubic meters (m^3): Three-dimensional measure of length. Although not an SI unit of measurement, volume is often measured in liters (L), where

   1 ml of H_2O = 1 cm^3

   1 L = 0.001 m^3

Density—kilogram/cubic meters (kg/m^3): Mass per unit volume.

Energy, work—joule (J): Energy denotes the capacity to perform work, and work refers to the application of a force over a distance.

   1 J = 1 N·m

   1 kcal = 4.183 kJ

   1 kpm = 9.807 J

Force—newton (N): One newton is a force that accelerates a 1-kg mass at a rate of 1 m/s^2.

   1 N = 1 kg·m/s^2

   1 kg-force = 9.81 N

   1 lb-force = 4.45 N

Impulse—newton·second (N·s): The application of a force over an interval of time; the area under a force-time curve.

Moment of inertia (kg·m^2): The resistance that an object offers to a change in its state of angular motion; a measure of the proximity of the mass of an object to an axis of rotation.

Power—watt (W): The rate of performing work.

   1 W = 1 J/s

   1 horsepower = 736 W

Base

3. **Time**—second (s): Defined in terms of one characteristic frequency of a cesium clock (9,192,631,770 cycles of radiation associated with a specified transition of the cesium-133 atom).

4. **Electric current**—ampere (A): Rate of flow of charged particles. The ampere is the constant current that would produce a force of 2×10^{-7} N/m between two conductors of infinite length and negligible circular cross section, and placed 1 m apart in a vacuum.

5. **Temperature**—kelvin (K): A measure of the velocity of vibration of the molecules of a body, which is the thermodynamic temperature. There is 100 K from ice point to steam point.

0 K = absolute zero

6. **Amount of substance**—mole (mol): The amount of substance containing the same number of particles as there are in 12 g (1 mol) of the nuclide ^{12}C.

7. **Luminous intensity**—candela (cd): The radiant intensity of 1/683 watt per steradian from a source that emits monochromatic radiation of frequency 540×10^{12} Hz.

Supplementary Unit

8. **Angle**—radian (rad): Measurement of an angle in a plane (i.e., two-dimensional angle).

1 rad = 57.3 degrees

Derived

Pressure—pascal (Pa): The force applied per unit area.

1 Pa = 1 N/m²

1 mm Hg = 133.3 Pa

Torque—moment of force (N·m): The rotary effect of a force.

1 ft-lb = 1.356 N·m

Acceleration (m/s²): Time rate of change in velocity. Gravity produces an acceleration of 9.807 m/s².

1 ft/s² = 0.3048 m/s²

Frequency—hertz (Hz): The number of cycles per second.

1 Hz = 1 cycle/s

Momentum (kg·m/s): Quantity of motion.

1 slug·ft/s = 4.447 kg·m/s

Speed, velocity (m/s): Time rate of change in position, where speed refers to the size of the change and velocity indicates its size and direction.

1 ft/s = 0.3048 m/s

1 mph = 0.447 m/s = 1.609 km/h

Capacitance—farad (F): The property of an electrical system of conductors and insulators that enables it to store electric charge when a potential difference exists between the conductors.

Conductance—Siemen (S): The reciprocal of resistance, thus the ease with which charged particles move through an object.

Resistance—ohm (Ω): The difficulty with which charged particles move through an object.

Voltage—volt (V): The difference in net distribution of charged particles between two locations.

Celsius (°C)

0° C = 273.15 K

Fahrenheit (°F)

32° F = 0° C = 273.15 K

°F = 1.8 °C + 32

Concentration (mol/m³): Amount of substance per unit volume.

Lumen (lm): Measure of light flux.

Steradian (sr): Three-dimensional angle, also known as a solid angle.

Conversion Factors

Acceleration

1 centimeter/second/second (cm/s²)	=	0.036 kilometers/hour/second (km/h/s)
1 centimeter/second/second (cm/s²)	=	0.01 meters/second/second (m/s²)
1 foot/second/second (ft/s²)	=	30.48 centimeters/second/second (cm/s²)
1 foot/second/second (ft/s²)	=	1.097 kilometers/hour/second (km/h/s)
1 foot/second/second (ft/s²)	=	0.3048 meters/second/second (m/s²)
1 kilometer/hour/second (km/h/s)	=	27.78 centimeters/second/second (cm/s²)
1 kilometer/hour/second (km/h/s)	=	0.2778 meters/second/second (m/s²)
1 meter/second/second (m/s²)	=	100 centimeters/second/second (cm/s²)
1 mile/hour/second	=	0.447 meters/second/second (m/s²)
1 revolution/minute/minute	=	0.001745 radians/second/second (rad/s²)
1 revolution/second/second	=	6.283 radians/second/second (rad/s²)

Angle

1 circumference	=	6.283 radians (rad)
1 degree (°)	=	0.01745 radians (rad)
1 degree (°)	=	$\dfrac{\pi}{180}$ radians (rad)
1 minute (′)	=	0.0002909 radians (rad)
1 radian (rad)	=	57.3 degrees (°)
1 revolution (rev)	=	360 degrees (°)
1 revolution (rev)	=	2π radians (rad)

Area

1 acre	=	4047 square meters (m²)
1 acre	=	0.4047 hectares (ha)
1 ares	=	100 square meters (m²)
1 barn	=	10^{-28} square meters (m²)
1 centare (ca)	=	1 square meter (m²)
1 hectare (ha)	=	10,000 square meters (m²)
1 shed	=	10^{-30} square meters (m²)
1 square centimeter (cm²)	=	0.0001 square meters (m²)
1 square centimeter (cm²)	=	100 square millimeters (mm²)
1 square degree	=	0.00030462 steradians (sr)
1 square foot (ft²)	=	929 square centimeters (cm²)

Area *(continued)*

1 square foot (ft²)	=	0.092903 square meters (m²)
1 square foot (ft²)	=	92,900 square millimeters (mm²)
1 square inch (in.²)	=	6.4516 square centimeters (cm²)
1 square inch (in.²)	=	645.16 square millimeters (mm²)
1 square inch (in.²)	=	0.0006452 square meters (m²)
1 square inch (in.²)	=	0.006944 square feet (ft²)
1 square kilometer (km²)	=	1,000,000 square meters (m²)
1 square meter (m²)	=	0.0001 hectare (ha)
1 square meter (m²)	=	10,000 square centimeters (cm²)
1 square mile (mile²)	=	2.590 square kilometers (km²)
1 square mile (mile²)	=	2,590,000 square meters (m²)
1 square millimeter (mm²)	=	10^8 square micrometers (μm²)
1 square millimeter (mm²)	=	0.01 square centimeters (cm²)
1 square yard (yd²)	=	8361 square centimeters (cm²)
1 square yard (yd²)	=	0.836127 square meters (m²)

Density

1 pound/cubic foot (lb/ft³)	=	16.01846 kilograms/cubic meter (kg/m³)
1 slug/cubic foot (slug/ft³)	=	515.3788 kilograms/cubic meter (kg/m³)
1 pound/gallon (UK)	=	99.77633 kilograms/cubic meter (kg/m³)
1 pound/gallon (USA)	=	119.8264 kilograms/cubic meter (kg/m³)

Electricity

1 biot (Bi)	=	10 ampere (A)
1 ampere/square inch (A/in.²)	=	1550 amperes/square meter (A/m²)
1 faraday/second	=	96,490 amperes (A)
1 faraday	=	96,490 coulombs (coulomb = ampere-second)
1 mho	=	1 Siemen (S)

Energy and Work

1 btu (British thermal unit)	=	1055 joules (J)
1 btu	=	1.0548 kilojoules (kJ)
1 btu	=	0.0002928 kilowatt-hours (kW-h)
1 calorie	=	4.184 joules (J)
1 erg	=	0.0001 millijoules (mJ)
1 foot-poundal	=	0.04214 joules (J)
1 foot-pound force	=	1.355818 joules (J)
1 gram-centimeter	=	0.09807 millijoules (mJ)
1 horsepower-hour	=	2684 kilojoules (kJ)
1 horsepower-hour	=	0.7457 kilowatt-hours (kW-h)
1 kilocalorie (International)	=	4.1868 kilojoules (kJ)
1 kilocalorie	=	4183 joules (J)
1 kilopond-meter (kp·m)	=	9.807 joules (J)
1 kilowatt-hour	=	3600 kilojoules (kJ)

Force

1 dyne	=	0.01 millinewtons (mN)
1 foot-pound (ft-lb)	=	1.356 joules (J)

1 foot-pound/second (ft-lb/s)	=	0.001356 kilowatts (kW)
1 gram (g)	=	9.807 millinewtons (mN)
1 kilogram-force (kg-f)	=	9.807 newtons (N)
1 kilopond (kp)	=	9.807 newtons (N)
1 poundal	=	0.138255 newtons (N)
1 pound-force (lb-f)	=	4.448222 newtons (N)
1 stone (weight)	=	62.275 newtons (N)
1 ton (long)	=	9964 newtons (N)
1 ton (metric)	=	9807 newtons (N)

Length

1 angstrom (Å)	=	0.0001micrometers (μm)
1 angstrom (Å)	=	10^{-10} meters (m)
1 bolt	=	36.576 meters (m)
1 centimeter (cm)	=	0.00001 kilometers (km)
1 centimeter (cm)	=	0.01 meters (m)
1 centimeter (cm)	=	10 millimeters (mm)
1 chain	=	20.12 meters (m)
1 fathom	=	1.8288 meters (m)
1 foot (ft)	=	30.48 centimeters (cm)
1 foot (ft)	=	0.3048 meters (m)
1 foot (ft)	=	304.8 millimeters (mm)
1 furlong	=	201.17 meters (m)
1 hand	=	10.16 centimeters (cm)
1 inch (in.)	=	2.54 centimeters (cm)
1 inch (in.)	=	0.0254 meters (m)
1 inch (in.)	=	25.4 millimeters (mm)
1 light year	=	9,460,910,000,000 kilometers (9.46×10^{12} km)
1 mile (nautical)	=	1.852 kilometers (km)
1 mile (nautical)	=	1852 meters (m)
1 mile (statute)	=	5280 feet (ft)
1 mile (statute)	=	1.609 kilometers (km)
1 mile (statute)	=	1609 meters (m)
1 mile (statute)	=	1760 yards (yd)
1 rod	=	5.029 meters (m)
1 sphere (solid angle)	=	12.57 steradians (sr)
1 yard (yd)	=	91.44 centimeters (cm)
1 yard (yd)	=	0.9144 meters (m)

Luminus Intensity

1 candela/square centimeter	=	10,000 candela/square meter (cd/m²)
1 candela/square foot	=	10.76 candela/square meter (cd/m²)
1 foot-candle	=	10.764 lumen/square meter (lm/m²)
1 foot-lambert (fL)	=	3.426 candela/square meter (cd/m²)
1 lambert (L)	=	3183 candela/square meter (cd/m²)
1 phot	=	10,000 lumen/square meter (lm/m²)

Moment of Inertia

1 slug-foot squared (slug-ft²)	=	1.35582 kilogram-square meters (kg·m²)
1 pound-foot squared (lb-ft²)	=	0.04214 kilogram-square meters (kg·m²)

Mass

1 hundredweight	=	50.8 kilograms (kg)
1 metric ton (tonne; T)	=	1000 kilograms (kg)
1 ounce (oz)	=	28.3495 grams (g)
1 pound (lb)	=	0.453592 kilograms (kg)
1 slug	=	14.59 kilograms (kg)
1 ton	=	1016 kilograms (kg)

Power

1 btu/hour	=	0.2931 watts (W)
1 btu/minute	=	17.57 watts (W)
1 calorie/second	=	4.187 watts (W)
1 erg/second	=	10^{-7} watts (W)
1 foot-pound/second	=	1.356 watts (W)
1 foot-poundal/second	=	0.04214 watts (W)
1 gram-calorie	=	0.001162 watt-hours
1 horsepower (UK)	=	745.7 watts (W)
1 horsepower (metric)	=	735.5 watts (W)
1 kilocalorie/minute (kcal/min)	=	69.767 watts (W)
1 kilogram-meter/second	=	9.807 watts (W)
1 kilopond-meter/minute (kpm/min)	=	0.1634 watts (W)

Pressure

1 atmosphere	=	760 millimeters of mercury (at 0° C)
1 atmosphere	=	101,340 pascals (Pa)
1 bar	=	100,031 pascals (Pa)
1 centimeter of mercury	=	1,333.224 pascals (Pa)
1 centimeter of water	=	0.738 millimeters of mercury
1 centimeter of water	=	98.3919 pascals (Pa)
1 dyne/square centimeter	=	0.10 pascals (Pa)
1 foot of water	=	2989 pascals (Pa)
1 inch of mercury	=	3386 pascals (Pa)
1 inch of water (4° C)	=	249 pascals (Pa)
1 kilogram-force/square meter	=	9.807 pascals (Pa)
1 millibar	=	100 pascals (Pa)
1 millimeter of mercury (1 torr)	=	133.322387 pascals (Pa)
1 pound-force/square foot (lb/ft^2)	=	47.88026 pascals (Pa)
1 pound-force/square inch ($lb/in.^2$)	=	6.8948 kilopascals (kPa)
1 poundal/square foot	=	1.488 pascal (Pa)
1 torr	=	1 mm Hg at 0° C
1 torr	=	133.3 pascals (Pa)

Speed, Velocity

1 centimeter/second (cm/s)	=	0.036 kilometers/hour (km/h, kph)
1 centimeter/second (cm/s)	=	0.6 meters/minute (m/min)
1 foot/minute (ft/min)	=	0.508 centimeters/second (cm/s)
1 foot/minute (ft/min)	=	0.01829 kilometers/hour (km/h, kph)
1 foot/minute (ft/min)	=	0.3048 meters/minute (m/min)
1 foot/second (ft/s)	=	30.48 centimeters/second (cm/s)
1 foot/second (ft/s)	=	1.097 kilometers/hour (km/h, kph)

1 foot/second (ft/s)	=	18.29 meters/minute (m/min)
1 foot/second (ft/s)	=	0.3048 meters/second (m/s)
1 kilometer/hour (km/h, kph)	=	16.67 meters/minute (m/min)
1 kilometer/hour (km/h, kph)	=	0.2778 meters/second (m/s)
1 knot	=	1.8532 kilometers/hour (km/h, kph)
1 knot	=	51.48 centimeters/second (cm/s)
1 knot	=	0.5155 meters/second (m/s)
1 meter/minute (m/min)	=	1.667 centimeters/second (cm/s)
1 meter/minute (m/min)	=	0.06 kilometers/hour (km/h, kph)
1 meter/second (m/s)	=	3.6 kilometers/hour (km/h, kph)
1 meter/second (m/s)	=	0.06 kilometers/minute (km/min)
1 mile/hour (mph)	=	44.7 centimeters/second (cm/s)
1 mile/hour (mph)	=	1.6093 kilometers/hour (km/h, kph)
1 mile/hour (mph)	=	0.447 meters/second (m/s)
1 mile/minute	=	2682 centimeters/second (cm/s)
1 mile/minute	=	1.6093 kilometers/minute (km/min)
1 revolution/minute	=	0.1047 radians/second (rad/s)
1 revolution/second	=	6.283 radians/second (rad/s)

Temperature

| 1 degree centigrade (°C) | = | (°C $\times$ 9/5) + 32 degrees Fahrenheit (°F) |
| 1 degree centigrade (°C) | = | °C + 273.18 degrees kelvin |

Time

1 minute (min)	=	60 seconds (s)
1 hour (h)	=	60 minutes (min)
1 hour (h)	=	3600 seconds (s)
1 day (d)	=	24 hours (h)
1 day (d)	=	86,400 seconds (s)
1 year (y)	=	365.2422 days (d)
1 year (y)	=	3.156×10^7 seconds (s)

Torque

| 1 foot-pound (ft-lb) | = | 1.356 newton-meters (N·m) |
| 1 kilopond-meter (kpm) | = | 9.807 newton-meters (N·m) |

Volume

1 barrel (UK)	=	0.1637 cubic meters (m^3)
1 barrel (USA)	=	0.11921 cubic meters (m^3)
1 bushel (UK)	=	0.03637 cubic meters (m^3)
1 bushel (USA)	=	0.03524 cubic meters (m^3)
1 bushel	=	35.24 liters (L)
1 cubic centimeter (cm^3)	=	0.000001 cubic meters (m^3)
1 cubic centimeter (cm^3)	=	0.001 liters (L)
1 cubic foot (ft^3)	=	0.02832 cubic meters (m^3)
1 cubic foot (ft^3)	=	28.32 liters (L)
1 cubic foot/minute (ft^3/min)	=	472 cubic centimeters/second (cm^3/s)
1 cubic foot/minute (ft^3/min)	=	0.472 liters/second (L/s)
1 cubic inch (in.^{3})	=	16.387 cubic centimeters (cm^3)
1 cubic inch (in.^{3})	=	0.0000164 cubic meters (m^3)

Volume *(continued)*

1 cubic inch (in.^{3})	=	0.0164 liters (L)
1 cubic meter (m^3)	=	1,000,000 cubic centimeters (cm^3)
1 cubic meter (m^3)	=	1000 liters (L)
1 cubic yard (yd^3)	=	0.7646 cubic meters (m^3)
1 cubic yard (yd^3)	=	764.6 liters (L)
1 cubic yard/minute (yd/min)	=	12.74 liters/second (L/s)
1 dram	=	3.6967 cubic centimeters (cm^3)
1 gallon (UK)	=	0.004546 cubic meters (m^3)
1 gallon (USA)	=	3785 cubic centimeters (cm^3)
1 gallon (USA)	=	0.003785 cubic meters (m^3)
1 gallon	=	3.785 liters (L)
1 gallon/minute	=	0.06308 liters/second (L/s)
1 gill (UK)	=	142.07 cubic centimeters (cm^3)
1 gill (USA)	=	118.295 cubic centimeters (cm^3)
1 gill (USA)	=	0.1183 liters (L)
1 liter (L)	=	1000 cubic centimeters (cm^3)
1 liter (L)	=	0.001 cubic meters (m^3)
1 ounce (fluid)	=	0.02957 liters (L)
1 ounce (fluid—UK)	=	28.413 cubic centimeters (cm^3)
1 ounce (fluid—USA)	=	29.573 cubic centimeters (cm^3)
1 peck (UK)	=	9.0919 liters (L)
1 peck (USA)	=	8.8096 liters (L)
1 pint	=	473.2 cubic centimeters (cm^3)
1 pint	=	0.4732 liters (L)
1 quart	=	946.4 cubic centimeters (cm^3)
1 quart	=	0.9463 liters (L)

Equations

$$\text{velocity} = \frac{\Delta \text{ position}}{\Delta \text{ time}} \tag{1.1}$$

$$\text{acceleration} = \frac{\Delta \text{ velocity}}{\Delta \text{ time}} \tag{1.2}$$

$$v_f = v_i + at \tag{1.3}$$

$$r_f - r_i = v_i t + \tfrac{1}{2} a t^2 \tag{1.4}$$

$$v_f{}^2 = v_i{}^2 + 2a(r_f - r_i) \tag{1.5}$$

$$\mathbf{d} \cdot \mathbf{F} = dF \cos \theta \tag{1.6}$$

$$\mathbf{r} \times \mathbf{F} = rF \sin \theta \tag{1.7}$$

$$s = r\theta \tag{1.8}$$

$$v = r\omega \tag{1.9}$$

$$\mathbf{v} = \boldsymbol{\omega} \times \mathbf{r} \tag{1.10}$$

$$a = \sqrt{\left(r\omega^2\right)^2 + (r\alpha)^2} \tag{1.11}$$

$$a = \frac{v^2}{r} \tag{1.12}$$

$$x(t) = a_0 + a_1 t + a_2 t^2 + \ldots + a_n t^n \tag{1.13}$$

$$x(t) = a_0 + \sum_{i=1}^{n} \left[a_i \cos\left(\frac{2\pi}{T} \cdot i\right) + b_i \sin\left(\frac{2\pi}{T} \cdot i\right) \right] \tag{1.14}$$

$$x'(i) = a_0 x_i + a_1 x_{i-1} + a_2 x_{i-2} + b_1 x'_{i-1} + b_2 x'_{i-2} \tag{1.15}$$

$$\dot{x}(t) = \sum_{i=1}^{n} \left\{ \left[-a_i \sin\left(\frac{2\pi t}{T} \cdot i\right)\left(\frac{2\pi}{T} \cdot i\right) \right] + \left[b_i \cos\left(\frac{2\pi t}{T} \cdot i\right)\left(\frac{2\pi}{T} \cdot i\right) \right] \right\} \tag{1.16}$$

$$\ddot{x}(t) = \sum_{i=1}^{n} \left\{ \left[-a_i \cos\left(\frac{2\pi t}{T} \cdot i\right)\left(\frac{2\pi}{T} \cdot i\right)^2 \right] + \left[-b_i \sin\left(\frac{2\pi t}{T} \cdot i\right)\left(\frac{2\pi}{T} \cdot i\right)^2 \right] \right\} \tag{1.17}$$

$$\dot{x}(i) = \frac{x_{i+1} - x_{i-1}}{2(\Delta t)} \tag{1.18}$$

$$\ddot{x}(i) = \frac{x_{i+1} - 2x_i + x_{i-1}}{\left(\Delta t\right)^2} \tag{1.19}$$

$$\text{EMG}_{\text{rms}} = \sqrt{\frac{1}{N} \sum_{i=1}^{N} x_i^2} \tag{1.20}$$

$$\text{average EMG} = \frac{1}{N} \sum_{i=1}^{N} |x_i| \tag{1.21}$$

$$F_c = \frac{mv^2}{r} \tag{2.1}$$

$$G = mv \tag{2.2}$$

$$F = ma \tag{2.3}$$

$$\boldsymbol{\tau} = \mathbf{r} \times \mathbf{F} \tag{2.4}$$

$$F \propto \frac{m_1 m_2}{r^2} \tag{2.5}$$

$$I = \sum_{i=1}^{n} m_i r_i^2 \tag{2.6}$$

$$I = \int r^2 dm \tag{2.7}$$

$$I_o = I_g + md^2 \tag{2.8}$$

$$I_o = \frac{F_w \cdot h \cdot T^2}{4\pi^2} \tag{2.9}$$

$$F_{s,max} = \mu F_{g,y} \tag{2.10}$$

$$F_f = kAv^2 \tag{2.11}$$

$$F_b = V_o\gamma \tag{2.12}$$

$$\text{Impulse} = \int_{t_1}^{t_2} \mathbf{F} dt \tag{2.13}$$

$$\int_{t_1}^{t_2} \mathbf{F} dt = \Delta\mathbf{G} \tag{2.14}$$

$$\sum \mathbf{F}t = \Delta m\mathbf{v} \ \text{ or } \ \overline{F} \cdot t = \Delta m\mathbf{v} \tag{2.15}$$

$$\left(m_A\mathbf{v}_A\right)_{before} + \left(m_B\mathbf{v}_B\right)_{before} = \left(m_A\mathbf{v}_A\right)_{after} + \left(m_B\mathbf{v}_B\right)_{after} \tag{2.16}$$

$$m_A\Delta v_A = m_B\Delta v_B \tag{2.17}$$

$$\frac{\Delta v_A}{\Delta v_B} = \frac{m_B}{m_A} \tag{2.18}$$

$$v_{B,a} - v_{b,a} = -e\left(v_{B,b} - v_{b,b}\right) \tag{2.19}$$

$$v_{b,a} = v_{B,a} + e\left(v_{B,b} - v_{b,b}\right) \tag{2.20}$$

$$v_{B,a} = v_{b,a} - e\left(v_{B,b} - v_{b,b}\right) \tag{2.21}$$

$$v_{B,a} = \frac{m_b v_{b,b}(1+e) + v_{B,b}\left(m_B - m_b e\right)}{m_b + m_B} \tag{2.22}$$

$$v_{B,a} = \frac{m_B v_{B,b}(1+e) + v_{b,b}\left(m_b - m_B e\right)}{m_B + m_b} \tag{2.23}$$

$$\int_{t_1}^{t_2} \left(\mathbf{r} \times \mathbf{F}\right) dt = \mathbf{H} \tag{2.24}$$

$$\mathbf{H}^{S/CS} = \mathbf{H}^{B1/C1} + \mathbf{H}^{B2/C2} + \mathbf{H}^{B3/C3} + \dots(\text{local terms}) \tag{2.25}$$

$$U = \int F \, dr \tag{2.26}$$

$$U = \sum_{i=1}^{N} F_i \, \Delta x \tag{2.27}$$

$$U = \int \mathbf{F} \cdot d\mathbf{r} \tag{2.28}$$

$$E_k = \tfrac{1}{2}mv^2 + \tfrac{1}{2}I\omega^2 \tag{2.29}$$

$$\Delta E_k = U \tag{2.30}$$

$$E_{p,g} = mgh \tag{2.31}$$

$$E_{p,s} = \tfrac{1}{2}kx^2 \tag{2.32}$$

$$\Delta E_k + \Delta E_p = U_{nc} \tag{2.33}$$

$$E_k + E_p = \text{constant} \tag{2.34}$$

$$\overline{P} = (9.81 \cdot m) \cdot \sqrt{r \cdot 4.9} \tag{2.35}$$

$$\overline{P} = \frac{\int F_{g,y} \, dt}{t} \cdot \frac{\int F_{net} \, dt}{2\,m} \tag{2.36}$$

$$\overline{P} = \frac{m\,g(r+h)}{t} \tag{2.37}$$

$$F_m = \text{specific tension} \times \text{cross-sectional area} \tag{3.1}$$

$$F_e = kx \tag{3.2}$$

$$E = \frac{\sigma}{\varepsilon} \tag{3.3}$$

$$\sum F_x = 0 \tag{3.4}$$

$$\sum F_y = 0 \tag{3.5}$$

$$\sum \tau_o = 0 \tag{3.6}$$

$$\sum F_x = ma_x \tag{3.7}$$

$$\sum F_y = ma_y \tag{3.8}$$

$$\sum \tau_o = I_o\alpha + mad \tag{3.9}$$

$$\sum F_n = mr\omega^2 \tag{3.10}$$

$$\sum F_t = mr\alpha \tag{3.11}$$

$$\sum \tau_g = I_g\alpha \tag{3.12}$$

$$s_M = s_{M/A} + s_{A/K} + s_{K/H} + s_H \tag{3.13}$$

$$v_M = r_f\omega_f + r_s\omega_s + r_t\omega_t + v_H \tag{3.14}$$

$$a_M = \sqrt{\left(r_f\omega_f^2\right)^2 + \left(r_f\alpha_f\right)^2} + \sqrt{\left(r_s\omega_s^2\right)^2 + \left(r_s\alpha_s\right)^2} + \\ \sqrt{\left(r_t\omega_t^2\right)^2 + \left(r_t\alpha_t\right)^2} + a_H \tag{3.15}$$

$$\mathbf{F}_{j,k} + \mathbf{F}_{w,s} = m_s \cdot \mathbf{a}_s \tag{3.16}$$

$$\mathbf{a}_s = \mathbf{a}_h + \left(\boldsymbol{\alpha}_t \times \mathbf{r}_{k/h}\right) + \left(\boldsymbol{\omega}_t \times \boldsymbol{\omega}_t \times \mathbf{r}_{k/h}\right) + \\ \left(\boldsymbol{\alpha}_s \times \mathbf{r}_{s/k}\right) + \left(\boldsymbol{\omega}_s \times \boldsymbol{\omega}_s \times \mathbf{r}_{s/k}\right) \tag{3.17}$$

$$\mathbf{F}_{j,k} = m_s \mathbf{a}_h + m_s \left(\boldsymbol{\alpha}_t \times \mathbf{r}_{k/h} \right) + m_s \left(\boldsymbol{\omega}_t \times \boldsymbol{\omega}_t \times \mathbf{r}_{k/h} \right) +$$
$$m_s \left(\boldsymbol{\alpha}_s \times \mathbf{r}_{s/k} \right) + m_s \left(\boldsymbol{\omega}_s \times \boldsymbol{\omega}_s \times \mathbf{r}_{s/k} \right) - \mathbf{F}_{w,s}$$
(3.18)

$$\boldsymbol{\tau}_{m,k} + \left(\mathbf{r}_{k/s} \times \mathbf{F}_{j,k} \right) = I_{g,s} \boldsymbol{\alpha}_s \tag{3.19}$$

$$\boldsymbol{\tau}_{m,h} - \boldsymbol{\tau}_{m,k} + \left(\mathbf{r}_{h,t} \times \mathbf{F}_{j,h} \right) - \left(\mathbf{r}_{k,s} \times \mathbf{F}_{j,k} \right) = I_{g,t} \boldsymbol{\alpha}_t \tag{3.20}$$

$$\text{peak } F_{g,y} \ (\text{BW}) = 0.856 \frac{T}{t_c} + 0.089 \tag{4.1}$$

$$\text{Centripetal force} = \frac{mv^2}{l} \tag{4.2}$$

$$\text{Froude number} = \frac{mv^2 / l}{mg} = \frac{v^2}{gl} \tag{4.3}$$

$$\kappa = \frac{\Delta \tau_m}{\Delta \theta} \tag{4.4}$$

$$k_{\text{leg}} = \frac{\text{peak } F_{g,y}}{\Delta l} \tag{4.5}$$

$$\% \ \text{recovery} = \frac{U_v + U_f - U_e}{U_v + U_f} \cdot 100 \tag{4.6}$$

$$v_x(t) = \int \frac{F_{g,x}}{m} dt + c \tag{4.7}$$

$$E_{k,f}(t) = \frac{m}{2} \left[v_x(t) \right]^2 \tag{4.8}$$

$$v_y(t) = \int \frac{F_{g,y} - F_w}{m} dt + c_1 \tag{4.9}$$

$$h(t) = \int v_y dt + c_2 \tag{4.10}$$

$$E_{p,g}(t) = mgh(t) \tag{4.11}$$

$$E_K = \frac{RT}{F} \log_e \frac{[K]_e}{[K]_i} \tag{6.1}$$

$$\text{fCSA} = \frac{\text{volume} \left(\text{cm}^3 \right) \cdot \cos \beta}{\text{fiber length (cm)}} \tag{6.2}$$

$$v = \frac{b \left(F_{m,o} - F_m \right)}{F_m + a} \tag{6.3}$$

$$F_m v + av = b F_{m,o} - b F_m \tag{6.4}$$

$$F_m v = \frac{v \left(b F_{m,o} - av \right)}{v + b} \tag{6.5}$$

$$\text{Gain} = \frac{\Delta \text{ control signal}}{\Delta \text{ controlled variable}} \tag{7.1}$$

$$P = \frac{0.5mv^2 + mgh}{\Delta t} \tag{9.1}$$

Glossary

A band—Anisotropic or dark striation in skeletal muscle due to the double refraction of light rays from a single source.

abduction—Movement away from the midline of the body or the body part.

absolute angle—The angle of a body segment relative to a fixed reference, such as a horizontal or vertical line.

acceleration—Rate of change in velocity with respect to time (m/s^2); the derivative of velocity with respect to time; the slope of a velocity-time graph.

accelerometer—A device that measures acceleration.

accommodation device—A training device in which the resistance varies to match the force exerted by the user.

accuracy—The closeness of the estimate to the true value.

acetylcholine—A chemical transmitter that is used by nerve terminals at, among other locations, the neuromuscular junction.

acetylcholine receptor—Protein in a muscle fiber membrane that combines with acetylcholine to produce excitation.

acetylcholinesterase—An enzyme that hydrolyzes the neurotransmitter acetylcholine after it has been released from the presynaptic terminal.

acoustomyography—The recording of muscle sounds during a contraction.

actin—A globular protein that combines to form filaments, such as the thin filament of the muscle fiber.

action potential—A brief electrical signal that travels along nerve and muscle fibers. Physically, it represents a patch of membrane that contains a transient reversal of the Na^+ and K^+ distribution.

action potential threshold—A trigger level that, when reached by the membrane potential, causes the cell (neuron or muscle fiber) to generate an action potential.

action tremor—Oscillations that occur at 3 to 5 Hz during a slow movement.

active touch—The exploration of the surroundings by reliance on the sensory receptors associated with the hand.

adaptation—A decline in the discharge rate of a neuron despite a constant excitatory input. The decline is due to the biophysical properties of the neuron.

adaptive controller—A control system that modifies the elements of the control system rather than causing immediate changes in the output.

adduction—Movement toward the midline of the body or the body part.

ADP—Adenosine diphosphate.

afferent—An axon that transmits signals from sensory receptors.

afterhyperpolarization—The trailing part of an action potential when the membrane is less excitable than in steady state conditions. A period of hyperpolarization on the final phase of the action potential.

agonist—A muscle whose activation produces the acceleration required for a movement.

agonist-contract stretch—A PNF-based stretch in which an assistant places the joint at the limit of rotation and then has the individual contract the agonist muscle (e.g., quadriceps femoris) to assist in further increasing the range of motion by stretching the antagonist muscle (e.g., hamstrings).

akinesia—An impaired ability to initiate movement as a consequence of a neurological deficit.

all-or-none—Events that either occur completely or not at all.

alpha chain—A sequence of about 1000 amino acids in a polypeptide chain of collagen.

alpha-gamma coactivation—Concurrent activation of alpha and gamma motor neurons during voluntary activation of a muscle.

alpha motor neuron—A motor neuron that innervates the muscle fibers that produce movements.

amnesia—Loss of memories.

AMP—Adenosine monophosphate.

angle-angle diagram—A graph that shows the changes in one angle (y-axis) as a function of another angle (x-axis).

angle of pull—The angle between the muscle force and the body segment.

angular—A form of motion in which not all parts of the object experience the same displacement.

angular impulse—The area under a torque-time curve. An angular impulse changes the angular momentum of a body.

angular momentum—The quantity of angular motion.

anion—A negatively charged atom or molecule in solution.

anisometric—A contraction that is not isometric, that is, a contraction in which there is a change in whole-muscle length.

antagonist—A muscle whose activation produces an acceleration in the direction opposite that required for a movement.

anterolateral pathway—An ascending pathway that conveys information mainly about pain and temperature with some tactile and proprioceptive information.

anthropometric—Referring to measurements of the human body.

anticipatory postural adjustment—A change in the activity of muscles that provides postural support prior to a movement that could disturb the stability of the individual.

antidromic conduction—Conduction of action potentials along an axon in the backward direction.

antigravity muscles—The muscles that exert a torque to oppose the action of gravity in an upright posture, such as the knee extensor and elbow flexor muscles.

aponeurosis—The connective tissue extension of the tendon into muscle.

arousal—An internal state of alertness.

articular cartilage—A tissue in a joint that comprises a viscoelastic gel reinforced with collagen.

ascending pathways—Neural connections that distribute information from sensory receptors and from the spinal cord to the brain.

assistance responses—Adjustments that stabilize the body prior to a movement.

assisted-locomotion training—The training of patients with spinal cord injuries to walk on a treadmill by partially supporting body weight and providing passive assistance with the leg displacements.

ataxia—An inability to perform voluntary movements.

athetosis—A condition characterized by slow, writhing, involuntary movements of the extremities.

ATP—Adenosine triphosphate.

ATP hydrolysis—The breakdown of ATP to ADP, P_i, and energy.

atrophy—Loss of muscle mass.

autogenesis—The process of degrading cellular structures. This occurs with the exercise-induced damage of muscle.

autonomic ganglia—Groups of terminal neurons (equivalent to motor neurons) involved in the autonomic nervous system. These groups of neurons lie outside the central nervous system but receive input directly from it.

autonomic nervous system—A system that innervates heart muscle, the smooth muscle of all organs, and exocrine glands and is generally not under voluntary control.

axon—A nerve fiber; a tubular process that arises from the soma of a neuron and functions as a cable for transmitting the electrical signals generated by the neuron.

axon hillock—The anatomical region where the axon leaves the soma.

axonal transport—The movement of proteins and organelles on the inside of an axon. This material can be moved in both the orthograde (soma to synapse) and retrograde (synapse to soma) directions.

axotomy—Transection of an axon.

Babinski reflex—A response in leg muscles to a tactile stimulation of the sole of the foot.

ballism—A disorder of the basal ganglia characterized by rapid involuntary movements that are irregular and have a large amplitude.

ballistic stretch—A technique to increase the range of motion about a joint by performing a series of rapid, bouncing stretches of the muscle.

band-pass filter—A filter that preserves the amplitude of the frequencies in a selected range and attenuates the other frequencies.

basal ganglia—Five closely related nuclei (caudate, putamen, globus pallidus, subthalamic nuclei, and substantia nigra) that receive input from the cerebral cortex and send most of their output, via the thalamus, back to the cerebral cortex.

basement membrane—Complex sheath investing nerve and muscle fibers.

Bernoulli's principle—Principle stating that fluid pressure is inversely related to fluid velocity.

beta motor neuron—A motor neuron that innervates both intrafusal and extrafusal muscle fibers.

bilateral deficit—The reduction in force that occurs during a concurrent bilateral contraction as compared with the force exerted during a unilateral contraction.

bilateral facilitation—The increase in force that occurs during a concurrent bilateral contraction as compared with the force exerted during a unilateral contraction.

biomechanics—The use of physics to study biological systems.

biophysics—The application of physical principles and methods to biological systems.

bipolar recording—Recording that yields the difference in the signals recorded by a pair of electrodes.

boundary layer—The streamline in fluid flow that is closest to the object.

bradykinesia—A condition in which voluntary movements have a reduced amplitude and velocity.

brainstem—The components of the central nervous system between the brain and the spinal cord, which includes the medulla oblongata, pons, and mesencephalon.

buoyancy force—An upward-directed force that depends on the weight of the fluid that has been displaced.

Butterworth filter—A type of digital filter.

Ca²⁺—Calcium ion.

calcium-activation curve—The relation between intracellular Ca^{2+} and muscle fiber tension.

cAMP—Cyclic AMP (adenosine monophosphate): a messenger molecule in the cell interior.

cartwheel axis—An axis of rotation that passes through the human body from front to back.

cation—A positively charged atom or molecule in solution.

caudate nucleus—One of the basal ganglia nuclei.

center of mass—The point about which the mass of the system is evenly distributed, sometimes referred to as the center of gravity.

center of percussion—The location along a bat where no reaction force is felt at the hands when the bat strikes a ball.

center of pressure—The point of application of the ground reaction force.

central command—The neural signal transmitted by the motor cortex to lower motor centers (brainstem, spinal cord) for the execution of a movement.

central drive—The excitation provided by supraspinal centers to motor neurons.

central fatigue—An impairment of the physiological processes that activate muscle during a fatiguing contraction.

central pattern generator—Neural network that is capable of generating behaviorally relevant patterns of motor output in the absence of afferent input.

centripetal force—A force directed toward the axis of rotation that is responsible for changing linear motion into angular motion.

cerebellar nuclei—Brainstem structures (dentate, fastigial, interpositus) that mediate most of the output from the cerebellum.

cerebellar peduncles—Six neural tracts connecting the cerebellum with the rest of the central nervous system.

cerebellar tremor—A low-frequency tremor (3-5 Hz) seen in patients with cerebellar disorders.

cerebellum—A brain structure involved in the control of movement. It is located inferior to the cerebral hemispheres and posterior to the brainstem.

cerebrocerebellum—The lateral hemispheres of the cerebellum, which receive input from the cerebral cortex and send output to the dentate nucleus.

chorea (Huntington's disease)—A disorder of the basal ganglia characterized by involuntary movements that are jerky and random.

chromatolysis—Dissolution of the Nissl substance (rough endoplasmic reticulum) and resynthesis of proteins that occur after axotomy.

chronic fatigue syndrome—A sustained feeling of exhaustion and an exaggerated sense of effort associated with performing any physical activity.

climbing fibers—One of the afferent pathways into the cerebellum.

clonus—A series of alternating bursts of activity (6-8 Hz) in limb flexor and extensor muscles.

Cl⁻—Chloride ion.

CNS—Central nervous system.

coactivation—Concurrent activation of the muscles around a joint, usually involving the agonist and antagonist muscles.

coefficient of restitution—A ratio that describes the speed of an object after a collision compared with its speed before the collision.

collateral—Referring to a branch of the axon that synapses onto other neurons.

collateral sprouting—The development of sprouts (neurites) by distal segments of an axon for the purpose of reinnervating a denervated target. This usually occurs after damage or an injury to a target cell (e.g., muscle fiber, neuron).

colliculus—A structure in the midbrain that is involved in the processing of visual and auditory information.

collinear—Lying on the same line. For example, two vectors whose lines of action are in the same direction are described as collinear.

collision—A brief contact between objects in which the force associated with the contact is much larger than the other forces acting on the objects.

command neuron—A neuron that activates a central pattern generator.

commisures—The axon bundles that connect the left and right cerebral hemispheres.

common drive—The correlated variation in average discharge rate of concurrently active motor units.

common input—Synaptic input that is delivered to motor neurons concurrently.

common mode rejection—The elimination of signals that are common to a pair of electrodes.

comparator—A device or structure that compares inputs provided by different sources, such as information about the desired position and the actual position.

compliance—The amount that a material can be forcibly stretched. This property is expressed as the amount of change in length per unit of force used to stretch the material (mm/N).

composition—The process of determining the resultant of several vectors.

compressive force—A pushing force.

computed tomography (CT)—A method of reconstructing three-dimensional images based on a series of two-dimensional X-ray images.

concentric contraction—A muscle contraction in which the muscle torque is greater than the load torque and as a consequence the active muscle shortens.

concentric needle electrode—A needle electrode containing one to four wires. The wires are connected to the barrel of the needle and present small detection surfaces to the surrounding tissue.

concurrent—Referring to vectors whose lines of action converge and intersect at a point.

conductance—A property of a membrane that depends on the permeability to an ion and the availability of the ion. Conductance is the inverse of electrical resistance.

conduction velocity—The speed at which an action potential is propagated along an excitable membrane.

conductivity—The ability of excitable membrane to propagate a wave of excitation.

conservation of mechanical energy—Principle stating that when there are no nonconstant opposing forces, such as friction, then the sum of the changes in kinetic and potential energy is equal to zero.

conservation of momentum—A state in which the quantity of motion remains constant.

constant load—A training load that remains constant (e.g., barbell) because the size of the load depends on gravity, which is a constant force.

contractile element—The component of the Hill model that accounts for the contractility of muscle.

contractility—The ability of a tissue to modify its length.

contraction—A state of activation in which the crossbridges of a muscle cycle in response to an action potential. Muscle length may shorten, stay the same, or lengthen during this state of activation.

contraction time—The time from force onset to the peak force during a twitch.

control system—A set of subsystems and interconnecting elements that process information. A subsystem receives incoming messages and performs computations on them before distributing the information throughout the system. There are three types of automatic control systems: feedback controller, feedforward controller, and adaptive controller (Houk, 1988). A control system that is mainly used to compensate for disturbances is called a *regulator*.

corollary discharge—Internal signals that arise from motor commands and that influence perception (Sperry, 1950).

corpus callosum—A major neural tract that connects the two cortical hemispheres.

cortex (cerebral, cerebellar)—The external layer of a component in the brain, which is thin and densely packed with neuron bodies.

corticobulbar tract—Axons in the corticospinal tract that terminate in the cranial nuclei and innervate facial muscles.

corticospinal tract—A descending pathway with input from the entire sensorimotor cortex.

cosecant—An angle in a triangle defined by the ratio of the hypotenuse to the side opposite the angle.

cosine—An angle in a triangle defined by the ratio between the side adjacent to the angle and the hypotenuse.

cost coefficient—The ratio of the rate of oxygen consumption to the speed of locomotion.

cotangent—For an acute angle in a triangle, the ratio of the adjacent side to the opposite side.

countermovement jump—A vertical jump that involves a lowering of the center of mass prior to the propulsive phase.

creep—The gradual increase in tissue length that is necessary to maintain a constant stress.

critical power—The maximum power that can be sustained for a set duration.

cross-bridge—The extension of the myosin molecule that can interact with actin and perform work.

cross-bridge cycle—The interaction of actin and myosin that occurs as a result of Ca^{2+} disinhibition.

cross-bridge theory of muscle contraction—A theory that explains the force exerted during a muscle contraction as due to the action of cross-bridges.

crossed-extensor reflex—An extension response in the contralateral limb to a noxious stimulus that elicits the withdrawal reflex.

cross education—An adaptation in motor capabilities that occurs in one limb as a consequence of physical training by the contralateral limb.

cross-links—Biochemical bonds that hold the collagen molecules together in connective tissue.

cross (vector) product—The procedure used to multiply two vectors to yield a vector product.

cross-sectional area—The area of the end-on view of an object (e.g., muscle) when it has been sectioned (cut) at right angles to its long axis.

cubic—Indicating a third-degree polynomial.

curve fitting—The derivation of a mathematical function to represent a data set.

cutaneous receptor—A sensory receptor that is sensitive to such stimuli as skin displacement, pressure on the skin, and temperature. These receptors include pacinian corpuscles, Merkel disks, Meissner corpuscles, and Ruffini endings.

cutoff frequency—A frequency that is specified for a filter (digital or electronic) to indicate the location in the frequency spectrum where the input signal should be reduced to one-half of its power. The rate at which the frequency spectrum is modified depends on the type of filter used.

cytoskeleton—The structural proteins that provide the physical framework for the organization and interaction of the contractile proteins.

deafferentation—State of a neuromuscular system that has been deprived of its afferent feedback, either due to an experimental intervention or as the result of a neurological disorder.

decerebrate preparation—An animal model in which the cerebral cortex has been disconnected from the brainstem and spinal cord.

decomposition—A technique the extracts identified action potentials from a multi-unit recording.

degree of freedom at a joint—An axis of rotation. A joint with three degrees of freedom permits rotation about three different axes.

delay—Time from a stimulus to the onset of a response.

delayed-onset muscle soreness—The perception of muscle soreness that is associated with subcellular damage and that occurs from 24 to 48 h after the exercise. The soreness may be due to the inflammatory response as a consequence of the damage.

demineralization—The excessive loss of salts from bone.

dendrite—A branch, other than the axon, that extends from the soma of a neuron.

denervation—A state in which the nerve has been cut so that the muscle is without its neural input.

dentate nucleus—One of the deep subcortical nuclei of the cerebellum.

depolarization—A reduction in the potential across the membrane.

derecruitment—The inactivation of a motor unit.

descending pathways—Neural pathways that transmit information from the brain to the brainstem and spinal cord. The major tracts include the corticospinal tract, corticobulbar tract, pyramidal tract, rubrospinal tract, vestibulospinal tract, reticulospinal tracts, and tectospinal tract.

desmin—A protein that is part of the cytoskeleton.

digital filter—A numerical procedure that manipulates the frequency spectrum of an input signal to produce an output signal containing a substantially attenuated frequency above the cutoff frequency.

digitizer—An instrument that determines the spatial coordinates *(xyz)* of selected landmarks.

direct pathway—The projection from the striatum to the internal part of globus pallidus, which is one of the output nuclei of the basal ganglia. The direct pathway facilitates movement.

directrix—A fixed line from which all the points in a parabola are equidistant.

discharge pattern—The timing of action potentials discharged by motor neurons.

discharge rate—The rate at which neurons discharge action potentials. The unit of measurement is hertz (Hz).

disinhibition—Inhibition of the inhibitor. For example, the Renshaw cell disinhibits the Ia inhibitory interneuron, and Ca^{2+} disinhibits the inhibitory effect of the regulatory proteins (troponin and tropomyosin).

displacement—A change in position. Displacement is measured in meters (m).

DNA—Deoxyribonucleic acid, the genetic material of the cell nucleus.

dopamine—A neurotransmitter whose deficiency leads to Parkinson's disease.

dorsal column-medial lemniscus pathway—An ascending pathway that distributes information on limb proprioception and tactile sensation.

dorsal root—The entry zone on the back side of the spinal cord. Afferent axons enter the spinal cord in the dorsal root.

double discharge—The occurrence of two action potentials discharged by a single motor unit within an interval of about 20 ms, a time that is much faster than usual.

drag force—The component of the fluid-resistance vector that acts parallel to the direction of fluid flow.

dual-strategy hypothesis—An explanation of activation strategies during voluntary movements that either involve or do not involve control of movement time.

dynamic analysis—Mechanical analysis dealing with a system in which the forces acting on the system are not balanced and hence the system experiences an acceleration. In a dynamic analysis the right-hand side of Newton's law of acceleration is nonzero.

dysdiadochokinesia—An inability to perform movements at a specified constant rhythm.

dysmetria—An inability to achieve a required final position in a goal-directed movement.

dystonia—A state in which there are involuntary movements that involve sustained abnormal postures and slow movements with coactivation of agonist and antagonist muscles.

eccentric contraction—A muscle contraction in which the load torque is greater than the muscle torque and as a consequence the active muscle is lengthened.

economy—Minimization of the energy needed to perform a prescribed quantity of work.

effective synaptic current—The net effect of input onto a neuron as measured by an intracellular microelectrode; presumably this represents the input that reaches the axon hillock.

efference copy—Internal, command-related signals that cancel sensory discharges due to motor commands (reafferent signals) and leave unaffected the sensory signals (exafferent signals) caused by external influences (Holst, 1954).

efferent—An axon that transmits signals from neurons.

efficiency—The ratio of the work done to the energy used. The more work performed per unit of energy expenditure, the more efficient the system.

elastic collision—A collision in which the objects bounce off one another.

elastic energy—The potential energy (J) stored by a system when it is stretched from a resting position.

elastic force—The passive property of a stretched material that tends to return it toward its original length.

elastic region—The initial linear part of a stress-strain or force-deformation graph.

electrical potential—Voltage.

electrode—A probe that can be used to measure a physical quantity, such as the concentration of a chemical (ion, metabolite, pH) or the flow of electricity (current).

electroencephalography (EEG)—A method of recording the waves of brain activity with electrodes placed over the skull.

electrogenic—Referring to the contribution of Na^+-K^+ pump activity to the electrical potential across an excitable membrane.

electromyography (EMG)—Measurement of action potentials in muscle fibers.

endomysium—A connective tissue matrix that surrounds individual muscle fibers.

endosarcomeric—Referring to the cytoskeletal proteins that maintain the orientation of the thick and thin filaments within the sarcomere.

end plate—Region of the muscle fiber underneath the motor nerve terminals.

end-plate potential—The synaptic potential that is generated in a muscle fiber in response to the release of acetylcholine.

epimysium—The outer layer of connective tissue that ensheathes an entire muscle.

equilibrium-point hypothesis—A formulation regarding the control strategy used by the nervous system to perform movement. It involves the control of equilibrium between the muscle forces and the load.

equilibrium potential of an ion—A potential at which there is no net movement of ion across the membrane.

equilibrium-trajectory hypothesis—A formulation regarding the scheme used by the central nervous system to control multi-joint movements; it involves specifying the virtual trajectory for the working point of the system.

error signal—Difference between a command signal and a controlled variable.

evoked potential—An electrical potential that is elicited by an external stimulus.

excitability—Responsiveness of an irritable membrane (e.g., axolemma, sarcolemma) to input signals.

excitation-contraction coupling—The electrochemical processes involved in converting a muscle action potential into mechanical work performed by the cross-bridges.

excitatory postsynaptic potential (EPSP)—A depolarizing (excitatory) synaptic potential that is elicited in the postsynaptic membrane (distal to the synapse).

exocytosis—The process of fusion by a vesicle to the presynaptic membrane and the subsequent release of neurotransmitter.

exosarcomeric—Referring to the cytoskeletal components that maintain the lateral alignment of the sarcomeres.

exponent—The mathematical power of a variable, which indicates the number of times the variable should be multiplied by itself; for example, y^4 has an exponent of 4, which indicates that y should be multiplied by itself four times.

exponential function—A function that has the general form $y = b^x$, where x is the independent variable.

extension—An increase in the angle between two adjacent body segments.

external work—The work done to displace the center of mass in locomotion.

exteroceptor—A sensory receptor that detects external stimuli from the surroundings.

extracellular—Outside the cell.

extrafusal fiber—A skeletal muscle fiber that is not part of the muscle spindle.

F actin—Fibrous actin; a strand of a few hundred G-actin molecules.

failure of activation—A decrease in the availability and efficacy of Ca^{2+} as an activation signal for muscle.

fastigial nucleus—One of the deep subcortical nuclei of the cerebellum.

fatigue—An exercise-induced reduction in the maximum force that a muscle can exert.

feedback—Signals arising from various peripheral receptors that provide information to the nervous system on the mechanical state of the neuromuscular system.

feedback control—A control system that generates forcing functions by comparing a desired performance (as dictated by command signals) with actual performance (sensed by feedback sensors).

feedforward control—A control system that generates command signals independently of the outcome.

FFT—Fast Fourier Transformation; the procedure used to determine the Fourier series for a given signal.

fibril—The basic load-bearing unit of tendon and ligament, which consists of bundles of microfibrils held together by cross-links. The number and state of the cross-links determine the strength of the connective tissue.

fictive—Referring to the output produced by a central pattern generator when the nerves have been disconnected from the muscles.

filtering—A signal-processing term that describes the alteration of the frequency content of a signal. For example, an EMG signal can be filtered to remove the high frequencies, making the resulting EMG signal much smoother.

final common pathway—The motor neuron considered as the route by which the nervous system controls muscle activity.

finite differences—A numerical technique for calculating the first and second derivations, such as velocity and acceleration from position.

first law of thermodynamics—A law stating that the performance of work requires the expenditure of energy; work = Δ energy.

flexibility—The range of motion about a joint.

flexion—A decrease in the angle between two adjacent body segments.

fluid resistance—The resistance that a fluid offers to any object that passes through it. The magnitude of the resistance depends on the physical characteristics of the fluid and the extent to which the motion of the object disturbs the fluid.

focal adhesion—Structures that connect intracellular proteins to extracellular space.

focus—A point about which all the points in a parabola are equidistant.

force—A mechanical interaction between an object and its surroundings. The SI unit of measurement for force is the newton (N).

force-frequency relation—The association between the rate of activation (e.g., discharge rate, electrical stimulation) and muscle force.

force-length relation—The association between maximum force and the length of a muscle. Also referred to as the length-tension relation.

force relaxation—The gradual decline in tissue stress while the tissue length remains constant.

force sharing—The contribution of each muscle in a group to the net force.

force-velocity relation—The effect that the rate of change in muscle length has on the maximum force a muscle can exert.

form drag—The drag due to a difference in the pressure between the front and back of the object, which increases as the flow becomes more turbulent.

forward dynamics—A dynamic analysis approach to determine the kinematics that will be exhibited by a system based on the forces and torques that it experiences.

Fourier analysis—The derivation of a series of sine and cosine terms to represent a signal.

Fourier series—The set of sine and cosine terms that describe a variable.

fraction—A ratio of two quantities.

free body diagram—A graphic-analysis technique that defines a system and indicates how the system interacts with its surroundings. A free body diagram is a graphic version of the left-hand side of Newton's law of acceleration.

free nerve ending—A termination of a small-diameter axon that senses abnormal mechanical stress and chemical agents.

frequency domain—A graph that has frequency (Hz) as the independent variable (x-axis).

friction—Contact resistance due to the relative motion of one body sliding, rolling, or flowing over another. In movements involving contacts with a support surface, friction is the resultant of the two horizontal components of the ground reaction force.

friction drag—The drag due to the friction between the boundary layer and the object.

frontal plane—A plane that divides the body into front and back for the purpose of describing movement direction.

Froude number—The ratio of centripetal force to gravitational force, which is used as an index of dimensionless speed.

functional cross-sectional area—The measure of muscle cross-sectional area that takes into account muscle fiber pennation. The measurement is made perpendicular to the long axis of the muscle fibers and is proportional to the maximal force that the fibers can exert.

functional electrical stimulation—The artificial activation of muscle with a protocol of electric shocks that enhances muscle function.

fundamental frequency—The single sine and cosine term that best describes how a signal varies during one cycle.

fused tetanus—The force evoked in muscle fibers, motor units, or muscle in response to activation at a high frequency.

fusimotor—Because the muscle spindle has a fusiform shape, gamma motor neurons are sometimes called fusimotor neurons, and their axons are referred to as fusimotor fibers.

F wave—A response in muscle that is evoked by stimulation of the axon to produce first an antidromic potential back to the soma and then an orthodromic potential out to the muscle.

G actin—Globular actin molecule.

gain—The amount by which the amplitude of an input signal is increased. In a control system, this is calculated as the ratio of the change in the control signal to the change in the controlled variable.

gamma-aminobutyric acid (GABA)—a neurotransmitter.

gamma motor neuron—A motor neuron that innervates the muscle fibers in a muscle spindle.

generator neuron—An endogenous pacemaker that provides the fundamental rhythm for a central pattern generator.

generator potential—The electrical potential that a sensory receptor generates in response to the stimulus to which it is sensitive.

globus pallidus—One of the basal ganglia nuclei.

Golgi ending—Thinly encapsulated, fusiform corpuscle that is similar to a tendon organ and may sense tension in ligament.

gravitational potential energy—The energy possessed by a system due to its location in a gravitational field above a baseline.

gravity—The force of attraction between an object and a planet, which is an object with large mass. The force of gravity causes an acceleration of 9.81 m/s^2 on Earth.

ground reaction force—The reaction force provided by the horizontal support surface.

Group A pathway—Descending pathway that includes the vestibulospinal, reticulospinal, and tectospinal tracts.

Group B pathway—Descending pathway that includes the crossed rubrospinal and crossed reticulospinal tracts.

Group Ia afferent—A muscle spindle afferent.

Group Ib afferent—The tendon organ afferent.

Group II afferent—Afferents with a diameter that is one class lower than that of the Group I afferents. The muscle spindle has a Group II afferent.

H$^+$—Hydrogen ion.

habituation—A decrease in a response to a stimulus seen with repeated presentation of the stimulus.

half-center model—A model of a central pattern generator in which two sets of neurons inhibit each other reciprocally.

half-relaxation time—The time it takes for twitch force to decline from the peak to one-half of the peak force.

harmonic—Multiple of the fundamental frequency.

H band—Hellerscheibe; the region of the A band that is devoid of thin filaments.

heavy chain—A protein with a high molecular weight, such as those in myosin.

heavy meromyosin—The head-end fragment of the myosin molecule. This fragment can be further subdivided into subfragments 1 and 2 (S1 and S2).

hemisection model—An experimental model in which one-half of the spinal cord is removed somewhere along the cord.

hindlimb suspension—An experimental protocol in which the hindlimbs of an experimental animal are lifted up off the ground for a few weeks so that they can still move but cannot contact the ground or any support surface.

Hoffmann reflex (H)—A response that is elicited artificially by electrical stimulation of a peripheral nerve and selective activation of the Group Ia (largest diameter) afferents. The afferent volley activates homonymous motor neurons and elicits an EMG and force response. The H reflex is used as a test of the level of excitability of the motor neuron pool.

hold-relax stretch—A PNF-based stretch that involves an initial maximum isometric contraction of the muscle to be stretched, followed by relaxation and stretch of the muscle to the limit of the range of motion.

hold-relax, agonist-contract stretch—A PNF-based stretch that combines the hold-relax and the agonist-contract techniques.

homogeneous—Of a similar kind or nature.

homonymous—Referring to an anatomical relation between sensory receptors and motor neurons that innervate the same muscle.

hypermetria—The overshoot of a target position during a goal-directed movement.

hypermobile joint—An exaggerated range of motion about a joint, sometimes described as double-jointedness.

hyperplasia—An increase in muscle mass due to an increase in the number of the muscle fibers.

hyperpolarization—An increase in the polarity across the cell membrane such that the inside of the cell becomes more negative with respect to the outside.

hypertonus—An increase in muscle tone, such as in spasticity and rigidity.

hypertrophy—An increase in muscle mass due to an increase in the cross-sectional area of the muscle fibers.

hypometria—A tendency to undershoot a target in a voluntary movement.

hypothalamus—A structure in the diencephalons, important in autonomic control and the expression of emotions.

hypotonus—A decrease in muscle tone, exhibited as a decreased resistance to a passive stretch.

hysteresis loop—A history-dependent relation in which the loading and unloading phases of a load-deformation graph do not coincide. For example, the change in length (deformation) of a tissue when a force is released does not retrace the curve obtained when the force was first applied.

H zone—Pale area in the center of the A band in the muscle fiber, indicating a region that contains only thick filaments.

Ia inhibitory interneuron—An interneuron that is excited by Group Ia afferents and by supraspinal input. This interneuron exerts an inhibitory effect on other neurons, especially motor neurons (e.g., reciprocal-inhibition reflex).

I band—Isotropic or light band of skeletal muscle, named for the single refraction of light rays from a single source. It contains predominantly thin filaments.

impact load—A brief contact force that has a magnitude much greater than other forces acting on the system.

impedance—The apparent opposition in an electrical circuit to the flow of alternating current.

impulse—The area under a force-time graph (N·s), which corresponds to the force-time integral.

indirect pathway—The projection from the striatum that goes to the external part of the globus pallidus and then to the output nuclei of the basal ganglia. The indirect pathway inhibits movement.

inertia—The resistance that an object offers to any changes in its motion.

inertial force—The force that an object exerts due to its motion.

inferior olive nucleus—The origin of the climbing fibers, which project from the medulla to the cerebellum.

inhibitory postsynaptic potential (IPSP)—A hyperpolarizing (inhibitory) synaptic potential that is elicited in the postsynaptic membrane (distal to the synapse).

innervation ratio—The number of muscle fibers innervated by a single motor neuron.

innervation zone—The area of a muscle that contains the neuromuscular junctions.

in parallel—Arranged side by side.

input resistance—The electrical resistance of a motor neuron to a current input that is injected by an intracellular microelectrode.

in series—Arranged end to end.

integration—A mathematical procedure for measuring the area under a curve, such as a voltage-time or force-time relationship. This procedure, often applied to a rectified EMG, results in a measure of the area under the EMG-time signal. Sometimes, however, a procedure that smooths (filters out the high frequencies) the rectified EMG is also called integration. This technique is more accurately referred to as "leaky integration"; however, the EMG signal is most frequently integrated by this procedure and described as integration.

integrin—Transmembrane protein that may serve to connect myofibrils to the extracellular matrix of connective tissue.

intention tremor—The large oscillations that occur when a limb approaches a target.

interelectrode distance—The space between a pair of electrodes.

interference EMG—The unprocessed EMG that involves the overlapping of hundreds of muscle fiber action potentials. This is sometimes referred to as the "raw" EMG.

intermediate fibers—One of the components of the exosarcomeric cytoskeleton. These fibers are arranged longitudinally along and transversely across sarcomeres to maintain the alignment of the sarcomeres.

interneuron—A neuron that receives information from other neurons and transmits its output to other neurons.

interposed nucleus—One of the deep subcortical nuclei of the cerebellum.

intersegmental dynamics—The inertial forces exerted by a moving body segment on its neighbors.

intra-abdominal pressure—The pressure (Pa) inside the abdominal cavity. The intra-abdominal pressure acts on the diaphragm and vertebral column to cause the trunk to extend.

intracellular—Inside the cell.

intradiscal pressure—The pressure inside the intervertebral disks.

intrafusal fiber—A miniature skeletal muscle fiber that forms part of the muscle spindle.

intramuscular pressure—The pressure inside muscle, which increases during a contraction.

intrathoracic pressure—The pressure (Pa) inside the thoracic cavity.

invariant characteristic—The association between muscle length and force for a constant command signal to the muscle.

inverse dynamics—A dynamic analysis approach to determine the forces and torques acting on a system based on the kinematics of the motion.

inverse relation—$y = \dfrac{k}{x}$. When x is positive and gets larger, y gets smaller.

inverted-pendulum model—A model of walking in which the leg is represented as a strut that rotates about the ankle joint.

inverted-U hypothesis—The shape of the relation between arousal (x-axis) and performance (y-axis), which indicates that performance is best at intermediate levels of arousal.

ion—Electrically charged atom or molecule.

ion channels—A class of membrane-bound proteins found in all cells in the body. Ion channels conduct ions, recognize and select specific ions, and open and close in response to specific signals.

irradiation—The overflow of activation among elements of the central nervous system.

irritability—The ability of a tissue to respond to a stimulus.

ischemia—A block of the blood flow to an area, which disrupts the transmission of action potentials along axons.

isoform—A functionally similar protein that is synthesized with a slightly different amino acid composition. Also referred to as isoenzyme.

isokinetic contraction—A movement in which the angular velocity of the displaced body segment is constant.

isometric contraction—A muscle contraction in which the muscle torque is equal to the load torque and as a consequence whole-muscle length does not change.

isotonic contraction—A muscle contraction in which a muscle contracts and does work against a constant load.

Jendrassik maneuver—The use of remote muscle activity to increase the excitability of a motor neuron pool and the size of the Hoffmann (H) reflex.

jerk—The derivative of acceleration with respect to time.

jitter—Variability in the arrival time of action potentials in two muscle fibers innervated by the same motor neuron.

joint capsule—A tissue that encloses the articulating surfaces of a synovial joint and separates the joint cavity from surrounding tissues.

joint reaction force—The net force transmitted from one segment to another due to muscle, ligament, and bony contacts that are exerted across a joint.

joint receptor—A class of sensory receptors that sense joint-related events.

joint stability—The ability of a joint to maintain an appropriate functional position throughout its range of motion.

joint stiffness—The ratio of the change in the resultant muscle torque to the change in angular displacement.

K$^+$—Potassium ion.

kilogram—The metric measurement for mass.

kinematic—Referring to a description of motion in terms of position, velocity, and acceleration.

kinesiology—The study of movement.

kinesthesia—The ability of the system to use information derived from sensory receptors to determine the position of the limbs, to identify the agent (itself or something else) that causes it to move, to distinguish the senses of effort and heaviness, and to perceive the timing of movements.

kinetic—Referring to a description of motion that includes consideration of force as the cause of motion.

kinetic diagram—A diagram that indicates the effects (mass × acceleration) of the forces acting on a body; a diagram of the right-hand side of the law of acceleration.

kinetic energy—The capacity of an object to perform work because of its motion.

kinetic tremor—Oscillations during movement.

Kohnstamm effect—The postcontraction activation of motor neurons that evokes a contraction in an apparently relaxed muscle.

lambda (λ) model—The concept that movements are controlled by variation in the threshold of the tonic stretch reflex.

Lambert-Eaton myasthenic syndrome—An immune disorder that results in the destruction of voltage-gated Ca^{2+} channels in the presynaptic motor nerve terminal.

laminar flow—Uniform flow of fluid (streamlines) around an object.

latency—The time delay between a stimulus and a response.

lateral corticospinal tract—Fibers in the corticospinal tract that cross the midline and project to interneurons and motor neurons innervating distal muscles on the contralateral side of the body.

lateral sac—The enlargement of the sarcoplasmic reticulum that is adjacent to the transverse tubules; also referred to as the terminal cisternae.

lateral vestibular nucleus—A nucleus located between the pons and medulla that gives rise to the vestibulospinal tract.

law of acceleration—F = ma.

law of action-reaction—Law stating that for every action there is an equal and opposite reaction.

law of gravitation—Law stating that all bodies attract one another with a force that is proportional to the product of their masses and inversely proportional to the square of the distance between them.

law of inertia—Law stating that a force is required to stop, start, or alter motion.

leg spring—A model of the leg muscles as behaving like springs during the stance phase of running.

length—A linear distance, which is measured in meters.

lift force—The component of the fluid-resistance vector that acts perpendicular to the direction of the fluid flow.

light chain—A protein with a low molecular weight, such as those on myosin.

light meromyosin—The tail-end fragment of the myosin molecule.

limbic circle—A set of forebrain structures (hypothalamus, hippocampus, amygdaloid nucleus, and cingulate gyrus) that participate in the generation of emotional responses.

limb immobilization—An experimental protocol in which a limb is prevented from moving for several weeks (e.g., cast, splint).

linear—A straight-line relation.

linear momentum—The quantity of linear motion.

line of action—The direction of a vector.

linked system—A system that is represented as a series of rigid links. In a biomechanical analysis, the human body is regarded as a linked system.

load-deformation relation—The changes in length (deformation) experienced by a tissue when it is subjected to various loads; the changes depend on the material properties of the tissue.

logarithm—The value (x) to which a number (b) must be raised to yield the specified number (n); for example, if $b^x = n$, then $\log_b n = x$.

lower motor neuron lesion—A lesion that disconnects a muscle from the motor neurons in the spinal cord.

low-frequency fatigue—Depression of the force evoked by low frequencies of activation.

M1—The short-latency component (~30 ms) of the stretch reflex.

M2—A long-latency component (50-60 ms) of the stretch reflex.

macro EMG—A needle electrode with a large recording area.

magnetic resonance imaging (MRI)—An imaging technique that involves the use of magnetic fields to determine the spatial localization of protons. Magnetic resonance imaging can be used to study the structure and function of the motor system.

magnetic stimulation—The use of a stimulator to generate a magnetic field that induces an electric field and elicits axonal action potentials.

magnitude—Size or amplitude.

Magnus force—The sideways pressure gradient across an object.

mantissa—The logarithm of the digits in a number.

mass—The amount of matter (kg).

maxima—The high points or peaks in a graph (e.g., position-time graph); at a maximum, the slope of a graph is zero.

maximum voluntary contraction—The maximum output of a muscle or a group of muscles during a voluntary isometric contraction.

M band—Mittelscheibe; intrasarcomere connection of two sets of thick filaments.

mean frequency—The central value of a frequency spectrum.

median frequency—The frequency that divides the spectrum into two equal halves based on the energy content of the signal.

medulla oblongata—The continuation of the brain into the spinal cord and the site of exit and entry for most of the cranial nerves into the brain.

Meissner corpuscle—A cutaneous mechanoreceptor that is sensitive to local, maintained pressure.

membrane—A biological structure that is semipermeable and that separates the inside structures of the cell from its surroundings.

Merkel disk—A cutaneous mechanoreceptor that is sensitive to local vertical pressure.

mesencephalon—The rostral component of the brainstem; merges anteriorly into the thalamus and hypothalamus.

meter—The SI unit of measurement for length.

MHC—Myosin heavy chain, which is part of the myosin molecule.

MHC-I, MHC-IIa, MHC-IId—Three types of muscle fibers that are identified by gel electrophoresis separation based on MHC migration.

microfibril—An elongated bundle composed of five parallel rows of three-stranded collagen molecules arranged in series.

microfilament—One of the cytoskeletal structures involved in axoplasmic transport.

microneurography—A technique that involves placing a needle inside a peripheral nerve to stimulate single axons or to record action potentials.

microtubule—A guiding structure involved in axonal transport.

miniature end-plate potential—Small synaptic potentials at the neuromuscular junction that occur in response to the spontaneous release of neurotransmitter.

minima—The low points or valleys in a graph (e.g., position-time graph); at a minimum, the slope of a graph is zero.

minimum jerk principle—Concept that the nervous system generates smooth trajectories by minimizing the jerk.

M line—A narrow, dark line in the center of the H zone.

modulus of elasticity—The slope of the elastic region of a stress-strain relation; the ratio of stress to strain.

moment arm—The shortest distance (perpendicular) from the line of action of a force vector to an axis of rotation.

moment of force—The rotary effect of a force; torque.

moment of inertia—The resistance that an object offers to any change in its angular motion; represents the distribution of the mass of the object about the axis of rotation. The symbol for moment of inertia is I, and the SI unit of measurement is $kg \cdot m^2$.

moment of momentum—Angular momentum.

momentum—The quantity of motion possessed by an object; a vector quantity. The SI units of measurement are $kg \cdot m/s$ for linear momentum (G) and $kg \cdot m^2/s$ for angular momentum (H).

monopolar recording—A recording made with a single electrode.

monosynaptic—Referring to a neural circuit that involves a single synapse.

morphology—A branch of biology that deals with the form and structure of animals and plants.

mossy fibers—One of the afferent pathways into the cerebellum.

motion—A change in position (m) that occurs over an interval of time.

motion-dependent interactions—Interactive forces between body segments during human movement. These are also called **motion-dependent effects**.

motor control—The control of movement by the nervous system.

motor neuron—A neuron that innervates muscle fibers.

motor neuron pool—The group of motor neurons that innervate a single muscle.

motor program—A stereotyped sequence of commands sent from the spinal cord to the muscles to elicit a specific behavior.

motor system—The neuromuscular elements involved in the production of movement.

motor unit—The cell body and dendrites of a motor neuron, the multiple branches of its axon, and the muscle fibers that it innervates.

motor unit synchronization—An increased coincidence in the timing of action potentials discharged by motor neurons.

motor unit territory—The subvolume of muscle where the muscle fibers belonging to a single motor unit are located.

movement strategies—The activation sequences and combinations of muscles that are used to perform various movements.

multiple sclerosis—A systemic disease that leads to a loss of the myelin sheath around axons in the central nervous system.

muscle—A tissue that contains contractile cells capable of converting chemical energy into mechanical energy and that has the properties of irritability, conductivity, contractility, and a limited growth and regenerative capacity.

muscle architecture—The design of muscle, including such factors as length, cross-sectional area, pennation, and the attachment points on the skeleton.

muscle cramp—A painful, involuntary shortening of muscle that appears to be triggered by peripheral stimuli.

muscle fatigue—An exercise-induced reduction in the maximum force that a muscle can exert.

muscle force—The force exerted by structural (passive) and active (cross-bridges) elements of muscle.

muscle mechanics—The study of the mechanical properties of the force-generating units of muscle.

muscle potentiation—An increase in the force evoked in muscle by a constant activation signal.

muscle power—The rate at which muscle can do work.

muscle soreness—See **delayed-onset muscle soreness.**

muscle spindle—An intramuscular sensory receptor that monitors unexpected changes in muscle length. It is arranged in parallel with skeletal muscle fibers.

muscle strain—A substantial strain of muscle that occurs as an acute and painful event and is immediately recognized as an injury. Muscle strains are also referred to as "pulls" and "tears."

muscle strength—The peak force or torque exerted by a limb during an isometric or isokinetic contraction, or the maximum load that can be lifted.

muscle synergy—A group of muscles and sequence of activity used to perform a task.

muscle tone—The passive resistance of muscle to a change in its length.

muscle wisdom—The reduction in discharge rate of motor neurons during a fatiguing contraction to match the change in the biochemically mediated reduction in relaxation rate.

musculoskeletal force—A force inside the human body that contributes to movement.

musculotendinous unit—The combination of muscle and associated connective tissue structures that is involved in transmitting the force exerted by muscle fibers to the skeleton.

MVC—Maximum voluntary contraction.

M wave—An EMG response that is evoked by activation of the alpha axons with electrical stimulation.

myasthenia gravis—An immunological disorder in which the acetylcholine receptors are targeted by the immune system.

myelin—A fatty, insulating sheath that surrounds axons.

myofibril—A subunit within a muscle fiber that consists of several rows of sarcomeres.

myofibrillar fatigue—A decline in the force exerted by individual cross-bridges.

myofilament—The thick and thin filaments of a muscle fiber that contain the contractile apparatus.

myogenic—Referring to an effect attributable to muscle.

myonucleus—A nucleus in a muscle fiber.

myosin—The major protein in the thick filament of the muscle fiber. It includes the cross-bridge.

myosin ATPase—Adenosine triphosphatase; the enzyme that catalyzes the actomyosin reaction associated with the cross-bridge cycle.

myotendinous junction—The connection between the myofibrils and the tendon.

Na$^+$—Sodium ion.

Na⁺-K⁺ pump—A membrane-bound protein that transports Na⁺ from the intracellular to the extracellular fluid and transports K⁺ in the reverse direction.

nebulin—A protein in the endosarcomeric cytoskeleton that may maintain the lattice array of actin.

negative feedback—Outcome information that decreases the magnitude of the command controlling the outcome.

negative work—The work done by the surroundings on a system. Energy is absorbed by the system from the surroundings during negative work. Muscle does negative work when the resultant muscle torque is less than the load torque.

Nernst equation—An equation for the equilibrium potential of an ion in the presence of an electrical field and a gradient in ion concentrations.

neurofilament—One of the cytoskeletal structures involved in axoplasmic transport.

neurogenic—Pertaining to an effect attributable to the nervous system.

neuroglia—One of two cell types in the nervous system. These cells provide structural, metabolic, and protective support for neurons.

neuromechanics—Interaction between the nervous system and the mechanical properties of the body.

neuromodulator—An agent that acts through a second messenger to alter the response of a neuron to an input signal.

neuromuscular compartment—The part of a muscle that is innervated by a primary branch of the muscle nerve.

neuromuscular electrical stimulation—A clinical or experimental procedure in which electric shocks are used to artificially generate axonal action potentials and to elicit a muscle contraction.

neuromuscular junction—The synapse between the motor axon and the muscle fiber, also known as the motor end plate.

neuromuscular propagation—The processes involved in the conversion of an axonal action potential into a sarcolemmal action potential.

neuron—One of two cell types in the nervous system; capable of generating and transmitting an electrical signal.

neuropathy—Disease of the nerves, which can prevent transmission of action potentials.

neurotransmitter—A chemical substance that is released from an ending of a nerve cell and that evokes a change in membrane potential in another cell.

neurotrophism—The sustaining influence that one biological element exerts on another.

nociceptor—Small sensory endings that generate action potentials in response to potentially damaging stimuli (temperature, pressure, and certain chemicals). These sensations contribute to the sense of pain.

normal component—A component that acts at a right angle to a surface.

normalization—The expression of an outcome measure relative to a factor that contributes to differences in the measure among individuals.

normalized muscle force—The net force relative to the cross-sectional area of the muscle.

nuclear bag fiber—An intrafusal fiber in which the nuclei cluster in a group.

nuclear chain fiber—An intrafusal fiber in which the nuclei are arranged end to end.

omphalion—The center of the navel.

one repetition-maximum (1-RM) load—The maximum load that can be lifted once, which is used as a measure of strength.

optimum—The value of an independent variable that provides the best outcome for the dependent variable.

orderly recruitment—The repeatable sequence of motor unit activation for a specific task.

orthodromic conduction—The conduction of action potentials in the forward direction, such as from the soma to the neuromuscular junction.

orthogonal—Perpendicular; independent.

orthograde transport—Axonal transport from the soma to the periphery.

osteon—Basic structural unit of bone that consists of a series of concentric layers of mineralized matrix surrounding a central canal.

osteoporosis—A decline in the mass and strength of bone.

osteotendinous junction—The connection between tendon and bone.

overlap of myofilaments—Interdigitation of the thick and thin filaments that allows the cross-bridges to cycle and to exert a force. The number of cross-bridges that can be formed, and hence the force that can be exerted, depends on the amount of overlap.

overload principle—A training principle stating that there is a threshold point that must be exceeded before an adaptive response will occur.

pacinian corpuscle—Thickly encapsulated receptor with a parent axon of 8 to 12 μm, a low threshold to mechanical stress, and the ability to detect acceleration of the joint.

parabola—A set of points that are equidistant from a fixed line (the directrix) and a fixed point not on the line (the focus). The vertex is midway between the focus and the directrix, and the graph is symmetrical about the axis, a line that connects the focus and the vertex.

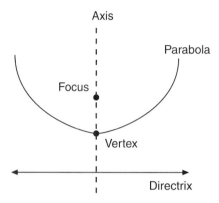

parallel axis theorem—A formula to determine the moment of inertia for a system about an axis that is parallel to the one for which the moment of inertia is known.

parallel elastic element—The component of the Hill model that accounts for the elasticity of muscle in parallel with the contractile element.

parallelogram law of combinations—A graphic procedure used to indicate the magnitude and direction of the resultant of two vectors or, conversely, two components of one vector.

parasympathetic nervous system—The components of the autonomic nervous system that originate from the thoracic spinal cord and upper two or three lumbar segments.

paresis—Partial loss of voluntary control of muscle function.

Parkinson's disease—A disorder that involves an impairment of the basal ganglia.

paw-shake response—A rapid, alternating flexion-extension movement of the paw for the purpose of removing an irritant (e.g., tape stuck to the skin).

PCr—Phosphocreatine.

pendulum method—A method that involves timing the period of oscillation of a suspended system in order to determine its moment of inertia.

pennation—The angle between the orientation of muscle fibers and the line of pull of the muscle.

perception—The recognition and interpretation of afferent input from sensory receptors.

perimysium—The connective tissue matrix that collects bundles of muscle fibers into fascicles.

permeabilized fiber—A preparation in which the outer membrane of a muscle fiber has been made more permeable than normal.

phase transition—The moment when a movement changes from one phase to another, such as from the stance phase to the swing phase in locomotion.

phasic—Intermittent.

P_i—Inorganic phosphate.

piezoelectric—Pertaining to the generation of electric potentials due to pressure.

pinocytosis—The closure and release of a vesicle from the membrane after exocytosis.

planar—Confined to a single plane.

planar law of intersegmental coordination—The association between the plane in which a movement is performed and the relative timing of the angular displacement of the involved body segments.

plasma membrane—A lipid bilayer that is semipermeable and excitable, also known as the plasmalemma.

plasticity—Functional changes in a system, such as a set of neurons or the fibers that comprise a muscle, due to the application of a stimulus.

plastic region—The part of a stress-strain or force-deformation graph where the tissue will not return to its original length when the force is removed.

plegia—Total loss of voluntary control of muscle.

plyometric training—Exercises for the stretch-shorten cycle. These involve sequences of eccentric and concentric contractions, such as hopping down a flight of stairs.

PNF—proprioceptive neuromuscular facilitation.

point-slope equation of a line—$y - y_1 = m(x - x_1)$.

polynomial—A sum of terms that are powers of a variable.

pons—The intermediate section of the brainstem between the medulla and the mesencephalon.

position—The location of an object relative to some reference.

positive feedback—Outcome information that increases the magnitude of the command controlling the outcome.

positive work—The work done by a system on its surroundings. Energy flows from the system to the surroundings during positive work. Muscle does positive work when the resultant muscle torque exceeds the load torque.

postcontraction sensory discharge—The increase in neural activity, primarily due to increased muscle spindle discharge, in the dorsal roots after a muscle contraction.

posterior parietal cortex—A component of the sensorimotor cortex that is posterior to the central sulcus; Brodman's areas 5 and 7.

postsynaptic—On the distal side of a synapse.

postsynaptic inhibition—An inhibitory response on the distal side of the synapse that is evoked by the release of a neurotransmitter.

post-tetanic potentiation—The transient increase in twitch force after a brief tetanus.

postural equilibrium—Maintenance of balance.

postural orientation—Positioning of the body relative to its surroundings.

postural set—The preparation of a group of muscles to provide postural support for a movement.

postural tremor—The oscillations that occur during a postural task.

posture—Orientation of the body for a task and the maintenance of equilibrium.

potential energy—The energy that a system possesses due to its location away from a more stable location. There are two forms of potential energy, gravitational and strain.

potentiation—An augmentation of a response (e.g., force, EMG) despite a constant input.

power—The rate of doing work; the rate of change in energy; the product of force and velocity.

power absorption—The flow of mechanical energy from the surroundings to the system. A system absorbs power when it does negative work.

power density spectrum—A graph of the relative contributions (y-axis) of different frequencies (x-axis) in a signal. The relative contribution is expressed as the power or amplitude of each frequency.

power production—The flow of mechanical energy from the system to the surroundings. A system produces power when it does positive work.

premotor cortex—A component of the sensorimotor cortex that is anterior to the central sulcus; Brodman's area 6.

pressure drag—The drag due to a difference in the pressure between the front and back of the object, which increases as the flow becomes more turbulent.

presynaptic—On the proximal side of a synapse.

presynaptic inhibition—An inhibitory influence, such as from another neuron, that acts on the presynaptic membrane of a neuron.

presynaptic terminal—An enlargement of an axon that is involved in a synapse.

primary motor area—A component of the sensorimotor cortex that is anterior to the central sulcus; Brodman's area 4.

primary somatosensory cortex—A component of the sensorimotor cortex that is posterior to the central sulcus; Brodman's areas 1–3.

principle of transmissibility—The property that makes it possible to slide a vector along its line of action without altering its mechanical effect on the rigid body.

progressive-resistance exercise—A training strategy in which the load increases progressively from one set of repetitions to the next.

projectile—An object that is displaced so that it has a phase of nonsupport and the only forces it experiences are those due to gravity and air resistance.

propagation—The conduction of an action potential by active, regenerative processes that tend to preserve the quantity of the potential.

proprioceptor—A sensory receptor (e.g., muscle spindle, tendon organ) that provides information on the actions that the body itself generates.

propriospinal axons—Interneurons that convey information between spinal segments.

psychophysics—The quantification of sensory experience; study of the relationship between a physical variable and its corresponding sensation.

Purkinje cell—Large inhibitory cells in the cerebellum that provide the output of the cerebellum.

putamen nucleus—One of the basal ganglia nuclei.

pyramidal cell—Large neurons in the cerebral cortex.

Pythagorean relationship—$a^2 = b^2 + c^2$.

quadratic—Indicating a second-degree polynomial.

qualitative analysis—Description of the type or kind.

quantitative analysis—Description of the quantity or how much.

quasistatic—Referring to a mechanical state in which the acceleration experienced by a system is small enough that we can assume it is zero.

radian—An angle defined as the quotient of a distance on the circumference of the circle relative to its radius. It is a dimensionless unit.

range of motion—The maximum angular displacement about a joint.

reaction time—The minimum time from the presentation of a stimulus to the onset of a response.

readiness potential—A slow, negative shift in the EEG that begins about 1.5 s prior to a voluntary movement.

rearfoot motion—The change in the angle between the shank and the heel during the stance phase of locomotion. The measurement is used as an index of the amount of pronation and supination experienced by the foot.

receptor potential—The electrical potential generated in a sensory receptor in response to a stimulus.

reciprocal-inhibition reflex—A decrease in the excitability of motor neurons innervating an antagonist muscle due to the stretch of the agonist muscle and activation of its Group Ia afferents and the Ia inhibitory interneuron.

recruitment—The process of motor unit activation.

recruitment threshold—The force at which a motor unit is recruited (activated).

rectification—A process that involves eliminating or inverting the negative phases in a signal. This process is frequently applied to the EMG interference pattern. Half-wave rectification refers to eliminating the negative phase, whereas full-wave rectification involves inverting the negative phases. Rectification may be accomplished numerically or electronically.

recurrent inhibition—A local reflex circuit whereby action potentials discharged by the motor neuron lead to activation, via axon collaterals, of the Renshaw cell and the subsequent generation of an inhibitory postsynaptic potential in the motor neuron.

red nucleus—A cluster of cells located in the mesencephalon that give rise to the rubrospinal tract.

reflex—A short-latency connection between an input signal (afferent feedback) and an output response (muscle activation).

refractory period—An interval when an excitable membrane is less excitable than normal.

regression analysis—The statistical process of finding a simple function, such as a line, to describe the relationship between two variables.

regulation—The process of maintaining a constant state with a system that can accommodate disturbances.

reinnervation—A state in which a muscle or muscle fiber is reconnected to the nervous system by the development of a functional connection (synapse).

relative angle—The angle between two adjacent body segments.

remodeling—The growth, reinforcement, and resorption experienced by living bone.

Renshaw cell—An interneuron in the spinal cord that elicits inhibitory postsynaptic potentials in other neurons. The Renshaw cell receives input from collateral branches of motor neuron axons and from supraspinal sources.

repolarization—A return of membrane potential (polarity) to steady state conditions.

residual analysis—A comparison between two sets of data to assess the adequacy of a numerical procedure. The two most common applications in biomechanics are (1) to compare the difference between the filtered and unfiltered signals and (2) to assign the remainder of a calculation to an unknown force (e.g., the joint reaction force).

residual moment of force—The term remaining in an equation of motion when all the other quantities have been determined. Use of this term is the most common procedure for calculating the resultant muscle force.

resistance reflex—A negative-feedback response.

resistance to fatigue—The ability of muscle (muscle fiber, motor unit, whole muscle) to sustain force with repetitive activation.

resolution—The process of breaking a vector down into several components.

resting length of muscle—The length at which a passive force is first detected when a muscle is stretched.

resting membrane potential—The transmembrane voltage during steady state conditions.

resultant muscle force (or **torque**)—The net force (torque) exerted by a group of muscles about a joint.

reticular formation—A diffuse cluster of cells in the brainstem with concentrations in the pons and the medulla that give rise to two reticulospinal tracts.

reticulospinal tract—Descending pathway from the reticular formation to the spinal cord.

retrograde transport—Axonal transport from the periphery to the soma.

rhabdomyolysis—Exaggerated muscle weakness and swelling that can occur after exercise involving strenuous eccentric contractions.

rheobase—A measure of neuron excitability as the amount of current that must be injected into the neuron in order for it to generate an action potential.

rheological model—Model used to study the deformation and flow of matter.

right-hand coordinate system—Standard positive directions for x (to the right)-, y (up)-, and z (out of page toward reader)-axes.

right-hand-thumb rule—A technique for determining the direction of a vector product. The direction of the product is always perpendicular to the plane in which the other two vectors lie.

rigidity—An increased resistance to passive movement that is independent of the movement velocity.

RM—Repetition maximum.

RNA—Ribonucleic acid; genetic material formed from DNA and used to construct proteins in the cytoplasm.

rotation—A motion in which all parts of the system are not displaced by a similar amount.

rubrospinal tract—A descending pathway from the red nucleus to motor neurons in the spinal cord.

Ruffini ending—Two to six thinly encapsulated, globular corpuscles with a single myelinated parent axon that has a diameter of 5 to 9 μm. These mechanoreceptors are capable of signaling joint position and displacement, angular velocity, and intra-articular pressure.

running—A mode of human locomotion that includes a phase when neither foot is on the ground.

ryanodine receptor—Calcium-releasing channel in the sarcoplasmic reticulum of the muscle fiber.

safety factor—A functional measure of tissue strength, which is expressed as the ratio of the typical forces encountered during activities of daily living to the maximum force that can be tolerated before failure.

sag—An unfused tetanus in which the force declines after the initial four to eight stimuli and then increases again.

sagittal plane—A plane that divides the body into right and left halves for the purpose of describing movement direction.

saltatory conduction—Propagation of an action potential along a myelinated axon by the depolarization of the axolemma that is exposed at each node of Ranvier.

sarcolemma—The excitable plasma membrane of a muscle fiber.

sarcomere—The components of a myofibril contained in the region from one Z band to the next.

sarcopenia—The decline in muscle mass with advancing age.

sarcoplasm—The fluid enclosed within a muscle fiber by the sarcolemma.

sarcoplasmic reticulum—A hollow membranous system within the muscle fiber that bulges into lateral sacs in the vicinity of the transverse tubules.

scalar—Variable that is defined by magnitude only.

scalar product—The procedure used to multiply vectors to produce a scalar quantity (product).

secant—An angle in a triangle defined by the ratio of the hypotenuse to the adjacent side.

segmental analysis—A biomechanical analysis that involves graphically separating body segments and drawing a free body diagram and equations of motion for each segment.

sense of effort—A perception based on the corollary discharge that indicates quantitative changes in the descending command.

sense of heaviness—The ability of the nervous system to integrate proprioceptive feedback and the centrally generated motor command to estimate the weight of an object.

sensory perception—The detection of a stimulus by a sensory receptor and the interpretation of the signal by the central nervous system.

series elastic element—The component of the Hill model that accounts for the elasticity of muscle in series with the contractile element.

servo—A feedback control system that enables a controller to achieve a desired output.

servo hypothesis—Notion that muscle length is maintained at a centrally specified value by means of the tonic stretch reflex.

shear force—A force that acts parallel to the contact surface.

shortening deactivation—Depression of muscle force after a shortening contraction.

shortening velocity—The rate at which a muscle shortens its length.

short-range stiffness—A mechanical property of muscle that produces a high initial stiffness during a stretch.

significant figures—The number of digits in a number that are used to indicate the accuracy of the measurement.

sine—An angle in a triangle defined by the ratio between the side opposite the angle and the hypotenuse.

single-joint system—A level of analysis that includes the neuromuscular components involved in producing movement about a single joint.

SI system—The international metric system; *Le Système Internationale d'Unites.*

Size Principle—The concept that the recruitment of motor units is based on motor neuron size, proceeding from the smallest to the largest.

skelemin—A protein that is part of the cytoskeleton.

sliding filament hypothesis—A concept describing the sliding of thick and thin myofilaments past one another during a contraction.

slope—The rate of change in one variable (dependent variable; y-axis variable) relative to another variable (independent variable; x-axis variable).

slope-intercept equation of a line—$y = mx + b$.

slow-to-fast conversion—An adaptation that involves a change in muscle fiber properties from slow twitch to fast twitch.

smoothing—The process of reducing the fluctuations in a signal, which has the effect of decreasing the higher-frequency components in the signal.

sodium-potassium pump—A molecular mechanism that maintains the difference in ion concentrations (Na^+ and K^+) across an excitable membrane.

soma—The cell body of a neuron.

somatosensory cortical areas—Areas 1, 2, 3a, and 3b in the parietal cortex, which receive inputs from the thalamus.

somatotopic—A body map that indicates organized connections between various parts of the nervous system.

somersault axis—An axis that passes through the human body from side to side; the term is used to describe the direction of a rotation.

space diagram—A schematic of the free body diagram that does not include the correct magnitudes of the force vectors.

spared-root preparation—An experimental model used to study sprouting in the CNS. In this model, all the dorsal roots innervating a hindlimb are transected except one. The dependent variables are recovery of motor function and the development of collateral sprouts in the spinal cord.

spasticity—Pathological disruption of transmission along descending pathways, which is manifested as uncontrolled spasms, increased muscle tone, and heightened excitability of the stretch reflex.

spatial summation—An increase in the combined effect of multiple concurrent inputs onto a neuron.

specificity principle—The concept that the adaptations experienced with physical training depend on the stress imposed during exercise.

specific tension—The intrinsic capacity of muscle to exert force (N/cm^2).

speed—The size of the velocity vector; expresses how fast.

speed-dependent strategy—Modulation of EMG amplitude to perform rapid movements with certain time constraints.

speed-independent strategy—Modulation of EMG duration to perform movements for which there is no time constraint.

spinal transection—Cutting of the spinal cord, which disconnects it from the brain. Also known as **spinalization**.

spinocerebellum—The vermis and intermediate hemispheres of the cerebellum. Receives input from the spinal cord and sends output to the fastigial and interposed nuclei.

spinocervical tract—An ascending pathway that ends in the cervical cord and contributes to the descending control of pain.

spinoreticular tract—An ascending pathway that conveys noxious and thermal information from the spinal cord to the reticular formation.

spinothalamic tract—An ascending pathway that conveys noxious and thermal information from the spinal cord to the thalamus.

spring-mass system—A simple model used to represent the elastic (spring) and inertial (mass) properties of a system.

stability—A state of equilibrium to which the system returns after it has been perturbed.

staggered muscle fibers—Serial attachment of muscle fibers that are shorter than whole-muscle length.

staircase effect—The progressive increase in twitch force that occurs when a series of twitches are elicited by electric shocks. Also known as **treppe**.

stance phase—The support phase of locomotion.

startle reaction—The response of the body to an unexpected auditory stimulus.

state-dependent response—A response that varies with the state of the system. Reflexes are described as state-dependent responses, which means that the amplitude varies depending on the activity of the individual—for example, walking versus standing, stance versus swing.

static analysis—Mechanical analysis in which the forces acting on the system are balanced and hence the system is not accelerating. The system is either stationary or moving at a constant velocity.

static stretch—A technique that attempts to increase the range of motion about a joint by sustaining a muscle stretch for 15 to 30 s.

steadiness—The ability to exert a constant muscle force.

step—Part of the human gait cycle, such as from left foot toe-off to right foot toe-off. There are two steps in one complete gait cycle (stride).

stiffness—The change in force per unit change in length (N/mm); the slope of a force-length graph.

strain—The change in length relative to the initial length (%).

strain energy—The potential energy (J) stored by a system when it is stretched from a resting position.

streamlines—The schematized lines of fluid flow around an object.

stress—Force applied per unit area (Pa).

stretch reflex—The response of a muscle to a sudden, unexpected increase in its length. The negative-feedback response activates the stretched muscle to minimize the increase in its length.

stretch-shorten cycle—A muscle activation scheme in which an activated muscle first lengthens before it shortens.

striatum—The caudate and putamen nuclei of the basal ganglia.

stride—One complete cycle of human gait, such as from left foot toe-off to left foot toe-off. A stride contains two steps.

stride length—The distance covered in a single stride.

stride rate—The frequency (Hz) at which strides are performed. The inverse of stride rate is the time it takes to complete a stride.

subfragment 1—The two globular heads of the myosin molecule. One globular head contains an ATP-binding site and the other an actin-binding site.

subfragment 2—The non-globular head region of heavy meromyosin.

substantia nigra—One of the basal ganglia nuclei.

subthalamic nuclei—Some of the basal ganglia nuclei.

supplementary motor area—A component of the sensorimotor cortex (area 6) that is anterior to the central sulcus.

supraspinal—The part of the central nervous system above (rostral) the spinal cord.

suprasternale—The most caudal point on the margin of the jugular notch of the sternum.

surface drag—The drag due to the friction between the boundary layer of the fluid and the object.

swing phase—The nonsupport phase of locomotion.

sympathetic nervous system—A branch of the autonomic nervous system that originates from the brainstem and the sacral segments and provides automatic regulation of various physiological processes.

synapse—The structure by which a neuron transmits its signals to a target cell.

synaptic cleft—The gap between the presynaptic and postsynaptic membranes of a synapse.

synaptic delay—The time it takes for an action potential to cross a synapse.

synaptic potential—A conducted (nonpropagated) excitatory or inhibitory electrical potential that is elicited in neurons and muscle fibers in response to a neurotransmitter. The amplitude of a synaptic potential is variable, depending on the excitability of the cell and the quantity of neurotransmitter released.

synaptogenesis—Formation of new synapses.

synchronization—See **motor unit synchronization.**

synergy—A combination of activation signals to a number of muscles for the purpose of assuring a certain movement or preserving a specific posture.

synovial membrane—A vascular membrane that secretes synovial fluid into the joint cavity.

T_1 relaxation time—An MRI measure of the time constant for the oscillations of atomic nuclei to return to an initial level of longitudinal magnetization after exposure to a radio-frequency pulse. The recovery rates vary across tissues, enabling MRI to differentiate between different types of tissue.

T_2 relaxation time—An MRI measure of the time constant for the oscillations of atomic nuclei to become random again after exposure to a radio-frequency pulse. The T_2 for a tissue largely depends on its chemical environment, which can change with exercise.

tangent—An angle in a triangle defined by the ratio between the side opposite the angle and the side adjacent to it.

tangential component—A component that acts parallel to and along a surface.

task dependency of muscle fatigue—The association between the demands of a task and the physiological processes that are impaired during a fatiguing contraction.

tectospinal tract—A descending pathway that arises from neurons in the superior colliculus, which is a mesencephalic area concerned with orientation to visual inputs.

temporal summation—The increase in the effect of an input when it follows another input after a brief delay.

tendon-tap reflex (T)—A subset of the stretch reflex that involves the response of muscle to the tap of its tendon. The afferents activated during the tendon tap are primarily the Group Ia afferents; a greater diversity of afferents is activated during the stretch reflex.

tensile force—A pulling force.

terminal velocity—The velocity of a falling object when the forces due to gravity and air resistance are equal in magnitude.

tetanus—A force evoked in muscle (single fiber, motor unit, or whole muscle) in response to a series of excitatory inputs (action potentials or electrical stimuli). The response represents a summation of twitch responses.

tetrodotoxin—A drug that blocks the propagation of action potentials by deactivating Na channels.

thalamus—A brain structure that integrates and distributes most of the sensory and motor information going to the cerebral cortex. It is important in coordination.

thixotropy—The property exhibited by various gels, such as muscle, of becoming fluid when shaken, stirred, or otherwise disturbed and of setting again when allowed to stand.

three-burst pattern of EMG—Alternating sequence of activity in agonist and antagonist muscles that is associated with a unidirectional movement to a target.

three-element model of muscle—A mechanical model of muscle that comprises three elements: parallel elastic, series elastic, and contractile elements.

time—A duration that, for human movement, is measured in seconds.

time domain—A graph that has time as the independent variable (*x*-axis).

titin—A protein in the endosarcomeric cytoskeleton that may be responsible for resting muscle elasticity.

TN-C—The component of troponin that binds calcium.

TN-I—The component of troponin that inhibits G actin from binding to myosin.

TN-T—The component of troponin that binds to tropomysin.

tonic—Continuous, sustained.

tonic stretch reflex—A polysynaptic reflex that increases the level of muscle activation in response to a slow muscle stretch.

tonic vibration reflex—A polysynaptic reflex that is elicited by small-amplitude, high-frequency (50-150 Hz) vibration of a muscle. The vibration activates the muscle spindles, which provide reflex activation of the motor neurons.

torque—The rotary effect of a force, which is quantified as the product of force and moment arm (N·m).

torque-angle relation—The variation in muscle torque as a function of joint angle.

torque-velocity relation—The variation in muscle torque as a function of joint angular velocity.

torsional spring—An angular spring, such as a snapping mousetrap.

torticollis—A dystonia that affects the neck muscles.

trajectory—A position-time record for a movement.

transcranial magnetic stimulation—A technique that activates brain cells by creating a magnetic field through the skull.

transduction—A process by which energy is converted from one form to another.

translation—A motion in which all parts of the system are displaced by a similar amount.

transmitter-gated channel—A pathway through an excitable membrane that is opened by a neurotransmitter.

transverse plane—A plane that divides the body into upper and lower.

transverse tubule—Invaginations of the sarcolemma that facilitate a rapid communication between sarcolemmal events (action potentials) and myofilaments located in the interior of the muscle fiber.

tremor—An oscillation of a body part that is produced by alternating muscle activity. The oscillations occur at about 3 to 5 Hz in patients with cerebellar disorders, at ~6 Hz in patients with Parkinson's disease, and at 8 to 12 Hz in healthy persons (physiological tremor).

treppe—The progressive increase in twitch force that occurs when a series of twitches are elicited. Also known as the staircase effect.

triad—One transverse tubule and the two adjacent lateral sacs of the sarcoplasmic reticulum.

trigonometry—A branch of mathematics dealing with the relations among the sides and angles of a triangle.

triphasic EMG pattern—A pattern that comprises three bursts of EMG, first in the agonist muscle, then in the antagonist muscle, and finally in the agonist muscle again.

triple helix of collagen—The three intertwined polypeptide chains that compose the collagen molecule.

tropomyosin—A thin-filament protein involved in regulating the interaction between actin and myosin.

troponin—A three-component molecule that forms part of the thin filament and is involved in the regulation of the interaction between actin and myosin.

T tubule—Transverse tubule of the muscle fiber.

turbulent flow—Non-uniform flow of fluid (streamlines) around an object.

twist axis—An axis that passes through the human body from head to toe.

twitch—The force response of muscle (single fiber, motor unit, or whole muscle) to a single excitatory input.

twitch superimposition—A technique used to test the maximality of a voluntary muscle contraction. The technique involves superimposing one to three supramaximal electric shocks to the muscle nerve during a voluntary contraction to determine whether the force increases. The technique is also known as "twitch interpolation" and "twitch occlusion."

two-joint muscle—A muscle whose attachment sites span two joints; examples are rectus femoris, the long head of biceps brachii, and gastrocnemius.

Type FF motor unit—A fast-twitch, fatigable motor unit. This type of unit is characterized by a sag response and a decline in force during a standard fatigue test.

Type FG muscle fiber—A fast-twitch, glycolytic muscle fiber that exists in type FF motor units.

Type FOG muscle fiber—A fast-twitch, oxidative-glycolytic muscle fiber that exists in type FR motor units.

Type FR motor unit—A fast-twitch, fatigue-resistant motor unit. This type of unit is characterized by a sag response and a minimal decline in force during a standard fatigue test.

Type I muscle fiber—A slow-twitch muscle fiber, as defined by a low level of myosin ATPase.

Type II muscle fiber—A fast-twitch muscle fiber, as defined by a high level of myosin ATPase.

Type S motor unit—A slow-twitch motor unit. This type of unit is characterized by a zero sag response and the absence of a decline in force during a standard fatigue test.

Type SO muscle fiber—A slow-twitch, oxidative muscle fiber that exists in type S motor units.

unfused tetanus—An irregular muscle force (muscle fiber, motor unit, whole muscle) elicited by a low frequency of activation. The peak forces of the individual twitch responses are evident.

unloading reflex—A decrease in muscle activity when a load is suddenly reduced.

unmasking—Exposing. The recovery of function following an injury to the nervous system can be due to the ability of a dormant pathway to assume the function of the injured pathway. In this scheme, the injury has unmasked the previously dormant pathway.

upper motor neuron lesion—A lesion that disconnects supraspinal centers from the spinal cord.

Valsalva maneuver—Voluntary pressurization of the abdominal cavity.

variable load—A training load that varies over a range of motion.

vector—Quantity that conveys both magnitude and direction.

velocity—The rate of change in position with respect to time (m/s); the derivative of position with respect to time; the slope of a position-time graph.

ventral corticospinal tract—Fibers in the corticospinal tract that do not cross the midline and that terminate on interneurons controlling axial muscles on both sides of the body.

ventral root—The exit zone on the front side of the spinal cord. Efferent axons exit the spinal cord in the ventral root.

ventrolateral thalamus—The ventral and lateral part of the thalamus, which receives input from the basal ganglia and the deep cerebellar nuclei and projects to the motor cortex.

vermis—Middle region of the cerebellum.

vertex—A point that is midway between the directrix and focus of a parabola.

vestibular nuclei—Nuclei located in the medulla that give rise to the vestibulospinal tracts.

vestibulocerebellum—Region occupying the flocculonodular lobe of the cerebellum; receives input from the vestibular nuclei and sends output back to the same nuclei.

vestibulospinal tract—A descending pathway from the lateral vestibular nucleus to ipsilateral motor neurons.

vimentin—A protein that is part of the cytoskeleton.

viscoelastic—Referring to a material that has both viscous and elastic properties.

viscosity—A measure of the shear stress that must be applied to a fluid to obtain a rate of deformation. Viscosity varies with temperature and depends on the cohesive forces between molecules as well as the momentum interchange between colliding molecules. The SI unit of measurement is $N \cdot s/cm^2$. Oil has a greater viscosity than water.

voltage-gated channel—A pathway through an excitable membrane that is opened by a decrease in the electrical potential across the membrane.

volume conduction—The spread of electrical signals in the body.

walking—A mode of human locomotion that is defined in either of two ways: (1) at least one foot is always in contact with the ground; or (2) the center of mass reaches a maximum height in the middle of the stance phase.

warm-up—An intervention that increases muscle temperature.

wave resistance—The resistive effects of waves encountered by a swimmer. The resistance is probably due to the difference in the densities of water and air.

weight—The amount of gravitational attraction between an object and Earth.

weighting coefficient—A coefficient used to modulate the amplitude of a variable and its contribution to a compound expression, for example, the harmonic terms of a Fourier analysis.

weightlessness—An environment in which gravity is close to zero.

Westphal phenomenon—An abrupt reflex excitation of muscle in response to an externally imposed shortening of the muscle.

withdrawal reflex—The withdrawal of a limb away from a noxious stimulus.

Wolff's law—Law stating that all changes in the function of bone are attended by alterations in internal structure.

work—A scalar quantity that describes the extent to which a force can move an object in a specified direction. The symbol for work is U, and its SI unit of measurement is the joule (J).

work loop—The force-length relation of muscle during a cyclic movement.

xyphion—The midpoint of the sulcus between the body of the sternum and the xyphoid process.

Z band—Zwischenscheibe; intrasarcomere connection of the two sets of thin filaments in adjacent sarcomeres.

References

Aagaard, P., Simonsen, E.B., Trolle, M., Bangsbo, J., & Klausen, K. (1994a). Effects of different strength training regimes on moment and power generation during dynamic knee extensions. *European Journal of Applied Physiology, 69,* 382–386.

Aagaard, P., Simonsen, E.B., Anderson, J.L., Magnusson, S.P., Halkaer-Kristensen, J., & Dhyre-Poulsen, P. (2000). Neural inhibition during maximal eccentric and concentric quadriceps contraction: effects of resistance training. *Journal of Applied Physiology, 89,* 2249–2257.

Aagaard, P., Simonsen, E.B., Trolle, M., Bangsbo, J., & Klausen, K. (1994b). Moment and power generation during maximal knee extensions performed at low and high speeds. *European Journal of Applied Physiology, 69,* 376–381.

Aagaard, P., Simonsen, E.B., Trolle, M., Bangsbo, J., & Klausen, K. (1996). Specificity of training velocity and training load on gains in isokinetic knee joint strength. *Acta Physiologica Scandinavica, 156,* 123–129.

Abelew, T.A., Miller, M.D., Cope, T.C., & Nichols, T.R. (2000). Local loss of proprioception results in disruption of interjoint coordination during locomotion in the cat. *Journal of Neurophysiology, 84,* 2709–2714.

Ackland, T.R., Blanksby, B.A., & Bloomfield, J. (1988). Inertial characteristics of adolescent male body segments. *Journal of Biomechanics, 21,* 319–327.

Adams, G.R., Duvoisin, M.R., & Dudley, G.A. (1992). Magnetic resonance imaging and electromyography as indexes of muscle function. *Journal of Applied Physiology, 73,* 1578–1583.

Adams, G.R., Harris, R.T., Woodard, D., & Dudley, G.A. (1993). Mapping of electrical muscle stimulation using MRI. *Journal of Applied Physiology, 74,* 532–537.

Adams, G.R., Hather, B.M., Baldwin, K.M., & Dudley, G.A. (1993). Skeletal muscle myosin heavy chain composition and resistance training. *Journal of Applied Physiology, 74,* 911–915.

Ahmed, A.M., & Burke, D.L. (1983). In vitro measurement of static pressure distribution in synovial joints. 1. Tibial surface of the knee. *Journal of Biomechanical Engineering, 105,* 216–225.

Akima, H., Takahashi, H., Kuno, S.-Y., Masuda, K., Masuda, T., Shimojo, H., Anno, I., Itai, Y., & Katsuta, S. (1999). Early phase adaptations of muscle use and strength to isokinetic training. *Medicine and Science in Sports and Exercise, 31,* 588–594.

Alexander, R.M. (1984a). Optimal strengths for bones liable to fatigue and accidental fracture. *Journal of Theoretical Biology, 109,* 621–636.

Alexander, R.M. (1984b). Walking and running. *American Scientist, 72,* 348–354.

Alexander, R.M. (1991). Optimum timing of muscle activation for simple models of throwing. *Journal of Theoretical Biology, 150,* 349–372.

Alexander, R.M. (1997). Optimum muscle design for oscillatory movements. *Journal of Theoretical Biology, 184,* 253–259.

Alexander, R.M., & Ker, R.F. (1990). The architecture of leg muscles. In J.M. Winters & S.L.-Y. Woo (Eds.), *Multiple muscle systems: Biomechanics and movement organization* (pp. 568–577). New York: Springer-Verlag.

Alexander, R.M., & Vernon, A. (1975). The dimensions of the knee and ankle muscles and the forces they exert. *Journal of Human Movement Studies, 1,* 115–123.

Al-Falahe, N.A., Nagaoka, M., & Vallbo, A.B. (1990). Response profiles of human muscle afferents during active finger movements. *Brain, 113,* 325–346.

Alford, E.K., Roy, R.R., Hodgson, J.A., & Edgerton, V.R. (1987). Electromyography of rat soleus, medial gastrocnemius, and tibialis anterior during hind limb suspension. *Experimental Neurology, 96,* 635–649.

Allaf, O., & Goubel, F. (1999). The rat suspension model is also a good tool for inducing muscle hyperactivity. *Pflügers Archive, 437,* 504–507.

Allen, D.G., Lee, J.A., & Westerblad, H. (1989). Intracellular calcium and tension during fatigue in isolated single muscle fibers from *Xenopus Laevis. Journal of Physiology, 415,* 433–458.

Allen, D.G., Westerblad, H., & Lännergren, J. (1995). The role of intracellular acidosis in muscle fatigue. In S.C. Gandevia, R.M. Enoka, A.J. McComas, D.G. Stuart, & C.K. Thomas (Eds.), *Fatigue: Neural and muscular mechanisms* (pp. 57–68). New York: Plenum Press.

Allen, G.M., Gandevia, S.C., & McKenzie, D.K. (1995). Reliability of measurement of muscle strength and voluntary activation using twitch interpolation. *Muscle and Nerve, 18,* 593–600.

Allen, G.M., McKenzie, D.K., & Gandevia, S.C. (1998). Twitch interpolation of the elbow flexor muscles at high forces. *Muscle & Nerve, 21,* 318–328.

Allum, J.H.J., Dietz, V., & Freund, H. (1978). Neuronal mechanisms underlying physiological tremor. *Journal of Neurophysiology, 41,* 557–571.

Almåsbakk, B., & Hoff, J. (1996). Coordination, the determinant of velocity specificity? *Journal of Applied Physiology, 80,* 2046–2052.

Almeida, G.L., Hong, D.-A., Corcos, D., & Gottlieb, G.L. (1995). Organizing principles for voluntary movement: Extending single-joint rules. *Journal of Neurophysiology, 74,* 1374–1381.

Almeida-Silveira, M.-I., Pérot, C., & Goubel, F. (1996). Neuromuscular adaptations in rats trained by muscle stretch-shortening. *European Journal of Applied Physiology, 72*, 261–266.

Alshuaib, W.B., & Fahim, M.A. (1991). Depolarization reverses age-related decrease of spontaneous transmitter release. *Journal of Applied Physiology, 70*, 2066–2071.

Alter, M.J. (1996). *Science of flexibility*. Champaign, IL: Human Kinetics.

Alway, S.E., Grumbt, W.H., Stray-Gundersen, J., & Gonyea, W.J. (1992). Effects of resistance training on elbow flexors of highly competitive bodybuilders. *Journal of Applied Physiology, 72*, 1512–1521.

Alway, S.E., MacDougall, J.D., & Sale, D.G. (1989). Contractile adaptations in the human triceps surae after isometric exercise. *Journal of Applied Physiology, 66*, 2725–2732.

Amar, J. (1920). *The human motor*. London: Routledge.

Amaral, D.G. (2000a). The anatomical organization of the central nervous system. In E.R. Kandel, J.H. Schwartz, & T.M. Jessell (Eds.), *Principles of neural science* (4th ed., pp. 317–336). New York: McGraw-Hill.

Amaral, D.G. (2000b). The functional organization of perception and movement. In E.R. Kandel, J.H. Schwartz, & T.M. Jessell (Eds.), *Principles of neural science* (4th ed., pp. 337–348). New York: McGraw-Hill.

Amiridis, I.G., Martin, A., Morlon, B., Martin, L., Cometti, G., Pousson, M., & van Hoecke, J. (1996). Co-activation and tension-regulating phenomena during isokinetic knee extension in sedentary and highly skilled humans. *European Journal of Applied Physiology, 73*, 149–156.

An, K.N., Hui, F.C., Morrey, B.F., Linscheid, R.L., & Chao, E.Y. (1981). Muscles across the elbow joint: A biomechanical analysis. *Journal of Biomechanics, 10*, 659–669.

An, K.N., Kwak, B.M., Chao, E.Y., & Morrey, B.F. (1984). Determination of muscle and joint forces: A new technique to solve the indeterminate problem. *Journal of Biomechanical Engineering, 106*, 364–367.

Andersen, J.L., Mohr, T., Biering-Sørensen, F., Galbo, H., & Kjær, M. (1996). Myosin heavy chain isoform transformation in single fibres from m. vastus lateralis in spinal cord injured individuals: Effects of long-term functional electrical stimulation (FES). *Pflügers Archive, 431*, 513–518.

Andersen, J.L., Terzis, G., & Kryger, A. (1999). Increase in the degree of coexpression of myosin heavy chain isoforms in skeletal muscle fibers of the very old. *Muscle & Nerve, 22*, 449–454.

Andersen, O.K., Sonnenborg, F.A., & Arendt-Nielsen, L. (1999). Modular organization of human leg withdrawal reflexes elicited by electrical stimulation of the foot sole. *Muscle & Nerve, 22*, 1520–1530.

Anderson, S.A., & Cohn, S.H. (1985). Bone demineralization during space flight. *Physiologist, 28*, 212–217.

Andersson, E.A., Nilsson, J., Ma, Z., & Thorstensson, A. (1996). Abdominal and hip flexor muscle activation during various training exercises. *European Journal of Applied Physiology, 75*, 115–123.

Andersson, G.B.J., Örtengren, R., & Nachemson, A. (1977). Intradiscal pressure, intra-abdominal pressure and myoelectric back muscle activity related to posture and loading. *Clinical Orthopedics Research, 129*, 156–164.

Angulo-Kinzler, R.M., Mynark, R.G., & Koceja, D.M. (1998). Soleus H-reflex gain in elderly and young adults: Modulation due to body position. *Journal of Gerontology, 53A*, M120–M125.

Antonio, J., & Gonyea, W.J. (1993). Skeletal muscle fiber hyperplasia. *Medicine and Science in Sports and Exercise, 25*, 1333–1345.

Arampatzis, A., Brüggemann, G.-P., & Metzler, V. (1999). The effect of speed on leg stiffness and joint kinetics in human running. *Journal of Biomechanics, 32*, 1349–1353.

Arampatzis, A., Knicker, A., Metzler, V., & Brüggemann, G.-P. (2000). Mechanical power in running: A comparison of different approaches. *Journal of Biomechanics, 33*, 457–463.

Aristotle. (1968). *Progression of animals*. (E.S. Forster, Trans.) Cambridge: Harvard University Press.

Armstrong, R.B. (1990). Initial events in exercise-induced muscular injury. *Medicine and Science in Sports and Exercise, 22*, 429–435.

Arsenault, A.B., & Chapman, A.E. (1974). An electromyographic investigation of the individual recruitment of the quadriceps muscles during isometric contraction of the knee extensors in different patterns of movement. *Physiotherapy of Canada, 26*, 253–261.

Aruin, A.S., Forrest, W.R., & Latash, M.L. (1998). Anticipatory postural adjustments in conditions of postural instability. *Electroencephalography and Clinical Neurophysiology, 109*, 350–359.

Aruin, A.S., Ota, T., & Latash, M.L. (2001). Anticipatory postural adjustments associated with lateral and rotational perturbations during standing. *Journal of Electromyography and Kinesiology, 11*, 39–51.

Asami, T., & Nolte, V. (1983). Analysis of powerful ball kicking. In H. Matsui & K. Kobayashi (Eds.), *Biomechanics VIII-B* (pp. 695–700). Champaign, IL: Human Kinetics.

Ashley, C.C., & Ridgway, E.B. (1968). Simultaneous recording of membrane potential, calcium transient and tension in single muscle fibres. *Nature, 219*, 1168–1169.

Ashley, C.C., & Ridgway, E.B. (1970). On the relationships between membrane potential, calcium transient and tension in single barnacle muscle fibres. *Journal of Physiology, 209*, 105–130.

Asmussen, E. (1952). Positive and negative muscular work. *Acta Physiologica Scandinavica, 28*, 365–382.

Asmussen, E. (1956). Observations on experimental muscle soreness. *Acta Rheumatologica Scandinavica, 1*, 109–116.

Atha, J. (1981). Strengthening muscle. *Exercise and Sport Sciences Reviews, 9*, 1–73.

Atwater, A.E. (1970). *Overarm throwing patterns: A kinematographic analysis*. Paper presented at the National Convention of the American Association for Health, Physical Education and Recreation, Seattle, WA.

Atwater, A.E. (1977). *Biomechanics of throwing: Correction of common misconceptions*. Paper presented at the Joint Meeting of the National College Physical Education Association for Men and the National Association for Physical Education of College Women, Orlando, FL.

Atwater, A.E. (1979). Biomechanics of overarm throwing movements and of throwing injuries. *Exercise and Sport Sciences Reviews, 7*, 43–85.

Babij P., & Booth, F.W. (1988). Sculpturing new muscle phenotypes. *News in Physiological Sciences, 3*, 100–102.

Bailey, A.J., Robins, S.P., & Balian, G. (1974). Biological significance of the intermolecular crosslinks of collagen. *Nature, 251*, 105–109.

Baker, J.R., Davey, N.J., Ellaway, P.H., & Friedland, C.L. (1992). Short-term synchrony of motor unit discharge during weak isometric contraction in Parkinson's disease. *Brain, 115,* 137–154.

Baker, L.L., Bowman, B.R., & McNeal, D.R. (1988). Effects of waveform on comfort during neuromuscular electrical stimulation. *Clinical Orthopaedics and Related Research, 233,* 75–85.

Baldissera, F., Cavallari, P., & Leocani, L. (1998). Cyclic modulation of the H-reflex in a wrist flexor during rhythmic flexion-extension movements of the ipsilateral foot. *Experimental Brain Research, 118,* 427–430.

Baldissera, F., Hultborn, H., & Illert, M. (1981). Integration of spinal neuronal systems. In V.B. Brooks (Ed.), *Handbook of physiology: Sec. 1. The nervous system. Vol. 2. Motor control* (Pt. I, pp. 509–595). Bethesda, MD: American Physiological Society.

Bandy, W.D., Irion, J.M., & Briggler, M. (1998). The effect of static stretching and dynamic range of motion on the flexibility of the hamstring muscles. *Journal of Orthopedic and Sports Physical Therapy, 27,* 295–300.

Bangsbo, J., Madsen, K., Kiens, B., & Richter, E.A. (1996). Effect of muscle acidity on muscle metabolism and fatigue during intense exercise in man. *Journal of Physiology, 495,* 587–596.

Bárány, M. (1967). ATPase activity of myosin correlated with speed of muscle shortening. *Journal of General Physiology, 50,* 197–218.

Baratta, R.V., Solomonow, M., Best, R., & D'Ambrosia, R. (1993). Isotonic length/force models of nine different skeletal muscles. *Medical & Biological Engineering & Computing, 31,* 449–458.

Baratta, R.V., Solomonow, M., Best, R., Zembo, M., & D'Ambrosia, R. (1995). Force-velocity relations of nine load-moving skeletal muscles. *Medical & Biological Engineering & Computing, 33,* 537–544.

Baratta, R., Solomonow, M., Zhou, B.H., Letson, D., Chuinard, R., & D'Ambrosia, R. (1988). Muscular coactivation. The role of the antagonist musculature in maintaining knee stability. *American Journal of Sports Medicine, 16,* 113–122.

Barbeau, H., & Rossignol, S. (1987). Recovery of locomotion after chronic spinalization in the adult cat. *Brain Research, 412,* 84–95.

Barclay, J.K. (1986). A delivery-independent blood flow effect on skeletal muscle fatigue. *Journal of Applied Physiology, 61,* 1084–1090.

Barr, J.O., Nielsen, D.H., & Soderberg, G.L. (1986). Transcutaneous electrical nerve stimulation characteristics for altering pain perception. *Physical Therapy, 66,* 1515–1521.

Bartee, H., & Dowell, L. (1982). A cinematographical analysis of twisting about the longitudinal axis when performers are free of support. *Journal of Human Movement Studies, 8,* 41–54.

Bassey, E.J. (1997). Measurement of muscle strength and power. *Muscle & Nerve* (Suppl. 5), S44–S46.

Bassey, E.J. (1998). Longitudinal changes in selected physical capabilities: Muscle strength, flexibility and body size. *Age and Ageing, 27,* 12–16.

Bastian, J., & Nakajima, S. (1974). Action potential in the transverse tubules and its role in the activation of skeletal muscle. *Journal of General Physiology, 63,* 257–278.

Bawa, P., & Calancie, B. (1983). Repetitive doublets in human flexor carpi radialis muscle. *Journal of Physiology (London), 339,* 123–132.

Bawa, P., & Jones, K.E. (1998). Do lengthening contractions represent a case of reversal of recruitment order? *Society for Neuroscience Abstracts, 24,* 675.

Bawa, P., & Sinkjær, T. (1999). Reduced short and long latency reflexes during voluntary tracking movement of human wrist movement. *Acta Physiologica Scandinavica, 167,* 241–246.

BeDell, K.K., Scremin, A.M.E., Perell, K.L., & Kunkel, C.F. (1996). Effects of functional electrical stimulation-induced lower extremity cycling on bone density of spinal cord-injured patients. *American Journal of Physical Medicine and Rehabilitation, 75,* 29–34.

Belanger, A.Y., & McComas, A.J. (1981). Extent of motor unit activation during effort. *Journal of Applied Physiology, 51,* 1131–1135.

Belanger, A.Y., McComas, A.J., & Elder, G.B.C. (1983). Physiological properties of two antagonistic human muscle groups. *European Journal of Applied Physiology, 51,* 381–393.

Belen'kii, V. Ye., Gurfinkel, V.S., & Pal'tsev, Ye. I. (1967). Elements of control of voluntary movements. *Biofizika, 12,* 135–141.

Belhaj-Saif, A., Fourment, A., & Maton, B. (1996). Adaptation of the precentral cortical command to elbow muscle fatigue. *Experimental Brain Research, 111,* 405–416.

Bell, J., Bolanowski, S., & Holmes, M.H. (1994). The structure and function of Pacinian corpuscles: A review. *Progress in Neurobiology, 42,* 79–128.

Bellemare, F., & Garzaniti, N. (1988). Failure of neuromuscular propagation during human maximal voluntary contraction. *Journal of Applied Physiology, 64,* 1084–1093.

Bellemare, F., Woods, J.J., Johansson, R.S., & Bigland-Ritchie, B. (1983). Motor-unit discharge rates in maximal voluntary contractions of three human muscles. *Journal of Neurophysiology, 50,* 1380–1392.

Bemben, M.G., Massey, B.H., Bemben, D.A., Misner, J.E., & Boileau, R.A. (1996). Isometric intermittent endurance of four muscle groups in men aged 20-74 yr. *Medicine and Science in Sports and Exercise, 28,* 145–154.

Bennett, D.J., De Serres, S.J., & Stein, R.B. (1996). Gain of the triceps surae stretch reflex in decerebrate and spinal cats during postural and locomotor activities. *Journal of Physiology, 496,* 837–850.

Bennett, M.B., Ker, R.F., Dimery, N.J., & Alexander, R.M. (1986). Mechanical properties of various mammalian tendons. *Journal of Zoology, 209A,* 537–548.

Bentley, S. (1996). Exercise-induced muscle cramp. Proposed mechanisms and management. *Sports Medicine, 21,* 409–420.

Berardelli, A., Hallett, M., Rothwell, R.C., Agostino, R., Manfredi, M., Thompson, P.D., & Marsden, C.D. (1996). Single-joint rapid arm movements in normal subjects and in patients with motor disorders. *Brain, 119,* 661–674.

Berg, H.E., Dudley, G.A., Häggmark, T., Ohlsén, H., & Tesch, P.A. (1991). Effects of lower limb unloading on skeletal muscle mass and function in humans. *Journal of Applied Physiology, 70,* 1882–1885.

Berg, H.E., Dudley, G.A., Hather, B., & Tesch, P.A. (1993). Work capacity and metabolic and morphologic characteristics of the human quadriceps muscle in response to unloading. *Clinical Physiology, 13,* 337–347.

Berg, H.E., & Tesch, P.A. (1996). Changes in muscle function in response to 10 days of lower limb unloading in humans. *Acta Physiologica Scandinavica, 157,* 63–70.

Berger, W., Quintern, J., & Dietz, V. (1984). Tension development and muscle activation in the leg during gait in spastic hemiparesis: The independence of muscle hypertonia and exaggerated stretch reflexes. *Journal of Neurology, Neurosurgery, and Psychiatry, 47,* 1029–1033.

Bergh, U., & Ekblom, B. (1979). Influence of muscle temperature on maximal muscle strength and power output in human skeletal muscles. *Acta Physiological Scandinavica, 107,* 33–37.

Bergmann, G., Graichen, F., & Rohlmann, A. (1993). Hip joint loading during walking and running, measured in two patients. *Journal of Biomechanics, 26,* 969–990.

Bernstein, N. (1984). Biodynamics of locomotion. In H.T.A. Whiting (Ed.), *Human motor actions: Bernstein reassessed* (pp. 171–222). New York: Elsevier.

Bertolasi, L., De Grandis, D., Bongiovanni, L.G., Zanette, G.P., & Gasperini, M. (1993). The influence of muscular lengthening on cramps. *Annals of Neurology, 33,* 176–180.

Best, T.M., Hasselman, C.T., & Garrett, W.E., Jr. (1997). Muscle strain injuries: Biomechanical and structural studies. In S. Salmon (Ed.), *Muscle damage* (pp. 145–167). Oxford: Oxford University Press.

Beverly, M.C., Rider, T.A., Evans, M.J., & Smith, R. (1989). Local bone mineral response to brief exercise that stresses the skeleton. *British Medical Journal, 299,* 233–235.

Beynnon, B.D., Johnson, R.J., Fleming, B.C., Peura, G.D., Renstrom, P.A., Nichols, C.E., & Pope, M.H. (1997). The effect of functional knee bracing on the anterior cruciate ligament in weightbearing and nonweightbearing knee. *American Journal of Sports Medicine, 25,* 353–359.

Bhagat, B., & Wheeler, N. (1973). Effect of amphetamine on the swimming endurance of rats. *Neuropharmacology, 12,* 711–713.

Bianchi, L., Angelini, D., Orani, G.P., & Lacquaniti, F. (1998). Kinematic coordination in human gait: Relation to mechanical energy cost. *Journal of Neurophysiology, 79,* 2155–2170.

Bichler, E. (2000). Mechanomyograms recorded during evoked contractions of single motor units in the rat medial gastrocnemius muscle. *European Journal of Applied Physiology, 83,* 310–319.

Biewener, A.A. (1991). Musculoskeletal design in relation to body size. *Journal of Biomechanics, 24*(Suppl. 1), 19–29.

Biewener, A.A. (1998). Muscle function in vivo: A comparison of muscles used as springs for elastic energy savings versus muscles used to generate mechanical power. *American Zoologist, 38,* 703–717.

Biewener, A.A., & Bertram, J.E.A. (1993). Skeletal strain patterns in relation to exercise training during growth. *Journal of Experimental Biology, 185,* 51–69.

Biewener, A.A., & Roberts, T.J. (2000). Muscle and tendon contributions to force, work, and elastic savings: A comparative perspective. *Exercise and Sport Sciences Reviews, 28,* 99–107.

Bigland, B., & Lippold, O.C.J. (1954). The relation between force, velocity and integrated electrical activity in human muscles. *Journal of Physiology (London), 123,* 214–224.

Bigland-Ritchie, B. (1981). EMG/force relations and fatigue of human voluntary contractions. *Exercise and Sport Sciences Reviews, 9,* 75–117.

Bigland-Ritchie, B., Cafarelli, E., & Vøllestad, N.K. (1986). Fatigue of submaximal static contractions. *Acta Physiologica Scandinavica, 556,* 137–148.

Bigland-Ritchie, B., Dawson, N.J., Johansson, R.S., & Lippold, O.C.J. (1986). Reflex origin for the slowing of motoneurone firing rates in fatigue of human voluntary contractions. *Journal of Physiology (London), 379,* 451–459.

Bigland-Ritchie, B., Fuglevand, A.J., & Thomas, C.K. (1998). Contractile properties of human motor units: Is man a cat? *Neuroscientist, 4,* 240–249.

Bigland-Ritchie, B., Furbush, F., & Woods, J.J. (1986). Fatigue of intermittent submaximal voluntary contractions: Central and peripheral factors. *Journal of Applied Physiology, 61,* 421–429.

Bigland-Ritchie, B., Johansson, R., Lippold, O.C.J., Smith, S., & Woods, J.J. (1983). Changes in motoneurone firing rates during sustained maximal voluntary contractions. *Journal of Physiology (London), 340,* 335–346.

Bigland-Ritchie, B., Johansson, R., Lippold, O.C.J., & Woods, J.J. (1983). Contractile speed and EMG changes during fatigue of sustained maximal voluntary contractions. *Journal of Neurophysiology, 50,* 313–324.

Bigland-Ritchie, B., Kukulka, C.G., Lippold, O.C.J., & Woods, J.J. (1982). The absence of neuromuscular transmission failure in sustained maximal voluntary contractions. *Journal of Physiology (London), 330,* 265–278.

Bigland-Ritchie, B., Rice, C.L., Garland, S.J., & Walsh, M.L. (1995). Task-dependent factors in fatigue of human voluntary contractions. In S.C. Gandevia, R.M. Enoka, A.J. McComas, D.G. Stuart, & C.K. Thomas (Eds.), *Fatigue: Neural and muscular mechanisms* (pp. 361–380). New York: Plenum Press.

Bilodeau, M., Keen, D.A., Sweeney, P.J., Shields, R.W., & Enoka, R.M. (2000). Strength training can improve steadiness in persons with essential tremor. *Muscle & Nerve, 23,* 771–778.

Binder, M.D., Heckman, C.J., & Powers, R.K. (1996). The physiological control of motoneuron activity. In L.B. Rowell & J.T. Shepherd (Eds.), *Handbook of physiology: Sec. 12. Exercise: Regulation and integration of multiple systems* (pp. 3–53). New York: Oxford University Press.

Binder, M.D., Kroin, J.S., Moore, G.P., & Stuart, D.G. (1977). The response of Golgi tendon organs to single motor unit contractions. *Journal of Physiology (London), 271,* 337–349.

Binder, M.D., & Mendell, L.M. (Eds.) (1990). *The segmental motor system.* New York: Oxford University Press.

Binder-Macleod, S.A., & Guerin, T. (1990). Preservation of force output through progressive reduction of stimulation frequency in human quadriceps femoris muscle. *Physical Therapy, 70,* 619–625.

Binder-Macleod, S.A., Lee, S.C.K., Russ, D.W., & Kucharski, L.J. (1998). Effects of activation pattern on human skeletal muscle fatigue. *Muscle & Nerve, 21,* 1145–1152.

Binder-Macleod, S.A., & Russ, D.W. (1999). Effects of activation frequency and force on low-frequency fatigue in human skeletal muscle. *Journal of Neurophysiology, 86,* 1337–1346.

Binkhorst, R.A., Hoofd, L., & Vissers, A.C.A. (1977). Temperature and force-velocity relationship of human muscles. *Journal of Applied Physiology, 42,* 471–475.

Binnie, C.D., & Prior, P.F. (1994). Electroencephalography. *Journal of Neurology, Neurosurgery, and Psychiatry, 57,* 1308–1319.

Birdsall, T.C. (1998). 5-hydroxytryptophan: A clinically-effective serotonin precursor. *Alternative Medicine Reviews, 3,* 271–280.

Bisdorff, A.R., Bronstein, A.M., & Gresty, M.A. (1994). Responses in neck and facial muscles to sudden free fall and a startling auditory stimulus. *Electromyography and Clinical Neurophysiology, 93,* 409–416.

Bisdorff, A.R., Bronstein, A.M., Wolsey, C., Gresty, M.A., Davies, A., & Young, A. (1999). EMG responses to free fall in elderly subjects and akinetic rigid patients. *Journal of Neurology, Neurosurgery, and Psychiatry, 66,* 447–455.

Bishop, B. (1974). Vibratory stimulation. Part I. Neurophysiology of motor responses evoked by vibratory stimulation. *Physical Therapy, 54,* 1273–1282.

Bishop, B. (1975a). Vibratory stimulation. Part II. Vibratory stimulation as an evaluation tool. *Physical Therapy, 55,* 28–34.

Bishop, B. (1975b). Vibratory stimulation. Part III. Possible applications of vibration in treatment of motor dysfunctions. *Physical Therapy, 55,* 139–143.

Bizzi, E., & Abend, W. (1983). Posture control and trajectory formation in single- and multi-joint arm movements. In J.E. Desmedt (Ed.), *Motor control mechanisms in health and disease* (pp. 31–45). New York: Raven Press.

Blackard, D.O., Jensen, R.L., & Ebben, W.P. (1999). Use of EMG analysis in challenging kinetic chain terminology. *Medicine and Science in Sports and Exercise, 31,* 443–448.

Blattner, S.E., & Noble, L. (1979). Relative effects of isokinetic and plyometric training on vertical jumping performance. *Research Quarterly, 50,* 583–588.

Blin, O., Ferrandez, A.M., Pailhouse, J., & Serratrice, G. (1991). Dopa-sensitive and Dopa-resistant gait parameters in Parkinson's disease. *Journal of Neurological Sciences, 103,* 51–54.

Blomstrand, E., Celsing, F., & Newsholme, E.A. (1988). Changes in plasma concentrations of aromatic and branched-chain amino acids during sustained exercise in man and their possible role in fatigue. *Acta Physiologica Scandinavica, 133,* 115–121.

Bloom, W., & Fawcett, D.W. (1968). *A textbook of histology* (9th ed.). Philadelphia: Saunders.

Bobath, B. (1978). *Adult hemiplegia: Evaluation and treatment.* London: Heinemann Medical Books.

Bobbert, M.F., Gerritsen, K.G.M., Litjens, M.C.A., & Soest, A.J. van. (1996). Why is the countermovement jump height greater than squat jump height? *Medicine and Science in Sports and Exercise, 28,* 1402–1412.

Bobbert, M.F., & Ingen Schenau, G.J. van. (1988). Coordination in vertical jumping. *Journal of Biomechanics, 21,* 249–262.

Bobbert, M.F., Schamhardt, H.C., & Nigg, B.M. (1991). Calculation of vertical ground reaction force estimates during running from positional data. *Journal of Biomechanics, 24,* 1095–1105.

Bodine, S.C., Garfinkel, A., Roy, R.R., & Edgerton, V.R. (1988). Spatial distribution of motor unit fibers in the cat soleus and tibialis anterior muscles: Local interactions. *Journal of Neuroscience, 8,* 2142–2152.

Bodine, S.C., Roy, R.R., Eldred, E., & Edgerton, V.R. (1987). Maximal force as a function of anatomical features of motor units in the cat tibialis anterior. *Journal of Neurophysiology, 57,* 1730–1745.

Bogert, A.J. van den, Read, L., & Nigg, B.M. (1996). A method for inverse dynamic analysis using accelerometry. *Journal of Biomechanics, 29,* 949–954.

Bogert, A.J. van den, Read, L., & Nigg, B.M. (1999). An analysis of hip joint loading during walking, running, and skiing. *Medicine and Science in Sports and Exercise, 31,* 131–142.

Bongiovanni, L.G., & Hagbarth, K.-E. (1990). Tonic vibration reflexes elicited during fatigue from maximal voluntary contractions in man. *Journal of Physiology (London), 423,* 1–14.

Bonnet, M., Bradley, M.M., Lang, P.J., & Requin, J. (1995). Modulation of spinal reflexes: Arousal, pleasure, action. *Psychophysiology, 32,* 367–372.

Booth, F.W., & Baldwin, K.M. (1996). Muscle plasticity: Energy demand and supply processes. In L.B. Rowell & J.T. Shepherd (Eds.), *Handbook of physiology: Sec. 12. Exercise: Regulation and integration of multiple systems* (pp. 1075–1123). New York: Oxford University Press.

Booth, F.W., Tseng, B.S., Flück, M., & Carson, J.A. (1998). Molecular and cellular adaptation of muscle in response to physical training. *Acta Physiologica Scandinavica, 162,* 343–350.

Borelli, A. (1680). *De motu animalium.* Rome: Superiorum Permissu.

Bosco, C., Cardinale, M., & Tsarpela, O. (1999). Influence of vibration on mechanical power and electromyogram activity in human arm flexor muscles. *European Journal of Applied Physiology, 79,* 306–311.

Botterman, B.R., Binder, M.D., & Stuart, D.G. (1978). Functional anatomy of the association between motor units and muscle receptors. *American Zoologist, 18,* 135–152.

Bottinelli, R., Canepari, M., Pellegrino, M.A., & Reggiani, C. (1996). Force-velocity properties of human skeletal muscle fibers: Myosin heavy chain isoform and temperature dependence. *Journal of Physiology, 495,* 573–586.

Bottinelli, R., Pellegrino, M.A., Canepari, M., Rossi, R., & Reggiani, C. (1999). Specific contributions of various muscle fibre types to human muscle performance: An in vitro study. *Journal of Electromyography and Kinesiology, 9,* 87–95.

Bottinelli, R., & Reggiani, C. (2000). Human skeletal muscle fibers: Molecular and functional diversity. *Progress in Biophysics and Molecular Biology, 73,* 195–262.

Bowditch, H.P. (1871). Ueber die Eigenthuemlichkeiten der Reizbarkeit, welch die Muskelfasern des Herzens zeigen. *Berichte Mathematische Physiologie, 23,* 652–689.

Brancazio, P.J. (1984). *Sport science: Physical laws and optimum performance.* New York: Simon & Schuster.

Brand, R.A., Crowninshield, R.D., Wittstock, C.E., Pedersen, D.R., Clark, C.R., & van Krieken, F.M. (1982). A model of lower extremity muscular anatomy. *Journal of Biomechanical Engineering, 104,* 304–310.

Brand, R.A., Pedersen, D.R., & Friederich, J.A. (1986). The sensitivity of muscle force predictions to changes in physiologic cross-sectional area. *Journal of Biomechanics, 19,* 589–596.

Braun, M. (1992). *Picturing time. The work of Etienne-Jules Marey (1830-1904).* Chicago: University of Chicago Press.

Breit, G.A., & Whalen, R.T. (1997). Prediction of human gait parameters from temporal measures of foot-ground contact. *Medicine and Science in Sports and Exercise, 29,* 540–547.

Bremner, F.D., Baker, J.R., & Stephens, J.A. (1991a). Correlation between the discharges of motor units recorded from the same and from different finger muscles in man. *Journal of Physiology (London), 432,* 355–380.

Bremner, F.D., Baker, J.R., & Stephens, J.A. (1991b). Effect of task on the degree of synchronization of intrinsic hand muscle motor units in man. *Journal of Neurophysiology, 66,* 2072–2083.

Bremner, F.D., Baker, J.R., & Stephens, J.A. (1991c). Variation in the degree of synchrony exhibited by motor units lying in different finger muscles in man. *Journal of Physiology (London), 432,* 381–399.

Brighton, C.T. (1981). Current concept review—the treatment of non-unions with electricity. *Journal of Bone and Joint Surgery, 63A,* 847–856.

Broberg, S., & Sahlin, K. (1989). Adenine nucleotide degradation in human skeletal muscle during prolonged exercise. *Journal of Applied Physiology, 67,* 116–122.

Brooke, J.D., Cheng, J., Collins, D.F., McIlroy, W.W., Misaszek, J.E., & Staines, R.E. (1997). Sensori-sensory afferent conditioning with leg movement: Gain control in spinal reflex and ascending paths. *Progress in Neurobiology, 51,* 393–421.

Brooke, M.H., & Kaiser, K.K. (1974). The use and abuse of muscle histochemistry. *Anals of the New York Academy of Sciences, 228,* 121–144.

Brooks, S.V., & Faulkner, J.A. (1991). Forces and powers of slow and fast skeletal muscle in mice during repeated contractions. *Journal of Physiology (London), 436,* 701–710.

Brown, D.A., & Kautz, S.A. (1998). Increased workload enhances force output during pedaling exercise in persons with poststroke hemiplegia. *Stroke, 29,* 598–606.

Brown, G.L., & von Euler, U.S. (1938). The after effects of a tetanus on mammalian muscle. *Journal of Physiology (London), 93,* 39–60.

Brown, P. (1995). Physiology of startle phenomena. *Advances in Neurology, 67,* 273–287.

Brown, P. (2000). Cortical drives to human muscle: The Piper and related rhythms. *Progress in Neurobiology, 60,* 97–108.

Brown, T.G. (1911). The intrinsic factors in the act of progression in the mammal. *Proceedings of the Royal Society of London, B84,* 308–319.

Bruton, J.D., Westerblad, H., Katz, A., & Lännergren, J. (1996). Augmented force output in skeletal muscle fibres of *Xenopus* following a preceding bout of activity. *Journal of Physiology, 493,* 211–217.

Buchanan, T.S., Rovai, G.P., & Rymer, W.Z. (1989). Strategies for muscle activation during isometric torque generation at the human elbow. *Journal of Neurophysiology, 62,* 1201–1212.

Buchthal, F. (1961). The general concept of the motor unit. Neuromuscular disorders. *Research Publication of the Association for Research on Nervous and Mental Disorders, 38,* 3–30.

Buchthal, F., & Schmalbruch, H. (1970). Contraction times of twitches evoked by the H-reflexes. *Acta Physiologica Scandinavica, 80,* 378–382.

Buchthal, F., & Schmalbruch, H. (1976). Contraction times of reflexly activated motor units and excitability cycle of the H-reflex. *Progress in Brain Research, 44,* 367–376.

Bulbulian, R., & Bowles, D.K. (1992). Effect of downhill running on motoneuron pool excitability. *Journal of Applied Physiology, 73,* 968–973.

Burgeson, R.E., & Nimni, M.E. (1992). Collagen types. Molecular structure and tissue distribution. *Clinical Orthopaedics, 282,* 250–272.

Burgess, P.R., Horch, K.W., & Tuckett, R.P. (1987). Mechanoreceptors. In G. Adelman (Ed.), *Encyclopedia of neuroscience* (Vol. II, pp. 620–621). Boston: Birkhäuser.

Burke, D. (1988). Spasticity as an adaptation to pyramidal tract injury. *Advances in Neurology, 47,* 401–422.

Burke, D., Hagbarth, K.-E., & Löfstedt, L. (1978). Muscle spindle activity in man during shortening and lengthening contractions. *Journal of Physiology, 277,* 131–142.

Burke, J.E., Kamen, G., & Koceja, D.M. (1989). Long-latency enhancement of quadriceps excitability from stimulation of skin afferents in young and old adults. *Journal of Gerontology, 44,* M158–163.

Burke, R.E. (1981). Motor units: Anatomy, physiology, and functional organization. In V.B. Brooks (Ed.), *Handbook of physiology: Sec. 1. The nervous system: Vol. II. Motor control* (Pt. 1, pp. 345–422). Bethesda, MD: American Physiological Society.

Burke, R.E. (1999). The use of state-dependent modulation of spinal reflexes as a tool to investigate the organization of spinal interneurons. *Experimental Brain Research, 128,* 263–277.

Burke, R.E., Levine, D.N., Tsairis, P., & Zajac, F.E. (1973). Physiological types and histochemical profiles in motor units of the cat gastrocnemius. *Journal of Physiology (London), 234,* 723–748.

Burke, R.E., Rudomin, P., & Zajac, F.E., III. (1970). Catch property in single mammalian motor units. *Science, 168,* 122–124.

Burke, R.E., & Tsairis, P. (1973). Anatomy and innervation ratios in motor units of cat gastrocnemius. *Journal of Physiology, 234,* 749–765.

Burnett, R.A., Laidlaw, D.H., & Enoka, R.M. (2000). Coactivation of the antagonist muscle does not covary with steadiness in old adults. *Journal of Applied Physiology, 89,* 61–71.

Burr, D.B. (1997). Bone, exercise, and stress fractures. *Exercise and Sport Sciences Reviews, 25,* 171–194.

Burstein, A.H., Reilly, D.T., & Martens, M. (1976). Aging bone tissue: Mechanical properties. *Journal of Bone and Joint Surgery, 58-A,* 82–86.

Büschges, A., & El Manira, A. (1998). Sensory pathways and their modulation in the control of locomotion. *Current Opinion in Neurobiology, 8,* 733–739.

Butler, D.L., Grood, E.S., Noyes, F.R., & Zernicke, R.F. (1978). Biomechanics of ligaments and tendons. *Exercise and Sport Sciences Reviews, 6,* 125–181.

Cady, E.B., Jones, D.A., Lynn, J., & Newham, D.J. (1989). The relationship between the fatigue of force and intracellular metabolites in human skeletal muscle. *Journal of Physiology (London), 418,* 311–325.

Cafarelli, E. (1988). Force sensation in fresh and fatigued human skeletal muscle. *Exercise and Sport Sciences Reviews, 16,* 139–168.

Caiozzo, V.J., Baker, M.J., Herrick, R.E., Tao, M., & Baldwin, K.M. (1994). Effect of spaceflight on skeletal muscle: Mechanical properties and myosin isoform content of a slow muscle. *Journal of Applied Physiology, 80,* 1503–1512.

Caiozzo, V.J., Haddad, F., Baker, M.J., & Baldwin, K.M. (1996). Influence of mechanical loading on myosin heavy-chain protein and mRNA isoform expression. *Journal of Applied Physiology, 80,* 1503–1512.

Caiozzo, V.J., Herrick, R.E., & Baldwin, K.M. (1991). Influence of hyperthyroidism on maximal shortening velocity and myosin isoform distribution in skeletal muscle. *American Journal of Physiology, 261,* C285–C295.

Caiozzo, V.J., Herrick, R.E., & Baldwin, K.M. (1992). Response of slow and fast muscle to hypothyroidism: Maximal shortening velocity and myosin isoforms. *American Journal of Physiology, 263,* C86–C94.

Calabrese, R.L. (1998). Cellular, synaptic network, and modulatory mechanisms involved in rhythm generation. *Current Opinion in Neurobiology, 8,* 710–717.

Calancie, B. (1991). Interlimb reflexes following cervical spinal cord injury in man. *Experimental Brain Research, 85,* 458–469.

Calancie, B., Lutton, S., & Broton, J.G. (1996). Central nervous system plasticity after spinal cord injury in man: Interlimb reflexes and the influence of cutaneous stimulation. *Electroencephalography and Clinical Neurophysiology, 101,* 304–315.

Calvert, T.W., & Chapman, A.E. (1977). Relationship between the surface EMG and force transients in muscle: Simulation and experimental studies. *Proceedings of the IEEE, 65,* 682–689.

Campbell, K.S., & Lakie, M. (1998). A cross-bridge mechanism can explain the thixotropic short-range elastic component of relaxed frog skeletal muscle. *Journal of Physiology, 510,* 941–962.

Campbell, M.J., McComas, A.J., & Petito, F. (1973). Physiological changes in ageing muscles. *Journal of Neurology, Neurosurgery, and Psychiatry, 36,* 174–182.

Campeau, S., Falls, W., Cullinan, W., Helmreich, D., Davis, M., & Watson, S. (1997). Elicitation and reduction of fear: Behavioral and neuroendocrine indices and brain induction of the immediate-early gene c-fos. *Neuroscience, 78,* 1087–1104.

Cao, C., Ashton-Miller, J.A., Schultz, A.B., & Alexander, N.B. (1997). Abilities to turn suddenly while walking: Effects of age, gender, and available response time. *Journal of Gerontology, 52A,* M88–M93.

Carlsöö, S. (1958). Motor units and action potentials in masticatory muscles. An electromyographic study of the form and duration of the action potentials and an anatomic study of the size of the motor units. *Acta Morphologica Neerlando-Scandinavica, 2,* 13–19.

Carolan, B., & Cafarelli, E. (1992). Adaptations in coactivation after isometric resistance training. *Journal of Applied Physiology, 73,* 911–917.

Carp, J.S., Herchenroder, P.A., Chen, X.Y., & Wolpaw, J.R. (1999). Sag during unfused tetanic contractions in rat triceps surae motor units. *Journal of Neurophysiology, 81,* 2647–2661.

Carp, J.S., & Wolpaw, J.R. (1994). Motoneuron plasticity underlying operant conditioned increase in primate H-reflex. *Journal of Neurophysiology, 72,* 431–442.

Carroll, T.J., Barry, B., Riek, S., & Carson, R.G. (2001). Resistance training enhances the stability of sensorimotor coordination. *Proceedings of the Royal Society of London B, 268,* 221–227.

Carson, J.A., & Wei, L. (2000). Integrin signaling's potential for mediating gene expression in hypertrophying skeletal muscle. *Journal of Applied Physiology, 88,* 337–343.

Carter, D.R. (1984). Mechanical loading histories and cortical bone remodeling. *Calcified Tissue International, 36,* S19–24.

Carter, D.R., Beaupré, G.S., Giori, N.J., & Helms, J.A. (1998). Mechanobiology of skeletal regeneration. *Clinical Orthopaedics, 355*(Suppl.), S41–S55.

Carter, D.R., & Spengler, D.M. (1978). Mechanical properties and composition of cortical bone. *Clinical Orthopaedics and Related Research, 135,* 192–217.

Castro, M.J., Apple, D.F., Staron, R.S., Campos, G.E.R., & Dudley, G.A. (1999). Influence of complete spinal cord injury on skeletal muscle within 6 mo of injury. *Journal of Applied Physiology, 86,* 350–358.

Cavagna, G.A. (1975). Force platforms as ergometers. *Journal of Applied Physiology, 39,* 174–179.

Cavagna, G.A. (1977). Storage and utilization of elastic energy in skeletal muscle. *Exercise and Sport Sciences Reviews, 5,* 89–129.

Cavagna, G.A., & Citterio, G. (1974). Effect of stretching on the elastic characteristics of the contractile component of the frog striated muscle. *Journal of Physiology (London), 239,* 1–14.

Cavagna, G.A., & Franzetti, P. (1986). The determinants of the step frequency in walking in humans. *Journal of Physiology, 373,* 235–242.

Cavagna, G.A., Heglund, B.C., & Taylor, C.R. (1977). Mechanical work in terrestrial locomotion: Two basic mechanisms for minimizing energy expenditure. *American Journal of Physiology, 233,* R243–R261.

Cavagna, G.A., Mantovani, M., Willems, P.A., & Musch, G. (1997). The resonant step frequency in human running. *Pflügers Archive, 434,* 678–684.

Cavagna, G.A., Saibene, F.P., & Margaria, R. (1964). Mechanical work in running. *Journal of Applied Physiology, 19,* 249–256.

Cavagna, G.A., Thys, H., & Zamboni, A. (1976). The sources of external work in level walking and running. *Journal of Physiology, 262,* 639–657.

Cavagna, G.A., Willems, P.A., & Heglund, N.C. (2000). The role of gravity in human walking: Pendular energy exchange, external work and optimal speed. *Journal of Physiology, 528,* 657–668.

Cavanagh, P.R., & Ae, M. (1980). A technique for the display of pressure distributions beneath the foot. *Journal of Biomechanics, 13,* 69–76.

Cavanagh, P.R., & Grieve, D.W. (1973). The graphical display of angular movement of the body. *British Journal of Sports Medicine, 7,* 129–133.

Cavanagh, P.R., & Kram, R. (1989). Stride length in distance running: Velocity, body dimensions, and added mass effects. *Medicine and Science in Sports and Exercise, 21,* 476–479.

Cavanagh, P.R., & Lafortune, M.A. (1980). Ground reaction forces in distance running. *Journal of Biomechanics, 13,* 397–406.

Cella, D.F., & Perry, S.W. (1986). Reliability and concurrent validity of three visual-analogue mood scales. *Psychological Reports, 59,* 827–833.

Chan, K.M., Andres, L.P., Polykovskaya, Y., & Brown, W.F. (1999). The effects of training through high-frequency electrical stimulation on the physiological properties of single human thenar motor units. *Muscle & Nerve, 22,* 186–195.

Chanaud, C.M., Pratt, C.A., & Loeb, G.E. (1987). A multiple-contact EMG recording array for mapping single muscle unit territories. *Journal of Neuroscience Methods, 21,* 105–112.

Chandler, R.F., Clauser, C.E., McConville, J.T., Reynolds, H.M., & Young, J.W. (1975). *Investigation of inertial properties of the human body* (AMRL-TR-74-137). Wright-Patterson Air Force Base, OH: Aerospace Medical Research Laboratories, Aerospace Medical Division (NTIS No. AD-A016 485).

Chang, Y.-H., & Kram, R. (1999). Metabolic cost of generating horizontal forces during human running. *Journal of Applied Physiology, 86,* 1657–1662.

Chaouloff, F., Berton, O., & Mormede, P. (1999). Serotonin and stress. *Neuropsychopharmacology, 21*(Suppl. 2), 28S–32S.

Chaouloff, F., Kennett, G.A., Serrurier, B., Merino, D., & Curson, G. (1986). Amino acid analysis demonstrates that increased plasma free tryptophan causes the increase of brain tryptophan during exercise in the rat. *Journal of Neurochemistry, 46,* 1647–1650.

Chase, P.B., & Kushmerick, M.J. (1988). Effects of pH on contraction of rabbit fast muscle slow skeletal muscle fibers. *Biophysical Journal, 53,* 935–946.

Cheney, P.D., & Fetz, E.E. (1980). Functional classes of primate corticomotoneuronal cells and their relation to active force. *Journal of Neurophysiology, 44,* 773–791.

Cheney, P.D., Fetz, E.E., & Mewes, K. (1991). Neural mechanisms underlying corticospinal and rubrospinal control of limb movements. *Progress in Brain Research, 87,* 213–252.

Child, R.B., Brown, S.J., Day, S.H., Saxton, J.M., & Donnelly, A.E. (1998). Manipulation of knee extensor force using percutaneous electrical myostimulation during eccentric actions: Effects on indices of muscle damage in humans. *International Journal of Sports Medicine, 19,* 468–473.

Chilibeck, P.D., Calder, A.W., Sale, D.G., & Webber, C.E. (1998). A comparison of strength and muscle mass increases during resistance training in young women. *European Journal of Applied Physiology, 77,* 170–175.

Chilibeck, P.D., Jeon, J., Weiss, C., Bell, G., & Burnham, R. (1999). Histochemical changes in muscle of individuals with spinal cord injury following functional electrical stimulated exercise training. *Spinal Cord, 37,* 264–268.

Chin, E.R., & Allen, D.G. (1996). The role of elevations in intracellular [Ca^{2+}] in the development of low frequency fatigue in mouse single muscle fibers. *Journal of Physiology, 491,* 813–824.

Cholewicki, J., Juluru, K., & McGill, S.M. (1999). Intra-abdominal pressure mechanism for stabilizing the lumbar spine. *Journal of Biomechanics, 32,* 13–17.

Cholewicki, J., McGill, S.M., & Norman, R.W. (1991). Lumbar spine loads during the lifting of extremely heavy weights. *Medicine and Science in Sports and Exercise, 23,* 1179–1186.

Chopard, A., Pons, F., & Marini, J.-F. (2001). Cytoskeletal protein contents before and after hindlimb suspension in a fast and slow rat skeletal muscle. *American Journal of Physiology, 280,* R323–R330.

Christakos, C.N. (1982). A study of the muscle force waveform using a population stochastic model of skeletal muscle. *Biological Cybernetics, 44,* 91–106.

Christakos, C.N., & Windhorst, U. (1986). Spindle gain increase during muscle unit fatigue. *Brain Research, 365,* 388–392.

Christensen, E. (1959). Topography of terminal motor innervation in striated muscles from stillborn infants. *American Journal of Physical Medicine, 38,* 65–78.

Christiansen, C. (1992). Prevention and treatment of osteoporosis: A review of current modalities. *Bone, 13,* S35–S43.

Christova, P., & Kossev, A. (1998). Motor unit activity during long-lasting intermittent muscle contractions in humans. *European Journal of Applied Physiology, 77,* 379–387.

Claassen, H., Gerber, C., Hoppeler, H., Lüthi, J.-M., & Vock, P. (1989). Muscle filament spacing and short-term heavy-resistance exercise in humans. *Journal of Physiology, 409,* 491–495.

Clancy, E.A., & Hogan, N. (1995). Multiple site electromyograph amplitude estimation. *IEEE Transactions on Biomedical Engineering, 42,* 203–211.

Clark, J.M., & Haynor, D.R. (1987). Anatomy of the abductor muscles of the hip as studied by computed tomography. *Journal of Bone and Joint Surgery, 69-A,* 1021–1031.

Clarkson, P.M., Cyrnes, W.C., McCarmick, K.M., Turcotte, L.P., & White, J.S. (1986). Muscle soreness and serum creatine kinase activity following isometric, eccentric, and concentric exercise. *International Journal of Sports Medicine, 7,* 152–155.

Clausen, T. (1996). Long- and short-term regulation of the Na^+-K^+ pump in skeletal muscle. *News in Physiological Sciences, 11,* 24–30.

Clausen, T., Nielsen, O.B., Harrison, A.P., Flatman, J.A., & Overgaard, E. (1998). The Na^+,K^+ pump and muscle excitability. *Acta Physiologica Scandinavica, 162,* 183–190.

Clauser, C.E., McConville, J.T., & Young, J.W. (1969). *Weight, volume and center of mass of segments of the human body* (AMRL-TR-69-70). Wright-Patterson Air Force Base, OH: Aerospace Medical Research Laboratories, Aerospace Medical Division.

Coggan, A.R., & Coyle, E.F. (1987). Reversal of fatigue during prolonged exercise by carbohydrate infusion or ingestion. *Journal of Applied Physiology, 63,* 2388–2395.

Coggan, A.R., Spina, R.J., King, D.S., Rogers, M.A., Bown, M., Nemeth, P.M., & Holloszy, J.O. (1992). Histochemical and enzymatic comparison of the gastrocnemius muscle of young and elderly men and women. *Journal of Gerontology, 47,* B71–B76.

Cole, J.D., & Sedgwick, E.M. (1992). The perceptions of force and movement in a man without large myelinated sensory afferents below the neck. *Journal of Physiology, 449,* 503–515.

Cole, K.J. (1991). Grasp force control in older adults. *Journal of Motor Behavior, 23,* 251–258.

Cole, K.J., Rotella, D.L., & Harper, J.G. (1999). Mechanisms for age-related changes of fingertip forces during precision gripping and lifting in adults. *Journal of Neuroscience, 19,* 3238–3247.

Colleti, L.A., Edwards, J., Gordon, L., Shary, J., & Bell, N.H. (1989). The effects of muscle-building exercise on bone mineral density of the radius, spine, and hip in young men. *Calcified Tissue International, 45,* 12–14.

Colliander, E.B., & Tesch, P.A. (1990). Effects of eccentric and concentric muscle actions in resistance training. *Acta Physiologica Scandinavica, 140,* 31–39.

Collins, J.J., De Luca, C.J., Burrows, A., & Lipsitz, L.A. (1995). Age-related changes in open-loop and closed-loop postural control mechanisms. *Experimental Brain Research, 104,* 480–492.

Colson, S., Pousson, M., Martin, A., & Van Hoecke, J. (1999). Isokinetic elbow flexion and coactivation following eccentric training. *Journal of Electromyography and Kinesiology, 9,* 13–20.

Condon, S.M., & Hutton, R.S. (1987). Soleus muscle electromyographic activity and ankle dorsiflexion range of motion during four stretching procedures. *Physical Therapy, 67,* 24–30.

Cooke, P. (1985). A periodic cytoskeletal lattice in striated muscle. In J.W. Shay (Ed.), *Cell and muscle motility* (Vol. 6, pp. 287–313). New York: Plenum Press.

Cooke, R. (1990). Force generation in muscle. *Current Opinion in Cell Biology, 2,* 62–66.

Cooke, R., Franks, K., Luciani, G.B., & Pate, E. (1988). The inhibition of rabbit skeletal muscle contraction by hydrogen ions and phosphate. *Journal of Physiology (London), 395,* 77–97.

Cope, T.C., Bodine, S.C., Fournier, M., & Edgerton, V.R. (1986). Soleus motor units in chronic spinal transected cat: Physiological and morphological alterations. *Journal of Neurophysiology, 55,* 1201–1220.

Cope, T.C., Bonasera, S.J., & Nichols, T.R. (1994). Reinnervated muscles fail to produce stretch reflexes. *Journal of Neurophysiology, 71,* 817–820.

Cope, T.C., & Pinter, M.J. (1995). The Size Principle: Still working after all these years. *News in Physiological Sciences, 10,* 280–286.

Corcos, D.M., Gottlieb, G.L., & Agarwal, G.C. (1989). Organizing principles for single-joint movements. II. A speed-sensitive strategy. *Journal of Neurophysiology, 62,* 358–368.

Corden, D.M., & Lippold, O.C.J. (1996). Age-related impaired reflex sensitivity in a human hand muscle. *Journal of Physiology, 76,* 2701–2706.

Cordo, P.J., & Nashner, L.M. (1982). Properties of postural adjustments associated with rapid arm movements. *Journal of Neurophysiology, 47,* 287–302.

Costill, D.L., & Hargreaves, M. (1992). Carbohydrate nutrition and fatigue. *Sports Medicine, 13,* 86–92.

Côté, L., & Crutcher, M.D. (1991). The basal ganglia. In E.R. Kandel, J.H. Schwartz, & T.M. Jessell (Eds.), *Principles of neural science* (3rd ed., pp. 647–659). New York: Elsevier.

Cowin, S.C. (1983). The mechanical and stress adaptive properties of bone. *Annals of Biomedical Engineering, 11,* 263–295.

Coyle, E.F., Coggan, A.R., Hemmert, M.K., & Ivy, J.L. (1986). Muscle glycogen utilization during prolonged strenuous exercise when fed carbohydrate. *Journal of Applied Physiology, 61,* 165–172.

Crago, P.E., Houk, J.C., & Hasan, Z. (1976). Regulatory actions of human stretch reflex. *Journal of Neurophysiology, 39,* 925–935.

Crenna, P., & Frigo, C. (1984). Evidence of phase-dependent nociceptive reflexes during locomotion in man. *Experimental Neurology, 85,* 336–345.

Crenna, P., & Frigo, C. (1987). Excitability of the soleus H-reflex arc during walking and stepping in man. *Experimental Brain Research, 66,* 49–60.

Crenshaw, A.G., Karlsson, S., Styf, J., Bäcklund, T., & Fridén, J. (1995). Knee extension torque and intramuscular pressure of the vastus lateralis muscle during eccentric and concentric activities. *European Journal of Applied Physiology, 70,* 13–19.

Cresswell, A.G., Grundström, H., & Thorstensson, A. (1992). Observations on intra-abdominal pressure and patterns of abdominal intra-muscular activity in man. *Acta Physiologica Scandinavica, 144,* 409–418.

Cresswell, A.G., Löscher, W.N., & Thorstensson, A. (1995). Influence of gastrocnemius muscle length on triceps surae torque development and electromyographic activity in man. *Experimental Brain Research, 105,* 283–290.

Crone, C., & Nielsen, J. (1989). Methodological implications of the post activation depression of the soleus H-reflex in man. *Experimental Brain Research, 78,* 28–32.

Cunnington, R., Iansek, R., Bradshaw, J.L., & Phillips, J.G. (1996). Movement-related potentials associated with movement preparation and motor imagery. *Experimental Brain Research, 111,* 429–436.

Currey, J.D., & Alexander, R.M. (1985). The thickness of walls of tubular bones. *Journal of Zoology, 206,* 453–468.

Czéh, G., Gallego, R., Kudo, N., & Kuno, M. (1978). Evidence for the maintenance of motoneurone properties by muscle activity. *Journal of Physiology (London), 281,* 239–252.

Daggfeldt, K., & Thorstensson, A. (1997). The role of intra-abdominal pressure in spinal unloading. *Journal of Biomechanics, 30,* 1149–1155.

Dagognet, F. (1992). *Etienne-Jules Marey. A passion for the trace.* New York: Zone Books.

Dahl, H.A., Aaserud, R., & Jensen, J. (1992). Muscle hypertrophy after light and heavy resistance training. *Medicine and Science in Sports and Exercise, 24,* S55.

Dahlkvist, N.J., Mayo, P., & Seedhom, B.B. (1982). Forces during squatting and rising from a deep squat. *Engineering in Medicine, 11,* 69–76.

Dainis, A. (1981). A model for gymnastics vaulting. *Medicine and Science in Sports and Exercise, 13,* 34–43.

Damiani, E., & Margreth, A. (1994). Characterization study of the ryanodine receptor and of calsequesterin isoforms of mammalian skeletal muscles in relation to fibre types. *Journal of Muscle Research and Cell Motility, 15,* 86–101.

Danieli-Betto, D., Betto, R., Megighian, A., Midrio, M., Salviati, G., & Larsson, L. (1995). Effects of age on sarcoplasmic reticulum properties and histochemical composition of fast- and slow-twitch rat muscles. *Acta Physiologica Scandinavica, 154,* 59–64.

Danube, J.R. (1995). Estimating the number of motor units in a muscle. *Journal of Clinical Neurophysiology, 12,* 585–594.

Darling, W.G., & Cole, K.J. (1990). Muscle activation patterns and kinetics of human index finger movements. *Journal of Neurophysiology, 63,* 1098–1108.

Darling, W.G., & Hayes, K.C. (1983). Human servo responses to load disturbances in fatigued muscle. *Brain Research, 267,* 345–351.

Datta, A.K., Farmer, S.F., & Stephens, J.A. (1991). Central nervous system pathways underlying synchronization of human motor unit firing during voluntary contraction. *Journal of Physiology, 432,* 401–425.

Datta, A.K., & Stephens, J.A. (1990). Synchronization of motor unit activity during voluntary contraction in man. *Journal of Physiology (London), 422,* 397–419.

Davies, C.T.M., Dooley, P., McDonagh, M.J.N., & White, M.J. (1985). Adaptation of mechanical properties of muscle to high force training in man. *Journal of Physiology, 365,* 277–284.

Davies, C.T.M., Rutherford, I.C., & Thomas, D.O. (1987). Electrically evoked contractions of the triceps surae during and following 21 days of voluntary leg immobilization. *European Journal of Applied Physiology, 56,* 306–312.

Davies, J., Parker, D.F., Rutherford, O.M., & Jones, D.A. (1988). Changes in strength and cross sectional area of elbow flexors as a result of isometric strength training. *European Journal of Applied Physiology, 57,* 667–670.

Davis, M. (1984). The mammalian startle response. In R.C. Eaton (Ed.), *Neural mechanisms of startle behavior* (pp. 287–351). New York: Plenum Press.

Day, B.L., Marsden, C.D., Obeso, J.A., & Rothwell, J.C. (1984). Reciprocal inhibition between the muscles of the human forearm. *Journal of Physiology (London), 349,* 519–534.

Degens, H., Yu, F., Li, X., & Larsson, L. (1998). Effects of age and gender on shortening velocity and myosin isoforms in single rat muscle fibres. *Acta Physiologica Scandinavica, 163,* 33–40.

de Haan, A. (1998). The influence of stimulation frequency on force-velocity characteristics of *in situ* rat medial gastrocnemius muscle. *Experimental Physiology, 83,* 77–84.

de Koning, F.L., Binkhorst, R.A., Vos, J.A., & van't Hof, M.A. (1985). The force-velocity relationship of arm flexion in untrained males and females and arm-trained athletes. *European Journal of Applied Physiology, 54,* 89–94.

de Koning, J.J., de Groot, G., & van Ingen Schenau, G.J. (1992). Ice friction during speed skating. *Journal of Biomechanics, 25,* 565–571.

de Leon, R.D., Hodgson, J.A., Roy, R.R., & Edgerton, V.R. (1998a). Full weight-bearing hindlimb standing following stand training in the adult spinal cat. *Journal of Neurophysiology, 79,* 83–91.

de Leon, R.D., Hodgson, J.A., Roy, R.R., & Edgerton, V.R. (1998b). Locomotor capacity attributable to step training versus spontaneous recovery after spinalization in adult cats. *Journal of Neurophysiology, 79,* 1329–1340.

de Leva, P. (1996). Adjustments to Zatsiorsky-Seluyanov's segment inertia parameters. *Journal of Biomechanics, 29,* 1223–1230.

Delitto, A., Brown, M., Strube, M.J., Rose, S.J., & Lehman, R.C. (1989). Electrical stimulation of quadriceps femoris in an elite weight lifter: A single subject experiment. *International Journal of Sports Medicine, 10,* 187–191.

Delitto, A., & Rose, S.J. (1986). Comparative comfort of three waveforms used in electrically eliciting quadriceps femoris muscle contractions. *Physical Therapy, 66,* 1704–1707.

DeLong M.R. (2000). The basal ganglia. In E.R. Kandel, J.H. Schwartz, & T.M. Jessell (Eds.), *Principles of neural science* (4th ed., pp. 853–867). New York: McGraw-Hill.

De Looze, M.P., Bussmann, J.B.J., Kingma, I., & Toussaint, H.M. (1992). Different methods to estimate total power and its components during lifting. *Journal of Biomechanics, 25,* 1089–1095.

DeLorme, T.L. (1945). Restoration of muscle power by heavy-resistance exercises. *Journal of Bone and Joint Surgery, 27,* 645–667.

Delp, S.L., Ringwelski, D.A., & Carroll, N.C. (1994). Transfer of the rectus femoris: Effects of transfer site on moment arms about the knee. *Journal of Biomechanics, 27,* 1201–1211.

De Luca, C.J., Foley, P.J., & Erim, Z. (1996). Motor unit control properties in constant-force isometric contractions. *Journal of Neurophysiology, 76,* 1503–1516.

De Luca, C.J., LeFever, R.S., McCue, M.P., & Xenakis, A.P. (1982a). Behaviour of human motor units in different muscles during linearly varying contractions. *Journal of Physiology, 329,* 113–128.

De Luca, C.J., LeFever, R.S., McCue, M.P., & Xenakis, A.P. (1982b). Control scheme governing concurrently active human motor units during voluntary contractions. *Journal of Physiology, 329,* 129–142.

De Luca, C.J., & Mambrito, B. (1987). Voluntary control of motor units in human antagonist muscles: Coactivation and reciprocal activation. *Journal of Neurophysiology, 58,* 525–542.

Delwaide, P.J., Sabatino, M., Pepin, J.L., & La Grutta, V. (1988). Reinforcement of reciprocal inhibition by contralateral movements in man. *Experimental Neurology, 99,* 10–16.

Delwaide, P.J., & Schepens, B. (1995). Auditory startle (audio-spinal) reaction in normal man: EMG responses and H reflex changes in antagonistic lower limb muscles. *Electroencephalography and Clinical Neurophysiology, 97,* 416–423.

Dempster, W.T. (1955). *Space requirements of the seated operator* (WADC-TR-55-159). Wright-Patterson Air Force Base, OH: Aerospace Medical Research Laboratory (NTIS No. AD-87892).

Dengler, R., Konstabzer, A., Hesse, S., Schubert, M., & Wolf, W. (1989). Collateral nerve sprouting and twitch forces of single motor units in conditions with partial denervation in man. *Neuroscience Letters, 97,* 118–122.

Denny-Brown, D., & Pennybacker, J.B. (1938). Fibrillation and fasciculation in voluntary muscle. *Brain, 61,* 311–334.

De Ruiter, C.J., De Haan, A., Jones, D.A., & Sargeant, A.J. (1998). Shortening-induced force depression in human adductor pollicis muscle. *Journal of Physiology, 507,* 583–591.

De Serres, S.J., & Enoka, R.M. (1998). Older adults can maximally activate the biceps brachii muscle by voluntary command. *Journal of Applied Physiology, 84,* 284–291.

De Serres, S.J., Yang, J.F., & Patrick, S.K. (1995). Mechanism for reflex reversal during walking in human tibialis anterior muscle revealed by single motor unit recording. *Journal of Physiology, 488,* 249–258.

Desmedt, J.E., & Godaux, E. (1977). Fast motor units are not preferentially activated in rapid voluntary contractions in man. *Nature, 267,* 717–719.

Desplanches, D. (1997). Structural and functional adaptations of skeletal muscle to weightlessness. *International Journal of Sports Medicine, 18,* S259–S264.

Dettmers, C., Fink, G.R., Lemon, R.N., Stephan, K.M., Passingham, R.E., Silbergsweig, D., Holmes, A., Ridding, M.C., Brooks, D.J., & Frackowiak, R.S.J. (1995). Relation between cerebral activity and force in the motor areas of the human brain. *Journal of Neurophysiology, 74,* 802–815.

DeVita, P., Blakenship, P., & Skelly, W.A. (1992). Effects of a functional knee brace on the biomechanics of running. *Medicine and Science in Sports and Exercise, 24,* 797–806.

DeVita, P., Hortobágyi, T., & Barrier, J. (1998). Gait biomechanics are not normal after anterior cruciate ligament reconstruction and accelerated rehabilitation. *Medicine and Science in Sports and Exercise, 30,* 1481–1488.

DeVita, P., Torry, M., Glover, K.L., & Speroni, D.L. (1996). A functional knee brace alters joint torque and power patterns during walking and running. *Journal of Biomechanics, 29,* 583–588.

De Vito, G., Bernardi, M., Forte, R., Pulejo, C., Macaluso, A., & Figura, F. (1998). Determinants of maximal instantaneous muscle power in women aged 50-75 years. *European Journal of Applied Physiology, 78,* 59–64.

De Wit, B., De Clercq, D., & Aerts, P. (2000). Biomechanical analysis of the stance phase during barefoot and shod running. *Journal of Biomechanics, 33,* 269–278.

De Wolf, S., Slijper, H., & Latash, M.L. (1998). Anticipatory postural adjustments during self-paced and reaction-time movements. *Experimental Brain Research, 121,* 7–19.

Dick, R.W., & Cavanagh, P.R. (1987). An explanation of the upward drift in oxygen uptake during prolonged sub-maximal downhill running. *Medicine and Science in Sports and Exercise, 19,* 310–317.

Dickinson, P. (1995). Interactions among neural networks for behavior. *Current Opinion in Neurobiology, 5,* 792–798.

Dietz, V. (1978). Analysis of the electrical muscle activity during maximal contraction and the influence of ischaemia. *Journal of the Neurological Sciences, 37,* 187–197.

Dietz, V. (1992). Human neuronal control of automatic functional movements: Interaction between central programs and afferent input. *Physiological Reviews, 72,* 33–69.

Dietz, V. (1997). Neurophysiology of gait disorders: Present and future applications. *Electroencephalography and Clinical Neurophysiology, 103,* 333–355.

Dietz, V., Colombo, G., & Jensen, L. (1994). Locomotor activity in spinal man. *Lancet, 344,* 1260–1263.

Dietz, V., Colombo, G., Jensen, L., & Baumgartner, L. (1995). Locomotor capacity of spinal cord in paraplegic patients. *Annals of Neurology, 37,* 574–582.

Dietz, V., Schmidtbleicher, D., & Noth, J. (1979). Neuronal mechanisms of human locomotion. *Journal of Neurophysiology, 42,* 1212–1222.

Dimitrijevic, M.R., Gersaimenko, Y., & Pinter, M.M. (1998). Evidence for a spinal pattern generator in humans. *Annals of the New York Academy of Sciences, 860,* 360–376.

Dimitrijevic, M.R., McKay, W.B., Sarjanovic, I., Sherwood, A.M., Svirtlih, L., & Vrbovà. (1992). Co-activation of ipsi- and contralateral muscle groups during contraction of ankle dorsiflexors. *Journal of the Neurological Sciences, 109,* 49–55.

Doherty, T., & Brown, W.F. (1997). Age-related changes in the twitch contractile properties of human thenar motor units. *Journal of Applied Physiology, 82,* 93–101.

Doherty, T.J., Vandervoort, A.A., Taylor, A.W., & Brown, W.F. (1993). Effects of motor unit losses on strength in older men and women. *Journal of Applied Physiology, 74,* 868–874.

Donelan, J.M., & Kram, R. (2000). Exploring dynamic similarity in human running using simulated reduced gravity. *Journal of Experimental Biology, 203,* 2405–2415.

Dooley, P.C., Bach, T.M., & Luff, A.R. (1990). Effect of vertical jumping on the medial gastrocnemius and soleus muscles of rats. *Journal of Applied Physiology, 69,* 2004–2011.

Dop Bär, P.R., Reijneveld, J.C., Wokke, J.H.J., Jacobs, S.C.J.M., & Bootsma, A.L. (1997). Muscle damage induced by exercise: Nature, prevention and repair. In S. Salmon (Ed.), *Muscle damage* (pp. 1–27). Oxford: Oxford University Press.

Dörge, H.C., Andersen, T.B., Sørensen, H., Simonsen, E.B., Dyhre-Poulsen, P., & Klausen, K. (1999). EMG activity of the iliopsoas muscle and leg kinetics during the soccer place kick. *Scandinavian Journal of Sports Medicine, 9,* 195–200.

Dorlöchter, M., Irintchev, A., Brinkers, M., & Wernig, A. (1991). Effects of enhanced activity on synaptic transmission in mouse extensor digitorum longus muscle. *Journal of Physiology (London), 436,* 283–292.

Dornay, M., Uno, Y., Kawato, M., & Suzuki, R. (1996). Minimum muscle tension change trajectories predicted using a 17-muscle model of the monkey's arm. *Journal of Motor Behavior, 28,* 88–100.

Duchateau, J., Carpentier, A., & Hainaut, K. (1999). Changes in motor units activation pattern and contractile properties during intermittent fatiguing contractions in human. *Proceedings of the XVIIth International Society of Biomechanics Congress,* p. 244.

Duchateau, J., & Hainaut, K. (1984). Isometric or dynamic training: Differential effects on mechanical properties of a human muscle. *Journal of Applied Physiology, 56,* 296–301.

Duchateau, J., & Hainaut, K. (1986). Nonlinear summation of contractions in striated muscle. I. Twitch potentiation in human muscle. *Journal of Muscle Research and Cell Motility, 7,* 11–17.

Duchateau, J., & Hainaut, K. (1987). Electrical and mechanical changes in immobilized human muscle. *Journal of Applied Physiology, 62,* 2168–2173.

Duchateau, J., & Hainaut, K. (1990). Effects of immobilization on contractile properties, recruitment and firing rates of human motor units. *Journal of Physiology, 422,* 55–65.

Duchateau, J., & Hainaut, K. (1991). Effects of immobilization on electromyogram power spectrum changes during fatigue. *European Journal of Applied Physiology, 63,* 458–462.

Duchateau, J., & Hainaut, K. (1993). Behaviour of short and long latency reflexes in fatigued human muscles. *Journal of Physiology (London), 471,* 787–799.

Duchêne, J., & Goubel, F. (1993). Surface electromyogram during voluntary contraction: Processing tools and relation to physiological events. *Critical Reviews in Biomedical Engineering, 21,* 313–397.

Duda, G.N., Schneider, E., & Chao, E.Y.S. (1997). Internal forces and moments in the femur during walking. *Journal of Biomechanics, 30,* 933–941.

Dudley, G.A., Castro, M.J., Rogers, S., & Apple, D.F., Jr. (1999). A simple means of increasing muscle size after spinal cord injury: A pilot study. *European Journal of Applied Physiology, 80,* 394–396.

Dudley, G.A., Duvoisin, M.R., Adams, G.R., Meyer, R.A., Belew, A.H., & Buchanan, P. (1992). Adaptations to unilateral lower limb suspension in humans. *Aviation, Space, and Environmental Medicine, 63,* 678–683.

Dudley, G.A., Tesch, P.A., Miller, B.J., & Buchanan, P. (1991). Importance of eccentric muscle actions in performance adaptations to resistance training. *Aviation, Space, and Environmental Medicine, 62,* 543–550.

Dum, R.P., & Kennedy, T.T. (1980). Physiological and histochemical characteristics of motor units in cat tibialis anterior and extensor digitorum longus muscles. *Journal of Neurophysiology, 43,* 1615–1630.

Dum, R.P., & Strick, P.L. (1996). The corticospinal system: A structural framework for the central control of movement. In L.B. Rowell & J.T. Shepherd (Eds.), *Handbook of physiology: Sec. 12. Exercise: Regulation and integration of multiple systems* (pp. 217–254). New York: Oxford University Press.

Dumitru, D. (2000). Physiologic basis of potentials recorded in electromyography. *Muscle & Nerve, 23,* 1667–1685.

Duncan, P.W., Chandler, J.M., Cavanaugh, D.K., Johnson, K.R., & Buehler, A.G. (1989). Mode and speed specificity of eccentric and concentric exercise training. *Journal of Orthopedic and Sports Physical Therapy, 11,* 70–75.

Dupont-Versteegden, E.E., Houlé, J.D., Gurley, C.M., & Peterson, C.A. (1998). Early changes in muscle fiber size and gene expression in response to spinal cord transection and exercise. *American Journal of Physiology, 275,* C1124–C1133.

Dutta, C., Hadley, E.C., & Lexell, J. (1997). Sarcopenia and physical performance in old age: An overview. *Muscle & Nerve* (Suppl. 5), S5–S9.

Dyck, P.J., Karnes, J., O'Brien, P.C., & Zimmerman, I.R. (1984). Detection thresholds of cutaneous sensation in humans. In P.J. Dyck, P.K. Thomas, E.H. Lambert, & R. Bunge (Eds.), *Peripheral Neuropathy* (Vol. I, pp. 1103–1138). Philadelphia: Saunders.

Dyhre-Poulsen, P., & Krogsgaard, M.R. (2000). Muscular reflexes elicited by electrical stimulation of the anterior cruciate ligament in humans. *Journal of Applied Physiology, 89,* 2191–2195.

Eccles, J.C., & Liley, A.W. (1959). Factors controlling the liberation of acetylcholine at the neuromuscular junction. *American Journal of Physical Medicine, 38,* 96–103.

Edgerton, V.R., Apor, P., & Roy, R.R. (1990). Specific tension of human elbow flexor muscles. *Acta Physiologica Hungarica, 75,* 205–216.

Edgerton, V.R., Bodine-Fowler, S., Roy, R.R., Ishihara, A., & Hodgson, J.A. (1996). Neuromuscular adaptation. In L.B. Rowell & J.T. Shepherd (Eds.), *Handbook of physiology: Sec. 12. Exercise: Regulation and integration of multiple systems* (pp. 54–88). New York: Oxford University Press.

Edgerton, V.R., Roy, R.R., de Leon, R., Tillakaratne, N., & Hodgson, J.A. (1997). Does motor learning occur in the spinal cord? *Neuroscientist, 3,* 287–294.

Edgerton, V.R., Roy, R.R., Gregor, R.J., & Rugg, S. (1986). Morphological basis of skeletal muscle power output. In N.L. Jones, N. McCartney, & A.J. McComas (Eds.), *Human muscle power* (pp. 43–64). Champaign, IL: Human Kinetics.

Edman, K.A.P. (1988). Double-hyperbolic force-velocity relation in frog muscle fibres. *Journal of Physiology, 404,* 301–321.

Edman, K.A.P. (1992). Contractile performance of skeletal muscle fibres. In P.V. Komi (Ed.), *Strength and power in sport* (pp. 96–114). Champaign, IL: Human Kinetics.

Edman, K.A.P. (1996). Fatigue vs. shortening-induced deactivation in striated muscle. *Acta Physiologica Scandinavica, 156,* 183–192.

Edman, K.A.P. (1995). Myofibrillar fatigue *versus* failure of activation. In S.C. Gandevia, R.M. Enoka, A.J. McComas, D.G. Stuart, & C.K. Thomas (Eds.), *Fatigue: Neural and muscular mechanisms* (pp. 29–43). New York: Plenum Press.

Edman, K.A.P., Elzinga, G., & Noble, M.I.M. (1978). Enhancement of mechanical performance by stretch during tetanic contractions of vertebral skeletal muscle fibres. *Journal of Physiology (London), 281,* 139–155.

Edman, K.A.P., & Lou, F. (1990). Changes in force and stiffness induced by fatigue and intracellular acidification in frog muscle fibres. *Journal of Physiology (London), 424,* 133–149.

Edman, K.A.P., Månsson, A., & Caputo, C. (1997). The biphasic force-velocity relationship in frog muscle fibres and its evaluation in terms of cross-bridge function. *Journal of Physiology, 503,* 141–156.

Edman, K.A.P., Reggiani, C., Schiaffino, S., & te Kronnie, G. (1988). Maximum velocity of shortening related to myosin isoform composition in frog skeletal muscle fibres. *Journal of Physiology, 95,* 679–694.

Edman, K.A.P., & Tsuchiya, T. (1996). Strain of passive elements during force enhancement by stretch in frog muscle fibres. *Journal of Physiology, 490,* 191–205.

Edwards, R.H.T., Hill, D.K., Jones, D.A., & Merton, P.A. (1977). Fatigue of long duration in human skeletal muscle after exercise. *Journal of Physiology (London), 272,* 769–778.

Edwards, R.H.T., Mills, K.R., & Newham, D.J. (1981). Measurement of severity and distribution of experimental muscle tenderness. *Journal of Physiology, 317,* 1–2P.

Eie, N., & Wehn, P. (1962). Measurements of the intra-abdominal pressure in relation to weight bearing of the lumbosacral spine. *Journal of Oslo City Hospitals, 12,* 205–217.

Elftman, H. (1938). The measurement of the external force in walking. *Science, 88,*152–153.

Elftman, H. (1939). Forces and energy changes in the leg during walking. *American Journal of Physiology, 125,* 339–356.

Elliott, B.C. (2000). Hitting and kicking. In V.M. Zatsiorsky (Ed.), *Biomechanics in Sport* (pp. 487–504). Oxford, UK: Blackwell Science.

Elson, P. (1974, December). Strength increases by electrical stimulation. *Track Technique,* p. 1856.

Emerson, N.D., & Zahalak, G.I. (1981). Longitudinal electrode array for electromyography. *Medical & Biological Engineering & Computing, 19,* 504–506.

Engelhorn, R. (1983). Agonist and antagonist muscle EMG activity pattern changes with skill acquisition. *Research Quarterly for Exercise and Sport, 54,* 315–323.

Engin, A.E., & Chen, S.-M. (1986). Statistical data base for the biomechanical properties of the human shoulder complex—I: Kinematics of the shoulder complex. *Journal of Biomechanical Engineering, 108,* 215–221.

Engin, A.E., & Chen, S.-M. (1987). Kinematic and passive resistive properties of human elbow complex. *Journal of Biomechanical Engineering, 109,* 318–323.

Engin, A.E., & Chen, S.-M. (1988). On the biomechanics of human hip complex in vivo—I: Kinematics for determination of the maximal voluntary hip complex sinus. *Journal of Biomechanics, 21,* 785–795.

English, A.W. (1984). An electromyographic analysis of compartments in cat lateral gastrocnemius during unrestrained locomotion. *Journal of Neurophysiology, 52,* 114–125.

English, A.W., & Ledbetter, W.D. (1982). Anatomy and innervation patterns of cat lateral gastrocnemius and plantaris muscles. *American Journal of Anatomy, 164,* 67–77.

Engstrom, C.M., Loeb, G.E., Reid, J.G., Forrest, W.J., & Avruch, L. (1991). Morphometry of the human thigh muscles. A comparison between anatomical sections and computer tomographic and magnetic resonance images. *Journal of Anatomy, 176,* 139–156.

Ennion, S., Sant'ana Pereira, J., Sargeant, A.J., Young, A., & Goldspink, G. (1995). Characterization of human skeletal muscle fibres according to the myosin heavy chains they express. *Journal of Muscle Research and Cell Motility, 16,* 35–43.

Enoka, R.M. (1979). The pull in Olympic weightlifting. *Medicine and Science in Sports, 11,* 131–137.

Enoka, R.M. (1983). Muscular control of a learned movement: The speed control system hypothesis. *Experimental Brain Research, 51,* 135–145.

Enoka, R.M. (1988a). Load- and skill-related changes in segmental contributions to a weightlifting movement. *Medicine and Science in Sports and Exercise, 20,* 178–187.

Enoka, R.M. (1988b). Muscle strength and its development. New perspectives. *Sports Medicine, 6,* 146–168.

Enoka, R.M. (1995). Morphological features and activation patterns of motor units. *Journal of Clinical Neurophysiology, 12,* 538–559.

Enoka, R.M. (1996). Eccentric contractions require unique activation strategies by the nervous system. *Journal of Applied Physiology, 81,* 2339–2346.

Enoka, R.M., & Fuglevand, A.J. (2001). Motor unit physiology: Some unresolved issues. *Muscle & Nerve, 24,* 4–17.

Enoka, R.M., Hutton, R.S., & Eldred, E. (1980). Changes in excitability of tendon tap and Hoffmann reflexes following voluntary contractions. *Electroencephalography and Clinical Neurophysiology, 48,* 664–672.

Enoka, R.M., Miller, D.I., & Burgess, E.M. (1982). Below-knee amputee running gait. *American Journal of Physical Medicine, 61,* 66–84.

Enoka, R.M., Robinson, G.A., & Kossev, A.R. (1989). Task and fatigue effects on low-threshold motor units in human hand muscle. *Journal of Neurophysiology, 62,* 1344–1359.

Enoka, R.M., & Stuart, D.G. (1984). Henneman's 'size principle': Current issues. *Trends in NeuroSciences, 7,* 226–228.

Enoka, R.M., & Stuart, D.G. (1992). Neurobiology of muscle fatigue. *Journal of Applied Physiology, 72,* 1631–1648.

Enoka, R.M., Trayanova, N., Laouris, Y., Bevan, L., Reinking, R.M., & Stuart, D.G. (1992). Fatigue-related changes in motor unit action potentials of adult cats. *Muscle & Nerve, 14,* 138–150.

Erim, Z., Beg, M.F., Burke, D.T., & De Luca, C.J. (1999). Effects of aging on motor-unit control properties. *Journal of Neurophysiology, 82,* 2081–2091.

Escamilla, R.F., Fleisig, G.S., Barrentine, S.W., Zheng, N., & Andrews, J.E. (1998). Kinematic comparisons of throwing different types of baseball pitches. *Journal of Applied Biomechanics, 14,* 1–23.

Escamilla, R.F., Fleisig, G.S., Zheng, N., Barrentine, S.W., Wilk, K.E., & Andrews, J.R. (1998). Biomechanics of the knee during closed kinetic chain and open kinetic chain exercises. *Medicine and Science in Sports and Exercise, 30,* 556–569.

Esser, K.A., & Hardeman, E.C. (1995). Changes in contractile protein mRNA accumulation in response to spaceflight. *American Journal of Physiology, 268,* C466–C471.

Etnyre, B.R., & Abraham, L.D. (1986). Gains in range of ankle dorsiflexion using three popular stretching techniques. *American Journal of Physical Medicine, 65,* 189–196.

Etnyre, B.R., & Abraham, L.D. (1988). Antagonist muscle activity during stretching: A paradox re-assessed. *Medicine and Science in Sports and Exercise, 20,* 285–289.

Ettema, G.J.C., Styles, G., & Kippers, V. (1998). The moment arms of 23 muscle segments of the upper limb with varying elbow and forearm positions: Implications for motor control. *Human Movement Science, 17,* 201–220.

Evans, W.J., & Cannon, J.G. (1991). The metabolic effects of exercise-induced muscle damage. *Exercise and Sport Sciences Reviews, 19,* 99–125.

Evarts, E.V. (1968). Relation of pyramidal tract activity to force exerted during voluntary movement. *Journal of Neurophysiology, 31,* 14–27.

Evatt, M.L., Wolf, S.L., & Segal, R.L. (1989). Modification of human spinal stretch reflexes: Preliminary studies. *Neuroscience Letters, 105,* 350–355.

Ewing, J.L., Wolfe, D.R., Rogers, M.A., Amundson, M.L., & Stull, G.A. (1990). Effects of velocity of isokinetic training on strength, power, and quadriceps muscle fibre characteristics. *European Journal of Applied Physiology, 61,* 159–162.

Faaborg-Andersen, K. (1957). Electromyographic investigation of intrinsic laryngeal muscles in humans. *Acta Physiologica Scandinavica, 41*(Suppl. 140), 1–149.

Falco, F.J., Hennessey, W.J., Braddom, R.L., & Goldberg, G. (1992). Standardized nerve conduction studies in the upper limb of the healthy elderly. *American Journal of Physical Medicine and Rehabilitation, 71,* 263–271.

Fallentin, N., Jørgensen, K., & Simonsen, E.B. (1993). Motor unit recruitment during prolonged isometric contractions. *European Journal of Applied Physiology, 67,* 335–341.

Fang, Z.-P., & Mortimer, J.T. (1991a). Alternate excitation of large and small axons with different stimulation waveforms: An application to muscle activation. *Medical & Biological Engineering & Computing, 29,* 543–547.

Fang, Z.-P., & Mortimer, J.T. (1991b). A method to effect physiological recruitment order in electrically activated muscle. *IEEE Transactions on Biomedical Engineering, 38,* 175–179.

Fang, Z.-P., & Mortimer, J.T. (1991c). Selective activation of small motor axons by quasitrapezoidal current pulses. *IEEE Transactions on Biomedical Engineering, 38,* 168–174.

Farley, C.T., & Gonzalez, O. (1996). Leg stiffness and stride frequency in human running. *Journal of Biomechanics, 29,* 181–186.

Farley, C.T., Houdijk, H.H.P., van Strien, C., & Louie, M. (1998). Mechanism of leg stiffness adjustment for hopping on surfaces of different stiffnesses. *Journal of Applied Physiology, 85,* 1044–1055.

Farley, C.T., & McMahon, T.A. (1992). Energetics of walking and running: Insights from simulated reduced-gravity experiments. *Journal of Applied Physiology, 73,* 2709–2712.

Farmer, S.F. (1998). Rhythmicity, synchronization and binding in human and primate motor systems. *Journal of Physiology, 509,* 3–14.

Farmer, S.F., Halliday, D.M., Conway, B.A., Stephens, J.A., & Rosenberg, J.R. (1997). A review of recent applications of cross-correlation methodologies to human motor unit recording. *Journal of Neuroscience Methods, 74,* 175–187.

Farmer, S.F., Sheean, G.L., Mayson, M.J., Rothwell, J.C., Marsden, C.D., Conway, B.A., Halliday, D.M., Rosenberg, J.R., & Stephens, J.A. (1998). Abnormal motor unit synchronization of antagonist muscles underlies pathological co-contraction in upper limb dystonia. *Brain, 121,* 801–814.

Favero, T.G. (1999). Sarcoplasmic reticulum Ca^{2+} release and muscle fatigue. *Journal of Applied Physiology, 87,* 471–483.

Feiereisen, P., Duchateau, J., & Hainaut, K. (1997). Motor unit recruitment order during voluntary and electrically induced contractions in the tibialis anterior. *Experimental Brain Research, 114,* 117–123.

Feige, B., Aertsen, A., & Kristeva-Feige, R. (2000). Dynamic synchronization between multiple cortical motor areas and muscle activity in phasic voluntary movements. *Journal of Neurophysiology, 84,* 2622–2629.

Feinstein, B., Lindegård, B., Nyman, E., & Wohlfart, G. (1955). Morphologic studies of motor units in normal human muscles. *Acta Anatomica, 23,* 127–142.

Feldman, A.G. (1966a). Functional tuning of the nervous system with control of movement or maintenance of a steady posture. II. Controllable parameters of the muscle. *Biophysics, 11,* 565–578.

Feldman, A.G. (1966b). Functional tuning of the nervous system with control of movement or maintenance of a steady posture. III. Mechanographic analysis of execution by man on the simplest motor tasks. *Biophysics, 11,* 766–775.

Feldman, A.G. (1986). Once more on the equilibrium-point hypothesis (λ model) for motor control. *Journal of Motor Behavior, 18,* 17–54.

Fellows, S.J., Kaus, C., Ross, H.F., & Thilmann, A.F. (1994). Agonist and antagonist EMG activation during isometric torque development at the elbow in spastic hemiparesis. *Electroencephalography and Clinical Neurophysiology, 93,* 106–112.

Fellows, S.J., & Rack, P.M.H. (1987). Changes in the length of the human biceps brachii muscle during elbow movements. *Journal of Physiology (London), 383,* 405–412.

Feltner, M.E. (1989). Three-dimensional interactions in a two-segment kinetic chain: 2. Application to the throwing arm in baseball pitching. *International Journal of Sport Biomechanics, 5,* 420-450.

Feltner, M., & Dapena, J. (1986). Dynamics of the shoulder and elbow joints of the throwing arm during a baseball pitch. *International Journal of Sport Biomechanics, 2,* 235–259.

Feltner, M.E., & Dapena, J. (1989). Three-dimensional interactions in a two-segment kinetic chain. Part I: General model. *International Journal of Sport Biomechanics, 5,* 403–419.

Feltner, M.E., & Taylor, G. (1997). Three-dimensional kinetics of the shoulder, elbow, and wrist during a penalty throw in water polo. *Journal of Applied Biomechanics, 13,* 347–372.

Fenn, W.O. (1924). The relation between the work performed and the energy liberated in muscular contraction. *Journal of Physiology (London), 58,* 373–395.

Fenn, W.O. (1930). Work against gravity and work due to velocity changes in running. *American Journal of Physiology, 93,* 433–462.

Feraboli-Lohnherr, D., Barthe, J.Y., & Orsal, D. (1999). Serotonin-induced activation of the network for locomotion in adult spinal rats. *Journal of Neuroscience Research, 55,* 87–98.

Ferris, D.P., Liang, K., & Farley, C.T. (1999). Runners adjust leg stiffness for their first step on a new running surface. *Journal of Biomechanics, 32,* 787–794.

Ferris, D.P., Louie, M., & Farley, C.T. (1998). Running in the real world: Adjusting leg stiffness for different surfaces. *Proceedings of the Royal Society of London, B265,* 989–994.

Fiatarone, M.A., Marks, E.C., Ryan, N.D., Meredith, C.N., Lipsitz, L.A., & Evans, W.J. (1990). High-intensity strength training in nonagenarians. *Journal of the American Medical Association, 263,* 3029–3034.

Fick, R. (1904). *Handbuch der anatomie des menschen* (Vol. 2). Stuttgart: Gustav Fischer Verlag.

Finni, T., Komi, P.V., & Lukkariniemi, J. (1998). Achilles tendon loading during walking: Application of a novel optic fiber technique. *European Journal of Applied Physiology, 77,* 289–291.

Finni, T., Komi, P.V., & Lepola, V. (2000). In vivo human triceps surae and quadriceps femoris muscle function in a squat jump and counter movement jump. *European Journal of Applied Physiology, 83,* 416–426.

Fisher, M.J., Meyer, R.A., Adams, G.R., Foley, J.M., & Potchen, E.J. (1990). Direct relationship between proton T2 and exercise intensity in skeletal muscle MR images. *Investigative Radiology, 25,* 480–485.

Fisher, W.J., & White, M.J. (1999). Training-induced adaptations in the central command and peripheral reflex components of the pressor response to isometric exercise of the human triceps surae. *Journal of Physiology, 520,* 621–628.

Fitts, R.H. (1996). Cellular, molecular, and metabolic basis of muscle fatigue. In L.B. Rowell & J.T. Shepherd (Eds.), *Handbook of physiology: Sec. 12. Exercise: Regulation and integration of multiple systems* (pp. 1151–1183). New York: Oxford University Press.

Fitts, R.H., Bodine, S.C., Romatowski, J.G., & Widrick, J.J. (1998). Velocity, force, power, and Ca^{2+} sensitivity of fast and slow monkey skeletal muscle fibers. *Journal of Applied Physiology, 84,* 1776–1787.

Fitts, R.H., Brimmer, C.J., Heywood-Cooksey, A., & Timmerman, R.J. (1989). Single muscle fiber enzyme shifts with hindlimb suspension and immobilzation. *American Journal of Physiology, 256,* C1082–C1091.

Fitts, R.H., Costill, D.L., & Gardetto, P.R. (1989). Effect of swim exercise training on human muscle fiber function. *Journal of Applied Physiology, 66,* 465–475.

Fitts, R.H., & Metzger, J.M. (1988). Mechanisms of muscular fatigue. In J.R. Poortmans (Ed.), *Principles of exercise biochemistry* (pp. 248–268). Basel: Karger.

Fitts, R.H., Metzger, J.M., Riley, D.A., & Unsworth, B.R. (1986). Models of disuse: A comparison of hindlimb suspension and immobilization. *Journal of Applied Physiology, 60,* 1946–1953.

Fitts, R.H., & Widrick, J.J. (1996). Muscle mechanics: Adaptations with exercise-training. *Exercise and Sport Sciences Reviews, 24,* 427–473.

Fitzpatrick, R.C., Taylor, J.L., & McCloskey, D.I. (1996). Effects of arterial perfusion pressure on force production in working human hand muscles. *Journal of Physiology, 495,* 885–891.

Fitzsimons, D.P., Herrick, R.E., & Baldwin, K.M. (1990). Isomyosin distribution in skeletal muscle: Effects of altered thyroid state. *Journal of Applied Physiology, 69,* 321–327.

Flanagan, J.R., Burstedt, M.K., & Johansson, R.S. (1999). Control of fingertip forces in multidigit manipulation. *Journal of Neurophysiology, 81,* 1706–1717.

Fleck, S.J., & Kraemer, W.J. (1987). *Designing resistance training programs.* Champaign, IL: Human Kinetics.

Fleckenstein, J.L., Canby, R.C., Parkey, R.W., & Peshock, R.M. (1988). Acute effects of exercise on MR imaging of skeletal muscle in normal volunteers. *American Journal of Roentgenology, 151,* 231–237.

Fleckenstein, J.L., & Shellock, F.G. (1991). Exertional muscle injuries: Magnetic resonance imaging evaluation. *Topics in Magnetic Resonance Imaging, 3,* 50–70.

Fleckenstein, J.L., Watumull, D., Bertocci, L.A., Parkey, R.W., & Peshock, R.M. (1992). Finger-specific flexor recruitment in humans: Depiction of exercise-enhanced MRI. *Journal of Applied Physiology, 72,* 1974–1977.

Foehring, R.C., & Munson, J.B. (1990). Motoneuron and muscle-unit properties after long-term direct innervation of soleus muscle by medial gastrocnemius nerve in cat. *Journal of Neurophysiology, 64,* 847–861.

Foehring, R.C., Sypert, G.W., & Munson, J.B. (1987a). Motor unit properties following cross-reinnervation of cat lateral gastrocnemius and soleus muscles with medial gastrocnemius nerve. I. Influence of motoneurons on muscle. *Journal of Neurophysiology, 57,* 1210–1226.

Foehring, R.C., Sypert, G.W., & Munson, J.B. (1987b). Motor unit properties following cross-reinnervation of cat lateral gastrocnemius and soleus muscles with medial gastrocnemius nerve. II. Influence of muscle on motoneurons. *Journal of Neurophysiology, 57,* 1227–1245.

Fortier, P.A., Kalaska, J.F., & Smith, A.M. (1989). Cerebellar neuronal activity related to whole-arm reaching movements in the monkey. *Journal of Neurophysiology, 62,* 198–211.

Forster, C., & Schmelz, M. (1996). New developments in microneurography of human C fibers. *News in Physiological Sciences, 11,* 170–175.

Fothergill, D.M., Grieve, D.W., & Pinder, A.D.J. (1996). The influence of task resistance on the characteristics of maximal one- and two-handed lifting exertions in men and women. *European Journal of Applied Physiology, 72,* 430–439.

Fournier, E., & Pierrot-Deseilligny, E. (1989). Changes in transmission in some reflex pathways during movement in humans. *News in Physiological Sciences, 4,* 29–32.

Fournier, M., Roy, R.R., Perham, H., Simard, C.P., & Edgerton, V.R. (1983). Is limb immobilization a model of muscle disuse? *Experimental Neurology, 80,* 147–156.

Frank, C.B. (1996). Ligament injuries: Pathophysiology and healing. In J.E. Zachazewski, D.J. Magee, & W.S. Quillen (Eds.), *Athletic injuries and rehabilitation* (pp. 9–26). Philadelphia: Saunders.

Freed, W.J., de Medinaceli, L., & Wyatt, R.J. (1985). Promoting functional plasticity in the damaged nervous system. *Science, 227,* 1544–1552.

Freund, H.J., Büdingen, H.J., & Dietz, V. (1975). Activity of single motor units from human forearm muscles during voluntary isometric contractions. *Journal of Neurophysiology, 38,* 933–946.

Fridén, J., Kjörell, U., & Thornell, L.-E. (1984). Delayed muscle soreness and cytoskeletal alterations: An immunocytological study in man. *International Journal of Sports Medicine, 5,* 15–18.

Fridén, J., & Lieber, R.L. (1992). Structural and mechanical basis of exercise-induced muscle injury. *Medicine and Science in Sports and Exercise, 24,* 521–530.

Fridén, J., & Lieber, R.L. (1997). Muscle damage induced by cyclic eccentric contraction: Biomechanical and structural studies. In S. Salmon (Ed.), *Muscle damage* (pp. 41–63). Oxford: Oxford University Press.

Fridén, J., & Lieber, R.L. (1998). Evidence for muscle attachment at relatively long lengths in tendon transfer surgery. *Journal of Hand Surgery, 23A,* 105–110.

Friederich, J.A., & Brand, R.A. (1990). Muscle fiber architecture in the human lower limb. *Journal of Biomechanics, 23,* 91–95.

Frohlich, C. (1980, March). The physics of somersaulting and twisting. *Scientific American,* pp. 154–164.

Frolkis, V.V., Tanin, S.A., Marcinko, V.I., Kulchitsky, O.K., & Yasechko, A.V. (1985). Axoplasmic transport of substances in motoneuronal axons of the spinal cord in old age. *Mechanisms of Ageing and Development, 29,* 19–28.

Frontera, W.R., Hughes, V.A., Fielding, R.A., Fiatarone, M.A., Evans, W.J., & Roubenoff, R. (2000). Aging of skeletal muscle: A 12-yr longitudinal muscle. *Journal of Applied Physiology, 88,* 1321–1326.

Fryer, M.W., Owen, V.J., Lamb, G.D., & Stephenson, D.G. (1995). Effects of creatine phosphate and P_i on Ca^{2+} movements and tension development in rat skinned skeletal muscle fibres. *Journal of Physiology, 482,* 123–140.

Fu, F.H., Harner, C.D., Johnson, D.L., Miller, M.D., & Woo, S.L.-Y. (1993). Biomechanics of knee ligaments. *Journal of Bone and Joint Surgery, 75-A,* 1716–1727.

Fuglevand, A.J., Macefield, V.G., & Bigland-Ritchie, B. (1999). Force-frequency and fatigue properties of motor units in muscles that control digits of the human hand. *Journal of Neurophysiology, 81,* 1718–1729.

Fuglevand, A.J., Winter, D.A., & Patla, A.E. (1993). Models of recruitment and rate coding organization in motor-unit pools. *Journal of Neurophysiology, 70,* 2470–2488.

Fuglevand, A.J., Winter, D.A., Patla, A.E., & Stashuk, D. (1992). Detection of motor unit action potentials with surface electrodes: Influence of electrode size and spacing. *Biological Cybernetics, 67,* 143–154.

Fuglevand, A.J., Zackowski, K.M., Huey, K.A., & Enoka, R.M. (1993). Impairment of neuromuscular propagation during human fatiguing contractions at submaximal forces. *Journal of Physiology, 460,* 549–572.

Fuglsang-Frederiksen, A. (2000). The utility of interference pattern analysis. *Muscle & Nerve, 23,* 18–36.

Fujiwara, M., & Basmajian, J.V. (1975). Electromyographic study of two-joint muscles. *American Journal of Physical Medicine, 54,* 234–242.

Fukashiro, S., & Komi, P.V. (1987). Joint moment and mechanical power flow of the lower limb during vertical jump. *International Journal of Sports Medicine, 8,* 15–21.

Fukashiro, S., Komi, P.V., Jarvinen, M., & Miyashita, M. (1995). In vivo Achilles tendon loading during jumping in humans. *European Journal of Applied Physiology, 71,* 453–458.

Fukunaga, T., Kuko, K., Kawakami, Y., Fukashiro, S., Kanehisa, H., & Maganaris, C.N. (2001). *In vivo* behaviour of human muscle tendon during walking. *Proceedings of the Royal Society, London B, 268,* 229–233.

Fukunaga, T., Roy, R.R., Shellock, F.G., Hodgson, J.A., & Edgerton, V.R. (1996). Specific tension of plantar flexors and dorsiflexors. *Journal of Applied Physiology, 80,* 158–165.

Fulco, C.S., Rock, P.B., Muza, S.R., Cymerman, A., Butterfield, G., Moore, L.G., Braun, B., & Lewis, S.F. (1999). Slower fatigue and faster recovery of the adductor pollicis muscle in women matched for strength with men. *Acta Physiologica Scandinavica, 167,* 233–239.

Funk, D.A., An, K.N., Morrey, B.F., & Daube, J.R. (1987). Electromyographic analysis of muscles across the elbow joint. *Journal of Orthopaedic Research, 5,* 529–538.

Gaffney, F.A., Sjøgaard, G., & Saltin, B. (1990). Cardiovascular and metabolic responses to static contraction in man. *Acta Physiologica Scandinavica, 138,* 249–258.

Galea, V., & Norman, R.W. (1985). Bone-on-bone forces at the ankle joint during a rapid dynamic movement. In D.A. Winter, R.W. Norman, R.P. Wells, K.C. Hayes, & A.E. Patla (Eds.), *Biomechanics IX-A* (pp. 71–76). Champaign, IL: Human Kinetics.

Galganski, M.E., Fuglevand, A.J., & Enoka, R.M. (1993). Reduced control of motor output in a human hand muscle of elderly subjects during submaximal contractions. *Journal of Neurophysiology, 69,* 2108–2115.

Galler, S., Schmitt, T.L., Hilber, K., & Pette, D. (1997). Stretch activation and isoforms of myosin heavy chain and troponin-T of rat skeletal muscle fibres. *Journal of Muscle Research and Cell Motility, 18,* 555–561.

Gamrin, L., Berg, H.E., Essen, P., Tesch, P.A., Hultman, E., Garlick, P.J., McNurlan, M.A., & Wernerman, J. (1998). The effect of unloading on protein synthesis in human skeletal muscle. *Acta Physiologica Scandinavica, 163,* 369–377.

Gandevia, S.C. (1996). Kinesthesia: Roles for afferent signals and motor commands. In L.B. Rowell & J.T. Shepherd (Eds.), *Handbook of physiology: Sec. 12. Exercise: Regulation and integration of multiple systems* (pp. 128–172). New York: Oxford University Press.

Gandevia, S.C. (1998). Neural control in human muscle fatigue: Changes in muscle afferents, motoneurones and motor cortical drive. *Acta Physiologica Scandinavica, 162,* 275–283.

Gandevia, S.C., Allen, G.M., Butler, J.E., & Taylor, J.L. (1996). Supraspinal factors in human muscle fatigue: Evidence for suboptimal output from the motor cortex. *Journal of Physiology, 490,* 529–536.

Gandevia, S.C., Enoka, R.M., McComas, A.J., Stuart, D.G., & Thomas, C.K. (1995). *Fatigue: Neural and muscular mechanisms.* New York: Plenum Press.

Gandevia, S.C., Herbert, R.D., & Leeper, J.B. (1998). Voluntary activation of human elbow flexor muscles during maximal concentric contractions. *Journal of Physiology, 512,* 595–602.

Gandevia, S.C., McCloskey, D.I., & Burke, D. (1992). Kinaesthetic signals and muscle contraction. *Trends in Neurosciences, 15,* 62–65.

Gandevia, S.C., & McKenzie, D.K. (1985). Activation of the human diaphragm during maximal static efforts. *Journal of Physiology (London), 367,* 45–56.

Gardetto, P.R., Schluter, J.M., & Fitts, R.H. (1989). Contractile function of single muscle fibers after hindlimb suspension. *Journal of Applied Physiology, 66,* 2739–2749.

Gardiner, P.F., & Seburn, K.L. (1997). The effects of tetrodotoxin-induced muscle paralysis on the physiological properties of muscle units and their innervating motoneurons in rat. *Journal of Physiology, 499,* 207–216.

Gardner, E. (1940). Decrease in human neurones with age. *Anatomical Record, 77,* 529–536.

Garfinkel, S., & Cafarelli, E. (1992). Relative changes in maximal force, EMG, and muscle cross-sectional area after isometric training. *Medicine and Science in Sports and Exercise, 24,* 1220–1227.

Garhammer, J. (1980). Power production by Olympic weightlifters. *Medicine and Science in Sports and Exercise, 12,* 54–60.

Garhammer, J., & Takano, B. (1992). Training for weightlifting. In P.V. Komi (Ed.), *Strength and power in sport* (pp. 357–369). Oxford: Blackwell Scientific.

Garland, S.J., Enoka, R.M., Serrano, L.P., & Robinson, G.A. (1994). Behavior of motor units in human biceps brachii during submaximal fatiguing contractions. *Journal of Applied Physiology, 76,* 2411–2419.

Garland, S.J., & Griffin, L. (1999). Motor unit double discharges: Statistical anomaly or functional entity? *Canadian Journal of Applied Physiology, 24,* 113–130.

Garland, S.J., & Kaufman, M.P. (1995). Role of muscle afferents in the inhibition of motoneurons during fatigue. In S.C.

Gandevia, R.M. Enoka, A.J. McComas, D.G. Stuart, & C.K. Thomas (Eds.), *Fatigue: Neural and muscular mechanisms* (pp. 271–278). New York: Plenum Press.

Garland, S.J., & Miles, T.S. (1997). Responses of human single motor units to transcranial magnetic stimulation. *Electroencephalography and Clinical Neurophysiology, 105,* 94–101.

Garner, S.H., Hicks, A.L., & McComas, A.J. (1989). Prolongation of twitch potentiating mechanism throughout muscle fatigue and recovery. *Experimental Neurology, 103,* 277–281.

Garnett, R., & Stephens, J.A. (1981). Changes in the recruitment threshold of motor units produced by cutaneous stimulation in man. *Journal of Physiology (London), 311,* 463–473.

Garnett, R.A.F., O'Donovan, M.J., Stephens, J.A., & Taylor, A. (1978). Motor unit organization of human medical gastrocnemius. *Journal of Physiology (London), 287,* 33–43.

Garrett, W.E. (1990). Muscle strain injuries: Clinical and basic aspects. *Medicine and Science in Sports and Exercise, 22,* 436–443.

Garrett, W.E., Califf, J.C., & Bassett, F.H. (1984). Histochemical correlates of hamstring injuries. *American Journal of Sports Medicine, 12,* 98–103.

Garrett, W.E., Safran, M.R., Seaber, A.V., Glisson, R.R., & Ribbeck, B.M. (1987). Biomechanical comparison of stimulated and nonstimulated skeletal muscle pulled to failure. *American Journal of Sports Medicine, 15,* 448–454.

Gatesy, S.M., & Biewener, A.A. (1991). Bipedal locomotion—effects of speed, size and limb posture in birds and humans. *Journal of Zoology (London) 224,* 127–147.

Gaviria, M., & Ohanna, F. (1999). Variability of the fatigue response of paralyzed skeletal muscle in relation to the time after spinal cord injury: mechanical and electrophysiological characteristics. *European Journal of Applied Physiology, 80,* 145-153.

Gebhard, J.S., Kabo, J.M., & Meals, R.A. (1993). Passive motion: The dose effects on joint stiffness, muscle mass, bone density, and regional swelling. *Journal of Bone and Joint Surgery, 75-A,* 1636–1647.

Gelfand, I.M., Orlovsky, G.N., & Shik, M.L. (1988). Locomotion and scratching in tetrapods. In A.H. Cohen, S. Rossignol, & S. Grillner (Eds.), *Neural control of rhythmic movements in vertebrates* (pp. 167–199). New York: Wiley.

Georgopoulos, A.P. (1988). Spatial coding of visually guided arm movements in primate motor cortex. *Canadian Journal of Physiology and Pharmacology, 66,* 518–526.

Georgopoulos, A.P., Caminiti, R., Kalaska, J.F., & Massey, J.T. (1983). Spatial coding of movement: A hypothesis concerning the coding of movement direction by motor cortical populations. *Experimental Brain Research, 7*(Suppl.), 327–336.

Georgopoulos, A.P., Kalaska, J.F., Caminiti, R., & Massey, J.T. (1982). On the relations between the direction of two-dimensional arm movements and cell discharge in primate motor cortex. *Journal of Neuroscience, 2,* 1527–1537.

Georgopoulos, A.P., Kettner, R.E., & Schwartz, A.B. (1988). Primate motor cortex and free arm movements to visual targets in three-dimensional space. II. Coding of the direction of movement by a neuronal population. *Journal of Neuroscience, 8,* 2928–2937.

Gergely, J. (1974). Some aspects of the role of the sarcoplasmic reticulum and the tropomyosin-troponin system in the control of muscle contraction by calcium ions. *Circulation Research, 34*(Suppl. 3), 74–82.

Gerilovsky, L., Tsvetinov, P., & Trenkova, G. (1989). Peripheral effects on the amplitude of monopolar and bipolar H-reflex potentials from the soleus muscle. *Experimental Brain Research, 76,* 173–181.

Gerrits, H.L., De Haan, A., Hopman, M.T.E., Van der Woude, L.H.V., Jones, D.A., & Sargeant, A.J. (1999). Contractile properties of the quadriceps muscle in individuals with spinal cord injury. *Muscle & Nerve, 22,* 1249–1256.

Gertler, R.A., & Robbins, N. (1978). Differences in neuromuscular transmission in red and white muscles. *Brain Research, 142,* 160–164.

Ghez, C. (1991a). The cerebellum. In E.R. Kandel, J.H. Schwartz, & T.M. Jessell (Eds.), *Principles of neural science* (3rd ed., pp. 626–646). New York: Elsevier.

Ghez, C. (1991b). Voluntary movement. In E.R. Kandel, J.H. Schwartz, & T.M. Jessell (Eds.), *Principles of neural science* (3rd ed., pp. 609–625). New York: Elsevier.

Ghez, C., & Krakauer, J. (2000). The organization of movement. In E.R. Kandel, J.H. Schwartz, & T.M. Jessell (Eds.), *Principles of neural science* (4th ed., pp. 653–673). New York: McGraw-Hill.

Ghez, C., & Thach, W.T. (2000). The cerebellum. In E.R. Kandel, J.H. Schwartz, & T.M. Jessell (Eds.), *Principles of neural science* (4th ed., pp. 832–852). New York: McGraw-Hill.

Gibala, M.J., MacDougall, J.D., Tarnopolsky, M.A., Stauber, W.T., & Elorriaga, A. (1995). Changes in human skeletal muscle ultrastructure and force production after acute resistance exercise. *Journal of Applied Physiology, 78,* 702–708.

Gibson, J.N.A., Halliday, D., Morrison, W.L., Stoward, P.J., Hornsby, G.A., Watt, P.W., Murdoch, G., & Rennie, M.J. (1987). Decrease in human quadriceps muscle protein turnover consequent upon leg immobilization. *Clinical Science, 72,* 503–509.

Giddings, V.L., Beaupré, G.A., Whalen, R.T., & Carter, D.R. (2000). Calcaneal loading during walking and running. *Medicine and Science in Sports and Exercise, 32,* 627–634.

Gielen, C.C.A.M., Ingen Schenau, G.J. van, Tax, T., & Theeuwen, M. (1990). The activation of mono- and bi-articular muscles in multi-joint movements. In J.M. Winters & S.L-Y. Woo (Eds.), *Multiple muscle systems: Biomechanics and movement organization* (pp. 302–311). New York: Springer-Verlag.

Gillard, D.M., Yakovenko, S., Cameron, T., & Prochazka, A. (2000). Isometric muscle length-tension curves do not predict angle-torque curves of human wrist in continuous active movements. *Journal of Biomechanics, 33,* 1341–1348.

Gleim, G.W., & McHugh, M.P. (1997). Flexibility and its effect on sports injury and performance. *Sports Medicine, 24,* 289–299.

Glitsch, U., & Baumann, W. (1997). The three-dimensional determination of internal loads in the lower extremity. *Journal of Biomechanics, 30,* 1123–1131.

Godard, M.P., Wygand, J.W., Carpinelli, R.N., Catalano, S., & Otto, R.M. (1998). Effects of accentuated eccentric exercise training on concentric knee extensor strength. *Journal of Strength and Conditioning Research, 12,* 26–29.

Godfrey, C.M., Jayawardena, A., & Welsh, P. (1986). Comparison of electro-stimulation and isometric exercise in strengthening the quadriceps muscle. *Physiotherapy (Canada), 31,* 265–267.

Goldberger, M., Murray, M., & Tessler, A. (1993). Sprouting and regeneration in the spinal cord: Their roles in recovery of function after spinal injury. In A. Gorio (Ed.), *Neuroregeneration* (pp. 241–264). New York: Raven Press.

Goldspink, G., Scutt, A., Loughna, P.T., Wells, D.J., Jaenicke, T., & Gerlach, G.F. (1992). Gene expression in skeletal muscle in response to stretch and force generation. *American Journal of Physiology, 262,* R356–R363.

Gollhofer, A., Horstmann, G.A., Berger, W., & Dietz, V. (1989). Compensation for translational and rotational perturbations in human posture: Stabilization of the centre of gravity. *Neuroscience Letters, 105,* 73–78.

Gordon, A.M., Huxley, A.F., & Julian, F.J. (1966). The variation in isometric tension with sarcomere length in vertebrate muscle fibres. *Journal of Physiology, 184,* 170–192.

Gordon, D.A., Enoka, R.M., Karst, G.M., & Stuart, D.G. (1990). Force development and relaxation in single motor units of adult cats during a standard fatigue test. *Journal of Physiology (London), 421,* 583–594.

Gordon, D.A., Enoka, R.M., & Stuart, D.G. (1990). Motor-unit force potentiation in adult cats during a standard fatigue test. *Journal of Physiology (London), 421,* 569–582.

Gordon, T., & Mao, J. (1994). Muscle atrophy and procedures for training after spinal cord injury. *Physical Therapy, 74,* 50–60.

Gordon, T., & Pattullo, M.C. (1993). Plasticity of muscle fiber and motor unit types. *Exercise and Sport Sciences Reviews, 21,* 331–362.

Gordon, T., Yang, J.F., Ayer, K., Stein, R.B., & Tyreman, N. (1993). Recovery potential of muscle after partial denervation: A comparison between rats and humans. *Brain Research Bulletin, 30,* 477–482.

Goslow, G.E., Reinking, R.M., & Stuart, D.G. (1973). The cat step cycle: Hind limb joint angles and muscle lengths during unrestrained locomotion. *Journal of Morphology, 141,* 1–41.

Gossard, J.-P. (1996). Control of transmission in muscle group Ia afferents during fictive locomotion in the cat. *Journal of Neurophysiology, 76,* 4104–4112.

Gottlieb, G.L. (1996). On the voluntary movement of compliant (inertial-viscous) loads by parcellated control mechanisms. *Journal of Neurophysiology, 76,* 3207–3229.

Gottlieb, G.L., Corcos, D.M., & Agarwal, G.C. (1989). Organizing principles for single-joint movements. I. A speed-insensitive strategy. *Journal of Neurophysiology, 62,* 342–357.

Gottlieb, G.L., Corcos, D.M., Agarwal, G.C., & Latash, M.L. (1990a). Organizing principles for single joint movements. III. Speed-insensitive strategy as a default. *Journal of Neurophysiology, 63,* 625–636.

Gottlieb, G.L., Corcos, D.M., Agarwal, G.C., & Latash, M.L. (1990b). Principles underlying single-joint movement strategies. In J.M. Winters & S.L-Y. Woo (Eds.), *Multiple muscle systems: Biomechanics and movement organization* (pp. 236–250). New York: Springer-Verlag.

Gowland, C., deBruin, H., Basmajian, J.V., Plews, N., & Burcea, I. (1992). Agonist and antagonist activity during voluntary upper-limb movement in patients with stroke. *Physical Therapy, 72,* 624–633.

Grabiner, M.D., & Enoka, R.M. (1995). Changes in movement capabilities with aging. *Exercise and Sport Sciences Reviews, 23,* 65–104.

Grabiner, M.D., & Jeziorowski, J.J. (1992). Isokinetic trunk extension discriminates uninjured subjects from subjects with previous low back pain. *Clinical Biomechanics, 7,* 195–200.

Grabiner, M.D., Koh, T.J., & Andrish, J.T. (1992). Decreased excitation of vastus medialis oblique and vastus lateralis in patellofemoral pain. *European Journal of Experimental Musculoskeletal Research, 1,* 33–39.

Grabiner, M.D., & Owings, T.M. (1999). Effects of eccentrically and concentrically induced unilateral fatigue on the involved and uninvolved limbs. *Journal of Electromyography and Kinesiology, 9,* 185–189.

Grange, R.W., & Houston, M.E. (1991). Simultaneous potentiation and fatigue in quadriceps after a 60-second maximal voluntary isometric contraction. *Journal of Applied Physiology, 70,* 726–731.

Grange, R.W., Vandenboom, R., Xeni, J., & Houston, M.E. (1998). Potentiation of in vitro concentric work in mouse fast muscle. *Journal of Applied Physiology, 84,* 236–243.

Gransberg, L., & Knutsson, E. (1983). Determination of dynamic muscle strength in man with acceleration controlled isokinetic movements. *Acta Physiologica Scandinavica, 119,* 317–320.

Grasso, R., Bianchi, L., & Lacquaniti, F. (1998). Motor patterns for human gait: Backward versus forward locomotion. *Journal of Neurophysiology, 80,* 1868–1885.

Graves, A.E., Kornatz, K.W., & Enoka, R.M. (2000). Older adults use a unique strategy to lift inertial loads with the elbow flexor muscles. *Journal of Neurophysiology, 83,* 2030–2039.

Green, H., Dahly, A., Shoemaker, K., Goreham, C., Bombardier, E., & Ball-Burnett, M. (1999). Serial effects of high-resistance and prolonged endurance training on Na^+-K^+ pump concentration and enzymatic activities in human vastus lateralis. *Acta Physiologica Scandinavica, 165,* 177–184.

Green, H., MacDougall, J., Tarnopolsky, M., & Melissa, N.L. (1999). Downregulation of Na^+-K^+-ATPase pumps in skeletal muscle with training in normobaric hypoxia. *Journal of Applied Physiology, 86,* 1745–1748.

Greensmith, L., & Vrbová, G. (1996). Motoneurone survival: A functional approach. *Trends in Neurosciences, 19,* 450–455.

Gregor, R.J., Cavanagh, P.R., & LaFortune, M. (1985). Knee flexor moments during propulsion in cycling—a creative solution to Lombard's paradox. *Journal of Biomechanics, 18,* 307–316.

Gregor, R.J., Komi, P.V., Browning, R.C., & Jarvinen, M. (1991). A comparison of the triceps surae and residual muscle moments at the ankle during cycling. *Journal of Biomechanics, 24,* 287–297.

Gregor, R.J., Komi, P.V., & Jarvinen, M. (1987). Achilles tendon forces during cycling. *International Journal of Sports Medicine, 8,* 9–14.

Gregor, R.J., Roy, R.R., Whiting, W.C., Lovely, R.G., Hodgson, J.A., & Edgerton, V.R. (1988). Mechanical output of the cat soleus during treadmill locomotion: *In vivo* vs *in situ* characteristics. *Journal of Biomechanics, 21,* 721–732.

Gregory, J.E. (1990). Relations between identified tendon organs and motor units in the medial gastrocnemius muscle of the cat. *Experimental Brain Research, 81,* 602–608.

Gregory, J.E., Morgan, D.L., & Proske, U. (1986). Aftereffects in the responses of cat muscle spindles. *Journal of Neurophysiology, 56,* 451–461.

Gribble, P.L., & Ostry, D.J. (1999). Compensation for interaction torques during single- and multijoint limb movement. *Journal of Neurophysiology, 82,* 2310–2326.

Griffin, L., Garland, S.J., & Ivanova, T. (1998). Discharge patterns in human motor units during fatiguing arm movements. *Journal of Applied Physiology, 85,* 1684–1692.

Griffin, L., Ivanova, T., & Garland, S.J. (2000). Role of limb movement in the modulation of motor unit discharge rate during fatiguing contractions. *Experimental Brain Research, 130,* 392–400.

Griffin, T.M., Tolani, N.A., & Kram, R. (1999). Walking in simulated reduced gravity: Mechanical energy fluctuations and exchange. *Journal of Applied Physiology, 86,* 383–390.

Griffiths, R.I. (1991). Shortening of muscle fibres during stretch of the active cat medial gastrocnemius muscle: The role of tendon compliance. *Journal of Physiology, 436,* 219–236.

Grillner, S. (1981). Control of locomotion in bipeds, tetrapods, and fish. In V.B. Brooks (Ed.), *Handbook of physiology: Sec. 1. The nervous system. Vol. 2. Motor control* (Pt. 1, pp. 1179–1236). Bethesda, MD: American Physiological Society.

Grillner, S., & Rossignol, S. (1978). On the initiation of the swing phase of locomotion in chronic spinal cats. *Brain Research, 146,* 269–277.

Grillner S., & Wallen, P. (1985). Central pattern generators for locomotion, with special reference to vertebrates. *Annual Reviews of Neuroscience, 8,* 233–261.

Grimby, G., Gustafsson, E., Peterson, L., & Renström, P. (1980). Quadriceps function and training after knee ligament surgery. *Medicine and Science in Sports and Exercise, 12,* 70–75.

Grimby, L., Hannerz, J., & Hedman, B. (1981). The fatigue and voluntary discharge properties of single motor units in man. *Journal of Physiology (London), 316,* 545–554.

Grood, E.S., Suntay, W.J., Noyes, F.R., & Butler, D.L. (1984). Biomechanics of the knee-extension exercise. *Journal of Bone and Joint Surgery, 66-A,* 725–734.

Gross, A.C., Kyle, C.R., & Malewicki, D.J. (1983, December). The aerodynamics of human-powered land vehicles. *Scientific American,* pp. 142–145, 148–152.

Gu, M.-J., Schultz, A.B., Shepard, N.T., & Alexander, N.B. (1996). Postural control in young and elderly adults when stance is perturbed: Dynamics. *Journal of Biomechanics, 29,* 319–329.

Guissard, N., Duchateau, J., & Hainaut, K. (1988). Muscle stretching and motoneuron excitability. *European Journal of Applied Physiology, 58,* 47–52.

Gunning, P., & Hardeman, E. (1991). Multiple mechanisms regulate muscle fiber diversity. *FASEB Journal, 5,* 3064–3070.

Gydikov, A.A., & Kosarov, D. (1974). Some features of different motor units in human biceps brachii. *Pflügers Archiv, 347,* 75–88.

Gydikov, A.A., Kossev, A.R., Kosarov, D.S., & Kostov, K.G. (1987). Investigations of single motor units firing during movements against elastic resistance. In B. Jonsson (Ed.), *Biomechanics X-A* (pp. 227–232). Champaign, IL: Human Kinetics.

Hagbarth, K.-E. (1962). Post-tetanic potentiation of myotatic reflexes in man. *Journal of Neurology, Neurosurgery, and Psychiatry, 25,* 1–10.

Hagbarth, K.-E., Hagglund, J.V., Nordin, M., & Wallin, E.U. (1985). Thixotropic behaviour of human finger flexor muscles with accompanying changes in spindle and reflex responses to stretch. *Journal of Physiology (London), 368,* 323–342.

Hainaut, K., & Duchateau, J. (1992). Neuromuscular electrical stimulation and voluntary exercise. *Sports Medicine, 14,* 100–113.

Häkkinen, K. (1985). Research overview: Factors influencing trainability of muscular strength during short term and prolonged training. *National Strength & Conditioning Association Journal, 7,* 32–37.

Häkkinen, K., Alén, M., & Komi, P.V. (1985). Changes in isometric force- and relaxation-time, electromyographic and muscle fibre characteristics of human skeletal muscle during strength training and detraining. *Acta Physiologica Scandinavica, 125,* 573–585.

Häkkinen, K., Kallinen, M., Izquierdo, M., Jokelainen, K., Lassila, H., Mälkiä, E., Kraemer, W.J., Newton, R.U., & Alen, M. (1998). Changes in agonist-antagonist EMG, muscle CSA, and force during strength training in middle-aged and older people. *Journal of Applied Physiology, 84,* 1341–1349.

Häkkinen, K., Kallinen, M., Linnamo, V., Pastinen, U.-M., Newton, R.U., & Kraemer, W.J. (1996). Neuromuscular adaptations during bilateral versus unilateral strength training in middle-aged and elderly men and women. *Acta Physiologica Scandinavica, 158,* 77–88.

Häkkinen, K., & Keskinen, K.L. (1989). Muscle cross-sectional area and voluntary force production characteristics in elite strength- and endurance-trained athletes and sprinter. *European Journal of Applied Physiology, 59,* 215–220.

Häkkinen, K., & Komi, P.V. (1986). Training-induced changes in neuromuscular performance under voluntary and reflex conditions. *European Journal of Applied Physiology, 55,* 147–155.

Häkkinen, K., Komi, P.V., & Alén, M. (1985). Effect of explosive type strength training on isometric force- and relaxation-time, electromyographic and muscle fibre characteristics of leg extensor muscles. *Acta Physiologica Scandinavica, 125,* 587–600.

Halbertsma, J.P.K., van Bolhuis, A.I., & Göeken, L.N.H. (1996). Sport stretching: Effect on passive muscle stiffness of short hamstrings. *Archives of Physical Medicine and Rehabilitation, 77,* 688–692.

Hallett, M. (1993). Physiology of basal ganglia disorders: An overview. *Canadian Journal of Neurological Sciences, 20,* 177–183.

Hallett, M., Berardelli, A., Delwaide, P., Freund, H.-J., Kimura, K., Lücking, C., Rothwell, J.C., Shahani, B.T., & Yanagisawa, N. (1994). Central EMG and tests of motor control. Report of an IFCN committee. *Electroencephalography and Clinical Neurophysiology, 90,* 404–432.

Halliday, D.M., Conway, B.A., Farmer, S.F., & Rosenberg, J.R. (1998). Using electroencephalography to study functional coupling between cortical activity and electromyograms during voluntary contractions in humans. *Neuroscience Letters, 241,* 1–4.

Hamill, J., & Knutzen, K.M. (1995). *Biomechanical basis of human movement.* Baltimore: Williams & Wilkins.

Hammond, P.H., Merton, P.A., & Sutton, G.G. (1956). Nervous gradation of muscular contraction. *British Medical Bulletin, 12,* 214–218.

Hanavan, E.P. (1964). *A mathematical model of the human body* (AMRL-TR-64-102). Wright Patterson Air Force Base, OH:

Aerospace Medical Research Laboratories (NTIS No. AD-608463).

Hanavan, E.P. (1966). A personalized mathematical model of the human body. *Journal of Spacecraft and Rockets, 3,* 446–448.

Hansen, P.D., Woollacott, M.H., & Debu, B. (1988). Postural responses to changing task conditions. *Experimental Brain Research, 73,* 627–636.

Haridas, C., Zehr, E.P., Sugajima, Y., & Gillies, E. (2000). Differential control of cutaneous reflexes during lengthening and shortening contractions of the human triceps surae. *Society for Neuroscience Abstracts, 26,* 1232.

Harman, E.A., Frykman, P.N., Clagett, E.R., & Kraemer, W.J. (1988). Intra-abdominal and intra-thoracic pressures during lifting and jumping. *Medicine and Science in Sports and Exercise, 20,* 195–201.

Harman, E.A., Rosenstein, R.M., Frykman, P.N., & Nigro, G.A. (1989). Effects of a belt on intra-abdominal pressure during weight lifting. *Medicine and Science in Sports and Exercise, 21,* 186–190.

Harre, E. (Ed.) (1982). *Principles of sports training: Introduction to the theory and methods of training.* East Berlin: Sportverlag.

Harridge, S.D.R., Bottinelli, R., Canepari, M., Pellegrino, M.A., Reggiani, C., Esbjörnsson, M., & Saltin, B. (1996). Whole-muscle and single-fibre contractile properties and myosin heavy chain isoforms in humans. *Pflügers Archive, 432,* 913–920.

Harridge, S.D.R., Bottinelli, R., Canepari, M., Pellegrino, M., Reggiani, C., Esbjörnsson, M., Balsom, P.D., & Saltin, B. (1998). Sprint training, in vitro and in vivo muscle function, and myosin heavy chain expression. *Journal of Applied Physiology, 84,* 442–449.

Harrison, R.N., Lees, A., McCullagh, P.J.J., & Rowe, W.B. (1986). A bioengineering analysis of human muscle and joint forces in the lower limbs during running. *Journal of Sports Sciences, 4,* 201–218.

Hartkopp, A., Murphy, R.J., Mohr, T., Kjær, M., & Biering-Sorensen, F. (1998). Bone fracture during electrical stimulation of the quadriceps in a spinal cord injured subject. *Archives of Physical Medicine and Rehabilitation, 79,* 1133–1136.

Hasan, Z. (1986). Optimized movement trajectories and joint stiffness in unperturbed, inertially loaded movements. *Biological Cybernetics, 53,* 373–382.

Hasan, Z. (1991). Biomechanics and the study of multijoint movements. In D.R. Humphrey & H.-J. Freund (Eds.), *Motor control: Concepts and issues* (pp. 75–84). Chichester: Wiley.

Hasan, Z., & Enoka, R.M. (1985). Isometric torque-angle relationship and movement-related activity of human elbow flexors: Implications for the equilibrium-point hypothesis. *Experimental Brain Research, 59,* 441–450.

Hasan, Z., & Stuart, D.G. (1984). Mammalian muscle receptors. In R.A. Davidoff (Ed.), *Handbook of the spinal cord* (pp. 559–607). New York: Dekker.

Hasan, Z., & Stuart, D.G. (1988). Animal solutions to problems of movement control: The role of proprioceptors. *Annual Review of Neurosciences, 11,* 199–223.

Hass, C.J., Garzarella, L., De Hoyos, D., & Pollock, M.L. (2000). Single versus multiple sets in long-term recreational weightlifters. *Medicine and Science in Sports and Exercise, 32,* 235–242.

Hather, B.M., Adams, G.R., Tesch, P.A., & Dudley, G.A. (1992). Skeletal muscle responses to lower limb suspension in humans. *Journal of Applied Physiology, 72,* 193–1498.

Hather, B.M., Tesch, P.A., Buchanan, P., & Dudley, G.A. (1991). Influence of eccentric actions on skeletal muscle adaptations to resistance training. *Acta Physiologica Scandinavica, 143,* 177–185.

Hatze, H. (1980). A mathematical model for the computational determination of parameter values of anthropomorphic segments. *Journal of Biomechanics, 13,* 833–843.

Hatze, H. (1981a). A comprehensive model for human motion simulation and its application to the take-off phase of the long jump. *Journal of Biomechanics, 14,* 135–141.

Hatze, H. (1981b). Estimation of myodynamic parameter values from observations on isometrically contracting muscle groups. *European Journal of Applied Physiology, 46,* 325–338.

Hatze, H. (1998). Validity and reliability of methods for testing vertical jumping performance. *Journal of Applied Biomechanics, 14,* 127–140.

Hatze, H. (2000). The inverse dynamics problem of neuromuscular control. *Biological Cybernetics, 82,* 133–141.

Hawk, L.W., & Cook, E.W. (1997). Affective modulation of tactile startle. *Psychophysiology, 34,* 23–31.

Hawkins, D., & Hull, M.L. (1990). A method for determining lower extremity muscle-tendon lengths during flexion/extension movements. *Journal of Biomechanics, 23,* 487–494.

Hay, J.G. (1993). *The biomechanics of sports techniques* (4th ed.). Englewood Cliffs, NJ: Prentice Hall.

Hay, J.G., Andrews, J.G., & Vaughan, C.L. (1980). The influence of external load on the joint torques exerted in a squat exercise. In J.M. Cooper & B. Haven (Eds.), *Proceedings of the Biomechanics Symposium* (pp. 286–293). Indiana University: Indiana State Board of Health.

Hay, J.G., Andrews, J.G., Vaughan, C.L., & Ueya, K. (1983). Load, speed and equipment effects in strength-training exercises. In H. Matsui & K. Kobayashi (Eds.), *Biomechanics VIII-B* (pp. 939–950). Champaign, IL: Human Kinetics.

Hay, J.G., Miller, J.A., & Cantera, R.W. (1986). The techniques of elite male long jumpers. *Journal of Biomechanics, 19,* 855–866.

Hay, J.G., Wilson, B.D., Dapena, J., & Woodworth, G.G. (1977). A computational technique to determine the angular momentum of the human body. *Journal of Biomechanics, 10,* 269–277.

Hay, L., Bard, C., Fleury, M., & Teasdale, N. (1996). Availability of visual and proprioceptive afferent messages and postural control in elderly adults. *Experimental Brain Research, 108,* 129–139.

He, S.Q., Dum, R.P., & Strick, P.L. (1993). Topographic organization of corticospinal projections from the frontal lobe: Motor areas on the lateral surface of the hemisphere. *Journal of Neurophysiology, 13,* 952–980.

Heckathorne, C.W., & Childress, D.S. (1981). Relationships of the surface electromyogram to the force, length, velocity, and contraction rate of the cineplastic human biceps. *American Journal of Physical Medicine, 60,* 1–19.

Heckman, C.J., & Binder, M.D. (1990). Neural mechanisms underlying the orderly recruitment of motoneurons. In M.D.

Binder & L.M. Mendell (Eds.), *The segmental motor system* (pp. 182–204). New York: Oxford University Press.

Heckman, C.J., & Binder, M.D. (1991). Computer simulation of the steady-state input-output function of the cat medial gastrocnemius motoneuron pool. *Journal of Neurophysiology, 65,* 952–967.

Henneman, E. (1957). Relation between size of neurons and their susceptibility to discharge. *Science, 126,* 1345–1347.

Henneman, E. (1979). Functional organization of motoneuron pools: The size-principle. In H. Asanuma & V.J. Wilson (Eds.), *Integration in the nervous system* (pp. 13–25). Tokyo: Igaku-Shoin.

Hennig, E.M., Cavanagh, P.R., Albert, H.T., & Macmillan, N.H. (1982). A piezoelectric method of measuring the vertical contact stress beneath the human foot. *Journal of Biomedical Engineering, 4,* 213–222.

Hennig, E.M., & Milani, T.L. (1995). In-shoe pressure distribution for running in various types of footwear. *Journal of Applied Biomechanics, 11,* 299–310.

Hennig, E.M., Valiant, G.A., & Liu, Q. (1996). Biomechanical variables and the perception of cushioning for running in various types of footwear. *Journal of Applied Biomechanics, 12,* 143–150.

Herbert, M.E., Roy, R.R., & Edgerton, V.R. (1988). Influence of one week of hindlimb suspension and intermittent high load exercise on rat muscles. *Experimental Neurology, 102,* 190–198.

Herbert, R.D., Dean, C., & Gandevia, S.C. (1998). Effects of real and imagined training on voluntary muscle activation during maximal isometric contractions. *Acta Physiologica Scandinavica, 163,* 361–368.

Herbert, R.D., & Gandevia, S.C. (1996). Muscle activation in unilateral and bilateral efforts assessed by motor nerve and cortical stimulation. *Journal of Applied Physiology, 80,* 1351–1356.

Hermansen, L., Hultman, E., & Saltin, B. (1967). Muscle glycogen during prolonged severe exercise. *Acta Physiologica Scandinavica, 71,* 129–139.

Hermens, H.J., v. Bruggen, T.A.M., Baten, C.T.M., Rutten, W.L.C., & Boom, H.B.K. (1992). The median frequency of the surface EMG power spectrum in relation to motor unit firing and action potential properties. *Journal of Electromyography and Kinesiology, 2,* 15–25.

Hernandez, C.J., Beaupré, G.S., & Carter, D.R. (2000). A model of mechanobiologic and metabolic influences on bone adaptation. *Journal of Rehabilitation Research and Development, 37,* 235–244.

Hershler, C., & Milner, M. (1980a). Angle-angle diagrams in above-knee amputee and cerebral palsy gait. *American Journal of Physical Medicine, 59,* 165–183.

Hershler, C., & Milner, M. (1980b). Angle-angle diagrams in the assessment of locomotion. *American Journal of Physical Medicine, 59,* 109–125.

Herzog, W. (1996). Force-sharing among synergistic muscles: Theoretical considerations and experimental approaches. *Exercise and Sport Sciences Reviews, 24,* 173–202.

Herzog, W. (1998). History dependence of force production in skeletal muscle: A proposal for mechanisms. *Journal of Electromyography and Kinesiology, 8,* 111–117.

Herzog, W., & Read, L.J. (1993). Lines of action and moment arms of the major force carrying structures that cross the human knee joint. *Journal of Anatomy, 182,* 213–230.

Hesselink, M.K.C., Kuipers, H., Guerten, P., & Van Straaten, H. (1996). Structural muscle damage and muscle strength after incremental number of isometric and forced lengthening contractions. *Journal of Muscle Research and Cell Motility, 17,* 335–341.

Hettinger, T. (1961). *Physiology of strength.* Springfield, IL: Charles C Thomas.

Heusler, E.J., Hepp-Reymond, M.C., & Dietz, V. (1998). Task-dependence of muscle synchronization in human hand muscles. *Neuroreport, 9,* 2167–2170.

Heyes, M.P., Garnett, E.S., & Coates, G. (1985). Central dopaminergic activity influences rats' ability to exercise. *Life Sciences, 36,* 671–677.

Heyes, M.P., Garnett, E.S., & Coates, G. (1988). Nigrostriatal dopaminergic activity is increased during exhaustive exercise stress in rats. *Life Sciences, 42,* 1537–1542.

Hicks, A.L., Cupido, C.M., Martin, J., & Dent, J. (1992). Muscle excitation in elderly adults: The effects of training. *Muscle & Nerve, 15,* 87–93.

Hicks, A., Fenton, J., Garner, S., & McComas, A.J. (1989). M wave potentiation during and after muscle activity. *Journal of Applied Physiology, 66,* 2606–2610.

Hicks, A., & McComas, A.J. (1989). Increased sodium pump activity following repetitive stimulation of rat soleus muscles. *Journal of Physiology, 414,* 337–349.

Hiebert, G.W., Whelan, R.J., Prochazka, A., & Pearson, K.G. (1996). Contribution of hind limb flexor muscle afferents to the timing of phase transitions in the cat step cycle. *Journal of Neurophysiology, 75,* 1126–1137.

Higbie, E.J., Cureton, K.J., Warren, G.L., & Prior, B.M. (1996). Effects of concentric and eccentric training on muscle strength, cross-sectional area, and neural activation. *Journal of Applied Physiology, 81,* 2173–2181.

Higgins, S. (1985). Movement as an emergent form: Its structural limits. *Human Movement Science, 4,* 119–148.

Hill, A.V. (1928). The air-resistance to a runner. *Proceedings of the Royal Society of London, B102,* 380–385.

Hill, A.V. (1938). The heat of shortening and the dynamic constraints of muscle. *Proceedings of the Royal Society of London, B126,* 136–195.

Hillegass, E.A., & Dudley, G.A. (1999). Surface electrical stimulation of skeletal muscle after spinal cord injury. *Spinal Cord, 37,* 251–257.

Hinrichs, R.N. (1987). Upper extremity function in running. II: Angular momentum considerations. *International Journal of Sport Biomechanics, 3,* 242–263.

Hinrichs, R.N., Cavanagh, P.R., & Williams, K.R. (1987). Upper extremity function in running. I: Center of mass and propulsion considerations. *International Journal of Sport Biomechanics, 3,* 222–241.

Hochman, S., & McCrea, D.A. (1994a). Effects of chronic spinalization on ankle extensor motoneurons. I. Composite Ia EPSPs in motoneurons separated into motor unit types. *Journal of Neurophysiology, 71,* 1480–1490.

Hochman, S., & McCrea, D.A. (1994b). Effects of chronic spinalization on ankle extensor motoneurons. I. Composite monosynaptic Ia EPSPs in four motoneuron pools. *Journal of Neurophysiology, 71,* 1452–1467.

Hochman, S., & McCrea, D.A. (1994c). Effects of chronic spinalization on ankle extensor motoneurons. II. Motoneuron electrical properties. *Journal of Neurophysiology, 71,* 1468–1479.

Hodges, P.W., & Gandevia, S.C. (2000). Changes in intra-abdominal pressure during postural and respiratory activation of the human diaphragm. *Journal of Applied Physiology, 89,* 967–976.

Hoehn-Saric, R., Hazlett, R.L., Pourmotabbed, T., & McLeod, D.R. (1997). Does muscle tension reflect arousal? Relationship between EMG and EEG recordings. *Psychiatry Research, 71,* 49–55.

Hof, A.L. (1984). EMG and muscle force: An introduction. *Human Movement Sciences, 3,* 119–153.

Hof, A.L. (1998). *In vivo* measurement of the series elasticity release curve of human triceps surae muscle. *Journal of Biomechanics, 31,* 793–800.

Hof, A.L., Pronk, C.N.A., & van Best, J.A. (1987). Comparison between EMG to force processing and kinetic analysis for the calf muscle moment in walking and stepping. *Journal of Biomechanics, 20,* 167–178.

Hof, A.L., & van den Berg, J.W. (1977). Linearity between the weighted sum of the EMGs of the human triceps surae and the total torque. *Journal of Biomechanics, 10,* 529–539.

Hof, A.L., & van den Berg, J. (1981a). EMG to force processing I: An electrical analogue of the Hill muscle model. *Journal of Biomechanics, 14,* 747–758.

Hof, A.L., & van den Berg, J. (1981b). EMG to force processing II: Estimation of parameters of the Hill muscle model for the human triceps surae by means of a calf ergometer. *Journal of Biomechanics, 14,* 759–770.

Hof, A.L., & van den Berg, J. (1981c). EMG to force processing III: Estimation of model parameters for the human triceps surae muscle and assessment of the accuracy by means of a torque plate. *Journal of Biomechanics, 14,* 771–785.

Hof, A.L., & van den Berg, J. (1981d). EMG to force processing IV: Eccentric-concentric contractions on a spring-flywheel setup. *Journal of Biomechanics, 14,* 787–792.

Hoffmann, P., Jonsdottir, I.H., & Thorén, P. (1996). Activation of different opioid systems by muscle activity and exercise. *News in Physiological Sciences, 11,* 223–228.

Hogan, N., & Flash, T. (1987). Moving gracefully: Quantitative theories of motor coordination. *Trends in Neuroscience, 10,* 170–174.

Högfors, C., Sigholm, G., & Herberts, P. (1987). Biomechanical model of the human shoulder—I. Elements. *Journal of Biomechanics, 20,* 157–166.

Hoh, J.F.Y. (1991). Myogenic regulation of mammalian skeletal muscle. *News in Physiological Sciences, 6,* 1–6.

Hoh, J.F.Y., & Hughes, S. (1988). Myogenic and neurogenic regulation of myosin gene expression in cat jaw-closing muscles regenerating in fast and slow limb muscles. *Journal of Muscle Research and Cell Motility, 9,* 57–72.

Hollerbach, J.M., & Flash, T. (1982). Dynamic interactions between limb segments during planar arm movement. *Biological Cybernetics, 44,* 67–77.

Holloszy, J.O., & Kohrt, W.M. (1995). Exercise. In E.J. Masoro (Ed.), *Handbook of physiology: Sec. 11. Aging* (pp. 633–666). New York: Oxford University Press.

Holst, E. von. (1954). Relations between the central nervous system and the peripheral organs. *British Journal of Animal Behavior, 2*, 89–94.

Hopper, B.J. (1973). *The mechanics of human movement.* New York: Elsevier.

Horak, F.B., & Macpherson, J.M. (1996). Postural orientation and equilibrium. In L.B. Rowell & J.T. Shepherd (Eds.), *Handbook of physiology: Sec. 12. Exercise: Regulation and integration of multiple systems* (pp. 255–292). New York: Oxford University Press.

Horak, F.B., Shupert, C.L., & Mirka, A. (1989). Components of postural dyscontrol in the elderly: A review. *Neurobiology of Aging, 10*, 727–738.

Horita, T., Kitamura, K., & Kohno, N. (1991). Body configuration and joint moment analysis during standing long jump in 6-yr-old children and adults males. *Medicine and Science in Sports and Exercise, 23*, 1068–1077.

Hortobágyi, T., Barrier, J., Beard, D., Braspennincx, J., Koens, P., DeVita, P., Dempsey, L., & Lambert, N.J. (1996). Greater initial adaptations to submaximal muscle lengthening than maximal shortening. *Journal of Applied Physiology, 81*, 1677–1682.

Hortobágyi, T., Dempsey, L., Fraser, D., Zheng, D., Hamilton, G., Lambert, J., & Dohm, L. (2000). Changes in muscle strength, muscle fibre size and myofibrillar gene expression after immobilization and retraining in humans. *Journal of Physiology, 524*, 293–304.

Hortobágyi, T., & DeVita, P. (2000). Muscle pre- and coactivity during downward stepping are associated with leg stiffness in aging. *Journal of Electromyography and Kinesiology, 10*, 117–126.

Hortobágyi, T., Hill, J.P., Houmard, J.A., Fraser, D.D., Lambert, N.J., & Israel, R.G. (1996). Adaptive responses to muscle lengthening and shortening in humans. *Journal of Applied Physiology, 80*, 765–772.

Hortobágyi, T., & Katch, F.I. (1990). Role of concentric force in limiting improvement in muscular strength. *Journal of Applied Physiology, 68*, 650–658.

Hortobágyi, T., Lambert, J.N., & Hill, J.P. (1997). Greater cross education following strength training with muscle lengthening than shortening. *Medicine and Science in Sports and Exercise, 29*, 107–112.

Hortobágyi, T., Scott, K., Lambert, J., Hamilton, G., & Tracy, J. (1999). Cross-education of muscle strength is greater with stimulated than voluntary contractions. *Motor Control, 3*, 205–219.

Houk, J.C. (1988). Control strategies in physiological systems. *Federation of American Societies for Experimental Biology Journal, 2*, 97–107.

Houk, J.C., & Rymer, W.Z. (1981). Neural control of muscle length and tension. In V.B. Brooks (Ed.), *Handbook of physiology: Sec. 1. The nervous system. Vol. II. Motor control* (Pt. 1, pp. 257–324). Bethesda, MD: American Physiological Society.

Houmard, J.A., Johns, R.A., Smith, L.L., Wells, J.M., Kobe, R.W., & McGoogan, S.A. (1991). The effect of warm-up on responses to intense exercise. *International Journal of Sports Medicine, 12*, 480–483.

Houmard, J.A., Weidner, M.L., Gavigan, K.E., Tyndall, G.L., Hickey, M.S., & Alshami, A. (1998). Fiber type and citrate synthase activity in the human gastrocnemius and vastus lateralis with aging. *Journal of Applied Physiology, 85*, 1337–1341.

Howard, J.D., & Enoka, R.M. (1991). Maximum bilateral contractions are modified by neurally mediated interlimb effects. *Journal of Applied Physiology, 70*, 306–316.

Howell, J.N., Chleboun, G., & Conaster, R. (1993). Muscle stiffness, strength loss, swelling and soreness following exercise-induced injury in humans. *Journal of Physiology, 464*, 183–196.

Howell, J.N., Fuglevand, A.J., Walsh, M.L., & Bigland-Ritchie, B. (1995). Motor unit activity during isometric and concentric-eccentric contractions of the human first dorsal interosseus muscle. *Journal of Neurophysiology, 74*, 901–904.

Hoy, M.G., Zajac, F.E., & Gordon, M.E. (1990). A musculoskeletal model of the human lower extremity: The effect of muscle, tendon, and moment arm on the moment-angle relationship of musculotendon actuators at the hip, knee, and ankle. *Journal of Biomechanics, 23*, 157–169.

Hoy, M.G., & Zernicke, R.F. (1986). The role of intersegmental dynamics during rapid limb oscillation. *Journal of Biomechanics, 19*, 867–879.

Hoy, M.G., Zernicke, R.J., & Smith, J.L. (1985). Contrasting roles of inertial and muscle moments at knee and ankle during paw-shake response. *Journal of Neurophysiology, 54*, 1282–1295.

Hoyle, G. (1983). *Muscles and their neural control.* New York: Wiley.

Hsieh, Y.-F., & Draganich, L.F. (1998). Increasing quadriceps loads affect the lengths of the ligaments and the kinematics of the knee. *Journal of Biomechanical Engineering, 120*, 750–756.

Hufschmidt, A., & Mauritz, K.-H. (1985). Chronic transformation of muscle in spasticity: A peripheral contribution to increased tone. *Journal of Neurology, Neurosurgery, and Psychiatry, 48*, 676–685.

Hubbard, M. (2000). The flight of sports projectiles. In V.M. Zatsiorsky (Ed.), *Biomechanics in Sport* (pp. 381–400). Oxford, UK: Blackwell Science.

Huijing, P.A. (1999). Muscle as a collagen fiber reinforced composite: A review of force transmission in muscle and whole limb. *Journal of Biomechanics, 32*, 329–345.

Huizar, P., Kuno, M., Kudo, N., & Miyata, Y. (1978). Reaction of intact spinal motoneurones to partial denervation of the muscle. *Journal of Physiology (London), 265*, 175–193.

Hulliger, M., Day, S.J., Guimaraes, A., Herzog, W., & Zhang, Y.T. (2001). A new method for experimental simulation of EMG using multi-channel independent stimulation of small groups of motor units. *Motor Control, 5*, 61-87.

Hultborn, H., Lindström, S., & Wigström, H. (1979). On the function of recurrent inhibition in the spinal cord. *Experimental Brain Research, 37*, 399–403.

Hultman, E., Bergström, M., Spriet, L.L., & Söderlund, K. (1990). Energy metabolism and fatigue. In A.W. Taylor, P.D. Gollnick, H.J. Green, C.D. Ianuzzo, E.G. Noble, G. Métivier, & J.R. Sutton (Eds.), *Biochemistry of exercise VII* (pp. 73–92). Champaign, IL: Human Kinetics.

Hultman, E., & Sjöholm, H. (1983). Electromyogram, force and relaxation time during and after continuous electrical stimulation of human skeletal muscle in situ. *Journal of Physiology (London), 339*, 33–40.

Hultman, E., Sjöholm, H., Jäderholm-Ek, I., & Krynicki, J. (1983). Evaluation of methods for electrical stimulation of human skeletal muscle in situ. *Pflügers Archive, 398,* 139–141.

Humphrey, D.R., & Reed, D.J. (1983). Separate cortical systems for control of joint movement and joint stiffness: Reciprocal activation and coactivation of antagonist muscles. *Advances in Neurology, 39,* 347–372.

Hunter, S., White, M., & Thompson, M. (1998). Techniques to evaluate elderly human muscle function: A physiological basis. *Journal of Gerontology, 53A,* B204–B216.

Hunter, S.K., Flagg, D.M., Fleshner, M., & Enoka, R.M. (2000). The endurance time of a submaximal fatiguing contraction is reliable for men and women. *Medicine and Science in Sports and Exercise, 32,* S184.

Hutton, R.S. (1984). Acute plasticity in spinal segmental pathways with use: Implications for training. In M. Kumamoto (Ed.), *Neural and mechanical control of movement* (pp. 90–112). Kyoto: Yamaguchi Shoten.

Hutton, R.S. (1992). Neuromuscular basis of stretching exercises. In P.V. Komi (Ed.), *Strength and power in sport* (pp. 29–38). Oxford: Blackwell Scientific.

Hutton, R.S., & Nelson, D.L. (1986). Stretch sensitivity of Golgi tendon organs in fatigued gastrocnemius muscle. *Medicine and Science in Sports and Exercise, 18,* 69–74.

Hutton, R.S., Smith, J.L., & Eldred, E. (1973). Postcontraction sensory discharge from muscle and its source. *Journal of Neurophysiology, 36,* 1090–1103.

Huxley, A.F. (1957). Muscle structure and theories of contraction. *Progress in Biophysics and Molecular Biology, 7,* 255–318.

Huxley, A.F. (2000). Mechanics and models of the myosin motor. *Philosophical Transactions of the Royal Society, B355,* 433–440.

Huxley, A.F., & Niedergerke, R. (1954). Structural changes in muscle during contraction. Interference microscopy of living muscle fibres. *Nature, 173,* 971–973.

Huxley, A.F., & Simmons, R.M. (1971). Proposed mechanism of force generation in striated muscle. *Nature, 233,* 533–538.

Huxley, H.E., & Hanson, J. (1954). Changes in cross-striations of muscle during contraction and stretch and their structural interpretation. *Nature, 173,* 973–976.

Ichinose, Y., Kawakami, Y., Ito, M., Kanehisa, H., & Fukunaga, T. (2000). In vivo estimation of contraction velocity of human vastus lateralis muscle during "isokinetic" action. *Journal of Applied Physiology, 88,* 851–856.

Ikai, M., & Steinhaus, A.H. (1961). Some factors modifying the expression of human strength. *Journal of Applied Physiology, 16,* 157–163.

Ikegawa, S., Finni, T., & Komi, P.V. (2000). Effect of pre-activation level on the force and length of muscle in eccentric actions. In J. Avela, P.V. Komi, & J. Komulainen (Eds.), *Proceedings of the 5th Annual Congress of the European College of Sport Science* (p. 342). Jyväskylä, Finland.

Iles, J.F. (1996). Evidence for cutaneous and corticospinal modulation of presynaptic inhibition of Ia afferents from the human lower limb. *Journal of Physiology, 491,* 197–207.

Imahori, Y., Fujii, R., Kondo, M., Ohmori, Y., & Nakajima, K. (1999). Neural features of recovery from CNS injury revealed by PET in human brain. *NeuroReport, 10,* 117–121.

Imms, F.J., Hackett, A.J., Prestidge, S.P., & Fox, R.H. (1977). Voluntary isometric muscle strength of patients undergoing rehabilitation following fractures of the lower limb. *Rheumatology and Rehabilitation, 16,* 162–171.

Imms, F.J., & MacDonald, I.C. (1978). Abnormalities of the gait occurring during recovery from fractures of the lower limb and their improvement during rehabilitation. *Scandinavian Journal of Rehabilitation Medicine, 10,* 193–199.

Ingalls, C.P., Warren, G.L., Williams, J.H., Ward, C.W., & Armstrong, R.B. (1998). E-C coupling failure in mouse EDL muscle after in vivo eccentric contractions. *Journal of Applied Physiology, 85,* 58–67.

Ingen Schenau, G.J. van (1990). On the action of bi-articular muscles, a review. *Netherlands Journal of Zoology, 40,* 521–540.

Ingen Schenau, G.J. van, Bobbert, M.F., & Haan, A. de. (1997). Does elastic energy enhance work and efficiency in the stretch-shortening cycle? *Journal of Applied Biomechanics, 13,* 389–415.

Ingen Schenau, G.J. van, Bobbert, M.F., Huijing, P.A., & Woittiez, R.D. (1985). The instantaneous torque-angular velocity relation in plantar flexion during jumping. *Medicine and Science in Sports and Exercise, 17,* 422–426.

Ingen Schenau, G.J. van, Bobbert, M.F., & Soest, A.J. van. (1990). The unique action of bi-articular muscles in leg extensions. In J.M. Winters & S.L-Y. Woo (Eds.), *Multiple muscle systems: Biomechanics and movement organization* (pp. 639–652). New York: Springer-Verlag.

Ingen Schenau, G.J. van, Boots, P.J.M., de Groot, G., Snackers, R.J., & Woenzel, W.W.L.M. (1992). The constrained control of force and position in multi-joint movements. *Neuroscience, 46,* 197–207.

Ingen Schenau, G.J. van, & Cavanagh, P.R. (1990). Power equations in endurance sports. *Journal of Biomechanics, 23,* 865–881.

Ingen Schenau, G.J. van, Woensel, W.W.L.M. van, Boots, P.J.M., Snackers, R.W., & de Groot, G. (1990). Determination and interpretation of mechanical power in human movement: Application to ergometer cycling. *European Journal of Applied Physiology, 61,* 11–19.

Ingjer, F., & Strømme, S.B. (1979). Effects of active, passive or no warm-up on the physiological response to heavy exercise. *European Journal of Applied Physiology, 40,* 273–282.

Inman, V.T., Ralston, H.J., Saunders, J.B. de C.M., Feinstein, B., & Wright, E.W. (1952). Relation of human electromyogram to muscular tension. *Electroencephalography and Clinical Neurophysiology, 4,* 187–194.

Iossifidou, A.N., & Baltzopoulos, V. (1998). Inertial effects on the assessment of performance in isokinetic dynamometry. *International Journal of Sports Medicine, 19,* 567–573.

Irving, M., & Piazzesi, G. (1997). Motions of the myosin heads that drive muscle contraction. *News in Physiological Sciences, 12,* 249–254.

Ishihara, A., Oishi, Y., Roy, R.R., & Edgerton, V.R. (1997). Influence of two weeks of non-weight bearing on rat soleus motoneurons and muscle fibers. *Aviation, Space, and Environmental Medicine, 68,* 421–425.

Ishijima, A., Kojima, H., Funatsu, T., Tokunaga, M., Higuchi, H., Tanaka, H., & Yanagida, T. (1998). Simultaneous observation of individual ATPase and mechanical events by a single myosin molecule during interaction with actin. *Cell, 92,* 161–171.

Issurin, V.B., Liebermann, D.G., & Tenenbaum, G. (1994). Effect of vibratory stimulation training on maximal force and flexibility. *Journal of Sports Sciences, 12,* 561–566.

Issurin, V.B., & Tenenbaum, G. (1999). Acute and residual effects of vibratory stimulation on explosive strength in elite and amateur athletes. *Journal of Sports Sciences, 17,* 177–182.

Ito, M., Kawakami, Y., Ichinose, Y., Fukashiro, S., & Fukunaga, T. (1998). Nonisometric behavior of fascicles during isometric contractions of a human muscle. *Journal of Applied Physiology, 85,* 1230–1235.

Iyengar, B.K.S. (1979). *Light on yoga.* New York: Schocken Books.

Izquierdo, M., Ibañez, J., Gorostiaga, E., Garrues, M., Zúñiga, A., Antón, A., Larrión, J.L., & Häkkinen, K. (1999). Maximal strength and power characteristics in isometric and dynamic actions of the upper and lower extremities in middle-aged and older men. *Acta Physiologica Scandinavica, 167,* 57–68.

Jackson, M.J., Jones, D.A., & Edwards, R.H.T. (1984). Experimental skeletal muscle damage: The nature of the calcium-activated degenerative processes. *European Journal of Clinical Investigation, 14,* 369–374.

Jacobs, B. (1994). Serotonin, motor activity, and depression-related disorders. *American Scientist, 82,* 456–463.

Jami, L., Murthy, K.S.K., Petit, J., & Zytnicki, D. (1983). Aftereffects of repetitive stimulation at low frequency on fast-contracting motor units of cat muscle. *Journal of Physiology (London), 340,* 129–143.

Jänkälä, H., Harjola, V.-P., Petersen, N.E., & Härkönen, M. (1997). Myosin heavy chain mRNA transform to faster isoforms in immobilized skeletal muscle: A quantitative PCR study. *Journal of Applied Physiology, 82,* 977–982.

Jankowska, E., & Odutola, A. (1980). Crossed and uncrossed synaptic actions on motoneurones of back muscles in the cat. *Brain Research, 194,* 65–78.

Jasmin, B.J., Lavoie, P.-A., & Gardiner, P.F. (1987). Fast axonal transport of acetylcholine in rat sciatic motoneurons is enhanced following prolonged daily running, but not following swimming. *Neuroscience Letters, 78,* 156–160.

Jenner, G., Foley, J.M., Cooper, T.G., Potchen, E.J., & Meyer, R.A. (1994). Changes in magnetic resonance images of muscle depend on exercise intensity and duration, not work. *Journal of Applied Physiology, 76,* 2119–2124.

Jensen, R.K., Doucet, S., & Treitz, T. (1996). Changes in segment mass and mass distribution during pregnancy. *Journal of Biomechanics, 29,* 251–256.

Jessell, T.M. (1991). Anatomy of the somatic sensory system. In E.R. Kandel, J.H. Schwartz, and T.M Jessell (Eds.), *Principles of Neural Science* (3rd ed., p. 259). New York: Elsevier.

Jiang, B., Roy, R.R., & Edgerton, V.R. (1990). Expression of a fast fiber enzyme profile in the cat soleus after spinalization. *Muscle & Nerve, 13,* 1037–1049.

Johansson, H., Sjölander, P., & Sojka, P. (1991). Receptors in the knee joint ligaments and their role in the biomechanics of the joint. *CRC Critical Reviews in Biomedical Engineering, 18,* 341–368.

Johansson, R.S. (1996). Sensory and memory information in the control of dextrous manipulation. In F. Lacquaniti & P. Viviani (Eds.), *Neural bases of motor behavior* (pp. 205–260). Netherlands: Kluwer Academic.

Johansson, R.S. (1998). Sensory input and control of grip. *Novartis Foundation Symposium, 218,* 45–59.

Johansson, R.S., Häger, C., & Bäckström, L. (1992). Somatosensory control of precision grip during unpredictable pulling loads. III. Impairments during digital anesthesia. *Experimental Brain Research, 89,* 204–213.

Johansson, R.S., Häger, C., & Riso, R. (1992). Somatosensory control of precision grip during unpredictable pulling loads. II. Changes in load force rate. *Experimental Brain Research, 89,* 192–203.

Johansson, R.S., Riso, R., Häger, C., & Bäckström, L. (1992). Somatosensory control of precision grip during unpredictable pulling loads. I. Changes in load force amplitude. *Experimental Brain Research, 89,* 181–191.

Jonas, D., Bischoff, C., & Conrad, B. (1999). Influence of different types of surface electrodes on amplitude, area and duration of the compound muscle action potential. *Clinical Neurophysiology, 110,* 2171–2175.

Jones, C., Allen, T., Talbot, J., Morgan, D.L., & Proske, U. (1997). Changes in the mechanical properties of human and amphibian muscle after eccentric exercise. *European Journal of Applied Physiology, 76,* 21–31.

Jones, D.A. (1993). How far can experiments in the laboratory explain the fatigue of athletes in the field? In A.J. Sargeant & D. Kernell (Eds.), *Neuromuscular fatigue* (pp. 100–108). Amsterdam: North-Holland.

Jones, D.A. (1996). High- and low-frequency fatigue revisited. *Acta Physiologica Scandinavica, 156,* 265–270.

Jones, D.A., & Round, J.M. (1997). Human muscle damage induced by eccentric exercise or reperfusion injury: A common mechanism? In S. Salmon (Ed.), *Muscle damage* (pp. 64–75). Oxford: Oxford University Press.

Jones, D.A., Rutherford, O.M., & Parker, D.F. (1989). Physiological changes in skeletal muscle as a result of strength training. *Quarterly Journal of Experimental Physiology, 74,* 233–256.

Jones, L.A. (1995). The senses of effort and force during fatiguing contractions. In S.C. Gandevia, R.M. Enoka, A.J. McComas, D.G. Stuart, & C.K. Thomas (Eds.), *Fatigue: Neural and muscular mechanisms* (pp. 305–313). New York: Plenum Press.

Jones, L.A., & Hunter, I.W. (1983). Effect of fatigue on force sensation. *Experimental Neurology, 81,* 640–650.

Jones, N.J., & Killian, K.J. (2000). Exercise limitation in health and disease. *New England Journal of Medicine, 343,* 632–641.

Jones, T.A., Chu, C.J., Grande, L.A., & Gregory, A.D. (1999). Motor skills training enhances lesion-induced structural plasticity in the motor cortex of adult rats. *Journal of Neuroscience, 19,* 10153–10163.

Josephson, R.K. (1985). Mechanical power output from striated muscle during cyclic contraction. *Journal of Experimental Biology, 114,* 493–512.

Josephson, R.K. (1993). Contraction dynamics and power output of skeletal muscle. *Annual Reviews in Physiology, 55,* 527–546.

Josephson, R.K. (1999). Dissecting muscle power. *Journal of Experimental Biology, 202,* 3369–3375.

Jovanovic, K., Petrov, T., Greer, J.J., & Stein, R.B. (1996). Serotonergic modulation of the mudpuppy (Necturus maculatus) locomotor pattern in vitro. *Experimental Brain Research, 111,* 57–67.

Joyce, G.C., Rack, P.M.H., & Westbury, D.R. (1969). The mechanical properties of cat soleus muscle during controlled lengthening and shortening movements. *Journal of Physiology, 204,* 461–474.

Kabbara, A.A., & Allen, D.G. (1999). The role of calcium stores in fatigue of isolated single muscle fibres from the cane toad. *Journal of Physiology, 519,* 169–176.

Kadhiresan, V.A., Hassett, C.A., & Faulkner, J.A. (1996). Properties of single motor units in medial gastrocnemius muscles of adult and old rats. *Journal of Physiology, 493,* 543–552.

Kagaya, H., Shimada, Y., Sato, K., & Sato, M. (1996). Changes in muscle force following therapeutic electrical stimulation in patients with complete paraplegia. *Paraplegia, 34,* 24–29.

Kakihana, W., & Suzuki, S. (in press). The EMG activity and mechanics of the running jump as a function of takeoff angle. *Journal of Electromyography and Kinesiology.*

Kakuda, N., & Nagaoka, M. (1998). Dynamic response of human muscle spindle afferents to stretch during voluntary contraction. *Journal of Physiology, 513,* 621–628.

Kalaska, J.F., & Crammond, D.J. (1992). Cerebral cortical mechanisms of reaching movements. *Science, 255,* 1517–1523.

Kamen, G., & DeLuca, C.J. (1989). Unusual motor unit firing behavior in older adults. *Brain Research, 482,* 136–140.

Kamen, G., & Roy, A. (2000). Motor unit synchronization in young and elderly adults. *European Journal of Applied Physiology, 81,* 403–410.

Kamen G., Sison S.V., Du C.C.D., & Patten, C. (1995). Motor unit discharge behavior in older adults during maximal-effort contractions. *Journal of Applied Physiology, 79,* 1908–1913.

Kanda, K., Burke, R.E., & Walmsley, B. (1977). Differential control of fast and slow twitch motor units in the decerebrate cat. *Experimental Brain Research, 29,* 57–74.

Kanda, K., & Hashizume, K. (1989). Changes in the properties of the rat medial gastrocnemius motor units in aging rats. *Journal of Neurophysiology, 61,* 737–746.

Kandarian, S.C., & White, T.P. (1990). Mechanical deficit persists during long-term muscle hypertrophy. *Journal of Applied Physiology, 69,* 861–867.

Kandarian, S.C., & Williams, J.H. (1993). Contractile properties of skinned fibers from hypertrophied muscle. *Medicine and Science in Sports and Exercise, 25,* 999–1004.

Kandel, E.R. (2000a). From nerve cells to cognition: The internal cellular representation required for perception and action. In E.R. Kandel, J.H. Schwartz, & T.M. Jessell (Eds.), *Principles of neural science* (4th ed., pp. 380–403). New York: McGraw-Hill.

Kandel, E.R. (2000b). Nerve cells and behavior. In E.R. Kandel, J.H. Schwartz, & T.M. Jessell (Eds.), *Principles of neural science* (4th ed., pp. 19–35). New York: McGraw-Hill.

Kandel, E.R., & Jessell, T.M. (1991). Touch. In E.R. Kandel, J.H. Schwartz, & T.M. Jessell (Eds.), *Principles of neural science* (3rd ed., pp. 367–384). New York: Elsevier.

Kandel, E.R., Schwartz, J.H., & Jessell, T.M. (Eds.) (1991). *Principles of neural sciences.* New York: Elsevier.

Kandel, E.R., & Siegelbaum, S. (1991). Directly gated transmission at the nerve-muscle synapse. In E.R. Kandel, J.H. Schwartz, & T.M. Jessell (Eds.), *Principles of neural science* (3rd ed., pp. 135–152). New York: Elsevier.

Kane, T.R., & Scher, M.P. (1969). A dynamical explanation of the falling cat phenomenon. *International Journal of Solids and Structures, 5,* 663–670.

Kanehisa, H., Ikegawa, S., & Fukunaga, T. (1994). Comparison of muscle cross-sectional area and strength between untrained women and men. *European Journal of Applied Physiology, 68,* 148–154.

Kannus, P., Parkkari, J., Koskinen, S., Niemi, S., Palvanen, M., Jarvinen, M., & Vuori, I. (1999). Fall-induced injuries and deaths among older individuals. *Journal of the American Medical Association, 281,* 1895–1899.

Kaplan, F.S., Hayes, W.C., Keaveny, T.M., Boskey, A., Einhorn, T.A., & Iannotti, J.P. (1994). Form and function of bone. In S.R. Simon (Ed.), *Orthopaedic basic science* (pp. 127–184). Park Ridge, IL: American Academy of Orthopaedic Surgeons.

Karst, G.M., & Hasan, Z. (1987). Antagonist muscle activity during human forearm movements under varying kinematic and loading conditions. *Experimental Brain Research, 67,* 391–401.

Katz, P.S. (1995). Intrinsic and extrinsic neuromodulation of motor circuits. *Current Opinion in Neurobiology, 5,* 799–808.

Katz, R., Mazzocchio, R., Penicaud, & Rossi, A. (1993). Distribution of recurrent inhibition in the human upper limb. *Acta Physiologica Scandinavica, 149,* 183–198.

Katz, R., Penicaud, A., & Rossi, A. (1991). Reciprocal Ia inhibition between elbow flexors and extensors in the human. *Journal of Physiology (London), 437,* 269–286.

Kaufman, K.R., An, K.-N., & Chao, E.Y.S. (1995). A comparison of intersegmental joint dynamics to isokinetic dynamometer measurements. *Journal of Biomechanics, 28,* 1243–1256.

Kaufman, M.P., Rybicki, K.J., Waldrop, T.G., & Ordway, G.A. (1983). Effect of ischemia on responses of group III and IV afferents to contraction. *Journal of Applied Physiology, 57,* 644–650.

Kawakami, Y., Abe, T., Kuno, S.Y., & Fukunaga, T. (1995). Training-induced changes in muscle architecture and specific tension. *European Journal of Applied Physiology, 72,* 37–43.

Kawakami, Y., & Lieber, R.L. (2000). Interaction between series compliance and sarcomere kinetics determines internal sarcomere shortening during fixed-end contraction. *Journal of Biomechanics, 33,* 1249–1255.

Kawakami, Y., Muraoka, T., Ito, S., Kanehisa, H., & Fukunaga, T. (2000). In vivo muscle-fiber behaviour reveal significant contribution of tendon elasticity in stretch-shortening cycle. *Medicine and Science in Sports and Exercise, 32,* S57.

Kawakami, Y., Nakazawa, K., Fujimoto, T., Nozaki, D., Miyashita, M., & Fukunaga, T. (1994). Specific tension of elbow flexor and extensor muscles based on magnetic resonance imaging. *European Journal of Applied Physiology, 68,* 139–147.

Kawato, M. (1999). Internal models of motor control and trajectory planning. *Current Opinion in Neurobiology, 9,* 718–727.

Kawato, M., Maeda, Y., Uno, Y., & Suzuki, R. (1990). Trajectory formation of arm movement by cascade neural network model based on minimum torque-change criterion. *Biological Cybernetics, 62,* 275–288.

Keen, D.A., Woodring, S.F., Schieber, M.H., & Fuglevand, A.J. (1998). Mechanical coupling of extensor digitorum communis motor units across digits of the human hand. *Society for Neuroscience Abstracts, 24,* 2110.

Keen, D.A., Yue, G.H., & Enoka, R.M. (1994). Training-related enhancement in the control of motor output in elderly humans. *Journal of Applied Physiology, 77,* 2648–2658.

Keller, A., Arissian, K., & Asanuma, H. (1992). Synaptic proliferation in the motor cortex of adult cats after long-term thalamic stimulation. *Journal of Neurophysiology, 68,* 295–308.

Kellis, E., & Baltzopoulos, V. (1995). Isokinetic eccentric exercise. *Sports Medicine, 19,* 202–222.

Kellis, E., & Baltzopoulos, V. (1998). Muscle activation differences between eccentric and concentric isokinetic exercise. *Medicine and Science in Sports and Exercise, 30,* 1616–1623.

Kelly, J.P. (1985). Reactions of neurons to injury. In E.R. Kandel & J.H. Schwartz (Eds.), *Principles of neural science* (2nd ed., pp. 187–195). New York: Elsevier.

Kent-Braun, J.A., & Le Blanc, R. (1996). Quantitation of central activation failure during maximal voluntary contractions in humans. *Muscle & Nerve, 19,* 861–869.

Kent-Braun, J.A., & Ng, A.V. (1999). Specific strength and voluntary muscle activation in young and elderly women and men. *Journal of Applied Physiology, 87,* 22–29.

Kern, H., Hofer, C., Strohhofer, M., Mayr, W., Richter, W., & Stohr, H. (1999). Standing up with denervated muscles in humans using functional electrical stimulation. *Artificial Organs, 23,* 447–452.

Kernell, D. (1992). Organized variability in the neuromuscular system: A survey of task-related adaptations. *Archives Italiennes de biologie, 130,* 19–66.

Kernell, D., Donselaar, Y., & Eerbeek, O. (1987). Effects of physiological amounts of high- and low-rate chronic stimulation on fast-twitch muscle of the cat hindlimb. II. Endurance-related properties. *Journal of Neurophysiology, 58,* 614–627.

Kernell, D., Eerbeek, O., & Verhey, B.A. (1983). Relation between isometric force and stimulus rate in cat's hindlimb motor units of different twitch contraction time. *Experimental Brain Research, 50,* 220–227.

Kernell, D., Eerbeek, O., Verhey, B.A., & Donselaar, Y. (1987). Effects of physiological amounts of high- and low-rate chronic stimulation on fast-twitch muscle of the cat hindlimb. I. Speed- and force-related properties. *Journal of Neurophysiology, 58,* 598–613.

Kernell, D., & Hultborn, H. (1990). Synaptic effects on recruitment gain: A mechanism of importance for the input-output relations of motoneurone pools? *Brain Research, 507,* 176–179.

Kernell, D., & Monster, A.W. (1982a). Motoneurone properties and motor fatigue. An intracellular study of gastrocnemius motoneurones of the cat. *Experimental Brain Research, 46,* 197–204.

Kernell, D., & Monster, A.W. (1982b). Time course and properties of late adaptation in spinal motoneurones of the cat. *Experimental Brain Research, 46,* 191–196.

Kiehn, O., Hounsgaard, J., & Sillar, K.T. (1997). Basic building blocks of vertebrate spinal central pattern generators. In P.S.G. Stein, S. Grillner, A.I. Selverston, & D.G. Stuart (Eds.), *Neurons, networks, and motor behavior* (pp. 47–59). Cambridge, MA: MIT Press.

Kiehn, O., & Kjaerulff, O. (1998). Distribution of central pattern generators for rhythmic motor outputs in the spinal cord of limbed vertebrates. *Annals of the New York Academy of Sciences, 860,* 110–129.

Kilbreath, S.L., & Gandevia, S.C. (1994). Limited independent flexion of the thumb and fingers in human subjects. *Journal of Physiology (London), 479,* 487–497.

Kilbreath, S.L., Raymond, J., Gorman, R.B., & Gandevia, S.C. (1998). Distribution of forces produced by single motor units in human flexor digitorum profundus. *Society for Neuroscience Abstracts, 24,* 672.

Kilgore, J.B., & Mobley, B.A. (1991). Additional force during stretch of single frog muscle fibres following tetanus. *Experimental Physiology, 76,* 579–588.

King, I. (1993). Plyometric training: In perspective. Part 2. *Science Periodical on Research and Technology in Sport, 13* (6). Coaching Association of Canada.

Kirkwood, P.A. (1989). On the use and interpretation of cross-correlation measurements in the mammalian central nervous system. *Journal of Neuroscience Methods, 1,* 107–132.

Kirkwood, P.A., & Sears, T.A. (1991). Cross-correlation analyses of motorneurone inputs in a coordinated motor act. In J. Krüger (Ed.), *Neuronal Cooperativity* (pp. 225–248). Berlin: Springer-Verlag.

Kirsch, R.F., Boskov, D., & Rymer, W.Z. (1994). Muscle stiffness during transient and continuous movements of cat muscle: Perturbation characteristics and physiological relevance. *IEEE Transactions on Biomedical Engineering, 41,* 758–770.

Kirsch, R.F., & Rymer, W.Z. (1987). Neural compensation for muscular fatigue: Evidence for significant force regulation in man. *Journal of Neurophysiology, 57,* 1893–1910.

Kirsch, R.F., & Rymer, W.Z. (1992). Neural compensation for fatigue-induced changes in muscle stiffness during perturbations of elbow angle in human. *Journal of Neurophysiology, 68,* 449–470.

Kirschbaum, C., & Hellhammer, D.H. (1994). Salivary cortisol in psychoneuroendocrine research: Recent developments and applications. *Psychoneuroendocrinology, 19,* 313–333.

Kitai, T.A., & Sale, D.G. (1989). Specificity of joint angle in isometric training. *European Journal of Applied Physiology, 58,* 744–748.

Kitamura, K., Tokunaga, M., Iwane, A.H., & Yanagida, T. (1999). A single myosin head moves along an actin filament with regular steps of 5.3 nanometres. *Nature, 397,* 129–134.

Klein, C., Fischer, B., Hartnegg, K., Heiss, W.H., & Roth, M. (2000). Optomotor and neuropsychological performance in old age. *Experimental Brain Research, 135,* 141–154.

Knott, M., & Voss, D.E. (1968). *Proprioceptive neuromuscular facilitation: Patterns and techniques* (2nd ed.). New York: Hoeber Medical Division, Harper & Row.

Koceja, D.M. (1995). Quadriceps mediated changes in soleus motoneuron excitability. *Electromyography and Clinical Neurophysiology, 35,* 25–30.

Koceja, D.M., & Kamen, G. (1991). Interactions in human quadriceps-triceps surae motoneuron pathways. *Experimental Brain Research, 86,* 433–439.

Koceja, D.M., & Raglin, J. (1992). Changes in neuromuscular characteristics during periods of overtraining and tapering. *Medicine and Science in Sports and Exercise, 24*(Suppl.), S80.

Koester, J. (1991). Membrane potential. In E.R. Kandel, J.H. Schwartz, & T.M. Jessell (Eds.), *Principles of neural science* (3rd ed., pp. 80–94). New York: Elsevier.

Koh, T.J., Grabiner, M.D., & Clough, C.A. (1993). Bilateral deficit is larger for step than for ramp isometric contractions. *Journal of Applied Physiology, 74,* 1200–1205.

Kohnstamm, O. (1915). Demonstration einer katatonieartigen Erscheinung beim esunden (Katatonusversuch). *Neurologisches Centralblatt, 34,* 290–291.

Komi, P.V. (1990). Relevance of *in vivo* force measurements to human biomechanics. *Journal of Biomechanics, 23*(Suppl.), 23–34.

Komi, P.V. (1992). Stretch-shortening cycle. In P.V. Komi (Ed.), *Strength and power in sport* (pp. 169–179). Champaign, IL: Human Kinetics.

Komi, P.V., Belli, A., Huttunen, V., Bonnefoy, R., Geyssant, A., & Lacour, J.R. (1996). Optic fibre as a transducer of tendomuscular forces. *European Journal of Applied Physiology, 72,* 278–280.

Komi, P.V., & Gollhofer, A. (1997). Stretch reflexes can have an important role in force enhancement during SSC exercise. *Journal of Applied Biomechanics, 13,* 451–460.

Komi, P.V., Linnamo, V., Silventoinen, P., & Sillanpää, M. (2000). Force and EMG power spectrum during eccentric and concentric actions. *Medicine and Science in Sports and Exercise, 32,* 1757–1762.

Komi, P.V., & Nicol. C. (2000). Stretch-shortening cycle of muscle function. In V.M. Zatsiorsky (Ed.), *Biomechanics in Sport* (pp. 87–102). Oxford, UK: Blackwell Science.

Komi, P.V., & Viitasalo, J.T. (1977). Changes in motor unit activity and metabolism in human skeletal muscle during and after repeated eccentric and concentric contractions. *Acta Physiologica Scandinavica, 100,* 246–254.

Komulainen, J., Koskinen, S.O.A., Kalliokoski, R., Takala, T.E.S., & Vihko, V. (1999). Gender differences in skeletal muscle fibre damage after eccentrically biased downhill running in rats. *Acta Physiologica Scandinavica, 165,* 57–63.

Konieczynski, D.D., Truty, M.J., & Biewener, A.A. (1998). Evaluation of a bone's in vivo 24-hour loading history for physical exercise compared with background loading. *Journal of Orthopaedic Research, 16,* 29–37.

Kornecki, S. (1992). Mechanism of muscular stabilization process in joints. *Journal of Biomechanics, 25,* 235–245.

Koshland, G.F., & Smith, J.L. (1989a). Mutable and immutable features of paw-shake responses after hindlimb deafferentation in the cat. *Journal of Neurophysiology, 62,* 162–173.

Koshland, G.F., & Smith, J.L. (1989b). Paw-shake responses with joint immobilization—EMG changes with atypical feedback. *Experimental Brain Research, 77,* 361–373.

Kossev, A., & Christova, P. (1998). Discharge pattern of human motor units during dynamic concentric and eccentric contractions. *Electroencephalography and Clinical Neurophysiology, 109,* 245–255.

Kossev, A.R., Siggelkow, S., Schubert, M., Wohlfarth, K., & Dengler, R. (1999). Muscle vibration: Different effects on transcranial magnetic and electrical stimulation. *Muscle & Nerve, 22,* 946–948.

Kots, J.M. (1971). Trenirovka mysecnoj sily metodom elektrostimuljacci. Soobscenie 1. Teoreticeshie predposylki. *Teoryai Praktika Fizicheskoi Kultury, 3,* 64–67.

Kouzaki, M., Shinohara, M., & Fukunaga, T. (2000). Decrease in maximal voluntary contraction by tonic vibration to a single synergist muscle in humans. *Journal of Applied Physiology, 89,* 1420–1424.

Kozhina, G.V., Person, R.S., Popov, K.E., Smetanin, B.N., & Shlikov, V.Y. (1996). Motor unit discharge during muscular after-contraction. *Journal of Electromyography and Kinesiology, 6,* 169–175.

Krakauer, J., & Ghez, C. (2000). Voluntary movement. In E.R. Kandel, J.H. Schwartz, & T.M. Jessell (Eds.), *Principles of neural science* (4th ed., pp. 756–781). New York: McGraw-Hill.

Kram, R. (2000). Muscular force or work: What determines the metabolic energy cost of running? *Exercise and Sport Sciences Reviews, 28,* 138–142.

Kram, R., Domingo, A., & Ferris, D.P. (1997). Effect of reduced gravity on the preferred walk-run transition speed. *Journal of Experimental Biology, 200,* 821–826.

Kram, R., & Taylor, C.R. (1990). Energetics of running: A new perspective. *Nature, 346,* 265–267.

Kranz, H., Williams, A.M., Cassell, J., Caddy, D.J., & Silberstein, R.B. (1983). Factors determining the frequency content of the electromyogram. *Journal of Applied Physiology, 55,* 392–399.

Krarup, C. (1981). Enhancement and diminution of mechanical tension evoked by staircase and by tetanus in rat muscle. *Journal of Physiology (London), 311,* 355–372.

Krnjevic, K., & Miledi, R. (1958). Failure of neuromuscular propagation in rats. *Journal of Physiology (London), 140,* 440–461.

Kubo, K., Kanehisa, H., Kawakami, Y., & Fukunaga, T. (2000). Elasticity of tendon structures of the lower limbs in sprinters. *Acta Physiologica Scandinavica, 168,* 327–335.

Kudina, L.P., & Alexeeva, N.L. (1992). After-potentials and control of repetitive firing in human motoneurones. *Electroencephalography and Clinical Neurophysiology, 85,* 345–353.

Kugelberg, E., & Lindegren, B. (1979). Transmission and contraction fatigue of rat motor units in relation to succinate dehydrogenase activity of motor unit fibres. *Journal of Physiology (London), 288,* 285–300.

Kugelberg, E., & Thornell, L.-E. (1983). Contraction time, histochemical type, and terminal cisternae volume of rat motor units. *Muscle & Nerve, 6,* 149–153.

Kukulka, C.G., & Clamann, H.P. (1981). Comparison of the recruitment and discharge properties of motor units in human brachial biceps and adductor pollicis during isometric contractions. *Brain Research, 219,* 45–55.

Kuno, M. (1964). Mechanism of facilitation and depression of the excitatory synaptic potential in spinal motoneurons. *Journal of Physiology (London), 175,* 100–112.

Kuno, S.-Y., Katsuta, S., Akisada, M., Anno, I., & Matsumoto, K. (1990). Effect of strength training on the relationship between magnetic resonance relaxation time and muscle fibre composition. *European Journal of Applied Physiology, 61,* 33–36.

Kuypers, H.G.J.M. (1985). The anatomical and functional organization of the motor system. In M. Swash & C. Kennard (Eds.), *Scientific basis of clinical neurology* (pp. 3–18). London: Churchill Livingstone.

Lacquaniti, F., Grasso, R., & Zago, M. (1999). Motor patterns in walking. *News in Physiological Sciences, 14,* 168–174.

Ladin, Z., & Wu, G. (1991). Combining position and acceleration measurements for joint force estimation. *Journal of Biomechanics, 24,* 1173–1187.

Laforest, S., St-Pierre, D.M.M., Cyr, J., & Guyton, D. (1990). Effects of age and regular exercise on muscle strength and endurance. *European Journal of Applied Physiology, 60,* 104–111.

Laidlaw, D.H., Bilodeau, M., & Enoka, R.M. (2000). Steadiness is reduced and motor unit discharge is more variable in old adults. *Muscle & Nerve, 23,* 600–612.

Laidlaw, D.H., Kornatz, K.W., Keen, D.A., Suzuki, S., & Enoka, R.M. (1999). Strength training improves the steadiness of slow lengthening contractions performed by old adults. *Journal of Applied Physiology, 87,* 1786–1795.

Lakatta, E.G. (1995). Cardiovascular system. In E.J. Masoro (Ed.), *Handbook of physiology: Sec. 11. Aging* (pp. 413–474). New York: Oxford University Press.

Lakie, M., & Robson, L.G. (1988a). Thixotropic changes in human muscle stiffness and the effects of fatigue. *Quarterly Journal of Experimental Physiology, 73,* 487–500.

Lakie, M., & Robson, L.G. (1988b). Thixotropy: The effect of stretch size in relaxed frog muscle. *Quarterly Journal of Experimental Physiology, 73,* 127–129.

Lakomy, H.K.A. (1987). Measurement of human power output in high intensity exercise. In B. Van Gheluwe & J. Atha (Eds.), *Current research in sport biomechanics* (pp. 46–57). Basel: Karger.

Lan, C., Lai, J-S., Chen, S-Y., & Wong, M-K. (1998). 12-month Tai Chi training in the elderly: Its effect on health fitness. *Medicine and Science in Sports and Exercise, 30,* 345–351.

Lance, J.W., Burke, D., & Andrews, C.J. (1973). The reflex effects of muscle vibration. In J.E. Desmedt (Ed.), *New developments in electromyography and clinical neurophysiology* (Vol. 3, pp. 444–462). Basel: Karger.

Lander, J.E., Bates, B.T., & DeVita, P. (1986). Biomechanics of the squat exercise using a modified center of mass bar. *Medicine and Science in Sports and Exercise, 18,* 468–478.

Lander, J.E., Hundley, J.R., & Simonton, R.L. (1992). The effectiveness of weight-belts during multiple repetitions of the squat exercise. *Medicine and Science in Sports and Exercise, 24,* 603–609.

Landis, C., & Hunt, W.A. (1939). *The startle pattern.* New York: Farrar and Rinehart.

Lännergren, J., & Westerblad, H. (1989). Maximum tension and force-velocity properties of fatigued, single *Xenopus* muscle fibres studied by caffeine and high K⁺. *Journal of Physiology (London), 409,* 473–490.

Lännergren, J., & Westerblad, H. (1991). Force decline due to fatigue and intracellular acidification in isolated fibres from mouse skeletal muscle. *Journal of Physiology (London), 434,* 307–322.

Lännergren, J., Westerblad, H., & Bruton, J.D. (1996). Slow recovery of force in single skeletal muscle fibres. *Acta Physiologica Scandinavica, 156,* 193–202.

Lanyon, L.E., & Rubin, C.T. (1984). Static vs dynamic loads as an influence on bone remodelling. *Journal of Biomechanics, 17,* 897–905.

Laouris, Y., Kalli-Laouri, J., & Schwartze, P. (1990). The postnatal development of the air-righting reaction in albino rats. Quantitative analysis of normal development and the effect of preventing neck-torso and torso-pelvis rotations. *Behavioral Brain Research, 37,* 37–44.

Larsson, L. (1983). Histochemical characteristics of human skeletal muscle during aging. *Acta Physiologica Scandinavica, 117,* 469–471.

Larsson, L., Li, X., Berg, H.E., & Frontera, W.R. (1996). Effects of removal of weight-bearing function on contractility and myosin isoform in single human skeletal muscle cells. *Pflügers Archive, 432,* 320–328.

Larsson, L., Li, X., & Frontera, W.R. (1997). Effects of aging on shortening velocity and myosin isoform composition in single human skeletal muscle cells. *American Journal of Physiology, 272,* C638–C649.

Latash, M.L. (1998). *Neurophysiological basis of movement.* Champaign, IL: Human Kinetics.

Lateva, Z.C., & McGill, K.C. (2001). Estimating motor-unit architectural properties by analyzing motor-unit action potential morphology. *Clinical Neurophysiology, 112,* 127–135.

Lauer, R.T., Peckham, P.H., & Kilgore, K.L. (1999). EEG-based control of a hand grasp neuroprosthesis. *NeuroReport, 10,* 1767–1771.

Laughman, R.K., Youdas, J.W., Garrett, T.R., & Chao, E.Y.S. (1983). Strength changes in the normal quadriceps femoris muscle as a result of electrical stimulation. *Physical Therapy, 63,* 494–499.

Lawrence, D.G., & Kuypers, H.G.J.M. (1968). The functional organization of the motor system in the monkey. II. The effects of lesions of the descending brain-stem pathways. *Brain, XCI,* 15–41.

Lawrence, J.H., & De Luca, C.J. (1983). Myoelectric signal versus force relationship in different human muscles. *Journal of Applied Physiology, 54,* 1653–1659.

Lawrence, J.H., Nichols, T.R., & English, A.W. (1993). Cat hindlimb muscles exert substantial torques outside the sagittal plane. *Journal of Neurophysiology, 69,* 282–285.

LeFever, R.S., & De Luca, C.J. (1982). A procedure for decomposing the myoelectric signal into its constituent action potential—Part I: Technique, theory, and implementation. *IEEE Transactions in Biomedical Engineering,* BME-29, 149–157.

LeFever, R.S., Xenakis, A.P., & De Luca, C.J. (1982). A procedure for decomposing the myoelectric signal into its constituent action potential—Part II: Execution and test for accuracy. *IEEE Transactions in Biomedical Engineering,* BME-29, 158–164.

Leijnse, J.N.A.L. (1997). Measuring force transfers in the deep flexors of the musician's hand: Theoretical analysis, clinical examples. *Journal of Biomechanics, 30,* 873–882.

Lennmarken, C., Bergman, T., Larsson, J., & Larsson, L.-E. (1985). Skeletal muscle function in man: Force, relaxation rate, endurance and contraction-time dependence on sex and age. *Clinical Physiology, 5,* 243–255.

Lesmes, G.R., Costill, D.L., Coyle, E.F., & Fink, W.J. (1978). Muscle strength and power changes during maximal isokinetic training. *Medicine and Science in Sports, 10,* 266–269.

Leterme, D., & Casasnovas, B. (1999). Adaptation of rat lateral gastrocnemius muscle motor units during hindlimb unloading. *European Journal of Applied Physiology, 79,* 312–317.

Leterme, D., & Falempin, M. (1996). Contractile properties of rat soleus motor units following 14 days of hindlimb unloading. *Pflügers Archive, 432,* 313–319.

Levin, M.F., & Hui-Chan, C.W.Y. (1992). Relief of hemiparetic spasticity by TENS is associated with improvement in reflex and voluntary motor functions. *Electroencephalography and Clinical Neurophysiology, 85,* 131–142.

Lexell, J., Downham, D.Y., Larsson, Y., Bruhn, E., & Morsing, B. (1995). Heavy-resistance training in older Scandinavian men and women: Short- and long-term effects on arm and leg muscles. *Scandinavian Journal of Medicine & Science in Sports, 5,* 329–341.

Lexell, J., & Taylor, C.C. (1991). Variability in muscle fibre areas in whole human quadriceps muscle: Effects of increasing age. *Journal of Anatomy, 174,* 239–249.

Li, C., & Atwater, A.E. (1984). *Temporal and kinematic analysis of arm motion in sprinters.* Paper presented at the Olympic Scientific Congress, Eugene, OR.

Li, Z.-M., Latash, M.L., & Zatsiorsky, V.M. (1998). Force sharing among fingers as a model of the redundancy problem. *Experimental Brain Research, 119,* 276–286.

Liao, H., & Belkoff, S.M. (1999). A failure model for ligaments. *Journal of Biomechanics, 32,* 183–188.

Liberson, W.T., Holmquest, H.J., Scot, D., & Dow, M. (1961). Functional electrotherapy: Stimulation of the peroneal nerve synchronized with the swing phase of the gait of hemiplegic patients. *Archives of Physical Medicine and Rehabilitation, 42,* 101–105.

Liddell, E.G.T., & Sherrington, C.S. (1925). Recruitment and some other factors of reflex inhibition. *Proceedings of the Royal Society of London, B97,* 488–518.

Lieber, R.L. (1992). *Skeletal muscle structure and function.* Baltimore: Williams & Wilkins.

Lieber, R.L., Fazeli, B.M., & Botte, M.J. (1990). Architecture of selected wrist flexor and extensor muscles. *Journal of Hand Surgery, 15A,* 244–250.

Lieber, R.L., & Fridén, J. (1997). Intraoperative measurement and biomechanical modeling of the flexor carpi ulnaris-to-extensor carpi radialis longus tendon transfer. *Journal of Biomechanical Engineering, 119,* 386–391.

Lieber, R.L., & Fridén, J. (1998). Musculoskeletal balance of the human wrist elucidated using intraoperative laser diffraction. *Journal of Electromyography and Kinesiology, 8,* 93–100.

Lieber, R.L., & Fridén, J. (2000). Functional and clinical significance of skeletal muscle architecture. *Muscle & Nerve, 23,* 1647–1666.

Lieber, R.L., Fridén, J.O., Hargens, A.R., Danzig, L.A., & Gershuni, D.H. (1988). Differential response of the dog quadriceps muscle to external skeletal fixation of the knee. *Muscle & Nerve, 11,* 193–201.

Lieber, R.L., & Kelly, M.J. (1991). Factors influencing quadriceps femoris muscle torque using transcutaneous neuromuscular electrical stimulation. *Physical Therapy, 71,* 715–723.

Lieber, R.L., Loren, G.J., & Fridén, J. (1994). In vivo measurement of human wrist extensor muscle sarcomere length changes. *Journal of Neurophysiology, 71,* 874–881.

Lieber, R.L., Schmitz, M.C., Mishra, D.V., & Fridén, J. (1994). Contractile and cellular remodeling in rabbit skeletal muscle after cyclic eccentric contractions. *Journal of Applied Physiology, 77,* 1926–1934.

Lieber, R.L., Silva, P.D., & Daniel, D.M. (1996). Equal effectiveness of electrical and volitional strength training for quadri-

ceps femoris muscles after anterior cruciate ligament surgery. *Journal of Orthopaedic Research, 14,* 131–138.

Lindstrom, B., Lexell, J., Gerdle, B., & Downham, D. (1997). Skeletal muscle fatigue and endurance in young and old men and women. *Journal of Gerontology, 52A,* B59–B66.

Linnamo, V., Bottas, R., & Komi, P.V. (2000). Force and EMG power spectrum during and after eccentric and concentric fatigue. *Journal of Electromyography and Kinesiology, 10,* 293–300.

Liu, R.H., Yamuy, J., Engelhardt, J.K., Xi, M.C., Morales, F.R., & Chase, M.H. (1996). Cell size and geometry of spinal cord motoneurons in the adult cat following the intramuscular injection of adriamycin: Comparison with data from aged cats. *Brain Research, 738,* 121–130.

Li Volsi, G., Lacata, F., Ciranna, L., Caserta, C., & Santangelo, F. (1998). Electromyographic effects of serotonin application into the lateral vestibular nucleus. *NeuroReport, 3,* 2539–2543.

Lloyd, A.R., Gandevia, S.C., & Hales, J.P. (1991). Muscle performance, voluntary activation, twitch properties and perceived effort in normal subjects and patients with chronic fatigue syndrome. *Brain, 114,* 85–98.

Lloyd, D.P.C. (1949). Post-tetanic potentiation of response in monosynaptic reflex pathways of the spinal cord. *Journal of General Physiology, 33,* 147–170.

Loeb, G.E., & Gans, C. (1986). *Electromyography for experimentalists.* Chicago: University of Chicago Press.

Loitz-Ramage, B.J., & Zernicke, R.F. (1996). Bone biology and mechanics. In J.E. Zachazewski, D.J. Magee, & W.S. Quillen (Eds.), *Athletic injuries and rehabilitation* (pp. 99–119). Philadelphia: Saunders.

Lombardi, V., & Piazzesi, G. (1990). The contractile response during lengthening of stimulated frog muscle fibres. *Journal of Physiology (London), 431,* 141–171.

Lømo, T., & Waerhaug, O. (1985). Motor endplates in fast and slow muscles of the rat: What determines their differences? *Journal of Physiology (Paris), 80,* 290–297.

Loren, G.J., & Lieber, R.L. (1995). Tendon biomechanical properties enhance human wrist muscle specialization. *Journal of Biomechanics, 28,* 791–799.

Loren, G.J., Shoemaker, S.D., Burkholder, T.J., Jacobson, M.D., Fridén, J., & Lieber, R.L. (1996). Influences of human wrist motor design on joint torque. *Journal of Biomechanics, 29,* 331–342.

Löscher, W.N., Cresswell, A.G., & Thorstensson, A. (1996a). Central fatigue during a long-lasting submaximal contraction of the triceps surae. *Experimental Brain Research, 108,* 305–314.

Löscher, W.N., Cresswell, A.G., & Thorstensson, A. (1996b). Recurrent inhibition of soleus ∝–motoneurons during a sustained submaximal plantar flexion. *Electroencephalography and Clinical Neurophysiology, 101,* 334–338.

Lotz, B.P., Dunne, J.W., & Daube, J.R. (1989). Preferential activation of muscle fibers with peripheral magnetic stimulation of the limb. *Muscle & Nerve, 12,* 636–639.

Lovely, R.G., Gregor, R.J., Roy, R.R., & Edgerton, V.R. (1990). Weight-bearing hindlimb stepping in treadmill-exercised adult spinal cats. *Brain Research, 514,* 206–218.

Lowey, S., Waller, G.S., & Trybus, K.M. (1993). Skeletal muscle myosin light chains are essential for physiological speeds of shortening. *Nature, 365,* 454–456.

Lowrie, M.B., & Vrbová, G. (1992). Dependence of postnatal motoneurones on their targets: Review and hypothesis. *Trends in Neurosciences, 15,* 80–84.

Lu, T.W., Taylor, S.J.G., O'Connor, J.J., & Walker, P.S. (1997). Influence of muscle activity on the forces in the femur: An in vivo study. *Journal of Biomechanics, 30,* 1101–1106.

Luhtanen, P. (1988). Kinematics and kinetics of serve in volleyball at different age levels. In G. de Groot, A.P. Hollander, P.A. Huijing, & G.J. van Ingen Schenau (Eds.), *Biomechanics XI-B* (pp. 815–819). Amsterdam: Free University Press.

Luthanen, P., & Komi, P.V. (1978). Mechanical factors influencing running speed. In E. Asmunssen & K. Jørgensen (Eds.), *Biomechanics VI-B* (pp.23–29). Baltimore: University Park Press.

Lund, J.P., Kolta, A., Westberg, K.-G., & Scott, G. (1998). Brainstem mechanisms underlying feeding behaviors. *Current Opinions in Neurobiology, 8,* 718–724.

Lusby, L.A., & Atwater, A.E. (1983). Speed-related position-time profiles of arm motion in trained women distance runners. *Medicine and Science in Sports and Exercise, 15,* 171.

Lüscher, H.-R., Ruenzel, P., & Henneman, E. (1979). How the size of motoneurones determines their susceptibility to discharge. *Nature, 282,* 859–861.

Lutz, G.J., & Lieber, R.L. (1999). Skeletal muscle myosin II structure and function. *Exercise and Sport Sciences Reviews, 27,* 63–77.

MacDougall, J.D., Webber, C.E., Martin, J., Ormerod, S., Chesley, A., Younglai, E.V., Gordon, C.L., & Blimkie, C.J.R. (1992). Relationship among running mileage, bone density, and serum testosterone in male runners. *Journal of Applied Physiology, 73,* 1165–1170.

Macefield, G., Hagbarth, K.-E., Gorman, R., Gandevia, S.C., & Burke, D. (1991). Decline in spindle support to ∝-motoneurones during sustained voluntary contractions. *Journal of Physiology (London), 440,* 497–512.

Macefield, V.G., Fuglevand, A.J., & Bigland-Ritchie, B. (1996). Contractile properties of single motor units in human toe extensors assessed by intraneural motor axon stimulation. *Journal of Neurophysiology, 75,* 2509–2519.

Macefield, V.G., Fuglevand, A.J., Howell, J.N., & Bigland-Ritchie, B. (2000). Discharge behavior of single motor units during maximal voluntary contractions of a human toe extensor. *Journal of Physiology, 528,* 227–234.

MacIntosh, B.R., Neptune, R.E., & Horton, J.F. (2000). Cadence, power, and muscle activation in cycle ergometry. *Medicine and Science in Sports and Exercise, 32,* 1281–1287.

MacIntosh, B.R., & Willis, J.C. (2000). Force-frequency relationship and potentiation in mammalian skeletal muscle. *Journal of Applied Physiology, 88,* 2088–2096.

Madsen, N., & McLaughlin, T. (1984). Kinematic factors influencing performance and injury risk in the bench press exercise. *Medicine and Science in Sports and Exercise, 16,* 376–381.

Magnus, R. (1922). Wie sich die fallende katze in der luft umdrecht. *Archives Neerlandaises de Physiologie de l'Homme et des Animaux, 7,* 218–222.

Magnusson, S.P. (1998). Passive properties of human skeletal muscle during stretch maneuvers. *Scandinavian Journal of Medicine & Science in Sports, 8,* 65–77.

Magnusson, S.P., Aagaard, P., Simonsen, E., & Bojsen-Møller, F. (1998). A biomechanical evaluation of cyclic and static stretch in human skeletal muscle. *International Journal of Sports Medicine, 19,* 310–316.

Magnusson, S.P., Simonsen, E.B., Aagaard, P., Dyhre-Poulsen, P., McHugh, M.P., & Kjær, M. (1996). Mechanical and physiological responses to stretching with and without preisometric contraction in human skeletal muscle. *Archives of Physical Medicine and Rehabilitation, 77,* 373–378.

Magnusson, S.P., Simonsen, E.B., Aagaard, P., Strensen, H., & Kjær, M. (1996). A mechanism for altered flexibility in human skeletal muscle. *Journal of Physiology, 497,* 291–298.

Magnusson, S.P., Simonsen, E.B., Dyhre-Poulsen, P., Aagaard, P., Mohr, T., & Kjær, M. (1996). Viscoelastic stress relaxation during static stretch in human skeletal muscle in the absence of EMG activity. *Scandinavian Journal of Medicine & Science in Sports, 6,* 323–328.

Malamud, J.G., Godt, R.E., & Nichols, T.R. (1996). Relationship between short-range stiffness and yielding in type-identified, chemically skinned muscle fibers from the cat triceps surae muscles. *Journal of Neurophysiology, 76,* 2280–2289.

Malm, C., Lenkel, R., & Sjödin, B. (1999). Effects of eccentric exercise on the immune system in men. *Journal of Applied Physiology, 86,* 461–468.

Mancini, D.M., Coyle, E., Coggan, A., Beltz, J., Ferraro, N., Montain, S., & Wilson, J.R. (1989). Contribution of intrinsic skeletal muscle changes to 31P NMR skeletal muscle metabolic abnormalities in patients with chronic heart failure. *Circulation, 80,* 1338–1346.

Mankin, H.J., Mow, V.C., Buckwalter, J.A., Iannotti, J.P., & Ratcliffe, A. (1994). Form and function of articular cartilage. In S.R. Simon (Ed.), *Orthopaedic basic science* (pp. 1–44). Park Ridge, IL: American Academy of Orthopaedic Surgeons.

Mann, R.V. (1981). A kinetic analysis of sprinting. *Medicine and Science in Sports and Exercise, 13,* 325–328.

Manter, J.T. (1938). The dynamics of quadrupedal walking. *Journal of Experimental Biology, 15,* 522–540.

Marder, E. (1998). From biophysics to models of network function. *Annual Reviews of Neuroscience, 21,* 25–45.

Maréchal, G., & Plaghki, L. (1979). The deficit of the isometric tetanic tension redeveloped after a release of frog muscle at a constant velocity. *Journal of General Physiology, 73,* 453–467.

Marey, E.-J. (1879). *Animal mechanism: A treatise on terrestrial and aerial locomotion.* New York: D. Appleton and Co.

Marey, E.J. (1894). Des mouvements que certains animaux executent pour retomber sur leurs pieds, lorsqu'ils sont precipites d'un lieu eleve. *Academie des Sciences, 119,* 714–718.

Margreth, A., Damiani, E., & Bortoloso, E. (1999). Sarcoplasmic reticulum in aged skeletal muscle. *Acta Physiologica Scandinavica, 167,* 331–338.

Marino, A.A. (1984). Electrical stimulation in orthopaedics: Past, present and future. *Journal of Bioelectricity, 3,* 235–244.

Marras, W.S., Joynt, R.L., & King, A.I. (1985). The force-velocity relation and intra-abdominal pressure during lifting activities. *Ergonomics, 28,* 603–613.

Marras, W.S., & Mirka, G.A. (1992). A comprehensive evaluation of trunk response to asymmetric trunk motion. *Spine, 17,* 318–326.

Marras, W.S., & Sommerich, C.M. (1991a). A three-dimensional motion model of loads on the lumbar spine: I. Model structure. *Human Factors, 33,* 123–137.

Marras, W.S., & Sommerich, C.M. (1991b). A three-dimensional motion model of loads on the lumbar spine: II. Model validation. *Human Factors, 33,* 139–149.

Marsden, C.D., & Meadows, J.C. (1970). The effect of adrenaline on the contraction of human muscle. *Journal of Physiology, 207,* 429–448.

Marsden, C.D., Meadows, J.C., & Merton, P.A. (1983). "Muscular wisdom" that minimized fatigue during prolonged effort in man: Peak rates of motoneuron discharge and slowing of discharge during fatigue. In J.E. Desmedt (Ed.), *Motor control mechanisms in health and disease* (pp. 169–211). New York: Raven Press.

Marsden, C.D., Merton, P.A., & Morton, H.B. (1976). Servo action in the human thumb. *Journal of Physiology (London), 257,* 1–44.

Marsden, C.D., Merton, P.A., & Morton, H.B. (1983). Rapid postural reactions to mechanical displacement of the hand in man. In J.E. Desmedt (Ed.), *Motor control mechanisms in health and disease* (pp. 645–659). New York: Raven Press.

Marsden, J.F., Farmer, S.F., Halliday, D.M., Rossenberg, J.R., & Brown, P. (1999). The unilateral and bilateral control of motor unit pairs in the first dorsal interosseous and paraspinal muscles in man. *Journal of Physiology, 521,* 553–564.

Marsh, E., Sale, D., McComas, A.J., & Quinlan, J. (1981). The influence of joint position on ankle dorsiflexion in humans. *Journal of Applied Physiology, 51,* 160–167.

Marsh, R.L. (1999). How muscles deal with real-world loads: The influence of length trajectory on muscle performance. *Journal of Experimental Biology, 202,* 3377–3385.

Martin, J.H., & Jessell, T.M. (1991). Anatomy of the somatic sensory system. In E.R. Kandel, J.H. Schwartz, & T.M. Jessell (Eds.), *Principles of neural science* (3rd ed., pp. 353–366). New York: Elsevier.

Martin, P.E., Mungiole, M., Marzke, M.W., & Longhill, J.M. (1989). The use of magnetic resonance imaging for measuring segment inertial properties. *Journal of Biomechanics, 22,* 367–376.

Martin, P.E., Sanderson, D.J., & Umberger, B.R. (2000). Factors affecting preferred rates of movement in cyclic activities. In V.M. Zatsiorsky (Ed.), *Biomechanics of Sport* (pp. 143–160). Oxford, UK: Blackwell Science.

Marvin, G., Sharma, A., Aston, W., Field, C., Kendall, M.J., & Jones, D.A. (1997). The effects of buspirone on perceived exertion and time to fatigue in man. *Experimental Physiology, 82,* 1057–1060.

Masakado, Y., Noda, Y., Nagata, M., Kimura, A., Chino, N., & Akaboshi, K. (1994). Macro-EMG and motor unit recruitment threshold: Differences between the young and aged. *Neuroscience Letters, 179,* 1–4.

Mathiassen, S.E., Winkel, J., & Hägg, G.M. (1995). Normalization of surface EMG amplitude from upper trapezius muscle in ergonomic studies—a review. *Journal of Electromyography and Kinesiology, 5,* 195–226.

Maton, B., & Gamet, D. (1989). The fatigability of two agonistic muscles in human isometric voluntary submaximal contraction: An EMG study. II. Motor unit firing rate and recruitment. *European Journal of Applied Physiology, 58,* 369–374.

Maton, B., Petitjean, M., & Cnockaert, J.C. (1990). Phonomyogram and electromyogram relationships with isometric force reinvestigated in man. *European Journal of Applied Physiology, 60,* 194–201.

Matsuo, A., Ozawa, H., Goda, K., & Fukunaga, T. (1995). Moment of inertia of whole body using an oscillating table in adolescent boys. *Journal of Biomechanics, 28,* 219–223.

Matthews, P.B.C. (1972). *Mammalian muscle receptors and their central actions.* Baltimore: Williams & Wilkins.

Matthews, P.B.C. (1987). Muscle sense. In G. Adelman (Ed.), *Encyclopedia of neuroscience* (Vol. II, pp. 720–721). Boston: Birkhäuser.

Matthews, P.B.C. (1990). The knee jerk: Still an enigma? *Canadian Journal of Physiology and Pharmacology, 68,* 347–354.

Matthews, P.B.C. (1991). The human stretch reflex and the motor cortex. *Trends in Neurosciences, 14,* 87–91.

Matyas, T.A., Galea, M.P., & Spicer, S.D. (1986). Facilitation of the maximum voluntary contraction in hemiplegia by concomitant cutaneous stimulation. *American Journal of Physical Medicine, 65,* 125–134.

Mayer, R.F., Burke, R.E., Toop, J., Hodgson, J.A., Kanda, K., & Walmsley, B. (1981). The effect of long-term immobilization on the motor unit population of the cat medial gastrocnemius muscle. *Neuroscience, 6,* 725–739.

McAuley, J.H., & Marsden, C.D. (2000). Physiological and pathological tremors and rhythmic central motor control. *Brain, 123,* 1545–1567.

McCall, G.E., Byrnes, W.C., Dickinson, A., Pattany, P.M., & Fleck, S.J. (1996). Muscle fiber hypertrophy, hyperplasia, and capillary density in college men after resistance training. *Journal of Applied Physiology, 81,* 2004–2012.

McCartney, N., Hicks, A.L., Martin, J., & Webber, C.E. (1996). A longitudinal trial of weight training in the elderly: Continued improvements in Year 2. *Journal of Gerontology, 51A,* B425–B433.

McCloskey, D.I. (1987). Kinesthesia, kinesthetic perception. In G. Adelman (Ed.), *Encyclopedia of neuroscience* (Vol. I, pp. 548–551). Boston: Birkhäuser.

McCloskey, D.I., Ebeling, P., & Goodwin, G.M. (1974). Estimation of weights and tensions and apparent involvement of a "sense of effort." *Experimental Neurology, 42,* 220–232.

McComas, A.J. (1991). Motor unit estimation: Methods, results, and present status. *Muscle & Nerve, 14,* 585–597.

McComas, A.J. (1995). Motor-unit estimation: The beginning. *Journal of Clinical Neurophysiology, 12,* 560–564.

McComas, A.J. (1996). *Skeletal muscle: Form and function.* Champaign, IL: Human Kinetics.

McComas, A.J. (1998). Motor units: How many, how large, what kind? *Journal of Electromyography and Kinesiology, 8,* 391–402.

McComas, A.J., Sica, R.E., Upton, A.R.M., & Aguilera, G.C. (1973). Functional changes in motoneurons of hemiparetic patients. *Journal of Neurology, Neurosurgery, and Psychiatry, 36,* 183–193.

McCrea, D.A., Shefchyk, S.J., Stephens, M.J., & Pearson, K.G. (1995). Disynaptic group I excitation of synergist ankle extensor motoneurones during fictive locomotion. *Journal of Physiology, 487*, 527–539.

McCully, K.K., & Faulkner, J.A. (1985). Injury to skeletal muscle fibers of mice following lengthening contractions. *Journal of Applied Physiology, 59*, 119–126.

McDonagh, M.J.N., & Davies, C.T.M. (1984). Adaptive response of mammalian skeletal muscle to exercise with high loads. *European Journal of Applied Physiology, 52*, 139–155.

McDonagh, M.J.N., Hayward, C.M., & Davies, C.T.M. (1983). Isometric training in human elbow flexor muscles: The effects on voluntary and electrically evoked forces. *Journal of Bone and Joint Surgery, 65B*, 355–358.

McDonald, K.S., & Fitts, R.H. (1995). Effect of hindlimb unloading on rat soleus fiber force, stiffness, and calcium sensitivity. *Journal of Applied Physiology, 79*, 1796–1802.

McGill, S.M., & Norman, R.W. (1993). Low back biomechanics in industry: The prevention of injury through safer lifting. In M.D. Grabiner (Ed.), *Current issues in biomechanics* (pp. 69–120). Champaign, IL: Human Kinetics.

McHugh, M.P., Kremenic, I.J., Fox, M.B., & Gleim, G.W. (1998). The role of mechanical and neural restraints to joint range of motion during passive stretch. *Medicine and Science in Sports and Exercise, 30*, 928–932.

McLaughlin, T.M., Dillman, C.J., & Lardner, T.J. (1977). A kinematic model of performance in the parallel squat by champion powerlifters. *Medicine and Science in Sports, 9*, 128–133.

McMahon, T.A., & Cheng, G.C. (1990). The mechanics of running: How does stiffness couple with speed? *Journal of Biomechanics, S1*, 65–78.

McMahon, T.A., Valiant, G., & Frederick, E.C. (1987). Groucho running. *Journal of Applied Physiology, 62*, 2326–2337.

McNulty, P.A., Falland, K.J., & Macefield, V.G. (2000). Comparison of contractile properties of single motor units in human intrinsic and extrinsic finger muscles. *Journal of Physiology, 526*, 445–456.

Melvill Jones, G. (2000). Posture. In E.R. Kandel, J.H. Schwartz, & T.M. Jessell (Eds.), *Principles of neural science* (4th ed., pp. 816–831). New York: McGraw-Hill.

Melvill-Jones, G., & Watt, D.G.D. (1971). Muscular control of landing from unexpected falls in man. *Journal of Physiology (London), 219*, 729–737.

Meriam, J.L., & Kraige, L.G. (1987). *Engineering mechanics.* New York: Wiley.

Merletti, R., Knaflitz, M., & De Luca, C.J. (1990). Myoelectric manifestations of fatigue in voluntary and electrically elicited contractions. *Journal of Applied Physiology, 69*, 1810–1820.

Merletti, R., & Lo Conte, L.R. (1997). Surface EMG signal processing during isometric contractions. *Journal of Electromyography and Kinesiology, 7*, 241–250.

Merletti, R., Rainoldi, A., & Farina, D. (2001). Surface EMG for the noninvasive characterization of muscle. *Exercise and Sport Sciences Reviews, 29*, 20–25.

Mero, A., & Komi, P.V. (1987). Electromyographic activity in sprinting at speeds ranging from sub-maximal to supra-maximal. *Medicine and Science in Sports and Exercise, 19*, 266–274.

Merton, P.A. (1953). Speculations on the servo-control of movement. In J.L. Malcolm & J.A.B. Gray (Eds.), *The spinal cord* (pp. 247–260). London: Churchill.

Merton, P.A. (1954). Voluntary strength and fatigue. *Journal of Physiology, 123*, 553–564.

Metter, E.J., Conwit, R., Tobin, J., & Fozard, J.L. (1997). Age-associated loss of power and strength in the upper extremities in women and men. *Journal of Gerontology, 52*, B267–B276.

Metzger, J.M., & Fitts, R.H. (1986). Fatigue from high- and low-frequency muscle stimulation: Role of sarcolemma action potentials. *Experimental Neurology, 93*, 320–333.

Meunier, S., Mogyoros, I., Kiernan, M.C., & Burke, D. (1996). Effects of femoral nerve stimulation on the electromyogram and reflex excitability of tibialis anterior and soleus. *Muscle & Nerve, 19*, 1110–1115.

Meunier, S., Pierrot-Deseilligny, E., & Simonetta, M. (1993). Pattern of monosynaptic heteronymous Ia connections in the human lower limb. *Experimental Brain Research, 96*, 534–544.

Meunier, S., Pierrot-Deseilligny, E., & Simonetta-Moreau, M. (1994). Pattern of heteronymous recurrent inhibition in the human lower limb. *Experimental Brain Research, 102*, 149–159.

Meyer, R.A., & Prior, B.M. (2000). Functional magnetic resonance imaging of muscle. *Exercise and Sport Sciences Reviews, 28*, 89–92.

Mikic, B., & Carter, D.R. (1995). Bone strain gage data and theoretical models of functional adaptation. *Journal of Biomechanics, 28*, 465–469.

Miles, T.S. (1999). Studies of stimulus-evoked responses in single motoneurones in humans. *Journal of Physiology (Paris), 93*, 61–69.

Miller, A.E.J., MacDougall, J.D., Tarnopolsky, M.A., & Sale, D.G. (1993). Gender differences in strength and muscle fiber characteristics. *European Journal of Applied Physiology, 66*, 254–262.

Miller, C., & Thépaut-Mathieu, C. (1993). Strength training by electrostimulation conditions for efficacy. *International Journal of Sports Medicine, 14*, 20–28.

Miller, D.I. (1976). A biomechanical analysis of the contribution of the trunk to standing vertical jump take-offs. In J. Broekhoff (Ed.), *Physical education, sports and the sciences* (pp. 355–374). Eugene, OR: Microform.

Miller, D.I. (1978). Biomechanics of running—what should the future hold? *Canadian Journal of Applied Sport Sciences, 3*, 229–236.

Miller, D.I. (1979). Modelling in biomechanics: An overview. *Medicine and Science in Sports, 11*, 115–122.

Miller, D.I. (1980). Body segment contributions to sport skill performance: Two contrasting approaches. *Research Quarterly for Exercise and Sport, 51*, 219–233.

Miller, D.I. (1981). *Biomechanics of Diving.* Report to the Canadian Amateur Diving Association.

Miller, D.I. (1990). Ground reaction forces in distance running. In P.R. Cavanagh (Ed.), *Biomechanics of distance running* (pp. 203–224). Champaign, IL: Human Kinetics.

Miller, D.I. (2000). Springboard and platform diving. In V.M. Zatsiorsky (Ed.), *Biomechanics in Sport* (pp. 326–348). Oxford, UK: Blackwell Science.

Miller, D.I., Enoka, R.M., McCulloch, R.G., Burgess, E.M., Hutton, R.S., & Frankel, V.H. (1979). *Biomechanical analysis of lower extremity amputee extra-ambulatory activities* (Contract No. V5244P-1540/VA). New York: Veterans Administration.

Miller, D.I., & Munro, C.F. (1984). Body segment contributions to height achieved during the flight of a springboard dive. *Medicine and Science in Sports and Exercise, 16,* 234–242.

Miller, D.I., & Munro, C.F. (1985). Greg Louganis' springboard takeoff: II. Linear and angular momentum considerations. *International Journal of Sport Biomechanics, 1,* 288–307.

Miller, D.I., & Nelson, R.C. (1973). *Biomechanics of sport.* London: Kimpton.

Miller, K.J., Garland, S.J., Ivanova, T., & Ohtsuki, T. (1996). Motor-unit behavior in humans during fatiguing arm movements. *Journal of Neurophysiology, 75,* 1629–1636.

Miller, R.G., Giannini, D., Milner-Brown, H.S., Layzer, R.B., Koretsky, A.P., Hooper, D., & Weiner, M.W. (1987). Effects of fatiguing exercise on high-energy phosphates, force, and EMG: Evidence for three phases of recovery. *Muscle & Nerve, 10,* 810–821.

Mills, K.R. (1991). Magnetic brain stimulation: A tool to explore the action of the motor cortex on single human spinal motoneurones. *Trends in Neuroscience, 14,* 401–405.

Milner-Brown, H., & Stein, R.B. (1975). The relation between the surface electromyogram and muscular force. *Journal of Physiology (London), 246,* 549–569.

Milner-Brown, H.S., & Miller, R.G. (1986). Muscle membrane excitation and impulse propagation velocity are reduced during muscle fatigue. *Muscle & Nerve, 9,* 367–374.

Milner-Brown, H.S., & Miller, R.G. (1989). Increased muscular fatigue in patients with neurogenic muscle weakness: Quantification and pathophysiology. *Archives of Physical Medicine and Rehabilitation, 70,* 361–366.

Milner-Brown, H.S., Stein, R.B., & Lee, R.G. (1975). Synchronization of human motor units: Possible roles of exercise and supraspinal reflexes. *Electroencephalography and Clinical Neurophysiology, 38,* 245–254.

Milner-Brown, H.S., Stein, R.B., & Yemm, R. (1973). The contractile properties of human motor units during voluntary isometric contractions. *Journal of Physiology (London), 228,* 285–306.

Mohr, T., Podenphant, J., Biering-Sorensen, F., Galbo, H., Thamsborg, G., & Kjær, M. (1997). Increased bone mineral density after prolonged electrically induced cycle training of paralyzed limbs in spinal cord injured man. *Calcified Tissue International, 61,* 22–25.

Mommersteeg, T.J.A., Huiskes, R., Blankevoort, L., Kooloos, J.G.M., & Kauer, J.M.G. (1997). An inverse dynamics modeling approach to determine the restraining function of human knee ligament bundles. *Journal of Biomechanics, 30,* 139–146.

Monster, A.W., & Chan, H.C. (1977). Isometric force production by motor units of extensor digitorum communis muscle in man. *Journal of Neurophysiology, 40,* 1432–1443.

Monster, A.W., Chan, H.C., & O'Connor, D. (1978). Activity patterns of human skeletal muscle: Relation to muscle fiber type composition. *Science, 200,* 314–317.

Monti, R.J., Roy, R.R., Hodgson, J.A., & Edgerton, V.R. (1999). Transmission of forces within mammalian skeletal muscles. *Journal of Biomechanics, 32,* 371–380.

Moore, J.C. (1975). Excitation overflow: An electromyographic investigation. *Archives of Physical Medicine and Rehabilitation, 56,* 115–120.

Moore, M.A., & Hutton, R.S. (1980). Electromyographic investigation of muscle stretching techniques. *Medicine and Science in Sports and Exercise, 12,* 322–329.

Moore, M.A., & Kukulka, C.G. (1991). Depression of Hoffmann reflexes following voluntary contraction and implications for proprioceptive neuromuscular facilitation therapy. *Physical Therapy, 71,* 321–333.

Morag, E., & Cavanagh, P.R. (1999). Structural and functional predictors of regional peak pressures under the foot during walking. *Journal of Biomechanics, 32,* 359–370.

Morasso, P. (1981). Spatial control of arm movements. *Experimental Brain Research, 42,* 223–237.

Moreno-Aranda, J., & Seireg, A. (1981a). Electrical parameters for over-the-skin muscle stimulation. *Journal of Biomechanics, 14,* 579–585.

Moreno-Aranda, J., & Seireg, A. (1981b). Force response to electrical stimulation of canine skeletal muscles. *Journal of Biomechanics, 14,* 595–599.

Moreno-Aranda, J., & Seireg, A. (1981c). Investigation of over-the-skin electrical stimulation parameters for different normal muscles and subjects. *Journal of Biomechanics, 14,* 587–593.

Morey, E.R. (1979). Spaceflight and bone turnover: Correlation with a new rat model of weightlessness. *Bioscience, 29,* 168–172.

Morgan, D.L. (1990). New insights into the behavior of muscle during active lengthening. *Biophysical Journal, 57,* 209–221.

Morgan, D.L., & Allen, D.G. (1999). Early events in stretch-induced muscle damage. *Journal of Applied Physiology, 87,* 2007–2015.

Moritani, T. (1992). Time course of adaptations during strength and power training. In P.V. Komi (Ed.), *Strength and power in sport* (pp. 266–278). Champaign. IL: Human Kinetics.

Morris, J.M., Lucas, D.B., & Bressler, B. (1961). Role of the trunk in stability of the spine. *Journal of Bone and Joint Surgery, 43A,* 327–351.

Morrissey, M.C., Harman, E.A., & Johnson, M.J. (1995). Resistance training modes: Specificity and effectiveness. *Medicine and Science in Sports and Exercise, 27,* 648–660.

Moss, B.M., Refsnes, P.E., Abildgaard, A., Nicolaysen, K., & Jensen, J. (1997). Effects of maximal effort strength training with different loads on dynamic strength, cross-sectional area, load-power and load-velocity relationships. *European Journal of Applied Physiology, 75,* 193–199.

Mow, V.C., Proctor, C.S., & Kelly, M.A. (1989). Biomechanics of articular cartilage. In M. Nordin & V.H. Frankel (Eds.), *Basic biomechanics of the musculoskeletal system* (pp. 31–58). Philadelphia: Lea & Febiger.

Müller, R.-A., Rothermel, R.D., Behen, M.E., Muzik, O., Chakraborty, P.K., & Chugani, H.T. (1997). Plasticity of motor organization in children and adults. *NeuroReport, 8,* 3103–3108.

Munro, C.F., Miller, D.I., & Fuglevand, A.J. (1987). Ground reaction forces in running: A reexamination. *Journal of Biomechanics, 20,* 147–155.

Munson, J.B., Foehring, R.C., Lofton, S.A., Zengel, J.E., & Sypert, G.W. (1986). Plasticity of medial gastrocnemius motor units following cordotomy in the cat. *Journal of Neurophysiology, 55,* 619–633.

Murray, W.M., Buchanan, T.S., & Delp, S.L. (2000). The isometric functional capacity of muscles that cross the elbow. *Journal of Biomechanics, 33,* 943–952.

Murray, W.M., Delp, S.L., & Buchanan, T.S. (1995). Variation of muscle moment arms with elbow and forearm position. *Journal of Biomechanics, 28,* 513–525.

Mynark, R.G., & Koceja, D.M. (1997). Comparison of soleus H-reflex gain from prone to standing in dancers and controls. *Electroencephalography and Clinical Neurophysiology, 105,* 135–140.

Nachemson, A.L., Andersson, G.B.J., & Schultz, A.B. (1986). Valsalva maneuver biomechanics. *Spine,* 11, 476–479.

Nakamura, E., Moritani, T., & Kanetaka, A. (1996). Effects of habitual physical exercise on physiological age in men aged 20-85 years as estimated using principal component analysis. *European Journal of Applied Physiology, 73,* 410–418.

Nakazawa, K., Kawakami, Y., Fukunaga, T., Yano, H., & Miyashita, M. (1993). Differences in activation patterns in elbow flexor muscles during isometric, concentric and eccentric contractions. *European Journal of Applied Physiology, 66,* 214–220.

Nardone, A., Romanò, C., & Schieppati, M. (1989). Selective recruitment of high-threshold human motor units during voluntary isotonic lengthening of active muscles. *Journal of Physiology, 409,* 451–471.

Nardone, A., & Schieppati, M. (1988). Shift of activity from slow to fast muscle during voluntary lengthening contractions of the triceps surae muscles in humans. *Journal of Physiology, 395,* 363–381.

Nardone, A., Siliotto, R., Grasso, M., & Schieppati, M. (1995). Influence of aging on leg muscle reflex responses to stance perturbation. *Archives of Physical Medicine and Rehabilitation, 76,* 158–165.

Narici, M. (1999). Human muscle skeletal architecture studied in vivo by non-invasive imaging techniques: Functional significance and applications. *Journal of Electromyography and Kinesiology, 9,* 97–103.

Narici, M.V., Bordini, M., & Cerretelli, P. (1991). Effect of aging on human adductor pollicis muscle function. *Journal of Applied Physiology, 71,* 1277–1281.

Narici, M.V., Hoppeler, H., Kayser, B., Landoni, L., Claassen, H., Gavardi, C., Conti, M., & Ceretelli, P. (1996). Human quadriceps cross-sectional area, torque and neural activation during 6 months strength training. *Acta Physiologica Scandinavica, 157,* 175–186.

Narici, M.V., Roi, G.S., & Landoni, L. (1988). Force of knee extensor and flexor muscles and cross-sectional area determined by nuclear magnetic resonance imaging. *European Journal of Applied Physiology, 57,* 39–44.

Narici, M.V., Roi, G.S., Landoni, L., Minetti, A.E., & Ceretelli, P. (1989). Changes in force, cross-sectional area and neural activation during strength training and detraining of the human quadriceps. *European Journal of Applied Physiology, 59,* 310–319.

Nashner, L.M. (1971). A model describing vestibular detection of body sway motion. *Acta Otolaryngology, 72,* 429–436.

Nashner, L.M. (1972). Vestibular postural control model. *Kybernetic, 10,* 106–110.

Nashner, L.M. (1976). Adapting reflexes controlling the human posture. *Experimental Brain Research, 26,* 59–72.

Nashner, L.M. (1977). Fixed patterns of rapid postural responses among leg muscles during stance. *Experimental Brain Research, 30,* 13–24.

Nashner, L.M. (1982). Adaptation of human movement to altered environments. *Trends in Neurosciences, 5,* 358–361.

Nelson, D.L., & Hutton, R.S. (1985). Dynamic and static stretch responses in muscle spindle receptors in fatigued muscle. *Medicine and Science in Sports and Exercise, 17,* 445–450.

Németh, G., & Ohlsén, H. (1986). Moment arm lengths of trunk muscles to the lumbosacral joint obtained in vivo with computed tomography. *Spine, 11,* 158–160.

Newham, D.J. (1988). The consequences of eccentric contractions and their relationship to delayed onset muscle pain. *European Journal of Applied Physiology, 57,* 353–359.

Newham, D.J., Jones, D.A., & Clarkson, P.M. (1987). Repeated high-force eccentric exercise: Effects on muscle pain and damage. *Journal of Applied Physiology, 63,* 1381–1386.

Nichols, T.R. (1994). A biomechanical perspective on spinal mechanisms of coordinated muscular action: An architectural principle. *Acta Anatomica, 151,* 1–13.

Nichols, T.R., Cope, T.C., & Abelew, T.A. (1999). Rapid spinal mechanisms of motor coordination. *Exercise and Sport Sciences Reviews, 27,* 255–284.

Nicks, D.K., Beneke, W.M., Key, R.M., & Timson, B.F. (1989). Muscle fibre size and number following immobilisation atrophy. *Journal of Anatomy, 163,* 1–5.

Nicol, C., & Komi, P.V. (1998). Significance of passively induced stretch reflexes on Achilles tendon force enhancement. *Muscle & Nerve, 21,* 1546–1548.

Nielsen, J., Crone, C., & Hultborn, H. (1993). H-reflexes are smaller in dancers from The Royal Danish Ballet than in well-trained athletes. *European Journal of Applied Physiology, 66,* 116–121.

Nielsen, J., Kagamihara, Y., Crone, C., & Hultborn, H. (1992). Central facilitation of Ia inhibition during tonic ankle dorsiflexion revealed after blockade of peripheral feedback. *Experimental Brain Research, 88,* 651–656.

Nielsen, J., & Pierrot-Deseilligny, E. (1996). Evidence of facilitation of soleus-coupled Renshaw cells during voluntary co-contraction of antagonistic ankle muscles in man. *Journal of Physiology, 493,* 603–611.

Nielsen, O.B., & Clausen, T. (2000). The Na$^+$/K$^+$-pump protects muscle excitability and contractility during exercise. *Exercise and Sport Sciences Reviews, 28,* 159–164.

Nielsen, O.B., & Harrison, A.P. (1998). The regulation of the Na$^+$,K$^+$ pump in contracting skeletal muscle. *Acta Physiologica Scandinavica, 162,* 191–200.

Nieuwenhuijzen, P.H.J.A., Schillings, A.M., Van Galen, G.P., & Duysens, J. (2000). Modulation of the startle response during human gait. *Journal of Neurophysiology, 84,* 65–74.

Nigg, B.M. (Ed.) (1986). *Biomechanics of running shoes.* Champaign, IL: Human Kinetics.

Nigg, B.M., & Herzog, W. (Eds.) (1994). *Biomechanics of the musculo-skeletal system.* New York: Wiley.

Nilsson, J., & Thorstensson, A. (1989). Ground reaction forces at different speeds of human walking and running. *Acta Physiologica Scandinavica, 136,* 217–228.

Nilsson, J., Thorstensson, A., & Halbertsma, J. (1985). Changes in leg movements and muscle activity with speed of locomotion and mode of progression in humans. *Acta Physiologica Scandinavica, 123,* 457–475.

Nishikawa, K., Murray, S.T., & Flanders, M. (1999). Do arm postures vary with speed of reaching? *Journal of Neurophysiology, 81,* 2582–2586.

Nissinen, M., Preiss, R., & Brüggemann, P. (1985). Simulation of human airborne movements on the horizontal bar. In D.A. Winter, R.W. Norman, R.P. Wells, K.C. Hayes, & A.E. Patla (Eds.), *Biomechanics IX-B* (pp. 373–376). Champaign, IL: Human Kinetics.

Nordstrom M.A., Enoka, R.M., Callister, R.J., Reinking, R.M., & Stuart, D.G. (1995). Effects of six weeks of limb immobilization on the cat tibialis posterior: 1. Motor units. *Journal of Applied Physiology, 78,* 901–913.

Nordstrom, M.A., Fuglevand, A.J., & Enoka, R.M. (1992). Estimating the strength of common input to motoneurons from the cross-correlogram. *Journal of Physiology (London), 453,* 547–574.

Nordstrom, M.A., & Miles, T.S. (1990). Fatigue of single motor units in human masseter. *Journal of Applied Physiology, 68,* 26–34.

Noreau, L., & Shephard, R.J. (1995). Spinal cord injury, exercise and quality of life. *Sports Medicine, 20,* 226–250.

Nøregaard, J., Lykkegaard, J.J., Bülow, P.M., & Danneskiold-Samsøe, B. (1997). The twitch interpolation technique for the estimation of true quadriceps muscle strength. *Clinical Physiology, 17,* 523–532.

Noteboom, J.T., & Enoka, R.M. (2000). Electrical shock increases physiological arousal and impairs motor performance. *Medicine and Science in Sports and Exercise, 32,* S282.

Noyes, F.R. (1977). Functional properties of knee ligaments and alterations induced by immobilization. *Clinical Orthopaedics and Related Research, 123,* 210–242.

Noyes, F.R., Butler, D.L., Grood, E.S., Zernicke, R.F., & Hefzy, M.S. (1984). Biomechanical analysis of human ligament grafts used in knee-ligament repairs and reconstructions. *Journal of Bone and Joint Surgery, 66-A,* 344–352.

Nussbaum, M.A., Chaffin, D.B., & Rechtien, C.J. (1995). Muscle lines-of-action affect predicted forces in optimization-based spine muscle modeling. *Journal of Biomechanics, 28,* 401–409.

Nygaard, E., Houston, M.E., Suzuki, Y., Jørgensen, K., & Saltin, B. (1983). Morphology of the brachial biceps muscle and elbow flexion in man. *Acta Physiologica Scandinavica, 117,* 287–292.

O'Brien, B., Payne, W., Gastin, P., & Burge, C. (1997). A comparison of active and passive warm ups on energy system contribution and performance in moderate heat. *Australian Journal of Science and Medicine in Sport, 29,* 106–109.

Ochs, S. (1987). Axoplasmic transport. In G. Adelman (Ed.), *Encyclopedia of neuroscience* (Vol. I, pp. 105–108). Boston: Birkhäuser.

O'Connor, P.J., & Cook, D.B. (1999). Exercise and pain: The neurobiology, measurement, and laboratory study of pain in relation to exercise in humans. *Exercise and Sport Sciences Reviews, 27,* 119–166.

O'Hagan, F.T., Sale, D.G., MacDougall, J.D., & Garner, S.H. (1995). Response to resistance training in young women and men. *International Journal of Sports Medicine, 16,* 313–321.

O'Hara, T.E., & Goshgarian, H.G. (1991). Quantitative assessment of phrenic nerve functional recovery mediated by the crossed phrenic reflex at various time intervals after spinal cord injury. *Experimental Neurology, 111,* 244–250.

Ohtsuki, T. (1983). Decrease in human voluntary isometric arm strength induced by simultaneous bilateral exertion. *Behavioural Brain Research, 7,* 165–178.

Oishi, Y., Ishihara, A., & Katsuta, S. (1992). Muscle fibre number following hindlimb immobilization. *Acta Physiological Scandinavica, 146,* 281–282.

Oishi, Y., Ishihara, A., Yamamoto, H., & Miyamoto, E. (1998). Hindlimb suspension induces the expression of multiple myosin heavy chain isoforms in single fibres of the rat soleus muscle. *Acta Physiologica Scandinavica, 162,* 127–134.

O'Leary, D.D., Hope, K., & Sale, D.G. (1997). Posttetanic potentiation of human dorsiflexors. *Journal of Applied Physiology, 83,* 2131–2138.

Orizio, C., Perini, R., Diemont, B., Figini, M.M., & Veicsteinas, A. (1990). Spectral analysis of muscular sound during isometric contraction of biceps brachii. *Journal of Applied Physiology, 68,* 508–512.

Orizio, C., Perini, R., & Veicsteinas, A. (1989). Changes in muscular sound during sustained isometric contraction up to exhaustion. *Journal of Applied Physiology, 66,* 1593–1598.

Oster, G. (1984). Muscle sounds. *Scientific American, 250,* 108–115.

O'Sullivan, M.C., Eyre, J.A., & Miller, S. (1991). Radiation of phasic stretch reflex in biceps brachii to muscles of the arm in man and its restriction during development. *Journal of Physiology, 439,* 529–543.

Otten, E. (1988). Concepts and models of functional architecture in skeletal muscle. *Exercise and Sport Sciences Reviews, 16,* 89–137.

Otter, M.W., McLeod, K.J., & Rubin, C.T. (1998). Effects of electromagnetic fields in experimental fracture repair. *Clinical Orthopedics, 355*(Suppl.), S90–S104.

Ouamer, M., Boiteux, M., Petitjean, M., Travens, L., & Salès, A. (1999). Acoustic myography during voluntary isometric contraction reveals non-propagative lateral vibration. *Journal of Biomechanics, 32,* 1279–1285.

Ounjian, M., Roy, R.R., Eldred, E., Garfinkel, A., Payne, J.R., Armstrong, A., Toga, A.W., & Edgerton, V.R. (1991). Physiological and developmental implications of motor unit anatomy. *Journal of Neurobiology, 22,* 547–559.

Owings, T.M., Pavol, M.J., Foley, K.T., & Grabiner, M.D. (2000). Measures of postural stability are not predictors of recovery from large postural disturbances in healthy older adults. *Journal of the American Geriatrics Society, 48,* 42–50.

Pacak, K., Palkovits, M., Yadid, G., Kvetnansky, R., Kopin, I.J., & Goldstein, D.S. (1998). Heterogeneous neurochemical responses to different stressors: A test of Selye's doctrine of nonspecificity. *American Journal of Physiology, 275,* R1247–R1255.

Pachter, B.R., & Eberstein, A. (1986). The effect of limb immobilization and stretch on the fine structure of the neuromuscular junction in rat muscle. *Experimental Neurology, 92,* 13–19.

Pai, Y.-C., Rogers, M.W., Patton, J., Cain, T.D., & Hanke, T.A. (1998). Static versus dynamic predictions of protective stepping following waist-pull perturbations in young and older adults. *Journal of Biomechanics, 31,* 1111–1118.

Palay, S.L., & Chan-Palay, V. (1987). Neuron. In G. Adelman (Ed.), *Encyclopedia of neuroscience* (Vol. II, pp. 812–815). Boston: Birkhäuser.

Palliyath, S., Hallett, M., Thomas, S.L., & Lebiedowska, M.K. (1998). Gait in patients with cerebellar ataxia. *Movement Disorders, 13,* 958–964.

Pancheri, P., & Biondi, M. (1990). Biological and psychological correlates of anxiety: The role of psychoendocrine reactivity as a marker of the anxiety response. In N. Sartorius (Ed.), *Anxiety: Psychobiological and clinical perspectives* (pp. 101–113). New York: Hemisphere Books.

Pandy, M.G., & Shelburne, K.B. (1997). Dependence of cruciate-ligament loading on muscle forces and external load. *Journal of Biomechanics, 30,* 1015–1024.

Panenic, R., & Gardiner, P.F. (1998). The case for adaptability of the neuromuscular junction to endurance exercise training. *Canadian Journal of Applied Physiology, 23,* 339–360.

Parkkola, R., Alanen, A., Kalimo, H., Lillsunde, I., Komu, M., & Kormano, M. (1993). MR relaxation times and fiber predominance of the psoas and multifidus muscle. *Acta Radiologica, 34,* 16–19.

Pasquet, B., Carpentier, S., Duchateau, J., & Hainaut, K. (2000). Muscle fatigue during concentric and eccentric contractions. *Muscle & Nerve, 23,* 1727–1735.

Patel, T.J., & Lieber, R.L. (1997). Force transmission in skeletal muscle: From actomyosin to external tendons. *Exercise and Sport Sciences Reviews, 25,* 321–363.

Patten, C., & Kamen, G. (2000). Adaptations in motor unit discharge activity with force control training in young and older human adults. *European Journal of Applied Physiology, 83,* 128–143.

Pawson, P.A., & Grinnell, A.D. (1990). Physiological differences between strong and weak frog neuromuscular junctions: A study involving tetanic and posttetanic potentiation. *Journal of Neuroscience, 10,* 1769–1778.

Pearson, K. (1993). Common principles of motor control in vertebrates and invertebrates. *Annual Reviews in Neuroscience, 16,* 265–297.

Pearson, K.G. (1995). Proprioceptive regulation of locomotion. *Current Opinion in Neurobiology, 5,* 786-791.

Pearson, K., & Gordon, J. (2000a). Locomotion. In E.R. Kandel, J.H. Schwartz, & T.M. Jessell (Eds.), *Principles of neural science* (4th ed., pp. 736–755). New York: McGraw-Hill.

Pearson, K., & Gordon, J. (2000b). Spinal reflexes. In E.R. Kandel, J.H. Schwartz, & T.M. Jessell (Eds.), *Principles of neural science* (4th ed., pp. 713–736). New York: McGraw-Hill.

Pearson, K.G., & Ramirez, J.-M. (1997). Sensory modulation of pattern-generating circuits. In P.S.G. Stein, S. Grillner, A.I. Selverston, & D.G. Stuart (Eds.), *Neurons, networks, and motor behavior* (pp. 225–235). Cambridge, MA: MIT Press.

Pepe, F.A. & Drucker, B. (1979). The myosin filament IV: Myosin content. *Journal of Molecular Biology, 130,* 379, 393.

Pereon, Y., Genet, R., & Guiheneuc, P. (1995). Facilitation of motor evoked potentials: Timing of Jendrassik maneuver effects. *Muscle & Nerve, 18,* 1427–1432.

Perl, E.R. (1957). Crossed reflexes of cutaneous origin. *American Journal of Physiology, 188,* 609–615.

Perry, J. (1993). Determinants of muscle function in the spastic lower extremity. *Clinical Orthopaedics and Related Research, 288,* 10–26.

Person, R.S. (1958). An electromyographic investigation on coordination of the activity of antagonist muscles in man during development of a motor habit. *Pavlov Journal of Higher Nervous Activity, 8,* 13–23.

Person, R.S. (1993). Spinal mechanisms of muscle contraction control. *Soviet Scientific Reviews, Section F. Physiology and General Biology Reviews, 6,* 1–83.

Person, R.S., & Kudina, L.P. (1972). Discharge frequency and discharge pattern of human motor units during voluntary contraction of muscle. *Electroencephalography and Clinical Neurophysiology, 32,* 471–483.

Peters, E.J.D., & Fuglevand, A.J. (1999). Cessation of human motor unit discharge during sustained maximal voluntary contraction. *Neuroscience Letters, 274,* 66–70.

Peters, S.E. (1989). Structure and function in vertebrate skeletal muscle. *American Zoologist, 29,* 221–234.

Petit, J., & Gioux, M. (1993). Properties of motor units after immobilization of cat peroneus longus muscle. *Journal of Applied Physiology, 74,* 1131–1139.

Petit, J., Scott, J.J.A., & Reynolds, K.J. (1997). Tendon organ sensitivity to steady-state isotonic contraction of in-series motor units in feline peroneus tertius muscle. *Journal of Physiology, 500,* 227–233.

Petrof, B.J., Shrager, J.B., Stedman, H.H., Kelly, A.M., & Sweeney, H.L. (1993). Dystrophin protects the sarcolemma from stresses developed during muscle contraction. *Proceedings of the National Academy of Sciences, 90,* 3710–3714.

Petrofsky, J.S., & Hendershot, D.M. (1984). The interrelationship between blood pressure, intramuscular pressure, and isometric endurance in fast and slow twitch skeletal muscle in the cat. *European Journal of Applied Physiology, 53,* 106–111.

Petrofsky, J.S., & Stacy, R. (1992). The effect of training on endurance and the cardiovascular responses of individuals with paraplegia during dynamic exercise induced by functional electrical stimulation. *European Journal of Applied Physiology, 64,* 487–492.

Pette, D., Peuker, H., & Staron, R.S. (1999). The impact of biochemical methods for single muscle fibre analysis. *Acta Physiologica Scandinavica, 166,* 261–277.

Pette, D., & Vrbová, G. (1992). Adaptation of mammalian skeletal muscle to chronic electrical stimulation. *Reviews of Physiology, Biochemistry, and Pharmacology, 120,* 115–202.

Pette, D., & Vrbová, G. (1999). What does chronic electrical stimulation teach us about muscle plasticity? *Muscle & Nerve, 22,* 666–677.

Phillips, C.G. (1986). *Movements of the hand.* Liverpool: Liverpool University Press.

Phillips, S.J., & Roberts, E.M. (1980). Muscular and non-muscular moments of force in the swing limb of Masters runners. In J.M. Cooper & B. Haven (Eds.), *Proceedings of the Biomechanics Symposium* (pp. 256–274). Bloomington, IN: Indiana State Board of Health.

Phillips, S.J., Roberts, E.M., & Huang, T.C. (1983). Quantification of intersegmental reactions during rapid swing motion. *Journal of Biomechanics, 16,* 411–418.

Piazza, S.J., & Delp, S.L. (1996). The influence of muscles on knee flexion during the swing phase of gait. *Journal of Biomechanics, 29,* 723–733.

Piazzesi, G., Reconditi, M., Dobbie, I., Linari, M., Boesecke, P., Diat, O., Irving, M., & Lombardi, V. (1999). Changes in conformation of myosin heads during the development of isometric contraction and rapid shortening in single frog muscle fibres. *Journal of Physiology, 514,* 305–312.

Pierotti, D.J., Roy, R.R., Hodgson, J.A., & Edgerton, V.R. (1994). Level of independence of motor unit properties from neuromuscular activity. *Muscle & Nerve, 17,* 1324–1335.

Pigeon, P., Yahia, H., & Feldman, A.G. (1996). Moment arms and lengths of human upper limb muscles as functions of joint angles. *Journal of Biomechanics, 29,* 1365–1370.

Pinder, A.D.J., & Grieve, D.W. (1997). Hydro-resistive measurement of dynamic lifting strength. *Journal of Biomechanics, 30,* 399–402.

Pitman, M.I., & Peterson, L. (1989). Biomechanics of skeletal muscle. In M. Nordin & V.H. Frankel (Eds.), *Basic biomechanics of the musculoskeletal system* (pp. 89–111). Philadelphia: Lea & Febiger.

Ploutz, L.L., Tesch, P.A., Biro, R.L., & Dudley, G.A. (1994). Effect of resistance training on muscle use during exercise. *Journal of Applied Physiology, 76,* 1675–1681.

Ploutz-Snyder, L.L., Tesch, P.A., Crittenden, D.J., & Dudley, G.A. (1995). Effect of unweighting on skeletal muscle use during exercise. *Journal of Applied Physiology, 79,* 168–175.

Polcyn, A.F., Lipsitz, L.A., Kerrigan, C., & Collins, J.J. (1998). Age-related changes in the initiation of gait: Degradation of central mechanisms for momentum generation. *Archives of Physical Medicine and Rehabilitation, 79,* 1582–1589.

Pope, R.P., Herbert, R.D., Kirwan, J.D., & Graham, B.J. (2000). A randomized trial of preexercise stretching for prevention of lower limb injury. *Medicine and Science in Sports and Exercise, 32,* 271–277.

Porter, M.M., Vandervoort, A.A., & Lexell, J. (1995). Aging of human muscle: Structure, function and adaptability. *Scandinavian Journal of Medicine & Science in Sports, 5,* 129–142.

Powers, R.K., Marder-Meyer, J., & Rymer, W.Z. (1989). Quantitative relations between hypertonia and stretch reflex threshold in spastic hemiparesis. *Annals of Neurology, 23,* 115–124.

Pratt, C. (1995). Evidence of positive force feedback among hindlimb extensors in the intact standing cat. *Journal of Neurophysiology, 73,* 2578–2583.

Prilutsky, B.I. (2000). Eccentric muscle action in sport exercise. In V.M. Zatsiorsky (Ed.), *Biomechanics in Sport* (pp. 56–86). Oxford, UK: Blackwell Science.

Prilutsky, B.I., Herzog, W., Leonard, T.R., & Allinger, T.L. (1996). Role of the muscle belly and tendon of soleus, gastrocnemius, and plantaris in mechanical energy absorption and generation during cat locomotion. *Journal of Biomechanics, 29,* 417–434.

Prilutsky, B.I., Petrova, L.N., & Raitsin, L.M. (1996). Comparison of mechanical energy expenditure of joint moments and muscle forces during human locomotion. *Journal of Biomechanics, 29,* 405–415.

Prilutsky, B.I., & Zatsiorsky, V.M. (1994). Tendon action of two-joint muscles: Transfer of mechanical energy between joints during jumping, landing, and running. *Journal of Biomechanics, 27,* 25–34.

Prior, B.M., Foley, J.M., Jayaraman, R.C., & Meyer, R.A. (1999). Pixel T2 distribution in functional magnetic resonance images of muscle. *Journal of Applied Physiology, 87,* 2107–2114.

Prochazka, A. (1989). Sensorimotor gain control: A basic strategy of motor systems? *Progress in Neurobiology, 33,* 281–307.

Prochazka, A. (1996). Proprioceptive feedback and movement regulation. In L.B. Rowell & J.T. Shepherd (Eds.), *Handbook of physiology: Sec. 12. Exercise: Regulation and integration of multiple systems* (pp. 89–127). New York: Oxford University Press.

Prochazka, A., Clarac, F., Loeb, G.E., Rothwell, J.C., & Wolpaw, J.R. (2000). What do reflex and voluntary mean? Modern views on an ancient debate. *Experimental Brain Research, 130,* 417–432.

Prochazka, A., Gillard, D., & Bennett, D.J. (1997). Positive force feedback control of muscles. *Journal of Neurophysiology, 77,* 3226–3236.

Proctor, D.N., Sinning, W.E., Walro, J.M., Sieck, G.C., & Lemon, P.W.R. (1995). Oxidative capacity of human muscle fiber types: Effects of age and training status. *Journal of Applied Physiology, 78,* 2033–2038.

Proske, U. (1997). The mammalian muscle spindle. *News in Physiological Sciences, 12,* 37–42.

Proske, U., Morgan, D.L., & Gregory, J.E. (1993). Thixotropy in skeletal muscle and in muscle spindles: A review. *Progress in Neurobiology, 41,* 705–721.

Proske, U., Wise, A.K., & Gregroy, J.E. (2000). The role of muscle receptors in the detection of movements. *Progress in Neurobiology, 60,* 85–96.

Psek, J.A., & Cafarelli, E. (1993). Behavior of coactive muscles during fatigue. *Journal of Applied Physiology, 74,* 170–175.

Putnam, C.A. (1983). Interaction between segments during a kicking motion. In H. Matsui & K. Kobayashi (Eds.), *Biomechanics VIII-B* (pp. 688–694). Champaign, IL: Human Kinetics.

Putnam, C.A. (1991). A segment interaction analysis of proximal-to-distal sequential segment motion patterns. *Medicine and Science in Sports and Exercise, 23,* 130–144.

Rab, G.T., Chao, E.Y. S., & Stauffer, R.N. (1977). Muscle force analysis of the lumbar spine. *Orthopedic Clinics of North America, 8,* 193–199.

Rack, P.M.H., & Westbury, D.R. (1969). The effects of length and stimulus rate on tension in the isometric cat soleus muscle. *Journal of Physiology (London), 204,* 443–460.

Rack, P.M.H., & Westbury, D.R. (1974). The short range stiffness of active mammalian muscle and its effect on mechanical properties. *Journal of Physiology (London), 240,* 331–350.

Rácz, L., Tihanyi, J., & Hortobágyi, T. (2000). Muscle fatigue during concentric and eccentric contraction. In J. Avela, P.V. Komi, & J. Komulainen (Eds.), *Proceedings of the 5th Annual Congress of the European College of Sport Science* (p. 600). Jyväskylä, Finland.

Rafuse, V.F., & Gordon, T. (1996). Self-reinnervated cat medial gastrocnemius muscles. I. Comparisons of the capacity for regenerating nerves to form enlarged motor units after extensive peripheral nerve injuries. *Journal of Neurophysiology, 75,* 268–281.

Rafuse, V.F., & Gordon, T. (1998). Incomplete matching of nerve and muscle properties in motor units after extensive nerve injuries in cat hindlimb muscle. *Journal of Physiology, 509,* 909–926.

Rafuse, V.F., Gordon, T., & Orozco, R. (1992). Proportional enlargement of motor units after partial denervation of cat triceps surae muscles. *Journal of Neurophysiology, 68,* 1261–1276.

Raglin, J.S. (1992). Anxiety and sport performance. *Exercise and Sport Sciences Reviews, 20,* 243–274.

Rall, W. (1987). Neuron, cable properties. In G. Adelman (Ed.), *Encyclopedia of neuroscience* (Vol. II, pp. 816–820). Boston: Birkhäuser.

Ralston, H.J., Inman, V.T., Strait, L.A., & Shaffrath, M.D. (1947). Mechanics of human isolated voluntary muscle. *American Journal of Physiology, 151,* 612–620.

Ranatunga, K.W., Sharpe, B., & Turnbull, B. (1987). Contractions of a human skeletal muscle at different temperatures. *Journal of Physiology (London), 390,* 383–395.

Rankin, L.L., Enoka, R.M., Volz, K.A., & Stuart, D.G. (1988). Coexistence of twitch potentiation and tetanic force decline in rat hindlimb muscle. *Journal of Applied Physiology, 65,* 2687–2695.

Rantanen, T., Guralnik, J.M., Ferrucci, L., Leveille, S., & Fried, L.P. (1999). Coimpairments: Strength and balance as predictors of severe walking disability. *Journal of Gerontology, 54A,* M172–M176.

Rasch, P.J., & Morehouse, L.E. (1957). Effect of static and dynamic exercises on muscular strength and hypertrophy. *Journal of Applied Physiology, 11,* 29–34.

Rassier, D.E., MacIntosh, B.R., & Herzog, W. (1999). Length dependence of active force production in skeletal muscle. *Journal of Applied Physiology, 86,* 1445–1457.

Ratkevicius, A., Mizuno, M., Povilonis, E., & Quistorff, B. (1998). Energy metabolism of the gastrocnemius and soleus muscles during isometric voluntary and electrically induced contractions in man. *Journal of Physiology, 507,* 593–602.

Ravn, S., Voigt, M., Simonsen, E.B., Alkjær, T., Bojsen-Møller, F., & Klausen, K. (1999). Choice of jumping strategy in two standard jumps, squat and countermovement jump—effect of training background or inherited preference? *Scandinavian Journal of Medicine & Science in Sports, 9,* 201–208.

Rayment, I., Holden, H.M., Whittaker, M., Yohn, C.B., Lorenz, M., Holmes, K.C., & Milligan, R.A. (1993). Structures of the actin-myosin complex and its implications for muscle contraction. *Science, 261,* 58–65.

Reich, T.E., Lindstedt, S.L., LaStayo, P.C., & Pierotti, D.J. (2000). Is the spring quality of muscle plastic? *American Journal of Physiology, 278,* R1661–R1666.

Reimers, C.D., Harder, T., & Saxe, H. (1998). Age-related muscle atrophy does not affect all muscles and can partly be compensated by physical activity: An ultrasound study. *Journal of the Neurological Sciences, 159,* 60–66.

Rho, R.-Y., Kuhn-Spearing, L., & Zioupos, P. (1998). Mechanical properties of bone and the hierarchical structure of bone. *Medical Engineering & Physics, 20,* 92–102.

Richardson, R.S., Frank, L.R., & Haseler, L.J. (1998). Dynamic knee-extensor and cycle exercise: Functional MRI of muscular activity. *International Journal of Sports Medicine, 19,* 182–187.

Rihet, P., Hasbroucq, T., Blin, O., & Possamai, C.A. (1999). Serotonin and human information processing: An electromyographic study of the effects of fluvoxamine on choice reaction time. *Neuroscience Letters, 16,* 143–146.

Riley, D.A., Bain, J.L.W., Thompson, J.L., Fitts, R.H., Widrick, J.J., Trappe, S.W., Trappe, T.A., & Costill, D.L. (2000). Increased thin filament density and length in human atrophic soleus muscle fibers after spaceflight. *Journal of Applied Physiology, 88,* 567–572.

Riley, D.A., Slocum, G.R., Bain, J.L.W., Sedlak, F.R., Sowa, T.E., & Mellender, J.W. (1990). Rat hindlimb unloading: Soleus histochemistry, ultrastructure, and electromyography. *Journal of Applied Physiology, 69,* 58–66.

Ríos, E., Ma, J., & González, A. (1991). The mechanical hypothesis of excitation-contraction (EC) coupling in skeletal muscle. *Journal of Muscle Research and Cell Motility, 12,* 127–135.

Ríos, E., & Pizarró, G. (1988). Voltage sensors and calcium channels of excitation-contraction coupling. *News in Physiological Sciences, 3,* 223–227.

Ritzmann, R.E., & Eaton, R.C. (1997). Neural substrates for the initiation of startle responses. In P.S.G. Stein, S. Grillner, A.I. Selverston, & D.G. Stuart (Eds.), *Neurons, Networks and Motor Behavior* (pp. 33–44). Cambridge, MA: MIT Press.

Roberts, T.J., Marsh, R.L., Weyand, P.G., & Taylor, C.R. (1997). Muscular force in running turkeys: The economy of minimizing work. *Science, 275,* 1113–1115.

Robinovitch, S.N., Hsiao, E.T., Sandler, R., Cortez, J., Liu, Q., & Paiement, G.D. (2000). Prevention of falls and fall-related fractures through biomechanics. *Exercise and Sport Sciences Reviews, 28,* 74–79.

Robinson, F.R. (1995). Role of the cerebellum in movement control and adaptation. *Current Opinion in Neurobiology, 5,* 755–762.

Robinson, G.A., Enoka, R.M., & Stuart, D.G. (1991). Immobilization-induced changes in motor unit force and fatigability in the cat. *Muscle & Nerve, 14,* 563–573.

Rodenburg, J.B., de Boer, R.W., Schiereck, P., van Echteld, C.J., & Bär, P.R. (1994). Changes in phosphorous compounds and water content in skeletal muscle due to eccentric exercise. *European Journal of Applied Physiology, 68,* 205–213.

Rodgers, M.M., Glaser, R.M., Figoni, S.F., Hooker, S.P., Ezenwa, B.N., Collins, S.R., Mathews, T., Suryaprasad, A.G., & Gupta, S. C. (1991). Musculoskeletal responses of spinal cord injured individuals to functional neuromuscular stimulation-induced knee extension exercise training. *Journal of Rehabilitation Research and Development, 28,* 19–26.

Roeleveld, K., Stegeman, D.F., Vingerhoets, H.M., & van Oosterom, A. (1997). Motor unit potential contribution to surface electromyography. *Acta Physiologica Scandinavica, 160,* 175–183.

Roesler, H. (1987). The history of some fundamental concepts in bone biomechanics. *Journal of Biomechanics, 20,* 1025–1034.

Rogers, M.W. (1991). Motor control problems in Parkinson's disease. In M.J. Lister (Ed.), *Contemporary management of motor control problems* (pp. 195–208). Alexandria, VA: Foundation for Physical Therapy.

Rogers, M.W., Kukulka, C.G., & Soderberg, G.L. (1992). Age-related changes in postural responses preceding rapid self-paced and reaction time arm movements. *Journal of Gerontology, 47,* M159–M165.

Rogers, M.W., & Pai, Y.-C. (1990). Dynamic transitions in stance support accompanying leg flexion movements in man. *Experimental Brain Research, 81,* 398–402.

Roland, P.E., & Zilles, K. (1996). Functions and structures of the motor cortices in humans. *Current Opinion in Neurobiology, 6*, 773–781.

Rome, L.C., Funke, R.P., Alexander, R.M., Lutz, G., Aldridge, H., Scott, F., & Freadman, M. (1988). Why animals have different muscle fibre types. *Nature, 335*, 824–827.

Roos, M.R., Rice, C.L., Connelly, D.M., & Vandervoort, A.A. (1999). Quadriceps muscle strength, contractile properties, and motor unit firing rates in young and old men. *Muscle & Nerve, 22*, 1094–1103.

Rose, C.R., Keen, D.A., Koshland, G.F., & Fuglevand, A.J. (1999). Coordination of multiple muscles in the elaboration of individual finger movements. *Society for Neuroscience Abstracts, 25*, 1149.

Ross, B.H., & Thomas, C.K. (1995). Human motor unit activity during induced muscle cramp. *Brain, 118*, 983–993.

Rossignol, S. (1996). Neural control of stereotypic limb movements. In L.B. Rowell & J.T. Shepherd (Eds.), *Handbook of physiology: Sec. 12. Exercise: Regulation and integration of multiple systems* (pp. 173–216). New York: Oxford University Press.

Rossignol, S. (2000). Locomotion and its recovery after spinal injury. *Current Opinion in Neurobiology, 10*, 708–716.

Rossignol, S., Julien, C., Gauthier, L., & Lund, J.P. (1981). State dependent responses during movements. In A. Taylor & A. Prochazka (Eds.), *Muscle receptors and movement* (pp. 389–402). London: Macmillan.

Rothwell, J.C. (1994). *Control of human voluntary movement* (2nd ed.). Kent, United Kingdom: Croom Helm.

Roy, R.R., Baldwin, K.M., & Edgerton, V.R. (1991). The plasticity of skeletal muscle: Effects of neuromuscular activity. *Exercise and Sport Sciences Reviews, 19*, 269–312.

Roy, R.R., & Edgerton, V.R. (1992). Skeletal muscle architecture and performance. In P.V. Komi (Ed.), *Strength and power in sport* (pp. 115–129). Champaign, IL: Human Kinetics.

Roy, R.R., Pierotti, D.J., Baldwin, K.M., Zhong, H., Hodgson, J.A., & Edgerton, V.R. (1998). Cyclical passive stretch influences the mechanical properties of the inactive cat soleus. *Experimental Physiology, 83*, 377–385.

Roy, R.R., Sacks, R.D., Baldwin, K.M., Short, M., & Edgerton, V.R. (1984). Interrelationships of contraction time, Vmax and myosin ATPase after spinal transection. *Journal of Applied Physiology, 56*, 1594–1601.

Roy, R.R., Talmadge, R.J., Hodgson, J.A., Oishi, Y., Baldwin, K.M., & Edgerton, V.R. (1999). Differential response of fast hindlimb extensor and flexor muscles to exercise in adult spinalized cats. *Muscle & Nerve, 22*, 230–241.

Roy, R.R., Talmadge, R.J., Hodgson, J.A., Zhong, H., Baldwin, K.M., & Edgerton, V.R. (1998). Training effects on soleus of cats spinal cord transected (T12-13) as adults. *Muscle & Nerve, 21*, 63–71.

Rube, N., & Secher, N.H. (1990). Effect of training on central factors in fatigue following two- and one-leg static exercise in man. *Acta Physiologica Scandinavica, 141*, 87–95.

Rüegg, J.C. (1983). Muscle. In R.F. Schmidt & F. Thews (Eds.), *Human physiology* (pp. 32–50). Berlin: Springer-Verlag.

Rugg, S.G., Gregor, R.J., Mandelbaum, B.R., & Chiu, L. (1990). *In vivo* moment arm calculations at the ankle using magnetic resonance imaging (MRI). *Journal of Biomechanics, 23*, 495–501.

Russell, B., Motlagh, D., & Ashley, W.W. (2000). Form follows function: How muscle shape is regulated by work. *Journal of Applied Physiology, 88*, 1127–1132.

Rutherford, O.M., & Jones, D.A. (1986). The role of learning and coordination in strength training. *European Journal of Applied Physiology, 55*, 100–105.

Ryaby, J.T. (1998). Clinical effects of electromagnetic and electric fields on fracture healing. *Clinical Orthopedics, 355*(Suppl.), S205–S215.

Sacco, P., Newberry, R., McFadden, L., Brown, T., & McComas, A.J. (1997). Depression of human electromyographic activity by fatigue of a synergistic muscle. *Muscle & Nerve, 20*, 710–717.

Sacco, P., Thickbroom, G.W., Byrnes, M.L., & Mastaglia, F.L. (2000). Changes in corticomotor excitability after fatiguing muscle contractions. *Muscle & Nerve, 23*, 1840–1846.

Sacco, P., Thickbroom, G.W., Thompson, M.L., & Mastaglia, F.L. (1997). Changes in corticomotor excitation and inhibition during prolonged submaximal muscle contractions. *Muscle & Nerve, 20*, 1158–1166.

Sahlin, K., Tonkonogi, M., & Söderlund, K. (1998). Energy supply and muscle fatigue in humans. *Acta Physiologica Scandinavica, 162*, 261–266.

Sahrmann, S.A., & Norton, B.J. (1977). The relationship of voluntary movement to spasticity in the upper motor neuron syndrome. *Annals of Neurology, 2*, 460–464.

Sainburg, R.L., Ghez, C., & Kalakanis, D. (1999). Intersegmental dynamics are controlled by sequential anticipatory, error correction, and postural mechanisms. *Journal of Neurophysiology, 81*, 1045–1056.

Sainburg, R.L., Ghilardi, M.F., Poizner, H., & Ghez, C. (1995). Control of limb dynamics in normal subjects and patients without proprioception. *Journal of Neurophysiology, 73*, 820–835.

Sainburg, R.L., Poizner, H., & Ghez, C. (1993). Loss of proprioception produces deficits in interjoint coordination. *Journal of Neurophysiology, 70*, 2136–2147.

Saito, M., Kobayashi, K., Miyashita, M., & Hoshikawa, T. (1974). Temporal patterns in running. In R.C. Nelson & C.A. Morehouse (Eds.), *Biomechanics IV* (pp. 106–111). Baltimore: University Park Press.

Sale, D.G. (1988). Neural adaptation to resistance training. *Medicine and Science in Sports and Exercise, 20*, S135–S145.

Sale, D.G., & MacDougall, J.D. (1981). Specificity in strength training: A review for the coach and athlete. *Canadian Journal of Applied Sport Sciences, 6*, 87–92.

Sale, D.G., MacDougall, J.D., Upton, A.R.M., & McComas, A.J. (1983). Effect of strength training upon motoneuron excitability in man. *Medicine and Science in Sports and Exercise, 125*, 57–62.

Sale, D.G., McComas, A.J., MacDougall, J.D., & Upton, A.R.M. (1982). Neuromuscular adaptation in human thenar muscles following strength training and immobilization. *Journal of Applied Physiology, 53*, 419–424.

Salinas, E., & Sejnowski, T.J. (2000). Impact of correlated synaptic input on output firing rate and variability in simple neuronal models. *Journal of Neuroscience, 20*, 6193–6209.

Salmons, S. (1997). *Muscle damage.* Oxford: Oxford University Press.

Saltiel, P., Tresch, M.C., & Bizzi, E. (1998). Spinal cord modular organization and rhythm generation: An NMDA iontophoretic study in the frog. *Journal of Neurophysiology, 80,* 2323–2339.

Sandercock, T.G., & Heckman, C.J. (1997). Doublet potentiation during eccentric and concentric contractions of cat soleus muscle. *Journal of Applied Physiology, 82,* 1219–1228.

Sanders, D.B., Stålberg, E.V., & Nandedkar, S.D. (1996). Analysis of the electromyographic interference pattern. *Journal of Clinical Neurophysiology, 13,* 385–400.

Sanes, J.N. (1987). Proprioceptive afferent information and movement control. In G. Adelman (Ed.), *Encyclopedia of neuroscience* (Vol. II, pp. 982–984). Boston: Birkhäuser.

Sanes, J.N., Donoghue, J.P., Thangaraj, V., Edelman, R.R., & Warach, S. (1995). Shared neural substrates controlling hand movements in human motor cortex. *Science, 23,* 1775–1777.

Sanes, J.N., & Evarts, E.V. (1984). Motor psychophysics. *Human Neurobiology, 2,* 217–225.

Sant'ana Pereira, J.A.A., Wessels, A., Nijtmans, L., Moorman, A.F.M., & Sargeant, A.J. (1994). New method for the accurate characterization of single human skeletal muscle fibres demonstrates a relation between mATPase and MyHC expression in pure and hybrid fibre types. *Journal of Muscle Research and Cell Motility, 16,* 21–34.

Saper, C.B., Iversen, S., & Frackowiak, R. (2000). Integration of sensory and motor function: The association areas of the cerebral cortex and the cognitive capabilities of the brain. In E.R. Kandel, J.H. Schwartz, & T.M. Jessell (Eds.), *Principles of neural science* (4th ed., pp. 349–380). New York: McGraw-Hill.

Sapirstein, M.R., Herman, R.C., & Wallace, G.B. (1937). A study of after-contraction. *American Journal of Physiology, 119,* 549–556.

Sargeant, A.J., & Boreham, A. (1981). Measurement of maximal short-term (anaerobic) power output during cycling. In J. Borms, M. Hebbelinck, & A. Venerando (Eds.), *Women and sport* (pp. 119–124). Basel: Karger.

Saugen, E., & Vøllestad, N.K. (1995). Nonlinear relationship between heat production and force during voluntary contractions in humans. *Journal of Applied Physiology, 79,* 2043–2049.

Saugen, E., Vøllestad, N.K., Gibson, H., Martin, P.A., & Edwards, R.H.T. (1997). Dissociation between metabolic and contractile responses during intermittent isometric exercise in man. *Experimental Physiology, 82,* 213–226.

Sayers, S.P., Clarkson, P.M., Rouzier, P.A., & Kamen, G. (1999). Adverse events associated with eccentric exercise protocols: Six case studies. *Medicine and Science in Sports and Exercise, 31,* 1697–1702.

Sayers, S.P., Harackiewicz, D.V., Harman, E.A., Frykman, P.N., & Rosenstein, M.T. (1999). Cross-validation of three jump power equations. *Medicine and Science in Sports and Exercise, 31,* 572–577.

Schechtman, H., & Bader, D.L. (1997). *In vitro* fatigue of human tendons. *Journal of Biomechanics, 30,* 829–835.

Schiaffino, S., & Reggiani, C. (1996). Molecular diversity of myofibrillar proteins: Gene regulation and functional significance. *Physiological Reviews, 76,* 371–423.

Schieber, M.H. (1995). Muscular production of individuated finger movements: The roles of extrinsic finger muscles. *Journal of Neuroscience, 15,* 284–297.

Schieber, M.H., & Hibbard, L.S. (1993). How somatotopic is the motor cortex hand area? *Science, 261,* 489–492.

Schieber, M.H., & Thach, W.T. (1985). Trained slow tracking. II. Bidirectional discharge patterns of cerebellar nuclear, motor cortex, and spindle afferent neurons. *Journal of Neurophysiology, 54,* 1228–1270.

Schieppati, M., Trompetto, C., & Abbruzzese, G. (1996). Selective facilitation of responses to cortical stimulation of proximal and distal arm muscles by precision tasks in man. *Journal of Physiology, 491,* 551–562.

Schiff, J.M. 1858. *Lehrbuch der Physiologie des Menschen. I. Muskelund Nervenphysiologie.* Lahr, Germany: Schauenburg.

Schluter, J.M., & Fitts, R.H. (1994). Shortening velocity and ATPase activity of rat skeletal muscle fibers: Effect of endurance exercise training. *American Journal of Physiology, 266,* C1699–C1713.

Schmidt, R.A., & Lee, T.D. (1999). *Motor control and learning.* Champaign, IL: Human Kinetics.

Schmidt, R.F., & Thews, G. (Eds.) (1983). *Human physiology.* Berlin: Springer-Verlag.

Schmidt, R.F., Wahren, L.K., & Hagbarth, K.-E. (1990). Multiunit neural responses to strong finger pulp vibration. I. Relationship to age. *Acta Physiologica Scandinavica, 140,* 1–10.

Schmied, A., Pagni, S., Sturm, H., & Vedel, J.-P. (2000). Selective enhancement of motoneurone short-term synchrony during an attention-demanding task. *Experimental Brain Research, 133,* 377–390.

Schmied, A., Pouget, J., & Vedel, J.-P. (1999). Electromechanical coupling and synchronous firing of single wrist extensor motor units in sporadic amyotrophic lateral sclerosis. *Clinical Neurophysiology, 110,* 960–977.

Schmied, A., Vedel, J.-P., & Pagni, S. (1994). Human spinal lateralization assessed from motoneurone synchronization: Dependence on handedness and motor unit type. *Journal of Neurophysiology, 480,* 369–387.

Schmied, A., Vedel, J.-P., Pouget, J., Forget, R., Lamarre, Y., & Paillard, J. (1995). Changes in motoneurone connectivity evaluated from neuronal synchronization analysis. In A. Taylor, M.H. Gladden, & R. Durbaba (Eds.), *Alpha and Gamma Motor Systems* (pp. 469–477). New York: Plenum.

Schneider, K., & Zernicke, R.F. (1992). Mass, center of mass, and moment of inertia estimates for infant limb segments. *Journal of Biomechanics, 25,* 145–148.

Schott, J., McCully, K., & Rutherford, O.M. (1995). The role of metabolites in strength training. II. Short versus long isometric contractions. *European Journal of Applied Physiology, 71,* 337–341.

Schouenborg, J., Weng, H.R., & Holmberg, H. (1994). Modular organization of spinal nociceptive reflexes: A new hypothesis. *News in Physiological Sciences, 9,* 261–265.

Schroeter, J.P., Bretaudiere, J.P., Sass, R.L., & Goldstein, M.A. (1996). Three-dimensional structure of the Z band in a normal mammalian skeletal muscle. *Journal of Cell Biology, 133,* 571–583.

Schultz, A.B. (1992). Mobility impairment in the elderly: Challenges for biomechanics research. *Journal of Biomechanics, 25,* 519–528.

Schwartz, J.H. (1985). Synthesis and distribution of neuronal protein. In E.R. Kandel & J.H. Schwartz (Eds.), *Principles of neural science* (2nd ed., pp. 37–48). New York: Elsevier.

Schwartz, J.H., & De Camilli, P. (2000). Synthesis and trafficking of neuronal protein. In E.R. Kandel, J.H. Schwartz, & T.M. Jessell (Eds.), *Principles of neural science* (4th ed., pp. 88–104). New York: McGraw-Hill.

Scott, J.J.A. (1996). The functional recovery of muscle proprioceptors after peripheral nerve lesions. *Journal of the Peripheral Nervous System, 1,* 19–27.

Scremin, A.M.E., Kurta, L., Gentili, A., Wiseman, B., Perell, K., Kunkel, C., & Scremin, O.U. (1999). Increasing muscle mass in spinal cord injured persons with a functional electrical stimulation protocol. *Archives of Physical Medicine and Rehabilitation, 80,* 1531–1536.

Sears, T.A., & Stagg, D. (1976). Short-term synchronization of intercostal motoneurone activity. *Journal of Physiology (London), 263,* 357–381.

Seburn, K.L., & Gardiner, P.F. (1996). Properties of sprouted rat motor units: Effects of period of enlargement and activity level. *Muscle & Nerve, 19,* 1100–1109.

Secher, N.H. (1975). Isometric rowing strength of experienced and inexperienced oarsmen. *Medicine and Science in Sports and Exercise, 7,* 280–283.

Secher, N.H., Rube, N., & Elers, J. (1988). Strength of two- and one-leg extension in man. *Acta Physiologica Scandinavica, 134,* 333–339.

Seger, J.Y., Arvidsson, B., & Thorstensson, A. (1998). Specific effects of eccentric and concentric training on muscle strength and morphology in humans. *European Journal of Applied Physiology, 79,* 49–57.

Sejrsted, O.M., & Sjøgaard, G. (2000). Dynamics and consequences of potassium shifts in skeletal muscle and heart during exercise. *Physiological Reviews, 80,* 1411–1481.

Selverston, A.I., Panchin, Y.V., Arshavsky, Y.I., & Orlovsky, G.N. (1997). Shared features of invertebrate central pattern generators. In P.S.G. Stein, S. Grillner, A.I. Selverston, & D.G. Stuart (Eds.), *Neurons, networks, and motor behavior* (pp. 105–117). Cambridge, MA: MIT Press.

Semmler, J.G., & Enoka, R.M. (2000). Neural contributions to changes in muscle strength. In V.M. Zatsiorsky (Ed.), *Biomechanics in sport: The scientific basis of performance* (pp. 3–20). Oxford, UK: Blackwell Science.

Semmler, J.G., Kutzscher, D.V., & Enoka, R.M. (1999). Gender differences in the fatigability of human skeletal muscle. *Journal of Neurophysiology, 82,* 3590–3593.

Semmler, J.G., Kutzscher, D.V., & Enoka, R.M. (2000). Limb immobilization alters muscle activation patterns during a fatiguing isometric contraction. *Muscle & Nerve, 23,* 1381–1392.

Semmler, J.G., Kutzscher, D.V., Zhou, J., & Enoka, R.M. (2000). Motor unit synchronization is enhanced during slow shortening and lengthening muscle contractions of the first dorsal interosseus muscle. *Society for Neuroscience Abstracts, 26,* 463.

Semmler, J.G., & Nordstrom, M.A. (1995). Influence of handedness on motor unit discharge properties and force tremor. *Experimental Brain Research, 104,* 115–125.

Semmler, J.G., & Nordstrom, M.A. (1998). Motor unit discharge and force tremor in skill- and strength-trained individuals. *Experimental Brain Research, 119,* 27–38.

Semmler, J.G., Nordstrom, M.A., & Wallace, C.J. (1997). Relationship between motor unit short-term synchronization and common drive in human first dorsal interosseus muscle. *Brain Research, 767,* 314–320.

Sergio, L.E., & Kalaska, J.F. (1998). Changes in the temporal pattern of primary motor cortex activity in a directional isometric force versus limb movement task. *Journal of Neurophysiology, 80,* 1577–1583.

Seyffarth, H. (1940). The behaviour of motor-units in voluntary contractions. *Avhandlinger Utgitt Norske Videnskap-Akap Oslo. I. Matematisk-Naturvidenskapelig Klasse, 4,* 1–63.

Shadwick, R.E. (1990). Elastic energy storage in tendons: Mechanical differences related to function and age. *Journal of Applied Physiology, 68,* 1033–1040.

Shanebrook, J.R., & Jaszczak, R.D. (1976). Aerodynamic drag analysis of runners. *Medicine and Science in Sports, 8,* 43–45.

Sheard, P.W. (2000). Tension delivery from short fibers in long muscles. *Exercise and Sport Sciences Reviews, 28,* 51–56.

Sheean, G.L., Murray, N.M.F., Rothwell, J.C., Miller, D.H., & Thompson, A.J. (1997). An electrophysiological study of the mechanism of fatigue in multiple sclerosis. *Brain, 120,* 299–315.

Sheetz, M.P., Steuer, E.R., & Schroer, T.A. (1989). The mechanism and regulation of fast axonal transport. *Trends in Neurosciences, 12,* 474–478.

Shelburne, K.B., & Pandy, M.G. (1997). A musculoskeletal model of the knee for evaluating ligament forces during isometric contractions. *Journal of Biomechanics, 30,* 163–176.

Shellock, F.G. (1986). Physiological, psychological, and injury prevention aspects of warm-up. *National Strength & Conditioning Association Journal, 8,* 24–27.

Shellock, F.G., Fukunaga, T., Mink, J.H., & Edgerton, V.R. (1991). Exertional muscle injury: Evaluation of concentric versus eccentric actions with serial MRI imaging. *Radiology, 179,* 659–664.

Shellock, F.G., & Prentice, W.E. (1985). Warming-up and stretching for improved physical performance and prevention of sports-related injuries. *Sports Medicine, 2,* 267–278.

Sherrington, C.S. (1910). Flexion-reflex of the limb, crossed extension-reflex and reflex stepping and standing. *Journal of Physiology, 40,* 28–121.

Shields, R.K. (1995). Fatigability, relaxation properties, and electromyographic responses of the human paralyzed soleus muscle. *Journal of Neurophysiology, 73,* 2195–2206.

Shirakura, K., Kato, K., & Udagawa, E. (1992). Characteristics of the isokinetic performance of patients with injured cruciate ligaments. *American Journal of Sports Medicine, 20,* 755–760.

Shumskii, V.V., Merten, A.A., & Dzenis, V.V. (1978). Effect of the type of physical stress on the state of the tibial bones of highly trained athletes as measured by ultrasound techniques. *Mekhanika Polimerov, 5,* 884–888.

Sica, R.E.P., & McComas, A.J. (1971). Fast and slow muscle units in a human muscle. *Journal of Neurology, Neurosurgery, and Psychiatry, 34,* 113–120.

Sieck, G.C., & Prakash, Y.S. (1995). Fatigue at the neuromuscular junction. In S.C. Gandevia, R.M. Enoka, A.J. McComas, D.G. Stuart, & C.K. Thomas (Eds.), *Fatigue: Neural and muscular mechanisms* (pp. 83–100). New York: Plenum Press.

Siegmund, G.P., Sanderson, D.J., & Inglis, J.T. (2000). Readiness to perform a ballistic head movement sculpts the acoustic startle response of neck muscles. *Society for Neuroscience Abstracts, 26,* 169.

Siff, M.C. (2000). Biomechanical foundations of strength and power training. In V.M. Zatsiorsky (Ed.), *Biomechanics in Sport,* (pp.103–139). Oxford, UK: Blackwell Science.

Sillar, K.T., Kiehn, O., & Kudo, N. (1997). Chemical modulation of vertebrate circuits. In P.S.G. Stein, S. Grillner, A.I. Selverston, & D.G. Stuart (Eds.), *Neurons, networks, and motor behavior* (pp. 183–193). Cambridge, MA: MIT Press.

Simard, C.P., Spector, S.A., & Edgerton, V.R. (1982). Contractile properties of rat hind limb muscles immobilized at different lengths. *Experimental Neurology, 77,* 467–482.

Simonsen, E.B., & Dyhre-Poulsen, P. (1999). Amplitude of the human soleus H reflex during walking and running. *Journal of Physiology, 515,* 929–939.

Singer, J.H., & Berger, A.J. (1996). Presynaptic inhibition by serotonin: A possible mechanism for switching motor output of the hypoglossal nucleus. *Sleep, 19,* S146–S149.

Sinkjær, T. (1997). Muscle, reflex and central components in the control of the ankle joint in healthy and spastic man. *Acta Neurologica Scandinavica, 96,* 1–28.

Sinkjær, T., Andersen, J.B., & Larsen, B. (1996). Soleus stretch reflex modulation during gait in humans. *Journal of Neurophysiology, 76,* 1112–1120.

Sjøgaard, G. (1996). Potassium and fatigue: The pros and cons. *Acta Physiologica Scandinavica, 156,* 257–264.

Sjøgaard, G., Kiens, B., Jørgensen, K., & Saltin, B. (1986). Intramuscular pressure, EMG and blood flow during low-level prolonged static contraction in man. *Acta Physiologica Scandinavica, 128,* 475–484.

Sjøgaard, G., Savard, G., & Juel, C. (1988). Muscle blood flow during isometric activity and its relation to muscle fatigue. *European Journal of Applied Physiology, 57,* 327–335.

Sjöstrom, M., Kidman, S., Larsén, K.H., & Ängquist, K.-A. (1982). Z- and M-band appearance in different histochemically defined types of human skeletal muscle fibers. *Journal of Histochemistry and Cytochemistry, 30,* 1–11.

Slawinska, U., Tyc, F., Kasicki, S., Navarrete, R., & Vrbová, G. (1998). Time course of changes in EMG activity of fast muscles after partial denervation. *Experimental Brain Research, 120,* 193–201.

Slifkin, A.B., & Newell, K.M. (1999). Noise, information transmission, and force variability. *Journal of Experimental Human Perception and Performance, 25,* 837–851.

Smerdu, V., Karch-Mizrachi, I., Campione, M., Leinwand, L., & Schiaffino, S. (1994). Type IIx myosin heavy chain transcripts are expressed in type IIb fibers of human skeletal muscle. *American Journal of Physiology, 267,* C1723–C1728.

Smith, A.M., Malo, S.A., Laskowski, E.R., Sabick, M., Cooney, W.P., III, Finnie, S.B., Crews, D.J., Eischen, J.J., Hay, I.D., Detling, N.J., & Kaufman, K. (2000). A multidisciplinary study of the "yip" phenomenon in golf. *Sports Medicine, 30,* 423–437.

Smith, C.A. (1994). The warm-up procedure: To stretch or not to stretch. A brief review. *Journal of Orthopedic and Sports Physical Therapy, 19,* 12–17.

Smith, F. (1982). Dynamic variable resistance and the Universal system. *National Strength & Conditioning Association Journal, 4,* 14–19.

Smith, J.L., Betts, B., Edgerton, V.R., & Zernicke, R.F. (1980). Rapid ankle extension during paw shakes: Selective recruitment of fast ankle extensors. *Journal of Neurophysiology, 43,* 612–620.

Smith, J.L., Carlson-Kuhts, P., & Trank, T.V. (1998). Forms of forward quadrupedal locomotion. III. A comparison of posture,

hindlimb kinematics, and motor patterns for downslope and level walking. *Journal of Neurophysiology, 79,* 1702–1716.

Smith, J.L., & Zernicke, R.F. (1987). Predictions for neural control based limb dynamics. *Trends in Neurosciences, 10,* 123–128.

Snow-Harter, C., & Marcus, R. (1991). Exercise, bone mineral density, and osteoporosis. *Exercise and Sport Sciences Reviews, 19,* 351–388.

Snyder-Mackler, L., Ladin, Z., Schepsis, A.A., & Young, J.C. (1991). Electrical stimulation of the thigh muscles after reconstruction of the anterior cruciate ligament. *Journal of Bone and Joint Surgery, 73-A,* 1025–1036.

Soechting, J.F., Buneo, C.A., Herrmann, U., & Flanders, M. (1995). Moving effortlessly in three-dimensions: Does Donder's law apply to arm movement? *Journal of Neuroscience, 15,* 6271–6280.

Soechting, J.F., & Flanders, M. (1998). Movement planning: Kinematics, dynamics, both or neither? In L. Harris & M. Jenkin (Eds.), *Vision and action* (pp. 352–371). New York: Cambridge University Press.

Soechting, J.F., & Lacquaniti, F. (1981). Invariant characteristics of a pointing movement in man. *Journal of Neuroscience, 1,* 710–720.

Søgaard, K., Christensen, K., Jensen, B.R., Finsen, L., & Sjøgaard, G. (1996). Motor control and kinetics during low level concentric and eccentric contractions in man. *Electroencephalography and Clinical Neurophysiology, 101,* 453–460.

Sokoloff, A.J., Siegel, S.G., & Cope, T.C. (1999). Recruitment order among motoneurons from different motor nuclei. *Journal of Neurophysiology, 81,* 2485–2492.

Sparrow, D., & Weiss, S.T. (1995). Respiratory system. In E.J. Masoro (Ed.), *Handbook of physiology: Sec. 11. Aging* (pp. 475–483). New York: Oxford University Press.

Spector, S.A., Simard, C.P., Fournier, M., Sternlicht, E., & Edgerton, V.R. (1982). Architectural alterations of rat hind-limb skeletal muscles immobilized at different lengths. *Experimental Neurology, 76,* 94–110.

Sperry, R.W. (1950). Neural basis of the spontaneous optokinetic response produced by visual neural inversion. *Journal of Comparative and Physiological Psychology, 43,* 482–489.

Spiegel, K.M., Stratton, J., Burke, J.R., Glendinning, D.S., & Enoka, R.M. (1996). The influence of age on the assessment of motor unit activation in a human hand muscle. *Experimental Physiology, 81,* 805–819.

Spielberger, C.D., Gorsuch, R.L., Lushene, R.E., Vagg, P.R., & Jacobs, G.A. (1983). *Manual for the State-Trait Anxiety Inventory STAI (Form Y).* Palo Alto, CA: Consulting Psychologists Press.

Spielberger, C.D., & Rickman, R.L. (1990). Assessment of state and trait anxiety. In N. Sartorius (Ed.), *Anxiety: Psychological and clinical perspectives* (pp. 69–83). New York: Hemisphere Books.

Spira, M.E., Yarom, Y., & Parnas, I. (1976). Modulation of spike frequency by regions of special axonal geometry and by synaptic inputs. *Journal of Neurophysiology, 39,* 882–899.

Spoor, C.W., van Leeuwen, J.L., Meskers, C.G.M., Titulaer, A.F., & Huson, A. (1990). Estimation of instantaneous moment arms of lower-leg muscles. *Journal of Biomechanics, 23,* 1247–1259.

Spring, E., Savolainen, S., Erkkilä, J., Hämäläinen, T., & Pihkala, P. (1988). Drag area of a cross-country skier. *International Journal of Sport Biomechanics, 4,* 103–113.

Stackhouse, S.K., Dean, J.C., Lee, S.C.K., & Binder-Macleod, S.A. (2000). Measurement of central activation failure of the quadriceps femoris in healthy adults. *Muscle & Nerve, 23,* 1706–1712.

Stainsby, W.N., Brechue, W.F., O'Drobinak, D.M., & Barclay, J.K. (1990). Effects of ischemic and hypoxic hypoxia on $\dot{V}O_2$ and lactic acid output during tetanic contractions. *Journal of Applied Physiology, 68,* 574–579.

Stålberg, E. (1980). Macro EMG, a new recording technique. *Journal of Neurology, Neurosurgery, and Psychiatry, 43,* 475–482.

Stålberg, E. (1986). Single fibre EMG, macro EMG, and scanning EMG. New ways of looking at the motor unit. *CRC Critical Reviews in Clinical Neurobiology, 2,* 125–167.

Stålberg, E., & Falck, B. (1997). The role of electromyography in neurology. *Electroencephalography and Clinical Neurophysiology, 103,* 579–598.

Stålberg, E., Nandedkar, S.D., Sanders, D.B., & Falck, B. (1996). Quantitative motor unit potential analysis. *Journal of Clinical Neurophysiology, 13,* 401–422.

Stamenovic, D., & Wang, N. (2000). Engineering approaches to cytoskeletal mechanics. *Journal of Applied Physiology, 89,* 2085–2090.

Stanish, W.D., & Hubley-Kozey, C.L. (1984). Separating fact from fiction about common sports activity: Can stretching prevent athletic injuries? *Journal of Musculoskeletal Medicine, 1,* 25–32.

Staron, R.S., Karapondo, D.L., Kraemer, W.J., Fry, A.C., Gordon, S.E., Falkel, J.E., Hagerman, F.C., & Hikida, R.S. (1994). Skeletal muscle adaptations during early phase of heavy-resistance training in men and women. *Journal of Applied Physiology, 76,* 1247–1255.

Staron, R.S., & Pette, D. (1986). Correlation between myofibrillar ATPase activity and myosin heavy chain composition in rabbit muscle fibres. *Histochemistry, 86,* 19–23.

Stauber, W.T. (1989). Eccentric actions of muscles: Physiology, injury, and adaptation. *Exercise and Sport Sciences Reviews, 17,* 157–185.

Stein, P.S.G., Grillner, S., Selverston, A.I., & Stuart, D.G. (Eds.) (1997). *Neurons, networks, and motor behavior.* Cambridge, MA: MIT Press.

Stein, P.S.G., & Smith, J.L. (1997). Neural and biomechanical control strategies for different forms of vertebrate hindlimb motor tasks. In P.S.G. Stein, S. Grillner, A.I. Selverston, & D.G. Stuart (Eds.), *Neurons, networks, and motor behavior* (pp. 61–73). Cambridge, MA: MIT Press.

Stein, R.B. (1995). Presynaptic inhibition in humans. *Progress in Neurobiology, 47,* 533–544.

Stein, R.B., & Capaday, C. (1988). The modulation of human reflexes during functional motor tasks. *Trends in Neurosciences, 11,* 328–332.

Stein, R.B., Gordon, T., Jefferson, J., Sharfenberger, A., Yang, J.F., Totosy de Zepetnek, J., & Belanger, M. (1992). Optimal stimulation of paralyzed muscle after human spinal cord injury. *Journal of Applied Physiology, 72,* 1393–1400.

Stein, R.B., & Yang, J.F. (1990). Methods for estimating the number of motor units in human muscles. *Annals of Neurology, 28,* 487–495.

Steinen, G.J.M., Kiers, J.L., Bottinelli, R., & Reggiani, C. (1996). Myofibrillar ATPase activity in skinned human skeletal muscle fibres: Fibre type and temperature dependence. *Journal of Physiology, 493,* 299–307.

Steinen, G.J.M., Roosemalen, M.C.M., Wilson, M.G.A., & Elzinga, G. (1990). Depression of force by phosphate in skinned skeletal muscle fibers of the frog. *American Journal of Physiology, 259,* C349–C357.

Stephens, M.J., & Yang, J.F. (1996). Short latency, non-reciprocal group I inhibition is reduced during the stance phase of walking in humans. *Brain Research, 743,* 24–31.

Stephenson, D.G., Lamb, G.D., Stephenson, G.M.M., & Fryer, M.W. (1995). Mechanisms of excitation-contraction coupling relevant to skeletal muscle fatigue. In S.C. Gandevia, R.M. Enoka, A.J. McComas, D.G. Stuart, & C.K. Thomas (Eds.), *Fatigue: Neural and muscular mechanisms* (pp. 45–56). New York: Plenum Press.

Stevens, E.D. (1993). Relation between work and power calculated from force-velocity curves to that done during oscillatory work. *Journal of Muscle Research and Cell Motility, 14,* 518–526.

Stevens, J.C., Cruz, L.A., Marks, L.E., & Lakatos, S. (1998). A multimodal assessment of sensory thresholds in aging. *Journal of Gerontology, 53,* B263–B272.

Stewart, I.B., & Sleivert, G.G. (1998). The effect of warm-up intensity on range of motion and anaerobic performance. *Journal of Orthopedic and Sports Physical Therapy, 27,* 154–161.

Stokes, I.A.F., Moffroid, M.S., Rush, S., & Haugh, L.D. (1988). Comparison of acoustic and electrical signals from erectores spinae muscles. *Muscle & Nerve, 11,* 331–336.

Stokes, M., & Young, A. (1984). The contribution of reflex inhibition to arthrogenous muscle weakness. *Clinical Science, 67,* 7–14.

Stokes, M.J., & Cooper, R.G. (1992). Muscle sounds during voluntary and stimulated contractions of the human adductor pollicis muscle. *Journal of Applied Physiology, 72,* 1908–1913.

Stone, M.H., & O'Bryant, H.S. (1987). *Weight training: A scientific approach.* Minneapolis: Bellweather Press.

Street, S.F. (1983). Lateral transmission of tension in frog myofibers: A myofibrillar network and transverse cytoskeletal connections are possible transmitters. *Journal of Cell Physiology, 114,* 346–364.

Strojnik, V. (1995). Muscle activation level during maximal voluntary effort. *European Journal of Applied Physiology, 72,* 144–149.

Stroup, F., & Bushnell, D.L. (1970). Rotation, translation, and trajectory in diving. *Research Quarterly, 40,* 812–817.

Stuart, D.G., & Enoka, R.M. (1983). Motoneurons, motor units, and the size principle. In R.N. Rosenberg (Ed.), *The clinical neurosciences* (pp. V:471–V:517). New York: Churchill Livingstone.

Stucke, H., Baudzus, W., & Baumann, W. (1984). On friction characteristics of playing surfaces. In E.C. Frederick (Ed.), *Sport shoes and playing surfaces* (pp. 87–97). Champaign, IL: Human Kinetics.

Suzuki, S., & Hutton, R.S. (1976). Postcontractile motoneuronal discharge produced by muscle afferent activation. *Medicine and Science in Sports, 8,* 258–264.

Svensson, P., Houe, L., & Arendt-Nielsen, L. (1997). Bilateral experimental muscle pain changes electromyographic activity of human jaw-closing muscles during mastication. *Experimental Brain Research, 116,* 182–185.

Sweeney, H.L., Bowman, B.F., & Stull, J.T. (1993). Myosin light chain phosphorylation in vertebrate striated muscle: Regulation and function. *American Journal of Physiology, 264,* C1085–C1095.

Sweeney, H.L., & Stull, J.T. (1990). Alteration of cross-bridge kinetics by myosin light chain phosphorylation in rabbit skeletal muscle: Implications for regulation of actin-myosin interaction. *Proceedings of the National Academy of Sciences, 87,* 414–418.

Takarada, Y., Hirano, Y., Ishige, Y., & Ishii, N. (1997). Stretch-induced enhancement of mechanical power output in human multijoint exercise with countermovement. *Journal of Applied Physiology, 83,* 1749–1755.

Talmadge, R.J., Roy, R.R., & Edgerton, V.R. (1995). Prominence of myosin heavy chain hybrid fibers is soleus muscle of spinal cord-transected rats. *Journal of Applied Physiology, 78,* 1256–1265.

Tal'nov, A.N., Serenko, S.G., Strafun, S.S., & Kostyukov, A.I. (1999). Analysis of the electromyographic activity of human elbow joint muscles during slow linear flexion movements in isotorque conditions. *Neuroscience, 90,* 1123–1136.

Tamaki, H., Kitada, K., Akamine, T., Murata, F., Sakou, T., & Kurata, H. (1998). Alternate activity in the synergistic muscles during prolonged low-level contractions. *Journal of Applied Physiology, 84,* 1943–1951.

Tanaka, H., & Seals, D.R. (1997). Age and gender interactions in physiological functional capacity: Insight from swimming performance. *Journal of Applied Physiology, 82,* 846–851.

Tang, A., & Rymer, W.Z. (1981). Abnormal force: EMG relations in paretic limbs of hemiparetic human subjects. *Journal of Neurology, Neurosurgery, and Psychiatry, 44,* 690–698.

Tang, P.-F., & Woollacott, M.H. (1998). Inefficient postural responses to unexpected slips during walking in older adults. *Journal of Gerontology, 53A,* M471–M480.

Taniguchi, Y. (1998). Relationship between the modifications of bilateral deficit in upper and lower limbs by resistance training in humans. *European Journal of Applied Physiology, 78,* 226–230.

Tanji, J., & Kato, M. (1973). Firing rate of individual motor units in voluntary contraction of abductor digiti minimi muscle in man. *Experimental Neurology, 40,* 771–783.

Tax, A.A.M., Denier van der Gon, J.J., & Erkelens, C.J. (1990). Differences in coordination of elbow flexor muscles in force tasks and in movement tasks. *Experimental Brain Research, 81,* 567–572.

Tax, A.A.M., Denier van der Gon, J.J., Gielen, C.C.A.M., & van den Tempel, C.M.M. (1989). Differences in activation of m. biceps brachii in the control of slow isotonic movement and isometric contractions. *Experimental Brain Research, 76,* 55–63.

Tax, A.A.M., Wezel, B.M.H. van, & Dietz, V. (1995). Bipedal reflex coordination to tactile stimulation of the sural nerve during human running. *Journal of Neurophysiology, 73,* 1947–1964.

Taylor, A., Durbaba, R., Ellaway, P.H., & Rawlinson, S. (2000). Patterns of fusimotor activity during locomotion in the decerebrate cat deduced from recordings from hindlimb muscle spindles. *Journal of Physiology, 522,* 515–532.

Taylor, C.R., Heglund, N.C., McMahon, T.A., & Looney, T.R. (1980). Energetic cost of generating muscular force during running. *Journal of Experimental Biology, 86,* 9–18.

Taylor, D.C., Dalton, J., Seaber, A.V., & Garrett, W.E. (1990). The viscoelastic properties of muscle-tendon units. *American Journal of Sports Medicine, 18,* 300–309.

Taylor, J.L., Butler, J.E., Allen, G.M., & Gandevia, S.C. (1996). Changes in motor cortical excitability during human muscle fatigue. *Journal of Physiology, 490,* 519–528.

Taylor, J.L, & Gandevia, S.C. (2001). Transcranial magnetic stimulation and human muscle fatigue. *Muscles & Nerve, 24,* 18–29.

ter Haar Romeny, B.M., Denier van der Gon, J.J., & Gielen, C.C.A.M. (1982). Changes in recruitment order of motor units in the human biceps brachii muscle. *Experimental Neurology, 78,* 360–368.

Tesch, P.A. (1992). Training for bodybuilding. In P.V. Komi (Ed.), *Strength and power in sport* (pp. 370–380). Oxford: Blackwell Scientific.

Tesch, P.A., Dudley, G.A., Duvoisin, M.R., Hather, B.M., & Harris, R.T. (1990). Force and EMG signal patterns during repeated bouts of concentric and eccentric muscle actions. *Acta Physiologica Scandinavica, 138,* 263–271.

Thelen, D.G., Brockmiller, C., Ashton-Miller, J.A., Schultz, A.B., & Alexander, N.B. (1998). Thresholds for detecting foot dorsi- and plantarflexion during upright stance: Effects of age and velocity. *Journal of Gerontology, 53A,* M33–M38.

Thelen, D.G., Muriuki, M., James, J., Schultz, A.B., Ashton-Miller, J.A., & Alexander, N.B. (2000). Muscle activities used by young and old adults when stepping to regain balance during a forward fall. *Journal of Electromyography and Kinesiology, 10,* 93–101.

Thelen, D.G., Schultz, A.B., Alexander, N.B., & Ashton-Miller, J.A. (1996). Effects of age on rapid ankle torque development. *Journal of Gerontology, 51A,* M226–M232.

Thelen, D.G., Wojcik, L.A., Schultz, A.B., Ashton-Miller, J.A., & Alexander, N.B. (1997). Age differences in using a rapid step to regain balance during a forward fall. *Journal of Gerontology, 52A,* M8–M13.

Thériault, R., Boulay, M.R., Thériault, G., & Simoneau, J.-A. (1996). Electrical stimulation-induced changes in performance and fiber type proportion of human knee extensor muscles. *European Journal of Applied Physiology, 74,* 311–317.

Thomas, C.K. (1997). Contractile properties of human thenar muscles paralyzed by spinal cord injury. *Muscle & Nerve, 20,* 788–799.

Thomas, C.K., Bigland-Ritchie, B., & Johansson, R.S. (1991). Force-frequency relationships of human thenar motor units. *Journal of Neurophysiology, 65,* 1509–1516.

Thomas, C.K., Broton, J.G., & Calancie, B. (1997). Motor unit forces and recruitment patterns after cervical spinal cord injury. *Muscle & Nerve, 20,* 212–220.

Thomas, C.K., Johansson, R.S., & Bigland-Ritchie, B. (1991). Attempts to physiologically classify human thenar motor units. *Journal of Neurophysiology, 65,* 1501–1508.

Thomas, C.K., Johansson, R.S., & Bigland-Ritchie, B. (1999). Pattern of pulses that maximize force output from single human thenar motor units. *Journal of Neurophysiology, 82,* 3188–3195.

Thomas, C.K., Ross, B.H., & Calancie, B. (1987). Human motor-unit recruitment during isometric contractions and repeated dynamic movements. *Journal of Neurophysiology, 57,* 311–324.

Thomas, C.K., Stein, R.B., Gordon, T., Lee, R.G., & Elleker, M.G. (1987). Patterns of reinnervation and motor unit recruitment in human hand muscles after complete ulnar and median nerve section and resuture. *Journal of Neurology, Neurosurgery, and Psychiatry, 50,* 259–268.

Thomas, C.K., Tucker, M.E., & Bigland-Ritchie, B. (1998). Voluntary muscle weakness and co-activation after chronic cervical spinal cord injury. *Journal of Neurotrama, 15,* 149–161.

Thomas, C.K., Woods, J.J., & Bigland-Ritchie, B. (1989). Impulse propagation and muscle activation in long maximal voluntary contractions. *Journal of Applied Physiology, 67,* 1835–1842.

Thomas, C.K., Zaidner, E.Y., Calancie, B., Broton, J.G., & Bigland-Ritchie, B.R. (1997). Muscle weakness, paralysis, and atrophy after human cervical spinal cord injury. *Experimental Neurology, 148,* 414–423.

Thomason, D.B., & Booth, F.W. (1990). Atrophy of the soleus muscle by hindlimb unweighting. *Journal of Applied Physiology, 68,* 1–12.

Thomason, D.B., Herrick, R.E., & Baldwin, K.M. (1987). Activity influences on soleus muscle myosin during rodent hindlimb suspension. *Journal of Applied Physiology, 63,* 138–144.

Thomis, M.A.I., Beunen, G.P., Van Leemputte, M., Maes, H.H., Blimkie, C.J., Claessens, A.L., Marchal, G., Willems, E., & Vlietinck, R.F. (1998). Inheritance of static and dynamic arm strength and some of its determinants. *Acta Physiologica Scandinavica, 163,* 59–71.

Thompson, L.V., Johnson, S.A., & Shoeman, J.A. (1998). Single soleus muscle fiber function after hindlimb unweighting in adult and aged rats. *Journal of Applied Physiology, 84,* 1936–1942.

Thornell, L.E., Carlsson, E., Kugelberg, E., & Grove, B.K. (1987). Myofibrillar M-band structure and composition of physiologically defined rat motor units. *American Journal of Physiology, 253,* C456–C468.

Thusneyapan, S., & Zahalak, G.I. (1989). A practical electrode-array myoprocessor for surface electromyography. *IEEE Transactions on Biomedical Engineering, 36,* 295–299.

Tidball, J.G. (1991). Force transmission across muscle cell membranes. *Journal of Biomechanics, 24*(Suppl.), 43–52.

Tipton, C.M., Matthes, R.D., Maynard, J.A., & Carey, R.A. (1975). The influence of physical activity on tendons and ligaments. *Medicine and Science in Sports and Exercise, 7,* 165–175.

Tomlinson, B.E., & Irving, D. (1977). The number of limb motor neurons in the human lumbosacral cord throughout life. *Journal of Neurological Sciences, 34,* 213–219.

Torre, M. (1953). Nombre et dimensions des unités motrices dans les muscles extrinsêques de l'œil et, en général, dans les muscles squélettiques reliés à des organes de sens. *Archives Suisses de Neurologie et de Psychiatrie, 72,* 362–376.

Tötösy de Zepetnek, J.E., Zung, H.V., Erdebil, S., & Gordon, T. (1992). Innervation ratio is an important determinant of force in normal and reinnervated rat tibialis anterior muscles. *Journal of Neurophysiology, 67,* 1385–1403.

Toussaint, H.M., van Baar, C.E., van Langen, P.P., de Looze, M.P., & van Dieën, J.H. (1992). Coordination of the leg muscles in backlift and leglift. *Journal of Biomechanics, 25,* 1279–1289.

Townend, M.S. (1984). *Mathematics in sport.* New York: Halstead.

Tracy, B.L., Pruitt, B.M., Butler, A.T., & Enoka, R.M. (2000). Knee extensor steadiness and strength is reduced in older adults. *Medicine and Science in Sports, 32,* S244.

Trappe, S., Williamson, D., Godard, M., Porter, D., Rowden, G., & Costill, D. (2000). Effect of resistance training on single muscle fiber contractile function in older men. *Journal of Applied Physiology, 89,* 143–152.

Trimble, M.H., & Enoka, R.M. (1991). Mechanisms underlying the training effects associated with neuromuscular electrical stimulation. *Physical Therapy, 71,* 273–282.

Trotter, J.A. (1990). Interfiber tension transmission in series-fibered muscles of the cat hindlimb. *Journal of Morphology, 206,* 351–361.

Trotter, J.A. (1993). Functional morphology of force transmission in skeletal muscle. *Acta Anatomica, 146,* 205–222.

Trotter, J.A., Richmond, F.J.R., & Purslow, P.P. (1995). Functional morphology and motor control of series-fibered muscles. *Exercise and Sport Sciences Reviews, 23,* 167–213.

Tsika, R.W., Herrick, R.E., & Baldwin, K.M. (1987). Subunit composition of rodent isomyosins and their distribution in hindlimb skeletal muscles. *Journal of Applied Physiology, 63,* 2101–2110.

Ulfhake, B., & Kellerth, J.-O. (1984). Electrophysiological and morphological measurements in cat gastrocnemius and soleus $\propto$-motoneurones. *Brain Research, 307,* 167–179.

Vallbo, Å.B. (1971). Muscle spindle response at the onset of isometric voluntary contractions in man. Time difference between fusimotor and skeletomotor effects. *Journal of Physiology, 218,* 405–431.

Vallbo, Å.B., & Wessberg, J. (1993). Organization of motor output in slow finger movements in man. *Journal of Physiology (London), 469,* 673–691.

Valls-Solé, J., Rothwell, J.C., Goulart, F., Cossu, G., & Muñoz, E. (1999). Patterned ballistic movements triggered by a startle in healthy humans. *Journal of Physiology, 516,* 931–938.

van Bolhuis, B.M., & Gielen, C.C. (1997). The relative activation of elbow-flexor muscles in isometric flexion and in flexion/extension movements. *Journal of Biomechanics, 30,* 803–811.

Van Cutsem, M., Duchateau, J., & Hainaut, K. (1998). Neural adaptations mediate increase in muscle contraction speed and change in motor unit behaviour after dynamic training. *Journal of Physiology, 513,* 295–305.

Van Cutsem, M., Feiereisen, P., Duchateau, J., & Hainaut, K. (1997). Mechanical properties and behaviour of motor units in the tibialis anterior during voluntary contractions. *Canadian Journal of Applied Physiology, 22,* 585–597.

Vandenborne, K.A., Elliott, M.A., Walter, G.A., Abdus, S., Okereke, E., Shaffer, M., Tahernia, D., & Esterhai, J.L. (1998). Longitudinal study of skeletal muscle adaptations during immobilization and rehabilitation. *Muscle & Nerve, 21,* 1006–1012.

Vandenburgh, H.H. (1992). Mechanical forces and their second messengers in stimulating cell growth in vitro. *American Journal of Physiology, 262,* R350–R355.

Vandenburgh, H.H., Hatfaludy, S., Sohar, I., & Shansky, J. (1990). Stretch-induced prostaglandins and protein turnover in cultured skeletal muscle. *American Journal of Physiology, 259,* C232–C240.

van der Helm, F.C.T., & Veenbaas, R. (1991). Modelling the mechanical effect of muscles with large attachment sites: Application to the shoulder mechanism. *Journal of Biomechanics, 24,* 1151–1163.

Vander Molen, M.A., Donahue, H.J., Rubin, C.T., & McLeod, K.J. (2000). Osteoblastic networks with deficient coupling: Differential effects of magnetic and electric field exposure. *Bone, 27,* 227–231.

Vanderthommen, M., Gilles, R., Carlier, P., Ciancabilla, F., Zahlan, O., Sluse, F., & Crielaard, J.M. (1999). Human muscle energetics during voluntary and electrically induced isometric contractions as measured by ^{31}P NMR spectroscopy. *International Journal of Sports Medicine, 20,* 279–283.

van der Vaart, A.J.M., Savelberg, H.H.C.M., de Groot, G., Hollander, A.P., Toussaint, H.M., & van Ingen Schenau, G.J. (1987). An estimation of drag in front crawl swimming. *Journal of Biomechanics, 20,* 543–546.

Vandervoort, A.A., & Hayes, K.C. (1989). Plantarflexor muscle function in young and elderly women. *European Journal of Applied Physiology, 58,* 389–394.

Vandervoort, A.A., Quinlan, J., & McComas, A.J. (1983). Twitch potentiation after voluntary contraction. *Experimental Neurology, 81,* 141–152.

van der Werf, S.P., Jongen, P.J.H., Lycklama à Nijeholt, G.J., Barkhof, F., Hommes, O.R., & Bleijenberg, G. (1998). Fatigue in multiple sclerosis: Interrelations between fatigue complaints, cerebral MRI abnormalities and neurological disability. *Journal of the Neurological Sciences, 160,* 164–170.

Van Eck, M.M.M., Nicolson, N.A., Berkhof, H., & Sulon, J. (1996). Individual differences in cortisol responses to a laboratory speech task and their relationship to responses to stressful daily events. *Biological Psychology, 43,* 69–84.

van Mameren, H., & Drukker, J. (1979). Attachment and composition of skeletal muscles in relation to their function. *Journal of Biomechanics, 12,* 859–867.

van Zuylen, E.J., Gielen, C.C.A.M., & Denier van der Gon, J.J. (1988). Coordination and inhomogeneous activation of human arm muscles during isometric torques. *Journal of Neurophysiology, 60,* 1523–1548.

Vaughan, C.L. (1984). Biomechanics of running gait. *CRC Critical Reviews in Biomedical Engineering, 12,* 1–48.

Veldhuizen, J.W., Verstappen, F.T.J., Vroemen, J.P.A.M., Kuipers, H., & Greep, J.M. (1993). Functional and morphological adaptations following four weeks of knee immobilization. *International Journal of Sports Medicine, 14,* 283–287.

Verburg, E., Hallén, J., Sejersted, O.M., & Vøllestad, N. (1999). Loss of potassium from muscle during moderate exercise in humans: A result of insufficient activation of the Na$^+$-K$^+$-pump? *Acta Physiologica Scandinavica, 165,* 357–367.

Videman, T. (1987). Connective tissue and immobilization: Key factors in musculoskeletal degeneration. *Clinical Orthopaedics and Related Research, 221,* 26–32.

Voigt, M., Chelli, F., & Frigo, C. (1998). Changes in the excitability of soleus muscle short latency stretch reflexes during human hopping after 4 weeks of hopping training. *European Journal of Applied Physiology, 78,* 522–532.

Voigt, M., Dyhre-Poulsen, P., & Simonsen, E.B. (1998). Modulation of short latency stretch reflexes during human hopping. *Acta Physiologica Scandinavica, 163,* 181–194.

Volkmann, N., Hanein, D., Ouyang, G., Trybus, K.M., DeRosier, D.J., & Lowey, S. (2000). Evidence for cleft closure in actomyosin upon ADP release. *Nature Structural Biology, 7,* 1147–1155.

Vøllestad, N.K. (1995). Metabolic correlates of fatigue from different types of exercise in man. In S.C. Gandevia, R.M. Enoka, A.J. McComas, D.G. Stuart, & C.K. Thomas (Eds.), *Fatigue: Neural and muscular mechanisms* (pp. 185–194). New York: Plenum Press.

Vorontsov, A.R., & Rumyantsev, V.A. (2000). Resistive forces in swimming. In V.M. Zatsiorsky (Ed.), *Biomechanics in Sport* (pp.184–204). Oxford, UK: Blackwell Science.

Vrbová, G., & Wareham, A.C. (1976). Effects of nerve activity on the postsynaptic membrane of skeletal muscle. *Brain Research, 118,* 371–382.

Wachholder, K., & Altenburger, H. (1926). Beiträge zur Physiologie der willkürlichen Bewegung: X. Mitteilung, Einzelbewegungen. *Pflügers Archiv für die Physiologie, 214,* 642–661.

Wade, A.J., Broadhead, M.W., Cady, E.B., Llewelyn, M.E., Tong, H.N., & Newham, D.J. (2000). Influence of muscle temperature during fatiguing work with the first dorsal interosseous muscle in man: A ^{31}P-NMR study. *European Journal of Applied Physiology, 81,* 203–209.

Wallin, D., Ekblom, B., Grahn, R., & Nordenborg, T. (1985). Improvement of muscle flexibility. A comparison between two techniques. *American Journal of Sports Medicine, 13,* 263–268.

Walmsley, B., Hodgson, J.A., & Burke, R.E. (1978). Forces produced by medial gastrocnemius and soleus muscles during locomotion in freely moving cats. *Journal of Neurophysiology, 41,* 1203–1216.

Walmsley, B., & Proske, U. (1981). Comparison of stiffness of soleus and medial gastrocnemius muscles in cats. *Journal of Neurophysiology, 46,* 250–259.

Walsh, E.G. (1992). *Muscles, masses and motion.* London: Mac Keith Press.

Walsh, M.L. (2000). Whole body fatigue and critical power. *Sports Medicine, 29,* 153–166.

Wang, F-C., de Pasqua, V., & Delwaide, P.J. (1999). Age-related changes in fastest and slowest conducting axons of thenar motor units. *Muscle & Nerve, 22,* 1022–1029.

Wang, K., McCarter, R., Wright, J., Beverly, J., & Ramirez-Mitchell, R. (1993). Viscoelasticity of the sarcomere matrix of skeletal muscles: The titin-myosin composite filament is a dual-stage molecular spring. *Biophysical Journal, 64,* 1161–1177.

Warabi, T., Noda, H., & Kato, T. (1986). Effect of aging on sensorimotor functions of eye and hand movements. *Experimental Neurology, 92,* 686–697.

Ward-Smith, A.J. (1985). A mathematical analysis of the influence of adverse and favourable winds on sprinting. *Journal of Biomechanics, 18,* 351–357.

Warren, G.L., Hayes, D.A., Lowe, D.A., & Armstrong, R.B. (1993). Mechanical factors in the initiation of eccentric contraction-induced injury in rat soleus muscle. *Journal of Physiology (London), 464,* 457–475.

Warren, G.L., Hayes, D.A., Lowe, D.A., Prior, B.M., & Armstrong, R.B. (1993). Materials fatigue initiates eccentric contraction-induced injury in rat soleus muscle. *Journal of Physiology (London), 464,* 477–489.

Warshaw, D.M. (1996). The in vitro motility assay: A window into the myosin molecular motor. *News in Physiological Sciences, 11*, 1–6.

Waterman-Storer, C.M. (1991). The cytoskeleton of skeletal muscle: Is it affected by exercise? A brief review. *Medicine and Science in Sports and Exercise, 23*, 1240–1249.

Webber, S., & Kriellaars, D. (1997). Neuromuscular factors contributing to in vivo eccentric moment generation. *Journal of Applied Physiology, 83*, 40–45.

Weeks, J.C., & McEwen, B.S. (1997). Modulation of neural circuits by steroid hormones in rodent and insect model systems. In P.S.G. Stein, S. Grillner, A.I. Selverston, & D.G. Stuart (Eds.), *Neurons, networks, and motor behavior* (pp. 195–207). Cambridge, MA: MIT Press.

Weinberg, R.S., & Hunt, V.V. (1976). The interrelationships between anxiety, motor performance and electromyography. *Journal of Motor Behavior, 8*, 219–224.

Weiss, T., Miltner, W.H.R., Dillmann, J., Meissner, W., Huonker, R., & Nowak, H. (1998). Reorganization of the somatosensory cortex after amputation of the index finger. *NeuroReport, 9*, 213–216.

West, S.P., Roy, R.R., & Edgerton, V.R. (1986). Fiber type and fiber size of cat ankle, knee and hip extensors and flexors following low thoracic spinal cord transection at an early age. *Experimental Neurology, 91*, 174–182.

Westerblad, H., Allen, D.G., Bruton, J.D., Andrade, F.H., & Lännergren, J. (1998). Mechanisms underlying the reduction of isometric force in skeletal muscle fatigue. *Acta Physiologica Scandinavica, 162*, 253–260.

Westing, S.H., Cresswell, A.G., & Thorstensson, A. (1991). Muscle activation during maximal voluntary eccentric and concentric knee extension. *European Journal of Applied Physiology, 62*, 104–108.

Westing, S.H., Seger, J.Y., & Thorstensson, A. (1990). Effects of electrical stimulation on eccentric and concentric torque-velocity relationships during knee extension in man. *Acta Physiologica Scandinavica, 140*, 17–22.

Wetzel, M.C., & Stuart, D.G. (1976). Ensemble characteristics of cat locomotion and its neural control. *Progress in Neurobiology, 7*, 1–98.

Weyand, P.G., Sternlight, D.B., Bellizzi, M.J., & Wright, S. (2000). Faster top running speeds are achieved with greater ground forces not more rapid leg movements. *Journal of Applied Physiology, 89*, 1991–1999.

Whalen, R.T., Carter, D.R., & Steele, C.R. (1988). Influence of physical activity on the regulation of bone density. *Journal of Biomechanics, 21*, 825–837.

Whelan, P.J., Hiebert, G.W., & Pearson, K.G. (1995). Stimulation of the group I extensor afferents prolongs the stance phase in walking cats. *Experimental Brain Research, 103*, 20–30.

Whitehead, N.P., Allen, T.J., Morgan, D.L., & Proske, U. (1998). Damage to human muscle from eccentric exercise after training with concentric exercise. *Journal of Physiology, 512*, 615–620.

Whiting, A.C., & Zernicke, R.F. (1998). *Biomechanics of musculoskeletal injury*. Champaign, IL: Human Kinetics.

Wickiewicz, T.L., Roy, R.R., Powell, P.L., & Edgerton, V.R. (1983). Muscle architecture of the human lower limb. *Clinical Orthopaedics and Related Research, 179*, 275–283.

Wickiewicz, T.L., Roy, R.R., Powell, P.L., Perrine, J.J., & Edgerton, V.R. (1984). Muscle architecture and force-velocity relationships in humans. *Journal of Applied Physiology, 57*, 435–443.

Widrick, J.J., Trappe, S.W., Costill, D.L., & Fitts, R.H. (1996). Force-velocity and force-power properties of single muscle fibers from elite master runners and sedentary men. *American Journal of Physiology, 271*, C676–C683.

Wiegner, A.W. (1987). Mechanism of thixotropic behaviour at relaxed joints in the rat. *Journal of Applied Physiology, 62*, 1615–1621.

Wiktorsson-Möller, M., Öberg, B., Ekstrand, J., & Gillquist, J. (1983). Effects of warming up, massage, and stretching on range of motion and muscle strength in the lower extremity. *American Journal of Sports Medicine, 11*, 249–252.

Williams, J.H., & Barnes, W.S. (1989). The positive inotropic effect of epinephrine on skeletal muscle: A brief review. *Muscle & Nerve, 12*, 968–975.

Williams, K.R. (1985). Biomechanics of running. *Exercise and Sport Sciences Reviews, 13*, 389–441.

Williams, R.A., Morrissey, M.C., & Brewster, C.E. (1986). The effect of electrical stimulation on quadriceps strength and thigh circumference in meniscectomy patients. *Journal of Orthopaedic and Sports Physical Therapy, 8*, 143–146.

Williams, R.F., & Neufer, P.D. (1996). Regulation of gene expression in skeletal muscle by contractile activity. In L.B. Rowell & J.T. Shepherd (Eds.), *Handbook of physiology: Sec. 12. Exercise: Regulation and integration of multiple systems* (pp. 1124–1150). New York: Oxford University Press.

Wilson, B.D. (1977). Toppling techniques in diving. *Research Quarterly, 48*, 800–804.

Wilson, D.R., Feikes, J.D., & O'Connor, J.J. (1998). Ligaments and articular contact guide passive knee flexion. *Journal of Biomechanics, 31*, 1127–1136.

Wilson, G.J., & Murphy, A.J. (1996). The use of isometric tests of muscular function in athletic assessment. *Sports Medicine, 22*, 19–37.

Wilson, G.J., Murphy, A.J., & Walshe, A. (1996). The specificity of strength training: The effect of posture. *European Journal of Applied Physiology, 73*, 346–352.

Wilson, G.J., Newton, R.U., Murphy, A.J., & Humphries, B.J. (1993). The optimal training load for the development of dynamic athletic performance. *Medicine and Science in Sports and Exercise, 25*, 1279–1286.

Windhorst, U. (1988). *How brain-like is the spinal cord?* Berlin: Springer-Verlag.

Windhorst, U. (1996). On the role of recurrent inhibitory feedback in motor control. *Progress in Neurobiology, 49*, 517–587.

Windhorst, U., Christakos, C.N., Koehler, W., Hamm, T.M., Enoka, R.M., & Stuart, D.G. (1986). Amplitude reduction of motor unit twitches during repetitive activation is accompanied by relative increase of hyperpolarizing membrane potential trajectories in homonymous $\propto$-motoneurones. *Brain Research, 398*, 181–184.

Windhorst, U., Hamm, T.M., & Stuart, D.G. (1989). On the function of muscle and reflex partitioning. *Behavioral and Brain Sciences, 12*, 629–682.

Wing, A.M., Haggard, P., & Flanagan, J.R. (Eds.) (1996). *Hand and brain. The neurophysiology and psychology of hand movements*. New York: Academic Press.

Winiarski, A.M., Roy, R.R., Alford, E.K., Chiang, P.C., & Edgerton, V.R. (1987). Mechanical properties of rat skeletal muscle after hindlimb suspension. *Experimental Neurology, 96,* 650–660.

Winter, D.A. (1983). Moments of force and mechanical power in jogging. *Journal of Biomechanics, 16,* 91–97.

Winter, D.A. (1990). *Biomechanics and motor control of human movement* (2nd ed.). New York: Wiley.

Winter, D.A., Fuglevand, A.J., & Archer, S.E. (1994). Crosstalk in surface electromyography: Theoretical and practical estimates. *Journal of Electromyography and Kinesiology, 4,* 15–26.

Winter, D.A., Sidwall, H.G., & Hobson, D.A. (1974). Measurement and reduction of noise in kinematics of locomotion. *Journal of Biomechanics, 7,* 157–159.

Winter, D.A., Wells, R.P., & Orr, G.W. (1981). Errors in the use of isokinetic dynamometers. *European Journal of Applied Physiology, 46,* 397–408.

Winters, J.M., & Woo, S.L-Y. (Eds.) (1990). *Multiple muscle systems: Biomechanics and movement organization.* New York: Springer-Verlag.

Wise, A.K., Morgan, D.L., Gregory, J.E., & Proske, U. (2001). Fatigue in mammalian skeletal muscle stimulated under computer control. *Journal of Applied Physiology, 90,* 189–197.

Wohl, G.R., Boyd, S.K., Judex, S., & Zernicke, R.F. (2000). Functional adaptation of bone to exercise and injury. *Journal of Science and Medicine in Sport, 3,* 313–324.

Wolf, S.L., Barnhart, H.X., Kutner, N.G., McNeely, E., Coogler, C., Xu, T., & Atlanta FICSIT Group (1996). Reducing frailty and falls in older persons: An investigation of Tai Chi and computerized balance training. *Journal of the American Geriatrics Society, 44,* 489–497.

Wolf, S.L., Segal, R.L., Heter, N.D., & Catlin, P.A. (1995). Contralateral and long latency effects of human biceps brachii stretch reflex conditioning. *Experimental Brain Research, 107,* 96–102.

Wolpaw, J.R. (1994). Acquisition and maintenance of the simplest motor skill: Investigation of CNS mechanisms. *Medicine and Science in Sports and Exercise, 26,* 1475–1479.

Wolpaw, J.R., & Carp, J.S. (1990). Memory traces in spinal cord. *Trends in Neurosciences, 13,* 137–142.

Wolpaw, J.R., Herchenroder, P.A., & Carp, J.S. (1993). Operant conditioning of the primate H-reflex: Factors affecting the magnitude of the change. *Experimental Brain Research, 97,* 31–39.

Wolpaw, J.R., & Lee, C.L. (1989). Memory traces in primate spinal cord produced by operant conditioning of H-reflex. *Journal of Neurophysiology, 61,* 563–572.

Wolpaw, J.R., McFarland, D.J., Neat, G.W., & Forneris, C.A. (1991). An EEG-based brain-computer interface for cursor control. *Electroencephalography and Clinical Neurophysiology, 78,* 252–259.

Wong, T.S., & Booth, F.W. (1990a). Protein metabolism in rat gastrocnemius muscle after stimulated chronic concentric exercise. *Journal of Applied Physiology, 69,* 1709–1717.

Wong, T.S., & Booth, F.W. (1990b). Protein metabolism in rat tibialis anterior muscle after stimulated chronic eccentric exercise. *Journal of Applied Physiology, 69,* 1718–1724.

Woo, S.L-Y., An, K-N., Arnoczky, S.P., Wayne, J.S., Fithian, D.C., & Myers, B.S. (1994). Anatomy, biology, and biomechanics of tendon, ligament, and meniscus. In S.R. Simon (Ed.), *Orthopaedic basic science* (pp. 45–87). Park Ridge, IL: American Academy of Orthopaedic Surgeons.

Woo, S.L., Debski, R.E., Withrow, J.D., & Janaushek, M.A. (1999). Biomechanics of knee ligaments. *American Journal of Sports Medicine, 27,* 533–543.

Wood, G.A. (1982). Data smoothing and differentiation procedures in biomechanics. *Exercise and Sport Sciences Reviews, 10,* 308–362.

Wright, J.R., McCloskey, D.I., & Fitzpatrick, R.C. (2000). Effects of systemic arterial blood pressure on the contractile force of a human hand muscle. *Journal of Applied Physiology, 88,* 1390–1396.

Wu, G., & Ladin, Z. (1993). The kinematometer—an integrated kinematic sensor for kinesiologic measurements. *Journal of Biomechanical Engineering, 115,* 53–62.

Xi, M.C., Liu, R.H., Engelhardt, J.K., Morales, F.R., & Chase, M.H. (1999). Changes in the axonal conduction velocity of pyramidal tract neurons in the aged cat. *Neuroscience, 92,* 219–225.

Yamaguchi, G.T., Moran, D.W., & Si, J. (1995). A computationally efficient method for solving the redundant problem in biomechanics. *Journal of Biomechanics, 28,* 999–1005.

Yamaguchi, G.T., Sawa, A.G.U., Moran, D.W., Fessler, M.J., & Winters, J.M. (1990). A survey of human musculotendon actuator parameters. In J.M. Winters & S.L-Y. Woo (Eds.), *Multiple muscle systems: Biomechanics and movement organization* (pp. 717–773). New York: Springer-Verlag.

Yamashita, N. (1988). EMG activities in mono- and bi-articular thigh muscles in combined hip and knee extension. *European Journal of Applied Physiology, 58,* 274–277.

Yang, J.F., & Stein, R.B. (1990). Phase-dependent reflex reversal in human leg muscles during walking. *Journal of Neurophysiology, 63,* 1109–1117.

Yang, J.F., Stein, R.B., Jhamandas, J., & Gordon, T. (1990). Motor unit numbers and contractile properties after spinal cord injury. *Annals of Neurology, 28,* 496–502.

Yao, W.X., Fuglevand, A.J., & Enoka, R.M. (2000). Motor-unit synchronization increases EMG amplitude and decreases force steadiness of simulated contractions. *Journal of Neurophysiology, 83,* 441–452.

Yarasheski, K.E., Campbell, J.A., Smith, K., Rennie, M.J., Holloszy, J.O., & Bier, D.M. (1992). Effect of growth hormone and resistance exercise on muscle growth in young men. *American Journal of Physiology, 262,* E261–E267.

Yeadon, M.R. (1990). The simulation of aerial movement—II. A mathematical inertia model of the human body. *Journal of Biomechanics, 23,* 67–74.

Yeadon, M.R. (1993a). The biomechanics of twisting somersaults Part I: Rigid body motions. *Journal of Sports Sciences, 11,* 187–198.

Yeadon, M.R. (1993b). The biomechanics of twisting somersaults Part II: Contact twist. *Journal of Sports Sciences, 11,* 199–208.

Yeadon, M.R. (1993c). The biomechanics of twisting somersaults Part III: Aerial twist. *Journal of Sports Sciences, 11,* 209–218.

Yeadon, M.R. (1993d). The biomechanics of twisting somersaults Part IV: Partitioning performances using the tilt angle. *Journal of Sports Sciences, 11,* 219–225.

Yeadon, M.R. (1993e). Twisting techniques used by competitive divers. *Journal of Sports Sciences, 11,* 337–342.

Yingling, V.R., Yack, H.J., & White, S.C. (1996). The effect of rearfoot motion on attenuation of the impulsive wave at impact during running. *Journal of Applied Biomechanics, 12,* 313–325.

Young, A., Stokes, M., & Iles, J.F. (1987). Effects of joint pathology on muscle. *Clinical Orthopaedics and Related Research, 219,* 21–27.

Young, J.L., & Mayer, R.F. (1981). Physiological properties and classification of single motor units activated by intramuscular microstimulation in the first dorsal interosseus muscle in man. In J.E. Desmedt (Ed.), *Motor unit types, recruitment and plasticity in health and disease* (pp. 17–25). Basel: Karger.

Young, K., McDonagh, M.J.N., & Davies, C.T.M. (1985). The effects of two forms of isometric training on the mechanical properties of the triceps surae in man. *Pflügers Archive, 405,* 384–388.

Young, R.R. (1994). Spasticity: A review. *Neurology, 44*(Suppl. 9), S12–S20.

Young, W.B., & Bilby, G.E. (1993). The effect of voluntary effort to influence speed of contraction on strength, muscular power, and hypertrophy development. *Journal of Strength and Conditioning Research, 7,* 172–178.

Yue, G., Alexander, A.L., Laidlaw, D.H., Gmitro, A.F., Unger, E.C., & Enoka, R.M. (1994). Sensitivity of muscle proton spin-spin relaxation time as an index of muscle activation. *Journal of Applied Physiology, 77,* 84–92.

Yue, G., & Cole, K.J. (1992). Strength increases from the motor program: A comparison of training with maximal voluntary and imagined muscle contractions. *Journal of Neurophysiology, 67,* 1114–1123.

Yue, G.H., Bilodeau, M., Hardy, P.A., & Enoka, R.M. (1997). Task-dependent effect of limb immobilization on the fatigability of the elbow flexor muscles in humans. *Experimental Physiology, 82,* 567–592.

Zajac, F.E. (1993). Muscle coordination of movement: A perspective. *Journal of Biomechanics, 26,* 109–124.

Zatsiorsky, V. (1997). The review is nice. I disagree with it. *Journal of Applied Biomechanics, 13,* 479–483.

Zatsiorsky, V., & Seluyanov, V. (1983). The mass and inertia characteristics of the main segments of the human body. In H. Matsui & K. Kobayashi (Eds.), *Biomechanics VIII-B* (pp. 1152–1159). Champaign, IL: Human Kinetics.

Zatsiorsky, V., Seluyanov, V., & Chugunova, L. (1990a). In vivo body segment inertial parameters determination using a gamma-scanner method. In N. Berme & A. Cappozzo (Eds.), *Biomechanics of human movement: Applications in rehabilitation, sports and ergonomics* (pp. 186–202). Ohio: Bertec.

Zatsiorsky, V.M. (1995). *Science and practice of strength training.* Champaign, IL: Human Kinetics.

Zatsiorsky, V.M., Li, Z.-M., & Latash, M.L. (1998). Coordinated force production in multi-finger tasks: Finger interaction and neural network modeling. *Biological Cybernetics, 79,* 139–150.

Zatsiorsky, V.M., Seluyanov, V.N., & Chugunova, L.G. (1990b). Methods of determining mass-inertial characteristics of human body segments. In G.G. Chernyi & S.A. Regirer (Eds.), *Contemporary problems of biomechanics* (pp. 272–291). Massachusetts: CRC Press.

Zemková, H., Teisinger, J., Almon, R.R., Vejsada, R., Hník, P., & Vyskocil, F. (1990). Immobilization atrophy and membrane properties in rat skeletal muscle fibres. *Pflügers Archive, 416,* 126–129.

Zernicke, R.F., & Smith, J.L. (1996). Biomechanical insights into neural control of movement. In L.B. Rowell & J.T. Shepherd (Eds.), *Handbook of physiology: Sec. 12. Exercise: Regulation and integration of multiple systems* (pp. 293–330). New York: Oxford University Press.

Zernicke, R.F., Vailis, A.C., & Salem, G.J. (1990). Biomechanical response of bone to weightlessness. *Exercise and Sport Sciences Reviews, 18,* 167–192.

Zhang, J.H., Sampogna, S., Morales, F.R., & Chase, M.H. (1997). Age-related alterations in immunoreactivity of the midsized neurofilament subunit in the brainstem reticular formation of the cat. *Brain Research, 769,* 196–200.

Zhang, L., Butler, J., Nishida, T., Nuber, G., Huang, H., & Rymer W.Z. (1998). In vivo determination of the direction of rotation and moment-angle relationship of individual elbow muscles. *Journal of Biomechanical Engineering, 120,* 625–633.

Zheng, N., Fleisig, G.S., Escamilla, R.F., & Barrentine, S.W. (1998). An analytical model of the knee for estimation of internal forces during exercise. *Journal of Biomechanics, 31,* 963–967.

Zhou, S. (2000). Chronic neural adaptations to unilateral exercise: Mechanisms of cross education. *Exercise and Sport Sciences Reviews, 28,* 177–184.

Zijdewind, I., & Kernell, D. (2001). Bilateral interactions during contractions of intrinsic hand muscles. *Journal of Neurophysiology, 85,* 1907-1913.

Zimny, M.L., & Wink, C.S. (1991). Neuroreceptors in the tissues of the knee joint. *Journal of Electromyography and Kinesiology, 3,* 148–157.

Zinovieff, A.N. (1951). Heavy-resistance exercise, the Oxford Technique. *British Journal of Physical Medicine, 14,* 159–162.

Zoladz, J.A., Rademaker, A.C.H.J., & Sargeant, A.J. (2000). Human muscle power generating capability during cycling at different pedalling rates. *Experimental Physiology, 85,* 117–124.

Zytnicki, D., Lafleur, J., Horcholle-Bossavit, G., Lamy, F., & Jami, L. (1990). Reduction of Ib autogenetic inhibition in motoneurons during contractions of an ankle extensor muscle in the cat. *Journal of Neurophysiology, 64,* 1380–1389.

Index

Note: Tables are indicated by an italicized t following the page number; figures by an italicized f.

Author

About the Author

Roger M. Enoka, PhD, is an internationally acclaimed teacher and researcher and author of the groundbreaking first edition of this book, *Neuromechanical Basis of Kinesiology*.

Dr. Enoka is a professor in the department of kinesiology and applied physiology at the University of Colorado at Boulder. He has been deeply involved in the field of the integration of biomechanics and neuromuscular physiology for 25 years and has been teaching many of the concepts described in this book since the 1970s. He has conducted an interdisciplinary research program that has been continuously funded by the National Institutes of Health for almost two decades.

Dr. Enoka was a biomechanist in the department of biomedical engineering at the Cleveland Clinic Foundation from 1993 to 1996 and was a professor in the department of physiology at the University of Arizona from 1981 to 1993.

Dr. Enoka is a member of the American Society of Biomechanics, which he served as president of from 1989 to 1990. Other professional affiliations include the American College of Sports Medicine, the American Physiological Society, and the Society of Neuroscience. He is a former member of the Advisory Panel on Research for the American Physical Therapy Association and the Respiratory and Applied Physiology Study Section of the National Institutes of Health.

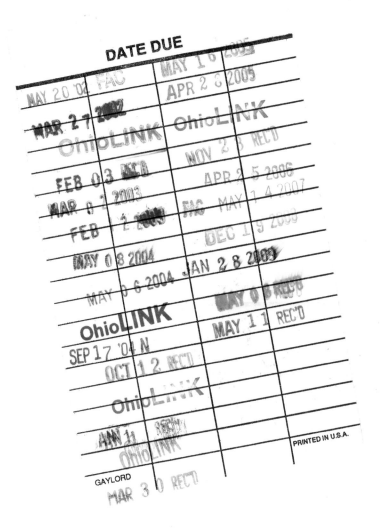